Western Canada & Alaska

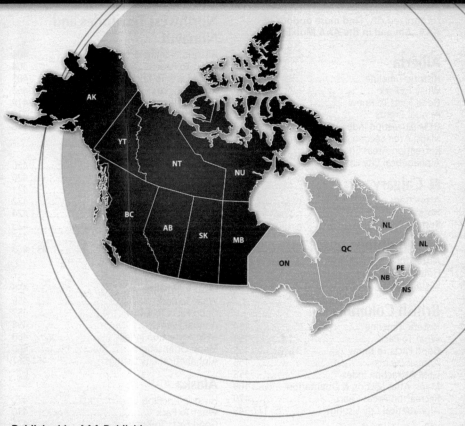

Published by AAA Publishing
1000 AAA Drive, Heathrow, FL 32746-5063
Copyright AAA 2016, All rights reserved

Advertising Rate and Circulation Information: (407) 444-8280

Printed in the USA by Quad/Graphics

This book is printed on paper certified by third-party standards for sustainably managed forestry and production.

 Printed on recyclable paper.
Please recycle whenever possible.

Stock #4601

CONTENTS

Attractions, hotels, restaurants and other travel experience information are all grouped under the alphabetical listing of the city in which those experiences are physically located—or the nearest recognized city. **Find more options at AAA.com and in the AAA Mobile app.**

To view these helpful tools, visit tdr.aaa.com/tb/4601/
• Using Your Guide & Just For Members
• Metric Equivalents Chart
• Driving Distances Map
• Points of Interest Index

Dream.
Plan.
Go.

Picture yourself ...
- At your ideal destination
- In a comfortable hotel
- Eating your favorite meals
- Exploring the sights

Turn your dreams into reality
with **TripTik® Travel Planner**.

explore

The card that gets you there™

Get the credit card that lets you earn **3x points** on qualifying AAA and travel purchases, **2x points** on gas, grocery store and drugstore purchases, and **1 point** per **$1** on all other purchases.*

Planning to explore the new world, or just visit your old stomping grounds? It's easier than ever to get there with a AAA Member Rewards Visa® credit card.

To apply for an account, visit a participating AAA branch or AAA.com/creditcard.

Using Your Guide

AAA TourBook guides are packed with travel insight, maps and listings of AAA Approved places to play, stay and eat. To unpack the details, revisit this section as you plan and explore.

A to Z City Listings

Cities and places are listed alphabetically within each state or province. Attractions, hotels and restaurants are listed once — under the city in which they are physically located.

Cities that are considered part of a larger destination city or area have an expanded city header. The header identifies the larger region and cross-references pages that contain shared trip planning resources:

- Destination map – outline map of the cities that comprise a destination city or area
- Attraction spotting map – regional street map marked with attraction locations
- Hotel/restaurant spotting map and index – regional street map numbered with hotel and restaurant locations identified in an accompanying index

Cities that are not considered part of a larger destination city or area but have a significant number of listings may have these resources within the individual city section:

- Attraction spotting map
- Hotel/restaurant spotting map and index

Location Abbreviations

Directions are from the center of town unless otherwise specified, using these highway abbreviations:

Bus. Rte.=business route
CR=county road
FM=farm to market
FR=forest road
Hwy.=Canadian highway
I=interstate highway
LR=legislative route
R.R.=rural route
SR/PR=state or provincial route
US=federal highway

About Listed Establishments

AAA/CAA Approved hotels and restaurants are listed on the basis of merit alone after careful evaluation and approval by full-time, professionally trained AAA/CAA inspectors. An establishment's decision to advertise in the TourBook guide has no bearing on its evaluation or rating; nor does inclusion of advertising imply AAA endorsement of products and services.

Information in this guide was believed accurate at the time of publication. However, since changes inevitably occur between annual editions, please contact your AAA travel professional, visit AAA.com or download the free AAA mobile app to confirm prices and schedules.

Attraction Listing Icons

SAVE AAA Discounts & Rewards® member discount

Electric vehicle charging station on premises. Domestic station information provided by the U.S. Department of Energy. Canadian station information provided by Plug'n Drive Ontario.

GT Guided Tours available

Camping facilities

Food on premises

Recreational activities

Pets on leash allowed

Picnicking allowed

In select cities only:

Mass transit station within 1 mile. Icon is followed by station name and AAA/CAA designated station number within listing.

GEM AAA/CAA travel experts may designate an attraction of exceptional interest and quality as a AAA GEM — a *Great Experience for Members®*. See *GEM Attraction Index (listed on CONTENTS page) for a complete list of locations.*

Consult the online travel guides at AAA.com or visit AAA Mobile for additional things to do if you have time.

Hotel Listing Icons

(May be preceded by CALL and/or SOME UNITS.)

SAVE Member rates: discounted standard room rate or lowest public rate available at time of booking for dates of stay.

ECO Eco-certified by government or private organization.

Electric vehicle charging station on premises. Domestic station information provided by the U.S. Department of

Energy. Canadian station information provided by Plug'n Drive Ontario.

⊠ Smoke-free premises

In select cities only:

🚉 Mass transit station within 1 mile. Icon is followed by station name and AAA/CAA designated station number within listing.

Services:

✈ Airport transportation

🐕 Pets allowed (Call property for restrictions.)

💲🐕 Pets allowed (Call property for restrictions and fees.)

🍴 Restaurant on premises

🍴+ Restaurant off premises

🍽 Room service for 2 or more meals

🍸 Full bar

🧸 Child care

BIZ Business area

♿M Accessible features (Call property for available services and amenities.)

Activities:

♠ Full-service casino

🏊 Pool

💪 Health club on premises

In-Room Amenities:

HS High-speed Internet service

$HS High-speed Internet service (Call property for fees.)

🛜 Wireless Internet service

💲🛜 Wireless Internet service (Call property for fees.)

🚫🛜 No wireless Internet service

🎬 Pay movies

🧊 Refrigerator

🔲 Microwave

☕ Coffee maker

🚫 No air conditioning

📺 No TV

☎ No telephones

Restaurant Listing Icons

SAVE AAA Discounts & Rewards® member discount

ECO Eco-certified by government or private organization.

🔌 Electric vehicle charging station on premises. Domestic station information provided by the U.S. Department of Energy. Canadian station information provided by Plug'n Drive Ontario.

🚫 No air conditioning

♿M Accessible features (Call property for available services and amenities.)

⊠ Designated smoking section

B Breakfast

L Lunch

D Dinner

24 Open 24 hours

LATE Open after 11 p.m.

🛏 Pet-friendly (Call property for restrictions.)

In select cities only:

🚉 Mass transit station within 1 mile. Icon is followed by station name and AAA/CAA designated station number within listing.

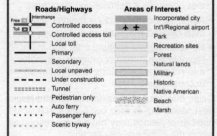

Map Legend

For attraction and hotel/ restaurant spotting maps, refer to the legend below to identify symbols and color coding.

Roads/Highways

Free	Interchange
Toll	Controlled access
	Controlled access toll
	Local toll
	Primary
	Secondary
	Local unpaved
	Under construction
	Tunnel
	Pedestrian only
	Auto ferry
	Passenger ferry
	Scenic byway

Areas of Interest

Incorporated city
✈ ✈ Int'l/Regional airport
Park
Recreation sites
Forest
Natural lands
Military
Historic
Native American
Beach
Marsh

Route Shields

				Primary	Secondary
Interstate	95	95 Business	Trans-Canada		
Federal	Primary 22	Secondary 22	Provincial Autoroute	22	22
State	1	1	Mexico	1	1
County	1	1	Historic	66	

Boundaries

International	Time zone
State	Continental Divide

Points of Interest

★ National capital   o Town

★ State/Prov capital   🏕 Campground

■ AAA/CAA club location   🍷 Winery

■ Feature of interest   🛂 Customs station

⚜ GEM attraction   ■ Historic

12 Hotel listing   △ Mountain peak

③ Restaurant listing   🔴 Rapid transit

🏛 College/University   Stations 🔴 Metromover

Understanding the Diamond Ratings

Hotel and restaurant evaluations are unscheduled to ensure our professionally trained inspectors encounter the same experience members do.

- When an establishment is Diamond Rated, it means members can expect a good fit with their needs. The inspector assigns a rating that indicates the type of experience to expect.
- While establishments at high levels must offer increasingly complex personalized services, establishments at every level are subject to the same basic requirements for cleanliness, comfort and hospitality. Learn more at AAA.com/Diamonds.

 Red Diamonds mark establishments that participate in the AAA/CAA logo licensing program for increased visibility to members.

 Black Diamonds identify all other AAA/CAA Approved and Diamond Rated establishments.

Hotels	Restaurants
Budget-oriented, offering basic comfort and hospitality.	Simple, economical food, often quick-serve, in a functional environment.
Affordable, with modestly enhanced facilities, décor and amenities.	Familiar food, often cooked to order, served in casual surroundings.
 Distinguished, multifaceted with enhanced physical attributes, amenities and guest comforts.	 Trendy cuisine, skillfully prepared and served, with expanded beverage options, in an enhanced setting.
Refined, stylish with upscale physical attributes, extensive amenities and high degree of hospitality, service and attention to detail.	Distinctive fine-dining. Creative preparations, skillfully served, often with wine steward, amid upscale ambience.
Ultimate luxury, sophistication and comfort with extraordinary physical attributes, meticulous personalized service, extensive amenities and impeccable standards of excellence.	Leading-edge cuisine of the finest ingredients, uniquely prepared by an acclaimed chef, served by expert service staff led by maître d' in extraordinary surroundings.

Guest Safety

Inspectors view a sampling of rooms during evaluations and, therefore, AAA/CAA cannot guarantee the presence of working locks and operational fire safety equipment in every guest unit.

Contacting AAA/CAA About Approved Properties

If your visit to a AAA/CAA Approved attraction, hotel or restaurant doesn't meet your expectations, please tell us about it — **during your visit or within 30 days**. Be sure to save your receipts and other documentation for reference.

Use the easy online form at AAA.com/TourBookComments to send us the details.

Alternatively, you can email your comments to: memberrelations@national.aaa.com or submit them via postal mail to: AAA Member Comments, 1000 AAA Dr., Box 61, Heathrow, FL 32746.

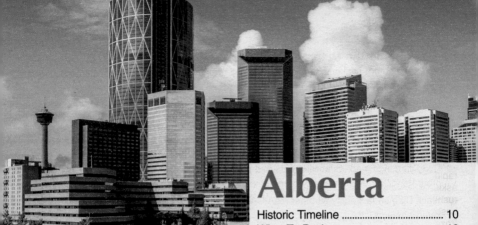

Calgary cityscape

Alberta

Alberta is the great outdoors personified. Mirror images of mountain peaks are reflected on the surface of glacially fed, brilliantly blue lakes. The twinkling, shimmering dance of lights known as aurora borealis provides a surreal sky show. Golden wheat and the bright yellow flowers of the canola plant create blankets of color across endlessly rolling countryside. Is this your typical version of the Wild West? Hardly—but Alberta urges you to stretch the definition of what the Canadian West is all about.

Plenty in Canada's fourth-largest province does fit neatly into the Western mold. Take Calgary, for instance. This former cow town's earliest roots were in ranching and meatpacking. Even the roof of the Scotiabank Saddledome is in the shape of you know what. The home of the National Hockey League's Calgary Flames, the Western Hockey League's Calgary Hitmen and the National Lacrosse

Scotiabank Saddledome, Calgary

League's Calgary Roughnecks also is the venue of choice for everyone from country superstar Kenny Chesney to the Dalai Lama of Tibet, who visited the city in 2009.

Thousands of folks decked out in cowboy boots and ten-gallon hats gather at Stampede Park every July to watch bull ridin', barrel racin' and other rough-and-tumble rodeo events at the Calgary Stampede, which celebrated its centennial in 2012. The city wears its Western heritage proudly, but Calgary also prides itself on being remarkably well-rounded.

Take the XV Olympic Winter Games in 1988, for instance. Besides showcasing the world's best athletes—including the memorable "Battle of the Brians" between Brian Boitano of the United States and Brian Orser of Canada—the city was in the glare of the world spotlight. Not to worry; five world-class facilities were built, and a concerted grassroots effort enlisted more than 10,000 resident volunteers to help stage the games.

From grizzly bears to wood bison, the Calgary Zoo, Botanical Garden & Prehistoric Park offers outstanding opportunities to view native wildlife. It also is home to more than 4,000 plants and a collection of life-size replicas of dinosaurs in a simulated Mesozoic landscape. In futuristic contrast are the elevated "pedways" that link many downtown buildings.

Such dichotomies are commonplace in this vast province. Hikers in Cypress Hills Interprovincial Park might catch the scent of pine and the subtle fragrance of wild orchids. But just to the northwest, Medicine Hat harnesses an extensive reserve of natural gas that once prompted Rudyard Kipling to describe the city, in an olfactory sense, as having "all hell for a basement."

Rafters steel themselves against the raging rapids of the Elbow, Highwood and Kananaskis rivers in Kananaskis Country. Turbulent rushes of water sweeping over rock at Athabasca and Sunwapta falls become imposing frozen challenges for ice climbers who chink away at them in winter. In serene contrast, canoeists play the placid, emerald waters of Banff National Park's Moraine Lake on still summer mornings, gazing at a backdrop of unspoiled wilderness.

A Canadian Melting Pot

Alberta's ethnic diversity is on display at places like the Ukrainian Cultural Heritage Village east of Edmonton, where costumed interpreters demonstrate what life was like for settlers from the 1890s to 1930. In Vegreville, the design of a famed bronze, gold and silver pysanka, or Ukrainian Easter egg, depicts the people's faith and commemorates the protection provided to them by the Royal Canadian Mounted Police. The Basilian Fathers Museum in Mundare chronicles the order's work in eastern Alberta and holds a collection of Canadian and Ukrainian religious and folk artifacts.

The history of native cultures comes alive at the Head-Smashed-In Buffalo Jump Interpretive Centre near Fort Macleod and in the petroglyphs and pictographs at Writing-on-Stone Provincial Park/Áísínai'pi National Historic Site, near Milk River. Indian Battle Park in Lethbridge details a dust-up between the Cree and Blackfoot, the last intertribal conflict in North America.

And let's not forget dinosaurs. They left their mark on the Red Deer Valley by way of fossils buried in walls of sediment. Drumheller pays tribute to that bygone age along the Dinosaur Trail (hwys. 838 and 837). To the southeast, a fertile fossil bed at Dinosaur Provincial Park, near Patricia, contains the remains of 39 species of extinct reptiles.

Recreation

Nature and outdoor lovers need only look to Alberta's five national parks. In fact Banff is Canada's first national park. Elk Island is an oasis for rare and endangered species. Jasper is a feast of glaciers. The Rockies and the prairie meet at Waterton Lakes. And Wood Buffalo reaches north into neighboring Northwest Territories.

But they're not the only popular outdoor destinations in untamed Alberta. Experienced guides lead trail riding expeditions through the Elbow and Sheep valleys in the Kananaskis high country, west of Calgary. Hiking, mountain climbing and mountain biking are ways to experience the challenging peaks of the Rockies.

White-water rafting fans gravitate to the Athabasca, Elbow, Highwood, Kananaskis, Kicking Horse, Red Deer and Sunwapta rivers. The Blackstone River, a hot spot for kayaking in inflatable boats, cuts through the foothills of the Rockies.

Or take advantage of one of North America's longest ski seasons. Some of the best downhill skiing and snowboarding Alberta has to offer is at Marmot Basin, south of Jasper; Lake Louise, northwest of Banff; Sunshine Village and Banff Mount Norquay, both within 15 minutes of Banff; Fortress Mountain, in Kananaskis Country; and Nakiska, west of Calgary.

Plus, there are opportunities galore for fishing. The Bow River offers exceptional trout fly-fishing, while notable fly-in trophy lakes are Gardiner and Namur, northwest of Fort McMurray, and Winefred, northeast of Lac La Biche.

Banff National Park

Historic Timeline

1670	The Hudson's Bay Co. obtains fur-trading rights to a portion of what is now Alberta.
1795	Fort Edmonton is founded as a Hudson's Bay trading post.
1875	Calgary is designated a North West Mounted Police fort.
1883	The Canadian Pacific Railway reaches Calgary.
1905	The province of Alberta is created.
1930	Jasper National Park is established.
1967	The Great Canadian Oil Sands Co. in Fort McMurray begins producing synthetic crude oil from large deposits of oil sands.
1981	West Edmonton Mall—now one of the world's largest shopping centers following three expansions—opens.
1988	Calgary hosts the XV Olympic Winter Games.
2005	Alberta celebrates its centennial.
2016	Vast forest fires around Fort McMurray cause mass evacuation from the city and surroundings.

What To Pack

Temperature Averages Maximum/Minimum (Celsius)	JANUARY	FEBRUARY	MARCH	APRIL	MAY	JUNE	JULY	AUGUST	SEPTEMBER	OCTOBER	NOVEMBER	DECEMBER
Banff NP	-5 / -15	0 / -11	4 / -8	9 / -3	14 / 2	19 / 6	22 / 7	22 / 7	16 / 3	10 / -1	1 / -8	-5 / -14
Calgary	-3 / -16	-1 / -12	3 / -8	11 / -2	17 / 3	21 / 7	23 / 9	23 / 9	17 / 4	13 / -1	3 / -9	-2 / -14
Edmonton	-8 / -17	-4 / -14	1 / -9	10 / -1	17 / 6	21 / 9	23 / 12	22 / 11	16 / 6	11 / 1	-1 / -9	-7 / -15
Fort McMurray	-15 / -25	-9 / -21	-1 / -15	9 / -4	17 / 3	21 / 7	23 / 10	22 / 8	15 / 3	8 / -2	-5 / -14	-13 / -22
Grande Prairie	-10 / -21	-6 / -18	-1 / -12	9 / -3	16 / 3	20 / 8	22 / 9	21 / 8	16 / 3	10 / -2	-2 / -12	-8 / -19
Jasper NP	-6 / -16	-1 / -12	4 / -8	10 / -3	15 / 2	19 / 6	22 / 8	22 / 7	16 / 3	10 / -1	0 / -9	-6 / -14

From the records of The Weather Channel Interactive, Inc.

Good Facts To Know

ABOUT THE PROVINCE

POPULATION: 3,645,257.

AREA: 640,045 sq km (247,123 sq mi.); ranks 6th.

CAPITAL: Edmonton.

HIGHEST POINT: 3,747 m (12,293 ft.), Mount Columbia.

LOWEST POINT: 152 m (499 ft.), Salt River at border with the Northwest Territories.

TIME ZONE(S): Mountain. DST.

GAMBLING

MINIMUM AGE FOR GAMBLING: 18.

REGULATIONS

TEEN DRIVING LAWS: For probationary licensees, driving is not permitted daily midnight-5 a.m. The minimum age for an unrestricted driver's license is 18. Phone (780) 427-8901 in Edmonton or (403) 297-6679 in Calgary for more information about Alberta driver's license regulations.

SEAT BELT/CHILD RESTRAINT LAWS: Seat belts are required for driver and all passengers ages 16 and over. Children ages 6-15 and 18 kilograms (40 lbs.) and over are required to be in a child restraint or seat belt. Appropriate child restraints are required for children under age 6 and under 18 kilograms (40 lbs.). AAA recommends the use of seat belts and appropriate child restraints for the driver and all passengers.

CELLPHONE RESTRICTIONS: The use of handheld cellphones and text messaging while driving are prohibited.

HELMETS FOR MOTORCYCLISTS: Required for all riders.

RADAR DETECTORS: Permitted.

MOVE OVER LAW: A motorist may not drive more than 60 kph (37 mph) or the maximum speed limit, whichever is lower, if traveling in the same direction in the lane immediately adjacent and passing a stopped emergency vehicle or tow truck using flashing signals.

FIREARMS LAWS: By federal law, all nonresidents entering Canada with a firearm must declare their weapon in writing and pay a fee of $25 (Canadian). Contact the Canadian Firearms Centre at (800) 731-4000 to receive a declaration form or for additional information.

ALCOHOL CONSUMPTION: Legal age 18.

HOLIDAYS

HOLIDAYS: Jan. 1 ▪ Family Day, Feb. (3rd Mon.) ▪ Good Friday ▪ Easter Monday ▪ Victoria Day, May 24 (if a Mon.) or the closest prior Mon. ▪ Canada Day, July 1 ▪ Heritage Day, Aug. (1st Mon.) ▪ Labour Day, Sept. (1st Mon.) ▪ Thanksgiving, Oct. (2nd Mon.) ▪ Remembrance Day, Nov. 11 ▪ Christmas, Dec. 25 ▪ Boxing Day, Dec. 26.

MONEY

TAXES: Alberta has no provincial sales tax. However, there is a 4 percent hotel tax, plus a 1-2 percent tourism levy in some areas. In addition there is a 5 percent national Goods and Service Tax (GST).

VISITOR INFORMATION

INFORMATION CENTERS: Travel Alberta Visitor Centres provide information about accommodations and campgrounds as well as maps. They are located at Canmore on Hwy. 1 ▪ Crowsnest Pass on Hwy. 3 ▪ Field, British Columbia, on Hwy. 1 ▪ Grande Prairie on 106th St. ▪ Hinton on Hwy. 16 ▪ Lloydminster on Hwy. 16 ▪ Milk River on Hwy. 4 ▪ Oyen at the junction of hwys. 9 and 41 ▪ Walsh on Hwy. 1 ▪ and West Glacier, Mont., at the junction of Hwy. 2 and Going-to-the-Sun Road. Most centers are open daily 9-6, mid-May through Labour Day. A tourism office is open year-round in Canmore.

FURTHER INFORMATION FOR VISITORS:
Travel Alberta
400, 1601 9th Ave. S.E.
Calgary, AB T2G 0H4
Canada
(403) 648-1000

FISHING AND HUNTING REGULATIONS:
Alberta Environment and Parks (AEP)
9920 108th St., Main Floor
Edmonton, AB T5K 2M4
Canada
(780) 944-0313
(877) 310-3773 (in Alberta)

RECREATION INFORMATION:
Alberta Tourism, Parks and Recreation
Parks & Protected Areas
9820 106th St., 2nd Floor
Edmonton, AB T5K 2J6
Canada
(866) 427-3582

Alberta Annual Events

Please call ahead to confirm event details.

JANUARY

- Ice on Whyte Festival
  Edmonton
  780-439-9166
- Jasper in January / Jasper
  780-852-3858
- Ice Magic Festival
  International Ice Sculpture
  Competition / Lake Louise
  403-762-0270

FEBRUARY

- Canadian Birkebeiner Ski
  Festival / Edmonton
  780-430-7153
- Silver Skate Festival
  Edmonton
  780-496-4000
- Calgary Midwinter Blues
  Festival / Calgary
  403-668-7144

MARCH

- Outdoor Adventure &
  Travel Show / Calgary
  403-261-0101
- Edmonton Home and
  Garden Show / Edmonton
  780-459-2008
- Edmonton Boat and
  Sportsmen's Show
  Edmonton
  888-800-7275

APRIL

- Edmonton Kiwanis Music
  Festival / Edmonton
  780-488-3498
- Red Deer Festival of the
  Performing Arts / Red Deer
  403-342-3526
- Aggie Days Family Fun
  Days / Calgary
  403-261-0162

MAY

- Calgary International
  Children's Festival / Calgary
  403-294-7414
- Lilac Festival at 4th Street
  Calgary
  403-229-0902
- Grande Prairie Stompede
  Grande Prairie
  780-532-4646

JUNE

- Edmonton International
  Jazz Festival / Edmonton
  780-990-0222
- Grande Prairie Highland
  Games / Grande Prairie
  780-513-2492
- Medicine Hat JazzFest
  Medicine Hat
  403-527-5214

JULY

- Medicine Hat Exhibition &
  Stampede / Medicine Hat
  403-527-1234
- Edmonton's K-Days
  Edmonton
  780-471-7210
- Calgary Stampede / Calgary
  403-261-0172

AUGUST

- Taste of Calgary / Calgary
  403-293-2888
- Edmonton International
  Fringe Theatre Festival
  Edmonton
  780-448-9000
- Edmonton Folk Music
  Festival / Edmonton
  780-429-1899

SEPTEMBER

- Masters Tournament
  Calgary
  403-974-4200
- Canmore Highland Games
  Canmore
  403-678-9454
- BBQ on the Bow / Calgary
  403-264-6450

OCTOBER

- Haunted Pumpkin Festival
  Bon Accord
  780-921-2272
- Great White North Pumpkin
  Fair and Weigh-Off
  Smoky Lake
  780-656-3674
- Rocky Mountain Wine and
  Food Festival / Calgary
  403-261-0101

NOVEMBER

- Spruce Meadows
  International Christmas
  Market / Calgary
  403-974-4200
- Canadian Finals Rodeo
  Edmonton
  888-800-7275
- Banff Mountain Film and
  Book Festival / Banff
  800-413-8368

DECEMBER

- Airdrie Festival of Lights
  Airdrie
  403-948-3249
- A Traditional Christmas
  Calgary
  403-571-0849
- Once Upon a Christmas at
  Heritage Park / Calgary
  403-268-8500

Banff Gondola

Cave and Basin National Historic Site, Banff National Park

Moraine Lake, Banff National Park

Lake Minnewanka, Banff National Park

Lilac Festival at 4th Street, Calgary

Index: Great Experience for Members

AAA editor's picks of exceptional note

Calgary Tower

TELUS World of
Science—Edmonton

Lake Louise

Icefields Parkway
(Hwy. 93)

See Orientation map on p. 20 for corresponding grid coordinates, if applicable.
*Indicates the GEM is temporarily closed.

Get maps, travel information and road service with the AAA and CAA Mobile apps

Alberta
Atlas Section

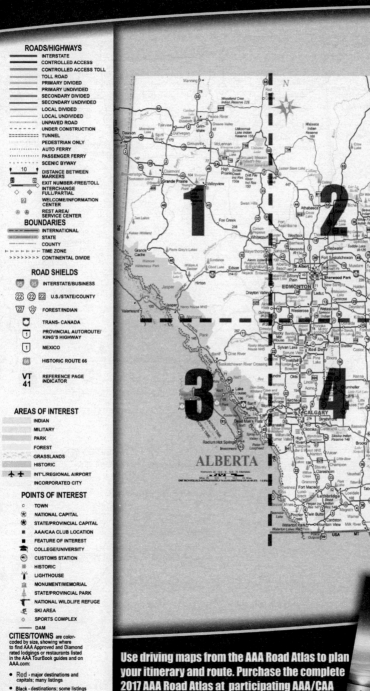

ROADS/HIGHWAYS
- INTERSTATE
- CONTROLLED ACCESS
- CONTROLLED ACCESS TOLL
- TOLL ROAD
- PRIMARY DIVIDED
- PRIMARY UNDIVIDED
- SECONDARY DIVIDED
- SECONDARY UNDIVIDED
- LOCAL DIVIDED
- LOCAL UNDIVIDED
- UNPAVED ROAD
- UNDER CONSTRUCTION
- TUNNEL
- PEDESTRIAN ONLY
- AUTO FERRY
- PASSENGER FERRY
- SCENIC BYWAY
- DISTANCE BETWEEN MARKERS
- EXIT NUMBER-FREE/TOLL
- INTERCHANGE FULL/PARTIAL
- WELCOME/INFORMATION CENTER
- REST AREA/ SERVICE CENTER

BOUNDARIES
- INTERNATIONAL
- STATE
- COUNTY
- TIME ZONE
- CONTINENTAL DIVIDE

ROAD SHIELDS
- 95 / 95 INTERSTATE/BUSINESS
- 22 / 22 / 22 U.S./STATE/COUNTY
- 127 / 27 FOREST/INDIAN
- TRANS- CANADA
- PROVINCIAL AUTOROUTE/ KING'S HIGHWAY
- 1 MEXICO
- 66 HISTORIC ROUTE 66
- VT 41 REFERENCE PAGE INDICATOR

AREAS OF INTEREST
- INDIAN
- MILITARY
- PARK
- FOREST
- GRASSLANDS
- HISTORIC
- ✈ INT'L/REGIONAL AIRPORT
- INCORPORATED CITY

POINTS OF INTEREST
- ○ TOWN
- ✹ NATIONAL CAPITAL
- ✹ STATE/PROVINCIAL CAPITAL
- ■ AAA/CAA CLUB LOCATION
- ■ FEATURE OF INTEREST
- COLLEGE/UNIVERSITY
- CUSTOMS STATION
- HISTORIC
- LIGHTHOUSE
- MONUMENT/MEMORIAL
- STATE/PROVINCIAL PARK
- NATIONAL WILDLIFE REFUGE
- SKI AREA
- SPORTS COMPLEX
- DAM

CITIES/TOWNS are color-coded by size, showing where to find AAA Approved and Diamond rated lodgings or restaurants listed in the AAA TourBook guides and on AAA.com.
- ● Red - major destinations and capitals; many listings
- ● Black - destinations; some listings
- ● Grey - no listings

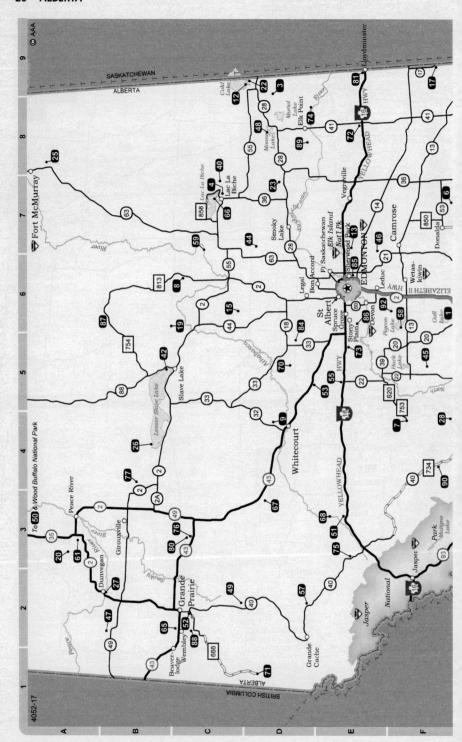

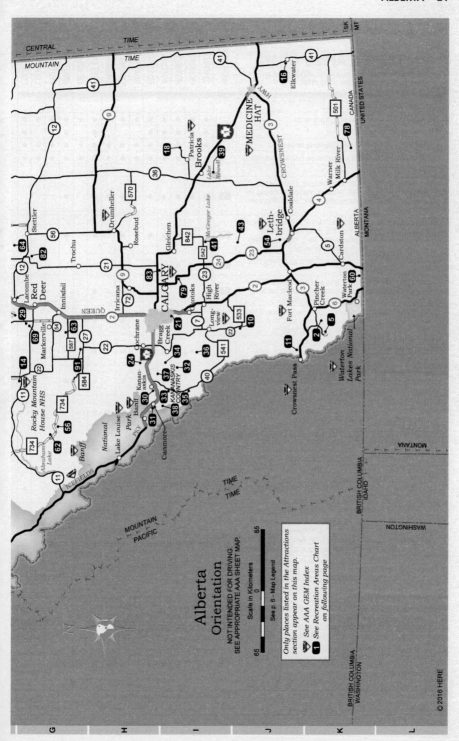

Alberta
Orientation
NOT INTENDED FOR DRIVING.
SEE APPROPRIATE AAA SHEET MAP.

Scale in Kilometers
65   0   65

See p. 6 Map Legend

*Only places listed in the Attractions
section appear on this map.*

🔻 See AAA GEM Index

1 See Recreation Areas Chart
on following page

© 2016 HERE

Recreation Areas Chart

The map location numerals in column 2 show an area's location on the preceding map.

	MAP LOCATION	CAMPING	PICNICKING	HIKING TRAILS	BOATING	BOAT RAMP	BOAT RENTAL	FISHING	SWIMMING	PETS ON LEASH	BICYCLE TRAILS	WINTER SPORTS	VISITOR CENTER	LODGE/CABINS	FOOD SERVICE
NATIONAL PARKS *(See place listings.)*															
Banff (G-5) 6,641 square kilometres. Horse rental.		•	•	•	•	•	•	•	•	•	•	•	•	•	•
Elk Island (E-7) 194 square kilometres.		•	•	•	•	•				•			•	•	•
Jasper (E-2) 11,228 square kilometres. Horse rental.		•	•	•	•	•	•	•	•	•	•	•	•	•	•
Waterton Lakes (K-5) 505 square kilometres. Golf; horse rental.		•	•	•	•	•	•	•	•	•		•	•	•	•
PROVINCIAL															
Aspen Beach (F-6) 214 hectares on Gull Lake, 17 km w. of Lacombe on Hwy. 12. Baseball, canoeing, cross-country skiing, ice fishing, kayaking, powerboating, water skiing, windsurfing; swimming beach.	**1**	•	•	•	•	•		•	•	•		•			
Beauvais Lake (K-5) 1,160 hectares 11 km w. of Pincher Creek on Hwy. 507, then 8 km s. on Hwy. 775. Backcountry camping, bird-watching, canoeing, cross-country skiing, ice fishing, kayaking, snowshoeing, windsurfing, winter camping.	**2**	•	•	•	•	•		•		•		•			
Beaverdam (D-9) 110 hectares 5 km e. of Nordegg on Hwy. 11. Canoeing, kayaking.	**3**	•	•	•				•		•					
Beaver Lake (C-7) 96 hectares 6 km s.e. of Lac La Biche off Hwy. 36, on the n.e. shore of Beaver Lake. Bird-watching, canoeing, kayaking, water skiing, windsurfing; swimming beach.	**4**	•			•	•	•	•	•	•					
Beaver Mines Lake (K-6) 118 hectares 20 km w. of Pincher Creek on Hwy. 507, 10 km s.w. on Hwy. 774, then 5 km s. on access road. Canoeing, horseback riding, ice fishing, kayaking.	**5**	•		•	•	•		•		•					
Big Knife (F-7) 295 hectares 8 km w. and 13 km s. of Forestburg on Hwy. 855. Canoeing, cross-country skiing, kayaking, snowshoeing; horseshoe pitch, playground.	**6**	•	•	•	•			•		•		•			
Brazeau Reservoir (F-4) 130 hectares 60 km s.w. of Drayton Valley along Hwy. 620. Bird-watching, canoeing, kayaking, sailing, water skiing, windsurfing.	**7**	•			•	•		•		•					
Calling Lake (C-6) 738 hectares 55 km n. of Athabasca on Hwy. 813. Bird-watching, canoeing, kayaking, powerboating, sailing, water skiing, water skiing, windsurfing; playground.	**8**	•	•		•	•		•	•	•			•		
Carson-Pegasus (D-4) 1,209 hectares 6 km w. of Whitecourt on Hwy. 43, 11 km n. on Hwy. 32, then 5 km e. on access road. Bird-watching, canoeing, cross-country skiing, ice fishing, kayaking, snowmobiling, wildlife observation; amphitheater, swimming beach.	**9**	•	•	•	•	•	•	•	•	•		•			•
Chain Lakes (J-6) 409 hectares 38 km s.w. of Nanton on Hwy. 533. Canoeing, ice fishing, kayaking, sailing, powerboating, windsurfing; horseshoe pitch, swimming beach.	**10**	•	•		•	•		•	•	•		•			
Chinook (J-5) 48 hectares 8 km w. of Crowsnest Pass off Hwy. 3. Canoeing, cross-country skiing, kayaking.	**11**	•	•	•				•		•	•	•			
Cold Lake (C-8) 5,849 hectares 3 km n.e. of Cold Lake off Hwy. 28. Bird-watching, canoeing, cross-country skiing, ice fishing, kayaking, sailing, water skiing, windsurfing; amphitheater, interpretive programs.	**12**	•	•	•	•	•		•	•	•		•	•		
Cooking Lake-Blackfoot (E-7) 9,700 hectares 24 km e. of Sherwood Park s. of Hwy. 16. Bird-watching, canoeing, cross-country skiing, dog sledding, horseback riding, hunting, ice-skating, kayaking, snowmobiling.	**13**	•	•							•	•	•			
Crimson Lake (G-5) 3,209 hectares 14 km w. of Rocky Mountain House on Hwy. 11, then 6 km n. on Hwy. 756. Bird-watching, canoeing, cross-country skiing, ice fishing, kayaking, sailing, volleyball, water skiing, windsurfing; horseshoe pitch, interpretive programs.	**14**	•		•	•	•		•	•	•					•
Cross Lake (C-6) 2,076 hectares 8 km n. and 19 km n.e. of Jarvie off Hwy. 663. Bird-watching, canoeing, cross-country skiing, ice fishing, kayaking, water skiing, windsurfing; horseshoe pitch.	**15**	•		•	•	•		•	•	•		•			
Cypress Hills (J-9) 20,451 hectares 1.5 km s. of Elkwater on Hwy. 41. Historic. Canoeing, cross-country skiing, golf, kayaking, sailing, windsurfing; amphitheater, interpretive programs.	**16**	•	•	•	•	•	•	•	•	•		•	•	•	•

Recreation Areas Chart

The map location numerals in column 2 show an area's location on the preceding map.

	MAP LOCATION	CAMPING	PICNICKING	HIKING TRAILS	BOATING	BOAT RAMP	BOAT RENTAL	FISHING	SWIMMING	PETS ON LEASH	BICYCLE TRAILS	WINTER SPORTS	VISITOR CENTER	LODGE/CABINS	FOOD SERVICE
Dillberry Lake (F-9) 1,205 hectares 15 km s.e. of Chauvin on Hwy. 17 at Alberta/Saskatchewan border. Bird-watching, canoeing, cross-country skiing, ice fishing, kayaking, powerboating, sailing, snowshoeing, windsurfing; playground, swimming beach.	17	•	•	•	•	•	•		•	•	•		•		
Dinosaur (I-8) 8,085 hectares 13 km n.e. of Patricia via Hwy. 210. Historic. Bird-watching, canoeing, kayaking, winter camping; amphitheater, interpretive programs.	18	•	•	•	•					•		•	•		•
Fawcett Lake (West) (C-6) 48 hectares 55 km s.e. of Slave Lake on Hwy. 2, 20 km n. on Hwy. 2A, then 18 km n. on access road. Canoeing, kayaking, snowmobiling; swimming beach.	19	•	•		•	•	•		•	•		•			
Figure Eight Lake (A-3) 90 hectares 25 km w. of Peace River off Hwy. 35. Canoeing, cross-country skiing, dog sledding, ice fishing, kayaking, snowmobiling, windsurfing.	20	•	•	•	•	•			•	•	•	•			
Fish Creek (I-6) 1,355 hectares in Calgary between 37th St. S.W. and the Bow River. Bird-watching, golf; amphitheater, beach, interpretive programs, playground.	21		•	•	•	•			•	•	•		•		•
French Bay (D-9) 449 hectares 11 km e. and 3 km n. of Cold Lake off Hwy. 55. Canoeing, skiing, kayaking, powerboating, sailing, water skiing, windsurfing; swimming beach.	22	•			•	•	•	•	•	•		•			
Garner Lake (D-7) 74 hectares 5 km n. of Spedden off Hwy. 28. Canoeing, cross-country skiing, ice fishing, kayaking, powerboating, sailing, volleyball, water skiing, windsurfing; swimming beach.	23	•	•	•	•	•		•	•	•		•			
Ghost Reservoir (H-5) 24 hectares 18 km w. of Cochrane on Hwy. 1A. Canoeing, ice fishing, kayaking, sailing, water skiing, windsurfing.	24	•	•		•	•	•	•		•		•			
Gregoire Lake (A-8) 696 hectares 19 km s. of Fort McMurray on Hwy. 63, then 10 km e. on Hwy. 881. Canoeing, cross-country skiing, ice fishing, sailing, snowmobiling, water skiing, windsurfing; horseshoe pitch, playground.	25	•	•	•	•	•		•	•	•		•			
Hilliard's Bay (B-4) 2,323 hectares 10 km e. of Grouard off Hwy. 750. Canoeing, ice fishing, kayaking, powerboating, sailing, water skiing, windsurfing; horseshoe pitch, playground, swimming beach.	26	•		•	•	•		•	•	•	•	•			
Historic Dunvegan (B-2) 9 hectares off Queen Elizabeth II Hwy. on the n. side of the Peace River beside Dunvegan Suspension Bridge. Historic. Canoeing, kayaking, wildlife viewing; playground.	27	•	•		•			•		•			•		
Jackfish Lake (F-4) 203 hectares 50 km w. of Rocky Mountain House on Hwy. 11, then 2 km n. on access road. Canoeing, ice fishing, kayaking, powerboating, snowmobiling.	28	•			•	•		•	•	•	•	•			
Jarvis Bay (G-6) 86 hectares 4 km n. of Sylvan Lake townsite on Hwy. 20. Cross-country skiing, snowshoeing; pier, playground.	29	•		•				•		•					
Kananaskis Country (I-4)															
Bow Valley (H-5) 3,129 hectares 25 km e. of Canmore on Hwy. 1 and .5 km n. on Hwy. 1X. Backcountry camping, canoeing, horseback riding, hunting, kayaking, rock climbing, snowshoeing.	30	•		•				•		•		•			•
Canmore Nordic Centre (H-4) 804 hectares 3 km s. of Canmore on Spray Lakes Rd. Cross-country skiing, disc golf, ice-skating, roller skating.	31		•	•						•	•	•	•	•	•
Elbow River (I-5) 245 hectares 20 km w. of Bragg Creek on Hwy. 66. Horseback riding; interpretive programs, playground.	32	•	•	•				•		•	•				
Evan-Thomas (I-5) 2,571 hectares 30 km e. of Canmore on Spray Lakes Rd. Cross-country skiing, horseback riding, hunting.	33			•				•		•				•	
Mclean Creek (I-5) 238 hectares 12 km w. of Bragg Creek on Hwy. 66, then 1.3 km s. on McLean Creek Trail. Snowmobiling.	34	•						•		•					
Peter Lougheed (I-5) 50,142 hectares 43 km s.e. of Canmore on Hwy. 40. Canoeing, cross-country skiing, ice fishing, kayaking, powerboating, sailing, snowshoeing, windsurfing; interpretive programs, playground.	35	•	•	•	•	•	•		•		•	•	•	•	•

Recreation Areas Chart

The map location numerals in column 2 show an area's location on the preceding map.

	MAP LOCATION	CAMPING	PICNICKING	HIKING TRAILS	BOATING	BOAT RAMP	BOAT RENTAL	FISHING	SWIMMING	PETS ON LEASH	BICYCLE TRAILS	WINTER SPORTS	VISITOR CENTER	LODGE/CABINS	FOOD SERVICE
Sheep River (I-5) 6,191 hectares 25 km w. of Turner Valley on Hwy. 546. Cross-country skiing, horseback riding, ice-skating.	36	●		●				●		●	●	●			
Sibbald Lake (I-5) 79 hectares 30 km e. of Canmore on Hwy. 1, 6 km s. on Hwy. 40, then 12 km e. on Hwy. 68. Canoeing, kayaking.	37	●	●	●				●		●		●			
Spray Valley (I-5) 27,471 hectares s.w. of Canmore, surrounding the Spray Lakes Reservoir. Backcountry camping, canoeing, cross-country skiing, ice fishing, kayaking, powerboating, sailing, windsurfing; interpretive programs.	38	●	●	●	●	●		●		●		●			
Kinbrook Island (I-8) 540 hectares 13 km s. of Brooks off Hwy. 873. Bird-watching, canoeing, cross-country skiing, ice fishing, ice-skating, kayaking, powerboating, sailing, snowmobiling, volleyball, water skiing, windsurfing; playground.	39	●			●	●		●	●	●	●				●
Lakeland (C-8) 59,030 hectares 13 km e. of Lac La Biche off Hwy. 663. Bird-watching, canoeing, dog sledding, ice fishing, kayaking, sailing, snowmobiling, snowshoeing, water skiing, windsurfing, winter camping; swimming beach.	40	●	●	●	●	●	●		●	●	●				●
Lake McGregor (I-7) 140 hectares 20 km n. of Vulcan on Hwy. 23, then 25 km e. on Hwy. 542. Bird-watching, canoeing, ice fishing, kayaking, powerboating, sailing, water skiing, windsurfing.	41	●			●	●		●	●	●					
Lesser Slave Lake (B-5) 7,566 hectares 6 km n. of Slave Lake on Hwy. 88. Bird-watching, cross-country skiing, ice fishing, sailing, snowshoeing, water skiing, windsurfing; horseshoe pitch, interpretive programs.	42	●	●	●	●			●	●	●		●			
Little Bow (J-7) 110 hectares 20 km s. of Vulcan on Hwy. 23, 16 km e. on Hwy. 529, then 1 km s. on access road. Bird-watching, canoeing, hunting, ice fishing, kayaking, powerboating, sailing, water skiing, windsurfing; horseshoe pitch, swimming beach.	43	●	●		●	●	●	●	●	●		●			●
Long Lake (D-7) 769 hectares 20 km s. of Boyle on Hwy. 831, then 2 km n.e. on access road. Canoeing, cross-country skiing, downhill skiing, skiing, golf (adjacent to park), ice fishing, kayaking, powerboating, sailing, snowmobiling, water skiing, windsurfing; horseshoe pitch.	44	●		●	●	●		●	●	●	●				●
Medicine Lake (F-5) 24 hectares 47 km n. of Rocky Mountain House on Hwy. 22, then 8 km s.e. on access road. Canoeing, kayaking, powerboating; horseshoe pitch, playground.	45	●	●		●			●	●	●					
Miquelon Lake (E-7) 1,299 hectares 3 km s. of New Sarepta on Hwy. 21, then 20 km e. on Hwy. 623. Baseball, bird-watching, canoeing, cross-country skiing, golf (adjacent to park), ice-skating, kayaking, sailing, snowshoeing, windsurfing, winter camping; horseshoe pitch, interpretive programs, swimming beach.	46	●	●	●				●	●			●	●		
Moonshine Lake (B-2) 1,103 hectares 27 km w. of Spirit River on Hwy. 49, then 7 km n. on Hwy. 725. Baseball, bird-watching, canoeing, cross-country skiing, ice fishing, ice-skating, power-boating, sailing, snowshoeing, windsurfing; horseshoe pitch, interpretive programs, playground, swimming beach.	47	●		●	●			●	●	●		●	●		
Moose Lake (D-8) 736 hectares 5 km n. of Bonnyville on Hwy. 41, 10 km w. on Hwy. 660, then 2 km s. on access road. Canoeing, kayaking, sailing, water skiing, windsurfing; swimming beach.	48	●	●	●	●	●		●	●	●					
Musreau Lake (C-2) 1,803 hectares 80 km s. of Grande Prairie on Hwy. 40, then 2 km e. on access road. Canoeing, kayaking, powerboating; swimming beach.	49	●	●		●			●	●	●					
Notikewin (A-3) 9,697 hectares 37 km n. of Manning via Hwy. 35, then 30 km e. on Hwy. 692. Bird-watching, canoeing, cross-country skiing, golf, kayaking, powerboating; swimming beach.	50	●	●	●	●			●	●				●		
Obed Lake (E-3) 3,402 hectares 55 km w. of Edson off Hwy. 16. Canoeing, ice fishing, kayaking, powerboating.	51	●			●	●		●							
O'Brien (C-2) 65 hectares 10 km s. of Grande Prairie on Hwy. 40. Canoeing, kayaking, powerboating; swimming beach.	52		●		●	●		●	●	●					
Paddle River Dam (E-5) 70 hectares 10 km n.w. of Sangudo on Hwy. 43. Canoeing, ice fishing, kayaking, powerboating, sailing, snowmobiling, tobogganing, water skiing, windsurfing.	53		●		●	●		●	●	●		●			

Recreation Areas Chart

The map location numerals in column 2 show an area's location on the preceding map.

	MAP LOCATION	CAMPING	PICNICKING	HIKING TRAILS	BOATING	BOAT RAMP	BOAT RENTAL	FISHING	SWIMMING	PETS ON LEASH	BICYCLE TRAILS	WINTER SPORTS	VISITOR CENTER	LODGE/CABINS	FOOD SERVICE
Park Lake (J-7) 224 hectares 17 km n.w. of Lethbridge on Hwy. 25, then 5 km n.w. on Hwy. 101. Canoeing, ice fishing, kayaking, sailing; playground, swimming beach.	54	•	•	•	•	•	•	•	•	•	•	•	•		
Pembina River (E-5) 167 hectares 2 km n.e. of Entwistle on Hwy. 16A. Canoeing, kayaking, volleyball.	55	•	•	•				•	•	•					
Peppers Lake (G-4) 18 hectares 84 km s.e. of Nordegg on Forestry Trunk Rd. (Hwy. 734). Canoeing, horseback riding, kayaking, powerboating.	56	•		•				•		•					
Pierre Grey's Lakes (D-2) 633 hectares 37 km s. of Grande Cache off Hwy. 40 on access road. Historic. Canoeing, ice fishing, kayaking, powerboating, snowmobiling, water skiing; swimming beach.	57	•	•	•	•	•		•	•	•		•			
Pigeon Lake (F-6) 443 hectares 5 km w. and 10 km n. of Westerose off Hwy. 771. Canoeing, cross-country skiing, ice fishing, kayaking, powerboating, sailing, snowmobiling, water skiing, windsurfing; horseshoe pitch, playground, swimming beach.	58	•	•	•	•	•		•	•	•	•	•	•		•
Poacher's Landing (C-7) 1,518 hectares 35 km n.e. of Athabasca on Hwy. 55, then 25 km n. on access road. Horseback riding; horse corrals, playground.	59	•	•	•				•		•					
Police Outpost (K-6) 223 hectares 10 km s. and 23 km w. of Cardston on Queen Elizabeth II Hwy. Bird-watching, canoeing, cross-country skiing, kayaking, powerboating; playground.	60	•	•	•	•	•		•		•		•			
Queen Elizabeth (A-3) 86 hectares 3 km n. and 5 km w. of Grimshaw off Hwy. 35. Bird-watching, canoeing, cross-country skiing, kayaking, powerboating, sailing, snowmobiling, snowshoeing, volleyball, water skiing, windsurfing, winter camping; horseshoe pitch, swimming beach.	61	•	•	•	•	•				•		•			
Ram Falls (G-4) 409 hectares 64 km s. of Nordegg on Forestry Trunk Rd. (Hwy. 734). Cross-country skiing, snowmobiling.	62	•	•	•						•		•			
Red Lodge (G-6) 129 hectares 15 km w. of Bowden on Hwy. 587. Canoeing, kayaking; horseshoe pitch.	63	•	•					•	•	•					
Rochon Sands (G-7) 119 hectares 12 km w. of Stettler on Hwy. 12, then 16 km n. on Hwy. 835. Bird-watching, canoeing, kayaking, powerboating, sailing, water skiing, windsurfing; swimming beach.	64	•	•		•			•		•					
Saskatoon Island (B-2) 101 hectares 21 km w. of Grande Prairie on Hwy. 43, then 4 km n. on an access road. Baseball, bird watching, canoeing, cross-country skiing, kayaking, snowshoeing, volleyball; interpretive programs, horseshoe pitch.	65	•	•	•	•	•				•	•	•			
Sir Winston Churchill (C-7) 662 hectares 11 km n.e. of Lac La Biche off Hwy. 881. Bird-watching, canoeing, cross-country skiing, kayaking, powerboating, sailing, snowshoeing, water skiing, windsurfing; interpretive programs, swimming beach.	66	•	•	•	•	•		•	•	•		•			
Smoke Lake (D-3) 102 hectares 9 km s.w. of Fox Creek off Hwy. 43. Canoeing, ice fishing, kayaking, snowmobiling, water skiing; swimming beach.	67				•	•		•	•	•		•			
Sundance (E-3) 151 hectares 56 km n.e. of Hinton on Emerson Creek Rd. Canoeing, ice fishing, kayaking, powerboating (electric motors only), snowmobiling.	68	•		•	•			•		•		•			
Sylvan Lake (G-5) 67 hectares 18 km n.w. of Red Deer on Hwy. 11 in the town of Sylvan Lake. Canoeing, golf, ice fishing, ice-skating, kayaking, powerboating, sailing, water skiing, windsurfing; swimming beach.	69		•		•			•	•	•			•		•
Thunder Lake (D-5) 208 hectares 21 km w. of Barrhead on Hwy. 18. Baseball, canoeing, ice fishing, kayaking, sailing, volleyball, water skiing, windsurfing; beach, playground.	70	•	•		•	•		•		•		•			
Two Lakes (D-1) 1,566 hectares 130 km s.w. of Grande Prairie on Two Lakes Rd. Canoeing, ice fishing, kayaking, powerboating.	71	•		•	•			•		•	•	•			
Vermilion (E-8) 759 hectares 1.5 km n. of Vermilion on Hwy. 41 from jct. Hwy. 16, then w. on 50th Ave. following signs. Baseball, canoeing, cross-country skiing, ice fishing, kayaking, sailing, tobogganing, winter camping.	72	•	•	•				•		•		•			

Recreation Areas Chart

The map location numerals in column 2 show an area's location on the preceding map.

Area	MAP LOCATION	CAMPING	PICNICKING	HIKING TRAILS	BOATING	BOAT RAMP	BOAT RENTAL	FISHING	SWIMMING	PETS ON LEASH	BICYCLE TRAILS	WINTER SPORTS	VISITOR CENTER	LODGE/CABINS	FOOD SERVICE
Wabamun Lake (E-5) 231 hectares 3 km e. and 1 km s. of Wabamun off Hwy. 16A. Baseball, bird-watching, canoeing, kayaking, sailing, water skiing, windsurfing.	73	●	●	●	●	●	●	●	●	●					
Whitney Lakes (D-8) 1,489 hectares 24 km e. of Elk Point off Hwy. 646. Historic. Bird-watching, canoeing, cross-country skiing, ice fishing, kayaking, powerboating, sailing, volleyball, water skiing, windsurfing; beach, horseshoe pitch, playground.	74	●	●	●	●	●	●	●	●	●	●	●	●		
William A. Switzer (E-3) 6,268 hectares 3 km w. of Hinton on Hwy. 16, then 19 km n. on Hwy. 40. Historic. Bird-watching, canoeing, cross-country skiing, ice fishing, kayaking, powerboating, winter camping; interpretive programs, swimming beach.	75	●	●	●	●	●	●	●	●	●	●	●	●	●	●
Williamson (C-3) 17 hectares 17 km w. of Valleyview on Hwy. 43, then 2 km n. on an access road. Canoeing, ice fishing, kayaking, sailing, snowmobiling, water skiing, windsurfing; horseshoe pitch, swimming beach.	76	●	●		●	●		●	●	●		●			
Winagami Lake (B-4) 6,542 hectares 20 km n. of High Prairie on Hwy. 749, 10 km w. on Hwy. 679, then 7 km n. on access road. Bird-watching, canoeing, cross-country skiing, ice fishing, kayaking, powerboating, sailing, snowshoeing, water skiing, windsurfing; playground, swimming beach.	77	●	●	●	●	●	●	●	●	●		●			
Writing-on-Stone (K-8) 1,718 hectares 35 km e. of Milk River off Hwy. 501. Historic. Bird-watching, canoeing, kayaking; interpretive programs.	78	●	●	●	●			●	●	●			●		
Wyndham-Carseland (I-6) 178 hectares 2 km e. and 2 km s. of Carseland on Hwy. 24. Canoeing, cross-country skiing, kayaking; horseshoe pitch, playground.	79	●	●	●	●	●		●	●	●		●			
Young's Point (B-3) 3,072 hectares 26 km w. of Valleyview on Hwy. 43, then 10 km n.e. on an access road. Canoeing, cross-country skiing, ice fishing, kayaking, sailing, snowshoeing, water skiing, windsurfing; beach, horseshoe pitch.	80	●	●	●	●	●	●	●	●	●		●			
OTHER															
Bud Miller All Seasons Park (E-9) 81 hectares at 2902 59th Ave. in Lloydminster. Bird-watching, cross-country skiing, disc golf, ice-skating, lawn bowling, miniature golf, soccer, tennis, volleyball; aquatic complex, horseshoe pitch, indoor pool, interpretive trails, playgrounds, skateboard park.	81		●	●					●	●		●	●		
Content Bridge (G-6) 12 hectares 6 km s. of Nevis on Hwy. 21. Baseball, canoeing, kayaking.	82	●	●		●			●							
Eagle Lake Park (H-6) 7 km e. and 6 km s. of Strathmore via Hwy. 1. Horseshoe pitch, playground.	83	●	●		●	●	●	●	●	●					●
Elks Beach (D-6) 14 km s. of Barrhead on Hwy. 33, then e. on Hwy. 651. Cross-country skiing, ice fishing; playground.	84	●	●		●	●		●	●	●	●				●
Half Moon Lake (E-6) 4 hectares 3 km e. of Sherwood Park on Hwy. 630. Canoeing, kayaking; beach, horseshoe pitch, paddleboats.	85	●	●	●	●		●	●	●	●					●
Hasse Lake (E-6) 81 hectares 5 km w. and 10 km s. of Stony Plain on Hwy. 16. Basketball, cross-country skiing, golf, volleyball; beach, playground.	86		●	●	●			●	●	●			●		
North Wabasca (B-6) 77 hectares 38 km n. of Slave Lake on Hwy. 88, 100 km n.e. on Hwy. 754, then 7 km. n. on access road.	87	●	●	●	●	●	●	●	●	●					
Pipestone Creek (C-2) 15 km s. of Wembley. Disc golf; dinosaur museum, interpretive trails, horseshoe pitch, playground.	88	●	●	●	●			●	●				●		
Stoney Lake (D-8) 158 hectares on Stony Lake, 16 km s.w. of Elk Point off Hwy. 646. Playground.	89	●	●	●	●			●	●	●					
Upper Shunda Creek (F-4) 47 hectares 3 km w. of Nordegg off Hwy. 11.	90	●		●				●				●	●		
Westward Ho (G-5) 8 km e. of Sundre on Hwy. 27. Baseball, canoeing, kayaking, volleyball; beach, horseshoe pitch, playgrounds.	91	●	●		●			●	●	●					●
Wizard Lake (E-6) 33 hectares 19 km s. of Calmar on Hwy. 795. Canoeing; playground, swimming beach.	92	●	●		●	●		●	●	●					●

AIRDRIE pop. 42,564, elev. 1,077m/3,533'
• Part of Calgary area — see map p. 42

BEST WESTERN AIRDRIE (403)948-3838

Hotel
$125-$200

 Best Western. **AAA Benefit:** Save 10% or more every day and earn 10% bonus points!

Address: 121 Edmonton Tr SE T4B 1S2 **Location:** Hwy 2 exit Airdrie/Irricana, just w, then 0.5 mi (0.9 km) s. **Facility:** 60 units. 3 stories, interior/exterior corridors. **Parking:** winter plug-ins. **Terms:** cancellation fee imposed. **Activities:** hot tub, exercise room. **Guest Services:** coin laundry.

COMFORT INN & SUITES AIRDRIE (403)948-3411

Hotel
$100-$143

Address: 133 Sierra Springs Dr SE T4B 3G7 **Location:** Hwy 2 exit 282 (Yankee Valley Blvd), just w. **Facility:** 103 units. 4 stories, interior corridors. **Parking:** winter plug-ins. **Terms:** check-in 4 pm. **Pool(s):** heated indoor. **Activities:** sauna, exercise room. **Guest Services:** valet and coin laundry. **Featured Amenity:** breakfast buffet.

HAMPTON INN & SUITES AIRDRIE (403)980-4477
Hotel. **Address:** 52 E Lake Ave NE T4A 2G8
AAA Benefit: Members save up to 10%!

HOLIDAY INN EXPRESS & SUITES AIRDRIE-CALGARY NORTH (403)912-1952
Hotel. **Address:** 64 E Lake Ave NE T4A 2G8

SUPER 8 AIRDRIE (403)948-4188
Hotel. **Address:** 815 E Lake Blvd T4A 2G4

WINGATE BY WYNDHAM AIRDRIE (587)775-6171
Hotel. **Address:** 513 Gateway Rd NE T4B 0J6

WHERE TO EAT

MR MIKES STEAKHOUSECASUAL 403/948-3701
American. Casual Dining. **Address:** 130 Sierra Springs Dr T4B 3G6

SMITTY'S 403/945-1225
American. Casual Dining. **Address:** 191 E Lake Cres T4A 1H3

SUSHI HARU 403/948-6373
Japanese Sushi. Casual Dining. **Address:** 400 Main St N, #100 T4B 1E1

ATHABASCA pop. 2,990

THE 49TH STREET GRILL 780/675-5418
International. Casual Dining. **Address:** 4901 49th St T9S 1C5

BANFF NATIONAL PARK (G-5)
• Attractions map p. 30

Elevations in the park range from 1,326
metres (4,350 ft.) around the Bow River to
3,612 metres (11,851 ft.) at Mount Forbes.
Refer to CAA/AAA maps for additional
elevation information.

Banff National Park sprawls across the jagged
backs of the Rocky Mountains, offering some of the
most beautiful alpine scenery in the world. It is a
land of breathtaking vistas no photo can do justice
to—no matter how gifted the photographer. Craggy,
snow-capped peaks encircle forested valleys and
glacier-fed lakes. Sheltered meadows wear a glorious mantle of wildflowers, vibrant with fireweed, Indian paintbrush, columbine and anemone. Rushing
streams sparkle in the crisp mountain air, flowing
through forests of lodgepole pine and Douglas fir.

Banff was established in 1885, 2 years after railway
workers discovered a misty cave containing thermal
springs, a find that led to a legal battle over who would
develop the springs as a bathing resort. The conflict
was resolved when the Canadian government set
aside the rugged land for the benefit of all its citizens,
creating what would become the country's first national park. Although bathing in these mineral springs
is no longer permitted, you can still see the natural
grotto where it all began at Cave and Basin National
Historic Site *(see attraction listing p. 32)*.

To attract wealthy tourists, the Canadian Pacific
Railway built the luxurious Banff Springs Hotel in 1888.
The castle-like stone-and-concrete building you see
today replaced the original wooden hotel after it
burned in 1926, but the idea of providing guests with
opulent accommodations while they enjoy the area's
scenic beauty remains unchanged. The image of the
hotel's stately, high-peaked roofline rising above the
surrounding evergreens is a fixture on postcards.

Known today as The Fairmont Banff Springs, the
hotel stands on the outskirts of the charming resort

This map shows cities in Banff
National Park where you will
find attractions, hotels and
restaurants. Cities are listed
alphabetically in this book on
the following pages.

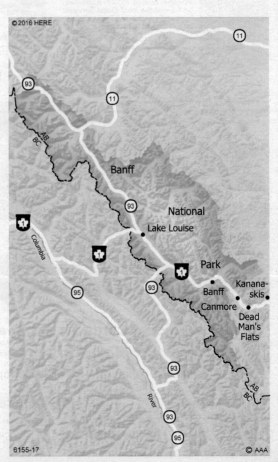

©2016 HERE

6155-17   © AAA

town of Banff *(see place listing p. 31)*, where most development within the park is focused and where you'll find the largest number of hotels. Rustic mountain lodge-style buildings house boutiques, sporting goods stores, gift shops and restaurants. In spring and summer the sidewalks—radiant with colorful annuals planted in window boxes and hanging baskets—are crowded with visitors; in winter the streets in the town center can be just as packed as in warm-weather months with the difference being roof racks now carry skis and winter gear instead of canoes and kayaks.

The village of Lake Louise *(see place listing p. 129)* is the park's second most developed area, where you'll find a small shopping center, cafes, hotels and a ski resort. The community takes its name from the beautiful lake nearby, which is fed by meltwater from Victoria Glacier. The runoff carries finely ground rock flour that gives the lake a striking milky turquoise color you'll see in the area's other glacially fed lakes. Facing the glacier on the opposite shore is The Fairmont Chateau Lake Louise, a grand hotel with more than 500 rooms. The hotel, lake and glacier together create one of the most photographed settings in the park.

Another highlight of Banff National Park is Bow Valley Parkway *(see attraction listing)*, a scenic roadway that parallels Trans-Canada Highway (Hwy. 1), connecting the towns of Banff and Lake Louise. Nestled in Valley of the Ten Peaks, Moraine Lake *(see attraction listing p. 31)* dazzles visitors with its sparkling blue waters, earning it the nickname, "Jewel of the Rockies."

Other sights for which the park is famous: Johnston Canyon *(see attraction listing p. 31)*, Crow Foot Glacier, the sawtooth profile of Mount Rundle reflected in the clear waters of Vermilion Lakes and, in winter, the frozen waterfall known as Weeping Wall. And while you make your way among these scenic points, you'll likely encounter Banff's abundant wildlife. Elk, deer and bighorn sheep are most common, and if you have binoculars you may catch sight of mountain goats and moose in the distance. If you should spot them, you may want to steer clear of the area's predators: bears, wolves, coyotes and lynx, but odds are they'll want to keep their distance from you, too.

General Information and Activities

The park, which is open all year, has about 354 kilometres (219 mi.) of scenic roads. Hwy. 1 to Vancouver and Calgary and Hwy. 93S (Banff-Windermere Hwy.) are open year-round, as is the northern end of Hwy. 93N (Icefields Parkway) from Lake Louise to Jasper; check locally for road conditions. One- or multiple-day bus tours of the park's major points of interest also are available.

More than 1,500 kilometres (932 mi.) of trails traverse the park. All activities involving an overnight stay in the backcountry require a wilderness permit that is available for purchase at visitor centers in the Banff and Lake Louise townsites. Some public campgrounds in the park are available on a first-come, first-served basis, but most are available by reservation; phone (877) 737-3783.

Lake Louise's waters, about 4 C (39 F), are too cold for swimming but are ideal for canoeing or kayaking. Motorboats may be used only on Lake Minnewanka. Cruises on Lake Minnewanka are offered during the summer. Skating, skiing, curling and hockey are available in the park in winter.

Park naturalists conduct interpretive programs at major campgrounds most evenings and at key attractions daily throughout the summer. Bankhead, a once-booming mining town 4.8 kilometres (3 mi.) northeast of Banff, has a self-guiding trail with explanatory signs and a mining exhibit.

Special events include the Banff Mountain Film and Book Festival, held late October through early November. From May through August, The Banff Centre, a performing arts venue off Tunnel Mountain Drive in the town of Banff, hosts the 🐾 Banff Summer Arts Festival.

Throughout the summer guides and outfitters offer fishing, hiking and float trips. Saddle horses are available for treks through the mountains to glacier-fed lakes. White-water rafting trips and helicopter tours can be arranged outside the park boundaries in Canmore and in Golden, British Columbia *(see place listings p. 77 and p. 194)*.

Information, interpretive program schedules and backcountry trail tips are available at Banff Visitor Information Centre, (403) 762-1550, 224 Banff Ave., and Lake Louise Visitor Information Centre, (403) 522-3833, 201 Village Rd.; topographical maps and trail guides are sold at both locations. Visitor center hours vary throughout the year; phone ahead for current schedules.

A free public shuttle runs to the viewpoint at Lake Louise July through early September and to Moraine Lake on weekends September 10-25 during larch season. Both shuttles run from Lake Louise Overflow Camping, 5.5 km (3.5 mi.) east of Lake Louise.

Fishing is permitted; national park fishing permits are sold at park visitor centers as well as at some boat concessionaires and tackle shops. Check at the visitor centers in Banff or Lake Louise for a summary of park fishing regulations.

Note: Hunting is strictly prohibited; visitors entering the area must have firearms dismantled. Motorists driving at dusk, dawn and during the nighttime should be attentive for wildlife on roadways. It is not only dangerous but also against national park regulations to feed, approach or harass any wildlife in a national park. *See Recreation Areas Chart.*

ADMISSION to the park is free in 2017 to celebrate Canada's 150th anniversary of Confederation. Otherwise admission is $9.33; $7.90 (ages 65+); $4.67 (ages 6-16); $18.67 (up to seven people arriving in a single vehicle). An annual pass, valid at most Canadian national parks, marine areas and historic sites, is available.

PETS are allowed in the park but must be leashed or physically contained at all times. Pets are restricted in some areas during winter months; phone ahead for more information.

ADDRESS inquiries to the Banff Visitor Centre, 224 Banff Ave., Town of Banff, AB, Canada T1L 1K2; phone (403) 762-1550.

BANFF LAKE CRUISE is on Lake Minnewanka, 8 km (5 mi.) n.e. of the town of Banff on Hwy. 1, then n. 7 km (4 mi.) from the beginning of Lake Minnewanka Loop. The interpretive sightseeing cruises, in glass-enclosed, heated boats, last 1 hour. Rental motorboats, paddleboats and charter fishing tours also are available. Visitors should arrive at least 30 minutes prior to departure time. **Hours:** Sightseeing cruises depart daily on the hour 10-6, early June to mid-Sept.; Mon.-Thurs. at 11, 1, 3, and 5, Fri.-Sun. on the hour 10-5, mid-May to early June; daily on the hour noon-5, mid-Sept. to early Oct. **Cost:** Sightseeing cruise $60; $30 (ages 6-15). **Phone:** (403) 762-6700 or (866) 606-6700. **GT**

BOW VALLEY PARKWAY (HWY. 1A) is 5 km (3 mi.) w. of the town of Banff off Hwy. 1. The parkway, the original road between the town of Banff and the village of Lake Louise, runs along the Bow River parallel to the Trans-Canada Hwy. The parkway's speed limit of 60 kph (37 mph) provides a slower, more scenic alternative to Hwy. 1. Each curve in the road brings postcardlike images of snow-capped mountains.

There are frequent pull-offs with viewpoints, interpretive panels, picnic sites and trailheads. Wildlife such as bears, bighorn sheep, elk and deer frequent the area. **Note:** In order to help protect wildlife, there is a seasonal travel restriction on driving a 17-kilometre (10.5-mi.) section of the parkway between Banff and Johnston Canyon daily 8 p.m.-8 a.m., Mar. 1-June 25. Use Hwy. 1 instead.

ICEFIELDS PARKWAY (HWY. 93) crosses Banff and Jasper national parks. The scenic highway parallels the Continental Divide for 230 kilometres (143 mi.) between Lake Louise and the town of Jasper, passing through a breathtaking landscape

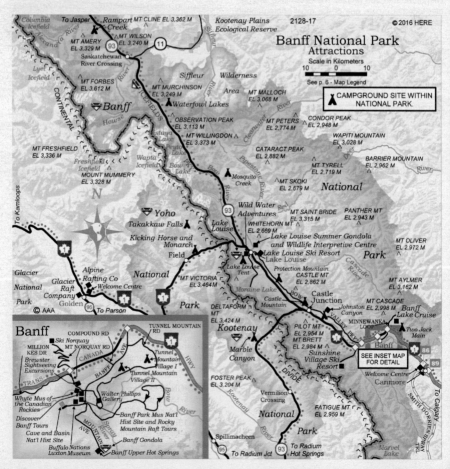

of snowcapped mountains, waterfalls, lakes and rivers. The park's most visited sights are either along the parkway or just a short distance from it. Driving this spectacular route—roughly a 4-hour trip one way—is an experience you shouldn't miss.

The parkway gets its chilly name from the vast bodies of ice you can see along its length, the most impressive being the massive Columbia Icefield *(see attraction listing p. 121)*, source of eight glaciers including the Athabasca Glacier, which is within walking distance of the parkway just inside Jasper National Park *(see place listing p. 120)*. For an up-close look at the glacier, climb aboard a specially designed Ice Explorer snowcoach departing from the Columbia Icefield Glacier Discovery Centre *(see attraction listing p. 121)* for a narrated excursion and walk out onto the glacier's frozen surface.

There are too many scenic overlooks and turnouts along the parkway to name, but some of the most outstanding include Bow Glacier, Peyto Lake from Bow Summit and Saskatchewan River Crossing, where several display panels explain the history of the Howse Pass and the fur trade. Farther north are viewpoints taking in the Weeping Wall, Bridal Veil Falls and Cirrus Mountain.

Many turnouts also serve as trailheads for day hikes to even more panoramas. One of the best: Parker Ridge just south of Banff's northern boundary. The trail leads up to a fantastic vista encompassing a narrow river valley with the Saskatchewan Glacier at one end. In Jasper National Park, you can enjoy amazing views at Wilcox Pass or Tangle Falls right from the parkway, and both Sunwapta and Athabasca falls are just a short drive off the main road. Popular viewpoints are Stutfield Glacier and Athabasca Pass, where interpretive panels explain the national importance of this remote location.

Note: Drivers should be alert for slow or stopped vehicles and animals. Snow tires and/or chains are mandatory in winter; check for weather and road conditions. **Cost:** Parkway free; drivers must pay the national park entrance fee regardless of whether they stop inside the park. **Phone:** (780) 852-6176.

JOHNSTON CANYON is 18 km (11 mi.) w. of the town of Banff on the Bow Valley Pkwy. (Hwy. 1A). An uphill hike to one or both of the two waterfalls at this canyon follows a paved pathway through a wooded area along Johnston Creek. Observation points along the way allow for scenic views of the rushing water. The pathway soon becomes more of a catwalk that is literally attached to the canyon wall.

The Lower Falls are reached after a hike of about 1.1 kilometres (.7 mi.); the trail continues another 1.7 kilometres (1 mi.) to the Upper Falls. **Note:** This is a popular day-use area, and the parking lot can become crowded.

LAKE LOUISE—see Lake Louise p. 129.

MORAINE LAKE is about 14 km (8.7 mi.) s. of the Lake Louise townsite and about 71 km (44 mi.) n.w. of the town of Banff. Though roughly half the size of better-known nearby Lake Louise, many believe blue-green Moraine Lake is equally beautiful. Known as "the jewel of the Rockies," the lake is in the Valley of the Ten Peaks, which provides the ten sawtoothed ridges that rise dramatically from the lakeshore. A number of hikes begin at the lake. A short trek to the top of a rockslide leads to panoramic views of the lake and valley. In addition, canoe rentals are available in summer, and cross-country skiing can be enjoyed in winter.

Note: Due to the risk of avalanches, the road to Moraine Lake is closed from early fall to late spring. The precise dates vary depending on weather conditions. Some trails may not be available in summer; phone ahead for current trail information. **Phone:** (403) 522-3833 for the Lake Louise Visitor Information Centre.

RECREATIONAL ACTIVITIES
Skiing
- **Sunshine Village Ski Resort** is just off Sunshine Road, 20 km (12.4 mi.) w. of the town of Banff via Hwy. 1. **Hours:** Daily 9-4, early Nov.-late May. **Phone:** (403) 705-4000 or (877) 542-2633.

BANFF (H-4) pop. 7,584

BANFF GONDOLA is at 1 Mountain Ave. An enclosed gondola journeys along the eastern slope of Sulphur Mountain. The lift rises 698 metres (2,290 ft.) from the 1,583-metre (5,194-ft.) level to the 2,281-metre (7,484-ft.) summit ridge in 8 minutes. The Summit Complex includes observation decks offering stunning panoramic views, an interpretive center with natural and cultural history exhibits and a multisensory theater that treats audiences to a thrilling flight over the surrounding mountains by simulating an eagle's point of view. A boardwalk affords more 360-degree vistas and leads to a historic cosmic ray station and weather observatory.

Time: Allow 1 hour, 30 minutes minimum. **Hours:** Daily 8 a.m.-10 p.m., July 1-early Oct.; 9-9 late May-June 30; 10-6, May 1-late May; 10-5, early Oct.-Dec. 31. Last ride up 1 hour prior to closing, and last ride down 30 minutes prior to closing. **Cost:** Round-trip fare $42; $21 (ages 6-15). **Phone:** (403) 762-2523.

BREWSTER SIGHTSEEING EXCURSIONS departs from several area hotels. Guides discuss local history during the 4.5-hour Explore Banff tour, which offers views of wildlife and such points of interest as the Banff Gondola and the Banff Lake Cruise. A variety of full- and half-day narrated excursions of and from Banff to Lake Louise, the Columbia Icefield and Jasper also are offered. **Hours:**

(See map & index p. 33.)

Tours are offered daily, early May to mid-Oct. Departure times vary; phone ahead. **Cost:** Explore Banff tour from $111; $56 (children). **Phone:** (403) 762-6700 or (866) 606-6700. GT

BUFFALO NATIONS LUXTON MUSEUM is just w. of Banff Ave. at 1 Birch Ave. This log-fort museum re-creates the era when Europeans first arrived on the Plains to find a culture rich in ceremonies, songs and legends. Arts, crafts, dioramas and displays showcase the historical journey of the Northern Plains people, their culture and the flora and fauna of the surrounding area.

Time: Allow 30 minutes minimum. **Hours:** Daily 10-7, May-Sept.; 11-5, rest of year. Closed Christmas. Phone ahead to confirm schedule. **Cost:** $9.52; $8.57 (ages 65+); $4.76 (ages 7-17). **Phone:** (403) 762-2388. GT

CAVE AND BASIN NATIONAL HISTORIC SITE is at 311 Cave Ave. The beginnings of Canada's national park system are founded on a cave and hot springs discovered in 1883 by three Canadian Pacific Railway workers. Disputes over the ownership of the area prompted the Canadian government to declare the area a national reserve 2 years later. The site consists of naturally occurring warm mineral springs inside the cave and an emerald-colored basin outside. A four-screen high-definition film presents the history of the springs and the development of Banff National Park and the Canadian national park system. Exhibits and interpretive trails also are offered.

Time: Allow 1 hour minimum. **Hours:** Daily 10-5, mid-May to early Sept.; Tues.-Sun. 10-5, early Sept. to early Oct.; Wed.-Sun. 11-5, rest of year. Guided tours are given daily at 11 and 2:30, mid-May to early Sept. Closed Jan. 1, Christmas and day after Christmas. **Cost:** Free in 2017 to celebrate Canada's 150th anniversary of Confederation, otherwise $3.71; $3.24 (ages 65+); $1.81 (ages 6-18); $9.33 (up to seven people arriving in a single vehicle). **Phone:** (403) 762-1566. GT

DISCOVER BANFF TOURS is at 215 Banff Ave. in the Sundance Mall. Passengers also are picked up at area hotels. Various year-round guided tours are offered, including ice walks, snowshoe treks, dog sled trips, sleigh rides, mountain hikes, wildlife safaris, horseback riding and white-water rafting. Some tours include lunch. Self-guiding tours also are available.

Inquire about cancellation policies. Allow 2-9 hours minimum, depending on tour. **Hours:** Tours depart daily (weather permitting) 8:30-6:30. Tour times vary; phone ahead. **Cost:** Fees vary, depending on activity. **Phone:** (403) 760-5007 or (877) 565-9372. GT

ROCKY MOUNTAIN RAFT TOURS has a launch point meeting area below Bow Falls on Golf Course Loop Rd. Tickets are available at a kiosk at the launch point. Scenic 1-hour Hoodoo Tours and 2.5-hour Bow River Safari guided raft tours travel the Bow Valley below Tunnel and Rundle mountains. Both tours end with a bus ride back to base. The River Safari also includes a 20-minute forest hike. **Hours:** Hoodoo Tours depart daily at 9:20, 11:20, 1:20, 3:20 and 5:20, mid-May to late Sept. Bow River Safaris depart daily at 3:30, June 1-late Aug. (weather permitting). Phone ahead to confirm schedule. **Cost:** Hoodoo Tour$47.62; $19.05 (ages 0-15). Bow River Safari $80.95; $38.10 (ages 4-15). Reservations are required. **Phone:** (403) 762-3632. GT

SAVE **WHYTE MUSEUM OF THE CANADIAN ROCKIES,** 111 Bear St., presents the heritage of the region through galleries exhibiting cultural and natural history displays and historic and contemporary artwork. Museum interpreters also guide visitors through two historic houses on-site, including the former residence of the museum's founders, Peter and Catharine Whyte.

Time: Allow 30 minutes minimum. **Hours:** Museum daily 10-5. Archives and library Tues.-Fri. 1-5; otherwise by appointment. Heritage Homes Tours at 11, 1 and 3, June-Aug.; by appointment, rest of year. Closed Jan. 1 and Christmas. Phone ahead to confirm schedule. **Cost:** $9.52; $8.57 (ages 65+); $3.81 (students with ID); free (ages 0-12). **Phone:** (403) 762-2291. GT

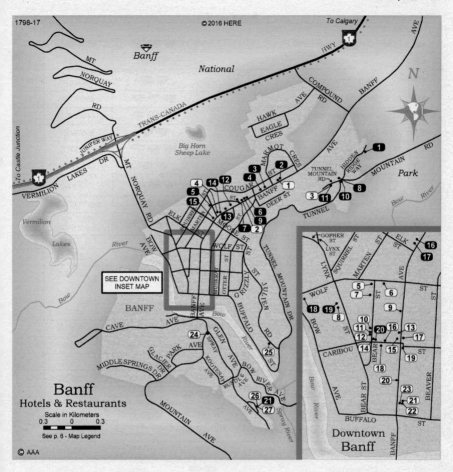

1798-17   © 2016 HERE

Banff

This index helps you "spot" where approved hotels and restaurants are located on the corresponding detailed maps. Hotel daily rate range is for comparison only. Restaurant price range is a combination of lunch and/or dinner. Turn to the listing page for more information and consult display ads for special promotions.

BANFF

Map Page	Hotels	Diamond Rated	Rate Range	Page
1 this page	Hidden Ridge Resort	▽▽▽	$129-$329	36
2 this page	Rundlestone Lodge	▽▽▽	$150-$350	37
3 this page	Banff Caribou Lodge	▽▽▽	Rates not provided	35
4 this page	Charlton's Banff *(See ad p. 35.)*	▽▽▽	$149-$344	36
5 this page	Buffaloberry Bed and Breakfast	▽▽▽▽	$345-$395	35
6 this page	Delta Banff Royal Canadian Lodge *(See ad p. 36.)*	▽▽▽	$143-$270	36
7 this page	**Best Western Plus Siding 29 Lodge**	▽▽▽	$120-$369 [SAVE]	35
8 this page	Tunnel Mountain Resort	▽▽	Rates not provided	37
9 this page	The Fox Hotel & Suites	▽▽▽	$129-$329	36
10 this page	**Douglas Fir Resort & Chalets**	▽▽	Rates not provided [SAVE]	36

BANFF (cont'd)

Map Page	Hotels (cont'd)	Diamond Rated	Rate Range	Page
⑪ p. 33	Buffalo Mountain Lodge	◆◆◆	$179-$349	35
⑫ p. 33	Irwin's Mountain Inn	◆◆	$229-$299	36
⑬ p. 33	Red Carpet Inn	◆◆	Rates not provided	37
⑭ p. 33	High Country Inn	◆◆◆	$99-$349	36
⑮ p. 33	**Banff Aspen Lodge**	◆◆◆	$144-$439 [SAVE]	35
⑯ p. 33	Banff Ptarmigan Inn	◆◆	$99-$269	35
⑰ p. 33	Elk + Avenue	◆◆◆	$99-$312	36
⑱ p. 33	Bow View Lodge	◆◆	$79-$299	35
⑲ p. 33	Banff Park Lodge Resort Hotel & Conference Centre	◆◆◆	$149-$399	35
⑳ p. 33	**Brewster's Mountain Lodge**	◆◆	$99-$425 [SAVE]	35
㉑ p. 33	**The Fairmont Banff Springs** *(See ad p. 37.)*	◆◆◆◆	Rates not provided [SAVE]	36

Map Page	Restaurants	Diamond Rated	Cuisine	Price Range	Page
① p. 33	Bumper's The Beef House	◆◆	Steak	$11-$44	38
② p. 33	The Evergreen *(See ad p. 36.)*	◆◆◆	International	$16-$39	38
③ p. 33	Sleeping Buffalo Restaurant	◆◆◆	Regional Canadian	$15-$40	38
④ p. 33	Ticino Swiss-Italian Restaurant	◆◆◆	International	$18-$42	38
⑤ p. 33	Masala Authentic Indian Cuisine	◆◆	Indian	$15-$20	38
⑥ p. 33	St. James's Gate Olde Irish Pub	◆◆	Irish	$13-$27	38
⑦ p. 33	The Bear Street Tavern	◆◆	Pizza	$11-$23	38
⑧ p. 33	La Terrazza	◆◆◆	Italian	$20-$40	38
⑨ p. 33	Park Distillery Restaurant + Bar	◆◆◆	New Canadian	$15-$36	38
⑩ p. 33	Saltlik A Rare Steakhouse	◆◆◆	Steak	$14-$35	38
⑪ p. 33	The Bison Restaurant & Terrace	◆◆◆	Regional Canadian	$19-$45	38
⑫ p. 33	Wild Flour Bakery Cafe	◆	Natural/Organic Breads/Pastries	$6-$12	38
⑬ p. 33	Nourish Bistro	◆◆	Vegetarian	$15-$26	38
⑭ p. 33	Sushi Bistro	◆◆	Sushi	$8-$24	38
⑮ p. 33	Block Kitchen and Bar	◆◆	Mediterranean Small Plates	$14-$26	38
⑯ p. 33	Coyotes Deli & Grill	◆◆	New Southwestern	$9-$31	38
⑰ p. 33	Grizzly House	◆◆	Fondue	$15-$64	38
⑱ p. 33	The Eddie Burger + Bar	◆◆	Burgers	$13-$18	38
⑲ p. 33	The Maple Leaf Grille & Spirits	◆◆◆	Canadian	$13-$50	38
⑳ p. 33	Elk & Oarsman	◆◆	International	$14-$35	38
㉑ p. 33	Tommy's Neighbourhood Pub	◆◆	American	$7-$13	38
㉒ p. 33	Banff Ave Brewing Co	◆◆	American	$14-$36	38
㉓ p. 33	Balkan The Greek Restaurant	◆◆	Greek	$11-$39	38
㉔ p. 33	**Silver Dragon Restaurant Banff**	◆◆	Chinese	$14-$26	38
㉕ p. 33	Three Ravens Restaurant & Wine Bar	◆◆◆	New Canadian	$32-$41	38
㉖ p. 33	1888 Chop House	◆◆◆	Steak	$38-$68	38
㉗ p. 33	**Grapes Wine Bar**	◆◆◆	Small Plates	$20-$32	38

(See map & index p. 33.)

BANFF ASPEN LODGE   (403)762-4401 15

Hotel
$144-$439

Address: 401 Banff Ave T1L 1A9 **Location:** Between Moose and Rabbit sts. **Facility:** 89 units. 3 stories, interior/exterior corridors. **Parking:** winter plug-ins. **Terms:** cancellation fee imposed. **Amenities:** safes. **Activities:** sauna, hot tub, steamroom. **Guest Services:** valet and coin laundry, area transportation. **Featured Amenity: breakfast buffet.**

BANFF CARIBOU LODGE   403/762-5887 3
 Hotel. **Address:** 521 Banff Ave T1L 1A4

BANFF PARK LODGE RESORT HOTEL & CONFERENCE CENTRE   (403)762-4433 19
Hotel. **Address:** 222 Lynx St T1L 1K5

BANFF PTARMIGAN INN   (403)762-2207 16
Hotel. **Address:** 337 Banff Ave T1L 1B1

BANFF ROCKY MOUNTAIN RESORT   403/762-5531
Resort Hotel. **Address:** 1029 Banff Ave T1L 1A2

BEST WESTERN PLUS SIDING 29 LODGE
(403)762-5575 7

Hotel
$120-$369

  AAA Benefit: Save 10% or more every day and earn 10% bonus points!

Address: 453 Marten St T1L 1B3 **Location:** 0.6 mi (1 km) ne, just off Banff Ave. Located in a residential area. **Facility:** 57 units, some kitchens. 3 stories, interior corridors. **Terms:** resort fee. **Pool(s):** heated indoor. **Activities:** hot tub. **Guest Services:** valet laundry. **Featured Amenity: breakfast buffet.**

BOW VIEW LODGE   (403)762-2261 18
Motel. **Address:** 228 Bow Ave T1L 1A5

BREWSTER'S MOUNTAIN LODGE   (403)762-2900 20

Hotel
$99-$425

Address: 208 Caribou St T1L 1C1 **Location:** Just w off Banff Ave; downtown. **Facility:** 77 units. 3 stories, interior corridors. **Parking:** on-site (fee). **Terms:** check-in 4 pm, 3 day cancellation notice-fee imposed. **Dining:** Sushi Bistro, see separate listing. **Activities:** sauna, hot tub, limited exercise equipment. **Guest Services:** valet and coin laundry, rental car service. **Featured Amenity: continental breakfast.**

BUFFALOBERRY BED AND BREAKFAST   (403)762-3750 5
Bed & Breakfast. **Address:** 417 Marten St T1L 1G5

BUFFALO MOUNTAIN LODGE   (403)762-2400 11
Hotel. **Address:** 700 Tunnel Mountain Rd T1L 1B3

▼ See AAA listing p. 36 ▼

(See map & index p. 33.)

CASTLE MOUNTAIN CHALETS   (403)762-3868
▼▼ Cabin. **Address:** Bow Valley Pkwy (Hwy 1A) & Hwy 93 S T1L 1B5

CHARLTON'S BANFF   (403)762-4485 **4**

▼▼▼ Motel. **Address:** 513 Banff Ave T1L 1B4 *(See ad p. 35.)*

DELTA BANFF ROYAL CANADIAN LODGE
                                (403)762-3307 **6**

> **AAA Benefit:**
> Members save 5% or more!

▼▼▼ Boutique Hotel. **Address:** 459 Banff Ave T1L 1B4 *(See ad this page.)*

DOUGLAS FIR RESORT & CHALETS
                                403/762-5591 **10**
▼▼ ▼▼
Condominium
Rates not provided
Address: 525 Tunnel Mountain Rd T1L 1B2 **Location:** Jct Banff Ave and Wolf St, 1 mi (1.6 km) ne. Located in a secluded area. **Facility:** 130 units, some cottages and condominiums. 2-3 stories (no elevator), interior/exterior corridors. **Parking:** winter plug-ins. **Terms:** check-in 4 pm. **Amenities:** safes. **Pool(s):** heated indoor. **Activities:** sauna, hot tub, steamroom, game room, trails, exercise room. **Guest Services:** coin laundry, area transportation.

SAVE ⊞ 🏊 🛜 ✕ 🖥 🍽 ▢ /SOME UNITS 🐾

ELK + AVENUE   (403)762-5666 **17**
▼▼▼ Hotel. **Address:** 333 Banff Ave T1L 1B1

THE FAIRMONT BANFF SPRINGS   403/762-2211 **21**

▼▼▼ ▼▼▼
Classic Historic
Resort Hotel
Rates not provided
Address: 405 Spray Ave T1L 1J4 **Location:** Just s on Banff Ave over the bridge, 0.3 mi (0.5 km) e. **Facility:** There are many impressive public areas to explore at this iconic jewel, which brings to mind a magnificent castle. Guest rooms range from upscale, compact units to extravagant suites. 764 units. 3-9 stories, interior corridors. **Parking:** on-site (fee) and valet, winter plug-ins. **Terms:** check-in 4 pm. **Amenities:** safes. **Dining:** 10 restaurants, also, 1888 Chop House, Grapes Wine Bar, see separate listings. **Pool(s):** heated outdoor, heated indoor. **Activities:** sauna, hot tub, steamroom, regulation golf, tennis, cross country skiing, sledding, ice skating, recreation programs, kids club, bicycles, playground, game room, lawn sports, trails, spa. **Guest Services:** valet laundry, rental car service. *(See ad p. 37.)*

SAVE ECO ⊞ 🏊 🍽 🛜 👪 BIZ HS 🛜 ✕
🎥 🖥 ▢ /SOME UNITS 🐾 🎿

THE FOX HOTEL & SUITES   (403)760-8500 **9**
▼▼▼ Hotel. **Address:** 461 Banff Ave T1L 1B1

HIDDEN RIDGE RESORT   (403)762-3544 **1**
▼▼▼ Condominium. **Address:** 901 Hidden Ridge Way T1L 1B7

HIGH COUNTRY INN   (403)762-2236 **14**
▼▼▼ Hotel. **Address:** 419 Banff Ave T1L 1A7

IRWIN'S MOUNTAIN INN   (403)762-4566 **12**
▼▼ Hotel. **Address:** 429 Banff Ave T1L 1B2

Request roadside assistance
in a click — online or using
the AAA or CAA apps

▼ *See AAA listing this page* ▼

(See map & index p. 33.)

JOHNSTON CANYON RESORT   403/762-2971

Historic Cabin
Rates not provided

Address: Hwy 1A T1L 1A9 **Location:** 15 mi (24 km) nw on Hwy 1A (Bow Valley Pkwy). Located at Johnston Canyon. **Facility:** This 1927 property is at the base of the trail to the iconic Johnston Canyon waterfalls and ink pots. Rustic yet charming wood cabins have a variety of décor and comfort levels. 36 cabins. 1 story, exterior corridors. **Terms:** check-in 4 pm. **Dining:** 2 restaurants. **Activities:** tennis, picnic facilities, trails.

SAVE ECO [icons] / SOME UNITS [icons]

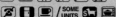

JOHNSTON CANYON RESORT

**7 spectacular waterfalls.
Scenic & wildlife photo opportunities.
All located at your doorstep.**

RED CARPET INN   403/762-4184 **13**
Hotel. **Address:** 425 Banff Ave T1L 1B6

THE RIMROCK RESORT HOTEL   (403)762-3356

Resort Hotel
$188-$488

Address: 300 Mountain Ave T1L 1J2 **Location:** 2.4 mi (4 km) s via Sulphur Mountain Rd; adjacent to Upper Hot Springs Pool. Located in a quiet secluded area. **Facility:** This luxury hotel is literally built on the slope of a mountain. Upscale rooms have two comfy armchairs and you'll find the best views on the highest floors. 343 units. 9 stories, interior corridors. **Parking:** on-site (fee) and valet, winter plug-ins. **Terms:** check-in 4 pm, 3 day cancellation notice-fee imposed. **Amenities:** video games, safes. **Dining:** 2 restaurants, also, Eden, see separate listing. **Pool(s):** heated indoor. **Activities:** sauna, hot tub, steamroom, cross country skiing, ice skating, trails, spa. **Guest Services:** valet laundry, area transportation.

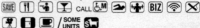

RUNDLESTONE LODGE   (403)762-2201 **2**
Hotel. **Address:** 537 Banff Ave T1L 1A6

SUNSHINE MOUNTAIN LODGE   (403)762-6500

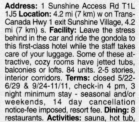
Resort Hotel
$360-$740

Address: 1 Sunshine Access Rd T1L 1J5 **Location:** 4.2 mi (7 km) w on Trans-Canada Hwy 1 exit Sunshine Village, 4.2 mi (7 km) s. **Facility:** Leave the stress behind in the car and ride the gondola to this first-class hotel while the staff takes care of your luggage. Some of these attractive, cozy rooms have jetted tubs, balconies or lofts. 84 units. 2-5 stories, interior corridors. **Terms:** closed 5/22-6/29 & 9/24-11/11, check-in 4 pm, 3 night minimum stay - seasonal and/or weekends, 14 day cancellation notice-fee imposed, resort fee. **Dining:** 8 restaurants. **Activities:** sauna, hot tub, downhill & cross country skiing, snowboarding, sledding, recreation programs in season, exercise room, spa. **Guest Services:** valet laundry, area transportation.

SAVE [icons]

TUNNEL MOUNTAIN RESORT   403/762-4515 **8**
Condominium. **Address:** 502 Tunnel Mountain Rd T1L 1B1

▼ See AAA listing p. 36 ▼

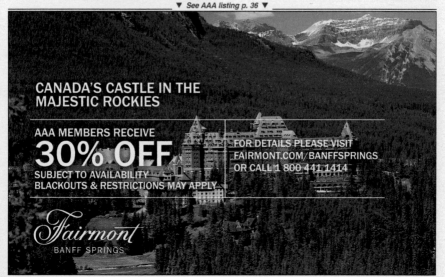

(See map & index p. 33.)

WHERE TO EAT

1888 CHOP HOUSE   403/762-6860   **26**
🍷🍷🍷 Steak. Fine Dining. **Address:** 405 Spray Ave T1L 1J4

BALKAN THE GREEK RESTAURANT   403/762-3454   **23**
🍷🍷 Greek. Casual Dining. **Address:** 120 Banff Ave T1L 1A4

BANFF AVE BREWING CO   403/762-1003   **22**
🍷🍷 American. Gastropub. **Address:** 110 Banff Ave T1L 1C9

THE BEAR STREET TAVERN   403/762-2021   **7**
🍷🍷 Pizza. Gastropub. **Address:** 211 Bear St T1L 1E4

THE BISON RESTAURANT & TERRACE   403/762-5550   **11**
🍷🍷🍷 Regional Canadian. Casual Dining. **Address:** 211 Bear St T1L 1E4

BLOCK KITCHEN AND BAR   403/985-2887   **15**
🍷🍷 Mediterranean Small Plates. Casual Dining. **Address:** 201 Banff Ave, #5 T1L 1C6

BUMPER'S THE BEEF HOUSE   403/762-2201   **1**
🍷🍷 Steak. Casual Dining. **Address:** 537 Banff Ave T1L 1A6

COYOTES DELI & GRILL   403/762-3963   **16**
🍷🍷 New Southwestern. Casual Dining. **Address:** 206 Caribou St T1L 1A2

THE EDDIE BURGER + BAR   403/762-2230   **18**
🍷🍷 Burgers. Casual Dining. **Address:** 137 Banff Ave, #6 T1L 1B7

EDEN   403/762-1840
🍷🍷🍷🍷🍷

New French Fine Dining
$85-$215

AAA Inspector Notes: A touch of something magical is in the air here where tastes, textures, creativity and imagination mingle to produce an exquisite meal. Hours will pass unnoticed as you unwind in comfy chairs, gazing out at the spectacular Rocky Mountains. Professional and engaging servers provide knowledgeable service with an impressive food delivery where entrées arrive in a perfectly synchronized fashion. An à la carte menu (minimum two courses) and tasting menus, including a vegetarian option, are offered. **Features:** full bar. **Reservations:** suggested. **Address:** 300 Mountain Ave T1L 1J2 **Location:** 2.4 mi (4 km) s via Sulphur Mountain Rd; adjacent to Upper Hot Springs Pool; in The Rimrock Resort Hotel. **Parking:** on-site and valet. D CALL 📞M

ELK & OARSMAN   403/762-4616   **20**
🍷 International. Gastropub. **Address:** 119 Banff Ave T1L 1B6

THE EVERGREEN   403/762-3307   **2**
🍷🍷🍷 International. Fine Dining. **Address:** 459 Banff Ave T1L 1B4 *(See ad p. 36.)*

GRAPES WINE BAR   403/762-6860   **27**
🍷🍷🍷

Small Plates Casual Dining
$20-$32

AAA Inspector Notes: During some renovation work in the 1980s a carved grape ceiling trim was discovered dating from 1926 and thus this wine bar was born. The intimate little spot, with dark wood and stone work, offers mainly fine charcuterie, cheeses and an array of candied nuts, pickles and chutneys along with artisan bread choices. They also feature cheese fondue. Reservations are not accepted. **Features:** full bar. **Address:** 405 Spray Ave T1L 1J4 **Location:** Just s on Banff Ave over the bridge, 0.3 mi (0.5 km) e; in The Fairmont Banff Springs. **Parking:** on-site and valet. D

GRIZZLY HOUSE   403/762-4055   **17**
🍷🍷 Fondue. Casual Dining. **Address:** 207 Banff Ave T1L 1B4

LA TERRAZZA   403/760-3271   **8**
🍷🍷🍷 Italian. Fine Dining. **Address:** 222 Lynx St T1L 1K5

THE MAPLE LEAF GRILLE & SPIRITS   403/760-7680   **19**
🍷🍷 Canadian. Casual Dining. **Address:** 137 Banff Ave T1L 1C8

MASALA AUTHENTIC INDIAN CUISINE   403/760-6612   **5**
🍷🍷 Indian. Casual Dining. **Address:** 229 Bear St T1L 1B7

NOURISH BISTRO   403/760-3933   **13**
🍷🍷 Vegetarian. Casual Dining. **Address:** 211 Banff Ave T1L 1B4

PARK DISTILLERY RESTAURANT + BAR   403/762-5114   **9**
🍷🍷🍷 New Canadian. Casual Dining. **Address:** 219 Banff Ave T1L 1A7

ST. JAMES'S GATE OLDE IRISH PUB   403/762-9355   **6**
🍷🍷 Irish. Casual Dining. **Address:** 207 Wolf St T1L 1C2

SALTLIK A RARE STEAKHOUSE   403/762-2467   **10**
🍷🍷🍷 Steak. Casual Dining. **Address:** 221 Bear St T1L 1B3

SILVER DRAGON RESTAURANT BANFF
                                  403/762-3939   **24**
🍷🍷

Chinese Casual Dining
$14-$26

AAA Inspector Notes: Make this a definite stop for those who crave Chinese food, as they have an excellent variety of classic dishes including ginger beef and Peking duck. The food is freshly prepared and served piping hot. Mountain views from the wide expanse of windows is an added bonus of the spacious, open dining room, which sports giant red hanging paper lanterns. **Features:** full bar. **Reservations:** suggested. **Address:** 109 Spray Ave T1L 1C4 **Location:** Just se of Banff Ave bridge. L D CALL 📞M ✗

SLEEPING BUFFALO RESTAURANT   403/760-4484   **3**
🍷🍷🍷 Regional Canadian. Casual Dining. **Address:** 700 Tunnel Mountain Rd T1L 1B3

SUSHI BISTRO   403/762-4000   **14**
🍷🍷 Sushi. Casual Dining. **Address:** 208 Caribou St T1L 1B4

THREE RAVENS RESTAURANT & WINE BAR
                                  403/762-6300   **25**
🍷🍷🍷 New Canadian. Casual Dining. **Address:** 107 Tunnel Mountain Dr T1L 1G7

TICINO SWISS-ITALIAN RESTAURANT   403/762-3848   **4**
🍷🍷🍷 International. Fine Dining. **Address:** 415 Banff Ave T1L 1B5

TOMMY'S NEIGHBOURHOOD PUB   403/762-8888   **21**
🍷🍷 American. Casual Dining. **Address:** 120 Banff Ave T1L 1A4

WILD FLOUR BAKERY CAFE   403/760-5074   **12**
🍷 Natural/Organic Breads/Pastries. Quick Serve. **Address:** 211 Bear St, #101 T1L 1E8

BEAVERLODGE (C-1) pop. 2,365

First settled in 1908, Beaverlodge derives its name from the Beaver First Nation who made their temporary home, or lodge, in the area. With the arrival of the railway in 1928, a new townsite was created about 1.6 kilometres (1 mi.) northwest of the original hamlet; many original buildings were moved. In the Beaverlodge Valley, the town serves as a gateway to Monkman Pass and is a large agricultural center.

Beaverlodge & District Chamber of Commerce: 508 5th Ave., P.O. Box 303, Beaverlodge, AB, Canada T0H 0C0. **Phone:** (780) 354-8785.

SOUTH PEACE CENTENNIAL MUSEUM AND INTERPRETIVE CENTER is 3 km (1.9 mi.) n.w. on Hwy. 43. With an emphasis on fully restored antique tractors, cars and trucks, the 16-hectare (40-acre) site displays pioneer items, equipment and furnishings used in the early 1900s. A 1928 pioneer house is furnished in period. Other exhibits include a trading post, a general store, a flour mill, a schoolhouse, an Anglican church and a railway caboose. Antique steam engines are fired up for the Pioneer Days festival in mid-July. **Hours:** Daily 10-6, mid-May to mid-Sept. **Cost:** $4.76; free (ages 0-6). Cash only. **Phone:** (780) 354-8869.

BLACKFALDS pop. 6,300

MICROTEL INN & SUITES BY WYNDHAM BLACKFALDS
(403)885-9797
Hotel. **Address:** 6021 Parkwood Rd T0M 0J0

BON ACCORD (E-6) pop. 1,488

PRAIRIE GARDENS & ADVENTURE FARM is at 56311 Lily Lake Rd. In addition to U-pick gardens and a garden center, this 14-hectare (35-acre) working farm has an all-encompassing kids' zone with over 50 activities. Included are playgrounds and a petting farm. Tykes also can take old-fashioned, tractor-pulled trackless train rides, find their way through three different corn mazes or pan for gems in the Lost Lemon Gem Mine. Various festivals and dinners showcasing farm-grown ingredients add to the fun, as do such seasonal features as a 2.8-hectare (7-acre) pumpkin patch and a haunted farm house.

Pets are not permitted. **Time:** Allow 2 hours minimum. **Hours:** Mon.-Sat. 10-8, Sun. 10-6, late Apr. to mid-June; daily 10-6, mid-June through Oct. 31. Phone ahead to confirm schedule. **Cost:** Mon.-Fri. day pass $9.50; free (ages 0-2). Sat.-Sun. and holidays day pass $14.30. Reservations are required for some activities. **Phone:** (780) 921-2272.

BONNYVILLE pop. 6,216

BEST WESTERN BONNYVILLE INN & SUITES
(780)826-6226

Hotel
$140-$170

Best Western. **AAA Benefit:** Save 10% or more every day and earn 10% bonus points!

Address: 5401 43rd St T9N 0H3 **Location:** Hwy 28, just n at 44th St. **Facility:** 94 units. 4 stories, interior corridors. **Parking:** winter plug-ins. **Terms:** check-in 4 pm, cancellation fee imposed. **Activities:** exercise room. **Guest Services:** valet and coin laundry.

COMFORT INN & SUITES BONNYVILLE (780)826-2020
Hotel. **Address:** 5404 Lakeland Rd T9N 0B2

BRAGG CREEK (I-5) pop. 595
• Part of Calgary area — see map p. 42

Bragg Creek, 40 kilometres (25 mi.) southwest of Calgary on Hwy. 22, was named after Albert Bragg, a rancher who settled in the area in 1894. Known as the "Gateway to the Kananaskis" for its proximity to the Northern Rockies, the town has been a popular weekend getaway and year-round recreation area since the 1920s. Bragg Creek offers picnic areas, hiking trails, cross-country skiing, campgrounds and scenic Elbow Falls. The area has evolved as an artist's community with sculptors, potters, weavers, painters and other artisans practicing their crafts.

Bragg Creek Chamber of Commerce: 3 Balsam Ave., P.O. Box 216, Bragg Creek, AB, Canada T0L 0K0. **Phone:** (403) 949-0004.

BROOKS (I-8) pop. 13,676

Brooks is surrounded by 105,222 hectares (260,000 acres) of irrigated farmland and more than 404,700 hectares (1 million acres) of rangeland used for cattle grazing. This semiarid shortgrass section of the province is the setting for wildlife and horticultural research centers.

Brooks Visitor Information Centre: 568 Sutherland Dr. E., Brooks, AB, Canada T1R 1C7. **Phone:** (403) 362-5073.

DINOSAUR PROVINCIAL PARK—see Patricia p. 139.

CANALTA HOTEL 403/363-0080
Hotel. **Address:** 115 15th Ave W T1R 1C4

HERITAGE INN & SUITES BROOKS (403)362-8688
Hotel. **Address:** 1239 2nd St W T1R 1P7

HERITAGE INN HOTEL & CONVENTION CENTRE BROOKS
(403)362-6666
Hotel. **Address:** 1217 2nd St W T1R 1P7

RAMADA BROOKS (403)362-6440
Hotel. **Address:** 1319 2nd St W T1R 1P7

WHERE TO EAT

THE MANGO TREE 403/501-0045
Indian. Casual Dining. **Address:** 1131 2nd St T1R 0N9

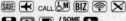

Calgary

Then & Now

Calgary, once considered a cow town, now is one of Canada's fastest-growing cities, with skyscrapers, light-rail transit, shopping complexes and contemporary houses. The city's economy began with—and still includes—ranching and the subsequent meatpacking industry, but the discovery of oil just south of the city in 1914 and just north in 1947 fueled a spurt of growth that turned an agricultural community into a metropolis.

Calgary today boasts the highest concentration of corporate offices in Canada. Energy, agriculture, tourism, manufacturing, research and development, and advanced technology comprise Calgary's industrial base.

The city's modern skyline, jagged with skyscrapers, makes a dramatic appearance on the vast expanse of Alberta prairie. To the west, almost mirroring Calgary's silhouette, are the Ca-

nadian Rockies, jutting into the sky just over an hour's drive away. The Trans-Canada Highway, a major national east-west roadway, runs through the heart of the city; in Calgary the highway also is known as 16th Avenue.

The region's history of human habitation began almost 10,000 years before the first 19th-century fur and whiskey traders arrived. First Nations tribes chose the confluence of the Bow and Elbow rivers as a campsite; emerging as the dominant tribe was the Blackfoot. Their acquisition of horses allowed them to hunt buffalo and fight almost every other prairie tribe with great success. As European settlement increased, so did the friction between the natives and the newcomers.

An 1877 treaty calmed the rough waters, and relative peace among all factions has existed since. Several reservations, including the Tsuu T'ina Reserve south of the city, are near Calgary. Native North Americans have sought to assimilate themselves into Canadian culture while retaining their native heritage.

Chinese were recruited abroad in the late 1800s to build railroads; once the trains were running, however, immigration was restricted. Oil and money lured Americans who brought technology and investment funds needed to get Calgary's petroleum industry started. But many of those who came for the money enjoyed the area and stayed, becoming Canadian citizens.

Calgary's modern sophistication is offset by a romantic perception of the past—a past in which the city was established as a North West Mounted Police fort in 1875. The Calgary Stampede, a 10-day Western wingding that celebrated its centennial in 2012, is attended by more than a million residents and visitors who relive the days of chuck wagons and

Calgary skyline

(Continued on p. 43.)

Destination Calgary

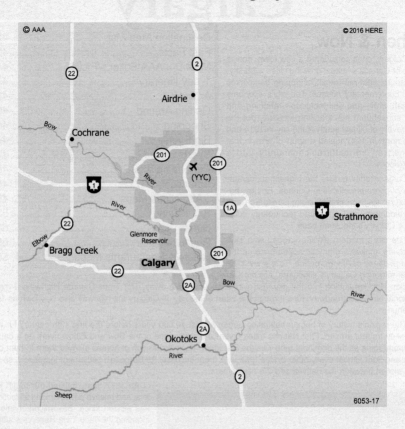

© AAA

©2016 HERE

6053-17

This map shows cities in the Calgary vicinity where you will find attractions, hotels and restaurants. Cities are listed alphabetically in this book on the following pages.

Fast Facts

ABOUT THE CITY

POP: 1,096,833 ▪ **ELEV:** 1,048 m/3,440 ft.

MONEY

SALES TAX: The federal Goods and Service Tax is 5 percent and applies to most goods, food/beverages and services, including lodgings. Alberta does not have a provincial sales tax but does impose a 4 percent tourism levy on hotel rooms.

WHOM TO CALL

EMERGENCY: 911

POLICE (non-emergency): (403) 266-1234

FIRE (non-emergency): 311

TEMPERATURE: (403) 299-7878

ROAD CONDITIONS: (877) 262-4997

HOSPITALS: Foothills Medical Centre, (403) 944-1110 ▪ Peter Lougheed Centre, (403) 943-4555 ▪ Rockyview General Hospital, (403) 943-3000.

WHERE TO LOOK AND LISTEN

NEWSPAPERS: Calgary's daily newspapers are the *Calgary Herald* and the *Calgary Sun,* both morning papers. The national newspapers are *The Globe and Mail* and the *National Post. Calgary Metro* is a free newspaper.

RADIO: Calgary radio station CBC (1010 AM) is a member of the Canadian Broadcasting Corp.

VISITOR INFORMATION

Tourism Calgary: 238 11th Ave. S.E., Room 200, Calgary, AB, Canada T2G 0X8. **Phone:** (403) 263-8510 or (800) 661-1678.

Visitor information also is available at the Calgary International Airport on the arrivals level and at the Riley & McCormick Western Store at 220 Stephen Ave. in the Eau Claire Market.

TRANSPORTATION

AIR TRAVEL: Calgary International Airport (YYC) is northeast of downtown off Hwy. 2 exit 266. Public bus transportation to and from the airport is offered by Calgary Transit via Route 300, with service to and from downtown for $9.05. Taxi service between the airport and downtown typically costs $38-$43. Many hotels also offer free shuttle service for their guests.

RENTAL CARS: Hertz, downtown or at the airport, offers discounts to CAA and AAA members; phone (403) 221-1676, (800) 654-3131.

RAIL SERVICE: The nearest VIA Rail stations are in Jasper and Edmonton; phone (888) 842-7245.

BUSES: Greyhound Lines Inc. operates from the depot at 850 16th St. S.W.; phone (403) 218-3000 or (800) 661-8747. Red Arrow Express operates luxury motor coaches between Calgary, Red Deer, Edmonton, Fort McMurray and Lethbridge; phone (403) 531-0350 or (800) 232-1958.

TAXIS: Taxi companies include Associated Cab, (403) 299-1111 ▪ Checker Yellow Cab, (403) 299-9999 ▪ and Mayfair Taxi, (403) 255-6555. Allied Limousine provides town car and limo service ▪ phone (403) 299-9555. Rates begin at $3.62 for the first 120 metres (about .074 mi.) or portion thereof, plus 19c for each additional 120 metres (about .074 mi.) or portion thereof (unless departing from Calgary International Airport, where rates are $7.90 for the first 120 metres, then 19c for each additional 120 metres). Cabs can be hailed on the street, but phoning ahead is recommended.

PUBLIC TRANSPORTATION: Calgary has both bus and light-rail transit (LRT) service; the latter, known as the CTrain, is free in the downtown core. Calgary Transit's office, 125 7th Ave. S.E., has schedules and maps and sells transit passes. Fare is $3; $2 (ages 6-17). A 1-day pass is $9.05; $6.43 (ages 6-17). Phone (403) 262-1000.

(Continued from p. 41.)

lassos. Those days existed more than a century ago, after the North West Mounted Police—the forerunner of today's Royal Canadian Mounted Police—and the railroad brought law, order and homesteaders to a region previously settled by trappers, buffalo hunters and whiskey traders. The festival, held each year since 1912, takes place in July.

Although Calgary's growth has been rapid, it has been practical. The bustling downtown district was designed to accommodate a large amount of activity, even during winter when below-freezing temperatures normally would inhibit commerce. Enclosed walkways called "plus-15s" (since they are 15 feet above street level) connect almost half the downtown buildings, making it possible to eat, work, shop or visit neighbors without donning so much as a mitten.

The Stephen Avenue Walk, a brick pedestrian mall in the city center lined with restored late 19th- and early 20th-century buildings, trees, statues and benches, is an urban refuge from traffic as well as a nice place to people watch and enjoy lunch or a stroll in warm weather.

Nearby is Olympic Plaza, the site of the awards ceremonies during the 15th Olympic Winter Games, held in Calgary in 1988, and now a popular venue for events and festivals.

Must Do: AAA Editor's Picks

- Zip to the top of ✈ **Calgary Tower** (101 9th Ave. S.W.) via high-speed elevator to take in a fantastic 360-degree view of the city, a great way to get your bearings. Built to commemorate Canada's centennial, the tower has been a distinctive city landmark since 1968.

- Pull on a pair of cowboy boots and celebrate all things wild and western during the ✈ **Calgary Stampede,** a rodeo-centered event attended by more than a million people. For 10 days every July, the Stampede puts on a tremendous show that not only includes barrel racing, bull riding and chuck wagon races, but also fireworks, parades, street parties, a carnival midway and a huge outdoor music festival.

- Walk in the footsteps of Olympic greats from the 1988 Winter Games at ✈ **Canada Olympic Park** (88 Canada Olympic Rd. S.W.), a year-round sports complex offering miniature golf, a zipline and bobsleigh runs in summer and skiing, snowboarding and luge rides in winter.

- Hop aboard a steam train or ride in a horse-drawn wagon as you explore nearly a century's worth of local history at ✈ **Heritage Park Historical Village** (1900 Heritage Dr. S.W.). You'll get a feel for life in the isolated prairie settlement that Calgary once was when you tour the historic buildings relocated to the park and chat with the costumed "townspeople" inside.

- Listen to birdsong as you wander through the **Inglewood Bird Sanctuary** (2425 9th Ave. S.E.), a lovely bit of wooded parkland just minutes from downtown Calgary. And once your inner peace has been restored, explore nearby Inglewood, one of the city's oldest neighborhoods. It's a place known for boutiques, art galleries and antique stores, especially along 9th Avenue S.E.

- At ✈ **TELUS Spark** (220 St. George's Dr. N.E.), get answers to such weighty questions as: What does it mean to be human? What natural forces have shaped our world? How can we harness energy for our use? The state-of-the-art science center is filled with high-tech displays that engage both children and adults. The two-level building houses exhibit galleries, the HD Digital Dome Theatre, learning labs, an interactive kids museum and more. The outdoor Brainasium, a .4-hectare (1-acre) park teaches young visitors about gravity and acoustics.

- Discover the bravery of Canada's military heroes at ✈ **The Military Museums** (4520 Crowchild Tr. S.W.), showcasing the nation's army, navy and air force as well as four army regiments. Tanks and a fighter jet seem poised for battle outside the museum, while inside dramatic dioramas and displays of weaponry, medals and photographs bring Canada's military history to life.

- Flip, fly and fall courtesy of thrill rides at **Calaway Park** (245033 Range Rd. 33), where the amusements range from tame to terrifying. The Adrenaline Test Zone, Chaos and the Vortex roller coaster are in the latter group, but there are plenty of rides designed for smaller children as well. Plus, with various carnival games on-site, the whole family can compete for plush prizes—and glory. The park also offers a miniature golf course, live shows and a 3-D theater.

- Trek back through time to the age of the dinosaurs at the ✈ **Calgary Zoo, Botanical Garden & Prehistoric Park** (1300 Zoo Rd. N.E.), home to a collection of fierce-looking dinosaur replicas, to say nothing of the even more impressive collection of living, breathing animals from all over the world. Such creatures as gentoo penguins, grizzly bears, cougars, bison, mountain goats and wolves thrive within their particular re-created habitats.

- Imagine rubbing elbows with one of 19th-century Calgary's wealthiest and most influential families when you enter **Lougheed House** (707 13th Ave. S.W.), their imposing sandstone mansion. Stroll through the formal gardens and you'll understand why the estate was named Beaulieu, French for "beautiful place."

Calgary Tower

Calgary 1-day Itinerary

AAA editors suggest these activities for a great short vacation experience.

Morning

- Start your day out and about in Calgary with breakfast at **Diner Deluxe** (804 Edmonton Tr. N.E.). This fun, 1950s retro-cool eatery serves classic eggs-and-toast breakfasts along with French toast stuffed with Gouda and Canadian bacon and a French-Canadian twist on hash browns involving cheese curds and hollandaise sauce.

- Diner Deluxe makes a good starting point not just for the hearty food or the mid-century modern ambience (picture Formica countertops and vinyl chairs) but also because it's just a few minutes from the ▼ **Calgary Zoo, Botanical Garden & Prehistoric Park** (1300 Zoo Rd. N.E.).

- You'll want to spend a few hours exploring the zoo's carefully designed animal enclosures and exhibits. Learn about grizzly bears and wolves in the zoo's Canadian Wilds section, or check out the life-size dinosaur models in Prehistoric Park. You also won't want to miss Penguin Plunge, where you'll witness four species of penguins waddling and shaking their tail feathers in an indoor-outdoor exhibit complete with a waterfall.

Calgary Zoo, Botanical Garden & Prehistoric Park

- In addition, the zoo offers such educational programs as zookeeper talks, nature walks and daily meet and greets with zoo residents that range from talkative parrots to laid-back turtles. If you're traveling with little ones, they'll love the zoo's storytime presentations and its game-filled kids' activity center.

Afternoon

- Cross the river into downtown to arrive at the ▼ **Glenbow Museum** (130 9th Ave. S.E.), a complex that includes both a history museum housing more than a million artifacts and an art gallery with thousands of works of art. Although the culture and heritage of Western Canada is the focus here, you'll also find cultures outside of Canada represented, for example, in the Asian Gallery and within an exhibition of West African cultural artifacts. There's also an extensive mineral collection with a dazzling assortment of sparkling gemstones.

- Across from the museum is ▼ **Calgary Tower** (101 9th Ave. S.W.), the place to go for stunning views of the city and on the horizon, the Rocky Mountains. The wraparound observation deck not only allows 360-degree panorama, but a glass-floored section lets you step out over a sheer drop to the street. The tower's restaurant, **Sky 360**, rotates once an hour, giving diners a complete tour of the scenery from the comfort of their table.

- Just a block north from the tower is Stephen Avenue Walk, a portion of 8th Avenue S.W. closed to car traffic from 6 a.m. to 6 p.m. The many examples of public art you'll see here include the towering steel tree sculptures that serve both to beautify and reduce gusting winds. Boutiques, bars, restaurants, shopping centers and historic buildings line the pedestrian mall, and during warm weather months, street performers entertain the crowds.

- As you stroll along Stephen Avenue, you'll notice pedestrian bridges spanning the street. These are part of the +15 Walkway System, so-called because they are generally 15 feet (4.6 metres) above street level. The network of enclosed walkways allows people to reach office buildings and shopping malls throughout a 50-block area in climate-controlled comfort, something Calgarians appreciate in the freezing cold of winter.

Evening

- Of course, dinner up in the air at the Calgary Tower's Sky 360 restaurant would be a spectacular conclusion to your day, but now that you've already seen Calgary from a bird's-eye perspective, head to the River Café on Prince's Island Park for a totally different but equally beautiful city view.

- Park at the **Eau Claire Market** (200 Barclay Parade S.W.) and take the Jaipur footbridge across to the island. The **River Café** (25 Prince's Island Park) occupies a rustic wood-and-stone building that evokes a cabin deep in the woods, yet looking out over the river from its patio, you see downtown's office towers. Make reservations because the café's lovely setting and fabulous dishes specializing in wild game and fish make it a popular dinner spot highly sought-after by both locals and visitors.

Arriving
By Car

Two major highways pass through Calgary. Queen Elizabeth II Hwy. runs north and south through the city; Trans-Canada Hwy. provides access from the east and west. Hwy. 1A, which connects Calgary and Cochrane, also serves as an alternate route between Calgary and the towns of Canmore and Banff. Hwy. 8 connects Calgary with Bragg Creek.

Getting Around
Street System

Calgary is divided into quadrants, with Centre Street separating the east and west sectors and the Bow River and Memorial Drive delineating north and south. Streets run north and south, avenues east and west. All are numbered from the intersection of Centre Street and Centre Avenue, just north of downtown. Roads in suburban areas are numbered where they form grids and named where they do not.

The speed limit is 50 kilometres per hour (30 mph) or as posted. A right turn on red after stopping is permitted unless otherwise posted; U-turns are not. Other restrictions apply during rush hours in certain areas; be aware of signs, especially in school and playground zones. Pedestrian crosswalks are designated by "X" signs, and motorists must yield to pedestrians.

Parking

Parking is not permitted on major roads in the downtown core during rush hours, between 6:30 and 9 a.m. and 3:30 and 6 p.m. Downtown metered street parking usually is limited to 2 hours at a maximum cost of $4.76 per hour. Pay parking for extended periods is available at numerous locations. Rates for downtown parking lots range from $1.67-$3.81 per half-hour during the day.

Shopping

Stephen Avenue Walk, a downtown pedestrian mall, extends from Bankers Hall to the city municipal buildings. This popular spot for people watching features shops, galleries and restaurants housed within historic buildings. Also downtown, a five-block shopping complex linked by an indoor walkway includes the more than 200 boutiques, department stores and retail chains of **The CORE - TD Square/Holt Renfrew** (324 8th Ave. S.W.), **Bankers Hall** (315 8th Ave. S.W.) and **Scotia Centre** (225 7th Ave. S.W.).

Unique specialty shops, kiosks and restaurants are the draw at **Eau Claire Market,** adjacent to the Bow River and Prince's Island Park at 2nd Avenue and 2nd Street S.W.

The trendy **Uptown 17th Avenue,** a scenic neighborhood and upscale shopping district, features stylish fashion shops, antiques stores and eclectic craft boutiques. The **Kensington district** features smaller stores in new and old buildings. Originally Atlantic Avenue, **Ninth Avenue S.E.** now is lined with antiques and home-furnishings stores, bookstores and cappuccino bars.

Major department stores and a wide variety of chain and specialty stores occupy the city's shopping centers: **Chinook Centre** (6455 Macleod Tr. S.W.), **Market Mall** (3625 Shaganappi Tr. N.W.), **North Hill Centre** (1632 14th Ave. N.W.), **Northland Village** (5111 Northland Dr. N.W.), **Southcentre Mall** (100 Anderson Rd. S.E.), **Sunridge Mall** (2525 36th St. N.E.) and **Willow Park Village** (10816 Macleod Tr. S.E.).

Big Events

The **Calgary Midwinter Blues Fest** takes place over 6 days in late February in venues throughout Calgary. The event features concerts by national blues performers; dance parties; and the Singing the Blues Vocal Camp, a workshop for aspiring singers.

Calgary International Children's Festival, which begins the third Wednesday in May and continues for 4 days, draws performers from such locales as Peru, Germany, Russia and Zimbabwe. The festival's many offerings include music, puppetry, dance and storytelling. Also in late May, the ▽ **Lilac Festival at 4th Street** features a parade and concerts—along with tons of vendors hawking artisan crafts.

Despite a focus on the modern oil and gas industry, Calgary citizens recall their past with the ▽ **Calgary Stampede,** held in July. This 10-day Wild West exhibition features a rodeo, chuck wagon races, livestock shows, beach-themed attractions, educational displays, shopping, extreme sports events and a midway. Parades, fireworks, street dancing, pancake breakfasts and other activities create a carnival-like atmosphere. Families enjoy the cultural and musical events that take place

Shop in downtown Calgary

during the 🎵 **Calgary Folk Music Festival**, held over 4 days in late July.

GlobalFest takes place in August and features such events as an international fireworks competition and a multicultural celebration. **Afrikadey!** celebrates African culture through traditional and contemporary music, crafts, food and special scheduled events. Venues for the popular August event are found throughout the area, with festivities concluding at **Prince's Island Park** with an all-day music festival. Visitors can sample fine foods and beverages at the **Eau Claire Market** during 🎵 **Taste of Calgary**, which also occurs in mid-August.

During Labour Day weekend **BBQ on the Bow** offers a barbecue competition, live performances by local bands, a children's craft tent, and vendors selling food samples and take-home goods. The **Masters Tournament** takes place in September at the **Spruce Meadows** outdoor equestrian center, off Hwy. 22X (Spruce Meadows Trail) and Macleod Trail. Other racing and dressage events are held at the center throughout the year.

Sports & Rec

Calgary was an appropriate choice as host of the 1988 Winter Olympic Games—opportunities for indoor and outdoor recreation abound. For information about recreational activities, programs and facilities visitors can phone the city's recreation department by dialing 311 in Calgary or (403) 268-2489.

In winter public **skiing** facilities at **Canada Olympic Park** *(see attraction listing p. 50)* and in numerous areas nearby are available. Canada Olympic Park also is where to go for other **winter sports**, such as bobsledding, luge, ski jumping and snowboarding.

At **Talisman Centre**, 2225 Macleod Tr. S., **swimming, track events** and **weight lifting** are among the popular activities; phone (403) 233-8393. Similar facilities are offered at the following leisure centers: **Gray Family Eau Claire YMCA**, 101 3rd St. S.W.; phone (403) 269-6701; **Southland Leisure Center**, 2000 Southland Dr. S.W.; phone (403) 648-6555; and **Village Square Leisure Center**, 2623 56th St. N.E.; phone (403) 366-3900. The latter two offer wave pools.

Ice-skating is featured during the winter at Olympic Plaza as well as year-round at more than two dozen other locations. The **Olympic Oval**, at 2500 University Dr. N.W., is the site of the 1988 Olympic speed-skating events; skate rentals are available.

Several parks are in the city, particularly along the **Bow River. Fish Creek Provincial Park** *(see Recreation Areas Chart)* has a visitor center and a small lake providing swimming in summer and ice-skating in winter. Joggers and bicyclists use the park's extensive trail system. Other recreation sites include **Bowness, Edworthy** and **Riley** parks in northwest Calgary and **Prince's Island Park** in the city center. The 145-hectare (360-acre) **Glenmore Reservoir**

Bike the trails

provides ample space for **sailing** and **canoeing**; the Dragon Boat races are held in late August.

With spectacular natural areas nearby, many visitors to Calgary will be lured to the wilds to enjoy canoeing, **camping, rafting, hiking** and other outdoor pursuits. **Walking** and **bicycling** trails meander through these regions, as do cross-country skiing routes. **Tennis** and swimming enthusiasts will find courts and pools throughout Calgary.

Golf lovers can play at more than 40 local courses, including 18 holes at **Maple Ridge**, 1240 Mapleglade Dr. S.E.; **McCall Lake**, 1600 32nd Ave. N.E.; **McKenzie Meadows**, 17215 McKenzie Meadows Dr.; and **Shaganappi Point**, 1200 26th St. S.W. Nine-hole courses are at **Confederation Park**, 3204 Collingwood Dr. N.W.; **Lakeview**, 5840 19th St. S.W.; and **Richmond Green**, 2539 33rd Ave. S.W. Some private courses accept visiting golfers; check locally for greens fees and restrictions.

With names like Flames, Stampeders **Roughnecks** and **Hitmen**, Calgary's major sports teams cannot help but be exciting. The **Flames** play **ice hockey** at **Scotiabank Saddledome**, 555 Saddledome Rise S.E. in Stampede Park; phone (407) 777-4646.

The local Canadian **Football** League team, the **Calgary Stampeders**, pounds the turf at **McMahon Stadium**, off 16th Avenue at 1817 Crowchild Tr. N.W. Tickets can be obtained by phoning the box office at (403) 289-0258 or (800) 667-3267. Ticket prices are $33.33-$111.43.

Spruce Meadows, an outdoor equestrian center and show jumping venue 3 kilometres (2 mi.) west on Hwy. 22X (Spruce Meadows Trail) from Macleod Trail at 18011 Spruce Meadows Way S.W., has world-class programs, including international show jumping events. On days when no shows are scheduled the grounds are open free to the public, daily 9-6. Visitors are invited to wander the grounds, picnic and view horses as they are exercised by the trainers; phone (403) 974-4200 for a schedule of Spruce Meadows events.

Performing Arts

Four of Calgary's most illustrious theater and music companies perform in the **Arts Commons** at 205 8th Ave. S.E. The center is shared by **Alberta Theatre Projects, Theatre Calgary, One Yellow Rabbit Performance Theatre, Calgary International Children's Festival,** Downstage and the **Calgary Philharmonic Orchestra.** In addition to four theaters and a concert hall, it contains shops, a restaurant and a coffee bar. For information about performance schedules and ticket sales phone the Arts Commons box office at (403) 294-9494.

Southern Alberta Jubilee Auditorium, 1415 14th Ave. N.W., stages a variety of performing arts, including touring companies of Broadway musicals and presentations by **Calgary Opera;** for details phone the opera company at (403) 262-7286 or the auditorium at (403) 297-8000.

Loose Moose Theatre Company, 1235 26th Ave. S.E., performs adult comedy and drama as well as children's theater; phone (403) 265-5682. **Pumphouse Theatre,** 2140 Pumphouse Ave. S.W., gets its name from the 1913 former pump house that the city converted into two theaters; phone (403) 263-0079, ext. 100, for schedule and ticket information. Midday performances take place in the aptly named **Lunchbox Theatre,** at the base of Calgary Tower at 160 9th Ave. S.E.; phone (403) 265-4292, ext. 0.

A popular dinner theater that often showcases well-known performers in its productions is **Stage West,** 727 42nd Ave. S.E.; phone (403) 243-6642. Other theater, dance and music companies operate locally; check newspapers for performance schedules.

⚑ ATTRACTIONS

SAVE **AERO SPACE MUSEUM OF CALGARY** is at 4629 McCall Way N.E. In a former Royal Air Force drill hall, the museum contains exhibits about western Canada's aviation history. Twenty-four aircraft are displayed, including an F86 Sabre jet, a

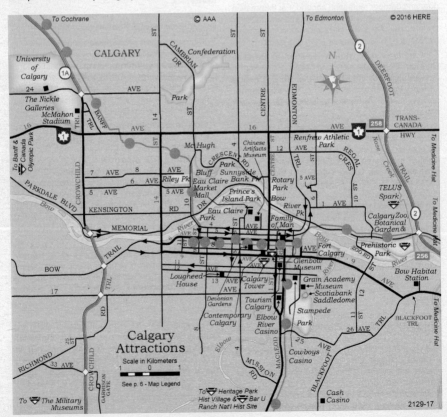

Calgary Attractions

Bell 47G helicopter and one of the few remaining World War II Avro Lancasters. Also featured are piston and jet aircraft engines, aviation artwork and a Martin Baker ejection seat.

Time: Allow 30 minutes minimum. **Hours:** Daily 10-4. Holiday hours in Dec. vary; phone ahead. Closed Jan. 1, Jan. 31 and Christmas. **Cost:** $9.52; $6.67 (ages 60+ and students 12-17 with ID); $4.76 (ages 6-11); $23.81 (family, two adults and up to four children ages 0-17). **Phone:** (403) 250-3752.

BOW HABITAT STATION is at 1440 17A St. S.E. in Pearce Estate City Park. Located along the Bow River, the site features a fish hatchery where six species of trout are raised, 8.5 hectares (21 acres) of interpretive wetland, a nature center and a trout pond. The Discovery Centre educates visitors about fish management, aquatic ecosystems and Alberta's wetlands through both interactive exhibits and aquariums that shelter a variety of local fish species. Highlights include a large model outlining the anatomy of a fish, an exhibit that explores the cycle of water and the 40-minute film "Wet Alberta."

A stocked fish pond is available for children to experience catch-and-release fishing. Interpretive trails allow for exploration of Pearce Estate Park Wetland. Guided tours of the Sam Livingston Fish Hatchery, one of the largest fish hatcheries in North America, last approximately 30 minutes.

Time: Allow 2 hours minimum. **Hours:** Discovery Centre Tues.-Sun. 10-4, mid-May through Oct. 31; Tues.-Sat. 10-4, rest of year. Fish hatchery tours are given at noon and 2. Trout pond and interpretive wetland daily 5 a.m.-11 p.m. (fishing season May 15-Oct. 31). Fish feedings at 11, 1 and 3. Closed major holidays. **Cost:** Discovery Centre $10; $8 (ages 65+ and students with ID); $6 (ages 4-17); $30 (family, two adults and up to four children). Fish

hatchery tour $5; $3 (ages 4-17); $15 (family, two adults and up to four children). Combination ticket $14; $12 (ages 65+ and students with ID); $8 (ages 4-17); $45 (family, two adults and up to four children). Fishing rod rental $5. **Phone:** (403) 297-6561. GT ⊼

BUTTERFIELD ACRES CHILDREN'S FARM is at 254077 Rocky Ridge Rd. At this whimsical, educational farm, visitors can meet and interact with many animals such as chicks and chickens, ducks, turkeys, horses, piglets, ponies, goats, lambs, rabbits, sheep, emus and yaks. In addition to interactive displays and pony and wagon rides, children also can try their hands at milking.

Note: Closed footwear with socks is required. Pets are not permitted. **Time:** Allow 2 hours minimum. **Hours:** Daily 10-4, July-Aug.; Mon.-Fri. 10-2, Sat.-Sun. 10-4, Apr.-June and in Sept. **Cost:** $14.99; $12.99 (ages 65+); $11.99 (ages 1-17). Pony ride $2, or three rides for $5. **Phone:** (403) 239-0638. ⊤⊤ ⊼

CALAWAY PARK, 10 km (6 mi.) w. off Trans-Canada Hwy. Springbank Rd. exit at 245033 Range Rd. 33, is said to be western Canada's largest outdoor amusement park. It features 32 rides, including a roller coaster, a log ride and bumper boats. Live stage shows are presented daily. The landscaped grounds also include an interactive maze, a miniature golf course and a fishing hole.

Kennel, stroller and wheelchair rentals are available. **Time:** Allow 4 hours minimum. **Hours:** Daily 10-7, July 1-Labour Day; Sat.-Sun. and Mon. holidays 10-7, Victoria Day weekend-June 30; Sat.-Sun. and Mon. holidays 11-6, day after Labour Day-Thanksgiving Day. **Cost:** $37.95; $31 (ages 3-6);

▼ See AAA listing this page ▼

$29 (ages 50+); $119.95 (family of four; $25 for each additional family member). After 2 p.m. $22.95; free (ages 0-2). Admission includes unlimited rides, attractions, stage shows and parking; prices for individual games, the maze, fishing and miniature golf vary. Phone ahead to confirm schedule and prices. **Phone:** (403) 240-3822. *(See ad p. 49.)*

THE CALGARY SPACEPORT is on the third floor of the Calgary International Airport off Hwy. 2 (Deerfoot Tr. N.E.) at 2000 Airport Rd. N.E. The entertaining educational facility offers exhibits focusing on space and aeronautics. Hands-on displays, NASA and Canadian Space Agency items, and a simulator ride are featured. Visitors can view a moon rock and learn about flight tracking systems. **Time:** Allow 30 minutes minimum. **Hours:** Mon.-Fri. 9-9, Sat.-Sun. 9-5. **Cost:** Admission free. Simulator ride prices vary; phone ahead. **Phone:** (403) 717-7678.

CALGARY TOWER is in Tower Centre at 101 9th Ave. S.W. at Centre St. S. The tower rises 191 metres (626 ft.) above the city. An observation deck and revolving restaurant provide a panorama of the city and the nearby Rocky Mountains. The observation deck features a glass floor and glass walls, which create in visitors the sensation of floating high above the city. A torch atop the tower burned nonstop during the 1988 Olympic Games; it is illuminated on special occasions.

Using multimedia, a self-guiding tour presents the history of Calgary as well as information about some of the landmarks visible from the tower. **Hours:** Daily 9 a.m.-10 p.m., July-Aug.; 9-9, rest of year. Hours may vary Oct.-May; phone ahead. **Cost:** $17.14; $15.24 (ages 65+); $8.57 (ages 4-12). **Phone:** (403) 266-7171.

CALGARY ZOO, BOTANICAL GARDEN & PREHISTORIC PARK is at 1000 Zoo Rd. N.E. at Memorial Dr. and 12th St. E. In themed areas like Destination Africa and Eurasia, visitors observe nearly 1,500 animals, including purring big cats, yawning river hippos and such rare and endangered species as the Amur tiger.

Basking in an icy, state-of-the-art habitat, five penguin species pretend not to notice the crowds of chilly onlookers drawn to the Penguin Plunge exhibit. Elsewhere, bold guests can thump their chests along with the resident western lowland gorilla troop and enjoy the antics of colobus monkeys. Nearby, Komodo dragons and Indian rhinos hold court in the Eurasia exhibit.

Black bears, cougars and bison are among the creatures children and parents can learn about in the Canadian Wilds. A 2.6-hectare (6.5-acre) prehistoric park dotted by life-size dinosaur replicas transports you to western Canada's bygone Mesozoic landscape. **Time:** Allow 3 hours minimum. **Hours:** Daily 9-6. Last admission 1 hour before closing. Closed Christmas. Phone ahead to confirm schedule. **Cost:** $23; $21 (ages 60+); $15 (ages 3-15). Prices may vary; phone ahead. **Parking:** $9.52. **Phone:** (403) 232-9300 or (800) 588-9993. *(See ad p. 51.)*

CANADA OLYMPIC PARK is at 88 Canada Olympic Rd. S.W. The park, the host area for ski jumping, freestyle skiing, bobsled and luge events at the 1988 Winter Olympic Games, remains a site for year-round sports activities. In winter visitors can learn to ski and snowboard, and in warmer weather, a mountain bike park with more than 25 kilometres (15 mi.) of trails can be enjoyed. The Markin MacPhail Centre, home to several national sports organizations including Hockey Canada, has one international-sized rink and three North American-sized rinks.

Also on-site are the Ice House, a training facility where bobsleigh, skeleton and luge athletes practice; the Olympic bobsleigh track; the 90-metre (295-ft.) ski-jump tower; and the Performance Training Centre. Summer activities include bobsleigh rides, a zipline and a luge ride. A chairlift offers breathtaking scenic views.

Time: Allow 2 hours minimum. **Hours:** Park main gate open daily 5 a.m.-1 a.m. Schedule for facilities and activities vary. **Cost:** Prices for activities and rides vary; phone ahead. **Phone:** (403) 247-5452.

Canada's Sports Hall of Fame is at 169 Canada Olympic Rd. S.W., at Canada Olympic Park. The facility highlights the inspiring achievements of more than 600 inducted athletes. Twelve interactive galleries—including the Motion, Bounce and Olympic & Paralympic galleries—house exhibits relating to 62 different sports, such as hockey, baseball, figure skating, horse racing, downhill and cross-country skiing, auto racing and football.

Visitors to the hall of fame are greeted by a sculpture of hockey legend Wayne Gretzky. In the 120-seat Riddell Family Theatre, an 11-minute film featuring rare Olympic footage about Canadian athletes over the years is shown every half-hour. Items on display include a skin suit worn by Olympic gold medalist skeleton racer Jon Montgomery and golf clubs and trophies belonging to Sandra Post, one of the youngest players to ever win the LPGA Championship. Rare videos, photographs and artifacts from 150 years of Canadian sporting history are on display in the Legends Gallery.

Interactive displays include 3-D hockey, shadowboxing, rowing and wheelchair racing. You also can find out what it feels like to ski jump or to catch a fast pitch. Videos of awe-inspiring moments in sports history are sure to get visitors' hearts pounding as well. **Time:** Allow 2 hours minimum. **Hours:** Daily 10-5, July-Aug.; Tues.-Sun. 10-5 (also Mon. holidays), rest of year. Closed Jan. 1 and Christmas. **Cost:** $12; $10 (ages 65+); $8 (ages 4-18); $35 (family, two adults and two children). **Phone:** (403) 776-1040.

SAVE **FORT CALGARY** is at 750 9th Ave. S.E. The 16-hectare (40-acre) riverside park marks the location of the 1875 North West Mounted Police fort and the Deane House Historic Site, the last remaining building from the site's days as a garrison. Interactive exhibits, hands-on activities and audiovisual presentations tell the story of the site, the settlement and the people of Calgary.

Hours: Daily 9-5. Closed Jan. 1, Good Friday, Christmas Eve, Christmas, day after Christmas and Dec. 31. **Cost:** $11.43; $10.48 (ages 65+ and college students with ID); $6.67 (ages 7-17); $4.76 (ages 3-6). Prices may vary; phone ahead. **Phone:** (403) 290-1875.

GEM **GLENBOW MUSEUM** is at 130 9th Ave. S.E., across from the Calgary Tower. The complex includes a museum, an art gallery, a library and archives. Fascinating men and women who contributed to the development of the province are highlighted in Mavericks: An Incorrigible History of Alberta. Niitsitapiisinni: Our Way of Life features artifacts and interactive displays illustrating Blackfoot traditions and values.

Other galleries feature contemporary art exhibitions, exhibits about warriors, gemstones and West Africa. An Asian sculpture gallery and a hands-on art studio also are on site. **Time:** Allow 2 hours minimum. **Hours:** Mon.-Sat. 9-5 (also 5-9 first

▼ See AAA listing p. 50 ▼

Thurs. of the month), Sun. noon-5, July-Aug.; Tues.-Sat. 9-5 (also 5-9 first Thurs. of the month), Sun. noon-5, rest of year. Closed Christmas. **Cost:** $16; $11 (senior citizens and college students with ID); $10 (ages 7-17); $40 (family, two adults and four children). **Phone:** (403) 268-4110. [⫠]

GRAIN ACADEMY MUSEUM is at Stampede Park off 4th St. S.E. on the second level of Round Up Centre. Visitors can learn about the processes of bringing grain from the field to the table. Highlights include a model grain elevator and a working model train that depicts the transportation of grain from the prairie to the Pacific coast. A movie theater and displays describing the history of grain also are featured. **Time:** Allow 1 hour minimum. **Hours:** Mon.-Fri. 10-4 (11-8 during the Calgary Stampede). Closed major holidays. **Cost:** Donations. **Parking:** $13-$15. **Phone:** (403) 263-4594.

HERITAGE PARK HISTORICAL VILLAGE is 2.5 km (1.5 mi.) w. off Queen Elizabeth II Hwy. to 1900 Heritage Dr. S.W. This living-history museum resembles a pre-1914 village and reflects the fur trade of the 1860s, the pre-railway settlements of the 1880s and businesses and residences 1900-14. Among the park's more than 200 exhibits and attractions are a ranch house, a saloon, pioneer farm machinery and a Hudson's Bay Co. trading post. Most of the buildings are originals that have been moved to the 51-hectare (127-acre) site.

An antique steam train circles the park, and a paddlewheel boat cruises Glenmore Reservoir. The Gasoline Alley Museum features interactive displays and a collection of vintage vehicles. Representing the 1930s, '40s and '50s, Heritage Town Square depicts the prairie's urban enclaves.

Hours: Historical village daily 9:30-5, late May-Labour Day; Sat.-Sun. 9:30-5, day after Labour Day to mid-Oct. Heritage Town Square and Gasoline Alley Museum daily 9:30-4, year-round. **Cost:** (includes unlimited rides) late May to mid-Oct. $26.25; $20.50 (ages 65+); $18.75 (ages 7-14); $13.50 (ages 3-6). Rest of year $10.75; $8.50 (ages 65+); $6.75 (ages 7-14); $5.50 (ages 3-6). Prices may vary; phone ahead. **Parking:** $5 for 7 hours. **Phone:** (403) 268-8500. *(See ad this page.)*

INGLEWOOD BIRD SANCTUARY is at 2425 9th Ave. S.E. on the Bow River. Self-guiding trails wind throughout the forest, where some 270 species of birds and 21 species of mammals have been sighted among the 347 species of plants. Natural history programs and guided nature walks also are offered. **Note:** Some of the sanctuary walking trails are still closed due to damage caused by the 2013 Alberta floods, and a new outdoor learning center is under construction; phone ahead for updates.

Time: Allow 1 hour minimum. **Hours:** Trails daily dawn-dusk. Nature center daily 10-4, May-Sept.; Tues.-Fri. 10-4, Sat. noon-4, rest of year. Tours are given Wed. at 2 and 7, Sat.-Sun. at 11 and 2, Tues. and Thurs. at 2, early June-early Sept. Closed Jan. 1, Easter, Nov. 11, Christmas Eve, Christmas and day after Christmas. **Cost:** Donations. **Phone:** (403) 268-2489. [GT]

[SAVE] **LOUGHEED HOUSE** is at 707 13th Ave. S.W. Built in 1891 and enlarged in 1907, the sandstone mansion was the residence of Sir James Alexander Lougheed, a cabinet minister and party leader in the Senate, and his family. It later served as a barracks for the Canadian Women's Army Corps and as a blood donor clinic and dormitory for the Canadian Red Cross Society; today it houses interpretive exhibits detailing the structure's history and architecture.

▼ *See AAA listing this page* ▼

The lovely 1.1-hectare (2.8-acre) estate includes the formal Beaulieu Gardens. Redesigned every year, the green space dazzles onlookers with such flora as yellow cannas and marigolds, red dahlias, and white and pink peonies. Guided tours by historical interpreters as well as self-guiding audio tours are available. **Time:** Allow 30 minutes minimum. **Hours:** House Wed.-Fri. 11-4, Sat.-Sun. 10-4. Gardens daily 7 a.m.-dusk. Closed major holidays. **Cost:** House $8.10; $6.19 (students with ID and ages 65+); $4.76 (ages 6-12); $23.81 (family, two adults and three children); free (Canadian military with ID). Gardens free. **Phone:** (403) 244-6333. GT ¶¶

THE MILITARY MUSEUMS, 4520 Crowchild Tr. S.W., off Flanders Ave. exit, is home to seven museums detailing the history of the Canadian Forces. On-site are the Naval Museum of Alberta, the Army Museum of Alberta and the Air Force Museum of Alberta as well as museums highlighting Lord Strathcona's Horse Regiment—the Royal Canadians, Princess Patricia's Canadian Light Infantry, The King's Own Calgary Regiment and the Calgary Highlanders.

Galleries re-create battle scenes and specific acts of heroism with audio and artifacts. Featured are an impressive collection of weapons, including guns, cannons and torpedoes; a Banshee Naval jet fighter; a submarine exhibit; and other equipment relating to life in the military. In addition, short videos are shown in two unique theaters: one a to-scale interior model of a C-130 Hercules transport aircraft and the other a period Nissen hut.

Visitors also can view a huge mural in the Queen Elizabeth II Atrium entry hall; videos explain what each mosaic piece represents. Outside, vintage tanks and carriers dot the landscaped grounds.

Time: Allow 3 hours minimum. **Hours:** Daily 9-5. Closed Jan. 1, Christmas and day after Christmas. **Cost:** $9.52; $4.76 (ages 65+); $3.81 (ages 7-17 and students with ID); free (ages 0-6 and veterans and active military with ID); $19.05 (family, six people). **Phone:** (403) 410-2340. 🏧

THE NICKLE GALLERIES is on the University of Calgary campus on the main floor of the Taylor Family Digital Library at 410 University Ct. N.W. The galleries were first established with an initial donation by Sam Nickle of one of the most comprehensive numismatic collections in Canada. In addition to its vast array of ancient coins and other types of money, the museum also possesses an impressive assemblage of rugs and textiles as well as a collection of Western art. Lectures, gallery talks and other events are offered during the school year.

Time: Allow 1 hour minimum. **Hours:** Mon.-Fri. 10-5 (also Thurs. 5-8), Sat. 11-4, Sept.-Apr.; Mon.-Fri. 10-5, rest of year. Closed major holidays. Phone ahead to confirm schedule. **Cost:** Free. **Phone:** (403) 210-6201.

TELUS SPARK is at 220 St. George's Dr. N.E. Science, engineering and art are at the core of this educational feast for the senses with more than 100 interactive displays. In Energy & Innovation, you can inspect a wind turbine and see how much energy your household electronics use. Create snowflakes or view distant galaxies in the Earth & Sky gallery. Check your mood on a special camera or monitor your reaction time in the Being Human exhibit area. In the Open Studio, you can build an invention using toothpicks, take apart a machine or digitally animate a story.

High-definition films and live planetarium shows are the highlight of the HD Digital Dome Theatre. The Creative Kids Museum offers hands-on activities geared toward children under age 8. Daily educational programs and performances connecting science and the arts take place in the 164-seat Presentation Theatre. Brainasium, an outdoor park, offers a 19-metre (63-ft.) slide and other activities for children.

Time: Allow 3 hours minimum. **Hours:** Daily 10-5, July-Aug.; Sun.-Fri. 10-4, Sat. 10-5, rest of year. Closed Aug. 31-Sept. 4 and Christmas. Closed Christmas. **Cost:** $19.95; $17.95 (ages 65+); $15.95 (ages 13-17); $12.95 (ages 3-12). Dome Theatre show additional $10 (40-minute show) or $7 (20-minute show). **Parking:** $5. **Phone:** (403) 817-6800. ¶¶

GAMBLING ESTABLISHMENTS

• SAVE **Century Casino** is at 1010 42nd Ave. S.E. **Hours:** Casino open daily 9:30 a.m.-3 a.m. Slot machines daily 10 a.m.-3 a.m. Table games daily 11 a.m.-3 a.m. Closed Christmas. **Phone:** (403) 287-1183.

Sightseeing
Bus, Train and Van Tours

Brewster Travel Canada offers trips around Banff, Lake Louise, Jasper and the Columbia Icefield; phone (403) 762-6700 or (866) 606-6700 for schedules and fares.

Rocky Mountaineer Vacations offers scenic vacation packages, including the Rocky Mountaineer, a 2-day, all-daylight, narrated rail tour between Canada's west and the Canadian Rockies. The Rocky Mountaineer tour departs mid-April to mid-October; phone (604) 606-7245 or (877) 460-3200.

Walking Tours

Free pamphlets detailing a self-guiding tour of Stephen Avenue, a heavily trafficked commercial thoroughfare, are available from the Calgary Downtown Association, 304 8th Ave. S.W., (403) 215-1570. A showcase for historical buildings, murals and sculptures, the mall extends along 8th Avenue S.W. between 1st Street S.E. and 4th Street S.W. and is open to pedestrians only from 6 a.m. to 6 p.m.

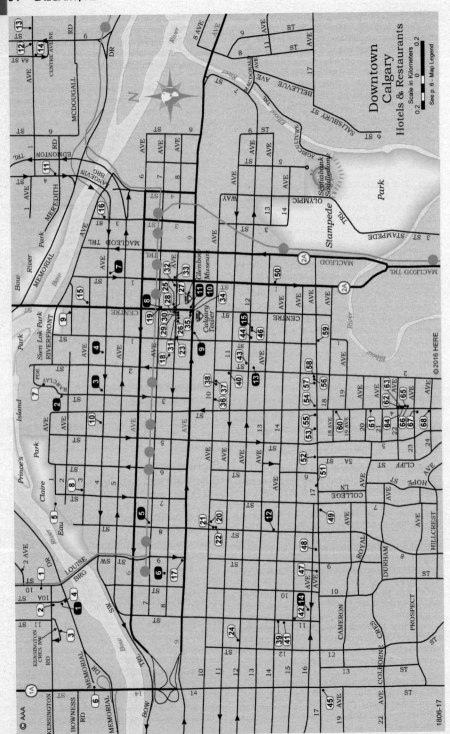

Downtown
Calgary
Hotels & Restaurants

Scale in Kilometers

See p. 6 - Map Legend

© 2016 HERE

1806-17

© AAA

Downtown Calgary

This index helps you "spot" where approved hotels and restaurants are located on the corresponding detailed maps. Hotel daily rate range is for comparison only. Restaurant price range is a combination of lunch and/or dinner. Turn to the listing page for more information and consult display ads for special promotions.

DOWNTOWN CALGARY

Map Page	Hotels	Diamond Rated	Rate Range	Page
1 p. 54	**Kensington Riverside Inn**	▽▽▽	$189-$409 (SAVE)	65
2 p. 54	**Sheraton Suites Calgary Eau Claire**	▽▽▽▽	$149-$789 (SAVE)	65
3 p. 54	**The Westin Calgary**	▽▽▽	$129-$399 (SAVE)	65
4 p. 54	International Hotel of Calgary	▽▽▽	Rates not provided	64
5 p. 54	Sandman Hotel Downtown Calgary	▽▽	Rates not provided	65
6 p. 54	Holiday Inn Express Hotel & Suites Calgary Downtown	▽▽▽	Rates not provided	64
7 p. 54	**Delta Calgary Downtown**	▽▽▽	$100-$301 (SAVE)	63
8 p. 54	**Hyatt Regency Calgary**	▽▽▽▽	$149-$709 (SAVE)	64
9 p. 54	**The Fairmont Palliser**	▽▽▽▽	$169-$699 (SAVE)	64
10 p. 54	**Hotel Le Germain Calgary**	▽▽▽▽	$209-$799 (SAVE)	64
11 p. 54	**Calgary Marriott Downtown**	▽▽▽	$92-$302 (SAVE)	63
12 p. 54	**Best Western Plus Suites Downtown** (See ad p. 63.)	▽▽▽	$149-$249 (SAVE)	63
13 p. 54	**Fairfield Inn & Suites by Marriott Calgary Downtown**	▽▽▽	$125-$240 (SAVE)	63
14 p. 54	Hotel Elan	▽▽▽	$229-$259	64
15 p. 54	Hotel Arts	▽▽▽	Rates not provided	64

Map Page	Restaurants	Diamond Rated	Cuisine	Price Range	Page
1 p. 54	Vero Bistro Moderne	▽▽▽	New Italian	$16-$39	67
2 p. 54	Winebar Kensington	▽▽▽	New World Small Plates	$14-$29	67
3 p. 54	Pulcinella	▽▽	Pizza	$13-$30	67
4 p. 54	**Chef's Table**	▽▽▽▽	New French	$26-$40	66
5 p. 54	Q Haute Cuisine	▽▽▽▽	New World	$15-$150	67
6 p. 54	Sultan's Tent	▽▽	Traditional Moroccan	$20-$29	67
7 p. 54	Prego Cucina Italiana	▽▽▽	Italian	$16-$34	67
8 p. 54	Buchanan's Chop House & Whisky Bar	▽▽▽	Steak	$19-$76	65
9 p. 54	Sakana Grill	▽▽	Japanese	$13-$20	67
10 p. 54	**Caesar's Steakhouse**	▽▽▽	Steak	$15-$52	65
11 p. 54	Whitehall	▽▽▽	New British	$27-$30	67
12 p. 54	La Brezza	▽▽	Italian	$13-$45	66
13 p. 54	Sushi Bar Zipang	▽▽	Japanese	$15-$25	67
14 p. 54	The Main Dish	▽	Deli	$8-$21	66
15 p. 54	**Silver Dragon Restaurant**	▽▽	Chinese	$12-$60	67
16 p. 54	Bookers BBQ Grill & Crab Shack	▽▽	Barbecue	$13-$43	65
17 p. 54	Atlas Specialty Supermarket & Persian Cuisine	▽▽	Persian	$8-$29	65
18 p. 54	Mango Shiva Indian Kitchen & Bar	▽▽▽	Indian	$18-$35	66
19 p. 54	Thomson's Restaurant	▽▽▽	American	$14-$39	67

Map Page	Restaurants (cont'd)	Diamond Rated	Cuisine	Price Range	Page
⑳ p. 54	The Holy Grill	◆	American	$7-$12	66
㉑ p. 54	Posto Pizzeria and Bar	◆◆	Pizza	$18-$24	67
㉒ p. 54	Bonterra Trattoria	◆◆◆	New Italian	$14-$44	65
㉓ p. 54	Murrieta's Bar & Grill	◆◆◆	Western Pacific Rim	$15-$40	67
㉔ p. 54	Pizzeria Gaga	◆	Pizza	$7-$9	67
㉕ p. 54	**Catch Restaurant**	◆◆◆	Seafood	$16-$45	65
㉖ p. 54	Divino Wine & Cheese Bistro	◆◆◆	New Canadian	$17-$42	66
㉗ p. 54	One18 Empire	◆◆◆	New World	$16-$36	67
㉘ p. 54	Catch Oyster Bar	◆◆◆	Seafood	$18-$28	65
㉙ p. 54	Blink Restaurant & Bar	◆◆◆	New World	$15-$39	65
㉚ p. 54	Saltlik A Rare Steakhouse	◆◆◆	Steak	$20-$37	67
㉛ p. 54	The Belvedere	◆◆◆	New Canadian	$22-$47	65
㉜ p. 54	**Centini Restaurant and Lounge**	◆◆◆	Italian	$18-$54	66
㉝ p. 54	Teatro	◆◆◆	New Italian	$18-$55	67
㉞ p. 54	CHARCUT Roast House	◆◆◆	New Canadian	$16-$38	66
㉟ p. 54	Sky 360	◆◆◆	American	$16-$42	67
㊱ p. 54	Craft Beer Market	◆◆	American	$14-$25	66
㊲ p. 54	Thai Sa-On Restaurant	◆◆	Thai	$15-$25	67
㊳ p. 54	Briggs Kitchen + Bar	◆◆◆	New International	$13-$24	65
㊴ p. 54	Myhre's Deli	◆	Sandwiches	$5-$11	67
㊵ p. 54	Vintage Chophouse & Tavern	◆◆◆	Steak	$12-$49	67
㊶ p. 54	Galaxie Diner	◆	Breakfast	$9-$16	66
㊷ p. 54	Good Earth Coffeehouse & Bakery	◆	Breads/Pastries Sandwiches	$6-$9	66
㊸ p. 54	Native Tongues Taqueria	◆◆	New Mexican Small Plates	$25-$53	67
㊹ p. 54	Yellow Door Bistro	◆◆◆	New Mediterranean	$15-$34	67
㊺ p. 54	Moti Mahal	◆◆	Northern Indian	$13-$17	67
㊻ p. 54	Raw Bar	◆◆◆	New Vietnamese Small Plates	$19-$31	67
㊼ p. 54	Cibo	◆◆◆	New Italian	$15-$24	66
㊽ p. 54	The Coup + Meet	◆◆	Vegetarian	$14-$16	66
㊾ p. 54	Manies Pizzaria and Greek Cuisine	◆◆	Greek	$14-$25	66
㊿ p. 54	Manuel Latruwe Belgian Patisserie & Bread Shop	◆◆	Breads/Pastries	$9-$17	66
(51) p. 54	MARKET	◆◆◆	New Canadian	$14-$30	66
(52) p. 54	Una Pizza + Wine	◆◆◆	Mediterranean Small Plates Pizza	$15-$20	67
(53) p. 54	Ox and Angela	◆◆◆	Spanish	$9-$27	67
(54) p. 54	Anju	◆◆◆	New Korean Small Plates	$25-$35	65
(55) p. 54	The Living Room	◆◆◆	New International	$12-$31	66
(56) p. 54	Pigeonhole	◆◆◆	New World Small Plates	$25-$39	67

Map Page	Restaurants (cont'd)	Diamond Rated	Cuisine	Price Range	Page
⑤⑦ p. 54	Cilantro	◈◈◈	California	$18-$44	66
⑤⑧ p. 54	Model Milk	◈◈◈	New World	$19-$38	67
⑤⑨ p. 54	**La Chaumiere Restaurant**	◈◈◈◈	French	$17-$40	66
⑥⓪ p. 54	Hana Sushi	◈◈	Japanese	$8-$19	66
⑥① p. 54	Fleur de Sel	◈◈	New French	$15-$45	66
⑥② p. 54	Sushi Kawa	◈◈	Japanese	$10-$20	67
⑥③ p. 54	Aida's	◈◈	Lebanese	$8-$35	65
⑥④ p. 54	Purple Perk	◈	Coffee/Tea	$9-$15	67
⑥⑤ p. 54	Mercato	◈◈◈	Italian	$15-$43	66
⑥⑥ p. 54	Suzette Brittany Bistro	◈◈◈	French	$16-$24	67
⑥⑦ p. 54	Famoso Neapolitan Pizzeria	◈◈	Pizza	$10-$17	66
⑥⑧ p. 54	The Joyce on 4th Irish Pub	◈◈	Irish	$14-$20	66

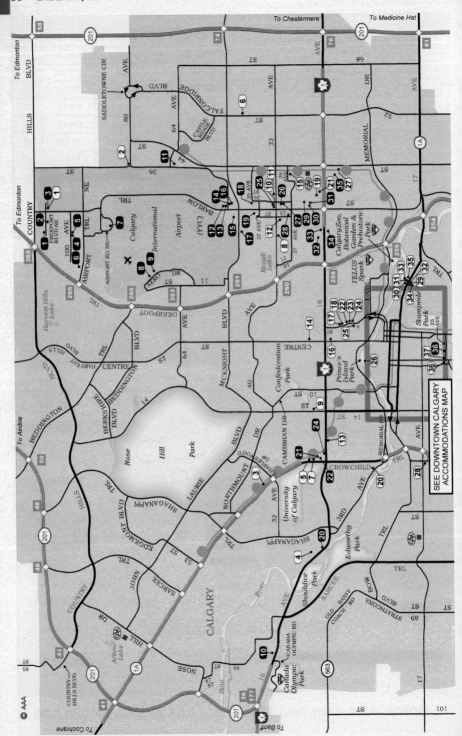

SEE DOWNTOWN CALGARY ACCOMMODATIONS MAP

© AAA

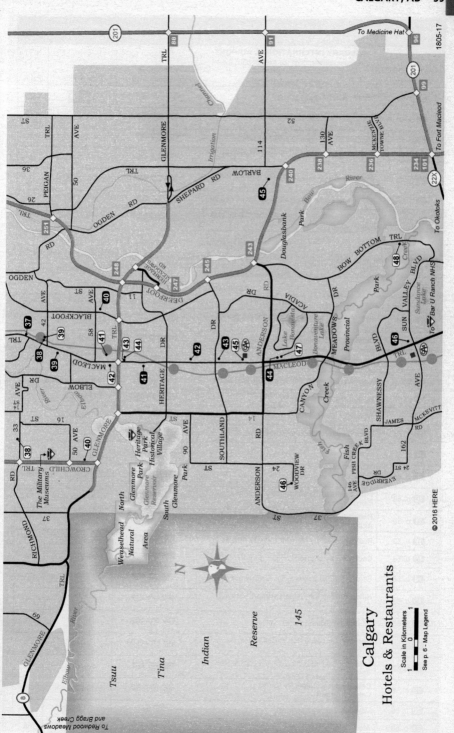

Calgary
Hotels & Restaurants

Scale in Kilometers

See p. 6 - Map Legend

© 2016 HERE

1805-17

✈ Airport Hotels

Map Page	CALGARY INTERNATIONAL AIRPORT (Maximum driving distance from airport: 2.6 mi (4.1 km))	Diamond Rated	Rate Range	Page
3 p. 58	Acclaim Hotel, 1.9 mi (3.0 km)	◈◈◈	Rates not provided	68
1 p. 58	Best Western Premier Freeport Inn & Suites, 2.2 mi (3.5 km)	◈◈◈	$115-$249 (SAVE)	68
2 p. 58	Comfort Inn & Suites, 2.6 mi (4.1 km)	◈◈◈	$94-$230 (SAVE)	69
7 p. 58	Delta Calgary Airport In-Terminal Hotel, on airport property	◈◈◈	$112-$244 (SAVE)	70
4 p. 58	Hampton Inn by Hilton Calgary Airport North, 1.7 mi (2.8 km)	◈◈◈	$99-$179 (SAVE)	71
5 p. 58	Homewood Suites Calgary Airport, 1.7 mi (2.8 km)	◈◈◈	$119-$189	73
6 p. 58	Wyndham Garden Calgary Airport, 2.5 mi (4.0 km)	◈◈◈	$90-$174 (SAVE)	74

Calgary

This index helps you "spot" where approved hotels and restaurants are located on the corresponding detailed maps. Hotel daily rate range is for comparison only. Restaurant price range is a combination of lunch and/or dinner. Turn to the listing page for more information and consult display ads for special promotions.

CALGARY

Map Page	Hotels	Diamond Rated	Rate Range	Page
1 p. 58	**Best Western Premier Freeport Inn & Suites** *(See ad p. 69.)*	◈◈◈	$115-$249 (SAVE)	68
2 p. 58	**Comfort Inn & Suites**	◈◈◈	$94-$230 (SAVE)	69
3 p. 58	Acclaim Hotel	◈◈◈	Rates not provided	68
4 p. 58	**Hampton Inn by Hilton Calgary Airport North**	◈◈◈	$99-$179 (SAVE)	71
5 p. 58	Homewood Suites Calgary Airport	◈◈◈	$119-$189	73
6 p. 58	Wyndham Garden Calgary Airport	◈◈◈	$90-$174 (SAVE)	74
7 p. 58	Delta Calgary Airport In-Terminal Hotel	◈◈◈	$112-$244 (SAVE)	70
8 p. 58	Hotel Clique	◈◈◈	Rates not provided	73
9 p. 58	Applause Hotel	◈◈◈	Rates not provided	68
10 p. 58	**Four Points by Sheraton Hotel & Suites, Calgary West**	◈◈◈	$129-$199 (SAVE)	71
11 p. 58	**Radisson Hotel & Conference Centre Calgary Airport**	◈◈◈	Rates not provided (SAVE)	73
12 p. 58	**Residence Inn by Marriott Calgary Airport**	◈◈◈	$95-$212 (SAVE)	73
13 p. 58	**Courtyard by Marriott Calgary Airport**	◈◈◈	$108-$239 (SAVE)	70
14 p. 58	Sandman Hotel Suites & Spa Calgary Airport	◈◈◈	Rates not provided	73
15 p. 58	**Hilton Garden Inn-Calgary Airport** *(See ad p. 72.)*	◈◈◈	Rates not provided (SAVE)	71
16 p. 58	Holiday Inn Express Airport Calgary	◈◈◈	Rates not provided	73
17 p. 58	**Best Western Plus Port O'Call Hotel** *(See ad p. 64.)*	◈◈◈	$120-$190 (SAVE)	68
18 p. 58	Lakeview Signature Inn *(See ad opposite inside front cover.)*	◈◈◈	$140-$310	73
19 p. 58	**Country Inn & Suites By Carlson, Calgary-Airport**	◈◈◈	$119-$299 (SAVE)	70
20 p. 58	Days Inn Calgary Northwest	◈◈	$113-$189	70
21 p. 58	**Aloft Calgary University**	◈◈◈	$129-$269 (SAVE)	68

CALGARY (cont'd)

Map Page	Hotels (cont'd)	Diamond Rated	Rate Range	Page
22 p. 58	**Best Western Village Park Inn**	◆◆◆	$129-$169 (SAVE)	68
23 p. 58	**Travelodge Calgary University**	◆◆	$109-$189 (SAVE)	74
24 p. 58	**Sheraton Cavalier Hotel**	◆◆◆	$129-$409 (SAVE)	74
25 p. 58	**Comfort Inn & Suites-Airport South**	◆◆	$95-$169 (SAVE)	70
26 p. 58	**Super 8 Calgary Airport**	◆◆	$99-$138 (SAVE)	74
27 p. 58	Executive Royal Hotel North Calgary	◆◆◆	Rates not provided	71
28 p. 58	Days Inn Calgary Airport	◆◆	$160-$189	70
29 p. 58	**Staybridge Suites Calgary Airport**	◆◆◆	$129-$199 (SAVE)	74
30 p. 58	**Four Points by Sheraton Calgary Airport**	◆◆◆	$109-$219 (SAVE)	71
31 p. 58	**Best Western Airport Inn**	◆◆	$139-$159 (SAVE)	68
32 p. 58	**Clarion Hotel & Conference Centre Calgary Airport**	◆◆	$89-$219 (SAVE)	69
33 p. 58	Holiday Inn Calgary-Airport *(See ad p. 73.)*	◆◆◆	Rates not provided	72
34 p. 58	**Coast Plaza Hotel & Conference Centre**	◆◆◆	$109-$289 (SAVE)	69
35 p. 58	**Calgary Westways Guest House**	◆◆◆	$110-$189 (SAVE)	68
36 p. 58	**Best Western Plus Calgary Centre Inn**	◆◆	$130-$180 (SAVE)	68
37 p. 58	**Holiday Inn Calgary-Macleod Trail South**	◆◆◆	$119-$289 (SAVE)	72
38 p. 58	**Comfort Inn & Suites-South**	◆◆◆	$119-$220 (SAVE)	70
39 p. 58	Hotel Blackfoot	◆◆◆	$129-$299	73
40 p. 58	**Econo Lodge South**	◆◆	$95-$190 (SAVE)	70
41 p. 58	**Carriage House Inn**	◆◆◆	$145-$369 (SAVE)	69
42 p. 58	Delta Calgary South	◆◆◆	$85-$182	70
43 p. 58	Holiday Inn Express Hotel & Suites Calgary-South	◆◆◆	$130-$300	73
44 p. 58	**Service Plus Inn & Suites Calgary**	◆◆◆	$139-$159 (SAVE)	74
45 p. 58	Wingate by Wyndham Calgary	◆◆◆	$169-$399	74

Map Page	Restaurants	Diamond Rated	Cuisine	Price Range	Page
1 p. 58	Pacini Pasta & Grill Ristorante	◆◆◆	Italian	$10-$32	76
2 p. 58	XS Lounge and Grill	◆◆	International	$13-$36	76
3 p. 58	Jamesons Irish Pub	◆◆	American	$14-$24	75
4 p. 58	NOtaBLE - The Restaurant	◆◆◆	New Canadian Comfort Food	$17-$42	75
5 p. 58	Nick's Steakhouse & Pizza	◆◆	Steak Pizza	$14-$60	75
6 p. 58	Alberta King of Subs	◆	Sandwiches	$7-$19	74
7 p. 58	Big T's BBQ	◆◆	Barbecue	$12-$32	74
8 p. 58	Misai Japanese Restaurant	◆◆	Japanese	$10-$16	75
9 p. 58	Jimmy's A & A Deli	◆	Mediterranean Deli	$7-$12	75
10 p. 58	Carver's Steakhouse	◆◆◆	Steak	$28-$55	75
11 p. 58	Basil	◆◆	Vietnamese	$6-$15	74
12 p. 58	Thai Boat	◆◆	Thai	$8-$15	76
13 p. 58	Juree's Thai Place Restaurant	◆◆	Thai	$10-$18	75

Map Page	Restaurants (cont'd)	Diamond Rated	Cuisine	Price Range	Page
⑭ p. 58	Lina's Italian Market	▽	Italian Deli	$5-$10	75
⑮ p. 58	Samosa Grill	▽▽	Eastern Indian	$11-$17	76
⑯ p. 58	Santorini Greek Taverna	▽▽	Greek	$15-$30	76
⑰ p. 58	Open Range Steaks & Chops	▽▽▽	New American	$16-$38	75
⑱ p. 58	Big Fish	▽▽▽	Seafood	$15-$32	74
⑲ p. 58	The Pita Basket Cafe	▽	Lebanese	$6-$13	76
⑳ p. 58	Pizza Bobs	▽	Pizza	$12-$25	76
㉑ p. 58	Pio Peruvian Rotisserie Chicken	▽▽	Peruvian	$11-$18	76
㉒ p. 58	Boogie's Burgers	▽	Burgers	$6-$18	75
㉓ p. 58	Oeb Breakfast Co.	▽▽	Breakfast	$13-$18	75
㉔ p. 58	Diner Deluxe	▽▽	American	$10-$23	75
㉕ p. 58	Carino Japanese Bistro	▽▽▽	Japanese Fusion	$9-$35	75
㉖ p. 58	River Cafe	▽▽▽	Regional Canadian	$16-$49	76
㉗ p. 58	Forbidden City Seafood & Dim Sum Restaurant	▽▽	Chinese Dim Sum	$8	75
㉘ p. 58	Cassis Bistro	▽▽▽	French	$15-$30	75
㉙ p. 58	Kane's Harley Diner	▽▽	Comfort Food	$7-$22	75
㉚ p. 58	Without Papers Pizza	▽▽	Pizza	$15-$21	76
㉛ p. 58	Sugo Italian Food & Wine	▽▽▽	Italian	$15-$39	76
㉜ p. 58	The Carmichael	▽▽	International	$14-$36	75
㉝ p. 58	Rouge Restaurant	▽▽▽▽	New French	$16-$46	76
㉞ p. 58	The Nash	▽▽▽	New World	$15-$43	75
㉟ p. 58	Spolumbo's Deli	▽	Deli	$8-$11	76
㊱ p. 58	La Boulangerie	▽	Breads/Pastries	$8-$14	75
㊲ p. 58	Rajdoot	▽▽	Indian	$13-$17	76
㊳ p. 58	Belmont Diner	▽	American	$9-$15	74
㊴ p. 58	Alloy	▽▽▽	New International	$17-$48	74
㊵ p. 58	**Pfanntastic Pannenkoek Haus**	▽▽	Dutch	$8-$18	76
㊶ p. 58	Bagolac Saigon Restaurant	▽▽	Vietnamese	$9-$22	74
㊷ p. 58	Globefish Sushi & Izakaya	▽▽	Sushi	$12-$35	75
㊸ p. 58	Open Sesame	▽▽	Asian	$13-$24	75
㊹ p. 58	Smuggler's Inn	▽▽	Steak	$13-$40	76
㊺ p. 58	Broken Plate Kitchen & Bar	▽▽	Greek	$10-$38	75
㊻ p. 58	Gus's Cafe & Pizzeria	▽▽	Pizza	$8-$24	75
㊼ p. 58	Fire Kirin	▽▽	Asian	$10-$22	75
㊽ p. 58	Bow Valley Ranche Restaurant	▽▽▽	Regional Canadian	$16-$39	75

DOWNTOWN CALGARY
- Restaurants p. 65
- Hotels & Restaurants map & index p. 54

BEST WESTERN PLUS SUITES DOWNTOWN
(403)228-6900

 Hotel
$149-$249

 **AAA Benefit:** Save 10% or more every day and earn 10% bonus points!

Address: 1330 8th St SW T2R 1B6 **Location:** Corner of 8th St and 13th Ave SW. **Facility:** 124 units, some two bedrooms, efficiencies and kitchens. 16 stories, interior corridors. **Amenities:** safes. **Activities:** sauna, exercise room. **Guest Services:** valet and coin laundry. **Featured Amenity:** breakfast buffet. *(See ad this page.)*

CALGARY MARRIOTT DOWNTOWN
(403)266-7331

 Contemporary Hotel
$92-$302

 AAA Benefit: Members save 5% or more!

Address: 110 9th Ave SE T2G 5A6 **Location:** Jct 9th Ave and Centre St; adjacent to TELUS Convention Centre. Across from Calgary Tower. **Facility:** 388 units. 22 stories, interior corridors. **Parking:** valet only. **Amenities:** safes. **Dining:** One18 Empire, see separate listing. **Pool(s):** heated indoor. **Activities:** hot tub, exercise room. **Guest Services:** valet laundry.

DELTA CALGARY DOWNTOWN
(403)266-1980

 Hotel
$100-$301

 **AAA Benefit:** Members save 5% or more!

Address: 209 4th Ave SE T2G 0C6 **Location:** Jct 1st St SE and 4th Ave SE. **Facility:** 394 units. 25 stories, interior corridors. **Parking:** on-site (fee) and valet. **Pool(s):** heated indoor. **Activities:** sauna, hot tub, exercise room. **Guest Services:** valet laundry.

FAIRFIELD INN & SUITES BY MARRIOTT CALGARY DOWNTOWN
(403)351-6500

 Hotel
$125-$240

AAA Benefit: Members save 5% or more!

Address: 239 12th Ave SW T2R 1H7 **Location:** Corner of 2nd St SW. **Facility:** 124 units. 11 stories, interior corridors. *Bath:* shower only. **Parking:** valet only. **Dining:** 2 restaurants. **Activities:** exercise room. **Guest Services:** valet and coin laundry. **Featured Amenity:** breakfast buffet.

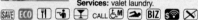

Choose real ratings you can trust from professional inspectors who've been there

▼ *See AAA listing this page* ▼

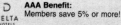

(See map & index p. 54.)

THE FAIRMONT PALLISER (403)262-1234 **9**

Historic Hotel
$169-$699

Address: 133 9th Ave SW T2P 2M3 **Location:** Jct 9th Ave SW and 1st St SW. **Facility:** The spacious lobby at this grand hotel has a stunning imperial theme. Rooms combine modern décor with distinctive historical elements to create an elegant upscale ambiance. 407 units, some kitchens. 12 stories, interior corridors. **Parking:** on-site (fee) and valet, winter plug-ins. **Terms:** check-in 4 pm, cancellation fee imposed. **Amenities:** safes. **Pool(s):** heated indoor. **Activities:** hot tub, steamroom, bicycles, in-room exercise equipment, spa. **Guest Services:** valet laundry.

[SAVE] [ECO] [icons] / [SOME UNITS] [icons]

HOLIDAY INN EXPRESS HOTEL & SUITES CALGARY
DOWNTOWN 403/269-8262 **6**
[icons] Hotel. **Address:** 1020 8th Ave SW T2P 1J2

HOTEL ARTS 403/266-4611 **15**
[icons] Boutique Contemporary Hotel. **Address:** 119 12th Ave SW T2R 0G8

HOTEL ELAN (403)229-2040 **14**
[icons] Boutique Contemporary Hotel. **Address:** 1122 16th Ave SW T2R 0T6

AAA Vacations® packages ...

exciting itineraries

and exclusive values

HOTEL LE GERMAIN CALGARY (403)264-8990 **10**

Boutique
Contemporary
Hotel
$209-$799

Address: 899 Centre St SW T2G 1B8 **Location:** Corner of 1st St SW and 9th Ave SW; center. **Facility:** This sleek, downtown hotel offers ultramodern guest rooms with desks you can really spread out on, luxurious bedding and a little sitting area with lounge chairs and a side table. 143 units. 12 stories, interior corridors. **Parking:** on-site (fee) and valet. **Terms:** cancellation fee imposed, resort fee. **Amenities:** safes. **Dining:** CHARCUT Roast House, see separate listing. **Activities:** sauna, exercise room, in-room exercise equipment, spa. **Guest Services:** valet laundry. **Featured Amenity: continental breakfast.**

[SAVE] [icons] / [SOME UNITS] [icons]

HYATT REGENCY CALGARY (403)717-1234 **8**

[icons]
Hotel
$149-$709

AAA Benefit: Members save 10%!

Address: 700 Centre St SE T2G 5P6 **Location:** Corner of Centre St and 7th Ave SW. Adjacent to TELUS Convention Centre. **Facility:** Standard rooms feature a handsome design with upholstered lounge chairs, ottomans and side tables. Make time to wander the gorgeous public areas to check out the hotel's amazing art collection. 355 units. 22 stories, interior corridors. **Parking:** on-site (fee) and valet. **Terms:** cancellation fee imposed. **Amenities:** safes. **Dining:** Catch Oyster Bar, Catch Restaurant, Thomson's Restaurant, see separate listings. **Pool(s):** heated indoor. **Activities:** hot tub, steamroom, bicycles, exercise room, in-room exercise equipment, spa. **Guest Services:** valet laundry, boarding pass kiosk.

[SAVE] [icons] CALL [icons] / [SOME UNITS] [icons]

INTERNATIONAL HOTEL OF CALGARY 403/265-9600 **4**
[icons] Hotel. **Address:** 220 4th Ave SW T2P 0H5

▼ See AAA listing p. 68 ▼

(See map & index p. 54.)

KENSINGTON RIVERSIDE INN

(403)228-4442 **1**

Boutique Hotel
$189-$409

Address: 1126 Memorial Dr NW T2N 3E3 **Location:** Just w of 10th St NW. Located in Kensington area. **Facility:** This exquisite little gem features original artwork, gourmet breakfasts and is near the trendy Kensington shopping area. Some of the elegant, modern suites have a private garden patio or a fireplace. 19 units. 2 stories, interior corridors. **Parking:** on-site (fee). **Terms:** cancellation fee imposed, resort fee. **Dining:** Chef's Table, see separate listing. **Activities:** bicycles, trails. **Guest Services:** valet laundry.

SAVE ⑪ ⑦ HS 📶 ✕

SANDMAN HOTEL DOWNTOWN CALGARY

403/237-8626 **5**

◆◆ Hotel. **Address:** 888 7th Ave SW T2P 3J3

SHERATON SUITES CALGARY EAU CLAIRE

(403)266-7200 **2**

◆◆◆
Hotel
$149-$789

Sheraton Ⓢ

AAA Benefit: Members save up to 15%, plus Starwood Preferred Guest® benefits!

Address: 255 Barclay Parade SW T2P 5C2 **Location:** At 3rd St SW and 2nd Ave SW. **Facility:** The downtown location here is prime being next to Eau Claire Market and Prince's Island Park. All of the upscale suites include separate living areas with plenty of seating and large two-sided desks. 323 units, some two bedrooms. 15 stories, interior corridors. **Parking:** valet only. **Terms:** cancellation fee imposed. **Amenities:** *Some:* safes. **Dining:** 2 restaurants. **Pool(s):** heated indoor. **Activities:** hot tub, trails, exercise room, massage. **Guest Services:** valet and coin laundry.

SAVE ECO ⑪ 👤 ⑦ CALL 🌙 🏊 BIZ SHS 📶 ✕ 🎦 🔒 📠 🖨 / SOME UNITS 🐾

THE WESTIN CALGARY

(403)266-1611 **3**

◆◆◆
Hotel
$129-$399

WESTIN HOTELS & RESORTS

AAA Benefit: Members save up to 15%, plus Starwood Preferred Guest® benefits!

Address: 320 4th Ave SW T2P 2S6 **Location:** Corner of 4th Ave SW and 3rd St. **Facility:** 525 units. 20 stories, interior corridors. **Parking:** on-site (fee) and valet. **Terms:** cancellation fee imposed. **Amenities:** safes. **Dining:** 2 restaurants. **Pool(s):** heated indoor. **Activities:** sauna, exercise room, in-room exercise equipment, massage. **Guest Services:** valet laundry.

SAVE ⑪ 👤 ⑦ CALL 🌙 🏊 BIZ HS 📶 ✕ 🎦 🔒 🖨 / SOME UNITS 🐾

WHERE TO EAT

AIDA'S

403/541-1189 **63**

◆ Lebanese. Casual Dining. **Address:** 2208 4th St SW T2S 1W9

ANJU

403/460-3341 **54**

◆◆◆ New Korean Small Plates. Casual Dining. **Address:** 344 17th Ave SW T2S 0A5

ATLAS SPECIALTY SUPERMARKET & PERSIAN CUISINE

403/230-0990 **17**

◆◆◆ Persian. Casual Dining. **Address:** 1000 9th Ave SW, #100 T2P 2Y6

THE BELVEDERE

403/265-9595 **31**

◆◆◆ New Canadian. Fine Dining. **Address:** 107 8th Ave SW T2P 1B4

BLINK RESTAURANT & BAR

403/263-5330 **29**

◆◆◆ New World. Casual Dining. **Address:** 111 8th Ave SW T2B 1B4

BONTERRA TRATTORIA

403/262-8480 **22**

◆◆◆ New Italian. Casual Dining. **Address:** 1016 8th St SW T2R 1K2

BOOKERS BBQ GRILL & CRAB SHACK

403/264-6419 **16**

◆◆ Barbecue. Casual Dining. **Address:** 316 3rd St SE T2G 2S4

BRIGGS KITCHEN + BAR

587/350-5015 **38**

◆◆ New International. Casual Dining. **Address:** 317 10 Ave SW, #100 T2R 0A5

BUCHANAN'S CHOP HOUSE & WHISKY BAR

403/261-4646 **8**

◆◆◆ Steak. Casual Dining. **Address:** 738 SW 3rd Ave T2P 0G7

CAESAR'S STEAKHOUSE

403/264-1222 **10**

◆◆◆
Steak
Fine Dining
$15-$52

AAA Inspector Notes: A trip to the West is not complete without a stop at this great steakhouse, one of the city's first and finest. The upscale room has intimate lighting, beautiful wood paneling, interesting Roman themed artwork and buzzes with downtown energy, although there are some cozy corners too. Service flows smoothly with a team of professional dressed servers. And what would a Calgary steakhouse be without wonderful Alberta AAA beef grilled and seasoned to perfection along with other classic menu choices? **Features:** full bar. **Reservations:** suggested. **Address:** 512 4th Ave SW T2P 0J6 **Location:** Just e of 5th St SW. **Parking:** valet and street only. L D

CATCH OYSTER BAR

403/206-0000 **28**

◆◆◆ Seafood. Casual Dining. **Address:** 100 8th Ave SE T2P 0K6

CATCH RESTAURANT

403/206-0000 **25**

◆◆◆
Seafood
Fine Dining
$16-$45

AAA Inspector Notes: On the second level above the oyster bar, this upscale, striking dining room—with lofty ceilings and exposed original stone—is where diners can enjoy a remarkable and changing offering of seafood lovers might find. Alaskan sable fish, Nova Scotia lobster, British Columbia oysters, spot prawns and wild ling cod are some of the choices seafood lovers might find. For the carnivores, Alberta AAA beef and other meats are also on the menu. An impressive wine list is presented on an iPad. **Features:** full bar. **Reservations:** suggested. **Address:** 100 8th Ave SE T2P 0K6 **Location:** Corner of Centre St and 7th Ave SW; in Hyatt Regency Calgary. **Parking:** on-site and street. L D

(See map & index p. 54.)

CENTINI RESTAURANT AND LOUNGE
403/269-1600 (32)

Italian
Fine Dining
$18-$54

AAA Inspector Notes: Experience new Italian cuisine fused with Asian and French influences enhanced with local ingredients. An excellent selection of wines, cognacs and aged scotches offers great complements. Menus change seasonally, so watch for fresh Italian truffles in the fall. While the dining room is upscale, the atmosphere remains quite informal. **Features:** full bar. **Reservations:** suggested. **Address:** 160 8th Ave SE T2G 0K6 **Location:** Corner of 8th Ave SE (Stephen Ave) and 1st St SE; in TELUS Convention Centre. **Parking:** street only. L D CALL M

CHARCUT ROAST HOUSE
403/984-2180 (34)
New Canadian. Casual Dining. **Address:** 899 Centre St SW T2G 1B8

CHEF'S TABLE
403/228-4442 (4)

New
French
Fine Dining
$26-$40

AAA Inspector Notes: In trendy Kensington, this tiny restaurant is one of the best in the city. Relax in the contemporary lounge before or after dinner to enjoy the fireplace and original artwork, and then head to the dining room, where an open-kitchen concept offers real insight into the inner workings of the kitchen. The chef has a creative and deft touch with flavor, so the food is delicious, and plates are beautifully presented. A tasting menu changes biweekly. **Features:** full bar, patio dining, Sunday brunch. **Reservations:** suggested. **Address:** 1126 Memorial Dr NW T2N 3E3 **Location:** Just w of 10th St NW; in Kensington Riverside Inn. **Parking:** street only. B D CALL M

Elegant cuisine, award winning with open kitchen design

CIBO
403/984-4755 (47)
New Italian. Casual Dining. **Address:** 1012 17th Ave SW T2T 0A5

CILANTRO
403/229-1177 (57)
California. Casual Dining. **Address:** 338 17th Ave SW T2S 0A8

THE COUP + MEET
403/541-1041 (48)
Vegetarian. Casual Dining. **Address:** 924 B 17th Ave SW T2T 0A2

CRAFT BEER MARKET
403/514-2337 (36)
American. Gastropub. **Address:** 345 10th Ave SW T2R 0A5

DIVINO WINE & CHEESE BISTRO
403/410-5555 (26)
New Canadian. Fine Dining. **Address:** 113 8th Ave SW T2P 1B4

EARLS KITCHEN + BAR
American. Casual Dining.
LOCATIONS:
Address: 2401 4th St SW T2S 1X5 **Phone:** 403/228-4141
Address: 315 8th Ave SW T2P 1C4 **Phone:** 403/265-3275

FAMOSO NEAPOLITAN PIZZERIA
403/455-3839 (67)
Pizza. Casual Dining. **Address:** 2303 4th St SW, #105 T2S 2S7

FLEUR DE SEL
403/228-9764 (61)
New French. Casual Dining. **Address:** 2015 4th St SW, #2 T2S 1W6

GALAXIE DINER
403/228-0001 (41)
Breakfast. Casual Dining. **Address:** 1413 11th St SW T3C 0M9

GOOD EARTH COFFEEHOUSE & BAKERY
403/228-9543 (42)
Breads/Pastries Sandwiches. Quick Serve. **Address:** 1502 11th St SW T2R 1G9

HANA SUSHI
403/229-1499 (60)
Japanese. Casual Dining. **Address:** 1807 4th St SW T2S 1W2

THE HOLY GRILL
403/261-9759 (20)
American. Quick Serve. **Address:** 827 10th Ave SW T2R 0B4

JOEY RESTAURANTS
403/263-6336
American. Casual Dining. **Address:** 200 Barclay Parade SW T2P 4R5

THE JOYCE ON 4TH IRISH PUB
403/541-9168 (68)
Irish. Casual Dining. **Address:** 506 24th Ave SW T2S 0K4

LA BREZZA
403/262-6230 (12)
Italian. Casual Dining. **Address:** 990 1st Ave NE T2E 4J9

LA CHAUMIERE RESTAURANT
403/228-5690 (59)

French
Fine Dining
$17-$40

AAA Inspector Notes: This upscale restaurant's impressive, almost château-like building has a peaked roof and elegant exterior, making it an ideal spot for fine French dining. Classic cuisine is offered with everything from appetizers of escargot and sautéed foie gras to entrées of salmon, duck breast, veal sweetbreads or Châteaubriand, to name a few. Grand Marnier soufflés are a dessert specialty. **Features:** full bar. **Reservations:** suggested. **Address:** 139 17th Ave SW T2S 0A1 **Location:** Corner of 1st St SW and 17th Ave SW. L D

THE LIVING ROOM
403/228-9830 (55)
New International. Casual Dining. **Address:** 514 17th Ave SW T5W 4X6

THE MAIN DISH
403/265-3474 (14)
Deli. Casual Dining. **Address:** 903 General Ave NE T2E 0P4

MANGO SHIVA INDIAN KITCHEN & BAR
403/290-1644 (18)
Indian. Casual Dining. **Address:** 218 8th Ave T2P 1B5

MANIES PIZZARIA AND GREEK CUISINE
403/228-9207 (49)
Greek. Casual Dining. **Address:** 819 17th Ave SW T2T 0A1

MANUEL LATRUWE BELGIAN PATISSERIE & BREAD SHOP
403/261-1092 (50)
Breads/Pastries. Quick Serve. **Address:** 1333 1st St SE T2G 5L1

MARKET
403/474-4414 (51)
New Canadian. Casual Dining. **Address:** 718 17 Ave SW T2S 0B7

MERCATO
403/263-5535 (65)
Italian. Casual Dining. **Address:** 2224 4th Rd SW T2S 1W9

(See map & index p. 54.)

MODEL MILK 403/265-7343 (58)
◆◆ New World. Casual Dining. **Address:** 308 17th Ave SW T2S 0A8

MOTI MAHAL 403/228-9990 (45)
◆◆ Northern Indian. Casual Dining. **Address:** 1805 14th St SW T2T 3P1

MOXIE'S CLASSIC GRILL 403/234-7507
◆◆ American. Casual Dining. **Address:** 888 7th Ave SW T2P 3J3

MURRIETA'S BAR & GRILL 403/269-7707 (23)
◆◆◆ Western Pacific Rim. Casual Dining. **Address:** 200-808 1st St SW T2P 1M9

MYHRE'S DELI 403/244-6602 (39)
◆ Sandwiches. Quick Serve. **Address:** 1411 11th St SW T2R 1G7

NATIVE TONGUES TAQUERIA 403/263-9444 (43)
◆◆ New Mexican Small Plates. Casual Dining. **Address:** 235 12th Ave SW T2R 1H7

ONE18 EMPIRE 403/269-0299 (27)
◆◆ New World. Casual Dining. **Address:** 820 Centre St SE T2G 5J2

ORIENTAL PHOENIX 403/262-3633
◆◆ Vietnamese. Casual Dining. **Address:** 401 9th Ave S, Unit 105 T2P 3C5

OX AND ANGELA 403/457-1432 (53)
◆◆ Spanish. Casual Dining. **Address:** 528 17th Ave SW T2S 0A9

PIGEONHOLE 403/452-4694 (56)
◆◆ New World Small Plates. Casual Dining. **Address:** 306 17 Ave SW T2S 1V5

PIZZERIA GAGA 403/264-2421 (24)
◆ Pizza. Quick Serve. **Address:** 1236 12 Ave SW T3C 1A7

POSTO PIZZERIA AND BAR 403/262-4876 (21)
◆◆ Pizza. Casual Dining. **Address:** 1014 8th St SW T2R 1K2

PREGO CUCINA ITALIANA 403/233-7885 (7)
◆◆◆ Italian. Casual Dining. **Address:** 200 Barclay Parade S, #218 T2P 4R5

PULCINELLA 403/283-1166 (3)
◆◆ Pizza. Casual Dining. **Address:** 1147 Kensington Cres NW T2N 1X7

PURPLE PERK 403/244-1300 (64)
◆ Coffee/Tea. Quick Serve. **Address:** 2212 4th St SW T2S 1W9

Q HAUTE CUISINE 403/262-5554 (5)
◆◆ ◆◆ New World. Fine Dining. **Address:** 100 La Caille Pl SW T2P 5E2

RAW BAR 403/206-9565 (46)
◆◆◆ New Vietnamese Small Plates. Casual Dining. **Address:** 119 12th Ave SW T2R 0G8

SAKANA GRILL 403/290-1118 (9)
◆◆ Japanese. Casual Dining. **Address:** 116 2nd Ave SW T2P 0B9

SALTLIK A RARE STEAKHOUSE 403/537-1160 (30)
◆◆◆ Steak. Fine Dining. **Address:** 101 8th Ave SW T2P 1B4

SILVER DRAGON RESTAURANT 403/264-5326 (15)
◆◆ ◆◆
Chinese
Casual Dining
$12-$60
AAA Inspector Notes: This restaurant specializes in Cantonese and Szechuan cuisine, including excellent ginger beef. A delicious dim sum selection is served each day. The contemporary decor comprises nouveau Oriental artwork. Servers are cordial. **Features:** full bar.
Reservations: suggested. **Address:** 106 3rd Ave SE T2G 0B6 **Location:** In Chinatown. **Parking:** street only. [L] [D]

SKY 360 403/532-7966 (35)
◆◆◆ American. Fine Dining. **Address:** 101 9th Ave SW T2P 1J9

SULTAN'S TENT 403/244-2333 (6)
◆◆ Traditional Moroccan. Casual Dining. **Address:** 4 14th St NW T2N 1Z4

SUSHI BAR ZIPANG 403/262-1888 (13)
◆◆ Japanese. Casual Dining. **Address:** 1010 1st Ave NE T2E 7W7

SUSHI KAWA 403/802-0058 (62)
◆◆ Japanese. Casual Dining. **Address:** 2204 4th St SW T2S 1W9

SUZETTE BRITTANY BISTRO 403/802-0036 (66)
◆◆◆ French. Casual Dining. **Address:** 2210 4 St T2S 1W9

TEATRO 403/290-1012 (33)
◆◆◆ New Italian. Fine Dining. **Address:** 200 8th Ave SE T2G 0K7

THAI SA-ON RESTAURANT 403/264-3526 (37)
◆◆ Thai. Casual Dining. **Address:** 351 10th Ave SW T2R 0A5

THOMSON'S RESTAURANT 403/537-4449 (19)
◆◆◆ American. Casual Dining. **Address:** 700 Centre St SE T2G 5P6

UNA PIZZA + WINE 403/453-1183 (52)
◆◆◆ Mediterranean Small Plates Pizza. Casual Dining. **Address:** 618 17th Ave SW T2S 0B4

VERO BISTRO MODERNE 403/283-8988 (1)
◆◆◆ New Italian. Casual Dining. **Address:** 209 10th St T2N 1V5

VINTAGE CHOPHOUSE & TAVERN 403/262-7262 (40)
◆◆◆ Steak. Fine Dining. **Address:** 322 11th Ave SW T2R 0C5

WHITEHALL 587/349-9008 (11)
◆◆◆ New British. Fine Dining. **Address:** 24 4 St NE T2E 3R7

WINEBAR KENSINGTON 403/457-1144 (2)
◆◆◆ New World Small Plates. Casual Dining. **Address:** 1131 Kensington Rd NW T2N 3P4

YELLOW DOOR BISTRO 403/206-9585 (44)
◆◆◆ New Mediterranean. Casual Dining. **Address:** 119 12 Ave SW T2R 0G8

CALGARY

- Restaurants p. 74
- Hotels & Restaurants map & index p. 58

ACCLAIM HOTEL   403/291-8000
 Hotel. **Address:** 123 Freeport Blvd NE T3N 0A3

ALOFT CALGARY UNIVERSITY   (403)289-1973

Contemporary Hotel
$129-$269

 AAA Benefit: Members save up to 15%, plus Starwood Preferred Guest® benefits!

Address: 2359 Banff Tr NW T2M 4L2 **Location:** Just n of jct Trans-Canada Hwy 1 and Crowfchild Tr. Located in Motel Village. **Facility:** 143 units. 3 stories, interior corridors. *Bath:* shower only. **Parking:** winter plug-ins. **Terms:** cancellation fee imposed. **Amenities:** safes. **Pool(s):** heated indoor. **Activities:** exercise room, spa. **Guest Services:** valet and coin laundry. **Featured Amenity: breakfast buffet.**

APPLAUSE HOTEL   403/460-9589
 Contemporary Hotel. **Address:** 22 Aero Cres NE T2E 7Y5

BEST WESTERN AIRPORT INN   (403)250-5015

Hotel
$139-$159

Best Western. **AAA Benefit:** Save 10% or more every day and earn 10% bonus points!

Address: 1947 18th Ave NE T2E 7T8 **Location:** 0.6 mi (1 km) e of jct Hwy 2 (Deerfoot Tr) and 16th Ave NE (Trans-Canada Hwy 1), just n on 19th St NE, then just w. **Facility:** 76 units. 3 stories, interior corridors. **Parking:** winter plug-ins. **Terms:** cancellation fee imposed. **Amenities:** *Some:* safes. **Pool(s):** heated indoor. **Activities:** hot tub, exercise room. **Guest Services:** valet and coin laundry. **Featured Amenity: continental breakfast.**

BEST WESTERN PLUS CALGARY CENTRE INN
                                                  (403)287-3900

Hotel
$130-$180

Best Western PLUS. **AAA Benefit:** Save 10% or more every day and earn 10% bonus points!

Address: 3630 Macleod Tr S T2G 2P9 **Location:** East side of Hwy 2A (Macleod Tr) at 36th Ave SE. **Facility:** 71 units. 4 stories, interior corridors. **Parking:** winter plug-ins. **Pool(s):** heated indoor. **Activities:** hot tub, exercise room. **Guest Services:** valet and coin laundry. **Featured Amenity: full hot breakfast.**

BEST WESTERN PLUS PORT O'CALL HOTEL
                                                  (403)291-4600

Hotel
$120-$190

Best Western PLUS. **AAA Benefit:** Save 10% or more every day and earn 10% bonus points!

Address: 1935 McKnight Blvd NE T2E 6V4 **Location:** 1.6 mi (2.5 km) ne of jct Hwy 2 (Deerfoot Tr); at 19th St NE. **Facility:** 201 units. 6-7 stories, interior corridors. **Amenities:** *Some:* safes. **Dining:** 2 restaurants. **Pool(s):** heated indoor. **Activities:** hot tub, steamroom, exercise room, massage. **Guest Services:** valet laundry. *(See ad p. 64.)*

BEST WESTERN PREMIER FREEPORT INN & SUITES
                                                  (403)264-9650

Hotel
$115-$249

PREMIER BEST WESTERN. **AAA Benefit:** Save 10% or more every day and earn 10% bonus points!

Address: 86 Freeport Blvd NE T3J 5J9 **Location:** 1 mi (1.6 km) n of Calgary International Airport on Barlow Tr, just w. **Facility:** 97 units. 4 stories, interior corridors. **Parking:** winter plug-ins. **Amenities:** safes. **Pool(s):** heated indoor. **Activities:** hot tub, exercise room. **Guest Services:** valet and coin laundry, area transportation. *(See ad p. 69.)*

BEST WESTERN VILLAGE PARK INN   (403)289-0241

Hotel
$129-$169

Best Western. **AAA Benefit:** Save 10% or more every day and earn 10% bonus points!

Address: 1804 Crowchild Tr NW T2M 3Y7 **Location:** Just ne of jct Trans-Canada Hwy 1 and Crowfchild Tr. Located in Motel Village. **Facility:** 160 units. 5 stories, interior corridors. **Amenities:** safes. **Pool(s):** heated indoor. **Activities:** hot tub, exercise room. **Guest Services:** valet and coin laundry.

CALGARY WESTWAYS GUEST HOUSE
                                                  (403)229-1758

Historic Bed & Breakfast
$110-$189

Address: 216 25th Ave SW T2S 0L1 **Location:** 1.1 mi (1.7 km) s on Hwy 2A (Macleod Tr); just w. Located in a residential area. **Facility:** This nicely furnished 1912 house has original woodwork in the dining area. Room sizes vary from quite cozy to the top-floor units which are the largest and most luxurious. 5 units. 3 stories (no elevator), interior corridors. **Parking:** winter plug-ins. **Terms:** 2 night minimum stay - seasonal, 4 day cancellation notice-fee imposed. **Activities:** bicycles. **Featured Amenity: full hot breakfast.**

(See map & index p. 58.)

CARRIAGE HOUSE INN

(403)253-1101 **42**

Hotel
$145-$369

Address: 9030 Macleod Tr S T2H 0M4 **Location:** On Hwy 2A (Macleod Tr); corner of 90th Ave SW. **Facility:** 157 units. 4-10 stories, interior corridors. **Parking:** winter plug-ins. **Dining:** 4 restaurants. **Pool(s):** heated outdoor. **Activities:** hot tub, steamroom, exercise room, massage. **Guest Services:** valet laundry. **Featured Amenity: breakfast buffet.**

SAVE ECO 🍴 👥 ⛱ 🏊 BIZ
HS 🛜 ✖ 🎥 🔋 💻
/SOME UNITS 🛏 🛎

COAST PLAZA HOTEL & CONFERENCE CENTRE

(403)248-8888 **35**

Hotel
$109-$289

Address: 1316 33rd St NE T2A 6B6 **Location:** Just s of jct 16th Ave (Trans-Canada Hwy 1) and 36th St NE, just w on 12th Ave NE. Adjacent to Pacific Place Mall. **Facility:** 248 units. 6-12 stories, interior corridors. **Parking:** winter plug-ins. **Terms:** 3 day cancellation notice-fee imposed. **Amenities:** safes. **Dining:** nightclub. **Pool(s):** heated indoor. **Activities:** sauna, hot tub, exercise room, massage. **Guest Services:** valet laundry, area transportation.

SAVE ECO ➡ 🍴 👥 ⛱ 🏊
BIZ HS 🛜 ✖ 🎥 🔋 💻
/SOME UNITS 🛏 🛎

CLARION HOTEL & CONFERENCE CENTRE CALGARY AIRPORT

(403)291-4666 **33**

Hotel
$89-$219

Address: 2120 16th Ave NE T2E 1L4 **Location:** Just e of jct Hwy 2 (Deerfoot Tr) and 16th Ave NE (Trans-Canada Hwy 1). **Facility:** 184 units. 10 stories, interior corridors. **Parking:** winter plug-ins. **Pool(s):** heated indoor. **Activities:** hot tub, exercise room. **Guest Services:** valet laundry.

SAVE ECO ➡ 🍴 👥 ⛱
CALL 📞💲M 🏊 BIZ HS 🛜 ✖
💻 /SOME UNITS 🛏 🔋 💻

COMFORT INN & SUITES

(587)349-7289 **2**

Hotel
$94-$230

Address: 147 Freeport Cres NE T3J 0T3 **Location:** Hwy 2 (Deerfoot Tr) exit 266, just ne. Located in an industrial area. **Facility:** 100 units. 4 stories, interior corridors. **Parking:** winter plug-ins. **Terms:** cancellation fee imposed. **Pool(s):** heated indoor. **Activities:** hot tub, exercise room. **Guest Services:** valet and coin laundry. **Featured Amenity: breakfast buffet.**

SAVE ➡ 🏊 BIZ HS 🛜 ✖
🔋 🛎 💻

▼ See AAA listing p. 68 ▼

Get up to 20 percent off Hertz rentals

PLUS exclusive everyday member benefits

(See map & index p. 58.)

COMFORT INN & SUITES-AIRPORT SOUTH
(403)735-1966 **26**

Hotel
$95-$169

Address: 3111 26th St NE T1Y 7E4 **Location:** Just se of jct 32nd Ave NE and Barlow Tr NE. **Facility:** 74 units. 4 stories, interior corridors. **Parking:** winter plug-ins. **Amenities:** safes. **Pool(s):** heated indoor. **Activities:** hot tub, exercise room. **Guest Services:** valet and coin laundry. **Featured Amenity: full hot breakfast.**

[SAVE] [⊀] [†]↑ [▧] [BIZ] [HS] [⇩]
[✕] [▭] / SOME UNITS [🛏] [🖼]

COMFORT INN & SUITES-SOUTH
(403)287-7070 **39**

Hotel
$119-$220

Address: 4611 Macleod Tr SW T2G 0A6 **Location:** Hwy 2A (Macleod Tr), w on 45th Ave. **Facility:** 93 units. 4 stories, interior corridors. **Parking:** winter plug-ins. **Amenities:** safes. **Pool(s):** heated indoor. **Activities:** hot tub, exercise room. **Guest Services:** valet and coin laundry, rental car service. **Featured Amenity:** breakfast buffet.

[SAVE] [†]↑ [▧] [BIZ] [HS] [⇩] [📹]
[🛏] [🖼] [▭]

COUNTRY INN & SUITES BY CARLSON, CALGARY-AIRPORT
(403)250-1800 **19**

Hotel
$119-$299

Address: 2481 39th Ave NE T2E 8V8 **Location:** Jct Barlow Tr and 39th Ave NE; access via 37th Ave. **Facility:** 106 units. 3 stories, interior corridors. **Parking:** winter plug-ins. **Pool(s):** heated indoor. **Activities:** hot tub, exercise room. **Guest Services:** valet and coin laundry. **Featured Amenity:** breakfast buffet.

[SAVE] [ECO] [⊀] [†]↑ [🚶] CALL [⇩M]

[▧] [BIZ] [HS] [⇩] [✕] [📹] [🛏]
[🖼] [▭]

COURTYARD BY MARRIOTT CALGARY AIRPORT
(403)238-1000 **13**

Hotel
$108-$239

COURTYARD Marriott
AAA Benefit: Members save 5% or more!

Address: 2500 48th Ave NE T3J 4V8 **Location:** Just n of jct Barlow Tr NE and McKnight Blvd NE. **Facility:** 171 units. 6 stories, interior corridors. **Parking:** winter plug-ins. **Terms:** check-in 4 pm. **Amenities:** safes. **Pool(s):** heated indoor. **Activities:** exercise room. **Guest Services:** valet and coin laundry, boarding pass kiosk.

[SAVE] [⊀] [†] [Y] CALL [⇩M] [▧]
[BIZ] [HS] [⇩] [✕] [🛏] [▭] / SOME UNITS [🖼]

COURTYARD BY MARRIOTT CALGARY SOUTH
(587)349-7599

Hotel
$126-$177

COURTYARD Marriott
AAA Benefit: Members save 5% or more!

Address: 3750 Market St SE T3M 1M4 **Location:** Hwy 2 (Deerfoot Tr) exit Seton Blvd SE, just e. Across from South Health Campus. **Facility:** 127 units. 7 stories, interior corridors. *Bath:* shower only. **Terms:** check-in 4 pm. **Pool(s):** heated indoor. **Activities:** hot tub, exercise room. **Guest Services:** valet and coin laundry.

[SAVE] [†] [Y] CALL [⇩M] [▧] [BIZ]
[⇩] [✕] [🛏] [▭] / SOME UNITS [🖼]

DAYS INN CALGARY AIRPORT
(403)250-3297 **29**

Hotel. **Address:** 2799 Sunridge Way NE T1Y 7K7

DAYS INN CALGARY NORTHWEST
(403)288-7115 **20**

Hotel. **Address:** 4420 16th Ave NW T3B 0M4

DELTA CALGARY AIRPORT IN-TERMINAL HOTEL
(403)291-2600 **7**

Hotel
$112-$244

D DELTA HOTELS
AAA Benefit: Members save 5% or more!

Address: 2001 Airport Rd NE T2E 6Z8 **Location:** At Calgary International Airport. **Facility:** 296 units. 3-8 stories, interior corridors. **Parking:** on-site (fee) and valet. **Pool(s):** heated indoor. **Activities:** hot tub, exercise room, in-room exercise equipment. **Guest Services:** valet laundry.

[SAVE] [ECO] [†] [🚶] [Y] CALL [⇩M]
[▧] [BIZ] [HS] [⇩] [✕] [📹] [🛏]
[▭] / SOME UNITS [S🛏]

DELTA CALGARY SOUTH
(403)278-5050 **43**

Hotel. **Address:** 135 Southland Dr SE T2J 5X5

AAA Benefit: Members save 5% or more!

ECONO LODGE SOUTH
(403)252-4401 **41**

Motel
$95-$190

Address: 7505 Macleod Tr SW T2H 0L8 **Location:** Corner of Hwy 2A (Macleod Tr) and 75th Ave SW. **Facility:** 73 units, some efficiencies and kitchens. 2-3 stories (no elevator), interior/exterior corridors. **Parking:** winter plug-ins. **Pool(s):** heated indoor. **Activities:** hot tub, limited exercise equipment. **Guest Services:** coin laundry. **Featured Amenity:** continental breakfast.

[SAVE] [ECO] [†]↑ [▧] [BIZ] [⇩] [🛏]
[🖼] [▭] / SOME UNITS [S🛏]

(See map & index p. 58.)

EXECUTIVE ROYAL HOTEL NORTH CALGARY
403/291-2003   **28**

 Hotel. **Address:** 2828 23rd St NE T2E 8T4

FOUR POINTS BY SHERATON CALGARY AIRPORT
(403)648-3180   **31**

Hotel
$109-$219

 AAA Benefit: Members save up to 15%, plus Starwood Preferred Guest® benefits!

Address: 2875 Sunridge Way NE T1Y 7K7 **Location:** Jct Trans-Canada Hwy 1 and Barlow Tr NE, 0.6 mi (1 km) n, just e. **Facility:** 159 units, some two bedrooms. 7 stories, interior corridors. **Parking:** winter plug-ins. **Amenities:** safes. **Pool(s):** heated indoor. **Activities:** sauna, hot tub, steamroom, exercise room, coin laundry. **Guest Services:** valet and coin laundry.

FOUR POINTS BY SHERATON HOTEL & SUITES, CALGARY WEST
(403)288-4441   **10**

Hotel
$129-$199

AAA Benefit: Members save up to 15%, plus Starwood Preferred Guest® benefits!

Address: 8220 Bowridge Cres NW T3B 2V1 **Location:** Opposite Canada Olympic Park. **Facility:** 150 units. 4 stories, interior corridors. **Parking:** winter plug-ins. **Amenities:** safes. **Pool(s):** heated indoor. **Activities:** hot tub, exercise room, spa. **Guest Services:** valet and coin laundry.

   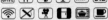 

HAMPTON INN BY HILTON CALGARY AIRPORT NORTH
(403)452-9888   **4**

Hotel
$99-$179

AAA Benefit: Members save up to 10%!

Address: 2000 2021 100th Ave NE T3J 0R3 **Location:** Hwy 2 (Deerfoot Tr) exit 266, 1.1 mi (1.8 km) e on Airport Tr NE, then just n on 19th St NE. **Facility:** 135 units. 10 stories, interior corridors. **Terms:** 1-7 night minimum stay, cancellation fee imposed. **Amenities:** safes. **Pool(s):** heated indoor. **Activities:** hot tub, exercise room. **Guest Services:** coin laundry.

    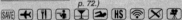

HILTON GARDEN INN-CALGARY AIRPORT
403/717-1999   **15**

Hotel
Rates not provided

AAA Benefit: Members save up to 10%!

Address: 2335 Pegasus Rd NE T2E 8C3 **Location:** Jct Barlow Tr and McKnight Blvd, just w, n on 19th St NE, then just e. **Facility:** 135 units. 5 stories, interior corridors. **Pool(s):** heated indoor. **Activities:** hot tub, exercise room, in-room exercise equipment. **Guest Services:** valet and coin laundry, area transportation. *(See ad p. 72.)*

Ask your AAA/CAA club about travel money and other financial services for travelers

---

Be Vacation Ready

Have your car checked out by a dependable AAA/CAA Approved Auto Repair facility.

AAA.com/Repair

(See map & index p. 58.)

HOLIDAY INN CALGARY-AIRPORT   403/230-1999 **34**

▼▼▼▼ Hotel. **Address:** 1250 McKinnon Dr NE T2E 7T7 *(See ad p. 73.)*

HOLIDAY INN CALGARY-MACLEOD TRAIL SOUTH
(403)287-2700 **38**

▼▼▼▼
Hotel
$119-$289

Address: 4206 Macleod Tr S T2G 2R7 **Location:** Corner of 42nd Ave SW and Macleod Tr S. **Facility:** 151 units. 4 stories, interior corridors. **Parking:** winter plug-ins. **Terms:** cancellation fee imposed, resort fee. **Pool(s):** heated indoor. **Activities:** exercise room. **Guest Services:** valet and coin laundry.

Recommend places you'd like us to inspect
at AAA.com/TourBookComments

▼ *See AAA listing p. 71* ▼

(See map & index p. 58.)

HOLIDAY INN EXPRESS AIRPORT CALGARY
403/769-1888 **16**
Hotel. **Address:** 45 Hopewell Way NE T3J 4V7

HOLIDAY INN EXPRESS HOTEL & SUITES CALGARY-SOUTH
(403)225-3000 **44**
Hotel. **Address:** 12025 Lake Fraser Dr SE (Macleod Tr S) T2J 7G5

HOMEWOOD SUITES CALGARY AIRPORT
(403)453-7888 **5**
Extended Stay Hotel. **Address:** 1000 2021 100th Ave NE T3J 0R3

AAA Benefit: Members save up to 10%!

HOTEL BLACKFOOT
(403)252-2253 **40**
Contemporary Hotel. **Address:** 5940 Blackfoot Tr SE T2H 2B5

HOTEL CLIQUE
403/460-9588 **8**
Contemporary Hotel. **Address:** 24 Aero Cres NE T2E 7Y5

LAKEVIEW SIGNATURE INN
(403)735-3336 **18**
Hotel. **Address:** 2622 39th Ave NE T1Y 7J9 *(See ad opposite inside front cover.)*

RADISSON HOTEL & CONFERENCE CENTRE CALGARY AIRPORT
403/475-1111 **11**

Contemporary Hotel
Rates not provided

Address: 6620 36th St NE T3J 4C8 **Location:** Jct McKnight Blvd NE and Barlow Tr NE, just n, then 1.6 mi (2.6 km) ne on 48th Ave NE. **Facility:** 120 units. 4 stories, interior corridors. **Parking:** winter plug-ins. **Amenities:** Some: safes. **Dining:** XS Lounge and Grill, see separate listing. **Pool(s):** heated indoor. **Activities:** sauna, hot tub, exercise room, spa. **Guest Services:** valet laundry, area transportation.

RESIDENCE INN BY MARRIOTT CALGARY AIRPORT
(403)278-1000 **12**

Extended Stay Hotel
$95-$212

Residence Inn Marriott

AAA Benefit: Members save 5% or more!

Address: 2530 48th Ave NE T3J 4V8 **Location:** Just n of jct Barlow Tr NE and McKnight Blvd NE. **Facility:** 158 units, some two bedrooms, efficiencies and kitchens. 6 stories, interior corridors. **Parking:** winter plug-ins. **Terms:** check-in 4 pm. **Amenities:** safes. **Pool(s):** heated indoor. **Activities:** picnic facilities, exercise room. **Guest Services:** valet and coin laundry, boarding pass kiosk. **Featured Amenity:** breakfast buffet.

RESIDENCE INN BY MARRIOTT CALGARY SOUTH
(587)349-8633

Extended Stay Hotel
$136-$200

Residence Inn Marriott

AAA Benefit: Members save 5% or more!

Address: 3710 Market St SE T3M 1M4 **Location:** Hwy 2 (Deerfoot Tr) exit Seton Blvd SE, just e. Across from South Health Campus. **Facility:** 98 two-bedroom units, some efficiencies and kitchens. 6 stories, interior corridors. **Terms:** check-in 4 pm. **Pool(s):** heated indoor. **Activities:** hot tub, exercise room. **Guest Services:** valet and coin laundry. **Featured Amenity:** breakfast buffet.

SANDMAN HOTEL SUITES & SPA CALGARY AIRPORT
403/219-2475 **14**
Hotel. **Address:** 25 Hopewell Way NE T3J 4V7

▼ *See AAA listing p. 72* ▼

(See map & index p. 58.)

SERVICE PLUS INN & SUITES CALGARY
(403)256-5352 **45**

Hotel
$139-$159

Address: 3503 114th Ave SE T2Z 3X2 **Location:** South end of Barlow Tr, just w. Located in an industrial area. **Facility:** 139 units. 4 stories, interior corridors. **Parking:** winter plug-ins. **Terms:** cancellation fee imposed. **Pool(s):** heated indoor. **Activities:** hot tub, exercise room. **Guest Services:** valet laundry, area transportation. **Featured Amenity:** full hot breakfast.

SHERATON CAVALIER HOTEL
(403)291-0107 **25**

Hotel
$129-$409

Sheraton

AAA Benefit: Members save up to 15%, plus Starwood Preferred Guest® benefits!

Address: 2620 32nd Ave NE T1Y 6B8 **Location:** Barlow Tr at 32nd Ave NE. **Facility:** 305 units. 7 stories, interior corridors. **Parking:** on-site and valet, winter plug-ins. **Amenities:** safes. **Dining:** 2 restaurants, also, Carver's Steakhouse, see separate listing. **Pool(s):** heated indoor. **Activities:** sauna, hot tub, exercise room. **Guest Services:** valet laundry.

STAYBRIDGE SUITES CALGARY AIRPORT
(403)204-7829 **30**

Extended Stay Hotel
$129-$199

Address: 2825 Sunridge Way NE T1Y 7K7 **Location:** Trans-Canada Hwy 1 exit Barlow Tr NE, just n, then just e. **Facility:** 96 efficiencies, some two bedrooms. 4 stories, interior corridors. **Parking:** winter plug-ins. **Terms:** cancellation fee imposed. **Pool(s):** heated indoor. **Activities:** hot tub, picnic facilities, exercise room. **Guest Services:** complimentary and valet laundry. **Featured Amenity:** breakfast buffet.

SUPER 8 CALGARY AIRPORT
(403)291-9888 **27**

Hotel
$99-$138

Address: 3030 Barlow Tr NE T1Y 1A2 **Location:** Corner of 32nd Ave NE and Barlow Tr NE. **Facility:** 61 units. 4 stories, interior corridors. **Parking:** winter plug-ins. **Terms:** cancellation fee imposed. **Amenities:** safes. **Guest Services:** valet and coin laundry. **Featured Amenity:** continental breakfast.

Enjoy great member rates and benefits

at AAA/CAA Preferred Hotels

TRAVELODGE CALGARY UNIVERSITY
(403)289-6600 **24**

Hotel
$109-$189

Address: 2227 Banff Tr NW T2M 4L2 **Location:** 16th Ave NW (Trans-Canada Hwy 1) and Banff Tr NW. Located in Motel Village. **Facility:** 64 units. 3 stories, interior corridors. **Parking:** winter plug-ins. **Pool(s):** heated outdoor. **Activities:** exercise room. **Featured Amenity:** breakfast buffet.

WINGATE BY WYNDHAM CALGARY
(403)514-0099 **46**
Hotel. **Address:** 400 Midpark Way SE T2X 3S4

WYNDHAM GARDEN CALGARY AIRPORT
(403)516-2266 **6**

Hotel
$90-$174

Address: 11 Freeport Cres NE T3J 0T4 **Location:** Hwy 2 (Deerfoot Tr) exit 266, just ne. Located in an industrial area. **Facility:** 156 units. 5 stories, interior corridors. **Parking:** winter plug-ins. **Terms:** check-in 4 pm. **Pool(s):** heated indoor. **Activities:** hot tub, bicycles, trails, exercise room. **Guest Services:** valet and coin laundry. **Featured Amenity:** continental breakfast.

WHERE TO EAT

ALBERTA KING OF SUBS
403/293-5809 **6**
Sandwiches. Quick Serve. **Address:** 7196 Temple Dr NE, #22 T1Y 4E8

ALLOY
403/287-9255 **39**
New International. Fine Dining. **Address:** 220 42 Ave SE T2G 1Y4

BAGOLAC SAIGON RESTAURANT
403/252-5588 **41**
Vietnamese. Casual Dining. **Address:** 6130 1A St SW, #8 T2H 0G3

BASIL
403/457-0808 **11**
Vietnamese. Casual Dining. **Address:** 2770 32nd Ave NE, #10 T1Y 5S5

BEARS DEN
403/241-7611
Regional Canadian. Fine Dining. **Address:** 254028 Bearspaw Rd NW T3L 2P7

BELMONT DINER
403/242-6782 **38**
American. Casual Dining. **Address:** 2008 33rd Ave W T2T 1Z6

BIG FISH
403/277-3403 **18**
Seafood. Casual Dining. **Address:** 1112 Edmonton Tr NE T2E 3K4

BIG T'S BBQ
403/284-5959 **7**
Barbecue. Casual Dining. **Address:** 2138 Crowchild Tr NW T2M 3Y7

(See map & index p. 58.)

BOOGIE'S BURGERS   403/230-7070   (22)
🔻 Burgers. Quick Serve. **Address:** 908 Edmonton Tr NE T2E 3K1

BOW VALLEY RANCHE RESTAURANT   403/476-1310   (48)
🔻🔻🔻 Regional Canadian. Fine Dining. **Address:** 15979 Bow Bottom Tr SE T2J 6T5

BROKEN PLATE KITCHEN & BAR   403/225-9650   (45)
🔻🔻 Greek. Casual Dining. **Address:** 590-10816 Macleod Tr SE T2J 5N8

CACTUS CLUB CAFE   403/250-1120
🔻🔻🔻 New American. Casual Dining. **Address:** 2612 39th Ave NE T1Y 7S9

CACTUS CLUB CAFE   403/255-1088
🔻🔻🔻 New American. Casual Dining. **Address:** 7010 Macleod Tr SE T2H 0L3

CARINO JAPANESE BISTRO   403/984-7534   (25)
🔻🔻🔻 Japanese Fusion. Casual Dining. **Address:** 709 Edmonton Tr NE T2E 3J4

THE CARMICHAEL   403/266-1005   (32)
🔻🔻 International. Casual Dining. **Address:** 1219 9th Ave SE T2G 0S9

CARVER'S STEAKHOUSE   403/250-6327   (10)
🔻🔻🔻 Steak. Fine Dining. **Address:** 2620 32nd Ave NE T1Y 6B8

CASSIS BISTRO   403/262-0036   (28)
🔻🔻🔻 French. Casual Dining. **Address:** 2505 17th Ave SW T3C 1J7

THE CHEESECAKE CAFE   403/255-7443
🔻🔻 American. Casual Dining. **Address:** 7600 Macleod Tr SE T2H 0L9

DINER DELUXE   403/276-5499   (24)
🔻🔻 American. Casual Dining. **Address:** 804 Edmonton Tr NE T2E 3J6

EARLS KITCHEN + BAR
🔻🔻 American. Casual Dining.
LOCATIONS:
Address: 3030 23rd St NE T2E 8R7 **Phone:** 403/291-6700
Address: 1110 16th Ave NW T2M 0K8 **Phone:** 403/289-2566

FIRE KIRIN   403/278-8018   (47)
🔻🔻 Asian. Casual Dining. **Address:** 12101 Lake Fraser Dr SE, Unit 500 T2J 7G4

FORBIDDEN CITY SEAFOOD & DIM SUM RESTAURANT
    403/250-1848   (27)
🔻🔻 Chinese Dim Sum. Casual Dining. **Address:** 999 36th St NE, #220 T2A 7X6

GLOBEFISH SUSHI & IZAKAYA   403/457-1500   (42)
🔻 Sushi. Casual Dining. **Address:** 6455 Macleod Tr SW, #130 T2H 0K3

GUS'S CAFE & PIZZERIA   403/282-4005   (46)
🔻🔻 Pizza. Casual Dining. **Address:** 1620 29th St NW, #180 T2W 4L7

JAMESONS IRISH PUB   403/220-9888   (3)
🔻🔻 American. Casual Dining. **Address:** 3790 Brentwood Rd NW T2L 1K8

JIMMY'S A & A DELI   403/289-1400   (9)
🔻 Mediterranean Deli. Quick Serve. **Address:** 1401 20th Ave NW T2M 1G6

JOEY RESTAURANTS
🔻🔻 American. Casual Dining.
LOCATIONS:
Address: 3026 23rd St NE T2E 8R7 **Phone:** 403/219-8465
Address: 50 Crowfoot Way NW T3G 4C8 **Phone:** 403/547-5639
Address: 6455 Macleod Tr SW, #100A T2H 0K8
Phone: 403/692-6626

JUREE'S THAI PLACE RESTAURANT   403/264-6477   (13)
🔻🔻 Thai. Casual Dining. **Address:** 2055 16th Ave NW T2M 0M3

KANE'S HARLEY DINER   403/269-7311   (29)
🔻🔻 Comfort Food. Casual Dining. **Address:** 1209 9th Ave SE T2G 3E8

LA BOULANGERIE   403/984-9294   (36)
🔻 Breads/Pastries. Quick Serve. **Address:** 2435 4th St SW T2S 2T4

LINA'S ITALIAN MARKET   403/277-9166   (14)
🔻 Italian Deli. Quick Serve. **Address:** 2202 Centre St NE T2E 2T4

MISAI JAPANESE RESTAURANT   403/250-1688   (8)
🔻🔻 Japanese. Casual Dining. **Address:** 1915 32nd Ave NE T2E 7C8

MOXIE'S CLASSIC GRILL   403/291-4636
🔻🔻 American. Casual Dining. **Address:** 29 Hopewell Way NE T3J 4V7

THE NASH   403/984-3365   (34)
🔻🔻🔻 New World. Casual Dining. **Address:** 925 11 St SE T2G 0R4

NICK'S STEAKHOUSE & PIZZA   403/282-9278   (5)
🔻🔻 Steak Pizza. Casual Dining. **Address:** 2430 Crowchild Tr NW T2M 4N5

NOTABLE - THE RESTAURANT   403/288-4372   (4)
🔻🔻🔻 New Canadian Comfort Food. Casual Dining. **Address:** 4611 Bowness Rd NW T3B 0B3

OEB BREAKFAST CO.   403/278-3447   (23)
🔻🔻 Breakfast. Casual Dining. **Address:** 824 Edmonton Tr NE T2E 3J6

OPEN RANGE STEAKS & CHOPS   403/277-3408   (17)
🔻🔻🔻 New American. Casual Dining. **Address:** 1114 Edmonton Tr NE T2E 3K4

OPEN SESAME   403/259-0123   (43)
🔻🔻 Asian. Casual Dining. **Address:** 6920 Macleod Tr S T2H 0L3

ORIENTAL PHOENIX   403/253-8189
🔻🔻 Vietnamese. Casual Dining. **Address:** 104 58th Ave SW, #80 T2H 0N7

(See map & index p. 58.)

PACINI PASTA & GRILL RISTORANTE   403/930-8080 ① \
▼▼▼ Italian. Casual Dining. **Address:** 123 Freeport Blvd NE T3N 0A3

PFANNTASTIC PANNENKOEK HAUS
                         403/243-7757 ④

Dutch \
Casual Dining \
$8-$18

AAA Inspector Notes: Ah crepes. Find at least 75 varieties of Dutch crepes served with all kinds of toppings cooked right into the pancake and if that's not enough of a choice you can build your own creation. A savoury crepe and a sweet choice for dessert make for a super tasty meal. Yummy Dutch inspired house soups and salads are also offered as well as omelettes and open-face sandwiches. You can rely on your super friendly, efficient server to recommend their own favourite and help you pronounce it! **Features:** full bar. **Address:** 2439 54th Ave SW T3E 1M4 **Location:** Just ne of jct Hwy 8 (Glenmore Tr) and Crowchild Tr; in small strip mall. Ⓑ ⒧ Ⓓ

PIO PERUVIAN ROTISSERIE CHICKEN   403/681-7378 ㉑ \
▼▼ Peruvian. Casual Dining. **Address:** 2929 Sunridge Way T1Y 7K7

THE PITA BASKET CAFE   403/219-2747 ⑲ \
▼ Lebanese. Quick Serve. **Address:** 3221 Sunridge Way NE, #140 T1Y 7M4

PIZZA BOBS   403/283-2041 ⑳ \
▼ Pizza. Casual Dining. **Address:** 2610 Kensington Rd T2N 4S5

RAJDOOT   403/245-0181 ㊲ \
▼▼ Indian. Casual Dining. **Address:** 2424 4th St SW T2S 2T4

RICKY'S ALL DAY GRILL   403/571-3220 \
▼▼▼ American. Casual Dining. **Address:** 3321 20th Ave NE T1Y 7A8

RIVER CAFE   403/261-7670 ㉖ \
▼▼▼▼ Regional Canadian. Fine Dining. **Address:** 25 Prince's Island Park T2P 0R1

ROUGE RESTAURANT   403/531-2767 ㉝ \
▼▼▼▼ New French. Fine Dining. **Address:** 1240 8th Ave SE T2G 0M7

SAMOSA GRILL   403/250-2515 ⑮ \
▼▼ Eastern Indian. Casual Dining. **Address:** 210-3393 26th Ave NE T1Y 6L4

SANTORINI GREEK TAVERNA   403/276-8363 ⑯ \
▼▼ Greek. Casual Dining. **Address:** 1502 Centre St N T2E 2R9

SMUGGLER'S INN   403/253-5355 ㊹ \
▼ Steak. Casual Dining. **Address:** 6920 Macleod Tr S T2H 0L3

SPOLUMBO'S DELI   403/264-6452 ㉟ \
▼ Deli. Quick Serve. **Address:** 1308 9th Ave SE T2G 0T3

SUGO ITALIAN FOOD & WINE   403/263-1115 ㉛ \
▼▼▼ Italian. Fine Dining. **Address:** 1214 9th Ave SE T2G 0S9

THAI BOAT   403/291-9887 ⑫ \
▼▼ Thai. Casual Dining. **Address:** 2323 32nd Ave NE, #108 T2E 6Z3

WHITE SPOT   403/278-8212 \
▼▼ American. Casual Dining. **Address:** 10440 Macleod Tr SE T2J 0P8

WITHOUT PAPERS PIZZA   403/457-1154 ㉚ \
▼▼ Pizza. Casual Dining. **Address:** 1216 9th Ave SE T2G 0T1

XS LOUNGE AND GRILL   403/475-1111 ② \
▼▼ International. Casual Dining. **Address:** 6625 36th St NE T3J 4C8

CAMROSE (F-7) pop. 17,286

Camrose, first settled around 1900 as a trading post, has a strong sense of its Scandinavian heritage. Known originally as the Hamlet of Sparling, its name was changed to Camrose in 1906. Camrose salutes country music during the 🎵 Big Valley Jamboree, a 4-day festival that typically begins in late July or early August.

Tourism Camrose: 4522 53rd St., Camrose, AB, Canada T4V 4E3. **Phone:** (780) 672-4255.

CAMROSE AND DISTRICT CENTENNIAL MUSEUM is 2 blks. s. of Hwy. 13 at 4522 53rd St. at jct. 46th Ave. The museum houses items from Camrose's pioneer days. Buildings include a country school; a fire hall; and a restored log pioneer house and church, both furnished in period. A steam engine, a replica of the first newspaper building and a working model of an early threshing machine are displayed. **Hours:** Wed.-Sun. 10-5, mid-May to early Sept.; by appointment rest of year. **Cost:** Donations. **Phone:** (780) 672-3298.

BEST WESTERN PLUS CAMROSE RESORT & CASINO \
                                       780/679-2376

▼▼▼ \
Hotel \
Rates not provided

Ⓑ🅦 **Best Western PLUS** **AAA Benefit:** Save 10% or more every day and earn 10% bonus points!

Address: 3201 48th Ave T4V 0K9 **Location:** Hwy 13 (48th Ave), just s of Correction Line Rd; eastern approach to city. **Facility:** Modern and sparkly, the public spaces show off some contemporary crystal ball light fixtures as well as cool seating and art pieces. Guest rooms are also lovely with a very nice design. 113 units, some efficiencies. 4 stories, interior corridors. **Parking:** winter plug-ins. **Amenities:** safes. **Pool(s):** heated indoor. **Activities:** hot tub, exercise room. **Guest Services:** coin laundry. **Featured Amenity:** full hot breakfast.

SAVE 🅘 ⒴⒧ 🅗 Ⓨ CALL 🄼 ➋ BIZ HS 📶 \
✕ 🄱 🄳 🄳 / SOME UNITS 🆂

CANALTA HOTEL CAMROSE   780/672-7303 \
▼▼▼ Hotel. **Address:** 4710 73rd St T4V 0E5

NORSEMEN INN   (780)672-9171 \
▼▼▼ Hotel. **Address:** 6505 48th Ave T4V 3K3

RAMADA INN CAMROSE   (780)672-5220 \
▼▼▼ Hotel. **Address:** 4702 73rd St T4V 0E5

WHERE TO EAT

THE CANADIAN BREWHOUSE   780/672-8880
◆◆ International. Sports Bar. **Address:** 6608 48th Ave T4V 4R1

THE LEFSE HOUSE SCANDINAVIAN BAKERY   780/672-7555
◆ Scandinavian. Casual Dining. **Address:** 5210 51st Ave T4V 4N5

MONTE CARLO RESTAURANT   780/672-1040
◆◆ American. Casual Dining. **Address:** 4907 48th Ave T4V 0J4

STOCKMEN'S CHOPHOUSE   780/672-7872
◆◆◆ Steak. Casual Dining. **Address:** 6404 48th Ave T4V 3A3

CANMORE (H-5) pop. 12,288, elev. 1,341m/4,400'
- **Restaurants p. 78**
- **Attractions map p. 30**
- **Part of Banff National Park area — see map p. 28**

Established in 1883 as a coal-mining center, Canmore was the first Canadian Pacific Railroad divisional point west of Calgary. The town also was the site of the biathlon and cross-country ski events of the 1988 Winter Olympics. Year-round recreational activities are abundant; fly-fishing, rock climbing, snowshoeing and dog sledding are just a few activities visitors can enjoy. Hiking, mountain biking and cross-country skiing are popular along the area's numerous trails. The Canmore Highland Games on Labour Day weekend also keeps sports enthusiasts entertained with a variety of athletic competitions. Scottish and Celtic dance and musical performances and sheep dog demonstrations take place during the daylong festival as well.

Tourism Canmore Kananaskis: 907A 7th Ave., P.O. Box 8608, Canmore, AB, Canada T1W 3K1. **Phone:** (855) 678-1295.

ALPINE HELICOPTERS LTD. is off Hwy. 1 Canmore exit, following signs to Canmore Municipal Heliport at 91 Bow Valley Tr. Scenic flights over the Canadian Rockies are offered. Passengers can view alpine valleys, glaciers, the Continental Divide, Banff National Park and towering Mount Assiniboine—"the Matterhorn of the Canadian Rockies." Helicopters carry four to six passengers.

Hours: Departures require a minimum of two passengers. Sightseeing flights are offered daily (weather permitting). Departure times vary. Closed Jan. 1 and Christmas. **Cost:** Marvel Pass 1-hour tour $849 (per two passengers). Mt. Assiniboine Glacier 30-minute tour $299 (per passenger). Royal Canadian 25-minute tour $249 (per passenger). Three Sisters Peaks 12-minute tour $124 (per passenger). Reservations are required. **Phone:** (403) 678-4802. GT

BANFF BOUNDARY LODGE   (403)678-9555

◆◆
Condominium
$109-$279

Address: 1000 Harvie Heights Rd T1W 2W2 **Location:** Trans-Canada Hwy 1 exit 86, just n. **Facility:** 26 condominiums. 1-2 stories (no elevator), exterior corridors. **Parking:** winter plug-ins. **Terms:** check-in 4 pm, cancellation fee imposed, resort fee. **Activities:** hot tub, picnic facilities, trails. **Guest Services:** coin laundry.

BEST WESTERN POCATERRA INN   (403)678-4334

◆◆◆
Hotel
$140-$355

AAA Benefit:
Save 10% or more every day and earn 10% bonus points!

Address: 1725 Mountain Ave T1W 2W1 **Location:** Trans-Canada Hwy 1 exit 86, 1.3 mi (2.1 km) e. **Facility:** 83 units. 4 stories, interior corridors. **Parking:** winter plug-ins. **Terms:** check-in 4 pm. **Pool(s):** heated indoor. **Activities:** sauna, hot tub, steamroom, exercise room. **Guest Services:** valet and coin laundry.

Best Western.
Pool & waterslide, Free Hot Breakfast, Banquet & Meeting Rooms.

BLACKSTONE MOUNTAIN LODGE   (403)609-8098
◆◆◆ Hotel. **Address:** 170 Kananaskis Way T1W 0A8

BOW VALLEY MOTEL   403/678-5085
◆◆ Motel. **Address:** 610 8th St T1W 2B5

CANADIAN ROCKIES CHALETS   403/678-3799
◆◆ Condominium. **Address:** 1206 Bow Valley Tr T1W 1N6

COAST CANMORE HOTEL & CONFERENCE CENTRE   (403)678-3625

◆◆◆
Hotel
$119-$399

Address: 511 Bow Valley Tr T1W 1N7 **Location:** Trans-Canada Hwy 1 exit 89, 1.4 mi (2.2 km) s. **Facility:** 164 units. 3 stories, interior corridors. **Parking:** winter plug-ins. **Terms:** check-in 4 pm, cancellation fee imposed, resort fee. **Amenities:** Some: safes. **Dining:** Table Food + Drink, see separate listing. **Pool(s):** heated indoor. **Activities:** hot tub, trails, exercise room. **Guest Services:** valet laundry.

DAYS INN CANMORE   (403)678-5488
◆◆ Hotel. **Address:** 1602 2nd Ave T1W 1M8

FALCON CREST LODGE   403/678-6150
◆◆◆ Condominium. **Address:** 190 Kananaskis Way T1W 3K5

FIRE MOUNTAIN LODGE   403/609-9949
◈◈◈ Condominium. **Address:** 121 Kananaskis Way T1W 2X2

THE GRANDE ROCKIES RESORT   (403)678-8880
◈◈◈◈ Hotel. **Address:** 901 Mountain St T1W 0C9

HOLIDAY INN CANMORE   403/609-4422

◈◈◈◈
Hotel
Rates not provided

Address: 1 Silver Tip Tr T1W 2Z7 **Location:** Trans-Canada Hwy 1 exit 89, just s. **Facility:** 99 units. 3 stories, interior corridors. **Parking:** winter plug-ins. **Activities:** hot tub, exercise room. **Guest Services:** valet and coin laundry.

[SAVE] [⊮] [⊻] CALL [⊙M] [BIZ] [⊚]
[✕] [⊠] [⊟] [⊡] [⊡] [⊡]

MYSTIC SPRINGS CHALETS & HOT POOLS   (403)609-0333
◈◈◈ Condominium. **Address:** 140 Kananaskis Way T1W 2X2

QUALITY RESORT-CHATEAU CANMORE   (403)678-6699
◈◈ Hotel. **Address:** 1720 Bow Valley Tr T1W 2X3

RAMADA INN & SUITES CANMORE   (403)609-4656
◈◈ Hotel. **Address:** 1402 Bow Valley Tr T1W 1N5

ROCKY MOUNTAIN SKI LODGE   (403)678-5445

◈◈◈
Motel
$109-$239

Address: 1711 Bow Valley Tr T1W 2T8 **Location:** Trans-Canada Hwy 1 exit 86, 0.5 mi (0.8 km) s. Located in a commercial area. **Facility:** 83 units, some two bedrooms and kitchens. 1-2 stories, exterior corridors. **Terms:** cancellation fee imposed, resort fee. **Activities:** sauna, hot tub, playground, picnic facilities, trails. **Guest Services:** coin laundry.

[SAVE] [ECO] [⊮+] [⊚] [✕] [⊟] [⊡]
[/SOME UNITS] [⊡] [⊡]

RUNDLE CLIFFS LODGE   (403)678-5108

◈◈◈◈
Condominium
$209-$959

Address: 375 Spring Creek Dr T1W 0G9 **Location:** Trans-Canada Hwy 1 exit 89, 1.2 mi (2 km) s; in Spring Creek Village. **Facility:** Marvelous, modern one- to three-bedroom suites feature designer kitchens, balconies or decks with a grill and great bathrooms. In-floor heating throughout the units will be welcomed in the ski season. 11 condominiums. 4 stories, interior corridors. **Terms:** check-in 4 pm, 2 night minimum stay - weekends, 3 day cancellation notice-fee imposed, resort fee. **Activities:** hot tub, ice skating, bicycles, playground, game room, trails, exercise room. **Guest Services:** complimentary laundry.

[SAVE] [HS] [⊚] [✕] [⊟] [⊡] [⊡]

SOLARA RESORT & SPA   (403)609-3600
◈◈◈◈ Condominium. **Address:** 187 Kananaskis Way T1W 0A3

STONERIDGE MOUNTAIN RESORT CANMORE   403/675-5000
◈◈◈◈ Condominium. **Address:** 30 Lincoln Park T1W 3E9

WHERE TO EAT

BEAMER'S COFFEE BAR   403/678-3988
◈ Coffee/Tea. Quick Serve. **Address:** 1702A Bow Valley Tr T1W 1N5

BOURBON STR   403/678-3612
◈◈ Cajun. Casual Dining. **Address:** 1005 Cougar Creek Dr, Unit 100 T1W 1E1

CHEF'S STUDIO JAPAN   403/609-8383
◈◈ Japanese. Casual Dining. **Address:** 709 8th St, #108 T1W 2B2

CHEZ FRANCOIS   403/678-6111
◈◈ French. Casual Dining. **Address:** 1602 2nd Ave T1W 1P7

COMMUNITEA CAFE   403/678-6818
◈◈ Vegetarian. Quick Serve. **Address:** 1001 6th Ave, #117 T1W 3L8

CRAZYWEED KITCHEN   403/609-2530
◈◈◈ New American. Casual Dining. **Address:** 1600 Railway Ave T1W 1P6

THE GRIZZLY PAW PUB & BREWING COMPANY
                                          403/678-9983
◈◈ Canadian. Gastropub. **Address:** 622 8th St T1W 2B5

HABITAT RESTAURANT & BAR   403/679-5228
◈◈◈ New World. Casual Dining. **Address:** 901 Mountain St T1W 0C9

INDOCHINE   403/675-3888
◈◈ Vietnamese. Casual Dining. **Address:** 190 Kananaskis Way T1W 3K5

THE IRON GOAT PUB & GRILL   403/609-0222
◈◈ Canadian. Casual Dining. **Address:** 703 Benchlands Tr T1W 3G9

LA BELLE PATATE   403/678-0077
◈ Canadian Specialty. Quick Serve. **Address:** 102 Boulder Cres, #4 T1W 1L2

LE FOURNIL BAKERY   403/675-5005
◈ French Breads/Pastries. Quick Serve. **Address:** 1205 Bow Valley Tr T1W 2G4

MOUNTAIN MERCATO SPECIALTY FOOD MARKET
                                          403/609-6631
◈ Deli. Quick Serve. **Address:** 817 Main St, #102 T1W 2B3

MURRIETA'S BAR & GRILL   403/609-9500
◈◈◈ Western Pacific Rim. Casual Dining. **Address:** 200-737 Main St T1W 2B2

PATRINOS STEAKHOUSE & PUB   403/678-4060

◈◈
International
Casual Dining
$10-$36

AAA Inspector Notes: This simple, family-run, roadside restaurant features a good selection of comfort foods, ranging from pizza and pasta to steaks. Guests can eat in the casual dining room or grab something in the lounge next door. Expect friendly, attentive service. **Features:** full bar, patio dining, Sunday brunch. **Reservations:** suggested. **Address:** 1602 Bow Valley Tr T1W 1N5 **Location:** Trans-Canada Hwy 1 exit 86, 0.6 mi (1 km) s.

[L] [D] CALL [⊙M]

ROCKY MOUNTAIN FLATBREAD COMPANY   403/609-5508
▼▼▼ Pizza. Casual Dining. **Address:** 838 10th St, Unit 101 T1W 2A8

RUSTICA STEAKHOUSE   403/678-1600
▼▼▼▼ Steak. Fine Dining. **Address:** 2000 Silvertip Tr T1W 3J4

SAGE BISTRO   403/678-4878
▼▼▼▼ New Canadian. Casual Dining. **Address:** 1712 Bow Valley Tr T1W 1P2

SANTA LUCIA TRATTORIA   403/678-3414
▼▼ Italian. Casual Dining. **Address:** 714 Main St T1W 2B6

TABLE FOOD + DRINK   403/609-5441
▼▼▼▼ New Canadian. Casual Dining. **Address:** 511 Bow Valley Tr T1W 1N7

TAPAS RESTAURANT   403/609-0583
▼▼▼ Mediterranean Small Plates. Casual Dining. **Address:** 633 10th St T1W 2A2

THE TROUGH DINING CO.   403/678-2820
▼▼▼▼ New American. Fine Dining. **Address:** 725 9th St T1W 2V7

CARDSTON (K-6) pop. 3,580, elev. 1,185m/3,888'

A son-in-law of Brigham Young, Charles Ora Card, led 10 Mormon families from Utah into Canada in 1887, hoping to find freedom from American anti-polygamy laws. Settling in Cardston, the immigrants founded the country's first Mormon settlement and named the town after their leader, who became its first mayor.

Today, a considerable percentage of Cardston residents are Mormon. Completed and dedicated in 1923, Cardston Alberta Temple of the Church of Jesus Christ of Latter-day Saints, 348 3rd St. W., was the first temple to be built in Canada. Non-Mormons are not permitted to enter the structure but can tour the grounds, where a visitor center offers information; phone (403) 653-3552.

Cardston & District Chamber of Commerce: 490 Main St., P.O. Box 1212, Cardston, AB, Canada T0K 0K0. **Phone:** (403) 795-1032.

REMINGTON CARRIAGE MUSEUM is at 623 Main St. More than 250 19th- and early 20th-century horse-drawn vehicles are showcased. Interactive displays and exhibit galleries provide the feeling of riding in the horse-drawn transportation of that era, and an introductory multimedia presentation provides an overview of that time.

The exhibit galleries, which include a blacksmith shop and livery stable, carriage factory, carriage dealership, working restoration shop, frontier settlement and racetrack, depict 19th-century society and its dependence on this mode of transportation. Sound effects, lighting and audiovisual presentations enhance many of the presentations. In summer visitors may schedule 15-minute rides on vintage and reproduction carriages.

Time: Allow 1 hour, 30 minutes minimum. **Hours:** Daily 9-5, July-Aug.; 9-4, rest of year. Carriage rides are offered daily 11-noon and 1-5, July-Aug.; 11-noon and 1-4, in June. Closed Jan. 1, Easter, Christmas Eve and Christmas. **Cost:** $12.38; $10.48 (ages 65+); $8.57 (ages 7-17); $33.33 (family, two adults and two children). Carriage ride $6.67; $4.76 (ages 4-17); $19.05 (family). **Phone:** (403) 653-5139. GT ⑪ 𝔸

CLAIRMONT pop. 1,652

RAMADA CLAIRMONT/GRAND PRAIRIE   (780)814-7448
▼▼ Hotel. **Address:** 7201 99th St T0H 0W0

CLARESHOLM pop. 3,758

BLUEBIRD MOTEL   403/625-3395
▼▼ Motel. **Address:** 5505 1st St W T0L 0T0

MOTEL 6 CLARESHOLM   403/625-4646
▼ Hotel. **Address:** 11 Alberta Rd (Hwy 2) T0L 0T0

COALDALE (J-7) pop. 7,493

THE ALBERTA BIRDS OF PREY CENTRE is at 2124 16th Ave. The facility, a working conservation center, rehabilitates injured and orphaned birds of prey and prepares them for release back into the wild. A self-guiding nature walk provides a close-up view of captive hawks, falcons, owls, eagles and vultures; visitors also can pose for photos with owls. Birds fly freely during daily demonstrations at this 28-hectare (70-acre) prairie wetland site.

Time: Allow 1 hour, 30 minutes minimum. **Hours:** Daily 9:30-5, May 10-Sept. 10. **Cost:** $9.05; $8.10 (ages 60+); $6.19 (ages 6-18); $5.24 (ages 3-5). Reservations are required for guided tours. **Phone:** (403) 345-4262. GT 𝔸

COCHRANE (H-5) pop. 17,580
• Hotels p. 80 • Restaurants p. 80
• Part of Calgary area — see map p. 42

Cochrane—named for Sen. Matthew Henry Cochrane, who began the first large-scale cattle ranch in the area in the 1880s—is known locally for its homemade ice cream, made by the same family since 1948; hang gliding; horseback riding; and canoe trips down the Bow River. Stoney First Nations Reserve, 16 kilometres (10 mi.) west on Hwy. 1A, was the filming site of several movies, including Arthur Penn's "Legends of the Fall" and "Little Big Man," and of the television series "Lonesome Dove."

Downtown Cochrane's Western-style architecture provides a backdrop for local arts and crafts and specialty shops. Of particular interest is Studio West, a foundry and art gallery where visitors can view the 3,000-year-old sculpting technique known as the "lost wax" process.

Also noteworthy is the town's "Trust" mural, on display at The Cochrane RancheHouse at 101

RancheHouse Rd. A montage of small paintings, the collective work of nearly 200 artists, forms a large Western image of a cowboy and his horse. The mural is accessible Mon.-Fri. 8:30-4:30. Closed holidays.

Cochrane Visitor Centre: 521 First St. W., Cochrane, AB, Canada T4C 0A4. **Phone:** (403) 851-2960.

DAYS INN & SUITES COCHRANE   (403)932-5588
 Hotel. **Address:** 5 West Side Dr T4C 1M1

SUPER 8 COCHRANE   (403)932-1410

Hotel
$120-$160

Address: 11 West Side Dr T4C 1M1 **Location:** Jct Hwy 1A and 22, 0.4 mi (0.6 km) s, just e on Quigley Dr, then just s. **Facility:** 49 units, some kitchens. 3 stories (no elevator), interior corridors. **Parking:** winter plug-ins. **Activities:** hot tub, steamroom, exercise room. **Guest Services:** valet and coin laundry. **Featured Amenity: continental breakfast.**

WHERE TO EAT

JAIPUR INDIA CUISINE   403/981-9988
Indian. Casual Dining. **Address:** 114 3rd Ave W T4C 1Z6

PORTOFINO ITALIAN RISTORANTE   403/932-1777
Italian. Casual Dining. **Address:** 205 1st St E, Bay 18 T4C 1X6

PRAIRIE SMOKE COUNTRY KITCHEN   403/932-9001
American. Casual Dining. **Address:** 19 West Side Dr T4C 1M1

COLD LAKE pop. 13,839, elev. 555m/1,820'

BEST WESTERN COLD LAKE INN   (780)594-4888

Hotel
$139-$249

 Best Western. **AAA Benefit:** Save 10% or more every day and earn 10% bonus points!

Address: 4815 52nd St T9M 1P1 **Location:** Corner of 55th Ave (Hwy 26 and 55) and 52nd St; south end of city. **Facility:** 137 units, some efficiencies. 2-4 stories, interior/exterior corridors. **Parking:** winter plug-ins. **Dining:** Sawmill Prime Rib & Steak House, see separate listing. **Pool(s):** heated indoor. **Activities:** hot tub, exercise room. **Guest Services:** valet laundry. **Featured Amenity: breakfast buffet.**

COURTYARD BY MARRIOTT COLD LAKE   (780)278-7709
fyi Hotel. Too new to rate, opening scheduled for December 2016. **Address:** Rt 28 & Hwy 897 T9M 1P4 *(See ad this page.)*

AAA Benefit: Members save 5% or more!

HOLIDAY INN EXPRESS & SUITES COLD LAKE   780/654-3688
Hotel. **Address:** 5315 48 Ave T9M 1P1

WHERE TO EAT

CLARKS GENERAL STORE & EATERY   780/639-4782
American. Casual Dining. **Address:** 701 Lakeshore Dr T9M 1N1

SAWMILL PRIME RIB & STEAK HOUSE   780/594-5985
Steak. Casual Dining. **Address:** 4815 52nd St T9M 1P1

Say YES to ERS text updates to stay posted when your tow truck is on the way

▼ *See AAA listing this page* ▼

COLUMBIA ICEFIELD—See Jasper National Park p. 120.

CONKLIN pop. 211

RAMADA INN CONKLIN   (780)559-0040
▼▼▼ Hotel. **Address:** 104 Northland Dr T0P 1H1

CROWSNEST PASS (J-5) pop. 5,565

An area of wild beauty and haunting legends, the municipality of Crowsnest Pass is an amalgamation of the former coal-mining towns of Bellevue, Blairmore, Coleman, Frank and Hillcrest. Scenic Hwy. 3 through Crowsnest Pass connects Burmis to Fernie, British Columbia, via the Rocky Mountain Range and the Continental Divide.

The area provides visitors with recreational opportunities and stimulates the imagination with such stories as the curse of the Lost Lemon Gold Mine, rum-running and the shoot-out at Bellevue Cafe.

The town of Frank made national headlines April 29, 1903, when close to 70 residents were killed in the dramatic slide of Turtle Mountain on the east side of the pass. Ninety million tons of limestone swept over 1.5 kilometres (.9 mi.) of the valley before dawn, destroying part of the town and burying a mine plant and railway. The old town was at the western edge of the slide; many cellars still are visible.

BELLEVUE UNDERGROUND MINE TOUR is n. off Hwy. 3 Bellevue exit, following signs to the Bellevue Underground Mine access road at 2531-213 St. Participants don a miner's helmet with a lamp and a battery pack and follow guides along the same path taken by coal miners 1903-61 when the coal mine was operational. The 1-hour tour provides insights into the lives of coal miners and the work they did in the mine.

Note: The temperature in the mine is around 1 C (35 F); dress in warm clothing and wear sturdy footwear, even in summer months. **Time:** Allow 1 hour minimum. **Hours:** Daily 10-6 July-Aug.; daily 9-5, May-June; Mon.-Fri. 9-4, Sept.-Oct. Last tour departs 30 minutes before closing. **Cost:** $15.24; $12.38 (ages 65+); $9.52 (ages 6-17); $38.10 (family, two adults and two children ages 6-17; additional children $4.76). **Phone:** (403) 564-4700. GT

FRANK SLIDE INTERPRETIVE CENTRE is 1.5 km (.9 mi.) n. off Hwy. 3 at w. edge of Frank Slide. The center overlooks the site of the 1903 rockslide. Visitors experience the impact of Canada's deadliest rockslide through interactive exhibits and multimedia presentations. Walkways outside the center provide spectacular views of the surrounding Canadian Rockies. A 1.5-kilometre (.9-mi.) self-guiding trail over the slide allows visitors to view the debris. Interpretive programs are offered in summer.

Time: Allow 1 hour, 30 minutes minimum. **Hours:** Daily 9-6, July-Labour Day; 10-5, rest of year.

Closed Jan. 1, Easter, Christmas Eve and Christmas. **Cost:** $12.38; $10.48 (ages 65+); $8.57 (ages 7-17); free (Canadian military and family with ID); $33.33 (family, two adults and children). **Phone:** (403) 562-7388.

DEAD MAN'S FLATS pop. 121
• **Part of Banff National Park area — see map p. 28**

COPPERSTONE RESORT HOTEL   403/678-0303
▼▼▼ Condominium. **Address:** 250 2nd Ave T1W 2W4

WHERE TO EAT

THE JUNCTION HOUSE CAFE AND MARKET   403/609-3671
▼▼ Indian. Casual Dining. **Address:** 120 1st Ave T1W 2W4

DEVON (E-6) pop. 6,510, elev. 680m/2,230'
• **Part of Edmonton area — see map p. 85**

Canada's first planned community, Devon was created by Imperial Oil Resources Ltd. in 1948 to provide accommodations for the workers employed in the company's oilfields. Imperial Leduc No. 1, the area's first well, had just put the town of Devon on the map. The town's name was derived from the Devonian formation, the oil's source, a stratum 1,524 metres (5,000 ft.) underground.

Devon is on the banks of the North Saskatchewan River, where fishing often yields northern pike, walleye and goldeye. Year-round recreational activities include canoeing, cross-country skiing, golf, hiking, ice-skating and swimming.

Town of Devon: 1 Columbia Ave. W., Devon, AB, Canada T9G 1A1. **Phone:** (780) 987-8300.

LEDUC #1 ENERGY DISCOVERY CENTRE is 2 km (1.2 mi.) s. on Hwy. 60 at 50339 Hwy. 60 S. The center not only provides insight into the workings of the oil industry but also looks at area history, the story behind Leduc No. 1 and how Canada became self-sufficient in oil production. A 15-minute video presentation, interactive energy displays, geological exhibits, equipment, artifacts, photographs, scale models, murals and an outdoor interpretive trail help explain how oil is produced and refined.

A 53-metre (174-ft.) replica of the original derrick has been erected on the discovery site. **Note:** The Living Energy Project, launched in 2016, will demonstrate renewable resources—including geothermal, solar and wind power—when it is completed. **Time:** Allow 1 hour minimum. **Hours:** Mon.-Fri. 9:30-6, Sat.-Sun. 11-6, mid-June to Sept. 1; Mon.-Fri. 9:30-4:30, rest of year. **Cost:** $10; $8 (ages 65+); $6 (ages 6-17); $25 (family, two adults and all children). **Phone:** (780) 987-4323 or (866) 987-4323.

DONALDA (F-7) pop. 259

Situated in the heart of Alberta, Donalda was established in 1911 and named after the niece of Donald A. Mann, an official with the Canadian National Railway. It overlooks the scenic Meeting Creek Coulee. The region's unusual Paskapoo sandstone rock formations attract sportsman, hikers, artists and photographers. Donalda also claims an unusual man-made distinction. A 12.8-metre (42-ft.) lamp, said to be the world's largest oil lamp replica, was built in the town center by local residents. It glows at the east end of Main Street each evening.

DRAYTON VALLEY pop. 7,049

BEST WESTERN PLUS EXECUTIVE RESIDENCY DRAYTON VALLEY   (780)621-2378

▼▼▼▼
Extended Stay
Contemporary
Hotel
$150-$180

 AAA Benefit: Save 10% or more every day and earn 10% bonus points!

Address: 2252 50th St T7A 1R5 **Location:** Just n on Hwy 39; south end of town. **Facility:** 90 efficiencies, some two bedrooms. 4 stories, interior corridors. **Parking:** winter plug-ins. **Terms:** cancellation fee imposed. **Amenities:** safes. **Activities:** game room, picnic facilities, exercise room. **Guest Services:** valet and coin laundry.

(SAVE) (¶→) CALL (&M) (BIZ) 🛜 (✕)

(🎦) (📠) (📶) (📺) /SOME UNITS (S🛏) (HS)

HOLIDAY INN EXPRESS HOTEL & SUITES   780/515-9888
▼▼▼▼ Hotel. **Address:** 5001 Brougham Dr T7A 0A1

LAKEVIEW INN & SUITES   780/542-3200
▼▼ Hotel. **Address:** 4302 50th St T7A 1M4 **(See ad opposite inside front cover.)**

RAMADA DRAYTON VALLEY   (780)514-7861
▼▼▼ Hotel. **Address:** 2051 50th St T7A 1S5

WHERE TO EAT

MR MIKES STEAKHOUSECASUAL   780/515-8433
▼▼ American. Casual Dining. **Address:** 2248 50th St T7A 0A1

THREE KNIGHTS STEAK HOUSE & PIZZA   780/542-5222
▼▼ American. Casual Dining. **Address:** 5211 50th St T7A 1R5

DRUMHELLER (H-7) pop. 8,029

About 65 million years before Sam Drumheller began promoting the 1910 townsite later named for him, the surrounding Red Deer Valley was the home of immense dinosaurs. Plant-eating hadrosaurs, flesh-eating tyrannosaurs and their formidable cousins stomped through the swampy lowlands and forests bordering the Mowry Sea, which once covered the North American plains. Fossils of prehistoric creatures often are discovered in the multi-layered sedimentary walls of the valley; several life-size dinosaur replicas can be seen in town.

A larger-than-life version of one of these prehistoric beings, a 25-metre-tall (84-ft.) facsimile of a tyrannosaurus rex, has been built over the top of the Drumheller & District Chamber of Commerce at 60 1st Ave. W. Visitors can climb up to a viewing platform in the dinosaur's mouth.

Although the local coal industry founded in 1911 by American Jesse Gouge has declined, remnants of old mines still exist. Six kilometres (3.7 mi.) w. on N. Dinosaur Trail (Hwy. 838), Midland Provincial Park features Badlands Trail, a self-guiding walking trail that leads to the former site of Midland Mine. Gas and oil wells sporadically dot the nearby rolling prairies, but the shortgrass country is occupied mostly by geese and antelope.

Hoodoos—mushroom-shaped pillars of rock that have been carved into unusual formations by centuries of wind and rain—can be seen 18 kilometres (11 mi.) southeast on Hwy. 10. Because of their fragile nature, climbing these formations is not permitted.

Another nearby remarkable natural site is Horseshoe Canyon, 17 kilometres (11 mi.) southwest on Hwy. 9. Deriving its name from its horseshoe shape, the canyon is in an area of badlands amidst the Alberta prairies. Viewpoints provide opportunities to survey multicolored canyon walls and unusual rock formations.

A natural amphitheater is the site in early July for 9 days of performances of The Canadian Badlands Passion Play. In a setting closely resembling the Holy Land, a cast of 150 and a 100-voice choir relate the life of Christ; phone (403) 823-2001 or (888) 823-2001.

Stretching over the Red Deer River, the Rosedale Suspension Bridge on Hwy. 10 originally was used to carry miners across the river to the now-abandoned Star Mine. In 1931 the swinging bridge replaced the original cable car system and was used until the mine closed in 1957. A park with picnic facilities is available.

Drumheller Visitor Information Centre: 60 1st Ave. W., P.O. Box 999, Drumheller, AB, Canada T0J 0Y0. **Phone:** (403) 823-1331 or (866) 823-8100.

ATLAS COAL MINE NATIONAL HISTORIC SITE is 18 km (11 mi.) s.e. on Hwy. 10 to 110 Century Dr. This site explores the coal mining history of the Drumheller Valley through exhibits and various guided tours. Visitors can see inside what is said to be the last remaining wooden tipple (coal screening plant) in Canada on the Tipple Tour; take a ride on a 1936 Mancha locomotive on the Mantrip Train Tour; learn about the darker side of mining life in the Unmentionables Tour; and walk through an inclined conveyor tunnel in the Underground Tunnel Tour. Visitors can also explore restored mine offices, a lamp house and a miner's shack; hike on interpretive trails; and climb on antique mining machines.

Note: Visitors should wear sturdy, closed-toe shoes for tours. The Underground Tunnel Tour includes steep uphill and downhill climbs. **Time:** Allow 1 hour, 30 minutes minimum. **Hours:** Daily 9:45-7:30, July 1-late Aug. and Labour Day weekend; 9:45-6, mid-May through June 30; 9:45-5, early to mid-May, late Aug.-day before Labour Day weekend and early Sept. to mid-Oct. Tipple tour is given daily at 10:30, 11:45, 2, 3:15 and 4:45, in summer; otherwise varies. Tunnel tour is given daily at 10:30, 11:30, 12:30, 1:15, 2, 2:45, 3:30, 4:15 and 5:30, in summer; otherwise varies. Phone ahead to confirm schedule.

Cost: Historic site (includes mine building and locomotive ride) $10; free (ages 0-5); $30 (family, two adults and all children under 18). Tunnel Tour (includes historic site) $25; free (ages 0-5); $75 (family, two adults and all children under 18). Tipple Tour or Unmentionables Tour (includes historic site) $20; free (ages 0-5); $60 (family, two adults and all children under 18). Day pass (includes train ride and all tours) $40; free (ages 0-5); $95 (family, two adults and all children under 18). Ages 0-4 are not permitted on the Tunnel Tour. Parental discretion advised on the Unmentionables Tour; minimum age 14 recommended. **Phone:** (403) 822-2220. GT

GEM SAVE **ROYAL TYRRELL MUSEUM** is 6 km (4 mi.) n.w. on N. Dinosaur Tr. (Hwy. 838) in Midland Provincial Park. The museum is in the badlands of the Red Deer River Valley, surrounded by one of the richest fossil deposits in the world. Dinosaurs that once roamed Alberta are now showcased in the museum's Dinosaur Hall, where more than 45 skeletons are displayed.

Fossils, a preparation laboratory, hands-on exhibits and an indoor garden illustrate millions of years of geological and biological development; educational programs also are offered. Fossils in Focus, a rotating exhibit, highlights some of the most scientifically significant fossils in the museum collection. The Cretaceous Garden contains plants that are virtually the same today as they were more than 65 million years ago. In addition the museum houses a research center and operates a field station near Patricia *(see attraction listing p. 139).*

Time: Allow 3 hours minimum. **Hours:** Daily 9-9, May 15-Aug. 31; daily 10-5, in Sept.; Tues.-Sat. 10-5 (also Mon. holidays), rest of year. Closed Jan. 1 and Christmas. **Cost:** $17.14; $13.33 (ages 65+); $9.52 (ages 7-17); $43.81 (family, two adults and all children); free (Canadian military with ID). Two-day tickets $25.71; $20 (ages 65+); $14.29 (ages 7-17);

$65.71 (family, two adults and all children). **Phone:** (403) 823-7707, or (888) 440-4240 out of Alberta.

CANALTA JURASSIC HOTEL   403/823-7700
▼▼▼ Hotel. **Address:** 1103 Hwy 9 S T0J 0Y0

INN AND SPA AT HEARTWOOD   (403)823-6495
▼▼▼ Country Inn. **Address:** 320 N Railway Ave E T0J 0Y4

RAMADA INN & SUITES   (403)823-2028
▼▼▼ Hotel. **Address:** 680 2nd St SE T0J 0Y0

SUPER 8 DRUMHELLER   (403)823-8887
▼▼ Hotel. **Address:** 600-680 2nd St SE T0J 0Y0

TASTE THE PAST BED & BREAKFAST   403/823-5889
▼ Historic Bed & Breakfast. **Address:** 281 2nd St W T0J 0Y0

WHERE TO EAT

BERNIE & THE BOYS   403/823-3318
▼ American. Quick Serve. **Address:** 305 4th St W T0J 0Y3

O'SHEA'S EATERY & ALE HOUSE   403/823-2460
▼▼ American. Casual Dining. **Address:** 2nd St SE, #600B T0J 0Y0

SUBLIME FOOD AND WINE   403/823-2344
▼▼▼ New American. Casual Dining. **Address:** 109 Centre St T0J 0Y0

DUNVEGAN (B-2)

SAVE **HISTORIC DUNVEGAN PROVINCIAL PARK** is on Queen Elizabeth Hwy. 2 on the n. side of the Peace River beside Dunvegan Suspension Bridge. The park was a fur-trading post and the site of one of the first Roman Catholic missions in Alberta. Four original buildings remain: the 1877-78 Factor's House, part of the Hudson's Bay Co.'s fort, along with the 1885 church of St. Charles Mission with its 1889 rectory and an early 1900s Revillon Frères trading post.

Historical interpreters lead guided walks and educational programs explain the site's history. A visitor center offers a small gallery and a theater featuring a short film about the history of Dunvegan. *See Recreation Areas Chart.* **Time:** Allow 1 hour, 30 minutes minimum. **Hours:** Daily 10-5, May 15-Labour Day. **Cost:** $4.76; $3.81 (ages 65+); $1.90 (ages 7-17); free (Canadian military and family with ID); $13.33 (family, two adults and up to six children). **Phone:** (780) 835-7150 or (866) 427-3582. GT 🅰 🐾 🅰

Edmonton

Then & Now

Few first-time visitors to Edmonton are prepared for what they discover when they arrive. From trading post to metropolis within some 200 years, Edmonton continues to surprise visitors by its size, quality of life, sophistication and beautiful river valley location.

Edmonton owes its existence to an abundant and varied supply of natural resources, which prompted each of its three major booms. In 1795 the Hudson's Bay Co. founded Fort Edmonton on the banks of the North Saskatchewan River. Traders bartered with Cree and Blackfoot First Nations for luxuriant and sought-after pelts of otters, beavers, muskrats, minks and foxes. A trading settlement developed and became the main stopping point on routes to the north and to the Pacific.

This stopping point became a starting point for gold seekers rushing to the Klondike; they gathered supplies in Edmonton for the harsh trip north. When gold failed to materialize and many prospectors realized they weren't going to get rich, let alone get rich quick, they returned to Edmonton to settle for a slower but surer way of life.

A bust for prospectors was a boom for Edmonton. The city grew to six times its previous size, making it a prime choice for the provincial capital when Alberta was formed in 1905.

In the years that followed, the capital city earned its nickname, "Gateway to the North," because of its status as a transportation hub and gateway to the regions beyond. In 1915 Edmonton became a major link in the Canadian Pacific Transcontinental Railroad, emerging as an important crossroads stop between east and west as well as north and south.

Edmonton skyline

The city's reputation as a transportation center was reinforced during the 1930s as bush pilots transported vital medical supplies, food and mail to northern communities. And when construction began on the Alaska Highway in 1942, Edmonton found itself again in the role of a major distribution and supply center.

In February 1947, the Leduc No. 1 Well gushed crude oil 40 kilometres (25 mi.) southwest of Edmonton. Since then more than 2,250 wells within a 40-kilometre (25-mi.) radius of Edmonton have coaxed the precious natural resource to the surface. Enormous industrial growth resulted; the city's population quadrupled in the 25 years following the Leduc gusher. Today more than 450,000 barrels of crude oil are refined daily in Greater Edmonton.

With about 938,000 residents in the greater metropolitan area, Edmonton has been careful not to sacrifice the natural resource that makes it livable—its green space. Edmonton's river valley parkland is reputed to be the

(Continued on p. 86.)

Destination Edmonton

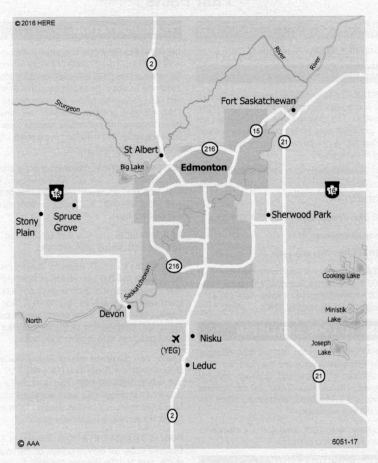

This map shows cities in the Edmonton vicinity where you will find attractions, hotels and restaurants. Cities are listed alphabetically in this book on the following pages.

Fast Facts

ABOUT THE CITY

POP: 812,201 ▪ **ELEV:** 670 m/2,198 ft.

MONEY

SALES TAX: The federal Goods and Service Tax is 5 percent and applies to most goods, food/beverages and services, including lodgings. Alberta does not have a provincial sales tax but does impose a 4 percent hotel tax. A 1-2 percent tourism levy also is charged in some areas.

WHOM TO CALL

EMERGENCY: 911

POLICE (non-emergency): (780) 423-4567

FIRE (non-emergency): 311

TEMPERATURE: (780) 468-4940

HOSPITALS: Grey Nuns Community Hospital, (780) 735-7000 ▪ Misericordia Community Hospital, (780) 735-2000 ▪ Royal Alexandra Hospital, (780) 735-4111 ▪ University of Alberta Hospital, (780) 407-8822.

WHERE TO LOOK AND LISTEN

NEWSPAPERS: Edmonton has two daily newspapers, the *Edmonton Journal* and the *Edmonton Sun,* both distributed in the morning. Canada's national newspapers, *The Globe and Mail* and the *National Post,* also are available at newsstands. *Metro Edmonton* is a free newspaper.

RADIO: Radio station CBC (740 AM) is a member of Canadian Broadcasting Corp.

VISITOR INFORMATION

Edmonton Welcome Centre: 9797 Jasper Ave. N.W., West Shaw Building, Edmonton, AB, Canada T5J 1P7. **Phone:** (780) 401-7696.

Visitor information also is available at the Edmonton International Airport.

TRANSPORTATION

AIR TRAVEL: Edmonton International Airport (YEG) is 29 kilometres (18 mi.) south of the city center; for information phone (780) 890-8382 or (800) 268-7134. Skyshuttle service to downtown costs $17.14 one way and $28.57 round-trip (phone to confirm fares); phone (780) 465-8515 or (888) 438-2342. Taxi service between the airport and downtown typically costs $55; a limousine costs $66. In addition many hotels offer free shuttle service for their guests.

RENTAL CARS: Hertz, downtown or at the airport, offers discounts to CAA and AAA members; phone (780) 423-3431 downtown, (780) 890-4435 at the airport, (800) 654-3131 in Canada or (800) 654-3001 outside of Canada.

RAIL SERVICE: The VIA Rail station is at 12360 121st St. N.W.; phone (888) 842-7245.

BUSES: The downtown depot for Greyhound Lines Inc. is at the VIA Rail train station at 12360 121st St. N.W.; phone (780) 420-2400 or (800) 661-8747. The south side depot is at 5723 104th St. N.W. Red Arrow Express offers luxury motor coach service between Edmonton, Calgary, Fort McMurray and Red Deer; phone (780) 433-1919 or (800) 232-1958.

TAXIS: Taxi companies include Alberta Co-Op Taxi, (780) 425-2525 ▪ Barrel Taxi (780) 489-7777 ▪ and Yellow Cab, (780) 462-3456. Taxi rates start at $3.43, plus $1.41 is charged for each additional kilometre (about 5/8 mile) or a portion thereof. Taxis can be hailed, but phoning is recommended.

PUBLIC TRANSPORTATION: Edmonton Transit System's Customer Service Centre, on the main floor of City Hall at 1 Sir Winston Churchill Sq., is open Mon.-Fri. 8-4:30; phone 331 within Edmonton or (780) 442-5311. Buses operate Mon.-Fri. 5:20 a.m.-1:30 a.m., Sat.-Sun. 6:30 a.m.-1:30 a.m. On holidays hours may be extended for special events. The Light-Rail Transit (LRT) operates daily 5:30 a.m.-1 a.m. Fare is $3.10. A 1-day pass is $8.81.

(Continued from p. 84.)
largest stretch of urban parkland in North America, encompassing 7,340 hectares (18,348 acres). The city contains more than 11,000 hectares (27,181 acres) of parkland, playgrounds and open areas. Stretches of parks along the North Saskatchewan River Valley let residents and visitors spend long summer days enjoying such warm-weather activities as golf, hiking and water sports. When the cold weather arrives, the park system provides a playground for cross-country skiing, ice-skating, dog sledding and snowshoeing.

An extensive system of underground and overhead "pedways" in the downtown area makes it possible to travel in climate-controlled comfort regardless of the weather. Those who'd rather play indoors head to West Edmonton Mall, which combines 800-plus retail stores with restaurants and such attractions as an amusement park, a water park, an aquarium and an ice-skating rink. The largest of its kind in North America, this shopping and entertainment center has undergone three major expansions since its 1981 opening and draws an estimated 28.4 million people each year.

Must Do: AAA Editor's Picks

- Travel back in time at  **Fort Edmonton Park** (7000 143rd St.), dubbed Canada's largest living-history park. Staffed by costumed interpreters, the site features both original and re-created historical structures—everything from a replicated Hudson's Bay Co. fort to a 1920s-style midway.

- Spend a few loonies at the **West Edmonton Mall** (8882 170th St. N.W.), the largest shopping and entertainment center in North America. The gargantuan complex boasts an amusement park, a water park, an aquarium, a shooting range and an ice rink.

- Attend a show at the **Francis Winspear Centre for Music** (4 Sir Winston Churchill Sq.). Built in 1997, the main performance space is a modern interpretation of such shoebox-style concert halls as the Tonhalle in Zurich and the Musikverein in Vienna. The downtown Edmonton facility is renowned for its acoustics as well as a stunning 6,551-pipe concert organ fashioned by Orgues Létourneau Limitée of Québec.

- Wrap your head around architect Randall Stout's **Art Gallery of Alberta** (2 Sir Winston Churchill Sq.), a curvy blend of steel and glass inspired by such undulating natural treasures as the aurora borealis and the North Saskatchewan River. When you're done ogling the ultra-modern exterior, head inside and admire the handiwork of such Canadian painters as Maxwell Bates, Emily Carr and David Milne.

- Scan the **Muttart Conservatory** (9626 96A St.). Readable by smartphones, matrix barcodes posted in four futuristic pyramid-shaped greenhouses put descriptions of walking tours and changing exhibitions in the palm of your hand. Low-tech printed tour brochures also are available, as are weekend guided tours. Located in the North Saskatchewan River valley, the botanical garden is one of the city's most iconic landmarks.

- Cheer on the National Hockey League's Edmonton Oilers at **Rogers Place** (10220 104 Ave. N.W.), which became the team's new, state-of-the-art home in 2016. Along with the Oilers, the 9-foot-tall, bronze statue of legendary player Wayne Gretzky was relocated as well. The monument honoring "The Great One," who led his team to four Stanley Cup victories, was erected in 1989 and has become a beloved city landmark.

- Eat, drink and be merry in **Old Strathcona,** a five-block historic district now dominated by bohemian java joints, funky stores, live performance venues, restaurants and bars. Whether the agenda calls for a bit of window-shopping or some late-night carousing, your best bet is to stick to the section of Whyte Avenue between 99th and 109th streets.

- Explore Edmonton's "Ribbon of Green," a 48-kilometre (30-mi.) stretch of the **North Saskatchewan River Valley** with bragging rights to more than 20 major parks and public facilities. In winter, strap on your cross-country skis and traverse 130-hectare (1.3-sq.-mi.) William Hawrelak Park (9930 Groat Rd. N.W.). Or, if the weather's warm, play a round at Victoria Golf Course (12130 River Valley Rd.), said to be the oldest municipal golf course in Canada.

- Party like an Edmontonian. An overbooked calendar filled with more than 30 annual events—including July's **Edmonton International Street Performers Festival,** August's **Edmonton Folk Music Festival** and November's **Canadian Finals Rodeo**— earned the provincial capital the nickname "The Festival City."

- Tour the 1912 Beaux Arts **Alberta Legislature Building** (10800 97th Ave.) for sure. But spend the bulk of your time strolling the handsome grounds—monuments dedicated to military veterans, immigrant groups and prominent Albertans dot the 23-hectare (57-acre) park. Wading pools and shooting water fountains are huge kid magnets in summer, and the holiday light and ice sculpture displays that arrive come winter dazzle visitors of all ages.

Ride a streetcar at Fort Edmonton Park

Edmonton 1-day Itinerary

AAA editors suggest these activities for a great short vacation experience.

Morning

- Operating from late May to mid-October, the **High Level Bridge Streetcar** *(see Sightseeing p. 95)* is a fun way to travel between downtown Edmonton (where you can browse Jasper Avenue boutiques or hit the slots at the **Baccarat Casino**) and Old Strathcona (a historic district now sheltering a bastion of independent businesses). As your vintage vehicle crosses the High Level Bridge, you'll catch a glimpse—and likely a shaky snapshot or two—of the idyllic North Saskatchewan River Valley.

- For eats, the **Blue Plate Diner** (10145 104th St. N.W.) is a few blocks east of the streetcar's northern terminus (downtown, south of Jasper Avenue and west of 109th Street). Your typical brunch dishes are doled out on weekends, as are more unconventional mid-morning morsels, like the Eggs Beneduckt served with duck confit.

- Along the streetcar line are three intermediary stops, including one in the Garneau neighborhood. Disembark here and try a specialty brew from **Transcend** (8708 109th St. N.W.), a local coffee chain that hawks gourmet blends and ethically sourced beans. Hankering for some java and something cakey to dunk? Look no further than the **Highlevel Diner** (10912 88th Ave. N.W.), an eclectic space known far and wide for its supersize cinnamon buns.

- At the High Level Bridge Streetcar's southern terminus (at 103rd Street and 84th Avenue) is the **Strathcona Streetcar Barn Museum**, where rail buffs can peruse antique model trains and ticket punches. The museum is at the north end of the **Old Strathcona Farmers' Market** (10310 83rd Ave. N.W.), open every Saturday from 10 a.m. to 2 p.m., Victoria Day weekend to Labour Day weekend.

Afternoon

- First-time visitors to Edmonton will no doubt want to check the ⧫ **West Edmonton Mall** (8882 170th St. N.W.) off their to-do lists. The mega mall is home to more than 800 stores and services, as well as a myriad of fashion-forward mannequins. After raiding the sales racks, strike a few cover model poses in the shopping center's three "theme streets": Bourbon Street, Chinatown and Europa Boulevard.

- There are plenty of places to grab a bite inside WEM. Or, skip the mall food court and head about 5 kilometres (3 mi.) north to family-owned **Fife N' Dekel** (10646 170th St. N.W.) for delectable deli meats sandwiched between slices of freshly baked sunflower bread. More importantly, for dessert, there's pie! Drool-worthy flavors run the gamut from banana cream to sour cream strawberry rhubarb.

- If The Mall is on your been-there, done-that list (*and* you're a sucker for geraniums and cacti),

Highlevel Diner

enjoy an afternoon at the ⧫ **Muttart Conservatory** (9626 96A St.). Changing displays of ornamental flowering plants as well as flora from tropical, temperate and arid regions keep so-called "floraphiles" content inside four glass pyramids. Hungry tree huggers will appreciate the on-site café, **Culina Muttart**, which offers breakfast, brunch and lunch menus that include greens and herbs grown in the Muttart greenhouse.

Evening

- If the menus at downtown darlings like the **Hardware Grill** (9698 Jasper Ave. N.W.) and **Khazana** (10177 107th St.) don't excite you, the views from **The Harvest Room** (10065 100th St. N.W.) and **La Ronde Revolving Restaurant** (10111 Bellamy Hill Rd. N.W.) surely will. After dinner, see a show at the **Citadel Theatre** (9828 101A Ave. N.W.), a five-theater multi-purpose complex that opened in 1976. In a city with a surplus of stages, this Arts District facility is acknowledged as Edmonton's premier performing arts venue.

- Before turning in, cab it back to Old Strathcona in south-central Edmonton. The entertainment district is centered on Whyte Avenue. An abundance of watering holes, tattoo shops, theaters and live music venues makes this area a popular late-night destination. If you're a serious lover of jazz, **Yardbird Suite** (11 Tommy Banks Way), founded in the 1950s, is without equal. Meanwhile, laid-back **Funky Buddha** (10341 Whyte Ave.) offers a jammed activities calendar with fun events like karaoke and Latin dance lessons.

Arriving
By Car

Two major highways run through Edmonton. The Trans-Canada Yellowhead Hwy. (Hwy. 16) provides access from the east and west; Queen Elizabeth II Hwy. runs north and south between Edmonton and Calgary.

Getting Around
Street System

Edmonton's street system is a grid with streets running north and south and avenues running east and west. Most streets and avenues are numbered starting from the southeast corner of the city; a few are named.

Edmonton's street plan includes several traffic circles. When approaching a traffic circle, make sure you are in the correct lane. Use the right lane if you plan to exit, the left lane if you are traveling around the circle. When in the circle, the vehicle on the outside must yield to the vehicle on the inside.

The city speed limit is 50 kilometres per hour (30 mph) or as posted. A right turn on red after stopping is permitted; U-turns are not. A sign that reads "Bus and Taxi Lane Only" means it is illegal to drive, park or stop any vehicle other than the above in that lane.

Parking

Street parking restrictions vary throughout the city; watch for and heed the signs. Parking is not permitted in the residential areas surrounding Northlands Park, TELUS Field and Commonwealth Stadium during major events; cars parked there will be towed.

Rates for city-operated parking meters are $2.50-$3.50 per hour. Most meters are free after 6 p.m. and on Sundays and holidays; however, there are some 24-hour meters. Rates for downtown parking lots range $2.50-$4 per half-hour during the day.

Shopping

For the intrepid shopper, there is nothing like ✈ West Edmonton Mall *(see attraction listing p. 94)*, which occupies a 44-hectare (110-acre) site at 8882 170th St. N.W. Inside are more than 800 stores and services.

South Edmonton Common (1978 99th St. N.W.) offers about 130 hectares (320 acres) of retail space. The massive outdoor shopping complex at 23rd Avenue and Calgary Trail is home to more than 155 businesses, including IKEA, Tommy Hilfiger, Nike Saks Fifth Avenue OFF 4TH. With more than 165 retailers, Southgate Centre (5015 111th St. N.W.) is South Edmonton's largest shopping center and includes Edmonton's largest Hudson's Bay store.

For those who want shopping on a less imposing scale, other popular malls include Kingsway Garden Mall (109 St. and Kingsway N.W.) and Londonderry Mall (258 137th Ave. at 66th Street).

Downtown offers boutiques and restaurants as well as covered shopping areas joined by enclosed walkways or pedways. The Edmonton City Centre

West Edmonton Mall

complex between 100th and 103rd streets on 102nd Avenue contains Hudson's Bay, 170 other shops and a nine-screen theater among its four glittering floors.

ManuLife Place (10180 101st St. N.W.) contains designer boutiques and Holt Renfrew, an elegant retail store with a quaint in-store café. Rice Howard Way, an attractive outdoor pedestrian area lined with sidewalk seating and eateries, is downtown at 100th Street and 101A Avenue. It is particularly popular in summer.

At 102nd Avenue and 97th Street, the Chinatown Gate symbolizes friendship and welcomes visitors to Chinatown, which features several ethnic restaurants, shops and outdoor vendors selling fresh produce.

The 124th Street & Area commercial district, which extends from Jasper Avenue north to 111th Avenue, is home to a wide variety of businesses, including the handful of art galleries comprising the 12-block Gallery Walk area.

Old Strathcona at Whyte Avenue (82nd Avenue from 99th to 109th streets), the main outdoor shopping street on the south side of the city, has the look of historic Edmonton and offers boutiques, specialty shops, restaurants, bistros and coffee bars.

Don't forget that the major museums have interesting shops with items sometimes impossible to find elsewhere. Of particular interest are the six period shops in Fort Edmonton Park *(see attraction listing p. 92)* and the shop in the interpretive center at the Alberta Legislature Building *(see attraction listing p. 91)*.

Big Events

Edmonton offers a smorgasbord of events. Concerts, workshops, club dates and outdoor events characterize the **Edmonton International Jazz Festival,** held late June to early July. Also beginning in late June, **The Works Art and Design Festival** brings together artists and artisans.

In June and July the **Freewill Shakespeare Festival** presents evening performances during the week and two shows on weekends at the **Myer Horowitz Theatre,** located in the Students' Union building on the University of Alberta campus. **Edmonton International Street Performers Festival** in early July offers 10 days of free performances by street acts including magicians, clowns, jugglers, mime artists, musicians and comics.

Two music venues, several parades, and midway entertainment keep the city alive with activities during ▽ **Edmonton's K-Days,** a 10-day celebration held in July. Kids can pan for gold and learn about the history and cultures of First Nations peoples in gold rush-themed Klondike Park. The fun comes to a close with a large fireworks display.

The ▽ **Edmonton Heritage Festival** during the first 3 days of August offers more than 60 outdoor ethnic pavilions showcasing international music, dance, art and cuisine. Also in August are the ▽ **Edmonton Folk Music Festival; Cariwest,** a Caribbean arts festival; the **Edmonton Blues Festival;** the **Edmonton Dragon Boat Festival;** and the ▽ **Edmonton International Fringe Theatre Festival,** an 11-day extravaganza of plays, dance, music, mime and street performances. The Edmonton Symphony Orchestra's 3-day **Symphony**

Under the Sky festival takes place at **William Hawrelak Park** in late August.

Post-summer events include the **Edmonton International Film Festival,** featuring independent short and feature-length movies in early October, the ▽ **Canadian Finals Rodeo** in early November, and **New Year's Eve special events.**

Sports & Rec

Whatever the season, there are opportunities for both indoor and outdoor recreation. The **North Saskatchewan River Valley** is an oasis of parkland, with 122 kilometres (76 mi.) of trails, four lake systems and 22 parks. Depending on the time of year, you can **golf, hike, jog, cycle, ride horseback, fish, ski (cross-country** and **downhill), skate** or even pan for gold in a park.

The largest park is **Capital City Recreation Park,** composed of many smaller areas in the center and on the east side of the city. Within the park are 30 kilometres (19 mi.) of paths for **bicycling** and **jogging.**

Playing host to three major sporting events—the Commonwealth Games in 1978, the World University Games in 1983 and the World Championships in Athletics in 2001—has provided Edmonton with a legacy of world-class sporting facilities. Several multiple-purpose centers—including **Kinsmen Sports Centre,** 9100 Walterdale Hill, and **Mill Woods Recreation Centre,** 7207 28th Ave.—offer such activities as **swimming, diving, racquetball, squash** and **track** events.

For information about activities and facilities at Edmonton parks, phone the central information line at (780) 442-5311 Monday through Friday.

Bring your set of clubs and try out one of more than 70 **golf** courses scattered about the Edmonton area. Three courses in the city's river valley are **Riverside,** on Rowland Road (106th Avenue) on the south side of the Dawson Bridge; **Rundle Park,** in the east end of Edmonton off 118th Avenue and Victoria Trail; and **Victoria,** said to be the oldest municipal golf course in Canada, on River Valley Road, accessible from Groat Road or from either 109th Street via the Walterdale Bridge from the south, or from 101st Street from the north. For information on all city-run golf courses, phone (780) 496-4710.

Spectator sports can be enjoyed throughout the year. **Castrol Raceway,** 2 kilometres (1.2 mi.) west of Queen Elizabeth II Hwy. on Hwy. 19, offers **motorsport racing** May through October; phone (780) 461-5801 or (877) 331-7223.

Home to four professional sports teams, Edmonton is referred to fondly as the City of Champions. The **Edmonton Oilers,** several-time Stanley Cup champions of the National **Hockey** League, play from September to April in **Rogers Place** on 102nd Street; phone (780) 414-5483. The **Edmonton Eskimos football** team, many times the Grey Cup champions of the Canadian Football League, play at **Commonwealth Stadium,** 111th

Ride the trails

Avenue and Stadium Road, from June to November; phone 311 within Edmonton or (780) 442-5311.

Performing Arts

Theater season runs from September through May. For live theater visit the **Citadel Theatre** complex, 99th Street and 101A Avenue, which consists of four theaters, an amphitheater and a beautiful atrium; phone (780) 425-1820 or (888) 425-1820. Family-themed theater, produced by **Fringe Theatre Adventures,** can be enjoyed by all ages from October through May at the STB Financial Arts Barns in Old Strathcona at 103rd Street and 84th Avenue; phone (780) 409-1910.

Prominent Canadian and American performers take to the stage at **Mayfield Dinner Theatre** at the Doubletree West Edmonton, 166th Street and 109th Avenue; phone (780) 483-4051 or (877) 529-7829. **Jubilations Dinner Theatre,** in the West Edmonton Mall at the intersection of 87th Avenue and 170th Street, features musical comedy; phone (780) 484-2424.

The **Alberta Ballet,** (780) 428-6839, and the **Edmonton Opera,** (780) 429-1000, perform in **Northern Alberta Jubilee Auditorium** on the University of Alberta campus at 87th Avenue and 114th Street; phone (780) 427-2760 for auditorium information. The **Edmonton Symphony Orchestra** performs at the **Francis Winspear Centre for Music,** 4 Sir Winston Churchill Sq.; phone (780) 428-1414 or (800) 563-5081 for concert information. The Winspear Centre also plays host to a variety of concerts ranging from classical music to rock, as do the **Shaw Conference Centre,** phone (780) 421-9797; **Rogers Place,** phone (780) 414-5483; and **Rexall Place,** phone (780) 471-7210.

The free publications *Vue Weekly* and *Where Edmonton* give detailed, up-to-date information about arts and entertainment in Edmonton, and local newspapers provide current performance information. Ticketmaster outlets handle ticket sales for most sports, recreation, theater and concert events; phone (855) 985-5000.

◢ ATTRACTIONS

ALBERTA AVIATION MUSEUM is at 11410 Kingsway Ave. This hangar was part of a training facility for air crews during World War II. The museum displays more than 30 historic aircraft including a carefully restored Fairchild 71, a fighter-bomber version of the de Havilland Mosquito, as well as 1920s biplanes and jet fighters from the Cold War era. Other displays detail the history of aviation in Edmonton and Alberta and include "story islands" featuring videos, dioramas, artifacts and the museum's most iconic aircraft.

Time: Allow 1 hour minimum. **Hours:** Mon.-Fri. 10-5, Sat.-Sun. and holidays 10-4. Closed Jan. 1, Christmas and day after Christmas. **Cost:** $12; $9.50 (ages 60+ and students with ID); $8.50 (ages 13-17); $7.50 (ages 6-12); $30 (family, two adults

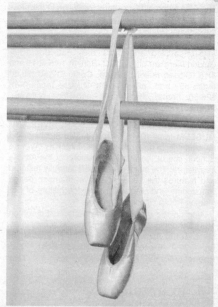

See a performance by the Alberta Ballet

and up to four children ages 6-18). **Phone:** (780) 451-1175.

ALBERTA LEGISLATURE BUILDING is at 10800 97th Ave. Public-use parkland, monuments, reflecting pools and fountains surround the building, which was built with sandstone and marble and completed in 1912. Displays outline Alberta's history and parliamentary traditions. Guided 45-minute tours begin in lower rotunda of the Legislature Building.

Time: Allow 1 hour minimum. **Hours:** Daily 10-5, June-Aug.; Mon.-Fri. 10-5 (also Thurs. 5-8), Sat.-Sun. noon-5, rest of year. Guided tours are offered on the hour year-round. Last tour is given at 4. Closed Jan. 1, Good Friday and Christmas. **Cost:** Free. **Phone:** (780) 427-7362. GT

Legislative Assembly Visitor Centre is on the main floor of the Edmonton Federal Building at 9820-107 St. The center houses galleries featuring changing exhibits describing Canadian history, culture and identity. **Hours:** Daily 10-5 (also Thurs. 5-8), June-Aug.; Mon.-Fri. 10-5 (also Thurs. 5-8), Sat.-Sun. noon-5, rest of year. Closed Jan. 1, Good Friday and Christmas. **Cost:** Free. **Phone:** (780) 427-7362.

ART GALLERY OF ALBERTA, 2 Sir Winston Churchill Sq., is dedicated to the development and presentation of contemporary and historical art from Canada and around the world. The gallery features three levels of exhibition space in a stunning four-level building—a work of art in and of itself—designed by Los Angeles architect Randall Stout.

The AGA is the oldest cultural institution in the province and offers a full range of cultural programming, educational classes and art exhibitions.

Time: Allow 2 hours minimum. **Hours:** Tues.-Fri. 11-5 (also Wed. and Thurs. 5-9), Sat.-Sun. 10-5. Guided tours are offered Sat.-Sun. at 1:15, 2:15 and 3:15. Closed major holidays. **Cost:** $12.50; $8.50 (ages 65+ and students with ID); free (ages 0-6); $26.50 (family, two adults and four children). **Phone:** (780) 422-6223. GT ¶

EDMONTON PUBLIC SCHOOLS ARCHIVES AND MUSEUM is at 10425 99th Ave. The archives and museum is in the historic 1904 McKay Avenue School, site of the first two sessions of the Alberta Legislature. The building has been carefully restored and features the 1906 legislative chamber, period classrooms and displays tracing the history of Edmonton Public Schools.

Also on the grounds is the restored Edmonton 1881 Schoolhouse, the first free public school in Alberta. **Time:** Allow 1 hour minimum. **Hours:** Mon.-Fri. 8:30-4. Closed major holidays. **Cost:** Free. **Phone:** (780) 422-1970.

FORT EDMONTON PARK is at jct. Fox and Whitemud drs. at 7000 143rd. St. Reputed to be Canada's largest living-history park, it depicts Edmonton in four eras: as an 1846 Hudson's Bay Co. fur-trading fort and Cree encampment, as an 1885 settlement, as a developing capital in 1905 and as a 1929 business community and midway.

Streets named for historical eras from the 1840s to the 1920s feature historically appropriate old-time activities. Visitors can visit a wheelwright shop, pump water for tea and play in a penny arcade. Costumed interpreters give demonstrations of pioneer activities such as beading, bannock making and fur pressing. A short 4-D film about the history and development of Edmonton is screened in a reconstructed 1929 cinema. Mini golf, a shooting gallery, wagon and pony rides, steam train and streetcar rides also are available. A 1920s-style midway—complete with Ferris wheel, fun house and other attractions—is included.

Pets are not permitted. **Time:** Allow 3 hours minimum. **Hours:** Daily 10-5, late June-Aug. 30;

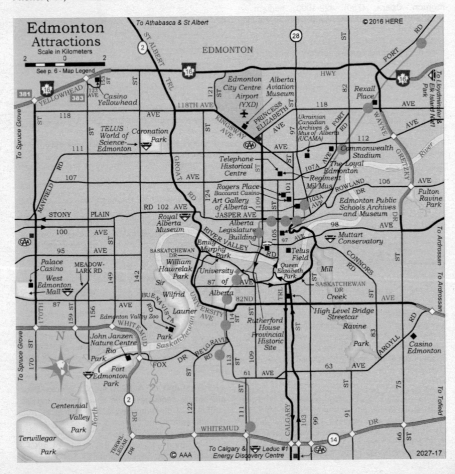

Edmonton Attractions

Mon.-Fri. 10-3, Sat.-Sun. 10-5, mid-May to late June; Sat.-Sun. 11-5, day after Labour Day-Sept. 28. Phone ahead to confirm schedule. **Cost:** (includes steam train, streetcar rides, 4-D film and more than 80 attractions) $26.20; $20.90 (ages 2-17 and 65+); $95 (family, two adults and up to four children). **Phone:** (780) 496-7381. [¶]

JOHN JANZEN NATURE CENTRE is at jct. Fox and Whitemud drs., adjacent to Fort Edmonton Park. The center has exhibits, self-guiding nature trails through the river valley, small animals, hands-on exhibits for children, and interpretive programs and events designed to promote awareness and appreciation of wildlife and the environment.

Time: Allow 1 hour minimum. **Hours:** Daily 10-5, early Jan.-late Dec.; 11-4, rest of year. Holiday hours vary; phone ahead. Closed Jan. 1 and Christmas. **Cost:** $6.43 (one parent and child ages 2+); $2.86 (one parent and child ages 0-23 months); $13.33 (family, maximum seven people of same household; $2.86 per additional parent or child). **Phone:** (780) 442-5311.

THE LOYAL EDMONTON REGIMENT MILITARY MUSEUM is at 10440 108th Ave. in the Prince of Wales Armouries Heritage Centre. The museum's two galleries examine the history of The Loyal Edmonton Regiment, Alberta's oldest infantry unit, and explore military life. Displays include weapons, military equipment, uniforms, medals and badges, photographs and documents. **Time:** Allow 1 hour minimum. **Hours:** Mon.-Fri. 10-4. Phone ahead to confirm schedule. **Cost:** Donations. **Phone:** (780) 421-9943.

MUTTART CONSERVATORY is at 9626 96A St., at the e. end of the James MacDonald Bridge. Four pyramid-shaped glass greenhouses showcase a variety of flora. Plants that thrive in warm, moist climates—including palm trees, orchids, hibiscus and a corpse flower—thrive in the rain forest atmosphere of the Tropical Pyramid, while the Arid Pyramid displays vegetation indigenous to parts of North America and Africa. The Temperate Pyramid exhibits plant life from temperate climates around the world, and the Feature Pyramid has seasonal floral displays. The conservatory's outdoor grounds can be enjoyed on a stroll.

Guided and self-guiding tours are available. **Time:** Allow 1 hour minimum. **Hours:** Daily 10-5 (also Thurs. 5-9). Guided tours of the Tropical, Arid and Temperate Pyramids are given Sat.-Sun. and Wed. Closed Christmas. Phone ahead to confirm schedule. **Cost:** (includes guided tours) $11.90; $10 (ages 13-17 and 65+); $6.10 (ages 2-12); $35.24 (family). Prices may vary. Reservations are required. **Phone:** (780) 442-5311. [GT] [¶]

ROYAL ALBERTA MUSEUM is at 9828 103A Ave. Alberta's natural and human history museum houses a permanent collection in three main galleries, with changing displays and events scheduled throughout the year.

Muttart Conservatory

The Natural History gallery offers specimens of plants, animals, birds, live insects, fossils and minerals depicting the 1 billion-year odyssey from dinosaurs to rare minerals and gems. Fossils: Creatures from the Depths of Time displays extinct beasts from ancient Alberta, while The Bug Room contains live specimens from around the world. The Syncrude Gallery of Aboriginal Culture tells the story of 11,000 years of aboriginal history. The Wild Alberta gallery encourages visitors to look at Alberta's environment from a different perspective.

CLOSURE INFORMATION: The Royal Alberta Museum is closed through early 2018 as its collections are moved from the museum's former home on 102nd Avenue to its new facility at 9828 103A Ave.; phone ahead for updates. **Phone:** (780) 453-9100.

[SAVE] **RUTHERFORD HOUSE PROVINCIAL HISTORIC SITE** is at 11153 Saskatchewan Dr. on the University of Alberta campus. The structure was home to A.C. Rutherford, Alberta's first premier and a founder of the University of Alberta. Completed in 1911, the elegant Jacobethan (a blend of Jacobean and Elizabethan styles) Revival house established a new standard in domestic architecture and marked the end of the pioneer style in Alberta. Historical interpreters in period dress conduct house tours upon request. Events are scheduled throughout the year.

Time: Allow 1 hour minimum. **Hours:** Daily 10-5, May 15-Labour Day; Tues.-Sun. noon-5, rest of year. Closed Jan. 1, Good Friday, Christmas Eve, Christmas and day after Christmas. **Cost:** $4.76; $3.81 (ages 65+); $2.86 (ages 7-17); $11.43 (family, two adults and two children). **Phone:** (780) 427-3995. [GT] [¶]

TELUS WORLD OF SCIENCE— EDMONTON is at 142nd St. and 111th Ave. Five galleries house exhibits that explain and explore science and technology. Space Place focuses on space exploration and life on a space station. The Body Fantastic includes large-scale 3-D models of body parts and the aptly named Gallery of the Gross. The Syncrude Environment Gallery features Science on a Sphere, a 1.8-metre (6-ft.) diameter globe staff scientists use to enhance presentations about the earth's environment. Discoveryland is a hands-on area designed for children ages 2 through 8.

The Science Garage is the center's newest permanent gallery, encouraging visitors to get hands

Take Your Imagination to New Destinations

Use AAA Travel Guides online to explore the possibilities.

❯ Tour popular places in the U.S., Canada, Mexico and the Caribbean from the comfort of your home.

❯ Read what AAA's professional inspectors say about area hotels, restaurants and attractions.

❯ Check out the best stuff to see and do, with itineraries to ensure you won't miss a thing.

Go to AAA.com/travelguide today to discover your next destination.

and minds busy with science and engineering. In the Maker Space, visitors use random materials to create, build and experiment, aided by staff scientists, and there are daily activities and challenges.

In addition you'll enjoy live science demonstrations, an outdoor observatory equipped with telescopes, an IMAX theater and full-dome shows presented in the Margaret Zeidler Star Theatre planetarium. On weekends, you can program your own robot in the Robotics Lab.

Hours: Building and galleries Sun.-Thurs. 9-6, Fri.-Sat. 9-8. Observatory Fri. 7-10, Sat.-Sun. 1-4 and 7-10 (weather permitting). IMAX and Robotics Lab hours vary. Closed Christmas. Phone ahead to confirm schedule.

Cost: Science center (includes planetarium shows) $19.95; $16.95 (ages 13-17 and 65+); $13.95 (ages 3-12); $79.95 (family, two adults and four children). IMAX film $13.95; $11.95 (ages 13-17 and 65+); $9.50 (ages 3-12); $54.95 (family, two adults and four children). Combination ticket (science center and IMAX film) $27.95; $23.95 (ages 13-17 and 65+); $19.95 (ages 3-12); $125.95 (family, two adults and four children). **Phone:** (780) 451-3344. 🍴

UKRAINIAN CULTURAL HERITAGE VILLAGE is 50 km (31 mi.) e. on Hwy. 16, 3 km e. of the entrance to Elk Island National Park. The lifestyle of the region's Ukrainian immigrant population is portrayed in a village re-created to resemble a typical east central Alberta settlement 1892-1930.

Living-history demonstrations center around more than 35 restored historical buildings, including houses, farm buildings, churches and stores. Costumed interpreters depicting a wide variety of characters from the turn of the 20th century re-create the lives of those who lived in each of the buildings, demonstrating the settlers' daily routines. Special events are held throughout the summer.

Time: Allow 2 hours minimum. **Hours:** Daily 10-5, Victoria Day weekend-Labour Day. **Cost:** $14.29; $12.38 (ages 65+); $6 (ages 7-17); $38.10 (family, two adults and children). **Phone:** (780) 662-3640. 🏞

WEST EDMONTON MALL is at 8882 170th St. N.W. The huge, two-level complex is North America's largest shopping and entertainment center. It contains more than 800 stores and services, more than 100 eateries and nine theme attractions. Galaxyland features 25 rides and attractions. World Waterpark offers more than 2 hectares (5 acres) of indoor fun, including a giant wave pool and surfing on an endless wave. Sea Life Caverns contains approximately 100 species of marine life, including South African penguins and California sea lions. The Ice Palace features an NHL-size ice rink, two miniature golf courses, a multilevel rope course, and a recreation center offering bowling and billiards.

Time: Allow a full day. **Hours:** Shops open Mon.-Sat. 10-9, Sun. 11-6, most holidays 10-6. Hours for attractions, theaters and restaurants vary; phone ahead. **Cost:** Prices for individual attractions vary. **Phone:** (780) 444-5321 for general mall information, (780) 444-5300, or (800) 661-8890 for more information about attractions, including hours of operation and prices. *(See ad this page.)* 🍴 ⊠

Sightseeing

Driving Tours
The most scenic areas in Edmonton are along the North Saskatchewan River Valley. On the south side, the drive north along Saskatchewan Drive from 76th Avenue and 120th Street to 99th Street offers a picturesque trip around the University of Alberta campus.

Streetcar Tours

HIGH LEVEL BRIDGE STREETCAR departs from the Old Strathcona stop at 103rd St. and 84th Ave. and from downtown s. of Jasper Ave. and w. of 109th St. A vintage streetcar takes passengers along the old Canadian Pacific Railway (CPR) line across the 49-metre (160-ft.) High Level Bridge, built 1910-13 to link Old Strathcona and downtown Edmonton. The narrated, 6-kilometre (3.7-mi.) trip offers excellent views of the city and the North Saskatchewan River Valley.

The Strathcona Streetcar Barn Museum features exhibits relating the history of the Edmonton Streetcar System; included are conductor uniforms, photographs and antique ticket punches. **Time:** Allow 45 minutes minimum. **Hours:** Streetcars operate Sun.-Fri. 11-4:20, Sat. 9-4:20, late May-Labour Day; Fri.-Sun. 11-4:20, day after Labour Day-early Oct. Hours extended to 10 p.m. during the Fringe Festival in Aug. Museum open Sat. 10-2, late May-early Oct. Phone ahead to confirm schedule. **Cost:** Round-trip streetcar fare $5.71; free (ages 0-5); $19.05 (family, two adults and children). Museum free. **Phone:** (780) 437-7721. GT

Walking Tours
Heritage Trail leads from the Shaw Conference Centre to the Alberta Legislature Building, a route that links government and industry by way of Edmonton's past. Old Strathcona, south of the North Saskatchewan River, offers a view of many original buildings and street scenes characteristic of an early 20th-century prairie town. Edmonton Gallery Walk joins nine private art galleries around Jasper Avenue and 124th Street.

Traveling across the border or abroad?
Begin painting beautiful memories right away.

Arrive ready with foreign currency.

Stop by your local AAA/CAA office.

Product not available at all locations.

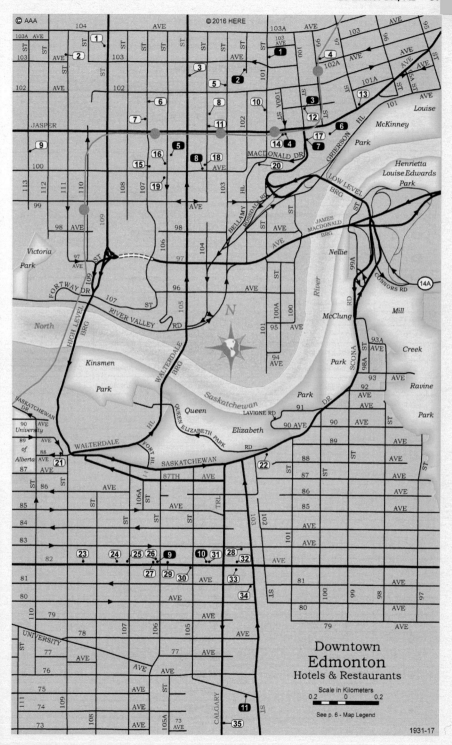

Downtown
Edmonton
Hotels & Restaurants

Scale in Kilometers
0.2   0   0.2

See p. 6 - Map Legend

1931-17

Downtown Edmonton

This index helps you "spot" where approved hotels and restaurants are located on the corresponding detailed maps. Hotel daily rate range is for comparison only. Restaurant price range is a combination of lunch and/or dinner. Turn to the listing page for more information and consult display ads for special promotions.

DOWNTOWN EDMONTON

Map Page	Hotels	Diamond Rated	Rate Range	Page
1 p. 97	The Sutton Place Hotel Edmonton	▽▽▽	Rates not provided	104
2 p. 97	**Delta Edmonton Centre Suite Hotel**	▽▽▽	$80-$187 [SAVE]	104
3 p. 97	**The Westin Edmonton**	▽▽▽▽	$129-$329 [SAVE]	105
4 p. 97	**Union Bank Inn**	▽▽▽	$209-$429 [SAVE]	105
5 p. 97	Days Inn Downtown Edmonton	▽▽	$101-$150	104
6 p. 97	Courtyard by Marriott Edmonton Downtown	▽▽▽	$98-$190	104
7 p. 97	**The Fairmont Hotel Macdonald** (See ad p. 104.)	▽▽▽▽	$189-$489 [SAVE]	104
8 p. 97	Holiday Inn Express Edmonton Downtown	▽▽▽	Rates not provided	104
9 p. 97	Varscona Hotel on Whyte	▽▽▽	Rates not provided	105
10 p. 97	Metterra Hotel on Whyte	▽▽▽	Rates not provided	104
11 p. 97	Days Inn Edmonton South	▽▽	$120-$139	104

Map Page	Restaurants	Diamond Rated	Cuisine	Price Range	Page
① p. 97	Mikado	▽▽	Japanese	$12-$30	106
② p. 97	Louisiana Purchase	▽▽	Cajun	$10-$28	105
③ p. 97	Characters Fine Dining	▽▽▽	New American	$18-$52	105
④ p. 97	Zinc Restaurant	▽▽▽	New American	$13-$30	106
⑤ p. 97	The Creperie	▽▽	French	$10-$30	105
⑥ p. 97	Khazana	▽▽	Indian	$13-$72	105
⑦ p. 97	Doan's Restaurant	▽▽	Vietnamese	$8-$17	105
⑧ p. 97	Blue Plate Diner	▽▽	International	$11-$26	105
⑨ p. 97	Bua Thai Restaurant	▽▽	Thai	$13-$27	105
⑩ p. 97	Lux steakhouse & bar	▽▽▽	Steak	$14-$89	105
⑪ p. 97	Tzin Wine and Tapas	▽▽	New World Small Plates	$15-$36	106
⑫ p. 97	Share	▽▽▽	American	$15-$35	106
⑬ p. 97	Hardware Grill	▽▽▽	Regional Canadian	$17-$50	105
⑭ p. 97	Madison's Grill	▽▽▽	New Canadian	$13-$47	105
⑮ p. 97	Wildflower Grill	▽▽▽	Northern Canadian	$15-$46	106
⑯ p. 97	Select	▽▽▽	Continental	$15-$55	106
⑰ p. 97	**The Harvest Room**	▽▽▽	New Canadian	$23-$51	105
⑱ p. 97	The Free Press Bistro	▽▽	American	$10-$26	105
⑲ p. 97	The Marc Restaurant	▽▽▽	French	$13-$29	105
⑳ p. 97	La Ronde Revolving Restaurant	▽▽▽	New Canadian	$31-$100	105
㉑ p. 97	Highlevel Diner	▽▽	American	$10-$23	105
㉒ p. 97	New Asian Village	▽▽	Eastern Indian	$12-$27	106
㉓ p. 97	Cafe Mosaics	▽	Vegetarian	$10-$15	105

Map Page	Restaurants (cont'd)	Diamond Rated	Cuisine	Price Range	Page
㉔ p. 97	Tokyo Noodle Shop	▼▼	Japanese	$10-$22	106
㉕ p. 97	The King & I	▼▼	Thai	$12-$25	105
㉖ p. 97	Ampersand 27	▼▼	American	$14-$32	105
㉗ p. 97	O'Byrne's Irish Pub	▼▼	Irish	$13-$23	106
㉘ p. 97	Packrat Louie's Kitchen & Bar	▼▼▼	New American	$12-$40	106
㉙ p. 97	Continental Treat Fine Bistro	▼▼	European	$20-$45	105
㉚ p. 97	Chianti Cafe & Restaurant	▼▼	Italian	$14-$25	105
㉛ p. 97	Yiannis Taverna	▼▼	Greek	$12-$44	106
㉜ p. 97	The Pourhouse Bier Bistro	▼▼	American	$11-$22	106
㉝ p. 97	Block 1912	▼	Coffee/Tea	$7-$13	105
㉞ p. 97	Von's Steak House & Oyster Bar	▼▼▼	Steak	$18-$58	106
㉟ p. 97	Billingsgate Seafood Market Lighthouse Cafe	▼▼	Seafood	$8-$20	105

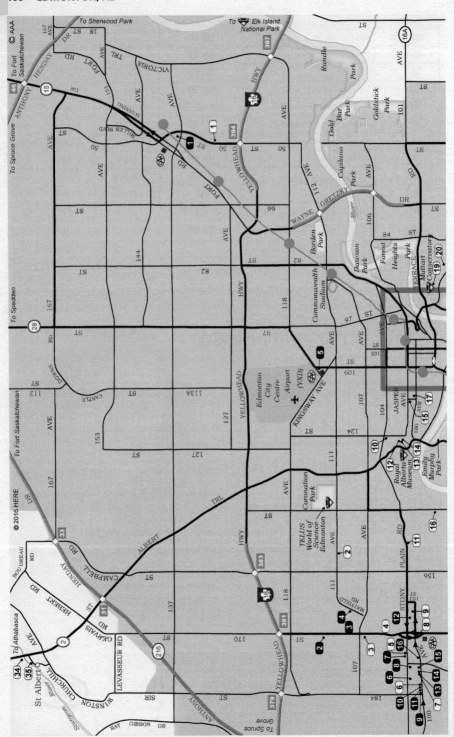

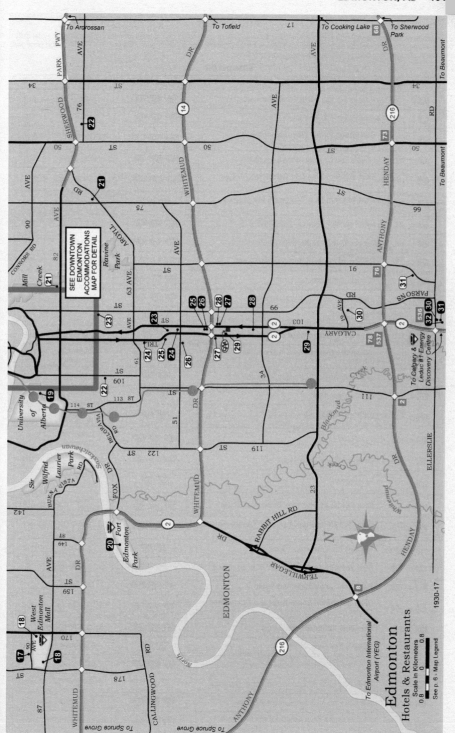

Edmonton
Hotels & Restaurants
Scale in Kilometers
See p. 6 - Map Legend

Edmonton

This index helps you "spot" where approved hotels and restaurants are located on the corresponding detailed maps. Hotel daily rate range is for comparison only. Restaurant price range is a combination of lunch and/or dinner. Turn to the listing page for more information and consult display ads for special promotions.

EDMONTON

Map Page	Hotels	Diamond Rated	Rate Range	Page
1 p. 100	Holiday Inn Express & Suites Edmonton North	◆◆◆	$139-$149	110
2 p. 100	Holiday Inn & Suites, West Edmonton	◆◆◆	$129-$249	110
3 p. 100	**Staybridge Suites West Edmonton** *(See ad p. 111.)*	◆◆◆	$152-$190 [SAVE]	111
4 p. 100	DoubleTree by Hilton West Edmonton	◆◆◆	$139-$169	109
5 p. 100	**Best Western Plus City Centre Inn** *(See ad p. 107.)*	◆◆◆	$155-$250 [SAVE]	107
6 p. 100	**Best Western Plus Westwood Inn** *(See ad p. 108.)*	◆◆	$109-$129 [SAVE]	108
7 p. 100	Hilton Garden Inn-West Edmonton	◆◆◆	$125-$179	110
8 p. 100	Quality Inn West Edmonton	◆◆◆	$114-$230	111
9 p. 100	**Courtyard by Marriott Edmonton West**	◆◆◆	$105-$160 [SAVE]	108
10 p. 100	Wingate Inn Edmonton West	◆◆◆	$129-$249	112
11 p. 100	Hampton Inn & Suites Edmonton West	◆◆◆	$139-$179	110
12 p. 100	Continental Inn	◆◆	$120-$145	108
13 p. 100	**Days Inn & Suites West Edmonton**	◆◆	$140-$159 [SAVE]	109
14 p. 100	Holiday Inn Express Hotel & Suites, West Edmonton	◆◆◆	Rates not provided	111
15 p. 100	Executive Royal Hotel West Edmonton	◆◆	$124-$200	109
16 p. 100	**Comfort Inn West**	◆◆	$99-$180 [SAVE]	108
17 p. 100	West Edmonton Mall Inn	◆◆	Rates not provided	111
18 p. 100	Fantasyland Hotel	◆◆◆	Rates not provided	110
19 p. 100	**Campus Tower Suite Hotel**	◆◆◆	$161-$195 [SAVE]	108
20 p. 100	Hotel Selkirk	◆◆	Rates not provided	111
21 p. 100	Four Points by Sheraton Edmonton South	◆◆◆	Rates not provided [SAVE]	110
22 p. 100	**Radisson Hotel and Convention Centre** *(See ad p. 110.)*	◆◆◆	Rates not provided [SAVE]	111
23 p. 100	Ramada Inn Edmonton South	◆◆	$92-$160	111
24 p. 100	**Best Western Cedar Park Inn** *(See ad p. 106.)*	◆◆	$119-$139 [SAVE]	106
25 p. 100	**Radisson Hotel Edmonton South**	◆◆◆	$119-$349 [SAVE]	111
26 p. 100	**Delta Edmonton South Hotel and Conference Centre**	◆◆◆	$113-$175 [SAVE]	109
27 p. 100	**Sawridge Inn Edmonton South**	◆◆◆	$109-$189 [SAVE]	111
28 p. 100	Super 8 Edmonton South	◆◆	$120-$134	111
29 p. 100	Holiday Inn Express & Suites Edmonton South	◆◆◆	$109-$169	110
30 p. 100	**Four Points by Sheraton Edmonton Gateway**	◆◆◆	$129-$209 [SAVE]	110
31 p. 100	Hampton Inn by Hilton Edmonton South	◆◆◆	$119-$189	110
32 p. 100	**Best Western Plus South Edmonton Inn & Suites**	◆◆◆	$139-$169 [SAVE]	107

Map Page	Restaurants	Diamond Rated	Cuisine	Price Range	Page
① p. 100	Franco's Steak & Pizza	◈◈	Italian	$9-$40	112
② p. 100	**Haus Falkenstein**	◈◈	German	$12-$28	112
③ p. 100	Fife N' Dekel	◈	Deli	$6-$11	112
④ p. 100	Phoenicia	◈◈	Lebanese	$12-$26	112
⑤ p. 100	Cha For Tea Palace	◈◈	Chinese Dim Sum Seafood	$8-$17	112
⑥ p. 100	Homefire Bar & Grill	◈◈	International	$12-$34	112
⑦ p. 100	ConYac's Bar & Grill	◈◈	American	$11-$28	112
⑧ p. 100	Guru Fine Indian Cuisine	◈◈◈	Indian	$15-$32	112
⑨ p. 100	Bucas & Pastas	◈	Italian	$7-$14	112
⑩ p. 100	The Dish Bistro	◈◈	American	$15-$24	112
⑪ p. 100	Tropika	◈◈	Thai	$12-$26	113
⑫ p. 100	Urban Diner	◈◈	American	$11-$19	113
⑬ p. 100	Violino Gastronomia Italiana	◈◈◈	Italian	$15-$39	113
⑭ p. 100	Manor Casual Bistro	◈◈	International	$14-$36	112
⑮ p. 100	Normand's Fine Regional Cuisine	◈◈◈	French	$20-$40	112
⑯ p. 100	Delux Burger Bar	◈◈	American	$10-$19	112
⑰ p. 100	Il Pasticcio Trattoria	◈◈	Italian	$12-$32	112
⑱ p. 100	Famoso Neapolitan Pizzeria	◈◈	Pizza	$7-$16	112
⑲ p. 100	Culina Muttart	◈◈	American	$11-$17	112
⑳ p. 100	Red Ox Inn	◈◈◈	New American	$29-$38	112
㉑ p. 100	Unheardof Restaurant	◈◈◈	American	$35-$45	113
㉒ p. 100	Parkallen Restaurant	◈◈◈	Lebanese	$10-$45	112
㉓ p. 100	Old Country Inn	◈◈	German	$9-$26	112
㉔ p. 100	Tropika	◈◈	Thai	$12-$26	113
㉕ p. 100	The Bothy Wine & Whisky Bar	◈◈◈	New American	$14-$26	112
㉖ p. 100	Lemongrass Cafe	◈◈	Vietnamese	$10-$19	112
㉗ p. 100	Tom Goodchilds Moose Factory	◈◈	Steak	$12-$50	113
㉘ p. 100	Creations Dining Room & Lounge	◈◈◈	New American	$11-$34	112
㉙ p. 100	Century Grill	◈◈◈	New Pacific Rim	$12-$41	112
㉚ p. 100	Local Public Eatery	◈◈	American	$10-$20	112
㉛ p. 100	Zaika Indian Bistro Bar	◈◈	Indian	$14-$19	113

ST. ALBERT

Map Page	Restaurants	Diamond Rated	Cuisine	Price Range	Page
㉞ p. 100	River House	◈◈◈	Regional Canadian	$11-$35	144
㉟ p. 100	Blue Rare Steak & Bar	◈◈◈	Steak Seafood	$12-$49	144

Ask about AAA/CAA Associate membership
to share the benefits you value

DOWNTOWN EDMONTON
• Hotels & Restaurants map & index p. 97

COURTYARD BY MARRIOTT EDMONTON DOWNTOWN
(780)423-9999 **6**
▼▼▼ Hotel. **Address:** 1 Thornton
Ct T5J 2E7

AAA Benefit: Members save 5% or more!

DAYS INN DOWNTOWN EDMONTON
(780)423-1925 **5**
▼▼ Hotel. **Address:** 10041 106th St T5J 1G3

DAYS INN EDMONTON SOUTH
(780)430-0011 **11**
▼▼ Hotel. **Address:** 10333 University Ave T6E 6N3

DELTA EDMONTON CENTRE SUITE HOTEL
(780)429-3900 **2**

▼▼▼ Hotel $80-$187

DELTA HOTELS

AAA Benefit: Members save 5% or more!

Address: 10222 102nd St NW T5J 4C5 **Location:** At 102nd St NW and 103rd Ave NW. Attached to a shopping centre. **Facility:** 169 units. 7 stories, interior corridors. **Parking:** on-site (fee) and valet, winter plug-ins. **Activities:** exercise room. **Guest Services:** complimentary and valet laundry.

SAVE ECO ⑪ 👶 ⒯ CALL 🅼 BIZ HS 📶 ✕ 🎥 🖬 💻 / SOME UNITS 🐾

THE FAIRMONT HOTEL MACDONALD
(780)424-5181 **7**

▼▼▼ ▼▼▼
Historic Hotel
$189-$489

Address: 10065 100th St T5J 0N6 **Location:** Just s of Jasper Ave. **Facility:** This landmark hotel with its majestic ambience is perched above the river valley, and the elegant lounge has a beautiful view. Guest rooms, available in a variety of sizes, have upscale décor. 198 units. 9 stories, interior corridors. **Parking:** on-site (fee) and valet, winter plug-ins. **Terms:** cancellation fee imposed. **Amenities:** safes. **Dining:** The Harvest Room, see separate listing. **Pool(s):** heated indoor. **Activities:** sauna, hot tub, steamroom, massage. **Guest Services:** valet laundry, boarding pass kiosk, area transportation. *(See ad this page.)*

SAVE ECO ⑪ 👶 ⒯ Ⓨ ⒤ CALL 🅼 🛏 👶 BIZ
$HS 📶 ✕ 🎥 💻 / SOME UNITS 🛏 🐾

HOLIDAY INN EXPRESS EDMONTON DOWNTOWN
780/423-2450 **8**
▼▼▼ Hotel. **Address:** 10010 104th St T5J 0Z1

METTERRA HOTEL ON WHYTE
780/465-8150 **10**
▼▼▼ Boutique Hotel. **Address:** 10454 82nd Ave (Whyte Ave) T6E 4Z7

THE SUTTON PLACE HOTEL EDMONTON
780/428-7111 **1**
▼▼▼ Hotel. **Address:** 10235 101st St T5J 3E9

▼ See AAA listing this page ▼

Visit the AAA and CAA senior driving websites

for tips to help you drive safely longer

(See map & index p. 97.)

UNION BANK INN   (780)423-3600   **4**

▼▲▼▲▼▲
Boutique Hotel
$209-$429

Address: 10053 Jasper Ave T5J 1S5 **Location:** Corner of 101st St. **Facility:** Originally built in 1911, this former bank was transformed to include a Heritage and Contemporary wing. Designer rooms include fireplaces, luxurious microfiber bedding, and wine and cheese service. 34 units. 3-5 stories, interior corridors. **Parking:** on-site (fee). **Terms:** cancellation fee imposed. **Amenities:** safes. **Dining:** Madison's Grill, see separate listing. **Activities:** limited exercise equipment. **Guest Services:** valet laundry.

[SAVE] [TI] [Y] CALL [&M] [BIZ] [HS]
[wifi] [X] [▢] / SOME UNITS [H]

VARSCONA HOTEL ON WHYTE   780/434-6111   **9**

▼▲▼▲▼▲ Hotel. **Address:** 8208 106th St T6E 6R9

THE WESTIN EDMONTON   (780)426-3636   **3**

▼▲▼ ▲▼▲ Hotel $129-$329

WESTIN HOTELS & RESORTS **AAA Benefit:** Members save up to 15%, plus Starwood Preferred Guest® benefits!

Address: 10135 100th St T5J 0N7 **Location:** Jct 101st Ave. **Facility:** Expect professional service at this elegant downtown hotel offering a mix of well-appointed guest rooms in two separate towers. My advice is to ask for the newly remodeled rooms. 416 units, some two bedrooms. 20 stories, interior corridors. **Parking:** on-site (fee) and valet. **Amenities:** safes. **Dining:** Share, see separate listing. **Pool(s):** heated indoor. **Activities:** sauna, exercise room, spa. **Guest Services:** valet laundry.

[SAVE] [ECO] [TI] [👶] [Y] CALL [&M] [➰] [BIZ] [📶] [X]
[📽] [▢] / SOME UNITS [🐕] [sHS] [H]

WHERE TO EAT

AMPERSAND 27   780/757-2727   **26**
▼▲ ▼▲ American. Casual Dining. **Address:** 10612 82 Ave NW T6E 2A7

BILLINGSGATE SEAFOOD MARKET LIGHTHOUSE CAFE
    780/433-0091   **35**
▼▲ ▼▲ Seafood. Casual Dining. **Address:** 7331 104th St T6E 4B9

BLOCK 1912   780/433-6575   **33**
▼▲ Coffee/Tea. Quick Serve. **Address:** 10361 82nd Ave NW T6E 1Z9

BLUE PLATE DINER   780/429-0740   **8**
▼▲ ▼▲ International. Casual Dining. **Address:** 10145 104th St T5J 0Z9

BUA THAI RESTAURANT   780/482-2277   **9**
▼▲ ▼▲ Thai. Casual Dining. **Address:** 10049 113th St NW T5K 1N9

CAFE MOSAICS   780/433-9702   **23**
▼▲ Vegetarian. Casual Dining. **Address:** 10844 82nd Ave T6E 2B3

CHARACTERS FINE DINING   780/421-4100   **3**
▼▲ ▼▲ ▼▲ New American. Fine Dining. **Address:** 10257 105th St T5J 1E3

CHIANTI CAFE & RESTAURANT   780/439-9829   **30**
▼▲ Italian. Casual Dining. **Address:** 10501 82nd Ave NW T6E 2A3

CONTINENTAL TREAT FINE BISTRO   780/433-7432   **29**
▼▲ ▼▲ European. Fine Dining. **Address:** 10560 82nd Ave NW T6E 2A4

THE CREPERIE   780/420-6656   **5**
▼▲ ▼▲ French. Casual Dining. **Address:** 10220 103rd St T5J 0Y8

DOAN'S RESTAURANT   780/424-3034   **7**
▼▲ ▼▲ Vietnamese. Casual Dining. **Address:** 10130 107th St NW T5J 1J4

THE FREE PRESS BISTRO   780/497-7784   **18**
▼▲ ▼▲ American. Casual Dining. **Address:** 10014 104th St, #80 T5J 0Z1

HARDWARE GRILL   780/423-0969   **13**
▼▲ ▼▲ Regional Canadian. Fine Dining. **Address:** 9698 Jasper Ave T5H 3V5

THE HARVEST ROOM   780/424-5181   **17**

▼▲ ▼▲ ▼▲
New
Canadian
Fine Dining
$23-$51

AAA Inspector Notes: The atmosphere is warm and vibrant in the elegant surroundings of this restaurant. Views of the North Saskatchewan River are beautiful. Creative Canadian Prairie cuisine is prepared in the open-concept kitchen. A true value is the executive lunch—an upscale, buffet-style presentation of gourmet sandwiches, salads and soups. **Features:** full bar, patio dining, Sunday brunch. **Reservations:** suggested. **Address:** 10065 100th St T5J 0N6 **Location:** Just s of Jasper Ave; in The Fairmont Hotel Macdonald. **Parking:** on-site (fee) and valet.

[B] [L] [D] CALL [&M]

HIGHLEVEL DINER   780/433-0993   **21**
▼▲ ▼▲ American. Casual Dining. **Address:** 10912 88th Ave NW T6G 0Z1

KHAZANA   780/702-0330   **6**
▼▲ Indian. Casual Dining. **Address:** 10177 107 St T5J 1J5

THE KING & I   780/433-2222   **25**
▼▲ ▼▲ Thai. Casual Dining. **Address:** 8208 107th St T6E 6P4

LA RONDE REVOLVING RESTAURANT   780/420-8366   **20**
▼▲ ▼▲ New Canadian. Fine Dining. **Address:** 10111 Bellamy Hill T5J 1N7

LOUISIANA PURCHASE   780/420-6779   **2**
▼▲ ▼▲ Cajun. Casual Dining. **Address:** 10320 111th St T5K 1L2

LUX STEAKHOUSE & BAR   780/424-0400   **10**
▼▲ ▼▲ Steak. Fine Dining. **Address:** 10150 101st St NW, Commerce Pl T5J 4G8

MADISON'S GRILL   780/401-2222   **14**
▼▲ ▼▲ New Canadian. Fine Dining. **Address:** 10053 Jasper Ave T5J 1S5

THE MARC RESTAURANT   780/429-2828   **19**
▼▲ ▼▲ French. Casual Dining. **Address:** 9940 106th St, 100 Sterling Pl T5K 2N2

(See map & index p. 97.)

MIKADO 780/425-8096 ①
♦♦ Japanese. Casual Dining. **Address:** 10350 109th St T5J 4X9

NEW ASIAN VILLAGE 780/433-3804 ㉒
♦♦ Eastern Indian. Casual Dining. **Address:** 10143 Saskatchewan Dr T6E 4R5

O'BYRNE'S IRISH PUB 780/414-6766 ㉗
♦♦ Irish. Casual Dining. **Address:** 10616 82nd Ave NW (Whyte Ave) T6E 2A7

PACKRAT LOUIE'S KITCHEN & BAR 780/433-0123 ㉘
♦♦♦ New American. Casual Dining. **Address:** 10335 83rd Ave T6E 2C6

THE POURHOUSE BIER BISTRO 780/757-7687 ㉜
♦♦ American. Gastropub. **Address:** 10354 82nd Ave NW T6E 1Z8

SELECT 780/428-1629 ⑯
♦♦♦ Continental. Casual Dining. **Address:** 10018 106th St T5J 1G1

SHARE 780/493-8994 ⑫
♦♦♦ American. Fine Dining. **Address:** 10135 100th St T5J 0N7

TOKYO NOODLE SHOP 780/430-0838 ㉔
♦♦ Japanese. Casual Dining. **Address:** 10736 82nd Ave T6E 6P4

TZIN WINE AND TAPAS 780/428-8946 ⑪
♦♦♦ New World Small Plates. Casual Dining. **Address:** 10115 104th St T5J 0Z9

VON'S STEAK HOUSE & OYSTER BAR 780/439-0041 �34
♦♦♦ Steak. Casual Dining. **Address:** 10309 81st Ave T6E 1X3

WILDFLOWER GRILL 780/990-1938 ⑮
♦♦♦ Northern Canadian. Fine Dining. **Address:** 10009 107th St NW T5J 1J1

YIANNIS TAVERNA 780/433-6768 ㉛
♦♦ Greek. Casual Dining. **Address:** 10444 82nd Ave NW (Whyte Ave) T6E 2A2

ZINC RESTAURANT 780/392-2501 ④
♦♦♦ New American. Casual Dining. **Address:** 2 Sir Winston Churchill Sq T5J 2C1

EDMONTON
- **Restaurants p. 112**
- **Hotels & Restaurants map & index p. 100**

BEST WESTERN CEDAR PARK INN
(780)434-7411 ㉔

♦♦ ♦♦
Hotel
$119-$139

AAA Benefit: Save 10% or more every day and earn 10% bonus points!

Address: 5116 Gateway Blvd T6H 2H4 **Location:** Hwy 2 (Gateway Blvd) at 51st Ave. **Facility:** 195 units. 4-5 stories, interior corridors. **Parking:** winter plug-ins. **Terms:** check-in 4 pm. **Amenities:** Some: safes. **Pool(s):** heated indoor. **Activities:** exercise room. **Guest Services:** valet laundry. (See ad this page.)

▼ See AAA listing this page ▼

Save more, earn more and spend less
with AAA/CAA financial products and services

(See map & index p. 100.)

BEST WESTERN PLUS CITY CENTRE INN
(780)479-2042

Hotel
$155-$250

Best Western PLUS.
AAA Benefit:
Save 10% or more every day and earn 10% bonus points!

Address: 11310 109th St T5G 2T7 **Location:** From Kingsway Ave NW, just n. **Facility:** 109 units. 2 stories, interior corridors. **Parking:** winter plug-ins. **Pool(s):** heated indoor. **Activities:** hot tub, exercise room. **Guest Services:** valet and coin laundry. *(See ad this page.)*

[SAVE] [ECO] [icons] CALL [icons] / SOME UNITS [HS] [icons]

BEST WESTERN PLUS SOUTH EDMONTON INN & SUITES
(780)801-3580

Hotel
$139-$169

Best Western PLUS.
AAA Benefit:
Save 10% or more every day and earn 10% bonus points!

Address: 1204 101st St T6X 0P1 **Location:** Hwy 2 (Gateway Blvd) exit Ellerslie Rd. **Facility:** 105 units. 4 stories, interior corridors. **Parking:** winter plug-ins. **Terms:** check-in 4 pm. **Pool(s):** heated indoor. **Activities:** hot tub, exercise room. **Guest Services:** valet and coin laundry. **Featured Amenity:** full hot breakfast.

[SAVE] [ECO] [icons] CALL [icons] [BIZ]
[HS] [icons]

▼ See AAA listing this page ▼

(See map & index p. 100.)

BEST WESTERN PLUS WESTWOOD INN
(780)483-7770

Hotel
$109-$129

Best Western PLUS.

AAA Benefit: Save 10% or more every day and earn 10% bonus points!

Address: 18035 Stony Plain Rd T5S 1B2 **Location:** Hwy 16A (Stony Plain Rd) at 180th St. **Facility:** 172 units. 3-6 stories, interior corridors. **Parking:** winter plug-ins. **Terms:** check-in 4 pm, resort fee. **Amenities:** Some: safes. **Pool(s):** heated indoor. **Activities:** exercise room. **Guest Services:** valet laundry. *(See ad this page.)*

CAMPUS TOWER SUITE HOTEL
(780)439-6060

Extended Stay Hotel
$161-$195

Address: 11145 87th Ave T6G 0Y1 **Location:** At 111th St and 87th Ave. Near university and hospital campuses. **Facility:** 90 units, some two bedrooms and efficiencies. 16 stories, interior corridors. **Parking:** winter plug-ins. **Terms:** check-in 4 pm, cancellation fee imposed. **Amenities:** safes. **Dining:** 3 restaurants. **Activities:** exercise room. **Guest Services:** valet and coin laundry.

COMFORT INN WEST
(780)484-4415

Hotel
$99-$180

Address: 17610 100th Ave T5S 1S9 **Location:** At 176th St. **Facility:** 100 units. 2 stories (no elevator), interior corridors. **Guest Services:** valet and coin laundry.

CONTINENTAL INN
(780)484-7751

 Hotel. **Address:** 16625 Stony Plain Rd T5P 4A8

COURTYARD BY MARRIOTT EDMONTON WEST
(780)638-6070

Hotel
$105-$160

COURTYARD Marriott

AAA Benefit: Members save 5% or more!

Address: 10011 184th St T5S 0C7 **Location:** From Anthony Henday Dr, 0.8 mi (1.3 km) e. **Facility:** 136 units. 5 stories, interior corridors. **Parking:** winter plug-ins. **Pool(s):** heated indoor. **Activities:** hot tub, exercise room. **Guest Services:** valet and coin laundry.

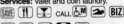

▼ See AAA listing this page ▼

Before you travel, ask your AAA/CAA club about identity theft monitoring products

(See map & index p. 100.)

DAYS INN & SUITES WEST EDMONTON
(780)444-4440   **13**

Hotel
$140-$159

Address: 10010 179A St T5S 2T1 **Location:** From Anthony Henday Dr, 1.2 mi (2 km) e. **Facility:** 108 units, some efficiencies. 4 stories, interior corridors. **Parking:** winter plug-ins. **Terms:** check-in 4 pm, cancellation fee imposed. **Dining:** ConYac's Bar & Grill, see separate listing. **Pool(s):** heated indoor. **Activities:** hot tub, exercise room. **Guest Services:** valet and coin laundry.

DELTA EDMONTON SOUTH HOTEL AND CONFERENCE CENTRE
(780)434-6415   **26**

Hotel
$113-$175

AAA Benefit:
Members save 5% or more!

Address: 4404 Gateway Blvd T6H 5C2 **Location:** Jct Hwy 2 (Gateway Blvd) and Whitemud Dr. **Facility:** 237 units. 11 stories, interior corridors. **Parking:** onsite and valet, winter plug-ins. **Pool(s):** heated indoor. **Activities:** hot tub, exercise room. **Guest Services:** valet laundry.

DOUBLETREE BY HILTON WEST EDMONTON
(780)484-0821   **4**

Hotel. **Address:** 16615 109th Ave T5P 4K8

AAA Benefit:
Members save 5% or more!

EDMONTON MARRIOTT AT RIVER CREE RESORT
(780)484-2121

Hotel
$97-$175

AAA Benefit:
Members save 5% or more!

Address: 300 E Lapotac Blvd T7X 3Y3 **Location:** 1 mi (1.6 km) w of jct Hwy 216 (Anthony Henday Dr) and Whitemud Dr W. **Facility:** This property is situated conveniently off Anthony Henday Drive and just a 10-minute drive to West Edmonton Mall. Contemporary décor adorns the good-size rooms which all have soft upscale bedding. 249 units. 9 stories, interior corridors. **Parking:** winter plug-ins. **Terms:** check-in 4 pm. **Dining:** Sage Restaurant, see separate listing. **Pool(s):** heated indoor. **Activities:** hot tub, exercise room. **Guest Services:** complimentary and valet laundry, area transportation. (See ad this page.)

EXECUTIVE ROYAL HOTEL WEST EDMONTON
(780)484-6000   **15**
Hotel. **Address:** 10010 178th St T5S 1T3

─────── ▼ See AAA listing this page ▼ ───────

Ask your AAA/CAA club about travel money
and other financial services for travelers

▼ *See AAA listing p. 111* ▼

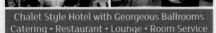

AAA.com/ TourBook Comments

Let Your Voice Be Heard

If your visit to a TourBook-listed property doesn't meet your expectations, tell us about it.

AAA.com/TourBookComments

FANTASYLAND HOTEL   780/444-3000 **18**
▼▼▼▼ Hotel. **Address:** 17700 87th Ave T5T 4V4

FOUR POINTS BY SHERATON EDMONTON GATEWAY
(780)801-4000 **30**

▼▼▼▼
Hotel
$129-$209

FOUR POINTS BY SHERATON — **AAA Benefit:** Members save up to 15%, plus Starwood Preferred Guest® benefits!

Address: 10010 12th Ave SW T6X 0P9 **Location:** Hwy 2 (Gateway Blvd) exit Ellerslie Rd. **Facility:** 154 units. 8 stories, interior corridors. **Parking:** winter plug-ins. **Amenities:** safes. **Pool(s):** heated indoor. **Activities:** hot tub, exercise room, spa. **Guest Services:** valet and coin laundry.

[SAVE] [♨] [🛁] [Y] CALL [M] [🛏] [BIZ] [HS] [📶] [✕] [🔌] [🖥] [📺]

FOUR POINTS BY SHERATON EDMONTON SOUTH
780/465-7931 **21**

▼▼▼▼
Hotel
Rates not provided

FOUR POINTS BY SHERATON — **AAA Benefit:** Members save up to 15%, plus Starwood Preferred Guest® benefits!

Address: 7230 Argyll Rd T6C 4A6 **Location:** Hwy 2 (Gateway Blvd), 2.3 mi (3.7 km) e at 63rd Ave (which becomes Argyll Rd); at 75th St. **Facility:** 139 units. 7 stories, interior corridors. **Parking:** winter plug-ins. **Pool(s):** heated indoor. **Activities:** steamroom, exercise room. **Guest Services:** valet laundry. **Featured Amenity:** full hot breakfast.

[SAVE] [♨] [🛁] [Y] CALL [M] [🛏] [BIZ] [HS] [📶] [✕] [🔌] [🖥] [📺] [SOME UNITS] [🐾]

HAMPTON INN & SUITES EDMONTON WEST
(780)484-7280 **11**
▼▼▼▼ Hotel. **Address:** 18304 100th Ave T5S 2V2   **AAA Benefit:** Members save up to 10%!

HAMPTON INN BY HILTON EDMONTON SOUTH
(780)801-2600 **31**
▼▼▼▼ Hotel. **Address:** 10020 12th Ave T6X 0P6   **AAA Benefit:** Members save up to 10%!

HILTON GARDEN INN-WEST EDMONTON
(780)443-2233 **7**
▼▼▼ Hotel. **Address:** 17610 Stony Plain Rd T5S 1A2   **AAA Benefit:** Members save up to 10%!

HOLIDAY INN & SUITES, WEST EDMONTON
(780)444-3110 **2**
▼▼▼ Hotel. **Address:** 11330 170th St T5S 2X1

HOLIDAY INN EXPRESS & SUITES EDMONTON NORTH
(780)476-9898 **1**
▼▼▼▼ Hotel. **Address:** 13742 50th St NW T5A 4Y3

HOLIDAY INN EXPRESS & SUITES EDMONTON SOUTH
(780)440-5000 **29**
▼▼▼▼ Hotel. **Address:** 2440 Calgary Tr NW T6J 5J6

(See map & index p. 100.)

HOLIDAY INN EXPRESS HOTEL & SUITES, WEST
EDMONTON   780/483-4000 **14**
▼▼▼▼ Hotel. **Address:** 10017 179A St T5S 2L4

HOTEL SELKIRK   780/496-7227 **20**
▼▼ ▼▼ Hotel. **Address:** 7000 143rd St T5J 2R7

QUALITY INN WEST EDMONTON   (780)484-8000 **8**
▼▼▼▼ Hotel. **Address:** 17803 Stony Plain Rd NW T5S 1B4

RADISSON HOTEL AND CONVENTION CENTRE
780/468-5400 **22**

▼▼▼▼
Hotel
Rates not provided

Address: 4520 76th Ave T6B 0A5 **Location:** Hwy 14, just s via 50th St exit, just e. **Facility:** 168 units. 6 stories, interior corridors. **Parking:** winter plug-ins. **Pool(s):** heated indoor. **Activities:** hot tub, steamroom, exercise room. **Guest Services:** valet and coin laundry. **Featured Amenity: full hot breakfast.** *(See ad p. 110.)*

[SAVE] [TI] [Y] CALL [&M] [≈]
[BIZ] [HS] [♥] [✕] [♣] [🖥]
[📷] [🖥]

RADISSON HOTEL EDMONTON SOUTH
(780)437-6010 **25**

▼▼▼▼
Hotel
$119-$349

Address: 4440 Gateway Blvd NW T6H 5C2 **Location:** Between Whitemud Dr and 45th Ave. **Facility:** 235 units. 4 stories, interior corridors. **Parking:** winter plug-ins. **Terms:** cancellation fee imposed. **Pool(s):** heated indoor. **Activities:** sauna, hot tub, steamroom, massage. **Guest Services:** valet and coin laundry, rental car service. **Featured Amenity: full hot breakfast.**

[SAVE] [ECO] [TI] [Y] CALL [&M] [≈]
[🐾] [BIZ] [HS] [♥] [✕] [♣] [🖥]
[📷] /SOME UNITS [🛏] [📷]

RAMADA INN EDMONTON SOUTH   (780)434-3431 **23**
▼▼ ▼▼ Hotel. **Address:** 5359 Calgary Tr T6H 4J9

SAWRIDGE INN EDMONTON SOUTH
(780)438-1222 **27**

▼▼▼▼
Hotel
$109-$189

Address: 4235 Gateway Blvd T6J 5H2 **Location:** Just s of Whitemud Dr. **Facility:** 136 units. 5 stories, interior corridors. **Parking:** winter plug-ins. **Terms:** 15 day cancellation notice-fee imposed. **Dining:** Creations Dining Room & Lounge, see separate listing. **Activities:** exercise room. **Guest Services:** valet and coin laundry. **Featured Amenity: full hot breakfast.**

[SAVE] [ECO] [TI] [🐾] [Y] CALL [&M]
[BIZ] [♥] [✕] [♣] [🖥]
/SOME UNITS [🛏] [🍴] [📷]

STAYBRIDGE SUITES WEST EDMONTON
(780)484-6223 **3**

▼▼▼▼
Extended Stay
Hotel
$152-$190

Address: 16929 109 Ave NW T5P 4P6 **Location:** Hwy 216 (Anthony Henday Dr) exit 21. **Facility:** 126 efficiencies, some two bedrooms. 4 stories, interior corridors. **Parking:** winter plug-ins. **Terms:** cancellation fee imposed. **Pool(s):** indoor. **Activities:** exercise room. **Guest Services:** complimentary and valet laundry. *(See ad this page.)*

[SAVE] [TI+] CALL [&M] [≈] [HS]
[♥] [✕] [🍴] [📷] [🖥]
/SOME UNITS [🛏]

SUPER 8 EDMONTON SOUTH   (780)433-8688 **28**
▼▼ Hotel. **Address:** 3610 Gateway Blvd T6J 7H8

WEST EDMONTON MALL INN   780/444-9378 **17**
▼▼ ▼▼ Hotel. **Address:** 17504 90th Ave T5T 6L6

▼ *See AAA listing this page* ▼

(See map & index p. 100.)

WINGATE INN EDMONTON WEST   (780)443-1000 **10**
▼▲▼▼ Hotel. **Address:** 18220 100th Ave T5S 2V2

WHERE TO EAT

THE BOTHY WINE & WHISKY BAR   780/761-1761 **25**
▼▼▼▼ New American. Gastropub. **Address:** 5482 Calgary Tr T6H 4J8

BUCAS & PASTAS   780/496-2461 **9**
▼ Italian. Quick Serve. **Address:** 16516 100th Ave T5P 4Y2

CENTURY GRILL   780/431-0303 **29**
▼▼▼▼ New Pacific Rim. Casual Dining. **Address:** 3975 Calgary Tr S T6J 6S6

CHA FOR TEA PALACE   780/443-2832 **5**
▼▼▼ Chinese Dim Sum Seafood. Casual Dining. **Address:** 17512 Stony Plain Rd T5S 1L1

THE CHEESECAKE CAFE   780/486-0440
▼▼▼ American. Casual Dining. **Address:** 17011 100th Ave NW T5S 1T9

CONYAC'S BAR & GRILL   780/483-2255 **7**
▼▼▼ American. Casual Dining. **Address:** 10010 179A St T5S 2T1

CREATIONS DINING ROOM & LOUNGE   780/989-4439 **28**
▼▼▼▼ New American. Casual Dining. **Address:** 4235 Gateway Blvd T6J 5H2

CULINA MUTTART   780/466-1181 **19**
▼▼▼ American. Casual Dining. **Address:** 9626 96A St T6C 4L8

DELUX BURGER BAR   780/420-0101 **16**
▼▼▼ American. Casual Dining. **Address:** 9682 142nd St T5N 4B2

THE DISH BISTRO   780/488-6641 **10**
▼▼▼ American. Casual Dining. **Address:** 12417 Stony Plain Rd T5N 3N3

EARLS KITCHEN + BAR   780/473-9008
▼▼▼ American. Casual Dining. **Address:** 13330 50th St T5A 4Z8

FAMOSO NEAPOLITAN PIZZERIA   780/487-0046 **18**
▼▼▼ Pizza. Casual Dining. **Address:** 8882 170th St, Unit 1951 St T5T 4M2

FIFE N' DEKEL   780/489-6436 **3**
▼ Deli. Quick Serve. **Address:** 10646 170th St T5S 1P3

FRANCO'S STEAK & PIZZA   780/476-4333 **1**
▼▼▼ Italian. Casual Dining. **Address:** 12981 50th St NE T5A 3P3

GURU FINE INDIAN CUISINE   780/484-4300 **8**
▼▼▼▼ Indian. Casual Dining. **Address:** 17021 100th Ave NW T5S 1T9

HAUS FALKENSTEIN   780-483-5904 **2**
▼▼ ▼▼
German
Casual Dining
$12-$28

AAA Inspector Notes: This small local restaurant has earned a Guinness world record for serving the largest variety of schnitzel—347 varieties to be precise. This place is a virtual pork machine focused on the eponymous pan-fried German breaded cutlets. If pork is not to your liking, with one day's advance notice, the chef would be happy to procure fresh chicken for your party. **Features:** full bar. **Reservations:** suggested. **Address:** 15215 111 Ave NW T5M 2R1 **Location:** Hwy 16 exit 383, 1.3 mi s, then just e. **Parking:** on-site and street. **D**

Largest variety of fresh, pan-fried schnitzel

HOMEFIRE BAR & GRILL   780/489-8086 **6**
▼▼ ▼▼ International. Casual Dining. **Address:** 18210 100th Ave T5S 2V2

IL PASTICCIO TRATTORIA   780/488-9543 **17**
▼▼ ▼▼ Italian. Casual Dining. **Address:** 11520 100th Ave T5K 0J7

JOEY RESTAURANTS   780/465-1880
▼▼ ▼▼ American. Casual Dining. **Address:** 9911 19th Ave NW T6N 1M4

LEMONGRASS CAFE   780/413-0088 **26**
▼▼ ▼▼ Vietnamese. Casual Dining. **Address:** 10417 51st Ave T6H 0K4

LOCAL PUBLIC EATERY   780/989-5898 **30**
▼▼ ▼▼ American. Gastropub. **Address:** 1820 99th St T6N 1M5

MANOR CASUAL BISTRO   780/482-7577 **14**
▼▼ ▼▼ International. Casual Dining. **Address:** 10109 125th St T5N 1S7

MOXIE'S CLASSIC GRILL
▼▼ ▼▼ American. Casual Dining.
LOCATIONS:
Address: 1670 8882-170th St T5T 4M2 **Phone:** 780/484-6669
Address: 17109 100th Ave NW T5S 2GS **Phone:** 780/484-2040
Address: 1739 102 St NW T6N 0B1 **Phone:** 780/468-3098

NORMAND'S FINE REGIONAL CUISINE   780/482-2600 **15**
▼▼▼▼ French. Casual Dining. **Address:** 11639A Jasper Ave NW T5K 0M9

OLD COUNTRY INN   780/433-3242 **23**
▼▼▼ German. Casual Dining. **Address:** 9906 72nd Ave NW T6E 0Z3

PARKALLEN RESTAURANT   587/520-6401 **22**
▼▼▼▼ Lebanese. Casual Dining. **Address:** 7018 109th St NW T6H 3C1

PHOENICIA   780/455-8855 **4**
▼▼ ▼▼ Lebanese. Casual Dining. **Address:** 10406 Mayfield Rd T5P 4P4

RED OX INN   780/465-5727 **20**
▼▼▼▼ New American. Casual Dining. **Address:** 9429 91st St T6C 3P4

RICKY'S ALL DAY GRILL   780/486-7109
▼▼ ▼▼ American. Casual Dining. **Address:** 9917 170th St T5P 4S2

(See map & index p. 100.)

SAGE RESTAURANT 780/930-2636
▼▼▼ Steak. Fine Dining. **Address:** 300 E Lapotac Blvd T7X 3Y3

THAI FLAVOURS 780/484-7911
▼▼ Thai. Casual Dining. **Address:** 2570 Guardian Rd NW T5T 1K8

TOM GOODCHILDS MOOSE FACTORY 780/437-5616 ㉗
▼▼ Steak. Casual Dining. **Address:** 4810 Calgary Tr S T6H 5H5

TROPIKA 780/439-6699 ㉔
▼▼ Thai. Casual Dining. **Address:** 6004 104th St T6H 2K3

TROPIKA 780/487-6668 ⑪
▼▼ Thai. Casual Dining. **Address:** 14921 Stony Plain Rd T5P 4W1

UNHEARDOF RESTAURANT 780/432-0480 ㉑
▼▼▼ American. Fine Dining. **Address:** 9602 82nd Ave T6C 1A1

URBAN DINER 780/488-7274 ⑫
▼▼ American. Casual Dining. **Address:** 12427 102nd Ave T5N 0M2

VIOLINO GASTRONOMIA ITALIANA 780/757-8701 ⑬
▼▼▼ Italian. Fine Dining. **Address:** 10133 125th St T5N 1S7

WHITE SPOT 780/485-3534
▼▼ American. Casual Dining. **Address:** 10010 12th Ave T6X 0P9

ZAIKA INDIAN BISTRO BAR 780/462-8722 ㉛
▼▼ Indian. Casual Dining. **Address:** 2303 Ellwood Dr SW T6X 0A9

EDSON pop. 8,475

BEST WESTERN HIGH ROAD INN (780)712-2378

▼▼ ▼▼
Hotel
$136-$170

BW **Best Western.** **AAA Benefit:** Save 10% or more every day and earn 10% bonus points!

Address: 300 52nd St T7E 1V8 **Location:** On 2nd Ave; center. **Facility:** 114 units. 4 stories, interior corridors. **Parking:** winter plug-ins. **Pool(s):** heated indoor. **Activities:** hot tub, exercise room. **Guest Services:** valet laundry.

(SAVE) 🍴 📶 🍸 CALL 📞 🚐 (BIZ) (HS) 📶 🛗 🖥 / SOME UNITS 🐕

COMFORT INN & SUITES EDSON (780)723-7303

▼▼ ▼▼
Hotel
$100-$140

Address: 5517 4th Ave T7E 1L6 **Location:** Hwy 16; west end of town. **Facility:** 40 units, some kitchens. 4 stories, interior corridors. **Parking:** winter plug-ins. **Activities:** exercise room. **Guest Services:** valet and coin laundry.

(SAVE) 🍴 CALL 📞 (BIZ) (HS) 📶 ✕ 🛗 🖥

HOLIDAY INN EXPRESS HOTEL & SUITES EDSON (780)723-4011
▼▼▼ Hotel. **Address:** 4520 2nd Ave T7E 1C3

LAKEVIEW INN & SUITES EDSON AIRPORT WEST 780/723-7508
▼▼ Hotel. **Address:** 528 63rd St T7E 1M1 **(See ad opposite inside front cover.)**

RAMADA EDSON (780)723-9797
▼▼▼ Hotel. **Address:** 4536 2nd Ave T7E 1C3

WHERE TO EAT

MOUNTAIN PIZZA & STEAK HOUSE 780/723-3900
▼▼ Steak. Pizza. Casual Dining. **Address:** 5102 4th Ave T7E 1T8

ORIGINAL JOE'S RESTAURANT & BAR 780/723-6445
▼▼ American. Gastropub. **Address:** 330 45th St T7E 1C3

ELK ISLAND NATIONAL PARK (E-7)

Elevations in the park range from 709 metres (2,326 ft.) at Goose Lake to 754 metres (2,475 ft.) at Tawayik Lake. Refer to CAA/AAA maps for additional elevation information.

About 35 kilometres (22 mi.) east of Edmonton, Elk Island National Park is reached by Hwy. 15 from the north and Hwy. 16 from the south. The lakes, ponds, forests and meadows of this 194-square-kilometre (75-sq.-mi.) park provide a haven for many species of animals and plants.

The park occupies the Beaver Hills region, which first was settled by Sarcee and Plains Cree First Nations. They trapped beavers and hunted bison and elk, as did the European fur traders who arrived between the late 18th and the mid-19th centuries. Soon the animals became nearly extinct, and the natives were forced to seek sustenance elsewhere.

In 1906 five local men asked that the government establish a wildlife refuge to preserve the remaining elk. A year later 400 plains bison were added, while another preserve near Wainwright was being established. Most of these animals later were transferred, but about 50 stayed and produced the plains bison herd of more than 300 that remains today north of Hwy. 16, and now provides bison to conservation projects in Canada and elsewhere. A herd of several hundred wood bison, a threatened subspecies, is kept separate from this herd south of Hwy. 16.

As the wildlife populations grew, so did the park's area; more land was added to the refuge in 1922, 1947, 1956 and 1978. Many small lakes dot the landscape, but the major bodies are Tawayik and Astotin, the latter being the larger. The lakes and marshes support the more than 250 bird species, including ducks, grebes, gulls, loons, pelicans, rare trumpeter swans and terns.

Marsh marigolds and several types of lilies are among several plants rarely seen outside the park. Song birds occupy the many aspen, spruce and birch forests, but few fish inhabit the waters due to low oxygen levels. The herd of elk for which the park was established flourish among the meadows and forests, as do reintroduced colonies of beavers. Deer, moose and coyotes also roam the park.

General Information and Activities

The park is open daily all year. Most recreation facilities center on Astotin Lake, which offers non-motorized boating, wildlife observations, picnic facilities, a nine-hole golf course, camping, hiking and walking trails. Canoe rentals are available June through August. Sandy Beach campground is on the east side of the lake. Interpretive talks, displays and events explain the park's history and features.

A visitor information center is .8 kilometres (.5 mi.) north of Hwy. 16 before the park's south gate entrance. Staff members and displays describe Elk Island and other national parks. The center is open daily 9:30-4:30, mid-May through Labour Day; phone (780) 922-5790 to confirm schedule.

Camping and picnicking are popular in summer. The park's approximately 80 kilometres (49 mi.) of trails are popular with hikers and cross-country skiers. Hunting and fishing are prohibited. *See Recreation Areas Chart.*

ADMISSION to the park is free in 2017 to celebrate Canada's 150th anniversary of Confederation, otherwise $7.43; $6.48 (ages 65+); $3.71 (ages 6-16); $18.67 (up to seven people arriving in a single vehicle). An annual pass, valid at all Canadian national parks, is available.

PETS must be kept on a leash at all times.

ADDRESS inquiries for additional information to Elk Island National Park, Site 4, R.R. 1, Fort Saskatchewan, AB, Canada T8L 2N7; phone (780) 922-5790.

 **UKRAINIAN CULTURAL HERITAGE VILLAGE**—see Edmonton p. 94.

ELK POINT (D-8) pop. 1,412, elev. 594m/1,948'

[SAVE] **FORT GEORGE AND BUCKINGHAM HOUSE PROVINCIAL HISTORIC SITE,** 13 km (8 mi.) s.e. on Hwy. 646, encompasses the archeological remains of two fur trade forts built in the late 18th century. A scenic interpretive trail complemented by wild flowers—including the rare yellow lady's slipper orchid—allows for closer inspection of the site and its various structural remains. Staff members at the visitor center are available to provide information about the area's heritage and fur trading industry.

Educational programs are offered. **Time:** Allow 2 hours minimum. **Hours:** Daily 10-5, May 15-Labour Day. **Cost:** $4.76; $3.81 (ages 65+); $1.90 (ages 7-17); $13.33 (family, two adults and up to six children); free (Canadian military and family with ID). **Phone:** (780) 724-2611, or (780) 645-6256 in the off-season. [GT] [⊞]

ELKWATER (J-9) pop. 50

Before Europeans came to the Elkwater region, Assiniboine, Blackfoot, Cree and Sioux shared the land with grizzly bears, wolves, bison and a large number of elk. After settlers and trappers arrived, the wolves and elk were hunted to extinction; the elk population since has been reintroduced. An 1873 massacre of Assiniboine people by wolf hunters and whiskey traders prompted the formation of the North West Mounted Police and the establishment of Fort Walsh.

The Cypress Hills area, shared by Alberta and Saskatchewan, is noted for its lodgepole pine forests, water resources and wildlife. The hills, which rise to more than 1,466 metres (4,810 ft.), offer visitors a cool climate, scenic views and diverse flora and fauna. Elkwater serves as the area's hub.

FORT MACLEOD (J-6) pop. 3,117, elev. 955m/3,133'

In 1874 at the end of their 1,126-kilometre (700-mi.) march through the prairie wilderness to rid western Canada of whiskey traders, the North West Mounted Police, now the Royal Canadian Mounted Police, chose the site of what is now Fort Macleod as their first headquarters.

A commanding view of the countryside and the natural protection afforded by the Oldman River made Fort Macleod an important outpost; a cairn at 2nd Avenue and 25th Street commemorates the fort's founding. Guided walking tours of the historic district, ranging from 30 minutes to 1 hour, can be arranged in advance during the summer by contacting The Fort Museum; phone (403) 553-4703.

The highland physical geography that made the Fort Macleod outpost successful also helped the Plains people survive long before the first traders appeared in the area. In order to kill the buffalo for food, the Plains hunters stampeded them over the high cliffs.

Self-guiding tours: A brochure describing a self-guiding tour of the Fort Macleod historic district is available at The Fort Museum, 219 25th St.

[GEM] [SAVE] **HEAD-SMASHED-IN BUFFALO JUMP INTERPRETIVE CENTRE** is 3 km (1.9 mi.) n. on Queen Elizabeth II Hwy., then 16 km (10 mi.) w. on Hwy. 785. For at least 6,000 years people of the Plains First Nations stampeded herds of buffalo over sandstone cliffs to their deaths. The hunters then butchered the kill at their campsite below the cliffs. This is one of the oldest, best-preserved buffalo jump sites. A theater screens a 12-minute film that re-creates the buffalo hunts. The hunting grounds are preserved, and short trails lead to the main areas.

The site's name is derived from a young brave who stood under a ledge of the cliff to watch the buffalo as they fell past him. As the number of carcasses multiplied, his skull was crushed as he became trapped between the animals and the cliff. Built into that cliff today is a seven-story interpretive center with displays. Exhibits focus on the geographical and climatic factors affecting these tribes as well as their lifestyle and history.

Time: Allow 2 hours minimum. **Hours:** Daily 9-5, May 15-Labour Day; 10-5, rest of year. Closed Jan. 1, Easter, Christmas Eve and Christmas. **Cost:** $14.29; $12.38 (ages 65+); $9.52 (ages 7-17); $38.10 (family, two adults and up to six children); free (Canadian military and family with ID). **Phone:** (403) 553-2731. 🍴

SUNSET MOTEL   403/553-4448
▼ Motel. **Address:** 104 Hwy 3 W T0L 0Z0

WHERE TO EAT

JOHNNY'S RESTAURANT   403/553-3939
▼▼ Chinese. Casual Dining. **Address:** 225 24th St (Main St) T0L 0Z0

FORT MCMURRAY (A-8) pop. 61,374

At the confluence of the Clearwater and Athabasca rivers in the fur country of northern Alberta, Fort McMurray began as the home of the Woodland Cree and Chipewyan First Nations. In 1778 explorers and fur traders led by Peter Pond opened the vast fur trade region of the Mackenzie River basin. In 1870 Henry John Moberly built a post and named it Fort McMurray after his chief factor, William McMurray of Hudson's Bay Co.

Soon after a steamboat terminus was established near Fort McMurray in 1884, the region's vast resources began to attract attention. Oil sands containing some 1.7 trillion barrels of oil were found around Lake Athabasca. The first commercially successful extractions, however, did not take place until the late 1960s. Since then Fort McMurray has boomed, serving oil recovery plants that now extract from the sands more than 600,000 barrels of synthetic crude oil per day.

The city is the southern terminus of the vast water transportation system that navigates Great Slave Lake and the Mackenzie River en route to the Arctic. Logging and tourism further bolster the economy. Fort McMurray is a service center for surrounding areas and the oil sands plants.

Note: In 2016, a devastating wildfire swept through Fort McMurray and the surrounding area prompting mass evacuations and destroying thousands of homes. Most attractions have returned to their normal schedules as of press time, but it's a good idea to phone ahead to confirm hours of operation.

Fort McMurray Tourism: 515 MacKenzie Blvd., Fort McMurray, AB, Canada T9H 4X3. **Phone:** (780) 791-4336 or (800) 565-3947.

 OIL SANDS DISCOVERY CENTRE is at 515 MacKenzie Blvd. Exhibits relate

the geology, history and technology of Alberta's Athabasca oil sands, said to be the world's single largest oil deposit. Oil sands extraction methods, history, science and technology, and new methods of exploration are explained through interpretive displays and films and interactive demonstrations. Outdoor exhibits include retired mining machines, research equipment and one of the largest land-based artifacts in Canada, a seven-story bucket-wheel excavator.

Time: Allow 1 hour minimum. **Hours:** Daily 9-5, mid-May through Labour Day; Tues.-Sun. 10-4, rest of year. Phone ahead to confirm schedule. **Cost:** $10.48; $7.62 (ages 65+); $6.67 (ages 7-17); $27.62 (family, two adults and up to six children); free (Canadian military and family with ID). Prices are subject to change; phone ahead. **Phone:** (780) 743-7167.

BEST WESTERN PLUS SAWRIDGE SUITES
        (780)799-4552

Hotel
$185-$299

 **Best Western PLUS.** **AAA Benefit:** Save 10% or more every day and earn 10% bonus points!

Address: 410 Taiganova Cres T9H 4W1 **Location:** Hwy 63 exit Taiganova Cres, then 0.6 mi (1 km) e. **Facility:** 151 efficiencies. 4 stories, interior corridors. **Parking:** winter plug-ins. **Amenities:** video games, safes. **Activities:** steamroom, exercise room. **Guest Services:** valet and coin laundry.

[SAVE] CALL [&M] [BIZ] [HS] 📶 ✕ 🎥 🔒 🍽 💻 / SOME UNITS 🐾

CLEARWATER SUITE HOTEL   780/799-7676
▼▼▼ Extended Stay Hotel. **Address:** 4 Haineault St T9H 1L6

FRANKLIN SUITE HOTEL   780/788-2199
▼▼▼ Hotel. **Address:** 10300 Franklin Ave T9H 0A5

MERIT HOTEL & SUITES   780/714-9444
▼▼ Hotel. **Address:** 8200 Franklin Ave T9H 2H9

VANTAGE INN & SUITES   (780)713-4111
▼▼ Hotel. **Address:** 200 Parent Way T9H 5E6

WHERE TO EAT

EARLS KITCHEN + BAR   780/791-3275
▼▼ American. Casual Dining. **Address:** 9802 Morrison St T9H 5B8

THE FISH PLACE   780/791-4040
▼▼ Seafood. Casual Dining. **Address:** 412 Thickwood Blvd T9K 1P1

MOXIE'S CLASSIC GRILL   780/791-1996
▼▼ American. Casual Dining. **Address:** 9521 Franklin Ave, #100 T9H 3Z7

Check DrivingLaws.AAA.com
for local motor vehicle laws
when traveling

FORT SASKATCHEWAN (E-6) pop. 19,051, elev. 622m/2,043'
• Part of Edmonton area — see map p. 85

Fort Saskatchewan is located along the North Saskatchewan River, about 25 kilometres (15.5 mi.) northeast of Edmonton. The city has more than 30 kilometres (18.6 mi.) of multiuse pathways and sidewalks and numerous parks and recreation areas. It is known for the flock of sheep that graze in Peter T. Ream Historic Park during the summer months. The historic park, at 101st Street and 101st Avenue, is home to the Fort Saskatchewan Museum, which encompasses such historical structures as the 1875-85 North West Mounted Police Fort and the 1937 Warden's House; phone (780) 998-1783.

BEST WESTERN PLUS FORT SASKATCHEWAN INN & SUITES
(587)285-8033

Hotel
$134-$174

Best Western PLUS

AAA Benefit: Save 10% or more every day and earn 10% bonus points!

Address: 50 Westpark Blvd T8L 0B2 **Location:** Just e of Hwy 15/21. **Facility:** 100 units, some two bedrooms and kitchens. 4 stories, interior corridors. **Parking:** winter plug-ins. **Pool(s):** indoor. **Activities:** sauna, hot tub, exercise room. **Guest Services:** valet and coin laundry.

SAVE ⓉⓉ+ CALL ⓈM ⊇ BIZ HS
🛜 ✕ 🏢 🖥 🖨

COMFORT INN & SUITES
(780)998-4000
WWW Hotel. **Address:** 120 Town Crest Rd T8L 0G7

HAMPTON INN BY HILTON FORT SASKATCHEWAN
(780)997-1001
WWW Hotel. **Address:** 8709 101st St T8L 0H9

AAA Benefit: Members save up to 10%!

HOLIDAY INN EXPRESS & SUITES
780/997-9700
WWW Hotel. **Address:** 10120 86th Ave T8L 0N6

THE KANATA
780/998-2770
WWW Hotel. **Address:** 9820 86th Ave T8L 4P4

LAKEVIEW INNS & SUITES
780/998-7888
WW Hotel. **Address:** 10115 88th Ave T8L 2T1 (See ad opposite inside front cover.)

SUPER 8 HOTEL-FORT SASKATCHEWAN
(780)998-2898
WW Hotel. **Address:** 8750 84th St T8L 4P5

ORIGINAL JOE'S RESTAURANT & BAR
780/998-0520
WW American. Gastropub. **Address:** 9372 Southfort Dr, #103 T8L 0C5

SAWMILL PRIME RIB & STEAK HOUSE
780/992-2255
WWW Steak. Casual Dining. **Address:** 21 Westpark Blvd T8L 4M5

FOX CREEK pop. 1,969

BEST WESTERN PLUS FOX CREEK
(780)548-3338

Hotel
$140-$170

Best Western PLUS

AAA Benefit: Save 10% or more every day and earn 10% bonus points!

Address: 313 1st Ave T0H 1P0 **Location:** Hwy 43, just n. **Facility:** 95 units, some efficiencies. 4 stories, interior corridors. **Parking:** winter plug-ins. **Pool(s):** heated indoor. **Activities:** steamroom, exercise room. **Guest Services:** coin laundry. **Featured Amenity:** continental breakfast.

SAVE ⓉⓉ+ CALL ⓈM ⊇ BIZ HS
🛜 🏢 🖥 🖨

COMFORT INN & SUITES
780/622-3311
WWW Hotel. **Address:** 317 1st Ave T0H 1P0

SUPER 8
(780)622-8333
WW Hotel. **Address:** 206 Highway Ave T0H 1P0

GIROUXVILLE (B-3) pop. 266

GIROUXVILLE MUSEUM is on Main St. (Hwy. 49). More than 6,000 artifacts tell the story of the indigenous people, devout missionaries and rugged pioneers who lived here. The museum also displays mounted birds and fur-bearing animals (the most famous being a five-legged squirrel) and the works of local artists Leon Tremblay and Alfred Gaboury.

Transportation Means of Yesterday includes sleighs, an antique snowmobile, a birch bark canoe, a 1927 Chevrolet truck and various other historic vehicles and machinery. **Time:** Allow 1 hour minimum. **Hours:** Mon.-Fri. 10-5, May-Aug.; by appointment rest of year. **Cost:** $2.86; $1.43 (ages 4-17). **Phone:** (780) 323-4252.

GLEICHEN (I-7) pop. 336, elev. 899m/2,952'

BLACKFOOT CROSSING HISTORICAL PARK is 11 km (7 mi.) e. on Hwy. 1, then 9.7 km (6 mi.) s. on Hwy. 842. Used by the Siksika (Blackfoot) First Nation as a wintering grounds, Blackfoot Crossing was the site of the signing of Treaty No. 7 by representatives of the Blackfoot Confederacy and the Canadian and British governments in 1877. An on-site cultural center offers several galleries describing the culture and history of the Siksika people, along with an introductory video in the Vision Quest Theatre.

Housed in a striking, eco-friendly edifice are exhibits about hunting, early life, societies, storytelling and warriors. The collection features such artifacts as tools, weapons, clothing and utensils as well as multimedia displays. The building's architectural features also document First Nations heritage, with tepee-shaped skylights and stained glass eagle feather fans incorporated into the structure's design.

Time: Allow 1 hour, 30 minutes minimum. **Hours:** Mon.-Fri. 9-5. Phone ahead to confirm schedule. **Cost:** $12; $8 (ages 8-17 and 65+). **Phone:** (403) 734-5171. GT ⓉⓉ 🏕

GRANDE CACHE (D-2) pop. 4,319

Grande Cache was named after a large shipment of furs cached nearby in 1821 by Ignace Giasson, an Iroquois working for Hudson's Bay Co. The Grande Cache area historically served as a major trading area for marten, lynx and beaver pelts.

Grande Cache is known for the many recreational activities available nearby. The town is surrounded on three sides by Willmore Wilderness Park, which has the Continental Divide and Jasper National Park as its western and southern borders, respectively; the park can be accessed only by horseback, mountain bike or by hiking.

Lakes, rivers and mountains are favorites with outdoor enthusiasts, who come for white-water rafting, horseback riding, hiking, kayaking, fishing, canoeing and mountain biking. Pacific Western Helicopter Tours offers various sightseeing trips; phone (780) 827-3911.

Local events accommodate those with an adventurous streak. During the Canadian Death Race, held the first weekend in August, runners must travel 125 kilometres (78 mi.) over rough mountain trails—with part of the race occurring after dusk—and then cross a major river by raft. An accompanying festival offers food, concerts and carnival rides and games.

Interpretive displays in the tourism center, on the south side of Grande Cache, feature dinosaur tracks, artifacts from the ice age and memorabilia from the fur trade era.

Grande Cache Tourism and Interpretive Centre: 9701 100th St., P.O. Box 300, Grande Cache, AB, Canada T0E 0Y0. **Phone:** (780) 827-3362 or (888) 827-3790.

DAYS HOTEL & SUITES GRANDE CACHE   (780)827-3303
♦♦ Hotel. **Address:** 9901 100th St T0E 0Y0

GRANDE PRAIRIE (C-2) pop. 55,032
• Restaurants p. 118

Surrounded by a colorful checkerboard of rich farmland along the gateway to the Alaska Hwy., Grande Prairie serves as the business and transportation center of Alberta's Peace River country.

Glimpses into the Peace River region's past are evident in the Kleskun Hills, just east via Hwy. 43. Erosion of the glacial drift of clay, sand, gravel and boulders has uncovered dinosaur tracks and aquatic fossils embedded in a prehistoric river delta formed more than 70 million years ago.

Muskoseepi Park has hiking and bicycling trails, picnicking areas and recreation facilities. Other area recreational pursuits include swimming, boating, bird-watching and fishing. A pioneer-oriented event is the Grande Prairie Stompede the last 5 days in May. Other festivals celebrated throughout the summer highlight the region's diversity.

Grande Prairie Regional Tourism Association: 11330 106th St., Suite 114, Grande Prairie, AB, Canada T8V 7X9. **Phone:** (780) 539-7688 or (866) 202-2202.

HERITAGE DISCOVERY CENTRE is at 11330-106 St. on the lower level of Centre 2000, Grand Prairie's Tourism Information Centre. The hands-on interpretive center depicts regional history through pioneer artifacts, a geology timeline, an animatronic dinosaur named Piper, a tepee, photographs, films, a caboose and interactive games. Changing exhibits also are featured.

Hours: Mon.-Fri. 8:30-6:30, Sat.-Sun. 10-6, late May-Labour Day; Mon.-Fri. 8:30-4:30, Sat.-Sun. 10-4:30, rest of year. Closed Jan. 1, third Mon. in Feb., Good Friday, Christmas and day after Christmas. **Cost:** Free. **Phone:** (780) 532-5790. GT

BEST WESTERN GRANDE PRAIRIE HOTEL & SUITES
(780)402-2378

♦♦ ♦♦
Hotel
$149-$199

BW **Best Western**

AAA Benefit: Save 10% or more every day and earn 10% bonus points!

Address: 10745 117th Ave T8V 7N6 **Location:** Corner of Hwy 43 (100th Ave) and 117th Ave. **Facility:** 100 units. 4 stories, interior corridors. **Parking:** winter plug-ins. **Dining:** Padrino's Italian Ristorante, see separate listing. **Pool(s):** heated indoor. **Activities:** hot tub, exercise room. **Guest Services:** valet and coin laundry.

SAVE ECO ♦ ♦ ♦ ♦ ♦
CALL ♦M ♦ BIZ HS ♦ ♦ ♦ ♦
/ SOME UNITS ♦ ♦

DAYS INN GRANDE PRAIRIE   (780)532-2773
♦♦ Hotel. **Address:** 10218 162nd Ave T8V 0P2

HOLIDAY INN HOTEL & SUITES   (780)402-6886
♦♦♦ Hotel. **Address:** 9816 107th St T8V 8E7

MOTEL 6 GRANDE PRAIRIE #5709   780/830-7744
♦♦ Hotel. **Address:** 15402 101st St T8V 0P7

PARADISE INN & CONFERENCE CENTRE GRANDE PRAIRIE AIRPORT   780/539-6000
♦♦ Hotel. **Address:** 11201 100th Ave T8V 5M6

PODOLLAN INN & SPA   780/830-2000
♦♦♦ Hotel. **Address:** 10612 99th Ave T8V 8E8

POMEROY HOTEL & CONFERENCE CENTRE   780/532-5221
♦♦♦ Hotel. **Address:** 11633 100th St T8V 3Y4

QUALITY INN & SUITES   (780)831-2999
♦♦♦ Hotel. **Address:** 11710 102nd St T8V 7S7

SERVICE PLUS INNS AND SUITES   780/538-3900
♦♦ Hotel. **Address:** 10810 107A Ave T8V 7A9

STANFORD HOTEL   780/539-5678
♦♦ Hotel. **Address:** 11401 100th St T8V 5M6

STONEBRIDGE HOTEL   (780)539-5561
WWW Hotel. **Address:** 12102 100th St T8V 5P1

SUPER 8   (780)532-8288
WWWW Hotel. **Address:** 10050 116th Ave T8V 4K5

ACROPOLIS   780/538-4424
WW Greek. Casual Dining. **Address:** 10011 101st Ave T8V 0X9

BURGER HEAVEN   780/814-7015
W Burgers. Casual Dining. **Address:** 9805 116th St, #103 T8V 2N1

THE CHOPPED LEAF   780/897-2562
W Specialty. Quick Serve. **Address:** 10902 105th Ave, #108 T8V 7Y5

GUERINO'S ITALIAN KITCHEN   780/513-3630
W Italian. Quick Serve. **Address:** 10635 West Side Dr, #103 T8V 8E6

HONG FAH THAI RESTAURANT   780/357-9988
WWW Thai. Casual Dining. **Address:** 11735 105th St T8V 8L1

JAX GRILL & LOUNGE   780/830-2000
WWW International. Casual Dining. **Address:** 10612 99th Ave T8V 8E8

JEFFERY'S CAFE COMPANY   780/830-0140
WWW American. Casual Dining. **Address:** 106-10605 West Side Dr T8V 8E6

MOXIE'S CLASSIC GRILL   780/532-4401
WWW American. Casual Dining. **Address:** 11801 100th St, #212 T8V 3Y2

PADRINO'S ITALIAN RISTORANTE   780/814-7171
WWW Italian Pizza. Casual Dining. **Address:** 10745 117th Ave T8V 7N6

TAJ GRILL & BAR   780/532-4500
WWW Eastern Indian. Casual Dining. **Address:** 9927 97th Ave, #103 T8V 0N3

TITO'S BISTRO & CAFE   780/539-4881
W Lebanese. Quick Serve. **Address:** 10006 101st Ave T8V 0Y1

GRIMSHAW pop. 2,515

POMEROY INN & SUITES   (780)332-2000
WWW Extended Stay Hotel. **Address:** 4311 51st St T0H 1W0

HIGH LEVEL pop. 3,641

BEST WESTERN PLUS MIRAGE HOTEL & RESORT
                                           (780)821-1000

 WWWW Hotel $90-$150

Best Western PLUS.

AAA Benefit: Save 10% or more every day and earn 10% bonus points!

Address: 9616 Hwy 58 T0H 1Z0 **Location:** Jct Hwy 35 and 58; north end of town. **Facility:** 92 units, some two bedrooms and kitchens. 2 stories, interior/exterior corridors. **Parking:** winter plug-ins. **Terms:** check-in 4 pm. **Dining:** Mirage Restaurant, see separate listing. **Pool(s):** heated indoor. **Activities:** hot tub, exercise room. **Guest Services:** valet and coin laundry. **Featured Amenity:** breakfast buffet.

SUPER 8 HIGH LEVEL   (780)841-3448
WWW Hotel. **Address:** 9502 114th Ave T0H 1Z0

MIRAGE RESTAURANT   780/821-1000
WWW Canadian. Casual Dining. **Address:** 9616 Hwy 58 T0H 1Z0

HIGH PRAIRIE pop. 2,600

DAYS INN HIGH PRAIRIE   (780)523-3050
WW Hotel. **Address:** 4125 52nd Ave T0G 1E0

PEAVINE INN & SUITES   780/523-2398
WW Hotel. **Address:** 3905 51st Ave T0G 1E0

HIGH RIVER (I-6) pop. 12,920

A ranching and farming town, High River hosts Guy Weadick Days, which encompasses a rodeo and WPCA chuckwagon races, in June. The Little Britches Rodeo and Parade is held in July. The winter holiday season is ushered in the first weekend in December with the evening Santa Claus Parade.

High River Visitor Information Centre: 228 12th Ave. S.E., Bob Snodgrass Recreation Complex, High River, AB, Canada T1V 1Z5. **Phone:** (403) 603-3101.

HIGH RIVER HISTORICAL MURALS are at various locations throughout town. Many colorful paintings illustrate area history. The murals present a variety of subjects, ranging from cattle ranching and polo to well-known residents, including author W.O. Mitchell and former Prime Minister Joe Clark. **Hours:** Muralsvisible daily 24 hours. Closed Jan. 1 and Christmas. **Cost:** Free. **Phone:** (403) 603-3101.

HERITAGE INN HOTEL & CONVENTION CENTRE
(403)652-3834
Hotel. **Address:** 1104 11th Ave SE T1V 1M4

RAMADA INN & SUITES HIGH RIVER   (403)603-3183
Hotel. **Address:** 1512 13th Ave SE T1V 2B1

SUPER 8   (403)652-4448
Hotel. **Address:** 1601 13th Ave SE T1V 2B1

WHERE TO EAT

EVELYN'S MEMORY LANE CAFE   403/336-1925
Sandwiches Desserts. Casual Dining. **Address:** 118 4th
Ave SW T1V 1P7

WHISTLESTOP CAFE   403/652-7026
American. Casual Dining. **Address:** 406 1st St SW T1V
1S2

HINTON pop. 9,640, elev. 1,049m/3,444'
• **Part of Jasper National Park area — see map**
p. 120

HOLIDAY INN EXPRESS & SUITES   780/865-2048
Hotel. **Address:** 462 Smith St T7V 2A1

HOLIDAY INN HINTON   (780)865-3321
Hotel. **Address:** 393 Gregg Ave T7V 1N1

WHERE TO EAT

GUS' PIZZA   780/865-4232
Pizza. Casual Dining. **Address:** 346 Hardisty Ave T7V
1E8

L & W FAMILY RESTAURANT   780/865-4892
American. Casual Dining. **Address:** 414 Carmichael Ln T7V
1X7

RANCHER'S SPORTS BAR & GRILL   780/865-9785
American. Casual Dining. **Address:** 438 Smith St T7V
2A1

SMITTY'S   780/865-6151
American. Casual Dining. **Address:** 445 Gregg Ave T7V
1X8

INNISFAIL (G-6) pop. 7,876, elev. 945m/3,100'

DISCOVERY WILDLIFE PARK is off Queen Elizabeth II Hwy. N. Innisfail exit; take Hwy. 2A 2 blks.
n.e., then just n.w. on 42nd Ave., following signs.
The 36-hectare (90-acre) park is home to a variety
of rescued exotic and native animals, including jag-
uars, bears, monkeys, tigers and wolves. Some of
the creatures are trained to work in show business
and have been featured in major film and television
productions. Educational shows and interactive programs are offered daily.

Time: Allow 1 hour, 30 minutes minimum. **Hours:**
Daily 10-7, May 1 to mid-Oct. Last admission 1 hour
before closing. **Cost:** $17; $15 (ages 13-17 and
60+); $11 (ages 3-12); $1 (ages 0-2). **Phone:** (403)
227-3211.

DAYS INN INNISFAIL   (403)227-4405

Hotel
$129-$159

Address: 5010 40th Ave T4G 1Z1 **Lo-**
cation: Hwy 2 exit Hwy 54
(Innisfail/Caroline), just w. **Facility:** 66
units. 3 stories, interior corridors.
Parking: winter plug-ins. **Pool(s):**
heated indoor. **Activities:** hot tub, picnic
facilities, exercise room. **Guest Ser-**
vices: coin laundry.

IRRICANA (H-6) pop. 1,162

PIONEER ACRES OF ALBERTA MUSEUM is off
Hwy. 9, 1 km n., then 1 km w. The museum features
one of the largest collections of antique farm equipment in western Canada. It also displays furniture,
tools, memorabilia, clothing and vehicles. A collection of early buildings includes a school, a steam-
engine shop and a blacksmith shop. **Time:** Allow 1
hour, 30 minutes minimum. **Hours:** Daily 9-5, May
15-Sept. 30. **Cost:** $7.62; $4.76 (ages 6-12).
Phone: (403) 935-4357.

JASPER NATIONAL PARK (E-2)
• Attractions map p. 122

Elevations in the park range from 1,067 metres (3,500 ft.) in the town of Jasper to 3,747 metres (12,293 ft.) at Mount Columbia. Refer to CAA/AAA maps for additional elevation information.

The largest of Canada's seven national parks in the Rocky Mountains, Jasper preserves a spectacular wilderness of forested glacial valleys, dazzling snow-capped peaks, roaring waterfalls and sparkling blue-green lakes. Jasper is less developed and less crowded than Banff National Park to the south, so it tends to attract those seeking the solitude and tranquility that are among the park's greatest assets. Nearly a thousand kilometres (600 mi.) of trails help visitors escape into the virtually pristine countryside.

The park's wildlife is as diverse as its peaks and valleys. Mountain goats and bighorn sheep inhabit the crags and highlands, although the sheep frequently wander down from the heights and into the camera viewfinders of tourists. The lower slopes and meadows are home to deer, elk and moose. Bears, coyotes, wolves, lynx and other predators usually avoid humans.

The Whistlers, whose peak looms above the town of Jasper *(see place listing p. 124)*, is named for the whistling call of the hoary marmot, which looks like something between a squirrel and a beaver. You might encounter marmots along Jasper National Park's trails, along with Columbian ground squirrels and tiny pikas, which look like mice but are actually related to rabbits, as you might guess from their other name: rock rabbits.

The park was named for Jasper Hawes who operated Jasper's House, an early 19th-century fur-trading post in the area. The town, originally called Fitzhugh, adopted the name of the surrounding park in 1913. It's a laid-back place with a surprisingly

This map shows cities in Jasper National Park where you will find attractions, hotels and restaurants. Cities are listed alphabetically in this book on the following pages.

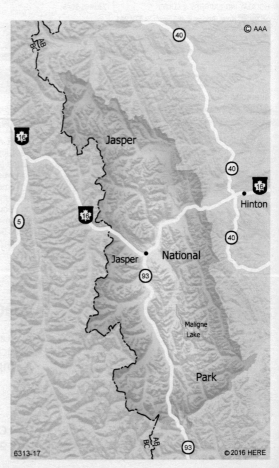

small-town feel despite catering to the millions who visit the park annually. You will find one of the park's two information centers in a rustic cobblestone building on the town's main street. Completed in 1914, it once housed the park's headquarters; its design established the style now common for national park buildings.

Looked at from above, the town's curved layout appropriately enough resembles the letter J. Take a look for yourself by making the 7-minute journey via the Jasper Tramway *(see attraction listing p. 124)* to the upper station on The Whistlers, 2,277 metres (7,472 ft.) above sea level. The view of the town, the Athabasca River Valley and surrounding mountains is unforgettable.

Strolling the streets of Jasper, you can't help but notice the distinctive profile of Mount Edith Cavell with its contrasting parallel bands of rock and snow. A half-hour drive will take you to the mountain, called "the White Ghost" by the people of the Stoney First Nation. Trails there lead to the wildflower-strewn Cavell Meadows and offer fantastic views of Angel Glacier, named for its outstretched "wings." Below the glacier, little icebergs bob in Cavell Pond, even in summer.

Other Jasper National Park highlights: the scenic Maligne Lake Road connecting Malign Canyon and lovely Medicine and Maligne lakes; thundering Athabasca and Sunwapta falls; Pyramid and Patricia lakes; Marmot Basin ski resort; and the breathtaking Icefields Parkway running south to the Columbia Icefield and the Athabasca Glacier, where a short trail leads from the parkway right up to the glacier.

General Information and Activities

The park is open all year, though weather conditions in winter make some portions inaccessible except to cross-country skiers and those on snowshoes. Some facilities are open only from May to June or September to October. A Parks Canada information center is in the townsite at 500 Connaught Dr. It's open daily late March to late October, and Wednesday through Sunday the rest of the year.

Many hiking trails, including the 11.2-kilometre (7-mi.) trip to Valley of Five Lakes and the loop to Lac Beauvert, depart from Old Fort Point, 1.6 kilometres (1 mi.) east of Jasper on Hwy. 93. The Valley of Five Lakes also can be accessed from the trailhead on the Icefields Parkway, 9 km (6 mi.) south of the townsite.

Hikers and skiers staying overnight in the backcountry must have a valid backcountry use permit. These permits are available at the Parks Canada information center in Jasper and at the Columbia Icefield Glacier Discovery Centre from early June to mid-September.

Campgrounds are open varying durations, and limited camping facilities are available in winter. For more information, phone (780) 852-6176.

There are many ways to explore the park's features, either alone or with a guide. One- or multiple-day bus tours to attractions within the park depart from Jasper. Several stables in the Jasper area offer 1-hour and half- and full-day trail rides from mid-May to mid-September and sleigh rides in winter.

Winter sports include curling, skating, tobogganing, ice climbing, snowshoeing and hockey. Cross-country skiing tours operate out of Jasper. Downhill skiing is available at Marmot Basin. Approximately 75 kilometres of cross-country trails traverse the park; trails are groomed from early December to March. Interpretive guides share their insights in theatrical productions. Wildlife and stand-up paddleboarding tours also are available. Self-guiding tour brochures are available at the Parks Canada information center, 500 Connaught Dr.; phone (780) 852-6176.

Note: Since hunting is illegal, some wildlife may have lost their natural fear of human contact. Be alert for animals on the highways both day and night, and never feed them. Fishing permits can be obtained at information centers, campgrounds and local sport fishing shops. Boats with electric motors are allowed on lakes unless signs indicate otherwise. *See Recreation Areas Chart.*

ADMISSION to the park is free in 2017 to celebrate Canada's 150th anniversary of Confederation, otherwise $9.33; $7.90 (ages 65+); $4.67 (ages 6-16); $18.67 (up to seven people arriving in a single vehicle). An annual pass, valid at Jasper and more than 100 other Canadian national parks and historic sites, is available.

PETS are allowed in some areas of the park but must be leashed, crated or physically restrained at all times. A fenced area for leashed pets is located on Sleepy Hollow Road adjacent to the industrial park.

ADDRESS inquiries to the Jasper National Park Information Centre, Jasper National Park, P.O. Box 10, Jasper, AB, Canada T0E 1E0; phone (780) 852-6176. For other area information contact Jasper Park Chamber of Commerce, P.O. Box 98, Jasper, AB, Canada T0E 1E0; phone (780) 852-3858.

COLUMBIA ICEFIELD, just inside the Jasper National Park boundary next to Banff National Park, is the largest ice mass in the Rocky Mountains. Its main bulk, about 16 by 24 kilometres (10 by 15 mi.), straddles the Great Divide, part of the British Columbia border and portions of Banff and Jasper national parks. The ice covers about 325 square kilometres (130 sq. mi.) to an estimated depth of 300 metres (984 ft.). Three glaciers—Stutfield, Athabasca and Dome—can be seen from Icefields Parkway.

Columbia Icefield Glacier Discovery Centre is 105 km (64 mi.) s. of the town of Jasper on Hwy. 93. The center overlooks Athabasca and Dome glaciers and offers views of major mountain peaks surrounding the Columbia Icefield. An interpretive

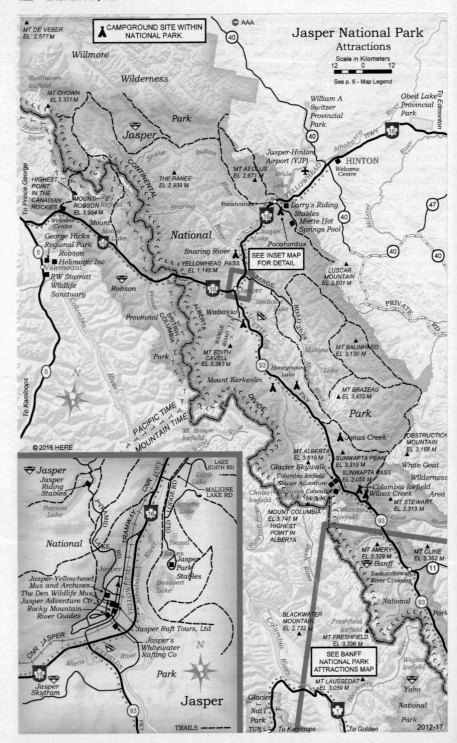

🏕 CAMPGROUND SITE WITHIN NATIONAL PARK.

© AAA

Jasper National Park
Attractions

Scale in Kilometers

12   0   12

See p. 6 - Map Legend

MT DE VEBER
EL 2,577 M

Willmore

Wilderness

Park

Jasper

Resthaven
Icefield

MT CHOWN
EL 3,331 M

Holmes
River

Snake
River

Indian
River

William A
Switzer
Provincial
Park

Obed Lake
Provincial
Park

To Edmonton

40

Athabasca Hwy

River

16

HIGHEST
POINT
IN THE
CANADIAN
ROCKIES

MOUNT
ROBSON
EL 3,954 M

CONTINENTAL

THE RANEE
EL 2,939 M

MT AEOLUS
EL 2,671 M

Jasper-Hinton
Airport (YJP)

HINTON

Welcome
Centre

To Prince George

Mount

Rigel
Icefield

Snaring
River

Brule
Lake

Pocahontas

Larry's Riding
Stables
Miette Hot
Springs Pool

40

McLeod
River

47

Welcome
Centre

George Hicks
Regional Park

Moose
Lake

National

Jasper
Lake

Pocahontas

16

Helimagic Inc

Valemount

5

15

Robson

RW Starratt
Wildlife
Sanctuary

Snaring River

YELLOWHEAD PASS
EL 1,146 M

16

Jasper

Medicine
Lake

LUSCAR
MOUNTAIN
EL 2,601 M

PRIVATE

RD

To Kamloops

5

Robson

Provincial

Fraser
River

BRITISH
COLUMBIA

ALBERTA

Wabasso

RANGE
ROAD 11

ICEFIELDS

ROAD 262A

Maligne
Lake

MT BALINHARD
EL 3,130 M

Park

Columbia
River

MT EDITH
CAVELL
EL 3,363 M

93

Honeymoon
Lake

Maligne
River

MT BRAZEAU
EL 3,470 M

Mount Kerkeslin

PKY

Park

© 2016 HERE

N

PACIFIC TIME

MOUNTAIN TIME

DIVIDE

Mt Brown
Icefield

Jonas Creek

OBSTRUCTION
MOUNTAIN
EL 3,168 M

White Goat

MT ALBERTA
EL 3,619 M

SUNWAPTA PEAK
EL 3,315 M

Wilderness
Area

Wood
River

Glacier Skywalk
Columbia Icefield
Glacier Adventure

SUNWAPTA PASS
EL 2,055 M

Columbia Icefield
Wilcox Creek

Chaba
Icefield

Athabasca
Icefield

Columbia
Icefield

MT STEWART
EL 3,313 M

Cline
River

MOUNT COLUMBIA
EL 3,747 M
HIGHEST
POINT IN
ALBERTA

Columbia
Icefield

93

Sunwapta River

Alexandra River

MT AMERY
EL 3,329 M

MT CLINE
EL 3,362 M

Banff

Saskatchewan
River Crossing

11

National

93

BLACKWATER
MOUNTAIN
EL 2,732 M

Freshfield
Icefield

MT FRESHFIELD
EL 3,336 M

Park

Bush River

Columbia River

River

Wapta
Icefield

SEE BANFF
NATIONAL PARK
ATTRACTIONS MAP

MT LAUSSEDAT
EL 3,059 M

1

To Kamloops

Glacier
Nat'l
Park

To Golden

Yoho

National

Park

2012-17

Inset map — Jasper

💎 Jasper
Jasper
Riding
Stables

LAKE
EDITH RD

Edith
Lake

MALIGNE
LAKE RD

Patricia
Lake

PYRAMID

CNR HWY

OLD LODGE RD

Annette
Lake

National

TRAMWAY

LAKE

YELLOWHEAD RD

Athabasca River

Trefoil
Lakes

Jasper
Park
Stables

Jasper-Yellowhead
Mus and Archives
The Den Wildlife Mus
Jasper Adventure Ctr
Rocky Mountain
River Guides

Jasper

Beauvert
Lake

16

CNR JASPER

Jasper Raft Tours, Ltd

Jasper's
Whitewater
Rafting Co

N

Miette River

ICEFIELDS

16

Jasper
Skytram

93 PKY

Park

Jasper

TRAILS ------

center contains exhibits about the icefield and local wildlife as well as a theater that screens the film "Through Ice and Time." Also inside the center is a Parks Canada information desk, which offers maps, information and details about interpretive programs. **Time:** Allow 30 minutes minimum. **Hours:** Daily 10-5. **Cost:** Free. **Phone:** (780) 852-5288 or (877) 423-7433. ⓘ

COLUMBIA ICEFIELD GLACIER ADVENTURE departs from Columbia Icefield Glacier Discovery Centre, 105 km (64 mi.) s. of the town of Jasper on Hwy. 93. Tours provide an opportunity to see and walk on a field of moving glacier ice formed by snow falling as long ago as 400 years. The bus driver provides anecdotes and information during this 80-minute excursion.

Time: Allow 1 hour, 30 minutes minimum. **Hours:** Tours depart every 15-30 minutes daily 9-6 (weather permitting), late May-early Sept.; 10-5, late Apr.-late May and early Sept.-early Oct.; 10-4, mid-Apr. to late Apr. and early Oct. to mid-Oct. **Cost:** $80; $40 (ages 6-15); free (ages 0-5 in lap). **Phone:** (403) 762-6700 or (877) 423-7433. ⃝ᴳᵀ

GLACIER SKYWALK is accessible via free shuttles departing from the Columbia Icefield Glacier Discovery Centre, 105 km (64 mi.) s. of the town of Jasper on Hwy. 93. Interpretive signs along the walkway running along the edge of the Sunwapta Valley educate visitors about the Canadian Rockies' ecology and geological and evolutionary history. The walkway leads to the site's showpiece, a glass-floored observation platform 280 metres (918 ft.) over spectacular glacier-formed valleys and rushing waterfalls.

Hours: Daily 10-6, late May to mid-July; 10-7, mid-July to early Sept.; 10-5:30, early Sept.-early Oct.; 10-4, early Oct. to mid-Oct. Shuttles depart daily every 15 minutes from the Columbia Icefield Glacier Discovery Centre (weather permitting). Phone ahead to confirm schedule. **Cost:** $32; $16 (ages 6-15). Combination tickets are available. **Phone:** (403) 762-6701 or (866) 816-2758.

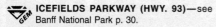 **ICEFIELDS PARKWAY (HWY. 93)**—see Banff National Park p. 30.

MALIGNE CANYON is 10 km (6.2 mi.) n.e. of Jasper via Maligne Lake Rd. A steep-walled ravine more than 50 metres (164 ft.) deep, this spectacular gorge carved by the rushing Maligne River is spanned by six footbridges. Evergreen-shaded trails hug the edge of the chasm, providing excellent views into its depths, and interpretive signs line the way. Nourished by cool mist from the river, bright green moss clings to the nearly vertical limestone walls. A parking lot at the Upper Canyon affords easy access to Maligne's most impressive waterfalls. **Time:** Allow 1 hour minimum. **Cost:** Free. **Phone:** (780) 852-6176 or (780) 852-6162. ⓘ

MALIGNE LAKE BOAT TOURS is 48 km (30 mi.) s.e. of the Jasper townsite via Maligne Lake Rd.; tickets can be purchased from the office at 616 Patricia St. in Jasper and at some area hotels. The 90-minute tours, which offer a brief stop at Spirit Island, provide exceptional views of Maligne Narrows as well as insight into area geology and wildlife. Hiking and trout-fishing trips along with boat, canoe and sea kayak rentals are available June to September. A 2.5-hour photography tour, accompanied by a professional photographer, runs July through mid-September.

Time: Allow 1 hour, 30 minutes minimum. **Hours:** Boat tours depart daily on the hour (weather permitting) 10-5, July 1-early Sept.; 10-4, early June-June 30 and early Sept.-early Oct.; 10-3, early May-early June. **Cost:** $65; $33 (ages 6-15). **Phone:** (780) 852-3370 for general information. ⃝ᴳᵀ

Ⓢᴬⱽᴱ **MIETTE HOT SPRINGS POOL** is e. on Hwy. 16 from the town of Jasper for 44 km (27.3 mi.) to the Pocahontas Bungalows and jct. Miette Rd., then s. 17 km (11 mi.) to the end of Miette Rd. Natural sulfur hot springs feed two man-made pools, with the water temperature ranging between 39 C (102 F) and 42 C (108 F). Pool depth ranges from .5 metres (18 in.) to 1.5 metres (5 ft.) deep. Visitors also can cool off in two plunge pools.

Wildlife viewing, hiking trails and picnic sites are available in the area. Changing rooms as well as swimsuit and towel rentals are available. **Time:** Allow 45 minutes minimum. **Hours:** Daily 9 a.m.-11 p.m., mid-June through Labour Day; 10:30-9, early May to mid-June and day after Labour Day to mid-Oct. **Cost:** $5.76; $4.90 (ages 3-17 and 65+); $17.48 (family, two adults and two children). Prices may vary; phone ahead. **Phone:** (780) 866-3939 or (800) 767-1611. ⓘ 🅿

RECREATIONAL ACTIVITIES

White-water Rafting

• **Jasper's Whitewater Rafting Co.** departs from the parking lot .3 km (.19 mi.) s. of Sunwapta Falls Resort off Hwy. 93. Other trips are available. **Hours:** Trips are offered May 1-early Oct. Schedule varies; phone ahead. **Phone:** (780) 852-7238. ⃝ᴳᵀ

JASPER (F-2) pop. 4,051
- Restaurants p. 126
- Part of Jasper National Park area — see map p. 120

JASPER ADVENTURE CENTRE is at 611 Patricia St. May through October and at 414 Connaught Dr. in winter. The company offers guided interpretive van tours, wildlife tours and walking tours. Summer adventures include exploration of the Columbia Icefield, Maligne Valley and Morro Peak. Winter activities include ice walks, train tours, dog sledding and cross-country skiing. Horseback riding trips, canoe and rafting tours, and wildlife tours also are offered seasonally. **Hours:** Daily 8-6, May-Oct.; 8-5, rest of year. Closed Christmas. **Cost:** Fares $61.90-$114.29. **Phone:** (780) 852-5595 May-Oct., (780) 852-4056 Nov.-Apr., or (800) 565-7547 year-round. GT

JASPER SKYTRAM is 3 km (1.8 mi.) s. on Hwy. 93, then 4 km (2.5 mi.) w. at Whistlers Mountain Rd. Take a 7-minute narrated ride in an enclosed tram car 973 metres (3,243 ft.) up into the alpine zone on Whistlers Mountain, where stunning scenic views await. From the aerial tram's upper station at 2,277 metres (7,470 ft.) you can see six surrounding mountain ranges, several glacial-fed lakes, the Athabasca River and the town of Jasper. On a clear day you may even see Mount Robson in British Columbia, the highest mountain in the Canadian Rockies.

Once at the upper station, you can stroll along the wooden boardwalk and read the interpretive panels posted along the way, or if you're feeling energetic, climb the remaining 189 metres (620 ft.) up to the summit where you'll have a breathtaking 360-degree view.

Step carefully here; the plants that cling to life in this harsh alpine climate are delicate, small and easily damaged. Several have tiny but beautiful flowers. Ptarmigans are the most common birds in this rugged environment, and other frequently seen inhabitants include the diminutive pika and the hoary marmot, although you may hear these creatures before you ever see them. Pikas make a recognizable "eep" sound while the hoary marmot's call resembles a whistle, which is how Whistlers Mountain got its name.

Time: Allow 1 hour minimum. **Hours:** Daily 8 a.m.-9 p.m., late June-early Sept.; 9-8, mid-May to late June; 10-5, late Mar. to mid-May and early Sept.-late Oct. **Cost:** $43; $21.50 (ages 6-15); $107.50 (family, two adults and two children). **Phone:** (780) 852-3093. *(See ad this page.)*

▼ *See AAA listing this page* ▼

ALPINE VILLAGE

Cabin
$140-$350

780-852-3285

Address: Hwy 93A T0E 1E0 **Location:** Waterfront. Jct Hwy 16 and 93, 0.9 mi (1.4 km) s on Hwy 93, just e. **Facility:** Stay outside town amid towering spruce trees along the river in one of the really lovely, smaller cabins or one of the larger upscale units. A large outdoor hot tub is great for easing muscle pains. 50 cabins, some kitchens. 1 story, exterior corridors. **Terms:** closed 11/16-4/17, check-in 4 pm, 2-3 night minimum stay - seasonal and/or weekends, 14 day cancellation notice-fee imposed. **Activities:** hot tub, playground, trails. **Guest Services:** valet laundry.

   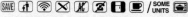

BECKER'S CHALETS

Cabin
$155-$215

780-852-3779

Address: Hwy 93 S T0E 1E0 **Location:** Waterfront. 4.3 mi (6.8 km) s. Located in a quiet rustic area. **Facility:** 118 units, some two bedrooms, three bedrooms, efficiencies, kitchens and cabins. 2 stories (no elevator), exterior corridors. **Terms:** closed 10/14-5/1, check-in 4 pm, 7 day cancellation notice. **Activities:** playground, trails. **Guest Services:** coin laundry. *(See ad this page.)*

BEST WESTERN JASPER INN & SUITES

(780)852-4461

Hotel
$108-$275

AAA Benefit:
Save 10% or more every day and earn 10% bonus points!

Address: 98 Geikie St T0E 1E0 **Location:** Corner of Geikie and Bonhomme sts. Located in a residential area. **Facility:** 143 units, some kitchens. 2-3 stories (no elevator), interior/exterior corridors. **Parking:** winter plug-ins. **Terms:** check-in 4 pm, 3 day cancellation notice-fee imposed. **Amenities:** safes. **Pool(s):** heated indoor. **Activities:** sauna, hot tub, steamroom, bicycles. **Guest Services:** coin laundry.

 Best Western.

Enjoy a quiet location away from the main street, but still close to convenient destinations.

CHATEAU JASPER   (780)852-5644
 Hotel. **Address:** 96 Geikie St T0E 1E0

▼ *See AAA listing this page* ▼

Visit AAA.com/searchfordiscounts to save on travel, shopping, dining and attractions

THE CRIMSON JASPER   780/852-3394
▼▼▼▼ Hotel. **Address:** 200 Connaught Dr T0E 1E0

THE FAIRMONT JASPER PARK LODGE 780/852-3301

▼▼▼▼
Resort Hotel
Rates not provided

Address: 1 Old Lodge Rd T0E 1E0 **Location:** 3 mi (4.8 km) ne via Hwy 16, 2 mi (3.2 km) se off highway via Maligne Rd, follow signs. **Facility:** It's said that at one time Marilyn Monroe frequented this resort set along the shore of gorgeous Lac Beauvert in its spectacular mountain setting. Rooms range from upscale rustic to fabulous décors. 446 units. 1-2 stories (no elevator), exterior corridors. **Parking:** on-site and valet, winter plug-ins. **Terms:** check-in 4 pm. **Amenities:** safes. **Dining:** 2 restaurants, also, The Moose's Nook Chophouse, Orso Trattoria, see separate listings. **Pool(s):** heated outdoor. **Activities:** sauna, hot tub, steamroom, self-propelled boats, boat dock, fishing, regulation golf, miniature golf, tennis, cross country skiing, sledding, ice skating, recreation programs, kids club, bicycles, playground, game room, lawn sports, trails, in-room exercise equipment, spa. **Guest Services:** valet laundry, area transportation. *(See ad this page.)*

SAVE ECO ⦿ ⦿ ⦿ ⦿ CALL ⦿ ⦿ ⦿ BIZ
⦿ ⦿ ⦿ ⦿ ⦿ ⦿ / SOME UNITS ⦿ SHS ⦿

JASPER HOUSE BUNGALOWS   780/852-4535
▼▼ Cabin. **Address:** Hwy 93 S T0E 1E0

LOBSTICK LODGE   780/852-4431
▼▼ Hotel. **Address:** 94 Geikie St T0E 1E0

MARMOT LODGE   780/852-4471
▼▼ Motel. **Address:** 86 Connaught Dr T0E 1E0

MOUNT ROBSON INN   (780)852-3327
▼▼ Motel. **Address:** 902 Connaught Dr T0E 1E0

PARK PLACE INN   780/852-9770
▼▼▼ Boutique Hotel. **Address:** 623 Patricia St T0E 1E0

PATRICIA LAKE BUNGALOWS   780/852-3560
▼▼ Cabin. **Address:** Pyramid Lake Rd T0E 1E0

PYRAMID LAKE RESORT   (780)852-4900
▼▼▼ Hotel. **Address:** Pyramid Lake Rd T0E 1E0

SAWRIDGE INN & CONFERENCE CENTRE JASPER
                                   (780)852-5111

▼▼▼▼
Hotel
$123-$402

Address: 76 Connaught Dr T0E 1E0 **Location:** 1.1 mi (1.7 km) e. **Facility:** 152 units. 3 stories, interior corridors. **Parking:** winter plug-ins. **Terms:** check-in 4 pm, 3 day cancellation notice-fee imposed, resort fee. **Amenities:** safes. **Dining:** 2 restaurants. **Pool(s):** heated indoor. **Activities:** hot tub, steamroom, bicycles, trails, exercise room, spa. **Guest Services:** valet and coin laundry, area transportation.

SAVE ECO ⦿ ⦿ ⦿ CALL ⦿
⦿ BIZ ⦿ ⦿ ⦿ ⦿ ⦿ / SOME UNITS ⦿

SUNWAPTA FALLS ROCKY MOUNTAIN LODGE 780/852-4852
▼▼ Cabin. **Address:** Hwy 93 T0E 1E0

TONQUIN INN   (780)852-4987
▼▼ Motel. **Address:** 100 Juniper St T0E 1E0

WHERE TO EAT

BEAR'S PAW BAKERY   780/852-3233
▼ Breads/Pastries. Quick Serve. **Address:** 4 Pyramid Ave T0E 1E0

▼ See AAA listing this page ▼

BECKER'S GOURMET RESTAURANT   780/852-3535

▼▼▼▼▼
Canadian
Fine Dining
$12-$42

AAA Inspector Notes: About a 10-minute drive from Jasper along the Icefields Parkway, this restaurant features a decidedly Canadian warm oak and firs décor and a large stone fireplace, where you can enjoy the views of Mount Kerkeslin and Mount Hardisty. The menu features Canadian and local meats, game and fish with slight international influences. Salmon and other ingredients are smoked in house. Oven-fired pizzas are also on the menu. **Features:** full bar. **Reservations:** suggested. **Address:** Hwy 93 T0E 1E0 **Location:** On Hwy 93, 4.3 mi (6.8 km) s. B D ✗

CAFE MONDO   780/852-9676

▼ Sandwiches. Quick Serve. **Address:** 616 Patricia St T0E 1E0

CASSIO'S ITALIAN RESTAURANT   780/852-4070

▼▼▼ Italian. Casual Dining. **Address:** 602 Connaught Dr T0E 1E0

DOWNSTREAM RESTAURANT & LOUNGE   780/852-9449

▼▼ International. Gastropub. **Address:** 620 Connaught Dr T0E 1E0

EARLS KITCHEN + BAR   780/852-2393

▼▼ American. Casual Dining. **Address:** 600 Patricia St T0E 1E0

EL MONDO LOCO   780/852-9676

▼ Mexican. Casual Dining. **Address:** 616 Patricia St T0E 1E0

EVIL DAVE'S GRILL   780/852-3323

▼▼▼ New International. Casual Dining. **Address:** 622 Patricia St T0E 1E0

FAMOSO NEAPOLITAN PIZZERIA   780/931-2840

▼▼ Pizza. Casual Dining. **Address:** 607 Patricia St T0E 1E0

FIDDLE RIVER RESTAURANT   780/852-3032

▼▼ Canadian. Casual Dining. **Address:** 620 Connaught Dr T0E 1E0

JASPER BREWING CO   780/852-4111

▼▼ American. Gastropub. **Address:** 624 Connaught Dr T0E 1E0

JASPER PIZZA PLACE   780/852-3225

▼▼ Pizza. Casual Dining. **Address:** 402 Connaught Dr T0E 1E0

KAROUZO'S STEAKHOUSE   780/852-4640

▼ Steak. Casual Dining. **Address:** 628 Connaught Dr T0E 1E0

KIMCHI HOUSE   780/852-5022

▼ Korean. Casual Dining. **Address:** 407 Patricia St T0E 1E0

L & W FAMILY RESTAURANT   780/852-4114

▼ International. Casual Dining. **Address:** 101 Pine Ave T0E 1E0

THE MOOSE'S NOOK CHOPHOUSE   780/852-6052

▼▼▼
Steak
Fine Dining
$29-$52

AAA Inspector Notes: This nook of a restaurant is cozy and intimate with an interesting mountain theme. The menu offers great cuts of AAA Alberta beef and bison and accompaniments that come a la carte. Other entrées include their own sides. All food is well-prepared and flavorful, and the chef incorporates fine ingredients. The service and ambience are upscale without being pretentious, laid-back yet classy. **Features:** full bar. **Reservations:** suggested. **Address:** 1 Old Lodge Rd T0E 1E0 **Location:** 3 mi (4.8 km) ne via Hwy 16, 2 mi (3.2 km) se off highway via Maligne Rd, follow signs; in The Fairmont Jasper Park Lodge. **Parking:** on-site and valet. D CALL ✆M ✗

OLIVE BISTRO & LOUNGE   780/852-5222

▼▼ International. Casual Dining. **Address:** 401 Patricia St T0E 1E0

ORSO TRATTORIA   780/852-6052

▼▼▼
New
Italian
Fine Dining
$25-$48

AAA Inspector Notes: The beautiful dining room includes big picture windows that offer lovely views of nearby Mount Edith Cavell and Lac Beauvert. Fresh high-quality ingredients with a focus on organic and sustainable items are crafted into beautifully prepared and tasty dishes with a Northern Italian slant. Almost all the pastas and the delicious desserts are made in house. There is a nice selection of Italian wine by the glass and the friendly servers bring the bottle over so guests can taste before committing. **Features:** full bar, patio dining. **Reservations:** suggested. **Address:** 1 Old Lodge Rd T0E 1E0 **Location:** 3 mi (4.8 km) ne via Hwy 16, 2 mi (3.2 km) se off highway via Maligne Rd, follow signs; in The Fairmont Jasper Park Lodge. **Parking:** on-site and valet. B D CALL ✆M

PAPA GEORGE'S RESTAURANT   780/852-2260

▼▼▼ International. Casual Dining. **Address:** 404 Connaught Dr T0E 1E0

PATRICIA STREET DELI   780/852-4814

▼ Deli. Quick Serve. **Address:** 606 Patricia St T0E 1E0

THE RAVEN BISTRO   780/852-5151

▼▼ International. Casual Dining. **Address:** 504 Patricia St T0E 1E0

SYRAHS OF JASPER   780/852-4559

▼▼▼ International. Casual Dining. **Address:** 606 Patricia St T0E 1E0

TREELINE RESTAURANT   780/852-3093

▼ American. Quick Serve. **Address:** Top of Whistler Mountain Rd T0E 1E0

VILLA CARUSO   780/852-3920

▼▼ Steak. Casual Dining. **Address:** 640 Connaught Dr T0E 1E0

KANANASKIS pop. 249
• **Part of Banff National Park area — see map p. 28**

DELTA LODGE AT KANANASKIS   (403)591-7711

AAA Benefit:
Members save 5% or more!

▼▼▼ Resort Hotel. **Address:** 1 Centennial Dr, Kananaskis Village T0L 2H0 *(See ad this page.)*

KANANASKIS COUNTRY (I-5)

Kananaskis Country is a four-season, multiuse recreation area encompassing more than 4,200 square kilometres (1,622 sq. mi.) of mountains and foothills. West of Calgary, the area contains Bow Valley, Bragg Creek, Canmore Nordic Centre, Peter Lougheed, Sheep River and Spray Valley provincial parks. In addition there are Blue Rock, Bow Valley, Don Getty and Elbow-Sheep wildland parks. There are also numerous provincial recreation areas with campgrounds, day use areas and trails *(see Recreation Areas Chart).*

Year-round recreational activities are offered, including hiking, horseback riding, snowmobiling, kayaking, mountain biking, fishing, snowshoeing and downhill and cross-country skiing. The area begins just south of Hwy. 1 and extends south to the intersection of hwys. 940 and 532. Animals, including elk, deer, bighorn sheep, lynx, moose, mountain goats, bears and porcupines, can be observed in the area.

Three major visitor information centers within Kananaskis Country provide brochures, maps, displays and other travel information. The Barrier Lake Visitor Information Centre is 6.5 kilometres (4 mi.) south of Hwy. 1 on Hwy. 40. Peter Lougheed Provincial Park Visitor Information Centre is 50 kilometres (31 mi.) south off Hwy. 40 on Kananaskis Lakes Trail. Elbow Valley Visitor Information Centre is 5 kilometres (3 mi.) west of Hwy. 22 on Hwy. 66. Phone (403) 678-0760 for information about all three locations. Several campground amphitheaters offer interpretive programs Wednesday through Sunday evenings in July and August. The area is open daily; however, Hwy. 40 is closed December 1 to June 15 between the Kananaskis Lakes Trail and the junction of hwys. 541 and 940.

Kananaskis Country General Inquiries: Provincial Building, 800 Railway Ave., Suite 201, Canmore, AB, Canada T1W 1P1. **Phone:** (403) 678-0760.

▼ *See AAA listing this page* ▼

Enhance your Kananaskis adventure in the Summit Spa and Fitness Centre with our indoor/outdoor whirlpool and our 17 metre indoor pool or with one of the many activities available in the Valley of Adventure.

Summer	Winter
• mountain biking	• downhill skiing
• climbing	• cross-country skiing
• hiking	• ice skating
• horseback riding	• snowshoeing
• whitewater rafting	• sleigh rides
• fly fishing	• tobogganing

DELTA
LODGE AT KANANASKIS

For more information call **1-866-432-4322** or visit: **www.deltalodgeatkananaskis.com**

Get up to 20 percent off Hertz rentals

PLUS exclusive everyday member benefits

LAC LA BICHE (C-7) pop. 2,544

South of town, Portage La Biche was discovered in 1798 by renowned geographer and explorer David Thompson of the North West Co. This area encompasses the land between the Churchill and Athabasca-Mackenzie basins. Soon after its discovery the portage became a key link in Canada's main fur trade routes and a passageway to the Pacific Ocean.

The 1853 founding of Lac La Biche Mission played a vital role in the settlement of the area, which quickly developed into a major transportation center of the north.

Lakeland Provincial Park *(see Recreation Areas Chart),* 13 kilometres (8 mi.) east off Hwy. 663, provides such recreational opportunities as bicycling, bird-watching, camping, cross-country skiing, fishing, hiking and swimming. The park also offers Alberta's only backcountry canoe circuit. Sir Winston Churchill Provincial Park *(see Recreation Areas Chart),* 11 kilometres (6.8 mi.) northeast off Hwy. 881, is the largest of the 12 islands on Lac La Biche and offers opportunities for camping, hiking and bird-watching.

Lac La Biche and District Chamber of Commerce: 10307 100th St., P.O. Box 804, Lac La Biche, AB, Canada T0A 2C0. **Phone:** (780) 623-2818.

RAMADA INN & SUITES LAC LA BICHE   (780)623-2250
▼▼▼▼ Hotel. **Address:** 9305 100 St T0A 2C0

LACOMBE (F-6) pop. 11,707, elev. 846m/2,775'

Lacombe is the site of the Canadian Agriculture Department's experimental farm; visitors can tour the facility. At Gull Lake 17 kilometres (11 mi.) west on Hwy. 12, Aspen Beach Provincial Park is a noteworthy area resort affording such recreational activities as cross-country skiing, ice fishing and water skiing *(see Recreation Areas Chart).*

ELLIS BIRD FARM, 8 km (5 mi.) e. on Hwy. 12, then 8 km (5 mi.) s. on Prentiss Rd., encourages the conservation of mountain bluebirds, purple martins and other native cavity-nesting birds. A wide variety of garden birds—including a large purple marlin colony and such species as house wrens, owls and warblers—are attracted to the vibrant grounds. A network of trails affords access to butterfly, native wildflower, hummingbird and water gardens. A visitor center featuring interpretive exhibits is on-site, as is a pier where children can try to net aquatic creatures.

Time: Allow 1 hour minimum. **Hours:** Tues.-Sat. and Mon. holidays 11-5, Victoria Day weekend-Labour Day. **Cost:** Admission by donation. Guided tour $2.86. Reservations are required for guided tours. **Phone:** (403) 885-4477. GT ⏹ ⏹

BEST WESTERN PLUS LACOMBE INN & SUITES
(403)782-3535

▼▼▼▼
Hotel
$159-$174

Best Western PLUS.
AAA Benefit:
Save 10% or more every day and earn 10% bonus points!

Address: 4751 63rd St T4L 1K7 **Location:** Hwy 2 exit 422, 1.5 mi (2.5 km) e. **Facility:** 83 units, some efficiencies. 4 stories, interior corridors. **Parking:** winter plug-ins. **Terms:** resort fee. **Pool(s):** heated indoor. **Activities:** hot tub, exercise room. **Guest Services:** valet and coin laundry.

/ SOME
  UNITS 🐕

LAKE LOUISE (H-4)

• Hotels p. 130 • Restaurants p. 130
• Part of Banff National Park area — see map p. 28

 LAKE LOUISE is 4 km (2.4 mi.) w. of Hwy. 1/93 behind The Fairmont Chateau Lake Louise hotel. Incredibly aqua in summer and glistening with snow and ice in winter, the lake has been the subject of countless photographs. Viewed from the hotel side of the lake, the milky blue water creates a striking foreground framed by steep, densely forested mountains on either side and at the far end, the rocky bulk of Mount Victoria blanketed by a sparkling layer of glacial ice. It's the grinding of this ice against the mountain that creates the fine rock particles that wash down into the lake, giving it the unusual hue.

Benches along the shore near the hotel offer a place to relax and take in the magnificent view, but if you're here in summer, especially in the late morning or early afternoon, you'll have plenty of competition for those seats. It's at this time when RVs and automobiles cruise the parking lots endlessly, searching for a coveted spot, while one bus after another disgorges throngs of tourists.

It's an amazingly beautiful place, but during the high season, not a very peaceful one. To escape the crowds, choose one of the several trails that begin near the hotel and make your escape. The easy Lakeshore Trail follows the northern edge of Lake Louise for about 2 kilometres (1.2 mi.) one way. If you continue another 3.3 kilometres (2 mi.), the trail becomes much more challenging, but eventually you'll reach the Plain of Six Glaciers, a rocky area created by advancing and retreating glaciers. A quaint teahouse sells refreshments here, and the view extends all the way to the other side of the valley. Another way to explore the lake is by canoe, which you can rent at the boathouse on the lake's west shore.

The Lake Louise Visitor Information Centre in nearby Samson Mall has maps and information. Nearby Moraine Lake *(see attraction listing p. 31)* is another spectacular Banff National Park location worth visiting. **Phone:** (403) 762-8421 for the visitor center.

LAKE LOUISE SUMMER GONDOLA AND WILDLIFE INTERPRETIVE CENTRE

LAKE LOUISE SUMMER GONDOLA AND WILDLIFE INTERPRETIVE CENTRE is just n. of Hwy. 1 interchange at 1 Whitehorn Rd. A lift offers an impressive aerial view of Lake Louise and the mountains of the Continental Divide. At the interpretive center staff members present a brief visitor orientation session; interpretive programs, including guided walks, are offered daily for an additional fee. Ride and dine packages also are offered. **Hours:** Daily 9-5, mid-May to late Sept.; otherwise varies. Phone ahead to confirm schedule. **Cost:** Gondola $32.95; $15.95 (ages 6-15). Interpretive center free. Guided walk $9. **Phone:** (403) 522-3555 or (877) 956-8473. GT ⑪

THE FAIRMONT CHATEAU LAKE LOUISE
(403)522-3511

Historic Resort Hotel
$309-$749

Address: 111 Lake Louise Dr T0L 1E0 **Location:** 1.8 mi (3 km) up the hill from the village. **Facility:** This château-style, grande dame hotel sits on a lake—considered by some to be a Wonder of the World—surrounded by ruggedly beautiful mountains and glaciers. Lovely rooms range in size and grandeur. 552 units, some two bedrooms. 8 stories, interior corridors. **Parking:** on-site (fee) and valet, winter plug-ins. **Terms:** check-in 4 pm, 7 day cancellation notice-fee imposed, resort fee. **Amenities:** safes. **Dining:** 5 restaurants, also, Chateau Deli, Fairview Dining Room, see separate listings. **Pool(s):** heated indoor. **Activities:** hot tub, steamroom, self-propelled boats, cross country skiing, ice skating, recreation programs, kids club, bicycles, trails, exercise room, spa. **Guest Services:** valet laundry, rental car service, area transportation. *(See ad this page.)*

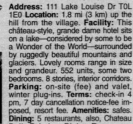

SAVE ECO 🍽 🛏 ⛄ 🏋 📶 ✈ BIZ SHS 📶
✕ 🎥 ⊟ 🖥 SOME UNITS 🐾 ⚒

LAKE LOUISE INN   403/522-3791
🏨🏨 Hotel. **Address:** 210 Village Rd T0L 1E0

MOUNTAINEER LODGE   (403)522-3844
🏨🏨 Hotel. **Address:** 101 Village Rd T0L 1E0

POST HOTEL & SPA   (403)522-3989
🏨🏨🏨🏨 Classic Hotel. **Address:** 200 Pipestone Rd T0L 1E0

WHERE TO EAT

CHATEAU DELI   403/522-3511
🏨 Deli. Quick Serve. **Address:** 111 Lake Louise Dr T0L 1E0

FAIRVIEW DINING ROOM   403/522-1818

New Canadian Fine Dining
$28-$49

AAA Inspector Notes: *Historic.* Oversize windows with commanding views of Lake Louise and the Victoria Glacier are found at this beautiful restaurant. From start to finish, diners can expect professional and knowledgeable service with a tantalizing menu that explores a diverse seasonal selection of cuisine utilizing top-notch ingredients. It is a good idea to check for off-season closures and there are times in season where dining is restricted to in-house guests. **Features:** full bar. **Reservations:** required. **Address:** 111 Lake Louise Dr T0L 1E0 **Location:** 1.8 mi (3 km) up the hill from the village; in The Fairmont Chateau Lake Louise. **Parking:** on-site and valet. D CALL

LAGGAN'S MOUNTAIN BAKERY & DELI   403/522-2017

Deli Quick Serve
$5-$12

AAA Inspector Notes: This popular bakery serves an extensive range of baked goods, freshly-made sandwiches and pizza as well as several soups of the day. Fast food items like chili cheese fries and chicken burgers also are offered. Giant cookies, yummy squares and other goodies satisfy those with a sweet tooth, and delicious Frog Friendly Wild coffee help wash it all down. **Address:** 101 Lake Louise Dr T0L 1E0 **Location:** Center; in Samson Mall.
B L D

LAKE LOUISE STATION   403/522-2600
🏨🏨 American. Casual Dining. **Address:** 200 Sentinel Rd T0L 1E0

▼ *See AAA listing this page* ▼

MOUNT FAIRVIEW DINING ROOM
403/522-4202

◇◇◇

Regional
Canadian
Fine Dining
$15-$39

AAA Inspector Notes: Located deep in the heart of the Rockies, this restaurant is tucked behind the lounge of a historic hotel. With windows on three sides, almost every seat has nice views of the mountains. The extraordinary wine list includes selections perfectly matched to the creative and artistic food, which blends the best seasonal and local ingredients. This place is well known for its preparations of game, most of which is raised on the property's ranch outside of Calgary. **Features:** full bar. **Reservations:** suggested. **Address:** 80 Lake Louise Dr T0L 1E0 **Location:** 1.8 mi (3 km) up the hill from village; in Deer Lodge Hotel. B L D 🅐🅒

POST HOTEL DINING ROOM
403/522-3989

◇◇◇◇

Continental
Fine Dining
$16-$54

AAA Inspector Notes: This restaurant has an exceptional reputation for delicious food which can be enjoyed in a dining room with an elegant, upscale cabin décor. The chef sources excellent quality ingredients, mainly from Alberta, but also from other Canadian regions, to prepare innovative European classics which are wonderfully flavored and colorfully presented. Service is refined and highly professional. A less extensive menu is offered at lunch. **Features:** full bar. **Reservations:** suggested, for dinner. **Address:** 200 Pipestone Rd T0L 1E0 **Location:** Just w of main intersection; in Lake Louise village; in Post Hotel & Spa. **Parking:** on-site and valet. B L D 🅐🅒

LEDUC (E-6) pop. 24,279, elev. 764m/2,509'
- Restaurants p. 132
- Part of Edmonton area — see map p. 85

Just south of Edmonton, Leduc is situated near two large lakes—Saunders Lake and Telford Lake—along with several smaller lakes where residents enjoy water sports. The city has more than 32 kilometres (20 mi.) of multiuse pathways, along with multiple golf courses and a ski hill. The Leduc Recreation Centre, 4330 Black Gold Dr., includes three NHL-size hockey rinks, an aquatic complex, a curling complex and track; it also hosts provincial and national sports tournaments. Phone (780) 980-7177. Leduc's Maclab Centre for the Performing Arts, 4308 50th St., presents a variety of music, theater and dance performances and other events in its 460-seat theater throughout the year; phone (780) 980-1866.

BEST WESTERN PLUS DENHAM INN & SUITES
(780)986-2241

◇◇◇

Hotel
$110-$190

Best Western PLUS. **AAA Benefit:** Save 10% or more every day and earn 10% bonus points!

Address: 5207 50th Ave T9E 6V3 **Location:** Hwy 2 exit Leduc/City Centre, just e. **Facility:** 95 units. 2-5 stories, interior corridors. **Parking:** winter plug-ins. **Terms:** check-in 4 pm. **Activities:** hot tub, exercise room. **Guest Services:** valet and coin laundry. (See ad this page.)

SAVE ECO 🔌 🍴 🏊 🍸 CALL 🔲 BIZ HS 📶 ✖ 🛗 🖨 / SOME UNITS 🖨

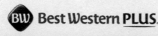

PLAN AN ADVENTURE
Visit AAA.com or CAA.ca
© LifeJourneys / Getty Images

▼ See AAA listing this page ▼

DAYS INN EDMONTON AIRPORT   (780)986-6550

Hotel
$111-$136

Address: 5705 50th St T9E 6Z8 **Location:** 1.2 mi (2 km) ne of jct Hwy 2 and 39. **Facility:** 116 units. 4 stories, interior corridors. **Terms:** check-in 4 pm. **Activities:** exercise room. **Guest Services:** coin laundry. **Featured Amenity:** full hot breakfast. *(See ad this page.)*

[SAVE] ✈ 🛏 ▼ BIZ

📶 ⊠ ▯ 🍽 📺

HAMPTON INN & SUITES BY HILTON EDMONTON INTERNATIONAL AIRPORT   (780)980-9775

Hotel
$102-$159

Hampton by HILTON

AAA Benefit: Members save up to 10%!

Address: 3916 84th Ave T9E 7G1 **Location:** Hwy 2 exit Edmonton International Airport, just e. **Facility:** 111 units. 4 stories, interior corridors. **Parking:** winter plug-ins. **Terms:** 1-7 night minimum stay, cancellation fee imposed. **Pool(s):** heated indoor. **Activities:** hot tub, exercise room. **Guest Services:** valet and coin laundry. **Featured Amenity:** full hot breakfast.

[SAVE] ✈ 🍴 CALL 🄼 🏊 BIZ HS 📶 ⊠ ▯

📺 / SOME UNITS 🍽

HILTON GARDEN INN EDMONTON INTERNATIONAL AIRPORT   (780)612-2350
 Hotel. **Address:** 8208 36th St T9E 0H7

AAA Benefit: Members save up to 10%!

RAMADA EDMONTON INTERNATIONAL AIRPORT   (780)980-0986
Hotel. **Address:** 8340 Sparrow Cres T9E 8B7

SUPER 8-EDMONTON INTERNATIONAL AIRPORT   (780)986-8898
Hotel. **Address:** 8004 Sparrow Cres T9E 7G1

WINGATE BY WYNDHAM LEDUC EDMONTON AIRPORT   (587)783-7179
Hotel. **Address:** 7120 Sparrow Dr T9E 8A5

WHERE TO EAT

HABANEROS MEXICAN GRILL   780/986-8017
Mexican. Casual Dining. **Address:** 5015 48 A St T9E 6Y2

ZAMBELLIS RESTAURANT   780/980-9669
International. Casual Dining. **Address:** 6210 50th St T9E 7G9

LEGAL (D-6) pop. 1,225

Best known for its collection of building-size historical murals, the small town of Legal is 50 kilometres (31 mi.) north of Edmonton. The Francophone community is named after Father Emile Legal, a French bishop, missionary and architect.

The town takes pride in its Francophone pioneer history, as is depicted by its huge outdoor murals. Subject matter ranges from the Grey Nuns—who built the first educational center for rural children—to Alexandre Lavoie, whose court battle helped French-Canadians throughout the country obtain federal services in French.

ACFA and Centralta Community Centre: 5109-46 St., P.O. Box 328, Legal, AB, Canada T0G 1L0. **Phone:** (780) 961-3665.

LETHBRIDGE (J-7) pop. 83,517,
elev. 930m/3,051'
• Restaurants p. 134

Founded in the 1870s, abundant agricultural resources helped Lethbridge to become one of Alberta's major feedlot and grain distribution centers. The region reportedly receives more hours of sunshine annually than any other spot in Canada and therefore requires irrigation to counterbalance the semi-arid climate; more than 400,000 hectares (988,000 acres) produce crops of grain and sugar beets. Livestock, oil and gas also support the economic base.

Numerous parks and green spaces complement the city's commercial enterprises. Two popular areas are Lethbridge Nature Preserve in Indian Battle Park at 3rd Avenue S. and Scenic Drive, and Henderson Lake Park at Parkside Drive S. and Mayor Magrath Drive S. The park has a golf course, a 24-hectare (60-acre) lake with tennis courts, a picnic area, playgrounds and a campground. Rose and Japanese gardens, a stadium and an ice-skating center are included. Lethbridge holds Whoop-Up Days in August.

Chinook Country Tourist Association: 2805 Scenic Dr. S., Lethbridge, AB, Canada T1K 5B7. **Phone:** (403) 320-1222 or (800) 661-1222.

Shopping: Park Place Mall (501 1st Ave. S.) has more than 100 stores, including Sears.

BREWERY GARDENS is just w. off 1st Ave. S. at Brewery Hill on Scenic Dr. Developed by a former brewery, the gardens present eight floral displays May through the first frost, as well as displays for Easter, Halloween, Remembrance Day and Christmas. The gardens are not walk-through gardens but are a 1-hectare (2.5-acre) plot on the side of a coulee. Visitors view them across the coulee. **Hours:** Daily dawn-dusk. **Cost:** Free. **Phone:** (403) 320-1222, or (800) 661-1222 (Chinook Country Tourist Association).

NIKKA YUKO JAPANESE GARDEN is on Mayor Magrath Dr. at 9th Ave. Five basic types of traditional Japanese gardens are incorporated into the overall design, which is one of the most authentic of its kind in North America. A pavilion, bridges, a bell tower imported from Japan and cypress wood structures from Taiwan are featured; paths punctuated by footbridges over ponds and streams weave through the gardens.

A variety of ongoing activities are offered, including cultural, historical and horticultural experiences. Visitors can take in art exhibitions or learn pruning and gardening techniques. Guides in traditional Japanese garments conduct tours daily. Special events, which take place regularly, include traditional Japanese art demonstrations of bonsai, flower arranging, origami, sand art and calligraphy. A tea ceremony is offered the second Sunday of every month.

Time: Allow 1 hour minimum. **Hours:** Daily 9-5:30, May-Oct. Phone ahead to confirm schedule. **Cost:** $8.57; $5.71 (ages 60+); $3.81 (ages 6-17). **Phone:** (403) 328-3511. GT

SOUTHERN ALBERTA ART GALLERY is at 601 3rd Ave. S. Exhibits showcase works of Canadian and international artists with an emphasis on contemporary art. **Time:** Allow 30 minutes minimum. **Hours:** Tues.-Sat. 10-5 (also Thurs. 5-7), Sun. 1-5. **Cost:** $4.76; $3.81 (students with ID and ages 60+); free (ages 0-11, to all on Sun. and on Thurs. from 5-7 p.m.). **Phone:** (403) 327-8770.

BEST WESTERN PLUS SERVICE INN & SUITES
(403)329-6844

Hotel
$150-$170

Best Western PLUS. **AAA Benefit:** Save 10% or more every day and earn 10% bonus points!

Address: 209 41st St S T1J 1Z3 **Location:** Hwy 3 (Crowsnest Tr), just s on 43rd St S. **Facility:** 113 units. 4 stories, interior corridors. **Parking:** winter plug-ins. **Terms:** resort fee. **Pool(s):** heated indoor. **Activities:** hot tub, exercise room. **Guest Services:** valet laundry. **Featured Amenity: full hot breakfast.**

SAVE / SOME UNITS

COAST LETHBRIDGE HOTEL & CONFERENCE CENTRE
(403)327-5701

Hotel
$134-$164

Address: 526 Mayor Magrath Dr S T1J 3M2 **Location:** Hwy 3 (Crowsnest Tr) exit Mayor Magrath Dr S, just s. **Facility:** 103 units. 3 stories, interior corridors. **Terms:** check-in 4 pm, cancellation fee imposed. **Dining:** Firestone Restaurant & Bar, see separate listing. **Pool(s):** heated indoor. **Activities:** hot tub, exercise room. **Guest Services:** valet laundry.

/ SOME UNITS

COMFORT INN   (403)320-8874
Hotel. **Address:** 3226 Fairway Plaza Rd S T1K 7T5

DAYS INN LETHBRIDGE   (403)327-6000
Hotel. **Address:** 100 3rd Ave S T1J 4L2

FAIRFIELD INN & SUITES BY MARRIOTT LETHBRIDGE
(587)425-0388
Hotel. **Address:** 4081 2 Ave S T1J 1Z2

AAA Benefit: Members save 5% or more!

HAMPTON INN & SUITES BY HILTON LETHBRIDGE
(403)942-2142
Hotel. **Address:** 4073 2nd Ave S T1J 1Z2

AAA Benefit: Members save up to 10%!

HOLIDAY INN EXPRESS HOTEL & SUITES LETHBRIDGE
(403)394-9292
Hotel. **Address:** 120 Stafford Dr S T1J 4W4

HOLIDAY INN HOTEL LETHBRIDGE   (403)380-5050

Hotel
$139-$199

Address: 2375 Mayor Magrath Dr S T1K 7M1 **Location:** Hwy 3 (Crowsnest Tr) exit Mayor Magrath Dr S, 1.8 mi (3 km) s, then just e on 22nd St. **Facility:** 119 units. 4 stories, interior corridors. **Parking:** winter plug-ins. **Terms:** cancellation fee imposed, resort fee. **Dining:** Mr Mikes SteakhouseCasual, see separate listing. **Pool(s):** heated indoor. **Activities:** hot tub, exercise room. **Guest Services:** valet and coin laundry.

LETHBRIDGE LODGE HOTEL AND CONFERENCE CENTRE
403/328-1123

Hotel. **Address:** 320 Scenic Dr T1J 4B4

MOTEL 6 LETHBRIDGE   403/328-4436

Motel. **Address:** 1142 Mayor Magrath Dr S T1K 2P8

PREMIER INN & SUITES   (403)380-6677

Hotel
$109-$150

Address: 2225 Mayor Magrath Dr S T1K 7M1 **Location:** Hwy 3 (Crowsnest Tr) exit Mayor Magrath Dr S, 1.8 mi (3 km) s, then just e on 22nd St. **Facility:** 50 units. 4 stories, interior corridors. **Parking:** winter plug-ins. **Terms:** cancellation fee imposed. **Activities:** hot tub, exercise room. **Guest Services:** coin laundry. **Featured Amenity:** continental breakfast.

QUALITY INN & SUITES   (403)331-6440

Hotel. **Address:** 4070 2nd Ave S T1J 3Z2

RAMADA LETHBRIDGE   (403)329-0555

Hotel. **Address:** 1303 Mayor Magrath Dr S T1K 2R1

SANDMAN HOTEL LETHBRIDGE   403/328-1111

Hotel. **Address:** 421 Mayor Magrath Dr S T1J 3L8

WHERE TO EAT

BAADSHAH ROYAL EAST INDIAN CUISINE   403/381-1353

Indian. Casual Dining. **Address:** 310 5th St S T1J 2B2

EL COMAL   403/380-6836

Mexican. Casual Dining. **Address:** 1020 Mayor Magrath Dr S T1K 2R2

FIRESTONE RESTAURANT & BAR   403/329-3473

American. Casual Dining. **Address:** 532 Mayor Magrath Dr S T1J 3M2

LIGHTHOUSE AKARI SUSHI JAPANESE RESTAURANT
403/328-4828

Japanese. Casual Dining. **Address:** 708 3rd Ave S T1J 0H6

MIRO BISTRO   403/394-1961

Continental. Casual Dining. **Address:** 212 5th St S T1J 2B3

MOCHA CABANA   403/329-6243

American. Casual Dining. **Address:** 317 4th St S T1J 1Z9

MR MIKES STEAKHOUSECASUAL   403/380-6453

American. Casual Dining. **Address:** 2375 Mayor Magrath Dr S T1K 7M1

NAMU GRILL & SUSHI   403/328-5077

Asian. Casual Dining. **Address:** 1303 Mayor Magrath Dr S T1K 2R1

O SHO JAPANESE RESTAURANT   403/327-8382

Sushi. Casual Dining. **Address:** 311 4th St S T1J 1Z9

PENNY COFFEE HOUSE   403/320-5282

Coffee/Tea. Quick Serve. **Address:** 331 5th St S T1J 2B4

PLUM   403/394-1200

New American. Casual Dining. **Address:** 330 6th St S T1J 2G2

STREATSIDE EATERY   403/328-8085

American. Casual Dining. **Address:** 317 8th St S T1J 2J5

TELEGRAPH TAP HOUSE   403/942-4136

American. Casual Dining. **Address:** 310 6 St S T1J 0H4

LLOYDMINSTER (E-9) pop. 18,032

Lloydminster is the province's only city with one foot planted in Saskatchewan and the other in Alberta. Four 31-metre-tall (100-ft.) border markers—shaped like the survey stakes used during the original survey of the border between the two provinces—represent four themes: oil and gas, agriculture, the Barr Colonists and native North Americans. The downtown monument, erected in 1994, denotes the city's bi-provincial status.

Many nearby lakes, regional parks and campgrounds offer opportunities for fishing, bird-watching and other pursuits. Other recreational opportunities include an 18-hole golf course and an aquatic leisure center with a wave pool and a waterslide.

Summer events include Canada Day celebrations, which are held July 1 in Bud Miller All Seasons Park; Colonial Days, a 4-day fair with a parade, agricultural exhibits and grandstand entertainment held in early July; and racing action at the Canadian Professional Chuckwagon Finals in mid-August.

Lloydminster Tourism: 5420 50th Ave., Lloydminster, AB, Canada T9V 0X1. **Phone:** (780) 875-8881 or (800) 825-6180.

DAYS HOTEL & SUITES LLOYDMINSTER   (780)875-4404
▼▼▼ Hotel. **Address:** 5411 44th St T9V 0A9

HAMPTON INN BY HILTON-LLOYDMINSTER   (780)874-1118
▼▼▼ Hotel. **Address:** 8288 44 St
T9V 2G8

HOLIDAY INN HOTEL & SUITES   (780)870-5050
▼▼▼ Hotel. **Address:** 5612 44th St T9V 0B6

RAMADA INN LLOYDMINSTER   (780)871-6940

Hotel
$109-$179

Address: 5610 44th St T9V 0B6 **Location:** Jct Hwy 16 and 17, 0.6 mi (1 km)
w. **Facility:** 61 units. 3 stories, interior
corridors. **Parking:** winter plug-ins.
Terms: check-in 4 pm. **Activities:** exercise room. **Guest Services:** valet
laundry.

SAVE (TI+) BIZ HS 📶 🖥 ▣
▣ / SOME
/ UNITS 🅂▦

ROYAL HOTEL   (780)875-6113
▼▼ Hotel. **Address:** 5620 44th St T9V 0B6

WHERE TO EAT

MR BILL'S FAMILY RESTAURANT   780/875-3388
▼▼ Continental. Casual Dining. **Address:** 5405 44th St,
Suite 10 T9V 0A9

ROCK CREEK TAP AND GRILL   780/874-7625
▼▼ American. Casual Dining. **Address:** 8120 44 St T9V
3L6

SPIRO'S   780/875-4241
▼▼ Mediterranean. Casual Dining. **Address:** 1408 50th Ave
T9V 0Y1

LONGVIEW   (I-6) pop. 307

 **BAR U RANCH NATIONAL HISTORIC SITE**
GEM is 13 km (9 mi.) s. on Hwy. 22. The site fo-
cuses on the history of ranching in Canada and the
role that occupation played in the country's development. Visitors learn the history of the Bar U Ranch,
from the days of open range ranching through its
prominence as a breeding center for cattle and Per-
cheron horses to its position as part of a multiple-
ranch cattle operation.

The visitor center has exhibits and a video presentation about the site, one of Canada's largest
ranching operations 1882-1950. Guests can tour the
ranch site on foot or via horse-drawn wagon shuttle.
Historic structures include the 1882-83 saddle horse
barn, blacksmith shop, stud horse barn, wintering
pens, 1910 cook house, storage sheds and ranch
office/post office. Ranch activities such as roping,
leather working and the making of cowboy coffee
also are demonstrated.

Hours: Daily 10-5, Victoria Day-Sept. 30. **Cost:**
Free in 2017 to celebrate Canada's 150th anniversary of Confederation, otherwise $7.43; $6.24 (ages
65+); $3.71 (ages 6-16); $18.67 (up to seven people
arriving in a single vehicle). **Phone:** (403) 395-2212
or (888) 773-8888. (TI)

MARKERVILLE   (G-6) pop. 42

On June 27, 1888, 50 Icelanders from the
drought-plagued Dakota Territory crossed the Red
Deer River to settle in Markerville, where they hoped
to maintain their language and customs. For a time
they produced woolen outerwear, pastries, sweets
and smoked mutton in the traditional Icelandic
manner.

During the 1920s, however, an increase in inter-
marriage with other ethnic groups and improved
transportation diluted their cultural isolation. Less
than 10 percent of the population is now of purely
Icelandic descent, but many traditional customs are
celebrated during heritage days.

HISTORIC MARKERVILLE CREAMERY MUSEUM
is off hwys. 781 and 592 at 114 Creamery Way.
Begun by 34 Icelandic farmers as a cooperative in
1899 and in operation until 1972, the creamery has
been restored to depict the operation as it was in the
1930s. Costumed guides offer tours. Special events
are scheduled throughout the year. **Time:** Allow 30
minutes minimum. **Hours:** Daily 10-5, mid-May to
early Sept. **Cost:** $4.76; $3.81 (ages 7-17 and 65+).
Phone: (403) 728-3006 or (877) 728-3007.
GT (TI) ⛱

**STEPHANSSON HOUSE PROVINCIAL HISTORIC
SITE** is 7 km (4 mi.) n. at 2230 Township Rd. 371.
The site includes the home of Stephan G. Stephansson, a prominent Icelandic poet and Canadian pioneer. The historic home has been restored to its
1927 appearance and contains many original furnishings. Costumed guides give 15- to 30-minute

tours and demonstrations of 1920s homemaking chores such as spinning wool and baking in a wood-burning oven.

Time: Allow 30 minutes minimum. **Hours:** Daily 10-5, May 15-Labour Day. **Cost:** $4.76; $3.81 (ages 65+); $1.90 (ages 7-17); free (Canadian military with ID); $13.33 (family, two adults and children ages 0-17). Cash only. **Phone:** (403) 728-3929 May 15-Labour Day, or (780) 431-2321 rest of year. GT 🎠

MEDICINE HAT (J-9) pop. 60,005, elev. 715m/2,346'

According to popular legend the name Medicine Hat originated because of a battle between Cree and Blackfoot Indians on the banks of a southern Alberta river. The Cree fought bravely until their medicine man deserted them, losing his headdress in midstream. Believing this to be a bad omen, the Cree put down their weapons and were killed by the Blackfoot. This site became known as "Saamis," which translates as "medicine man's hat."

A buried prehistoric river, or aquifer, serves as a source of unlimited cool water. More than 20 billion cubic metres (26 billion cu. yd.) of natural gas reserves inspired Rudyard Kipling in 1907 to describe Medicine Hat as possessing "all hell for a basement."

Outdoor opportunities include swimming and fishing at Echo Dale Regional Park. Circuit cowboys and spectators gather for 3 days in mid-July for the Medicine Hat Exhibition & Stampede.

Tourism Medicine Hat: 330 Gehring Rd. S.W., Medicine Hat, AB, Canada T1B 4W1. **Phone:** (403) 527-6422 or (800) 481-2822.

Shopping: Medicine Hat Mall (3292 Dunmore Rd. S.E.) features Hudson's Bay and Sears among its more than 100 stores.

ESPLANADE ARTS & HERITAGE CENTRE, 401 First St. S.E., houses an art gallery featuring works by both local and national artists, a museum with a permanent gallery, two theaters and archives containing more than 1 million documents and photos.

The museum presents audiovisual displays detailing the region's cultural heritage as well as a collection encompassing more than 25,000 artifacts. Included are pioneer items and pieces related to the area's petroleum industry.

Time: Allow 1 hour minimum. **Hours:** Galleries and box office Mon.-Fri. 10-5, Sat. noon-5. Closed major holidays. **Cost:** Galleries $5.15; $3.85 (ages 7-17 and students with ID); free (ages 0-6 and to all Thurs.); $15.50 (family, up to four people). Prices for Esplanade Theatre shows vary; phone ahead. **Phone:** (403) 502-8580. 🎭

MEDALTA is at 713 Medalta Ave. S.E. Brick, tile and pottery manufacturing were prominent industries in Medicine Hat starting in the late 19th century due to a supply of clay deposits, natural gas and the availability of railroad transportation. The city once boasted several potteries, such as Medalta Potteries and Medicine Hat Potteries (later Hycroft China Ltd.). Today only the brick industry remains.

At the Medalta Potteries National Historic Site, visitors can watch pottery demonstrations and view beehive kilns constructed in the early 1920s, a large collection of Medicine Hat pottery and contemporary ceramic art. Artifacts and production machines also are displayed. **Time:** Allow 1 hour minimum. **Hours:** Daily 10-5 (also Thurs. 5-8:30). Guided tours are offered Thurs.-Sun. in summer; self-guiding tours are available rest of year. Closed Nov. 11. **Cost:** $12; $10 (ages 6-17, ages 60+ and students with ID); $30 (family, two adults and two children). **Phone:** (403) 529-1070. GT

SAAMIS TEEPEE is at jct. Hwy. 1 and South Ridge Dr. Made of steel, the tepee stands approximately 20 stories high. Storyboards incorporated in the tepee stand 3.6 metres (12 ft.) high and depict First Nations history. Used during the 1988 Olympics in Calgary, the tepee was moved to Medicine Hat where it now stands above the Saamis Archaeological Site—the location of a 16th-century buffalo camp. **Time:** Allow 1 hour minimum. **Hours:** Daily 24 hours. **Cost:** Free. **Phone:** (403) 527-6422 (Tourism Medicine Hat).

BEST WESTERN PLUS SUN COUNTRY   (403)527-3700

Hotel
$109-$129

 Best Western PLUS. **AAA Benefit:** Save 10% or more every day and earn 10% bonus points!

Address: 722 Redcliff Dr T1A 5E3 **Location:** Just w of Trans-Canada Hwy 1, access on 7th St SW. **Facility:** 121 units, some efficiencies and kitchens. 2 stories (no elevator), interior/exterior corridors. **Parking:** winter plug-ins. **Pool(s):** heated indoor. **Activities:** sauna, hot tub, exercise room. **Guest Services:** valet and coin laundry.

COMFORT INN & SUITES   (403)504-1700

Hotel
$79-$259

Address: 2317 Trans-Canada Way SE T1B 4E9 **Location:** Trans-Canada Hwy 1, just n on Dunmore Rd, just w. Opposite Medicine Hat Mall. **Facility:** 100 units. 3 stories, interior corridors. **Parking:** winter plug-ins. **Terms:** check-in 4 pm. **Pool(s):** heated indoor. **Activities:** hot tub, exercise room. **Guest Services:** valet and coin laundry. **Featured Amenity:** full hot breakfast.

Comfort INN & SUITES **CHOICE**

- Free Hot Deluxe Breakfast
- High Speed Internet
- Pet Friendly Rooms
- Close to Major Attractions

DAYS INN MEDICINE HAT   (403)580-3297
Hotel. **Address:** 24 Strachan Ct SE T1B 4R7

HAMPTON INN & SUITES BY HILTON MEDICINE HAT
403/548-7818
Hotel. **Address:** 2510 Box Springs Blvd T1C 0C8

AAA Benefit: Members save up to 10%!

HOLIDAY INN EXPRESS HOTEL & SUITES   403/504-5151
Hotel. **Address:** 9 Strachan Bay SE T1B 4Y2

HOME INN EXPRESS MEDICINE HAT   403/527-1749
Contemporary Hotel. **Address:** 20 Strachan Ct SE T1B 4R7

Enjoy great member rates

and benefits at AAA/CAA

Preferred Hotels

MEDICINE HAT LODGE RESORT, CASINO & SPA
(403)529-2222

Hotel
$139-$159

Address: 1051 Ross Glen Dr SE T1B 3T8 **Location:** Trans-Canada Hwy 1 exit Dunmore Rd, just ne. **Facility:** Many of the attractive rooms are poolside or have views of the pool, where a large waterslide will get your kids excited. Tower rooms are farthest away from the pool, but are closest to the casino. 221 units. 4 stories, interior corridors. **Parking:** winter plug-ins. **Terms:** check-in 4 pm, resort fee. **Amenities:** video games. Some: safes. **Pool(s):** heated indoor. **Activities:** hot tub, exercise room, spa. **Guest Services:** valet and coin laundry. **Featured Amenity:** full hot breakfast.

WHERE TO EAT

EARLS KITCHEN + BAR   403/528-3275
American. Casual Dining. **Address:** 3215 Dunmore Rd SE T1B 2H2

THE GARAGE PUB AND EATERY   403/580-2588
American. Casual Dining. **Address:** 710 Gershaw Dr SW T1A 5C8

HAT'S RESTAURANT   403/529-9739
Chinese. Casual Dining. **Address:** 1701 Dunmore Rd SE T1A 1Z8

MADHATTER COFFEE ROASTERY   403/529-2344
Coffee/Tea. Quick Serve. **Address:** 513 3rd St SE T1A 0H2

RUSTIC KITCHEN + BAR   403/525-9938
New Canadian. Casual Dining. **Address:** 925 7th St SW T1A 7R8

THAI ORCHID ROOM   403/580-8210
Thai. Casual Dining. **Address:** 3-36 Strachan Ct SE T1B 4R7

TWIST WINE & TAPAS BUSTRO   403/528-2188
International. Casual Dining. **Address:** 531 3rd St SE T1A 0H2

THE ZUCCHINI BLOSSOM MARKET AND CAFE   403/526-1630
Deli. Quick Serve. **Address:** 62 3rd St NE T1A 5L8

MILK RIVER (K-7) pop. 811

Milk River is on the east side of Milk River Ridge, an area more than 1,200 metres (3,900 ft.) high, 39 kilometres (24 mi.) long and 29 kilometres (18 mi.) wide. Quartzite, granite and gneiss rock formations indicate prehistoric glacial action; meltwater carved the Milk River Valley 10,000 years ago. The river, formed from small streams and springs in southwest Alberta and northern Montana, joins the Missouri and Mississippi rivers to flow to the Gulf of Mexico.

Throughout the area and predominantly in Writing-on-Stone Provincial Park/Áísínai'pi National Historic Site are mushroom-shaped sandstone hoodoos, odd rock formations that once led First Nations people to believe spirits inhabited the valley.

The Alberta Tourism Information Centre: Hwy. 4, Milk River, AB, Canada T0K 1M0. Phone: (403) 647-3938.

MORLEY

STONEY NAKODA RESORT & CASINO   (403)881-2830

Hotel
$89-$199

Address: Jct Trans-Canada Hwy 1 and Hwy 40 T0L 1N0 **Location:** Jct Hwy 40, just s. Located in a rural area. **Facility:** Guests will be intrigued immediately by the striking art and murals in the lobby of this modern hotel. Comfortable, well-appointed guest rooms have soft seating and provide a respite from the casino. 111 units. 4 stories, interior corridors. **Parking:** winter plug-ins. **Terms:** check-in 4 pm, cancellation fee imposed. **Amenities:** safes. **Dining:** 2 restaurants. **Pool(s):** heated indoor. **Activities:** hot tub, exercise room. **Guest Services:** coin laundry. **Featured Amenity:** full hot breakfast.

MOUNTAIN VIEW pop. 80

ROCKY RIDGE COUNTRY LODGE   (403)653-2350
Bed & Breakfast. **Address:** 523 2nd St N T0K 1N0

NISKU
• Part of Edmonton area — see map p. 85

FOUR POINTS BY SHERATON EDMONTON INTERNATIONAL AIRPORT   (780)770-9099

Hotel
$99-$149

AAA Benefit: Members save up to 15%, plus Starwood Preferred Guest® benefits!

Address: 403 11th Ave T9E 7N2 **Location:** Hwy 2 exit Edmonton International Airport/Nisku Business Park (10th Ave), 0.5 mi (0.9 km) e. **Facility:** 112 units. 4 stories, interior corridors. **Parking:** winter plug-ins. **Terms:** cancellation fee imposed. **Amenities:** safes. **Pool(s):** heated indoor. **Activities:** hot tub, exercise room. **Guest Services:** valet and coin laundry.

HOLIDAY INN AND SUITES EDMONTON AIRPORT AND CONFERENCE CENTER   (780)979-0839

Hotel
$109-$230

Address: 1100 4th St T9E 8E2 **Location:** Hwy 2 exit Edmonton International Airport/Nisku Business Park (10th Ave), 0.5 mi (0.9 km) e. **Facility:** 97 units. 5 stories, interior corridors. **Bath:** shower only. **Parking:** winter plug-ins. **Terms:** cancellation fee imposed. **Dining:** Eclipse Restaurant & Lounge, see separate listing. **Pool(s):** heated indoor. **Activities:** hot tub, exercise room. **Guest Services:** valet and coin laundry.

Use travel time to share driving tips and rules of the road with your teens

HOLIDAY INN EXPRESS & SUITES EDMONTON INT'L AIRPORT   (780)955-1000

Hotel
$104-$229

Address: 1102 4th St T9E 8E2 **Location:** Hwy 2 exit Edmonton International Airport/Nisku Business Park (10th Ave), 0.5 mi (0.9 km) e. **Facility:** 120 units. 4 stories, interior corridors. **Parking:** winter plug-ins. **Terms:** cancellation fee imposed. **Pool(s):** heated indoor. **Activities:** hot tub, exercise room. **Guest Services:** valet and coin laundry. **Featured Amenity:** breakfast buffet.

QUALITY INN & SUITES-AIRPORT   (780)955-3001
Hotel. **Address:** 501 11th Ave T9E 7N5

RENAISSANCE EDMONTON AIRPORT HOTEL   (780)488-7159

Hotel
$121-$224

R
RENAISSANCE®
HOTELS

AAA Benefit: Members save 5% or more!

Address: 4236 36th St E Edmonton International Airport T9E 0A4 **Location:** Connected to Edmonton International Airport. **Facility:** With soundproof windows and upscale décor, it is easy to forget the airport is just a short walk from the lobby. There is sleek, custom furniture and unique artwork in the public areas and rooms. 213 units. 2-8 stories, interior corridors. **Parking:** on-site (fee), winter plug-ins. **Terms:** check-in 4 pm. **Amenities:** safes. **Pool(s):** heated indoor. **Activities:** sauna, hot tub, exercise room. **Guest Services:** valet laundry, area transportation.

WHERE TO EAT

ECLIPSE RESTAURANT & LOUNGE   780/770-9131
American. Casual Dining. **Address:** 1100 4th St T9E 8E2

OKOTOKS (I-6) pop. 24,511, elev. 1,036m/3,400'
• Part of Calgary area — see map p. 42

Incorporated in 1904, Okotoks thrived on brick making, lumber and oil distribution in its early days. Today Okotoks is a commuter community of Calgary. The town gets its name from the Blackfoot name *okatoks,* meaning "rocks." Big Rock, 7 kilometres (4 mi.) west, is the continent's largest known glacial boulder, having been carried here during an ice age.

A popular recreational retreat, Okotoks offers such leisure pursuits as fishing and hiking. Events include Spirit of Okotoks Children's Festival, held in mid-June in conjunction with the Spirit of Okotoks Parade, as well as the Okotoks Pro Rodeo on Labour Day weekend.

Okotoks Visitor Information Centre: 53 N. Railway St., Okotoks, AB, Canada T1S 1K1. **Phone:** (403) 938-3204.

Self-guiding tours: Heritage Walking Tour brochures are available from the visitor information center.

BEST WESTERN PLUS OKOTOKS INN & SUITES
(403)995-6262

Hotel
$149-$194

Best Western PLUS. **AAA Benefit:** Save 10% or more every day and earn 10% bonus points!

Address: 100 Southbank Rd T1S 0N3 **Location:** Hwy 2 exit 209 (Hwy 7), 2.7 mi (4.5 km) w. **Facility:** 82 two-bedroom units, some efficiencies. 4 stories, interior corridors. **Parking:** winter plug-ins. **Amenities:** safes. **Pool(s):** indoor. **Activities:** hot tub, exercise room. **Guest Services:** coin laundry. **Featured Amenity: full hot breakfast.**

OLDS pop. 8,235

BEST WESTERN OF OLDS
(403)556-5900

Hotel
$113-$179

Best Western. **AAA Benefit:** Save 10% or more every day and earn 10% bonus points!

Address: 4520 46th St T4H 1P7 **Location:** Hwy 2 exit 340B (Hwy 27), 3 mi (5 km) w. **Facility:** 41 units. 2 stories (no elevator), interior corridors. **Parking:** winter plug-ins. **Pool(s):** heated indoor. **Activities:** hot tub, exercise room. **Guest Services:** complimentary laundry. **Featured Amenity: full hot breakfast.**

POMEROY INN & SUITES AT OLDS COLLEGE   403/556-8815
Extended Stay Hotel. **Address:** 4601 46 Ave T4H 1P5

RAMADA OLDS   (403)507-8349
Hotel. **Address:** 500 6700 46th St T4H 0A2

PATRICIA (I-8) pop. 108

DINOSAUR PROVINCIAL PARK is 13 km (8 mi.) n.e. via Hwy. 210, following signs. The park, declared a UNESCO World Heritage Site in 1979, covers 81 square kilometres (31 sq. mi.) of badlands and prairie along the Red Deer River. One of the richest Cretaceous Period fossil sites in the world, it contains the remains of 49 species of dinosaurs from 75 million years ago as well as crocodile, fish, flying reptile, small mammal and turtle fossils.

Five self-guiding trails explore three habitats: prairie grassland, badlands and riverside. Each offers opportunities for bird-watching. A variety of interpretive programs, bus tours and guided hikes are offered May to mid-October. Outdoor fossil displays and self-guiding walking trails are available year-round. *See Recreation Areas Chart.*

Time: Allow a full day. **Hours:** Grounds daily 24 hours. Visitor center Sun.-Thurs. 9-5, Fri.-Sat. 9-7, mid-May through Sept. 1; daily 9-4, late Mar. to mid-May and early Sept. to mid-Oct., Mon.-Fri. 9-4, rest of year. **Cost:** Park free. Visitor center exhibit gallery $5.71; $4.76 (ages 65+); $2.86 (ages 7-17); $14.29 (family). Prices for interpretive programs and other programs vary; phone ahead. **Phone:** (403) 378-4344 for guided hike and tour information, or (877) 537-2757 for camping reservations.

Dinosaur Provincial Park Visitor Centre and Field Station, 13 km (8 mi.) n.e. via Hwy. 210, contains dinosaur skeletons and an 80-seat theater. Interpretive displays depict the park's geological and paleontological resources and cultural history as well as the flora and fauna of the badlands and the prairie environment. **Hours:** Sun.-Thurs. 9-5, Fri.-Sat. 9-7, mid-May through Sept. 1; daily 9-4, late Mar. to mid-May and early Sept. to mid-Oct., Mon.-Fri. 9-4, rest of year. Phone ahead to confirm schedule. **Cost:** Exhibit gallery $5.71; $4.76 (ages 65+); $2.86 (ages 7-17); $14.29 (family). **Phone:** (403) 378-4342.

PEACE RIVER (A-3) pop. 6,744
• Hotels p. 140 • Restaurants p. 140

Formed by the confluence of the Smoky and Heart rivers, the Peace River flows north and east of the town of the same name to Lake Athabasca and to the west into British Columbia. The area was known as "The Forks" by trappers and traders in the 1700s and "Sagitawa" (meeting of the waters) by the Cree Indians. On his historic trek across the northern continent, Alexander Mackenzie explored the region and built a fort and wintered here 1792-93.

A wooden statue honors prospector and local legend Henry Fuller "Twelve-Foot" Davis. The Vermont native, known for his generosity and hospitality, achieved great social stature when he mined $15,000 worth of gold from a 3.5-metre (12-ft.) plot between two gold claims. Davis said on his deathbed that he was not afraid to die because "I never kilt nobody, I never stole from nobody and I kept open house for travelers all my life." His grave overlooks the confluence of the Peace, Heart and Smoky rivers.

Nearby forests, rivers and streams make Peace River a popular center for year-round recreation in northern Alberta. Golfing, swimming, canoeing, downhill skiing and dog sledding are all options.

Peace River and District Chamber of Commerce: 9309 100th St., P.O. Box 6599, Peace River, AB, Canada T8S 1S4. **Phone:** (780) 624-4166.

BEST WESTERN PLUS PEACE RIVER HOTEL & SUITES
(780)617-7600

Hotel
$115-$169

Best Western PLUS AAA Benefit: Save 10% or more every day and earn 10% bonus points!

Address: 8016 99th Ave T8S 1R2 **Location:** Hwy 2 (Queen Elizabeth II), w of town center, just n. **Facility:** 98 units, some efficiencies. 4 stories, interior corridors. **Activities:** sauna, hot tub, exercise room. **Guest Services:** coin laundry. **Featured Amenity:** breakfast buffet.

WHERE TO EAT

MR MIKES STEAKHOUSECASUAL   780/624-8803
American. Casual Dining. **Address:** 8006 99 Ave T8S 0A4

PINCHER CREEK (K-6) pop. 3,685

Pincher Creek was established in 1878 by the North West Mounted Police as a horse farm to provide remounts for Fort Macleod *(see place listing p. 114)*. The town was named for a pair of pincers that presumably were left behind by prospectors. After hearing that the area had ample grassland, other settlers soon arrived.

Pincher Creek Visitor Information Centre: 1037 Bev McLachlin Dr., Pincher Creek, AB, Canada T0K 1W0. **Phone:** (403) 627-3684.

HERITAGE INN & HOTEL CONVENTION CENTRE PINCHER CREEK   (403)627-5000
Hotel. **Address:** 919 Waterton Ave (Hwy 6) T0K 1W0

RAMADA INN & SUITES   (403)627-3777
Hotel. **Address:** 1132 Table Mountain St T0K 1W0

WHERE TO EAT

HARVEST COFFEEHOUSE   403/904-4000
Coffee/Tea. Quick Serve. **Address:** 766 Main St T0K 1W0

RED DEER (G-6) pop. 90,564, elev. 905m/2,969'
• Restaurants p. 142

Red Deer's name comes from the Cree Indian word *waskasoo,* meaning "elk." Early Scottish settlers mistook the native elk for the red deer of their homeland and the name stuck. A creek and park running through Red Deer still bear the name Waskasoo.

The original settlement was several kilometres upstream on the Red Deer River where the water was shallow and easy to cross. Dr. Leonard Gaetz, a Methodist minister who arrived in 1884, persuaded the Calgary and Edmonton Railway to cross the river on his property by donating half of his land for use as a townsite. The trains came through, and the

town took root at its current site. Agriculture and petroleum products are the major local industries.

City Hall Park, 48th Avenue and Ross Street, is a landscaped oasis known for its Christmas light and flower displays. West of town is Sylvan Lake, which accommodates Jarvis Bay and Sylvan Lake provincial parks *(see Recreation Areas Chart).*

Red Deer Visitor Information Centre: 101-4200 Queen Elizabeth II Hwy. (Hwy. 2), Red Deer, AB, Canada T4N 1E3. **Phone:** (403) 346-0180.

Self-guiding tours: A brochure outlining a walking tour of the historic downtown is available from the Red Deer Museum + Art Gallery and from the visitor information center west of Heritage Ranch in Waskasoo Park *(see attraction listings).*

Shopping: Bower Place, Gaetz Avenue and Molly Banister Drive, has 115 stores and is anchored by Hudson's Bay and Sears. Parkland Mall, 67th Street and Gaetz Avenue, has more than 100 shops.

ALBERTA SPORTS HALL OF FAME & MUSEUM is n. of 32nd St. by Heritage Ranch at 102-4200 Queen Elizabeth II Hwy. (Hwy. 2). Alberta's sports history and heroes are celebrated through the display of 12,000 artifacts, archival material and interactive exhibits. Visitors can play an Alpine ski racer game in the Ice and Snow—the Spirit of Winter gallery or try out five different sports via a virtual computer system. Also on-site are a climbing wall and a putting green.

Time: Allow 1 hour, 30 minutes minimum. **Hours:** Mon.-Fri. 9-5, Sat.-Sun. and Mon. holidays 10-5. Closed Jan. 1, Good Friday, Easter, Christmas and day after Christmas. **Cost:** $5; $3 (ages 4-17); $12 (family, two adults and children). **Phone:** (403) 341-8614.

BAYMONT INN & SUITES AND CONFERENCE CENTER
(403)346-8841
Hotel. **Address:** 4311 49th Ave T4N 5Y7

BEST WESTERN PLUS RED DEER INN & SUITES
(403)346-3555

Hotel
$120-$186

Best Western PLUS AAA Benefit: Save 10% or more every day and earn 10% bonus points!

Address: 6839 66th St T4P 3T5 **Location:** Hwy 2 exit 401 (67th St), just e. **Facility:** 92 units. 4 stories, interior corridors. **Parking:** winter plug-ins. **Terms:** check-in 4 pm. **Amenities:** *Some:* safes. **Pool(s):** heated indoor. **Activities:** hot tub, exercise room. **Guest Services:** valet and coin laundry. **Featured Amenity:** full hot breakfast.

COMFORT INN & SUITES   (403)348-0025
Hotel. **Address:** 6846 66th St T4P 3T5

DAYS INN RED DEER   (403)340-3297
 Hotel. **Address:** 1000 5001 19th St T4R 3R1

HAMPTON INN & SUITES BY HILTON RED DEER
                                                     (403)346-6688
Hotel. **Address:** 128 Leva   **AAA Benefit:**
Ave T4N 5E2   Members save up to
                                     10%!

HOLIDAY INN EXPRESS RED DEER   (403)343-2112
Hotel. **Address:** 2803 50th Ave T4R 1H1

HOLIDAY INN HOTEL & SUITES RED DEER SOUTH
                                                     (403)348-8485
Hotel. **Address:** 33 Petrolia Dr T4E 1B3

MICROTEL INN & SUITES BY WYNDHAM RED DEER
                                                     (403)967-0320
                  Address: 126 Leva Ave T4E 1B9 **Loca-**
Hotel   **tion:** Hwy 2 exit 391 (Gasoline Alley),
$107-$175   just w. **Facility:** 100 units, some efficien-
                                       cies. 4 stories, interior corridors.
                                       Parking: winter plug-ins. **Pool(s):**
                                       heated indoor. **Activities:** hot tub, exer-
                                       cise room. **Guest Services:** valet and
                                       coin laundry. **Featured Amenity:** conti-
                                       nental breakfast.

MOTEL 6 RED DEER   403/340-1749
Hotel. **Address:** 900-5001 19th St T4R 3R1

QUALITY INN & CONFERENCE CENTRE (403)343-8800
Hotel   **Address:** 7150 50th Ave T4N 6A5 **Lo-**
$108-$179   **cation:** Hwy 2 exit 401 (67th St), 1.7 mi
                                       (2.9 km) e, then 0.5 mi (0.8 km) n. **Fa-**
                                       cility: 114 units. 3 stories, interior corri-
                                       dors. **Parking:** winter plug-ins. **Dining:**
                                       nightclub. **Pool(s):** indoor. **Activities:**
                                       hot tub. **Guest Services:** valet and coin
                                       laundry. **Featured Amenity:** full hot
                                       breakfast.

RADISSON RED DEER   (403)342-6567
Hotel   **Address:** 6500 67th St T4P 1A2 **Lo-**
$109-$169   **cation:** Hwy 2 exit 401 (67th St), 0.5
                                       mi (0.8 km) e. **Facility:** 142 units. 4
                                       stories, interior corridors. **Parking:**
                                       winter plug-ins. **Terms:** cancellation
                                       fee imposed. **Amenities:** safes.
                                       Some: video games. **Pool(s):** heated
                                       indoor. **Activities:** sauna, hot tub,
                                       steamroom. **Guest Services:** valet
                                       and coin laundry. **Featured Amenity:**
                                       breakfast buffet. *(See ad this
                                       page.)*

RAMADA RED DEER HOTEL & SUITES   403/342-4445
Hotel   **Address:** 6853 66th St T4P 3T5 **Loca-**
$118-$145   **tion:** Hwy 2 exit 401 (67th St), just e. **Fa-**
                                       cility: 90 units. 2-4 stories, interior
                                       corridors. **Parking:** winter plug-ins.
                                       Pool(s): heated indoor. **Activities:** hot
                                       tub, exercise room. **Guest Services:**
                                       valet and coin laundry. **Featured Ame-**
                                       nity: full hot breakfast.

SANDMAN HOTEL RED DEER   (403)343-7400
Hotel. **Address:** 2818 Gaetz Ave T4R 1M4

SHERATON RED DEER HOTEL   (403)346-2091

Hotel
$149-$299

Sheraton

AAA Benefit: Members save up to 15%, plus Starwood Preferred Guest® benefits!

Address: 3310 50th Ave T4N 3X9 **Location:** 1.3 mi (2 km) n on Hwy 2A (Gaetz Ave). **Facility:** 241 units, some two bedrooms. 2-14 stories, interior corridors. **Parking:** winter plug-ins. **Terms:** cancellation fee imposed. **Amenities:** Some: safes. **Dining:** 2 restaurants, nightclub. **Pool(s):** indoor. **Activities:** sauna, steamroom, exercise room. **Guest Services:** valet laundry.

SUPER 8 CITY CENTRE   (403)358-7722
WW Hotel. **Address:** 4217 50th Ave T4N 3Z4

TOWNEPLACE SUITES BY MARRIOTT RED DEER
(403)341-3589

Extended Stay Hotel
$97-$161

TOWNEPLACE — SUITES — MARRIOTT

AAA Benefit: Members save 5% or more!

Address: 6822 66th St T4P 3T5 **Location:** Hwy 2 exit 401 (67th St), just e. **Facility:** 92 units, some two bedrooms, efficiencies and kitchens. 4 stories, interior corridors. **Parking:** winter plug-ins. **Terms:** check-in 4 pm. **Amenities:** safes. **Pool(s):** heated indoor. **Activities:** hot tub, picnic facilities, exercise room. **Guest Services:** valet and coin laundry. **Featured Amenity:** breakfast buffet.

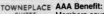

WHERE TO EAT

BOULEVARD RESTAURANT + LOUNGE   403/314-2583
WW International. Casual Dining. **Address:** 33 Petrolia Dr T4E 1B3

EARLS KITCHEN + BAR   403/342-4055
WW American. Casual Dining. **Address:** 2111 Gaetz Ave T4R 1Z4

FAMOSO NEAPOLITAN PIZZERIA   587/273-3744
WW Pizza. Casual Dining. **Address:** 5016 51 Ave, Bld B T4N 4H5

FUSION CAFE   403/348-5268
WW Asian. Casual Dining. **Address:** 6842 50th Ave, Unit 6 T4N 4E3

INDIA FEAST   403/346-9300
WW Indian. Casual Dining. **Address:** 3235D 50th Ave T4N 3Y1

LA CASA PERGOLA   403/342-2404
WW Italian. Casual Dining. **Address:** 4909 48th St T4N 1S8

MOXIE'S CLASSIC GRILL   403/340-0111
WW American. Casual Dining. **Address:** 2828 Gaetz Ave T4R 1M4

MR MIKES STEAKHOUSECASUAL   403/356-0056
WW American. Casual Dining. **Address:** 6701 Gaetz Ave T4N 4C9

ORIGINAL JOE'S   403/343-6793
WW American. Gastropub. **Address:** 4720 51st St T4N 4H1

QUEEN'S DINER   403/340-3302
W Comfort Food. Casual Dining. **Address:** 34 Burnt Basin St T4P 0J2

REDSTONE GRILL   403/342-4980
WWW New American. Fine Dining. **Address:** 5018 45th St T4N 1K9

THE RUSTY PELICAN   403/347-1414
WW International. Casual Dining. **Address:** 2079 50th Ave T4R 1Z4

SHISO JAPANESE RESTAURANT   403/341-5502
WW Japanese. Casual Dining. **Address:** 3731 50th Ave T4N 3Y7

TANDOOR 'N' FLAME   403/347-7600
WW Indian Vegetarian. Casual Dining. **Address:** 4807 50th Ave T4N 4A5

REDWATER   pop. 1,915

BEST WESTERN PLUS REDWATER INN & SUITES
(780)580-6201

Hotel
$115-$150

Best Western PLUS

AAA Benefit: Save 10% or more every day and earn 10% bonus points!

Address: 4710 58th St T0A 2W0 **Location:** Hwy 38, west of town center. **Facility:** 89 units, some efficiencies. 3 stories, interior corridors. **Parking:** winter plug-ins. **Amenities:** safes. **Pool(s):** heated indoor. **Activities:** hot tub, steamroom, exercise room. **Guest Services:** coin laundry.

RIMBEY   pop. 2,378

BEST WESTERN RIMSTONE RIDGE HOTEL
(403)843-2999

Hotel
$126-$225

AAA Benefit: Save 10% or more every day and earn 10% bonus points!

Address: 5501 50th Ave T0C 2J0 **Location:** Jct Hwy 20 and 20A (50th Ave), 1.2 mi (2 km) w; west end of town. **Facility:** 60 units, some efficiencies. 3 stories, interior corridors. **Parking:** winter plug-ins. **Pool(s):** heated indoor. **Activities:** hot tub, exercise room. **Guest Services:** coin laundry. **Featured Amenity:** full hot breakfast.

BW Best Western.

This Hotel goes above & beyond expectations. Offering free hot breakfast, pool, hot tub & waterslide.

ROCKY MOUNTAIN HOUSE pop. 6,933

BEST WESTERN ROCKY MOUNTAIN HOUSE INN & SUITES   (403)844-3100

Hotel
$139-$169

Best Western

AAA Benefit: Save 10% or more every day and earn 10% bonus points!

Address: 4407 41st Ave T4T 1A5 **Location:** Hwy 11 and 22, just w on 42nd Ave, just s; east end of town. **Facility:** 81 units. 4 stories, interior corridors. **Parking:** winter plug-ins. **Pool(s):** heated indoor. **Activities:** hot tub, exercise room. **Guest Services:** valet and coin laundry. **Featured Amenity:** full hot breakfast.

[SAVE] [ECO] [📶] CALL [📞] [🚗] [BIZ]

[HS] [📶] [📱] [📺] [📋] /SOME UNITS [🚽]

ROCKY MOUNTAIN HOUSE CANALTA   403/846-0088
Hotel. **Address:** 4406 41st Ave T4T 1J6

WHERE TO EAT

CUCINA   403/844-2173
International. Casual Dining. **Address:** 5207 48th St T4T 0B1

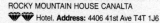

ROCKY MOUNTAIN HOUSE NATIONAL HISTORIC SITE (G-5)

In west central Alberta about 80 kilometres (50 mi.) west of Red Deer on Hwy. 11 and 6 kilometres (4 mi.) west from the town of Rocky Mountain House via Hwy. 11A, following signs, Rocky Mountain House National Historic Site tells the story of the fur trade era that existed 1799-1875. The site, on the banks of the North Saskatchewan River, protects the remains of four fur-trading posts.

Both the North West Co. and Hudson's Bay Co. were expanding in an attempt to reach the area's native peoples. The two rivals arrived here within a week of each other in 1799, their goal being to stimulate trade with the Kootenai, who were on the western side of the Rocky Mountains. The Blackfoot people blocked the planned trade. Rocky Mountain House traded with eight different aboriginal groups in its 76 years of operation.

Well-known cartographer and fur trader David Thompson used Rocky Mountain House for a time as a base for exploring routes over the mountains. Thompson was the first person of European descent to cross Howse Pass, accomplishing this feat in 1807.

Trade competition remained intense between the two companies until their merger in 1821. The influx of illegal whiskey traders into southern Alberta in 1869 disrupted trade with the aboriginal people, and in 1875 the last of the four posts was abandoned.

Two walking trails along the North Saskatchewan River and through a scenic wooded area connect the remains of the four forts. Eight listening stations and illustrated interpretive panels are spaced along the trail system. A 30-minute walk leads past the two later forts, the reconstructed chimneys at the last

fort site, a replica flat-bottom York boat, a Red River cart and a fur press. A longer 90-minute walk travels to the first two forts built at Rocky Mountain House, passing tepees, the 1967 Centennial Canoe Race exhibit and a buffalo viewing area. Visitors often can see deer, coyotes, bluebirds and hawks along the trails.

The visitor center contains exhibits of trade items and aboriginal objects and a theater presenting films. Interpretive programs and special events are offered in summer; phone ahead for current schedule.

The visitor center is open daily 10-5, mid-May to early Sept.; Thurs.-Sun. 10-5, early Sept. to Sept. 30. Admission is free in 2017 to celebrate Canada's 150th anniversary of Confederation, otherwise $3.71; $3.24 (ages 65+); $1.81 (ages 6-16); $9.33 (family, up to seven people including two adults).

ROSEBUD (H-7) pop. 88

A pioneer ranching settlement founded in the 1880s, Rosebud has become a thriving cultural center. The community participates in the activities of Rosebud School of the Arts. Rosebud Theatre offers dinner and theater entertainment. Evening shows and matinees are offered; phone (403) 677-2350 or (800) 267-7553 for the performance schedule and ticket information.

Among Rosebud's historical buildings is an early 20th-century Chinese laundry, which now is home to Centennial Museum. The museum displays local memorabilia and an array of western Canadiana. Works by Alberta artists are exhibited in Akokiniskway Art Gallery and other shops along the town's self-guiding historical walking tour.

ST. ALBERT (E-6) pop. 61,466
• Hotels p. 144 • Restaurants p. 144
• Hotels & Restaurants map & index p. 100
• Part of Edmonton area — see map p. 85

Alberta's oldest non-fortified community, St. Albert was established in 1861. The city is the site of the first cathedral west of Winnipeg. Its founder—Father Albert Lacombe—devoted 62 years to acting as a peacemaker between the Cree and the Blackfoot and as a negotiator between the Blood Tribe and the Canadian Pacific Railway.

St. Albert lays claim to western Canada's largest outdoor farmers market, which operates every Saturday mid-June to early October, as well as a vibrant arts community. The town also boasts both natural and man-made outdoor features, including Big Lake, just west of Ray Gibbon Drive, and the Woodlands Water Play Park, a small interactive water playground at 165 Sturgeon Rd.

The St. Albert Kinsmen Rainmaker Rodeo & Exhibition takes place the fourth weekend in May. The International Children's Festival—a showcase for performers in theater, music, dance, storytelling and

(See map & index p. 100.)

puppetry—is traditionally held the weekend after the rodeo.

St. Albert Visitor Welcome Centre: 71 St. Albert Tr., St. Albert, AB, Canada T8N 6L5. **Phone:** (780) 459-2797.

BEST WESTERN PLUS THE INN AT ST. ALBERT
(780)470-3800

Hotel
$140-$180

 Best Western PLUS AAA Benefit: Save 10% or more every day and earn 10% bonus points!

Address: 460 St. Albert Tr T8N 5J9 **Location:** Hwy 2 (St. Albert Tr), just w at Lennox Dr. **Facility:** 90 units. 4 stories, interior corridors. **Parking:** winter plug-ins. **Terms:** check-in 4 pm, cancellation fee imposed. **Pool(s):** heated indoor. **Activities:** hot tub, exercise room. **Guest Services:** valet and coin laundry. **Featured Amenity:** full hot breakfast.

WHERE TO EAT

BLUE RARE STEAK & BAR   780/460-2233 **35**
Steak Seafood. Casual Dining. **Address:** 24 Perron St T8N 1E7

RIVER HOUSE   780/458-2232 **34**
Regional Canadian. Casual Dining. **Address:** 8 Mission Ave T8N 1H4

ST. PAUL pop. 5,400

CANALTA HOTEL   (780)645-5581
Hotel. **Address:** 5008 43rd St T0A 3A2

Explore
BIG Savings
Around the Globe

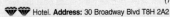

SHERWOOD PARK (E-6) pop. 65,475, elev. 764m/2,509'
• Part of Edmonton area — see map p. 85

Sherwood Park is located just outside the eastern boundary of Edmonton. Though designated a hamlet, it is Alberta's seventh-largest municipality. Primarily residential, Sherwood Park offers typical suburban amenities such as restaurants, shops, and fitness and recreation facilities. At the heart of the community is Centre in the Park, a multiuse recreational area featuring a scenic walkway. The path links a central plaza area with Festival Place, a performing arts venue at 100 Festival Way, and Sherwood Park's Heritage Trail System. Phone (780) 449-3378 for the Festival Place box office.

BEST WESTERN PLUS SHERWOOD PARK INN & SUITES
(780)416-7800

Hotel
$140-$180

Best Western PLUS AAA Benefit: Save 10% or more every day and earn 10% bonus points!

Address: 300 Lakeland Dr T8H 0N6 **Location:** Hwy 16 exit 400B westbound; exit 400C (Broadmoor Blvd) eastbound, 0.9 mi (1.5 km) s, then just e. **Facility:** 90 units. 4 stories, interior corridors. **Parking:** winter plug-ins. **Terms:** check-in 4 pm, cancellation fee imposed. **Pool(s):** heated indoor. **Activities:** hot tub, exercise room. **Guest Services:** valet and coin laundry.

DAYS INN & SUITES SHERWOOD PARK   (780)570-8080

Extended Stay Hotel
$125-$145

Address: 201 Palisades Way T8H 0N3 **Location:** Hwy 16 exit 403 (Sherwood Dr), 0.9 mi (1.5 km) s. **Facility:** 118 efficiencies. 4 stories, interior corridors. **Parking:** winter plug-ins. **Activities:** exercise room. **Guest Services:** valet and coin laundry, area transportation. **Featured Amenity:** continental breakfast.

HAMPTON INN BY HILTON   (780)449-1609
Hotel. **Address:** 950 Emerald Dr T8H 0N3

AAA Benefit: Members save up to 10%!

HOLIDAY INN EXPRESS & SUITES   780/417-3388
Hotel. **Address:** 11 Portage Ln T8H 2R7

HOLIDAY INN SHERWOOD PARK - CONFERENCE CENTRE
780/464-4900
Hotel. **Address:** 2100 Premier Way T8H 2G4

RAMADA-EDMONTON EAST/SHERWOOD PARK
(780)467-6727
Hotel. **Address:** 30 Broadway Blvd T8H 2A2

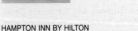

SUPER 8 SHERWOOD PARK/EDMONTON AREA
(780)464-1000

Hotel
$120-$129

Address: 26 Strathmoor Dr T8H 2B6 **Location:** Hwy 16 exit Broadmoor Blvd, just sw. Next to truck stop. **Facility:** 120 units. 2 stories, interior corridors. **Parking:** winter plug-ins. **Dining:** 2 restaurants. **Activities:** exercise room. **Guest Services:** coin laundry. **Featured Amenity:** full hot breakfast.

CAFE HAVEN   780/417-5523
Coffee/Tea. Quick Serve. **Address:** 9 Sioux Rd T8A 4C7

JOEY RESTAURANTS   780/449-1161
American. Casual Dining. **Address:** 250-222 Baseline Rd T8H 1S8

THE SOUP & SANDWICH CO.   780/467-8530
Soup Sandwiches. Quick Serve. **Address:** 2833 Broadmoor Blvd, Unit 144 T8H 2H3

SUMO SUMO SUSHI BAR & GRILL   780/416-7866
Sushi. Casual Dining. **Address:** 220 Lakeland Dr, #300 T8H 0N6

VICKY'S BISTRO WINE BAR   780/417-1750
International. Casual Dining. **Address:** 100 501 Festival Ave T8A 4X3

SLAVE LAKE (C-5) pop. 6,782

Slave Lake is on the southeast shore of Lesser Slave Lake, the second-largest lake in Alberta. Popular with bird-watchers and recreationalists, the expansive body of water is easily accessible by automobile. Six kilometres (4 mi.) north on Hwy. 88, Lesser Slave Lake Provincial Park *(see Recreation Areas Chart)* hugs the lake's east shore and provides snowshoeing and cross-country skiing opportunities in winter as well as camping and hiking during the summer. The park also is home to the Lesser Slave Lake Bird Observatory and the Boreal Centre for Bird Conservation. Riverboat Daze takes place in early July. Sand sculptors compete during the Sand Blast Competition, held the third weekend in July.

In 2011 a devastating fire that originated in a nearby forest ravaged the Slave Lake community, necessitating the complete evacuation of the town. At the time, the displacement of nearly 7,000 residents was reported to be the largest in Alberta's history. Although about a third of Slave Lake was destroyed in the fire—which gutted the town hall, library and radio station—the community has since made what is considered to be a remarkable recovery and has rebuilt most of what was lost.

HOLIDAY INN EXPRESS   (780)849-4819
Hotel. **Address:** 1551 Main St SE T0G 2A0

LAKEVIEW INNS & SUITES   (780)849-9500
Hotel. **Address:** 1550 Holmes Tr SE T0G 2A3 *(See ad opposite inside front cover.)*

MR MIKES STEAKHOUSECASUAL   780/849-6452
American. Casual Dining. **Address:** 1500 Holmes Tr T0G 2A0

TAO RESTAURANT & LOUNGE   780/849-6658
Asian. Casual Dining. **Address:** 109 2nd Ave NW T0G 2A1

SMOKY LAKE (D-7) pop. 1,022

VICTORIA SETTLEMENT PROVINCIAL HISTORIC SITE is 10 km (6 mi.) s. on Hwy. 855 and 6 km (3.6 mi.) e. on Victoria Tr. to 58161 Range Rd. 171A. Settlement began in 1862 as a Methodist mission. A Hudson's Bay Co. fur-trading post soon followed, and by the beginning of the 20th century the village was known as Pakan. Guided tours are offered of the 1906 Methodist Church and the 1864 Clerk's Quarters, which is furnished with pioneer articles. A video presentation describes local history.

Time: Allow 1 hour minimum. **Hours:** Thurs.-Tues. 10-5, May 15-Labour Day. **Cost:** $4.76; $3.81 (ages 65+); $1.90 (ages 7-17); $13.33 (family, two adults and their children). **Phone:** (780) 656-2333. GT

SPRUCE GROVE (E-6) pop. 26,171
• Part of Edmonton area — see map p. 85

Olympic gold medalist Jennifer Heil, a freestyle skier, hails from Spruce Grove, as does Carla MacLeod, a retired member of Canada's national women's hockey team. Located just 35 kilometres (22 mi.) west of downtown Edmonton, the city also attracts athletic day-trippers from the provincial capital with such impressive recreational features as the state-of-the-art TransAlta Tri Leisure Centre, the adjacent Bruce and Jeannette Fuhr Sports Park, and Heritage Grove Park, a network of bicycle paths that connects several neighborhoods.

Other local draws include the Horizon Stage Performing Arts Centre, 1001 Calahoo Rd., (780) 962-8995, and the Spruce Grove Grain Elevator Museum, 120 Railway Ave., home to one of the last wood grain elevators in the province. The museum hosts a farmers market on Saturdays from April through December and also contains the Spruce Grove Archives; phone (780) 960-4600.

TRAVELODGE INN & SUITES SPRUCE GROVE
(780)962-6050
Hotel. **Address:** 20 Westgrove Dr T7X 3X3

STETTLER (G-7) pop. 5,748
• Hotels p. 146

Stettler is named after Carl Stettler, a Swiss immigrant who arrived in Alberta in 1903. He helped establish a Swiss community known as Blumenau not far from present-day Stettler. With the arrival of the railroad, the Stettler settlement was established and the residents of Blumenau relocated there.

ALBERTA PRAIRIE RAILWAY EXCURSIONS depart the train station at 4611 47th Ave. Steam- and diesel-powered rail excursions are offered through the Alberta countryside in vintage passenger coaches. Trips last 5 to 6 hours; all include a buffet-style meal at the destination as well as live on-board entertainment, and may include staged train robberies. Theme trips also are scheduled.

Hours: Trains operate Sat.-Sun. and selected weekdays, May-Oct. Departure times vary. **Cost:** Fares $100-$165; $70-$145 (ages 11-17); $40-$140 (ages 4-10). Prices may vary. Reservations are required. **Phone:** (403) 742-2811, or (800) 282-3994 in Canada. [GT]

RAMADA INN & SUITES   (403)742-6555
♦♦♦ Hotel. **Address:** 6711 49th Ave T0C 2L1

STONY PLAIN (E-6) pop. 15,051
• Part of Edmonton area — see map p. 85

Plentiful water and abundant fish and game attracted the first settlers to the region in 1881. By 1892 the name of the community itself was changed from Dog Creek to Stony Plain. The Stony Plain of today is an agricultural community.

Murals depicting historical remembrances, events and pioneers prominent in the early settlement of Stony Plain have been painted by local artists on 26 buildings in town. Memories of an early 1900s Christmas from a child's point of view are the basis for one mural, while another shows the multiculturalism of the area's early residents. The Heritage Walk Murals can be seen on a walking tour.

Stony Plain Visitor Information Centre: 4815 44th Ave., Stony Plain, AB, Canada T7Z 1V5. **Phone:** (780) 963-4545.

BEST WESTERN SUNRISE INN & SUITES
                                       (780)968-1716

Hotel
$120-$180

 Best Western. **AAA Benefit:** Save 10% or more every day and earn 10% bonus points!

Address: 3101 43rd Ave T7Z 1L1 **Location:** Hwy 16A (Township Rd 530), just s at S Park Dr, just e. **Facility:** 110 units. 4 stories, interior corridors. **Parking:** winter plug-ins. **Terms:** check-in 4 pm, resort fee. **Amenities:** safes. **Pool(s):** heated indoor. **Activities:** hot tub, steamroom, exercise room. **Guest Services:** valet and coin laundry. **Featured Amenity:** continental breakfast.

MOTEL 6 STONY PLAIN   780/968-5123
♦♦ Hotel. **Address:** 66 Boulder Blvd T7Z 1V7

RAMADA INN & SUITES   (780)963-0222
♦♦♦ Hotel. **Address:** 3301 43rd Ave T7Z 1L1

TRAVELODGE STONY PLAIN   (780)963-1161

Hotel
$90-$118

Address: 74 Boulder Blvd T7Z 1V7 **Location:** Hwy 16A exit N 35th St, just n, then just e. **Facility:** 59 units. 3 stories, interior corridors. **Activities:** exercise room. **Guest Services:** coin laundry. **Featured Amenity:** continental breakfast.

 / SOME UNITS

WHERE TO EAT

SAWMILL PRIME RIB AND STEAKHOUSE   780/968-1130
♦♦♦ Steak. Casual Dining. **Address:** 3201 43 Ave T7Z 1L1

STRATHMORE pop. 12,305
• Part of Calgary area — see map p. 42

BEST WESTERN STRATHMORE INN   (403)934-5777

Hotel
$99-$169

BW Best Western. **AAA Benefit:** Save 10% or more every day and earn 10% bonus points!

Address: 550 Hwy 1 T1P 1M6 **Location:** Jct Trans-Canada Hwy 1 and 817; center. **Facility:** 81 units, some two bedrooms. 3 stories (no elevator), interior corridors. **Parking:** winter plug-ins. **Terms:** check-in 4 pm. **Pool(s):** heated indoor. **Activities:** hot tub, exercise room. **Guest Services:** coin laundry.

 / SOME UNITS

DAYS INN & SUITES   (403)934-1134
♦♦♦ Hotel
$140-$170

Address: 400 Ranch Market T1P 0B2 **Location:** Trans-Canada Hwy 1, just n at Lakeside Blvd (Centre St). **Facility:** 102 units. 4 stories, interior corridors. **Parking:** winter plug-ins. **Pool(s):** heated indoor. **Activities:** hot tub, exercise room. **Guest Services:** coin laundry. **Featured Amenity:** continental breakfast.

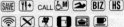 / SOME UNITS

TRAVELODGE STRATHMORE   (403)901-0000
♦♦♦ Hotel. **Address:** 350 Ridge Rd T1P 1B5

WHERE TO EAT

ORIGINAL JOE'S RESTAURANT & BAR   403/934-4715
♦♦ American. Gastropub. **Address:** 100 Ranch Market T1P 1W2

STRATHMORE STATION RESTAURANT & PUB   403/934-0000
♦♦ Comfort Food. Casual Dining. **Address:** 380 Ridge Rd T1P 1B5

SUNDRE pop. 2,610

BEST WESTERN PLUS MOUNTAINVIEW INN & SUITES
(403)638-0002

Hotel
$150-$170

Best Western PLUS

AAA Benefit: Save 10% or more every day and earn 10% bonus points!

Address: 706 Main Ave E T0M 1X0 **Location:** Hwy 22/27, just e of Bergen Rd. **Facility:** 80 units. 3 stories, interior corridors. **Parking:** winter plug-ins. **Pool(s):** heated indoor. **Activities:** hot tub, exercise room. **Guest Services:** coin laundry. **Featured Amenity:** breakfast buffet.

SYLVAN LAKE pop. 12,327

BEST WESTERN PLUS CHATEAU INN SYLVAN LAKE
(403)887-7788

Hotel
$144-$170

Best Western PLUS

AAA Benefit: Save 10% or more every day and earn 10% bonus points!

Address: 5027 Lakeshore Dr T4S 1R3 **Location:** Jct Hwy 11 and 781 (50th St), 1.9 mi (3.1 km) n, just e. **Facility:** 72 units. 4 stories, interior corridors. **Parking:** winter plug-ins. **Terms:** check-in 4 pm. **Pool(s):** heated indoor. **Activities:** hot tub, exercise room. **Guest Services:** coin laundry. **Featured Amenity:** full hot breakfast.

WHERE TO EAT

LOKAL KITCHEN
403/864-9996
International. Casual Dining. **Address:** 4923 33rd St T4S 1A7

TABER pop. 8,104

HERITAGE INN HOTEL & CONVENTION CENTRE TABER
(403)223-4424
Hotel. **Address:** 4830 46th Ave T1G 2A4

THREE HILLS pop. 3,198

BEST WESTERN DIAMOND INN
(403)443-7889

Hotel
$119-$145

Best Western

AAA Benefit: Save 10% or more every day and earn 10% bonus points!

Address: 351 7th Ave N T0M 2A0 **Location:** Jct Hwy 21/27 and 583, 1.1 mi (1.9 km) w. **Facility:** 52 units. 3 stories, interior corridors. **Parking:** winter plug-ins. **Activities:** hot tub, exercise room. **Guest Services:** coin laundry. **Featured Amenity:** continental breakfast.

TROCHU (G-6) pop. 1,072

ST. ANN RANCH TRADING CO. PROVINCIAL HISTORIC SITE is .5 km (.3 mi.) s. to 331062A Range Rd. 234 (King George Ave.). This reconstructed 1905 French settlement contains restored historic houses and reproductions of period buildings. The site has seven buildings, including a small school, post office, hospital and chapel.

An interpretive center contains displays recounting the history of the settlement, which was founded by aristocratic officers from the French cavalry. **Time:** Allow 30 minutes minimum. **Hours:** Museum and interpretive center open daily 9-9. **Cost:** $1.90. **Phone:** (403) 442-3924, or (888) 442-3924 in Canada.

TWIN BUTTE pop. 10

TWIN BUTTE COUNTRY GENERAL STORE
403/627-4035
Mexican. Casual Dining. **Address:** Hwy 6 T0K 2J0

VALLEYVIEW pop. 1,761
• Hotels p. 104 • Restaurants p. 105

WESTERN VALLEY INN
(780)524-4000

Motel
$120-$180

Address: 5402 Highway St T0H 3N0 **Location:** Just w of jct Hwy 43 and 49. **Facility:** 50 units, some efficiencies. 2 stories (no elevator), exterior corridors. **Parking:** winter plug-ins. **Terms:** cancellation fee imposed. **Activities:** exercise room. **Guest Services:** coin laundry. **Featured Amenity:** full hot breakfast.

VEGREVILLE (E-7) pop. 5,717

The center of eastern Alberta's Ukrainian culture, Vegreville has the distinction of possessing the largest known pysanka, or Easter egg, in the world. The 9.4-metre-high (31-ft.) egg, decorated to reflect Ukrainian folk art, was erected in 1975 for the centennial of the formation of the Royal Canadian Mounted Police in Alberta.

The egg's bronze, gold and silver design, made from more than 3,500 pieces of aluminum, illustrates the local settlers' struggles and the protection the mounted police provided them. Queen Elizabeth and Prince Phillip unveiled the plaque next to the giant egg in Elks/Kinsmen Park during their visit in 1978. The Ukrainian Pysanka Festival is held in early July.

Vegreville Tourist Information Centre: 4500 Pysanka Ave., P.O. Box 640, Vegreville, AB, Canada T9C 1K8. **Phone:** (780) 632-6800.

HOTELLO BY POMEROY
780/632-2878
Hotel. **Address:** 6529 Hwy 16A W T9C 0A3

VEGREVILLE POMEROY INN & SUITES
780/632-2094
Hotel. **Address:** 6359 Hwy 16A W T9C 0A3

WAINWRIGHT pop. 5,925

BEST WESTERN WAINWRIGHT INN & SUITES
(780)845-9934

Hotel
$160-$180

 Best Western. AAA Benefit: Save 10% or more every day and earn 10% bonus points!

Address: 1209 27th St T9W 0A2 **Location:** Jct Hwy 14 and 41, just e. **Facility:** 85 units. 4 stories, interior corridors. **Parking:** winter plug-ins. **Terms:** check-in 4 pm, cancellation fee imposed. **Pool(s):** heated indoor. **Activities:** hot tub, exercise room. **Guest Services:** coin laundry.

RAMADA WAINWRIGHT
(780)842-5010
▼▼▼▼ Hotel. **Address:** 1510 27th St T9W 0A4

WHERE TO EAT

THE HONEY POT EATERY & PUB
780/842-4094
▼▼ American. Casual Dining. **Address:** 823 2nd Ave T9W 1C5

WARNER (K-7) pop. 331, elev. 1,017m/3,336'

DEVIL'S COULEE DINOSAUR & HERITAGE MUSEUM is in the County of Warner Administration Building w. off Hwy. 4, following signs to 300 County Rd. Embryonic fossils in their nests were found on the Milk River Ridge in 1987. The specimens were from a hadrosaur (a duck-billed dinosaur); the location was the first nesting site found in Canada. A 2-hour walking tour allows for first-hand inspection of the dinosaur egg site, where ongoing excavations often yield new scientific discoveries. Museum displays feature a hadrosaur nest, embryo, fossils and models of dinosaurs. Also included are hands-on activities for all ages and an exhibit about early area settlement.

Note: The guided hikes are organized at the museum, but visitors must drive their own private vehicles to the dig site. The nesting site is in a primitive area not suitable for small children or those with mobility or medical problems. Allow 30 minutes minimum for the museum, 3 hours minimum for tour and museum.

Hours: Museum Tues.-Sat. and holiday Mon. 9-5, Victoria Day-Labour Day. Tours of the nesting site are given Tues.-Sat. at 10 and 1, July-Sept.; Fri.-Sat. at 10 and 1, May-June (weather permitting). Phone ahead to confirm schedule. **Cost:** Museum $8; $6 (ages 6-17 and 60+); $25 (family, two adults and three children ages 6-17). Tour of dig site, including museum tour, $20; $18 (ages 6-17 and 60+); $55 (family, two adults and three children ages 6-17). **Phone:** (403) 642-2118. GT

Upgrade to Plus or Premier membership for *more* of the benefits you need most

---

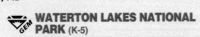

WATERTON LAKES NATIONAL PARK (K-5)

Elevations in the park range from 1,279 metres (4,200 ft.) in the town of Waterton Park to 2,920 metres (9,580 ft.) at Mount Blakiston. Refer to CAA/AAA maps for additional elevation information.

The most direct approach into the national park from the south is over Chief Mountain International Hwy. (SR 17/Hwy. 6) from Glacier National Park in Montana; the park also is accessible via Hwy. 5 from Cardston or Hwy. 6 from Pincher Creek. Covering 505 square kilometres (195 sq. mi.), Waterton Lakes National Park adjoins Glacier National Park. Together the two parks form Waterton-Glacier International Peace Park. The Chief Mountain border crossing customs office is open daily 7 a.m.-10 p.m., June 1-Sept. 1; 9-6, Victoria Day weekend-May 31 and Sept. 2-30.

Still considered aboriginal territory, the area was home to the Kootenai and Blackfoot aboriginal tribes for thousands of years. In 1858 Lt. Thomas Blakiston became the first European on record to explore the area; he named the lakes for Charles Waterton, an 18th-century English naturalist.

Local rancher Fred Godsal, American journalist and naturalist George Bird Grinnell and others lobbied their respective governments in the late 19th century to set aside parts of this wilderness area for future generations. They succeeded, and Waterton Lakes and Glacier national parks were established in 1895 and 1910, respectively.

Waterton Lake is divided into three parts: Upper, Middle and Lower Waterton lakes. The townsite is on the north shore of Upper Waterton Lake, which juts 4.7 kilometres (3 mi.) into Glacier National Park. The mountains on either side tower up to 1,200 metres (3,937 ft.) above the lake. Mount Crandell rises to the north; Sofa Mountain and Vimy Peak are east across the lake.

Wildlife ranging from squirrels and marmots to deer and bears inhabits the park. A small herd of plains bison can be viewed in a paddock on the northern boundary, 1.6 kilometres (1 mi.) north of the Waterton River Bridge on Hwy. 6. Thousands of waterfowl visit the lakes during spring and fall migrations.

Among the many rare wildflowers that grace prairie and mountain landscapes are bear grass, pygmy poppy and mountain lady-slipper. Evergreens blanket the slopes and peaks below mountain goat country.

General Information and Activities

The park is open all year, though most concessions operate only from Victoria Day weekend through the second Monday in October. Red Rock Canyon, 15 kilometres (11 mi.) up the Red Rock Parkway, offers a .7-kilometre (.4-mi.) loop trail along the canyon and a 1-kilometre (.6-mi.) trail to Blakiston Falls. Riding stables are 2.5 kilometres

(1.5 mi.) north of town off the main entrance road; guided trail rides are available.

Just north of the townsite is an 18-hole public golf course that is open daily, Victoria Day weekend through the second Monday in October. A public four-court tennis facility is on Cameron Falls Drive.

The park visitor center, at the junction of the entrance road and Prince of Wales Road, is open daily 8-7, mid-June through Labour Day; 9-5, early May to mid-June and day after Labour Day-second Mon. in Oct. Interpretive display centers at Cameron Lake and the Waterton townsite describe the park's subalpine forest and the history of the International Peace Park. All are open daily 24 hours.

Interpretive talks are given most evenings at 8 at the park's indoor theaters from Canada Day to Labour Day. There also are guided walks and other interpretive programs; phone (403) 859-5133.

Those wishing to camp in Waterton's backcountry campsites must obtain a park use permit ($9.80 per person, per night) at the visitor center. You also can register your outing with the Park Warden Service.

Hunting is prohibited. Anglers need a national park fishing license, which can be obtained along with fishing regulations at the park offices, information center, campgrounds, from park wardens and at the service station in the townsite. Motorboats are permitted on both Upper and Middle Waterton lakes with a boat permit; water skiing, however, is permitted only on Middle Waterton Lake. *See Recreation Areas Chart.*

ADMISSION is free in 2017 to celebrate Canada's 150th anniversary of Confederation, otherwise $7.43; $6.48 (ages 65+); $3.71 (ages 6-16); $18.67 (up to seven people arriving in a single vehicle) per day, May-Oct.; $5.52; $4.67 (ages 65+); $2.76 (ages 6-16); $14 (up to seven people arriving in a single vehicle) per day, rest of year. An annual pass, valid at all Canadian national parks, is available.

PETS must be leashed at all times while in the park.

ADDRESS inquiries to the Superintendent, Waterton Lakes National Park, P.O. Box 200, Waterton Park, AB, Canada T0K 2M0; phone (403) 859-2224.

WATERTON INTER-NATION SHORELINE CRUISE CO. departs from the Waterton Marina. Narrated sightseeing trips lasting 2.25 hours cross Waterton Lake, which is surrounded by the majestic scenery of the Rocky Mountains. From early June through late September the cruise includes a 30-minute stop at Goat Haunt in Montana; passengers also may stay at Goat Haunt for daylong hiking trips and return on a later boat. Hikes to Crypt Lake also may be enjoyed, with a shuttle picking up and dropping off patrons at Crypt Landing mid-May to early October.

Note: A passport must be presented by any passenger choosing to disembark at Goat Haunt for the day-long hiking trips. **Hours:** Sightseeing trips landing at Goat Haunt depart daily at 10, 1 and 4,

early June-late Sept. (also at 7 p.m., July-Aug.). Non-landing sightseeing trips depart daily at 10 and 1, early May-early June and late Sept.-second Mon. in Oct. Crypt Landing shuttle trips depart daily at 10, mid-May to early Oct. (also at 9, July 1-early Sept.). Phone ahead to confirm schedule. **Cost:** Sightseeing trip $44.76; $22.86 (ages 13-17); $15.24 (ages 1-12); free (under 12 months, but a ticket is required). Crypt Landing shuttle $22.86; $11.43 (ages 4-12). **Phone:** (403) 859-2362. [GT]

RECREATIONAL ACTIVITIES
Horseback Riding
- **Alpine Stables** is in Waterton Lakes National Park, following signs. **Hours:** Daily 9-5. Phone ahead to confirm schedule. **Phone:** (403) 859-2462 May-Sept., or (403) 653-2449 Oct.-Apr. [GT]

WATERTON PARK (K-6) pop. 88, elev. 1,282m/4,209'
- Restaurants p. 150

Waterton Park, commonly referred to as Waterton, is a hamlet located just north of the Montana border in southwestern Alberta, within Waterton Lakes National Park *(see place listing p. 148).* The park, which borders Montana's Glacier National Park, is part of the Waterton-Glacier Peace Park, designated by the United Nations Educational, Scientific and Cultural Organization as a World Heritage Site.

ASPEN VILLAGE INN   403/859-2255

Motel
Rates not provided

Address: 111 Windflower Ave T0K 2M0 **Location:** Center. **Facility:** 51 units, some two bedrooms, efficiencies, kitchens and cottages. 1-2 stories (no elevator), exterior corridors. **Terms:** check-in 4 pm.

[SAVE] 🍴 📶 ✕ 🎿 🖥 / SOME UNITS 🛏 🍴 🖼

BAYSHORE INN RESORT & SPA   (403)859-2211
Motel. **Address:** 111 Waterton Ave T0K 2M0

CRANDELL MOUNTAIN LODGE   403/859-2288

Hotel
Rates not provided

Address: 102 Mt. View Rd T0K 2M0 **Location:** Center. **Facility:** 17 units, some two bedrooms, efficiencies and kitchens. 2 stories (no elevator), interior corridors. **Terms:** check-in 4 pm.

[SAVE] 📶 ✕ 🎿 🖥 / SOME UNITS 🍴 🖼

WATERTON GLACIER SUITES   (403)859-2004

Hotel. **Address:** 107 Windflower Ave T0K 2M0

WATERTON LAKES RESORT   403/859-2150

Hotel
Rates not provided

Address: 101 Clematis Ave T0K 2M0 **Location:** Center. **Facility:** 80 units, some efficiencies and kitchens. 2 stories (no elevator), interior/exterior corridors. **Parking:** winter plug-ins. **Terms:** check-in 4 pm. **Dining:** Vimy's Lounge & Grill, see separate listing. **Pool(s):** heated indoor. **Activities:** sauna, hot tub, steamroom, cross country skiing, game room, trails.

WHERE TO EAT

BAYSHORE LAKESIDE CHOPHOUSE   403/859-2211
International. Casual Dining. **Address:** 111 Waterton Ave T0K 2M0

VIMY'S LOUNGE & GRILL   403/859-2150
American. Casual Dining. **Address:** 101 Clematis Ave T0K 2M0

WIENERS OF WATERTON   403/859-0007
Hot Dogs. Quick Serve. **Address:** 301 Windflower Ave T0K 2M0

ZUM'S EATERY & MERCANTILE   403/859-2388
Comfort Food. Casual Dining. **Address:** 116 Waterton Ave T0K 2M0

WEMBLEY (C-2) pop. 1,383

SAVE **PHILIP J. CURRIE DINOSAUR MUSEUM** is just off Hwy. 43 at 9301 112th Ave. Named after Canada's leading paleontologist, the state-of-the-art facility showcases fossils, core samples and other artifacts from the Pipestone Creek bone bed, which was discovered by a high-school teacher in 1973. The museum's galleries also include dinosaur reconstructions, displays about oil and gas extraction in Alberta, and temporary exhibits. Other features of the 10-acre complex are the 60-seat Aykroyd Family Theater, an outdoor fossil walk and a children's playground. Helicopter tours over the bone bed are available.

Hours: Tues.-Fri. 10-8, Sat.-Mon. 10-6, July-Aug.; Tues.-Fri. 10-8, Sat.-Sun. 10-6, May-June and Sept.-Oct.; Tues.-Sun. 10-6 (also Fri. 6-8 p.m.), rest of year. Closed Jan. 1, Christmas Eve, Christmas and Dec. 31. **Cost:** Museum $14; $11 (senior citizens and veterans with ID); $7 (ages 5-17 and students with ID); family $40 (two adults and up to four children). Film or special exhibition additional $2. Film only $5; $2.50 (students with ID). Helicopter tours $195. **Phone:** (587) 771-0662.

WESTEROSE

VILLAGE CREEK COUNTRY INN   780/586-0006
Hotel. **Address:** 15 Village Dr, RR 2 T0C 2V0

WHERE TO EAT

DAISY MCBEANS ICE CREAM & COFFEE   780/586-0771
American. Quick Serve. **Address:** 22 Village Dr, RR 2 T0C 2V0

ECO CAFE   780/586-2627
International. Casual Dining. **Address:** 10 Village Dr T0C 2V0

WESTLOCK pop. 4,823

BEST WESTERN WESTLOCK   (780)349-4102

Hotel
$104-$170

 Best Western. **AAA Benefit:** Save 10% or more every day and earn 10% bonus points!

Address: 10520 100th St T7P 2C6 **Location:** Jct Hwy 18 and 44, just e. **Facility:** 59 units. 2 stories (no elevator), interior/exterior corridors. **Parking:** winter plug-ins. **Activities:** exercise room. **Guest Services:** valet laundry.

RAMADA INN & SUITES WESTLOCK   (780)349-2245
Hotel. **Address:** 11311 100 St T7P 2R8

WETASKIWIN (F-6) pop. 12,525

Wetaskiwin got its name from a Cree phrase meaning "the hills where peace was made." It is believed that a peace agreement between the warring Cree and Blackfoot tribes was made in the area. A stop between the growing outposts of Calgary and Edmonton, Wetaskiwin flourished due to its proximity to the Canadian Pacific Railway; the city was incorporated in 1906. Today Wetaskiwin boasts progressive commercial, agricultural and industrial ties, while a restored downtown area highlights the community's historic roots.

Wetaskiwin Visitor Information Centre: 4910 55A Ave., Wetaskiwin, AB, Canada T9A 2E9. **Phone:** (780) 361-4417.

REYNOLDS-ALBERTA MUSEUM is 2 km (1.2 mi.) w. on Hwy. 13 to 6426 40th Ave. Displays interpret the history of ground and air transportation, agriculture and industry in Alberta. Audiovisual presentations, displays and demonstrations supplement the actual operation of vintage automobiles, bicycles, and farm and industrial machinery. One area features a reproduction of a small drive-in theater, complete with old films, metal speakers and seats shaped like the back end of 1950-era automobiles.

The museum also is home to Canada's Aviation Hall of Fame, situated in a separate exhibit building. Vintage aircraft are displayed. Canadians who have contributed significantly to aviation history are recognized. **Time:** Allow 2 hours minimum. **Hours:** Daily 10-5, Victoria Day-Labour Day; Tues.-Sun. and Mon. holidays 10-5, rest of year. Closed Jan. 1,

Christmas Eve and Christmas. **Cost:** $12.38; $10.48 (ages 65+); $8.57 (ages 7-17); $33.33 (family, two adults and up to six children under 17). **Phone:** (780) 312-2065.

WETASKIWIN & DISTRICT HERITAGE MUSEUM is at 5007 50th Ave. Housed in a historic building, the museum depicts local history and includes displays about the military, hospitals, early businesses, and Swedish and Chinese immigrants. The Origins Exhibit offers interactive games as well as such archeological finds as dinosaur fossils and Plains Cree artifacts. Women of Aspenland profiles notable women from the community.

A hands-on gallery for children features a one-room schoolhouse, a general store and a pioneer kitchen. **Time:** Allow 30 minutes minimum. **Hours:** Tues.-Sat. 10-5, May-Sept.; Tues.-Fri. 10-5, rest of year. Closed major holidays. Phone ahead to confirm schedule. **Cost:** Donations. Reservations are required for guided tours. **Phone:** (780) 352-0227. GT

BEST WESTERN WAYSIDE INN   (780)312-7300

Hotel
$130-$150

Best Western. **AAA Benefit:** Save 10% or more every day and earn 10% bonus points!

Address: 4103 56th St T9A 1V2 **Location:** On Hwy 2A, just n of jct Hwy 13 W. **Facility:** 28 units. 2 stories, interior corridors. **Terms:** check-in 4 pm. **Dining:** 2 restaurants. **Activities:** exercise room.

SUPER 8 WETASKIWIN   (780)361-3808
Hotel. **Address:** 3820 56th St T9A 2B2

HUCKLEBERRY'S CAFE   780/352-3111
International. Casual Dining. **Address:** 103-3840 56th St T9A 2B2

WHITECOURT (D-4) pop. 9,605, elev. 732m/2,404'

Whitecourt Visitor Information Centre: 3002 33rd St., Whitecourt, AB, Canada T7S 1N6. **Phone:** (780) 778-3433 or (800) 313-7383.

HOLIDAY INN EXPRESS & SUITES WHITECOURT   780/778-2512
Hotel. **Address:** 4721 49th St T7S 1N5

THE KANATA   780/706-3390
Hotel. **Address:** 3315 33rd St T7S 0A2

LAKEVIEW INNS & SUITES   (780)706-3349
Hotel. **Address:** 3325 Caxton St T7S 1P2 *(See ad opposite inside front cover.)*

MICROTEL INN & SUITES BY WYNDHAM
          (780)396-0990

Hotel
$109-$189

Address: 4915 49th Ave T7S 1N5 **Location:** Hwy 43, just n on 51st St, then just e. **Facility:** 104 units, some two bedrooms and efficiencies. 4 stories, interior corridors. **Parking:** winter plug-ins. **Guest Services:** valet and coin laundry. **Featured Amenity: continental breakfast.**

SUPER 8   (780)778-8908
Hotel. **Address:** 4121 Kepler St T7S 0A3

MOUNTAIN PIZZA & STEAK HOUSE   780/778-3600
Steak. Casual Dining. **Address:** 3827 Caxton St T7S 1P3

ORIGINAL JOE'S   780/778-1981
American. Gastropub. **Address:** 5004 Dahl #100A Dr T7S 1X6

WOOD BUFFALO NATIONAL PARK—
See Northwest Territories and Nunavut p. 415

Kootenay National Park

British Columbia

Sailing along Vancouver Island's untamed coast in 1842, James Douglas visited the site of present-day Victoria and reported: "The place itself appears a perfect Eden...one might be pardoned for supposing it had been dropped from the clouds..."

Today, Edenic gardens are the province's forte: From Victoria's renowned, blossom-loaded Butchart Gardens to lush Queen Elizabeth Park atop Vancouver's tallest hill, horticultural delights are everywhere.

And if a single apple was enough to tempt Adam and Eve, they would no doubt have found BC's fertile Okanagan Valley irresistible. Its orchards produce more than a third of Canada's apples, and the valley also lures vacationers with sunny weather, sandy lakefront beaches and picturesque rolling hills striped by orderly rows of grapevines.

If you were searching for the Garden of Eden on Earth, British Columbia wouldn't be a bad place to start.

Totem pole in Stanley Park, Vancouver

Into the Woods

Indeed, a trip here just might recapture a lost youthful expectation of adventure. BC's snowcapped mountains and mist-filled rain forests seem to have sprung from the pages of a novel full of exciting new experiences.

Take a walk among centuries-old Douglas firs in MacMillan Provincial Park's Cathedral Grove; you'll feel child-size by comparison. Look up at the high, dim ceiling of needle-heavy boughs arching overhead and you'll understand how this grove got its name. Stands of old-growth forests continue to thrive in Pacific Rim National Park Reserve and Strathcona Provincial Park.

Another of these sylvan sanctuaries is Vancouver's Stanley Park, an evergreen woodland so extensive that while wandering its paths you might forget you're in the heart of Canada's third largest city.

Especially intriguing are the stylized figures carved into totem poles. A thicket of these cedar columns is at the park's eastern edge, each one communicating its own story—possibly a family history, notable event or age-old myth. More examples carved by the Bella Coola, Haida, Kwakwaka'wakw, Nootka, Salish, Tlingit and Tsimshian peoples rise along the province's mainland coast or offshore islands.

In the Canadian Rockies, Kootenay National Park preserves land that seems equally imbued with magic. At the park's southern end are the Radium Hot Springs, which bubble forth hot, mineral water no matter what time of year.

On the other hand, changing seasons at Victoria's Butchart Gardens make a huge difference. As some plants bloom, others fade, producing a dramatic shift in hues. Meandering paths among blossoming trees and shrubs pass softly splashing fountains and countless flower beds in this floral heaven.

Vancouver's VanDusen Botanical Garden is also endowed. This former golf course is now a showplace of lakes, streams, hedge mazes and whimsical topiaries.

Recreation

The Rocky Mountain and Cascade ranges, a lush valley and rivers, lakes and protected ocean waterways are the hallmarks of British Columbia's natural beauty and the sources of unlimited recreational possibilities.

Extended canoeing trips await you on the Outside Trail, a chain of lakes in the Kootenay region's Champion Lakes Provincial Park, and the coast's Powell Forest Canoe Route, eight lakes connected by portage routes.

The 116-kilometre (72-mi.) canoeing and kayaking circuit (plus portage routes) in Bowron Lake Provincial Park is so popular that reservations are required and daily access is limited to 25 boats. Paddling through this unspoiled wildlife sanctuary could take up to 7 days, depending on the weather or how much time you spend gawking at wildlife or the beautiful Cariboo Mountains.

In addition to spectacular mountain scenery, canoeists will find calm, turquoise glacial lakes nestled in the snowcapped Rockies; two of these, O'Hara and Emerald, are in Yoho National Park.

If rushing water is more your speed, try negotiating the Thompson and Fraser rivers. They converge near Lytton, said to be Canada's white-water rafting capital; outfitters and guides are plentiful.

Hiking trails throughout BC bring you up close with its natural wonders. One of the best coastal hikes is in Pacific Rim National Park Reserve. The Long Beach Unit near Ucluelet offers eight moderately challenging hiking venues ranging from beaches to rain forests. The park's pride and joy, the rugged West Coast Trail, follows the shoreline from Port Renfrew to Bamfield.

But that's just the tip of the iceberg. A National Marine Conservation Area as well as seven national and nearly 650 provincial parks and recreation areas await your discovery.

You can swim, water ski or windsurf at one of Okanagan Lake's seven provincial beach parks or at Osoyoos Lake, the province's warmest; both are in the desertlike Okanagan Valley. The valley's climate and terrain also invite other activities. The Kettle Valley Railway bed, west of Penticton, provides easy mountain biking; tougher trails cross nearby Campbell Mountain and Ellis Ridge.

The skiing amenities at Whistler and Blackcomb mountains north of Vancouver—39 high-speed lifts, 200 trails and 12 alpine bowls—are world renowned and make up one of North America's largest ski resorts. Off the slopes, unlimited après ski options exist in Whistler Village's eclectic mix of pubs, dance clubs and culinary nightspots, shops, spas and art galleries.

The Okanagan Valley's gentle slopes and rolling hills draw snowboarders and cross-country skiers. Resorts and ski areas near Osoyoos, Oliver, Penticton, West Kelowna (Westbank) and Kelowna have quite a following; most offer night skiing, too. Some of western Canada's best cross-country skiing is farther north, from 100 Mile House to Quesnel west of the Cariboo Mountains.

Bowron Lake Provincial Park, Quesnel

Historic Timeline

1750	The Queen Charlotte Islands are occupied by Haida First Nation.
1774	Spanish explorers first sight the coast of Vancouver Island.
1792	George Vancouver, an English explorer, surveys the British Columbian coast.
1820	The powerful Hudson's Bay Co. controls fur trading in the Pacific Northwest.
1849	Vancouver Island becomes a crown colony.
1858	Gold is discovered in the Fraser River Valley.
1871	British Columbia becomes the sixth province of the Dominion of Canada.
1885	A transcontinental railroad links British Columbia with eastern Canada.
1986	Vancouver celebrates its centennial with a world's fair, Expo '86.
1998	The Nisga'a Treaty ends 20 years of negotiations with the Nisga'a nation over land, resources and self-government.
2010	Vancouver and Whistler host the 2010 Olympic Winter Games.

What To Pack

Temperature Averages Maximum/Minimum (Celsius)	JANUARY	FEBRUARY	MARCH	APRIL	MAY	JUNE	JULY	AUGUST	SEPTEMBER	OCTOBER	NOVEMBER	DECEMBER
Fort St. John	-11 / -19	-7 / -16	-1 / -11	8 / -2	15 / 3	19 / 8	21 / 10	20 / 9	14 / 4	8 / -1	-3 / -11	-9 / -18
Kamloops	-2 / -9	3 / -5	10 / -2	16 / 2	21 / 7	25 / 11	28 / 13	28 / 13	22 / 8	14 / 3	5 / -2	0 / -7
Prince George	-6 / -14	-1 / -11	4 / -6	11 / -2	16 / 3	19 / 6	22 / 8	21 / 7	16 / 3	9 / -1	1 / -7	-5 / -13
Prince Rupert	4 / -3	6 / -1	7 / 0	9 / 1	12 / 4	14 / 7	16 / 9	16 / 10	15 / 7	11 / 4	7 / 1	4 / -2
Vancouver	6 / 0	8 / 1	9 / 2	12 / 4	16 / 8	19 / 11	22 / 12	22 / 13	18 / 10	13 / 6	9 / 3	6 / 1
Victoria	6 / 0	8 / 1	10 / 2	13 / 3	16 / 6	19 / 9	22 / 11	22 / 11	19 / 8	14 / 5	9 / 2	7 / 1

From the records of The Weather Channel Interactive, Inc.

Good Facts To Know

POPULATION: 4,400,057.

AREA: 944,735 sq km (364,762 sq mi.); ranks 5th.

CAPITAL: Victoria.

HIGHEST POINT: 4,663 m (15,295 ft.), Mount Fairweather.

LOWEST POINT: Sea level, Pacific Ocean.

TIME ZONE(S): Mountain/Pacific. DST in portions of the province.

GAMBLING

MINIMUM AGE FOR GAMBLING: 19.

REGULATIONS

TEEN DRIVING LAWS: The minimum age for an unrestricted driver's license is 19 (18 years, 3 months with approved driver's ed). No more than one unrelated passenger is permitted unless accompanied by a driver age 25 or older. For more information about British Columbia driver's license regulations, phone (800) 663-3051.

SEAT BELT/CHILD RESTRAINT LAWS: Seat belts are required for driver and all passengers ages 16 and over. Children ages 9-15 or 145 cm (57 in.) tall and over are required to use a booster seat or seat belt; appropriate booster or forward-facing child seats are required for children under age 9 or under 145 cm (57 in.) tall. Infants under 20 pounds must be in a rear-facing seat until they are 12 months old and must not be placed in front of an air bag. AAA recommends the use of seat belts and appropriate child restraints for the driver and all passengers.

CELLPHONE RESTRICTIONS: The use of handheld phones and text messaging while driving are prohibited.

HELMETS FOR MOTORCYCLISTS: Required for all riders.

RADAR DETECTORS: Permitted.

MOVE OVER LAW: Drivers approaching a stopped emergency vehicle displaying flashing lights must slow down and, if traffic permits, move over into the adjacent lane in order to pass by.

FIREARMS LAWS: By federal law, all nonresidents entering Canada with a firearm must declare their weapon in writing and pay a fee of $25 (Canadian). Contact the Canadian Firearms Centre at (800) 731-4000 to receive a declaration form or for additional information.

ALCOHOL CONSUMPTION: Legal age 19.

HOLIDAYS

HOLIDAYS: Jan. 1 ▪ Family Day, Feb. (2nd Mon.) ▪ Good Friday ▪ Easter Monday ▪ Victoria Day, Mon. prior to May 25 ▪ Canada Day, July 1 ▪ British Columbia Day, Aug. (1st Mon.) ▪ Labour Day, Sept. (1st Mon.) ▪ Thanksgiving, Oct. (2nd Mon.) ▪ Remembrance Day, Nov. 11 ▪ Christmas, Dec. 25 ▪ Boxing Day, Dec. 26.

MONEY

TAXES: British Columbia has a 5 percent goods and services tax (GST) and a 7 percent provincial sales tax (PST). Hotel accommodations with more than four rooms are subject to a PST of 8 percent and an additional Municipal and Regional District Tax (MRDT) of up to 3 percent. The PST for alcohol is 10 percent. Restaurants and admission fees are exempt from the 7 percent PST. Automobile rental sales tax is $1.50 per day, or portion of a day, for rentals of more than 8 consecutive hours and up to 28 consecutive days.

VISITOR INFORMATION

INFORMATION CENTERS: British Columbia has more than 138 visitor information centers throughout the province. Of these more than 80 are open all year and can be found in all major cities including Victoria and Vancouver. The smaller community travel information centers are open June through August. For further information phone Hello BC at (800) 435-5622.

ROAD CONDITIONS: DriveBC provides current information about road conditions; phone (800) 550-4997 in British Columbia or anywhere in North America.

FURTHER INFORMATION FOR VISITORS:
1-800-HELLO BC
1166 Alberni St., Unit 600
Vancouver, BC V6C 3L6
Canada
(800) 435-5622

FISHING AND HUNTING REGULATIONS:
British Columbia Ministry of Environment
Fish and Wildlife Branch
P.O. Box 9391, Stn. Prov. Gov't.
Victoria, BC V8W 9M8
Canada
(250) 387-9771
(877) 855-3222

RECREATION INFORMATION:
BC Parks
P.O. Box 9398, Stn. Prov. Gov't.
Victoria, BC V8W 9M9
Canada
(800) 689-9025 (camping reservations)

British Columbia Annual Events
Please call ahead to confirm event details.

JANUARY

- Polar Bear Swim
  Vancouver
  604-665-3424
- Winter Carnival / Rossland
  250-362-5666
- Brackendale Winter Eagle
  Festival and Count
  Brackendale
  604-898-3333

FEBRUARY

- Vernon Winter Carnival
  Vernon
  250-545-2236
- BC Home and Garden
  Show / Vancouver
  905-951-4051
- Maple Sugar Festival
  Nanaimo
  250-729-2776

MARCH

- CelticFest Vancouver
  Vancouver
  604-727-3984
- Pacific Rim Whale Festival
  Ucluelet
  250-726-4641
- Cowboy Festival
  Kamloops
  888-763-2224

APRIL

- Okanagan Fest-of-Ale
  Penticton
  800-663-1900
- World Ski & Snowboard
  Festival / Whistler
  604-664-5614
- Goodbye Chums!
  Maple Ridge
  604-462-8643

MAY

- Cloverdale Rodeo and
  Country Fair / Surrey
  604-576-9461
- Victoria Highland Games &
  Celtic Festival / Victoria
  250-598-8961
- Fire & Ice Street Festival
  Qualicum Beach
  250-228-0199

JUNE

- Sam Steele Days
  Cranbrook
  250-426-4161
- Vancouver International
  Children's Festival
  Vancouver
  604-708-5655
- Seafest / Prince Rupert
  250-624-9118

JULY

- Bella Coola Music Festival
  Bella Coola
  800-663-5885
- Celebration of Light
  Vancouver
  604-641-1193
- Billy Barker Days / Quesnel
  250-992-1234

AUGUST

- Parksville Beach Festival
  Parksville
  250-248-4819
- Abbotsford Airshow
  Abbotsford
  604-852-8511
- Victoria Dragon Boat
  Festival / Victoria
  250-472-2628

SEPTEMBER

- Coho Festival
  West Vancouver
  604-925-7194
- Pender Harbour Jazz
  Festival / Madeira Park
  604-883-2561
- Vancouver International
  Fringe Festival / Vancouver
  604-257-0350

OCTOBER

- The Mane Event--Equine
  Education and Trade Fair
  Chilliwack
  250-578-7518
- Ghosts of Victoria Festival
  Victoria
  250-384-6698
- Okanagan Fall Wine
  Festival / Kelowna
  250-861-6654

NOVEMBER

- Kris Kringle Craft Market
  Nanaimo
  250-758-9750
- Heritage Christmas at
  Burnaby Village / Burnaby
  604-297-4565
- Cornucopia--Whistler's
  Celebration of Wine and
  Food / Whistler
  604-932-2394

DECEMBER

- Festival of Lights
  Vancouver
  604-257-8665
- WinterFest / Prince Rupert
  250-624-9118
- Magic of Christmas
  Brentwood Bay
  250-652-4422

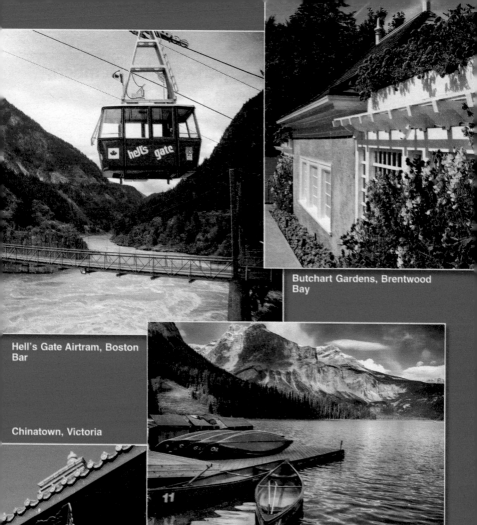

Butchart Gardens, Brentwood Bay

Hell's Gate Airtram, Boston Bar

Chinatown, Victoria

Emerald Lake, Yoho National Park

Science World at TELUS World of Science, Vancouver

Index: Great Experience for Members

AAA editor's picks of exceptional note

Barkerville Historic Town

Historic Hat Creek Ranch

Fort St. James National Historic Site

Fort Steele Heritage Town

See Orientation map on p. 168 for corresponding grid coordinates, if applicable.
*Indicates the GEM is temporarily closed.

Stay connected with #AAA and #CAA

on your favorite social media sites

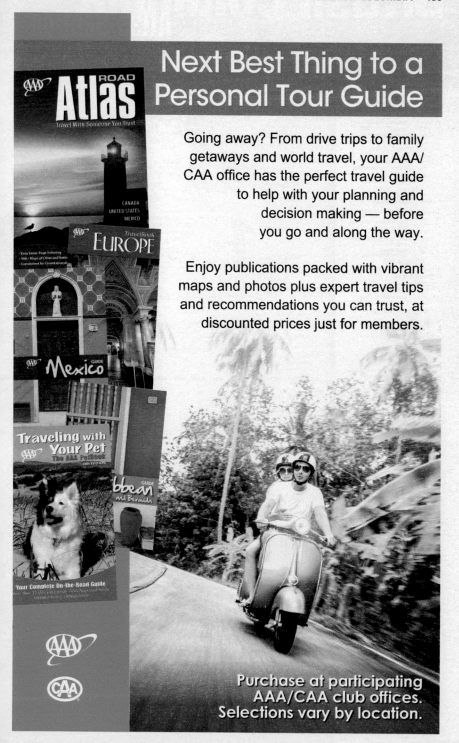

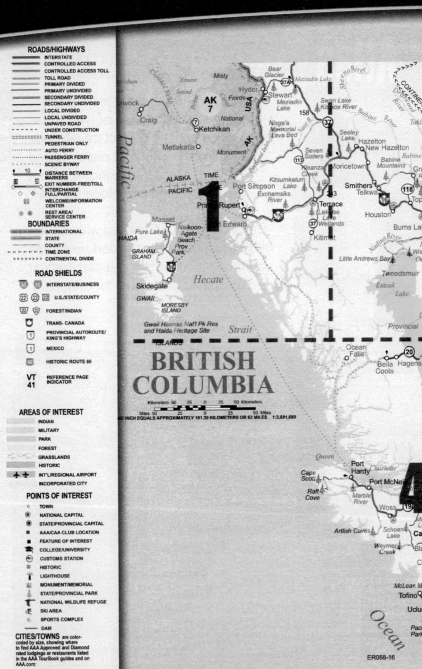

BRITISH COLUMBIA

ROADS/HIGHWAYS

	INTERSTATE
	CONTROLLED ACCESS
	CONTROLLED ACCESS TOLL
	TOLL ROAD
	PRIMARY DIVIDED
	PRIMARY UNDIVIDED
	SECONDARY DIVIDED
	SECONDARY UNDIVIDED
	LOCAL DIVIDED
	LOCAL UNDIVIDED
	UNPAVED ROAD
	UNDER CONSTRUCTION
	TUNNEL
	PEDESTRIAN ONLY
	AUTO FERRY
	PASSENGER FERRY
	SCENIC BYWAY
10	DISTANCE BETWEEN MARKERS
	EXIT NUMBER-FREE/TOLL
	INTERCHANGE FULL/PARTIAL
	WELCOME/INFORMATION CENTER
	REST AREA/ SERVICE CENTER

BOUNDARIES

	INTERNATIONAL
	STATE
	COUNTY
	TIME ZONE
>>>>>>>>	CONTINENTAL DIVIDE

ROAD SHIELDS

95 95	INTERSTATE/BUSINESS
22 22 22	U.S./STATE/COUNTY
127	FOREST/INDIAN
	TRANS- CANADA
1	PROVINCIAL AUTOROUTE/ KING'S HIGHWAY
1	MEXICO
66	HISTORIC ROUTE 66
VT 41	REFERENCE PAGE INDICATOR

AREAS OF INTEREST

	INDIAN
	MILITARY
	PARK
	FOREST
	GRASSLANDS
	HISTORIC
✈ ✈	INT'L/REGIONAL AIRPORT
	INCORPORATED CITY

POINTS OF INTEREST

○	TOWN
✷	NATIONAL CAPITAL
✶	STATE/PROVINCIAL CAPITAL
■	AAA/CAA CLUB LOCATION
■	FEATURE OF INTEREST
	COLLEGE/UNIVERSITY
	CUSTOMS STATION
	HISTORIC
	LIGHTHOUSE
	MONUMENT/MEMORIAL
	STATE/PROVINCIAL PARK
	NATIONAL WILDLIFE REFUGE
	SKI AREA
	SPORTS COMPLEX
	DAM

CITIES/TOWNS are color-coded by size, showing where to find AAA Approved and Diamond rated lodgings or restaurants listed in the AAA TourBook guides and on AAA.com:

- ● Red - major destinations and capitals; many listings
- ● Black - destinations; some listings
- ○ Grey - no listings

Kilometers 50 25 0 25 50 Kilometers
Miles 50 25 0 25 50 Miles
ONE INCH EQUALS APPROXIMATELY 101.39 KILOMETERS OR 63 MILES 1:3,991,680

ER068-16

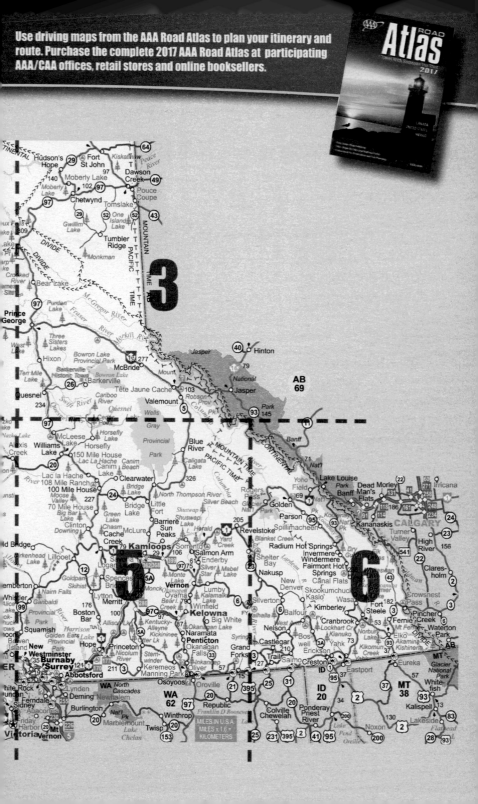

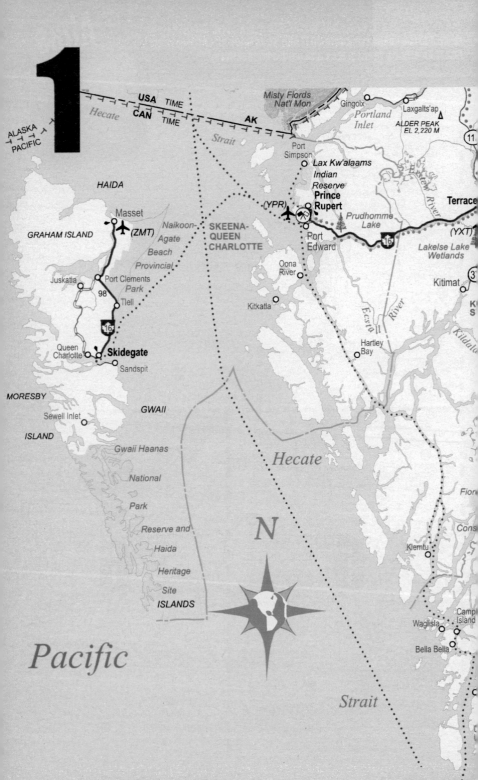

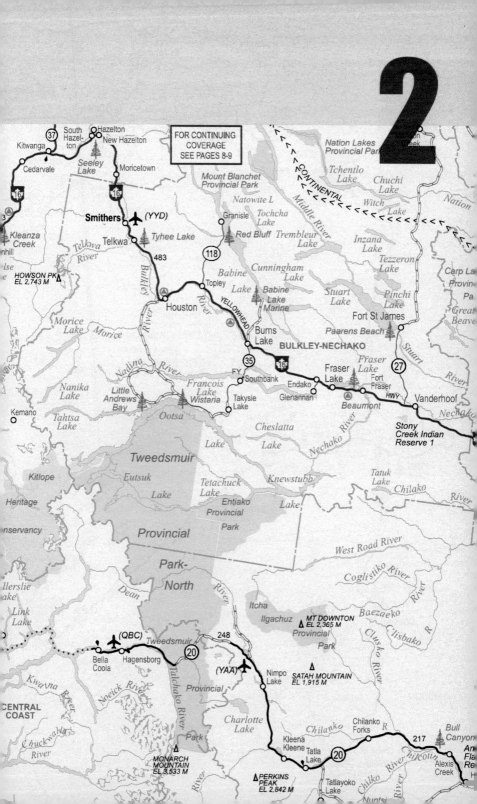

2

FOR CONTINUING COVERAGE SEE PAGES 8-9

Kitwanga

37

Cedarvale

Hazelton
South Hazel-ton
New Hazelton

Moricetown

16

Seeley Lake

16

Mount Blanchet Provincial Park

Natowite L

Nation Lakes Provincial Park

CONTINENTAL

Tchentlo Lake

Chuchi Lake

Witch Lake

Nation

3

Kleanza Creek

nhill

Smithers ✈ *(YYD)*

Telkwa

Tyhee Lake

Granisle

Red Bluff

Tochcha Lake

Trembleur Lake

Middle River

Inzana Lake

Tezzeron Lake

Carp La
Provi
Pa

HOWSON PK
EL 2,743 M

Telkwa River

Bulkley River

483

118

Topley

Babine Lake

Babine Lake Marine

Cunningham Lake

Stuart Lake

Pinchi Lake

Grea
Beave

ise

Morice Lake

Morice River

Houston

YELLOWHEAD

River

Burns Lake

Paarens Beach

Fort St James

Stuart River

27

Kemano

Nadina River

Nanika Lake

Little Andrews Bay

Francois Lake Wistaria

35

FY.

Southbank

Takysie Lake

Endako

Glenannan

BULKLEY-NECHAKO

16

Fraser Lake

Beaumont

HWY

Fraser Lake

Fort Fraser

Vanderhoof

Nechako

Tahtsa Lake

Ootsa Lake

Cheslatta Lake

Nechako River

Chilako River

Stony Creek Indian Reserve 1

Heritage

Kitlope

Tweedsmuir

Eutsuk Lake

Tetachuck Lake

Entiako Provincial Park

Knewstubb Lake

Tatuk Lake

H

nservancy

Provincial

West Road River

llerslie
ake

Link Lake

Dean River

Park-

North

Coglistiko River

Itcha

Ilgachuz

MT DOWNTON
EL 2,365 M

Baezaeko River

Clisbako R

Clusko River

(QBC) ✈

Bella Coola

Hagensborg

Tweedsmuir

248

20

Provincial Park

Satah Mountain Provincial Park

(YAA) ✈

Nimpo Lake

SATAH MOUNTAIN
EL 1,915 M

Kwatna

Noeick River

Talchako River

Charlotte Lake

Chilanko R

Chilanko Forks

217

Bull Canyon

CENTRAL COAST

Chuckwalla River

MONARCH MOUNTAIN
EL 3,533 M

PERKINS PEAK
EL 2,842 M

Tatlayoko Lake

Kleena Kleene

Tatla Lake

20

Chilko Lake

Chilko River

Chilcotin River

Alexis Creek

An
Fla
Re
H

Nuntsi

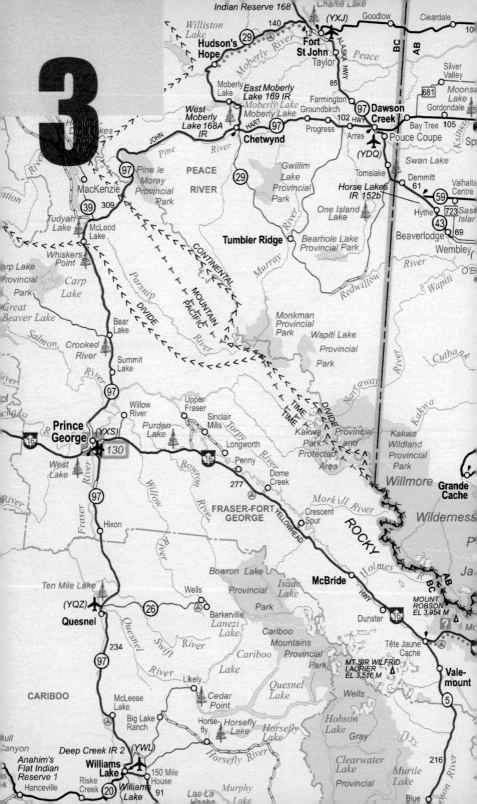

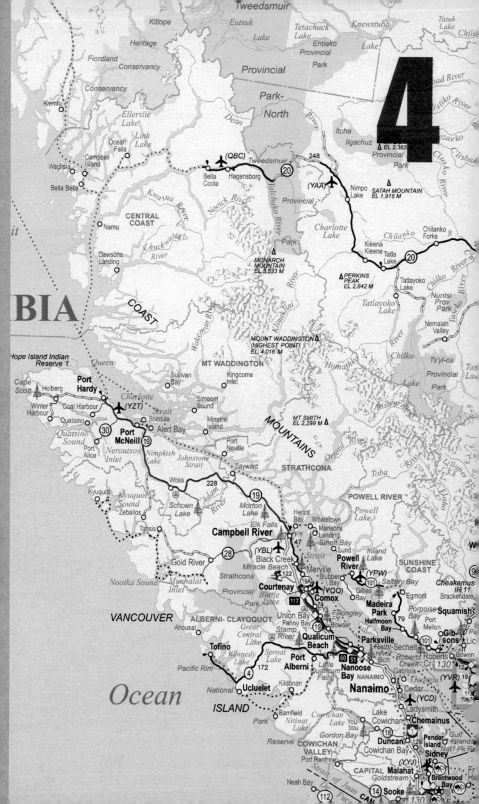

4054-17

British Columbia
Orientation

NOT INTENDED FOR DRIVING.
SEE APPROPRIATE AAA SHEET MAP.

Scale in Kilometers

120   0   120

See p. 6 - Map Legend

© 2016 HERE

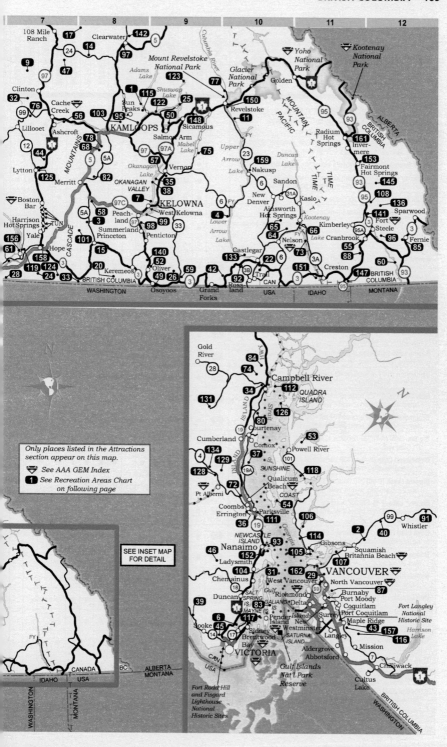

*Only places listed in the Attractions
section appear on this map.*

See AAA GEM Index

1 *See Recreation Areas Chart
on following page*

SEE INSET MAP
FOR DETAIL

Recreation Areas Chart

The map location numerals in column 2 show an area's location on the preceding map.

	MAP LOCATION	CAMPING	PICNICKING	HIKING TRAILS	BOATING	BOAT RAMP	BOAT RENTAL	FISHING	SWIMMING	PETS ON LEASH	BICYCLE TRAILS	WINTER SPORTS	VISITOR CENTER	LODGE/CABINS	FOOD SERVICE
NATIONAL PARKS *(See place listings.)*															
Glacier (A-10) 1,350 square kilometres. Camping, caving, mountaineering.		•	•	•						•	•	•	•	•	•
Gulf Islands (I-10) 33 square kilometres. Golf, kayaking, scuba diving. Recreational activities vary on each island.		•	•	•	•		•		•	•					
Gwaii Haanas (F-1) 1,495 square kilometres. Kayaking.		•		•	•			•					•		
Kootenay (A-11) 1,406 square kilometres. Horseback riding, mountain biking, wildlife viewing. Power boats prohibited.		•	•	•				•	•	•	•	•	•	•	•
Mount Revelstoke (A-9) 260 square kilometres.		•	•	•					•		•	•	•		
Pacific Rim (I-3) 510 square kilometres.		•	•	•				•	•	•			•		
Yoho (A-11) 1,310 square kilometres. Cross-country skiing; horseback riding. Power boats prohibited.		•	•	•	•		•	•	•	•	•	•	•	•	
PROVINCIAL															
Adams Lake (A-8) 56 hectares 30 km n. of Chase off Hwy. 1. Archeological sites. Canoeing, scuba diving, water skiing, windsurfing; beach.	1	•		•	•	•		•	•	•	•				
Alice Lake (G-11) 396 hectares 13 km n. of Squamish on Hwy. 99. Canoeing.	2	•	•	•				•	•	•	•				
Allison Lake (C-8) 23 hectares 28 km n. of Princeton on Hwy. 5A. Canoeing, water skiing.	3	•	•					•	•	•	•				
Arrow Lakes (Shelter Bay) (C-9) 93 hectares on Hwy. 23. Canoeing, horseback riding.	4	•	•		•	•		•	•	•	•				
Babine Lake-Pendleton Bay Marine (E-3) 37 hectares 45 km n. of Burns Lake off Hwy. 16.	5	•			•	•		•		•	•				
Bamberton (H-9) 28 hectares 45 km n. of Victoria off Hwy. 1. Canoeing, windsurfing.	6	•	•	•				•	•	•					
Bear Creek (C-8) 178 hectares 9 km n. off Hwy. 97 w. of Kelowna. Canoeing, water skiing, wildlife viewing.	7	•	•	•				•	•	•	•				
Beaumont (E-4) 192 hectares 134 km w. of Prince George on Hwy. 16. Canoeing, water skiing, wildlife viewing, windsurfing.	8	•	•	•	•	•		•	•	•	•				
Big Bar Lake (A-7) 332 hectares 42 km n.w. of Clinton off Hwy. 97. Canoeing.	9	•	•	•	•			•	•	•	•				
Birkenhead Lake (H-4) 10,439 hectares 54 km n.e. of Pemberton. Canoeing, wildlife viewing, windsurfing.	10	•	•	•	•			•	•	•	•			•	
Blanket Creek (B-10) 318 hectares 25 km s. of Revelstoke on Hwy. 23. Canoeing, wildlife viewing.	11	•	•	•				•	•	•	•				
Bowron Lake (F-5) 149,207 hectares 120 km e. of Quesnel via a gravel access road off Hwy. 26. Water circuit of connecting lakes. Canoeing.	12	•		•	•	•		•	•	•	•	•			
Boya Lake (B-2) 4,597 hectares 150 km n. of Dease Lake. Canoeing, hunting, kayaking, wildlife viewing.	13	•		•	•	•		•	•	•	•				
Bridge Lake (A-8) 405 hectares 51 km e. of 100 Mile House off Hwy. 24.	14	•	•		•	•		•	•						
Bromley Rock (C-8) 149 hectares 21 km e. of Princeton on Hwy. 3. Canoeing.	15	•	•					•	•	•	•				
Bull Canyon (G-4) 369 hectares 6 km w. of Alexis Creek off Hwy. 20.	16	•	•	•				•		•	•				
Canim Beach (A-7) 6 hectares on Canim Lake, 43 km n.e. of 100 Mile House off Hwy. 97. Canoeing, kayaking.	17		•	•	•			•	•	•					
Cape Scott (G-2) 22,294 hectares 64 km w. of Port Hardy. Camping (rustic), canoeing, hunting, kayaking, wildlife viewing.	18	•		•	•	•		•	•				•		
Carp Lake (E-4) 38,149 hectares 32 km s.w. of McLeod Lake off Hwy. 97. Canoeing, hunting, ice fishing, kayaking, wildlife viewing.	19	•	•	•	•	•		•	•	•	•	•			
Cathedral (D-8) 33,272 hectares 24 km w. of Keremeos off Hwy. 3. Canoeing, climbing, hunting, mountaineering, wildlife viewing.	20	•	•	•				•	•					•	

Recreation Areas Chart

The map location numerals in column 2 show an area's location on the preceding map.

	MAP LOCATION	CAMPING	PICNICKING	HIKING TRAILS	BOATING	BOAT RAMP	BOAT RENTAL	FISHING	SWIMMING	PETS ON LEASH	BICYCLE TRAILS	WINTER SPORTS	VISITOR CENTER	LODGE/CABINS	FOOD SERVICE
Cedar Point (F-5) 8 hectares 118 km n.e. of Williams Lake off Hwy. 97 on Quesnel Lake. Canoeing, water skiing; mining displays.	21	●	●	●	●	●	●	●	●	●	●				
Champion Lakes (C-10) 1,426 hectares 10 km s. of Castlegar off Hwy. 3B. Canoeing, cross-country skiing, ice fishing, wildlife viewing, windsurfing. Power boats prohibited.	22	●	●	●	●	●	●	●	●	●	●	●			
Charlie Lake (D-5) 176 hectares 11 km n. of Fort St. John off Hwy. 97.	23	●	●	●	●	●	●	●	●	●	●				
Chilliwack Lake (D-7) 9,528 hectares 64 km s.e. of Chilliwack via an access road off Hwy. 1. Canoeing, hunting, water skiing. ATVs or unlicensed motorbikes prohibited.	24	●	●	●	●	●	●	●	●	●	●	●			
Cinnemousun Narrows (A-9) 176 hectares 22.5 km n. of Sicamous via boat. Camping (walk-in only), canoeing, houseboating, scuba diving, water skiing, windsurfing.	25	●	●	●	●	●	●	●	●	●					
Conkle Lake (D-9) 587 hectares 28 km n.e. of Osoyoos via Hwy. 3, then 26 km to entrance. Canoeing, windsurfing.	26	●	●	●	●	●	●	●	●						
Crooked River (E-4) 970 hectares 70 km n. of Prince George on Hwy. 97. Canoeing, cross-country skiing, ice fishing, wildlife viewing, windsurfing.	27	●	●	●				●	●	●	●				
Cultus Lake (D-7) 2,561 hectares 11 km s.w. of Chilliwack off Hwy. 1. Canoeing, horseback riding, water skiing, wildlife viewing, windsurfing.	28	●	●	●	●	●	●	●	●	●	●	●	●		
Cypress (G-11) 3,012 hectares off Hwy. 1 exit 8 in West Vancouver, then w. following signs. Camping (wilderness only), cross-country and downhill skiing, snowmobiling, wildlife viewing.	29	●	●	●						●		●	●		
Diana Lake (E-1) 233 hectares 16 km e. of Prince Rupert on Hwy. 16. Canoeing, kayaking and paddling.	30		●	●				●	●	●					
Dionisio Point (G-10) 142 hectares on Galiano Island via car ferry. Camping (walk-in only), scuba diving, wildlife viewing.	31	●						●	●	●					
Downing (A-7) 100 hectares 18 km s.w. of Clinton off Hwy. 97. Canoeing.	32	●	●	●				●		●					
E.C. Manning (D-7) 70,844 hectares on Hwy. 3 between Hope and Princeton. Scenic. Boating (no motors), canoeing, cross-country and downhill skiing, horseback riding, hunting, kayaking, mountain biking, paddleboarding, snowshoeing, wildlife viewing.	33	●	●	●	●	●	●	●	●	●		●	●	●	●
Elk Falls (E-10) 1,087 hectares 3 km n.w. of Campbell River off Hwy. 28. Camping (winter), mountain biking (on designated trails), wildlife viewing; waterfall.	34	●	●	●				●		●	●				
Ellison (B-9) 200 hectares on Okanagan Lake, 16 km s.w. of Vernon off Hwy. 97. Canoeing, scuba diving, rock climbing.	35	●	●	●				●	●	●					
Englishman River Falls (G-10) 97 hectares 13 km s.w. of Parksville off Hwy. 4. Wildlife viewing.	36	●	●	●						●					
Fillongley (F-10) 23 hectares on Denman Island via ferry from Buckley Bay. Camping (winter), canoeing, kayaking, wildlife viewing.	37	●	●	●						●					
Fintry (C-9) 361 hectares 34 km n. of Kelowna off Hwy. 97. Canoeing, hunting, scuba diving, water skiing, wildlife viewing, windsurfing.	38	●	●	●	●	●	●	●	●	●					
French Beach (H-9) 59 hectares 20 km w. of Sooke off Hwy. 14. Wildlife viewing, windsurfing.	39	●	●	●				●	●	●					
Garibaldi (G-12) 194,650 hectares accessible by five trails from Hwy. 99 in Squamish. Camping (backcountry), climbing, cross-country skiing, kayaking. Snowmobiling prohibited.	40	●	●	●						●		●	●	●	
Giscome Portage Trail (E-4) 160 hectares 40 km n. of Prince George. Historic. Cross-country skiing, snowshoeing.	41		●									●	●		
Gladstone (Texas Creek) (D-9) 39,387 hectares 5 km e. of Christina Lake on Hwy. 3. Canoeing, cross-country skiing, horseback riding, hunting, scuba diving, snowshoeing, water skiing.	42	●	●	●	●	●	●	●	●	●	●				
Golden Ears (H-12) 62,540 hectares 11 km n. of Maple Ridge off Hwy. 7. Canoeing, rock climbing, water skiing, windsurfing; horse rental.	43	●	●	●	●	●	●	●	●	●	●				●

Recreation Areas Chart

The map location numerals in column 2 show an area's location on the preceding map.

Area	MAP LOCATION	CAMPING	PICNICKING	HIKING TRAILS	BOATING	BOAT RAMP	BOAT RENTAL	FISHING	SWIMMING	PETS ON LEASH	BICYCLE TRAILS	WINTER SPORTS	VISITOR CENTER	LODGE/CABINS	FOOD SERVICE
Goldpan (B-7) 5 hectares 10 km s. of Spences Bridge adjacent to Hwy. 1 on the e. bank of the Thompson River. Canoeing, kayaking, wildlife viewing.	44	•	•					•	•	•					
Goldstream (H-9) 477 hectares 16 km n.w. of Victoria via Hwy. 1. Camping (winter), wildlife viewing. Salmon spawning in fall.	45	•	•	•				•	•	•					
Gordon Bay (G-9) 51 hectares 14 km w. of Lake Cowichan off Hwy. 18. Camping (winter), canoeing, freshwater diving, waterskiing, windsurfing.	46	•	•	•	•	•	•	•	•	•					
Green Lake (A-7) 347 hectares 16 km n.e. of Hwy. 97 at 70 Mile House. Canoeing, horseback riding, water skiing.	47	•	•	•	•	•		•	•	•					
Gwillim Lake (E-5) 32,326 hectares 56 km. s.e. of Chetwynd on Hwy. 29. Canoeing, horseback riding, hunting, kayaking, rock climbing, scuba diving, water skiing, wildlife viewing, windsurfing.	48	•	•	•	•	•		•	•	•	•	•			
Haynes Point (D-9) 38 hectares 2 km s. of Osoyoos on Hwy. 97. Canoeing, water skiing, wildlife viewing.	49	•	•	•	•	•		•	•	•					
Herald (B-9) 79 hectares 14 km e. of Tappen off Hwy. 1. Canoeing, scuba diving, water skiing, windsurfing.	50	•	•	•	•	•		•	•	•					
Horsefly Lake (G-5) 148 hectares 65 km e. of 150 Mile House off Hwy. 97. Canoeing, scuba diving, water skiing, wildlife viewing, windsurfing.	51	•	•	•	•	•		•	•	•					
Inkaneep (C-9) 21 hectares 6 km n. of Oliver on Hwy. 97. Canoeing, kayaking, wildlife viewing.	52	•		•	•			•		•	•				
Inland Lake (F-11) 2,763 hectares 12 km n. of Powell River on Inland Lake Rd. Canoeing, hunting, kayaking, wildlife viewing; wheelchair accessible trail.	53	•	•	•	•	•		•	•	•	•				
Jedediah Island Marine (G-10) 243 hectares between Lasqueti and Texada islands in the Sabine Channel of the Strait of Georgia. Accessible only via boat from Lasqueti Island. Camping (wilderness walk-in only), canoeing, kayaking; sandy bays.	54	•		•				•	•	•					
Jimsmith Lake (C-11) 14 hectares 5 km e. of Cranbrook off Hwy. 3. Canoeing. Power boats prohibited.	55	•	•	•	•			•	•	•					
Juniper Beach (B-8) 260 hectares 19 km e. of Cache Creek on Hwy. 1. Canoeing.	56	•	•					•	•						
Kalamalka Lake (B-9) 4,209 hectares 8 km s. of Vernon off Hwy. 6. Canoeing, cross-country skiing, fishing, horseback riding, kayaking, snowshoeing, water skiing, wildlife viewing.	57		•	•				•	•	•	•	•	•		
Kentucky Alleyne (C-8) 144 hectares 38 km s. of Merritt on Hwy. 5A. Horsepower restriction for boats.	58	•		•	•	•		•	•	•					
Kettle River (D-9) 179 hectares 5 km n. of Rock Creek on Hwy. 33. Cross-country skiing, snowshoeing.	59	•	•	•				•	•	•		•			
Kikomun Creek (C-12) 682 hectares 64 km s.e. of Cranbrook via Hwy. 3, then 11 km s. to entrance. Canoeing, hunting; playground.	60	•	•	•	•	•		•	•	•		•			
Kilby (C-7) 3 hectares 2 km e. of Harrison Mills on Hwy. 7. Historic. Water skiing, wildlife viewing.	61	•			•	•		•	•						
Kinaskan Lake (C-2) 1,800 hectares on Hwy. 37 100 km s. of Dease Lake. Canoeing.	62	•	•	•	•	•		•	•						
Kleanza Creek (E-2) 269 hectares 15 km e. of Terrace on Hwy. 16. Canoeing, snowshoeing, wildlife viewing.	63	•	•	•						•		•			
Kokanee Creek (C-10) 260 hectares 19 km e. of Nelson on Hwy. 3A. Cross-country skiing, snowshoeing, water skiing, canoeing, wildlife viewing, windsurfing; adventure playground.	64	•	•	•				•	•	•		•	•		•
Kokanee Glacier (C-10) 32,035 hectares 19 km n.e. of Nelson on Hwy. 3A. Back- and cross-country skiing, snowshoeing. Non-motorized boats allowed. No pets allowed.	65	•	•					•				•		•	
Kootenay Lake (Davis Creek/Lost Ledge) (C-11) 343 hectares n. of Kaslo on Hwy. 31. Camping (wilderness walk-in only), canoeing, water skiing, windsurfing.	66	•	•		•	•		•	•	•					
Lac La Hache (G-5) 24 hectares 13 km n. of Lac la Hache on Hwy. 97. Canoeing, water skiing; adventure playground.	67	•	•	•				•	•	•		•			

Recreation Areas Chart

The map location numerals in column 2 show an area's location on the preceding map.

Area	MAP LOCATION	CAMPING	PICNICKING	HIKING TRAILS	BOATING	BOAT RAMP	BOAT RENTAL	FISHING	SWIMMING	PETS ON LEASH	BICYCLE TRAILS	WINTER SPORTS	VISITOR CENTER	LODGE/CABINS	FOOD SERVICE
Lac Le Jeune (B-8) 213 hectares 37 km s. of Kamloops off Hwy. 5. Nature programs. Canoeing, cross-country skiing, ice skating, snowshoeing; wildlife viewing; playground.	68	•	•	•	•	•	•	•	•	•	•	•			
Lakelse Lake (E-2) 354 hectares 20 km s. of Terrace on Hwy. 37. Canoeing, water skiing, windsurfing.	69	•	•	•	•	•	•	•	•	•	•	•			
Liard River Hot Springs (B-4) 1,082 hectares at Liard River at Km-post 765 on Hwy. 97 (Alaska Hwy.). Camping (winter), wildlife viewing; playground.	70	•	•	•				•	•	•			•		
Little Andrews Bay Marine (E-3) 45 hectares 95 km s. of Houston on Oosta Lake. Canoeing.	71	•	•		•	•		•	•						
Little Qualicum Falls (F-10) 440 hectares 19 km w. of Parksville off Hwy. 4. Canoeing, kayaking, scuba diving, water skiing, windsurfing; adventure playground.	72	•	•	•				•	•	•					
Lockhart Beach (C-11) 3 hectares 40 km n. of Creston on Hwy. 3A. Canoeing.	73	•	•	•	•			•	•	•					
Loveland Bay (E-10) 30 hectares 16 km w. of Campbell River off Hwy. 28. Canoeing, waterskiing, windsurfing.	74	•			•	•		•	•						
Mabel Lake (B-9) 187 hectares 60 km n.e. of Vernon via an access road off Hwy. 6. Canoeing, water skiing, wildlife viewing.	75	•	•	•	•	•		•	•	•					
Marble Canyon (B-7) 355 hectares 40 km n.w. of Cache Creek off Hwy. 99. Canoeing, rock climbing, scuba diving, wildlife viewing.	76	•	•	•				•	•	•					
Martha Creek (A-9) 71 hectares 20 km n. of Revelstoke on Hwy. 23. Canoeing, kayaking.	77	•	•	•	•	•		•	•	•					
McConnell Lake (B-8) 102 hectares 35 km s. of Kamloops off Hwy. 5. Canoeing, ice fishing, kayaking, snowshoeing.	78		•	•	•			•	•	•	•		•		
Meziadin Lake (D-2) 335 hectares 50 km e. of Stewart off Hwy. 37. Canoeing, wildlife viewing.	79	•	•	•				•	•	•					
Miracle Beach (F-10) 137 hectares 22 km n. of Courtenay off Hwy. 19. Camping (winter), canoeing, wildlife viewing.	80	•	•	•				•	•	•	•				•
Moberly Lake (D-5) 98 hectares 25 km n.w. of Chetwynd on Hwy. 29. Canoeing, water skiing, windsurfing; playground.	81	•	•	•	•	•		•	•	•					
Monck (B-8) 92 hectares 22 km n. of Merritt off Hwy. 5A. Canoeing, water skiing, wildlife viewing, windsurfing; playground.	82	•	•	•	•	•		•	•	•	•				
Montague Harbour Marine (H-10) 97 hectares on Galiano Island via car ferry. Middens. Canoeing.	83	•	•	•	•	•		•	•	•	•		•		
Morton Lake (E-10) 74 hectares 27 km n.w. of Campbell River on Hwy. 19. Camping (winter), canoeing.	84	•	•	•	•			•	•	•					
Mount Fernie (C-12) 259 hectares 3 km s. of Fernie on Hwy. 3.	85	•	•	•				•		•		•			
Mount Robson (F-6) 224,866 hectares bordering Jasper National Park on Hwy. 16. Camping (winter), canoeing, rock climbing, spelunking; horse rental, playground.	86	•	•	•	•			•	•	•	•	•	•	•	•
Mount Seymour (H-12) 3,508 hectares 24 km n.e. of North Vancouver off Hwy. 1. Camping (backcountry only), cross-country skiing, horseback riding.	87	•	•	•					•	•	•	•		•	•
Moyie Lake (C-11) 91 hectares 20 km s. of Cranbrook on Hwy. 3. Canoeing, ice fishing, kayaking, windsurfing; playground.	88	•	•	•	•	•		•	•	•	•				
Muncho Lake (B-3) 86,079 hectares on Hwy. 97 at Muncho Lake at Km-post 681 of the Alaska Hwy. Canoeing, hunting, kayaking, scuba diving, water skiing, wildlife viewing.	89	•	•	•	•	•	•	•	•	•		•		•	
Naikoon (E-1) 69,961 hectares on n. tip of Graham Island in Haida Gwaii. Canoeing, hunting.	90	•	•	•				•	•	•	•		•		
Nairn Falls (G-12) 170 hectares 32 km n. of Whistler on Hwy. 99. Wildlife viewing.	91	•	•					•		•					
Nancy Greene (D-10) 203 hectares 29 km n.w. of Rossland via Hwy. 3B. Canoeing, cross-country skiing, windsurfing.	92	•	•	•				•	•	•		•			
Newcastle Island Marine (G-10) 336 hectares e. of Nanaimo via foot passenger ferry. Camping (walk-in only).	93	•	•	•				•	•	•	•				•

Recreation Areas Chart

The map location numerals in column 2 show an area's location on the preceding map.

	MAP LOCATION	CAMPING	PICNICKING	HIKING TRAILS	BOATING	BOAT RAMP	BOAT RENTAL	FISHING	SWIMMING	PETS ON LEASH	BICYCLE TRAILS	WINTER SPORTS	VISITOR CENTER	LODGE/CABINS	FOOD SERVICE
Nisga'a Memorial Lava Bed (D-2) 17,683 hectares 100 km n. of Terrace on Nisga'a Hwy. (first 70 km is paved). Canoeing, hunting, wildlife viewing.	94	•	•	•	•	•		•	•	•	•	•			
Niskonlith Lake (B-8) 238 hectares 8 km n.w. of Chase off Hwy. 1. Cross-country skiing, ice fishing, scuba diving, snowshoeing, windsurfing, wildlife viewing.	95	•			•	•		•	•	•	•	•			
Norbury Lake (C-12) 97 hectares 16 km s. of jct. hwys. 93 and 95 at Fort Steele. Canoeing.	96	•	•	•	•	•		•	•	•	•	•			
North Thompson River (A-8) 126 hectares 5 km s. of Clearwater off Hwy. 5. Playground.	97	•	•	•				•		•	•				
Okanagan Lake (C-9) 98 hectares 11 km n. of Summerland off Hwy. 97. Canoeing, water skiing, windsurfing, wildlife viewing; playground.	98	•	•	•	•			•	•	•	•	•			•
Okanagan Mountain (C-9) 11,038 hectares 25 km n. of Penticton off Hwy. 97. Camping (walk-in only), canoeing, horseback riding, hunting, kayaking, water skiing, wildlife viewing.	99	•	•	•	•			•	•	•	•				
One Island Lake (E-5) 59 hectares 30 km s. of Tupper off Dawson Creek-Tupper Hwy. (Hwy. 2) and Heritage Hwy. (Hwy. 52). Canoeing, kayaking, scuba diving, water skiing, windsurfing; playground.	100	•	•	•		•	•		•	•	•				
Otter Lake (C-8) 51 hectares on Otter Lake, 33 km w. of Princeton off Hwy. 5A. Canoeing, ice fishing, water skiing.	101	•	•	•	•	•		•	•	•	•	•	•		
Paarens Beach (E-4) 43 hectares 11 km s.w. of Fort St. James off Hwy. 27. Canoeing, water skiing, windsurfing; playground.	102	•	•	•	•	•		•	•	•	•	•			
Paul Lake (B-8) 670 hectares 5 km n. of Kamloops off Hwy. 5. Canoeing, cross-country skiing, snowshoeing, wildlife viewing.	103	•	•	•	•			•	•	•	•		•		
Pirates Cove Marine (G-10) 31 hectares 16 km s.e. of Nanaimo on DeCourcy Island via boat. Camping (walk-in only), canoeing, wildlife viewing.	104	•	•	•	•			•		•	•				
Plumper Cove Marine (G-11) 66 hectares on Keats Island. Boat and ferry access only. Camping (winter), canoeing.	105	•	•	•	•			•	•	•	•				
Porpoise Bay (G-11) 61 hectares 4 km n. of Sechelt off US 101. Canoeing; playground.	106	•	•	•	•			•	•	•	•				
Porteau Cove (G-11) 56 hectares 38 km n. of Vancouver on Hwy. 99. Camping (winter), canoeing, scuba diving, windsurfing, wildlife viewing.	107	•	•	•	•			•		•	•				
Premier Lake (C-12) 662 hectares 12 km s. of Skookumchuck via Hwy. 95. Camping (winter), canoeing, hunting, wildlife viewing; playground.	108	•	•	•	•	•		•	•	•	•				
Prudhomme Lake (E-2) 7 hectares 16 km e. of Prince Rupert on Hwy. 16. Canoeing.	109	•			•			•		•					
Purden Lake (F-5) 2,521 hectares 64 km e. of Prince George off Hwy. 16. Canoeing, hunting, water skiing, wildlife viewing, windsurfing; playground.	110	•	•	•	•	•		•	•	•	•				
Rathtrevor Beach (G-10) 347 hectares 3 km s. of Parksville on Hwy. 19A. Nature programs. Camping (winter), canoeing, wildlife viewing, windsurfing; playground.	111	•	•	•				•	•	•	•	•			
Rebecca Spit Marine (E-10) 177 hectares on Quadra Island via ferry from Campbell River, then 5 km e. on Heriot Bay Rd. Canoeing, scuba diving, windsurfing.	112		•	•	•			•	•	•	•	•			
Red Bluff (E-3) 148 hectares 45 km n. of Topley via Hwy. 118. Canoeing, wildlife viewing.	113	•	•	•	•			•	•	•	•	•			
Roberts Creek (G-11) 40 hectares 9 km s. of Sechelt on Hwy. 101.	114		•	•					•	•	•				
Roderick Haig-Brown (A-8) 1,076 hectares 5 km n. of Squilax off Hwy. 1 on both sides of the Adams River. Salmon spawning beds. Non-motorized boats only. Canoeing, wildlife viewing.	115		•	•	•			•		•	•	•	•		
Rolley Lake (H-12) 115 hectares 23 km n.w. of Mission off Hwy. 7. Canoeing, wildlife viewing.	116	•	•	•	•			•	•	•	•	•			

Recreation Areas Chart

The map location numerals in column 2 show an area's location on the preceding map.

	MAP LOCATION	CAMPING	PICNICKING	HIKING TRAILS	BOATING	BOAT RAMP	BOAT RENTAL	FISHING	SWIMMING	PETS ON LEASH	BICYCLE TRAILS	WINTER SPORTS	VISITOR CENTER	LODGE/CABINS	FOOD SERVICE
Ruckle (H-10) 529 hectares at Beaver Point on Salt Spring Island via ferry from Swartz Bay. Camping (winter), canoeing, scuba diving, wildlife viewing, windsurfing.	117	•	•	•				•	•	•	•				
Saltery Bay (F-11) 69 hectares 1 km n. of Saltery Bay ferry landing on Hwy. 101. Canoeing, kayaking, scuba diving, wildlife viewing.	118	•	•	•	•			•	•	•	•				
Sasquatch (D-7) 1,217 hectares 6.4 km n. of Harrison Hot Springs via an access road off Hwy. 7. Canoeing, water skiing, windsurfing, wildlife viewing; playground.	119	•	•	•	•	•		•	•	•	•				
Schoen Lake (H-3) 8,775 hectares 45 km s. of Sayward, 12 km off of Hwy. 19 via Davie Road. Backcountry skiing, canoeing, hunting, snowshoeing.	120	•	•	•	•	•		•	•	•	•	•			
Seeley Lake (E-3) 24 hectares 10 km w. of Hazelton on Hwy. 16. Electric motors only.	121	•	•	•	•			•	•	•	•				
Shuswap Lake (A-9) 149 hectares 19 km n. of Squilax. Nature programs. Canoeing, cross-country skiing, kayaking, snorkeling, snowshoeing, water skiing, windsurfing; playground.	122	•	•	•	•	•	•	•	•	•	•				
Silver Beach (A-9) 130 hectares at n. end of Shuswap Lake at Seymour Arm. Canoeing, scuba diving, water skiing, windsurfing.	123	•		•	•	•		•	•	•	•				
Skagit Valley (D-7) 27,948 hectares 3 km w. of Hope via Hwy. 1, then 37 km s. on entrance portal via Silver Skagit Rd. Interpretive programs. Canoeing, hunting; horse trails, playground.	124	•	•	•	•	•		•	•	•	•				
Skihist (B-7) 386 hectares 6 km e. of Lytton on Hwy. 1. Canoeing, wildlife viewing.	125	•	•	•				•		•	•				
Smelt Bay (E-10) 16 hectares on s.w. side of Cortes Island via ferry from Campbell River. Canoeing, kayaking.	126	•	•		•	•		•	•	•	•				
Sowchea Bay (E-4) 13 hectares on Stuart Lake, 20 km w. of Fort St. James off Hwy. 27. Canoeing, water skiing, windsurfing.	127	•			•	•		•	•	•					
Sproat Lake (F-9) 43 hectares 13 km n.w. of Port Alberni on Sproat Lake Rd. Canoeing, scuba diving, water skiing, windsurfing. Prehistoric petroglyphs (K'ak'awin).	128	•	•	•	•	•		•	•	•	•				
Stamp River (F-10) 327 hectares 14 km w. of Port Alberni on Stamp River Rd. Camping (winter).	129	•		•				•		•	•				
Stone Mountain (B-4) 25,690 hectares 140 km w. of Fort Nelson on Hwy. 97. Canoeing, horseback riding, kayaking, wildlife viewing.	130	•	•	•	•	•	•	•	•	•	•				
Strathcona (E-9) 245,807 hectares 48 km w. of Campbell River via Hwy. 28. Cross-country skiing, horseback riding, mountain biking, snowshoeing, water skiing, wildlife viewing, windsurfing. Snowmobiles prohibited.	131	•	•	•	•	•		•	•	•	•	•	•		•
Swan Lake (D-5) 82 hectares at Tupper, 35 km s.e. of Dawson Creek via Hwy. 2. Canoeing, kayaking, scuba diving, water skiing, windsurfing; playground.	132	•	•	•	•	•	•	•	•	•	•				
Syringa (C-10) 4,417 hectares 19 km n.w. of Castlegar off Hwy. 3. Canoeing, hunting, kayaking, water skiing, windsurfing; playground.	133	•	•	•	•	•		•	•	•	•				
Taylor Arm (F-9) 71 hectares 23 km n.w. of Port Alberni on Hwy. 4.	134		•	•	•			•	•		•				
Ten Mile Lake (F-4) 260 hectares 12 km n. of Quesnel on Hwy. 97. Canoeing; cross-country and water skiing.	135	•	•	•				•	•	•	•	•	•		
Top of the World (C-12) 8,790 hectares 48 km n.e. of Kimberley off Hwy. 93. Camping (winter), cross-country skiing, hunting, mountain biking, snowshoeing; horse trails.	136	•		•				•		•	•	•			
Tudyah Lake (E-4) 56 hectares 9 km n. of McLeod Lake on Hwy. 97. Canoeing, ice fishing, water skiing.	137	•	•					•	•	•	•		•		
Tweedsmuir (South and North) (G-3) 989,616 hectares 365 km n.w. of Williams Lake on Hwy. 20. Canoeing circuit, cross-country and downhill skiing, horseback riding, hunting.	138	•	•	•	•	•	•	•	•	•	•	•			

Recreation Areas Chart

The map location numerals in column 2 show an area's location on the preceding map.

Area	MAP LOCATION	CAMPING	PICNICKING	HIKING TRAILS	BOATING	BOAT RAMP	BOAT RENTAL	FISHING	SWIMMING	PETS ON LEASH	BICYCLE TRAILS	WINTER SPORTS	VISITOR CENTER	LODGE/CABINS	FOOD SERVICE
Tyhee Lake (E-3) 33 hectares 10 km e. of Smithers off Hwy. 16. Canoeing, cross-country skiing, ice skating, kayaking, water skiing, wildlife viewing.	139	•	•	•	•	•	•	•	•	•	•	•			
Vaseux Lake (C-9) 12 hectares 25 km s. of Penticton on Hwy. 97. Canoeing, ice skating, kayaking, wildlife viewing.	140	•	•	•	•			•	•	•	•	•			
Wasa Lake (C-12) 144 hectares 21 km n. of Fort Steele off Hwy. 93/95. Canoeing, water skiing, windsurfing; playground.	141	•	•	•	•	•		•	•	•	•				
Wells Gray (A-8) 540,000 hectares just n. of Clearwater via an access road off Hwy. 5. Interpretive programs. Canoeing, cross-country skiing, horseback riding, hunting, kayaking, snowshoeing, wildlife viewing.	142	•	•	•	•	•	•	•	•	•	•	•	•	•	•
West Lake (F-4) 256 hectares 22 km s.w. of Prince George off Hwy. 16. Canoeing, cross-country skiing, water skiing, wildlife viewing, windsurfing.	143		•	•	•	•		•	•	•		•			
Whiskers Point (E-4) 116 hectares 130 km n. of Prince George off Hwy. 97. Canoeing, hunting, kayaking, water skiing, windsurfing; nature trail, playground.	144	•	•	•	•	•		•	•	•		•			
Whiteswan Lake (B-12) 1,994 hectares 22 km s.e. of Canal Flats off Hwy. 93/95. Canoeing.	145	•	•	•	•	•		•	•	•	•				
Wistaria (E-3) 40 hectares 60 km w. of Hwy. 35, s.w. of Burns Lake on Ootsa Lake.	146		•		•	•		•		•					
Yahk (D-11) 9 hectares on Hwy. 3/93 at Yahk. Canoeing.	147	•	•	•		•		•		•		•			
Yard Creek (B-9) 175 hectares 15 km e. of Sicamous on Hwy. 1.	148	•	•	•				•	•	•					
OTHER															
Berman Lake (F-4) 38 hectares 45 km w. of Prince George. Canoeing.	149		•	•				•	•						
Canyon Hot Springs (A-10) Hot mineral springs 35 km e. of Revelstoke on Hwy. 1.	150	•	•	•	•			•	•	•				•	•
Creston Valley Wildlife Management Area (D-11) 7,000 hectares 13 km w. of Creston on Hwy. 3. Bird-watching, hunting.	151		•	•				•	•	•	•	•			
Descanso Bay Regional Park (G-10) 16 hectares 1 km e. of Nanaimo on Gabriola Island via ferry. Kayaking.	152	•	•	•	•			•	•	•					
Fairmont Hot Springs (B-12) Hot mineral springs on Hwy. 95 in Fairmont Hot Springs. Downhill skiing, fly fishing, ice fishing, rock climbing, snowshoeing, wildlife viewing, winter camping; horse rental.	153	•	•	•	•			•	•	•	•	•		•	•
Ferry Island (E-2) 61 hectares 1 km e. of Terrace off Hwy. 16. Cross-country skiing, fly-fishing, snowshoeing.	154	•	•	•				•	•	•		•			
Harold Mann (E-4) 13 hectares 50 km n.e. of Prince George. Canoeing; nature trail.	155		•	•				•	•	•			•		
Harrison Hot Springs (C-7) Hot mineral springs on Harrison Lake, 5 km n. of Hwy. 7 on Hwy. 9. Canoeing, golf, hunting, rock hunting; horse rental.	156	•	•	•	•	•	•	•	•	•			•		•
Kanaka Creek (H-12) 400 hectares 2 km e. of Haney. Canoeing, kayaking; fish hatchery, horse trails.	157		•	•	•			•	•	•					
Kawkawa Lake (C-7) 7 hectares 2.5 km e. of Hope off Hwy. 5. Canoeing, jet skiing, kayaking, tubing. Buggy rentals.	158	•	•	•	•	•		•	•						
Nakusp Hot Springs (B-10) Hot mineral springs 14 km n. of Nakusp on Nakusp Hot Springs Rd. Cross-country skiing, kayaking, mountain biking, snowmobiling.	159	•	•	•	•			•	•			•	•	•	
Ness Lake (E-4) 14 hectares 35 km n.w. of Prince George. Canoeing, cross-country skiing, ice fishing.	160		•	•				•	•	•					
Radium Hot Springs (B-11) Hot mineral springs near the w. entrance of Kootenay National Park. Hunting, skiing; horse rental.	161	•	•	•	•			•	•	•	•	•	•	•	
Whytecliff Park (G-11) 16 hectares near Horseshoe Bay in West Vancouver. Scuba diving; playground.	162		•	•	•			•	•	•					
Wilkins Park (E-4) 57 hectares 15 km w. of Prince George. Cross-country skiing; nature trail.	163		•	•	•	•				•		•			

100 MILE HOUSE pop. 1,886

HAPPY LANDING RESTAURANT   250/395-5359
 Traditional Swiss. Casual Dining. **Address:** 725 Alder Ave V0K 2E0

SMITTY'S   250/395-4655
 American. Casual Dining. **Address:** 451 Caribou Hwy V0K 2E0

108 MILE RANCH (A-7) pop. 2,559

South Cariboo Visitor Info Centre: 155 Airport Rd., Box 340, 100 Mile House, BC, Canada V0K 2E0. **Phone:** (250) 395-5353 or (877) 511-5353.

ABBOTSFORD (H-11) pop. 133,497, elev. 58m/190'

Abbotsford is the regional shopping center as well as the center of trade and industry for the fruit, livestock, poultry and dairy farms of the surrounding Fraser Valley. Several area industries and farms offer tours, including Clayburn Industries Ltd., at Railway and Pine streets, which produces refractory products. Castle Park Golf and Games Amusement Park, 36165 N. Parallel Rd., provides a range of family entertainment.

The city is also the site of the Abbotsford International Air Show, held in early August. In addition to more than 2 dozen planes on display, more than 30 planes, both military and civilian, take to the air.

Tourism Abbotsford Visitor Centre: 34561 Delair Rd., Abbotsford, BC, Canada V2S 2E1. **Phone:** (604) 859-1721 or (888) 332-2229.

BEST WESTERN BAKERVIEW INN   (604)859-1341

Motel
$109-$169

Best Western. **AAA Benefit:** Save 10% or more every day and earn 10% bonus points!

Address: 1821 Sumas Way V2S 4L5 **Location:** Trans-Canada Hwy 1 exit 92 (Town Centre), just n on Hwy 11. **Facility:** 61 units, some efficiencies. 2 stories (no elevator), exterior corridors. **Parking:** winter plug-ins. **Terms:** check-in 4 pm. **Pool(s):** heated indoor. **Activities:** hot tub. **Guest Services:** coin laundry.

Take your imagination to new destinations with the online AAA/CAA Travel Guides

BEST WESTERN PLUS REGENCY INN & CONFERENCE CENTRE   (604)853-3111

Hotel
$109-$300

 Best Western PLUS. **AAA Benefit:** Save 10% or more every day and earn 10% bonus points!

Address: 32110 Marshall Rd V2T 1A1 **Location:** Trans-Canada Hwy 1 exit 87 (Clearbrook Rd), just e. Located behind an elementary school. **Facility:** 128 units, some efficiencies and kitchens. 2-3 stories, interior corridors. **Pool(s):** heated indoor. **Activities:** hot tub, exercise room. **Guest Services:** valet and coin laundry.

WHERE TO EAT

MILESTONES GRILL AND BAR   604/381-1222
 American. Casual Dining. **Address:** 3122 Mount Lehman Rd V4X 2M9

RESTAURANT 62   604/855-3545
 New Canadian. Fine Dining. **Address:** 2001 McCallum Rd V2S 3N5

AINSWORTH HOT SPRINGS (C-11) elev. 538m/1,766'

AINSWORTH HOT SPRINGS RESORT is at 3609 Hwy. 31. Overlooking Kootenay Lake, the springs feature a natural, odorless mineral cave pool with an average temperature of 40-44 C (104-111 F), and a main pool averaging 35 C (97 F). The cold plunge pool, fed by a natural spring, has an average temperature of 4 C (40 F). Towels can be rented. **Hours:** Daily 10-9:30. Last admission 30 minutes before closing. **Cost:** $11.43; $10.48 (ages 13-17 and 60+ and students with ID); $9.05 (ages 3-12); $36.19 (family, two adults and two children). **Phone:** (250) 229-4212 or (800) 668-1171.

AINSWORTH HOT SPRINGS RESORT   (250)229-4212
 Hotel. **Address:** 3609 Hwy 31 V0G 1A0

WHERE TO EAT

KTUNAXA GRILL   250/229-4212
 American. Casual Dining. **Address:** 3609 Balfour-Kaslo-Galena Bay Hwy V0G 1A0

ALDERGROVE (H-11) elev. 61m/200'
• Hotels p. 178 • Restaurants p. 178
• Part of Vancouver area — see map p. 263

A small town on the Lower Fraser Valley's southern side, Aldergrove is near the Fraser River and the Canada-United States border. Dairy, chicken, strawberry and raspberry farms dot the surrounding area. Just northeast of Aldergrove, Bradner grows about 400 varieties of daffodils.

GREATER VANCOUVER ZOO is at 5048 264th St. The 49-hectare (120-acre) zoo is devoted to the preservation of endangered species. More than 600 animals represent 121 species from around the world, including hippopotami, monkeys, giraffes, cougars, coyotes, black bears, elk, reptiles, raptors, bison, tigers and a rescued grizzly bear named Shadow. A narrated miniature train ride takes passengers around the zoo's perimeter; guests can also pedal 2-seater quadra-cycles on a self-guiding tour. Interpretive talks are offered.

Time: Allow 2 hours minimum. **Hours:** Daily 9-7, Apr.-Sept.; 9-4, rest of year. Closed Christmas. **Cost:** $23.81; $21.90 (ages 16+ with student ID); $18.10 (ages 3-15 and 65+); $76.19 (family, two adults and three children). Train ride $4.76. Quadra-cycle $18 per hour. **Parking:** Parking $6. Rates may vary; phone ahead. **Phone:** (604) 856-6825.

BEST WESTERN PLUS COUNTRY MEADOWS INN
(604)856-9880

Hotel
$119-$359

 Best Western PLUS

AAA Benefit: Save 10% or more every day and earn 10% bonus points!

Address: 3070 264th St V4W 3E1 **Location:** Trans-Canada Hwy 1 exit 73 (264th St/Aldergrove), 3.1 mi (5 km) s on 264th St (Hwy 13). **Facility:** 77 units, some efficiencies and kitchens. 2 stories, interior corridors. **Terms:** check-in 4 pm, cancellation fee imposed. **Pool(s):** heated indoor. **Activities:** hot tub, exercise room. **Guest Services:** valet and coin laundry.

 **WHERE TO EAT**

FOX & HOUNDS PUB & RESTAURANT   604/856-8111
International. Casual Dining. **Address:** 26444 32 Ave V4W 3E8

TOMO SUSHI   604/856-8998
Sushi. Casual Dining. **Address:** 26391 Fraser Hwy V4W 2Z7

ALERT BAY (H-2) pop. 445, elev. 15m/49'

On crescent-shaped Cormorant Island off Vancouver Island's northeast coast, Alert Bay is a fishing village reached by ferry from Port McNeill (see place listing p. 237). The influence of indigenous cultures is evident in the many totem poles, including a memorial pole for totem carver Chief Mungo Martin.

Christ Church on Front Street is an 1881 cedar church with stained-glass windows that reflect the blending of native and European cultures; phone the Travel InfoCentre for information.

Alert Bay Visitor Centre: 118 Fir St., Bag Service 2800, Alert Bay, BC, Canada V0N 1A0. **Phone:** (250) 974-5024.

ARMSTRONG pop. 4,815
• Part of Okanagan Valley area — see map p. 222

VILLAGE CHEESE COMPANY   250/546-8651
Soup Sandwiches. Quick Serve. **Address:** 3475 Smith Dr V0E 1B0

ASHCROFT (B-7) pop. 1,628, elev. 305m/1,000'

Ashcroft Manor, a roadside house on Cariboo Waggon Road, was named for the English home of its settlers, Clement and Henry Cornwall. The Cornwalls established themselves as cattlemen in 1862 and lived the pioneer life in the style of gentlemen, practicing such rituals as afternoon tea and riding to hounds through sagebrush and scrub in pursuit of coyotes. The manor is south of town on Hwy. 1.

BARKERVILLE HISTORIC TOWN (F-5)

Barkerville is approximately 80 kilometres (50 mi.) east of Quesnel via Hwy. 26. The restored 1870s gold rush town once had the largest population north of San Francisco and west of Chicago. In those days when more than $50 million of gold—at $16 per ounce—had been mined from the area, soap cost $1 a bar and a dance with a hurdy-gurdy girl cost $1 a whirl.

The town was named for Billy Barker, a Cornish miner who first found gold in large quantities in the early 1860s. Barkerville became a virtual ghost town a few years later when the gold ran out.

The Barkerville Hotel, St. Saviours Church, the Mason and Daly General Store and the Wake Up Jake Cafe are just a few of the 125 original or reconstructed buildings in the town; many are manned by attendants in period dress. A replica of Billy Barker's Barker & Co. Discovery Shaft and Shaft House is complete with working windlass and sluice box displays. Board sidewalks and dirt streets help preserve the essence of the original site.

Theatre Royale presents period melodrama, dance and music Victoria Day through September 30. Treasure seekers can pan for gold at Eldorado Mine. A visitor center presents videos and exhibits about the history of Barkerville. Guided town, Chinatown and cemetery tours as well as living-history programs are offered.

Pets are not permitted. The townsite is open daily 8-8. Full visitor services operate daily, mid-May to late Sept. Admission mid-May to late Sept., $15.25; $14.15 (ages 65+); $9.65 (ages 13-18); $4.70 (ages 6-12); $5 (second-day admission with first-day receipt); $36.75 (family, two adults and four children). Rest of year free. Phone (250) 994-3332 or (888) 994-3332.

BARRIERE pop. 1,326

MOUNTAIN SPRINGS MOTEL & RV PARK   250/672-0090
Motel. **Address:** 4253 Yellowhead Hwy V0E 1E0

BOSTON BAR (C-7) pop. 206,
elev. 309m/1,013'

Boston Bar, which began as a gold mining town, was named for a Dutchman who came from Boston to prospect in the 1860s. Because Boston was the home port to many of the ships bringing prospectors, local First Nations people called the newcomers Boston men. Boston Bar is a logging and trade center, with the Canadian National Railway passing through town. The Canadian Pacific Railway parallels the National on the other side of Fraser River Canyon and passes through the village of North Bend.

Boston Bar is the access point for the Nahatlatch Valley, which features the Nahatlatch River and a chain of lakes. Recreation includes camping, fishing and white-water rafting.

HELL'S GATE AIRTRAM is 11 km (7 mi.) s. on Hwy. 1 to 43111 Trans-Canada Hwy. in Fraser River Canyon. The 25-passenger gondola descends 153 metres (502 ft.) across the river to the narrowest part of Fraser Canyon and across Hell's Gate Fishways, where millions of salmon annually swim upstream to their spawning grounds. Visitors can see eight fishways from the lower observation decks or a suspension bridge.

A film about the life cycle of the salmon is shown at the education center, along with stories about early explorer Simon Fraser and the Fraser River Gold Rush. Panning for gold is available.

Time: Allow 1 hour minimum. **Hours:** Daily 10-6, July-Oct.; 10-4, Apr.-June. Phone ahead to confirm schedule. **Cost:** $23.10; $21 (ages 65+ and students with ID); $16.80 (ages 6-18); $63 (family). **Phone:** (604) 867-9277.

BRENTWOOD BAY (H-10)
• Hotels p. 180 • Restaurants p. 180
• Part of Victoria area — see map p. 317

BUTCHART GARDENS is 2 km (1.2 mi.) s. on W. Saanich Rd., then w. to 800 Benvenuto Ave. The magnificent floral displays of Butchart Gardens owe their existence to Jennie Butchart, wife of Robert Pim Butchart, a successful Portland cement pioneer.

When the limestone quarry near their home became depleted in the early 1900s, Jennie lined the empty pit with topsoil and the gardens began to take shape. The Sunken Garden, the site of the former quarry, was soon joined on the 22-hectare (55-acre) site with the Rose Garden, Japanese Garden and Italian Garden as well as the Star Pond and Ross Fountain. The Butcharts named their estate *Benvenuto*, Italian for "welcome."

The spring season brings azaleas, tulips, daffodils and other delicate blossoms. Breathtaking roses, annuals and perennials bloom in summer, while bursts of colorful foliage appear in autumn; subtle colored lighting illuminates the gardens June 15 through Sept. 15.

Two electrically operated boats offer 45-minute tours of the local coastline, including the location of the now-gone factory that produced cement from the limestone quarried in what is now the Sunken Garden. The cruise along Tod Inlet and Brentwood Bay often provides sightings of seals, herons, eagles and otters. The Rose Carousel in the Children's Pavilion offers old-fashioned rides on 30 hand-carved animals and two chariots.

July through August, nightly entertainment is offered with fireworks displays Saturday nights. The sparkle of holiday lights and decorations complement the colorful berries on shrubs and trees from Dec. 1 to Jan. 6 during Christmas at Butcharts. An outdoor skating rink, with skate rental, also is available in Waterwheel Square.

Time: Allow 2 hours minimum. **Hours:** Gardens open daily at 9 (at 1 on Christmas). Closing times vary depending on the season; phone ahead. Boat tours depart the dock daily every half-hour 11-5, mid-June to mid-Sept.; 11-4, late May to mid-June.

Cost: June 15-Sept. 30, $32.10; $16.05 (ages 13-17); $3 (ages 5-12). Admission in Oct., $26.85; $13.45 (ages 13-17); $2 (ages 5-12). Admission in Nov. $20.80; $10.40 (ages 13-17); $2 (ages 5-12). Admission Dec. 1-Jan. 6, $26.60; $13.30 (ages 13-17); $3 (ages 5-12). Admission Jan. 7-Jan. 14, $17.75; $8.90 (ages 13-17); $2 (ages 5-12). Admission Jan. 15-Mar. 19, $23.80; $11.90 (ages 13-17); $2 (ages 5-12). Admission Mar. 20-June 14, $29.90; $14.95 (ages 13-17); $2 (ages 5-12). Boat tours $17.25; $13.25 (ages 13-17); $10.50 (ages 5-12). Carousel rides $2. Rates may vary; phone ahead. **Phone:** (250) 652-5256 or (866) 652-4422.

VICTORIA BUTTERFLY GARDENS is 2 km (1.2 mi.) s. at jct. Benvenuto Ave. and Keating Cross Rd. at 1461 Benvenuto Ave. This 1,110-square-metre (12,000-sq.-ft.) indoor tropical garden was designed specifically for the housing and breeding of more than 75 exotic butterfly and moth species.

Guided tours and a video presentation explain the transformations the butterflies undergo during their life cycle. Between 600 and 1,200 pupae are imported each week and displayed in the Emerging Room.

Up to 6,000 butterflies—from the 2.5-centimetre-long (1-in.) helicon to the 30.5-centimetre-long (1-ft.) atlas moth—fly free among tropical plants and flowers, including an orchid exhibit and a carnivorous bog. Water falls into a stream that is home to koi fish and tropical ducks. Parrots, flamingos, songbirds and rare species such as the South African turacos also call the gardens home. Other garden residents include poison dart frogs, geckos, chameleons and sulcata tortoises.

Time: Allow 1 hour minimum. **Hours:** Daily 10-5, Jan.-Nov.; 10-7, in Dec. Last admission 1 hour before closing. Closed Jan. 1 and Christmas. Phone ahead to confirm schedule. **Cost:** All-day admission $16.50; $11 (ages 13-17, ages 65+ and students with ID); $6 (ages 5-12). **Phone:** (250) 652-3822 or (877) 722-0272.

BRENTWOOD BAY RESORT & SPA   (250)544-2079

Contemporary
Resort Hotel
$149-$899

Address: 849 Verdier Ave V8M 1C5 **Location:** Oceanfront. Jct Brentwood Dr and Verdier Ave. **Facility:** This is a luxury retreat where every room offers a water view, private sun decks, deep soaker tubs, gas fireplaces and soft, fine linens on every bed. The spa offers fine couples' treatments. 35 units, some condominiums. 3 stories, exterior corridors. **Terms:** 2 night minimum stay - seasonal and/or weekends, 7 day cancellation notice. **Amenities:** safes. **Dining:** The Dining Room at Brentwood Bay, see separate listing. **Pool(s):** heated outdoor. **Activities:** hot tub, self-propelled boats, marina, fishing, scuba diving, exercise room, spa. **Guest Services:** valet and coin laundry.

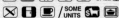

THE DINING ROOM AT BRENTWOOD BAY   250/544-2079
Pacific Northwest. Fine Dining. **Address:** 849 Verdier Ave V8M 1C5

ZANZIBAR CAFE   250/652-1228
Breakfast Sandwiches. Casual Dining. **Address:** 1164 Stelly's Cross Rd V8M 1H3

BRITANNIA BEACH (G-11) pop. 254, elev. 6m/20'

From 1930 to 1935 the Britannia Mine at Britannia Beach was the largest producer of copper in the British Empire. No longer in operation, the mine is now part of the Britannia Mine Museum.

Shopping: At the CRS Trading Post on Hwy. 99 the wood and soapstone carvings, silver jewelry, spirit masks, jade pieces, handcrafted walking sticks, moccasins and other items are created by Coast Salish artists in British Columbia. Look for the rocks displaying hand-painted scenes by well-known local artist Ken Skoda.

BRITANNIA MINE MUSEUM is off Hwy. 99/Sea to Sky Hwy., following signs. The Britannia Mine was an important 20th-century copper mining site during its 70-year existence. The company town included libraries, swimming pools and a gym, and social events were held throughout the year.

The towering 20-story 1923 mill building, through which the ore would move as it was crushed and the valuable minerals separated from the rest of the rock, is now a museum. Fourteen other historic buildings also can be seen. Mining artifacts document the history of the site, and other items depict the social history of mining communities. The Canadian Mining Hall of Fame and a theater are on-site.

An underground mine tunnel ride is a highlight of the museum, which chronicles mining history through hands-on demonstrations and exhibits. On site is a 235-ton super mine truck. Gold panning is included with admission.

Note: The tunnel temperature is a constant 12 C (54 F); warm clothing and comfortable walking shoes are recommended. Hard hats are provided. **Time:** Allow 1 hour, 30 minutes minimum. **Hours:** Tours daily at 10 and every half-hour until 5, July 1-Labour Day. Arrive 20 minutes before tour time. Closed major holidays. Phone ahead to confirm schedule. **Cost:** $29; $26.50 (ages 65+); $23 (ages 13-18); $18.50 (ages 5-12); $105 (family, two adults and up to three children). **Phone:** (604) 896-2233 or (800) 896-4044. GT

BURNABY (H-11) pop. 223,218, elev. 40m/130'

Burnaby is more than just a suburban, bedroom community of hills, ridges, valleys, plain, and stunning views; it is an urban center which is home to Simon Fraser University and the British Columbia Institute of Technology. It's also home to Playground of the Gods, a stunning collection of 25 non-typical totem poles made by artist Nuburi Toko and his son in the Japanese Ainu animist tradition, in Burnaby Mountain Park, 100 Centennial Way; phone (604) 294-7450.

ACCENT INNS   604/473-5000 **14**
Hotel. **Address:** 3777 Henning Dr V5C 6N5

BEST WESTERN PLUS KINGS INN & CONFERENCE CENTER   (604)438-1383 **19**

Motel
$119-$159

Best Western PLUS

AAA Benefit: Save 10% or more every day and earn 10% bonus points!

Address: 5411 Kingsway V5H 2G1 **Location:** Trans-Canada Hwy 1 exit 29 (Willingdon Ave), 1.9 mi (3 km) s to Kingsway, then 1.2 mi (2 km) e. Royal Oak, 23. **Facility:** 137 units, some efficiencies and kitchens. 2 stories (no elevator), exterior corridors. **Pool(s):** heated outdoor. **Guest Services:** valet and coin laundry. **Featured Amenity:** breakfast buffet.

(See ad p. 181.)

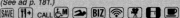

(See map & index p. 290.)

DELTA BURNABY HOTEL AND CONFERENCE CENTRE
(604)453-0750 **15**

Contemporary
Hotel
$125-$252

DELTA HOTELS

AAA Benefit: Members save 5% or more!

Address: 4331 Dominion St V5G 1B2
Location: Trans-Canada Hwy 1 exit 29 (Willingdon Ave), just w on Canada Way, then n on Sumner St. Gilmore, 9. **Facility:** Rich hues of purple accent the striking décor of the outstanding lobby here. Guest rooms are upscale in design, but the suites on the top floor are especially swanky and glitzy. 195 units. 21 stories, interior corridors. **Parking:** on-site and valet. **Amenities:** safes. **Dining:** 2 restaurants, also, Ebo Restaurant and Lounge, see separate listing. **Activities:** hot tub, steamroom, exercise room. **Guest Services:** valet laundry, area transportation.

ELEMENT VANCOUVER METROTOWN
(604)568-3696 **16**

Extended Stay
Contemporary
Hotel
$189-$349

AAA Benefit: Members save up to 15%, plus Starwood Preferred Guest® benefits!

Address: 5988 Willingdon Ave V5H 2A7
Location: Trans-Canada Hwy 1 exit 29 (Willingdon Ave), 2 mi (3.3 km) s. Metrotown, 22. **Facility:** 169 units, some efficiencies. 18 stories, interior corridors. *Bath:* shower only. **Parking:** on-site (fee). **Terms:** cancellation fee imposed. **Amenities:** safes. **Dining:** Trattoria, see separate listing. **Pool(s):** heated outdoor. **Activities:** sauna, hot tub, bicycles, picnic facilities, exercise room. **Guest Services:** valet and coin laundry. **Featured Amenity:** breakfast buffet.

EXECUTIVE HOTELS & RESORTS
604/298-2010 **13**

Hotel. **Address:** 4201 Lougheed Hwy V5C 3Y6

▼ See AAA listing p. 180 ▼

(See map & index p. 290.)

HILTON VANCOUVER METROTOWN

(604)438-1200 **17**

Hotel
$119-$284

AAA Benefit: Members save 5% or more!

Address: 6083 McKay Ave V5H 2W7 **Location:** Trans-Canada Hwy 1 exit 29 (Willingdon Ave), 1.8 mi (3 km) s to Kingsway, then just e. Next to Metrotown Shopping Mall. Metrotown, 22. **Facility:** 283 units. 18 stories, interior corridors. **Parking:** on-site (fee) and valet. **Terms:** 1-7 night minimum stay, cancellation fee imposed. **Amenities:** safes. **Dining:** Reflect Social Dining + Lounge, see separate listing. **Pool(s):** heated outdoor. **Activities:** hot tub, exercise room. **Guest Services:** valet laundry.

HOLIDAY INN EXPRESS METROTOWN   604/438-1881 **18**
Hotel. **Address:** 4405 Central Blvd V5H 4M3

WHERE TO EAT

CACTUS CLUB CAFE   604/291-6606
New American. Casual Dining. **Address:** 4219B Lougheed Hwy V5C 3Y6

COCKNEY KINGS FISH & CHIPS   604/291-1323 **35**
Fish & Chips. Casual Dining. **Address:** 6574 E Hastings V5B 1S2

EARLS KITCHEN + BAR   604/205-5025
American. Casual Dining. **Address:** 3850 Lougheed Hwy V5C 6N4

EBO RESTAURANT AND LOUNGE   604/453-0788 **37**
Pacific Northwest. Casual Dining. **Address:** 4331 Dominion St V5G 1B2

HART HOUSE RESTAURANT   604/298-4278 **38**
Pacific Northwest. Fine Dining. **Address:** 6664 Deer Lake Ave V5E 4H3

HORIZONS   604/299-1155 **36**
Pacific Rim. Fine Dining. **Address:** 100 Centennial Way V5A 2X9

THE PEAR TREE RESTAURANT   604/299-2772 **34**
Regional Canadian. Fine Dining. **Address:** 4120 E Hastings St V5C 2J4

REFLECT SOCIAL DINING + LOUNGE   604/438-1200 **40**
American. Casual Dining. **Address:** 6083 McKay Ave V5H 2W7

SWISS CHALET   604/299-1761
Chicken. Casual Dining. **Address:** 3860 Lougheed Hwy V5C 6N4

TRATTORIA   604/424-8778 **39**
Italian. Casual Dining. **Address:** 4501 Kingsway V5H 2A9

CACHE CREEK (B-7) pop. 1,040, elev. 450m/1,500'

HISTORIC HAT CREEK RANCH is 11 km (7 mi.) n. on Hwy. 99 at Hwy. 97 jct. The 130-hectare (320-acre) ranch, on one of the few sections of the Cariboo Waggon Road still accessible to the public, consists of more than 20 historic buildings constructed 1863-1915 when the ranch served as a roadhouse for the horse-drawn stagecoaches and freight wagons of the B.C. Express line (known as the B.X.).

Docents in period costumes conduct guided tours of the 1860s roadhouse, and visitors can explore a heritage apple orchard, a Shuswap native village, a blacksmith shop and a collection of pioneer agricultural machinery. Visitors also can enjoy stagecoach rides and try their hand at gold panning.

Hours: Daily 9-5 (stagecoach and tours 9:30-4:30), May-Sept. **Cost:** $13.50; $12 (ages 55+); $8 (ages 6-12); $30 (family, two adults and two children). **Phone:** (250) 457-9722 or (800) 782-0922.

CAMPBELL RIVER (E-10) pop. 31,186, elev. 18m/59'

An important lumber, mining and commercial fishing center, Campbell River is near a noted Vancouver Island timber stand. The Elk Falls Pulp and Paper Mill offers tours in the summer. Campbell River is headquarters of the Tyee Club, whose members must catch a salmon of 14 kilograms (30 lbs.) or more while fishing from a rowboat in the raging waters of Discovery Passage.

Provincial parks preserve the area's natural beauty, typified by waterfalls and mountainous wilderness. At Elk Falls Provincial Park the Campbell River drops 27 metres (90 ft.) into a deep canyon. Strathcona Provincial Park contains Mount Golden Hinde, at 2,200 metres (7,218 ft.) the highest mountain on Vancouver Island, and 440-metre (1,445-ft.) Della Falls, the highest waterfall in Canada. Scuba diving is popular during the winter when the waters are particularly clear. *See Recreation Areas Chart.*

The 183-metre-long (600-ft.) Campbell River Fishing Pier, 655 Island Hwy., is available for fishing, strolling or watching the cruise ships pass through the Strait of Georgia.

Campbell River Visitor Centre: 1235 Shoppers Row, Tyree Plaza, Campbell River, BC, Canada V9W 2C7. **Phone:** (250) 286-6901 or (877) 286-5705.

BEST WESTERN AUSTRIAN CHALET   (250)923-4231

Hotel
$114-$169

AAA Benefit:
Save 10% or more every day and
earn 10% bonus points!

Address: 462 S Island Hwy V9W 1A5 **Location:** 2 mi (3.2 km) s on Island Hwy 19A. **Facility:** 60 units, some efficiencies. 2-3 stories (no elevator), interior/exterior corridors. **Terms:** cancellation fee imposed. **Pool(s):** heated indoor. **Activities:** sauna, hot tub, exercise room. **Guest Services:** coin laundry. **Featured Amenity: continental breakfast.**

Best Western.

Panoramic ocean and mountain view rooms. Complimentary deluxe continental breakfast.

COMFORT INN & SUITES-CAMPBELL RIVER   (250)914-5117
Hotel. **Address:** 1351 Shoppers Row V9W 2C9

OCEAN RESORT   250/923-4281
Motel. **Address:** 4384 S Island Hwy V9H 1E8

WHERE TO EAT

BAAN THAI RESTAURANT   250/286-4850
Thai. Casual Dining. **Address:** 1090B Shoppers Row V9W 2C6

BEST WOK   250/287-2831
Chinese. Casual Dining. **Address:** 968 Alder St V9W 2P9

THE DRIFTWOOD RESTAURANT   250/923-5505
Chinese. Casual Dining. **Address:** 4329 S Island Hwy V9H 1B7

FUSILLI GRILL   250/830-0090
Pacific Northwest. Casual Dining. **Address:** 1760 N Island Hwy V9W 1B8

MOXIE'S CLASSIC GRILL   250/830-1500
American. Casual Dining. **Address:** 1360 Island Hwy V9W 8C9

QUAY WEST KITCHEN & CATERING   250/286-9988
Pacific Northwest. Casual Dining. **Address:** 921 Island Hwy V9W 2C2

RICKY'S ALL DAY GRILL   250/286-3448
American. Casual Dining. **Address:** 811 13th Ave V9W 4G9

CASTLEGAR (C-10) pop. 7,816, elev. 494m/1,620'

At the junction of hwys. 3 and 3A, Castlegar is considered the crossroads of the Kootenays. Just north is the 51-metre-high (167-ft.) Hugh Keenleyside Dam. The upper and lower Arrow Lakes, created by the dam, offer popular summer recreation areas including Arrow Lakes Provincial Park (Shelter Bay) and Syringa Provincial Park *(see Recreation Areas Chart)*.

Castlegar Chamber of Commerce: 1995 Sixth Ave., Castlegar, BC, Canada V1N 4B7. **Phone:** (250) 365-6313.

CANADAS BEST VALUE INN & SUITES CASTLEGAR
(250)365-2177
Hotel. **Address:** 1935 Columbia Ave V1N 2W8

SUPER 8-CASTLEGAR   (250)365-2700
Hotel. **Address:** 651 18th St V1N 2N1

WHERE TO EAT

BLACK ROOSTER CLASSIC BAR & GRILL   250/365-7779
American. Casual Dining. **Address:** 651 18th St V1N 2N1

ELEMENT CLUB BAR GRILL   250/365-8066
American. Casual Dining. **Address:** 292 Columbia Ave V1N 1G4

CHASE pop. 2,495

CHASE COUNTRY INN MOTEL   250/679-3333
Motel. **Address:** 576 Coburn St V0E 1M0

QUAAOUT LODGE & SPA, TALKING ROCK GOLF
(250)679-3090

Resort Hotel
$116-$215

Address: 1663 Little Shuswap Lake Rd V0E 1M0 **Location:** Trans-Canada Hwy 1 exit Squilax Bridge, 1.5 mi (2.5 km) w; on Little Shuswap Lake Rd. Located in a quiet secluded area. **Facility:** Native interpretive trails criss-cross the grounds of this lovely lodge; there is also a sprawling beach. The tastefully decorated rooms feature balconies or patios. 70 units. 3 stories, interior corridors. **Terms:** check-in 4 pm, cancellation fee imposed. **Pool(s):** heated indoor. **Activities:** hot tub, steamroom, self-propelled boats, boat dock, regulation golf, recreation programs, lawn sports, trails, exercise room, spa. **Guest Services:** valet laundry.

CHEMAINUS (H-10) pop. 3,035, elev. 6m/20'
• Hotels p. 184 • Restaurants p. 184

A lumber and manufacturing town, Chemainus added tourism to its economy with the creation of murals. More than 40 professional paintings on the walls of buildings portray the history of the Chemainus Valley. Subjects range from First Nations people to dramatic depictions of the logging industry.

Begun by local artists, the series of murals has attracted artists from around the world. Recent additions include interpretations of images created by noted Canadian artist Emily Carr, including a trompe l'oeil mural on the wall of the Chemainus Theatre. Walking tour maps can be bought at the kiosk in the central parking area. Prearranged guided tours and horse-drawn carriage tours also are available for a fee; phone (250) 246-5055 or (250) 246-0063.

The Chemainus Theatre offers dramas, comedies and musical productions; phone (250) 246-9820 or (800) 565-7738.

Chemainus Visitor Centre: 102-9799 Waterwheel Crescent, P.O. Box 575, Chemainus, BC, Canada V0R 1K0. **Phone:** (250) 246-3944.

BEST WESTERN PLUS CHEMAINUS INN (250)246-4181

Hotel
$143-$175

 Best Western PLUS **AAA Benefit:** Save 10% or more every day and earn 10% bonus points!

Address: 9573 Chemainus Rd V0R 1K5 **Location:** Trans-Canada Hwy 1 exit Henry Rd, 0.9 mi (1.4 km) e. **Facility:** 75 units, some two bedrooms and efficiencies. 4 stories, interior corridors. **Terms:** check-in 4 pm, resort fee. **Amenities:** safes. **Pool(s):** heated indoor. **Activities:** hot tub, exercise room, massage. **Guest Services:** coin laundry.

[SAVE] [ECO] [⏏] CALL [&M] [≈] [BIZ]

[HS] [🛜] [✕] [🔌] [💻] /SOME UNITS [S🛏] [🍽]

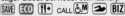
WHERE TO EAT

ODIKA CAFE   250/324-3303
▼▼ ▼▼ International. Casual Dining. **Address:** 2976 Mill St V0R 1K0

CHETWYND pop. 2,635

DAYS INN CHETWYND   (250)788-3344
▼▼ ▼▼ Motel. **Address:** 4401 53rd Ave V0C 1J0

LAKEVIEW INNS & SUITES   250/788-3000
▼▼ ▼▼ Hotel. **Address:** 4820 N Access Rd V0C 1J0 **(See ad opposite inside front cover.)**

POMEROY INN & SUITES   250/788-4800
▼▼ ▼▼ ▼ Extended Stay Hotel. **Address:** 5200 N Access Rd V0C 1J0

CHILLIWACK (H-12) pop. 77,936, elev. 10m/33'

In the heart of the upper Fraser River Valley, Chilliwack is the center of a prosperous farming and dairy region. The surrounding lakes, rivers, mountains and nearby provincial parks offer such varied recreation as skiing, hiking, fishing, rock hunting and white-water rafting. Scenic views and picnic facilities are available at Chilliwack Lake Provincial Park, 84 kilometres (54 mi.) southeast off Hwy. 1 *(see Recreation Areas Chart)*, and Cultus Lake Provincial Park, 11 kilometres (7 mi.) southwest off Hwy. 1 *(see Recreation Areas Chart)*.

Tourism Chilliwack Visitor Information Centre: 44150 Luckakuck Way, Chilliwack, BC, Canada V2R 4A7. **Phone:** (604) 858-8121 or (800) 567-9535.

GREAT BLUE HERON NATURE RESERVE is at 5200 Sumas Prairie Rd. This 130-hectare (321-acre) site includes an interpretive center, an observation tower, fish-spawning channels and a self-guiding interpretive walking trail. More than 90 herons build nests here; painted turtles, tailed frogs, beavers, bald eagles and a variety of other birds also dwell at the reserve.

Time: Allow 1 hour minimum. **Hours:** Nature reserve open daily 8-dusk. Interpretive center open daily 10-4, Feb.-Oct.; 10-2, rest of year. Phone ahead to confirm schedule in winter. **Cost:** Donations. **Phone:** (604) 823-6603.

BEST WESTERN RAINBOW COUNTRY INN
(604)795-3828

Hotel
$110-$300

 Best Western **AAA Benefit:** Save 10% or more every day and earn 10% bonus points!

Address: 43971 Industrial Way V2R 3A4 **Location:** Trans-Canada Hwy 1 exit 116 (Lickman Rd). **Facility:** 74 units. 2 stories, interior corridors. **Terms:** resort fee. **Pool(s):** heated indoor. **Activities:** hot tub. **Guest Services:** valet and coin laundry. **Featured Amenity:** breakfast buffet.

[SAVE] [ECO] [⏏] [🍴] [🍸] CALL [&M] [≈]

[BIZ] [🛜] [✕] [🔌] [💻]

/SOME UNITS [S🛏] [HS] [🍽]

THE COAST CHILLIWACK HOTEL   604/792-5552
▼▼▼ ▼▼ Hotel. **Address:** 45920 First Ave V2P 7K1

TRAVELODGE HOTEL CHILLIWACK (604)792-4240

▼▼ ▼▼
Hotel
$89-$149

 Address: 45466 Yale Rd W V2R 3Z8 **Location:** Trans-Canada Hwy 1 exit 119, just n. **Facility:** 82 units, some two bedrooms and efficiencies. 2 stories (no elevator), interior corridors. **Terms:** 3 day cancellation notice. **Pool(s):** heated indoor. **Activities:** hot tub, picnic facilities, limited exercise equipment. **Guest Services:** coin laundry.

[SAVE] [ECO] [➕] [🍴] CALL [&M] [≈]

[BIZ] [HS] [🛜] [✕] [💻]

/SOME UNITS [S🛏] [🔌] [🍽]

WHERE TO EAT

EARLS KITCHEN + BAR   604/858-3360
▼▼ ▼▼ American. Casual Dining. **Address:** 45585 Luckakuck Way V2R 1A1

PRESTONS   604/701-3070
▼▼▼ ▼▼ American. Casual Dining. **Address:** 45920 First Ave V2P 7K1

RICKY'S ALL DAY GRILL   604/858-5663
▼▼ ▼▼ American. Casual Dining. **Address:** 45389 Luckakuck Way V2R 3C7

SHANDHAR HUT INDIAN CUISINE   604/793-0188
▼▼ ▼▼ Indian. Casual Dining. **Address:** 8835 Young Rd V2P 4P6

VITA BELLA ITALIAN BISTRO   604/846-5001
▼▼▼▼ Italian. Casual Dining. **Address:** 45355 Luckakuck Way V2R 3C7

CHRISTINA LAKE pop. 1,168

NEW HORIZON MOTEL   250/447-9312
▼▼ **Motel. Address:** 2037 Hunter Frontage Rd (Hwy 3) V0H 1E2

CLEARWATER (A-8) pop. 2,331

Clearwater gets its name from the clear waters of the nearby Clearwater River. Opportunities for riding, hiking, canoeing, skiing and fishing abound in the surrounding North Thompson Valley.

Wells Gray Provincial Park, north off Hwy. 5, offers a variety of scenery, particularly with regard to water. Scattered throughout its boundaries are five large lakes, two river systems, many streams and waterways and a multitude of waterfalls. Helmcken Falls, which drops 141 metres (465 ft.), is said to be the fourth highest in Canada. At Bailey's Chute Loop in late summer, visitors can view salmon jumping upstream to spawn. Extinct volcanoes and lava beds recall the region's fiery past. *See Recreation Areas Chart.*

Clearwater & District Chamber of Commerce: 416 Eden Rd., Clearwater, BC, Canada V0E 1N1. **Phone:** (250) 674-3530.

CLINTON (A-7) pop. 636, elev. 274m/898'

During the gold rush of the late 1850s and early 1860s Clinton was the junction of several wagon roads leading to northern goldfields. In 1863 Queen Victoria changed the town's name from Junction to Clinton. Retaining much of its frontier look, Clinton is a supply center for surrounding resorts, fishing camps and ranches. Summer activities include boating, fishing and camping at area lakes, which also attract various wildlife.

The Village of Clinton: 1423 Cariboo Hwy., P.O. Box 309, Clinton, BC, Canada V0K 1K0. **Phone:** (250) 459-2261.

COMOX (F-10) pop. 13,627

Comox was founded in the mid-1800s, taking its name from the Salish word *Koumuckthay,* meaning "land of plenty." Once an important port for ships of the Royal Navy, the east coast village became the home of a Royal Air Force base in 1942. CFB Comox maintains search-and-rescue operations, maritime patrols and support of naval and air force defense.

PORT AUGUSTA INN & SUITES   250/339-2277
▼▼ **Motel. Address:** 2082 Comox Ave V9M 1P8

WHERE TO EAT

BLACKFIN PUB AT THE MARINA   250/339-5030
▼▼ American. Gastropub. **Address:** 132 Port Augusta St V9M 3N7

SMITTY'S   250/339-3911
▼▼▼▼ American. Casual Dining. **Address:** 1747 Comox Ave V9M 3M2

COOMBS (G-10) pop. 1,547

Coombs retains the atmosphere of a quaint village settled around 1910. The Coombs General Store, which has operated continuously since the settlement days, and the Old Country Market, which is unusual for the goats that are kept on the roof in summer, are two landmarks.

The town is on Vancouver Island, midway between Little Qualicum Falls Provincial Park *(see Recreation Areas Chart)* and Englishman River Falls Provincial Park *(see Recreation Areas Chart),* where there are many recreational opportunities.

COQUITLAM (H-11) pop. 126,456,
elev. 137m/449'
* **Restaurants p. 186**
* **Attractions map p. 278**
* **Hotels & Restaurants map & index p. 290**
* **Part of Vancouver area — see map p. 263**

Named for a type of landlocked salmon, Coquitlam borders Pitt Lake and encompasses Burke Mountain. Recreational opportunities, including swimming, canoeing, hiking and fishing, are available throughout the area.

Nearby parks and lakes include Mundy Park, 4 kilometres (2.5 mi.) south off Mariner Way; Belcarra Park, 15 kilometres (9 mi.) northwest off Ioco and Bedwell Bay roads; Buntzen Lake, 12 kilometres (7 mi.) northwest off East and Sunnyside roads; Minnekhada Regional Park, 13 kilometres (8 mi.) northeast off Victoria Drive and Quarry Road; Town Centre Park and Lafarge Lake, on Pinetree Way just north of Lougheed Highway; and Burke Mountain, 11 kilometres (7 mi.) northeast off Coast Meridian and Harper roads.

Coquitlam Tourist/Visitor Info Booth: 1209 Pinetree Way, Coquitlam, BC, Canada V3B 7Y3. **Phone:** (604) 464-2716.

BEST WESTERN CHELSEA INN (604)525-7777 ㉓

▼▼▼ Hotel $109-$139

Ⓑ Best Western **AAA Benefit:** Save 10% or more every day and earn 10% bonus points!

Address: 725 Brunette Ave V3K 6A6 **Location:** Trans-Canada Hwy 1 exit 40B (Brunette Ave N). (🚇) Braid, 16. **Facility:** 61 units, some efficiencies. 3 stories, interior corridors. **Pool(s):** heated outdoor. **Activities:** sauna, exercise room. **Guest Services:** valet and coin laundry. **Featured Amenity:** continental breakfast.

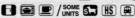

(See map & index p. 290.)

BEST WESTERN PLUS COQUITLAM INN CONVENTION CENTRE
(604)931-9011

Hotel
$139-$209

Best Western PLUS **AAA Benefit:** Save 10% or more every day and earn 10% bonus points!

Address: 319 North Rd V3K 3V8 **Location:** Trans-Canada Hwy 1 exit 37 (Cariboo Rd/Gaglardi Way), 1.2 mi (2 km) e on Lougheed Hwy (Hwy 7), then just s. Lougheed Town Centre, 15. **Facility:** 105 units, some two bedrooms and kitchens. 2 stories (no elevator), interior/exterior corridors. **Amenities:** safes. **Dining:** 2 restaurants. **Pool(s):** heated indoor. **Activities:** sauna, hot tub, exercise room. **Guest Services:** valet laundry.

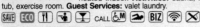

WHERE TO EAT

CACTUS CLUB CAFE   604/777-0440
New American. Casual Dining. **Address:** 110-101 Schoolhouse St V3K 4X8

JOEY RESTAURANTS   604/939-3077
American. Casual Dining. **Address:** 550 Lougheed Hwy V3K 3S3

JOHN B NEIGHBORHOOD PUB   604/931-5115 43
International. Casual Dining. **Address:** 1000 Austin Ave V3K 3P1

RICKY'S ALL DAY GRILL   604/468-8000
American. Casual Dining. **Address:** 2929 Barnet Hwy, Unit 2660 V3B 5R5

COURTENAY (F-10) pop. 24,099, elev. 25m/82'

Courtenay was established in the late 1860s when settlers began a major farming community near the Comox Valley. Known for a garden called the Mile of Flowers, the town is now a year-round recreation area with good skiing and sailing nearby.

The 1989 Puntledge River discovery of the fossilized intact skull of a 14-metre-long (46-ft.) elasmosaur, a long-necked Cretaceous marine reptile 80 million years old, brought Courtenay to the attention of the world of paleontology.

Courtenay is the terminus of the Powell River Ferry, which makes round-trip excursions to the mainland.

Vancouver Island Visitor Centre: 101-3607 Small Rd., Cumberland, BC, Canada V9N 3Z8. **Phone:** (250) 400-2882 or (855) 400-2882.

COURTENAY AND DISTRICT MUSEUM AND PALEONTOLOGY CENTRE is at 207 Fourth St., downtown at jct. Fourth St. and Cliffe Ave. Permanent exhibits, enhanced by audiovisuals, focus on native history, exploration, agriculture, logging and pioneer life. A reconstruction of an elasmosaur is displayed along with locally excavated fossil evidence from the age of dinosaurs. The museum has archival material pertaining to the nearby Comox Valley. Guided fossil discovery tours are available.

Time: Allow 1 hour minimum. **Hours:** Mon.-Sat. 10-5, Sun. noon-4, Victoria Day-Labour Day; Tues.-Sat. 10-5, rest of year. Closed Jan. 1, Easter, Victoria Day, Civic Day, Labour Day, Thanksgiving, Christmas Eve, Christmas and day after Christmas. **Cost:** Donations. **Phone:** (250) 334-0686.

KITTY COLEMAN WOODLAND GARDENS is at 6183 Whittaker Rd. The gardens, created by Bryan Zimmerman to share the beauty of the area with others, showcase rhododendrons, with more than 3,000 varieties and sizes planted throughout the landscape. The peak viewing season is mid-April through fall. The gardens host the Kitty Coleman Arts and Bloom Festival over the Victoria Day weekend in mid-May.

Ponds, walking paths lined with granite rocks, a creek, a gazebo, benches and driftwood sculptures add to the beauty of the site. **Hours:** Daily 9-dusk. **Cost:** $7.62; $2.86 (ages 5-12). Cash only. **Phone:** (250) 338-6901. GT

ANCO INN   (250)334-2451
Motel. **Address:** 1885 Cliffe Ave V9N 2K9

BEST WESTERN THE WESTERLY HOTEL & CONVENTION CENTRE   (250)338-7741

Hotel
$129-$199

Best Western. **AAA Benefit:** Save 10% or more every day and earn 10% bonus points!

Address: 1590 Cliffe Ave V9N 2K4 **Location:** Corner of Cliffe Ave and Island Hwy 19A N. **Facility:** 142 units. 3-4 stories, interior corridors. **Pool(s):** heated indoor. **Activities:** sauna, hot tub, game room, exercise room. **Guest Services:** valet and coin laundry.

CROWN ISLE RESORT & GOLF COMMUNITY   (250)703-5050
Resort Hotel. **Address:** 399 Clubhouse Dr V9N 9G3

HOLIDAY INN EXPRESS & SUITES COMOX VALLEY
(778)225-0010
Hotel. **Address:** 2200 Cliffe Ave V9N 2L4

KINGFISHER OCEANSIDE RESORT & SPA   (250)338-1323
Hotel. **Address:** 4330 S Island Hwy V9N 9R9

TRAVELODGE COURTENAY   (250)334-4491
Motel. **Address:** 2605 Cliffe Ave V9N 2L8

WHERE TO EAT

ATLAS CAFE   250/338-9838
International. Casual Dining. **Address:** 250 6th St V9N 1M1

THE BREAKWATER RESTAURANT 250/338-1323
▼▼▼ Pacific Northwest. Casual Dining. **Address:** 4330 S Island Hwy V9N 9R9

LOCALS RESTAURANT 250/338-6493
▼▼▼ Canadian. Fine Dining. **Address:** 1760 Riverside Ln V9N 8C7

RICKY'S ALL DAY GRILL 250/334-9638
▼▼ American. Casual Dining. **Address:** 795 Ryan Rd V9N 3R6

WHITE WHALE PUBLIC HOUSE 250/338-1468
▼▼ American. Casual Dining. **Address:** 975 Comox Rd V9N 3P7

COWICHAN BAY pop. 203

COW CAFE 250/597-4353
▼▼ American. Casual Dining. **Address:** 1765 Cowichan Bay Rd V0R 1N0

CRANBROOK (C-11) pop. 19,319, elev. 940m/3,083'

Cranbrook is the key city of the eastern Kootenays *(see Kootenay National Park p. 210)* and the center of many circle tours. Nearby lakes, rivers and mountains provide such recreational opportunities as swimming, fishing, hiking, hunting and skiing. A scenic portion of Hwy. 93 runs north from Cranbrook through Kootenay National Park into Banff National Park to the junction with Hwy. 16 in Jasper National Park. (A valid park pass is required to travel on the Icefields Parkway section of Hwy. 93.)

Cranbrook Chamber of Commerce & Visitor Centre: 2279 Cranbrook St. N. (Hwy. 3/95), P.O. Box 84, Cranbrook, BC, Canada V1C 4H6. **Phone:** (250) 426-5914 or (800) 222-6174.

Self-guiding tours: Information about driving and walking tours is available from the chamber of commerce.

CRANBROOK HISTORY CENTRE is at 57 Van Horne St. S. (Hwy. 3/95). The museum restores and preserves vintage Canadian Pacific Railway passenger train sets, including cars from the luxury Trans-Canada Limited. The lifestyle of rail travel is reflected in trains from 1880 to 1955, including cars of state, business and royalty. On display are a model railway, the Cranbrook Centennial Quilt, the 1864 Broadwood grand piano display room and the train restoration display. Also inside is the Cranbrook Museum, which features exhibits about life in the 1800s and First Nations history as well as 500-million-year-old trilobites.

On the grounds is the original three-story café from the Canadian Pacific Railway's Royal Alexandra Hotel of Winnipeg. Several guided tours, ranging from 15 to 35 minutes in length, are available and can be taken in various combinations. The 90-minute Grand Tour includes 17 railcars.

Time: Allow 1 hour, 30 minutes minimum. **Hours:** Museum Tues.-Sat. 10-5 (also Sun.-Mon. 10-5, mid-May through Aug. 31). Closed Canadian and British Columbia statutory holidays. **Cost:** Museum exhibits by donation. Grand Tour $15; $14 (ages 65+); $4 (ages 6-12). **Phone:** (250) 489-3918 to verify tour schedule and rates. GT

BEST WESTERN CRANBROOK HOTEL (250)417-4002

▼▼▼
Hotel
$149-$219

 Best Western. **AAA Benefit:** Save 10% or more every day and earn 10% bonus points!

Address: 1019 Cranbrook St N V1C 3S4 **Location:** Hwy 3 and 95; center. **Facility:** 94 units, some two bedrooms and efficiencies. 4 stories, interior corridors. **Parking:** winter plug-ins. **Pool(s):** indoor. **Activities:** game room, exercise room. **Guest Services:** valet and coin laundry.

/ SOME UNITS

DAYS INN CRANBROOK (250)426-6683
▼▼ Hotel. **Address:** 600 Cranbrook St N V1C 3R7

HERITAGE INN HOTEL & CONVENTION CENTRE CRANBROOK (250)489-4301
▼▼ Hotel. **Address:** 803 Cranbrook St N V1C 3S2

ST. EUGENE GOLF RESORT & CASINO 250/420-2000

▼▼▼
Hotel
Rates not provided

Address: 7731 Mission Rd V1C 7E5 **Location:** Hwy 3 exit Kimberley/Airport (Hwy 95A) to Mission Rd, 2.8 mi (4.5 km) n. **Facility:** This vine-covered hotel has lovely rooms, but those in the heritage wing are more upscale and feature amenities like robes and wine glasses. The outdoor pool and hot tubs are open year-round. 125 units. 3 stories, interior corridors. **Terms:** check-in 4 pm. **Amenities:** safes. **Dining:** 2 restaurants. **Pool(s):** heated outdoor. **Activities:** sauna, hot tub, steamroom, regulation golf, trails, exercise room, spa. **Guest Services:** valet laundry.

WHERE TO EAT

ALLEGRA MEDITERRANEAN CUISINE 250/426-8812
▼▼▼ Mediterranean. Casual Dining. **Address:** 1225B Cranbrook St N V1C 3S6

MR MIKES STEAKHOUSECASUAL 250/417-2542
▼▼ American. Casual Dining. **Address:** 1028 Cranbrook St N V1C 3S3

CRESTON (D-11) pop. 5,306, elev. 636m/2,086'
• Hotels p. 188 • Restaurants p. 188

The unusual Kutenai canoe, which has a bow and stern that both meet the waterline, was used by First Nations people in the area around Creston in pre-pioneer days. The only other place such a canoe has been found is the Amur River region in south-eastern Russia. The canoe's use in this area supports the theory that Asians migrated to North America over a frozen Bering Strait.

In the 1930s about 8,100 hectares (20,000 acres) of land were reclaimed from the Kootenay Delta for agriculture. The Creston Valley floor is now quilted with a variety of seed and root crops, grains and fruit orchards. Other Creston industries include forestry, dairying and brewing.

The Columbia Brewing Co., 1220 Erickson St., offers narrated tours of its facilities Mon.-Fri., mid-May to mid-October, Sat.-Sun., July-Aug. Closed toe shoes are mandatory. Complimentary beer is available at the end of the tour; phone (250) 428-1238. Free guided tours of a candlemaking factory are offered year-round by appointment only at Kootenay Candles, 1511 Northwest Blvd.; phone (250) 428-9785 or (866) 572-9785.

Hikers can trek along the old Dewdney Trail, which carried gold seekers from Hope to the Wild Horse goldfields in the 1860s.

Creston Visitor Centre: 121 Northwest Blvd., Creston, BC, Canada V0B 1G0. **Phone:** (250) 428-4342.

RAMADA CRESTON　　　　　　　　　(250)254-1111
▼▼▼ Hotel. **Address:** 1 1809 Hwy 3A V0B 1G8

WHERE TO EAT

A BREAK IN TIME CAFFE　　　　　　　250/428-5619
▼▼ ▼▼ International. Casual Dining. **Address:** 1417 Canyon St V0B 1G0

CHATKA FAMILY RESTAURANT　　　　　250/428-7200
▼▼ ▼▼ Polish. Casual Dining. **Address:** 2808 Hwy 3 V0B 1G1

REAL FOOD CAFE　　　　　　　　　　250/428-8882
▼▼ ▼▼ International. Casual Dining. **Address:** 223 10th Ave N V0B 1G0

CULTUS LAKE　(I-12) pop. 15, elev. 45m/150'

Cultus Lake Provincial Park, 11 kilometres (7 mi.) southwest of Chilliwack off Hwy. 1, is a popular recreational area and offers camping, boating, fishing, horseback riding and hiking (see Recreation Areas Chart). Cultus Lake Waterpark, Hwy. 1 exit 119A, has giant waterslides, twisting tunnels, pools and inner tube rides and is open daily early June to early September; phone (604) 858-7241 for more information.

CUMBERLAND　(F-10) pop. 3,398

Cumberland's origins are rooted in the rigors of coal mining. From 1888 until the last of its nine mines closed in 1966, the village produced some 25 million tons of high-grade coal. The lucrative enterprise solidified Cumberland's economy and contributed to its multi-ethnic mix, drawing miners from locations as diverse as England, Scotland, Italy,

China and Japan. The village and many of its streets were named for the mining region in England known as Cumbria.

Nestled in the foothills of the Beaufort Mountains and a stone's throw from Comox Lake, Cumberland offers ample snow skiing, hiking, fishing and boating opportunities.

Vancouver Island Visitor Centre: 101-3607 Small Rd., Cumberland, BC, Canada V9N 3Z8. **Phone:** (250) 400-2882 or (855) 400-2882.

DAWSON CREEK　(D-6) pop. 11,583, elev. 655m/2,148'

Named for George Mercer Dawson of the Geological Survey of Canada, Dawson Creek was settled in 1912. Growth accelerated during World War II, as this was the southern terminus of the Alaska Highway. The highway was then called the Alcan Military Highway, and it served as a supply road to bases in Alaska. The Mile Zero Cairn, which marks the start of the Alaska Highway, and the Zero Milepost are in the center of town. Alpine skiing, camping, hiking and fishing are popular recreational activities.

Dawson Creek Visitor's Centre: 900 Alaska Ave., Dawson Creek, BC, Canada V1G 4T6. **Phone:** (250) 782-9595 or (866) 645-3022.

DAWSON CREEK SUPER 8　　　　　　(250)782-8899
◆◆ ◆◆
Hotel
$146-$170

Address: 1440 Alaska Ave V1G 1Z5 **Location:** Jct Hwy 2 and 49, 0.5 mi (0.8 km) ne. **Facility:** 66 units, some efficiencies. 2 stories (no elevator), interior corridors. **Parking:** winter plug-ins. **Dining:** Sola's Bar & Grill, see separate listing. **Activities:** exercise room. **Guest Services:** coin laundry. **Featured Amenity:** full hot breakfast.

DAYS INN DAWSON CREEK　　　　　　(250)782-8887
◆◆ ◆◆
Hotel
$140

Address: 640 122nd Ave V1G 0A4 **Location:** Hwy 2, just n on 7th St; southeast end of town. Next to Walmart. **Facility:** 85 units. 4 stories, interior corridors. **Parking:** winter plug-ins. **Activities:** game room, exercise room. **Guest Services:** valet and coin laundry. **Featured Amenity:** continental breakfast.

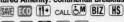

POMEROY INN & SUITES　　　　　　　250/782-3700
▼▼▼ Extended Stay Hotel. **Address:** 540 Hwy 2 V1G 0A4

STONEBRIDGE HOTEL DAWSON CREEK　250/782-6226
▼▼▼ Hotel. **Address:** 500 Hwy 2 V1G 0A4

WHERE TO EAT

BROWNS SOCIAL HOUSE   250/782-2400
♦♦ International. Gastropub. **Address:** 1100 Alaska Ave, #104 Ave V1G 4V8

MR MIKES STEAKHOUSECASUAL   250/782-1577
♦♦ American. Casual Dining. **Address:** 1501 Alaska Ave V1G 1Z8

SOLA'S BAR & GRILL   250/782-8890
♦♦ American. Casual Dining. **Address:** 1440 Alaska Ave V1G 1Z5

DELTA (H-11) pop. 99,863, elev. 10m/33'
- **Hotels & Restaurants map & index p. 290**
- **Part of Vancouver area — see map p. 263**

Delta, composed of the three distinct communities of Ladner, Tsawwassen and North Delta, is an amalgam of commerce, fisheries, industry, farmland, beaches and suburban residences. The warm-water beaches on Boundary Bay and Tsawwassen are popular spots for swimming and sunbathing. Other recreational opportunities in the area include fishing for salmon and boating on the Fraser River and the Strait of Georgia.

Delta Visitor Centre: 6201 60th Ave., Delta, BC, Canada V4K 4E2. **Phone:** (604) 946-4232.

THE COAST TSAWWASSEN INN   (604)943-8221 **51**
♦♦♦ Hotel. **Address:** 1665 56th St V4L 2B2

DELTA TOWN & COUNTRY INN   (604)946-4404 **50**
♦♦♦ Hotel
$102-$115
Address: 6005 Hwy 17A V4K 5B8 **Location:** Hwy 99 exit 28 (River Rd). Located in a quiet rural area. **Facility:** 49 units. 2 stories (no elevator), interior corridors. **Terms:** cancellation fee imposed. **Pool(s):** heated outdoor. **Activities:** tennis, exercise room. **Guest Services:** valet and coin laundry.

WHERE TO EAT

CACTUS CLUB CAFE   604/591-1707
♦♦ New American. Casual Dining. **Address:** 7907 120th St V4C 6P6

MARIO'S KITCHEN   604/943-4442 **68**
♦♦ International. Casual Dining. **Address:** 1105 56th St V4L 2A2

RICKY'S ALL DAY GRILL   604/599-1784
♦♦ American. Casual Dining. **Address:** 7135 120th St V4E 2A9

DUNCAN (H-10) pop. 4,932, elev. 15m/49'

Founded in 1887 as Alderlea, Duncan was renamed in 1912 in honor of farmer William Duncan, who gave his land for the original townsite. Settlers were attracted by the promise of copper and coal on nearby Mount Sicker, where abandoned mines and original homesteads still can be seen. The growth of the logging and farming industries brought increasing numbers to Duncan and the Cowichan Valley.

The area around Duncan is known for the handspun woolen sweaters produced by the Cowichan people. West on Hwy. 18 is the Cowichan Valley Demonstration Forest with scenic viewpoints and signs describing forest management practices and ecology. More than 80 totem poles dot the town of Duncan.

Duncan-Cowichan Chamber of Commerce: 381 Trans-Canada Hwy., Duncan, BC, Canada V9L 3R5. **Phone:** (250) 746-4636 or (888) 303-3337.

Shopping: Whippletree Junction, a group of shops and boutiques with late 1800s storefronts, is 5 kilometres (3 mi.) south on the Trans-Canada Highway. A Sunday market with local artisans and food producers is open April through October.

PACIFIC NORTHWEST RAPTOR VISITOR CENTRE 5 km (3 mi.) n. on Trans-Canada Hwy. 1 and 4 km (2 mi.) w. on 1877 Herd Rd. Birds of prey, some captive bred and others non-releasable, can be seen up close and personal at this facility. Those born in captivity are allowed to fly outside their pens during the day, returning home at night. Birds such as hawks, bald eagles, owls and falcons can be seen in daily flying demonstrations.

Time: Allow 1 hour, 30 minutes minimum. **Hours:** Center open daily 10:30-5, May-Sept.; daily noon-3, Mar.-Apr. and Oct.; Thurs.-Sun. noon-3, Nov.-Dec. Demonstrations are given daily at 11:30 and 1:30, Victoria Day weekend-Labour Day; daily at 1:30, early Mar.-day before Victoria Day weekend and day after Labour Day-Sept. 30. Phone ahead to confirm schedule. **Cost:** $15.24; $13.33 (ages 13-17 and 65+); $7.62 (ages 3-12); $41.90 (family, two adults and two children); $47.62 (family, two adults and three children). **Phone:** (250) 746-0372.

BEST WESTERN COWICHAN VALLEY INN   (250)748-2722
♦♦ Hotel
$119-$180

 Best Western. **AAA Benefit:** Save 10% or more every day and earn 10% bonus points!

Address: 6474 Trans-Canada Hwy V9L 6C6 **Location:** 1.8 mi (3 km) n. **Facility:** 42 units. 2 stories (no elevator), interior corridors. **Pool(s):** heated outdoor. **Activities:** exercise room. **Guest Services:** valet laundry.

WHERE TO EAT

DOGHOUSE A FAMILY RESTAURANT   250/746-4614
♦♦ American. Casual Dining. **Address:** 271 Trans-Canada Hwy V9L 3R1

ERRINGTON (G-10) pop. 2,678

NORTH ISLAND WILDLIFE RECOVERY ASSO-CIATION is at 1240 Leffler Rd. Bald eagles, owls, hawks, swans and black bears are among the animals that can be viewed at this 3-hectare (8-acre) rehabilitation facility. An eagle flight cage houses eagles waiting to be released into the wild. A nature museum, wildlife learning center and public viewing area are on the grounds. Special Event Days are held in July and August.

Time: Allow 30 minutes minimum. **Hours:** Daily 9-5, mid-Mar. through Dec. 19. Raptor presentation Wed.-Fri. at 1:30, July-Aug. **Cost:** $8; $5 (ages 3-12). **Phone:** (250) 248-8534.

FAIRMONT HOT SPRINGS (B-11) pop. 476, elev. 810m/2,657'

At the north end of Columbia Lake, Fairmont Hot Springs were discovered about 1840. This popular resort area offers four hot mineral springs with temperatures averaging 35 to 45 C (95 to 113 F). Water sports and alpine and cross-country skiing also are available. *See Recreation Areas Chart.*

FAIRMONT HOT SPRINGS RESORT   (250)345-6070

★★ (Resort Hotel)
$145-$225

Address: 5225 Fairmont Resort Rd V0B 1L1 **Location:** 1 mi (1.6 km) e off Hwy 93 and 95. **Facility:** All the elements are in place for a relaxing stay here with the natural hot springs and the appealing rooms equipped with bathrobes and wine glasses. Bathrooms however, have an older décor. 143 units, some two bedrooms, efficiencies, cabins and cottages. 3 stories (no elevator), interior/exterior corridors. **Parking:** winter plug-ins. **Terms:** check-in 4 pm, 3 day cancellation notice-fee imposed, resort fee. **Dining:** 2 restaurants. **Pool(s):** heated outdoor. **Activities:** sauna, hot tub, steamroom, self-propelled boats, fishing, regulation golf, par 3 golf, miniature golf, tennis, downhill & cross country skiing, snowboarding, ice skating, recreation programs in summer, bicycles, lawn sports, playground, picnic facilities, trails, exercise room, spa. **Guest Services:** coin laundry.

[SAVE] [ECO] [†↑] [🛄] [🍽] [🛗] [🏊] [HS] [🛜] [✕] [📷]
[🔌] [💻] / SOME UNITS [🔔] [🖨]

WHERE TO EAT

FROM SCRATCH-A MOUNTAIN KITCHEN   250/345-0008
★★ American. Casual Dining. **Address:** 5019 Fairmont Resort Rd, #8 V0B 1L1

FERNIE (C-12) pop. 4,448

At the foot of Trinity Mountain in the British Columbia Rockies, Fernie is a year-round recreation center. The many surrounding lakes and mountains provide opportunities for boating, fishing, hiking, camping and skiing. Mount Fernie Provincial Park is 4.8 kilometres (3 mi.) east *(see Recreation Areas Chart).* Prentice and Rotary parks are downtown.

Fernie Chamber of Commerce: 102 Commerce Rd. (Hwy. 3), Fernie, BC, Canada V0B 1M5. **Phone:** (250) 423-6868.

BEST WESTERN PLUS FERNIE MOUNTAIN LODGE
(250)423-5500

★★★ Hotel
$181-$265

AAA Benefit: Save 10% or more every day and earn 10% bonus points!

Address: 1622 7th Ave V0B 1M0 **Location:** Jct Hwy 3 and 7th Ave; east end of town. **Facility:** 95 units, some efficiencies. 3 stories, interior corridors. **Parking:** winter plug-ins. **Pool(s):** heated indoor. **Activities:** hot tub, exercise room, massage. **Guest Services:** coin laundry, area transportation. **Featured Amenity:** full hot breakfast.

[SAVE] [ECO] [†↑] [🍽] [🏊] [BIZ] [HS]
    / SOME UNITS [🔔]

CORNERSTONE LODGE   250/423-9211
★★ Condominium. **Address:** 5339 Ski Hill Rd V0B 1M6

LIZARD CREEK LODGE AND CONDOMINIUMS AT FERNIE ALPINE RESORT   250/423-2057
★★★ Condominium. **Address:** 5346 Highline Dr V0B 1M6

PARK PLACE LODGE   250/423-6871
★★★ Hotel. **Address:** 742 Hwy 3 V0B 1M0

WHERE TO EAT

THE BLUE TOQUE DINER   250/423-4637
★★ Breakfast. Casual Dining. **Address:** 601 1st Ave V0B 1M0

FERNIE CATTLE CO.   250/423-7498
★★★ Steak. Casual Dining. **Address:** 561 Hwy 3 V0B 1M0

KELSEY'S   250/423-2444
★★ American. Casual Dining. **Address:** 5339 Ski Hill, Fernie Alpine Resort Rd V0B 1M0

LOAF BAKERY & RESTAURANT   250/423-7702
★★ Breads/Pastries. Casual Dining. **Address:** 641 2nd Ave V0B 1M0

LUNCH BOX FRESH MARKET & SMOOTHIE BAR
250/423-4500
★ American. Quick Serve. **Address:** 561A 2nd Ave V0B 1M0

MUGSHOTS CAFE   250/423-8018
★ Coffee/Tea. Quick Serve. **Address:** 592 3rd Ave V0B 1M0

NEVADOS   250/423-5566
★★ New Latin American Small Plates. Casual Dining. **Address:** 531 2nd Ave V0B 1M0

YAMAGOYA JAPANESE RESTAURANT   250/430-0090
★★ Japanese. Casual Dining. **Address:** 741 7th Ave V0B 1M6

FORT LANGLEY NATIONAL HISTORIC SITE (H-11)

• **Part of Vancouver area — see map p. 263**

Fort Langley National Historic Site is 6.5 kilometres (4 mi.) north of Langley off Hwy. 1 at 23433 Mavis Ave. On the bank of the Fraser River, the 19th-century Hudson's Bay Company trading post was an important supply link in the company's network of fur trading forts west of the Rockies. British Columbia was proclaimed a colony at the site in 1858.

The site preserves an original 1840 storehouse and reconstructed wooden buildings, including a cooperage and blacksmith's shop and a log palisade. Interpreters in period costumes demonstrate fur-trading activities daily. A visitor center displays contemporary exhibits. Special events are presented throughout the year.

Picnicking is permitted. Allow 1 hour minimum. Daily 10-5. Closed Jan. 1, Christmas and day after Christmas. Admission to the park is free through 2017 to celebrate Canada's 150th anniversary of Confederation. Otherwise admission is $7.43; $6.24 (ages 65+); $3.71 (ages 6-16); $18.67 (family, two adults and four children). Prices may vary; phone (604) 513-4777. An annual pass, valid at most Canadian national parks, marine areas and historic sites, is available.

FORT NELSON (B-5) pop. 3,902, elev. 405m/1,350'

Originally a fur-trading post, Fort Nelson thrived with the building of the Alaska Highway during World War II. Nearby mountains, lakes, parks, forests and diverse wildlife populations make Fort Nelson a destination for adventurous tourists, anglers and hunters.

Fort Nelson Visitor Centre: 5500 Alaska Hwy., Fort Nelson, BC, Canada V0C 1R0. **Phone:** (250) 774-6400.

LAKEVIEW INN & SUITES   (250)233-5001
♦♦ Hotel. **Address:** 4507 50th Ave S V0C 1R0 *(See ad opposite inside front cover.)*

WOODLANDS INN & SUITES   (250)774-6669

♦♦♦♦
Hotel
$144-$154

Address: 3995 50th Ave S V0C 1R0 **Location:** On Hwy 97 (Alaska Hwy). **Facility:** 202 units, some efficiencies and kitchens. 4-6 stories, interior/exterior corridors. **Parking:** winter plug-ins. **Dining:** The One, see separate listing. **Activities:** exercise room. **Guest Services:** coin laundry.

WHERE TO EAT

THE ONE   250/774-6669
♦♦♦
American
Casual Dining
$12-$39

AAA Inspector Notes: You'll find friendly service and a contemporary flair in this dining room, with comfortable banquettes and great lighting which enhances the dark wood accents. Menu highlights include Alberta beef, salmon, stir-fry dishes, burgers, pasta and pizza. **Features:** full bar. **Address:** 3995 50th Ave S V0C 1R0 **Location:** On Hwy 97 (Alaska Hwy); in Woodlands Inn & Suites.
B D CALL 🍴

FORT RODD HILL AND FISGARD LIGHTHOUSE NATIONAL HISTORIC SITES (I-9)

• **Part of Victoria area — see map p. 317**

Fourteen kilometres (9 mi.) west of Victoria via Hwy. 1A, Fort Rodd Hill was a coastal artillery fort 1895-1956. Of interest are the loophole walls, underground magazines, artillery stores, command posts, barracks and gun and searchlight emplacements. Audio and video presentations, along with period rooms, depict life at the fort. The 1860 Fisgard Lighthouse, restored to its 1873 appearance, was the first built on this part of the coast. Still operational, the lighthouse has two floors of historical exhibits. A nature trail follows the paths formerly used by soldiers. Historical exhibits also are featured. Picnic facilities are available. Pets are not allowed on the grounds.

Allow 1 hour, 30 minutes minimum. Grounds daily 10-5:30, Mar. 1 to mid-Oct.; 10-4:30, rest of year. Exhibits daily 10-5, mid-May to mid-Oct.; Wed.-Sun. 10-5, Mar. 1 to mid-May; Sat.-Sun. 10-4, rest of year. Closed Jan. 1 and Dec. 25-26. Admission to the park (includes fort and lighthouse) is free in 2017 to celebrate Canada's 150th anniversary of Confederation. Otherwise admission is $3.71; $3.24 (ages 65+); $1.81 (ages 6-16); $9.33 (family, two adults and five children). An annual pass, valid at most Canadian national parks, marine areas and historic sites, is available. Phone (250) 478-5849.

FORT ST. JAMES (E-4) pop. 1,691, elev. 680m/2,230'

Established in 1806 by Simon Fraser and John Stuart, the fur-trading post of Fort St. James became the capital of New Caledonia in 1821. Furs from outlying New Caledonia posts were brought overland to Fort St. James by dog sled and then shipped south during the spring thaw to the coast by canoe and horse.

During this time George Simpson, governor of the Hudson's Bay Co.'s vast empire, visited the fort. Determined to impress the Carrier First Nation, Simpson organized a flamboyant procession complete with flute, bugle and bagpipe players in Highland dress, accompanied by a dog with a music box around its neck. Thereafter, the awe-struck population reverently referred to Simpson as the "great chief whose dog sings."

A Roman Catholic mission was founded at the fort in 1843. Services continue to be held in Our Lady of Good Hope Church, which was built in 1873 and is one of the oldest churches in British Columbia.

Mining activity supplemented the capital's trapping enterprises after the discovery of gold in the Omineca region in 1869. Interest in mining rekindled during World War II when the Pinchi Mine a few kilometres north yielded more mercury than any other mine in the British Commonwealth.

A lack of highways and railways prompted Fort St. James to pioneer bush flying as a means of transportation; it has served as an air base since the earliest days of charter flight.

The north shore of Stuart Lake, 16 kilometres (10 mi.) west, features some of the earliest signs of habitation in the form of prehistoric rock paintings just above the high-water mark. Although Fort St. James has emerged from relative wilderness, its surrounding evergreen forests continue to be among the best big-game hunting areas in the province. Alpine skiing is available nearby.

Fort St. James Visitor Centre: 115 Douglas Ave., P.O. Box 1164, Fort St. James, BC, Canada V0J 1P0. **Phone:** (250) 996-7023.

FORT ST. JAMES NATIONAL HISTORIC SITE is 2 blks. w. of Hwy. 27 at 280 Kwah Rd. W. Established on the southern shore of Stuart Lake by the North West Co. in 1806, Fort St. James contains one of the largest groups of original wooden buildings from Canada's fur trade. A massive fur warehouse is a noted example of Red River framing. The fully restored Hudson's Bay Co. post on the site served as a hub of commerce between fur traders and the indigenous peoples—and as the capital of New Caledonia, now central British Columbia.

The visitor center provides pictorial displays, artifacts and an audiovisual presentation. Changing exhibits are offered seasonally. Interpreters in period costume provide living-history demonstrations throughout the day. **Time:** Allow 2 hours minimum. **Hours:** Daily 9-5, June 1 through mid-Sept.; by appointment rest of year. **Cost:** Admission is free in 2017 to celebrate Canada's 150th anniversary of Confederation. Otherwise admission is $7.43; $6.24 (ages 65+); $3.71 (ages 6-16); $18.67 (family, two adults and five children). An annual pass, valid at most Canadian national parks, marine areas and historic sites, is available. Prices may vary; phone to confirm. **Phone:** (250) 996-7191. ⏍

FORT ST. JOHN (D-5) pop. 18,609, elev. 695m/2,280'

One of the oldest European settlements in the province, Fort St. John was established in 1793 as a fur-trading outpost called Rocky Mountain Fort. Residents engage in gas and oil exploration as well as the lumber industry and cattle ranching. There are coalfields to the south and west.

Recreational activities include fishing for Arctic grayling and gray trout in nearby Charlie Lake *(see Recreation Areas Chart)*, canoeing the rapids of the Peace River, skiing, and hunting for mountain caribou, mountain goats and black bears in the Rocky Mountain foothills. Floatplanes operating out of Charlie Lake provide access to the wilderness surrounding Fort St. John, and Hwy. 29 provides scenic driving to Chetwynd.

Fort St. John Visitor Centre: 9523 96th St., Fort St. John, BC, Canada V1J 6V5. **Phone:** (250) 785-3033 or (877) 785-6037.

HOLIDAY INN EXPRESS FORT ST. JOHN   250/787-7737
♦♦♦ Hotel. **Address:** 9504 Alaska Rd V1J 6L5

MICROTEL INN & SUITES BY WYNDHAM   (250)794-3100
♦♦ Hotel. **Address:** 8407 93 St V1J 6Y3

NORTHERN GRAND HOTEL   250/787-0521
♦♦♦ Hotel. **Address:** 9830 100th Ave V1J 1Y5

POMEROY HOTEL & CONFERENCE CENTRE   250/262-3233
♦♦♦ Hotel. **Address:** 11308 Alaska Rd V1J 5T5

POMEROY INN & SUITES   250/262-3030
♦♦ Extended Stay Hotel. **Address:** 9320 Alaska Rd V1J 6L5

SUPER 8-FORT ST. JOHN   (250)785-7588
♦♦♦ Hotel $159-$160. **Address:** 9500 W Alaska Rd V1J 6L5 **Location:** Just s on Hwy 97 (Alaska Hwy). **Facility:** 101 units. 4 stories, interior corridors. **Parking:** winter plug-ins. **Terms:** cancellation fee imposed. **Pool(s):** heated indoor. **Activities:** hot tub, exercise room. **Guest Services:** valet and coin laundry. **Featured Amenity:** breakfast buffet.
(SAVE) (ECO) (⏍) CALL (☎) (BIZ) (HS) (📶) (🔒) (🗖) (🖥) / SOME UNITS (🐾)

WHERE TO EAT

MASTARO SUSHI   250/261-6595
♦♦ Japanese. Casual Dining. **Address:** 9823 100th St V1J 3Y2

MONDO RESTAURANT   250/787-1454
♦♦ International. Casual Dining. **Address:** 10403 100th Ave V1J 1Z1

MR MIKES STEAKHOUSECASUAL   250/262-4151
♦♦ American. Casual Dining. **Address:** 9324 Alaska Rd V1J 6L5

OVERTIME SPORTS BAR AND GRILL   250/261-6961
♦♦ International. Casual Dining. **Address:** 9830 100th Ave V1J 1Y5

WHOLE WHEAT 'N' HONEY CAFE & COFFEEHOUSE   250/787-9866
♦ American. Quick Serve. **Address:** 10003 100th St V1J 1Y5

FORT STEELE (C-12) elev. 771m/2,529'

Founded during the 1864 Kootenay gold rush, Fort Steele, then known as Galbraith's Ferry, became the site of the first North West Mounted Police west of the Rockies. In 1888 the settlement's name was changed to honor police superintendent Samuel Steele, who peacefully settled tensions between European settlers and the Ktunaxa people.

As a result of the mining boom of the 1890s the town became a thriving center of trade, transportation, communication and social activity, with a population of more than 2,000. In 1898 the British Columbia Southern Railroad bypassed Fort Steele in favor of Cranbrook, 16 kilometres (10 mi.) southwest, and the town began its decline. At the end of World War II Fort Steele had fewer than 50 residents.

FORT STEELE HERITAGE TOWN is 3 km (1.9 mi.) s.w. at 9851 Hwy. 93/95. The 11-hectare (27-acre) site preserves an 1890s boomtown. More than 60 restored, reconstructed or original buildings include an operating bakery, restaurant, tinsmith shop, blacksmith shop and newspaper office. Street dramas and demonstrations such as quilting, horse farming and ice cream making help re-create life in the era.

Fort Steele's Clydesdales give wagon rides daily mid-June through Labour Day and perform a six-horse hitch show on July 1. Live entertainment is presented in the Wild Horse Theatre late June through Labour Day. Steam train rides are available during this time. A visitor reception center contains exhibits about the town's history.

Hours: Grounds open daily 10-5, mid-June through Labour Day; 10-4, rest of year. Last admission 1 hour before closing. Programs, including street skits depicting daily life of the late 1890s, are presented daily 10-4:30, mid-June to mid-Oct. Closed Christmas. **Cost:** mid-June to mid-Oct. $12; $10 (ages 65+); $5 (ages 6-17 and 65+). Cost rest of year $7; $5 (ages 6-17 and 65+). **Phone:** (250) 417-6000 or (250) 426-7352.

BULL RIVER GUEST RANCH   250/429-3760
Resort Ranch. **Address:** 2975 Bull River Rd V1C 4H7

GALIANO ISLAND (H-10) pop. 1,138

Named after Spanish explorer Dionisio Alcala Galiano, Galiano Island, part of the Gulf Islands chain, is a long narrow island that is a haven for bird watchers and naturalists. Bicycling, horseback riding, kayaking, fishing, sailing, diving, swimming and hiking are popular recreational activities. The efforts of hikers and cyclists are rewarded with grand vistas and viewpoints. Mount Galiano provides climbers with eye-catching views of the southern Gulf Islands and the Olympic Mountains.

Montague Harbour Marine Provincial Park has 3,000-year-old middens; camping facilities are available at the park as well as at Dionisio Point Provincial Park. The Descanso Bay Regional Park offers 30 camping sites. *See Recreation Areas Chart.*

GALIANO OCEANFRONT INN & SPA   250/539-3388
Hotel. **Address:** 134 Madrona Dr V0N 1P0

WHERE TO EAT

ATREVIDA RESTAURANT   250/539-3388
Pacific Northwest. Fine Dining. **Address:** 134 Madrona Dr V0N 1P0

GALIANO GRAND CENTRAL EMPORIUM   250/539-9885
American. Casual Dining. **Address:** 2470 Sturdies Bay Rd V0N 1P0

HUMMINGBIRD INN PUB   250/539-5472
American. Casual Dining. **Address:** 47 Sturdies Bay Rd V0N 1P0

GIBSONS (G-11) pop. 4,437

SUNSHINE COAST MUSEUM & ARCHIVES is at 716 Winn Rd. Two floors of exhibits explore the history of the Sunshine Coast. Highlights include a Squamish Nation stone tool exhibit and an extensive butterfly collection as well as displays about the area's logging, homesteading and fishing heritage. Events include workshops and film screenings. **Time:** Allow 1 hour minimum. **Hours:** Tues.-Sun. 10:30-4:30, July-Aug.; Tues.-Sat. 10:30-4:30, rest of year. Closed statutory holidays. **Cost:** Donations. **Phone:** (604) 886-8232.

MOLLY'S REACH RESTAURANT   604/886-9710
American. Casual Dining. **Address:** 647 School Rd V0N 1V0

GLACIER NATIONAL PARK (A-10)

Elevations in the park range from 800 metres (2,625 ft.) at the lower portion of the Beaver River to 3,380 metres (11,089 ft.) at Hasler Peak on Mount Dawson. Refer to CAA/AAA maps for additional elevation information.

West of the Rockies in the southeast interior of British Columbia, Glacier National Park and its smaller counterpart Mount Revelstoke National Park *(see place listing p. 214)* encompass portions of the rugged Columbia Mountains. The park's 1,350 square kilometres (521 sq. mi.) of hard rock terrain present a jagged profile of angular mountains with narrow steep-walled valleys. The steep mountain slopes and enormous snowfall make this region susceptible to avalanches.

Rogers Pass National Historic Site, located in the heart of the park became the scene of a pitched 19th-century battle between the railroad engineers and the surrounding mountains. Sheer walls, numerous slide areas and severe weather proved almost insurmountable obstacles to the completion of

Canada's first transcontinental railroad. Some of the largest railroad trestles then known were built to carry the line across raging streams to the summit of this pass.

The tracks crossed to the southern wall of the valley on several loops to avoid the numerous avalanche slopes and reduce the steep downgrade. Despite the ingenuity of its engineers, the new railroad eventually had to be abandoned to the area's devastating winter forces. Avalanches attaining speeds of up to 325 kilometres (202 mi.) per hour tore up sections of the new track and left other sections buried under tons of snow.

Thirty-one snowsheds were built to shield the track, but even this was not enough. In 1910, 58 men were killed by an avalanche as they were clearing snow from an earlier slide. This incident, mounting costs and the dangerous grades of this section convinced the railroad to tunnel under Mount MacDonald.

The Trans-Canada Highway met similar obstacles as it crossed the pass, but the use of mobile howitzers to dislodge potential slides and other methods of controlling avalanches have held the road's position. Evidence of the struggle to build the railroad is visible from the road and the park's various campgrounds.

Several short trails follow the railroad's progress, winding past the ruins of Glacier House, a 19th-century resort hotel, remains of former snow sheds and the stone pillars that once supported the railroad trestles.

History is only part of the park's attractions. Twelve percent of the park is covered perpetually by snow and ice; more than 400 glaciers are scattered throughout the park. The contrast of the deep green forests and meadows with the glacial whites of these crags makes the park especially scenic.

Towering above the richly wooded valleys, the 3,284-metre (10,774-ft.) Mount Sir Donald rises to the east of the campgrounds, with Eagle and Uto peaks to the north. Day-hiking trails lead toward the Illecillewaet and Asulkan glaciers.

General Information and Activities

The park is open all year, although many visitor facilities are closed due to heavy snowfall October through May. In the winter, ski touring enthusiasts take advantage of the park's world-class ski touring opportunities. During the summer months, some of the popular activities include camping, hiking and mountaineering. Camping is offered at three in-park campgrounds: Illecillewaet campground is open June 21-Sept. 30, and Loop Brook and Mount Sir Donald campgrounds are open July 1-Sept. 2.

Parks Canada staff lead a variety of interpretive programs from Illecillewaet campground in July and August.

In addition, an extensive network of challenging day-hiking trails leads to such attractions as the Illecillewaet and Asulkan glaciers; Abbott Ridge; and the

Hermit. Grizzly and black bears are common in Glacier National Park; be cautious and make noise frequently as you hike. Climbers and overnight hikers may voluntarily register at the Rogers Pass Discovery Centre before and after every trip. Park entry passes also can be purchased at the Rogers Pass Discovery Centre. *See Recreation Areas Chart.*

ADMISSION to the park is free in 2017 to celebrate Canada's 150th anniversary of Confederation. Otherwise admission is $7.43; $6.24 (ages 65+); $3.71 (ages 6-16); $18.67 (all occupants of a private vehicle with up to seven people). An annual pass, valid at most Canadian national parks, marine areas and historic sites, is available.

PETS are permitted in the park provided they are on a leash at all times.

ADDRESS inquiries to the Superintendent, Glacier and Mount Revelstoke National Parks, P.O. Box 350, Revelstoke, BC, Canada V0E 2S0; phone (250) 837-7500.

ROGERS PASS DISCOVERY CENTRE is 1.3 km (.8 mi.) e. of the Rogers Pass summit. Modeled after the snowsheds that once protected the railroad from avalanches, the discovery center includes a theatre, an exhibit hall with railway models and displays about natural history. **Time:** Allow 30 minutes minimum. **Hours:** Daily 8-7, mid-June to mid-Sept.; daily 9-5, May 1 to mid-June and mid-Sept. to mid-Nov.; Tues.-Fri. 7-12:30 and 1:30-4, Sat.-Mon. 7-4, mid-Nov. to mid-Apr. Closed Christmas. Phone ahead to confirm schedule. **Cost:** Free with park entry; park admission free through 2017. Admission beginning Jan. 1, 2018: $7.43; $6.24 (ages 65+); $3.71 (ages 6-16); $18.67 (all occupants of a private vehicle with up to seven people). **Phone:** (250) 837-7500.

GOLD BRIDGE pop. 10

TYAX WILDERNESS RESORT & SPA	250/238-2221
▼▼▼ Resort Hotel. **Address:** 1 Tyaughton Lake Rd V0K 1P0	

WHERE TO EAT

TYAX RESTAURANT & LOUNGE	250/238-2221
▼▼▼ Regional Canadian. Casual Dining. **Address:** 1 Tyaughton Lake Rd V0K 1P0	

GOLDEN (A-11) pop. 3,701, elev. 785m/2,575'

On the Trans-Canada Highway at the confluence of the Columbia and Kicking Horse rivers, Golden is between Glacier *(see place listing p. 193)* and Yoho national parks *(see place listing p. 349)* and located west of Banff National Park *(see place listing in Alberta p. 28)*. The community also is an outfitting point for sports enthusiasts.

The Golden and District Museum is at 11th Avenue and 13th Street. The museum is housed in a restored one-room schoolhouse and contains local historical items.

Kicking Horse Country Chamber of Commerce: 500 10th Ave. N., P.O. Box 1320, Golden, BC, Canada V0A 1H0. **Phone:** (250) 344-7125 or (800) 622-4653.

BEST WESTERN MOUNTAINVIEW INN   (250)344-2333

Hotel
$130-$240

 Best Western. **AAA Benefit:** Save 10% or more every day and earn 10% bonus points!

Address: 1024 11th St N V0A 1H2 **Location:** Just w of jct Hwy 95 and Trans-Canada Hwy 1; on S Service Rd. **Facility:** 72 units. 3 stories, interior corridors. **Parking:** winter plug-ins. **Pool(s):** heated indoor. **Guest Services:** coin laundry.

DAYS INN GOLDEN   (250)344-2216
Motel. **Address:** 1416 Golden View Rd V0A 1H1

RAMADA LIMITED GOLDEN   (250)439-1888
Hotel. **Address:** 1311 12th St N V0A 1H1

WHERE TO EAT

CEDAR HOUSE RESTAURANT & CHALETS   250/344-4679
Canadian. Casual Dining. **Address:** 735 Hefti Rd V0A 1H2

ELEVEN 22 GRILL & LIQUIDS   250/344-2443
International. Casual Dining. **Address:** 1122 10th Ave S V0A 1H0

THE ISLAND RESTAURANT   250/344-2400
New Canadian. Casual Dining. **Address:** 101 Gould's Island, 10th Ave V0A 1H0

LEGENDZ DINER   250/344-5059
American. Casual Dining. **Address:** 1405 N Trans-Canada Hwy V0A 1H0

WHITETOOTH MOUNTAIN BISTRO   250/344-5120
New Canadian. Casual Dining. **Address:** 427 9th Ave N V0A 1H0

THE WOLF'S DEN   250/344-9683
Burgers Steak. Casual Dining. **Address:** 1105 9th St S V0A 1H0

GOLD RIVER   (E-9) pop. 1,267, elev. 122m/400'

At the joining of the Gold and Heber rivers, the town of Gold River was built in 6 months in 1965 for employees of a pulp mill. The town, with its beautiful untamed countryside, has become popular with fishermen, photographers, hikers and campers.

The MV *Uchuck III* departs from the dock on Hwy. 28. The full-day and overnight cruises explore Tahsis, Nootka Sound and Friendly Cove, where Capt. James Cook met Chief Maquinna and the Nootka First Nation when he landed on Vancouver Island in 1778; phone (250) 283-2418 for the tourist information center or (250) 283-2207 for the municipal office during off-season.

GRAND FORKS   (D-9) pop. 3,985

Settlement at the confluence of the Kettle and Granby rivers began in the late 1800s when copper, gold and silver were discovered in the area. After 20 years of prosperity, Grand Forks suffered reverses when the local copper smelter—said to be the largest in the British Empire—closed due to faltering copper prices. The logging industry and seed-growing operations later restored stability to the community.

The downtown Boundary District contains preserved historic homes, stores and civic buildings from the settlement period. It is flanked on the south and east by rivers, on the west by 5th Avenue and on the north by 75th Avenue. A walking tour map is available at the Boundary Museum *(see attraction listing)*.

Chamber of Commerce of the City of Grand Forks: 524 Central Ave., P.O. Box 2140, Grand Forks, BC, Canada V0H 1H0. **Phone:** (250) 442-5835.

BOUNDARY MUSEUM AND INTERPRETIVE CENTRE is at 6145 Reservoir Rd. The museum depicts the area's history from the late 1800s. Artifacts, maps and photographs show the lifestyles of the native peoples as well as the Doukhobor. Other exhibits include a scale model and display of Grand Forks' Chinatown in the 1900s, a wildlife exhibit and a 1929 fire truck.

Hours: Tues.-Sat. 10-4. Guided tours are available by appointment outside of regular hours. Phone ahead to confirm schedule. **Cost:** Donations. **Phone:** (250) 442-3737.

WESTERN TRAVELLER MOTEL   (250)442-5566

Motel
$74-$144

Address: 1591 Central Ave V0H 1H0 **Location:** West end of town on Hwy 3. **Facility:** 34 units, some efficiencies and kitchens. 2 stories (no elevator), exterior corridors. **Terms:** cancellation fee imposed. **Activities:** picnic facilities.

WHERE TO EAT

THE WOODEN SPOON BISTRO & BAKE SHOP   250/442-5005
Breakfast Sandwiches. Quick Serve. **Address:** 211 Market Ave V0H 1H0

GULF ISLANDS

Separated from the San Juan Islands in Washington only by an international boundary, the almost 200 islands of various shapes and sizes that make up the Gulf Islands nestle against the southeast coast of Vancouver Island. Formed by a series of moving land masses beginning about 100 million years ago, today's Gulf Islands are the result of a mass collision of land that produced the long ridges of sandstone, conglomerate and shale that constitute the islands' geology.

The area was discovered by Capt. George Vancouver while on a quest to find a northwest passage to the Orient in 1792. Erroneously named Gulf of Georgia by Vancouver, the water separating Vancouver Island from the southwestern portion of British Columbia was later correctly termed the Strait of Georgia. The islands, however, retained the designation Gulf Islands.

The area features a climate that is sunnier and milder than that found on the nearby mainland. The quiet waters promote a much quieter lifestyle as well, and the islands are a haven from the frantic pace of nearby cities. Each island, though similar in many respects, has its own distinct identity. Easily reached from the mainland, they have become popular weekend retreats offering varying degrees of amenities and activities. Artists and professionals have joined the population of local fishermen and farmers who relish the peaceful lifestyle created by the sparkling waters, cliffs, winding roads and parks.

The main components of the southern Gulf Islands are Galiano, Mayne, North and South Pender, Salt Spring and Saturna islands. The islands can be explored by automobile; cycling is treacherous due to narrow winding and hilly roads. The Islands Trust, a governmental agency, is charged with preserving and protecting the islands and waters in the Strait of Georgia.

BC Ferries provides year-round service to the main islands from Tsawwassen, south of Vancouver, and Swartz Bay, near Victoria. Vehicle reservations are recommended for travel between the mainland and the islands, but are not available for travel between Vancouver Island and the Gulf Islands or for inter-island travel. It is advisable to make reservations as far in advance as possible for summer and holiday travel. For schedule information and reservations phone (250) 386-3431 from the Victoria area and outside British Columbia or (888) 223-3779 from elsewhere in the province. Air service also is available.

GULF ISLANDS NATIONAL PARK RESERVE (I-10)

Elevations in the park range from sea level to 401 metres (1,316 ft.) at Mt. Warburton Pike on Saturna Island. Refer to CAA/AAA maps for additional elevation information.

Gulf Islands National Park Reserve protects an island landscape of rocky headlands, forested hills and shorelines studded with colorful tide pools. The park encompasses areas of lands scattered over fifteen larger islands and includes many smaller islets and reefs. Waters adjacent to park lands, extending 200 metres (650 ft.) seaward, also are under Parks Canada management.

The park shares the larger populated islands of Mayne, Saturna and the Penders with communities that offer a range of tourist amenities. Facilities and services inside the national park reserve include camping, moorage, hiking trails, day use/picnic areas and regularly scheduled interpretation programs from May 15-Sept. 30. The populated larger islands are accessible by vehicle, bicycle and BC Ferries from Vancouver and Victoria. The smaller islands are accessible by only boat or kayak. Water taxis also operate in several areas. In the summer, a passenger ferry takes visitors from the main pier in Sidney to a popular white sand beach and camping area on Sidney Island in Gulf Islands National Park Reserve. Many local tour operators offer such recreational opportunities as cycling, kayaking, scuba diving, whale-watching or hiking. Comfortable, sturdy shoes and water are recommended for all hiking excursions.

The islands are a haven for various wildlife, including such endangered species as the anatum peregrine falcon, the sharp-tailed snake, Townsend's big-eared bat, the olive-sided flycatcher, the western meadowlark and the Orca whale. The southern Gulf Islands are home to the endangered Garry Oak ecosystem. Various shorebirds, waterfowl, great blue herons, seals and sea lions also inhabit the area. There are two important bird areas in and around the park at Sidney Channel (near Sidney Island) and Active Pass near Mayne Island.

For more information, contact the Gulf Islands National Park Reserve InfoCentre at (250) 654-4000 or (866) 944-1744. For campground reservations, phone (877) 737-3783. *See Recreation Areas Chart.*

GWAII HAANAS NATIONAL PARK RESERVE AND HAIDA HERITAGE SITE
(F-1)

Elevations in the park range from sea level along Kunghit and Moresby islands to 1,123 metres (696 ft.) at Mount de la Touche. Refer to CAA/AAA maps for additional elevation information.

Off the British Columbia coast west of Prince Rupert, Gwaii Haanas National Park Reserve, National Marine Conservation Area Reserve, and Haida Heritage Site is in the southern part of Haida Gwaii, a remote island chain formerly known as the Queen Charlotte Islands *(see place listing p. 197).* Haida Gwaii translates to "islands of the people." This protected area is jointly managed by the Government of Canada and the Council of the Haida Nation. In 2010, Gwaii Haanas became the only area in the world protected from mountain top to ocean floor.

The 1,470 square kilometres (912 sq. mi.) of Gwaii Haanas offer a rich and fascinating diversity of flora, sea creatures and wildlife. Whales, bald eagles, nesting seabirds, black bears, sea lions and river otters are commonly seen.

Remnants of Haida village sites on the 138 islands capture the history of the Haida. Haida Gwaii Watchmen basecamps have been established at major sites of cultural significance. Watchmen act as hosts and also provide site security and protection of the cultural features.

Access is challenging: The only way to and around Gwaii Haanas is by air or sea. Solo travel is recommended only for the experienced outdoor traveler. Licensed tour operators provide a variety of excursions. Sea kayaking, sailboat and powerboat charters are the most popular ways to tour Gwaii Haanas. There are no maintained trails or designated campsites, and only limited visitor facilities are provided within the protected area.

Haida Gwaii can be reached by air from Vancouver and Prince Rupert. BC Ferries also provides year-round service between the islands and Prince Rupert. Arrangements for ferry transportation should be made well in advance and reservations are highly recommended; phone (250) 386-3431 from the Victoria area and outside British Columbia or (888) 223-3779 from elsewhere in the province.

Single-day admission is free in 2017 to celebrate Canada's 150th anniversary of Confederation. Otherwise admission is $18.67; $15.81 (ages 65+); $9.33 (ages 6-16); $46.67 (all occupants of a private vehicle with up to seven people). Reservations are required to visit the reserve May through September. Regulations allow for no more than 12 people on shore in one place at one time. An annual pass, valid at most Canadian national parks, marine areas and historic sites, is available.

Note: If traveling independently (without a guide), visitors must participate in one 60-minute orientation session offered at visitor centers in Sandspit and Queen Charlotte; phone (250) 559-8818 to guarantee a place. For more information, phone (250) 559-8818 or (877) 559-8818. *See Recreation Areas Chart.*

HAIDA GWAII (E-1)

Haida Gwaii ("islands of the people"), formerly the Queen Charlotte Islands, were occupied by Haida First Nation when Spanish sea captain Juan Pérez sighted the archipelago in 1774. A seafaring and artistic people, the Haida traded sea otter pelts with European traders during the early 1800s. By the late 19th century, however, the Haida had to vacate many of their ancestral villages to escape a devastating smallpox epidemic.

Only a fraction of their original number still inhabit the islands—at Haida, near Masset, and Skidegate, near Queen Charlotte City. Continuing their cultural traditions, they carve elaborate works of art from argillite, a black slatelike stone found only in mountain deposits off the coast.

A group of about 150 islands forming an elongated triangle, Haida Gwaii stretches 250 kilometres (157 mi.) from north to south, 90 kilometres (56 mi.) off the coast of British Columbia. Characterized by fog and low clouds, these islands also are known as the Misty Islands. The towns are small and decidedly rural; the entire population of Haida Gwaii is about 5,000.

The two main islands are Graham and Moresby. The largest and most populated is Graham. In the north on its broad and flat eastern side are most of the archipelago's communities—Masset, Old Masset, Port Clements, Queen Charlotte City, Skidegate, and Tlell—which are linked by a paved road. An airport is at Masset as well as at Sandspit, on the northeastern tip of Moresby Island. A 20-minute ferry ride connects the two islands.

A temperate marine climate supports dense coniferous forests, which, as the basis of the islands' economy, have been logged extensively. The fish and shellfish in the coastal waters supply the islands' important commercial fishing industry.

Visitors are attracted by the pristine wilderness, the hunting and fishing prospects, kayaking and hiking opportunities, and the handicrafts and art of the Haida. In fact the main destination of many travelers to Haida Gwaii is Gwaii Haanas National Park Reserve, National Marine Conservation Area Reserve and Haida Heritage Site *(see place listing p. 196)*, in the southern part of the island chain on Moresby Island.

Wildlife is abundant here; tiny Sitka deer and bald eagles frequent the shores, and seals, sea lions, porpoises and migrating whales often appear in the inlets. Bird-watching, wildlife viewing, hiking, kayaking and freshwater and saltwater fishing are popular activities.

Points of interest include Naikoon Provincial Park *(see Recreation Areas Chart)* on Graham Island, the remote Haida village sites, the Delkatla Wildlife Sanctuary in Masset, the Haida Heritage Centre at Kaay LInagaay *(see attraction listing p. 251)* in Skidegate and the various carving sheds in Skidegate and Old Masset.

Permission to visit Haida unoccupied village sites must be obtained from Band Council offices; phone (250) 559-8225.

The islands' main visitor center in Queen Charlotte City has videos and interactive displays that provide information about life on the islands and in the waters that surround them, including craft galleries and a touch-tank saltwater aquarium. The center is open year-round.

Haida Gwaii can be reached by air from Prince Rupert and Vancouver and by ferry from Prince Rupert. Phone BC Ferries at (250) 386-3431 or (888) 223-3779 for ferry reservations. Kayak rentals, fishing charters and various guided boat and land tours are available.

Queen Charlotte Visitor Centre: 3220 Wharf St., P.O. Box 819, Queen Charlotte City, BC, Canada V0T 1S0. **Phone:** (250) 559-8316.

HALFMOON BAY pop. 396

ROCKWATER SECRET COVE RESORT DINING ROOM
604/885-7038
▼▼▼ Pacific Northwest. Fine Dining. **Address:** 5356 Ole's Cove Rd V0N 1Y2

HARRISON HOT SPRINGS (C-7)
pop. 1,468, elev. 11m/36'

At the foot of Harrison Lake, Harrison Hot Springs *(see Recreation Areas Chart)* is a well-known health and vacation resort with two mineral springs and a sandy beach on the lakeshore. Strong area winds make this a favorite spot for windsurfing. The surrounding mountains are known as Sasquatch country, where sightings of the legendary apelike creature twice the size of a man have been reported dozens of times.

More likely to be found in the mountains are mutton-fat jades, garnets, agates, fossils and gold; the area is renowned among rock hounds.

Harrison Hot Springs Visitor InfoCentre: 499 Hot Springs Rd., P.O. Box 255, Harrison Hot Springs, BC, Canada V0M 1K0. **Phone:** (604) 796-5581.

HARRISON BEACH HOTEL   (604)796-1111
▽▽▽ Extended Stay Hotel. **Address:** 160 Esplanade Ave V0M 1K0

HARRISON HOT SPRINGS RESORT & SPA
                                        (604)796-2244

▽▽ ▽▽
Resort Hotel
$119-$429

Address: 100 Esplanade Ave V0M 1K0 **Location:** Jct Hwy 9 (Hot Springs Rd) and Esplanade Ave, just w. **Facility:** Guest rooms here range from modest units in the original main hotel to a plethora of other types scattered among the sections, including the favored units with a walk-out patio to the hot springs. 342 units, some cottages. 1-8 stories, interior corridors. **Parking:** on-site (fee) and valet. **Terms:** check-in 4 pm, 2 night minimum stay - seasonal and/or weekends, 3 day cancellation notice-fee imposed. **Amenities:** video games. **Dining:** The Copper Room, see separate listing, entertainment. **Pool(s):** heated outdoor, heated indoor. **Activities:** hot tub, steamroom, motor boats, self-propelled boats, marina, fishing, regulation golf, tennis, game room, trails, exercise room, spa. **Guest Services:** valet laundry.

[SAVE] [ECO] [🍽] [☂] CALL [⬇M] [🛥] [📶] [✕] [🐾] [🔒]
[▭] / SOME UNITS [⬛] [🛏] [⚷]

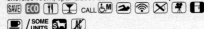
WHERE TO EAT

THE COPPER ROOM   604/796-2244
▽▽▽ Continental. Fine Dining. **Address:** 100 Esplanade Ave V0M 1K0

KITAMI JAPANESE RESTAURANT   604/796-2728
▽▽ Japanese. Casual Dining. **Address:** 318 Hot Springs Rd V0M 1K0

MUDDY WATERS ESPRESSO BAR & CAFE   604/796-5563
▽ American. Quick Serve. **Address:** 328 Esplanade Ave V0M 1K0

HAZELTON (D-3) pop. 270, elev. 306m/1,004'

A showplace of indigenous culture, Hazelton originally was called Git-an-maks, meaning "where people fish by torchlight." European settlers arriving in 1872 renamed the area Hazelton, after the profusion of hazelnut trees covering the fertile farmland.

Considered holy by the Gitxsan First Nation, the forest land within a 64.4-kilometre (40-mi.) radius of Hazelton has the province's greatest concentration of standing totem poles, many portrayed in paintings by British Columbia artist Emily Carr.

HOPE (C-7) pop. 5,969, elev. 39m/127'

At the entrance to the Fraser River Valley, Hope dates from 1848 when the Hudson's Bay Co. established a fort. The town developed rapidly, especially during the gold rush of 1858. The 1859 Anglican Christ Church is one of the province's oldest churches.

From Hope the Trans-Canada Highway leads north to Fraser Canyon. Kawkawa Lake *(see Recreation Areas Chart)*, Lake of the Woods, Mount Hope, Mount Ogilvie and Skagit Valley *(see Recreation Areas Chart)* are just some of the nearby places that offer year-round recreational opportunities.

The result of the 1965 Hope Slide is evident about 16 kilometres (10 mi.) east beside Hwy. 3. A plaque at the edge of the present roadway explains the collapse of the side of Johnson Peak, which buried the highway under 45 metres (148 ft.) of rubble.

The Hope Museum, inside the Hope Visitor Info-Centre, portrays the town's history through native artifacts and historical settings; phone (604) 869-2021. Hope was the location of several films, including "Rambo: First Blood," "Shoot to Kill" with Sidney Poitier, and Disney's "Far From Home: The Adventures of Yellow Dog."

The Hope Arts Gallery, 349 Fort St., features the work of more than 20 artists; phone (604) 869-2408. More art can be found scattered throughout downtown Hope. Wood carvings in such shapes as a gold prospector with his horse to a bald eagle holding a salmon in his talons were created from dying trees with a chainsaw; most are on the grounds of Memorial Park. Brochures about the more than two dozen carvings can be picked up at the Hope Visitor InfoCentre.

Hope Visitor Centre and Museum Complex: 919 Water Ave., P.O. Box 370, Hope, BC, Canada V0X 1L0. **Phone:** (604) 869-2021.

HELL'S GATE AIRTRAM—see Boston Bar p. 179.

OTHELLO-QUINTETTE TUNNELS are off Hwy. 3 exit 170 in Coquihalla Canyon Provincial Park; take 6th St. 1 blk. n. to Kawkawa Lake Rd., then 5 km (3 mi.) e. to Tunnels Rd. Five tunnels were built 1911-16 to complete a railroad through Coquihalla Canyon. The Coquihalla River zigzags through the canyon, presenting a challenge to engineer Andrew McCulloch, who used dynamite to blast through the canyon walls to create the narrow tunnels.

The railway ceased operations in 1959; wooden walkways now bridge the river's serpentine course between the tunnels and allow close-up views of the rushing waters.

Note: Wear shoes with good traction, as the gravel path through the tunnels may be wet, slippery and uneven. A flashlight is recommended. **Time:** Allow 1 hour, 30 minutes minimum. **Hours:** Daily dawn-dusk, Apr.-Oct. **Cost:** Free. **Parking:** $1 per hour, $3 per day. **Phone:** (604) 986-9371.

ALPINE MOTEL   (604)869-9931

Motel
$85-$135

Address: 505 Old Hope-Princeton Way V0X 1L0 **Location:** Trans-Canada Hwy 1 exit 173 westbound; exit 170 eastbound, just n from lights. **Facility:** 14 units, some kitchens. 1 story, exterior corridors. **Terms:** cancellation fee imposed.

BEST CONTINENTAL MOTEL   (604)869-9726

Motel
$64-$83

Address: 860 Fraser Ave V0X 1L0 **Location:** Trans-Canada Hwy 1 exit 170 to downtown; at Fort St. **Facility:** 14 units, some efficiencies. 2 stories (no elevator), exterior corridors. **Terms:** cancellation fee imposed.

HERITAGE INN   (604)869-7166

Motel. **Address:** 570 Old Hope-Princeton Way V0X 1L0

TRAVELODGE HOPE   (604)869-9951

Motel
$90-$110

Address: 350 Old Hope-Princeton Way V0X 1L0 **Location:** Trans-Canada Hwy 1 exit 173 westbound; exit 170 eastbound, just n from lights. **Facility:** 25 units, some efficiencies. 2 stories (no elevator), interior corridors. **Pool(s):** heated indoor. **Activities:** hot tub. **Featured Amenity:** continental breakfast.

WHERE TO EAT

293 WALLACE STREET RESTAURANT   604/860-0822

New American. Casual Dining. **Address:** 293 Wallace St V0X 1L0

BLUE MOOSE COFFEE HOUSE   604/869-0729

Coffee/Tea Sandwiches. Quick Serve. **Address:** 322 Wallace St V0X 1L0

HOPE DRIVE-IN & RESTAURANT   604/869-5380

American. Casual Dining. **Address:** 590 Old Hope-Princeton Way V0X 1L0

HUDSON'S HOPE (D-5) pop. 970,
elev. 520m/1,706'
• Hotels p. 200

Hudson's Hope is one of the oldest settlements in the province: Only two communities on Vancouver Island have been continuously occupied from earlier dates. First discovered in 1793 by Alexander Mackenzie, the area was the site of a small fur-trading post built in 1805. In 1900 the post was moved to the present site of Hudson's Hope on the north side of the Peace River, where it flourished as a center of trade for the Hudson's Bay Co.

Hudson's Hope is an important supplier of hydroelectricity; its two dams generate about 38 percent of the hydropower used in British Columbia. The dams also are major recreation centers for the area.

Hudson's Hope Visitor Centre: 9555 Beattie Dr., P.O. Box 330, Hudson's Hope, BC, Canada V0C 1V0. **Phone:** (250) 783-9154 May-Oct., or (250) 783-9901 rest of year.

PEACE CANYON DAM is 4 km (2.5 mi.) s. on Hwy. 29. Completed in 1980, the dam is 50 metres (165 ft.) high and 533 metres (1,750 ft.) long. It reuses water that has generated electricity at the W.A.C. Bennett Dam, 23 kilometres (14 mi.) upstream on the Peace River. Nearby recreational facilities include a campground, picnic facilities and a boat launch to Dinosaur Lake, the dam's reservoir. **Hours:** Daily 8-4, mid-May through Labour Day.

Peace Canyon Dam Visitor Centre is next to the powerhouse. Exhibits reflect the area's natural history, its pioneer past and the Peace Canyon Project. Highlights include a replica of the stern-wheeler SS *Peace River,* a large-scale model of a generating unit, displays about the damming of the Peace River, and mammoth tusks found during excavation. Visitors can view the project's central control system, walk across the dam or visit the observation area on the main floor and a viewing deck.

Guided tours of the visitor center are available. **Hours:** Daily 8-4, mid-May through Labour Day; Mon.-Fri. 8-4, rest of year. Closed Jan. 1, Easter, second Mon. in Oct., Nov. 11, Christmas and day after Christmas. **Cost:** Free. **Phone:** (250) 783-7418 or (888) 333-6667.

W.A.C. BENNETT DAM is 21 km (13 mi.) w. on Canyon Dr. following signs. A major hydroelectric project on the Peace River, the dam was completed in 1967 to produce electrical power for British Columbia. It is 183 metres (600 ft.) high, 2 kilometres (1.2 mi.) long and .8 kilometre (.5 mi.) thick at the base. Backup water from the dam forms 164,600-hectare (406,727-acre) Williston Lake, British Columbia's largest lake. Its shoreline stretches for 1,770 kilometres (1,100 mi.).

W.A.C. Bennett Dam Visitor Centre is about 1 km (.6 mi.) s.e. of the dam. Photographs and artifacts chronicle the history and geology of the region and the construction of the dam and powerhouse. A participatory exhibit demonstrates the generation of electricity and magnetism. Underground bus tours into the powerhouse and manifold chambers are available. A 40-minute multimedia presentation also is offered in the theater.

Note: Cameras, purses and bags are not permitted on the tour. **Hours:** Visitor center daily 10-5, mid-May through Labour Day; by appointment rest of year. Underground powerhouse tours are available 10:30-3:30. Phone ahead to confirm times for tours. **Cost:** $5.71; $4.76 (ages 6-18 and 55+); $14.24 (family, two adults and two children). Reservations are required for the tour. **Phone:** (250) 783-5048 or (888) 333-6667. [T]

SIGMA INN & SUITES (250)783-2300

▼▼ Extended Stay Hotel. **Address:** 9006 Clark Ave V0C 1V0

INVERMERE (B-11) pop. 2,955

Nestled in the "Valley of a Thousand Peaks" between the Rocky and Purcell mountain ranges, Invermere's bucolic location on Lake Windermere's north shore makes it the ideal spot for summer recreation, including hiking, camping, fishing, boating and sailboarding. Hang gliders frequently take flight off nearby Mount Swansea.

Birds of a different feather fly freely at Wilmer National Wildlife Area, about 5 kilometres (3 mi.) north of town; bring your binoculars to peep at songbirds, woodpeckers, waterfowl and birds of prey as well as four-legged creatures including deer, elk, muskrats and beavers.

Roam down Main Street in Invermere's downtown, where flowers bloom in abundance and small-town charm pervades the boutiques, antique shops and cafés. Take in a first-run flick at the 1952 Toby Theatre.

Invermere Visitor Centre: 651 Hwy. 93/95 or 1046 7th Ave., P.O. Box 1019, Invermere, BC, Canada V0A 1K0. **Phone:** (250) 342-2844.

BEST WESTERN INVERMERE INN (250)342-9246

Hotel
$129-$180

 Best Western. **AAA Benefit:** Save 10% or more every day and earn 10% bonus points!

Address: 1310 7th Ave V0A 1K0 **Location:** Hwy 93 and 95 exit Invermere, 1.8 mi (3 km) w; center. **Facility:** 46 units. 3 stories, interior corridors. **Parking:** winter plug-ins. **Terms:** check-in 4 pm. **Activities:** hot tub, exercise room. **Guest Services:** coin laundry. **Featured Amenity:** breakfast buffet.

COPPERPOINT RESORT (250)341-4000

▼▼▼ Contemporary Resort Hotel. **Address:** 760 Cooper Rd V0A 1K2

WHERE TO EAT

BLACK FOREST STEAK & SCHNITZEL HOUSE
250/342-9417

▼▼ ▼▼
Continental
Casual Dining
$17-$39

AAA Inspector Notes: Step into another world at this restaurant with its lovely and airy Bavarian décor. Servers sport matching garb and offer proficient and friendly service. On the menu is a good selection of tasty schnitzels, bratwurst, steak and seafood finely prepared with a respect for tradition. Table d'hotes are offered daily. The aviary on view is a nice spot for birders to enjoy watching the owner's pets while dining. **Features:** full bar, early bird specials. **Reservations:** suggested. **Address:** 540 Hwy 93 & 95 V0A 1K0 **Location:** Center. [D]

BLUE DOG CAFE 250/342-3814

▼ American. Casual Dining. **Address:** 1213 7th Ave V0A 1K0

ELEMENTS GRILL 250/341-4000

▼▼▼▼ International. Casual Dining. **Address:** 760 Cooper Rd V0A 1K2

STRAND'S OLD HOUSE RESTAURANT 250/342-6344

▼▼▼▼ Continental. Casual Dining. **Address:** 818 12th St V0A 1K0

KAMLOOPS (H-5) pop. 85,678, elev. 345m/1,131'
• Restaurants p. 204

Founded in 1812 as a North West Co. depot, Kamloops later was a Hudson's Bay Co. post. Developed where the north and south branches of the Thompson River converge to form Kamloops Lake, Kamloops was named after a Secwepemc (Shuswap) word, *Tk'emlúps,* or "the meeting of the waters" or, alternatively, a similar French phrase, *camp des loups,* or "camp of wolves." During the gold rush of the 1860s the Overlanders reached the city by rafting down the North Thompson. A bronze statue at city hall commemorates their arrival and their contributions to the city.

Since the Cariboo's gold supply disappeared in the 1860s, Kamloops has developed as a center of cattle and sheep ranching, forestry and lumber and, in more recent years, tourism.

In summer, Kamloops Heritage Railway, #6-510 Lorne St., operates a sightseeing tour on *The Spirit of Kamloops,* a restored 1912 steam locomotive with hayrack cars, heritage coaches and caboose. The train departs the Canadian National Railway station, passing St. Joseph's Church along the way, and features a train robbery reenactment on the return trip; phone (250) 374-2141.

With an abundance of lakes in the area, Kamloops offers good fishing. In fact, local trout are known to jump a few feet in the air after being hooked. Outdoor enthusiasts also enjoy golfing, nature trails, wildlife viewing, boating, kayaking, canoeing, hiking and mountain biking. Many urban parks also offer recreational activities, including hiking, biking, picnicking and strolling, and skiing can be enjoyed on nearby slopes.

Culturally speaking, Western Canada Theatre and Project X Theatre Productions stage plays virtually year-round; phone (250) 372-3216 and (250) 374-5483 respectively. And the Kamloops Symphony, (250) 372-5000, presents orchestral and chamber music performances September to May.

Kamloops Visitor Centre: 1290 W. Trans-Canada Hwy., Kamloops, BC, Canada V2C 6R3. **Phone:** (250) 374-3377 or (800) 662-1994.

Self-guiding tours: Kamloops is the site of several historical attractions, including the provincial courthouse and several old houses and churches. Self-guiding tour brochures are available from Kamloops Museum and Archives.

ACCENT INNS   250/374-8877
 Motel. **Address:** 1325 Columbia St W V2C 6P4

BEST WESTERN PLUS KAMLOOPS HOTEL
(250)374-7878

Hotel
$145-$195

Best Western PLUS.

AAA Benefit: Save 10% or more every day and earn 10% bonus points!

Address: 660 Columbia St W V2C 1L1 **Location:** Trans-Canada Hwy 1 exit 369 (Columbia St) eastbound; exit 370 (Summit Dr) westbound to Columbia St via City Centre, 1.1 mi (1.8 km) n. **Facility:** 81 units. 4 stories, interior corridors. **Parking:** winter plug-ins. **Pool(s):** heated indoor. **Activities:** hot tub, exercise room. **Guest Services:** valet and coin laundry. **Featured Amenity:** breakfast buffet. *(See ad this page.)*

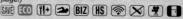

 **Get the App**

Stay mobile with maps, travel information
and road service on the go.

AAA.com/mobile • CAA.ca/mobile

CANADAS BEST VALUE INN AND SUITES   (250)374-8100
 Motel. **Address:** 1200 Rogers Way V1S 1N5 *(See ad p. 204.)*

THE COAST KAMLOOPS HOTEL & CONFERENCE CENTRE
(250)828-6660
 Hotel. **Address:** 1250 Rogers Way V1S 1N5 *(See ad p. 202.)*

COMFORT INN & SUITES   (250)372-0987
Hotel
$124-$209
Address: 1810 Rogers Pl V1S 1T7 **Location:** Trans-Canada Hwy 1 exit 368 (Hillside Ave), just s. **Facility:** 87 units. 3 stories, interior corridors. **Pool(s):** heated indoor. **Activities:** hot tub, exercise room. **Guest Services:** valet laundry. **Featured Amenity: breakfast buffet.** *(See ad p. 202.)*
  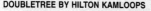

DOUBLETREE BY HILTON KAMLOOPS   (250)851-0026
Hotel
$109-$159

AAA Benefit: Members save 5% or more!
Address: 339 St. Paul St V2C 2J5 **Location:** Between 3rd and 4th Aves; downtown. **Facility:** 100 units. 5 stories, interior corridors. **Terms:** 1-7 night minimum stay, cancellation fee imposed. **Amenities:** safes. **Pool(s):** heated outdoor. **Activities:** sauna, hot tub, limited exercise equipment. **Guest Services:** valet laundry. **Featured Amenity: breakfast buffet.**

FAIRFIELD INN & SUITES BY MARRIOTT KAMLOOPS
(778)471-0902
Hotel
$65-$144
AAA Benefit: Members save 5% or more!
Address: 1475 Hugh Allan Dr V1S 1J3 **Location:** Trans-Canada Hwy 1 exit 367 (Pacific Way), just e. **Facility:** 114 units. 5 stories, interior corridors. **Pool(s):** indoor. **Activities:** hot tub, exercise room. **Guest Services:** valet and coin laundry. **Featured Amenity: breakfast buffet.**

FOUR POINTS BY SHERATON KAMLOOPS
250/374-4144
Hotel
Rates not provided

AAA Benefit: Members save up to 15%, plus Starwood Preferred Guest® benefits!
Address: 1175 Rogers Way V1S 1R5 **Location:** Trans-Canada Hwy 1 exit 368 (Hillside Ave), just s. **Facility:** 78 units, some two bedrooms, efficiencies and kitchens. 4 stories, interior corridors. **Parking:** winter plug-ins. **Amenities:** safes. **Pool(s):** heated indoor. **Activities:** sauna, hot tub, exercise room. **Guest Services:** valet and coin laundry. **Featured Amenity: full hot breakfast.**

HAMPTON INN BY HILTON   (250)571-7897
Hotel
$109-$179

AAA Benefit: Members save up to 10%!
Address: 1245 Rogers Way V1S 1R9 **Location:** Trans-Canada Hwy 1 exit 368 (Hillside Ave), just s via Hillside Way. **Facility:** 81 units. 3 stories, interior corridors. **Terms:** 1-7 night minimum stay, cancellation fee imposed. **Pool(s):** heated indoor. **Activities:** hot tub, exercise room. **Guest Services:** valet and coin laundry. **Featured Amenity: breakfast buffet.**

HOLIDAY INN & SUITES   (250)376-8288
Hotel
$99-$169
Address: 675 Tranquille Rd V2B 3H7 **Location:** Trans-Canada Hwy 1 exit 374 (Jasper Ave), 2.5 mi (4 km) w on Halston Connector Rd, 1.8 mi (3 km) s on 8th St to Fortune Dr, then just s. **Facility:** 89 units. 4 stories, interior corridors. **Parking:** winter plug-ins. **Terms:** cancellation fee imposed. **Pool(s):** heated indoor. **Activities:** hot tub, exercise room. **Guest Services:** valet and coin laundry.

HOLIDAY INN EXPRESS KAMLOOPS   250/372-3474
 Hotel. **Address:** 1550 Versatile Dr V1S 1X4

HOTEL 540   (250)372-2281
Hotel. **Address:** 540 Victoria St V2C 2B2

KAMLOOPS TRAVELODGE MOUNTVIEW   (250)374-4788
Motel. **Address:** 1225 Rogers Way V1S 1R9

MAVERICK MOTOR INN & WATERSLIDE   250/374-9666
◆◆◆ ◆◆ Motel. **Address:** 1250 W Trans-Canada Hwy 1 V2C 6R3

PACIFIC INN & SUITES   250/372-0952

◆◆◆ ◆◆ ◆◆◆
Hotel
Rates not provided

Address: 1820 Rogers Pl V1S 1T7 **Location:** Trans-Canada Hwy 1 exit 368 (Hillside Ave), just w. **Facility:** 39 units, some kitchens. 3 stories, interior corridors. **Pool(s):** heated outdoor. **Activities:** hot tub, exercise room. **Guest Services:** valet and coin laundry. **Featured Amenity: continental breakfast.**

[SAVE] [Ⓣ] CALL [⑃M] [⊿] [📶] [✕]
[▯] [▱] [▱] /SOME UNITS [🐕] [▣]

QUALITY INN   (250)851-0111

◆◆◆ ◆◆ ◆◆◆
Motel
$79-$189

Address: 1860 Rogers Pl V1S 1T7 **Location:** Trans-Canada Hwy 1 exit 368 (Hillside Ave). **Facility:** 63 units, some kitchens. 2 stories (no elevator), interior corridors. **Pool(s):** heated outdoor. **Activities:** sauna, hot tub. **Guest Services:** coin laundry. **Featured Amenity: full hot breakfast.**

[SAVE] [Ⓣ+] CALL [⑃M] [⊿] [📶] [▯]
[▱] [▱] /SOME UNITS [🐕]

RAMADA KAMLOOPS   (250)374-0358
◆◆◆ ◆◆ Hotel. **Address:** 555 W Columbia St V2C 1K7

RANCHLAND INN   (250)828-8787
◆◆ Motel. **Address:** 2357 Trans-Canada Hwy 1 E V2C 4A8

Crossing borders or traveling abroad?
Arrive ready with foreign currency

SCOTT'S INN & RESTAURANT   250/372-8221

◆◆◆ ◆◆ ◆◆◆
Motel
Rates not provided

Address: 551 11th Ave V2C 3Y1 **Location:** Trans-Canada Hwy 1 exit City Center (from eastern approach), 0.5 mi (0.9 km) w on Battle St, then just s. Located in residential area across from a playground. **Facility:** 51 units, some two bedrooms and kitchens. 2 stories (no elevator), exterior corridors. **Parking:** winter plug-ins. **Pool(s):** heated indoor. **Activities:** hot tub, picnic facilities. **Guest Services:** coin laundry. **Featured Amenity: continental breakfast.**

[SAVE] [Ⓣ] CALL [⑃M] [⊿] [📶] [✕]
[▯] [▱] /SOME UNITS [🐕] [▣]

THE THOMPSON HOTEL   250/374-1999

◆◆◆ ◆◆ ◆◆◆
Hotel
Rates not provided

Address: 650 Victoria St V2C 2B4 **Location:** Between 6th and 7th aves; downtown. **Facility:** 96 units, some efficiencies. 3 stories, interior corridors. **Parking:** on-site (fee), winter plug-ins. **Terms:** check-in 4 pm. **Dining:** The Noble Pig Brewhouse, see separate listing. **Pool(s):** heated indoor. **Activities:** hot tub, game room, exercise room. **Guest Services:** valet laundry.

[SAVE] [ECO] [Ⓣ] [Y] [⊿] [BIZ] [📶]
[✕] [▯] [▱] /SOME UNITS [🐕] [▣]

WINGATE BY WYNDHAM - KAMLOOPS   236/425-1986
[fyi] Hotel. Too new to rate, opening scheduled for January 2017. **Address:** 1200 Rogers Way V1S 1N5 **(See ad this page.)**

WHERE TO EAT

ARIGATO SUSHI   250/314-1185
◆◆ ◆◆ Japanese. Casual Dining. **Address:** 1395 Hillside Dr V2E 2R7

BEIJING RESTAURANT   250/372-3355
◆◆ ◆◆ Chinese. Casual Dining. **Address:** 1250 W Trans-Canada Hwy 1 V2C 6R3

BLUE DINING + LOUNGE   778/471-8035
▼▼▼ American. Casual Dining. **Address:** 540 Victoria St V2C 2B2

BOLD FIRE INSPIRED PIZZERIA   780/471-2653
▼▼ Pizza. Casual Dining. **Address:** 945 Columbia St W, #196 W V2C 1L5

BROWNSTONE RESTAURANT   250/851-9939
▼▼ New American. Fine Dining. **Address:** 118 Victoria St V2C 1Z7

BURGER & CAFE JOY   250/377-0049
▼ Japanese Burgers Fusion. Quick Serve. **Address:** 945 Columbia St W, #140 V2C 1L5

CHEZ CORA   778/471-5944
▼▼ Breakfast Sandwiches. Casual Dining. **Address:** 1801 Princeton-Kamloops Hwy V2E 2J7

EARLS KITCHEN + BAR   250/372-3275
▼▼ American. Casual Dining. **Address:** 1210 Summit Dr V2C 6M1

HELLO TOAST   250/372-9322
▼▼ American. Casual Dining. **Address:** 428 Victoria St V2C 2A7

MAURYA'S FINE INDIAN CUISINE   250/377-4969
▼▼ Indian. Casual Dining. **Address:** 165 Victoria St V2C 1Z4

MITTZ KITCHEN   778/471-5050
▼▼▼ New International. Casual Dining. **Address:** 227 Victoria St V2C 2A1

THE NOBLE PIG BREWHOUSE   778/471-5999
▼▼ American. Gastropub. **Address:** 650 Victoria St V2C 2B4

ON THE ROCKS PUB & GRILL   250/374-9761
▼▼ International. Sports Bar. **Address:** 1265 Rogers Way V1S 1R9

ORIENTAL GARDENS RESTAURANT   250/372-2344
▼▼ Chinese. Casual Dining. **Address:** 545 Victoria St V2C 2B1

ORIGINAL JOE'S RESTAURANT & BAR   778/471-6116
▼▼ American. Gastropub. **Address:** 1801 Princeton-Kamloops Hwy, #203 V2E 2J7

QUILAS MEXICAN RESTAURANT   778/471-6364
▼▼ Mexican. Casual Dining. **Address:** 330 Victoria St V2C 2A5

ROMEO'S KITCHEN + SPIRITS   250/372-5312
▼▼ International. Casual Dining. **Address:** 1250 Rogers Way V1S 1N5 **(See ad p. 202.)**

TERRA RESTAURANT   250/374-2913
▼▼▼ New Canadian. Casual Dining. **Address:** 326 Victoria St V2C 2A5

KASLO (C-11) pop. 1,026, elev. 588m/1,929'

Kaslo began as a mill site in 1888. Following large silver strikes in 1893 the town quickly expanded to city proportions. A village once again, Kaslo is a distribution center for the Lardeau Valley.

Duncan Dam, 42 kilometres (26 mi.) north, was the first of the three dams constructed by B.C. Hydro

in accordance with the Columbia River Treaty, ratified by British Columbia and the United States in 1964. Southwest of the dam is the Kokanee Spawning Channel, built to compensate for the loss of natural spawning areas resulting from the dam's construction. The 3.2-kilometre (2-mi.) channel, one of the longest in the world, is said to be the first constructed for freshwater fish.

KELOWNA (H-6) pop. 117,312,
elev. 420m/1,387'
• Hotels p. 206 • Restaurants p. 208
• Hotels & Restaurants map & index p. 226
• Part of Okanagan Valley area — see map p. 222

Kelowna is the center of a fruit and vineyard region around Lake Okanagan, from which one-third of all apples harvested in Canada are shipped. The lake also is known for its legendary monster, the Ogopogo, a Loch Ness type beast reportedly 9 to 21 metres (30-69 ft.) long with a head resembling that of a horse, goat or sheep.

The Kelowna Community Theatre stages productions during fall and winter; phone (250) 763-9018. The Okanagan Symphony Orchestra is another prominent cultural feature; phone (250) 763-7544.

Recreation in the area includes water sports, fishing and golf. City Park on Lake Okanagan is the city's largest park, with a beach, tennis courts and a children's water park. The Kelowna Princess II sets sail from the park's lakefront (end of Bernard Street). Departures are subject to weather conditions; for information and sailing times phone (250) 317-5628.

The fall grape harvest is celebrated for 11 days in early October at the ▽ Okanagan Fall Wine Festival. Wine and food lovers congregate to take in more than 165 events that take place throughout the Okanagan Valley.

Kelowna Visitor Centre: 544 Harvey Ave., Kelowna, BC, Canada V1Y 6C9. **Phone:** (250) 861-1515 or (800) 663-4345.

B.C. ORCHARD INDUSTRY MUSEUM is at 1304 Ellis St. Housed in the historic Laurel Packing House, the museum explores the Okanagan's roots in the orchard industry. A 15-metre (50-ft.) model train layout is displayed. Other displays explain fruit production from planting to processing and preserving. The Apple Tree Activities Centre is available for children. **Time:** Allow 30 minutes minimum. **Hours:** Tues.-Sat. 10-5, Sun. 11-4. Phone for holiday hours. Closed Jan. 1, Christmas and day after Christmas. **Cost:** Donations. **Phone:** (778) 478-0347.

The BC Wine Museum & Gift Shop is at 1304 Ellis St. Housed in a converted 1917 packing house, the museum displays machines used for pressing and bottling as well as exhibits featuring the history of wine production in the area. Guided tours are available by appointment. **Hours:** Mon.-Fri. 10-6, Sat. 10-5, Sun. and holidays 11-5. Closed Jan. 1,

(See map & index p. 226.)

Christmas and day after Christmas. **Cost:** Donations. **Phone:** (778) 478-0325.

ELYSIUM GARDENS is at 2834 Belgo Rd. The site covers 1.2 hectares (3 acres) and includes organically grown perennial gardens and a Japanese garden. Featured are herb gardens, cut flower and kitchen gardens, xeriscape gardens, ornamental grasses and rock and scree beds.

Dependent on the season, visitors will discover peonies, roses, primroses, tulips, day lilies and hydrangeas in full, fragrant bloom. Mountains and countryside views provide a backdrop for the gardens. **Time:** Allow 1 hour minimum. **Hours:** Tues.-Sat. 10-5, Sun. noon-5, May-Sept. Closed early to mid-July. **Cost:** $11.43. **Phone:** (250) 491-1368.

KELOWNA ART GALLERY is at 1315 Water St. This architecturally striking museum offers changing exhibitions in its four galleries as well as art classes and lectures. **Time:** Allow 1 hour minimum. **Hours:** Tues.-Sat. 10-5 (also Thurs. 5-9), Sun. 1-4. Closed major holidays. **Cost:** $4.76; $3.81 (ages 65+ and students with ID); $9.52 (family); free (to all Thurs.). **Parking:** Metered street parking and pay lot are nearby. **Phone:** (250) 762-2226.

OKANAGAN MILITARY MUSEUM is at 1424 Ellis St. between Queensway and Doyle Ave. Permanent exhibits focus on the contributions of Okanagan Valley residents in the military. Items from the Boer War, World War I, World War II and others are on display. A reference library holds books on military history, and volunteer veterans are on-site to answer questions. **Time:** Allow 30 minutes minimum. **Hours:** Tues.-Sat. 10-5, May-Sept.; Tues., Thurs. and Sat. 10-5, rest of year. Phone ahead to confirm holiday schedule. **Cost:** Donations. **Phone:** (250) 763-9292.

WINERIES

- **CedarCreek Estate Winery** is 12 km (7 mi.) s. at 5445 Lakeshore Rd., following signs. **Hours:** Tastings daily 10-7, July 1-Sept. 4; 11-6, May-June; 11-5, rest of year. Tours daily at 11, 1 and 3, May 15-Sept. 4. Closed Jan. 1, Christmas and day after Christmas. **Phone:** (778) 738-1020 in Canada. GT

- **Summerhill Pyramid Winery** is at 4870 Chute Lake Rd. **Hours:** Tastings daily 9-8, May 19-Oct. 9; 10-6, rest of year. Tours are given daily at 2, 4 and 6. **Phone:** (250) 764-8000 or (800) 667-3538. GT

▼ See AAA listing p. 207 ▼

(See map & index p. 226.)

BEST WESTERN PLUS KELOWNA HOTEL & SUITES
(250)860-1212 **21**

Hotel
$140-$250

 Best Western PLUS.

AAA Benefit:
Save 10% or more every day and earn 10% bonus points!

Address: 2402 Hwy 97 N V1X 4J1 **Location:** 0.6 mi (1 km) s of jct Hwy 97 N (Harvey Ave) and 33; corner of Leckie Rd. **Facility:** 176 units, some two bedrooms, efficiencies and kitchens. 2-8 stories, interior corridors. **Terms:** check-in 4 pm. **Pool(s):** heated indoor. **Activities:** hot tub, picnic facilities, exercise room, spa. **Guest Services:** valet and coin laundry. **Featured Amenity:** breakfast buffet. *(See ad p. 206.)*

COMFORT SUITES
(250)861-1110 **16**

Hotel
$142-$349

Address: 2656 Hwy 97 N V1X 4J4 **Location:** Jct Hwy 97 N (Harvey Ave) and 33, 0.5 mi (0.9 km) n. **Facility:** 83 units, some two bedrooms. 4 stories, interior corridors. **Parking:** winter plug-ins. **Amenities:** safes. **Pool(s):** heated indoor. **Activities:** hot tub, exercise room. **Guest Services:** valet and coin laundry. **Featured Amenity:** full hot breakfast.

COMFORT SUITES

2014 GOLD CHOICE AWARD
• **FREE HOT Breakfast**
• **Free Internet**
• **Indoor water-slide**
• **Some pet rooms**

DELTA GRAND OKANAGAN RESORT & CONFERENCE CENTRE
(250)763-4500 **12**
Resort Hotel. **Address:** 1310 Water St V1Y 9P3

AAA Benefit:
Members save 5% or more!

FAIRFIELD INN & SUITES BY MARRIOTT KELOWNA
(250)763-2800 **19**
Hotel. **Address:** 1655 Powick Rd V1X 4L1

AAA Benefit:
Members save 5% or more!

Use travel time to share

driving tips and rules

of the road with your teens

▼ See AAA listing p. 208 ▼

RAMADA
Hotel and Conference Centre
Kelowna, BC

Comfortable *Enjoyable* *Relaxing*

TF 1.800.665.2518
PH 250.860.9711
ramadalodgehotelkelowna.com
ramadalodge@rpbhotels.com

2170 Harvey Ave (Hwy 97 N)
Kelowna, BC V1Y 6G8

(See map & index p. 226.)

FOUR POINTS BY SHERATON KELOWNA AIRPORT
(250)807-2000 **11**

Hotel
$129-$389

AAA Benefit: Members save up to 15%, plus Starwood Preferred Guest® benefits!

Address: 5505 Airport Way V1V 3C3 **Location:** Hwy 97 (Harvey Ave), just w. **Facility:** 120 units, some efficiencies. 6 stories, interior corridors. **Amenities:** safes. **Pool(s):** heated indoor. **Activities:** hot tub, exercise room. **Guest Services:** valet and coin laundry, area transportation. **Featured Amenity:** full hot breakfast.

HOLIDAY INN EXPRESS KELOWNA CONFERENCE CENTRE
250/763-0500 **20**

Hotel
Rates not provided

Address: 2429 Hwy 97 N V1X 4J2 **Location:** 0.6 mi (1 km) s of jct Hwy 97 N (Harvey Ave) and 33. **Facility:** 190 units. 4-7 stories, interior corridors. **Terms:** check-in 4 pm. **Pool(s):** heated indoor. **Activities:** hot tub, exercise room. **Guest Services:** valet and coin laundry.

HOTEL ELDORADO (250)763-7500 **25**
Classic Boutique Hotel. **Address:** 500 Cook Rd V1W 3G9

KELOWNA INN & SUITES 250/762-2533 **15**
Motel. **Address:** 1070 Harvey Ave V1Y 8S4

MANTEO RESORT-WATERFRONT HOTEL & VILLAS
250/860-1031 **24**
Resort Hotel. **Address:** 3762 Lakeshore Rd V1W 3L4

RAMADA HOTEL & CONFERENCE CENTRE
(250)860-9711 **22**
Hotel. **Address:** 2170 Harvey Ave V1Y 6G8 *(See ad p. 207.)*

THE ROYAL ANNE HOTEL (250)763-2277 **14**
Hotel. **Address:** 348 Bernard Ave V1Y 6N5

SIESTA SUITES (250)763-5013 **23**
Motel. **Address:** 3152 Lakeshore Rd V1W 3T1

SUPER 8 KELOWNA (250)762-8222 **18**
Motel. **Address:** 2592 Hwy 97 N V1X 4J4

WHERE TO EAT

BAI TONG 250/763-8638 **22**
Thai. Casual Dining. **Address:** 275 Bernard Ave V1X 6N2

BLUETAIL SUSHI & BISTRO 778/484-5900 **21**
Sushi. Casual Dining. **Address:** 1675 Commerce Ave, #102 V1X 8A9

BOUCHONS BISTRO 250/763-6595 **11**
French. Fine Dining. **Address:** 105-1180 Sunset Dr V1Y 9W6

BREAD CO. FINE BAKED GOODS & EATERY
250/762-3336 **14**
Breads/Pastries Sandwiches. Quick Serve. **Address:** 363 Bernard Ave V1Y 6N6

CEDAR CREEK WINERY TERRACE RESTAURANT
778/738-1027 **33**
New Canadian. Casual Dining. **Address:** 5445 Lakeshore Rd V1W 4S5

DAWETT FINE INDIAN CUISINE 250/717-1668 **12**
Indian. Casual Dining. **Address:** 1435 Ellis St V1Y 2A3

DUNNENZIES PIZZA CO. 250/763-2420 **16**
Pizza. Quick Serve. **Address:** 1559 Ellis St V1Y 2A7

EARLS KITCHEN + BAR 250/763-2777
American. Casual Dining. **Address:** 211 Bernard Ave V1Y 6N2

ELDORADO DINING ROOM & BAR 250/763-7500 **31**
Regional Canadian. Fine Dining. **Address:** 500 Cook Rd V1W 3G9

THE FIXX CAFE & PASTA BAR 250/861-3499 **29**
International. Casual Dining. **Address:** 3275 Lakeshore Rd, #101 V1W 3S9

THE JAMMERY 250/766-1139 **9**
American. Casual Dining. **Address:** 8038 Hwy 97 N V1X 6A6

JOEY RESTAURANTS 250/860-8999
American. Casual Dining. **Address:** 300-2475 Hwy 97 N V1X 4J2

LITTLE HOBO 778/478-0411 **17**
Soup Sandwiches. Quick Serve. **Address:** 438 Lawrence Ave V1Y 6L5

MABUI 250/868-8852 **24**
Japanese Small Plates Sushi. Casual Dining. **Address:** 2070 Harvey Ave, #8 V1Y 8P8

MAMMA ROSA RESTAURANT 250/763-4114 **19**
Italian. Casual Dining. **Address:** 561 Lawrence Ave V1Y 6L8

THE MARMALADE CAT CAFE 250/861-4158 **27**
Sandwiches Desserts. Quick Serve. **Address:** 2903 Pandosy St, #103 V1Y 1W1

MIZU JAPANESE RESTAURANT 250/862-8022 **26**
Sushi. Casual Dining. **Address:** 2684 Pandosy St V1Y 1V6

MOXIE'S CLASSIC GRILL 250/861-6110
American. Casual Dining. **Address:** 1730 Cooper Rd V1Y 8V5

PEARSON'S EUROPEAN DELI 250/762-0800 **25**
Deli. Quick Serve. **Address:** 2070 Harvey Ave, Unit 30 V1Y 8P8

RAUDZ REGIONAL TABLE 250/868-8805 **15**
New Canadian. Casual Dining. **Address:** 1560 Water St V1Y 1J7

(See map & index p. 226.)

SALTED BRICK   778/484-3234   (13)
♦ Canadian. Casual Dining. **Address:** 243 Bernard Ave V1Y 6N2

SMACK DAB   250/860-4488   (30)
♦♦♦ American. Gastropub. **Address:** 3762 Lakeshore Rd V1W 3L4

SUMMERHILL SUNSET ORGANIC BISTRO
       250/764-8000   (32)
♦♦♦ New Canadian. Casual Dining. **Address:** 4870 Chute Lake Rd V1W 4M3

VALOROSO FOODS   250/860-3641   (23)
♦ Italian Deli. Quick Serve. **Address:** 1467 Sutherland Ave V1Y 5Y4

WATERFRONT WINES   250/979-1222   (10)
♦♦♦ New Canadian. Fine Dining. **Address:** 104-1180 Sunset Dr V1Y 9W6

YAMAS TAVERNA GREEK RESTAURANT   250/763-5823   (20)
♦♦ Greek. Casual Dining. **Address:** 1630 Ellis St V1Y 8L1

THE YELLOWHOUSE RESTAURANT   250/763-5136   (18)
♦♦♦ New International. Fine Dining. **Address:** 526 Lawrence Ave V1Y 6L7

ZABB THAI RESTAURANT   778/484-3988   (28)
♦♦ Thai. Casual Dining. **Address:** 3009 Pandosy St V1Y 1W3

KEREMEOS (D-8) pop. 1,330, elev. 430m/1,414'

The rich soil and desert climate of the Similkameen Valley drew early settlers, who planted the first fruit trees there in 1880. Today Keremeos is considered one of the best fruit-growing regions in British Columbia. Cherries, apples, grapes, peaches and apricots are among the area's bounties.

Keremeos Visitor Centre: 427 7th Ave., Keremeos, BC, Canada V0X 1N0. **Phone:** (250) 499-5225.

THE GRIST MILL AND GARDENS AT KEREMEOS is 1.5 km (.9 mi.) n.e. on Hwy. 3A, then .8 km (.5 mi.) e. on Upper Bench Rd. Demonstrations of the principles of milling and restoration are offered at this 1877 flour mill, which features a working waterwheel and flume. A visitor center provides a schedule of living-history presentations for the Apple House Theatre and the summer kitchen. On the grounds are Victorian-era gardens, an heirloom apple orchard, heritage wheat fields and a tearoom.

Time: Allow 1 hour minimum. **Hours:** Daily 9-5, Victoria Day-Thanksgiving Sunday; Fri.-Sun. 10-3, Mon. after Thanksgiving-Christmas Eve. **Cost:** $6.67; $4.76 (ages 5-19 and ages 65+). **Phone:** (250) 499-2888. (▲)

KIMBERLEY (C-11) pop. 6,652

Kimberley is a winter sports center with a Bavarian theme and a pedestrian mall—the Platzl—complete with wandering minstrels and a huge

cuckoo clock. The Kimberley Community Gardens present colorful views June through October.

Built on the slopes of Sullivan and North Star hills, Kimberley is one of Canada's highest cities. It is perhaps best known as the site of the Sullivan Mine, one of the world's largest underground silver, lead and zinc mines. The mine closed in 2001 after 92 years of production, yielding more than $20 billion in ore.

In keeping with the Bavarian theme, the city presents the ♦ Kimberley Old Time Accordion Championships for a week each year in early July.

Kimberley Visitor Centre: 270 Kimberley Ave., Kimberley, BC, Canada V1A 0A3. **Phone:** (778) 481-1891.

KIMBERLEY'S UNDERGROUND MINING RAILWAY departs the lower train station, 2 blks. n.w. of the Platzl. The railway offers narrated 1-hour train rides, transporting passengers through the Mark Creek Valley on a narrow-gauge mine track. Interactive mining displays are offered in an underground tunnel.

Hours: Mine tours daily at 11, 1 and 3, late June-Labour Day weekend. Resort Express rides Sat.-Sun. and holiday Mon. at 10, late June-Labour Day weekend. Phone ahead to confirm schedule. **Cost:** Mine tours $23.81; $14.24 (ages 13-18); $9.52 (ages 4-12). Resort Express $14.24; $9.52 (ages 4-12); $38.10 (family, two adults and two children, or one adult and three children). **Phone:** (250) 427-0022 or (250) 427-7365.

MOUNTAIN SPIRIT RESORT   250/432-6000
♦♦♦ Condominium. **Address:** 400 Stemwinder Dr V1A 2Y9

TRICKLE CREEK LODGE   250/427-5175
♦♦ Extended Stay Hotel. **Address:** 500 Stemwinder Dr V1A 2Y6

WHERE TO EAT

THE BEAN TREE   250/427-7889
♦ Coffee/Tea Sandwiches. Quick Serve. **Address:** 295 Spokane St V1A 2E6

BEAR'S EATERY   250/427-3412
♦♦ Comfort Food. Casual Dining. **Address:** 324 Archibald St V1A 1M9

KITIMAT (E-2) pop. 8,335, elev. 130m/426'

Kitimat is a planned city built in the early 1950s by Alcan Smelters and Chemicals Ltd. The company chose the wilderness site for a new plant because of the area's deepwater harbor, flat land and hydroelectric plant.

Kitimat Chamber of Commerce: 2109 Forest Ave., P.O. Box 214, Kitimat, BC, Canada V8C 2G7. **Phone:** (250) 632-6294 or (800) 664-6554.

KOOTENAY NATIONAL PARK
(A-11)

Elevations in the park range from 901 metres (2,956 ft.) at the park's west gate to 3,424 metres (11,235 ft.) at Deltaform Mountain. Refer to CAA/AAA maps for additional elevation information.

Straddling the Banff-Windermere Highway (Hwy. 93) from the Continental Divide to the Rocky Mountain Trench, Kootenay National Park encompasses 1,406 square kilometres (543 sq. mi.) of Rocky Mountain landscape. Following the Vermilion and Kootenay river valleys, this slender 94-kilometre-long (63-mi.) park embraces several significant geologic features and is part of the Canadian Rocky Mountain Parks UNESCO World Heritage Site.

Kootenay's western entrance provides one of the most dramatic gateways to any of the national parks in Canada. The highway clings to a sheer cliff before snaking through a narrow gorge and running along an iron-red rock face where bighorn sheep are a frequent sight. Visitors driving this scenic highway will see dramatic landscapes as they travel the Golden Triangle or Hot Springs routes.

Wildfires and prescribed burns in the northern part of the park have left charred trees visible from the road, but nature's renewal is visible through stunning wildflower displays in the burn areas during the summer.

Extensive faults created two of the park's most significant features: the Radium Hot Springs and the Paint Pots. Located in the southern end of the park, Radium Hot Springs is a result of rainwater and runoff being vaporized deep underground. The steam returns to the surface and is condensed in these clear, odorless springs. First used by the indigenous peoples in the area, the hot springs were later popularized by health buffs at the turn of the 20th century.

At the opposite end of the park are the Paint Pots, cold springs with a spiritual significance to the region's inhabitants. These iron-rich mineral springs bubble up into small, emerald green pools before staining the surrounding earth red. The Siksika, Nakoda and Ktunaxa First Nations once used the bright bronze mud called ochre to decorate their homes and draw the rock paintings once visible near Sinclair Canyon.

Good grazing conditions bring herds of bighorn sheep. Bears, deer, mountain goats, mountain goats, elk and countless species of birds are commonly seen throughout the park.

General Information and Activities

The park is open year-round. Parks Canada's facilities, including three frontcountry campgrounds—Redstreak, Marble Canyon and McLeod Meadows—are open during the summer months, with Redstreak staying open the longest. Phone ahead to confirm the schedule.

Kootenay provides a variety of trails ranging from easy hikes to multiday backcountry treks. In July and August, Parks Canada offers guided hikes to the recently discovered Burgess Shale Fossil Beds near Stanley Glacier. Hidden in the mountains near the continental divide, the Burgess Shale fossils continue to help scientists unravel the mystery of life on earth 505 million years ago. Fees range from $27.50-$55 and reservations are required; phone (877) 737-3783.

All backcountry campers must obtain a wilderness pass. Information about trails, park features and facilities can be obtained from the visitor center in the village of Radium Hot Springs from the Victoria Day weekend through Labour Day and at the park's west gate during the remainder of the year.

Nonmotorized watercraft are permitted on all lakes and rivers in the park. *See Recreation Areas Chart.*

ADMISSION to the park is free in 2017 to celebrate Canada's 150th anniversary of Confederation. Otherwise admission is $9.33; $7.90 (ages 65+); $4.67 (ages 6-16); $18.67 (all occupants of a private vehicle with up to seven people). An annual pass, valid at most Canadian national parks, marine areas and historic sites, is available.

PETS must be leashed at all times. Pets are permitted in the backcountry overnight.

ADDRESS inquiries to the Superintendent, Kootenay National Park, Box 220, Radium Hot Springs, BC, Canada V0A 1M0; phone (250) 347-9505.

MARBLE CANYON is on Hwy. 93 at the northern end of Kootenay National Park and close to the Alberta border. The walls of marble-like gray limestone make this one of the most beautiful canyons in the Rockies. Tokumm Creek has cut a sheer, narrow cleft to the depth of about 40 metres (130 ft.). A self-guiding trail follows the top edge of the canyon and leads to a waterfall. Interpretive signs describe the power of water in shaping the canyon's features. **Time:** Allow 30 minutes minimum. **Phone:** (250) 347-9505.

 RADIUM HOT SPRINGS is just n. of the w. entrance to Kootenay National Park. Water temperatures range from 37 to 40 C (98 to 104 F). There is a hot pool, a cool pool and a 372-square-metre (4,000-sq.-ft.) day spa. Iron oxide also colors the towering sandstone cliffs, giving a perpetual sunset quality. *See Recreation Areas Chart.*

Hours: Pools open daily 9 a.m.-11 p.m., mid-May to mid-Oct. Hot pools Sun.-Thurs. noon-9, Fri.-Sat. noon-10, mid-Oct. to mid-May. Cool pools Fri. 6-9 p.m., Sat.-Sun. noon-9, mid-Oct. to mid-May. **Cost:** $6; $5.14 (ages 3-17 and 65+); $18.19

(family, two adults and two children; each additional child $3.24). **Phone:** (250) 347-9485, (250) 343-6783 in southeastern British Columbia or (888) 347-9331.

LADYSMITH (G-10) pop. 7,921, elev. 40m/131'

On the 49th parallel, Ladysmith is noted for its scenic position between mountain and sea. Founded during the Boer War, Ladysmith was named for a sister city in South Africa. Transfer Beach Park offers a playground, picnic tables and a swimming area watched by lifeguards.

Ladysmith Visitor Centre: 33 Roberts St., Ladysmith, BC, Canada V9G 1A4. **Phone:** (250) 245-2112.

LANGLEY (H-11) pop. 25,081, elev. 10m/33'
• Restaurants p. 212
• Hotels & Restaurants map & index p. 290
• Part of Vancouver area — see map p. 263

Langley, the site of a Hudson's Bay Co. fort built in 1840 *(see Fort Langley National Historic Site p. 191)*, is also an important farming and wine-growing region. Orchards, berry farms, horse ranches, vineyards and lavender and heirloom vegetable farms make a patchwork of the countryside.

The city's position on the banks of the Fraser River makes it an easy proposition to enjoy water-based activities. Kayaks and voyageur canoes can be rented and launched at the Fort Langley Marina.

Langley Visitor Centre: 7888 200th St., Unit 2, Langley, BC, Canada V2Y 3J4. **Phone:** (604) 371-1477.

BEST WESTERN PLUS LANGLEY INN
(604)530-9311 66

Hotel
$132-$192

Best Western PLUS.
AAA Benefit: Save 10% or more every day and earn 10% bonus points!

Address: 5978 Glover Rd V3A 4H9 **Location:** Trans-Canada Hwy 1 exit 66 (232nd St), 3.6 mi (6 km) se on Hwy 10, follow signs. **Facility:** 78 units, some two bedrooms, efficiencies and kitchens. 2 stories, interior corridors. **Pool(s):** heated indoor. **Activities:** hot tub, limited exercise equipment. **Guest Services:** valet and coin laundry. **Featured Amenity: continental breakfast.**

  CALL
 /SOME UNITS

COAST HOTEL & CONVENTION CENTRE
(604)530-1500 67

Hotel
$112-$169

Address: 20393 Fraser Hwy V3A 7N2 **Location:** Trans-Canada Hwy 1 exit 58 (200th St/Langley City), 3.9 mi (6.3 km) s on 200th St, then just e. **Facility:** The lobby here has a coffee shop to help get you going in the morning and there is also an entry to the casino. Guest rooms feature large TVs and a comfortable lounge chair. 77 units. 6 stories, interior corridors. **Terms:** 3 day cancellation notice. **Dining:** 2 restaurants. **Activities:** exercise room, spa. **Guest Services:** valet laundry.

CALL /SOME UNITS

DAYS INN & SUITES LANGLEY (604)539-0100 65
Hotel. **Address:** 20250 Logan Ave V3A 4L6

▼ *See AAA listing p. 212* ▼

(See map & index p. 290.)

HOLIDAY INN EXPRESS HOTEL & SUITES LANGLEY
(604)882-2000 **64**

Hotel
$115-$499

Address: 8750 204th St V1M 2Y5 **Location:** Trans-Canada Hwy 1 exit 58 (200th St/Langley City), just e on 88th Ave. **Facility:** 85 units. 4 stories, interior corridors. **Terms:** cancellation fee imposed. **Pool(s):** heated indoor. **Activities:** sauna, hot tub, steamroom, exercise room. **Guest Services:** valet and coin laundry. **Featured Amenity: breakfast buffet.** (See ad p. 211.)

WHERE TO EAT

AKANE JAPANESE RESTAURANT 604/882-1134 **78**
Japanese. Casual Dining. **Address:** 20349 88th Ave V1M 2K5

AN INDIAN AFFAIR 604/539-8114 **79**
Indian. Casual Dining. **Address:** 19653 Willowbrook Dr V2Y 1A5

BAN CHOK DEE THAI CUISINE 778/278-3088 **82**
Thai. Casual Dining. **Address:** 20563 Douglas Cres V3A 4B6

C-LOVERS FISH & CHIPS 604/532-9747 **81**
Seafood. Casual Dining. **Address:** 20251 Fraser Hwy V3A 4E7

KOSTAS GREEK RESTAURANT 604/530-9531 **80**
Greek. Casual Dining. **Address:** 20080 Fraser Hwy V3A 4E5

RICKY'S ALL DAY GRILL
American. Casual Dining.
LOCATIONS:
Address: 8720 204th St V3A 8G5 **Phone:** 604/888-4211
Address: 22314 Fraser Hwy V3A 8M6 **Phone:** 604/530-4317

LILLOOET (B-7) pop. 2,322, elev. 290m/951'

Lillooet, on the Fraser River, marked the first leg of the Cariboo Waggon Road and was therefore sometimes referred to as "Mile 0." The trail reached north to such destinations as 100 Mile House and 150 Mile House, named for their distances from the start of the trail. In 1859, during the Cariboo Gold Rush, the 15,000 inhabitants of Lillooet made it the most populous city north of San Francisco and west of Chicago. The surrounding area now is of particular interest to rock hounds.

MIYAZAKI HOUSE is at 642 Russell Ln., near jct. Main St. and 6th Ave., following signs. Originally owned by prominent citizens Caspar and Cerise Phair, the late 19th-century house is an exceptional example of Victorian architecture. In the late 1940s Dr. Masajiro Miyazaki and his family purchased the house. Visitors will learn about both families and

local history through photographs and antiques. The doctor's office also is in the house. Local art, cultural and community events are held here.

Time: Allow 30 minutes minimum. **Hours:** Thurs.-Mon. 10-4, June-Sept. Outdoor concerts are offered Wed. at 7, July-Aug. **Cost:** Donations. **Phone:** (250) 256-6808. **GT**

LYTTON (B-7) pop. 228, elev. 199m/650'

At the junction of the Thompson and Fraser rivers, Lytton derives its livelihood from its location. Native peoples harvested salmon from this river junction. Their trail along the Fraser became a major route to the gold fields, with Lytton as a base of supplies. This community calls itself the Rafting Capital of Canada and claims some of the warmest weather in the country.

Lytton & District Chamber of Commerce: 400 Fraser St., P.O. Box 460, Lytton, BC, Canada V0K 1Z0. **Phone:** (250) 455-2523.

MADEIRA PARK

PAINTED BOAT RESORT SPA & MARINA (604)883-2456
Resort Condominium. **Address:** 12849 Lagoon Rd V0N 2H0

SUNSHINE COAST RESORT & MARINA (604)883-9177
Cottage. **Address:** 12695 Sunshine Coast Hwy V0N 2H0

WHERE TO EAT

THE RESTAURANT AT PAINTED BOAT 604/883-3000
Pacific Northwest. Casual Dining. **Address:** 12849 Lagoon Rd V0N 2H0

MAPLE RIDGE (H-11) pop. 76,052, elev. 30m/98'
• Part of Vancouver area — see map p. 263

Maple Ridge lies on the north shore of the Fraser River, with the Coast Mountains to the north and the Stave and Pitt Rivers forming its east and west boundaries. Snow-capped peaks overlook this Fraser Valley community.

The Fraser River Heritage Walk, which starts at Port Haney Wharf, passes many of the town's notable spots. The Haney House at 11612 224th St. was built in 1876 and contains many furnishings and artifacts owned by three generations of the Haney family; phone (604) 463-1377. Displays at Maple Ridge Museum, 22520 116th Ave., reflect the history and geography of the area; phone (604) 463-5311.

Kanaka Creek Regional Park (see Recreation Areas Chart) offers hiking and horseback riding trails as well as canoeing, kayaking, fishing and picnic facilities. A fish hatchery is on the grounds. Phone (604) 530-4983. Maple Ridge also has a large per capita horse population and an extensive riding trail system.

Maple Ridge-Pitt Meadows Chamber of Commerce: 20214 Lougheed Hwy., #6, Maple Ridge, BC, Canada V2X 2P7. **Phone:** (604) 460-8300, or (877) 465-8300 in Canada.

BEST WESTERN MAPLE RIDGE   (604)467-1511

Hotel
$109-$139

 Best Western.

AAA Benefit: Save 10% or more every day and earn 10% bonus points!

Address: 21650 Lougheed Hwy V2X 2S1 **Location:** 1.2 mi (2 km) w on Lougheed Hwy (Hwy 7). Port Haney, 1. **Facility:** 56 units, some efficiencies. 2 stories, interior corridors. **Pool(s):** heated indoor. **Activities:** sauna, hot tub, exercise room. **Guest Services:** coin laundry.

QUALITY INN   (604)463-5111

Motel
$89-$600

Address: 21735 Lougheed Hwy V2X 2S2 **Location:** 1.2 mi (2 km) w on Lougheed Hwy (Hwy 7). Port Haney, 1. **Facility:** 61 units. 2 stories (no elevator), exterior corridors. **Activities:** limited exercise equipment. **Guest Services:** valet and coin laundry.

WHERE TO EAT

BILLY MINER ALEHOUSE CAFE   604/467-6002

Burgers Pizza. Casual Dining. **Address:** 22355 River Rd V2X 2C5

MAYNE ISLAND (H-10) pop. 1,074

Although visited by the Spanish in the 1790s, it was not until the 1850s that British Capt. George Richards surveyed and mapped the area. Capt. Richards named Mayne Island after his lieutenant, Richard Charles Mayne. During the gold rush of the mid-1800s the island, in the Gulf Islands group halfway between Victoria and the mouth of the Fraser River, was a stopping point for miners heading for the riches to be found at the gold fields along the river.

The island is known as a haven for artists and artisans. Small and sparsely settled, Mayne offers quiet beaches and hiking trails; wildflowers; a landscape heavy with trees; seals, sea lions, salmon and sole offshore; and a large variety of birds, from tiny hummingbirds to soaring bald eagles.

Mayne Island Community Chamber of Commerce: P.O. Box 2, Mayne Island, BC, Canada V0N 2J0.

MERRITT (C-8) pop. 7,113, elev. 858m/2,814'

Merritt is known for its many lakes. Of particular interest is Nicola Lake, a large warm-water lake 10 kilometres (6 mi.) north of town. For a view of the landmarks, including a giant Canadian flag, hike to the Merritt Lookout from Juniper Drive. Recreational activities in the area include swimming, fishing, sailing, water skiing and windsurfing. Monck Provincial Park, on the west side of the lake, offers camping and picnic facilities.

Merritt Visitor Centre: 2250 Voght St., P.O. Box 1105, Merritt, BC, Canada V1K 1B8. **Phone:** (250) 378-0349.

QUALITY INN MERRITT   (250)378-4253

Motel
$96-$186

Address: 4025 Walters St V1K 1K1 **Location:** Hwy 5 exit 290, 0.6 mi (1 km) w. **Facility:** 56 units. 2 stories (no elevator), exterior corridors. **Parking:** winter plug-ins. **Pool(s):** heated indoor. **Activities:** hot tub, limited exercise equipment. **Guest Services:** coin laundry. **Featured Amenity:** continental breakfast.

RAMADA LIMITED   (250)378-3567

Motel
$80-$149

Address: 3571 Voght St V1K 1C5 **Location:** Hwy 5 exit 290, just w. **Facility:** 52 units, some two bedrooms and kitchens. 3 stories (no elevator), exterior corridors. **Parking:** winter plug-ins. **Pool(s):** heated indoor. **Activities:** sauna, hot tub, exercise room. **Guest Services:** coin laundry. **Featured Amenity:** continental breakfast.

SUPER 8 MERRITT   (250)378-9422

Motel. **Address:** 3561 Voght St V1K 1C5

WHERE TO EAT

HOME RESTAURANT   250/378-9112

American Comfort Food. Casual Dining. **Address:** 3561 Voght St V1K 1C5

MISSION (H-11) pop. 36,426, elev. 55m/180'

- Hotels p. 214 • Restaurants p. 214
- Part of Vancouver area — see map p. 263

Mission developed from a Roman Catholic mission built in 1861 to serve First Nations tribes. The site became a popular stopping place for trappers, settlers and other river travelers.

The Fraser River provides opportunities for swimming, fishing, boating and water sports; its sandbars are good for rock hounds in search of agates, jades and garnets. Motocross and boat races are held at Mission Raceway from March through October.

Mission Regional Chamber of Commerce: 34033 Lougheed Hwy., Mission, BC, Canada V2V 5X8. **Phone:** (604) 826-6914.

FRASER RIVER SAFARI departs from the harborfront at 33428 Harbour Ave. A 3-hour narrated cruise along the Fraser River in a fully covered jet boat comes complete with scenic mountain views; possible sightings of bears, seals, deer and birds; and entertaining folklore about native legends, fur traders, gold miners and Sasquatch. A stop is made at Kilby Historic Site in Harrison Mills. Eagle-watching tours are available in November and December.

Time: Allow 3 hours, 30 minutes minimum. **Hours:** Trips depart daily at 9:30 and 2, July 15-Dec. 15; at 10, rest of year. Arrive 15 minutes before departure. Closed Christmas. **Cost:** $104.76; $95.24 (ages 60+); $71.43 (ages 5-16); $320 (family, two adults and two children). Reservations are required. **Phone:** (604) 826-7361 or (866) 348-6877.

POWER HOUSE AT STAVE FALLS is 1.3 km (.8 mi.) w. on Ferndale Ave. from jct. Stave Lake St. and Ferndale Ave., then 12.9 km (8 mi.) n.w. on Dewdney Trunk Rd. to 31338 Dewdney Trunk Rd. Through interactive science exhibits and historic displays in Electrica, the facility tells the story of how power helped build British Columbia. Within a 50-seat theater, visitors may start their self-guiding tour with a 9-minute video that gives an overview of the history of Stave Falls and tells why electricity is important in our daily lives. On display in the Generator Hall are generators and turbines within a 1912 generating station. History Hall contains electrical gadgets from yesteryear. There also are outdoor exhibits and walking trails.

Time: Allow 1 hour minimum. **Hours:** Daily 10-4, mid-Sept. to mid-Oct.; Thurs.-Mon. 10-4, Mar. 1 to mid-Sept. Phone ahead to confirm schedule. **Cost:** $5.71; $4.76 (ages 6-17, ages 55+ and students with ID); $14.24 (family, two adults and two children). Guided tour $3.81; reservations are required. **Phone:** (604) 462-1222.

WESTMINSTER ABBEY is 1.5 km (.9 mi.) e., .7 km (.5 mi.) n. of Hwy. 7 to 34224 Dewdney Trunk Rd. The Seminary of Christ the King is managed by Benedictine monks. Of interest are the view and architecture. Modest dress is required. **Time:** Allow 30 minutes minimum. **Hours:** Mon.-Sat. 1:30-4:30, Sun. 2-4:30. Grounds open daily 8-8. **Cost:** Free. **Phone:** (604) 826-8975.

BEST WESTERN PLUS MISSION CITY LODGE
(604)820-5500

Hotel
$110-$150

AAA Benefit: Save 10% or more every day and earn 10% bonus points!

Address: 32281 Lougheed Hwy V2V 1A3 **Location:** Just w of Hwy 11; corner of Lougheed Hwy (Hwy 7) and Hurd St. **Facility:** 80 units, some kitchens. 4 stories, interior corridors. **Pool(s):** heated indoor. **Activities:** sauna, hot tub, exercise room. **Guest Services:** valet and coin laundry. **Featured Amenity:** full hot breakfast.

THE SWEET SPOT CAFE   604/287-2800
♦ American. Quick Serve. **Address:** 33057 1st Ave V2V 1G2

MORICETOWN (E-3) elev. 411m/1,348'

Moricetown is a Wet'suwet'en community that still practices the traditional hereditary system of governance. Originally known as Kyah Wiget, it was once the largest village of the Bulkley River Carrier tribe, a settlement built some 4,000 years ago. The town later took the name of Father A.G. Morice, a missionary who lived among the Carrier First Nation in the late 19th century.

MOUNT REVELSTOKE NATIONAL PARK (A-9)

Elevations in the park range from 480 metres (1,575 ft.) at the bottom of Mount Revelstoke to 2,639 metres (8,658 ft.) at the Mount Revelstoke summit at the Inverness Peaks. Refer to CAA/AAA maps for additional elevation information.

On the western edge of the Selkirk Range in southeastern British Columbia, Mount Revelstoke National Park is 260 square kilometres (100 sq. mi.) of sharp peaks, heavily timbered slopes and flowering meadows. The Selkirk Range, flanked on the east by the Purcell Range and on the west by the Monashee Range, are distinguished by their height and geologic complexity.

Erosion by glaciers and the heavy rainfall of the region have carved the rock of the Selkirks into jagged forms. Complementing the park's dense green forests and lush wildflower meadows are glacier-fed streams and lakes as well as the deep snows that blanket the slopes until late June.

Deer inhabit the lower slopes; black and grizzly bears and mountain caribou also may be seen in the park. Most mountain species of birds are represented, including Fox Sparrows, Hermit Thrushes and Northern Hawk Owls.

The Trans-Canada Highway (Hwy. 1) passes through the southeastern portion of the park for 13 kilometres (8 mi.) and parallels its southern boundary for 18 kilometres (11 mi.).

General Information and Activities

Visitor facilities and accommodations are available in the city of Revelstoke at the western park entrance. Park passes are available at the park kiosks at the base of the Meadows in the Sky Parkway and Giant Cedars Boardwalk Trail as well as the Rogers Pass Discovery Centre in Glacier National Park. Phone ahead for schedule.

From Hwy. 1, the Meadows in the Sky Parkway, a 26-kilometre (16-mi.) hard surface road that is open only in summer leads to the summit of Mount Revelstoke and provides an excellent panoramic view. Along its length are 16 switchbacks and several viewpoints. Picnic areas are available at Monashee, the 8-kilometre (5-mi.) viewpoint on this road, and at Balsam Lake, 1 kilometre (.6 mi.) from the summit. Other picnic areas and nature trails are along the Trans-Canada Highway.

Recreation includes subalpine hiking, mountain climbing and catch-and-release fishing. August is the best time to view wildflowers. More than 60 kilometres (37 mi.) of hiking trails lead to such sites as Miller and Jade lakes. Voluntary registration for backcountry travelers is available. Fishing is by permit, available at the park kiosk at the base of the Meadows in the Sky Parkway or the park administrative office in Revelstoke. See Recreation Areas Chart.

ADMISSION to the park is free in 2017 to celebrate Canada's 150th anniversary of Confederation. Otherwise admission is $7.43; $6.48 (ages 65+); $3.71 (ages 6-16); $18.67 (all occupants of a private vehicle with up to seven people). An annual pass, valid at most Canadian national parks, marine areas and historic sites, is available. Buses and trailers are not permitted on the Meadows in the Sky Parkway. Class A motor homes are not recommended as parking is extremely limited at the summit of the mountain.

PETS are permitted in the park provided they are on leashes at all times.

ADDRESS inquiries to the Superintendent, Mount Revelstoke and Glacier National Parks, P.O. Box 350, Revelstoke, BC, Canada V0E 2S0; phone (250) 837-7500.

NAKUSP (B-10) pop. 1,569, elev. 914m/2,998'

Nakusp, on the shore of Upper Arrow Lake between the Selkirk and Monashee mountain ranges, is named for a First Nation word meaning "bay of quiet waters." Arrow Lake, part of the Columbia River system, is a popular destination for trout and dolly fishing. A waterfront walkway with gardens and a beach as well as a campground are nearby.

Heli-skiing, snowmobiling, cross-country skiing, winter fishing and a small ski hill are among the many cold-weather attractions offered.

Nakusp & District Chamber of Commerce: 92 6th Ave. N.W., P.O. Box 387, Nakusp, BC, Canada V0G 1R0. **Phone:** (250) 265-4234, or (800) 909-8819 within British Columbia.

NANAIMO (G-10) pop. 83,810, elev. 30m/98'
• Hotels p. 216 • Restaurants p. 216

Some 120 kilometres (75 mi.) north of Victoria, Nanaimo began as a Hudson's Bay Co. outpost called Colviletown, established for miners brought from England and Scotland to mine coal. A thriving forest and marine products industry replaced coal's influence, and the economy of contemporary Nanaimo is centered on technology, service, manufacturing, tourism and recreation.

Offshore islands and nearby mountains and lakes provide a variety of recreational opportunities including hiking, swimming, camping and picnicking. Charter companies offer wildlife tours year-round to view animals such as the area's bald eagles and sea lions.

For a touch of wilderness in the middle of the city, check out Bowen Park, on the Millstone River just north of downtown. This 36-hectare (89-acre) expanse provides an outlet for a variety of activities. Trails wind through forests of fir, hemlock, cedar and maple, and kids enjoy the 4-H barnyard open July through August. A rhododendron grove, a nature center, duck pond, picnic shelters, swimming pool and sports fields complete the complex. In winter, tobogganers take to the park's big hills.

Exotic trees provide a setting for picnicking at Harmac Arboretum, 11 kilometres (7 mi.) south at Harmac Pulp Mill and Duke Point roads. Newcastle Island (see Recreation Areas Chart) is a marine provincial park accessible by a 10-minute ferry ride from Maffeo-Sutton Park on the harborfront. Automobiles are not permitted; the ferry operates daily every 30 minutes on the half hour and hour from spring through mid-October. Round-trip fare is $9.

In addition to the ferry, salmon sport fishing, scuba diving, windsurfing and sailing are also available from Nanaimo's natural harbor. An intertidal park with three lighted water curtains and a 4-kilometre (2.5-mi.) walkway along the seawall graces Nanaimo's waterfront. St. Jean's Custom Cannery is one of three factories where fishing enthusiasts can have their catch canned or smoked.

On a landscaped hillside, Vancouver Island University offers views of the city and harbor below and also is the site of Nanaimo Art Gallery (see attraction listing). Visitors interested in prehistoric art can see sandstone carvings at Petroglyph Provincial Park, 3.25 kilometres (2 mi.) south on scenic Hwy. 1. Other cultural endeavors can be enjoyed at The Port Theatre, an 800-seat performing arts center at 125 Front St. that hosts local, national and international events; phone (250) 754-8550 for ticket information.

Nanaimo is accessible from the mainland by BC Ferries, which sails from Horseshoe Bay to Departure Bay and from Tsawwassen to Duke Point, 8 kilometres (5 mi.) south of Nanaimo. For more information phone (250) 386-3431 or (888) 223-3779.

Tourism Nanaimo: 2450 Northfield Rd., Nanaimo, BC, Canada V9S 0B2. **Phone:** (250) 756-0106, (250) 751-1556 or (800) 663-7337.

NANAIMO MUSEUM is at 100 Museum Way on the second floor of the Vancouver Island Conference Centre. Nanaimo's history is explored through exhibits depicting life for the city's earliest settlers, its days as a 19th-century mining center and its transition into the 21st century. Visitors can discover stories about the Snunéymuxw First Nation and check out a replica coal mine to feel what it was like to be an underground miner.

Time: Allow 1 hour minimum. **Hours:** Daily 10-5, May-Sept.; Mon.-Sat. 10-5, rest of year. Closed Jan. 1, Nov. 11, Christmas and day after Christmas. Phone ahead to confirm schedule. **Cost:** $1.90; $1.67 (ages 55+ and students with ID); 71c (ages 6-12). **Phone:** (250) 753-1821.

The Bastion is on Front St. across from the Coast Bastion Inn. The small fort was built in 1853 to protect early settlers. A display shows how the bastion was used in the 1860s. A noon ceremonial cannon firing is conducted by staff dressed in period costumes. **Hours:** Daily 10-5, Victoria Day weekend-Labour Day. **Cost:** Donations. **Phone:** (250) 753-1821.

BEST WESTERN DORCHESTER HOTEL   (250)754-6835

Hotel
$129-$199

Best Western. AAA Benefit: Save 10% or more every day and earn 10% bonus points!

Address: 70 Church St V9R 5H4 **Location:** Hwy 19A (Island Hwy) to Comox Rd; downtown. **Facility:** 70 units. 4 stories, interior corridors. **Terms:** cancellation fee imposed. **Amenities:** safes. **Activities:** bicycles, exercise room. **Guest Services:** complimentary and valet laundry.

BEST WESTERN NORTHGATE INN   (250)390-2222

Hotel
$109-$399

Best Western. AAA Benefit: Save 10% or more every day and earn 10% bonus points!

Address: 6450 Metral Dr V9T 2L8 **Location:** Hwy 19A (Island Hwy), just w on Aulds Rd, just s. **Facility:** 72 units, some efficiencies. 3 stories, interior corridors. **Terms:** cancellation fee imposed. **Amenities:** safes. **Activities:** exercise room. **Guest Services:** valet and coin laundry.

BUCCANEER INN   (250)753-1246
Motel. **Address:** 1577 Stewart Ave V9S 4E3

DAYS INN NANAIMO HARBOURVIEW   (250)754-8171
Hotel. **Address:** 809 Island Hwy S V9R 5K1

INN ON LONG LAKE   250/758-1144

Hotel
Rates not provided

Address: 4700 Island Hwy N V9T 1W6 **Location:** Waterfront. 3.1 mi (5 km) n on Hwy 19A (Island Hwy) from Departure Bay Ferry Terminal. **Facility:** 62 units, some efficiencies and kitchens. 3 stories, exterior corridors. **Activities:** sauna, hot tub, boat dock, fishing, limited exercise equipment. **Guest Services:** valet and coin laundry. **Featured Amenity:** continental breakfast.

TRAVELODGE NANAIMO   (250)754-6355
Hotel. **Address:** 96 Terminal Ave N V9S 4J2

BLUE GINGER RESTAUARANT   250/751-8238
Asian. Casual Dining. **Address:** 5769 Turner Rd, Unit 1 V9T 6L8

CACTUS CLUB CAFE   250/729-0011
New American. Casual Dining. **Address:** 801-5800 Turner Rd V9T 6J4

GINA'S MEXICAN CAFE   250/753-5411
Mexican. Casual Dining. **Address:** 47 Skinner St V9R 5K4

LONGWOOD BREWPUB   250/729-8225
American. Gastropub. **Address:** 5775 Turner Rd V9T 6L8

POWER HOUSE LIVING FOODS CO.   250/591-7873
Raw Foods. Casual Dining. **Address:** 200 Commercial St V9R 5G6

POWER HOUSE LIVING FOODS CO.   250/933-3733
Raw Foods. Casual Dining. **Address:** 6560 Metral Dr V9T 2L8

RICKY'S ALL DAY GRILL   250/390-1227
American. Casual Dining. **Address:** 6550 Island Hwy N V9V 1K8

SMITTY'S   250/716-8887
American. Casual Dining. **Address:** 50 10th St V9R 6L1

ZOUGLA   250/716-3233
Mediterranean. Casual Dining. **Address:** 2021 Estevan Rd V9S 3Y9

NANOOSE BAY pop. 5,471

SMOKE N' WATER RESTAURANT   250/468-2400
Regional Barbecue. Casual Dining. **Address:** 1-1600 Stroulger Rd V9P 9B7

NARAMATA pop. 1,647
• **Hotels & Restaurants map & index p. 226**
• **Part of Okanagan Valley area — see map p. 222**

THE VILLAGE MOTEL   250/496-5535 **35**
Motel. **Address:** 244 Robinson Ave V0H 1N0

THE PATIO AT LAKE BREEZE   250/496-7502 **41**
Mediterranean. Casual Dining. **Address:** 930 Sammet Rd V0H 1N0

NELSON (C-10) pop. 10,230, elev. 535m/1,755'

An old iron and silver mining town, Nelson was settled by prospectors in the late 1880s. With the depletion of its mines, the town turned to logging, sawmilling and area trade. However, the legacy of the bonanza days lives on in the more than 350 heritage sites. Most of Nelson's historic commercial buildings are open to the public, but homes are private and closed to visitors. If Fido comes along with you, be sure to follow Nelson's dog ordinance and keep him out of restricted zones.

Nearby parks, lakes, streams and mountains offer all types of summer and winter recreation. Kokanee Creek and Kokanee Glacier provincial parks *(see Recreation Areas Chart)* are 19 kilometres (12 mi.) northeast on Hwy. 3A.

Nelson Chamber of Commerce: 225 Hall St., Nelson, BC, Canada V1L 5X4. **Phone:** (250) 352-3433 or (877) 663-5706.

Self-guiding tours: Maps detailing walking and driving tours are available from the chamber of commerce.

INTERNATIONAL SELKIRK LOOP is a 450-kilometre (280-mi.) scenic byway through southeastern British Columbia and adjoining parts of Washington and Idaho. From Nelson the main route follows Hwy. 6 south to the U.S. border at Nelway. The other leg of the loop heads east on Hwy. 3A to Balfour, where what is said to be the world's longest free ferry service transports vehicles and passengers across Kootenay Lake. Hwy. 3A continues south along the lake's east shore to Creston, where Hwy. 21 connects with the U.S. border at Rykerts.

One 166-kilometre (103-mi.) side route follows Hwys. 3A, 6 and 22 from Nelson to Castlegar and Trail, then Hwy. 3B and 3 from Rossland to Salmo. Another 217-kilometre (135-mi.) side route connects Nelson with Slocan Lake via Hwys. 3A and 6, then continues east from New Denver to Kaslo on Hwy. 31, completing the loop back to Nelson following Hwys. 31 and 3A.

Scenic highlights of the loop include Kootenay Lake, thick coniferous forests, snowcapped peaks and the lush Creston Valley. Museums, historic mining towns, heritage architecture, crafts villages and seasonal produce stands beckon travelers.

Recreational activities abound, including golf, fishing, boating, swimming, hunting, camping, hiking, mountain biking, horseback riding, skiing and snowmobiling. You also can tour a ghost town and soak in a hot spring.

Towns with attraction listings on the loop and its side routes include Ainsworth Hot Springs, Boswell, Castlegar, Creston, Kaslo, Nelson, New Denver, Rossland, Sandon and Trail.

Chambers of commerce and visitor centers on the loop provide maps and more information. Visitors also can write the International Selkirk Loop, P.O. Box 920, Bonners Ferry, ID 83805, United States; or in Canada, P.O. Box 2079, Creston, BC V0B 1G0. **Phone:** (208) 267-0822 or (888) 823-2626.

TOUCHSTONES NELSON: MUSEUM OF ART AND HISTORY is at s.e. corner of jct. Vernon and Ward sts. at 502 Vernon St. This renovated building features permanent visual and interactive exhibitions which examine the area's cultural, developmental and economic history. The Shawn Lamb Archives houses a thorough collection of materials relating to the region's diversified origins. Temporary exhibits and galleries also are available and change monthly.

Hours: Mon.-Sat. 10-5 (also Thurs. 5-8), Sun. 10-4, mid-May to mid-Sept.; Wed.-Sat. 10-5 (also Thurs. 5-8), Sun. 10-4, rest of year. Closed major holidays. **Cost:** $7.62; $5.71 (ages 60+ and college students with ID); $3.81 (ages 7-18); by donation (Thurs. 5-8); $20.95 (family). **Phone:** (250) 352-9813.

BEST WESTERN PLUS BAKER STREET INN & CONVENTION CENTRE   (250)352-3525

Hotel
$150-$220

Best Western PLUS

AAA Benefit: Save 10% or more every day and earn 10% bonus points!

Address: 153 Baker St V1L 4H1 **Location:** Jct Hwy 3A and 6. **Facility:** 70 units. 4 stories, interior corridors. **Terms:** check-in 4 pm. **Activities:** hot tub, exercise room. **Guest Services:** coin laundry.

NORTH SHORE INN   (250)352-6606
Motel. **Address:** 687 Hwy 3A V1L 5P7

WHERE TO EAT

ALL SEASONS CAFE   250/352-0101
American. Casual Dining. **Address:** 620 Herridge Ln V1L 6A7

BIBO   250/352-2744
New Canadian. Casual Dining. **Address:** 518 Hall St V1L 1Z2

OSO NEGRO COFFEE   250/352-7661
Coffee/Tea. Quick Serve. **Address:** 604 Ward St V1L 7B1

THE OUTER CLOVE   250/354-1667
American. Casual Dining. **Address:** 526 Stanley St V1L 1N2

REL-ISH   250/352-5232
New American. Casual Dining. **Address:** 301 Baker St V1L 4H6

THOR'S PIZZA   250/352-1212
Pizza. Quick Serve. **Address:** 303 Victoria St V1L 4K3

NEW DENVER (C-10) pop. 504,
elev. 555m/1,850'

In 1891 prospectors poured into the area; New Denver sprang up as a supply point on the shores of Slocan Lake. Here goods and passengers switched from rail to lake stern-wheelers. The town also provided a more sedate environment to raise a family and conduct business than the rowdy mining camps of the so-called Silvery Slocan.

The Kohan Reflection Garden, at the foot of First Avenue, honors the Japanese-Canadians interned here during World War II. Shacks that formerly housed internees can still be seen around town. The Silvery Slocan Historical Society Museum, housed in the 1897 former Bank of Montreal Building on Sixth Avenue, contains artifacts and exhibits about the town's history; phone (250) 358-2719.

NIKKEI INTERNMENT MEMORIAL CENTRE is at 306 Josephine St. Dedicated to remembering the Japanese internment experience during World War II, the center commemorates the 22,000 Nikkei (people of Japanese descent) removed from their British Columbia homes and relocated to camps. Exhibits include a typical two-family shack, an outhouse and a peace garden. Tribute also is paid to the first generation of Japanese who arrived in Canada in 1877.

Time: Allow 30 minutes minimum. **Hours:** Daily 10-5, May-Sept. **Cost:** $8.57; $6.67 (ages 6-17, ages 60+ and students with ID); free (ages 0-5); $19.05 (family). **Phone:** (250) 358-7288. GT

NEW WESTMINSTER (H-11) pop. 65,976, elev. 75m/246'

- Attractions map p. 278
- Hotels & Restaurants map & index p. 290
- Part of Vancouver area — see map p. 263

The oldest incorporated city in Western Canada, New Westminster—also known as the Royal City—was named by Queen Victoria. Transformed into a boomtown by the lure of gold in 1857, it plunged into a depression when the gold rush subsided in the late 1860s. The city was the provincial capital until 1868.

New Westminster also is known for its architecture. Parts of the city were built by the Royal Engineers, sent in 1855 to keep order in the new crown colony. Former members of this organization later formed the New Westminster Regiment, whose history is recounted in the Museum of the Royal Westminster Regiment at Sixth Street and Queens Avenue; phone (604) 666-4069.

Other places of interest include old houses in a variety of styles, some of which survived a devastating fire in 1898. The houses can be toured in late May. Tickets must be purchased in advance; for information phone the New Westminster Heritage Preservation Society at (604) 525-4868.

Westminster Quay Public Market, on the waterfront, maintains a tradition started in 1892 when farmers, hunters and settlers came to barter for goods. Fresh meat, baked goods, produce and local crafts can be purchased daily.

Antique Alley, on historic Front Street, is known for its heritage buildings housing stores featuring an array of antiques and collectibles.

Also of interest is *Sampson V* Maritime Museum aboard the stern-wheeler berthed on the Fraser River at 880 Quayside Dr. The stern-wheeler, the last steam-powered paddle wheeler to operate on the Fraser, can be toured; phone (604) 522-6894. The Canadian Lacrosse Hall of Fame, which celebrates Canada's national summer sport, is at 777 Columbia St. in the Anvil Centre; phone (604) 515-3830.

New Westminster Visitor Centre: 777 Columbia St., New Westminster, BC, Canada V3M 1B6. **Phone:** (604) 526-1905 or (604) 551-4974.

IRVING HOUSE, 302 Royal Ave., is an 1865 mansion built with San Francisco Gothic Revival influences for Capt. William Irving, a pioneer of the riverboat trade on the Fraser River. Furnished in period, the 14-room residence is bedecked in Victorian Christmas decor during December. **Hours:** Wed.-Thurs. 3-8, Fri.-Sun. noon-5, May-Sept.; Sat.-Sun. noon-4, rest of year. **Cost:** Donations. **Phone:** (604) 527-4640. ⊞ Columbia, 27

PADDLEWHEELER RIVERBOAT TOURS departs from the boardwalk of the New Westminster Quay Public Market at 788 Quayside Dr. Narrated sightseeing tours of various lengths are offered aboard an authentic paddlewheeler. The MV *Native* is a replica of a late 19th-century riverboat that carried passengers on the historic Gold Rush Trail via the Fraser River. Evening entertainment cruises also are available.

Hours: Cruises depart daily year-round. Phone ahead to confirm schedule. **Cost:** Fare $49.95-$94.95; $44.95-$94.95 (ages 60+); $39.95-$69.95 (ages 13-17); $24.95-$59.95 (ages 6-12). Some fares may include meals. Reservations are required. **Phone:** (604) 525-4465 or (800) 825-1302. ⊞ New Westminster, 26

INN AT THE QUAY	604/520-1776	26
▼▼▼ Boutique Hotel. **Address:** 900 Quayside Dr V3M 6G1		

WHERE TO EAT

THE BOATHOUSE RESTAURANT	604/525-3474
▼▼ Seafood. Casual Dining. **Address:** 900 Quayside Dr V3M 6G1	

BURGER HEAVEN	604/522-8339	46
▼▼ Burgers Sandwiches. Casual Dining. **Address:** 77 10th St V3M 3X4		

WILD RICE MARKET BISTRO	778/397-0028	47
▼▼ New Chinese. Casual Dining. **Address:** 810 Quayside Dr, #122 V3M 6B9		

NORTH VANCOUVER (H-11) pop. 48,196, elev. 99m/325'

- Hotels p. 220 • Restaurants p. 221
- Attractions map p. 278
- Hotels & Restaurants map & index p. 290
- Part of Vancouver area — see map p. 263

North Vancouver is a city, and it's also a district. All visitors really need to know, however, is that this North Shore destination is definitely worth checking out.

(See map & index p. 290.)

Lumbering and shipbuilding were important early on, and by the early 20th century the town across Burrard Inlet from Vancouver had incorporated. Today there are no discernible distinctions among the various municipalities that make up the North Shore. The city of North Vancouver does have its own impressive skyline, easily visible from the downtown Vancouver waterfront, while the district of North Vancouver is a bit of a hodgepodge, with pockets of industry and commercial development mixed in with parks and green spaces. It's also the location of Grouse Mountain and the Capilano Suspension Bridge Park (see attraction listings), two of the North Shore's most popular tourist attractions.

From Vancouver, take either the Lions Gate Bridge or the Ironworkers Memorial Second Narrows Crossing (Hwy. 1) to North Vancouver. (The bridge's name honors 27 workers who were killed when several spans collapsed during construction.) But the most scenic approach is aboard TransLink's SeaBus, with terminals on Vancouver's downtown waterfront (near Canada Place) and in North Vancouver next to the Lonsdale Quay Market. These 400-passenger catamaran ferries make the one-way trip across Burrard Inlet in about 12 minutes. Ferries depart from the Vancouver waterfront every 15 minutes Mon.-Fri. 6:16 a.m.-7:46 p.m. (then every 30 minutes until 1:22 a.m.); Sat. every 30 minutes 6:16 a.m.-10:16 a.m. and 6:46 p.m.-1:22 a.m. (every 15 minutes 10:16 a.m.-6:46 p.m.); Sun. every 30 minutes 8:16 a.m.-11:16 p.m. Service from Lonsdale Quay to the Vancouver waterfront follows a similar schedule, with last ferries departing Mon.-Sat. at 1 a.m. and Sun at 11:02 p.m. TransLink's Compass fare system allows passengers to travel freely between buses, the SeaBus and the SkyTrain rapid transit system. For additional schedule and fare information phone (604) 953-3333.

If you arrive via the SeaBus, the first place you must explore is the Lonsdale Quay Market. It's a classic Vancouver fresh market, open daily 9-7, Sun. 9-6 with an abundance of vendors selling fruit, veggies, flowers, seafood and baked goods, plus yummy soups, sauces and other specialty items. You'll be hard pressed to decide on something to go from one of the international food bars—the choices are many and tempting, from noodle stir fries to seafood chowder—but once the decision is made, eat outside on the deck so you can watch the ferry boats come and go with downtown Vancouver as a backdrop. A farmers market sets up on the East Plaza at the Quay Saturdays from 10 to 3, early May-late Oct. Organic farmers, bakers, jam and salsa makers and crafters all peddle their wares.

If peace and quiet are what you're seeking, head to Cates Park. From Vancouver, take the first exit off the Second Narrows bridge, following the signs for Deep Cove; then proceed east on Dollarton Highway about 8 kilometres (5 mi.) to the park entrance (on the right). There are grassy areas, a playground for kids and a pebble-sand beach. Watch the boats heading from Burrard Inlet into Indian Arm, check out the totem pole and indigenous canoe, hike a waterfront trail through stands of Douglas fir and big-leaf maple, or stretch out and take a nap under one of the huge cedar trees near the parking lot.

From Cates Park, get back on Dollarton Highway and continue north a couple of kilometres to the residential community of Deep Cove. The cove in question is a natural indentation of Indian Arm, a fiord-like extension of Burrard Inlet. In the 18th century Northwest tribes traveled up and down Indian Arm hunting and fishing, and lumbering was an important industry in this area in the first half of the 20th century.

What strikes you immediately about Deep Cove is how incredibly picturesque it is. Gallant Avenue is a quaint 2 blocks of eateries (fish and chips followed by a cone from Orca's Favourite Ice Cream makes a nice lunch combo), a shop or three and the Deep Cove Cultural Centre, which includes the Seymour Art Gallery and the Deep Cove Heritage Society, the Deep Cove Shaw Theatre and the First Impressions Theatre Company; phone (604) 929-3200 or (604) 929-9456. The street ends at nicely landscaped Panorama Park, bright with flower beds in the summer. Walk down the stairs to the beach and then out onto the pier.

Sheltered, serene Deep Cove harbor will take your breath away. Trees frame the cove on both sides. Rising beyond the water to the left are the thickly forested slopes of Mount Seymour Provincial Park (see attraction listing and Recreation Areas Chart). The wooded hillsides to the right are speckled with houses that undoubtedly have views to die for. Across Indian Arm loom the Coast Mountains, dark masses in the distance. Sailboats bob on the cove's tranquil surface. Kayakers slice through the water. Canoeists paddle gracefully. It's quite an enchanting vista, one you'll likely end up gazing out on all afternoon.

CAPILANO SUSPENSION BRIDGE PARK is off Hwy. 1 exit 14, then 2 km (1.2 mi.) n. to 3735 Capilano Rd.; a free shuttle is available from several locations in downtown Vancouver. The swinging 137-metre-long (450-ft.) footbridge spans a 70-metre-deep (230-ft.) densely wooded gorge above the Capilano River. George Grant Mackay, a Scottish civil engineer, built the original bridge in 1889 from hemp rope and cedar planks; the fourth structure on the site is reinforced with steel cables and concrete.

The park also features gardens; a totem park; Treetops Adventure, a series of seven suspension bridges high in the treetops; Cliffwalk, a cliffside walkway with a rock-climber's view of the canyon; and a story center that displays artifacts of the bridge. The Living Forest includes interactive displays and naturalist exhibits which guide visitors through a West Coast rain forest. Each year, from late November through Christmas, "Canyon Lights" has the bridge, Treetops Adventure, Cliffwalk and rainforest twinkling with lights, and visitors can view what may be the world's tallest living Christmas tree.

(See map & index p. 290.)

Wheelchairs are not permitted on the bridge. **Time:** Allow 1 hour minimum. **Hours:** Daily 8:30-8, late May-Labour Day; 9-7, late Apr.-late May; 9-6, mid-Mar. to late Apr. and day after Labour Day to mid-Oct.; 11-9, late Nov.-early Jan.; 9-5, rest of year. Closed Christmas. Phone ahead to confirm schedule. **Cost:** $39.95; $36.95 (ages 65+); $32.95 (students ages 17+ with ID); $26.95 (ages 13-16); $13.95 (ages 6-12). **Phone:** (604) 985-7474 or (877) 985-7474. *(See ad p. 280.)*

 GROUSE MOUNTAIN is at 6400 Nancy Greene Way. Step into The Skyride, an aerial tramway, for a 1.6-kilometre (1-mi.) ride over Grouse Mountain's lofty Douglas firs to the mountaintop where, from a height of 1,100 metres (4,100 ft.), you'll see a breathtaking panorama of downtown Vancouver. On clear nights, gaze at the city's floodlit buildings and twinkling lights reflected in the harbor.

Crowd-pleasing winter activities include skiing, snowshoeing, snowboarding, ice skating, sleigh rides, a Sliding Zone and Light Walk. In the summer, take in a helicopter tour, paragliding, ziplining and disc golf; a 45-minute lumberjack show; a Birds in Motion demonstration featuring free-flying birds of prey; and guided or self-guiding interpretive walks that inform about area flora, fauna and geology.

The Grouse Mountain Refuge for Endangered Wildlife, a 2-hectare (5 acre) habitat also open year-round, is home to two orphaned grizzly bears and a gray wolf.

Competitive locals and visitors can do the Grouse Grind (commonly referred to as "Mother Nature's Stairmaster"), a grueling 2.9-kilometre (1.8-mi.) climb up the mountain.

Complimentary bus service from Canada Place to Grouse Mountain is available with purchase of Experience ticket. **Time:** Allow 1 hour, 30 minutes minimum. **Hours:** Grouse Mountain open daily 8:45 a.m.-10 p.m. The Skyride departs every 15 minutes. Bus service from Canada Place is offered May-Sept. on a first-come, first-served basis; phone for schedule. Activity hours vary; phone ahead for schedule. **Cost:** Experience ticket $43.95-$57.95; $39.95-$53.95 (ages 65+); $24.95-$38.95 (ages 13-18); $14.95 (ages 5-12); $113.95-$139.95 (family, two adults and two children ages 0-18). Individual activity tickets also are available. Cash only. **Parking:** $2-$8. **Phone:** (604) 980-9311. GT ⑪ ⌧ ⌖

The Eye of the Wind is on top of Grouse Mountain at 6400 Nancy Greene Way. This 65-metre (215-ft.) wind turbine on the mountaintop is reportedly the only one in the world that allows you to stand in a glass viewPOD at the top of the tower (just 10 feet from its massive, rotating blades), giving an awe-inspiring 360-degree view of Vancouver, the harbor, the Coastal Mountains and, on a clear day, mounts Baker, Rainier and Garibaldi. The turbine provides

approximately 20 percent of Grouse Mountain's energy requirement.

Time: Allow 1 hour minimum. **Hours:** Grouse Mountain open daily 8:45 a.m.-10 p.m. The Eye of the Wind drop-in visits daily 10:30-8, mid-May to mid-Oct. Eye of the Wind tours available mid-May to mid-Oct. Phone ahead to confirm schedule. **Cost:** Grouse Mountain $43.95; $39.95 (ages 65+); $24.95 (ages 13-18); $14.95 (ages 5-12); $113.95 (family, two adults and two children). The Eye of the Wind tour (includes Grouse Mountain and chair lift) $57.95; $53.95 (ages 65+); $38.95 (ages 13-18); $14.95 (ages 5-12); $139.95 (family, two adults and two children). Various combination tours are also available. Fares may vary; phone ahead. Reservations are recommended. **Phone:** (604) 980-9311. ⑪

LYNN CANYON ECOLOGY CENTRE is off Lynn Valley Rd. to the end of Peters Rd., following signs to 3663 Park Rd. The center is in a municipal park that features hiking trails, canyons, natural streams and waterfalls and a 50-metre-high (166-ft.) suspension bridge spanning the canyon. The ecology center offers films, children's activities and nature displays. Interactive exhibits highlight the plants and animals of the coastal temperate rain forest.

Hours: Park open daily dawn-dusk. Center open daily 10-5, June-Sept.; Mon.-Fri. 10-5, Sat.-Sun. noon-4, rest of year. Closed Christmas-Jan. 1. **Cost:** $1.90. **Phone:** (604) 990-3755. ⑪

PARK & TILFORD GARDENS is at jct. Cotton Rd. and Brooksbank Ave. at 333 Brooksbank Ave. The 2.8-acre botanical site consists of eight interconnected theme gardens. A variety of both native and exotic floral arrangements leads through arboreal displays and to aviaries, where visitors may see parrots and other tropical birds.

An aromatic blend of plant and flower enclosures composes the Rose Garden, home to 24 varieties and more than 250 rose plants. **Time:** Allow 1 hour minimum. **Hours:** Daily 9:30-dusk. **Cost:** Free. **Phone:** (604) 984-8200. GT

(See map & index p. 290.)

COMFORT INN & SUITES   (604)988-3181 **7**

Motel
$109-$399

Address: 1748 Capilano Rd V7P 3B4 **Location:** Trans-Canada Hwy 1 exit 14 (Capilano Rd), 0.9 mi (1.5 km) s; from north end of Lions Gate Bridge, 0.6 mi (1 km) e on Marine Dr, just n. **Facility:** 95 units, some two bedrooms, efficiencies and kitchens. 2 stories (no elevator), exterior corridors. **Terms:** check-in 4 pm. **Pool(s):** heated outdoor. **Activities:** hot tub. **Guest Services:** valet and coin laundry. **Featured Amenity: full hot breakfast.**

[SAVE] [ECO] [†↓] CALL [&M] [➾] [BIZ]
[HS] [📶] [✕] [▣]
/SOME UNITS [🍴] [🍽]

HOLIDAY INN & SUITES NORTH VANCOUVER
                                     (604)985-3111 **10**

Hotel
$159-$209

Address: 700 Old Lillooet Rd V7J 2H5 **Location:** Trans-Canada Hwy 1 exit 22 (Mount Seymour Pkwy), follow signs. **Facility:** 162 units, some efficiencies. 6 stories, interior corridors. **Terms:** cancellation fee imposed. **Amenities:** safes. **Dining:** 2 restaurants. **Pool(s):** heated indoor. **Activities:** sauna, hot tub, exercise room, spa. **Guest Services:** valet and coin laundry.

[SAVE] [ECO] [†↓] [🛁] [Y]
CALL [&M] [➾] [BIZ] [HS] [📶]
[✕] [🐾] [🍴] [🍽] [▣]
/SOME UNITS [🍴]

Nestled at the foot of the majestic North Shore mountains, the perfect place to work, rest and play

---

NORTH VANCOUVER HOTEL   604/987-4461 **6**
[▽▽] Motel. **Address:** 1800 Capilano Rd V7P 3B6

PINNACLE HOTEL AT THE PIER   (604)986-7437 **9**

Contemporary Hotel
$149-$399

Address: 138 Victory Ship Way V7L 0B1 **Location:** Corner of Esplanade St and Lonsdale Ave. **Facility:** 106 units. 8 stories, interior corridors. **Parking:** on-site (fee). **Terms:** cancellation fee imposed. **Amenities:** safes. **Dining:** The Lobby Restaurant, see separate listing. **Pool(s):** heated indoor. **Activities:** sauna, hot tub, steamroom, bicycles, trails. **Guest Services:** valet laundry.

[SAVE] [ECO] [†↓] [🛁] [Y] [➾] [†]
[BIZ] [HS] [📶] [✕] [🎥] [🍴] [🍽]
[▣] /SOME UNITS [🍴]

WHERE TO EAT

ARMS REACH BISTRO   604/929-7442 **31**
[▽▽▽] Regional American. Casual Dining. **Address:** 4390 Gallant Ave, #107C V7G 1L2

CACTUS CLUB CAFE   604/986-5776
[▽▽] New American. Casual Dining. **Address:** 1598 Pemberton Ave V7P 2S2

FISHWORKS   778/340-3449 **27**
[▽▽▽] New Seafood. Casual Dining. **Address:** 91 Lonsdale Ave V7M 2E5

GUSTO DI QUATTRO   604/924-4444 **29**
[▽▽▽] Italian. Fine Dining. **Address:** 1 Lonsdale Ave V7M 2E4

JAGERHOF   604/980-4316 **28**
[▽▽] Continental. Casual Dining. **Address:** 71 Lonsdale Ave V7M 2E5

LA CUCINA   604/986-1334 **26**
[▽▽] Italian. Casual Dining. **Address:** 1509 Marine Dr V7P 1T8

THE LOBBY RESTAURANT   604/973-8000 **30**
[▽▽▽] Pacific Northwest. Casual Dining. **Address:** 138 Victory Ship Way V7L 0B1

OAK BAY pop. 18,015

- Hotels & Restaurants map & index p. 328
- Part of Victoria area — see map p. 317

OAK BAY BEACH HOTEL   (250)598-4556 **34**

Hotel
$219-$284

Address: 1175 Beach Dr V8S 2N4 **Location:** Oceanfront. In Oak Bay district. **Facility:** This outstanding seaside property whisks you back to the days of grand elegant hotels while offering all the modern conveniences of today. Each Tuesday is movie night complete with gourmet popcorn. 100 units, some efficiencies and kitchens. 8 stories, interior corridors. **Parking:** on-site and valet. **Terms:** check-in 4 pm, cancellation fee imposed. **Amenities:** safes. **Dining:** 4 restaurants, entertainment. **Pool(s):** heated outdoor. **Activities:** hot tub, steamroom, regulation golf, recreation programs, bicycles, trails, exercise room, spa. **Guest Services:** valet laundry, boarding pass kiosk.

[SAVE] [†↓] [🛁] [Y] [🏌] [➾] [BIZ] [HS] [📶] [✕] [🍴]
[🍽] [▣] /SOME UNITS [🍴]

WHERE TO EAT

THE MARINA RESTAURANT   250/598-8555 **30**
[▽▽▽] Pacific Northwest. Fine Dining. **Address:** 1327 Beach Dr V8S 2N4

OTTAVIO ITALIAN BAKERY & DELICATESSEN
                                     250/592-4080 **29**
[▽] Italian Deli Breads/Pastries. Quick Serve. **Address:** 2272 Oak Bay Ave V8R 1G7

PADELLA ITALIAN BISTRO   250/592-7424 **27**
[▽▽] Italian. Casual Dining. **Address:** 2524 Estevan Ave V8R 2S7

PENNY FARTHING ENGLISH PUB   250/370-9008 **28**
[▽▽] Canadian. Gastropub. **Address:** 2228 Oak Bay Ave V8R 1G5

OKANAGAN VALLEY

It's one thing to read about a place; it's quite another to experience it in person. Evocatively written guides and glossy photo books can pique the curiosity and whet the appetite of almost any traveler, but when it comes down to it you really need to get out of the armchair and go. This is certainly true of the Okanagan (oh-ka-NOG-an) Valley; in a province almost embarrassingly gifted with scenic riches, it still manages to stand out.

British Columbia—like much of Canada—is notable for its sheer ruggedness: lofty mountains, expansive forests, rushing rivers. The valley, in contrast, is an anomaly; it could almost be Italy or some other sun-kissed land. The sun does indeed shine warmly, and the azure sky is huge. Tawny bluffs rise from the shores of steel-blue lakes. Scraggly pine trees and compact mounds of silvery gray sagebrush cloak hillsides. Parts of the Okanagan are arid enough to meet the meteorological criteria of a desert, but irrigation has transformed it into one of the most productive fruit- and vegetable-growing regions in North America.

A Land Created by Glaciers

This long, narrow valley was shaped over time by glacial movement. Layers of ice more than a mile thick began retreating some 10,000 years ago, scraping the surface of the land and leaving behind deposits of sediment. Flowing mountain rivers caused innumerable cycles of flooding and erosion. All this water action contributed to a slow but steady accumulation of nutrient-rich soils that over time formed fertile deltas, setting the stage for the valley's eventual blossoming as an agricultural powerhouse.

Impressive mountains, with some peaks topping 3,000 metres (9,800 ft.), flank both sides of the Okanagan Valley—the Monashee range to the east, the Cascades to the west. The mountain systems in this part of North America are oriented in a north-south direction paralleling the Pacific coast, and the intervening valleys follow suit. The entire area is part of

This map shows cities in Okanagan Valley where you will find attractions, hotels and restaurants. Cities are listed alphabetically in this book on the following pages.

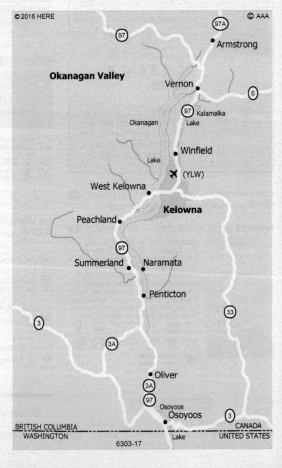

the vast Interior Plateau, an uplifted section of the Earth's crust that covers much of British Columbia's southern interior.

One of the Okanagan Valley's many virtues is its topographical variety—everything from desert to grassland to forest. The northern end is wetter and greener, with a panorama of snowcapped mountains rising off in the distance. As you head south into the heart of the valley the trees become more scattered; ponderosa pines speckling the hills are replaced by shrubs like antelope bush and hardy plants like bunch grass (so named because it grows in individual clumps or tufts rather than forming a uniform carpet), both of which are adapted to a drier climate.

Farther south the Okanagan verges on true desert. In and around Osoyoos the landscape is austere; towering cliffs and bare hillsides flaunt a palette of browns, beiges and grays, and the grasses and other low-growing plants are buffeted by persistent dry winds. The desert plants and animals that inhabit this arid environment are found nowhere else in Canada; the far southern end of the Okanagan Valley lies just above the northernmost reach of the Sonoran Desert, which extends south all the way into Mexico. This also is the country's warmest region, with relatively mild winters, hot summers and abundant sunshine, an ideal combination for irrigation-assisted agriculture.

Between Osoyoos to the east and Princeton to the west is the Similkameen Valley, nestled between steep rocky hills and threaded by the Similkameen River. Although a geographically separate region, it shares the southern Okanagan Valley's dramatic scenery and climatological characteristics. Similkameen country is known for its cattle ranches, horse farms and fruit orchards, and bills itself variously as the "Fruit Stand Capital of Canada" and "BC's Garden of Eden" in an attempt to step out of the better-known Okanagan's shadow.

Hwy. 3, also called the Crowsnest Highway, meanders along the province's southern border from Hope east to the Alberta border. Between Keremeos and Osoyoos the highway traverses an area that climatologists classify as a mid-altitude steppe, although it certainly *looks* like a desert. Away from the sweep of the ever-present irrigation sprinklers, this little portion of extreme southern British Columbia—known as Canada's "pocket desert"—is home to sagebrush, prickly pear cactus, Western rattlesnakes and even the odd scorpion, all of which thrive in these desert-like conditions.

The bracing beauty of the Similkameen countryside is particularly evident in the vicinity of Hedley, a small village about 76 kilometres (47 mi.) west of Osoyoos on Hwy. 3. Here the waters of Hedley Creek rush into the Similkameen River. Stemwinder Mountain looms to the west, Nickel Plate Mountain to the east. Marbled cliffs rise up on both sides of the highway (the Similkameen First Nation named this area Sna-za-ist, meaning "the striped rock place"). Notes of color are supplied by a bright blue sky, the deep green of flourishing fruit trees and (in season) the gold and purple hues of ripening apricots, peaches, plums and grapes.

About 9 kilometres (5.5 mi.) west of Osoyoos is Spotted Lake, which gets its name from one of the world's highest concentrations of magnesium sulfate, calcium, sodium sulfates and other minerals. In summer much of the lake's water evaporates and the minerals crystallize into circles on the surface that can be white, pale yellow, green or blue, depending on the mineral composition. The lake is on private land, but you can view it from the highway.

The Okanagan Valley's distinguishing feature, in fact, is its chain of long, narrow lakes that stretch from north to south. Created by receding glaciers, they are kept fresh and full by snowmelt and runoff from the mountains that flank both sides of the valley. The largest is Okanagan Lake, which stretches north to south for some 111 kilometres (69 mi.) while averaging just 5 kilometres (3 mi.) wide. Skaha, Vaseux and Osoyoos lakes continue the chain to the south. To the east of Okanagan Lake are Kalamalka and Wood lakes; just north is little Swan Lake.

Cattle, Gold, Fruit and Wine

These valleys were first inhabited by the Okanagan First Nation, an Interior Salish tribe. They hunted wild game, fished salmon runs, foraged for roots and berries and traded with other nations. The first European arrivals were fur traders searching for accessible routes to transport their goods to the Pacific. In the early 19th century they ventured north from Fort Okanogan, a Pacific Fur Co. trading post at the confluence of the Okanagan and Columbia rivers in present-day Washington state. Fur caravans were soon heading in and out of the valley region.

When the Oregon Treaty designated the 49th parallel as the border between the United States and the Canadian territory, Osoyoos became a port of entry, and vast herds of cattle were trailed through customs to supply food for miners who panned for placer gold along the Similkameen River. The bunch grass that grew along the river valley provided abundant forage, and ranches began to be established.

Father Charles Pandosy, an Oblate priest, founded a mission in 1859 on the eastern shore of Okanagan Lake. He and his followers endured a harsh first winter—they were forced to shoot their horses for food—but went on to build other missions in the Okanagan Valley, where Father Pandosy instructed the native people in European agricultural techniques in addition to performing baptisms, marriages and funerals.

The discovery of gold on the Fraser River in 1858 resulted in a full-fledged gold rush. British Columbia's southern interior was further opened up with the building of the Caribou Road (now Hwy. 97) and the Dewdney Trail (now Hwy. 3). By the late 19th century the Okanagan and Similkameen valleys were buzzing with gold camps and boom towns that began to spring up along the shores of the region's lakes.

The fruit industry that today is a hallmark of the Okanagan began with difficulty. Apple orchards were planted as early as 1892, but it wasn't until the 1920s that fruit crops proved economically successful. The valley's warm temperatures and long growing season—besides providing Canadians with approximately one-third of their apples—nurtures verdant orchards of apricots, cherries, peaches, pears and plums.

Commercial grape plantings near Kelowna supplied the Okanagan's first wineries. The local wine industry has grown exponentially since the introduction of large-scale irrigation, and almost all of British Columbia's wine comes from the Okanagan region. The diversity of growing conditions—from the hot, sandy desert soils of the south to the deep topsoil and clay of the cooler north, plus distinct microclimates created by the valley's lakes—help ensure a diversity of wines.

Vineyards at the southern end of the valley produce such vintages as Chardonnay, Merlot, Cabernet Sauvignon, Pinot Gris and Pinot Noir, while vineyards in the central and northern valley specialize in Pinot Blanc, Riesling and Gewürztraminer wines. Some grapes are left to freeze on the vine to produce icewine, a rich, sweet dessert wine. One of the Okanagan's most picturesque sights is orderly rows of grapevines, often covering a hillside that overlooks a deep blue lake.

Hwy. 97, which runs the length of British Columbia from the U.S. border just south of Osoyoos north to Watson Lake at the Yukon border, is the principal route through the Okanagan Valley. From Osoyoos it travels north to Penticton, then follows the western shore of Okanagan Lake before crossing the lake on a floating bridge (the largest in the country) that is scheduled to be replaced with an overhead bridge.

Okanagan Lake is said to be the home of Ogopogo, the best known of Canada's unexplained lake creatures. Sightings of the mythical beast—most often described as 5 to 6 metres (15 to 20 ft.) long, shaped like a log and with a head resembling that of a horse or goat—date back as far as 1872. Okanagan aboriginals believed that Ogopogo's home was small, barren Rattlesnake Island; they claimed that the island's rocky beaches were sometimes strewn with animal parts, presumably dinner remains, and when crossing the lake during bad weather always took along a small animal that would be thrown overboard in order to appease the monster. Interestingly, there are similarities between Okanagan Lake and Scotland's Loch Ness, home of the famed Loch Ness Monster; both bodies of water are long and narrow, and both lie at about the same latitude.

East of the lake Hwy. 97 winds north to Enderby, the unofficial northern end of the valley, before continuing on toward Sicamous. But whether you proceed from south to north or north to south, this 211-kilometre (131 mi.) journey through the heart of the Okanagan is utterly delightful. One minute the highway is running tantalizingly close to a sparkling lakeshore; the next it's in the shadow of a soaring, sagebrush-dotted bluff or looking down on checkerboard farmland. Each bend and turn reveals a new view, and each one is lovely. The scenery alone would be more than enough to recommend this drive, even if you didn't make a single stop.

Year-Round Fun

But of course you *will* want to stop, because this is Canada's No. 1 year-round recreation destination. Dozens of parks ring Okanagan Lake, offering myriad opportunities for hiking, backpacking, mountain biking and camping. Bear Creek Provincial Park, about 9 kilometres (6 mi.) west of Kelowna off Hwy. 97, has many hiking trails to explore, all beginning from a common trailhead at the park entrance. Bear Creek runs through the bottom of a tree-walled canyon, and the trails above wind past ponderosa pine, Douglas fir, juniper and prickly pear cactus that frame expansive lake views.

The lakes are, of course, ideal for water recreation, whether it's sailing, paddle boating, water skiing, jet skiing, kayaking, canoeing or freshwater fishing. Okanagan Lake is ringed with sandy beaches and sheltered coves, and numerous marina facilities provide equipment rentals.

For a northern Okanagan getaway head out to Kalamalka Lake Provincial Park, about 8 kilometres (5 mi.) southeast of Vernon off Hwy. 6. Kalamalka is known as a "marl lake," a process that begins when the water warms, forming calcium carbonate and limestone crystals that reflect sunlight. The water's distinctive blue-green color is often shot through with ribbons of deep blue, earning it the nickname "lake of a thousand colors." This largely undeveloped park encompasses rolling grasslands and forested ridges where Douglas fir and lodgepole pine grow; a paved trail leads to secluded beaches. Wildlife ranges from mule deer and minks to bobcats and western painted turtles. Bird-watching is rewarding, and the spring wildflower display is spectacular.

Nearly 40 golf courses are scattered from Vernon south to Osoyoos, with many of them concentrated around Kelowna. Due to the mild climate most courses open as early as March, and golfers frequently play into November. And this being the Okanagan, it's only natural that water and fruit trees figure into course layouts; the grounds of the Kelowna Springs Golf Club include seven spring-fed lakes, while fairways at the Harvest Golf Club are set in the midst of a huge hillside apple orchard and have prime views of Okanagan Lake.

Kelowna is the Okanagan Valley's largest city and a big summer vacation destination. Water sports—sailing, kayaking, windsurfing, fishing—rule the summer calendar, but downtown Kelowna also offers museums, art galleries, pretty lakeside parks, all kinds of restaurants and a lively nightlife. It makes a convenient base for touring the many small wineries in the vicinity.

Breezy Penticton has the best of both worlds; the north end of town fronts the southern tip of Okanagan Lake, while the south end brushes up against the north shore of Skaha Lake. Lakeside beaches give the city a summery feel, and families flock to Penticton's amusement centers, go-cart tracks, miniature golf course and waterslides. Stroll along Front Street, the original business corridor, which is lined with restaurants and funky little shops.

Situated between Swan, Kalamalka and Okanagan lakes, Vernon started out as a camp on the Okanagan Valley trail during the fur trade years; by the turn of the 20th century it was a bustling ranching center. Downtown Vernon truly earns the description "quaint": The tree-lined, flower-filled streets are packed with historic old buildings and specialty stores selling everything from Victorian crafts to homemade jams. Be sure to search out the 27 outdoor murals—some up to 91 metres (300 ft.) long—that depict Okanagan history, folklore and landscapes.

Just a stone's throw from the U.S. border, Osoyoos (oh-SOY-yoos) means, in the local Inkaneep native dialect, "where the water narrows"—a reference to its location spanning a narrow portion of Osoyoos Lake. Vineyards and orchards abound in the surrounding countryside, and the lake is one of Canada's warmest. Stroll along one of the lakeside parks in town while watching windsurfers and parasailing enthusiasts do their thing under sunny summer skies, and it's not that hard to believe you've happened onto some undiscovered Mediterranean resort.

The Okanagan Valley has something to offer regardless of the season. Downhill and cross-country skiers, snowboarders and other winter sports enthusiasts can choose from four ski resorts: Silver Star Mountain Resort, north of Vernon; Big White Ski Resort near Kelowna; Crystal Mountain resort near West Kelowna (Westbank); and Apex Mountain Resort, southwest of Penticton.

Spring and summer are seasons to experience the valley's agricultural bounty. In the spring fruit trees are in full glorious bloom. Spring into early summer also is the time when wildflowers make their appearance in the Okanagan's wilderness parks.

Harvest time for the region's famous fruits and vegetables begins in late June and lasts until mid-October. If you're here in the summer or fall stop at one of the ubiquitous roadside fruit stands, which seem almost as plentiful as the trees themselves. Cherries are first in the fruit parade, ripening from late June through mid-July. Peaches appear from mid-July through September; pears in August and September; plums in September; and apples from August through October.

Practically every town in the valley has a farmers market, and you'll want to check out every single one. In addition to all sorts of fruit, the markets offer tomatoes, pumpkins, squash, asparagus, organic preserves, homemade pies, artisanal cheeses, honey, herbs, flowers—just about everything. Most are open April or May through October.

Grapes are harvested September through mid-October, an ideal time to go winery hopping. Most of the Okanagan's roughly 100 wineries can be visited, many have an intriguing history to share, and practically all of them enjoy a picturesque rural setting. Before hitting the tasting bars, pick up information and maps at any local visitor center.

So when should you plan a trip? Come to think of it, just about any time is right.

Destinations in this region listed under their own names are Kelowna, Oliver, Osoyoos, Peachland, Penticton, Summerland, Vernon and West Kelowna (Westbank).

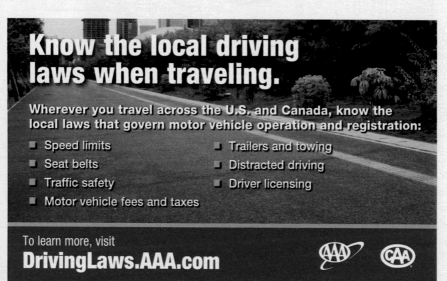

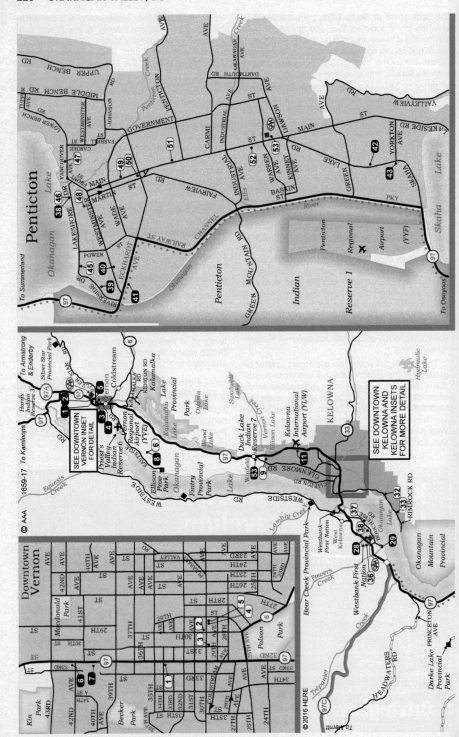

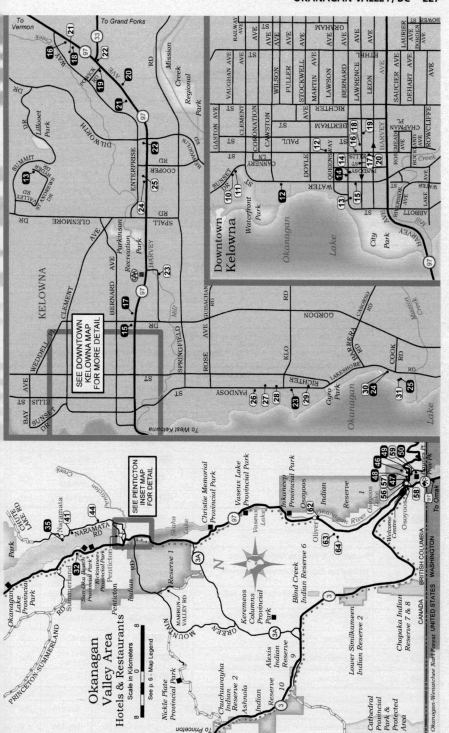

Okanagan Valley Area

This index helps you "spot" where approved hotels and restaurants are located on the corresponding detailed maps. Hotel daily rate range is for comparison only. Restaurant price range is a combination of lunch and/or dinner. Turn to the listing page for more information and consult display ads for special promotions.

VERNON

Map Page	Hotels	Diamond Rated	Rate Range	Page
1 p. 226	Fairfield Inn & Suites by Marriott	◆◆◆	$98-$165	313
2 p. 226	**Days Inn Vernon**	◆◆	$85-$165 [SAVE]	313
3 p. 226	**Best Western Pacific Inn** *(See ad p. 313.)*	◆◆◆	$99-$229 [SAVE]	313
4 p. 226	**Holiday Inn Express Hotel & Suites Vernon** *(See ad p. 314.)*	◆◆◆	Rates not provided [SAVE]	315
5 p. 226	**Village Green Hotel**	◆◆	$79-$159 [SAVE]	315
6 p. 226	Super 8 Vernon	◆◆	$79-$149	315
7 p. 226	**Vernon Atrium Hotel & Conference Centre** *(See ad p. 314.)*	◆◆	$124-$249 [SAVE]	315
8 p. 226	**Sparkling Hill Resort**	◆◆◆◆	Rates not provided [SAVE]	315

Map Page	Restaurants	Diamond Rated	Cuisine	Price Range	Page
① p. 226	Intermezzo Restaurant	◆◆◆	Italian	$17-$34	315
② p. 226	Naked Pig	◆◆	Barbecue	$12-$29	315
③ p. 226	Amarin Thai Restaurant	◆◆	Thai	$12-$18	315
④ p. 226	Los Huesos	◆◆	Mexican	$12-$18	315
⑤ p. 226	The Italian Kitchen Company	◆◆	Italian	$11-$29	315
⑥ p. 226	**PeakFine**	◆◆◆	Pacific Northwest	$13-$45	315

KELOWNA

Map Page	Hotels	Diamond Rated	Rate Range	Page
11 p. 226	**Four Points by Sheraton Kelowna Airport**	◆◆◆	$129-$389 [SAVE]	208
12 p. 226	Delta Grand Okanagan Resort & Conference Centre	◆◆◆	$149-$362	207
13 p. 226	A Vista Villa Couples Retreat	◆◆◆	$229-$379	206
14 p. 226	The Royal Anne Hotel	◆◆◆	$89-$500	208
15 p. 226	Kelowna Inn & Suites	◆◆	Rates not provided	208
16 p. 226	**Comfort Suites**	◆◆◆	$142-$349 [SAVE]	207
17 p. 226	Accent Inns	◆◆	Rates not provided	206
18 p. 226	Super 8 Kelowna	◆◆	$81-$145	208
19 p. 226	Fairfield Inn & Suites by Marriott Kelowna	◆◆◆	$85-$191	207
20 p. 226	**Holiday Inn Express Kelowna Conference Centre**	◆◆◆	Rates not provided [SAVE]	208
21 p. 226	**Best Western Plus Kelowna Hotel & Suites** *(See ad p. 206.)*	◆◆◆	$140-$250 [SAVE]	207
22 p. 226	Ramada Hotel & Conference Centre *(See ad p. 207.)*	◆◆◆	$119-$229	208
23 p. 226	Siesta Suites	◆◆	$92-$279	208
24 p. 226	Manteo Resort-Waterfront Hotel & Villas	◆◆◆	Rates not provided	208
25 p. 226	Hotel Eldorado	◆◆◆	$119-$299	208

Map Page	Restaurants	Diamond Rated	Cuisine	Price Range	Page
⑨ p. 226	The Jammery	◆◆	American	$11-$16	208
⑩ p. 226	Waterfront Wines	◆◆◆	New Canadian	$26-$36	209

Map Page	Restaurants (cont'd)	Diamond Rated	Cuisine	Price Range	Page
⑪ p. 226	Bouchons Bistro	◆◆◆	French	$23-$43	208
⑫ p. 226	Dawett Fine Indian Cuisine	◆◆	Indian	$12-$15	208
⑬ p. 226	Salted Brick	◆◆	Canadian	$13-$16	209
⑭ p. 226	Bread Co. Fine Baked Goods & Eatery	◆	Breads/Pastries Sandwiches	$8-$10	208
⑮ p. 226	RauDZ Regional Table	◆◆◆	New Canadian	$16-$45	208
⑯ p. 226	Dunnenzies Pizza Co.	◆	Pizza	$10-$25	208
⑰ p. 226	Little Hobo	◆	Soup Sandwiches	$6-$10	208
⑱ p. 226	The Yellowhouse Restaurant	◆◆◆	New International	$17-$29	209
⑲ p. 226	Mamma Rosa Restaurant	◆◆	Italian	$16-$36	208
⑳ p. 226	Yamas Taverna Greek Restaurant	◆◆	Greek	$18-$39	209
㉑ p. 226	Bluetail Sushi & Bistro	◆◆	Sushi	$10-$23	208
㉒ p. 226	Bai Tong	◆◆	Thai	$13-$17	208
㉓ p. 226	Valoroso Foods	◆	Italian Deli	$8-$15	209
㉔ p. 226	Mabui	◆◆	Japanese Small Plates Sushi	$9-$25	208
㉕ p. 226	Pearson's European Deli	◆	Deli	$7-$15	208
㉖ p. 226	Mizu Japanese Restaurant	◆◆	Sushi	$8-$17	208
㉗ p. 226	The Marmalade Cat Cafe	◆	Sandwiches Desserts	$7-$9	208
㉘ p. 226	Zabb Thai Restaurant	◆◆	Thai	$11-$13	209
㉙ p. 226	The Fixx Cafe & Pasta Bar	◆◆	International	$7-$38	208
㉚ p. 226	Smack DAB	◆◆◆	American	$11-$28	209
㉛ p. 226	Eldorado Dining Room & Bar	◆◆◆	Regional Canadian	$12-$46	208
㉜ p. 226	Summerhill Sunset Organic Bistro	◆◆◆	New Canadian	$17-$38	209
㉝ p. 226	Cedar Creek Winery Terrace Restaurant	◆◆◆	New Canadian	$21-$36	208

WEST KELOWNA

Map Page	Hotels	Diamond Rated	Rate Range	Page
㉘ p. 226	**Best Western Plus Wine Country Hotel & Suites**	◆◆◆	$149-$259 SAVE	337
㉙ p. 226	The Cove Lakeside Resort	◆◆◆	Rates not provided	337

Map Page	Restaurants	Diamond Rated	Cuisine	Price Range	Page
㊱ p. 226	Kekuli Cafe	◆	Canadian Specialty	$5-$11	337
㊲ p. 226	Old Vines The Restaurant at Quails' Gate	◆◆◆	Regional Canadian	$18-$48	337
㊳ p. 226	The Terrace Restaurant	◆◆◆	New Canadian	$27-$29	337

SUMMERLAND

Map Page	Hotel	Diamond Rated	Rate Range	Page
㉜ p. 226	Summerland Motel	◆◆	$69-$170	254

NARAMATA

Map Page	Hotel	Diamond Rated	Rate Range	Page
㉟ p. 226	The Village Motel	◆◆	$130-$157	216

Map Page	Restaurant	Diamond Rated	Cuisine	Price Range	Page
㊶ p. 226	The Patio at Lake Breeze	◆◆◆	Mediterranean	$17-$28	216

PENTICTON

Map Page	Hotels	Diamond Rated	Rate Range	Page
38 p. 226	Penticton Lakeside Resort, Convention Centre & Casino (See ad p. 234.)	◆◆◆	$141-$261	235
39 p. 226	Days Inn & Conference Centre Penticton	◆◆	$104-$199	235
40 p. 226	Coast Penticton Hotel	◆◆	Rates not provided	234
41 p. 226	Ramada Inn & Suites	◆◆◆	$99-$304	235
42 p. 226	**Best Western Inn at Penticton**	◆◆	$109-$239 (SAVE)	234
43 p. 226	Empire Motel	◆◆	$74-$179	235

Map Page	Restaurants	Diamond Rated	Cuisine	Price Range	Page
44 p. 226	Hillside Winery Bistro	◆◆◆	New Canadian	$19-$35	235
45 p. 226	Salty's Beach House	◆◆	Caribbean	$13-$24	235
46 p. 226	Hooded Merganser Bar & Grill (See ad p. 234.)	◆◆◆	Pacific Northwest	$11-$30	235
47 p. 226	The Bench Artisan Food Market	◆	Regional Deli Sandwiches	$9-$13	235
48 p. 226	Bad Tattoo Brewing Company	◆◆	Pizza	$18-$24	235
49 p. 226	Lachi Fine Indian Cuisine	◆◆	Indian	$8-$15	235
50 p. 226	Theo's Restaurant	◆◆	Greek	$12-$30	235
51 p. 226	La Casa Ouzeria	◆◆	Greek	$10-$45	235
52 p. 226	Shades on Main Family Restaurant	◆◆	American	$8-$17	235
53 p. 226	Buy the Sea	◆	Fish & Chips	$10-$19	235

OSOYOOS

Map Page	Hotels	Diamond Rated	Rate Range	Page
46 p. 226	Spirit Ridge Vineyard Resort & Spa	◆◆◆	Rates not provided	231
47 p. 226	Watermark Beach Resort	◆◆◆	$107-$476	232
48 p. 226	**The Coast Osoyoos Beach Hotel**	◆◆	$79-$539 (SAVE)	231
49 p. 226	**Best Western Plus Sunrise Inn**	◆◆◆	$119-$280 (SAVE)	231
50 p. 226	Walnut Beach Resort	◆◆◆	$149-$279	232

Map Page	Restaurants	Diamond Rated	Cuisine	Price Range	Page
56 p. 226	Wildfire Grill	◆◆	Continental	$16-$25	232
57 p. 226	Jojo's Cafe	◆	Coffee/Tea Sandwiches	$6-$9	232
58 p. 226	Watermark Wine Bar & Patio	◆◆◆	International Small Plates	$20-$35	232
59 p. 226	Campo Marina	◆◆	Italian	$16-$25	232

WINFIELD

Map Page	Hotel	Diamond Rated	Rate Range	Page
53 p. 226	Super 8 Motel Lake Country	◆◆	$115-$125	348

OLIVER

Map Page	Restaurants	Diamond Rated	Cuisine	Price Range	Page
62 p. 226	Cock & Bull Cappucino Bar	◆	American	$6-$11	231
63 p. 226	Miradoro at Tinhorn Creek	◆◆◆	New Mediterranean	$17-$31	231
64 p. 226	Terrafina at Hester Creek	◆◆◆	New Italian	$17-$35	231

OLIVER (D-8) pop. 4,824, elev. 307m/1,007'
• Hotels & Restaurants map & index p. 226
• Part of Okanagan Valley area — see map p. 222

The northern tip of the American Great Basin Desert, which extends to Mexico, begins at Oliver. Irrigation begun in the 1920s converted the once desertlike valley floor and arid hillsides surrounding the town into productive orchards and vineyards. Abundant sunshine and little rain provide ideal conditions for growing wine grapes.

The area's climate also promotes numerous recreational activities. An 18-kilometre (11-mi.) paved bicycle trail travels through Oliver's rolling hills and along the Okanagan River. The valley lakes and streams offer boating and fishing. Vaseux Lake and Inkaneep provincial parks *(see Recreation Areas Chart)* are nearby, as are Bear and Madden lakes, known for excellent trout fishing.

The Fairview Townsite, 3 kilometres (1.9 mi.) west on Fairview Road, formerly was the site of an 1880s boomtown. The town disappeared along with the gold in 1906; plaques at the site provide historical information.

Oliver Visitor Centre: 6431 Station St., P.O. Box 460, Oliver, BC, Canada V0H 1T0. **Phone:** (778) 439-2363 or (844) 896-3300.

COCK & BULL CAPPUCINO BAR   250/498-6261 **62**
American. Quick Serve. **Address:** 6041 Main St V0H 1T0

MIRADORO AT TINHORN CREEK   250/498-3237 **63**
New Mediterranean. Casual Dining. **Address:** 537 Tinhorn Creek Rd V0H 1T0

TERRAFINA AT HESTER CREEK   250/498-2229 **64**
New Italian. Casual Dining. **Address:** 877 Rd 8 V0H 1T1

OSOYOOS (D-9) pop. 4,845, elev. 335m/1,099'
• Restaurants p. 232
• Hotels & Restaurants map & index p. 226
• Part of Okanagan Valley area — see map p. 222

From Osoyoos on the east side of Osoyoos Lake, an area of desert sand extends 48 kilometres (30 mi.) north to Skaha Lake and 24 kilometres (15 mi.) west along the Similkameen River. The area's similarity to Spain in climate and terrain inspired the citizens to adopt an Iberian style in their buildings. Despite its arid surroundings, Osoyoos has 19 kilometres (12 mi.) of sandy beach lining one of Canada's warmest freshwater lakes.

Man-made recreational facilities include Wild Rapids on E. Lakeshore Drive, with three large waterslides, five giant hot tubs and two minislides. Skiing is available nearby.

A heavy concentration of minerals, including evaporated copper, silver, gold and sulfate and Epsom salts, can be found at Spotted Lake, west on Crowsnest Hwy. 3, which provides 446 kilometres (277 mi.) of scenic driving all the way to Hope.

Destination Osoyoos Visitor Services Centre: 236-15 Park Place, Watermark Beach Resort, Osoyoos, BC, Canada V0H 1V0. **Phone:** (778) 699-2044.

NK'MIP DESERT CULTURAL CENTRE is at 1000 Rancher Creek Rd. Visitors will experience a desert ecosystem and the traditions of the Okanagan people through interactive exhibits, artifacts, a recreated Okanagan village and self-guiding walking trails. The Village Trail is 1.4 kilometres (.9 mi.) long and has interpretive signs, benches and ramadas; the Loop Trail is 2 kilometres (1.2 mi.) and includes several uphill segments.

Time: Allow 1 hour minimum. **Hours:** Daily 9:30-4:30, Mar.-Oct. Phone ahead for Nov.-Feb. hours and guided tour information. **Cost:** $14; $13 (ages 65+); $10 (ages 5-18); $38 (family, two adults and two or more children). **Phone:** (250) 495-7901 or (888) 495-8555. **GT**

WINERIES
• **Nk'Mip Cellars** is at 1400 Rancher Creek Rd. **Hours:** Tastings daily 9-8, July-Aug.; 9-6, Apr.-June and Sept.-Oct.; 10-5, rest of year. Phone ahead to confirm schedule. **Phone:** (250) 495-2985. **GT**

BEST WESTERN PLUS SUNRISE INN
(250)495-4000 **49**
Hotel $119-$280
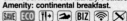
BW Best Western PLUS AAA Benefit: Save 10% or more every day and earn 10% bonus points!
Address: 5506 Main St V0H 1V0 **Location:** Jct Hwy 97, 1.9 mi (3 km) on Hwy 3 (Main St). **Facility:** 66 units, some efficiencies and kitchens. 3 stories, interior corridors. **Terms:** check-in 4 pm, 2 night minimum stay - seasonal. **Pool(s):** heated indoor. **Activities:** hot tub, exercise room. **Guest Services:** coin laundry. **Featured Amenity:** full hot breakfast.

THE COAST OSOYOOS BEACH HOTEL
(250)495-6525 **48**
Hotel $79-$539

Address: 7702 Main St V0H 1V0 **Location:** Waterfront. Jct Hwy 97, 1.2 mi (2 km) e. **Facility:** 60 units, some two bedrooms and kitchens. 3 stories (no elevator), interior/exterior corridors. **Terms:** check-in 4 pm, 14 day cancellation notice-fee imposed. **Pool(s):** heated indoor. **Activities:** hot tub, exercise room. **Guest Services:** coin laundry. **Featured Amenity:** continental breakfast.

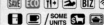

SPIRIT RIDGE VINEYARD RESORT & SPA
250/495-5445 **46**
Resort Condominium. **Address:** 1200 Rancher Creek Rd V0H 1V6

(See map & index p. 226.)

WALNUT BEACH RESORT   (250)495-5400 **50**
▼▼▼ Resort Hotel. **Address:** 4200 Lakeshore Dr V0H 1V6

WATERMARK BEACH RESORT   (250)495-5500 **47**
▼▼▼ Resort Condominium. **Address:** 15 Park Pl V0H 1V0

WHERE TO EAT

CAMPO MARINA   250/495-7650 **59**
▼▼ Italian. Casual Dining. **Address:** 5907 Main St (Hwy 3)
V0H 1V3

JOJO'S CAFE   250/495-6652 **57**
▼ Coffee/Tea Sandwiches. Quick Serve. **Address:** 8316 Main
St V0H 1T0

WATERMARK WINE BAR & PATIO   250/495-5508 **58**
▼▼▼ International Small Plates. Casual Dining. **Address:**
15 Park Pl V0H 1V0

WILDFIRE GRILL   250/495-2215 **56**
▼▼ Continental. Casual Dining. **Address:** 8526 Main St
V0H 1V0

PACIFIC RIM NATIONAL PARK RESERVE (I-3)

Elevations in the park range from sea level
along the Long Beach area to 140 metres
(459 ft.) at Radar Hill. Refer to CAA/AAA
maps for additional elevation information.

On the west coast of Vancouver Island, Pacific
Rim National Park Reserve consists of three geographically distinct sections with different entry
points: the Long Beach unit between Ucluelet and
Tofino; the Broken Group Island unit, a cluster of islands in Barkley Sound; and the 75-kilometre-long
(47-mi.) West Coast Trail unit between Bamfield and
Port Renfrew.

Numerous contrasts exist in the 510-square-
kilometre (197-sq.-mi.) reserve, which has sandy
beaches, tranquil estuaries and lakes, rugged headlands, dense rain forests and rocky islands. Wildflowers nurtured by the area's moist and temperate
climate thrive in an immense old-growth rain forest.

A stopping place for geese and ducks during their
yearly migrations, the shoreline zone also accommodates colonies of sea birds and wildlife. Each
spring some 20,000 gray whales migrate through
the reserve's waters.

General Information and Activities

The reserve is open all year, although many facilities are seasonal. The Long Beach Unit, about 16
kilometres (10 mi.) west of the junction of Hwy. 4
and the Ucluelet highway, has 19 kilometres (12 mi.)
of sandy beach and shoreline which are popular
year-round with surfers and beachwalkers;
wheelchair-accessible trails are available. Pacific
Rim Visitor Centre, open mid-March to mid-October,
is located at the junction of Hwy. 4 and Pacific Rim
Hwy. There are self-guiding nature trails in the surrounding rain forest and other interpretive programs.

The Kwisitis Visitor Centre features displays and
films chronicling marine life of the Pacific.

The Broken Group Islands, accessible only by
boat, offer pristine wilderness spread over a 100-
island cluster in the center of Barkley Sound. Eagles
and sea lions are abundant, while varied sea life and
sunken ships create a diver's paradise. Camping is
available in designated areas on eight islands.

The West Coast Trail, which had its beginnings as
a telegraph line and then an avenue of rescue for
shipwrecked sailors, follows the national park's
rugged coastline between Port Renfrew and Bamfield. The trail is recommended to experienced
hikers only and offers spectacular coastal scenery
along its challenging path. Remnants of former
settlements and shipwrecks can be seen along the
shoreline.

The West Coast Trail Information and Registration Centres at Pachena Bay near Bamfield and at
Port Renfrew are open daily 9-4, May through September. Reservations to hike the trail may be made,
beginning mid-March, for June 15 through September 15 dates; phone (877) 737-3783 within
Canada and the U.S. See Recreation Areas Chart.

ADMISSION to the Long Beach area is free in 2017
to celebrate Canada's 150th anniversary of Confederation. Otherwise admission is $7.43; $6.48 (ages
65+); $3.71 (ages 6-16); $18.67 (all occupants of a
private vehicle with up to seven people). Camping
fee at Long Beach is $22.38-$30.95 per person per
night. Camping fee at other designated sites is
$9.33 per person per night. West Coast Trail use
permit $121.43; reservation fee $23.33 (non-
refundable). Ferry fee $15.24. An annual pass, valid
at most Canadian national parks, marine areas and
historic sites, is available.

PETS are permitted in the Long Beach Unit of the
park provided they are on a leash at all times. Pets
are not permitted in the Broken Group Islands or the
West Coast Trail.

ADDRESS inquiries to the Superintendent, Pacific
Rim National Park Reserve, P.O. Box 280, Ucluelet,
BC, Canada V0R 3A0; phone (250) 726-3500, or
(250) 726-4212 June 1 to mid-Sept.

PARKSVILLE (G-10) pop. 11,977, elev. 80m/262'

With its 1.6-kilometre-long (1-mi.) sandy beach on
the Strait of Georgia, Parksville is a popular summer
resort. Nearby Englishman and Little Qualicum
rivers and parks, with scenic waterfalls, provide
many opportunities for recreation, as do other area
lakes, streams, mountains and parks. Rathtrevor
Beach Provincial Park offers a beach, camping and
picnicking. See Recreation Areas Chart.

Artistic endeavors in sand are the main focus of
the ▼ Parksville Beach Festival. Elaborate sand
sculptures compete for prizes in July and August,
and attendees can also enjoy fireworks, children's
activities and a volleyball tournament.

Parksville & District Chamber of Commerce:
1275 E. Island Hwy., P.O. Box 99, Parksville, BC,
Canada V9P 2G3. **Phone:** (250) 248-3613.

ARBUTUS GROVE MOTEL   250/248-6422
◆◆ Motel. **Address:** 1182 E Island Hwy V9P 1W3

THE BEACH CLUB RESORT   250/248-8999
◆◆◆◆ Contemporary Resort Hotel. **Address:** 181 Beachside
Dr V9P 2H5

OCEANSIDE VILLAGE RESORT   250/248-8961
◆◆◆◆ Vacation Rental Cottage. **Address:** 1080 Resort Dr V9P
2E3

QUALITY RESORT BAYSIDE   (250)248-8333

Hotel
$99-$199

Address: 240 Dogwood St V9P 2H5
Location: Island Hwy 19 exit 51
(Parksville/Coombs), 1.3 mi (2 km) e,
then 0.6 mi (1 km) n on Hwy 19A. **Facility:** 59 units. 3 stories, interior corridors. **Pool(s):** heated indoor. **Activities:**
hot tub, beach access, exercise room.

SANDCASTLE INN   250/248-2334
◆ Hotel. **Address:** 374 W Island Hwy V9P 1K8

SUNRISE RIDGE WATERFRONT RESORT   (250)248-4674
◆◆◆ Vacation Rental Hotel. **Address:** 1175 Resort Dr V9P
2E3

TIGH-NA-MARA SEASIDE SPA RESORT & CONFERENCE
CENTRE   250/248-2072
◆◆◆ Resort Hotel. **Address:** 1155 Resort Dr V9P 2E3

TRAVELODGE PARKSVILLE   (250)248-2232
◆◆ Hotel. **Address:** 424 W Island Hwy V9P 1K8

V.I.P. MOTEL   (250)248-3244
◆ Motel. **Address:** 414 W Island Hwy V9P 1K8

WHERE TO EAT

AMRIKKO'S FINE INDIAN CUISINE   250/951-0682
◆◆ Indian. Casual Dining. **Address:** 487 E Island Hwy V9P
2H6

THE CEDARS RESTAURANT   250/248-2333
◆◆◆ Pacific Northwest. Casual Dining. **Address:** 1155
Resort Dr V9P 2E3

KALVAS RESTAURANT   250/248-6933
◆◆ Steak Seafood. Casual Dining. **Address:** 180 Moilliet
St, Island Hwy N V9P 2H4

LEFTY'S FRESH FOOD RESTAURANT   250/954-3886
◆ American. Casual Dining. **Address:** 101-280 E Island
Hwy V9P 2G3

PACIFIC PRIME STEAK AND CHOP RESTAURANT
                                       250/947-2109
◆◆◆ Pacific Northwest. Fine Dining. **Address:** 181
Beachside Dr V9P 2H5

PEACHLAND (C-8) pop. 5,200,
elev. 366m/1,200'
• Part of Okanagan Valley area — see map p. 222

Peachland's rolling green countryside is a prosperous fruit-growing, farming, lumber-producing and
mining area. The mining of molybdenum and copper
from the Brenda Mines complex in the hills above
Hwy. 97 spurred significant growth during the 1970s.

Nearby mountains, rivers and lakes, including
Okanagan Lake *(see Recreation Areas Chart)*, offer
abundant opportunities for skiing, hiking, fishing and
water sports.

PENDER ISLANDS (H-10)

Part of the Gulf Islands *(see place listing p. 196)*,
the Penders, consisting of North and South Pender
islands, are connected by a one-lane wooden bridge
that spans the canal linking Bedwell and Browning
harbors. An archeological dig conducted at the time
the bridge was built found evidence of island occupation dating back 4,000 years. The Pender Islands
Museum, set on national park lands at Roseland, offers an overview of area history on Saturday and
Sunday 10-4 in July and August; Saturday and
Sunday 1-4, Easter weekend-Thanksgiving
weekend. Phone (250) 629-6935.

The island's 20 public ocean access points and
many coves allow ample opportunities for swimming
and picnicking. Hiking, boating, fishing, golfing, bicycling, kayaking and scuba diving are other available
recreational activities. Camping is available at Prior
Centennial Campground in Gulf Islands National
Park Reserve from May 15-Sept. 30. Roadside
stands offer locally grown produce. The view from
the summit of Mount Norman, part of Gulf Islands
National Park Reserve, is worth the climb.

POETS COVE RESORT & SPA   (250)629-2100
◆◆◆ Hotel. **Address:** 9801 Spalding Rd V0N 2M3

PENTICTON (C-8) pop. 32,877,
elev. 345m/1,131'
• Hotels p. 234 • Restaurants p. 235
• Hotels & Restaurants map & index p. 226
• Part of Okanagan Valley area — see map p. 222

The first orchards in Okanagan Valley were
planted by the Oblates at Okanagan Mission
1860-61, and the fruits, especially peaches, became
a staple of the area. Tom Ellis established the first
cattle ranch in 1865 and it was an empire when he
sold it for a hefty sum in 1905; by 1909 orchards had
replaced cattle in the agricultural economy. Today
Penticton's fruit industry combines with tourism and
lumber industries to keep the community strong.

Okanagan and Skaha lakes, at opposite ends of
the city, offer ample expanses of shoreline for recreational pursuits. A popular summer activity is floating
down the 8-kilometre (5-mi.) river channel from the
mouth of Okanagan Lake *(see Recreation Areas
Chart)* to Skaha Lake. The channel has rest and
picnic areas and is paralleled by a bicycle path and

(See map & index p. 226.)

a jogging trail. The *Casabella Princess*, a 48-passenger paddlewheeler departing from Penticton Marina, takes passengers on a 1-hour cruise of the south end of Okanagan Lake or on a 2-hour dinner cruise (June-Sept.); phone (250) 215-2779.

Penticton & Wine Country Visitor Centre: 553 Vees Dr. (at 400 Alberni St. through Feb. 2017), Penticton, BC, Canada V2A 8S3. **Phone:** (250) 276-2170 or (800) 663-5052.

WINERIES

- **Hillside Winery and Bistro** is 3 km (2 mi.) n. of jct. McMillan Ave. and Naramata Rd. at 1350 Naramata Rd. **Hours:** Tastings and self-guiding tours daily 10-7, July-Aug.; 10-6, Apr.-June and Sept.-Oct.; Mon.-Fri. 9-4, rest of year. **Phone:** (250) 493-6274 or (888) 923-9463. GT

BEST WESTERN INN AT PENTICTON

(250)493-0311 42

Hotel
$109-$239

Best Western. **AAA Benefit:** Save 10% or more every day and earn 10% bonus points!

Address: 3180 Skaha Lake Rd V2A 6G4 **Location:** From downtown, 2.5 mi (4 km) s. **Facility:** 67 units, some two bedrooms, efficiencies and kitchens. 2 stories (no elevator), exterior corridors. **Terms:** cancellation fee imposed. **Pool(s):** heated outdoor, heated indoor. **Activities:** hot tub, playground, picnic facilities, exercise room. **Guest Services:** valet and coin laundry. **Featured Amenity:** continental breakfast.

COAST PENTICTON HOTEL   250/492-0225 40
Hotel. **Address:** 950 Westminster Ave W V2A 1L2

▼ *See AAA listing p. 235* ▼

PENTICTON
LAKESIDE
RESORT
AND
CONFERENCE CENTRE

The **Barking Parrot** BAR

250.493.9753
barkingparrot.com

21 Lakeshore Drive West
Penticton, BC V2A 7M5
1.800.663.9400
pentictonlakesideresort.com

250.487.4663
hoodedmerganser.ca

Turn your road trip dreams into reality

with the TripTik® Travel Planner

(See map & index p. 226.)

DAYS INN & CONFERENCE CENTRE PENTICTON
(250)493-6616 **39**
▼▼ Hotel. **Address:** 152 Riverside Dr V2A 5Y4

EMPIRE MOTEL (250)493-2323 **43**
▼▼ Motel. **Address:** 3495 Skaha Lake Rd V2A 6G6

PENTICTON LAKESIDE RESORT, CONVENTION CENTRE &
CASINO (250)493-8221 **38**

 ▼▼▼ Resort Hotel. **Address:** 21
Lakeshore Dr W V2A 7M5 *(See ad
p. 234.)*

RAMADA INN & SUITES (250)492-8926 **41**
▼▼▼ Hotel. **Address:** 1050 Eckhardt Ave W V2A 2C3

WHERE TO EAT

BAD TATTOO BREWING COMPANY 250/493-8686 **48**
▼▼ Pizza. Brewpub. **Address:** 169 Estabrook Ave V2A 1G2

THE BENCH ARTISAN FOOD MARKET 250/492-2222 **47**
▼ Regional Deli Sandwiches. Quick Serve. **Address:** 368
Vancouver Ave V2A 1A5

BUY THE SEA 250/492-3474 **53**
▼ Fish & Chips. Quick Serve. **Address:** 2100 Main St V2A
5H7

HILLSIDE WINERY BISTRO 250/493-6274 **44**
▼▼▼ New Canadian. Casual Dining. **Address:** 1350
Naramata Rd V2A 8T6

HOODED MERGANSER BAR & GRILL 250/487-4663 **46**
▼▼▼ Pacific Northwest. Casual Dining. **Address:** 21
Lakeshore Dr W V2A 7M5 *(See ad p. 234.)*

LA CASA OUZERIA 250/492-9144 **51**
▼▼ Greek. Casual Dining. **Address:** 1090 Main St V2A 5E5

LACHI FINE INDIAN CUISINE 778/476-5665 **49**
▼▼ Indian. Casual Dining. **Address:** 510 Main St V2A 5C7

RICKY'S ALL DAY GRILL 250/490-0375
▼▼ American. Casual Dining. **Address:** 2111 Main St V2A
6W6

SALTY'S BEACH HOUSE 250/493-5001 **45**
▼▼ Caribbean. Casual Dining. **Address:** 1000 Lakeshore Dr
W V2A 1C1

SHADES ON MAIN FAMILY RESTAURANT 250/493-0465 **52**
▼▼ American. Casual Dining. **Address:** 1909 Main St V2A
5H5

THEO'S RESTAURANT 250/492-4019 **50**
▼▼ Greek. Casual Dining. **Address:** 687 Main St V2A 5C9

PITT MEADOWS pop. 17,736
• Hotels & Restaurants map & index p. 290
• Part of Vancouver area — see map p. 263

RAMADA INN PITT MEADOWS (604)460-9859 **73**
▼▼ Hotel. **Address:** 19267 Lougheed Hwy V3Y 2J5

PORT ALBERNI (F-9) pop. 17,743,
elev. 60m/197'
• Hotels p. 236 • Restaurants p. 236

A deepwater port and important fishing and
lumber shipping center, Port Alberni was discovered
in 1791 by Don Pedro Alberni, a Spanish sea captain. Industry began in 1860 when nine workmen arriving on the schooner *Meg Merrilees* built a sawmill
on the harbor's edge.

Port Alberni's harbor remains the city's focal
point, enhanced by the Alberni Harbour Quay at the
foot of Argyle Street. The facility includes shops, an
arts and crafts outlet and the Lady Rose Marine Services office *(see attraction listing)*. From the 1912
CPR Train Station, a logging locomotive takes visitors on a 35-minute journey along the waterfront to
McLean Mill National Historic Site *(see attraction
listing)*.

Surrounded by mountains, lakes and forests, the
city is a good base for naturalists and outdoors enthusiasts. Alpine and cross-country skiing are available nearby. Sproat Lake Provincial Park *(see
Recreation Areas Chart)* features First Nations carvings of mythological beasts. There are hundreds of
giant Douglas firs, many that date from the late 12th
century, at Cathedral Grove in MacMillan Provincial
Park, 16 kilometres (10 mi.) east.

The region's natural wonders are protected by the
Martin Mars Water Bombers based at Sproat Lake.
Designed to combat forest fires, these huge aircraft
carry 6,000 imperial gallons (7,206 U.S. gallons) of
water.

Port Alberni Visitor Centre: 2533 Port Alberni
Hwy., Port Alberni, BC, Canada V9Y 8P2. **Phone:**
(250) 724-6535.

ALBERNI VALLEY MUSEUM is at 4255 Wallace St.
in the Echo Centre building. The community museum features collections relating to First Nations as
well as community and industrial history. Feature exhibits include Nuu chah nulth basketry, folk art and
textiles.

Visitors also can see displays about the area's industrial past in logging, fishing, mining and farming.
An exhibit about the West Coast Trail tells of its
early uses as a telegraph line and a rescue trail for
shipwrecked sailors. Changing exhibitions also are
offered. **Time:** Allow 30 minutes minimum. **Hours:**
Tues.-Sat. 10-5 (also Thurs. 5-8 p.m.), Mon. noon-5,
July-Aug.; Tues.-Sat. 10-5 (also Thurs. 5-8 p.m.),
rest of year. Closed statutory holidays. **Cost:** Donations. **Phone:** (250) 723-2181.

MCLEAN MILL NATIONAL HISTORIC SITE
is 6 km (10 mi.) w. on Beaver Creek Rd.,
then 3 km (1.8 mi.) n. to 5633 Smith Rd., following
signs. The 13-hectare (32-acre) site preserves a
working 1926 steam sawmill that was operated by
the R.B. McLean family until 1965. Thirty structures
from the early days of British Columbia's forest industry include the camp where loggers and mill employees lived and worked. Interactive guided tours

and stage shows and sawmill demonstrations are given Thursday through Monday.

Time: Allow 1 hour, 30 minutes minimum. **Hours:** Grounds daily 10:30-5:15, late June-Labour Day. Sawmill demonstrations Thurs. and Sat. at 11:30 and 3:30, Fri. at 11:30 and 1, Sun. at 1, late June-Labour Day. Train departs Thurs.-Mon. at 10 (also Thurs. and Sat. at 2), late June-Labour Day. Phone ahead to confirm schedule. **Cost:** Mill and train tours $34.95; $26.50 (ages 13-18, ages 60+ and students with ID); $22 (ages 5-12); $89.95 (family of seven, maximum two adults). Mill only Thurs.-Sun. $16; $11.25 (ages 60+ and students with ID); $9.50 (ages 5-12); $40.75 (family of seven, maximum two adults). Mill only Mon.-Wed. $10; $7.50 (ages 60+ and students with ID); $6.25 (ages 5-12); $26.75 (family of seven, maximum two adults). Rates may vary; phone ahead. Reservations are recommended. **Phone:** (250) 723-1376 or (855) 866-1376. 🍴

Alberni Pacific Railway departs from the CPR Station at Argyle and Kingsway sts. Passengers embark upon a 35-minute train ride to McLean Mill National Historic Site. **Hours:** Trips depart Thurs.-Sun. at 10 (also Thurs. and Sat. at 2), late June-Labour Day. Phone ahead to confirm schedule. **Cost:** Round-trip fare (includes mill admission) $34.95; $26.50 (ages 13-18, ages 60+ and students with ID); $22 (ages 5-12); $89.95 (family of seven, maximum two adults). Rates may vary; phone ahead. **Phone:** (250) 723-2118 or (250) 723-1376.

BEST WESTERN PLUS BARCLAY HOTEL
(250)724-7171

Hotel
$110-$170

 Best Western PLUS. **AAA Benefit:** Save 10% or more every day and earn 10% bonus points!

Address: 4277 Stamp Ave V9Y 7X8 **Location:** Johnston Rd (Hwy 4), just s on Gertrude St. **Facility:** 84 units. 5 stories, interior corridors. **Pool(s):** heated outdoor. **Activities:** sauna, hot tub, exercise room. **Guest Services:** valet laundry.

SAVE 🍴 ▥ ⛉ ⌖ BIZ HS
📶 ✕ 🛗 ▤
/ SOME UNITS 🅢 ▦

THE HOSPITALITY INN
(250)723-8111

Hotel
$99-$159

Address: 3835 Redford St V9Y 3S2 **Location:** 2 mi (3.2 km) sw of jct Hwy 4 via City Centre/Port Alberni south route. **Facility:** 50 units. 2 stories (no elevator), interior corridors. **Pool(s):** heated outdoor. **Activities:** hot tub, exercise room. **Guest Services:** valet laundry. **Featured Amenity:** continental breakfast.

SAVE ECO 🍴 ▥ ⌖ ⛉ BIZ
HS 📶 ✕ 🛗 ▤ ▦
/ SOME UNITS 🅢

RIVERSIDE MOTEL
250/724-9916
Motel. **Address:** 5065 Roger St V9Y 3Y9

SOMASS MOTEL AND RV
250-724-3236
Motel. **Address:** 5279 River Rd V9Y 6Z3

WHERE TO EAT

BARE BONES FISH & CHIPS
250/720-0900
Fish & Chips. Casual Dining. **Address:** 4824 Johnston Rd V9Y 5M1

THE CLAM BUCKET RESTAURANT
250/723-1315
Seafood. Casual Dining. **Address:** 4479 Victoria Quay V9Y 5G1

LITTLE BAVARIA RESTAURANT
250/724-4242

German
Casual Dining
$12-$23

AAA Inspector Notes: Ask anyone in town about this quaint restaurant with pleasant Bavarian décor, and they'll gladly point the way to this long-established spot serving good old-fashioned German food. Schnitzel, Hungarian goulash, cabbage rolls and fondue are just some of the items you simply must try. Dinner is served nightly, however lunch is only available on weekdays. **Features:** full bar. **Reservations:** suggested. **Address:** 3035 4th Ave V9Y 2B8 **Location:** Between Argyle and Angus sts. **Parking:** street only. L   D

SMITTY'S
250/724-5022
American. Casual Dining. **Address:** 3426 3rd Ave V9Y 7M8

PORT COQUITLAM (H-11) pop. 56,342,
elev. 10m/33'
• **Attractions map p. 278**
• **Part of Vancouver area — see map p. 263**

Port Coquitlam is bordered by the Pitt and Fraser rivers to the east and south and mountains to the north. The rivers were coveted fishing grounds, and in fact, Coquitlam is derived from the Salish word *kwayhquitlum*, which means "red fish in the river," referring to the annual salmon spawning run. Before the 1800s, the area was occupied by the ancestors of the Kwayhquitlum First Nations tribe. With the arrival of the first European settlers, Port Coquitlam began its growth as a farming and logging community.

Opportunities for recreational activities abound. The 29-kilometre (18-mi.) PoCo Trail passes through wooded areas and runs alongside the Pitt River, providing plenty of opportunities to observe waterfowl and other wildlife; the Pitt Dikes can be seen from the trail. Activities such as hiking, jogging, bicycling and horseback riding also can be enjoyed.

EARLS KITCHEN + BAR
604/941-1733
American. Casual Dining. **Address:** 2850 Shaughnessy St V3C 6K5

PORT EDWARD (E-1) pop. 544

Port Edward, on the Tsimpsean Peninsula, was named after King Edward VI. The town was founded in 1908 and incorporated in 1966.

The river of mists, as the First Nations called the Skeena River, bursts through the Coast Range and empties into the Pacific Ocean near Port Edward.

The river provides the community's major commodity, fish, which is processed by local canneries. Salmon and steelhead trout, besides being economic staples, also offer a recreational challenge to anglers. Because of the area's proximity to luxuriant rain forests, mountain ranges and the river, sporting types also will find ample opportunities for canoeing, kayaking, camping, hunting and hiking.

NORTH PACIFIC CANNERY NATIONAL HISTORIC SITE is 10 km (6 mi.) s. of Hwy. 16 at 1889 Skeena Dr. For almost 100 years (1889-1980) this cannery, one of more than 200 such businesses operating along the West Coast at the industry's peak, processed and canned salmon from the Skeena River.

The site consists of 29 buildings and structures representing the factory operations and employee living quarters of a multiethnic workforce in one of the formative industries of British Columbia. The village includes the main cannery, reduction plant, staff housing and mess house. Artifacts of the fishing industry, such as boats, tools and machinery original to the shops as well as some of the workers' personal items are displayed throughout the complex. Guided tours feature a working canning line, stories of cannery life, and a walk along the riverfront boardwalk.

Time: Allow 1 hour minimum. **Hours:** Daily 9:30-5, May-June and in Sept.; Tues.-Sun. 9:30-5, July-Aug. Phone ahead to arrange tours. **Cost:** $11.43; $9.52 (ages 65+); $7.62 (ages 6-18); $23.81 (family of seven, maximum two adults). **Phone:** (250) 628-3538. [GT] [ᵀᵀ]

PORT HARDY pop. 4,008

AIRPORT INN	250/949-9434
▼ Hotel. **Address:** 4030 Byng Rd V0N 2P0	

GLEN LYON INN	(250)949-7115
▼▼ Hotel. **Address:** 6435 Hardy Bay Rd V0N 2P0	

QUARTERDECK INN & MARINA	(250)902-0455
▼▼ Hotel. **Address:** 6555 Hardy Bay Rd V0N 2P0	

WHERE TO EAT

MARKET STREET CAFE	250/949-8110
▼ Breakfast Sandwiches. Quick Serve. **Address:** 7030 Market St V0N 2P0	

PORT MCNEILL (H-2) pop. 2,505,
elev. 15m/49'

In the scenic, untamed wilderness of northern Vancouver Island, Port McNeill occupies a rich lumber and fishing region popular with adventurous hikers, campers, spelunkers, fishermen and other sports enthusiasts.

Of interest to rock collectors and geologists are several nearby natural phenomena, including the Vanishing River, which plunges underground into a maze of caves and tunnels; the Devil's Bath, a huge

rock bowl continuously filled by an underground spring; and the Eternal Fountain, which gushes from a rock crevice and then disappears underground again. All are reached by logging roads that are accessible only in summer.

An inter-island ferry operates a shuttle service between Port McNeill, Sointula and Alert Bay (see place listing p. 178).

Port McNeill Visitor Centre: 1594 Beach Dr., P.O. Box 129, Port McNeill, BC, Canada V0N 2R0. **Phone:** (250) 956-3131 or (888) 956-3131.

BLACK BEAR RESORT	250/956-4900
▼▼ Motel. **Address:** 1812 Campbell Way V0N 2R0	

HAIDA-WAY MOTOR INN	250/956-3373
▼ Motel. **Address:** 1817 Campbell Way V0N 2R0	

WHERE TO EAT

NORTHERN LIGHTS RESTAURANT	250/956-3263
▼▼ Canadian. Casual Dining. **Address:** 1817 Campbell Way V0N 2R0	

PORT MOODY (H-11) pop. 32,975,
elev. 10m/33'
• **Attractions map p. 278**
• **Part of Vancouver area — see map p. 263**

Port Moody once was the terminus of the Canadian Pacific Railway—the first train from Montréal to the Pacific arrived July 4, 1886. A year later the line was extended 20 kilometres (12 mi.) west to Vancouver. Rocky Point Park on Burrard Inlet offers picnicking, swimming, boating and nature trails.

POUCE COUPE (D-6) pop. 738,
elev. 652m/2,139'

The village of Pouce Coupe is referred to as the gateway to Peace country because it is one of the first communities travelers will see when entering British Columbia from Alberta.

POWELL RIVER (F-10) pop. 13,165,
elev. 55m/180'
• **Hotels p. 238** • **Restaurants p. 238**

Rich forests and abundant water brought the founders of the Powell River Company to the area in the early 1900s. The townsite is one of the oldest company-built communities in western Canada.

Separated from the mainland by Jervis Inlet, the area offers year-round recreation including freshwater and saltwater fishing, scuba diving, boating, kayaking, hiking and bicycling. The Powell Forest Canoe Route connects eight lakes around the Upper Sunshine Coast region with camping areas along the scenic circuit.

A panorama of the Strait of Malaspina unfolds from the Mount Valentine viewpoint, reached by a rock stairway in the heart of town. Bald eagles can be observed at any time of year, especially in late fall when they are attracted by salmon spawning in channels and small streams. Also of interest are Sliammon Fish Hatchery and Powell River Salmon Society Spawning Channel.

Guided 2-hour tours of the Catalyst Paper Mill are offered through the visitor center. Part of the tour is outdoors; appropriate dress and low-heeled, closed footwear are advised. For information and reservations phone (604) 485-4701 or (877) 817-8669.

Powell River Visitor Centre: 4760 Joyce Ave., Powell River, BC, Canada V8A 3B6. **Phone:** (604) 485-4701 or (877) 817-8669.

POWELL RIVER TOWN CENTRE HOTEL   604/485-3000
◆◆ Hotel. **Address:** 4660 Joyce Ave V8A 3B6

WHERE TO EAT

COSTA DEL SOL LATIN CUISINE   604/414-7463
◆◆ Latin American. Casual Dining. **Address:** 4578 Marine Ave V8A 2K6

THE SHINGLEMILL PUB & BISTRO   604/483-2001
◆◆ Canadian. Casual Dining. **Address:** 6233 Powell Pl V8A 4S6

PRINCE GEORGE (E-4) pop. 71,974, elev. 691m/2,267'

At the confluence of the Nechako and Fraser rivers, the area was visited in 1793 by Alexander Mackenzie in his trek down the Fraser to the Pacific. In 1807 it became the site for Simon Fraser's North West Co. fort. Fraser's canoe brigades soon gave way to paddlewheelers and then railroads, which converged on this important northern crossroads. Prince George remains a major transportation and trade center, a role enhanced by a thriving forest industry.

Despite its urban transformation, the city has retained much of its natural heritage in its 116 parks. Of interest are Fort George Park, which contains a replica of Fraser's trading post; Connaught Park's manicured gardens and scenic views; and Cottonwood Island Park, which includes the Prince George Railway & Forestry Museum and its collection of railroad artifacts and cars.

Prince George blends its pastoral features with such cultural centers as Studio 2880 and Vanier Hall. Studio 2880, home to six craft guilds, is the site of craft markets and special events throughout the year. Concerts by the Prince George Symphony and by visiting performers are held in Vanier Hall.

These cultural amenities coexist with the more rugged recreational opportunities available in the wilderness that surrounds the city. Nearby lakes, rivers and mountains present an array of activities ranging from rugged back-country hikes and fishing to skiing and ice skating.

Prince George Visitor Centre: 1300 First Ave., Suite 201, Prince George, BC, Canada V2L 2Y3. **Phone:** (250) 562-3700 or (800) 668-7646.

[SAVE] **THE EXPLORATION PLACE MUSEUM & SCIENCE CENTRE** is at the end of 20th Ave. at 333 Becott Pl. in Fort George Park. Fort George's history and development are explored through such topics as transportation, lumber and the indigenous culture. The Children's Gallery houses life-size dinosaur sculptures, skeletons and a dig pit. The Explorations Gallery features live animals and interactive computers. A steam locomotive ride is offered on weekends and holidays.

Time: Allow 1 hour minimum. **Hours:** Daily 9-5. Closed Jan. 1, Christmas and day after Christmas. **Cost:** Museum $11; $9 (ages 65+ and students with ID); $8 (ages 3-12); $25 (family, two adults and up to four children ages 0-18). **Phone:** (250) 562-1612 or (866) 562-1612.

HUBLE HOMESTEAD HISTORIC SITE is 38 km (24 mi.) n. on Hwy. 97, then 6 km (4 mi.) e. on Mitchell Rd. The site features several replicas of historic buildings as well as the original home of Al and Annie Huble. Along with his business partner Ed Seebach, Huble was instrumental in establishing a community within the Giscome Portage area. The homestead also offers weekend special events that feature demonstrations, live entertainment, games and contests.

Time: Allow 1 hour minimum. **Hours:** Daily 10-5, Victoria Day-Labour Day; Sat.-Sun. 10-5, day after Labour Day-Thanksgiving. Phone ahead to confirm schedule. **Cost:** $4.76; $2.86 (children and ages 65+); $9.52 (family). **Phone:** (250) 564-7033.
[GT] [♨] [🍴]

PRINCE GEORGE RAILWAY & FORESTRY MUSEUM is at 850 River Rd. The museum houses one of the largest collection of railway-related artifacts in British Columbia. Items, circa 1899-1960s, include a wooden snow plow, locomotives, box cars and cabooses.

Time: Allow 1 hour minimum. **Hours:** Daily 10-5, Victoria Day weekend-Labour Day weekend; daily 11-8, Dec. 18-23; 11-6 on Christmas Eve; Tues.-Sat. 11-4, rest of year. Closed Nov. 11. Phone ahead to confirm schedule. **Cost:** $8; $7 (ages 13-17, students with ID and senior citizens); $5 (ages 3-12). **Phone:** (250) 563-7351. [🛤]

BON VOYAGE INN   250/964-2333
◆ Motel. **Address:** 4222 Hwy 16 W V2N 5N7

CARMEL INN   250/564-6339
◆◆ Motel. **Address:** 1502 Hwy 97 S V2L 5L9

FOUR POINTS BY SHERATON PRINCE GEORGE
(250)564-7100

Hotel
$114-$160

FOUR POINTS BY SHERATON   **AAA Benefit:** Members save up to 15%, plus Starwood Preferred Guest® benefits!

Address: 1790 Hwy 97 S V2L 5L3 **Location:** Hwy 97 exit Spruce northbound; exit City Center southbound via Queensway. **Facility:** 74 units. 3 stories, interior corridors. **Parking:** winter plug-ins. **Pool(s):** heated indoor. **Activities:** hot tub, exercise room. **Guest Services:** valet laundry.

/ SOME UNITS

PRESTIGE TREASURE COVE PRINCE GEORGE
(250)614-9111

Hotel. **Address:** 2005 Hwy 97 S V2N 7A3

RAMADA PRINCE GEORGE
(250)563-0055

Hotel. **Address:** 444 George St V2L 1R6

SANDMAN SIGNATURE HOTEL & SUITES PRINCE GEORGE
250/645-7263

Hotel. **Address:** 2990 Recreation Place Dr V2N 0B2

WHERE TO EAT

CIMO MEDITERRANEAN GRILL
250/564-7975

Italian. Casual Dining. **Address:** 601 Victoria St V2L 2K3

THE COPPER PIG BBQ HOUSE
250/596-2006

Barbecue. Casual Dining. **Address:** 363 George St V2L 1R4

EARLS KITCHEN + BAR
250/562-1527

American. Casual Dining. **Address:** 1440 E Central St V2M 3C1

MOXIE'S CLASSIC GRILL
250/564-4700

American. Casual Dining. **Address:** 1804 E Central St V2M 3C3

NORTH 54
250/564-5400

American. Fine Dining. **Address:** 1493 3rd Ave V2L 3S1

THE SALTED CRACKER
250/562-1110

Soup Sandwiches. Quick Serve. **Address:** 1485 10th Ave V2L 2L2

THE TWISTED CORK RESTAURANT
250/561-5550

International. Casual Dining. **Address:** 1157 5th Ave V2L 3L1

WHITE GOOSE BISTRO
250/561-1002

American. Casual Dining. **Address:** 1205 3rd Ave V2L 1T6

PRINCE RUPERT (E-1) pop. 12,508,
elev. 50m/164'
• Restaurants p. 240

At the turn of the 20th century Prince Rupert existed only in the imagination of Charles Hays, manager of the Grand Trunk Pacific Railway. Hays died with the sinking of the SS *Titanic,* but the Grand Trunk Pacific Railway carried out his intention to build a port to rival Vancouver on this rugged, uninhabited island bordered by a natural harbor. The new site was expected to be successful because it was closer to the Far East than Vancouver and would provide an outlet for the untapped resources of Canada's far north.

Prince Rupert has fulfilled that potential and is now one of Canada's major seaports. It is the southernmost port of the Alaska Ferry System, the northern terminus of the British Columbia Ferry Corp. and the western terminus of the Canadian National Railway. Cruise ships en route to coastal glaciers and fjords also stop at Prince Rupert's harbor, said to be the world's third largest natural ice-free deep-sea harbor.

Before the coming of the railroad the northern coast was home to the Tsimpsean and Haida, cultures whose ancestors inhabited the area for almost 5,000 years. Both are renowned for their stylized artworks, the most familiar of which are totem poles. Many of these graceful monuments are shown in such city parks as Service Park, the colorful terraced Sunken Gardens, and Roosevelt Park with its sweeping views of the Pacific.

On the waterfront, Kwinitsa Railway Station is a relic of the modern era. Restored and moved from its original location, Kwinitsa is one of the last of the Grand Trunk Pacific Railway stations; inside are exhibits about the railroad's history.

Just beyond the city, climate and soil have stunted and twisted lodgepole pines into a natural bonsai garden at Oliver Lake Provincial Park. Another interesting phenomenon is Butze Rapids, a series of reversing rapids between Wainwright and Morse basins that rival the reversing falls at Saint John, New Brunswick. A dramatic view of the rapids occurs during a falling tide and can be seen from a viewing point on Hwy. 16, which offers scenic driving east to Terrace *(see place listing p. 258).*

Guided tours are offered during the summer by Farwest Bus Lines Ltd., 225 Second Ave. W. Trans-Provincial Airlines and Northcoast Air Services offer flight tours of the region.

Prince Rupert Visitor Centre: 200-215 Cowbay Rd. (Atlin Terminal), Prince Rupert, BC, Canada V8J 1A2. **Phone:** (250) 624-5637 or (800) 667-1994.

Self-guiding tours: A walking tour that includes sunken gardens, the harbor, sections of the downtown area and various attractions is detailed on maps and brochures available from the visitor bureau at the Museum of Northern British Columbia *(see attraction listing).*

INN ON THE HARBOUR
250/624-9107

Hotel. **Address:** 720 1st Ave W V8J 3V6

WHERE TO EAT

DOLLY'S FISH MARKET   250/624-6090
♦♦ ♦♦ Seafood. Casual Dining. **Address:** 7 Cow Bay Rd V8J 1A4

OPA SUSHI   250/627-4560
♦♦ ♦♦ Japanese Sushi. Casual Dining. **Address:** 34 Cow Bay Rd V8J 1A5

PRINCETON (C-8) pop. 2,724

Named "Vermilion Forks" by fur traders in the early 1800s, Princeton developed as a ranching and mining outpost in the foothills of the Cascade Mountains. In 1860 the town was renamed to honor a visit by the Prince of Wales. Revitalized downtown storefronts boast murals and facades in keeping with Princeton's Western heritage.

Princeton & District Chamber of Commerce: 105 Hwy. 3E, P.O. Box 540, Princeton, BC, Canada V0X 1W0. **Phone:** (250) 295-3103.

Self-guiding tours: Maps detailing walking tours are available from the chamber of commerce.

PRINCETON & DISTRICT MUSEUM AND ARCHIVES is at 167 Vermilion Ave. A tunnel complete with a replica dinosaur fossil welcomes visitors into the museum and provides a thematic preview. The Pollard Collection of fossils and minerals, considered one of the best in British Columbia, offers eye-catching displays and a glow-in-the-dark section. Additional exhibits include indigenous art and basketry as well as a hand-carved canoe, 1880s cabin and other artifacts from the pioneer era.

Time: Allow 1 hour minimum. **Hours:** Daily 10-6, July-Aug.; by appointment rest of year. Phone ahead to confirm schedule. **Cost:** Donations. Cash only. **Phone:** (250) 295-7588.

CANADAS BEST VALUE PRINCETON INN & SUITES
     250/295-3537

Motel
Rates not provided

Address: 169 Hwy 3 V0X 1W0 **Location:** Hwy 3, just n on Vermilion Ave. **Facility:** 45 units, some kitchens. 2 stories (no elevator), exterior corridors. **Pool(s):** heated outdoor. **Activities:** sauna, hot tub. **Featured Amenity:** continental breakfast.

WHERE TO EAT

COWBOY COFFEE   250/295-3431
♦♦ Coffee/Tea Sandwiches. Quick Serve. **Address:** 255 Vermilion Ave V0X 1W0

QUADRA ISLAND (E-11)

Totem poles are found within the Cape Mudge Reserve on Quadra Island, part of the Gulf Islands group, which is reached by a 15-minute ferry ride from Campbell River *(see place listing p. 182)*.

TAKU RESORT & MARINA   250/285-3031
♦♦ ♦♦ Motel. **Address:** 616 Taku Rd V0P 1H0

TSA-KWA-LUTEN LODGE   (250)285-2042
♦♦ ♦♦ Hotel. **Address:** 1 Lighthouse Rd V0P 1N0

WHERE TO EAT

HAMA ELAS DINING ROOM   250/285-2042
♦♦♦ ♦♦♦ Pacific Northwest. Casual Dining. **Address:** 1 Lighthouse Rd V0P 1N0

QUALICUM BEACH (G-10) pop. 8,687, elev. 9m/30'

A popular resort and arts community, Qualicum Beach is known for its white sand beaches. Nearby Little Qualicum Falls *(see Recreation Areas Chart)*, Englishman River Falls *(see Recreation Areas Chart)* and Horne Lake Caves provincial parks also present abundant recreational opportunities. Salmon and trout are raised at fish hatcheries on the Big and Little Qualicum rivers.

Qualicum Beach Visitor Information Centre: 2711 W. Island Hwy., Qualicum Beach, BC, Canada V9K 2C4. **Phone:** (250) 752-9532.

⬥GEM HORNE LAKE CAVES is 15 km (9 mi.) n. on Hwy. 19 to exit 75 (Horne Lake Rd.), then 14 km (9 mi.) w. on a gravel rd., following signs to the parking lot. A part of the Horne Lake Caves Provincial Park, the cave system is considered to be one of the best in Canada. Tours are guided and highlights include crystal formations, ancient fossils and a waterfall.

The 1.5-hour Main Cave Experience teaches about the geology and history of the caves. The interpretive tour starts with a 25-minute walk to the entrance. Once inside the cave, visitors explore the easy passages; no crawling or maneuvering in tight spaces is necessary.

Other 3-, 4-, and 5-hour tours, some of which include climbing and rappeling, are offered. Self-guiding exploration is available in Horne Lake Main and Lower caves year-round. A helmet and two sources of light are required. Helmets may be rented for $5 each during the summer only.

Note: The caves are mostly undeveloped and do not provide lighting. Floors are rocky and uneven; children ages 0-4 are not permitted on the tour and visitors with mobility issues could encounter difficulty walking. Warm clothing and comfortable boots or shoes are highly recommended, as the caves remain cool even in hot weather. Cameras are permitted.

Time: Allow 1 hour, 30 minutes minimum. **Hours:** Tours require a minimum of three people. Main Cave Experience is given on a first-come, first-served basis daily at 10:30, 11:30, 12:30, 2:30 and 5, late June-early Sept.; at 10:30, 12:30, 2:30 and 4:30, May 1-late June; at 10 and 2 in Apr. Schedule and age limits vary for other tours; phone ahead. Closed Jan. 1 and Christmas. **Cost:** Main Cave Experience $24 (ages 5+). Other tours $39-$165 (various age restrictions apply). Phone ahead to confirm rates. **Phone:** (250) 248-7829.

MILNER GARDENS AND WOODLAND, 2179 W. Island Hwy., comprises 24 hectares (60 acres) of Douglas fir woodland and 4 hectares (10 acres) of garden surrounding a gabled heritage house. Visitors may view the dining, sitting and drawing rooms as well as the library. Historical photos, artifacts and keepsakes of visits by members of the Royal family also are displayed.

Time: Allow 1 hour minimum. **Hours:** Daily 10-4:30, Apr. 27-Sept. 4; Thurs.-Sun. 10-4:30, Mar. 30-Apr. 23 and Sept. 7-Oct. 8; Sun. 11-3, Feb.-Mar. Phone ahead to confirm schedule. **Cost:** Apr. 27-Sept. 4, $10.48; $6.19 (ages 13-18); free (ages 0-12 with adult). Admission Mar. 30-Apr. 23 and Sept. 7-Oct. 8, $7.86; $4.05 (ages 13-18); free (ages 0-12 with an adult). Admission Feb.-Mar. $5; $3.10 (ages 13-18); free (ages 0-12 with adult). **Phone:** (250) 752-6153.

QUALICUM BEACH INN   (250)752-6914
▼▼▼▼ Hotel. **Address:** 2690 Island Hwy W V9K 1G8

WHERE TO EAT

CVIEW   250/752-6914
▼▼▼ American. Fine Dining. **Address:** 2690 Island Hwy W V9K 1G8

GARY'S BISTRO   250/752-5800
▼▼ American. Casual Dining. **Address:** 115 W Second Ave V9K 1S7

THE SHADY REST WATERFRONT PUB RESTAURANT
                                       250/752-9111
▼▼ American. Casual Dining. **Address:** 3109 Island Hwy W V9K 2C5

QUESNEL (F-5) pop. 10,007, elev. 545m/1,788'

Discovery of gold in the surrounding area in the 1860s contributed to Quesnel's growth. The city is the center of a popular hunting and fishing region at the junction of the Fraser and Quesnel rivers. Lumber, pulp and plywood manufacturing, tourism, cattle ranching and mining are the city's primary sources of income.

East of the city on Hwy. 26 is a historic remnant of the gold rush days, Barkerville Historic Town *(see place listing p. 178)*, a restored boomtown of that era. Just beyond Barkerville is Bowron Lake Provincial Park *(see Recreation Areas Chart)*, which has a 116-kilometre (72-mi.) canoe circuit of interconnecting lakes. Alpine skiing is available nearby.

Quesnel Visitor Centre: 703 Carson Ave., Quesnel, BC, Canada V2J 2B6. **Phone:** (250) 992-8716 or (800) 992-4922.

BEST WESTERN PLUS TOWER INN   (250)992-2201

Hotel
$118-$138

Best Western PLUS. **AAA Benefit:** Save 10% or more every day and earn 10% bonus points!

Address: 500 Reid St V2J 2M9 **Location:** Hwy 97, just e on Shepherd Ave; downtown. **Facility:** 63 units. 4 stories, interior corridors. **Parking:** winter plug-ins. **Activities:** exercise room. **Guest Services:** valet laundry.

[SAVE] [▯▯] [▯] [▯] [BIZ] [HS] [📶]
[✕] [🛢] [▯] /SOME UNITS [🐕]

QUALITY INN & SUITES   (250)992-7247

Hotel
$89-$189

Address: 753 Front St V2J 2L2 **Location:** Hwy 97, 0.6 mi (1 km) n of Carson Ave. **Facility:** 83 units, some efficiencies and kitchens. 2 stories (no elevator), interior corridors. **Parking:** winter plug-ins. **Activities:** hot tub, picnic facilities, exercise room. **Guest Services:** coin laundry. **Featured Amenity:** full hot breakfast.

[SAVE] [BIZ] [📶] [✕] [🛢] [▯] [▯]
/SOME UNITS [🐕] [HS]

TRAVELODGE QUESNEL   (250)992-7071

Motel
$80

Address: 524 Front St V2J 2K6 **Location:** Hwy 97, 0.5 mi (0.8 km) n of Carson Ave. **Facility:** 34 units, some efficiencies and kitchens. 2 stories (no elevator), exterior corridors. **Parking:** winter plug-ins. **Pool(s):** heated indoor. **Activities:** sauna. **Guest Services:** coin laundry. **Featured Amenity:** continental breakfast.

[SAVE] [ECO] [▯▯] [🛒] [BIZ] [📶] [🛢]
[▯] /SOME UNITS [🐕] [HS]

WHERE TO EAT

BLISS   250/992-7066
▼ Indian. Quick Serve. **Address:** 462B Anderson Dr V2J 1G2

GRANVILLE'S COFFEE   250/992-3667
▼ Breakfast Sandwiches. Quick Serve. **Address:** 383 Reid St V2J 2M5

SAVALAS STEAK HOUSE   778/414-9050
▼▼ International. Casual Dining. **Address:** 240 Reid St V2J 2M2

RADIUM HOT SPRINGS (B-11) pop. 777, elev. 805m/2,641'
• Hotels p. 242 • Restaurants p. 242

Renowned for its mineral hot springs *(see Kootenay National Park p. 210 and Recreation Areas Chart)*, the Village of Radium Hot Springs also is a popular departure point for scenic hikes and white-water river excursions. More than 10 golf courses are in the vicinity.

BEST WESTERN PLUS PRESTIGE INN RADIUM HOT SPRINGS
(250)347-2300

Hotel
$129-$249

 Best Western PLUS **AAA Benefit:** Save 10% or more every day and earn 10% bonus points!

Address: 7493 Main St W V0A 1M0 **Location:** Jct Hwy 93 and 95. **Facility:** 87 units, some efficiencies and kitchens. 3 stories, interior corridors. **Parking:** winter plug-ins. **Pool(s):** heated indoor. **Activities:** hot tub, exercise room. **Guest Services:** coin laundry.

BIGHORN MEADOWS RESORT   (250)347-2323
Condominium. **Address:** 10 Bighorn Blvd V0A 1M0

BIGHORN MOTEL
250/347-9111

Motel
$70-$80

Address: 4881 St. Mary's St E V0A 1M0 **Location:** Jct Hwy 93 and 95, just s on Main St W, just w. **Facility:** 20 units, some efficiencies. 1 story, exterior corridors. **Parking:** winter plug-ins. **Activities:** picnic facilities.

CEDAR MOTEL   (250)347-9463
Motel. **Address:** 7593 Main St W V0A 1M0

LIDO MOTEL   (250)347-9533
Motel. **Address:** 4876 McKay St V0A 1M0

WHERE TO EAT

BACK COUNTRY JACKS   250/347-0097
American. Casual Dining. **Address:** 7555 W Main St V0A 1M0

THE OLD SALZBURG RESTAURANT
250/347-6553

Austrian
Casual Dining
$17-$31

AAA Inspector Notes: This Alpine-style restaurant boasts a warm, mountain-village ambience. With traditional Austrian and European influences, the menu lists hearty portions of schnitzel, spaetzle, pasta, chicken and steak. A few prime window seats have views of the surrounding valley and mountain ranges. It's closed for lunch in the off-season. **Features:** full bar, patio dining. **Reservations:** suggested, in summer. **Address:** 4943 Hwy 93 V0A 1M0 **Location:** Hwy 93 and 95, just w; center.

AAA Vacations® packages ...

exciting itineraries

and exclusive values

REVELSTOKE (A-10) pop. 7,139, elev. 440m/1,433'

Revelstoke is located on the Trans-Canada Highway between Rogers and Eagle passes—some of the world's most scenic mountain roads. Downhill skiing is available near the city.

Revelstoke Visitor Centre: 301 Victoria Rd. W., P.O. Box 490, Revelstoke, BC, Canada V0E 2S0. **Phone:** (250) 837-5345 or (800) 487-1493.

CRAZY CREEK HOT POOLS is 38 km (24 mi.) w. on Hwy. 1. Four pools—three geothermal heated pools (temperatures 99, 102 and 104 F) and a cold plunge pool—are part of Crazy Creek Resort. In addition to taking a dip, visitors can use the pedestrian overpass to access the suspension bridge and boardwalks to view the two-stage waterfall, visit the high mountain patio and hike the gorge trail above the waterfall.

Note: When entering from the resort side of property, the trail over the pedestrian overpass to the suspension bridge and high mountain patio is stair free. **Hours:** Pools open daily 11-8:45, mid-June to early Sept.; 9-8:45, rest of year. Boardwalk, bridge and waterfalls open daily 11-4:30, mid-Apr. to mid-Oct. **Cost:** Pools *or* boardwalk, bridge and waterfalls $9.50; $5.70 (ages 3-16). All-day pool pass $16; $9.55 (ages 3-16). **Phone:** (250) 836-4097 or (855) 836-4097.

 ENCHANTED FOREST is 32 km (20 mi.) w. on Hwy. 1 to 7060 Trans-Canada Hwy. More than 350 handmade figurines include Old World fairy folk, dragons and dungeons in a natural forest setting with giant cedars, a stump house, a fish pond and a towering tree house that is reputedly one of the province's tallest. Tree houses, swamp boat rides and a wetland boardwalk including lush vegetation, beaver dams and spawning salmon beds also are offered.

Hours: Daily 8-8, mid-June through Aug. 31; 9-5, May 1 to mid-June and Sept. 1 to mid-Oct. **Cost:** $11; $8.50 (ages 3-15). **Phone:** (250) 837-9477 or (866) 944-9744.

REVELSTOKE RAILWAY MUSEUM is at 719 Track St. W. off Victoria Rd. The building of the Canadian Pacific Railway is traced with artifacts, photographs and original equipment. One of the company's largest steam locomotives is displayed beside a restored 1929 solarium car inside the museum, while the yard features such rolling stock as a caboose, a snow plow and a flange car. A diesel cabin simulator allows visitors to experience the feeling of driving a train.

Time: Allow 30 minutes minimum. **Hours:** Daily 9-5, May 1 to mid-Oct.; Wed.-Sat. 11-4, rest of year. Closed Jan. 1, Christmas Eve, Christmas and some winter days. Phone ahead to confirm schedule. **Cost:** $9.52; $7.62 (ages 60+ and students with ID); $4.76 (ages 8-16); $1.90 (ages 4-7); $20.95 (family). **Phone:** (250) 837-6060 or (877) 837-6060.

BEST WESTERN PLUS REVELSTOKE   (250)837-2043

Hotel
$199-$299

 Best Western PLUS.   **AAA Benefit:** Save 10% or more every day and earn 10% bonus points!

Address: 1925 Laforme Blvd V0E 2S0 **Location:** Trans-Canada Hwy 1, just n. **Facility:** 87 units. 4 stories, interior corridors. **Parking:** winter plug-ins. **Amenities:** safes. **Pool(s):** heated outdoor. **Activities:** hot tub, exercise room, massage. **Guest Services:** complimentary laundry.

/ SOME UNITS

COAST HILLCREST HOTEL   (250)837-3322

Hotel
$129-$249

Address: 2100 Oak Dr V0E 2S0 **Location:** 2.7 mi (4.3 km) e on Trans-Canada Hwy 1, 0.6 mi (1 km) sw. **Facility:** 75 units. 3 stories, interior corridors. **Terms:** 3 day cancellation notice-fee imposed. **Amenities:** safes. **Dining:** Begbie Room, see separate listing. **Activities:** sauna, hot tub, steamroom, trails, exercise room, spa. **Guest Services:** valet laundry, area transportation.

 / SOME UNITS

COAST hillcrest hotel

Lodge style Lobby.
Rock Fireplace.
Patio dining with
Mountain Views.
Repose Day Spa.
Free Wi-Fi.

SWISS CHALET MOTEL   250/837-4650
Motel. **Address:** 1101 W Victoria Rd V0E 2S0

WHERE TO EAT

BEGBIE ROOM   250/837-3322
American. Casual Dining. **Address:** 2100 Oak Dr V0E 2S0

THE NOMAD FOOD CO.   250/837-4211
Chicken Sandwiches. Quick Serve. **Address:** 1601 Victoria Rd W V0E 3K0

WOOLSEY CREEK BISTRO   250/837-5500
New Canadian. Casual Dining. **Address:** 604 2nd St W V0E 2S0

RICHMOND (H-11) pop. 190,473, elev. 5m/16'

• **Hotels p. 245** • **Restaurants p. 247**
• **Attractions map p. 278**
• **Hotels & Restaurants map & index p. 290**
• **Part of Vancouver area — see map p. 263**

On an island at the mouth of the Fraser River, Richmond first was settled in 1879. The town grew and prospered with its farming, fishing and waterborne trade industries. Today, Richmond's major industries include aviation, berry farming, high technology and manufacturing.

Golden Village, in central Richmond, affords visitors the opportunity to experience the Asian culture through shopping, dining and festivals.

The Richmond Nature Park, 44 hectares (109 acres) at 11851 Westminster Hwy., has a bird pond, beehive displays, mounted birds, a quaking bog and plants identified by markers. A naturalist conducts hour-long tours of the park on Sunday.

Steveston, tucked away in Richmond's southwest corner, is a bit of a contradiction. It has a historic past, but it's also a residential neighborhood. Commercial fishing was once this area's lifeblood, but today you're just as likely to sample fish that's battered and sharing a plate with a pile of fries at a local restaurant as you are seeing one freshly caught. And while weather-beaten buildings hint at a hardscrabble past, there's also a Starbucks.

Sitting at the confluence of two major bodies of water—the Strait of Georgia and the Fraser River—Steveston's first flush of success was as a salmon canning center. The Fraser's south arm was a fertile fishing ground, and a settlement grew up around this favored coastal location in the 1880s. Salmon turned Steveston into a classic turn-of-the-20th-century boom town: It became one of the busiest fishing ports in the world, with windjammers loading up canned salmon bound for far-flung markets.

The town was boisterous with a capital "B." Saloons and gambling dens thrived, and on Saturday nights crowds of sailors, indigenous peoples and European, Chinese and Japanese immigrants—most of them fishermen and cannery workers—thronged the boardwalks. In the years leading up to World War I eager boosters dubbed Steveston "Salmonopolis," but the boom was not to last. The internment during World War II of Japanese-Canadian citizens, who made up a large part of the town's population, struck a serious blow. The canning industry slowly declined, finally coming to an end by the early 1990s. You can learn more about this aspect of town history at the Gulf of Georgia Cannery National Historic Site *(see attraction listing).*

Steveston, still an active fishing port that to a large degree has retained its salty character, makes a good day trip. From downtown Vancouver it's about a 30-minute drive. Take Granville Street south to Hwy. 99 (via 70th Avenue W.), then take Hwy. 99 south to exit 32 (Steveston Highway) and turn right (west). Summer, when the weather is usually sunny and a couple of annual festivals are on tap, is the time to go; during the chilly, rainy winter months many restaurants and attractions reduce their hours.

So what do you do? For starters, just explore where your feet take you. Follow the planked wooden boardwalk along the shore of Cannery Channel; interpretive panels provide background about Steveston's fishing and canning past. Have your picture taken sitting on a bench in the garden outside the Prickly Pear Garden Centre (on No. 1 Road, just off Bayview Street). In addition to lovely hanging flower baskets, the large, emerald-green leaves of a banana tree will have you scratching

(See map & index p. 290.)

your head and reminding yourself that yes, you are in Canada.

Tramp around Garry Point Park (at the end of Moncton Street). Fronting the Strait of Georgia, it's basically undeveloped and has a wild and windswept look. Sunsets over the water can be showstoppers here, and the flat, open spaces bring out kite flyers. Stop at the Fisherman's Memorial, which takes the shape of a giant net-mending needle and is inscribed with a poem, "Spawning Cycle":

> These spring days grow longer
>
> Until the dark comes closing
>
> What tides disclose they again conceal
>
> We're out to fish until again
>
> It's time to be ashore
>
> Because the geese go by
>
> I'll be here with you
>
> 'Till it's time to be alone: the way out,
>
> The way back, and all ways this one.

Stroll the boardwalk along bustling Fisherman's Wharf, where seiners, trawlers and other vessels cruise in and out of the harbor. Depending on the season, some of the boats docked along the boardwalk sell fresh catches of salmon, cod, octopus and prawns.

The Steveston Museum, 3811 Moncton St., resembles a one-room country schoolhouse with its red-and-yellow clapboard exterior and steep gabled roof. This former Northern Bank building has a general store layout with displays of late 19th-century furniture and office equipment. It's also a working post office. Phone (604) 271-6868.

For lunch, it really has to be fish and chips. And there's a choice: Dave's Fish & Chips (3460 Moncton St.) or Pajo's (two locations—on the wharf at the corner of Bayview Street and 3rd Avenue, and a takeout stand in the large administrative building at Garry Point Park). Although the menus at both include such non-fishy items as burgers, do the right thing and order fish and chips (aficionados will go for the halibut over cod or salmon). Mushy peas are a veddy British accompaniment.

The big event of the year is the Steveston Salmon Festival, held on July 1 in conjunction with Canada Day. Floats, marching bands, vintage vehicles and local community groups are part of a big parade that begins at 10 a.m. There's a craft fair, an art show, a Japanese cultural show, carnival rides and a midway, martial arts demonstrations and a youth festival. The main attraction, though, is a salmon barbecue; hundreds of fillets are grilled to succulent perfection over open fire pits.

Summer in Steveston can get crowded, especially on nice sunny weekends. But there are several free parking lots in town, plenty of parking at Garry Point Park, and street parking if you're lucky enough to snag a space.

Tourism Richmond: 3811 Moncton St., Richmond, BC, Canada V7E 3A7. **Phone:** (604) 271-8280 or (877) 247-0777.

GULF OF GEORGIA CANNERY NATIONAL HISTORIC SITE is at 12138 Fourth Ave. in Steveston Village. The 1894 salmon cannery on the waterfront of a historic fishing village has been restored to serve as an interpretive center for Canada's West Coast fishing industry. During its heyday, this cannery earned the title of the Monster Cannery, a reference to its size in comparison to about 15 other canneries on Steveston's Cannery Row.

Interactive exhibits of the herring reduction plant and replicated 1930s-50s canning line, a children's activity area, a harbor viewing deck and a 15-minute film about the West Coast fishing industry are offered year-round. The full cannery experience is offered May through October and includes guided tours, salmon tastings and canning machine demonstrations.

Hours: Daily 10-5. Closed Jan. 1, Nov. 11 and Dec. 24-26. **Cost:** Free in 2017 to celebrate Canada's 150th anniversary of Confederation. Otherwise admission is May-Sept. $9.71; $8.52 (ages 65+); $6 (ages 6-16); $25.52 (family, up to seven people with maximum two adults). Rest of year $7.43; $6.24 (ages 65+); $3.71 (ages 6-16); $18.67 (family, up to seven people, maximum two adults). **Phone:** (604) 664-9009.

STEVESTON SEABREEZE ADVENTURES is at 12551 #1 Rd., Bldg. 43. A narrated whale-watching tour departs from historic Steveston village and transits the Fraser River Delta, Strait of Georgia and Gulf Islands. Hydrophones are used to listen to the whales vocalizing. The scenic trip affords passengers an opportunity to view other marine animals and wildlife.

Time: Allow 3 hours minimum. **Hours:** Departures daily at 9 and 2, mid-June to early Sept.; at noon, early Apr. to mid-June; at 11, early Sept.-late Oct. **Cost:** $130 (includes snack); $105 (ages 65+ and students with ID); $80 (ages 3-12). Reservations are recommended. **Phone:** (604) 272-7200 or (888) 272-7203.

VANCOUVER WHALE WATCH is at 210-12240 Second Ave. Two 40-passenger, semi-covered vessel transports visitors through the Gulf Islands and the San Juan Islands. Led by a wildlife guide, the narrated tour focuses on killer whales and humpback whales. Hydrophones are used to listen to the whales communicating. Other wildlife such as porpoises, sea lions, seals and eagles also may be seen. Sightings are guaranteed.

Time: Allow 3 hours minimum. **Hours:** Tours depart daily at 9 and 2, mid-June through Aug. 31; at 11, Apr. 1 to mid-June and Sept.-Oct. **Cost:** $130 (includes water and snack); $100 (students with ID

(See map & index p. 290.)

and senior citizens); $75 (ages 4-12). Reservations are recommended. **Phone:** (604) 274-9565 or (844) 474-9565.

ACCENT INNS   604/273-3311 **40**
 Hotel. **Address:** 10551 St Edwards Dr V6X 3L8

BEST WESTERN PLUS ABERCORN INN
(604)270-7576 **36**

Hotel
$109-$309

 Best Western PLUS **AAA Benefit:** Save 10% or more every day and earn 10% bonus points!

Address: 9260 Bridgeport Rd V6X 1S1 **Location:** Hwy 99 exit 39 (Bridgeport Rd/Airport) northbound; exit 39A (Richmond/Airport) southbound. Bridgeport, 35. **Facility:** 100 units. 3 stories, interior corridors. **Amenities:** *Some:* safes. **Activities:** exercise room. **Guest Services:** valet laundry.

THE FAIRMONT VANCOUVER AIRPORT
(604)207-5200 **29**

Hotel
$249-$949

Address: 3111 Grant McConachie Way V7B 0A6 **Location:** In Vancouver International Airport. YVR Airport, 38. **Facility:** This beautiful airport hotel has lovely rooms featuring sound-insulated windows and high-tech temperature and lighting controls. The jetted lap pool adds extra weight to the high tech fitness center. 392 units. 14 stories, interior corridors. **Parking:** on-site (fee) and valet. **Terms:** cancellation fee imposed. **Amenities:** safes. **Dining:** Globe@YVR Restaurant, see separate listing. **Pool(s):** heated indoor. **Activities:** sauna, hot tub, bicycles, in-room exercise equipment, spa. **Guest Services:** valet laundry, boarding pass kiosk, rental car service, luggage security pick-up. *(See ad p. 299.)*

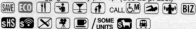
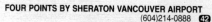

FOUR POINTS BY SHERATON VANCOUVER AIRPORT
(604)214-0888 **42**

Hotel
$140-$280

FOUR POINTS BY SHERATON **AAA Benefit:** Members save up to 15%, plus Starwood Preferred Guest® benefits!

Address: 8368 Alexandra Rd V6X 4A6 **Location:** No. 3 Rd, just e on Alderbridge Way, just n on Hazelbridge Way. Lansdowne, 40. **Facility:** 140 units. 6 stories, interior corridors. **Parking:** on-site (fee). **Amenities:** safes. **Activities:** exercise room. **Guest Services:** valet laundry.

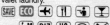

HAMPTON INN BY HILTON VANCOUVER AIRPORT
(604)232-5505 **33**

Hotel
$139-$199

AAA Benefit: Members save up to 10%!

Address: 8811 Bridgeport Rd V6X 1R9 **Location:** Hwy 99 exit 39 (Bridgeport Rd/Airport) northbound; exit 39A (Richmond/Airport) southbound, just w. Bridgeport, 35. **Facility:** 109 units. 5 stories, interior corridors. **Terms:** 1-7 night minimum stay, cancellation fee imposed. **Activities:** exercise room. **Guest Services:** valet laundry. **Featured Amenity:** breakfast buffet.

2km from Vancouver airport, near Canada line Skytrain and just 15 minutes from downtown Vancouver.

HILTON VANCOUVER AIRPORT
(604)273-6336 **43**

Hotel
$229-$489

Hilton HOTELS & RESORTS **AAA Benefit:** Members save 5% or more!

Address: 5911 Minoru Blvd V6X 4C7 **Location:** Corner of Minoru Blvd and Westminster Hwy. Lansdowne, 40. **Facility:** 237 units, some two bedrooms. 15 stories, interior corridors. **Parking:** on-site (fee). **Terms:** 1-7 night minimum stay, cancellation fee imposed. **Amenities:** safes. **Dining:** CAVU Kitchen Bar, see separate listing. **Pool(s):** heated outdoor. **Activities:** hot tub, exercise room. **Guest Services:** valet laundry, rental car service.

HOLIDAY INN EXPRESS & SUITES RIVERPORT
604/241-1830 **47**
Hotel. **Address:** 10688 No. 6 Rd V6W 1E7

HOLIDAY INN EXPRESS VANCOUVER-AIRPORT
604/273-8080 **35**
Hotel. **Address:** 9351 Bridgeport Rd V6X 1S3

HOLIDAY INN VANCOUVER AIRPORT-RICHMOND
604/821-1818 **41**
Hotel. **Address:** 10720 Cambie Rd V6X 1K8

HOTEL AT RIVER ROCK   (604)247-8900 **30**
Hotel. **Address:** 8811 River Rd V6X 3P8

(See map & index p. 290.)

PACIFIC GATEWAY HOTEL AT VANCOUVER AIRPORT
(604)278-1241 **32**

Hotel
$149-$499

Address: 3500 Cessna Dr V7B 1C7 **Location:** Waterfront. Just s of island airport interchange; at Russ Baker Way. Templeton, 36. **Facility:** 382 units. 10 stories, interior corridors. **Parking:** on-site (fee) and valet. **Terms:** cancellation fee imposed. **Dining:** Pier 73 Restaurant, see separate listing. **Pool(s):** heated outdoor. **Activities:** trails, exercise room. **Guest Services:** valet laundry, boarding pass kiosk.

RADISSON HOTEL VANCOUVER AIRPORT
(604)276-8181 **39**

Hotel
$159-$309

Address: 8181 Cambie Rd V6X 3X9 **Location:** Corner of No. 3 and Cambie rds. Aberdeen, 39. **Facility:** 200 units. 12 stories, interior corridors. **Parking:** on-site (fee). **Terms:** cancellation fee imposed, resort fee. **Amenities:** safes. **Pool(s):** heated indoor. **Activities:** hot tub, exercise room. **Guest Services:** valet laundry, boarding pass kiosk. **Featured Amenity: breakfast buffet.** (See ad this page.)

QUALITY HOTEL AIRPORT (SOUTH)
(604)244-3051 **44**

Hotel
$105-$240

Address: 7228 Westminster Hwy V6X 1A1 **Location:** Between Gilbert Rd and Alderbridge Way. Richmond-Brighouse, 41. **Facility:** 70 units. 4 stories, interior corridors. **Guest Services:** valet laundry. **Featured Amenity: full hot breakfast.**

▼ *See AAA listing this page* ▼

(See map & index p. 290.)

RIVER ROCK CASINO RESORT   (604)247-8900   [31]

Resort Hotel
$209-$459

Address: 8811 River Rd V6X 3P8 **Location:** Waterfront. Hwy 99 exit 39 (Bridgeport Rd/Airport) northbound; exit 39A (Richmond/Airport) southbound, just w on Bridgeport Rd, then just n on Great Canadian Way. 🚇 Bridgeport, 35. **Facility:** Beautiful one-bedroom suites with high tech features are the entry level rooms here. They have custom made mattresses and amazing bedding you will not want to get out of. 203 units, some two bedrooms. 9-11 stories, interior corridors. **Parking:** on-site and valet. **Terms:** check-in 4 pm, cancellation fee imposed. **Amenities:** safes. **Dining:** 2 restaurants, also, Tramonto, see separate listing. **Pool(s):** heated indoor. **Activities:** hot tub, marina, trails, exercise room, spa. **Guest Services:** valet laundry.

SANDMAN HOTEL VANCOUVER AIRPORT
604/303-8888   [38]

 Hotel. **Address:** 3233 St Edwards Dr V6X 3K4

SHERATON VANCOUVER AIRPORT HOTEL
(604)273-7878   [45]

Hotel
$199-$549

Sheraton

AAA Benefit: Members save up to 15%, plus Starwood Preferred Guest® benefits!

Address: 7551 Westminster Hwy V6X 1A3 **Location:** Corner of Minoru Blvd and Westminster Hwy. 🚇 Richmond-Brighouse, 41. **Facility:** 390 units. 2-8 stories, interior corridors. **Parking:** on-site (fee) and valet. **Terms:** cancellation fee imposed. **Amenities:** safes. **Pool(s):** heated outdoor. **Activities:** hot tub, exercise room. **Guest Services:** valet laundry, rental car service.

TRAVELODGE HOTEL VANCOUVER AIRPORT
(604)278-5155   [37]

Hotel
$70-$181

Address: 3071 St Edwards Dr V6X 3K4 **Location:** Hwy 99 exit 39 (Bridgeport Rd/Airport) northbound to St Edwards Dr; exit 39A (Richmond/Airport) southbound. 🚇 Bridgeport, 35. **Facility:** 160 units. 10 stories, interior corridors. **Terms:** cancellation fee imposed. **Amenities:** Some: safes. **Pool(s):** heated indoor. **Activities:** hot tub, limited exercise equipment.

Get your vehicle vacation ready at a AAA/CAA Approved Auto Repair facility

---

VANCOUVER AIRPORT MARRIOTT   (604)276-2112   [46]

Hotel
$150-$347

MARRIOTT

AAA Benefit: Members save 5% or more!

Address: 7571 Westminster Hwy V6X 1A3 **Location:** Corner of Minoru Blvd and Westminster Hwy. 🚇 Richmond-Brighouse, 41. **Facility:** 237 units, some two bedrooms. 18 stories, interior corridors. **Parking:** on-site (fee). **Dining:** The American Grille, see separate listing. **Pool(s):** heated outdoor. **Activities:** hot tub, exercise room. **Guest Services:** valet and coin laundry, boarding pass kiosk.

THE WESTIN WALL CENTRE VANCOUVER AIRPORT
(604)303-6565   [34]

Hotel
$149-$549

WESTIN HOTELS & RESORTS

AAA Benefit: Members save up to 15%, plus Starwood Preferred Guest® benefits!

Address: 3099 Corvette Way V6X 4K3 **Location:** Hwy 99 exit 39 (Bridgeport Rd/Airport) northbound; exit 39A (Richmond/Airport) southbound, just w to No. 3 Rd. 🚇 Bridgeport, 35. **Facility:** 188 units. 15 stories, interior corridors. **Parking:** on-site (fee) and valet. **Amenities:** safes. **Pool(s):** heated indoor. **Activities:** hot tub, exercise room, massage. **Guest Services:** valet laundry.

WHERE TO EAT

THE AMERICAN GRILLE   604/232-2804   [60]
New American. Casual Dining. **Address:** 7571 Westminster Hwy V6X 1A3

THE BOATHOUSE RESTAURANT   604/273-7014   [53]
Seafood. Casual Dining. **Address:** 8331 River Rd, #100 V6X 1Y1

CACTUS CLUB CAFE   604/244-9969
New American. Casual Dining. **Address:** 5500 No. 3 Rd V6X 2C8

CAVU KITCHEN BAR   604/232-5001   [59]
New International. Casual Dining. **Address:** 5911 Minoru Blvd V6X 4C7

CHARCOAL SUSHI & BBQ RESTAURANT   778/297-7255   [63]
Sushi. Casual Dining. **Address:** 7997 Westminster Hwy, #250 V6X 1A4

EMPIRE SEAFOOD RESTAURANT   604/249-0080   [61]
Chinese. Casual Dining. **Address:** 5951 No. 3 Rd, #200 V6X 2E3

FELICOS RESTAURANT   604/276-8282   [57]
Greek. Casual Dining. **Address:** 8140 Leslie Rd V6X 4A8

FLYING BEAVER BAR & GRILL   604/273-0278   [55]
American. Gastropub. **Address:** 4760 Inglis Dr V7B 1W4

(See map & index p. 290.)

FOGG N' SUDS   604/273-0776   58
◆◆ International. Casual Dining. **Address:** 10720 Cambie Rd V6X 1K8

GLOBE@YVR RESTAURANT   604/207-5200   50
◆◆◆ Pacific Northwest. Fine Dining. **Address:** 3111 Grant McConachie Way V7B 1X9

MAN RI SUNG KOREAN RESTAURANT   604/821-9922   56
◆◆ Korean. Casual Dining. **Address:** 4151 Hazelridge Way, #3600 V6X 4J7

MOXIE'S CLASSIC GRILL   604/303-1111
◆◆ American. Casual Dining. **Address:** 3233 St Edwards Dr V6X 3K4

PIER 73 RESTAURANT   604/276-1954   52
◆◆◆ International. Casual Dining. **Address:** 3500 Cessna Dr V7B 1C7

RED STAR SEAFOOD RESTAURANT   604/261-8389   54
◆◆ Chinese. Casual Dining. **Address:** 8181 Cambie Rd, #2200 V6X 3X9

RICKY'S ALL DAY GRILL   604/233-7705
◆◆ American. Casual Dining. **Address:** 9100 Blundell Rd, #490 V6V 1K3

SHANGHAI RIVER RESTAURANT   604/233-8885   62
◆◆ Chinese. Casual Dining. **Address:** 7831 Westminster Hwy V6X 4J4

STEVESTON SEAFOOD HOUSE   604/271-5252   64
◆◆◆ Seafood. Casual Dining. **Address:** 3951 Moncton St V7E 3A2

TAPENADE BISTRO   604/275-5188   65
◆◆◆ New Mediterranean. Casual Dining. **Address:** 3711 Bayview St V7E 3B6

TRAMONTO   604/247-8900   51
◆◆◆ Italian. Fine Dining. **Address:** 8811 River Rd V6X 3P8

ROSSLAND (D-10) pop. 3,556,
elev. 1,039m/3,408'

The 1890 gold rush on Red Mountain spurred the growth of Rossland from a prospectors' camp to a bustling town with 42 saloons, 17 law firms, four breweries and two distilleries. The area's vast mineral wealth, which supported a booming mining industry for 40 years, produced more than 6 million tons of ore valued at about $125 million.

Fishing, swimming and canoeing are available at Nancy Greene Provincial Park, 26 kilometres (16 mi.) northwest at hwys. 3 and 3B. *See Recreation Areas Chart.*

Rossland Visitor Centre: 1100 Hwy. 3B, Rossland, BC, Canada V0G 1Y0. **Phone:** (250) 362-7722 or (888) 448-7444.

CASA ALPINA   (250)362-7364
◆ Motel. **Address:** 1199 Nancy Greene Hwy V0G 1Y0

SALMON ARM (B-9) pop. 17,464,
elev. 415m/1,364'

R.J. HANEY HERITAGE VILLAGE & MUSEUM is nearly 3 kilometres (2 mi.) e. on Hwy. 1, then just s. on Hwy. 97B. The village grew around the Haney House, built in 1910. Among the buildings in the community, all built in the early 20th century, are Salmon Arm's first gas station, a blacksmith shop, a Methodist church, a fire station and a schoolhouse.

In addition, the Beamish Building contains what is said to be Western Canada's largest collection of records and cylinders. A small museum, which changes displays every 2 years, focuses on local Shuswap history, and a 2-kilometre (1.2-mi.) nature walk, a tea house and a dinner theatre also are on the property. Guided tours of the Haney House are available.

Time: Allow 1 hour minimum. **Hours:** Village, museum and office open daily 10-5, July-Aug.; Wed.-Sun. 10-4, mid-May through June 30 and Sept. 1-20; Mon.-Fri. 10-4, rest of year. Dinner theatre Wed., Fri. and Sun., July-Aug. Archives room Tues.-Thurs. 10-4, year-round. Phone ahead to confirm schedule. **Cost:** Donations. Reservations are required for the dinner theatre. **Phone:** (250) 832-5243. ⬤ ⬤

BEST WESTERN SALMON ARM INN   (250)832-9793
◆◆ Motel
$110-$170

Best Western   **AAA Benefit:** Save 10% or more every day and earn 10% bonus points!

Address: 61 10th St SW V1E 1E4 **Location:** 0.7 mi (1.1 km) w on Trans-Canada Hwy 1. **Facility:** 75 units. 2 stories (no elevator), exterior corridors. **Parking:** winter plug-ins. **Pool(s):** heated indoor. **Activities:** hot tub. **Guest Services:** valet laundry. **Featured Amenity:** full hot breakfast.

COMFORT INN & SUITES   (250)832-7711
◆◆ Hotel. **Address:** 1090 22nd St NE V1E 2V5

PODOLLAN INN   (250)832-6025
◆◆ Hotel. **Address:** 1460 Trans-Canada Hwy NE V1E 4N1

WHERE TO EAT

CHIANG MAI ORCHID THAI RESTAURANT   250/832-0699
◆◆ Northern Thai. Casual Dining. **Address:** 131 Hudson Ave NE V1E 4N7

SHUSWAP PIE COMPANY   250/832-7992
◆ Breads/Pastries. Quick Serve. **Address:** 331 Alexander St NE V1E 4P1

TABLE 24 RESTAURANT   250/832-5024
◆◆◆ Pacific Northwest. Casual Dining. **Address:** 1460 Trans-Canada Hwy NE V1E 4N1

SALT SPRING ISLAND (H-10) pop. 10,322

Originally called Chuan Island, then Admiral Island, Salt Spring Island is the largest of the Gulf Island group and a popular spot for yachting, cycling, fishing and golfing. Bicycle and kayak rentals are available.

Although it is one of the most developed of the islands, it retains a rural feel. Mount Maxwell Park has a scenic drive leading to 610-metre (2,001-ft.) Baynes Peak. Ruckle Provincial Park *(see Recreation Areas Chart)* offers 7 kilometres (4.3 mi.) of shoreline and has walking trails; bicycling, fishing, kayaking and picnicking are permitted.

The island also features popular Saturday farmers markets and arts and crafts, and is home to many fine artists such as Robert Bateman and Carol Evans.

Ganges is the island's largest village and its commercial hub. Much of the seaside community's charm is the result of its status as an artist's colony. Visitors are welcome at many artists' studios, and locally made arts and crafts such as ceramics, jewelry, furniture, stained glass and woodcraft, are sold at many village shops.

A local Ganges landmark is a retired buoy that has been painted with a marine-themed mural. Marine life such as salmon, orcas, cod and octopus seals—all creatures that can be found near Salt Spring Island—join a Coast Guard cutter and kayaks as the mural's focal points.

Ferries operate daily from the island's three ferry terminals—between Swartz Bay and Fulford Harbour, between Crofton and Vesuvius Bay and between Long Harbour (the largest of the terminals) and Tsawwassen. For schedules and information phone BC Ferries, (250) 386-3431 from the Victoria area or outside British Columbia, or (888) 223-3779 from elsewhere in the province.

Salt Spring Island Visitor InfoCentre: 121 Lower Ganges Rd., Salt Spring Island, BC, Canada V8K 2T1. **Phone:** (250) 537-5252 or (866) 216-2936.

Self-guiding tours: Maps describing self-guiding tours to the studios of more than 30 resident artists are available at the island's visitor infocenter as well as at lodgings, the marina and on BC Ferries.

HARBOUR HOUSE HOTEL   250/537-5571
▼▼ ▼▼ Hotel. **Address:** 121 Upper Ganges Rd V8K 2S2

WHERE TO EAT

AUNTIE PESTO'S CAFE & DELICATESSEN   250/537-4181
▼▼ ▼▼ Pacific Northwest Sandwiches. Casual Dining. **Address:** 115 Fulford-Ganges Rd V8K 1E2

BARB'S BAKERY & BISTRO   250/537-4491
▼▼ Breads/Pastries. Quick Serve. **Address:** 1-121 McPhillips Ave V8K 2T6

HASTINGS HOUSE DINING ROOM   250/537-2362
▼▼▼ ▼▼▼

Pacific Northwest
Fine Dining
$80-$95

AAA Inspector Notes: This restaurant offers a truly wonderful dining experience. Dinner guests receive their own personalized menu that features a three- or four-course chef's tasting menu with or without wine pairings. Ingredients are the freshest possible as many are produced on site. Guests are welcome to come earlier for drinks in the lounge. **Features:** full bar. **Reservations:** required. **Address:** 160 Upper Ganges Rd V8K 2S2 **Location:** 0.6 mi (1 km) n on Lower Ganges Rd, just e, towards Long Harbour Ferry Terminal; in Hastings House Country House Hotel. [D] [X]

SALT SPRING INN RESTAURANT   250/537-5339
▼▼ American. Casual Dining. **Address:** 132 Lower Ganges Rd V8K 2S9

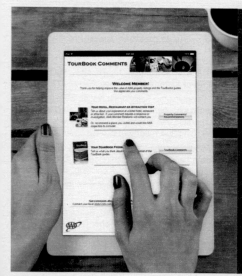

SANDON (C-10)

The remnants of one of western Canada's greatest mining towns nestle in the deep, wooded ravine of Carpenter Creek, high in the Selkirk Mountains. Pioneer prospectors Eli Carpenter and Jack Seaton discovered rich deposits of silver-lead ore here in 1891, triggering a rush. At its peak in the late 1890s, Sandon had over 5,000 residents, 29 hotels, 28 saloons, three breweries, theaters, an opera house, a school and a hospital.

Fire destroyed the central business district on May 3, 1900. The town was quickly rebuilt, channeling Carpenter Creek into a flume and converting its former course into the main street. The 1900s, however, ushered in a long decline. Rising metal prices during World War I briefly renewed prosperity, but the town disincorporated in 1920.

During World War II Sandon housed nearly 1,000 Japanese-Canadians, relocated from the Pacific coast, but by the early 1950s fewer than 200 residents remained. Much of the town remained intact until a major flood devastated the canyon in 1955.

Since the 1970s, volunteers have worked to preserve and restore the old mining town and to protect its heritage from souvenir hunters. Visitors are welcome to wander Sandon's scattered remnants. An old locomotive and other railroad rolling stock idle on a restored section of track. A steep gravel road (a high clearance vehicle is required) leads from the far end of town to Idaho Peak, where a short trail accesses a panoramic view. Galena Trail and K & S Railgrade Trail follow the former railroad routes. The Sandon Historical Society Museum acts as a visitor center.

SATURNA ISLAND (H-10) pop. 335

Saturna Island—remote, rugged and sparsely populated—is probably the least visited of the Gulf Islands as well as the southernmost isle. Forty-three percent of the island is protected by Gulf Islands National Park Reserve. Explore via hiking and boating, or hop on a bicycle, but proceed with caution as the narrow winding roads offer no shoulders. Saturna's bays, beaches and tidal pools offer glimpses of many varieties of marine life.

Walk-in or cycle-in camping is offered at Narvaez Bay as part of Gulf Islands National Park Reserve (see place listing p. 196). The seven-site camping area is nestled by a tranquil bay where you can often spot and hear harbour seals. However, the best wildlife viewing is offered at East Point, also in the park reserve; it is the easternmost point of the islands surrounded by active currents where Orcas, sea lions and porpoises can often be spotted. East Point is also one of the best places in the area for land-based whale watching.

SICAMOUS (B-9) pop. 2,441, elev. 352m/1,155'

Flanked by Mara and Shuswap lakes, Sicamous has abundant recreational opportunities, including swimming, fishing, boating and other water sports.

Full- and half-day cruises on Shuswap Lake (see Recreation Areas Chart) and 2- and 3-hour evening excursions on Mara Lake depart from the public wharf at the foot of Finlayson Street. Houseboats, which can be rented, are a popular way of touring the arms of Shuswap Lake.

At nearby Adams River almost 10 million scarlet sockeye salmon bury their eggs each October; it is one of the largest spawning grounds in the country. Several spawning grounds can be seen at Roderick Haig-Brown Provincial Park, 85 kilometres (53 mi.) northwest off Hwy. 1.

Sicamous Visitor Centre: 3-446 Main St., Sicamous, BC, Canada V0E 2V0. **Phone:** (250) 836-3313 or (866) 205-4055.

WHERE TO EAT

BLONDIES CAFE   250/515-2000
Sandwiches. Quick Serve. **Address:** 302 Finlayson St V0E 2V0

SIDNEY (H-10) pop. 11,178, elev. 9m/30'
• Part of Victoria area — see map p. 317

People of the Salish First Nation were the earliest known inhabitants of the area now called Sidney. Incorporated into a town in 1967, Sidney is known for its fishing and waterfront activity.

Booktown, the town's nickname, is the result of a dozen book shops concentrated in a five-block area around Beacon Avenue. Picnicking, beachcombing and camping are popular at Sidney Spit Marine Provincial Park.

Sidney Visitor Centre: 2281 Beacon Ave., Sidney, BC, Canada V8L 1W9. **Phone:** (250) 665-7362.

SHAW OCEAN DISCOVERY CENTRE is at 9811 Seaport Pl. The main concentration of this waterfront aquarium and marine education center is the inland Salish Sea ecosystem. After experiencing the sensation of descending into the ocean in a simulated "elevator," visitors reach the Gallery of the Drifters to view plankton, algae and jellyfish.

The Ocean's Heartbeat, a classroomlike environment, has microscopes and live Internet links to undersea sites. The Gallery of the Salish Sea is where you'll find large aquarium habitats that are home to local marine life as well as works by native artists that depict the peoples' relationship with the ocean; an octopus den can be seen overhead.

Touch pools provide an opportunity to get up-close to some of the sea creatures such as sea urchins and sea stars, and docents, called "oceaneers," are available to answer questions. The diverse population of the center's 17 aquariums include wolf eels, rockfish, sea cucumbers and anemones.

Time: Allow 1 hour minimum. **Hours:** Daily 10-5. Last admission 30 minutes before closing. Closed Jan. 1, Christmas Eve and Christmas. Phone ahead to confirm schedule. **Cost:** $15; $8 (ages 7-17); $5 (ages 3-6). **Phone:** (250) 665-7511.

BEACON INN AT SIDNEY   (250)655-3288
 Bed & Breakfast. **Address:** 9724 3rd St V8L 3A2

BEST WESTERN PLUS EMERALD ISLE MOTOR INN
                                            (250)656-4441

Hotel
$129-$199

AAA Benefit:
Save 10% or more every day and earn 10% bonus points!

Address: 2306 Beacon Ave V8L 1X2 **Location:** Hwy 17 exit 28 (Sidney), just e. **Facility:** 64 units, some kitchens. 2 stories, interior corridors. **Terms:** check-in 4 pm. **Dining:** Smitty's, see separate listing. **Activities:** exercise room. **Guest Services:** valet and coin laundry.

/ SOME UNITS

THE CEDARWOOD INN & SUITES   250/656-5551
 Hotel. **Address:** 9522 Lochside Dr V8L 1N8

THE SIDNEY PIER HOTEL & SPA   (250)655-9445
Contemporary Hotel
$144-$344

Address: 9805 Seaport Pl V8L 4X3 **Location:** Hwy 17 exit 28 (Beacon Ave), 0.6 mi (1 km) e. **Facility:** 55 units, some kitchens. 3 stories, interior corridors. **Parking:** on-site (fee). **Terms:** check-in 4 pm, cancellation fee imposed. **Amenities:** safes. **Dining:** Haro's Restaurant & Bar, see separate listing. **Activities:** steamroom, exercise room, spa. **Guest Services:** valet and coin laundry, area transportation.

/ SOME UNITS

WHERE TO EAT

DEEP COVE CHALET   250/656-3541
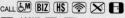 French. Fine Dining. **Address:** 11190 Chalet Rd V8L 4R4

HARO'S RESTAURANT & BAR   250/655-9700
Pacific Northwest. Casual Dining. **Address:** 9805 Seaport Pl V8L 4X3

SEA GLASS WATERFRONT GRILL   778/351-3663
Northern Pacific Northwest. Casual Dining. **Address:** 2320 Harbour Rd V8L 2P6

SMITTY'S   250/656-2423

American
Casual Dining
$8-$17

AAA Inspector Notes: The family-oriented restaurant satisfies patrons with its ever-popular all-day breakfast items, as well as tasty and wholesome soups and salads at lunchtime. A relaxed mood characterizes the dining space. **Features:** full bar. **Address:** 2306 Beacon Ave V8L 1X2 **Location:** Hwy 17 exit 28 (Sidney), just e; in Best Western Plus Emerald Isle Motor Inn.

B L D CALL

THIRD STREET CAFE   250/656-3035
American Breakfast. Casual Dining. **Address:** 2466 Beacon Ave V8L 1X8

SKIDEGATE (E-1)

HAIDA HERITAGE CENTRE AT KAAY LLNAGAAY is just n. of the BC Ferries terminal on Second Beach Rd. The center, on the site of the old Haida seaside village of Kaay Llnagaay, celebrates the relationship of the Haida people with the land and examines, through audiovisuals and interactive displays, Haida art, history and culture.

Traditional totem poles representing the 14 clans front the facility; three ancient poles are inside. A canoe house, a performing house and a carving shed also may be seen. The Haida Gwaii Museum includes exhibits about plants and wildlife as well as the Haida's belief in the natural and supernatural. A collection of argillite carvings and contemporary art is showcased.

Time: Allow 1 hour minimum. **Hours:** Sun.-Wed. 10-6, Thurs.-Sat. 10-8, July-Aug.; Mon.-Sat. 10-8, in June; Tues.-Sat. 10-5, rest of year. Phone ahead to confirm schedule. **Cost:** $15.24 (includes the heritage center and Haida Gwaii Museum); $14.24 (ages 65+); $9.52 (students with ID); $4.76 (ages 5-12). **Phone:** (250) 559-7885 or (877) 559-8818. GT

JAGS BEANSTALK ROOMS   250/559-8826
Motel. **Address:** 100 Hwy 16 V0T 1S1

WHERE TO EAT

JAGS BEANSTALK ESPRESSO & BISTRO   250/559-8826
Coffee/Tea Sandwiches. Quick Serve. **Address:** 100 Hwy 16 V0T 1S1

KAY BISTRO   250/559-7885
American. Quick Serve. **Address:** 2 Second Beach Rd V0T 1S1

SMITHERS (E-3) pop. 5,404, elev. 520m/1,706'

Named for A.W. Smithers, one-time chairman of the Grand Trunk Pacific Railway, Smithers owes its location to railway construction crews who in 1913 selected the scenic spot at the base of Hudson Bay Mountain. It became a village in 1921 and officially a town in 1967. Today it is a distribution and supply center for local farms, mills and mines. Murals adorn many buildings within its alpine-style Main Street district.

Smithers is popular as a year-round skiing center thanks to 2,652-metre (8,700-ft.) Hudson Bay Mountain. The town also is a convenient starting point for fossil hunting, fishing, mountain climbing and trail riding.

Smithers Visitor Centre: 1411 Court St., P.O. Box 2379, Smithers, BC, Canada V0J 2N0. **Phone:** (250) 847-5072 or (800) 542-6673.

Self-guiding tours: Information about driving and walking tours is available at the chamber of commerce.

ASPEN INN & SUITES   250/847-4551
◆◆ Motel. **Address:** 4628 Yellowhead Hwy V0J 2N0

SUNSHINE INN   250/847-6668
◆◆ Hotel. **Address:** 3880 Fourth Ave V0J 2N0

WHERE TO EAT

ALPENHORN BISTRO AND BAR   250/847-5366
◆◆ American. Casual Dining. **Address:** 1261 Main St V0J 2N0

SOOKE (H-9) pop. 11,435, elev. 38m/125'
• Part of Victoria area — see map p. 317

A natural harbor off the Juan de Fuca Strait, Sooke was discovered and claimed by the Spanish in 1790. The area, soon traded to the British by treaty, was named after a local First Nation tribe, T'Soke. It is a popular fishing site and the center of a large forest industry. A scenic portion of Hwy. 14 runs 43 kilometres (27 mi.) east from Sooke to Victoria.

Sooke Visitor Centre: 2070 Phillips Rd., Sooke, BC, Canada V9Z 0Y3. **Phone:** (250) 642-6351 or (866) 888-4748.

BEST WESTERN PREMIER PRESTIGE OCEANFRONT RESORT   (250)642-0805

◆◆◆◆
Contemporary Hotel
$120-$300

BW Premier —COLLECTION—

AAA Benefit: Members save 5% to 15% and earn 10% bonus Best Western Rewards® points!

Address: 6929 W Coast Rd V9Z 0V1 **Location:** 1 mi (1.6 km) w on Hwy 14. **Facility:** 122 units, some kitchens. 5 stories, interior corridors. **Terms:** check-in 4 pm. **Amenities:** safes. **Dining:** West Coast Grill, see separate listing. **Pool(s):** heated indoor. **Activities:** hot tub, exercise room, spa. **Guest Services:** valet and coin laundry.

[SAVE] [⊞] [🛁] [🍽] CALL [&M] [➔]
[BIZ] [HS] [📶] [✕] [🔌] [🖥] /SOME UNITS [🐟] [📺]

OCEAN WILDERNESS INN   (250)646-2116
◆◆ Bed & Breakfast. **Address:** 9171 W Coast Rd V9Z 1G3

SOOKE HARBOUR RESORT AND MARINA   (250)642-3236
◆◆◆ Condominium. **Address:** 6971 W Coast Rd V9Z 0V1

WHERE TO EAT

STONE PIPE GRILL   250/642-0566
◆◆ American. Casual Dining. **Address:** 2038 Otter Point Rd V9Z 0S9

WEST COAST GRILL   778/425-0888
◆◆ Pacific Northwest. Casual Dining. **Address:** 6929 W Coast Rd V9Z 0V1

WILD MOUNTAIN FOOD & DRINK   (250)642-3596
◆◆◆ Pacific Northwest. Casual Dining. **Address:** 1831 Maple Ave S V9Z 0N9

SPARWOOD (C-12) pop. 3,667

Once known as a mining town, Sparwood offers guided tours of the Elkview Coal Mine during summer. Popular area recreational activities include fly-fishing, white-water rafting, hiking and mountain biking.

Sparwood Visitor Centre: 141A Aspen Dr., P.O. Box 1448, Sparwood, BC, Canada V0B 2G0. **Phone:** (250) 425-2423 or (877) 485-8185.

SQUAMISH (G-11) pop. 17,158, elev. 5m/16'

Overshadowed by Stawamus Chief Mountain and other snowcapped peaks, Squamish was named for the First Nation's word meaning "mother of the wind." It is a popular stopover for tourists and recreation seekers. Rock climbing and windsurfing are popular activities.

Picnic facilities are available 3 kilometres (1.9 mi.) south at Shannon Falls, and camping facilities are available at Alice Lake Provincial Park *(see Recreation Areas Chart)* 13 kilometres (8 mi.) to the north.

Squamish Visitor Centre: 38551 Loggers Ln., Squamish, BC, Canada V8B 0H2. **Phone:** (604) 815-4994 or (877) 815-5084.

EXECUTIVE SUITES HOTEL & RESORT   604/815-0048

Extended Stay Hotel
Rates not provided

Address: 40900 Tantalus Rd V8B 0R3 **Location:** Hwy 99, just e on Garibaldi Way, 0.6 mi (1 km) n. **Facility:** 111 units, some two bedrooms, efficiencies and kitchens. 4 stories, interior corridors. **Terms:** check-in 4 pm. **Dining:** Living Room Restaurant & Lounge, see separate listing. **Pool(s):** heated outdoor. **Activities:** hot tub, exercise room. **Guest Services:** complimentary laundry.

MOUNTAIN RETREAT HOTEL & SUITES   (604)815-0883

Hotel
$1

Address: 38922 Progress Way V8B 0K5 **Location:** 0.9 mi (1.5 km) n on Hwy 99; at Industrial Way. **Facility:** 87 units, some efficiencies. 4 stories, interior corridors. **Terms:** cancellation fee imposed. **Dining:** Timberwolf Restaurant & Lounge, see separate listing. **Pool(s):** heated indoor. **Activities:** hot tub, exercise room. **Guest Services:** coin laundry.

SEA TO SKY HOTEL   (604)898-4874

Hotel
$89-$189

Address: 40330 Tantalus Rd V0N 1T0 **Location:** 2.9 mi (4.5 km) n on Hwy 99; at Garibaldi Way. **Facility:** 52 units. 3 stories, interior corridors. **Terms:** cancellation fee imposed. **Activities:** sauna, hot tub, exercise room. **Guest Services:** valet and coin laundry. *(See ad this page.)*

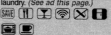

WHERE TO EAT

LIVING ROOM RESTAURANT & LOUNGE   604/815-0999
American. Casual Dining. **Address:** 40900 Tantalus Rd V8B 0R3

TIMBERWOLF RESTAURANT & LOUNGE   604/815-4424
American. Casual Dining. **Address:** 38922 Progress Way V8B 0K5

SUMMERLAND (C-8) pop. 11,280, elev. 454m/1,489'

- Hotels & Restaurants map & index p. 226
- Part of Okanagan Valley area — see map p. 222

Surrounded by lush orchards and vineyards, Summerland depends on fruit cultivation as its main industry. Overlooking Okanagan Lake (see Recreation Areas Chart), the first commercial orchard in the Okanagan Valley was planted in 1890. Fruit stands are still the best way to sample the region's bountiful produce.

Summerland also was the first town on the lake to employ electricity as an energy source; it was generated by a small hydroelectric plant built on the lakeshore in 1905. These and other historical landmarks are the focus of Summerland Museum at 9521 Wharton St.; phone (250) 494-9395.

Giants Head Park on 910-metre (2,986-ft.) Giants Head Mountain offers picnic facilities and views of Summerland, the valley below and Okanagan Lake.

Many beaches, including Sunoka, Peach Orchard, Powell and Rotary, line the shores of Okanagan Lake. Also of interest is the Summerland Trout Hatchery, 13405 Lakeshore Dr. S., where rainbow, brook and kokanee trout are raised; phone (250) 494-0491.

Summerland Visitor Centre: 15600 Hwy. 97, P.O. Box 130, Summerland, BC, Canada V0H 1Z0. **Phone:** (250) 494-2686.

KETTLE VALLEY STEAM RAILWAY is 5 km (3 mi.) w. on Prairie Valley Rd. to 18404 Bathville Rd. Passengers take a 1-hour, 30-minute narrated tour on the only preserved portion of the original Kettle Valley Railway Line, which ran from Midway to Hope.

Hours: The train departs from Prairie Valley Station Thurs.-Mon. at 10:30 and 1:30, late June-early Sept.; Sat.-Mon. at 10:30 and 1:30, mid-May to late June and mid-Sept. to mid-Oct. Departs at 10:30 and 1:30 on Easter and Mother's Day. **Cost:** $24.50; $22.50 (ages 65+); $19.50 (ages 13-18); $15.50 (ages 3-12). Fares may vary; phone ahead. **Phone:** (250) 494-8422, or (877) 494-8424 in Canada.

NIXDORF CLASSIC CARS, INC. is at 15809 Logie Rd. An inventory of more than 100 restored vehicles dating from 1936 to 1970 is rotated so that no fewer than half reside in the facility at one time. The cars, all of which are two-door hardtops or convertibles, may also be rented for chauffeured wine tours. **Time:** Allow 1 hour minimum. **Hours:** Daily 9-5, May 1 to mid-Oct.; by appointment rest of year. **Cost:** $19.05; free (ages 0-11 with adult). **Phone:** (250) 494-4111.

WINERIES

- **Sumac Ridge Estate Winery** is 1 km (.6 mi.) n. at 17403 Hwy. 97N. **Hours:** Tastings daily 10-6, July 1-Labour Day; 10-5, Mar.-June and day after Labour Day-Oct. 31; 11-4, rest of year. Tours are given daily at 11 and 2, year-round. Closed Jan. 1-2, Christmas and day after Christmas. **Phone:** (250) 494-0451 or (877) 433-0451. GT

SUMMERLAND MOTEL   (250)494-4444 **32**
▼▼ Motel. **Address:** 2107 Tait St V0H 1Z4

SUN PEAKS (B-8)

The resort community of Sun Peaks nestles amid firs and aspen at the base of Tod Mountain and Mount Morrisey in central British Columbia. The core of the village, 31 kilometres (19 mi.) east of Hwy. 5 at Heffley Creek, consists of three- to five-story alpine motif buildings clustered along pedestrian walkways.

With nearly 1,497 hectares (3,700 acres) of terrain, Sun Peaks is reportedly the third largest ski area in Canada, offering both alpine and Nordic skiing as well as a tube park, ice skating, sleigh rides, snowmobiling and dog sledding. Summer activities include golf, tennis, hiking, mountain biking, kayaking, canoeing, fishing and trail rides.

RECREATIONAL ACTIVITIES

Skiing

- SAVE **Sun Peaks Resort** is 54 km (32 mi.) n. on Hwy. 5 at 1280 Alpine Rd. Other activities are available. **Hours:** Daily 8-4:30, mid-Nov. to mid-Apr. Chairlifts open for summer activities daily 10-7, late June-Sept. 1. Hours may vary; phone ahead to confirm schedule. **Phone:** (250) 578-5474 or (800) 807-3257.

COAST SUNDANCE LODGE   250/578-0200
▼▼ ▼▼ Extended Stay Hotel. **Address:** 3160 Creekside Way V0E 5N0

HEARTHSTONE LODGE   250/578-6969
▼▼ ▼▼ Extended Stay Hotel. **Address:** 3170 Creekside Way V0E 5N0

HEFFLEY BOUTIQUE INN   (250)578-8343
▼▼ Extended Stay Hotel. **Address:** 3185 Creekside Way V0E 5N0

THE SUN PEAKS GRAND HOTEL & CONFERENCE CENTER   (250)578-6000

◆◆◆ Hotel
$99-$649

Address: 3240 Village Way V0E 5N0 **Location:** Hwy 5, 19.4 mi (31 km) ne on Todd Mountain Rd, follow signs to village. **Facility:** 262 units, some two bedrooms and kitchens. 4-5 stories, interior corridors. **Parking:** on-site (fee) and valet. **Terms:** check-in 4 pm, 3 day cancellation notice-fee imposed. **Dining:** Mantles Restaurant, see separate listing, nightclub. **Pool(s):** heated outdoor. **Activities:** sauna, hot tub, downhill & cross country skiing, snowboarding, sledding, ice skating, recreation programs in winter, bicycles, game room, trails, exercise room. **Guest Services:** coin laundry.

BELLA ITALIA RISTORANTE   250/434-0282
▼▼▼ Italian. Casual Dining. **Address:** 3170 Creekside Way V0E 5N0

BOLACCO CAFE   250/578-7588
▼ Coffee/Tea Sandwiches. Quick Serve. **Address:** 3160 Creekside Way, #109 V0E 5N0

MANTLES RESTAURANT   250/578-6060
🔻🔻🔻 American. Casual Dining. **Address:** 3240 Village Way
V0E 5N0

SUNSHINE COAST (F-10)

Lining the western edge of the British Columbia mainland, the Sunshine Coast offers a wide variety of marine and land habitats, from coastal rain forests and rocky beaches to an alpine wilderness with peaks reaching 2,500 metres (8,000 ft.).

Powell River *(see place listing p. 237)*, with more than 100 regional dive sites, exceptionally clear water and deep ocean currents, is called the "Dive Capital of Canada." Desolation Sound's warm, sheltered waters also contribute to the destination's popularity with scuba divers and kayakers. Sechelt is known for its rich artisan community, while Gibsons *(see place listing p. 193)* is home to up to 200 bird species throughout the year.

SURREY (H-11) pop. 468,251, elev. 80m/262'

- Restaurants p. 257
- Hotels & Restaurants map & index p. 290
- Part of Vancouver area — see map p. 263

Surrey's sights are popular with nature buffs. Bear Creek Park features a garden area that includes rhododendrons, azaleas, ornamental grasses and bulb displays. A shoreline walk extends from Crescent Beach to Peace Arch Park. Walkers can observe tide pools, dig for clams or watch the myriad native birds.

Surrey Visitor Centre: 730 176th St., Surrey, BC, Canada V3S 9S6. **Phone:** (604) 531-6646 or (888) 531-6646.

NEWTON WAVE POOL is in the Newton Recreation Centre at 13730 72nd Ave. The indoor aquatic center houses, in addition to the wave pool, two water slides, an interactive water fortress and a three-station water cannon platform. The complex also includes an exercise, a steam and 465-square-metre (5,000-sq.-ft.) weight room as well as a whirlpool.

Hours: Mon.-Sat. 6 a.m.-9 p.m., Sun. 8-8. Phone ahead for leisure swim times. **Cost:** Single drop-in swims $5.95; $4.52 (students with ID and ages 60+); $3.10 (ages 2-18). Prices may vary; phone ahead. **Phone:** (604) 501-5543.

SURREY MUSEUM is at 17710-56A Ave. Interactive exhibits and a 42-seat theater portray the history of Surrey. A textile library and weaving studio are featured on-site. Changing exhibits are offered. Also on the grounds are the Anderson cabin, the oldest remaining pioneer-era structure in Surrey. The cabin was built in 1872 by Eric Anderson, a Swedish immigrant and one of the first settlers in the area.

Time: Allow 1 hour minimum. **Hours:** Tues.-Fri. 9:30-5:30, Sat. 10-5, early Feb.-late Dec. Closed most major holidays. **Cost:** Donations. **Phone:** (604) 592-6956. 🔳

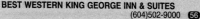

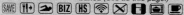

(See map & index p. 290.)

BEST WESTERN PEACE ARCH INN
(604)541-8100 **61**

Hotel
$109-$199

AAA Benefit:
Save 10% or more every day and earn 10% bonus points!

Address: 2293 King George Blvd V4A 5A4 **Location:** Hwy 99 exit 10 southbound, 2.8 mi (4.5 km) s; exit 2 northbound, 2.1 mi (3.5 km) n. **Facility:** 42 units. 3 stories, interior corridors. **Terms:** cancellation fee imposed. **Pool(s):** indoor. **Activities:** sauna, hot tub, limited exercise equipment. **Guest Services:** coin laundry. **Featured Amenity:** continental breakfast.

BW **Best Western.**

100% Non-Smoking. Free Continental Breakfast, Parking & Wi-Fi, Indoor Pool, Sauna, Fitness Centre!

Multiply the Value

Upgrade to **Plus** or **Premier**.

AAA.com/CAA.ca
800-Join-AAA

COMFORT INN & SUITES SURREY
(604)576-8888 **57**

Hotel. **Address:** 8255 166th St V4N 5R8

FOUR POINTS BY SHERATON SURREY
(604)930-4700 **55**

Hotel
$110-$179

 FOUR POINTS BY SHERATON

AAA Benefit: Members save up to 15%, plus Starwood Preferred Guest® benefits!

Address: 10410 158th St V4N 5C2 **Location:** Trans-Canada Hwy 1 exit 50 (160th St), just w on 104th Ave. **Facility:** 77 units. 3 stories, interior corridors. **Terms:** cancellation fee imposed. **Amenities:** safes. **Pool(s):** heated outdoor. **Activities:** exercise room. **Guest Services:** valet laundry.

HAMPTON INN & SUITES LANGLEY/SURREY
(604)530-6545 **59**

Hotel
$139-$199

Hampton by HILTON

AAA Benefit: Members save up to 10%!

Address: 19500 Langley Bypass V3S 7R2 **Location:** Trans-Canada Hwy 1 exit 58 (200th St/Langley City), 3.1 mi (5 km) s, then 0.7 mi (1.2 km) w on Hwy 10. **Facility:** 96 units, some efficiencies. 4 stories, interior corridors. **Terms:** 1-7 night minimum stay, cancellation fee imposed. **Pool(s):** heated indoor. **Activities:** hot tub, exercise room. **Guest Services:** valet and coin laundry. **Featured Amenity:** breakfast buffet.

▼ See AAA listing p. 257 ▼

Sheraton Vancouver Guildford Hotel

- Located across from Guildford Town Centre, BC's 2nd largest shopping mall
- Minutes away from the area's top golf courses
- Amenities: Sueno Spa, Outdoor Pool, Fitness Centre, Fresh Restaurant and Lounge

15269 104th Ave • Surrey, BC V3R 1N5
(604) 582-9288

1.888.627.8063

Sheraton
Vancouver Guildford
HOTEL

Rewards

www.sheratonguildford.com

(See map & index p. 290.)

HOLIDAY INN & SUITES
604/576-8862 **58**

WWWWWW
Hotel
Rates not provided

Address: 17530 64th Ave V3S 1Y9 **Location:** Trans-Canada Hwy 1 exit 53 (176th St/Hwy 15), 4.2 mi (7 km) s, then just w. Located in Cloverdale area. **Facility:** 76 units. 4 stories, interior corridors. **Pool(s):** heated indoor. **Activities:** exercise room. **Guest Services:** valet and coin laundry. **Featured Amenity: full hot breakfast.**

[SAVE] [🍴] [👶] [Y] CALL [&M] [🏊]

[BIZ] [HS] [📶] [✕] [🔌] [🖥]

/ SOME UNITS [📷]

RAMADA LANGLEY-SURREY
(604)576-8388 **60**

WWWW
Hotel
$110-$230

Address: 19225 Hwy 10 (56 Ave) V3S 8V9 **Location:** Trans-Canada Hwy 1 exit 58 (200th St/Langley City), 3.1 mi (5 km) s on 200th St, then 1.2 mi (2 km) w on Hwy 10 (56th Ave); corner of 192nd St and Hwy 10. **Facility:** 83 units, some efficiencies. 3 stories, interior corridors. **Terms:** cancellation fee imposed. **Amenities:** safes. **Pool(s):** heated indoor. **Activities:** hot tub, exercise room. **Guest Services:** valet and coin laundry.

[SAVE] [🍴] CALL [&M] [🏊] [BIZ]

[📶] [✕] [🔌] [🖥] [🖨]

/ SOME UNITS [S🔌] [HS]

🌀
RAMADA

Recipient of a Certificate of Excellence; newly renovated; award winning; value priced.

SHERATON VANCOUVER GUILDFORD HOTEL
(604)582-9288 **54**

WWWW
Hotel
$139-$249

Ⓢ
Sheraton

AAA Benefit: Members save up to 15%, plus Starwood Preferred Guest® benefits!

Address: 15269 104th Ave V3R 1N5 **Location:** Trans-Canada Hwy 1 exit 48 eastbound, 0.6 mi (1 km) s on 152nd St, then just e; exit 50 westbound, just w. **Facility:** 279 units. 20 stories, interior corridors. **Parking:** on-site (fee) and valet. **Terms:** cancellation fee imposed. **Pool(s):** heated outdoor. **Activities:** hot tub, exercise room, spa. **Guest Services:** valet laundry, area transportation. *(See ad p. 256.)*

[SAVE] [ECO] [🍴] [👶] [Y] CALL [&M] [🏊] [BIZ] [📶] [✕]

[🎬] [🖥] / SOME UNITS [🔌] [🔌] [📷]

WHERE TO EAT

CRESCENT BEACH BISTRO
604/531-1882 **73**
WW Mediterranean. Casual Dining. **Address:** 12251 Beecher St V4A 3A4

MAGUROGUY
604/560-1424 **74**
WW Japanese. Casual Dining. **Address:** 2670 152nd St, #320 V4P 1M8

MOXIE'S CLASSIC GRILL
604/495-7020
WW American. Casual Dining. **Address:** 10608 151A St V3R 1J8

RICKY'S ALL DAY GRILL
WW American. Casual Dining.
LOCATIONS:
Address: 3189 King George Hwy V4P 1B8 **Phone:** 604/535-1789
Address: 8958 152nd St V3R 4L7 **Phone:** 604/581-3212
Address: 1076 Central City V3T 2W1 **Phone:** 604/582-2545

SABAI THAI RESTAURANT
604/588-9819 **71**
WWW Thai. Casual Dining. **Address:** 10391 150th St V3R 4B1

SWISS CHALET
604/583-0883
WW Chicken. Casual Dining. **Address:** 9666 King George Hwy V3T 2V4

THE TURKEY HOUSE & DELI
604/531-6222 **75**
W Sandwiches Deli. Quick Serve. **Address:** 1433 King George Hwy V4A 4Z5

VILLA VERDI RISTORANTE ITALIANO
604/591-2123 **72**
WWWW Northern Italian. Casual Dining. **Address:** 13620 80th Ave V3W 6M1

TELEGRAPH COVE (H-3)

The bay community served as the northern terminus of the telegraph line along the coast of Vancouver Island and later became a logging and salmon fishing area. Whale watching, fishing and camping are popular during the summer.

STUBBS ISLAND WHALE WATCHING departs from the end of the #24 boardwalk. For excursions on the Johnstone Strait, vessels are equipped with underwater microphones for listening to whale vocalizations. Multiday tours also are available.

Warm clothing is recommended. **Time:** Allow 3 hours, 30 minutes minimum. **Hours:** Daily departures May 1-early Oct. Phone ahead to confirm schedule. **Cost:** $99; $89 (ages 65+); $84 (ages 1-12). Reservations are required. **Phone:** (250) 928-3185 or (800) 665-3066.

WHALE INTERPRETIVE CENTRE is at the end of the boardwalk. Interpreters provide hands-on presentations and share information about and promote awareness of the marine environment. Exhibits include whale skeletons and artifacts. **Time:** Allow 45 minutes minimum. **Hours:** Daily 9-6, July-Aug.; 9-5, May-June and in Sept.; by appointment rest of year. Phone ahead to confirm schedule. **Cost:** $4.76; $2.86 (children). **Phone:** (250) 928-3129, or (250) 928-3187 in the off-season.

TELEGRAPH COVE MARINA & RV PARK
250/928-3163
WW Vacation Rental Condominium. **Address:** 1642 Telegraph Cove Rd V0N 3J0

TERRACE (E-2) pop. 11,486, elev. 215m/705'

On the banks of the Skeena River, Terrace and its surrounding area provide excellent recreational opportunities ranging from hiking on a variety of trails to fishing in nearby rivers and creeks. Among the region's wildlife is a rare species of black bear, the white Kermodei. Native to the area, it is the city's symbol.

Among the most popular recreation areas are Lakelse Lake Provincial Park *(see Recreation Areas Chart)*; Lakelse River, a tributary of the Skeena River that harbors record-size salmon; and Williams Creek, which teems with spawning sockeye each August.

Several places of natural interest are nearby. At the eastern entrance to the city is Ferry Island Provincial Park, where you can hike trails and go fishing, swimming and camping *(see Recreation Areas Chart)*. Look closely at the cottonwood trees on the island's trails; more than 50 have faces carved into them by a local artist.

About 20 kilometres (12 mi.) south of Terrace is Mount Layton Hot Springs Resort, which has waterslides and a pool filled with natural hot spring mineral water. Hwy. 16 offers a scenic drive west along the Skeena River to Prince Rupert.

Terrace Visitor Centre: 4511 Keith Ave., Terrace, BC, Canada V8G 1K1. **Phone:** (250) 635-4944 or (877) 635-4944.

BEST WESTERN TERRACE INN   (250)635-0083

Hotel
$149-$189

Best Western **AAA Benefit:** Save 10% or more every day and earn 10% bonus points!

Address: 4553 Greig Ave V8G 1M7 **Location:** Hwy 16, just e on Greig Ave, follow City Centre signs. **Facility:** 68 units. 5 stories, interior corridors. **Amenities:** safes. **Activities:** exercise room. **Guest Services:** valet laundry. **Featured Amenity:** full hot breakfast.

DAYS INN TERRACE   (250)638-8141
Hotel. **Address:** 4620 Lakelse Ave V8G 1R1

WHERE TO EAT

DON DIEGO'S   250/635-2307
International. Casual Dining. **Address:** 3212 Kalum St V8G 2M9

NORTHERN DHABA HOT HOUSE RESTAURANT
250/615-5800
Indian. Casual Dining. **Address:** 4728 Lazelle Ave V8G 1T2

Stay connected with #AAA and #CAA
on your favorite social media sites

TOFINO (I-3) pop. 1,876

A fishing and resort village with sandy beaches, Tofino is on the western side of Vancouver Island at the end of Hwy. 4. The area was the site of Fort Defiance, where Boston fur trader Robert Gray and his men spent the winter of 1791. The fort was stripped and abandoned the next spring, and all that remains are scattered bricks and ruins.

Near Clayoquot Sound and the northern end of Pacific Rim National Park Reserve, the town's shoreline and waters are popular with scuba divers and beachcombers. In the spring whales often can be seen migrating along the coast. The Whale Centre and Museum, 411 Campbell St., exhibits scientific and artistic displays, photographs and artifacts depicting past and present whale encounters.

Several companies, including Adventure Tofino Wildlife Tours, (250) 725-2895; Remote Passages Marine Excursions *(see attraction listing)*, (250) 725-3330; and The Whale Centre, (250) 725-2132, offer whale-watching excursions on Clayoquot Sound. Tours lasting up to 3 hours may afford sightings of sea lions, porpoises and eagles. Combination whale-watching and hot springs cruises that last approximately 6.5 hours also are available.

Tofino Visitor Centre: 1426 Pacific Rim Hwy., Tofino, BC, Canada V0R 2Z0. **Phone:** (250) 725-3414 or (888) 720-3414.

REMOTE PASSAGES MARINE EXCURSIONS departs from Tofino harbor off Main St. at 51 Wharf St. Passengers have a choice of an open-air zodiac or a boat with an enclosed cabin and a viewing deck for their 2.5- to 3-hour journey through Clayoquot Sound to spot gray and humpback whales (and occasionally killer whales), sea otters, sea lions, seals, porpoises, sea birds and bald eagles. March through May encompasses the gray whale migration, while June through October is when gray and humpback whales linger in the area. Bear-watching tours, daily trips to Hot Springs Cove and sea kayaking trips also are available.

Warm clothing is recommended. **Hours:** Trips are offered daily in zodiacs and an enclosed-cabin boat early Mar.-Oct. 31 (weather permitting). Phone ahead to confirm schedule. **Cost:** Cabin fare $105; $79 (ages 3-12). Zodiac fare $99; $79 (ages 5-12). A fuel surcharge may apply. Fare may vary; phone ahead. **Phone:** (250) 725-3330 or (800) 666-9833.

TOFINO BOTANICAL GARDENS is at 1080 Pacific Rim Hwy. This site consists of 5 hectares (12 acres) of gardens that include a children's garden, a medicinal herb garden, 1,000-year-old cedar trees, an orchard and a berry patch, and a bird-watching area. An old homestead also is on the grounds. Pets and smoking are not permitted. **Time:** Allow 1 hour minimum. **Hours:** Daily 9-dusk. **Cost:** $11.43; $9.52 (senior citizens); $7.62 (students); free (ages 0-12). **Phone:** (250) 725-1220.

BEST WESTERN TIN WIS RESORT LODGE

(250)725-4445

Hotel
$119-$406

 Best Western. **AAA Benefit:** Save 10% or more every day and earn 10% bonus points!

Address: 1119 Pacific Rim Hwy V0R 2Z0 **Location:** 1.8 mi (3.5 km) s on Hwy 4. **Facility:** 85 units, some efficiencies. 2-3 stories, interior/exterior corridors. **Terms:** check-in 4 pm. **Activities:** hot tub, limited beach access, recreation programs, exercise room, massage. **Guest Services:** coin laundry, area transportation.

LONG BEACH LODGE RESORT

(250)725-2442

Contemporary Hotel. **Address:** 1441 Pacific Rim Hwy V0R 2Z0

PACIFIC SANDS BEACH RESORT

250/725-3322

Extended Stay Hotel. **Address:** 1421 Pacific Rim Hwy V0R 2Z0

TOFINO MOTEL

(250)725-2055

Motel. **Address:** 542 Campbell St V0R 2Z0

WICKANINNISH INN

(250)725-3100

Contemporary Hotel
$340-$600

Address: 500 Osprey Ln at Chesterman Beach V0R 2Z0 **Location:** 2.7 mi (4.3 km) e on Hwy 4. Located in a quiet area. **Facility:** One of the hotel buildings is built on the rocks overlooking the ocean. Rooms have many extras, ranging from locally made soaps in the bathrooms to back packs to beach blankets. 75 units, some kitchens. 3 stories, interior corridors. **Parking:** on-site and valet. **Terms:** closed 1/2-2/3, check-in 4 pm, 2-3 night minimum stay - seasonal and/or weekends, 14 day cancellation notice-fee imposed. **Amenities:** safes. **Dining:** The Pointe Restaurant, see separate listing. **Activities:** steamroom, beach access, recreation programs, bicycles, exercise room, spa. **Guest Services:** valet laundry, area transportation.

WHERE TO EAT

THE POINTE RESTAURANT

250/725-3106

Pacific Northwest Fine Dining
$28-$48

AAA Inspector Notes: Built above the rocks and jutting out into the ocean, this restaurant offers breathtaking scenery. In winter, wild waves crash on the rocks right outside the windows. Since opening in 1996, the restaurant has focused mainly on Canadian West Coast cuisine that reflects the bounty and tastes of Vancouver Island, especially its fresh seafood and amazing selection of B.C. wines. Walk-ins are welcome at breakfast and lunch. **Features:** full bar, Sunday brunch. **Reservations:** required, for dinner. **Address:** 500 Osprey Ln at Chesterman Beach V0R 2Z0 **Location:** 2.7 mi (4.3 km) e on Hwy 4; in Wickaninnish Inn. **Parking:** on-site and valet.

RESTAURANT AT LONG BEACH LODGE RESORT

250/725-2442

Pacific Northwest. Fine Dining. **Address:** 1441 Pacific Rim Hwy V0R 2Z0

SCHOONER RESTAURANT

250/725-3444

Pacific Northwest. Casual Dining. **Address:** 331 Campbell St V0R 2Z0

SHELTER RESTAURANT

250/725-3353

Pacific Northwest. Casual Dining. **Address:** 601 Campbell St V0R 2Z0

SOBO RESTAURANT

250/725-2341

Pacific Rim. Casual Dining. **Address:** 311 Neill St V0R 2Z0

TRAIL (D-10) pop. 7,681, elev. 430m/1,410'

At City Hall a sculptured screen titled "City of Lead and Zinc" illustrates how Trail's mineral and industrial strength steadily developed since the discovery of gold and copper in the area about 1890. Hydroelectric dams along the Kootenay River power extensive mining and smelting operations, dominated by Teck Cominco Ltd. Enjoy free concerts at Gyro Park, 1090 Charles Lakes Dr., on Thursday evenings in July and August.

Trail and District Chamber of Commerce and Visitor Centre: 1199 Bay Ave., Suite 200, Trail, BC, Canada V1R 4A4. **Phone:** (250) 368-3144, or (877) 636-9569 within British Columbia.

Self-guiding tours: Brochures for walking tours are available at the chamber of commerce.

BEST WESTERN PLUS COLUMBIA RIVER HOTEL

(250)368-3355

Hotel
$140-$180

 Best Western PLUS. **AAA Benefit:** Save 10% or more every day and earn 10% bonus points!

Address: 1001 Rossland Ave V1R 3N7 **Location:** On Hwy 3B; just n of center. **Facility:** 58 units. 4 stories, interior corridors. **Dining:** Foxy's Fine Food & Drinks, see separate listing. **Activities:** hot tub, exercise room. **Guest Services:** valet laundry. **Featured Amenity:** breakfast buffet.

WHERE TO EAT

COLANDER RESTAURANT

250/364-1816

Italian. Casual Dining. **Address:** 1475 Cedar Ave V1R 4C5

FOXY'S FINE FOOD & DRINKS

250/368-3355

American. Casual Dining. **Address:** 1001 Rossland Ave V1R 3N7

TUMBLER RIDGE pop. 2,710

TREND MOUNTAIN HOTEL & CONFERENCE CENTRE

250/242-2000

Extended Stay Hotel. **Address:** 375 Southgate St V0C 2W0

Take your imagination to new destinations with the online AAA/CAA Travel Guides

UCLUELET (I-3) pop. 1,627

On Barkley Sound, Ucluelet was named for a First Nation's word meaning "safe harbor." Charter boats for salmon fishing, whale watching, skin diving and nature excursions are available; phone the chamber of commerce. Lady Rose Marine Services makes round trips between Port Alberni and Ucluelet June through September; phone (250) 723-8313, or (800) 663-7192 Apr.-Sept., for reservations.

He Tin Kis Park allows visitors to experience a Canadian rain forest and follow a boardwalk trail that leads to the ocean. The 5-kilometre (3-mi.) Wild Pacific Trail passes a lighthouse en route to cliffside ocean views.

Ucluelet Visitor Centre: 2791 Pacific Rim Hwy., Ucluelet, BC, Canada V0R 3A0. **Phone:** (250) 726-4600.

BLACK ROCK OCEANFRONT RESORT   (250)726-4800
▼▼▼ Contemporary Hotel. **Address:** 596 Marine Dr V0R 3A0

THORNTON MOTEL   (250)726-7725
▼▼ Motel. **Address:** 1861 Peninsula Rd V0R 3A0

WHERE TO EAT

FETCH RESTAURANT   250/726-4800
▼▼▼ Pacific Northwest. Fine Dining. **Address:** 596 Marine Dr V0R 3A0

MATTERSON HOUSE RESTAURANT   250/726-2200
▼▼ American. Casual Dining. **Address:** 1682 Peninsula Rd V0R 3A0

OFFSHORE SEAFOOD RESTAURANT   250/726-2111
▼▼ Seafood. Casual Dining. **Address:** 2082 Peninsula Rd V0R 3A0

VALEMOUNT (F-6) pop. 1,020, elev. 792m/2,600'

Valemount, the valley in the mountains, offers many activities for outdoor enthusiasts. The village, where the Rocky, Cariboo and Monashee mountain ranges meet, is popular for both summer and winter pursuits, including hiking, rafting, skiing and snowmobiling. The area is rich with birds and other wildlife. Off Hwy. 16 is Mount Terry Fox Provincial Park. A viewing area affords vistas of the peak named for the late athlete.

Valemount Visitor Centre: 785 Cranberry Lake Rd., P.O. Box 146, Valemount, BC, Canada V0E 2Z0. **Phone:** (250) 566-9893.

GEORGE HICKS REGIONAL PARK is off Hwy. 5 at 785 Cranberry Lake Rd. The site offers a bird's-eye view of Chinook salmon as they near the end of a 1,280-kilometre (768-mi.) upstream trip from mid-August to mid-September. **Hours:** Daily May 1 to mid-Oct. **Cost:** Donations. **Phone:** (250) 566-9893.

MOUNT ROBSON PROVINCIAL PARK is on Hwy. 16. Mount Robson, at 3,954 metres (12,972 ft.) is the highest peak in the Canadian Rockies. Other park highlights include glacier-fed lakes, valleys, canyons, waterfalls, rivers and streams. More than 180 species of birds reside here along with deer, moose, bears, elk and caribou. Fishing, camping, horseback riding and hiking are just a few of the outdoor activities to be enjoyed.

Scenic views abound on the many walking and hiking trails. A visitor center is at the Mount Robson viewpoint. *See Recreation Areas Chart.* **Hours:** Park open daily 24 hours. Visitor center open May 1 to mid-Oct. **Cost:** Donations. **Phone:** (250) 566-4325. ▲ ⊠ 🐟 🏞

ROBSON HELIMAGIC INC. tours depart from the Yellowhead Helicopters hangar, 5 km (3 mi.) n. on Hwy. 5 to 3010 Selwyn Rd. Helicopters take passengers on 12-36 minute tours of the Valemount and Mount Robson areas, providing breathtaking views of glaciers, snow-covered mountains, alpine meadows, valleys, waterfalls, lakes and rivers.

Heli-skiing, heli-snowshoeing and heli-snowboarding also are offered in winter. Summer activities are available. **Hours:** Daily 8-7, June-Aug.; Mon.-Fri. 8-5, rest of year. Phone ahead to confirm schedule. **Cost:** $94.29-$232.38. **Phone:** (250) 566-4401 or (877) 454-4700.

R.W. STARRATT WILDLIFE SANCTUARY is 1 km (.6 mi.) s. on Hwy. 5. The refuge, also known as Cranberry March, is home to more than 140 species of songbirds, waterfowl and other animals. Informational signs line 7 kilometres (4 mi.) of trails and walkways to two viewing platforms. There are 6 kilometres (3.7 mi.) of trails and walkways in the sanctuary, or if you prefer your sightseeing from a boat, you can canoe through.

Time: Allow 30 minutes minimum. **Hours:** Daily 9-9, July-Aug.; 9-8, mid-June through June 30; 10-6, June 1 to mid-June; 9-5, Sept. 1-Labour Day; 10-5, late May-May 31 and day after Labour Day-Sept. 30; 10-4, early May to mid-May. Phone ahead to confirm schedule. **Cost:** Free. **Phone:** (250) 566-4846.

CANADAS BEST VALUE INN   250/566-8222

Hotel
Rates not provided

Address: 1501 Swift Creek Rd V0E 2Z0 **Location:** Just e of Hwy 5 (Yellowhead Hwy). **Facility:** 67 units, some kitchens. 2 stories, interior corridors. **Parking:** winter plug-ins. **Amenities:** safes. **Pool(s):** heated indoor. **Activities:** hot tub, exercise room. **Guest Services:** coin laundry. **Featured Amenity:** continental breakfast.

CARIBOU GRILL   250/566-8244

American. Casual Dining. **Address:** 1002 5th Ave V0C 2Z0

THE GATHERING TREE   250/566-0154

Sandwiches. Quick Serve. **Address:** 1150 5th Ave V0E 2Z0

Vancouver

Then & Now

You're hiking along a wide, bark-mulched trail through an old-growth forest of towering Western red cedar, Douglas fir and Western hemlock. Salmonberry, huckleberry and bog buckbean grow together in one luxurious tangle. A raccoon ambles by, giving you an inquisitive look. A goose honks in the distance. You stop and ask out loud, "Wait a minute—am I really in a city?" That question is answered a few minutes later when you emerge from Stanley Park to the hustle and bustle of Georgia Street.

There's no denying the beauty of Vancouver's natural setting. Vistas of green coastal mountains and the deep blue Strait of Georgia were tailor-made to grace a postcard. And downtown is a marvel: skyscrapers, human hubbub and quiet, tree-lined residential streets all coexisting harmoniously in one tightly packed urban cityscape. If that pocket description sounds a bit like San Francisco, it's an apt comparison, but there really is no place like Vancouver.

No doubt the southwestern British Columbia wilderness impressed Capt. George Vancouver.

An officer in the British Royal Navy, he sailed into Burrard Inlet on June 13, 1792, while searching for the Northwest Passage, the sea route that connects the Atlantic and Pacific oceans. Vancouver named the inlet after his friend Sir Harry Burrard, a member of Parliament, but lent his own moniker to the city and the large island that lies between the mainland and the Pacific.

Vancouver was incorporated in 1886, quite a young city given its present-day status. A Canadian Pacific Railway passenger train arrived the following year, showering exuberant spectators with soot and cinders. By the 1890s transpacific shipping inaugurated the city as a major world port, and the future was looking rosy indeed.

That era produced colorful characters like John Deighton, aka "Gassy Jack," a saloon owner who set up shop in Gastown, the city's oldest section and a popular tourist hangout. The name is a reference not to excessive flatulence but to Deighton's vaunted reputation for tall-tale bluster. His likeness stands at the circle where Water, Alexander, Powell and Carrall streets converge, and having your picture snapped in front of the old salt is a prime Vancouver photo op.

Mandarin and Cantonese are the mother tongues in almost a third of Vancouver's homes, and only San Francisco's and New York's Chinatowns are bigger. The Millennium Gate at Pender and Taylor streets is a symbolic entryway that incorporates both eastern and western symbols. Between 1890 and 1920 Asian immigrants settled on

Gastown's steam clock

(Continued on p. 264.)

Destination Vancouver

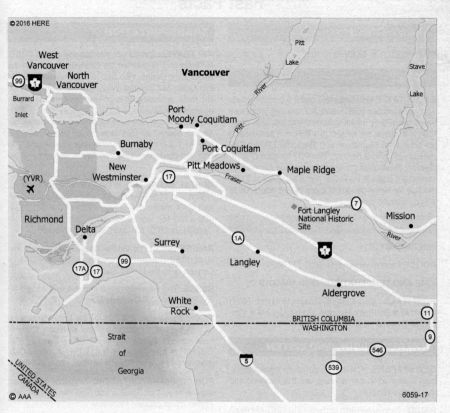

© 2016 HERE

West Vancouver
North Vancouver
Burrard Inlet
Vancouver
Pitt Lake
Stave Lake
Port Moody Coquitlam
Burnaby
Port Coquitlam
New Westminster
Pitt Meadows
Maple Ridge
(YVR)
Richmond
Delta
Surrey
Langley
Fort Langley National Historic Site
Mission
Aldergrove
White Rock
BRITISH COLUMBIA
WASHINGTON
Strait of Georgia
UNITED STATES
CANADA
© AAA
6059-17

This map shows cities in the Vancouver vicinity where you will find attractions, hotels and restaurants. Cities are listed alphabetically in this book on the following pages.

Fast Facts

POP: 603,502 ▪ **ELEV:** 3 m/10 ft.

MONEY

SALES TAX: British Columbia has a 5 percent goods and services tax (GST) and a 7 percent provincial sales tax (PST). Hotel accommodations with more than four rooms are subject to a PST of 8 percent and an additional Municipal and Regional District Tax (MRDT) of up to 3 percent. The PST for alcohol is 10 percent. Restaurants and admission fees are exempt from the 7 percent PST. Car rental sales tax is $1.50 per day for rental periods of more than 8 hours, up to 27 consecutive days.

WHOM TO CALL

EMERGENCY: 911

POLICE (non-emergency): (604) 717-3321

TIME AND TEMPERATURE: (604) 664-9010

HOSPITALS: Mount Saint Joseph Hospital, (604) 874-1141 ▪ St. Paul's Hospital, (604) 682-2344 ▪ Vancouver General Hospital, (604) 875-4111.

WHERE TO LOOK AND LISTEN

NEWSPAPERS: The two major daily newspapers, both published in the morning, are the *Province* and the *Vancouver Sun*.

RADIO: Vancouver radio stations CBU/CBC-AM (690) ▪ CBU-FM (105.7) ▪ CHQM-FM (103.5) ▪ CKCL-FM (104.9) ▪ CKLG-FM (96.9) ▪ CKNW-FM (980) ▪ and CKWX News-AM (1130) have news and weather reports.

VISITOR INFORMATION

Vancouver Tourist InfoCentre: 200 Burrard St., Plaza Level, Vancouver, BC, Canada V6C 3L6. **Phone:** (604) 683-2000 or (604) 682-2222.

Maps, lodging reservations and literature about attractions as well as tickets for tours are available at the Vancouver Tourist InfoCentre which is open daily 8:30-6, Victoria Day weekend to mid-Sept.; Mon.-Sat. 8:30-5, rest of year.

TRANSPORTATION

AIR TRAVEL: Vancouver International Airport (YVR), in Richmond, is reached via Granville Street and the Arthur Lang Bridge, then Sea Island Way, which leads into Grant McConachie Way. Taxi rates are fixed on flat rates according to a zoning system. The trip to downtown/Kitsilano is $31; Canada Place is $35. TransLink's Canada Line rapid transit operates rail service every 7 to 15 minutes, from approximately 5 a.m. to 1 a.m., between Vancouver International Airport and downtown. One-way fare is $5; phone (604) 953-3333.

RENTAL CARS: Hertz, at the Vancouver International Airport and 1128 Seymour St., offers discounts to AAA and CAA members; phone (604) 606-4711, (604) 606-3785 for airport location, (800) 263-0600 in Canada, or (800) 654-3131 in North America.

RAIL SERVICE: The Via Rail passenger train terminal is at 1150 Station St.; phone (888) 842-7245 in Canada or in the United States.

BUSES: The Greyhound bus terminal is at 1150 Station St.; phone (604) 483-8133.

TAXIS: Fares start at $3.25 for the first kilometre (.6 mi.), plus $1.88 for each additional kilometre. Companies include Black Top & Checker Cabs, (604) 731-1111 ▪ MacLure's, (604) 831-1111 ▪ Yellow Cab, (604) 681-1111 ▪ and Vancouver Taxi, (604) 871-1111.

PUBLIC TRANSPORTATION: TransLink offers bus service as well as SeaBus and SkyTrain service. *See Public Transportation for details.*

BOATS: BC Ferries links Vancouver and other points on the mainland with Vancouver Island operating 36 vessels serving 47 ports of call. Nanaimo and Sunshine Coast ferries leave from Horseshoe Bay, 21 kilometres (13 mi.) west of the city in West Vancouver. From Tsawwassen south of Vancouver automobile/passenger ferries make frequent trips to the southern Gulf Islands, Nanaimo and Swartz Bay, near the town of Sidney north of Victoria; Vancouver-Victoria bus service is available on most sailings.

For schedules phone the British Columbia Automobile Association, (604) 268-5555; British Columbia Ferries Information Centre, (250) 386-3431 outside British Columbia; (888) 223-3779 in British Columbia; or Tourism Vancouver, (604) 683-2000.

(Continued from p. 262.)

back streets like Shanghai Alley off Pender Street; wall panels tell the story of their lives. Holding out your arms is almost enough to embrace the Sam Kee Building at 8 Pender St., which is a mere 6 feet wide.

Just as the city is a cosmopolitan blend of cultures, Vancouverites represent a melting pot of nationalities.

The original inhabitants of coastal British Columbia were the Northwestern peoples, and their descendants live in urban areas as well as reserve communities located within ancestral territories. Diversity is the keynote, whether preserved in street names like Barclay and Granville, or in neighborhoods like Little Italy or the East Indian community.

Not bad for a former lumber town, eh?

Must Do: AAA Editor's Picks

- One of the world's great food markets, **Granville Island Public Market** (1689 Johnston St.) is the place to go for a slice of Vancouver life as well as the freshest fruits, vegetables, cheeses, meats, candy, baked goods and flowers.

- Enjoy fabulous waterside views while strolling, bicycling or in-line skating around the perimeter sea wall of ▽ **Stanley Park** (main entrance at west end of Georgia St.). Or tour the park in a horse-powered trolley provided by **Stanley Park Horse-drawn Tours** (735 Stanley Park Dr.). The park also has tennis courts, a pool, a golf course, woodland trails, playgrounds, totem poles and a miniature steam train. Beaches, gardens and woodland glades complete this 405-hectare (1,000-acre) urban sanctuary.

- Adorable white beluga whales steal the show at ▽ **Vancouver Aquarium Marine Science Centre** (845 Avison Way) in Stanley Park; competing for attention are the center's thousands of marine animals including sea lions, sharks and walruses as well as rain forest creatures such as iguanas and crocodiles. Go behind the scenes in close encounters with dolphins, belugas, sea turtles, penguins, Steller sea lions and sea otters.

- Downtown's **Robson Street** (between Burrard and Jervis streets) beckons shoppers with its trendy designer boutiques, bookstores, jewelry shops and more. When you need a break, grab a seat and a cappuccino at a bistro or coffee shop and watch the world go by.

- On a clear day, you can see forever at ▽ **Grouse Mountain** (6400 Nancy Greene Way) in North Vancouver; the Skyride, an aerial cable car, presents a breathtaking view of Vancouver and the harbor. Spend the day here without running out of things to do: Go skiing, zipline above an alpine rain forest, go paragliding or go on a sleigh ride, strap on snowshoes for a wintry hike, watch lumberjacks show off their axe and log-rolling skills, visit grizzly bears and a grey wolf and get a 360-degree view of Vancouver from the top of a 20-story-high wind turbine. Those without skiing skills can travel along trails and enjoy sensational views in a chauffeured Sno-Limo. After you've worked up an appetite, feast on fine cuisine at The Observatory or British Columbian dishes at Altitudes Bistro.

- Spot pods of orcas and other sea creatures on a scenic whale-watching cruise. Both **Steveston Seabreeze Adventures** (12551 #1 Rd., Bldg. 43) and **Vancouver Whale Watch** (210-12240 Second Ave.) in Richmond offer the opportunity to hear whales vocalize through hydrophones, see marine animals like sea lions and porpoises and travel through the Fraser River Delta, Strait of Georgia and the Gulf Islands.

- Dine in restaurants that rival New York's; an array of multicultural cuisines is available, but don't leave town without savoring mouth-watering Pacific Northwest and Asian cuisine featuring freshly caught seafood. Try such favorites as **CinCin** (1154 Robson St.) and **Joe Fortes Seafood & Chop House** (777 Thurlow St.).

- Discover one of Vancouver's trendiest neighborhoods; **Yaletown** (bordered by Homer and Robson streets) has earned comparisons to New York's SoHo, and rightfully so. Once a warehouse district, the area now attracts the young and hip with its of-the-moment shops, galleries, loft apartments, pubs and outdoor cafés.

- Confront your fear of heights with a walk through the tops of evergreens at ▽ **Capilano Suspension Bridge Park** (3735 Capilano Rd.) in North Vancouver; the 137-metre (450-foot) bridge sways 70 metres (230 ft.) above the Capilano River Canyon. View the Totem Park and learn about the area's indigenous culture through storytelling, weaving and beadwork demonstrations.

- Take in ▽ **VanDusen Botanical Garden** (5251 Oak St.), which takes full advantage of the local climate. Wander the meandering paths of the 22-hectare (5-acre) paradise to find 40 themed gardens. A highlight is a hedge maze made of 3,000 pyramidal cedars.

Yaletown

Vancouver 1-day Itinerary

AAA editors suggest these activities for a great short vacation experience. Those staying in the area for a longer visit can access a 3-day itinerary at AAA.com/TravelGuide.

Morning

- Kick off your tour at the **Vancouver Lookout at Harbour Centre Tower** (555 W. Hastings St.). A glass elevator zips to the top of this 167-metre-tall (553-ft.) building, where 360-degree views of the skyline, the North Shore Mountains, English Bay, Coal Harbour and Stanley Park take your breath away.

- Head to North America's second-largest **Chinatown** (between Carrall and Gore streets). Snap up souvenirs at colorful emporiums; choose from Chinese curios, jewelry and fashions and bamboo, jade and silk goods.

- Escape bustling crowds at **Dr. Sun Yat-Sen Classical Chinese Garden** (578 Carrall St.). Experience peace and harmony in this Ming Dynasty-style garden accented with pagodas, plum trees, bamboo and jade-hued ponds.

Afternoon

- Take your pick of three museums in Vanier Park, home to the **Museum of Vancouver**, **H.R. MacMillan Space Centre** (both at 1100 Chestnut St.), and the **Vancouver Maritime Museum** (1905 Ogden Ave.), where you can tour a 1960s submarine and a 1940s schooner, the first vessel to circumnavigate North America.

- The Museum of Vancouver has a wealth of exhibits focusing on the region's art and history. Or stargaze at the H.R. MacMillan Space Centre's planetarium.

- Grab lunch at **Vera's Burger Shack** (1925 Cornwall Ave.), half a kilometre (.3 mi.) south of Vanier Park. Expect a well-worth-it wait; the award-winning hamburgers are so popular they can't make them fast enough.

- Explore some of downtown's distinctive neighborhoods. You'll find funky boutiques, bookstores and coffee shops on Kitsilano's West Fourth Avenue, while antique shops, art galleries, pubs and street vendors line Gastown's cobblestone streets along Water Street. Trendy Yaletown (bordered by Homer and Robson streets) houses swank furniture shops, cafés and hip nightclubs. Robson Street (between Burrard and Jervis streets) has such mall chains as Banana Republic and Zara.

Evening

- For your evening repast, choose from an array of fine restaurants, many with picturesque waterfront views. Try **The Sandbar Seafood Restaurant** (1535 Johnston St.) on Granville Island.

- After dinner, catch a hockey game when the Canucks take to the ice at **General Motors Place** (800 Griffiths Way).

- Do you love the nightlife? Vancouver clubs run the gamut from frenetic discos, intimate lounges

Dr. Sun Yat-Sen Classical Chinese Garden

and swanky cabarets to beery pubs, sports bars and stadium concerts. Downtown's Granville Street is where the 24-hour party people go. Try **The Roxy** (932 Granville St.) or **Caprice Nightclub** (967 Granville St.) for starters.

- Drink, dance and be merry at Gastown's **The Metropole Pub** (320 Abbott St.) and **The Lamplighter Public House** (92 Water St.). In Kitsilano, the scene centers around local pubs, including **Elwood's** (3145 W. Broadway) and **The Wolf & Hound** (3617 W. Broadway). Watch flamenco dancers at **Kino Café** (3456 Cambie St.); sip sangria and clap along to the music.

- You'll find hipper-than-thou hangouts in Yaletown, home base for the city's young, stylish professionals. **Bar None** (1222 Hamilton St.) is a SoHo-style spot with a cigar lounge and martini bar, while homey **Yaletown Brewing Company** (1111 Mainland St.), with a fireplace and pool tables, is popular with the 9-to-5 crowd for microbrews and burgers. You may find celebs at au courant **AuBAR** (674 Seymour St.), since Vancouver is known as Hollywood North. Masculine yet modern décor, pool tables, a shark tank, big-screen TVs and hockey fans fill **The Shark Club**, a sports bar in the Sandman Hotel Vancouver City Centre (180 W. Georgia St.). After 10 p.m., live DJs and go-go dancers get the party started.

- Not a club-hopper? Wrap up your day with a dinner cruise provided by **Harbour Cruises** (501 Denman St.). Marvel at downtown's nighttime skyline ablaze with lights as you're treated to a West Coast-style buffet and live music.

Top Picks for Kids

Under 13

- **Granville Island** (1689 Johnston St.) lures adults to its many markets and shops, but it also has specialty shops that appeal directly to youngsters. Under a rainbow-colored sign, the **Granville Island Kids Market** (1496 Cartwright St.) is a miniature mall for little ones. From the moment they step through the diminutive door, kids can eyeball goodies in 23 shops that cater to their every whim, cavort in the arcade and make a splash in the water park (open in summer months).

- What kid doesn't enjoy face painting, storytelling, jugglers, stilt-walkers, clowns, puppet shows, comedy, dance and music? Find all this and more during May's weeklong **Vancouver International Children's Festival,** also on Granville Island.

- When it's time to quiet growling tummies, longtime local favorite **White Spot** is the right spot; it has several locations throughout the city. Small fries can get a burger, grilled cheese sandwich or spaghetti in a ship-shaped Pirate Pak, complete with a chocolate coin.

Teens

- The flight simulator ride at **FlyOver Canada** (201-999 Canada Pl.) will elicit screams and gasps of delight as it sweeps and soars from east to west over icebergs, Niagara Falls, the Rocky Mountains and other unforgettable landmarks of the Canadian countryside.

- Go on a full-day adventure on a **Prince of Whales Whale Watching** tour (1601 Bayshore

Stanley Park

Dr.). Your family will have a whale of a time as they gaze in awe at pods of glistening tuxedoed orcas and grey humpbacks leaping out of the Georgia Strait. The trip includes a stop in Victoria and a visit to Butchart Gardens, which features an orca on its carousel.

- For adventure, nature and animal lovers, and those who aren't afraid of heights, head to **Grouse Mountain** (6400 Nancy Greene Way) in **North Vancouver.** Ascend to the peak in an enclosed gondola, skimming over treetops on the way up. Brave souls can ride to the top of a 215-foot wind turbine for views that go on for miles. For a yummy treat, get a beavertail, a pastry covered in cinnamon sugar.

- **Capilano Suspension Bridge Park** (3735 Capilano Rd.), also in **North Vancouver,** yields more adventure for the daring. Tread slowly along a swaying 137-metre-long (450-ft.) footbridge above the treetops and the Capilano River, which spans 70 metres deep (230 feet). But don't fear, Mom and Dad: The bridge is reinforced with steel cables and concrete, so it's perfectly safe. After you cross the bridge, head for Cliffwalk, a 650-foot cliffside walkway with bridges and viewing platforms suspended from Douglas fir trees with a stunning canyon view.

All Ages

- Combining manicured gardens with West Coast rainforests, beaches, forest trails and surrounded on three sides by water, **Stanley Park** (main entrance at west end of Georgia St.) offers amazing views of the mountains, the city and English Bay. Rent a bike and pedal along the 10-kilometre (6.5-mi.) seawall. The park also has totem poles, a miniature train, playgrounds, a pool and a water park.

- Need a break from walking? Hop on a trolley on **Stanley Park Horse-drawn Tours** (735 Stanley Park Dr.) and see the 400-hectare (1,000-acre) park at a leisurely pace.

- Meet the most adorable sea creatures at Stanley Park's **Vancouver Aquarium Marine Science Centre** (845 Avison Way). Ogle rascally otters, beguiling belugas, pudgy sea lions, spotted harbor seals and chatty dolphins, just some of the more than 70,000 marine animals that call the aquarium home. Get super close at animal encounters, where you can feed and help train sea lions, otters and beluga whales.

- From the moment they set eyes on **Science World at TELUS World of Science** (1455 Quebec St.), kids will be psyched; housed in a huge geodesic dome, the science center is even cooler inside. There's something for every age group. Tykes under age 7 can learn about water, color, light and movement in the Kidspace Gallery, and the entire family will enjoy live shows, hands-on exhibits and IMAX films that bring out their inner scientist.

Arriving
By Car

Hwy. 1 (Trans-Canada Highway) and hwys. 1A and 7 are the major east-west routes to Vancouver. Tolls on Port Mann Bridge on Hwy. 1 and Golden Ears Bridge require electronic payment; there are no cash lanes. The toll is $3.55 each way. Phone (604) 516-8736 or toll-free (855) 888-8736 outside the Lower Mainland.

To reach downtown on the Trans-Canada Highway, use the First Avenue exit or continue to Hastings Street.

Hwy. 99 to S.W. Marine West becomes the major downtown artery, Granville Street. Before becoming a city street, Hwy. 99 begins its journey as I-5 at the Mexican border and crosses through California and the Pacific Northwest; beyond Vancouver it continues beyond Whistler to meet Hwy. 97, the main north-south route.

Getting Around
Street System

All streets and avenues in downtown Vancouver are named; many are one-way. Outside the business section, east-west avenues are numbered beginning with First Avenue, and north-south streets are named. Addresses begin at Ontario-Carrall streets for all east-west numbering and at Powell-Dundas streets for all north-south numbering.

The downtown peninsula is connected to western Vancouver by the Burrard, Granville and Cambie bridges and to North Vancouver and West Vancouver by the Lions Gate and the Iron Workers Memorial (Second Narrows) bridges.

SkyTrain

Rush hours are 6-9:30 a.m. and 3-6:30 p.m. Right turns on red are permitted after a stop, unless otherwise posted; drivers must yield to pedestrians and vehicles in the intersection and to city buses pulling into traffic.

Some intersections in the metropolitan area have a blinking green light. This is used when there is a stop sign, not a signal, on the cross street and allows pedestrians or bicyclists to turn the main street's light red so they can go through the intersection safely. When driving on a cross street, you must wait for a gap in traffic before you proceed.

Parking

On-street parking, controlled by meter, is restricted on many thoroughfares during rush hours; violators' cars will be towed. When parking at a meter, you can pay by credit card, coins or even by phone if you download the PayByPhone mobile app; phone (604) 909-7275 for information. Off-street parking is available in lots and garages at rates ranging from $1.25 per half-hour to $11 or more per day. Parking in a school zone between 8 and 5 on any school day is strictly prohibited unless otherwise posted.

Public Transportation

TransLink, Metro Vancouver's regional transportation authority, offers an integrated system utilizing bus, rail, SeaBus, cycling paths, custom transit services and roads to points throughout Vancouver and all suburban areas. Conventional buses, community shuttles, trolleys and HandyDART custom transit link tourist destinations, transit exchanges and SkyTrain stations

SeaBus is a passenger-only ferry that crosses Burrard Inlet, connecting downtown Vancouver with the North Shore. The downtown Waterfront terminal connects with buses, SkyTrain. The West Coast Express and the Lonsdale Quay terminal connects with an extensive North Shore bus network.

SkyTrain, Vancouver's light rail rapid transit system, runs from Waterfront Station through downtown Vancouver to the suburbs of Burnaby and New Westminster and across the Fraser River to the suburb of Surrey.

SkyTrain is one of the longest and oldest automated, driverless light rapid transit systems in the world and has three lines. The 19-kilometre (12-mi.) Canada Line, connects downtown with Richmond and Vancouver International Airport and has 16 stations, including stops at Vancouver City Centre, Olympic Village, Broadway-City Hall, Marine Drive, Vancouver International Airport and four Richmond locations. The train ride from downtown to the airport takes 26 minutes. The Expo Line and Millennium Line connect downtown with the cities of Burnaby, New Westminster and Surrey.

Trains operate every 7 to 15 minutes Mon.-Fri. 5:30 a.m.-midnight, Sat. 6:50 a.m.-12:30 a.m., Sun. 7:50 a.m.-11:30 p.m. Fares are the same for any TransLink service and a single fare covers travel for up to 90 minutes across Metro Vancouver. A 1-zone fare Monday through Friday until 6:30 p.m. is $2.75, a 2-zone fare is $4 and a 3-zone fare is $5.50; for ages 5-13, students ages 14-19 with a valid GoCard and ages 65+ a 1-zone fare is $1.75, a 2-zone fare is $2.75 and a 3-zone fare is $3.75. The fare for weekdays after 6:30 p.m. and Saturday, Sunday and holidays for all zones is $2.50; for ages 5-13, students ages 14-19 with a valid GoCard and ages 65+ the fare for all zones is $1.75. A trip to or from the airport adds an additional $5.

Every SkyTrain station has information panels. A 1-day pass, available from SkyTrain and SeaBus ticket machines, Safeway food stores and 7-11 stores, costs $9.75 and covers all zones; for ages 5-13, students ages 14-19 with a valid GoCard and ages 65+ the cost is $7.50. If you pay by cash on buses, exact change is required. Phone (604) 953-3333 daily 6:30 a.m.-11:30 p.m. for more information.

Aquabus Ltd., (604) 689-5858, provides ferry service with departures every five minutes between Hornby Street, Granville Island, David Lam Park, Stamps Landing, Spyglass Place, Yaletown, Plaza of Nations and The Village daily 6:48 a.m.-9:30 p.m. Times vary according to destination. Fare ranges from $3.25-$5.50 one-way or $25 for 20 tickets, $15 for a day pass, and $60 for a monthly pass, with discounts for ages 4-12 and ages 65+. The four Cyquabuses are equipped to carry wheelchairs and bicycles.

Daily bus service between Vancouver International Airport and Whistler is provided by Pacific Coach's YVR Whistler SkyLynx. Passengers can be picked up and dropped off at major Vancouver and Whistler lodgings; reservations are required. Phone (604) 662-7575 or (800) 661-1725 for information. To reach the airport from Vancouver by public transit, take Bus 90 B-line from Burrard station to Richmond Centre, then transfer to bus 424 to the airport.

Shopping

When you set out on a Vancouver shopping expedition be sure to bring along the AAA street map, because you're definitely going to want to hang out in every one of this town's cool and distinctively different urban neighborhoods.

Yaletown, reached via Davie Street, is the *de rigueur* downtown residential address for successful young professionals (just look at all those glass-walled condo towers). This former 19th-century rail yard district has morphed into an uber-stylish urban enclave; the industrial brick warehouses of yore are now hip clothing boutiques and designer furniture outlets.

Art galleries are concentrated along Homer and Mainland streets. Yaletown's many dog owners shop for trendy canine accessories at **barking babies** (1188 Homer St.); phone (604) 647-2275. Keep your head stylishly warm and dry with a fedora, derby or cloche from **Goorin Bros.** (1188 Hamilton St.), a cool hat shop that may remind you of your grandfather's living room, complete with Victrola and leather sofa; phone (604) 683-1895. For a lovely souvenir

John Fluevog Shoes

that doesn't feature a maple leaf, pick up a flowery Royal Albert teapot or some Cristal D'Arques stemware at **The Cross Decor & Design** (1198 Homer St.); phone (604) 689-2900.

Robson Street, however, is downtown's shopping central. Stand at the intersection of Robson and Burrard on any given day and it's a sea of shopping bag-toting humanity. From Burrard up to Jervis Street Robson offers an uninterrupted stretch of window gazing: men's and women's fashions and accessories, shoes, jewelry, eyewear, gifts, chocolates, cosmetics and luggage, plus more restaurants than you can shake a stick at. For high-quality outdoor wear go to **Roots**, a popular Canadian chain. There are two locations, one for adults (1001 Robson St.), phone (604) 683-4305, and one for kids (1153 Robson St.), phone (604) 684-8801.

Very touristy but always enjoyable **Gastown**, the oldest section of the city, runs for several blocks along Water Street. The atmosphere is turn-of-the-20th-century renovated, with handsome brick buildings and white-globed lamp posts bedecked with flowery hanging baskets. There are lots of art galleries, antique shops, fashion boutiques and places to buy Canadian souvenirs. But Gastown isn't all about maple candy or a moose in a can; trendy home furnishings stores sell sleekly contemporary furniture by well-known Canadian and international designers.

Standout shops in Gastown include cutting-edge **John Fluevog Shoes** (65 Water St.) which combines a vintage vibe with Dr Marten-esque cool, and **Dream** (45 Water St., Suite 145), where local fashionistas shop for locally designed apparel and jewelry; phone (604) 688-6228 and (604) 683-7326, respectively. Stop in at **Kit and Ace** (151 Water St.) and pick up a couple of their affordable, comfy *and* machine-washable cashmere-blend T-shirts; phone (844) 548-6223.

There's a **Coastal Peoples Fine Arts Gallery** here as well (312 Water St.); phone (604) 684-9222. **Gallery Gachet** (88 E. Cordova St.) is a non-profit artist-run center with exhibitions; phone (604) 687-2468. There also are specialty shops like **Button Button** (318 Homer St.), with buttons in all shapes and sizes from around the world, and **Jade Mine** (4-375 Water St.), which stocks a big selection of sculptures and jewelry carved from jade mined in northern British Columbia. Phone (604) 687-0067 and (604) 687-5233, respectively. Pet lovers will be drawn to **EZ Dog** (56 Powell St.), packed with goodies for your "best friend"; phone (604) 559-5606.

Walk a few blocks down Carrall Street into **Chinatown** *(see attraction listing)*, another neighborhood made for sidewalk exploration. You'll probably look rather than buy, since most of the businesses are where residents do their shopping. The produce and food markets lining Keefer and Main streets are fascinating, with unusual vegetables and bins full of dried fish, mushrooms and other foodstuffs. You'll also find a couple of jewelry shops selling bead necklaces and various trinkets.

Note: While the main thoroughfares in Gastown and Chinatown are fun to visit during the day, use big-city common sense regarding any encounters with panhandlers and street people, and avoid wandering around side streets after dark.

Granville Island Public Market

Downtown certainly isn't the only place to shop. In **Kitsilano**, along the south shore of English Bay, the blocks of West 4th Avenue between Fir and Larch streets are filled with grocers, wine shops and stores selling fashions, sportswear and sports gear from bikes to skis to snowboards.

The 10-block stretch of Granville Street between 6th and 16th avenues—dubbed **South Granville**—is where old-money families do their shopping; think expensive clothing boutiques, upscale furniture retailers and a plethora of home accessories stores like **18 Karat** (3039 Granville St. at 14th Avenue W.); phone (604) 742-1880. **Urbanity** (2412 Granville St.) sells beautiful knit sweaters, coats and blankets, most bought direct from Scandinavian designers; phone (604) 801-6262.

Much more down to earth is **Commercial Drive**, east of Main Street from Venables Street to East Broadway, one of Vancouver's funkiest shopping experiences. Most of the shops and businesses are owner-operated; chains are few, which means that it's really fun to explore. Hit "the Drive" on a Saturday or Sunday afternoon. The heart of Commercial Drive is between Venables Street and 6th Avenue E. Books, CDs, vintage clothing and unusual gifts are all good bets.

You could easily spend an entire day doing **Granville Island**, but shoppers and foodies should focus on the **Granville Island Public Market**. The big building is crammed with vendors: produce, meat, seafood, baked goods, coffee and a head-spinning array of specialty foods. Take advantage of fresh B.C. salmon, artisanal cheeses and ripe, regionally grown fruit. Have lunch here, too; takeaway fast food counters offer Asian, Mexican, Indian, sushi, pizza and just about everything else. Phone (604) 666-6655.

There also are plenty of shops outside the market selling regionally produced art, food, jewelry, clothing, kids' toys and the like. And don't drive—it's much easier to take the False Creek Ferry. It's a 10-minute ride to Granville Island from the Aquatic Centre dock just off Beach Drive in the West End (ferries also depart from the dock at the foot of Davie Street in Yaletown).

Another popular destination is the **Lonsdale Quay Market**, 123 Carrie Cates Ct. at the foot of Lonsdale Avenue in North Vancouver; phone (604) 985-6261. The lower level is a fresh market with vendors selling produce, seafood, baked goods and delicatessen items; specialty boutiques are on the upper level. Get a crab roll, fish and chips or a panini sandwich from one of the numerous stands at the international food bar and enjoy it outside on the dock, which has a great view of downtown and the harbor (don't feed the seagulls; they'll snitch a bite at any opportunity). There's a parkade for market customers—enter your car license plate number at one of the machines (2 hours of free parking with proof of purchase, $2.50 per additional hour, free after 6 p.m. and on weekends), but it often fills up;

you also can take the SeaBus, which shuttles between the downtown and North Vancouver terminals every 15 minutes. Conveniently, the SeaBus terminal is just a few minutes walk from the market.

Malls? Vancouver has several, if that's your shopping thing. Downtown, upscale **Pacific Centre** (corner of Georgia and Howe streets) is anchored by tony Holt Renfrew; in September 2015, Nordstrom's flagship store opened here in the space once occupied by Sears. The center's 60-plus other stores offer men's and ladies' wear, casual clothing, fashion accessories, shoes, electronics, sporting goods, handbags and cosmetics; shops include American Eagle Outfitters, bebe, Club Monaco, Ermenegildo Zegna, Express, SGH Sunglass Hut and Sony. The mall is open Mon.-Tues. and Sat. 10-7, Wed.-Thurs. 10-9, Fri. and Sun. 11-6; phone (604) 688-7235.

On the North Shore in West Vancouver, the city's second largest mall, **Park Royal** (on either side of Marine Drive, just west of Taylor Way and the Lions Gate Bridge) consists of two enclosed malls with anchor La Maison Simons plus more than 275 stores and restaurants as well as **The Village**, specialty shops and cafés in an open-air setting. It is open Mon.-Tues. 10-7, Wed.-Fri. 10-9, Sat. 9:30-6, Sun and holidays 11-6; phone (604) 922-3211. Park Royal's expanded and modernized south section is now open, while the north section is nearing completion of its renovations; in the south section are such stores as Anthropologie, Bath & Body Works, Free People, J. Crew, Sephora and Zara, among many others.

McArthurGlen Designer Outlet Mall, next to Vancouver International Airport in Richmond (1000-7899 Templeton Station Rd.), next to the Canada Line station, opened in July 2015; the European-style, open-air mall has more than 60 stores with a focus on designer brands such as Armani, Coach, Cole Haan and Polo Ralph Lauren; hours are Mon.-Sat. 10-9, Sun. and statutory holidays 10-10. The mall also has flight arrival and departure screens for those who are shopping pre-flight. From downtown Vancouver, take the Canada Line to Templeton Station; from there, it's a 3-minute walk. Phone (604) 231-5525.

For a true mega-mall experience, head to **Burnaby** and **Metropolis at Metrotown**, 4700 Kingsway (Hwy. 1A/99A) between Willingdon and Royal Oak avenues; phone (604) 438-4700. It's the province's largest shopping center, with The Bay (outfitters for the Canadian Olympic team), Sears and nearly 400 other stores on three sprawling levels. Expect the usual chains and specialty outlets—everything from American Eagle Outfitters to Zuri—plus a food court and the latest box-office biggies at Famous Players SilverCity. The mall is open Mon.-Sat. 10-9, Sun. and certain holidays 11-7, although a few stores may vary. Parking (plenty of it) is free.

Built in 1959, **Oakridge Centre**, 650 W. 41st Ave. at Cambie Street, is Vancouver's oldest mall, but that doesn't mean it's not packed with popular mall retailers. *Au contraire*, it has about 100 stores, including perennial favorites Apple, Banana Republic,

McArthurGlen Designer Outlet Mall

BCBGMAXAZRIA, Coach, Crabtree & Evelyn, Crate & Barrel, Gymboree, MAC Cosmetics, Michael Kors and Tiffany & Co.; The Bay is its anchor. The center is open Mon.-Tues. and Sat. 9:30-7, Wed.-Fri. 9:30-9, Sun. 11-6 (holiday hours may vary). Future plans for the mall include a $1.5-billion expansion, part of a massive area redevelopment that will enhance the shopping experience and also include residential and office buildings and green spaces, with the first phase expected to open in 2019. Phone (604) 261-2511.

Nightlife

Hip, cosmopolitan Vancouver has a buzzing nightlife, with plenty of spots where the young and beautiful congregate—and there are even a few options for the rest of us. Among the latter are several sophisticated hotel lounges where you can relax over drinks in a quiet, elegant atmosphere. Downtown is a prime spot for these given its assortment of business-class hotels. The bar inside **YEW Seafood + Bar**, the restaurant at the Four Seasons Hotel Vancouver (downtown at 791 W. Georgia St.) is a lovely place to put a capper on a busy day. A 12-metre (40-ft.) ceiling makes this a breathtakingly lofty space, warmed by wood-paneled walls and a big sandstone fireplace. The bar is open until midnight Sun.-Wed., 1 a.m. Thurs.-Sat.; phone (604) 692-4939.

Bacchus Piano Lounge, in The Wedgewood Hotel & Spa (downtown at 845 Hornby St.), is an equally elegant spot to enjoy a glass of B.C. wine or a martini in surroundings that exude luxury—subdued lighting, antique furniture and vases of fresh flowers, with a softly tinkling piano in the background. There's live entertainment Thursday through Saturday evenings. Do dress up. Phone (604) 608-5319.

You'll find a lively vibe at **The Shark Club** in the Sandman Hotel Vancouver City Centre (180 W. Georgia St.). This stylishly renovated sports bar has two massive TVs and DJs on Thursdays, and it's just a 5-minute walk from BC Place, so you can stop in before or after a concert or Canucks game; phone (604) 687-4275.

Opus Bar, in the Opus Hotel (322 Davie St.), is a cool, sleek lounge in hot-to-trot **Yaletown**. The decor is stylish with a capital "S": designer furniture, iridescent mood lighting, shimmer screens and live video feeds that allow you to keep an eye on the action at the bar and in the lounge. DJs spin dance music for a fashionably dressed, upwardly mobile crowd, and there's live music every Wednesday; phone (604) 642-6787.

Baby boomers will feel right at home in **The Cascade Room** (2616 Main St.), also in Yaletown. This restaurant and bar is a transplanted bit of British pub culture: Lampshades feature Queen Victoria's likeness, and a large glass panel advises patrons to "Keep calm and carry on"—a World War II slogan uttered by stiff-upper-lip Brits. Slide into one of the horseshoe-shaped booths for a cocktail, a beer or a pint of lager; phone (604) 709-8650.

Also hipper-than-thou is **Yaletown Brewing Company** (1111 Mainland St.), where suit-and-ties gather after business hours to shoot some pool and sup on microbrews and burgers; sit by the fireplace or on the spacious patio, depending on the weather; phone (604) 681-2739.

Granville Street is hopping with nightclubs, all with reasonable cover charges. **The Caprice** (967 Granville St.), a multi-level venue, has a large dance floor, VIP area, lounge with an outdoor patio and TV screens showing sporting events. Special event nights augment DJ music (Wednesday through Saturday) that tends toward Top 40, R&B and dance hits; phone (604) 685-3288.

The Roxy (932 Granville St.) draws a young, ready-to-party crowd with house bands pumping out rock and Top 40 and bartenders who put on their own show. If you don't feel like dancing, watch TV or play pool. It's open 7 p.m.-3 a.m. nightly; phone (604) 331-7999.

The **Commodore Ballroom** (868 Granville St.) is an old-time dance hall that books everything from gospel choirs to death metal quadruple bills. This is the place to see up-and-coming bands as well as established acts that don't sell out arenas. The dance floor is in front of the stage and table seating is limited; arrive early unless you don't mind standing in the back of the room. Phone (604) 739-4550.

Touristy **Gastown** pulses with nightspots. The **Steamworks Pub & Brewery** (375 Water St.) is named for the Gastown steam line that runs through the premises. The hoist of choice here is beer (brewed on-site), from signature Lions Gate lager and Cascadia cream ale to such concoctions as Heroica oatmeal stout and sour cherry ale. Coffee drinkers will appreciate the Steamworks Grand, a combo of espresso and stout. The basement looks like a Bavarian-style drinking hall, while upstairs the atmosphere is clubbier, with leather chairs and windows overlooking the harbor; phone (604) 689-2739. Energetic live bands tear it up at **The Revel Room** (238 Abbott St.), as they crank out rockabilly, blues, old country, Texas swing, boogie woogie and jump blues Tues.-Thurs. and Sun. nights beginning at 7 p.m., and there's daily boogie piano during "Sour Hour" (4-6 p.m.); phone (604) 687-4088.

You'll literally have to go underground to get to Gastown's **Guilt & Co.** (1 Alexander St.), as it's down a flight of stairs under the restaurant Chill Winston on Gassy Jack Square. This *boîte* has the feel of a bunker or an unfinished rec room, but reeks of cool. The evening's band plays on a small stage backed by a stone wall, a small dance floor sandwiched between it and round tables holding burning candles. You'd almost expect to see beatniks in berets snapping their fingers in time to the music, but the clientele is mostly smartly dressed young professionals. Guilt & Co. serves up expertly mixed cocktails with whimsically wicked names like Devil Inside, Desire and Little White Lies; phone (604) 288-1704.

Cool club kids hang at **Celebrities** (1022 Davie St.) in Davie Village. Visiting DJs like David Guetta and Boy George take advantage of state-of-the-art sound and lighting, and the dance floor is invariably packed with chiseled, often shirtless young men. It's open every night but Monday; phone (604) 681-6180.

If you're into casino games *and* live bands, lucky you! In addition to the usual slot machines and poker tables, the **Hard Rock Casino Vancouver** in nearby Coquitlam has three listening rooms: the intimate Asylum Sound Stage, where performers range from local bands to burlesque to comedy; the 100-seat Unlisted Lounge, with DJ'd jazz and electro-groove music and the occasional live act; and The Molson Canadian Theatre, a 1,000-seat venue hosting tribute bands, performers like singer-songwriter Rob Thomas or Roger Hodgson (ex-Supertramp), and 1980s heavy metal bands. Phone (604) 523-6888.

If you're in the Kitsilano area, go a little further southeast to the **Shameful Tiki Room** (4362 Main St.), a modern-day Trader Vic's. The room is decked out in Polynesian decor from floor to ceiling in painstaking detail, with a thatched ceiling, carved wood Tiki gods, puffer fish lamps, vintage postcards permanently lacquered onto tables and vintage Tiki memorabilia. Sip a mai tai, snack on small plates, or go for the volcano bowl, a potent blend of liquors served in a huge clamshell meant for sharing with three of your closest friends (the drink is accompanied by thunder, lightning and smoke from the bar's erupting volcano). Unlike most clubs, the tunes are played at lower decibels so you can carry on a conversation, and the overall ambience is relaxing yet fun.

And here's a beautifully simple suggestion. On a balmy summer evening, head down to **English Bay Beach** (just off Beach Avenue at the south end of Denman Street). First, stop and get an ice cream cone or something from Starbucks (there's one at the corner of Davie and Denman). Then sit on a beach log or a bench, or stroll along the seawall promenade, and watch the sun set over the bay and the mountains rising beyond the North Shore, turning the water a pale luminescent blue or perhaps streaking the clouds fiery orange or crimson. It's just you and nature—plus the company of similar-minded souls.

The *Georgia Straight,* a news and entertainment weekly that comes out on Thursday, has extensive arts and entertainment listings for greater Vancouver.

Big Events

Vancouver is an energetic city with plenty to celebrate, and its citizens know how to start the year off right. On January 1, more than 1,000 fearless swimmers brave the icy waters of English Bay in the annual **Polar Bear Swim.** The event includes a 91-metre (100-yd.) race and attracts thousands of spectators, some dressed in wild costumes.

Kung Hay Fat Choy! You'll probably hear this traditional Chinese blessing over and over during Chinese New Year. Vancouver, home to its own Chinatown, hosts an event honoring this Chinese holiday which occurs between late January and mid-February. The ⚡ **Vancouver Chinese New Year Parade** in **Chinatown** begins with activities at the **Dr. Sun Yat-Sen Classical Chinese Garden;** have your fortune told, learn calligraphy, watch martial artists and listen to storytellers. A parade winds through the streets of Chinatown in the afternoon.

Celebrate the return of spring in April with the **Vancouver Sun Run,** reputedly the second largest 10K run in North America. Cheer on tens of thousands of participants as they sprint or stroll through downtown, enjoying views of English Bay and Stanley Park with live music played along the route.

In May, the **Vancouver International Children's Festival** is a weeklong party for kids on **Granville Island.** Entertainers from around the globe put on plays and puppet shows as well as dance and musical performances. Activities include face painting, kite flying and playing in clay; jugglers, stilt-walkers, clowns and wandering minstrels create a carnival-like atmosphere.

You'll fall in love with Shakespeare at the **Bard on the Beach Shakespeare Festival** from early June through late September. Watch tragedies and comedies staged in front of the mountains and English Bay in **Vanier Park.** Select performances include a salmon Bard-B-Q during intermission and fireworks after the show.

Cultural entertainment sails into **False Creek** with the **Rio Tinto Alcan Dragon Boat Festival** in mid-June. Also held in June is the **Vancouver International Jazz Festival.** Bop 'til you drop at the festival, which features legendary jazz musicians and vocalists from around the globe playing at various jazz joints, parks and public places. Past performers include Miles Davis, Wynton Marsalis, Tito Puente and Diana Krall.

Has all that jazz put you in the mood for more music? The **Vancouver Folk Music Festival** at **Jericho Beach Park** draws fans from as far away as Los Angeles for concerts during mid-July.

Celebration of Light features 3 nights of fireworks displays and is held at English Bay the last week of July and the first week in August.

In late August, your childhood memories of the county fair will come rushing back at **The Fair at Pacific National Exhibition.** Ride the merry-go-round, root for your favorite swine at a pig race, bite into a crisp candy apple and try your luck on the midway. You'll also find live music, agricultural exhibits, a beer garden, talent contests and much more.

For 11 days in September, step outside of the norm at the **Vancouver International Fringe Festival.** Uncensored theatrical shows by about 100 international groups and performers defy the rules of conventional theater. Most of the shows take place on Granville Island.

December brings several holiday-themed events to the city. During the **Carol Ships Parade of Lights,** vessels adorned with Christmas lights and decorations sail in **Vancouver Harbor** almost every night, passing many Vancouver neighborhoods. Landlubbers celebrate with live music, craft workshops, bonfires and hot chocolate.

Vancouver Chinese New Year Parade

Bright Nights in Stanley Park, a holiday tradition of more than 30 years, turns the forest and the train into a wonderland with more than 2 million lights and animated displays.

More than a million shimmering lights greet you at ⚘ **VanDusen Botanical Garden** during the **Festival of Lights.** Dancing lights on Livingstone Lake twinkle in time to holiday music, and a water terrace is turned into a "magic marsh" complete with fiber-optic lights and whimsical creatures. Choral music and a storytelling Santa add to the magic.

Commemorate the beginning of winter at the **Winter Solstice Lantern Festival,** held on a late-December evening. Join a procession of lantern-holding revelers accompanied by drummers, beginning at either ⚘ **Science World at TELUS World of Science** or **Strathcona Community Centre** and ending at Dr. Sun Yat-Sen Classical Chinese Garden, where you'll enjoy ethereal music and enchanting lighted gardens.

Sports & Rec

Vancouver offers such a diversity of recreational opportunities that anyone with a yen for variety can ski on Grouse Mountain in the morning, golf on the banks of the Fraser River in the afternoon, fish for salmon in Horseshoe Bay at dusk and top off the day with a dip in English Bay.

Vancouver's park system has tennis courts, swimming pools, putting greens, golf courses, lawn bowling greens, hiking paths and a comprehensive bike route. For park information phone the city's Parks and Recreation Department at 311 (within the city) or (605) 873-7000.

Bicyclists will have a field day in Vancouver, which is practically a mecca for two-wheeling types. There are about 400 kilometres (249 mi.) of bike paths in the city. The Stanley Park Seawall, 9 kilometres (6 mi.) long, may be the most well-known bike route in the area, and for good reason. There's no shortage of eye candy—Burrard Inlet, Coal Harbour, rocky beaches, the North Shore mountains, totem poles, downtown Vancouver—for riders or pedestrians while circling Stanley Park. Want more? The seawall is just one section of the 30-kilometre (18 mi.) Seaside Greenway, which begins at the convention center, runs along Coal Harbour, around Stanley Park to Granville Island and Kitsilano Beach, then west along the Point Grey Road Greenway to Jericho Beach and Spanish Banks Beach Park. Note that bike helmets are required by law.

Head for the hills of the North Shore Mountains to practice your **extreme mountain biking** skills. Burnaby Mountain also comes equipped with structures and a 28-kilometre (17-mi.) network of trails where you can practice stunts. For tamer rides, coast flat trails through heavily wooded forests in Pacific Spirit Regional Park. Bicycle rentals (mountain, comfort, cruiser, hybrid and tandem) can be had at Bayshore Rentals, 745 Denman St.; phone (604) 688-2453. In North Vancouver, rent all-mountain, cross-country, trail and freeride bikes at

Endless Biking, 1401 Hunter St.; phone (604) 985-2519 or (604) 836-2517 after hours.

Go **swimming** in English Bay, which is bordered by beaches from West Point Grey to Stanley Park, most with lifeguards in summer and various amenities. Beaches are easily accessible from Northwest Marine Drive in West Point Grey, Point Grey Road in Vancouver West and from Beach Avenue downtown. In addition to Vancouver's nine indoor swimming pools, there are outdoor pools at Kitsilano, Maple Grove, New Brighton and Stanley Park's Second Beach.

White-water rafting is available April through September on the nearby Chilliwack River and a little farther afield on the Fraser and Thompson rivers, including the Devil's Gorge. Vancouver rafting companies offering day trips as well as multiday trips include REO Rafting Adventure Resort, (604) 461-7238 or (800) 736-7238, and Kumsheen Rafting Resort, (250) 455-2296 or (800) 663-6667. Lotus Land Tours offers **sea kayaking** trips on Indian Arm, Zodiac tours of Howe Sound and **whale-watching** tours; phone (604) 684-4922 or (800) 528-3331.

Winter visitors with a penchant for **skiing** can head for the hills in North Vancouver to tackle the challenging slopes of Grouse Mountain or Mount Seymour Provincial Park *(see attraction listings).* East of Vancouver are Hemlock Valley and Manning Park ski resorts, offering both downhill and cross-country treks. Cypress Provincial Park in West Vancouver also has cross-country and downhill skiing *(see Recreation Areas Chart).* Serious skiers and snowboarders will want to head north of Vancouver to Whistler and Blackcomb mountains.

When the waters sparkle from the summer sun, Vancouver becomes a **boating** paradise. For visitors without a boat, several companies have craft for hourly or daily rental. For **fishing** charters and boat rentals phone Sewell's Marina, (604) 921-3474, at Horseshoe Bay or Granville Island Boat Rentals, (877) 688-2628.

Vancouver residents love spectator sports, especially **football, hockey** and **soccer.** The BC Lions of the Canadian Football League usually play before capacity crowds at [SAVE] BC Place Stadium, 777 Pacific Blvd. S. Fans of Major League Soccer can watch the Vancouver Whitecaps FC get their kicks at the same stadium. The Canucks of the National Hockey League compete in Rogers Arena, 800 Griffiths Way; phone (604) 899-7444 for the event hotline. The Vancouver Giants, a junior hockey team, play at the Pacific Coliseum, 2901 E. Hastings St.; if you can't get tickets for the Canucks, who often sell out, Giants tickets cost less and offer just as many thrills; phone (604) 252-3700. For more football, soccer and hockey ticket information, phone Ticketmaster, (855) 985-5000 or the automated ticket sales line (855) 985-5500.

Baseball is played by the Vancouver Canadians at Scotiabank Field at Nat Bailey Stadium, 4601 Ontario St.; phone (604) 872-5232 for schedule and ticket information. Indoor **lacrosse** can be enjoyed at Bill Copeland Sports Centre, 3676 Kensington

Ave. in Burnaby, (604) 297-4521 or the 24-hour info line (604) 298-0533; and at Queens Park Arena at First Street and Third Avenue in New Westminster, (604) 777-5111.

Thoroughbred racing with pari-mutuel betting is held at Hastings Park Race Course on the grounds of the Pacific National Exhibition; phone (604) 254-1631 or (877) 977-7702 *(see attraction listing p. 281).*

Note: Policies concerning admittance of children to pari-mutuel betting facilities vary. Phone for information.

Performing Arts

The 2,765-seat **Queen Elizabeth Theatre** at the intersection of Hamilton and Georgia streets, (604) 665-3050 or (800) 840-9227, is home to **Ballet British Columbia**, (604) 732-5003, and the **Vancouver Opera**, (604) 683-0222 and also hosts touring shows. The adjacent **Vancouver Playhouse** presents professional theater, dance, recitals, some opera and chamber music; phone (604) 665-3050. The **Vancouver Symphony Orchestra** performs at the **Orpheum Theatre**, Smithe and Granville streets; phone (604) 665-3050 for ticket information.

Other prominent metropolitan theaters presenting dramatic productions include the **Arts Club Theatre**, on Johnston Street on **Granville Island**, (604) 687-1644; the **Metro Theatre**, 1370 S.W. Marine Dr., (604) 266-7191; **Langara College's Studio 58**, 100 W. 49th Ave., (604) 323-5227; and **The Cultch**, 1895 Venables St., (604) 251-1363.

During the summer concerts and musicals are presented in Stanley Park's Malkin Bowl. **Kitsilano Showboat** at **Kitsilano Beach** presents outdoor variety shows and concerts Monday, Wednesday, Friday and Saturday at 7:30 p.m. from early July to late August (weather permitting). For more information phone (604) 734-7332.

Concerts in such genres as classical, country, pop and rock are presented year-round at the 17,500-seat **Pacific Coliseum**, 100 N. Renfrew St. in Hastings Park, (604) 253-2311, and **Rogers Arena**, 800 Griffiths Way, (604) 899-7400.

The daily papers carry listings of cultural events, as do weekly and monthly magazines. Ticket outlets include **Tickets Tonight**, 210-200 Burrard St., inside the Tourism Vancouver Visitor Centre, and **Collector's Den**, a Ticketmaster outlet, in the Metrotown Mall in Burnaby. Tickets must be bought in person and sales usually end at 4 p.m.; there's a limit of four tickets per customer.

INSIDER INFO:
A Stanley Park Jaunt

Stanley Park is the crown jewel in a city uncommonly blessed with scenic attributes. It is not only paradise for walkers, hikers and outdoor recreation enthusiasts but a truly delightful wooded retreat that's all the more special for being only a stone's throw away from downtown Vancouver's skyscrapers and urban congestion. And one of the best

Orpheum Theatre

ways to experience the park is to walk the seawall promenade around its perimeter, a distance totaling a bit more than 9 kilometres (6 mi.) that you can take at a leisurely or vigorous pace.

A good starting point is English Bay Beach in the West End neighborhood; just follow the paved seawall path. (There are designated lanes for walkers and for cyclists and roller bladers.) One of the best things about this walk is that it offers an uninterrupted series of scenic water views. To your left, keep an eye out for the stone sculptures that people construct when the rocky beach is accessible during low tide; some of them are quite elaborate.

Once past the swimming pool and assorted recreational facilities at Second Beach you'll leave many of the casual strollers behind. Between Second Beach and Third Beach the waters of English Bay sparkle in the sun as the seawall runs along sandstone cliffs and conifer-covered hillsides. Third Beach is a good place to go beachcombing at low tide, when the receding waters reveal barnacle-encrusted rocks and pieces of driftwood.

Siwash Rock is a distinctive landmark you can't miss. This sea stack—a geologic feature formed when volcanic action caused a portion of rock to break free from the park foundation—is between 15 and 18 metres (50 and 60 ft.) tall. A small Douglas fir stands at its summit. Past Siwash Rock the seawall rounds the northern end of the park. At Prospect Point you'll be treated to outstanding views of the Lions Gate Bridge and mountains rising from the opposite North Shore.

On the other side of Prospect Point the seawall runs along Burrard Inlet. Stands of Douglas fir, western hemlock and western red cedar are in full view on this stretch of the walk. The fierce-looking green dragon arching toward the water is the Empress of Japan Figurehead, a replica of a prow ornament that once graced the RMS *Empress of Japan* ocean liner. Just beyond the dragon is "Girl in Wet Suit," a sculpture of a woman sitting on top of a rock about 9 metres (30 ft.) offshore. Although at first glance you might think she's a mermaid, this girl is wearing flippers and has a scuba mask atop her head.

Before reaching Brockton Point you'll see Stanley Park's totem poles standing in a clearing to your right. Interpretive plaques explain the significance of each pole's symbolic figures. Beyond the totems sits the squat Brockton Point Lighthouse. The 9 O'Clock Gun is an old cannon near the tip of Brockton Point; it used to be fired at 6 p.m. to signal the end of the fishing day. Although it goes off electronically these days, the sound is still loud enough to make you jump.

After curving around Brockton Point the seawall runs along the shore of Coal Harbour. There are superb views of the downtown skyline and the yachts and other pleasure craft docked at the harbor. Keep following the paved walkway until you reach the Georgia Avenue park entrance, which will take you back to the West End. Relaxing at one of the cafes or casual restaurants along Denman Street is a perfect way to end this Stanley Park jaunt. You've earned it.

ATTRACTIONS

BC SPORTS HALL OF FAME AND MUSEUM is at jct. Beatty and Robson sts., Gate A of BC Place Stadium. British Columbia sports history is traced from native traditions to the modern Olympic games. Honorees include amateur and professional teams, athletes, journalists and sports pioneers. Interactive galleries provide opportunities for running, climbing, throwing, riding, rowing and even mini hockey. The All Access Experience includes a behind-the-scenes tour of areas the public does not normally see, including team locker rooms, the media lounge and the field.

2221-16

© 2015 HERE

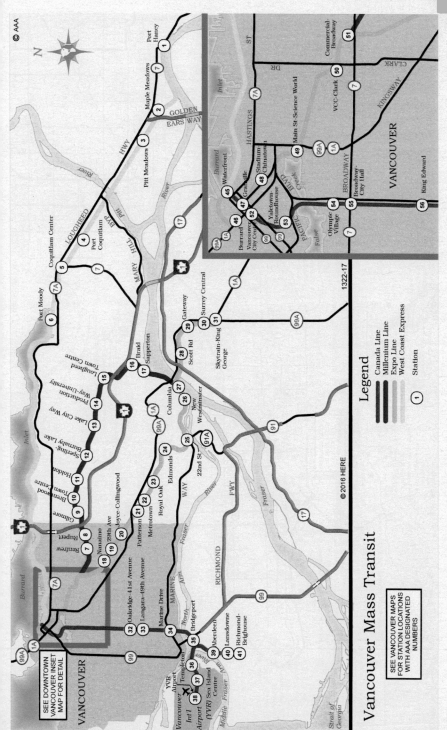

© AAA

N

Vancouver Mass Transit

Legend

Canada Line
Millenium Line
Expo Line
West Coast Express
① Station

SEE VANCOUVER MAPS
FOR STATION LOCATIONS
WITH AAA DESIGNATED
NUMBERS

SEE DOWNTOWN
VANCOUVER INSET
MAP FOR DETAIL

VANCOUVER

© 2016 HERE

1322-17

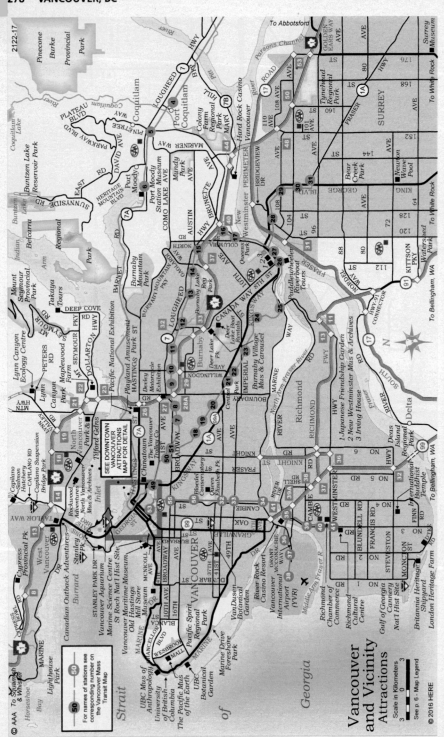

Vancouver and Vicinity Attractions

Scale in Kilometers

See p. 6 - Map Legend

© 2016 HERE

Hours: Daily 10-5. All Access Experience is offered on various days; phone ahead to confirm schedule. Closed Jan. 1 and Christmas. **Cost:** $15; $12 (ages 6-17, ages 65+ and students with ID); $25 (one adult and one child age 6-17); $40 (family, two adults and two children). All Access Experience $20. **Phone:** (604) 687-5520. [image] Stadium-Chinatown, 48

BILL REID GALLERY OF NORTHWEST COAST ART is downtown at 639 Hornby St. between W. Georgia and Dunsmuir sts. The museum is dedicated to Bill Reid, one of Canada's finest artists and a passionate proponent of Northwest Coast art. Reid was a master Haida goldsmith as well as a noted sculptor, carver, broadcaster, writer and spokesman for his native people.

His gold and silver jewelry forms the basis of the museum's permanent collection. Other highlights include his masterpiece, an 8.5-metre (28-ft.) bronze frieze titled "Mythic Messengers," and a massive 6.7-metre (22 ft.) totem pole carved in honor of the artist. Video displays alongside Reid's art allow visitors to watch him at work at different stages of his life. The gallery also hosts changing exhibitions of contemporary Aboriginal art of the Northwest Coast.

Time: Allow 1 hour minimum. **Hours:** Daily 10-5, late May-late Sept.; Wed.-Sun. 11-5, rest of year.

▼ See AAA listing p. 297 ▼

Closed major holidays. **Cost:** $10; $7 (students ages 18+ with ID and senior citizens); $5 (ages 13-17); free (ages 0-12); $25 (family, two adults and their children). Phone ahead to confirm hours and rates. **Phone:** (604) 682-3455. 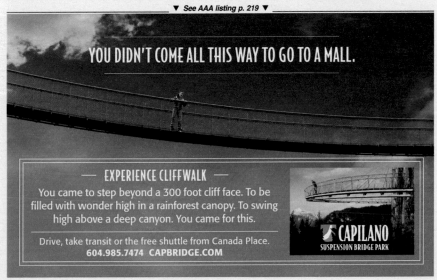 Burrard, 46

BLOEDEL CONSERVATORY—see Queen Elizabeth Park p. 281.

DR. SUN YAT-SEN CLASSICAL CHINESE GARDEN is at 578 Carrall St. What this walled garden lacks in size it more than makes up for in serene beauty. Located in the heart of Chinatown, it's a delightful respite from the surrounding hustle and bustle. Modeled after private gardens in the city of Suzhou, the garden embodies the Taoist philosophy of yin and yang, where every element—light, texture, vegetation—is balanced.

The architecture of the pavilions, covered walkways, terraces and viewing platforms evokes Ming Dynasty classical design. Rocks and water are integral elements, while trees and plants—from pine trees and bamboo to graceful weeping willows and winter-flowering plum trees—all have symbolic connotations. The Jade Water Pavilion is graced with beautiful woodwork. Two of the garden's most intriguing elements are the 43 leak windows (each one has a different lattice pattern) and the groupings of Tai Hu rocks, interestingly shaped stones from China's Lake Tai that lend themselves to all sorts of artistic interpretations.

Visitors can walk through the garden on their own, but the guided tour offers historical perspective and encourages you to reflect on the design elements in different ways. Afterward, take a stroll through the adjacent public park, where pathways wind through clumps of bamboo and other plantings.

Art and horticultural exhibits and demonstrations also are offered. Festivals and concerts are featured throughout the year. **Time:** Allow 1 hour minimum. **Hours:** Daily 9:30-7, June 15-Aug. 31; daily 10-6, May 1-June 14 and in Sept.; Tues.-Sun. 10-4:30 (10-2, Dec. 24 and 31), rest of year. Closed Jan. 1 and Christmas. **Cost:** $13.30 (includes guided tour and tea); $10.45 (ages 6-17, ages 65+ and students with ID); $9.50 (students with ID); $26.67 (family, two adults and two children ages 0-17). **Phone:** (604) 662-3207. 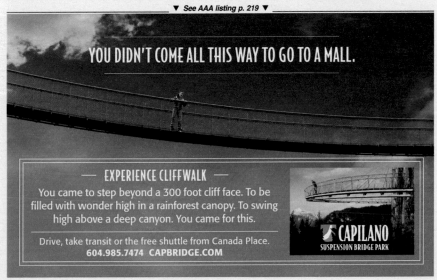 Stadium-Chinatown, 48

FLYOVER CANADA is at 999 Canada Pl. on the Canada Place pier. A 65-foot spherical screen shows a film of Canada while guests sit in moving state-of-the-art seats on an 8-minute whirlwind "flight" soaring across the country. Along with mountainside vistas, urban streetscapes and expansive prairies, visitors will experience sensations such as wind, mist and scents for an all-encompassing and fully immersive journey across Canada.

Note: The ride is not recommended for pregnant women or those with heart conditions, chronic neck or back problems, photosensitive epilepsy or other physical impairments. **Time:** Allow 30 minutes minimum. **Hours:** Daily 10-9. **Cost:** $21.95; $18.95 (ages 13-17 and 65+); $14.95 (ages 0-12). A $2 fee per ticket is charged for "fast lane" admission. Under 12 must be accompanied by a guardian 14+. Under 30 centimetres (40 in.) tall are not permitted. **Phone:** (604) 620-8455. 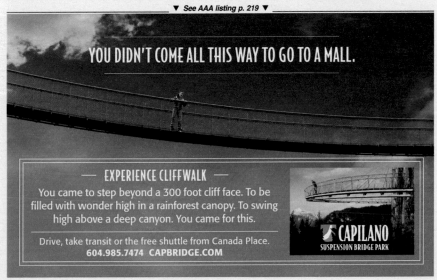 Waterfront, 45

HOLY ROSARY CATHEDRAL is at 646 Richards St. The church has stained-glass windows and eight bells hung in the rare English ringing style. **Hours:** Cathedral open Mon.-Sat. 6:30-6, Sun. 7:30 a.m.-9 p.m. Bell ringing Sun. at 10:30, Tues. at 7:30 p.m. **Cost:** Free. **Phone:** (604) 682-6774. 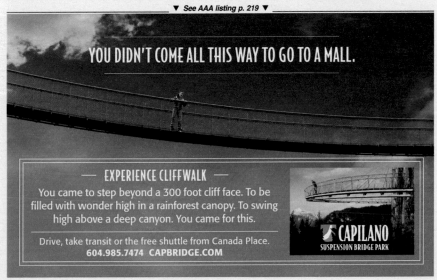 Granville, 47

▼ See AAA listing p. 219 ▼

SAVE **H.R. MACMILLAN SPACE CENTRE** is at 1100 Chestnut St. in Vanier Park. The center's Planetarium Star Theatre presents full dome tours of astronomy and space exploration. Other features include GroundStation Canada, which uses live science demonstrations to explain the latest discoveries; Cosmic Courtyard, which features interactive exhibits and one of only five touchable moon rocks in the world; an observatory with a 0.5-metre (1.6-ft.) telescope; and hands-on exhibits.

Time: Allow 1 hour, 30 minutes minimum. **Hours:** Daily 10-5, July-Aug.; Mon.-Fri. 10-3, Sat. 10-5, Sun. noon-5, rest of year. Planetarium shows Sat. at 7:30 p.m. and 9 p.m. Observatory open Sat. 8 p.m.-midnight. Hours and show times may vary; phone ahead. Closed Christmas. **Cost:** $19.20; $16 (ages 12-18 and 55+); $13.87 (ages 5-11); $59.73 (family, two adults and up to three children). Evening planetarium shows (includes planetarium and observatory) $13.87; $10.67 (ages 12-18 and 55+); $8.53 (ages 5-11); $40.53 (family, two adults and up to three children). **Phone:** (604) 738-7827.

SAVE **MUSEUM OF VANCOUVER,** on the s.w. end of Burrard St. in Vanier Park at 1100 Chestnut St., creates area-focused displays and programs that encourage dynamic conversations about what was, is, and can be Vancouver. Permanent exhibitions present the city's story 1900-1979, and are complemented by contemporary feature exhibits.

Hours: Daily 10-5 (also Thurs. 5-8), July 1-Labour Day weekend; Tues.-Sun. 10-5 (also Thurs. 5-8), rest of year. Closed Christmas. **Cost:** $15; $11 (ages 12-18, ages 65+ and students with ID); $5 (ages 5-11); donations (last Thurs. of the month 5-8). **Phone:** (604) 736-4431.

PACIFIC NATIONAL EXHIBITION is on E. Hastings St. between Renfrew and Cassiar sts. The site occupies 58 hectares (144 acres) and is home to Pacific Coliseum, a tradeshow and entertainment complex, and a skateboard park. Various trade and hobby shows, rock concerts and sporting events are scheduled throughout the year. The annual Fair at the PNE has been an end of summer highlight since it began in 1910.

Hours: Fair daily 11 a.m.-midnight (weather permitting), mid- to late Aug. through Labour Day. Last admission 1 hour, 30 minutes before closing. **Cost:** Fair admission $17; $8.50 (ages 65+); free (up to five children ages 0-13 per paying adult age 21+). $1.75 per ride coupon; $44.75 for 30 coupons (each ride requires 4-8 coupons). Ride pass $44.75 (over 48 in. tall); $31.75 (under 48 in. tall). Rates may vary; phone ahead. **Phone:** (604) 253-2311.

Playland Amusement Park is between Renfrew and Cassiar sts. at 2901 E. Hastings St. The 4-hectare (10-acre) park features games, miniature golf and more than 30 rides, including a vintage wooden roller coaster and four "extreme" rides.

Hours: Daily 11 a.m.-midnight, Aug. 1-15 (weather permitting); Sat.-Sun. 10-6, early May to

mid-June; Mon.-Fri. 10-3, Sat.-Sun. 10-6, mid-June through June 30; Mon.-Fri. 10-6, Sat.-Sun. and holidays 10-7, in July; daily 10-7, Aug. 16-31; Sat.-Sun. 10-5, Sept. 1 to mid-Sept. Phone ahead to confirm schedule. **Cost:** $34.29 (over 122 centimetres or 48 in. tall); $23.57 (under 122 centimetres or 48 in. tall); $25.48 (two adults ages 21+ when accompanied by a paying child ages 0-12); free (ages 0-3 and 65+). Rates may vary; phone ahead. **Phone:** (604) 253-2311 or (604) 252-3620.

QUEEN ELIZABETH PARK is off Cambie St. and W. 33rd Ave. On 152-metre (499-ft.) Little Mountain, the highest point in Vancouver, the park offers magnificent views of the city, harbor and North Shore Mountains. Other highlights include an arboretum; rose, sunken and quarry gardens; dancing fountains; tennis courts; and pitch and putt greens. **Hours:** Daily 24 hours. **Cost:** Free. **Parking:** $3.25 per hour, $11 per day, May-Sept.; $2.25 per hour, $6 per day, rest of year. **Phone:** (604) 873-7000. Oakridge-41st Avenue, 32

Bloedel Conservatory is at 4600 Cambie St. Climatically varied species of plants grow in a climate-controlled, illuminated triodetic dome 43 metres (141 ft.) in diameter and 21 metres (70 ft.) high. More than 200 free-flying tropical birds and a fish pond are other highlights. **Time:** Allow 30 minutes minimum. **Hours:** Mon.-Fri. 9-8, Sat.-Sun. 10-8, May 1-Labour Day; daily 10-5, rest of year. Closed Christmas. Phone ahead to confirm schedule. **Cost:** $6.43; $4.29 (ages 13-18 and 65+); $3.10 (ages 3-12); $14.52 (family, 2 adults and children). **Phone:** (604) 257-8584. King Edward, 56

GEM SAVE **SCIENCE WORLD AT TELUS WORLD OF SCIENCE,** 1455 Quebec St., is housed in a geodesic dome and features hands-on exhibits and demonstrations that explain scientific phenomena. Water, air and motion are some of the physical sciences explored in the Eureka! Gallery. The Wonder Gallery is a new space for young learners up to the age of five. Live, zany science demonstrations with audience participation take place daily in the Peter Brown Family Centre Stage. Watch films in the OMNIMAX Theatre, which projects nature and science films onto a dome screen that's 5 stories high and 27 metres (88 ft.) in diameter; or take a seat in the high-definition Science Theatre, which offers films and live shows.

Human performance and nature are the subjects of additional galleries. Learn about sustainable communities in Our World: BMO Sustainability Gallery, explore human life sciences in BodyWorks and discover the wonders of nature in Search: Sara Stern Gallery. Science World also has two outdoor galleries. In the Ken Spencer Science Park, you can plant seeds and gather eggs from chickens. On the TD Environmental Trail, discover exhibits about environmental issues on a hike around the building.

Note: BodyWorks is closed until May 2017. **Time:** Allow 2 hours minimum. **Hours:** Daily 10-6, July

1-Labour Day and during spring and winter breaks; Tues.-Fri. 10-5 (also Mon. 10-5, day after spring break-late June), Sat.-Sun. 10-6, rest of year. Open 10-3, Dec. 31; noon-6, Jan. 1. Closed Christmas. Phone ahead to confirm schedule. **Cost:** Exhibits and one OMNIMAX film $31.75; $27 (ages 13-18, ages 65+ and students with ID); $23.75 (ages 3-12). Exhibits only $25.75; $21 (ages 13-18, ages 65+ and students with ID); $17.75 (ages 3-12). **Parking:** $4-$15. Rates may vary; phone ahead. **Phone:** (604) 443-7440. ⏹ ⏹ Main St-Science World, 49

STANLEY PARK shares the peninsula where the city's business district is located. Vancouver's first City Council made a momentous decision in 1886, when it petitioned the government to lease 400 hectares (1,000 acres) of largely logged-over land for public and recreation purposes. The result of this wise move was the creation of one of North America's largest urban parks—a cool, lush evergreen oasis right at downtown's doorstep.

Named for Lord Frederick Stanley, Governor General of Canada when the park officially opened in 1888, Stanley Park was once land hunted and foraged by the Musqueam and Squamish First Nations peoples. And a large part of what makes it such a special place is the lush West Coast rain forest growth. One of the park's great pleasures, in fact, is exploring the network of bark-mulched trails that wind through Douglas fir, western hemlock and western red cedar trees. These giants create a hushed environment of subdued light and cool air that is all the more remarkable given such close proximity to downtown's hurly-burly.

Stanley Park

Such a magnificent setting, of course, offers plenty of inspiring views, and there are more than 27 kilometres (16.7 mi.) of trails. For example, follow Prospect Point Trail, an invigorating uphill trek, to Prospect Point at the northern tip of the peninsula; from this elevated perspective the vista of Burrard Inlet, the Lions Gate Bridge, the North Shore and the mountains beyond is a stunner. For a more relaxed jaunt, amble along Stanley Park Drive, the seawall that encircles the peninsula. The route totals about 9 kilometres (5.5 mi.), and you'll be gazing out over water essentially the entire time. There are separate lanes for walkers and cyclists/inline skaters.

There are other ways to enjoy nature. Walk to Beaver Lake, a body of water that is in the process of shrinking as it transitions from lake to bog (and may in time lose its watery aspects completely and become a meadow). Its surface is covered with yellow water lilies in summer. Or take a spin around Lost Lagoon, off the Georgia Street entrance to the park. This man-made body of water (created when the Stanley Park Causeway was built in 1916) provides a nesting ground for ducks, swans and Canada geese. The lagoon is located on the Pacific Flyway, which makes it a favorite haunt of bird watchers as well as one of the park's most popular strolls.

Standing near the Brockton Oval (where you can watch a cricket match), just in from the seawall, are nine totem poles. They make a distinctive photo op, and you can learn about their history by reading the interpretive panels. Another example of First Nations art is the "Raven: Spirit of Transformation" sculpture, created from the stump of a Douglas fir felled by a destructive 2006 windstorm. It stands at Klahowya Village at the Miniature Railway Plaza. You'll also want to take a ride in a horse-drawn carriage *(see attraction listing)*; breathing in the scent of the cedar trees while listening to the gentle clip-clop of a Clydesdale's hooves is an eminently relaxing way to tour the park.

There are free tennis courts near Lost Lagoon and the Beach Avenue entrance. The Second Beach Pool has English Bay as a backdrop. An 18-hole pitch-and-putt golf course also is located at Second Beach. At low tide, explore the rocky shoreline along Second and Third beaches. For kids there are three playgrounds—including the Variety Kids Water Park (June 1–Sept. 1) at Lumberman's Arch, Second Beach and near the park's Rose Garden—as well as a miniature steam train *(see attraction listing)*.

Shows take place at the open-air Malkin Bowl/Theatre Under the Stars in July and August. A park information booth is just inside the Georgia Street entrance, next to the seawall.

Hours: Park open daily 24 hours. Information booth open 9:30-7:30, June 15-Labour Day; hours vary rest of year, phone ahead. **Cost:** Park free. **Parking:** $2.25-$3.25 per hour; $6-$11 per day. **Phone:** (604) 681-6728. ⏹ ⏹

Miniature Train is near the Georgia St. entrance of Stanley Park off Pipeline Rd. Visitors can take a scenic ride through the park on this miniature train. The trip runs over trestles and through tunnels on its 2-kilometre (1.25-mi.) journey. Special excursions operate during Easter, Halloween and the Christmas season.

Klahowya Village appears during the summer. Klahowya comes from a greeting in the Chinook trade language meaning "welcome." The summer village presents handmade items, performances and interactive activities, including a spirit-washing ceremony in which a person holding an eagle feather wafts sage smoke over participants. The Spirit Catcher Train takes visitors on a 13-minute scenic ride through the forest as an audio soundtrack narrates a traditional story.

Time: Allow 1 hour minimum. **Hours:** Daily 10-5, July 1-Labour Day; Sat.-Sun. 10-4, Apr.-June and day after Labour Day-Sept. 30. Phone ahead to confirm special holiday excursion schedules. **Cost:** $7; $4 (ages 13-18 and 65+); $3.50 (ages 3-12); $20 (family, two adults and two children ages 3-18). **Phone:** (604) 257-8531. ⒯ ⒜

Stanley Park Horse-drawn Tours depart from beside the information booth at the Coal Harbour parking lot on Park Dr. off the Georgia St. entrance. The narrated, 1-hour tour highlights the park's points of interest. **Hours:** Tours depart daily every 20-30 minutes 9:30-5:30, July 1-Labour Day; 9:40-5, Apr.-June and day after Labour Day-Sept. 30; 9:40-4, Mar. 15-31 and in Oct. **Cost:** $38.09; $35.71 (ages 13-18, ages 65+ and students with ID); $19.04 (ages 3-12). **Phone:** (604) 681-5115 or (888) 681-5110.

Vancouver Aquarium Marine Science Centre is at 845 Avison Way. Visitors are greeted by "Chief of the Undersea World," a bronze sculpture by Haida artist Bill Reid. The center is home to more than 70,000 marine animals, with emphasis on such diverse habitats as the Canadian Arctic, the Amazon Rain Forest and the Pacific Northwest. Sharks, moray eels and colorful fish populate the Tropic Zone, while the Strait of Georgia exhibit features divers interacting with marine life.

Interactive multimedia displays in the Canada's Arctic exhibit allow visitors to meet the people of this region and explain the effects and impact of climate change on them and the area's marine life. Programs allowing animal encounters with sea lions, seals, otters and beluga whales are available for an additional fee. Teck Connections Gallery offers state-of-the-art wraparound screens of digital projections while the Engagement Gallery is available for talks and educational programs.

Walk the BC Hydro Salmon Stream in Stanley Park to learn about a salmon's incredible life journey. Other highlights include daily whale and dolphin shows, shark dives and sea otter feedings as well as exhibits that feature sea lions and harbor seals.

Time: Allow 2 hours minimum. **Hours:** Daily 9:30-6, July-Aug.; 10-5, rest of year. **Cost:** June 18-Labour Day $34.29; $25.71 (ages 13-18, ages 65+ and students ages 18+ with ID); $20 (ages 4-12). Cost rest of year $27.62; $19.05 (ages 13-18, ages 65+ and students ages 18+ with ID); $14.24 (ages 4-12). **Parking:** Apr.-Sept. $3.25 per hour, $11 per day; rest of year $2.25 per hour, $6 per day. **Phone:** (604) 659-3400 or (604) 659-3474. ⒯

UNIVERSITY OF BRITISH COLUMBIA is on Point Grey. Encompassing 2,470 hectares (6,103 acres) overlooking the Strait of Georgia, the university is the largest in the province. **Phone:** (604) 822-2211.

Beaty Biodiversity Museum is at 2212 Main Mall on the University of British Columbia campus. This natural history museum exhibits more than 2 million specimens divided among six collections: the Cowan Tetrapod Collection, The Herbarium, the Spencer Entomological Collection, the Fish Collection, the Marine Invertebrate Collection and the Fossil Collection. A highlight is Canada's largest blue whale skeleton, which is suspended in the museum's two-story glass atrium.

Note: Pay parking is available at the Health Sciences Parkade, one block south across East Mall, and near the UBC Bookstore. **Time:** Allow 1 hour, 30 minutes minimum. **Hours:** Tues.-Sun. 10-5. Guided tours are given daily at 3, Sat.-Sun. at 11:30. Closed Christmas. **Cost:** $12; $10 (ages 13-17, ages 65+ and non-UBC students with ID); $8 (ages 5-12); $35 (family, two adults and up to four children under 18). Combination ticket (UBC Museums and Gardens Pass) with UBC Botanical Garden, UBC Museum of Anthropology and Nitobe Memorial Garden $33; $28 (ages 13-17, ages 65+ and non-UBC students with ID); $85 (family, two adults and up to four children). **Phone:** (604) 827-4955. ⒯

The Pacific Museum of the Earth is just off the West Mall of the university on the main floor of the Earth and Ocean Science Building at 6339 Stores Rd. A highlight of the 30,000-piece mineral and fossil collection is an 80 million-year-old Lambeosaurus dinosaur. Also featured are a 2-metre-long (7-ft.) amethyst tube, a large sedimentary structure and the OmniGlobe, a spherical interactive display with real-time information. **Time:** Allow 30 minutes minimum. **Hours:** Mon.-Fri. 10-5. OmniGlobe and gem gallery Mon.-Fri. 10-4. Closed statutory holidays, Jan. 1-3 and Dec. 20-31. **Cost:** $5. **Phone:** (604) 822-6992.

UBC Botanical Garden is at 6804 S.W. Marine Dr. More than 10,000 plants from around the world are cultivated on 28 hectares (69 acres). Themed gardens include Asian, alpine, perennial, food, medicinal and native plantings. Within the Asian garden is the Greenheart TreeWalk, a 308-metre (1,010-ft.) aerial trail through a West Coast forest canopy. Guided tours take participants across eight bridges more than 15 metres (49 ft.) above ground level to view plants and animals that live in this environment.

Nitobe Memorial Garden, one of the most accurately represented Japanese gardens in North America, features a tea garden and stroll garden with seasonal displays of irises, Japanese maples and flowering cherries.

Pets are not permitted. **Time:** Allow 1 hour minimum. **Hours:** Main garden and Nitobe Memorial Garden open daily 9:30-5. **Cost:** Main garden $9; $7 (ages 13-17, ages 65+ and non-UBC students with ID); $5 (ages 5-12); $21 (family, two adults and up to four children). Nitobe Memorial Garden $7; $5.50 (ages 13-17, ages 65+ and non-UBC students with ID); $4 (ages 5-12); $16 (family, two adults and up to four children). Main garden plus Nitobe Memorial Garden $13; $11 (ages 13-17, ages 65+ and non- UBC students with ID); $7 (ages 5-12); $31 (family, two adults and up to four children). Main garden plus Greenheart TreeWalk $20; $15 (ages 13-17, ages 65+ and non-UBC students with ID); $10 (ages 5-12); $44 (family, two adults and up to four children). Main garden plus Nitobe and Greenheart TreeWalk $24; $18 (ages 13-17, ages 65+ and non-UBC students with ID); $12 (ages 5-12); $50 (family, two adults and up to four children). Combination ticket (UBC Museums and Gardens Pass) with Beaty Biodiversity Museum, Nitobe Memorial Garden and UBC Museum of Anthropology $33; $28 (ages 13-17, ages 65+ and non-UBC students with ID); $85 (family, two adults and four children). **Parking:** free for 3 hours, then $2 per hour (maximum $6 per day). **Phone:** (604) 822-4208.

UBC Museum of Anthropology is at 6393 N.W. Marine Dr. on the Point Grey Cliffs. Traditional post and beam construction is utilized in this concrete and glass building designed by Canadian architect Arthur Erickson. The Great Hall, the main exhibition area, has soaring glass walls that let in natural light. It provides a striking setting for a major collection of Northwest Coast First Nations artwork, which includes totem poles, house posts, carved figures, feast dishes and other objects.

The Rotunda features some of the museum's highlights, "The Raven and the First Men" by Canadian artist Bill Reid. Reid, whose mother was a Haida, developed an interest in tribal folklore, and this carving—fashioned from a single block of laminated yellow cedar—powerfully depicts a Haida human creation myth. Four accompanying display cases contain more of Reid's works in gold, silver and argillite, a fine-grained sedimentary rock frequently used in Haida carvings.

In marked contrast to the often-monumental scale of the indigenous art is the 600-piece collection of 15th to 19th-century European ceramics—stoneware, lead-glazed earthenware and tin-glazed ware—on display in the Koerner Ceramics Gallery.

Time: Allow 1 hour minimum. **Hours:** Daily 10-5 (also Tues. 5-9), mid-May to mid-Oct.; Tues.-Sun. 10-5 (also Tues. 5-9), rest of year. Closed Christmas and day after Christmas. **Cost:** $17.14; $15.24 (ages 7-18, ages 65+ and non-UBC students with ID); $44.76 (family, two adults and four children).

Combination ticket (UBC Museums and Gardens Pass) with Beaty Biodiversity Museum, Nitobe Memorial Garden and UBC Botanical Garden $33; $28 (ages 13-17, ages 65+ and non-UBC students with ID); $85 (family, two adults and four children). **Phone:** (604) 822-5087. GT

VANCOUVER AQUARIUM MARINE SCIENCE CENTRE—see Stanley Park p. 283.

VANCOUVER ART GALLERY is downtown at 750 Hornby St.; the museum encompasses a city block bounded by Georgia, Howe, Robson and Hornby sts. One of the largest art museums in Western Canada occupies a turn-of-the-20th-century building that originally was intended to serve as a provincial courthouse. Its stately exterior is a contrast to much of the art inside, which tends to reflect the creative energy and hip, progressive style that the city itself embodies.

While historical masters are given their due, the focus of the gallery's changing thematic exhibitions is on contemporary artists and works from groundbreaking new visionaries that veer toward the cutting edge. The museum's four floors of mixed-media installations contain works by Emily Carr and other well-known Canadian artists.

Time: Allow 1 hour minimum. **Hours:** Daily 10-5 (also Tues. 5-9). Guided tours depart Thurs. and Sat. 11-2:30. Closed Jan. 1 and Christmas. **Cost:** $22.85; $17.14 (ages 65+ and students with ID); $6.19 (ages 5-12); free (ages 5-12 on Sun.); $52.38 (family, two adults and four children); donations (Tues. 5-9). Rates may vary; phone ahead. **Phone:** (604) 662-4719. 🍴 🚇 Burrard, 46

VANCOUVER LOOKOUT AT HARBOUR CENTRE TOWER is at 555 W. Hastings St. Two glass elevators ascend the outside of this 168-metre (553 ft.) tower, which is crowned with an observation deck that offers a spectacular panoramic view of the city and outlying districts. Hourly guided tours point out the city's landmarks. The complex includes a revolving restaurant and a shopping mall.

Time: Allow 30 minutes minimum. **Hours:** Daily 8:30 a.m.-10:30 p.m., early May-late Sept.; 9-9, rest of year. **Cost:** $16.25; $13.25 (ages 60+); $11.25 (ages 13-18 and students with ID); $8.25 (ages 6-12); $41 (family, two adults and two children ages 6-12). Rates may vary; phone ahead. **Phone:** (604) 689-0421. GT 🚇 Waterfront, 45

VANDUSEN BOTANICAL GARDEN is at 5251 Oak St. (between Oak and Granville sts.) at W. 37th Ave. One benefit of Vancouver's benevolent maritime climate is that it creates a favorable environment for gardening, and the plant collections at VanDusen Botanical Garden offer spectacular proof. The 22-hectare (55-acre) site, once owned by the Canadian Pacific Railway and logged at the turn of the 20th century, was nurtured into a garden in the early 1970s in order to prevent the land from being developed for housing.

This is a botanical garden, as much scientifically organized and carefully labeled as it is visually pleasing. Trees, shrubs and perennials dominate the plantings, and there's something beautiful to see regardless of the season. Camellias, cherry trees, azaleas, magnolias and rhododendrons bloom from March through May. The Rose Garden begins flowering in June. Late July and August find flowering summer annuals and perennials at their peak. Japanese maples flaunt crimson fall foliage from September into October. And during the winter months, 140 different kinds of hollies along the Holly Trail are bright with berries.

Special gardens include the Perennial Garden, the Canadian Heritage Garden (where there is a lovely Korean Pavilion built from red cedar posts), the peaceful retreat that is the Meditation Garden, and the dark-leaved plants in the intriguing Black Garden. Rocks and water are integral elements as well, and the lakes and ponds are lovely spots to stop and reflect. Kids can puzzle their way around the hedges that form the Elizabethan Maze.

Time: Allow 1 hour, 30 minutes minimum. **Hours:** Daily 9-8:30, June-Aug.; 9-8, in May; 10-6, in Sept.; 10-7, in Apr.; 10-5 in Mar. and Oct.; 10-3, rest of year. Closed Christmas. **Cost:** Admission Apr.-Sept. $10.04; $7.59 (ages 13-18 and 65+); $5.75 (ages 3-12); $23.44 (family, two adults and children under 19). Admission rest of year $7.37; $5.13 (ages 13-18 and 65+); $3.79 (ages 3-12); $15.40 (family, two adults and children under 19). **Phone:** (604) 257-8335. ⑪ 🚇 Oakridge-41st Avenue, 32

Sightseeing

Opportunities to watch bustling harbor activities are available at several vantage points in Vancouver. Seaplanes, barges, tugboats, cargo ships, ferries and the SeaBus can be observed from Granville Square at the foot of Granville Street; from Canada Place at the foot of Howe St.; from Lonsdale Quay at the foot of Lonsdale Ave.; and from Stanley Park. Breathtaking views of the city, sea and mountains are available at Cypress Bowl, Simon Fraser University atop Burnaby Mountain, Grouse Mountain and Queen Elizabeth Park.

Bus Tours

Westcoast Sightseeing Ltd. features six narrated sightseeing trips of the city and its surrounding natural areas. Full-day trips to Victoria and Whistler also are available; phone (604) 451-1600 or (877) 451-1777.

Gray Line offers guided tours that include Butchart Gardens, Capilano Suspension Bridge Park and Grouse Mountain; phone (604) 451-1600 or (877) 451-1777.

Plane Tours

Another way to see Vancouver and its surroundings is by air. Harbour Air offers flights lasting from 35 minutes to 1.25 hours plus day-long packages, including whale-watching or bus tours; departure is from downtown on Coal Harbour Road, one block west of Canada Place. Fares vary, and reservations are required; phone (604) 274-1277 or (800) 655-0212 for reservations.

Train Tours

Rocky Mountaineer Vacations offers scenic, 2-day, all daylight, narrated rail tours between Vancouver or Whistler, British Columbia, and Banff, Calgary, or Jasper, Alberta. Westbound or eastbound departures are offered mid-April to mid-October, with winter rail trips available in December. Onboard meals and snacks as well as accommodations in Kamloops or Quesnel are included. A 3-hour trip on the Whistler Mountaineer also is available and runs between Vancouver and Whistler May through October. Phone (604) 606-7245 or (877) 460-3200, or (888) 687-7245 for information about Whistler trips.

Trolley Tours

Trolley tours provide a look at the city at a relaxed pace. The Downtown Historic Railway, comprised of two electric interurban railcars, skirts False Creek between Science World at TELUS World of Science and Granville Island and runs from mid-May to mid-October; phone (604) 665-3903.

Walking Tours

ROCKWOOD ADVENTURES departs from downtown hotels. Half- and full-day guided nature walks are offered to area ecological destinations including Lynn Canyon, a rain forest in Capilano River Canyon, a coastal forest at Burrard Inlet and Mount Gardner on Bowen Island. The urban city tour explores such sights as Chinatown, the shopping district, Stanley Park and Gastown. All trips include a snack or lunch and pick-up at downtown hotels.

Hours: Half-day tours offered daily 9-4, Apr. 15-Oct. 15. **Cost:** $115; $90 (students ages 12-25 with ID and ages 65+); $60 (ages 4-11). Rates may vary depending on tour. Reservations are required. **Phone:** (604) 913-1621, or (888) 236-6606 in Canada. 🚇 Stadium-Chinatown, 48

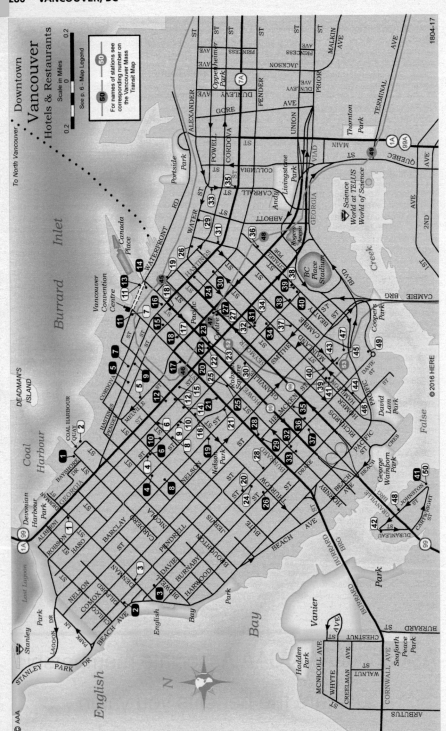

Downtown
Vancouver
Hotels & Restaurants

Scale in Miles

See p. 6 - Map Legend

For names of stations see
corresponding number on
the Vancouver Mass
Transit Map

To North Vancouver

© AAA

© 2016 HERE

1804-17

Downtown Vancouver

This index helps you "spot" where approved hotels and restaurants are located on the corresponding detailed maps. Hotel daily rate range is for comparison only. Restaurant price range is a combination of lunch and/or dinner. Turn to the listing page for more information and consult display ads for special promotions.

DOWNTOWN VANCOUVER

Map Page	Hotels	Diamond Rated	Rate Range	Page
1 p. 286	**The Westin Bayshore Vancouver**	◆◆◆◆	$199-$549 SAVE	308
2 p. 286	Sylvia Hotel	◆◆	$120-$350	307
3 p. 286	**Best Western Plus Sands** (See ad p. 279.)	◆◆◆	$99-$450 SAVE	297
4 p. 286	West End Guest House	◆◆◆	Rates not provided	308
5 p. 286	The Coast Coal Harbour Hotel	◆◆◆	$194-$484	298
6 p. 286	The Listel Hotel Vancouver	◆◆◆	$189-$329	303
7 p. 286	**Pinnacle Vancouver Harbourfront Hotel** (See ad p. 305.)	◆◆◆	$159-$699 SAVE	305
8 p. 286	Barclay House Bed and Breakfast	◆◆◆	Rates not provided	297
9 p. 286	**Vancouver Marriott Pinnacle Downtown**	◆◆◆◆	$115-$477 SAVE	307
10 p. 286	**Blue Horizon Hotel**	◆◆◆	$129-$349 SAVE	297
11 p. 286	**Fairmont Pacific Rim** (See ad p. 299.)	◆◆◆◆	$349-$1199 SAVE	298
12 p. 286	**Shangri-La Hotel Vancouver** (See ad p. 306.)	◆◆◆◆◆	$320-$800 SAVE	306
13 p. 286	**Pan Pacific Vancouver** (See ad p. 304.)	◆◆◆◆	$219-$729 SAVE	303
14 p. 286	**The Fairmont Waterfront** (See ad p. 299.)	◆◆◆◆	$239-$999 SAVE	298
15 p. 286	**Days Inn Vancouver Downtown**	◆◆	$113-$312 SAVE	298
16 p. 286	Auberge Vancouver Hotel	◆◆	Rates not provided	297
17 p. 286	**Hyatt Regency Vancouver**	◆◆◆◆	$199-$559 SAVE	302
18 p. 286	**Executive Hotel Le Soleil**	◆◆◆◆	Rates not provided SAVE	298
19 p. 286	'O Canada' House B&B	◆◆◆	Rates not provided	303
20 p. 286	**The Fairmont Hotel Vancouver** (See ad p. 299.)	◆◆◆◆	$269-$999 SAVE	298
21 p. 286	**The Sutton Place Hotel**	◆◆◆◆	$164-$495 SAVE	307
22 p. 286	**Rosewood Hotel Georgia**	◆◆◆◆	$329-$834 SAVE	306
23 p. 286	**Four Seasons Hotel Vancouver**	◆◆◆◆	$315-$775 SAVE	300
24 p. 286	**Delta Vancouver Suites**	◆◆◆	$85-$312 SAVE	298
25 p. 286	**The Wedgewood Hotel & Spa**	◆◆◆◆	$298-$718 SAVE	308
26 p. 286	**Sunset Inn & Suites** (See ad p. 307.)	◆◆◆	$199-$599 SAVE	307
27 p. 286	St. Regis Hotel	◆◆◆	Rates not provided	306
28 p. 286	**Sheraton Vancouver Wall Centre Hotel**	◆◆◆	$169-$649 SAVE	307
29 p. 286	The Burrard	◆◆	$150-$350	298
30 p. 286	Ramada Limited Downtown Vancouver	◆◆	$90-$400	305
31 p. 286	L'Hermitage Hotel	◆◆◆◆	Rates not provided	303
32 p. 286	**The Landis Hotel & Suites**	◆◆◆	$225-$399 SAVE	303
33 p. 286	**Residence Inn by Marriott Vancouver Downtown**	◆◆◆	$128-$367 SAVE	305

DOWNTOWN VANCOUVER (cont'd)

Map Page	Hotels (cont'd)	Diamond Rated	Rate Range	Page
34 p. 286	**The Westin Grand, Vancouver**	◆◆◆	$299-$499 [SAVE]	308
35 p. 286	**Best Western Plus Chateau Granville Hotel & Suites & Conference Centre** (See ad p. 297.)	◆◆◆	$139-$350 [SAVE]	297
36 p. 286	Howard Johnson Hotel Downtown Vancouver	◆◆	$109-$329	302
37 p. 286	Ramada Vancouver Downtown	◆◆	$79-$388	305
38 p. 286	**Hotel BLU Vancouver** (See ad p. 302.)	◆◆◆◆	$230-$600 [SAVE]	302
39 p. 286	**Georgian Court Hotel**	◆◆◆	$199-$599 [SAVE]	300
40 p. 286	**Hampton Inn & Suites by Hilton Downtown Vancouver**	◆◆◆	$169-$249 [SAVE]	300
41 p. 286	**Granville Island Hotel** (See ad p. 301.)	◆◆◆	$209-$650 [SAVE]	300

Map Page	Restaurants	Diamond Rated	Cuisine	Price Range	Page
1 p. 286	Ciao Bella Ristorante	◆◆	Italian	$18-$30	308
2 p. 286	Cardero's Restaurant	◆◆◆	Seafood	$14-$39	308
3 p. 286	España	◆◆◆	New Spanish Small Plates	$20-$30	309
4 p. 286	Forage	◆◆◆	New Canadian	$20-$30	309
5 p. 286	Tableau Bar Bistro	◆◆◆	New French	$16-$25	310
6 p. 286	Kirin Mandarin Restaurant	◆◆◆	Chinese	$18-$68	309
7 p. 286	Oru Cuisine	◆◆◆	Pacific Northwest	$18-$45	310
8 p. 286	Breka Bakery & Cafe	◆	Breads/Pastries	$3-$8	308
9 p. 286	CinCin	◆◆◆	Mediterranean	$29-$42	308
10 p. 286	Zefferelli's Restaurant	◆◆	Italian	$13-$28	310
11 p. 286	**Five Sails Restaurant**	◆◆◆◆	New European	$38-$42	309
12 p. 286	**Market by Jean-Georges**	◆◆◆◆	Pacific Northwest	$16-$36	310
14 p. 286	**Joe Fortes Seafood & Chop House**	◆◆◆	Seafood Steak	$17-$50	309
15 p. 286	The Urban Tea Merchant	◆◆◆	Specialty	$14-$42	310
16 p. 286	Guu Original	◆◆	Japanese Small Plates	$10-$20	309
17 p. 286	Copper Chimney	◆◆◆	Indian	$17-$28	309
18 p. 286	Scoozis Mediterranean Bar & Grill	◆◆	Mediterranean	$11-$31	310
19 p. 286	Miku	◆◆◆	Japanese	$19-$38	310
20 p. 286	India Bistro	◆◆	Indian	$10-$16	309
21 p. 286	**Le Crocodile**	◆◆◆◆	French	$17-$48	309
22 p. 286	Hawksworth Restaurant	◆◆◆	New Pacific Northwest	$23-$55	309
23 p. 286	YEW Seafood + Bar	◆◆◆	Seafood	$19-$41	310
24 p. 286	Stepho's Souvlaki Greek Taverna	◆◆	Greek	$8-$15	310
25 p. 286	**Bacchus Restaurant**	◆◆◆	French	$17-$44	308
26 p. 286	Al Porto Ristorante	◆◆◆	Northern Italian	$15-$43	308
27 p. 286	Gotham Steakhouse & Cocktail Bar	◆◆◆	Steak	$16-$63	309
28 p. 286	Banana Leaf Malaysian Cuisine	◆◆	Asian	$11-$24	308

Map Page	Restaurants (cont'd)	Diamond Rated	Cuisine	Price Range	Page
㉙ p. 286	Water St. Cafe	◇◇◇	International	$12-$31	310
㉚ p. 286	ShuRaku Sake Bar + Bistro	◇◇	Japanese	$8-$24	310
㉛ p. 286	Meat & Bread	◇	Sandwiches	$7-$13	310
㉜ p. 286	Kingston Taphouse & Grille	◇◇	American	$12-$24	309
㉝ p. 286	**L'Abattoir**	◇◇◇	New American	$25-$44	309
㉞ p. 286	Medina Cafe	◇◇	Mediterranean	$13-$19	310
㉟ p. 286	PiDGiN	◇◇◇	Fusion	$15-$33	310
㊱ p. 286	Chambar	◇◇◇	New Belgian	$13-$36	308
㊲ p. 286	Lupo Restaurant	◇◇◇	Italian	$18-$40	309
㊳ p. 286	Frankie's Italian Kitchen & Bar	◇◇◇	Italian	$13-$29	309
㊴ p. 286	Brix Restaurant & Wine Bar	◇◇◇	Pacific Northwest	$19-$29	308
㊵ p. 286	Blue Water Cafe + Raw Bar	◇◇◇◇	Seafood Sushi	$28-$46	308
㊶ p. 286	**Cioppino's Mediterranean Grill**	◇◇◇◇	Italian	$25-$48	309
㊷ p. 286	Bridges	◇◇	American	$15-$50	308
㊸ p. 286	Yaletown Brewing Company	◇◇	International	$15-$31	310
㊹ p. 286	Simply Thai	◇◇	Thai	$10-$19	310
㊺ p. 286	Minami	◇◇◇◇	New Japanese	$20-$38	310
㊻ p. 286	Rodney's Oyster House	◇◇	Seafood	$17-$35	310
㊼ p. 286	La Terrazza	◇◇◇	Northern Italian	$24-$42	309
㊽ p. 286	The Sandbar Seafood Restaurant	◇◇◇	Seafood	$15-$47	310
㊾ p. 286	Provence Marinaside	◇◇◇	Mediterranean Seafood	$14-$42	310
㊿ p. 286	Dockside Restaurant *(See ad p. 301.)*	◇◇◇	New American	$16-$34	309

© AAA

1803-17

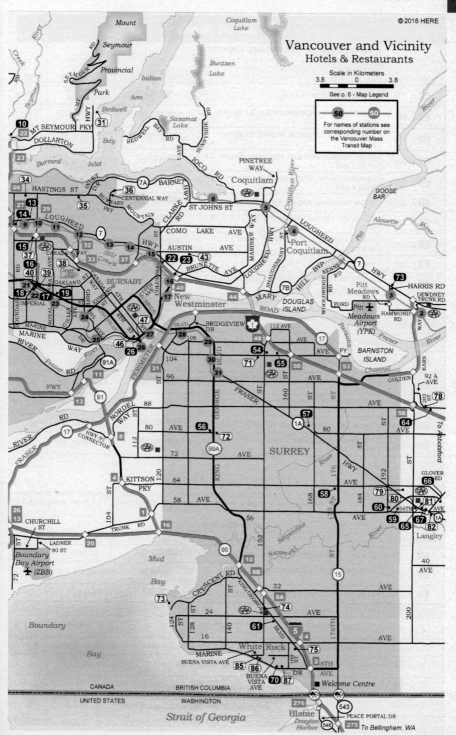

Vancouver and Vicinity
Hotels & Restaurants

© 2016 HERE

Scale in Kilometers
3.8   0   3.8

See p. 6 - Map Legend

For names of stations see
corresponding number on
the Vancouver Mass
Transit Map

✈ Airport Hotels

Map Page	VANCOUVER INTERNATIONAL AIRPORT (Maximum driving distance from airport: 4.2 mi (6.8 km))	Diamond Rated	Rate Range	Page
40 p. 290	Accent Inns, 4.0 mi (6.4 km)	◆◆	Rates not provided	245
36 p. 290	**Best Western Plus Abercorn Inn, 3.1 mi (4.9 km)**	◆◆◆	$109-$309 (SAVE)	245
29 p. 290	**The Fairmont Vancouver Airport, on airport property**	◆◆◆◆	$249-$949 (SAVE)	245
42 p. 290	**Four Points by Sheraton Vancouver Airport, 3.8 mi (6.1 km)**	◆◆◆	$140-$280 (SAVE)	245
33 p. 290	**Hampton Inn by Hilton Vancouver Airport, 2.8 mi (4.4 km)**	◆◆◆	$139-$199 (SAVE)	245
43 p. 290	**Hilton Vancouver Airport, 4.0 mi (6.4 km)**	◆◆◆	$229-$489 (SAVE)	245
35 p. 290	Holiday Inn Express Vancouver-Airport, 3.8 mi (6.1 km)	◆◆◆	Rates not provided	245
41 p. 290	Holiday Inn Vancouver Airport-Richmond, 4.2 mi (6.8 km)	◆◆◆	Rates not provided	245
30 p. 290	Hotel at River Rock, 3.1 mi (5.0 km)	◆◆◆	$269-$459	245
32 p. 290	**Pacific Gateway Hotel at Vancouver Airport, 2.9 mi (4.7 km)**	◆◆◆	$149-$499 (SAVE)	246
44 p. 290	**Quality Hotel Airport (South), 4.0 mi (6.4 km)**	◆◆	$105-$240 (SAVE)	246
39 p. 290	**Radisson Hotel Vancouver Airport, 3.1 mi (5.0 km)**	◆◆◆	$159-$309 (SAVE)	246
31 p. 290	**River Rock Casino Resort, 3.0 mi (4.9 km)**	◆◆◆◆	$209-$459 (SAVE)	247
38 p. 290	Sandman Hotel Vancouver Airport, 3.6 mi (5.8 km)	◆◆◆	Rates not provided	247
45 p. 290	**Sheraton Vancouver Airport Hotel, 4.1 mi (6.6 km)**	◆◆◆	$199-$549 (SAVE)	247
37 p. 290	**Travelodge Hotel Vancouver Airport, 3.6 mi (5.7 km)**	◆◆	$70-$181 (SAVE)	247
46 p. 290	**Vancouver Airport Marriott, 4.1 mi (6.5 km)**	◆◆◆	$150-$347 (SAVE)	247
34 p. 290	**The Westin Wall Centre Vancouver Airport, 2.5 mi (4.0 km)**	◆◆◆	$149-$549 (SAVE)	247

Vancouver and Vicinity

This index helps you "spot" where approved hotels and restaurants are located on the corresponding detailed maps. Hotel daily rate range is for comparison only. Restaurant price range is a combination of lunch and/or dinner. Turn to the listing page for more information and consult display ads for special promotions.

VANCOUVER

Map Page	Hotels	Diamond Rated	Rate Range	Page
1 p. 290	Holiday Inn Vancouver-Centre (Broadway)	◆◆◆	$119-$399	311
2 p. 290	**Best Western Plus Uptown Hotel** *(See ad p. 311.)*	◆◆	$99-$309 (SAVE)	311
3 p. 290	Days Inn-Vancouver Metro	◆◆	$59-$311	311

Map Page	Restaurants	Diamond Rated	Cuisine	Price Range	Page
① p. 290	Teahouse in Stanley Park	◆◆◆	Pacific Northwest	$16-$44	312
② p. 290	Provence Mediterranean Grill	◆◆◆	Mediterranean	$19-$34	312
③ p. 290	Bishop's	◆◆◆◆	Pacific Northwest	$35-$40	311
④ p. 290	Sophie's Cosmic Cafe	◆◆	American	$9-$16	312
⑤ p. 290	Las Margaritas Restaurante & Cantina	◆◆	Mexican	$13-$23	311
⑥ p. 290	Lombardo's Pizzeria & Ristorante	◆◆	Pizza	$12-$21	311

Map Page	Restaurants (cont'd)	Diamond Rated	Cuisine	Price Range	Page
⑦ p. 290	Maenam	◆◆◆	New Thai	$14-$21	311
⑧ p. 290	Romer's Burger Bar	◆◆	Burgers	$12-$19	312
⑨ p. 290	Cafe Salades de Fruits	◆◆	French	$9-$32	311
⑩ p. 290	Gramercy Grill	◆◆	Pacific Northwest	$14-$34	311
⑪ p. 290	Maurya Indian Cuisine	◆◆	Indian	$15-$23	311
⑫ p. 290	Trafalgars Bistro	◆◆	Regional Continental	$13-$36	312
⑬ p. 290	Tojo's Restaurant	◆◆◆	Japanese	$25-$45	312
⑭ p. 290	Salmon n' Bannock	◆◆	New Canadian	$12-$45	312
⑮ p. 290	West Restaurant	◆◆◆◆	Pacific Northwest	$17-$40	312
⑯ p. 290	Bistro Absinthe	◆◆◆	French	$33-$41	311
⑰ p. 290	The Ouisi Bistro	◆◆	Cajun	$10-$23	312
⑱ p. 290	Chutney Villa	◆◆	Southern Indian	$10-$22	311
⑲ p. 290	Vij's Restaurant	◆◆◆	New Indian	$19-$29	312
⑳ p. 290	Sawasdee Thai Restaurant	◆◆	Thai	$10-$16	312
㉑ p. 290	Shaughnessy Restaurant At VanDusen Garden	◆◆◆	Pacific Northwest	$15-$30	312
㉒ p. 290	Seasons in the Park Restaurant	◆◆◆	Pacific Northwest	$13-$39	312
㉓ p. 290	Milltown Bar & Grill	◆◆	American	$12-$24	312

NORTH VANCOUVER

Map Page	Hotels	Diamond Rated	Rate Range	Page
❻ p. 290	North Vancouver Hotel	◆◆	Rates not provided	221
❼ p. 290	**Comfort Inn & Suites**	◆◆	$109-$399 [SAVE]	221
❽ p. 290	**Best Western Capilano Inn & Suites**	◆◆	$80-$190 [SAVE]	220
❾ p. 290	**Pinnacle Hotel at the Pier**	◆◆◆	$149-$399 [SAVE]	221
❿ p. 290	**Holiday Inn & Suites North Vancouver**	◆◆◆	$159-$209 [SAVE]	221

Map Page	Restaurants	Diamond Rated	Cuisine	Price Range	Page
㉖ p. 290	La Cucina	◆◆	Italian	$10-$30	221
㉗ p. 290	Fishworks	◆◆◆	New Seafood	$12-$29	221
㉘ p. 290	Jagerhof	◆◆	Continental	$12-$26	221
㉙ p. 290	Gusto di Quattro	◆◆◆	Italian	$14-$34	221
㉚ p. 290	The Lobby Restaurant	◆◆◆	Pacific Northwest	$14-$35	221
㉛ p. 290	Arms Reach Bistro	◆◆◆	Regional American	$14-$38	221

BURNABY

Map Page	Hotels	Diamond Rated	Rate Range	Page
⓭ p. 290	Executive Hotels & Resorts	◆◆◆	Rates not provided	181
⓮ p. 290	Accent Inns	◆◆	Rates not provided	180
⓯ p. 290	**Delta Burnaby Hotel and Conference Centre**	◆◆◆◆	$125-$252 [SAVE]	181
⓰ p. 290	**Element Vancouver Metrotown**	◆◆◆	$189-$349 [SAVE]	181
⓱ p. 290	**Hilton Vancouver Metrotown**	◆◆◆	$119-$284 [SAVE]	182

BURNABY (cont'd)

Map Page	Hotels (cont'd)	Diamond Rated	Rate Range	Page
18 p. 290	Holiday Inn Express Metrotown	◆◆◆	Rates not provided	182
19 p. 290	Best Western Plus Kings Inn & Conference Center (See ad p. 181.)	◆◆	$119-$159 [SAVE]	180

Map Page	Restaurants	Diamond Rated	Cuisine	Price Range	Page
34 p. 290	The Pear Tree Restaurant	◆◆◆◆	Regional Canadian	$30-$39	182
35 p. 290	Cockney Kings Fish & Chips	◆	Fish & Chips	$9-$21	182
36 p. 290	HORIZONS	◆◆◆	Pacific Rim	$14-$36	182
37 p. 290	Ebo Restaurant and Lounge	◆◆◆	Pacific Northwest	$13-$39	182
38 p. 290	Hart House Restaurant	◆◆◆	Pacific Northwest	$15-$36	182
39 p. 290	Trattoria	◆◆◆	Italian	$13-$27	182
40 p. 290	Reflect Social Dining + Lounge	◆◆	American	$16-$29	182

COQUITLAM

Map Page	Hotels	Diamond Rated	Rate Range	Page
22 p. 290	Best Western Plus Coquitlam Inn Convention Centre	◆◆◆	$139-$209 [SAVE]	186
23 p. 290	Best Western Chelsea Inn	◆◆	$109-$139 [SAVE]	185

Map Page	Restaurant	Diamond Rated	Cuisine	Price Range	Page
43 p. 290	John B Neighborhood Pub	◆◆	International	$12-$20	186

NEW WESTMINSTER

Map Page	Hotel	Diamond Rated	Rate Range	Page
26 p. 290	Inn at the Quay	◆◆◆	Rates not provided	218

Map Page	Restaurants	Diamond Rated	Cuisine	Price Range	Page
46 p. 290	Burger Heaven	◆◆	Burgers Sandwiches	$12-$30	218
47 p. 290	Wild Rice Market Bistro	◆◆	New Chinese	$8-$18	218

RICHMOND

Map Page	Hotels	Diamond Rated	Rate Range	Page
29 p. 290	The Fairmont Vancouver Airport (See ad p. 299.)	◆◆◆◆	$249-$949 [SAVE]	245
30 p. 290	Hotel at River Rock	◆◆◆	$269-$459	245
31 p. 290	River Rock Casino Resort	◆◆◆◆	$209-$459 [SAVE]	247
32 p. 290	Pacific Gateway Hotel at Vancouver Airport	◆◆◆	$149-$499 [SAVE]	246
33 p. 290	Hampton Inn by Hilton Vancouver Airport	◆◆	$139-$199 [SAVE]	245
34 p. 290	The Westin Wall Centre Vancouver Airport	◆◆◆	$149-$549 [SAVE]	247
35 p. 290	Holiday Inn Express Vancouver-Airport	◆◆◆	Rates not provided	245
36 p. 290	Best Western Plus Abercorn Inn	◆◆◆	$109-$309 [SAVE]	245
37 p. 290	Travelodge Hotel Vancouver Airport	◆◆	$70-$181 [SAVE]	247
38 p. 290	Sandman Hotel Vancouver Airport	◆◆◆	Rates not provided	247
39 p. 290	Radisson Hotel Vancouver Airport (See ad p. 246.)	◆◆◆	$159-$309 [SAVE]	246
40 p. 290	Accent Inns	◆◆	Rates not provided	245
41 p. 290	Holiday Inn Vancouver Airport-Richmond	◆◆◆	Rates not provided	245

RICHMOND (cont'd)

Map Page	Hotels (cont'd)	Diamond Rated	Rate Range	Page
42 p. 290	**Four Points by Sheraton Vancouver Airport**	◈◈◈	$140-$280 SAVE	245
43 p. 290	**Hilton Vancouver Airport**	◈◈◈	$229-$489 SAVE	245
44 p. 290	**Quality Hotel Airport (South)**	◈◈	$105-$240 SAVE	246
45 p. 290	**Sheraton Vancouver Airport Hotel**	◈◈◈	$199-$549 SAVE	247
46 p. 290	**Vancouver Airport Marriott**	◈◈◈	$150-$347 SAVE	247
47 p. 290	Holiday Inn Express & Suites Riverport	◈◈◈	Rates not provided	245

Map Page	Restaurants	Diamond Rated	Cuisine	Price Range	Page
50 p. 290	Globe @ YVR Restaurant	◈◈◈	Pacific Northwest	$15-$42	248
51 p. 290	Tramonto	◈◈◈	Italian	$25-$45	248
52 p. 290	Pier 73 Restaurant	◈◈◈	International	$14-$29	248
53 p. 290	The Boathouse Restaurant	◈◈	Seafood	$15-$50	247
54 p. 290	Red Star Seafood Restaurant	◈◈	Chinese	$15-$30	248
55 p. 290	Flying Beaver Bar & Grill	◈◈	American	$12-$22	247
56 p. 290	Man Ri Sung Korean Restaurant	◈◈	Korean	$11-$38	248
57 p. 290	Felicos Restaurant	◈◈	Greek	$12-$40	247
58 p. 290	Fogg n' Suds	◈◈	International	$9-$29	248
59 p. 290	CAVU Kitchen Bar	◈◈◈	New International	$13-$30	247
60 p. 290	The American Grille	◈◈◈	New American	$14-$32	247
61 p. 290	Empire Seafood Restaurant	◈◈	Chinese	$15-$50	247
62 p. 290	Shanghai River Restaurant	◈◈	Chinese	$12-$50	248
63 p. 290	Charcoal Sushi & BBQ Restaurant	◈◈	Sushi	$10-$35	247
64 p. 290	Steveston Seafood House	◈◈	Seafood	$20-$40	248
65 p. 290	Tapenade Bistro	◈◈◈	New Mediterranean	$12-$32	248

DELTA

Map Page	Hotels	Diamond Rated	Rate Range	Page
50 p. 290	**Delta Town & Country Inn**	◈◈	$102-$115 SAVE	189
51 p. 290	The Coast Tsawwassen Inn	◈◈◈	$122-$275	189

Map Page	Restaurant	Diamond Rated	Cuisine	Price Range	Page
68 p. 290	Mario's Kitchen	◈◈	International	$11-$33	189

SURREY

Map Page	Hotels	Diamond Rated	Rate Range	Page
54 p. 290	**Sheraton Vancouver Guildford Hotel** (See ad p. 256.)	◈◈◈	$139-$249 SAVE	257
55 p. 290	**Four Points by Sheraton Surrey**	◈◈◈	$110-$179 SAVE	256
56 p. 290	**Best Western King George Inn & Suites** (See ad p. 255.)	◈◈	$99-$199 SAVE	255
57 p. 290	Comfort Inn & Suites Surrey	◈◈	$104-$239	256
58 p. 290	**Holiday Inn & Suites**	◈◈◈	Rates not provided SAVE	257
59 p. 290	**Hampton Inn & Suites Langley/Surrey**	◈◈◈	$139-$199 SAVE	256
60 p. 290	**Ramada Langley-Surrey**	◈◈	$110-$230 SAVE	257

SURREY (cont'd)

Map Page	Hotels (cont'd)	Diamond Rated	Rate Range	Page
61 p. 290	**Best Western Peace Arch Inn**	◆◆	$109-$199 [SAVE]	256

Map Page	Restaurants	Diamond Rated	Cuisine	Price Range	Page
71 p. 290	Sabai Thai Restaurant	◆◆	Thai	$11-$18	257
72 p. 290	Villa Verdi Ristorante Italiano	◆◆◆	Northern Italian	$17-$37	257
73 p. 290	Crescent Beach Bistro	◆◆	Mediterranean	$12-$35	257
74 p. 290	Maguroguy	◆◆	Japanese	$10-$25	257
75 p. 290	The Turkey House & Deli	◆	Sandwiches Deli	$10-$13	257

LANGLEY

Map Page	Hotels	Diamond Rated	Rate Range	Page
64 p. 290	**Holiday Inn Express Hotel & Suites Langley** (See ad p. 211.)	◆◆◆	$115-$499 [SAVE]	212
65 p. 290	Days Inn & Suites Langley	◆◆	$99-$169	211
66 p. 290	**Best Western Plus Langley Inn**	◆◆◆	$132-$192 [SAVE]	211
67 p. 290	**Coast Hotel & Convention Centre**	◆◆	$112-$169 [SAVE]	211

Map Page	Restaurants	Diamond Rated	Cuisine	Price Range	Page
78 p. 290	Akane Japanese Restaurant	◆◆	Japanese	$9-$17	212
79 p. 290	An Indian Affair	◆◆	Indian	$11-$17	212
80 p. 290	Kostas Greek Restaurant	◆◆	Greek	$13-$23	212
81 p. 290	C-Lovers Fish & Chips	◆	Seafood	$8-$19	212
82 p. 290	Ban Chok Dee Thai Cuisine	◆◆	Thai	$11-$19	212

WHITE ROCK

Map Page	Hotel	Diamond Rated	Rate Range	Page
70 p. 290	Ocean Promenade Hotel	◆◆◆	Rates not provided	348

Map Page	Restaurants	Diamond Rated	Cuisine	Price Range	Page
85 p. 290	Uli's Restaurant	◆◆	International	$15-$29	348
86 p. 290	Giraffe	◆◆◆	International	$25-$34	348
87 p. 290	La Baia Italian Restaurant	◆◆	Italian	$15-$27	348

PITT MEADOWS

Map Page	Hotel	Diamond Rated	Rate Range	Page
73 p. 290	Ramada Inn Pitt Meadows	◆◆	$93-$235	235

WEST VANCOUVER

Map Page	Restaurant	Diamond Rated	Cuisine	Price Range	Page
90 p. 290	Salmon House on the Hill	◆◆◆	Seafood	$28-$39	338

DOWNTOWN VANCOUVER

- Restaurants p. 308
- Hotels & Restaurants map & index p. 286

AUBERGE VANCOUVER HOTEL   604/678-8899 **16**
 Hotel. **Address:** 837 W Hastings St V6C 1B6

BARCLAY HOUSE BED AND BREAKFAST   604/605-1351 **8**
 Historic Bed & Breakfast. **Address:** 1351 Barclay St V6E 1H6

BEST WESTERN PLUS CHATEAU GRANVILLE HOTEL & SUITES & CONFERENCE CENTRE
(604)669-7070 **35**

Hotel
$139-$350

Best Western PLUS. **AAA Benefit:** Save 10% or more every day and earn 10% bonus points!

Address: 1100 Granville St V6Z 2B6 **Location:** Between Davie and Helmcken sts. Yaletown-Roundhouse, 53. **Facility:** 118 units. 3-15 stories, interior corridors. **Parking:** on-site (fee). **Terms:** resort fee. **Activities:** exercise room. **Guest Services:** valet laundry. *(See ad this page.)*

BEST WESTERN PLUS SANDS
(604)682-1831 **3**

Hotel
$99-$450

Best Western PLUS **AAA Benefit:** Save 10% or more every day and earn 10% bonus points!

Address: 1755 Davie St V6G 1W5 **Location:** Between Bidwell and Denman sts. Burrard, 46. **Facility:** 121 units. 6 stories, interior corridors. **Parking:** on-site (fee). **Terms:** check-in 4 pm, cancellation fee imposed, resort fee. **Dining:** 2 restaurants. **Activities:** sauna, exercise room. **Guest Services:** valet and coin laundry. *(See ad p. 279.)*

BLUE HORIZON HOTEL
(604)688-1411 **10**

Hotel
$129-$349

Address: 1225 Robson St V6E 1C3 **Location:** Between Jervis and Bute sts. Burrard, 46. **Facility:** 214 units. 31 stories, interior corridors. **Parking:** on-site (fee). **Terms:** cancellation fee imposed. **Amenities:** safes. **Pool(s):** heated indoor. **Activities:** sauna, hot tub, limited exercise equipment. **Guest Services:** valet laundry.

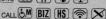

(See map & index p. 286.)

THE BURRARD (604)681-2331 **29**
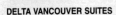 Hotel. **Address:** 1100 Burrard St V6Z 1Y7

THE COAST COAL HARBOUR HOTEL (604)697-0202 **5**
Hotel. **Address:** 1180 W Hastings St V6E 4R5

DAYS INN VANCOUVER DOWNTOWN (604)681-4335 **15**

Hotel
$113-$312

Address: 921 W Pender St V6C 1M2 **Location:** Between Burrard and Hornby sts. Located in the financial district. Waterfront, 45. **Facility:** 85 units. 9 stories, interior corridors. **Parking:** no self-parking. **Terms:** cancellation fee imposed. **Amenities:** safes. **Guest Services:** valet and coin laundry.

DELTA VANCOUVER SUITES (604)689-8188 **24**

Hotel
$85-$312

DELTA HOTELS

AAA Benefit:
Members save 5% or more!

Address: 550 W Hastings St V6B 1L6 **Location:** Between Seymour and Richards sts; entrance in alley way. Waterfront, 45. **Facility:** 225 units. 23 stories, interior corridors. **Parking:** on-site (fee) and valet. **Amenities:** safes. **Activities:** exercise room. **Guest Services:** valet laundry, boarding pass kiosk.

EXECUTIVE HOTEL LE SOLEIL 604/632-3000 **18**

Boutique Hotel
Rates not provided

Address: 567 Hornby St V6C 2E8 **Location:** Between Dunsmuir and Pender sts. Burrard, 46. **Facility:** As you step into the opulent lobby you'll see the staff is all about pampering guests. In the rooms and suites, every piece of art, furniture and fabric has been hand-picked from European designers. 113 units. 16 stories, interior corridors. **Parking:** valet only. **Terms:** check-in 4 pm. **Amenities:** safes. **Dining:** Copper Chimney, see separate listing. **Activities:** bicycles, limited exercise equipment. **Guest Services:** valet laundry.

THE FAIRMONT HOTEL VANCOUVER (604)684-3131 **20**

Classic Historic
Hotel
$269-$999

Address: 900 W Georgia St V6C 2W6 **Location:** Corner of Burrard at W Georgia St; enter from Hornby St. Across from Vancouver Art Gallery. Burrard, 46. **Facility:** Built in 1939, this landmark building was officially opened by the Queen Mother and her husband, King George. The rooms are currently being renovated, so some have a more up-to-date design. 557 units. 15 stories, interior corridors. **Parking:** on-site (fee) and valet. **Terms:** cancellation fee imposed. **Amenities:** safes. **Pool(s):** heated indoor. **Activities:** sauna, hot tub, bicycles, exercise room, spa. **Guest Services:** valet laundry. (See ad p. 299.)

FAIRMONT PACIFIC RIM (604)695-5300 **11**

Contemporary
Hotel
$349-$1199

Address: 1038 Canada Pl V6C 0B9 **Location:** Between Burrard and Thurlow sts. Waterfront, 45. **Facility:** Guests are pampered at this luxury tower, which has a beautiful, innovative design. Gorgeous rooms with super views are rigged with all the latest technological bells and whistles. 367 units. 48 stories, interior corridors. **Parking:** on-site (fee) and valet. **Terms:** 3 day cancellation notice-fee imposed, resort fee. **Amenities:** safes. **Dining:** 2 restaurants, also, Oru Cuisine, see separate listing, entertainment. **Pool(s):** heated outdoor. **Activities:** sauna, hot tub, steamroom, cabanas, bicycles, in-room exercise equipment, spa. **Guest Services:** valet laundry, boarding pass kiosk, area transportation. (See ad p. 299.)

THE FAIRMONT WATERFRONT (604)691-1991 **14**

Hotel
$239-$999

Address: 900 Canada Place Way V6C 3L5 **Location:** Waterfront. Between Howe and Burrard sts. Opposite Canada Place. Waterfront, 45. **Facility:** The staff is highly attune to guests' needs and the lovely rooms have great floor-to-ceiling windows with harbor or city views. The hotel is across from the cruise ship terminal and convention center. 489 units. 23 stories, interior corridors. **Parking:** on-site (fee) and valet. **Terms:** cancellation fee imposed. **Amenities:** safes. **Pool(s):** heated outdoor. **Activities:** hot tub, steamroom, bicycles, massage. **Guest Services:** valet laundry. (See ad p. 299.)

2:39PM

The moment when you saw the mountains rise from the sea.

FAIRMONT VANCOUVER AIRPORT

FAIRMONT HOTEL VANCOUVER

FAIRMONT PACIFIC RIM

FAIRMONT WATERFRONT

**FAIRMONT HOTELS IN VANCOUVER.
SIMPLY UNRIVALLED.**
Fairmont features extraordinary properties in Vancouver, a destination that combines natural beauty with a cosmopolitan city scene. Each hotel is unique, capturing the essence of Vancouver. Choose the one to suit your style.

Gateway to your moment in over 20 countries.
fairmont.com

UNFORGETTABLE. SINCE 1907.

(See map & index p. 286.)

FOUR SEASONS HOTEL VANCOUVER

(604)689-9333 **23**

Hotel
$315-$775

Address: 791 W Georgia St V6C 2T4 **Location:** Between Howe and Granville sts. 🚇 Vancouver City Centre, 52. **Facility:** Impeccable service is the norm here. The rooms are lovely with upscale bedding and if you need more space ask for one of the corner rooms. Make sure to check out the hidden gem garden at the pool. 372 units. 28 stories, interior corridors. **Parking:** on-site (fee) and valet. **Terms:** cancellation fee imposed. **Amenities:** safes. **Dining:** YEW Seafood + Bar, see separate listing. **Pool(s):** heated outdoor, heated indoor. **Activities:** sauna, hot tub, cabanas, in-room exercise equipment, massage. **Guest Services:** valet laundry.

SAVE ECO ⊘ ⊘ ⊘ CALL ⊘M ⊘ ⊘ BIZ HS
⊘ ⊘ ⊘ ⊘ / SOME UNITS ⊘ ⊘ ⊘

GEORGIAN COURT HOTEL

(604)682-5555 **39**

Boutique Hotel
$199-$599

Address: 773 Beatty St V6B 2M4 **Location:** Between Georgia and Robson sts. Opposite BC Place Stadium. 🚇 Stadium-Chinatown, 48. **Facility:** Close to many attractions like Robson Street and Queen Elizabeth Theatre, this lovely property's guest rooms exude charm with extra amenities like robes and slippers and windows that open. 180 units. 12 stories, interior corridors. **Parking:** on-site (fee). **Terms:** cancellation fee imposed. **Amenities:** safes. **Dining:** Frankie's Italian Kitchen & Bar, see separate listing. **Activities:** hot tub, steamroom, bicycles, exercise room. **Guest Services:** valet laundry, area transportation.

SAVE ⊘ ⊘ ⊘ CALL ⊘M BIZ HS ⊘ ⊘ ⊘
⊘ / SOME UNITS ⊘ ⊘

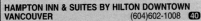

GEORGIAN
COURT
HOTEL

Downtown boutique hotel located near entertainment, shopping & sports venues. Luxury within reach!

GRANVILLE ISLAND HOTEL

(604)683-7373 **41**

Boutique Hotel
$209-$650

Address: 1253 Johnston St V6H 3R9 **Location:** Granville Island; below the bridge, follow signs. 🚇 Yaletown-Roundhouse, 53. **Facility:** Rooms are lovely at this distinctive hotel and feature fineries like super soft Italian cotton linens. Just steps from Granville Island Market, there are tons of shopping and entertainment options. 82 units. 3-4 stories, interior corridors. **Parking:** on-site (fee). **Terms:** cancellation fee imposed. **Amenities:** safes. **Dining:** Dockside Restaurant, see separate listing. **Activities:** sauna, hot tub, bicycles, trails, exercise room. **Guest Services:** valet laundry. *(See ad p. 301.)*

SAVE ⊘ ⊘ ⊘ CALL ⊘M BIZ HS ⊘ ⊘
⊘ / SOME UNITS ⊘ ⊘ ⊘

HAMPTON INN & SUITES BY HILTON DOWNTOWN VANCOUVER

(604)602-1008 **40**

Hotel
$169-$249

AAA Benefit:
Members save up to 10%!

Address: 111 Robson St V6B 2A8 **Location:** Between Cambie and Beatty sts. Opposite BC Place Stadium. 🚇 Stadium-Chinatown, 48. **Facility:** 132 units, some efficiencies. 16 stories, interior corridors. **Parking:** on-site (fee). **Terms:** 1-7 night minimum stay, cancellation fee imposed. **Amenities:** safes. **Activities:** sauna, hot tub, bicycles, exercise room. **Guest Services:** valet and coin laundry, area transportation. **Featured Amenity:** breakfast buffet.

SAVE ECO ⊘ ⊘ ⊘ CALL ⊘M BIZ ⊘ ⊘
⊘ ⊘ ⊘ ⊘ / SOME UNITS ⊘ HS ⊘

Our hotel is just steps from the city's best shops, eateries, entertainment & sports events venues.

▼ *See AAA listing p. 300* ▼

VANCOUVER'S BEST KEPT SECRET...

Granville Island HOTEL

GJH
GRANVILLE ISLAND HOTEL
VANCOUVER'S ISLAND OASIS

ART ~ NATURE ~ RELAXATION

All in a waterfront hotel
steps from downtown.

THE GRANVILLE ISLAND HOTEL
1253 Johnston Street, Vancouver, BC
Toll free: 1·800·663·1840 or 604·683·7373
www.granvilleislandhotel.com

(See map & index p. 286.)

HOTEL BLU VANCOUVER (604)620-6200 38

▼▼▼ ▼▼▼ Hotel

Boutique Contemporary Hotel

$230-$600

Address: 177 Robson St V6B 0N3 **Location:** Jct Cambie St. Stadium-Chinatown, 48. **Facility:** This upscale hotel has beautiful, bright décor. The comfortable rooms also boast a lovely design, plus many high-tech features like smart TVs and your own in-room tablet. 75 units. 4 stories, interior corridors. **Parking:** on-site (fee) and valet. **Terms:** cancellation fee imposed. **Amenities:** safes. **Pool(s):** heated indoor. **Activities:** sauna, hot tub, bicycles, exercise room. **Guest Services:** complimentary and valet laundry, area transportation. *(See ad this page.)*

HOWARD JOHNSON HOTEL DOWNTOWN VANCOUVER
(604)688-8701 36

▼▼ ▼▼ Hotel. **Address:** 1176 Granville St V6Z 1L8

HYATT REGENCY VANCOUVER (604)683-1234 17

▼▼▼ ▼▼▼ Hotel

$199-$559

AAA Benefit: Members save 10%!

Address: 655 Burrard St V6C 2R7 **Location:** Between W Georgia and Melville sts. Connected to shopping center. Burrard, 46. **Facility:** In the heart of downtown, there are lots of bright and beautiful areas in which to lounge at this large, convention-oriented hotel. Many of its spacious, modern rooms boast fantastic city views. 644 units. 34 stories, interior corridors. **Parking:** on-site (fee) and valet. **Terms:** check-in 4 pm, cancellation fee imposed. **Amenities:** safes. **Dining:** 2 restaurants. **Pool(s):** heated outdoor. **Activities:** hot tub, exercise room, in-room exercise equipment. **Guest Services:** valet laundry.

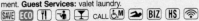

▼ See AAA listing this page ▼

(See map & index p. 286.)

THE LANDIS HOTEL & SUITES (604)681-3555 **32**

Extended Stay Hotel
$225-$399

Address: 1200 Hornby St V6Z 1W2 **Location:** Between Davie and Drake sts. Yaletown-Roundhouse, 53. **Facility:** 52 two-bedroom kitchen units. 18 stories, interior corridors. **Parking:** on-site (fee). **Terms:** cancellation fee imposed, resort fee. **Amenities:** safes. **Pool(s):** heated indoor. **Activities:** hot tub, picnic facilities, exercise room. **Guest Services:** valet and coin laundry, area transportation. **Featured Amenity:** continental breakfast.

THE LANDIS
HOTEL & SUITES

Located in the heart of downtown, offering large 2 bedroom suites, ideal for short or extended stays.

L'HERMITAGE HOTEL 778/327-4100 **31**
Boutique Hotel. **Address:** 788 Richards St V6B 3A4

THE LISTEL HOTEL VANCOUVER (604)684-8461 **6**
Boutique Contemporary Hotel. **Address:** 1300 Robson St V6E 1C5

'O CANADA' HOUSE B&B 604/688-0555 **19**
Historic Bed & Breakfast. **Address:** 1114 Barclay St V6E 1H1

PAN PACIFIC VANCOUVER (604)662-8111 **13**

Hotel
$219-$729

Address: 300-999 Canada Pl V6C 3B5 **Location:** Between Howe and Burrard sts. Located at Canada Place. Waterfront, 45. **Facility:** This waterfront landmark hotel connects to the convention center, cruise ship terminal, Skytrain and Flyover Canada. Members with advance reservations get complimentary room upgrades on availability. 503 units, some two bedrooms and kitchens. 23 stories, interior corridors. **Parking:** on-site (fee) and valet. **Terms:** check-in 4 pm, cancellation fee imposed. **Amenities:** safes. **Dining:** Five Sails Restaurant, see separate listing. **Pool(s):** heated outdoor. **Activities:** sauna, hot tub, steamroom, in-room exercise equipment, spa. **Guest Services:** valet laundry, boarding pass kiosk. (See ad p. 304.)

▼ See AAA listing p. 303 ▼

Inviting You To See Things Differently

Call toll-free for reservations:
Canada 1.800.663.1515 USA: 1.800.937.1515

Pan Pacific Vancouver, 999 Canada Place
Vancouver, British Columbia CANADA
Visit: www.panpacific.com/vancouver

PAN PACIFIC
VANCOUVER

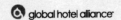 global hotel alliance

(See map & index p. 286.)

PINNACLE VANCOUVER HARBOURFRONT HOTEL
(604)689-9211 **7**

Hotel
$159-$699

Address: 1133 W Hastings St V6E 3T3 **Location:** Between Thurlow and Bute sts. ⊞ Burrard, 46. **Facility:** 442 units. 19 stories, interior corridors. **Parking:** on-site (fee) and valet. **Amenities:** safes. **Pool(s):** heated indoor. **Activities:** hot tub, bicycles. **Guest Services:** valet laundry. *(See ad this page.)*

SAVE ECO ❘❘ 🛁 ❨❩
CALL ♿M 🛬 📶 BIZ HS
🛜 ✕ 🎦 ▯
/ SOME UNITS 🛏 🧳 🚲

RAMADA LIMITED DOWNTOWN VANCOUVER
(604)488-1088 **30**
♦♦ Hotel. **Address:** 435 W Pender St V6B 1V2

RAMADA VANCOUVER DOWNTOWN   (604)685-1111 **37**
♦♦♦ Hotel. **Address:** 1221 Granville St V6Z 1M6

RESIDENCE INN BY MARRIOTT VANCOUVER DOWNTOWN
(604)688-1234 **33**

♦♦♦
Extended Stay Contemporary Hotel
$128-$367

  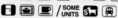

AAA Benefit: Members save 5% or more!

Address: 1234 Hornby St V6Z 1W2 **Location:** Between Drake and Davie sts. ⊞ Yaletown-Roundhouse, 53. **Facility:** 201 units, some efficiencies and kitchens. 22 stories, interior corridors. **Parking:** on-site (fee). **Terms:** check-in 4 pm, resort fee. **Amenities:** safes. **Pool(s):** heated indoor. **Activities:** hot tub, exercise room. **Guest Services:** valet and coin laundry. **Featured Amenity:** full hot breakfast.

SAVE ECO ❘❘ ❨❩ CALL ♿M 🛬 BIZ HS 🛜 ✕
🧳 📦 ▯ / SOME UNITS 🛏 🚲

▼ See AAA listing this page ▼

Enjoy great member rates and benefits
at AAA/CAA Preferred Hotels

(See map & index p. 286.)

ROSEWOOD HOTEL GEORGIA   (604)682-5566 **22**

Historic Boutique Hotel
$329-$834

Address: 801 W Georgia St V6C 1P7 **Location:** Between Hornby and Howe sts, entrance on Howe St. Across from Vancouver Art Gallery. Vancouver City Centre, 52. **Facility:** Since 1927, British royalty and celebrities have graced this stunning hotel with their presence. You too can sleep in a sumptuous room and enjoy the amazingly luxurious bedding. 156 units. 12 stories, interior corridors. **Parking:** valet only. **Terms:** cancellation fee imposed. **Amenities:** safes. **Dining:** Hawksworth Restaurant, see separate listing. **Pool(s):** heated indoor. **Activities:** exercise room, spa. **Guest Services:** valet laundry, area transportation.

ST. REGIS HOTEL   604/681-1135 **27**
Boutique Hotel. **Address:** 602 Dunsmuir St V6B 1Y6

SHANGRI-LA HOTEL VANCOUVER
  (604)689-1120 **12**

Boutique Contemporary Hotel
$320-$800

Address: 1128 W Georgia St V6E 0A8 **Location:** Between Thurlow and Bute sts. Burrard, 46. **Facility:** The unique underground drive-up entry for this stunning hotel is found along Alberni Street. Luxurious rooms have beautiful African rosewood walls, Italian marble bathrooms and the latest technology. 119 units. 15 stories, interior corridors. **Parking:** on-site (fee) and valet. **Terms:** cancellation fee imposed. **Amenities:** safes. **Dining:** Market by Jean-Georges, see separate listing. **Pool(s):** heated outdoor. **Activities:** sauna, hot tub, steamroom, bicycles, in-room exercise equipment, spa. **Guest Services:** valet laundry, boarding pass kiosk, area transportation. (See ad this page.)

▼ See AAA listing this page ▼

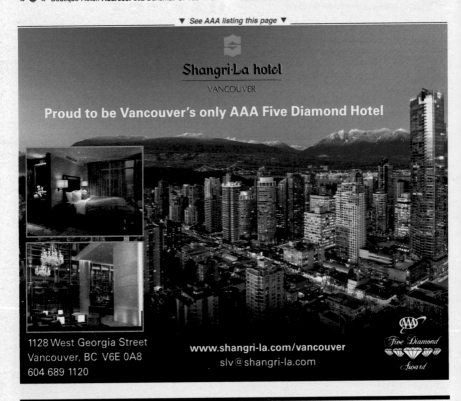
Say YES to ERS text updates to stay

posted when your tow truck is on the way

(See map & index p. 286.)

SHERATON VANCOUVER WALL CENTRE HOTEL
(604)331-1000

Hotel
$169-$649

Sheraton

AAA Benefit: Members save up to 15%, plus Starwood Preferred Guest® benefits!

Address: 1088 Burrard St V6Z 2R9 **Location:** Between Helmcken and Nelson sts. Vancouver City Centre, 52. **Facility:** 746 units, some two bedrooms. 27-35 stories, interior corridors. **Parking:** on-site (fee) and valet. **Amenities:** safes. **Pool(s):** heated indoor. **Activities:** sauna, hot tub, in-room exercise equipment. **Guest Services:** valet laundry, boarding pass kiosk, area transportation.

SUNSET INN & SUITES
(604)688-2474

Extended Stay Hotel
$199-$599

Address: 1111 Burnaby St V6E 1P4 **Location:** Between Thurlow and Bute sts. Located in a residential neighborhood. Yaletown-Roundhouse, 53. **Facility:** 50 kitchen units. 11 stories, interior corridors. **Terms:** check-in 4 pm, cancellation fee imposed. **Amenities:** safes. **Activities:** exercise room. **Guest Services:** coin laundry. **Featured Amenity:** continental breakfast. *(See ad this page.)*

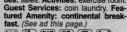

Ask about on-the-spot vehicle battery testing and replacement

THE SUTTON PLACE HOTEL
(604)682-5511

Hotel
$164-$495

Address: 845 Burrard St V6Z 2K6 **Location:** Between Smithe and Robson sts. Burrard, 46. **Facility:** The lovely lobby has a classic design with antique-style furnishings; the theme spills over to attractive rooms with luxurious bedding. You will find the staff highly attune to your needs. 397 units. 21 stories, interior corridors. **Parking:** on-site (fee) and valet. **Terms:** cancellation fee imposed, resort fee. **Amenities:** safes. **Pool(s):** heated indoor. **Activities:** hot tub, steamroom, spa. **Guest Services:** valet and coin laundry, boarding pass kiosk, area transportation.

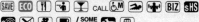

SYLVIA HOTEL
(604)681-9321

Historic Hotel. **Address:** 1154 Gilford St V6G 2P6

VANCOUVER MARRIOTT PINNACLE DOWNTOWN
(604)684-1128

Hotel
$115-$477

MARRIOTT

AAA Benefit: Members save 5% or more!

Address: 1128 W Hastings St V6E 4R5 **Location:** Between Thurlow and Bute sts. Burrard, 46. **Facility:** Just a few blocks from the Convention Centre in the heart of the downtown business district, classy and comfortable guest rooms offer breathtaking views of the mountains, water and downtown Vancouver. 438 units. 31 stories, interior corridors. **Parking:** on-site (fee) and valet. **Terms:** check-in 4 pm. **Amenities:** safes. **Pool(s):** heated indoor. **Activities:** sauna, hot tub, steamroom, exercise room. **Guest Services:** valet laundry, boarding pass kiosk.

▼ See AAA listing this page ▼

(See map & index p. 286.)

THE WEDGEWOOD HOTEL & SPA   (604)689-7777

Boutique Hotel
$298-$718

Address: 845 Hornby St V6Z 1V1 **Location:** Between Smithe and Robson sts. Vancouver City Centre, 52. **Facility:** This wonderfully intimate, stylish hotel offers beautiful rooms with gorgeous, classic furnishings. You will also find the service to be warm and highly personalized. 83 units. 13 stories, interior corridors. **Parking:** valet only. **Terms:** cancellation fee imposed, resort fee. **Amenities:** safes. **Dining:** Bacchus Restaurant, see separate listing, entertainment. **Activities:** steamroom, exercise room, spa. **Guest Services:** valet laundry. **Featured Amenity:** continental breakfast.

SAVE ▯▯ ▯▯ ▯▯ CALL ▯M BIZ ▯ ▯ ▯ ▯ ▯

WEST END GUEST HOUSE   604/681-2889 **4**
Historic Bed & Breakfast. **Address:** 1362 Haro St V6E 1G2

THE WESTIN BAYSHORE VANCOUVER
(604)682-3377 **1**

WESTIN HOTELS & RESORTS

Hotel
$199-$549

AAA Benefit: Members save up to 15%, plus Starwood Preferred Guest® benefits!

Address: 1601 Bayshore Dr V6G 2V4 **Location:** Waterfront. Jct W Georgia and Cardero sts. Burrard, 46. **Facility:** Enjoy your own little oasis in the city, where wonderful grounds surround this sprawling hotel. Each of the tasteful rooms and suites offer spectacular harbor, city and mountain views. 511 units. 9-16 stories, interior corridors. **Parking:** on-site (fee) and valet. **Terms:** cancellation fee imposed. **Amenities:** safes. **Dining:** 2 restaurants. **Pool(s):** heated outdoor, heated indoor. **Activities:** sauna, hot tub, steamroom, self-propelled boats, marina, trails, exercise room, in-room exercise equipment, spa. **Guest Services:** valet laundry, boarding pass kiosk.

SAVE ECO ▯▯ ▯▯ ▯▯ CALL ▯M ▯ BIZ ▯▯ ▯
▯ ▯ ▯ / SOME UNITS ▯ SHS ▯

THE WESTIN GRAND, VANCOUVER
(604)602-1999 **34**

WESTIN HOTELS & RESORTS

Hotel
$299-$499

AAA Benefit: Members save up to 15%, plus Starwood Preferred Guest® benefits!

Address: 433 Robson St V6B 6L9 **Location:** Between Homer and Richards sts. Vancouver City Centre, 52. **Facility:** 206 units. 26 stories, interior corridors. **Parking:** on-site (fee) and valet. **Terms:** cancellation fee imposed, resort fee. **Amenities:** safes. **Pool(s):** heated outdoor. **Activities:** sauna, hot tub, steamroom, massage. **Guest Services:** valet laundry.

SAVE ECO ▯▯ ▯▯ ▯▯ CALL ▯M ▯ ▯ BIZ SHS
▯ ▯ ▯ ▯ ▯ / SOME UNITS ▯ ▯ ▯ ▯

WHERE TO EAT

AL PORTO RISTORANTE   604/683-8376 **26**
Northern Italian. Fine Dining. **Address:** 321 Water St V6B 1B8

BACCHUS RESTAURANT   604/608-5319 **25**

French
Fine Dining
$17-$44

AAA Inspector Notes: Here you'll enjoy a fine meal in a luxurious, elegant setting, presided over by a superb painting of Bacchus himself. The chef has created a wonderful menu to match, employing superb ingredients and delicious preparations. You can usually find items like foie gras, Nova Scotia lobster, Fraser Valley duck, venison and plenty of BC seafood. The lounge is also a beautiful spot to unwind and people-watch when they open the street-side windows in nice weather. **Features:** full bar, Sunday brunch. **Reservations:** suggested. **Address:** 845 Hornby St V6Z 1V1 **Location:** Between Smithe and Robson sts; in The Wedgewood Hotel & Spa. Vancouver City Centre, 52. **Parking:** valet and street only. B L D CALL ▯M ▯

BANANA LEAF MALAYSIAN CUISINE   604/669-3389 **28**
Asian. Casual Dining. **Address:** 1043 Davie St V6E 1M5

BLUE WATER CAFE + RAW BAR   604/688-8078 **40**
Seafood Sushi. Fine Dining. **Address:** 1095 Hamilton St V6B 5T4

THE BOATHOUSE RESTAURANT   604/669-2225
Seafood Steak. Casual Dining. **Address:** 1795 Beach Ave V6G 1Y9

BREKA BAKERY & CAFE   604/620-8200 **8**
Breads/Pastries. Quick Serve. **Address:** 818 Bute St V6E 1Y4

BRIDGES   604/687-4400 **42**
American. Casual Dining. **Address:** 1696 Duranleau St V6H 3S4

BRIX RESTAURANT & WINE BAR   604/915-9463 **39**
Pacific Northwest. Fine Dining. **Address:** 1138 Homer St V6B 2X6

CACTUS CLUB CAFE   604/687-3278
New American. Casual Dining. **Address:** 1136 Robson St V6E 1B2

CACTUS CLUB CAFE   604/685-8070
New American. Casual Dining. **Address:** 357 Davie St V6B 1R2

CACTUS CLUB CAFE   604/681-2582
New American. Casual Dining. **Address:** 1790 Beach Ave V6G 1Y9

CARDERO'S RESTAURANT   604/669-7666 **2**
Seafood. Casual Dining. **Address:** 1583 Coal Harbour Quay V6G 3E7

CHAMBAR   604/879-7119 **36**
New Belgian. Fine Dining. **Address:** 568 Beatty St V6B 2L3

CIAO BELLA RISTORANTE   604/688-5771 **1**
Italian. Casual Dining. **Address:** 703 Denman St V6G 2L6

CINCIN   604/688-7338 **9**
Mediterranean. Fine Dining. **Address:** 1154 Robson St V6E 1B5

(See map & index p. 286.)

CIOPPINO'S MEDITERRANEAN GRILL
604/688-7466 (41)

Italian
Fine Dining
$25-$48

AAA Inspector Notes: The talented chef at this restaurant has a real knack for creating amazing, flavorful food using only high-quality ingredients. The expansive menu features items like Digby scallops with black truffle froth, wonderful handmade pastas and wild Alberta boar served two ways. The warm and inviting dining room showcases wine cabinets throughout, and hospitable servers go out of their way to make sure you have a wonderful dining experience. **Features:** full bar. **Reservations:** suggested. **Address:** 1133 Hamilton St V6B 5P6 **Location:** Between Helmcken and Davie sts. Yaletown-Roundhouse, 53. **Parking:** on-site (fee) and valet. D CALL M

COPPER CHIMNEY
604/689-8862 (17)

Indian. Fine Dining. **Address:** 567 Hornby St V6C 2E8

DOCKSIDE RESTAURANT
604/685-7070 (50)

New American. Casual Dining. **Address:** 1253 Johnston St V6H 3R9 **(See ad p. 301.)**

EARLS KITCHEN + BAR

American. Casual Dining.
LOCATIONS:
Address: 1185 Robson St V6E 1B5 **Phone:** 604/669-0020
Address: 905 Hornby St V6Z 1V3 **Phone:** 604/682-6700

ESPAÑA
604/558-4040 (3)

New Spanish Small Plates. Casual Dining. **Address:** 1118 Denman St V6G 2M8

FIVE SAILS RESTAURANT
604/844-2855 (11)

New
European
Fine Dining
$38-$42

AAA Inspector Notes: Whether it's the sight of cruise ships docked at the adjoining piers or the beautiful harbor and mountain vistas, every table gets a view. The menu is driven by seasonal market availability, and the chef celebrates the bounty by staying true to his European roots. Depending on what the market bears, look for offerings to include a variety of seafood, domestic and game meats, sweetbreads and exotics like truffles and sturgeon roe, and artisanal cheeses stashed away in the kitchen. **Features:** full bar. **Reservations:** suggested. **Address:** 999 Canada Pl, Suite 410 V6C 3E1 **Location:** Between Howe and Burrard sts; in Pan Pacific Vancouver. Waterfront, 45. **Parking:** on-site (fee) and valet. D CALL M

FORAGE
604/661-1400 (4)

New Canadian. Casual Dining. **Address:** 1300 Robson St V6E 1C5

FRANKIE'S ITALIAN KITCHEN & BAR
604/688-6368 (38)

Italian. Casual Dining. **Address:** 765 Beatty St V6B 2M4

GOTHAM STEAKHOUSE & COCKTAIL BAR
604/605-8282 (27)

Steak. Fine Dining. **Address:** 615 Seymour St V6B 3K3

GUU ORIGINAL
604/685-8817 (16)

Japanese Small Plates. Casual Dining. **Address:** 838 Thurlow St V6E 1W2

HAWKSWORTH RESTAURANT
604/673-7000 (22)

New Pacific Northwest. Fine Dining. **Address:** 801 W Georgia St V6C 1P7

INDIA BISTRO
604/684-6342 (20)

Indian. Casual Dining. **Address:** 1157 Davie St V6E 1N2

JOE FORTES SEAFOOD & CHOP HOUSE
604/669-1940 (14)

Seafood
Steak
Casual Dining
$17-$50

AAA Inspector Notes: *Classic.* A San Francisco-style seafood grill on trendy Robson Street, this restaurant features delightful rooftop garden dining in season. It also has a popular oyster bar and fireplace lounge. Be sure to ask about the restaurant's namesake, turn-of-the-century legend Joe Fortes. Valet parking is available weekdays and after 6 pm on Saturday and Sunday. **Features:** full bar, Sunday brunch, happy hour. **Reservations:** suggested. **Address:** 777 Thurlow St V6E 3V5 **Location:** Between Robson and Alberni sts. Burrard, 46. **Parking:** valet and street only. L D CALL M

KINGSTON TAPHOUSE & GRILLE
604/681-7011 (32)

American. Gastropub. **Address:** 755 Richards St V6B 3A6

KIRIN MANDARIN RESTAURANT
604/682-8833 (6)

Chinese. Fine Dining. **Address:** 1172 Alberni St V6E 3Z3

L'ABATTOIR
604/568-1701 (33)

New
American
Casual Dining
$25-$44

AAA Inspector Notes: The food here is truly inspirational as are the excellent libations from the bar. Capable servers can help you navigate the creative menu; it changes often and examples like veal tartare with smoked yolk or duck breast with whipped foie gras give you an idea of the quality. In a building which housed Vancouver's first jail, the space reflects a chic, industrial design. The vibe is casual and lively with seating either in the upstairs loft area or a glass-enclosed patio at the back. **Features:** full bar, Sunday brunch. **Reservations:** suggested. **Address:** 217 Carrall St V6B 2J2 **Location:** Just s of jct Water, Alexander and Powell sts; in Gastown. Stadium-Chinatown, 48. **Parking:** street only. D

Creative food; eclectic wine list; unique cocktails

LA TERRAZZA
604/899-4449 (47)

Northern Italian. Fine Dining. **Address:** 1088 Cambie St & Pacific Blvd V6B 6J5

LE CROCODILE
604/669-4298 (21)

French
Fine Dining
$17-$48

AAA Inspector Notes: This wonderful restaurant has an impressive menu featuring perfectly prepared classic cuisine. Ingredients are of the highest quality and you will find everything from sautéed frog legs to veal with sumptuous sauce and morels. Foie gras is featured in several dishes and pan-fried Dover sole is filleted tableside. The atmosphere is bustling when the place is full, which is nearly every night, and service is finely tuned. Valet parking is available at dinner only. **Features:** full bar, patio dining. **Reservations:** suggested. **Address:** 909 Burrard St (at Smithe St), Suite 100 V6Z 2N2 **Location:** Jct Smithe and Burrard sts. Burrard, 46. **Parking:** on-site (fee) and valet. L D CALL M

LUPO RESTAURANT
604/569-2535 (37)

Italian. Fine Dining. **Address:** 869 Hamilton St V6B 2R7

(See map & index p. 286.)

MARKET BY JEAN-GEORGES   604/695-1115   (12)

▼▼ ▼▼◆
**Pacific Northwest
Fine Dining**
$16-$36

AAA Inspector Notes: Internationally acclaimed chef Jean-Georges Vongerichten has put his name on this restaurant on the third floor of the hotel. You can choose from three distinct, stylish dining areas: the heated terrace, the fine-dining room or the lounge. Overall this is an informal environment and the staff is more than happy to assist you in choosing from the interesting menu. Examples include heirloom tomato salad with fresh burrata cheese or braised beef short ribs with cocoa spaetzle. **Features:** full bar, patio dining, Sunday brunch. **Reservations:** suggested. **Address:** 1115 Alberni St V6E 4T9 **Location:** Between Thurlow and Bute sts; in Shangri-La Hotel Vancouver. 🚇 Burrard, 46. **Parking:** on-site (fee) and valet.

B L D CALL 🔊M 🚭

MEAT & BREAD   604/566-9003   (31)
▼ Sandwiches. Quick Serve. **Address:** 370 Cambie St V6E 2M6

MEDINA CAFE   604/879-3114   (34)
▼▼ Mediterranean. Casual Dining. **Address:** 780 Richards V6B 3A4

MIKU   604/568-3900   (19)
▼▼▼ Japanese. Casual Dining. **Address:** 200 Granville St, #70 V6C 1S4

MILESTONES GRILL AND BAR
▼▼ American. Casual Dining.
LOCATIONS:
Address: 1145 Robson St V6E 1B5 **Phone:** 604/682-4477
Address: 1109 Hamilton St V6B 5P6 **Phone:** 604/684-9111

MINAMI   604/685-8080   (45)
▼▼▼▼ New Japanese. Casual Dining. **Address:** 1118 Mainland St V6B 2T9

MOXIE'S CLASSIC GRILL   604/678-8043
▼ American. Casual Dining. **Address:** 1160 Davie St V6E 1N1

ORU CUISINE   604/695-5500   (7)
▼▼▼ Pacific Northwest. Fine Dining. **Address:** 1038 Canada Pl V6C 0B9

PIDGIN   604/620-9400   (35)
▼▼▼ Fusion. Casual Dining. **Address:** 350 Carrall St V6B 2J3

PROVENCE MARINASIDE   604/681-4144   (49)
▼▼▼ Mediterranean Seafood. Fine Dining. **Address:** 1177 Marinaside Cres V6Z 2Y3

RICKY'S ALL DAY GRILL   604/602-9233
▼▼ American. Casual Dining. **Address:** 111 Dunsmuir St, #1 V6B 6A3

RODNEY'S OYSTER HOUSE   604/609-0080   (46)
▼▼▼ Seafood. Casual Dining. **Address:** 1228 Hamilton St V6B 2S8

THE SANDBAR SEAFOOD RESTAURANT   604/669-9030   (48)
▼▼▼ Seafood. Casual Dining. **Address:** 1535 Johnston St, Creekhouse #102 V6H 3R9

SCOOZIS MEDITERRANEAN BAR & GRILL   604/684-1009   (18)
▼▼ Mediterranean. Casual Dining. **Address:** 445 Howe St V6C 2X4

SHURAKU SAKE BAR + BISTRO   604/687-6622   (30)
▼▼ Japanese. Casual Dining. **Address:** 833 Granville St V6Z 1K7

SIMPLY THAI   604/642-0123   (44)
▼▼ Thai. Casual Dining. **Address:** 1211 Hamilton St V6Z 2Y3

STEPHO'S SOUVLAKI GREEK TAVERNA   604/683-2555   (24)
▼▼ Greek. Casual Dining. **Address:** 1124 Davie St V6E 1N1

TABLEAU BAR BISTRO   604/639-8692   (5)
▼▼▼ New French. Casual Dining. **Address:** 1181 Melville St V6E 0A3

THE URBAN TEA MERCHANT   604/692-0071   (15)
▼▼▼ Specialty. Casual Dining. **Address:** 1070 W Georgia St V6E 2Y2

VERA'S BURGER SHACK   604/228-8372
▼ Burgers Hot Dogs. Quick Serve. **Address:** 1925 Cornwall Ave V6J 1C8

VERA'S BURGER SHACK   604/893-8372
▼ Burgers. Quick Serve. **Address:** 1030 Davie St V6E 1M3

WATER ST. CAFE   604/689-2832   (29)
▼▼▼ International. Casual Dining. **Address:** 300 Water St V6B 1B6

WHITE SPOT
▼▼ American. Casual Dining.
LOCATIONS:
Address: 718 Drake St V6Z 2W6 **Phone:** 604/605-0045
Address: 1616 W Georgia St V6G 2V5 **Phone:** 604/681-8034

YALETOWN BREWING COMPANY   604/681-2739   (43)
▼▼ International. Casual Dining. **Address:** 1111 Mainland St V6B 2T9

YEW SEAFOOD + BAR   604/692-4939   (23)
▼▼▼ Seafood. Fine Dining. **Address:** 791 W Georgia St V6C 2T4

ZEFFERELLI'S RESTAURANT   604/687-0655   (10)
▼▼ Italian. Casual Dining. **Address:** 1136 Robson St V6E 1B2

Upgrade to Plus or Premier membership

for *more* of the benefits you need most

VANCOUVER
• Hotels & Restaurants map & index p. 290

BEST WESTERN PLUS UPTOWN HOTEL
(604)267-2000

Hotel
$99-$309

Best Western PLUS. AAA Benefit: Save 10% or more every day and earn 10% bonus points!

Address: 205 Kingsway V5T 3J5 **Location:** Corner of E 10th St. Broadway-City Hall, 55. **Facility:** 69 units. 4 stories, interior corridors. **Activities:** exercise room. **Guest Services:** valet laundry. **Featured Amenity:** breakfast buffet. (See ad this page.)

SAVE [TI] [🛗] [Y] CALL [M] BIZ [HS] 🛜 [X] [🖵]

/SOME UNITS

DAYS INN-VANCOUVER METRO   (604)876-5531
Motel. **Address:** 2075 Kingsway V5N 2T2

HOLIDAY INN VANCOUVER-CENTRE (BROADWAY)
(604)879-0511
Hotel. **Address:** 711 W Broadway V5Z 3Y2

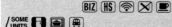
WHERE TO EAT

BISHOP'S   604/738-2025
Pacific Northwest. Fine Dining. **Address:** 2183 W 4th Ave V6K 1N7

BISTRO ABSINTHE   604/566-9053
French. Casual Dining. **Address:** 1260 Commercial Dr V5L 3X4

CACTUS CLUB CAFE   604/714-6000
New American. Casual Dining. **Address:** 575 W Broadway V5Z 1E6

CACTUS CLUB CAFE   604/733-0434
New American. Casual Dining. **Address:** 1530 W Broadway V6J 5K9

CAFE SALADES DE FRUITS   604/714-5987
French. Casual Dining. **Address:** 1551 W 7th Ave V6J 1S1

CHUTNEY VILLA   604/872-2228
Southern Indian. Casual Dining. **Address:** 147 E Broadway V5T 1W1

GRAMERCY GRILL   604/730-5666
Pacific Northwest. Casual Dining. **Address:** 2685 Arbutus St V6J 3Y4

LAS MARGARITAS RESTAURANTE & CANTINA
604/734-7117
Mexican. Casual Dining. **Address:** 1999 W 4th Ave V6J 1M7

LOMBARDO'S PIZZERIA & RISTORANTE   604/251-2240
Pizza. Casual Dining. **Address:** 120 1641 Commercial Dr V5L 3A4

MAENAM   604/730-5589
New Thai. Casual Dining. **Address:** 1938 W 4th Ave V6J 1M5

MAURYA INDIAN CUISINE   604/742-0622
Indian. Casual Dining. **Address:** 1643 W Broadway V6J 1W9

MEMPHIS BLUES BARBEQUE HOUSE
Barbecue. Casual Dining.
LOCATIONS:
Address: 1465 W Broadway V6H 1H6 **Phone:** 604/738-6806
Address: 1342 Commercial Dr V5L 3X6 **Phone:** 604/215-2599

MILESTONES GRILL AND BAR   604/678-8488
American. Casual Dining. **Address:** 2425 Cambie St V5Z 4M5

▼ See AAA listing this page ▼

(See map & index p. 290.)

MILLTOWN BAR & GRILL   604/269-2348 ㉓
♥♥ American. Gastropub. **Address:** 9191 Bentley St, Suite 101 V6P 6G2

THE OUISI BISTRO   604/732-7550 ⑰
♥♥ Cajun. Casual Dining. **Address:** 3014 Granville St V6H 3J8

PROVENCE MEDITERRANEAN GRILL   604/222-1980 ②
♥♥♥ Mediterranean. Fine Dining. **Address:** 100-4473 W 10th Ave V6R 2H2

ROMER'S BURGER BAR   604/732-9545 ⑧
♥♥ Burgers. Gastropub. **Address:** 1873 W 4th Ave V6J 1M4

SALMON N' BANNOCK   604/568-8971 ⑭
♥♥ New Canadian. Casual Dining. **Address:** 1128 W Broadway V6H 1G5

SAWASDEE THAI RESTAURANT   604/876-4030 ⑳
♥♥ Thai. Casual Dining. **Address:** 4250 Main St V5V 3P9

SEASONS IN THE PARK RESTAURANT   604/874-8008 ㉒
♥♥♥ Pacific Northwest. Fine Dining. **Address:** W 33rd Ave & Cambie St V6G 3E7

SHAUGHNESSY RESTAURANT AT VANDUSEN GARDEN
604/261-0011 ㉑
♥♥♥ Pacific Northwest. Casual Dining. **Address:** 5251 Oak St V6M 4H1

SOPHIE'S COSMIC CAFE   604/732-6810 ④
♥♥ American. Casual Dining. **Address:** 2095 W 4th Ave V6J 1N3

SWISS CHALET   604/732-8100
♥♥ Chicken. Casual Dining. **Address:** 3204 W Broadway V6K 2H4

TEAHOUSE IN STANLEY PARK   604/669-3281 ①
♥♥♥ Pacific Northwest. Fine Dining. **Address:** 7501 Stanley Park Dr V6G 3E2

TOJO'S RESTAURANT   604/872-8050 ⑬
♥♥♥ Japanese. Fine Dining. **Address:** 1133 W Broadway V6H 1G1

TRAFALGARS BISTRO   604/739-0555 ⑫
♥♥ Regional Continental. Casual Dining. **Address:** 2603 W 16th Ave V6K 3C2

VIJ'S RESTAURANT   604/736-6664 ⑲
♥♥♥ New Indian. Casual Dining. **Address:** 3106 Cambie St V5Z 2W2

WEST RESTAURANT   604/738-8938 ⑮
♥♥♥ Pacific Northwest. Fine Dining. **Address:** 2881 Granville St V6H 3J4

WHITE SPOT   604/261-2820
♥♥ American. Casual Dining. **Address:** 613A-650 41st Ave V5Z 2M9

VANDERHOOF (E-4) pop. 4,480, elev. 915m/2,050'

When the last spike of the railroad was driven in 1914, the Grand Trunk Pacific Development Company offered land for sale. The decision of where to put the new settlement in the wilderness was decided by Herbert Vanderhoof, a railroad employee, and a town was built in just a few weeks. The site, unfortunately, was a poor choice, as the land flooded every spring. In 1919 the townspeople moved to higher ground on the opposite side of the tracks.

Mr. Vanderhoof's legacy to the town is its name, Dutch for "of the farm." The name is fitting, as farming has always been an economic mainstay in the area.

Vanderhoof District Chamber of Commerce: 2353 Burrard Ave., P.O. Box 126, Vanderhoof, BC, Canada V0J 3A0. **Phone:** (250) 567-2124 or (800) 752-4094.

VERNON (B-9) pop. 38,150, elev. 383m/1,256'

• Restaurants p. 315
• Hotels & Restaurants map & index p. 226
• Part of Okanagan Valley area — see map p. 222

At the confluence of five valleys and bounded by three lakes, Vernon is an important shipping and trading center for the Okanagan region. The town's history is portrayed in 26 large murals painted on downtown buildings. On Hwy. 97 at 25th Avenue, Polson Park encompasses a Japanese garden, a Chinese tea house, a floral clock made of 3,500 plants and a children's water park.

Boating, fishing, hiking, mountain biking and golf are popular in summer; winter activities include skiing, dogsledding and snowshoeing. Several recreational opportunities are available at nearby Ellison Provincial Park *(see Recreation Areas Chart)* and Kalamalka Lake Provincial Park *(see attraction listing and Recreation Areas Chart).*

Silver Star Provincial Park offers mountain biking tours from late June to mid-September. A chairlift to the top of Silver Star Mountain operates daily, July 1 to mid-September.

For relaxation, the Kalamalka Lake viewpoint, 5 kilometres (3 mi.) south of 25th Avenue on Hwy. 97, provides an excellent view of the lake.

Tourism Greater Vernon: 3004 39th Ave., Vernon, BC, Canada V1T 3C3. **Phone:** (250) 542-1415 or (800) 665-0795.

ALLAN BROOKS NATURE CENTRE is on a ridgetop at 250 Allan Brooks Way in the old Vernon Upper Air Weather Station. The center—named after naturalist and illustrator Allan Brooks—features a habitat exhibit about the Northern Okanagan region's ecosystems, the Discovery Room with hands-on exhibits and an active beehive to view. The Grassland Trail, Naturescape Gardens and scenic views can be enjoyed outdoors. To overlook the countryside and see wildlife, climb the hill for a quiet spot.

Comfortable walking shoes are recommended. **Time:** Allow 1 hour minimum. **Hours:** Mon.-Sat. 9-4. Closed statutory holidays. **Cost:** $7.62; $4.76 (ages 3-18 and 65+); $21.43 (family, two adults and up to

(See map & index p. 226.)

four children ages 3-18); donations (viewpoint and grounds only). **Phone:** (250) 260-4227.

HISTORIC O'KEEFE RANCH is at 9380 Hwy 97N. One of the earliest cattle empires in the Okanagan Valley, the 1867 O'Keefe homestead includes a dozen restored structures. Guided tours are offered of the family's Victorian mansion. Other buildings include a log house, a church, a general store, a blacksmith shop, a cowboy bunk house, barns and tool sheds. A museum depicts the family's history and the ranching way of life and features a model train display.

Time: Allow 1 hour, 30 minutes minimum. **Hours:** Daily 10-6, July-Aug.; 10-5, May-June and Sept. 1-second Mon. in Oct. **Cost:** $13.50; $12 (ages 60+); $10 (ages 13-18); $8.50 (ages 6-12); $33 (family, two adults and children ages 6-18). Prices may vary; phone ahead. **Phone:** (250) 542-7868.

RECREATIONAL ACTIVITIES
Skiing

• **Silver Star Mountain Resort** is at 123 Shortt St. **Hours:** Daily 8-6 (also Fri.-Sat. 6-8 p.m. and daily 8-8, Dec. 21-Jan. 5), mid-Nov. to early Apr. Other activities are available daily 10-5 (also Wed. and Fri. 5-7:30), late June-early Sept. **Phone:** (250) 542-0224 for information, or (800) 663-4431 for reservations.

BEST WESTERN PACIFIC INN   (250)558-1800

Hotel
$99-$229

AAA Benefit: Save 10% or more every day and earn 10% bonus points!

Address: 4790 34th St V1T 5Y9 **Location:** Hwy 97 (32nd St); corner of 48th Ave. **Facility:** 61 units, some kitchens. 4 stories, interior corridors. *Bath:* shower only. **Terms:** cancellation fee imposed. **Activities:** exercise room. **Guest Services:** valet and coin laundry. *(See ad this page.)*

/ SOME UNITS

DAYS INN VERNON   (250)549-2224

Motel
$85-$165

Address: 5121 26th St V1T 8G4 **Location:** Hwy 97 (32nd St), 0.4 mi (0.7 km) e, just n on 27th St. Across from Village Green Mall. **Facility:** 53 units, some efficiencies. 2 stories (no elevator), exterior corridors. **Pool(s):** heated indoor. **Activities:** hot tub. **Featured Amenity:** continental breakfast.

/ SOME UNITS

FAIRFIELD INN & SUITES BY MARRIOTT   (250)260-7829

Hotel. **Address:** 5300 Anderson Way V1T 9V2

AAA Benefit: Members save 5% or more!

Keep your focus safely on the road when driving

Stay connected with #AAA and #CAA
on your favorite social media sites

(See map & index p. 226.)

HOLIDAY INN EXPRESS HOTEL & SUITES VERNON
250/550-7777 **4**

Hotel
Rates not provided

Address: 4716 34th St V1T 5Y9 **Location:** Hwy 97 (32nd St); corner of 48th Ave. **Facility:** 85 units. 3 stories, interior corridors. **Pool(s):** heated indoor. **Activities:** hot tub, exercise room. **Guest Services:** valet and coin laundry. *(See ad p. 314.)*

SPARKLING HILL RESORT
250/275-1556 **8**

Boutique
Contemporary
Hotel
Rates not provided

Address: 888 Sparkling Pl V1H 2K7 **Location:** 6 mi (10 km) s on Hwy 97, 1.1 mi (1.9 km) n on Bailey Rd, 2.4 mi (4 km) nw on Commonage Rd, then 1.8 mi (3 km) w on Predator Ridge Dr, follow signs. **Facility:** Be dazzled by the more than $10 million in Swarovski crystals throughout this one-of-a-kind spa retreat, which features suites with crystal fireplaces. Access to sauna and steam rooms is included. 149 units. 3 stories, interior corridors. **Parking:** valet only. **Terms:** check-in 4 pm. **Amenities:** safes. **Dining:** PeakFine, see separate listing. **Pool(s):** heated outdoor, heated indoor. **Activities:** sauna, hot tub, steamroom, regulation golf, trails, exercise room, in-room exercise equipment, spa. **Guest Services:** valet laundry, area transportation.

SUPER 8 VERNON
(250)542-4434 **6**

Hotel. **Address:** 4204 32nd St V1T 5P4

VERNON ATRIUM HOTEL & CONFERENCE CENTRE
(250)545-3385 **7**

Hotel
$124-$249

Address: 3914 32nd St V1T 5P1 **Location:** 1 mi (1.6 km) n on Hwy 97 (32nd St). **Facility:** 124 units. 3 stories (no elevator), interior corridors. **Terms:** cancellation fee imposed. **Dining:** 2 restaurants. **Pool(s):** heated indoor. **Activities:** hot tub, exercise room. **Guest Services:** valet and coin laundry. *(See ad p. 314.)*

VILLAGE GREEN HOTEL
(250)542-3321 **5**

Hotel
$79-$159

Address: 4801 27th St V1T 4Z1 **Location:** Hwy 97 (32nd St), 0.4 mi (0.7 km) e on 48th Ave. **Facility:** 128 units, some kitchens. 2-7 stories (no elevator), interior corridors. **Terms:** 3 day cancellation notice-fee imposed. **Pool(s):** heated indoor. **Activities:** sauna, hot tub, exercise room. **Guest Services:** valet laundry. **Featured Amenity: full hot breakfast.**

WHERE TO EAT

AMARIN THAI RESTAURANT 250/542-9300 **3**
Thai. Casual Dining. **Address:** 2903 31st St V1T 5H6

INTERMEZZO RESTAURANT 250/542-3853 **1**
Italian. Fine Dining. **Address:** 3206 34th Ave V1T 7E2

THE ITALIAN KITCHEN COMPANY 250/558-7899 **5**
Italian. Casual Dining. **Address:** 2916 30th Ave V1T 2B7

LOS HUESOS 250/275-4820 **4**
Mexican. Casual Dining. **Address:** 2918 30th Ave V1T 2B7

NAKED PIG 778/475-5475 **2**
Barbecue. Casual Dining. **Address:** 2933 30th Ave V1T 2B8

PEAKFINE 250/275-1556 **6**

Pacific Northwest
Fine Dining
$13-$45

AAA Inspector Notes: Almost every table here offers views of Okanagan Lake and the surrounding hillsides. The upscale menu changes with the seasons, and the chef sources meat and produce from the many area farmers. They try to offer some more healthful options in addition to rich and hearty dishes, and you will certainly be enticed by the delightful desserts. When making your reservation, ask for the front dining room so you sit near the beautiful, sparkling Swarovski crystal chandelier and a long, gas fireplace. **Features:** full bar. **Reservations:** required. **Address:** 888 Sparkling Pl V1H 2K7 **Location:** 6 mi (10 km) s on Hwy 97, 1.1 mi (1.9 km) n on Bailey Rd, 2.4 mi (4 km) nw on Commonage Rd, then 1.8 mi (3 km) w on Predator Ridge Dr, follow signs; in Sparkling Hill Resort. B L D CALL

Victoria

Then & Now

"To realize Victoria," Rudyard Kipling wrote, "you must take all that the eye admires in Bournemouth, Torquay, the Isle of Wight, the Happy Valley at Hong Kong, the Doon, Sorrento, Camp's Bay, add reminiscences of the Thousand Islands and arrange the whole around the Bay of Naples with some Himalayas for the background."

Yet the capital of British Columbia remains quintessentially British. Along with its tearooms, double-decker buses, horse-drawn tallyho carriages and shops that sell china and woolens, Victoria proudly claims another, much older culture. Totem poles can be seen throughout local parks, reflecting the city's dual heritage.

Regarded as Canada's gentlest city, Victoria has uncluttered streets, gardens that bloom year-round and hotels that have been serving high tea for decades. Sharing a passion for gardening, Victoria residents tend their prim English-style gardens. The city's innumerable flower beds and hanging baskets, nurtured by its mild climate, bloom in bright displays while the rest of Canada shivers.

The heart of the city curves around the stone-walled Inner Harbour, alive with bobbing pleasure craft, fishing boats and coastal shipping vessels. Facing the harbor are the parliament buildings and the block-long, ivy-covered Empress Hotel.

Emily Carr, a native of Victoria, devoted her artistic career to capturing on canvas the majestic totem poles carved by the vanishing First Nations civilizations of the Pacific coast. Like those she found in deserted tribal villages, the emblematic totems in Thunderbird Park evoke the highly developed ancient culture that dominated the area long before Victoria was settled in the mid-19th century.

Fort Victoria was built by Hudson's Bay Co. in 1843. Six years later Vancouver Island became a crown colony, and as British Columbia's only port, it became a passage to the Fraser Canyon goldfields on the mainland in 1858. Thousands of European and Asian miners descended on the city, forming the nucleus of today's diverse citizenry.

Violence around Bastion Square was so commonplace during this rowdy boomtown period that the *Victoria Gazette* reported no deaths "from natural causes in the city during the last 30 days." Local politicians supposedly settled their debates with fist fights.

After the gold fever broke, Victoria began to assume its characteristic cool reserve. Lured by modest land prices, English settlers developed their queen's namesake city into a thriving government and commercial center. In 1868 Victoria became the capital of the newly

The Fairmont Empress hotel and the Inner Harbour

(Continued on p. 318.)

Destination Victoria

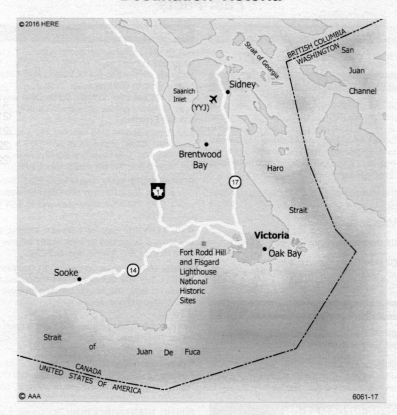

This map shows cities in the Victoria vicinity where you will find attractions, hotels and restaurants. Cities are listed alphabetically in this book on the following pages.

Fast Facts

ABOUT THE CITY

POP: 80,017 ▪ **ELEV:** 17m/56 ft.

MONEY

SALES TAX: British Columbia has a 5 percent goods and services tax (GST) and a 7 percent provincial sales tax (PST). Hotel accommodations are subject to an additional 3.5 percent and alcohol to an additional 3 percent. Restaurants and admission fees are exempt from the 7 percent PST. Automobile rental sales tax is $1.50 per day.

WHOM TO CALL

EMERGENCY: 911

POLICE (non-emergency): (250) 995-7654

HOSPITALS: Gorge Road Hospital, (250) 519-3500 ▪ Royal Jubilee Hospital, (250) 370-8000 ▪ Victoria General Hospital, (250) 727-4212.

WHERE TO LOOK AND LISTEN

NEWSPAPERS: Victoria's daily paper is the *Times Colonist,* which is distributed in the morning.

RADIO: Victoria radio stations CBC (90.5 FM) ▪ CIOC (98.5 FM) ▪ CFUV (101.9 FM) ▪ and C-FAX (1070 AM) have news and weather reports.

VISITOR INFORMATION

Tourism Victoria Visitor Centre: 812 Wharf St., Victoria, BC, Canada V8W 1T3. **Phone:** (250) 953-2033 or (800) 663-3883.

The center provides maps and brochures outlining self-guiding walking and driving tours. Open daily 8:30-8:30, mid-May to early Sept.; 9-5, rest of year.

TRANSPORTATION

AIR TRAVEL: Victoria International Airport (YYJ) is 22 kilometres (12 mi.) north on Hwy. 17 (Patricia Bay Highway). Air Canada flys to Victoria from Calgary, Seattle, Toronto and Vancouver. WestJet and Pacific Coastal Airlines offer domestic flights. Delta and Horizon Air/Alaska Airlines provide service from Seattle and San Francisco.

YYJ Airport Shuttle runs between the airport and downtown hotels; phone (778) 351-4995 or (855) 351-4995. Main Line Route fare $25; $15 (ages 3-17); free (ages 0-2) or $15 per person after 9 p.m.

RENTAL CARS: Hertz, 1640 Electra Blvd., Sidney, phone (250) 656-2312; and 548 David St., Victoria, phone (250) 952-3765, offers discounts to AAA and CAA members.

RAIL SERVICE: Service between Victoria and Courtenay is suspended for track repairs but may resume by early 2017; phone (888) 842-7245.

BUSES: The BC Ferries Connector, 721 Douglas St., provides daily bus service between Vancouver and Victoria via ferry. The vessels transport personal vehicles; reservations are required. Phone (778) 265-9474.

Greyhound & Pacific provides bus transportation between Victoria and Campbell River; stops include Duncan and Nanaimo. Phone (250) 385-4411.

TAXIS: Taxis charge $3.25 minimum plus $1.88 per kilometre (.6 mi.). Companies include Blue Bird Cabs, (250) 382-2222 ▪ Yellow Cab of Victoria, (250) 381-2222 ▪ and Victoria Taxi, (250) 383-7111.

PUBLIC TRANSPORTATION: BC Transit buses serve Greater Victoria's downtown area 6:30 a.m.-midnight. Fare $2.50 (single boarding); $5 (day pass); free (ages 0-5). Buses run frequently between downtown and the ferry terminal. For route information, phone (250) 382-6161.

BOATS: Several ferry systems make connections with mainland Canada and the U.S. *See Arriving, By Boat.*

(Continued from p. 316.)
joined crown colonies of Vancouver Island and British Columbia and, a short time later in 1871 when British Columbia joined the Canadian Confederation, it became the capital of the province.

Since commercial supremacy passed to Vancouver after the completion of the Canadian Pacific Railway, Victoria has adopted a slower pace with few heavy industries. The city is a center for commercial trade as well as the home of Canada's West Coast naval operations. Lumber and fishing also contribute to the bustle of this port.

The city's strong tourism industry is buoyed by the stream of travelers who come by ferry from Washington and throughout British Columbia. Those travelers come year round, thanks to Victoria's scenic setting and delightful climate. Flowers bloom all year, and the city only occasionally sees snow.

Victoria's climate and proximity to the Pacific Ocean also provide its citizens an opportunity for an active lifestyle. Marine-based activities such as fishing, sailing, kayaking, canoeing and whale watching are popular, as are bicycling, hiking and exploring neighborhoods and parks.

Whether or not Victoria is more British than Britain remains an ongoing debate among Victoria's residents. Few would contest, however, that nature's blessings have endowed the city with ample charm in its own right. No one understood this better than its native First Nations, whose awesome totems continue to speak the land's wonder.

Must Do: AAA Editor's Picks

- 🌿 **Butchart Gardens** (800 Benvenuto Ave., Brentwood Bay) attracts gardeners and nature lovers from around the world. Thousands of spring bulbs and flowering trees offer an extravagant show of color from late March to mid-June—but October and November, when the Japanese Garden takes center stage, matches spring's glory with a stunning autumn parade of reds, russets and golds, plus dozens of varieties of chrysanthemums.

- There's more beauty at 🌿 **Victoria Butterfly Gardens** (1461 Benvenuto Ave., Brentwood Bay) where more than 3,000 free-flying butterflies inhabit a 12,000-square-foot enclosure replete with tropical plants and koi-filled ponds. Swallowtails, brilliantly iridescent blue morphos and the impressively large Atlas moth are just a few of the species you'll see.

- Victoria's **Chinatown** (enter at Government and Fisgard streets) isn't as large as Vancouver's, but it is no less authentic, founded by Chinese immigrants in 1858. Wander up and down Fisgard Street, where vibrant wall murals depict turn-of-the-20th century Chinese families and the opium dens, gambling houses and brothels of yore that are now restaurants and local businesses. Hunt for souvenirs in the novelty shops along Fan Tan Alley, reputedly Canada's narrowest street.

- 🌿 **Miniature World** (649 Humboldt St.) isn't always what you might think—two dollhouses furnished in exquisite detail, as well as a model of the Great Canadian Railway, are among the largest of their kind in the world. But there's also a miniscule, operational sawmill, a tiny circus and scaled-down European castles. What makes this themed fantasyland particularly enthralling is that it's hands-on; push a button and something, somewhere, will start moving.

- Minutes away from the Inner Harbour, **Government Street** is packed with stores and art galleries. Do some shopping before settling into a booth at Bard and Banker, a convivial pub housed in a grand old bank building where you can tuck into beer-battered fish and chips.

- Those who don't feel like walking can ride in elegant style on a horse-drawn carriage tour. **Victoria Carriage Tours** (Belleville and Menzies streets) offers a 30-minute narrated excursion along the Inner Harbour that includes a peek at the architecturally grand homes in the historic James Bay neighborhood.

- 🌿 **Craigdarroch Castle** (1050 Joan Crescent), the home of 19th-century coal mining magnate Robert Dunsmuir, is a must-see. The interior of this massive estate, capped with a distinctive red slate roof, is a feast of oak paneling, stained glass and period room furnishings.

- A sylvan retreat in the middle of downtown Victoria, beautifully landscaped **Beacon Hill Park** (Douglas and Dallas streets) is named for a pair of masts placed atop a hill that acted as navigational aids for mariners approaching Victoria's Inner Harbour. Quiet and tree shaded, it's a stroller's delight right down to the freely roaming peacocks.

- From Kwakwaka'wakw ceremonial masks to Northern sea lions, 🌿 **The Royal BC Museum** (675 Belleville St.) explores every facet of British Columbia's natural and human history. Just how vast is this province? The Big Map, an animated audiovisual experience, provides a dramatic answer to that question.

- Indulge in afternoon tea on the lawn at **Point Ellice House** (2616 Pleasant St.), which overlooks the scenic Gorge Waterway. The former home of Irish emigrant Peter O'Reilly is filled with family possessions that comprise one of Canada's largest collections of Victoriana.

- The **Swiftsure International Yacht Race** (Clover Point Park off Dallas Rd.) has been a springtime tradition for more than 80 years. Thousands of people gather along the Dallas Road waterfront to watch fleets of sporting craft navigate the tricky waters of the Strait of Juan de Fuca. The competition is known for exciting starts and nail-biting finishes.

Butchart Gardens

Government House and Gardens

Victoria 1-day Itinerary

AAA editors suggest these activities for a great short vacation experience.

Morning

- Visit several gardens that serve as reminders of the city's British heritage (we'll get to the horse-drawn carriages and tearooms later in the day). Head to the Oak Bay neighborhood to **Abkhazi Garden** (1964 Fairfield Rd.). Though petite in size, the garden is resplendent in its beauty. Set on a rocky slope, the dramatic landscape is planted in rhododendrons, Japanese maples, azaleas, evergreens and alpine plants.

- Nearby is **Government House and Gardens** (1401 Rockland Ave.), home to the province's lieutenant governor. The formal gardens include spaces devoted to heather, iris and roses and plantings typical of an English country garden.

- A turreted, 39-room, four-story estate is next on your list. ▽▽ **Craigdarroch Castle** (1050 Joan Crescent) was built in the 1880s by a Scottish immigrant from a coal mining family who became one of the richest men in British Columbia. The impressive staircase, oak paneling, period furnishings and stained glass reflect 19th-century elegance.

- By this point, you've probably worked up an appetite. Stop at **Bin 4 Burger Lounge** (911 Yates St.) for lipsmacking gourmet burgers made from hormone-free beef, chicken, tofu, bison, lamb, pork or Ahi tuna. Refreshing salads and lettuce wraps are tempting options.

Afternoon

- Spend the rest of the day in the lovely Inner Harbor area. Cultural and natural provincial history is the focus of ▽▽ **The Royal BC Museum** (675 Belleville St.), a treasure trove of information about the province's development. Start at the First Peoples Gallery with its ceremonial masks and a full-size chief's house. Hear what a mammoth might have sounded like as well as other sounds from the Ice Age in a gallery devoted to natural history. Step outside to **Thunderbird Park** (Douglas and Belleville streets) to see a collection of Northwest Coast totem poles.

- Practically around the corner in **The Fairmont Empress** (721 Government St.) hotel is ▽▽ **Miniature World** (649 Humboldt St.). Incredible attention to detail is obvious in more than 80 dioramas, all intricately created in miniature. The world of the circus is elaborately crafted in teensy elements, as are dollhouses, castles, battle scenes and a 17th-century London cityscape.

- The palatial Fairmont Empress itself is worth a visit. Resembling a castle, the hotel is a Victoria landmark and known for its afternoon teas, a tradition since the hotel opened in 1908. Have a seat in the Tea Lobby and treat yourself to the English ritual (advance reservations are necessary). In addition to tea, sandwiches and pastries (think mango and curried chicken sandwiches and berry tarts) and raisin scones with heavy cream and strawberry preserves are served. Although worth a splurge, other options offer less expensive versions of the afternoon tea experience; try **White Heather Tea Room** (1885 Oak Bay Ave.).

- After the formal tea ceremony, a stroll and shopping on Government Street are in order. Victorian lampposts and colorful hanging baskets add to the city's charm. Browse through the 19th-century shops selling English woolens, fine china and other British imports; chocolates; Northwestern First Nations and Canadian art; clothing; and jewelry.

Evening

- For a very British way to begin the evening, there's a horse-drawn carriage awaiting. Head over to the corner of Belleville and Menzies streets where the carriages queue up.

- If enticing aromas from waterside restaurants beckon, there are many options near the harbor. Depending on your taste and pocketbook, you might want to consider **Pagliacci's** (1011 Broad St.) or **Restaurant Matisse** (512 Yates St.).

- After satisfying your appetite, take a romantic walk alongside the stone walls of the Inner Harbor. Enjoy the soothing breezes, the boats bobbing in the marinas and the lights illuminating the classic lines of the **Legislative Assembly of British Columbia** (501 Belleville St.).

Arriving
By Car

Victoria is the western terminus of the 7,821-kilometre (4,860-mi.) Trans-Canada Highway. The highway traverses the mainland to Horseshoe Bay in West Vancouver and resumes at the Departure Bay Ferry Terminal (Nanaimo). It then proceeds south along the island's eastern shore to Victoria. Hwy. 17, the other major artery into the city, connects Victoria with the ferry terminals at Swartz Bay and Sidney on the Saanich Peninsula.

By Boat

Several ferry systems connect Vancouver Island and Victoria with mainland Canada and the United States. The most direct route is the Tsawwassen-Swartz Bay automobile/passenger ferry service used by the intercity buses between Vancouver and Victoria. BC Ferries also connects Nanaimo, 111 kilometres (69 mi.) north of Victoria, to Horseshoe Bay in West Vancouver, and departs from the north end of the island at Port Hardy to travel through the Inside Passage to Prince Rupert, where they connect with the Alaska State Ferry system. Contact British Columbia Ferries for more information; phone (250) 386-3431 outside Canada and the U.S. or (888) 223-3779 within Canada and the U.S.

Ferries linking the southern end of the island and Victoria with the United States include Black Ball Transport Inc., (250) 386-2202 or (888) 993-3779, from Port Angeles, Wash., or (800) 265-6475 for the Victoria terminal; and Washington State Ferries, (206) 464-6400 or (888) 808-7977, from Anacortes, Wash., to Sidney. Reservations are available for the Anacortes, Wash., to Sidney route; phone 1 day in advance to determine estimated waiting time.

For a 2.75-hour trip to Seattle, take the Victoria Clipper, a high-speed passenger ferry; phone (250) 382-8100 for the Victoria terminal, (206) 448-5000 for the Seattle terminal, or (800) 888-2535.

Getting Around
Street System

Most traffic activity is on Wharf, Government and Belleville streets, which embrace the Inner Harbour. Ferries arrive from both Port Angeles and Seattle, Wash. all year. The main east-west streets are Yates, Fort and Johnson. Pandora Avenue, renamed Oak Bay Avenue in midtown, crosses the city from the Inner Harbour to Oak Bay.

Major north-south thoroughfares are Blanshard Street (Hwy. 17) and Douglas Street (Hwy. 1), which begins at Victoria's southern coast along the Juan de Fuca Strait. Dallas Road borders the shore and continues as Beach Drive along Victoria's eastern coast. Many Victoria streets are one-way.

Parking

On-street parking is controlled by meters and posted restrictions Mon.-Sat. 9-6; rates range from $1.50 to $3 per hour (free from 6-9 p.m. and on Sundays and holidays). Vehicles parked on specially posted blocks are subject to towing during rush hours. Downtown off-street parking is available in five city parkades, three surface parking lots and shopping center lots. Rates for city-run parking are $2 per hour, charged in 15-minute increments, or $12 per day ($14 at Bastion Square Parkade). At city parkades, the first hour is free; parking also is free Mon.-Sat. from 6-8 p.m. and on Sundays and holidays. During free parking periods, drivers need their entry ticket to exit the parking facility.

Shopping

Lined with shops carrying English tweeds and fine china, **Government Street** maintains Victoria's heritage as a trading post of the British Empire. Such shops as **Old Morris Tobacconist**, phone (250) 382-4811 or (888) 845-6111, have distinguished Government Street since the 19th century. Established in 1833, **Rogers' Chocolate** is a Victoria institution that counts British royalty in its clientele. The Rogers' factory, behind the store at 913 Government St., still produces its renowned bittersweet chocolate according to a guarded recipe; phone (250) 384-7021 or (800) 663-2220.

Shoppers determined to bring home something other than a few extra pounds might want to explore the craft and specialty shops in the renovated squares and malls off Government Street. More than 35 quaint stores and restaurants in revitalized old buildings highlight **Market Square**, bounded by Johnson, Pandora and Store streets; phone (250) 386-2441.

Trounce Alley, in the downtown core, is a hideaway of eclectic shops. Shops of mid-19th-century architecture display modern items in **Bastion Square**, once a hangout for prospectors and

Market Square

Swiftsure International Yacht Race

drifters. An attractive shopping arcade is in **Centennial Square** off Douglas Street. **Nootka Court** between Courtney and Humboldt streets contains small arts and crafts shops.

Popular items available in Victoria include hand-woven woolens from Ireland and England, hand-knit Cowichan sweaters, Inuit jade sculpture and Northwest First Nations masks and prints. **The Hudson's Bay** department store in The Bay Centre on Douglas Street, sells authentic Cowichan sweaters. Also in Victoria are **Hillside Shopping Centre**, 1644 Hillside Ave.; **Mayfair Shopping Centre**, 3147 Douglas St.; and **Sears**, 3190 Shelbourne St.

In keeping with its Victorian image, Victoria has more than 50 antiques shops. Many are found along Government and Fort streets and Oak Bay Avenue.

Big Events

In addition to its many cultural and historic landmarks, this destination hosts a number of outstanding festivals and events that may coincide with your visit.

As a city of traditions, Victoria celebrates many events and festivals year after year. The weekend following Victoria Day features the classic ❦ **Swiftsure International Yacht Race**, which has drawn an armada of more than 185 sailboats from all over the world since 1930. The **Victoria Highland Games & Celtic Festival** takes place in mid-May.

Boating enthusiasts will enjoy the **Victoria Classic Boat Festival** at **Inner Harbour** over Labour Day weekend. There will be a steamboat cruise, rowing regatta, boat races and lots of nautical fun.

Autumn shows off its best colors along the rural **Saanich Peninsula**, where the **Saanich Fair** has been held Labour Day weekend for more than a century. Fall's lower temperatures provide an energy boost for the mid-October **GoodLife Fitness Victoria Marathon**. During the first two weeks of October, however, guests can experience a chill that has nothing to do with the weather at the **Ghosts of Victoria Festival**.

Wrap up an incredible holiday journey in late November with the "jolly old elf" himself at **Santa's Light Parade** in the streets of Victoria.

Sports & Rec

The English spirit still is manifest in such games as **lawn bowling** and **cricket**, both played at various venues throughout the city, including Beacon Hill Park. Any notion, however, that Victoria's sports are too staid is dispelled quickly by a **box lacrosse** game. This offspring of the First Nations game of *baggataway* is a rough-and-tumble version of field lacrosse confined to a smaller, enclosed area. Canada's Parliament designated lacrosse, or boxla, as it also is called, the national sport in 1867 (hockey became the official national winter sport in 1994). Lacrosse is played from April to August at various venues, including the Q Centre, 1767 Old Island Hwy.

All-star **wrestling** and **ice hockey**, two other spectator sports that hardly could be considered sedate, also are held at the arena.

Water sports have obvious appeal in this island city. The wide variety of game fish around southern Vancouver Island includes rockfish, lingcod, sole and flounder; fishing licenses are required. Surf **fishing** often yields rewarding catches of salmon and black sea bass. Clamming and oyster harvesting are popular activities on any of the Gulf Islands, which are accessible by ferry from Swartz Bay.

Oak Bay Marina, 1327 Beach Dr., offers fishing charters at an hourly rate. Fishing equipment, a tackle shop and marine store are available; phone (250) 598-3369. Other nearby marinas include Anglers Anchorage Marina, 905 Grilse Ln. in Brentwood Bay, phone (250) 652-3531; North Saanich Marina, 1949 Marina Way in Sidney, phone (250) 656-5558; and the Westbay Marine Village, 453 Head St., phone (250) 385-1831 or (866) 937-8229.

Boating is enjoyed in the Strait of Georgia and the Saanich Inlet. Uplands Park on Oak Bay is equipped with boat ramps. Fine beaches border Dallas Road and Beach Drive.

With its scenic coastal location and balmy climate, Victoria offers excellent playing conditions for **golf**. On a peninsula jutting into the Juan de Fuca Strait, Victoria Golf Club, 1110 Beach Dr., is open to members of other clubs.

Other golf clubs include Ardmore (nine holes), 930 Ardmore Dr., North Saanich; Cedar Hill (18 holes), 1400 Derby Rd., Saanich; Cordova Bay (18 holes), 5333 Cordova Bay Rd.; Glen Meadows (18 holes),

1050 McTavish Rd., North Saanich; Green Acres (nine holes), 3970 Metchosin Rd.; Henderson Park (nine holes), 2291 Cedar Hill Crossroad; Mount Douglas (nine holes), 4225 Blenkinsop Rd.; Olympic View Golf Course (18 holes), 643 Latoria Rd.; Prospect Lake (nine holes), 4633 Prospect Lake Rd.; and Royal Oak Golf Club (nine holes), 540 Marsett Pl.

Many parks are scattered throughout Victoria and its surrounding municipalities of Oak Bay, Saanich and Esquimalt. Some offer **swimming,** such as Elk/Beaver Lake Park, Island View Beach Park, Mount Work Park, Thetis Lake Park and Willows Beach Park. Swimmers also might wish to try the Crystal Pool in Central Park.

Hiking, nature and horse trails are found at several parks. For more information contact Victoria Parks, Recreation & Culture; phone (250) 361-0600. Bamberton Provincial Park *(see Recreation Areas Chart)* offers developed recreational facilities, including **camping.**

Swan Lake-Christmas Hill Nature Sanctuary, 6.5 kilometres (4 mi.) north via the Patricia Bay Highway, can be explored by hiking trails and floating walkways weaving through the area. Excellent views of Victoria and the sea are at Mount Douglas, Mount Tolmie and Beacon Hill Park.

Performing Arts

McPherson Playhouse in Centennial Square is the center of Vancouver Island's regional and professional theater. The restored 1914 theater regularly presents noontime concerts and musical comedy productions in the evening; phone (250) 386-6121 or (888) 717-6121. The **Pacific Opera Victoria,** (250) 385-0222, performs at the **Royal Theatre.**

The Royal Theatre on Broughton Street is also the home of the **Victoria Symphony Orchestra,** (250) 385-6515, which offers a pop and masterworks series September through May. The **Victoria Conservatory of Music** sometimes offers performances; phone (250) 386-5311.

Contemporary plays, with an emphasis on Canadian works, are staged at the **Belfry,** (250) 385-6815, 1291 Gladstone Ave., while shows at the Royal Theatre, (250) 386-6121 or (888) 717-6121, 805 Broughton, range from touring musicians to classical concerts and ballet. The **University Centre Farquhar Auditorium,** 3800 Finnerty Rd., presents comedy, dance and other cultural events; phone (250) 721-8480. **Butchart Gardens** mounts concerts and musical stage shows during the summer. **Kaleidoscope Theatre,** an open-air theater at the Inner Harbour, also offers summer productions.

Top-name entertainers, rock groups and other performers draw large audiences to **Save-on-Foods Memorial Centre,** 1925 Blanshard; phone (250) 220-2600. A carillon at the **parliament buildings,** Government and Belleville sts., can be heard daily on the hour. The Royal BC Museum's **IMAX Victoria Theatre** offers big-screen films complementing the museum's natural and human history themes; phone (250) 356-7226 or (888) 447-7977.

ATTRACTIONS

ABKHAZI GARDEN is e. at 1964 Fairfield Rd. at Shotbolt Rd. This small, residential garden was created and nurtured by an Englishwoman and an exiled Georgian prince. The two met in Paris in the 1920s, spent time in separate World War II internment camps, reunited after the war, married and settled in Victoria.

Prince Nicholas and Princess Peggy Abkhazi built their home and developed this garden along rocky slopes meticulously planted with rhododendrons, Garry oaks and Japanese maples. The Abkhazis' home now houses The Teahouse, open for lunch and late afternoon tea.

Time: Allow 1 hour, 30 minutes minimum. **Hours:** Daily 11-5, Mar.-Oct.; Wed.-Sun. 11-4, rest of year. Last admission 1 hour before closing. Closed Jan. 1 and Christmas. Phone ahead to confirm schedule. **Cost:** $10. **Phone:** (778) 265-6466 or (250) 479-8053.

BUTCHART GARDENS—see Brentwood Bay p. 179.

CHRIST CHURCH CATHEDRAL is at 911 Quadra St., between Burdett and Rockland sts. The Anglican-Episcopal cathedral is reminiscent of the great Gothic churches of the Middle Ages. Originally founded in 1856, the present cathedral is the third church built on this site. Started in the late 1920s and completed in 1986, it is one of Canada's largest cathedrals. The bells are replicas of those at Westminster Abbey in

Parliament buildings

London, England. A labyrinth is on the grounds. **Hours:** Daily 8:30-5:30. **Cost:** Free. **Phone:** (250) 383-2714.

CRAIGDARROCH CASTLE is at 1050 Joan Crescent St. The sandstone mansion was built in the late 1880s for Robert Dunsmuir, a Scottish immigrant who attained wealth and fame through politics and coal mining. Dunsmuir died before the 39-room castle was completed. The building later served as a military hospital, a college and a music conservatory.

Visitors can appreciate the castle's stained-glass windows, intricate woodwork, ceiling murals and Victorian furnishings. There are numerous staircases, but no elevators. A self-guiding tour includes four floors of the castle and an 87-step climb to the tower, which offers stunning views of Victoria, the strait and the Olympic Mountains. An audio tour also is available.

Time: Allow 1 hour minimum. **Hours:** Daily 9-7, June 15-Sept. 6; 10-4:30, rest of year. Closed Jan. 1 and Dec. 25-26. **Cost:** $13.29; $12.33 (ages 65+); $8.52 (ages 13-18 and students with ID); $4.76 (ages 6-12). Prices may vary; phone ahead. **Phone:** (250) 592-5323.

THE GARDENS AT HORTICULTURE CENTRE OF THE PACIFIC are at 505 Quayle Rd. More than 3 hectares (9 acres) of educational gardens feature more than 10,000 plant varieties and sculptures. Highlights of the developing site include the Winter Garden and the Takata Japanese Garden. The surrounding 36 hectares (90 acres) include forests, wetlands and a haven for migratory birds.

Time: Allow 1 hour minimum. **Hours:** Daily 9-7, May-Sept.; 9-5, rest of year. Closed Jan. 1, Christmas Eve, Christmas and day after Christmas. **Cost:** $11.43; $8.57 (ages 60+ and students with ID); free (ages 0-16). **Phone:** (250) 479-6162.

GOVERNMENT HOUSE AND GARDENS is at 1401 Rockland Ave. Government House is the official residence of the Lieutenant Governor and the ceremonial home of all British Columbians. The grounds embrace 14.5 hectares (36 acres), including formal gardens and a rare Garry oak ecosystem. The Cary Castle Mews Interpretive Centre is a good place to explore the history of this National Historic Site. **Hours:** Gardens daily dawn-dusk. Cary Castle Mews Interpretive Centre and Tea Room Tues.-Sat. 10-4, May-Sept. House tours are scheduled for one Sat. each month at 10 and 11,

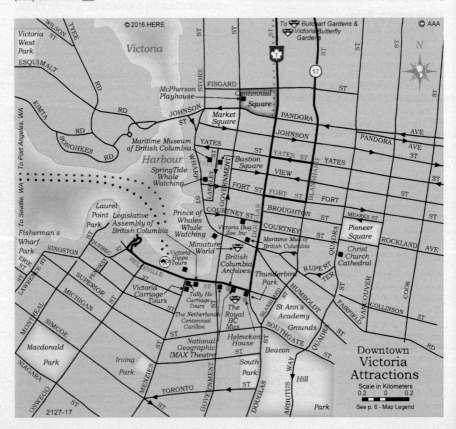

Downtown
Victoria
Attractions

Scale in Kilometers
0.2   0   0.2

See p. 6 - Map Legend

May-Oct.; phone ahead to confirm schedule. **Cost:** Free. **Phone:** (250) 387-2080, or (250) 356-5139 for tour reservations. GT ⁜ ⊞

LEGISLATIVE ASSEMBLY OF BRITISH CO-LUMBIA overlooks the Inner Harbour. The seat of British Columbia's parliament, the buildings have elaborately carved facades and are surrounded by 5 hectares (12 acres) of lawns, gardens, fountains and statues of dignitaries. The rooms have mosaic tile floors, rotundas, stained-glass windows, wood-carvings and murals.

Guided 30- to 45-minute tours, conducted in several languages, are offered. Self-guiding tours also are available weekdays; a booklet can be picked up at the tour desk. **Hours:** Daily 9-5, mid-May through Labour Day; Mon.-Fri. 9-5, rest of year. Phone ahead to confirm schedule. **Cost:** Free. **Phone:** (250) 387-3046.

MINIATURE WORLD is in The Fairmont Empress hotel at 649 Humboldt St. Animation, lighting, commentary and sound effects enhance more than 80 highly detailed miniature scenes. Displays include Circus World, one of the world's largest dollhouses, a Swiss Family Robinson tree house, a classic car rally and a futuristic space diorama. Scenes illustrate historic battles, fairy tales, nursery rhymes, "Gulliver's Travels" and novels by Charles Dickens. Eleven exhibits depict King Arthur's Camelot. The Great Canadian Railway exhibit re-creates rail transportation in late 19th-century Canada.

Time: Allow 1 hour minimum. **Hours:** Daily 9-9, mid-May through mid-Sept.; 9-7, early May to mid-May and mid-Sept. to late Sept.; 9-5, rest of year. Closed Christmas. **Cost:** $15; $11 (ages 65+); $10 (ages 12-17 and students with ID); $8 (ages 5-11). **Phone:** (250) 385-9731.

PRINCE OF WHALES WHALE WATCHING is at 812 Wharf St. Three-hour tours narrated by a marine biologist provide information about marine life. Passengers have a choice of sitting either outside on an open-air deck or inside in a heated cabin aboard either the 19-metre (62-ft.) *Ocean Magic* or *Ocean Magic II* cruiser. High-speed open-boat whale-watching tours in a Zodiac also are available. Hydrophones allow passengers to hear the whales vocalize. Sightseeing tours also are available.

Time: Allow 3 hours minimum. **Hours:** *Ocean Magic* or *Ocean Magic II* tours depart daily at 9, 12:15 and 3:30, May-Oct.; schedule varies, rest of year. Zodiac tours depart daily every half hour 9-5, year-round. Passengers should arrive 30 minutes prior to departure. **Cost:** Whale-watching $120; $95 (ages 13-17); $85 (ages 7-12). Combination ticket with Butchart Gardens $150; $125 (ages 13-17); $100 (ages 5-12). Phone ahead to confirm tour prices and schedule. Reservations are required. **Phone:** (250) 383-4884 or (888) 383-4884.

Craigdarroch Castle

THE ROYAL BC MUSEUM is on the Inner Harbour at 675 Belleville St. at Government St. Two floors of displays reflect the human and natural history of British Columbia. The early 1900s Old Town Gallery has a theater with silent movies, a saloon, shops and a hotel. The Natural History Gallery showcases several different exhibits including a coastal rain forest diorama highlighted by live plants and tidal-pool animals, and a climate change exhibit which explores the province's future climate. The First Peoples Gallery includes an exhibit focusing on the historic Nisga'a agreement and the present-day Nisga'a community, and Haida argillite carvings.

"Our Living Languages: First Peoples' Voices in BC" is an award-winning feature exhibition. The on-site IMAX Victoria Theatre offers films to complement the natural and human history theme of the museum as well as other exciting IMAX footage. Feature exhibits are presented annually.

Hours: Daily 10-5 (also Fri.-Sat. 5-10, early June-early Oct.). Closed Jan. 1 and Christmas. **Cost:** Museum $22.86; $16.19 (ages 6-18, ages 65+ and students ages 19+ with ID); $5.40 (ages 3-5). IMAX $11.38; $9.29 (ages 6-18 and 65+); $10.24 (students ages 19+ with ID); $5.40 (ages 3-5). Combination and discounted multi-day tickets are available. Admission may increase for feature exhibits. **Phone:** (250) 356-7226 or (888) 447-7977.

British Columbia Archives is at 655 Belleville St. Extensive public and private records are available to those conducting historical, genealogical or other research. Gardens containing native plants surround the building. **Note:** A photo identification is required for registration. **Hours:** The archives are open to the public Mon.-Fri. 10-8 (full services available 10-4), Sat. 1-5 (limited services). Closed major holidays. **Cost:** Free. **Phone:** (250) 387-1952.

Helmcken House is on the grounds of the Royal BC Museum. One of the oldest houses in British Columbia still on its original site, the 1852 log structure was the home of John Sebastian Helmcken, a surgeon for Hudson's Bay Co. at Fort Victoria and a Father of Confederation. The restored house displays many original furnishings and an impressive collection of period medical instruments.

Time: Allow 30 minutes minimum. **Hours:** Daily noon-4, May 18-Labour Day; by appointment rest of year. Phone ahead to confirm schedule. **Cost:** Donations. **Phone:** (250) 356-7226.

The Netherlands Centennial Carillon is on the grounds of the Royal BC Museum at the corner of Government and Belleville sts. The largest carillon in Canada houses 62 bells donated by British Columbians of Dutch origin in celebration of the 1967 Canadian Confederation Centennial and in recognition of Canada's role in the liberation of the Netherlands during World War II. **Hours:** Carillon chimes ring hourly 10-8, Mar.-Sept.; 10-5, rest of year. Phone ahead to confirm summer Sun. carillon concert schedule. **Cost:** Free. **Phone:** (250) 356-7226.

Thunderbird Park is at the corner of Douglas and Belleville sts. on the grounds of the Royal BC Museum. The park's collection of Northwest Coast totem poles was established in 1941 and recarved via the Totem Restoration Program 1950-90, when the originals began to decay beyond repair. A new Kwakwaka'wakw Honouring Pole was carved and raised in 1999.

Also showcased is Wawadit'la, the ceremonial bighouse built by noted carver and artist Mungo Martin in 1953 that bears the hereditary crests of his family. **Hours:** Park open daily dawn-dusk. **Cost:** Free. **Phone:** (250) 356-7226.

SPRINGTIDE WHALE WATCHING is at 1119 Wharf St. In addition to killer whales, visitors also may encounter sea lions; seals; porpoises; humpback, grey and minke whales as well as a variety of birds. Tours are given on a 19-metre (61-ft.) motor yacht as well as on high-speed, open Zodiacs. A harbor tour and sport fishing trips are available year-round.

Time: Allow 3 hours minimum. **Hours:** Whale-watch tours are given daily at 10 and 2, Apr.-Oct. Other times are available; phone for schedule. **Cost:** Whale-watch tour $109; $99 (ages 65+); $89 (ages 13-18 and students with ID); $79 (ages 3-12); A $2 Wildlife Conservation Fee is charged per person. Reservations are recommended. **Phone:** (250) 384-4444, (250) 386-6016 or (800) 470-3474.

Sightseeing

VICTORIA HIPPO TOURS depart from the Black Ball Ferry Line Terminal, 470 Belleville St. Take a 90-minute guided tour of Victoria by land and by sea on an amphibious vehicle. The Olympic Mountains, Bastion Square, the Fairmont Empress, Chinatown, Fan Tan Alley, parliament buildings and Beacon Hill Park are some of the sights you'll see.

Hours: Tours depart daily on the hour (weather and tide permitting) 11-4, May-Sept; additional tours may be added July-Aug. Departures at 4 require a minimum of four passengers. Boarding begins 10 minutes before departure. Phone ahead to confirm schedule. **Cost:** $42.86; $33.33 (ages 3-12 and 60+); $9.52 (ages 1-2); $142.86 (family, two adults and two children ages 3-12). Reservations are recommended. **Phone:** (250) 590-5290 or (844) 477-6877. GT

Boat Tours

Sightseers using Victoria as a base for their travels can explore the Gulf Islands and Vancouver by ferry from Swartz Bay, north of Victoria via Hwy. 17; for schedule and toll phone the BC Ferries at (250) 386-3431 or (888) 223-3779.

Opportunities for whale watching are offered by several boating companies, the oldest of which is Orca Spirit, 146 Kingston St.; phone (250) 800-3747 or (877) 815-7255.

Bus and Carriage Tours

Guided tours of the city in red double-decker buses from London enhance Victoria's British atmosphere. Many of these tour operators are found along Belleville and Menzies streets by the harbor. Gray Line, 4196 Glanford Ave., (250) 385-6553 or (855) 385-6553, conducts bus tours, including a hop-on, hop-off service; tickets can be purchased at a kiosk at 721 Government St.

Whale-watching tour

Narrated horse-drawn carriage tours of the city are offered by several companies, including Tally Ho Carriage Tours, phone (250) 514-9257, and Victoria Carriage Tours, phone (250) 383-2207 or (877) 663-2207. All tours leave from the corner of Belleville and Menzies streets.

Driving Tours

The Visitor Centre has information about such scenic routes as Marine Drive along the shoreline, a trip to Sooke Harbour on the west coast and the Malahat Drive, which runs along the east coast and reaches an elevation of 381 metres (1,250 ft.). The trip to Butchart Gardens is one of the most popular drives, following Hwy. 17 and Hwy. 17A through the rural communities and pastoral valleys of the Saanich Peninsula.

Walking Tours

Victoria is the perfect size for visitors keen on walking. A favorite thoroughfare of strollers and shoppers is Government Street, graced by banners and five-globe Victorian lampposts supporting baskets of geraniums and petunias. Stop in at the Visitor Centre for details.

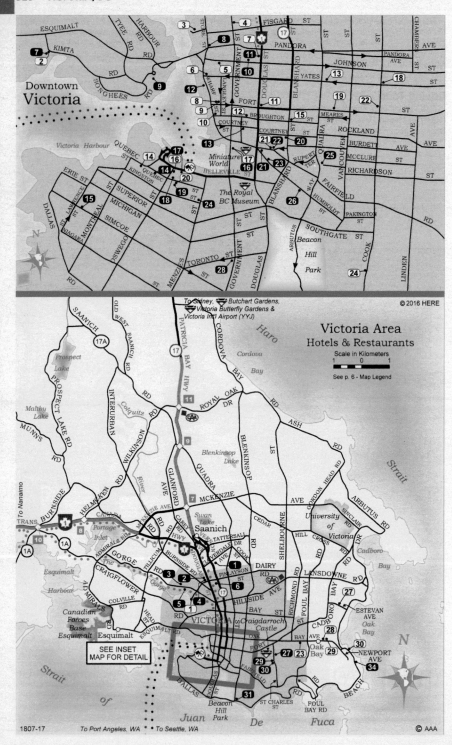

Downtown
Victoria

Victoria Harbour

Miniature
World

The Royal
BC Museum

Beacon
Hill
Park

ROCKLAND

© 2016 HERE

To Sidney, Butchart Gardens,
Victoria Butterfly Gardens &
Victoria Int'l Airport (YYJ)

Victoria Area
Hotels & Restaurants

Scale in Kilometers
See p. 6 - Map Legend

Prospect
Lake

Maltby
Lake

Cordova
Bay

Haro

Strait

Blenkinsop
Lake

Swan
Lake
Saanich

University
of
Victoria

Cadboro
Bay

To Nanaimo

Portage
Inlet

Esquimalt
Harbour

Canadian
Forces
Base
Esquimalt

VICTORIA

Craigdarroch Castle

Oak
Bay

ESTEVAN
AVE

Oak
Bay

NEWPORT
AVE

SEE INSET
MAP FOR DETAIL

Beacon
Hill
Park

Strait

of

Juan

De

Fuca

Victoria

This index helps you "spot" where approved hotels and restaurants are located on the corresponding detailed maps. Hotel daily rate range is for comparison only. Restaurant price range is a combination of lunch and/or dinner. Turn to the listing page for more information and consult display ads for special promotions.

VICTORIA

Map Page	Hotels	Diamond Rated	Rate Range	Page
1 p. 328	Accent Inns	◆◆	Rates not provided	330
2 p. 328	Mayfair Motel	◆◆	$69-$150	335
3 p. 328	Robin Hood Motel (See ad p. 334.)	◆◆	$70-$179	335
4 p. 328	Hotel Zed	◆◆	Rates not provided	334
5 p. 328	**Days Inn Victoria Uptown**	◆◆	$65-$230 SAVE	332
6 p. 328	**Comfort Inn & Suites Victoria**	◆◆◆	$129-$229 SAVE	331
7 p. 328	Spinnakers Gastro Brewpub & Guesthouses	◆◆◆	Rates not provided	335
8 p. 328	Swans Hotel and Brewpub	◆◆◆	Rates not provided	335
9 p. 328	**Delta Victoria Ocean Pointe Resort and Spa**	◆◆◆◆	$99-$340 SAVE	332
10 p. 328	**Best Western Plus Carlton Plaza Hotel**	◆◆◆	$89-$399 SAVE	330
11 p. 328	Hotel Rialto	◆◆◆	$139-$219	334
12 p. 328	**Victoria Regent Waterfront Hotel & Suites**	◆◆◆	$259-$339 SAVE	335
13 p. 328	**The Magnolia Hotel & Spa**	◆◆◆◆	Rates not provided SAVE	335
14 p. 328	**Harbour Towers Hotel & Suites (See ad p. 334.)**	◆◆	$100-$450 SAVE	334
15 p. 328	Heathergate House Bed & Breakfast	◆◆	$135-$175	334
16 p. 328	**The Fairmont Empress (See ad p. 333.)**	◆◆◆	$239-$699 SAVE	332
17 p. 328	**Days Inn Victoria on the Harbour**	◆◆	$93-$200 SAVE	332
18 p. 328	**Best Western Plus Inner Harbour (See ad p. 331.)**	◆◆◆	$129-$310 SAVE	331
19 p. 328	**Royal Scot Hotel & Suites**	◆◆◆	$99-$399 SAVE	335
20 p. 328	**Quality Inn Downtown Inner Harbour Victoria**	◆◆	$119-$299 SAVE	335
21 p. 328	**DoubleTree by Hilton Hotel & Suites Victoria**	◆◆◆	$139-$269 SAVE	332
22 p. 328	Chateau Victoria Hotel and Suites	◆◆◆	$125-$259	331
23 p. 328	**Victoria Marriott Inner Harbour**	◆◆◆◆	$112-$306 SAVE	335
24 p. 328	Embassy Inn (See ad p. 333.)	◆◆	$99-$379	332
25 p. 328	Abigail's Hotel	◆◆◆	Rates not provided	330
26 p. 328	Humboldt House Bed & Breakfast	◆◆◆	$165-$295	334
27 p. 328	Villa Marco Polo Inn	◆◆◆◆	$195-$365	336
28 p. 328	**James Bay Inn Hotel, Suites & Cottage**	◆◆	$79-$139 SAVE	335
29 p. 328	Abbeymoore Manor Bed & Breakfast Inn	◆◆◆	$139-$289	330
30 p. 328	Fairholme Manor	◆◆◆	$149-$355	332
31 p. 328	Dashwood Manor Seaside Bed & Breakfast Inn	◆◆◆	$109-$279	331

Map Page	Restaurants	Diamond Rated	Cuisine	Price Range	Page
① p. 328	Glo Restaurant & Lounge	◆◆◆	Canadian	$14-$30	336
② p. 328	Spinnakers Gastro Brewpub & Restaurant	◆◆	American	$11-$25	336
③ p. 328	Canoe Brewpub Marina Restaurant	◆◆	American	$14-$26	336

Map Page	Restaurants (cont'd)	Diamond Rated	Cuisine	Price Range	Page
④ p. 328	Brasserie L'Ecole	▽▽▽	French	$21-$50	336
⑤ p. 328	Il Terrazzo	▽▽▽	Northern Italian	$12-$36	336
⑥ p. 328	Restaurant Matisse	▽▽▽	French	$25-$40	336
⑦ p. 328	Veneto Tapa Lounge	▽▽▽	Pacific Northwest	$12-$30	336
⑧ p. 328	Koto Sushi Izakaya	▽▽	Japanese	$9-$32	336
⑨ p. 328	Siam Thai Restaurant	▽▽	Thai	$9-$21	336
⑩ p. 328	Nautical Nellie's Steak & Seafood Restaurant	▽▽▽	Steak Seafood	$14-$55	336
⑪ p. 328	Cactus Club Cafe	▽▽▽	New American	$12-$37	336
⑫ p. 328	Pagliacci's	▽▽	Italian	$14-$27	336
⑬ p. 328	Bin 4 Burger Lounge	▽▽	Burgers	$12-$18	336
⑭ p. 328	Nourish Kitchen and Cafe	▽▽	Natural/Organic	$12-$24	336
⑮ p. 328	The Pink Bicycle	▽▽	Burgers	$11-$16	336
⑯ p. 328	Victoria Harbour House Restaurant	▽▽	Steak Seafood	$18-$49	336
⑰ p. 328	Q at the Empress	▽▽▽	Pacific Northwest	$24-$55	336
⑱ p. 328	Ithaka Greek Restaurant	▽▽	Greek	$14-$32	336
⑲ p. 328	Cafe Brio	▽▽▽	Pacific Northwest	$23-$32	336
⑳ p. 328	Jonathan's Restaurant	▽▽	American	$16-$30	336
㉑ p. 328	Vista 18	▽▽▽	Regional Canadian	$28-$46	336
㉒ p. 328	Pluto's	▽▽	American	$10-$30	336
㉓ p. 328	White Heather Tea Room	▽▽	Desserts Sandwiches	$13-$24	336
㉔ p. 328	Pizzeria Primastrada	▽▽	Pizza	$12-$19	336

OAK BAY

Map Page	Hotel	Diamond Rated	Rate Range	Page
㉞ p. 328	**Oak Bay Beach Hotel**	▽▽▽▽	$219-$284 [SAVE]	221

Map Page	Restaurants	Diamond Rated	Cuisine	Price Range	Page
㉗ p. 328	Padella Italian Bistro	▽▽▽	Italian	$19-$30	221
㉘ p. 328	Penny Farthing English Pub	▽▽	Canadian	$14-$29	221
㉙ p. 328	Ottavio Italian Bakery & Delicatessen	▽	Italian Deli Breads/Pastries	$7-$14	221
㉚ p. 328	The Marina Restaurant	▽▽▽	Pacific Northwest	$19-$48	221

VICTORIA

• Restaurants p. 336
• Hotels & Restaurants map & index p. 328

ABBEYMOORE MANOR BED & BREAKFAST INN
(250)370-1470 ㉙
▽▽▽ Historic Bed & Breakfast. **Address:** 1470 Rockland Ave V8S 1W2

ABIGAIL'S HOTEL   250-388-5363 ㉕
▽▽▽ Boutique Hotel. **Address:** 906 McClure St V8V 3E7

ACCENT INNS   250/475-7500 ❶
▽▽ Hotel. **Address:** 3233 Maple St V8X 4Y9

BEST WESTERN PLUS CARLTON PLAZA HOTEL
(250)388-5513 ❿

Hotel
$89-$399

Best Western PLUS. **AAA Benefit:** Save 10% or more every day and earn 10% bonus points!

Address: 642 Johnson St V8W 1M6 **Location:** Between Douglas and Broad sts. **Facility:** 103 units, some efficiencies and kitchens. 7 stories, interior corridors. **Parking:** valet only. **Amenities:** safes. **Activities:** bicycles, exercise room. **Guest Services:** valet and coin laundry.

(See map & index p. 328.)

BEST WESTERN PLUS INNER HARBOUR
(250)384-5122

Extended Stay Hotel
$129-$310

 Best Western PLUS
AAA Benefit: Save 10% or more every day and earn 10% bonus points!

Address: 412 Quebec St V8V 1W5 **Location:** Between Oswego and Menzies sts. **Facility:** 74 kitchen units. 8 stories, interior corridors. **Terms:** check-in 4 pm. **Amenities:** safes. **Pool(s):** heated outdoor. **Activities:** sauna, hot tub, steamroom, exercise room. **Guest Services:** valet and coin laundry. **Featured Amenity:** breakfast buffet. *(See ad this page.)*

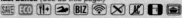

CHATEAU VICTORIA HOTEL AND SUITES
(250)382-4221
 Hotel. **Address:** 740 Burdett Ave V8W 1B2

COMFORT INN & SUITES VICTORIA
(250)382-4400

Hotel
$129-$229

Address: 3020 Blanshard St V8T 5C7 **Location:** 1.6 mi (2.6 km) n on Hwy 17 (Blanshard St), just s of Finlayson St. **Facility:** 151 units. 1-5 stories, interior/exterior corridors. **Terms:** check-in 4 pm. **Activities:** exercise room. **Guest Services:** valet and coin laundry. **Featured Amenity:** breakfast buffet.

DASHWOOD MANOR SEASIDE BED & BREAKFAST INN
(250)385-5517
Historic Bed & Breakfast. **Address:** 1 Cook St V8V 3W6

▼ See AAA listing this page ▼

Dream. Plan. Go.
TripTik® Travel Planner
AAA.com/ttp

(See map & index p. 328.)

DAYS INN VICTORIA ON THE HARBOUR
(250)386-3451 **17**

Hotel
$93-$200

Address: 427 Belleville St V8V 1X3 **Location:** Between Oswego and Menzies sts. **Facility:** 71 units, some kitchens. 4 stories, interior corridors. **Amenities:** safes. **Pool(s):** heated outdoor. **Activities:** hot tub. **Guest Services:** valet laundry.

Perfect Downtown Inner Harbour location, & walk to almost everything Victoria has to offer.

DAYS INN VICTORIA UPTOWN
(250)388-6611 **5**

Hotel
$65-$230

Address: 229 Gorge Rd E V9A 1L1 **Location:** From Douglas St, 1.2 mi (2 km) w at Washington Ave. **Facility:** 73 units, some efficiencies and kitchens. 3 stories (no elevator), exterior corridors. **Terms:** cancellation fee imposed. **Amenities:** safes. **Pool(s):** heated indoor. **Activities:** sauna, bicycles, exercise room. **Guest Services:** valet and coin laundry.

Overlooking Victoria's Upper Harbour. Close to Downtown. Pet-Friendly Rooms. Kitchen Suites Available.

DELTA VICTORIA OCEAN POINTE RESORT AND SPA
(250)360-2999 **9**

Contemporary Hotel
$99-$340

AAA Benefit:
Members save 5% or more!

Address: 100 Harbour Rd V9A 0G1 **Location:** Waterfront. Just w of Johnson St Bridge; jct Esquimalt and Harbour rds. **Facility:** Watch sea planes land and take off or witness the arrival of the M/V Coho, a U.S. ferry, all from the comfort of your room or from one of the outside patios at this inner harbour hotel. 240 units. 8 stories, interior corridors. **Parking:** onsite (fee) and valet. **Terms:** check-in 4 pm. **Dining:** 2 restaurants. **Pool(s):** heated indoor. **Activities:** sauna, hot tub, tennis, spa. **Guest Services:** valet laundry, area transportation.

DOUBLETREE BY HILTON HOTEL & SUITES VICTORIA
(250)940-3100 **21**

Hotel
$139-$269

AAA Benefit:
Members save 5% or more!

Address: 777 Douglas St V8W 2B5 **Location:** Between Blanshard (Hwy 17) and Douglas sts; downtown. **Facility:** 181 units, some two bedrooms and efficiencies. 17 stories, interior corridors. **Parking:** valet only. **Terms:** check-in 4 pm, 1-7 night minimum stay, cancellation fee imposed. **Amenities:** safes. **Dining:** 2 restaurants. **Activities:** limited exercise equipment. **Guest Services:** valet laundry. **Featured Amenity:** full hot breakfast.

EMBASSY INN
(250)382-8161 **24**

Hotel. **Address:** 520 Menzies St V8V 2H4 *(See ad p. 333.)*

FAIRHOLME MANOR
(250)598-3240 **30**

Bed & Breakfast. **Address:** 638 Rockland Pl V8S 3R2

THE FAIRMONT EMPRESS
(250)384-8111 **16**

Classic Historic Hotel
$239-$699

Address: 721 Government St V8W 1W5 **Location:** Between Belleville and Humboldt sts. Located on Inner Harbour. **Facility:** Renowned for its tradition of afternoon tea, this landmark Victorian-style hotel was built in 1908. Rooms vary in size with some bathrooms being compact. Don't miss taking a stroll of the shops. 464 units, some two bedrooms. 8 stories, interior corridors. **Parking:** onsite (fee) and valet. **Terms:** check-in 4 pm, 3 day cancellation notice-fee imposed. **Amenities:** safes. **Dining:** 3 restaurants, also, Q at the Empress, see separate listing. **Pool(s):** heated indoor. **Activities:** sauna, hot tub, exercise room, spa. **Guest Services:** valet laundry, area transportation. *(See ad p. 333.)*

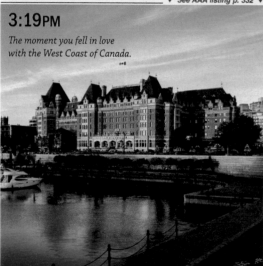

(See map & index p. 328.)

HARBOUR TOWERS HOTEL & SUITES
(250)385-2405 **14**

Hotel
$100-$450

Address: 345 Quebec St V8V 1W4 **Location:** Between Oswego and Pendray sts. **Facility:** 196 units, some two bedrooms, efficiencies and kitchens. 12 stories, interior corridors. **Parking:** on-site (fee). **Terms:** check-in 4 pm, resort fee. **Pool(s):** heated indoor. **Activities:** sauna, hot tub. **Guest Services:** valet and coin laundry, area transportation. *(See ad this page.)*

HEATHERGATE HOUSE BED & BREAKFAST
(250)383-0068 **15**
Bed & Breakfast. **Address:** 122 Simcoe St V8V 1K4

HOTEL RIALTO (250)383-4157 **11**
Boutique Contemporary Hotel. **Address:** 653 Pandora Ave V8W 1N8

HOTEL ZED 250/388-4345 **4**
Retro Hotel. **Address:** 3110 Douglas St V8Z 3K4

HUMBOLDT HOUSE BED & BREAKFAST (250)383-0152 **26**
Historic Bed & Breakfast. **Address:** 867 Humboldt St V8V 2Z6

▼ *See AAA listing this page* ▼

▼ *See AAA listing p. 335* ▼

(See map & index p. 328.)

JAMES BAY INN HOTEL, SUITES & COTTAGE
(250)384-7151

▼▼▼
Historic Hotel
$79-$139

Address: 270 Government St V8V 2L2 **Location:** Between Toronto and Marifield sts. **Facility:** In the heart of Victoria's heritage residential district, the hotel's lobby and public areas are full of antiques. Due to the building's historic nature, rooms are colorful but some are rather compact. 45 units, some kitchens. 4 stories (no elevator), interior corridors. **Terms:** cancellation fee imposed. **Guest Services:** valet laundry.

SAVE ECO ❙❙ ☗ BIZ 📶 ✕
🐾 / SOME UNITS 🔲 🔲

THE MAGNOLIA HOTEL & SPA
250/381-0999

▼▼▼ ▼▼▼
Boutique Hotel
Rates not provided

Address: 623 Courtney St V8W 1B8 **Location:** Corner of Courtney and Gordon sts. Located on Inner Harbour. **Facility:** This luxury hotel provides a convenient base for those interested in visiting downtown Victoria and its popular attractions. The elegant guest rooms have large bay windows. 64 units. 7 stories, interior corridors. **Parking:** valet only. **Terms:** check-in 4 pm. **Amenities:** safes. **Activities:** sauna, bicycles, exercise room, spa. **Guest Services:** valet laundry. **Featured Amenity:** continental breakfast.

SAVE ECO ❙❙ 🛁 ☗ CALL 🅼

BIZ HS 📶 ✕ 🔲 🔲 / SOME UNITS 🔲

MAYFAIR MOTEL
(250)388-7337 **2**
▼▼ Extended Stay Hotel. **Address:** 650 Speed Ave V8Z 1A4

QUALITY INN DOWNTOWN INNER HARBOUR VICTORIA
(250)385-6787 **20**

▼▼
Hotel
$119-$299

Address: 850 Blanshard St V8W 2H2 **Location:** Between Courtney St and Burdett St. **Facility:** 63 units, some efficiencies. 3 stories, interior corridors. **Parking:** on-site (fee). **Pool(s):** heated indoor. **Activities:** steamroom, limited exercise equipment. **Guest Services:** valet and coin laundry.

SAVE ECO ❙❙ ☗ 🔲 📶

✕ 🐾 🔲 🔲 🔲
/ SOME UNITS 🔲 HS

ROBIN HOOD MOTEL
(250)388-4302 **3**

 ▼▼ Motel. **Address:** 136 Gorge Rd E V9A 1L4 *(See ad p. 334.)*

ROYAL SCOT HOTEL & SUITES
(250)388-5463 **19**

▼▼▼
Hotel
$99-$399

Address: 425 Quebec St V8V 1W7 **Location:** Between Menzies and Oswego sts. **Facility:** 177 units, some two bedrooms and kitchens. 4 stories, interior corridors. **Parking:** on-site (fee). **Terms:** cancellation fee imposed. **Amenities:** safes. **Dining:** Jonathan's Restaurant, see separate listing. **Pool(s):** heated indoor. **Activities:** sauna, hot tub, game room, exercise room. **Guest Services:** valet and coin laundry, area transportation.

SAVE ECO ❙❙ 🛁 ☗ 🛥 BIZ

HS 📶 ✕ 🐾 🔲 🔲
/ SOME UNITS 🔲 🔲

SPINNAKERS GASTRO BREWPUB & GUESTHOUSES
250/386-2739 **7**
 Bed & Breakfast. **Address:** 308 Catherine St V9A 3S8

SWANS HOTEL AND BREWPUB
250/361-3310 **8**
▼▼▼ Extended Stay Hotel. **Address:** 506 Pandora Ave V8W 1N6

VICTORIA MARRIOTT INNER HARBOUR
(250)480-3800 **23**

▼▼▼ ▼▼▼
Hotel
$112-$306

MARRIOTT

AAA Benefit: Members save 5% or more!

Address: 728 Humboldt St V8W 3Z5 **Location:** Between Blanshard (Hwy 17) and Douglas sts. **Facility:** Close to the Inner Harbour and downtown, the full-service hotel offers spacious rooms and lots of attractions within walking distance. For a view, ask for a room on a higher floor. 236 units. 16 stories, interior corridors. **Parking:** on-site (fee) and valet. **Terms:** check-in 4 pm. **Amenities:** safes. **Pool(s):** heated indoor. **Activities:** hot tub, steamroom, exercise room, massage. **Guest Services:** valet and coin laundry.

SAVE ❙❙ 🛁 ☗ CALL 🅼 🛥 BIZ HS 📶 ✕
🔲 🔲 / SOME UNITS 🔲 🔲

VICTORIA REGENT WATERFRONT HOTEL & SUITES
(250)386-2211 **12**

▼▼▼
Vacation Rental Condominium
$259-$399

Address: 1234 Wharf St V8W 3H9 **Location:** Waterfront. Between Yates and Fort sts. Located on the Inner Harbour. **Facility:** These amazing condo units sit right at the water's edge, where the harbor views are simply spectacular. Modern full kitchens and super large bedrooms are in the many condo units. 42 units, some condominiums. 8 stories, interior corridors. **Terms:** check-in 4 pm, cancellation fee imposed. **Amenities:** safes. **Guest Services:** valet and coin laundry. **Featured Amenity:** breakfast buffet.

SAVE ECO ❙❙ CALL 🅼 BIZ

HS 📶 ✕ 🔲 🔲 / SOME UNITS 🐾 🔲

VR
VICTORIA REGENT
WATERFRONT HOTEL & SUITES

Combine your 10% AAA Member Discount with our free breakfast for great value & exceptional comfort.

(See map & index p. 328.)

VILLA MARCO POLO INN (250)370-1524 **27**
♦♦♦ ♦♦♦ Historic Bed & Breakfast. **Address:** 1524 Shasta Pl V8S 1X9

WESTIN BEAR MOUNTAIN GOLF RESORT & SPA
(250)391-7160

WESTIN HOTELS & RESORTS

Hotel
$149-$589

AAA Benefit: Members save up to 15%, plus Starwood Preferred Guest® benefits!

Address: 1999 Country Club Way V9B 6R3 **Location:** Trans-Canada Hwy 1 exit 14 (Langford/Highlands), 1.1 mi (1.7 km) n on Millstream Rd, then 1.9 mi (3 km) ne on Bear Mountain Pkwy, follow signs. **Facility:** 156 units, some kitchens. 3-5 stories, interior corridors. **Parking:** on-site (fee) and valet. **Terms:** resort fee. **Amenities:** safes. **Dining:** 2 restaurants. **Pool(s):** heated outdoor.
Activities: sauna, hot tub, regulation golf, tennis, bicycles, trails, exercise room, spa. **Guest Services:** valet and coin laundry, area transportation.

SAVE ECO ⬅ 🍴 🛎 🍽 CALL 🅼 🏊 BIZ HS
🛜 ✕ 🎥 🔒 🖨 💻 /SOME UNITS 🅢

WHERE TO EAT

BIN 4 BURGER LOUNGE 250/590-4154 **13**
♦♦ Burgers. Casual Dining. **Address:** 911 Yates St, #180 V8V 4X3

BRASSERIE L'ECOLE 250/475-6260 **4**
♦♦♦ French. Fine Dining. **Address:** 1715 Government St V8W 1Z4

CACTUS CLUB CAFE 250/361-3233 **11**
♦♦♦ New American. Casual Dining. **Address:** 1125 Douglas St V8W 3L7

CAFE BRIO 250/383-0009 **19**
♦♦♦ Pacific Northwest. Casual Dining. **Address:** 944 Fort St V8V 3K2

CANOE BREWPUB MARINA RESTAURANT
250/361-1940 **3**
♦♦♦ American. Gastropub. **Address:** 450 Swift St V8W 1S3

GLO RESTAURANT & LOUNGE 250/385-5643 **1**
♦♦♦ Canadian. Casual Dining. **Address:** 104-2940 Jutland Rd V8T 5K6

IL TERRAZZO 250/361-0028 **5**
♦♦♦ Northern Italian. Casual Dining. **Address:** 555 Johnson St V8W 1M2

ITHAKA GREEK RESTAURANT 250/384-6474 **18**
♦♦ Greek. Casual Dining. **Address:** 1102 Yates St V8V 3M8

JONATHAN'S RESTAURANT 250/383-5103 **20**
♦♦ American. Casual Dining. **Address:** 425 Quebec St V8V 1W7

KOTO SUSHI IZAKAYA 250/382-1514 **8**
♦♦ Japanese. Casual Dining. **Address:** 510 Fort St V8W 1E6

MILESTONES GRILL AND BAR 250/381-2244
♦♦ American. Casual Dining. **Address:** 812 Wharf St V8W 1T3

MOXIE'S CLASSIC GRILL 250/360-1660
♦♦ American. Casual Dining. **Address:** 1010 Yates St, #1 V8V 3M7

NAUTICAL NELLIE'S STEAK & SEAFOOD RESTAURANT
250/380-2260 **10**
♦♦♦ Steak Seafood. Casual Dining. **Address:** 1001 Wharf St V8W 1T6

NOURISH KITCHEN AND CAFE 250/590-3426 **14**
♦♦ Natural/Organic. Casual Dining. **Address:** 225 Quebec St V8V 1W2

PAGLIACCI'S 250/386-1662 **12**
♦♦ Italian. Casual Dining. **Address:** 1011 Broad St V8W 2A1

THE PINK BICYCLE 250/384-1008 **15**
♦♦ Burgers. Casual Dining. **Address:** 1008 Blanshard St V8W 2H5

PIZZERIA PRIMASTRADA 250/590-8595 **24**
♦♦ Pizza. Casual Dining. **Address:** 230 Cook St V8V 3X3

PLUTO'S 250/385-4747 **22**
♦♦ American. Casual Dining. **Address:** 1150 Cook St V8V 3Z9

Q AT THE EMPRESS 250/384-8111 **17**
♦♦♦ Pacific Northwest. Fine Dining. **Address:** 721 Government St V8W 1W5

RESTAURANT MATISSE 250/480-0883 **6**
♦♦♦ French. Fine Dining. **Address:** 512 Yates St V8W 1K8

SIAM THAI RESTAURANT 250/383-9911 **9**
♦♦ Thai. Casual Dining. **Address:** 512 Fort St V8W 1E6

SPINNAKERS GASTRO BREWPUB & RESTAURANT
250/386-2739 **2**
♦♦♦ American. Gastropub. **Address:** 308 Catherine St V9A 3S8

SWISS CHALET 250/475-0334
♦♦ Chicken. Casual Dining. **Address:** 3233 Douglas St V8Z 3K8

VENETO TAPA LOUNGE 250/383-7310 **7**
♦♦♦ Pacific Northwest. Fine Dining. **Address:** 1450 Douglas St V8W 2G1

VICTORIA HARBOUR HOUSE RESTAURANT
250/386-1244 **16**
♦♦ Steak Seafood. Fine Dining. **Address:** 607 Oswego St V8V 4W9

VISTA 18 250/382-4221 **21**
♦♦♦ Regional Canadian. Fine Dining. **Address:** 740 Burdett Ave V8W 1B2

WHITE HEATHER TEA ROOM 250/595-8020 **23**
♦♦ Desserts Sandwiches. Casual Dining. **Address:** 1885 Oak Bay Ave V8R 1C6

WEST KELOWNA (C-8) pop. 30,892, elev. 411m/1,348'
• Hotels & Restaurants map & index p. 226
• Part of Okanagan Valley area — see map p. 222

West Kelowna (Westbank) was a link on the fur-trading route from the north-central part of the province, called New Caledonia, to the Columbia River. In the early 1860s fortune seekers en route to the

(See map & index p. 226.)

Cariboo gold mines followed the old trail through the Okanagan Valley.

Ideal climatic conditions in the Okanagan Valley nurture the city's many orchards and vineyards. Vacationers also are drawn by the favorable weather in the valley. Downhill and cross-country skiing in the surrounding countryside are popular in winter.

West Kelowna Visitor Centre: 2376 Dobbin Rd., Suite 4, West Kelowna, BC, Canada V4T 2H9. **Phone:** (250) 768-2712.

WINERIES

• **Mission Hill Family Estate** is 4.5 km (3 mi.) e. off Hwy. 97 via Boucherie Rd. to 1730 Mission Hill Rd. **Hours:** Daily 9:30-7, early July-early Sept.; 10-6, early Sept. to mid-Oct.; 10-5, mid-Oct. through late Oct.; 11-5, late Oct.-Dec. 31. Tours are offered daily; phone for schedule. Reservations are required for some peak season and holiday weekends. Closed Jan. 1, Christmas and day after Christmas. Phone ahead to confirm schedule. **Phone:** (250) 768-6483 or (250) 768-6448. GT

THE COVE LAKESIDE RESORT   250/707-1800 29
▼▼▼▼ Resort Hotel. **Address:** 4205 Gellatly Rd V4T 2K2

WHERE TO EAT

KEKULI CAFE   250/768-3555 36
▼ Canadian Specialty. Quick Serve. **Address:** 3041 Louie Dr, #505 V4T 3E2

OLD VINES THE RESTAURANT AT QUAILS' GATE
                                    250/769-4451 37
▼▼▼▼ Regional Canadian. Fine Dining. **Address:** 3303 Boucherie Rd V1Z 2H3

THE TERRACE RESTAURANT   250/768-6467 38
▼▼▼▼ New Canadian. Casual Dining. **Address:** 1730 Mission Hill Rd V4T 2E4

WEST VANCOUVER (H-11) pop. 42,694
• **Restaurants p. 338**
• **Attractions map p. 278**
• **Hotels & Restaurants map & index p. 290**
• **Part of Vancouver area — see map p. 263**

If you're not a Vancouverite—or you're unfamiliar with British Columbia's Lower Mainland—you might think that the North Shore is simply one more spectacularly scenic backdrop to a city already blessed with loads of scenic allure. And you would be wrong. The North Shore is not only uncommonly beautiful; it's also teeming with things to do.

The city and district of North Vancouver are east of the Lions Gate Bridge; the district of West Vancouver spreads along the northern shore of Burrard Inlet from the bridge west to Horseshoe Bay. There's no manufacturing or industry here; "West Van" is primarily residential. It's also affluent, and there are many gorgeous and expensive homes tucked away on winding little streets or perched high on hillsides. All of West Vancouver is situated on slopes of the Coast Mountains, which means that most of these homes enjoy enviable vistas of water, trees, mountains or all three.

The Lions Gate Bridge, which connects Stanley Park and the North Shore, is the gateway to West Vancouver. This suspension bridge crosses the first narrows of Burrard Inlet, which accounts for its official name, the First Narrows Bridge; "lions gate" is a reference to two mountains known as the Lions.

Construction of the 1,795-metre (5,890-ft.) span began in 1937, and the bridge opened to traffic in 1938. It's similar in appearance to San Francisco's Golden Gate Bridge (although bright green rather than bright orange). Another similarity it shares with Golden Gate is the view from the bridge—it's gorgeous whether you're coming or going. The Guinness family (of beer fame), who for a time owned land on the North Shore, purchased decorative white lights for the bridge in 1986 as a gift to Vancouver, turning it into a distinctive nighttime landmark.

Marine Drive is West Vancouver's main thoroughfare. It runs from the bridge west to Horseshoe Bay, usually within sight of water, passing lovely neighborhoods and commercial blocks packed with shops and restaurants. Ambleside, between 11th and 23rd streets, is one of West Vancouver's oldest neighborhoods. The Centennial Seawalk in Ambleside Park is a breezy waterfront promenade that's a favorite spot for walkers, joggers or anyone who loves to gaze out onto the water and contemplate the awesome views of the bridge and Stanley Park. There's a long, sandy beach and a concession stand where you can grab a cheeseburger or an ice cream cone.

Ambleside also has art galleries and antique shops. The Silk Purse Gallery, 1570 Argyle Ave. (on the waterfront near John Lawson Park), is a comfy

(See map & index p. 290.)

old cottage that used to be a haven for honeymooners. It's now home to the West Vancouver Community Arts Council, which presents rotating art exhibits and a series of summer concerts; for ticket information phone (604) 925-7292. Local artists exhibit at the Ferry Building Gallery, a lovingly restored heritage building at 1414 Argyle Ave.; phone (604) 925-7290.

Dundarave is another exceedingly picturesque little seaside community. Stroll along the water once again at Dundarave Park, at the foot of 25th Street, with Cypress Mountain looming in the distance. Old-fashioned lamp posts are installed on Marine Drive between 23rd and 25th streets, flowers cascade from hanging baskets, and the 2 blocks are filled with eateries and specialty shops. It's a nice area to spend an hour or two. Have lunch at the Red Lion Bar & Grill (2427 Marine Dr.), a classic British-style pub—think dark wood walls, stained glass and several fireplaces when the weather's nippy—or stop for coffee and a muffin at Delaney's Coffee House (2424 Marine Dr.).

Marine Drive presses on to Caulfeild (yes, that spelling is correct), an exclusive residential community of narrow, precipitously winding streets and expensive homes shielded by tall privacy hedges. Almost every bend and curve of the road offers a brief, tantalizing water view. Walking the trails in Lighthouse Park *(see attraction listing)*, a protected stand of old-growth coastal forest, is well worth your time.

Past the Lighthouse Park turnoff Marine Drive winds north toward Horseshoe Bay. Side streets lead to tucked-away little green spaces like Kew Park (accessed via Kew Cliff Road and Seaside Place). The multimillion-dollar homes along Kew Cliff Road have stunning views of the Strait of Georgia. A bit farther north Marine Drive winds around Fisherman's Cove, bristling with the masts of pleasure craft moored at the West Vancouver Yacht Club.

Follow the signs to Horseshoe Bay, the North Shore's western bookend. This is where ferries depart for Vancouver Island and the Lower Mainland's "Sunshine Coast." The little community is another North Shore jewel. Take Nelson Avenue off Marine Drive, which leads to the ferry terminal and marina. BC Ferries chug in and out of port while sea gulls wheel overhead. Tree-covered slopes frame Horseshoe Bay, houses perch high above the water and the Coast Mountains loom in the distance. Charming really doesn't begin to describe it.

"Downtown" Horseshoe Bay has just a couple of streets, which makes it perfect for strolling. Browse a few art galleries. Lean against a dock piling and watch the waterfront activity. Get fish and chips or an oyster burger from one of the takeout restaurants on Bay Street and take your feast to Horseshoe Bay Park, where there are picnic tables, a little gravel beach, a playground, two totem poles and a massive cast-bronze propeller that came off a whaling

ship. Listen to the gulls and breathe in the sea air. Now *this* is an afternoon outing.

Backtrack to Marine Drive and turn right instead of left (which will take you back to Hwy. 99). Stay on Marine Drive and you'll reach Whytecliff Park *(see Recreation Areas Chart)*. Designated Canada's first salt water Marine Protected Area (MPA) in 1993, it's located at the entrance to Howe Sound and is known for excellent scuba diving. Seals frolic along this rugged stretch of coastline, and there's a pebbly beach to explore. Or just relax at the park's observation pavilion and—you guessed it—admire the view.

LIGHTHOUSE PARK is off Marine Dr. (watch for the park sign at the turnoff), then a short distance s. via Beacon Ln. to the parking area. Capt. George Vancouver sailed past the rocky peninsula at the entrance to Burrard Inlet in 1792 and named the site Point Atkinson. Today this lush remnant of old growth coastal rainforest encompassing 75 hectares (185 acres) is a peaceful haven and wonderful place to hike. The lofty first-growth Douglas firs and other conifers are up to 500 years old.

Several kilometres of trails crisscross the park; to get to the Point Atkinson Lighthouse take the Beacon Lane Trail south from the parking area. It's about a 15-minute walk to a viewpoint with an expansive vista (on clear days) of the lighthouse (a working one and therefore closed to the public), the inlet and downtown Vancouver on the opposite shore. From the lighthouse viewpoint, short East Beach Trail leads down to the rugged, rocky beach along Starboat Cove.

The group of buildings near the lighthouse were barracks during World War II, when a number of B.C. light stations were used for surveillance purposes. **Time:** Allow 30 minutes minimum. **Hours:** Daily dawn-dusk. **Cost:** Free. **Phone:** (604) 925-7275.

THE BOATHOUSE RESTAURANT   604/921-8188
▼▼ Seafood. Steak. Casual Dining. **Address:** 6695 Nelson Ave V7W 2B2

CACTUS CLUB CAFE   604/922-1707
▼▼ New American. Casual Dining. **Address:** 855 Main St V7T 2Z3

SALMON HOUSE ON THE HILL   604/926-3212   (90)
▼▼▼ Seafood. Fine Dining. **Address:** 2229 Folkestone Way V7S 2Y6

WHISTLER (G-12) pop. 9,824, elev. 640m/2,009'
• Hotels p. 344 • Restaurants p. 346
• Hotels & Restaurants map & index p. 342

Whistler would be a special place even without the whole enchilada it offers when it comes to winter sports. It would be special without the superb system of hiking and mountain biking trails that provide outdoor activity when the sun is warm and the snow isn't swirling. And it would be special without the amenities—all sorts of lodgings from basic to luxury, plenty of restaurants (and a few of culinary

(See map & index p. 342.)

distinction), a nice selection of specialty shops, evening entertainment from mild to wild—that combine to create this covers-every-base active vacation destination.

The reason why has a lot to do with an old adage: location, location, location. About 2 hours north of Vancouver, Whistler snuggles in a Coast Mountains valley amid a cluster of shimmering small lakes, the reflection of forested slopes etched on their surfaces. Rivers rush through steep-walled canyons. Waterfalls plunge. The stark white of glacier ice contrasts with the black of mountain peaks, framed against a brilliantly blue sky. The wilderness is rugged and unspoiled, the air bracingly fresh. Given such a spectacular setting, it's easy to see why it has become one of Canada's best all-season resorts.

Although the 2010 Olympic Winter Games are now history, Whistler remains a pretty exciting place—and getting there is part of the fun. From Vancouver, the major road link is the Sea-to-Sky Highway (Hwy. 99). The primary road link between Vancouver and Whistler was widened and improved for the games. The approximately 2-hour drive offers a full plate of scenic views as the highway climbs from a coastal rain forest environment in the vicinity of Horseshoe Bay to the rugged mountain landscapes around Whistler. Even so, it's always a good idea to check road conditions before heading to Whistler; for information and traffic updates phone (800) 944-7853.

Between Horseshoe Bay and Squamish the road runs along the eastern edge of Howe Sound, punctuated by a series of fjords. From a distance, islands in the bay look like plump green mounds floating on water that is invitingly blue in sunny weather and a brooding gray on overcast days.

Just south of Squamish water is left behind as the highway veers inland. If you want to take a break or need to make a pit stop before reaching Whistler, there are gas stations and a scattering of fast-food outlets at the intersection of Hwy. 99 and Cleveland Road. Past Squamish, Hwy. 99 twists and turns around tree-covered granite crags and sheer rock faces that rise almost straight up from the side of the road. Be sure to pull off and stop at the designated viewpoints; great views are guaranteed.

Whistler has no grand entrance; there are just two primary access roads off Hwy. 99 (Village Gate Drive and Lorimer Road). Whistler Village may seem small, but it's compact. Sitting at the base of Whistler Mountain's ski runs, this is where lots of hotels, restaurants and shops are concentrated. Blackcomb Way divides Whistler Village from the Upper Village, which lies at the base of Blackcomb Mountain's ski runs. Distinctions are pretty much a moot point, although the Upper Village tends to have more upscale accommodations and Whistler Village a livelier scene after dark.

You can walk between the two villages in about 5 minutes along Fitzsimmons Trail, which crosses burbling Fitzsimmons Creek via a covered bridge.

Branching off Fitzsimmons Trail is Bridge Meadows Trail, a pleasant walk through the woods that follows the creek and ends up near the new Squamish Lil'wat Cultural Centre *(see attraction listing)*. Pick up a copy of the tear-off Whistler walking map at your hotel's front desk, fold it up and stash it in your pocket.

Whistler Mountain and Blackcomb Mountain are Whistler's twin peaks. Each mountain has more than 1,524 metres (5,000 ft.) of vertical rise and more than 100 marked runs that are serviced by multiple lifts; together they offer more than 3,238 hectares (8,000 acres) of ski-worthy terrain. Challenge your thighs on downhill runs, negotiate spectacular alpine bowls or embark on a cross-country trek through deep powder. You can even ski on a glacier. There are lessons and instruction for every skill level, all sorts of equipment rentals and a variety of ski packages to choose from. If skiing doesn't strike your fancy, go snowshoeing, snowboarding, ice skating or snowmobiling. And if you're not the active sort, sit back and relax under a comfy blanket with a mug of hot chocolate on a Blackcomb Mountain sleigh ride. Even active sorts would enjoy this.

Whistler boasts North America's first gondola connecting two mountain peaks, the Peak 2 Peak Gondola at Whistler-Blackcomb Resort. The gondola's passenger cabins travel the 4.4-kilometre (2.7-mi.) distance between the two towers at the summit of Whistler and Blackcomb mountains in 11 minutes, allowing skiers to take advantage of cruising both mountains in the same day. Each gondola cabin holds up to 28 people, and two of them feature glass floors for a dizzying bird's-eye view of Fitzsimmons Valley 435 metres (1,427 ft.) below. Purchase of a regular lift ticket includes gondola transportation.

But Whistler isn't just about winter sports. Summer is prime time for hiking, mountain biking, windsurfing and canoeing, among other activities. Ski lifts take hikers up the two mountains to explore trails free of snow, but if you'd rather go down a different path, walk to Lost Lake. It takes about 30 minutes to get there from Whistler Village (trail access is off Lorimer Road), a good jaunt if you want to leave the hustle and bustle behind for an afternoon.

This tranquil lake is surrounded by Lost Lake Park's evergreen forests, with lovely views of mountains in the distance. The shallow water makes for good swimming on warm days. Numerous hiking trails crisscross this wooded area. There's no parking at the lake, but free shuttle bus service departs from the Gondola Transit Exchange on Blackcomb Way in July and August.

Walkers, hikers, cyclists and inline skaters all take advantage of the paved Valley Trail, which wends its way for some 30.5 kilometres (19 mi.) around the greater Whistler area, connecting parks, residential neighborhoods and the villages. It's a popular commuter biking route.

Adrenaline junkies head to Whistler Mountain Bike Park, a lift-accessed mountain biking haven. The terrain here covers the bases from gently

(See map & index p. 342.)

banked trails through a lush coastal forest environment to single-track trails twisting in a series of tight turns to death-defying descents down the side of steep rock faces (which sounds a bit like skiing on wheels). Access is by lift tickets or park passes; bikes and accessories can be rented. The park is open from mid-May to mid-October.

With four championship courses, Whistler's got some very good golf. The Whistler Golf Club, (604) 932-3280 or (800) 376-1777, is the first course in Canada designed by Arnold Palmer. Robert Trent Jones Jr. was the course architect for the Fairmont Chateau Whistler Golf Club, (604) 938-2092 or (877) 938-2092, at The Fairmont Chateau Whistler. The Golden Bear designed the Nicklaus North Golf Course, (604) 938-9898 or (800) 386-9898. Big Sky Golf and Country Club, (604) 894-6106 or (800) 668-7900, is near Pemberton, about a 25-minute drive north of Whistler. With a Bob Cupp-designed layout along the Green River, you can be assured that water will come into play.

For pure sightseeing fun, take the Whistler Village Gondola up Whistler Mountain. The bird's-eye views of alpine lakes, meadows full of wildflowers (in summertime) and mountain slopes from the enclosed gondola are breathtaking. The ride up takes about 25 minutes. Once at the top, hike back-country trails or have a leisurely lunch at the Roundhouse Lodge, a cool 1,850 metres (6,069 ft.) above sea level, while taking in the scenery all around you. More intrepid souls can continue ascending on the Peak Chair to the 2,182-metre (7,160-ft.) level, where a 360-degree panorama of the Coast Mountains awaits.

And what do you do après skiing or otherwise testing your physical endurance? You stroll around Whistler Village. It's pedestrian-only, it's done in the style of a German mountain village, and it's *cute*. In winter the atmosphere is all woolen caps, puffy ski parkas and oversize mittens; summer brings out the hanging flower baskets and umbrella-shaded tables for outdoor cafe dining. Mogul's Coffee House, next to the drugstore at Village Square, is a funky little place to hang out for a spell.

Four large day-use lots between the two villages offer free parking. Whistler and Valley Express (WAVE) public buses operated by BC Transit provide service to the greater area. Various bus lines serve the resort; shuttle lines 5 and 6 are the most useful if you're staying in or near Whistler Village. The fare is $2.50; free (ages 0-5). Exact change is required. Tickets (ten tickets $22.50; day pass $7) that are good for multiple rides can be purchased at the Whistler Visitor Centre, 4320 Gateway Dr. (as well as at Whistler Village stores and Meadow Park Sports Centre).

Tourism Whistler: 4230 Gateway Dr., Whistler, BC V0N 1B4. **Phone:** (604) 935-3357 or (877) 991-9988.

Shopping: With all kinds of specialty boutiques and eateries, Whistler Village is where it's at. Whistler's Marketplace (entrance off Lorimer Road) is the main shopping center. It has a ski lodge ambiance and retailers like the Escape Route, which carries a full lineup of outdoor recreation wear and accessories—body wear, head wear, hand wear, footwear, snowshoes, backpacks, you name it. Let kids loose in the Great Glass Elevator Candy Shop with its head-turning display of sweets. It just may be enough to drive you to the more adult-oriented Upper Village Market, where you can stock up on gourmet groceries (they'll also deliver to your hotel room).

Also in the Upper Village is Snowflake (in The Fairmont Chateau Whistler), with a selection of Canadian-designed fur and leather jackets, cashmere sweaters, scarves, shawls, boots and accessories for women. Bring lots of money. Back in Whistler Village, New Agers will want to waft into The Oracle at Whistler (on Main Street) and check out the jewelry, candles, incense and gifts. Tarot card and palm readings are given, or you can give in to a relaxing reiki massage.

The Whistler Village Art Gallery exhibits contemporary paintings, sculpture and art and has two locations, in the Four Seasons Whistler and at the Hilton Whistler Resort & Spa's Gallery Row. A popular and long-established showcase for Canadian artists is Adele Campbell Fine Art Gallery in the Westin Resort & Spa. Mountain Galleries at the Fairmont, in The Fairmont Chateau Whistler, exhibits museum-quality work—paintings, glass pieces, bronze sculptures, stone carvings—by respected Canadian artists.

Nightlife: Whistler's a family-oriented kind of place, but that doesn't mean it lacks hotspots for those itching to get down and *party*. Maxx Fish, below the Amsterdam Cafe in Village Square, has plush booths and plasma-screen TVs, plus a light show choreographed to the slammin' beats cooked up by resident and visiting DJs. A similar uninhibited mood and young, good-looking crowd prevails at Tommy Africa's Bar, not far away on Gateway Drive next to the taxi loop.

Garfinkels Night Club, on Main Street in Whistler Village, throws club night bashes on different days of the week; locals and visitors alike flock to "Happy Thursdays," and Saturday is another big party night. The music is DJ dance mixes, augmented by occasional live hip-hop shows. "Garf's" also has VIP hosts and table service, so reservations are a good idea; phone (604) 932-2323. Also in the village is Buffalo Bills Bar and Grill, a high-energy nightspot that packs 'em in with drink specials, a huge dance floor and a mix of mainstream and classic rock.

On the other hand, if crowded clubs and ear-splitting music isn't your cup of tea, you could catch a movie at the Village 8 Cinemas in Whistler Village. Or better yet, pick up a to-go pie at Avalanche Pizza (locals say it's the best in town) and chill out in your room, because you just might want to save your energy for the slopes.

HARBOUR AIR is 3 km (1.9 mi.) n. on Hwy. 99, following signs. The company offers 30-minute to 2-hour carbon-neutral floatplane tours over glaciers,

(See map & index p. 342.)

ice caps or alpine lakes. **Hours:** Trips depart daily Apr.-Oct. (weather permitting). **Cost:** $103.81-$341.90; $52.38-$176.19 (ages 2-11); free (ages 0-1 on parent's lap). Schedule and rates may vary; phone ahead. Reservations are required. **Phone:** (604) 932-6615 or (800) 665-0212.

SQUAMISH LIL'WAT CULTURAL CENTRE is at 4584 Blackcomb Way, just s. of Whistler's Upper Village. Conceived as a joint venture between the Squamish and Lil'wat First Nations, this facility is a showcase meant to share and preserve the culture and heritage of these two peoples. The spectacular building, with its rounded contours, was constructed to resemble a traditional Squamish longhouse and a Lil'wat *istken* (an earthen dwelling with a fire pit). Whistler and Blackcomb mountains are on view from the outdoor deck.

Inside, the Great Hall has soaring 22-foot ceilings, cedar wood walls and beautiful polished stone floors inlaid with different patterns. Among the exhibits are two Squamish canoes, traditional clothing and regalia, wall weavings, textiles and baskets. Visitors can watch artists at work and learn how to make a craft. Make sure you see the 15-minute film "Where Rivers, Mountains and People Meet," which provides some fascinating historical and cultural context to what is on display.

Parking is available in Day Lot 4 adjacent to the center. **Time:** Allow 1 hour minimum. **Hours:** Daily 9:30-5; winter and holiday hours are subject to change. **Cost:** $18; $13.50 (ages 65+ and students with ID); $8 (ages 6-12); $49 (family, two adults and two children ages 6-18). **Phone:** (866) 441-7522. 🍴

WHISTLER MUSEUM is at 4333 Main St. behind the public library. Exhibits and videos about Whistler's natural and human history as well as the 2010 Winter Olympics document aspects of mountain life in the area. **Time:** Allow 1 hour minimum. **Hours:** Daily 11-5 (also Thurs. 5-9). Closed Jan. 1 and Christmas. **Cost:** Donations. **Phone:** (604) 932-2019.

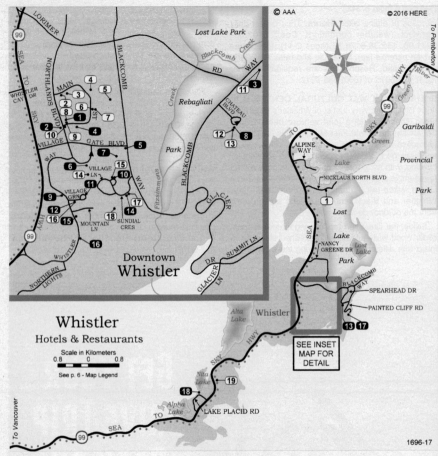

Whistler
Hotels & Restaurants
Scale in Kilometers

0.8   0   0.8

See p. 6 - Map Legend

Downtown **Whistler**

© AAA   ©2016 HERE

1696-17

Whistler

This index helps you "spot" where approved hotels and restaurants are located on the corresponding detailed maps. Hotel daily rate range is for comparison only. Restaurant price range is a combination of lunch and/or dinner. Turn to the listing page for more information and consult display ads for special promotions.

WHISTLER

Map Page	Hotels	Diamond Rated	Rate Range	Page
1 this page	**Whistler Pinnacle Hotel**	▽▽	$129-$779 SAVE	346
2 this page	Whistler Cascade Lodge	▽▽	Rates not provided	346
3 this page	**Four Seasons Resort and Residences Whistler**	▽▽▽▽	$239-$1250 SAVE	345
4 this page	**Delta Whistler Village Suites**	▽▽▽	$135-$534 SAVE	344
5 this page	Pan Pacific Whistler Village Centre	▽▽▽	Rates not provided	345
6 this page	**Blackcomb Lodge**	▽▽	$99-$619 SAVE	344
7 this page	Whistler Peak Lodge	▽▽	$129-$369	346
8 this page	**The Fairmont Chateau Whistler** (See ad p. 344.)	▽▽▽▽	$199-$1049 SAVE	344
9 this page	Aava Whistler Hotel	▽▽▽	Rates not provided	344
10 this page	Whistler Village Inn & Suites	▽▽	Rates not provided	346

WHISTLER (cont'd)

Map Page	Hotels (cont'd)	Diamond Rated	Rate Range	Page
11 p. 342	Crystal Lodge & Suites	◆◆◆	Rates not provided	344
12 p. 342	The Listel Hotel Whistler	◆◆	$89-$629	345
13 p. 342	The Aspens On Blackcomb	◆◆	$119-$569	344
14 p. 342	Pan Pacific Whistler Mountainside	◆◆◆	Rates not provided	345
15 p. 342	**Hilton Whistler Resort & Spa**	◆◆◆	Rates not provided [SAVE]	345
16 p. 342	**The Westin Resort & Spa, Whistler**	◆◆◆◆	$189-$1299 [SAVE]	346
17 p. 342	The Coast Blackcomb Suites at Whistler	◆◆◆	$169-$365	344
18 p. 342	**Nita Lake Lodge** *(See ad p. 345.)*	◆◆◆◆	$159-$650 [SAVE]	345

Map Page	Restaurants	Diamond Rated	Cuisine	Price Range	Page
① p. 342	Table Nineteen Lakeside Eatery	◆◆◆	American	$15-$30	346
② p. 342	Peaked Pies	◆	Australian Specialty	$6-$10	346
③ p. 342	Splitz Grill	◆	Burgers	$7-$14	346
④ p. 342	Purebread	◆	Breads/Pastries	$7-$8	346
⑤ p. 342	The Brewhouse	◆◆	American	$15-$37	346
⑥ p. 342	Elements Urban Tapas Lounge	◆◆	International Small Plates	$9-$30	346
⑦ p. 342	Sachi Sushi	◆◆	Sushi	$7-$25	346
⑧ p. 342	Quattro at Whistler	◆◆◆	Italian	$22-$43	346
⑨ p. 342	Alta Bistro	◆◆◆	New Canadian	$26-$30	346
⑩ p. 342	Hy's Steakhouse	◆◆◆	Steak	$25-$70	346
⑪ p. 342	Sidecut	◆◆◆◆	Steak Seafood	$27-$59	346
⑫ p. 342	The Wildflower	◆◆◆	International	$24-$40	346
⑬ p. 342	**The Grill Room**	◆◆◆◆	Steak	$22-$59	346
⑭ p. 342	Araxi Restaurant & Oyster Bar	◆◆◆◆	Pacific Northwest	$20-$45	346
⑮ p. 342	21 Steps Kitchen & Bar	◆◆	International	$15-$35	346
⑯ p. 342	Bearfoot Bistro	◆◆◆◆	New World	$78-$148	346
⑰ p. 342	Dubh Linn Gate Pub	◆◆	Irish	$13-$25	346
⑱ p. 342	Sushi Village Japanese Cuisine	◆◆	Japanese	$11-$38	346
⑲ p. 342	Rimrock Cafe	◆◆◆	Continental	$37-$53	346

AAVA WHISTLER HOTEL 604/932-2522 **9**
Hotel. **Address:** 4005 Whistler Way V0N 1B4

THE ASPENS ON BLACKCOMB (604)932-7222 **13**
Vacation Rental Condominium. **Address:** 4800 Spearhead Dr V0N 1B4

BLACKCOMB LODGE (604)932-4155 **6**
Hotel $99-$619

Address: 4220 Gateway Dr V0N 1B4 **Location:** Hwy 99, just e on Village Gate Blvd, just s. **Facility:** 71 units, some efficiencies and kitchens. 3 stories, interior corridors. **Parking:** on-site (fee). **Terms:** check-in 4 pm, 2-5 night minimum stay - seasonal and/or weekends, 30 day cancellation notice-fee imposed, resort fee. **Amenities:** safes. **Pool(s):** heated indoor. **Activities:** sauna, hot tub. **Guest Services:** coin laundry.

THE COAST BLACKCOMB SUITES AT WHISTLER (604)905-3400 **17**
Condominium. **Address:** 4899 Painted Cliff Rd V0N 1B4

CRYSTAL LODGE & SUITES 604/932-2221 **11**
Hotel. **Address:** 4154 Village Green V0N 1B4

DELTA WHISTLER VILLAGE SUITES (604)905-3987 **4**
Extended Stay Hotel $135-$534
 AAA Benefit: Members save 5% or more!

Address: 4308 Main St V0N 1B4 **Location:** Hwy 99, just e on Village Gate Blvd, just n on Northlands Blvd, then just e. **Facility:** 207 units, some two bedrooms and kitchens. 6 stories, interior corridors. **Parking:** on-site (fee) and valet. **Terms:** check-in 4 pm. **Dining:** Hy's Steakhouse, see separate listing. **Pool(s):** heated outdoor. **Activities:** sauna, hot tub, bicycles, exercise room. **Guest Services:** complimentary and valet laundry, area transportation.

THE FAIRMONT CHATEAU WHISTLER (604)938-8000 **8**
Resort Hotel $199-$1049

Address: 4599 Chateau Blvd V0N 1B4 **Location:** Hwy 99, 0.6 mi (1 km) e on Lorimer Rd (Upper Village), just s on Blackcomb Way, then just e. **Facility:** Near the Blackcomb Mountain chair lift, this inspiring château offers a lovely outdoor pool area that is open year round. Elegant floral arrangements and a huge fireplace adorn the vast lobby lounge. 550 units, some two bedrooms. 12 stories, interior corridors. **Parking:** on-site (fee) and valet. **Terms:** check-in 4 pm, 3 day cancellation notice-fee imposed, resort fee. **Amenities:** safes. **Dining:** 3 restaurants, also, The Grill Room, The Wildflower, see separate listings, entertainment. **Pool(s):** heated outdoor. **Activities:** sauna, hot tub, steamroom, cabanas, regulation golf, tennis, downhill & cross country skiing, snowboarding, recreation programs, bicycles, lawn sports, trails, in-room exercise equipment, spa. **Guest Services:** valet and coin laundry, area transportation. *(See ad this page.)*

(See map & index p. 342.)

FOUR SEASONS RESORT AND RESIDENCES
WHISTLER   (604)935-3400 **3**

Resort Hotel
$239-$1250

Address: 4591 Blackcomb Way V0N 1B4 **Location:** Hwy 99, 0.6 mi (1 km) e on Lorimer Rd (Upper Village), just n. **Facility:** Gorgeous public areas feature a unique collection of local art and beautiful wood accents. Spacious suites have a warm and rustic elegance with fireplaces and huge bathrooms. 291 units, some two bedrooms, three bedrooms and kitchens. 6-9 stories, interior corridors. **Parking:** valet only. **Terms:** check-in 4 pm, cancellation fee imposed. **Amenities:** safes. **Dining:** Sidecut, see separate listing. **Pool(s):** heated outdoor. **Activities:** hot tub, steamroom, downhill & cross country skiing, snowboarding, recreation programs, bicycles, trails, in-room exercise equipment, spa. **Guest Services:** valet laundry, area transportation.

HILTON WHISTLER RESORT & SPA   604/932-1982 **15**

Hotel
Rates not provided

AAA Benefit: Members save 5% or more!

Address: 4050 Whistler Way V0N 1B4 **Location:** Hwy 99, just e on Village Gate Blvd, just s. **Facility:** 287 units, some two bedrooms and efficiencies. 5-8 stories, interior corridors. **Parking:** on-site (fee) and valet. **Terms:** check-in 4 pm. **Amenities:** safes. **Pool(s):** heated outdoor. **Activities:** sauna, hot tub, downhill & cross country skiing, snowboarding, trails, exercise room, spa. **Guest Services:** valet and coin laundry.

THE LISTEL HOTEL WHISTLER   (604)932-1133 **12**
Hotel. **Address:** 4121 Village Green V0N 1B4

NITA LAKE LODGE   (604)966-5700 **18**

Boutique Contemporary Hotel
$159-$650

Address: 2131 Lake Placid Rd V0N 1B2 **Location:** 1.8 mi (3 km) s on Hwy 99, just w. **Facility:** This impressive hotel has gorgeous lobby décor and wonderful large, modern suites with upscale comfortable seating and furnishings. Huge bathrooms feature rain shower heads and separate soaker tubs. 77 units. 4 stories, interior corridors. **Parking:** on-site (fee) and valet. **Terms:** check-in 4 pm, 2-5 night minimum stay - seasonal and/or weekends, 14 day cancellation notice-fee imposed. **Amenities:** safes. **Dining:** 3 restaurants. **Pool(s):** heated outdoor. **Activities:** hot tub, self-propelled boats, boat dock, fishing, recreation programs in season, bicycles, trails, spa. **Guest Services:** valet and coin laundry, area transportation. (*See ad this page.*)

PAN PACIFIC WHISTLER MOUNTAINSIDE   604/905-2999 **14**
Extended Stay Contemporary Hotel. **Address:** 4320 Sundial Cres V0N 1B4

PAN PACIFIC WHISTLER VILLAGE CENTRE
          604/966-5500 **5**
Extended Stay Contemporary Hotel. **Address:** 4299 Blackcomb Way V0N 1B4

Enjoy great member rates and benefits
at AAA/CAA Preferred Hotels

▼ See AAA listing this page ▼

(See map & index p. 342.)

THE WESTIN RESORT & SPA, WHISTLER
(604)905-5000 **16**

▼◆▼ ▼◆▼
Extended Stay Hotel
$189-$1299

WESTIN® HOTELS & RESORTS **AAA Benefit:** Members save up to 15%, plus Starwood Preferred Guest® benefits!

Address: 4090 Whistler Way V0N 1B4 **Location:** Hwy 99, just e on Village Gate Blvd, just s. **Facility:** You get a great first impression as you enter the gorgeous lobby here. The units range from moderate size studios to expansive suites. You'll love the convenience of the ski-in, ski-out location. 419 units, some two bedrooms and kitchens. 9-11 stories, interior corridors. **Parking:** on-site (fee) and valet. **Terms:** check-in 4 pm, 2-5 night minimum stay - seasonal and/or weekends, cancellation fee imposed. **Amenities:** safes. **Dining:** 2 restaurants. **Pool(s):** heated outdoor. **Activities:** sauna, hot tub, steamroom, downhill & cross country skiing, snowboarding, bicycles, trails, spa. **Guest Services:** valet and coin laundry, area transportation.

[SAVE] [ECO] 🍴 🏋 ⦿ CALL 🔊M 🛏 👷 [BIZ] [SHS] 📶 ✕ 🎿 🧳 🖥 💻 / SOME UNITS 🐾

WHISTLER CASCADE LODGE   604/905-4875 **2**
▼◆▼ Vacation Rental Condominium. **Address:** 4315 Northlands Blvd V0N 1B4

WHISTLER PEAK LODGE   (604)938-0878 **7**
▼◆▼ Extended Stay Hotel. **Address:** 4295 Blackcomb Way V0N 1B4

WHISTLER PINNACLE HOTEL
(604)938-3218 **1**

▼◆▼ ▼◆▼
Extended Stay Hotel
$129-$779

Address: 4319 Main St V0N 1B4 **Location:** Hwy 99, just e on Village Gate Blvd, just n on Northlands Blvd, then just e. **Facility:** 84 kitchen units. 4 stories, interior corridors. **Parking:** on-site (fee). **Terms:** check-in 4 pm, 14 day cancellation notice-fee imposed. **Dining:** 2 restaurants, also, Alta Bistro, Quattro at Whistler, see separate listings. **Pool(s):** heated outdoor. **Activities:** hot tub, bicycles, limited exercise equipment. **Guest Services:** valet and coin laundry.

[SAVE] 🍴 ⦿ CALL 🔊M 🛏 [HS] 📶 ✕ 🧳 🖥 💻 / SOME UNITS 🔊[S]

WHISTLER VILLAGE INN & SUITES   604/932-4004 **10**
▼◆▼ Hotel. **Address:** 4429 Sundial Pl V0N 1B4

WHERE TO EAT

21 STEPS KITCHEN & BAR   604/966-2121 **15**
▼◆▼ International. Casual Dining. **Address:** 4433 Sundial Pl, RR 4 V0N 1B4

ALTA BISTRO   604/932-2582 **9**
▼◆▼ New Canadian. Casual Dining. **Address:** 4319 Main St, #104 V0N 1B4

ARAXI RESTAURANT & OYSTER BAR   604/932-4540 **14**
▼◆▼ ▼◆▼ Pacific Northwest. Fine Dining. **Address:** 4222 Village Square V0N 1B4

BEARFOOT BISTRO   604/932-3433 **16**
▼◆▼ ▼◆▼ New World. Fine Dining. **Address:** 4121 Village Green V0N 1B4

THE BREWHOUSE   604/905-2739 **5**
▼◆▼ American. Brewpub. **Address:** 4355 Blackcomb Way V0N 1B4

DUBH LINN GATE PUB   604/905-4047 **17**
▼◆▼ Irish. Casual Dining. **Address:** 4320 Sundial Cres V0N 1B4

EARLS KITCHEN + BAR   604/935-3222
▼◆▼ American. Casual Dining. **Address:** 4295 Blackcomb Way, Unit 220 V0N 1B4

ELEMENTS URBAN TAPAS LOUNGE   604/932-5569 **6**
▼◆▼ International Small Plates. Casual Dining. **Address:** 102B-4359 Main St V0N 1B7

THE GRILL ROOM
604/938-8000 **13**

▼◆▼ ▼◆▼
Steak Fine Dining
$22-$59

AAA Inspector Notes: From the moment you're seated, you'll feel like a specially invited guest due to the first-rate service and refinement not usually found at a traditional steakhouse. The menu changes seasonally, offering some perfectly grilled cuts of beef, bison and other meats. Special care is taken to provide sustainable and locally sourced seafood. The appetizers are all enticing, but my first choice is always going to be the mouth-watering tomato and gin soup, which is flambéed at the table. **Features:** full bar. **Reservations:** suggested. **Address:** 4599 Chateau Blvd V0N 1B4 **Location:** Hwy 99, 0.6 mi (1 km) e on Lorimer Rd (Upper Village), just s on Blackcomb Way, then just e; in The Fairmont Chateau Whistler. **Parking:** on-site (fee) and valet. [D] CALL 🔊M

HY'S STEAKHOUSE   604/905-5555 **10**
▼◆▼ ▼◆▼ Steak. Fine Dining. **Address:** 4308 Main St V0N 1B4

PEAKED PIES   604/962-4115 **2**
▼◆▼ Australian Specialty. Quick Serve. **Address:** 4369 Main St, #105 V0N 1B4

PUREBREAD   604/962-1182 **4**
▼◆▼ Breads/Pastries. Quick Serve. **Address:** 4338 Main St V0N 1B4

QUATTRO AT WHISTLER   604/905-4844 **8**
▼◆▼ ▼◆▼ Italian. Fine Dining. **Address:** 4319 Main St V0N 1B4

RIMROCK CAFE   604/932-5565 **19**
▼◆▼ ▼◆▼ Continental. Fine Dining. **Address:** 2117 Whistler Rd V0N 1B0

SACHI SUSHI   604/935-5649 **7**
▼◆▼ Sushi. Casual Dining. **Address:** 106-4359 Main St V0N 1B4

SIDECUT   604/966-5280 **11**
▼◆▼ ▼◆▼ Steak Seafood. Fine Dining. **Address:** 4591 Blackcomb Way V0N 1B4

SPLITZ GRILL   604/938-9300 **3**
▼◆▼ Burgers. Quick Serve. **Address:** 4369 Main St, #104 V0N 1B4

SUSHI VILLAGE JAPANESE CUISINE   604/932-3330 **18**
▼◆▼ Japanese. Casual Dining. **Address:** 4340 Sundial Crescent V0N 1B4

TABLE NINETEEN LAKESIDE EATERY   604/938-9898 **1**
▼◆▼ ▼◆▼ American. Casual Dining. **Address:** 8080 Nicklaus North Blvd V0N 1B8

THE WILDFLOWER   604/938-8000 **12**
▼◆▼ ▼◆▼ International. Fine Dining. **Address:** 4599 Chateau Blvd V0N 1B4

A Few Good Reasons to Know When Help Will Arrive

When a road trip stalls and you request AAA/CAA assistance, opt to receive text updates. Messages:

- Confirm receipt of your service request

- Alert you when a service vehicle is en route

- Provide the service vehicle's estimated arrival time

Opt in and stay informed.

AAA.com/mobile | CAA.ca/mobile

WHITE ROCK   pop. 19,339

- Hotels & Restaurants map & index p. 290
- Part of Vancouver area — see map p. 263

OCEAN PROMENADE HOTEL   604/542-0102   **70**
▼▼▼▼ Hotel. **Address:** 15611 Marine Dr V4B 1E1

WHERE TO EAT

GIRAFFE   604/538-6878   **86**
▼▼▼ International. Casual Dining. **Address:** 15053 Marine Dr V4B 1C5

LA BAIA ITALIAN RESTAURANT   604/531-6261   **87**
▼▼ Italian. Casual Dining. **Address:** 15791 Marine Dr V4B 1E5

ULI'S RESTAURANT   604/538-9373   **85**
▼▼ International. Casual Dining. **Address:** 15021 Marine Dr V4B 1C3

WILLIAMS LAKE   (G-5) pop. 10,832

The rush for gold brought prospectors to the heart of the Cariboo in the 1860s, but it was the 1920s Canadian Railway push that put Williams Lake on the map. Cattle ranching and timber production now are the economic mainstays. Twenty kilometres (12 mi.) north of Williams Lake, Bull Mountain Trails offers 30 kilometres (19 mi.) of trails for cross-country skiing, hiking and mountain biking.

Williams Lake and District Chamber of Commerce: 1660 S. Broadway, Williams Lake, BC, Canada V2G 2W4. **Phone:** (250) 392-5025 or (877) 967-5253.

BEST WESTERN WILLIAMS LAKE HOTEL
(778)412-9000

▼▼▼▼ Hotel $115-$143

Best Western. **AAA Benefit:** Save 10% or more every day and earn 10% bonus points!

Address: 1850 S Broadway Ave V2G 5G8 **Location:** 1.3 mi (2.1 km) s on Hwy 97. **Facility:** 64 units, some kitchens. 3 stories, interior corridors. **Parking:** winter plug-ins. **Pool(s):** heated indoor. **Activities:** hot tub, exercise room. **Guest Services:** complimentary laundry. **Featured Amenity:** continental breakfast.

[SAVE] [ⅠⅠ+] [🛏] [BIZ] [HS] [🛜] [✕]
[📶] [🖥] [📠] /SOME UNITS [🛏🔒]

DRUMMOND LODGE MOTEL   250/392-5334
▼ Motel. **Address:** 1405 Cariboo Hwy V2G 2W3

RAMADA WILLIAMS LAKE   (250)392-3321
▼▼ Hotel. **Address:** 1118 Lakeview Cres V2G 1A3

SUPER 8 WILLIAMS LAKE   (250)398-8884
▼▼ Motel $105-$120

Address: 1712 Broadway Ave S V2G 2W4 **Location:** 1.2 mi (2 km) s on Hwy 97. **Facility:** 53 units. 3 stories (no elevator), interior corridors. **Parking:** winter plug-ins. **Guest Services:** coin laundry. **Featured Amenity:** continental breakfast.

[SAVE] [ⅠⅠ+] [BIZ] [HS] [🛜] [✕] [📶]
[🖥] /SOME UNITS [🛏🔒] [📠]

WHERE TO EAT

CARMENS   250/392-3321
▼▼ American. Casual Dining. **Address:** 1118 Lakeview Cres V2G 1A3

WINDERMERE   pop. 1,019

WINDERMERE CREEK BED AND BREAKFAST CABINS
(250)342-0356
▼▼▼▼ Cabin. **Address:** 1658 Windermere Loop Rd V0B 2L2

WINFIELD

- Hotels & Restaurants map & index p. 226
- Part of Okanagan Valley area — see map p. 222

SUPER 8 MOTEL LAKE COUNTRY   (250)766-5244   **53**
▼▼ Motel. **Address:** 9564 Hwy 97 N V4V 1T7

YALE   (C-7) pop. 136

Settled at the southern entrance to Fraser Canyon, Yale was a major steamship port during the gold rush. The town was established in 1848 as a Hudson's Bay Co. fort, taking its name from the commander of Fort Langley. After gold was discovered on Hill's Bar in 1858, Yale's population swelled to 30,000. In later years the number dwindled to 200. Several buildings from the mid-1800s still stand, and a pioneer cemetery contains Victorian monuments to early settlers.

The Alexandra Suspension Bridge, 22 kilometres (14 mi.) north of town, was constructed in 1863 to ferry miners across the Fraser River. From the bridge, which was rebuilt in 1926 with the original foundations, the original wagon road to the Cariboo goldfields is visible and is home to a small 22.25-hectare (55-acre) provincial park. A hiking trail leading to the nearby Spirit Caves offers views of the canyon.

YOHO NATIONAL PARK (A-11)

Elevations in the park range from 1,090 metres (3,576 ft.) at the west boundary to 3,562 metres (11,686 ft.) at the top of Mount Goodsir at the South Tower. Refer to CAA/AAA maps for additional elevation information.

Reached by hwys. 1 and 93, Yoho National Park covers 1,310 square kilometres (507 sq. mi.) and is west of the Great Divide and Banff National Park. In the Cree language, *yoho* is an exclamation of wonder appropriate to the park's spectacular rock walls and towering waterfalls.

At the center of the park's history is Canada's first trans-continental railway. Following the route originally discovered by Sir James Hector, the Canadian Pacific Railway laid tracks through Kicking Horse Pass in 1884. The park was established two years later as a tourist destination for passengers on the newly completed rail line. In 1962, the Trans-Canada Highway opened along this same route.

Takakkaw Falls ("magnificent" in Cree) drops 380 metres (1,265 ft.) in all. Its highest sheer fall is 254 metres (833 ft.), making it one of the highest waterfalls in Canada and a visible landmark along the well-known Iceline trail.

Other highlights in the park include Natural Bridge, Emerald Lake, Wapta Falls and the Canadian Pacific Railway's Spiral Tunnels. Twisting their way under Mount Ogden and Cathedral Mountain, trains can be seen entering and exiting the Spiral Tunnels from the viewpoints on the Yoho Valley Road and the Trans-Canada Highway, 8 kilometres (5 mi.) east of Field.

Nestled high in the mountains are the famous Burgess Shale fossil beds. Discovered in 1909, these exquisitely preserved 505 million-year-old soft-bodied fossils draw visitors to Yoho National Park each year. The park's visitor center, located in Field, hosts an interactive exhibit and display of some of the many fossils found in the park.

General Information and Activities

The park is open all year; Parks Canada operates facilities during the spring, summer and fall. In winter it is popular with ice climbers, and cross-country and backcountry skiers as well as hikers and backpackers in other seasons. During the summer months, canoes and rowboats are available for rent at Emerald Lake.

The park's visitor center, located on Hwy. 1 in Field, is open May 1 to mid-October; phone (250) 343-6783 for schedule, or (888) 773-8888 rest of year. The adjoining washrooms are open year-round.

The Trans-Canada Highway traverses the park and provides access to most attractions. The 13-kilometre (7.8-mi.) Yoho Valley Road leading to Takakkaw Falls is open mid-June to mid-October, weather permitting.

Access to Burgess Shale fossil beds is restricted to guided hikes July-September. Parks Canada offers two guided hike programs: Walcott Quarry, at 22 kilometers (14 mi.), and Mount Stephen Fossil Beds, at 9 kilometres (6 mi.). Fees range from $52.38-$66.67 and reservations are required (reservation fees $10.48-$12.86); phone (877) 737-3783.

Yoho has four front-country campgrounds with site prices between $16.76-$26.10 per night. Firewood and permits are an additional $8.38. Visitors venturing into the backcountry require a wilderness pass to stay overnight; passes are available from the visitor center for $9.33 per person per night.

Fishing, particularly rewarding to those in search of a variety of trout, requires a $32.67 annual permit or a $9.80 1-day permit from the visitor center. Anglers are allowed to fish in most lakes and rivers in the park. *See Recreation Areas Chart.*

ADMISSION to the park is free in 2017 to celebrate Canada's 150th anniversary of Confederation. Otherwise admission is $9.33; $7.90 (ages 65+); $4.67 (ages 6-16); $18.67 (all occupants of a private vehicle with up to seven people). An annual pass, valid at most Canadian national parks, marine areas and historic sites, is available.

PETS are permitted in the park provided they are on a leash at all times.

ADDRESS inquiries to the Superintendent, Yoho National Park, P.O. Box 99, Field, BC, Canada V0A 1G0; phone (250) 343-6783.

Lake Winnipeg, Gimli

Manitoba

Waves pound a rock-strewn shore at the narrows of Lake Manitoba, producing a noise oddly like a beating drum. To the people of the Cree Nation, this sound was the great spirit Manitou, whose name was given to the lake and, in 1870, the entire province.

From clear water lapping in giant lakes—Winnipeg, Winnipegosis and Manitoba—to the rustling sigh of wind across golden seas of wheat, the great spirit of this province speaks with many voices and conveys many moods.

It echoes in the plaintive cry of migrating geese winging south and the hoarse chuffing of a protective mother polar bear herding her cubs along Hudson Bay's icy shore.

The spirit sings within a chorus of steel wheels as trains carry freight across the prairies. It proclaims itself in the bustling streets of Winnipeg, where sundry languages—French, English, Ukrainian, Chinese and others—blend

Polar bear and cub

into a rich, evocative murmur, and laughs amid the joyous din of the city's various celebrations.

Gem of the Prairies

Look north into the night sky. There. See it? A faint glow high above the horizon....

Watch as an arc of yellow light gradually forms. As it drifts upward, shimmering yellow-green streamers rise from it, rippling like a breeze-blown curtain. New arcs appear lined with bright amber streaks that curl like wisps of smoke. Eventually the swirls of color fade and darkness returns, ending your encounter with the aurora borealis.

In Manitoba you won't have to wait long for a repeat performance. This far north you can count on basking in the aurora's eerie luminescence nearly 90 nights a year. Even citizens of Winnipeg, the capital, are often treated to this celestial light show, despite living in the province's extreme south.

Sky-obscuring pollution may be the bane of many cities, but Winnipeg's clean air isn't likely to spoil your auroral view. And while multihued lights dance overhead, visitors to the "Gem of the Prairies" can enjoy an equally colorful cultural spectrum spread out before them. Home to more than half of all Manitobans, Winnipeg is a city of surprising diversity. It's not unusual to find a German butcher shop sandwiched between an Italian clothing store and a Vietnamese restaurant, all within a few steps of a Portuguese café.

In the 18th century, when conflicts escalated between French voyageurs and their English rivals, Fort Rouge—site of modern Winnipeg—was established where the Red and Assiniboine rivers meet. Now known as The Forks, this riverfront park is where you can take a tree-shaded stroll past splashing fountains and vibrantly hued flower beds.

The Great White North

Follow your compass farther north and the chances of seeing Mother Nature's silent fireworks multiply. The northern lights not only occur more frequently in Manitoba's subarctic areas, but are brighter, too.

But the real stars in this small community are its big, furry neighbors: polar bears. Sightings of the great white animals are common in October, when they migrate onto freezing Hudson Bay to fish, and late June, when thawing ice forces a return to shore.

The best way to meet these deceptively cuddly looking carnivores is safely ensconced in a specially designed, balloon-tired tundra vehicle. Climb aboard one for an unforgettable in-the-wild encounter. And when you're ready to thaw out, visit Churchill's Eskimo Museum, which is filled with ancient Inuit tools and other artifacts.

Well-acquainted with the aurora's haunting glow, the Inuits crafted stories as elaborate as their carvings to explain what they saw. According to one tale, the lights are torches lit by spirits to guide those who will follow across the narrow bridge to heaven.

But you don't have to study Inuit mythology to appreciate the northern lights' otherworldly beauty; all you really need to know is that the skies are perfect for admiring them.

Recreation

The overwhelming bulk of Manitoba's populace resides in a thin strip just above the U.S. border, which leaves a vast region of unspoiled territory farther north that's prime for exploration.

Colorful sails glide across the surface of Lake Winnipeg as windsurfing enthusiasts take advantage of breezy days. Canoeing down the Grass River, near the junction of hwys. 10 and 39, gives you the opportunity to see the beauty of the northern frontier.

Manitoba's lakes are home to dozens of species of fish, including walleye, northern pike, arctic grayling, sturgeon and channel catfish. Fly-in fishing—at such isolated spots as Aikens and Dogskin lakes, northeast of Bissett in Atikaki Provincial Park; Gods River, Knee Lake, and Island Lake, all in northeast Manitoba; and Big Sand, Egenolf, and Nueltin lakes in the northwest region—

attracts anglers of all skill levels.

When the lakes freeze over, ice fishing and ice-skating are favored pursuits. Smooth blankets of snow—at such places as Assiniboine Park in Winnipeg—are irresistible for snowshoeing and cross-country skiing.

Many adventurers, too, can't resist the snowmobiling trails that crisscross the province. Kick up some powder in Duck Mountain and Turtle Mountain provincial parks.

Although downhill skiing is hard to come by in a province that's known mostly for its lowlands, skiers can take on 25 runs at Asessippi Winter Park ski area.

For tobogganing fun, head for the hills and slides at Kildonan Park and more than a dozen park locations in Winnipeg.

Riding Mountain National Park rises from the flat prairie to provide a wealth of opportunity for activity. Self-guiding hiking trails range from the easy Beach Ridges Trail to the difficult Bald Hill Trail, named for the barren hill towering over scores of lush, green trees. Most memorable is the grueling but beautiful Ochre River Trail, which entices both trekkers and cross-country skiers.

Mountain bikers favor the exhilarating J.E.T. Trail, which rewards risk-takers with great views. The multiuse Central Trail, the longest at 73 kilometres (45 miles), is especially popular for horseback riding.

Aurora borealis

Historic Timeline

1612	Capt. Thomas Button winters at Port Nelson on Hudson Bay and claims the land for England.
1690	Henry Kelsey of the Hudson's Bay Co. sets out on a 2-year exploration of the province.
1738	French fur-trader Pierre Gaultier de la Vérendrye arrives at the site now known as Winnipeg.
1812	The Red River Colony, one of Manitoba's earliest settlements, is established with a land grant from the Hudson's Bay Co.
1869	The Métis, native people of mixed ancestry, are led by Louis Riel in the Red River Rebellion.
1870	Manitoba becomes the fifth Canadian province.
1887	The Winnipeg Grain and Produce Exchange is established.
1912	Manitoba's boundary is extended north to Hudson Bay.
1986	The Supreme Court rules that all provincial laws passed since 1870 are invalid because they were written only in English.
1999	The Pan Am Games are held in Winnipeg.
2007	A tornado in Elie is Canada's first officially documented F5 tornado, the highest possible rating on the Fujita scale.

What To Pack

Temperature Averages Maximum/Minimum (Celsius)	JANUARY	FEBRUARY	MARCH	APRIL	MAY	JUNE	JULY	AUGUST	SEPTEMBER	OCTOBER	NOVEMBER	DECEMBER
Churchill	-23 / -32	-22 / -31	-16 / -26	-7 / -17	1 / -6	9 / 1	16 / 7	14 / 7	8 / 2	0 / -6	-10 / -19	-19 / -28
Hecla Island	-14 / -25	-9 / -21	-2 / -13	8 / -3	17 / 3	22 / 9	24 / 12	23 / 10	17 / 5	9 / -1	-2 / -10	-11 / -21
Swan River	-10 / -23	-6 / -19	1 / -12	9 / -5	17 / 2	22 / 7	24 / 10	24 / 8	17 / 3	9 / -2	-2 / -12	-9 / -20
The Pas	-17 / -26	-12 / -23	-4 / -17	6 / -6	15 / 2	21 / 9	23 / 12	22 / 11	14 / 5	7 / -1	-4 / -12	-14 / -22
Thompson	-19 / -31	-14 / -28	-6 / -21	4 / -10	13 / -1	19 / 5	22 / 8	21 / 7	12 / 2	4 / -4	-7 / -17	-17 / -27
Winnipeg	-13 / -23	-10 / -21	-2 / -13	9 / -3	18 / 4	23 / 10	26 / 13	24 / 12	18 / 6	11 / 0	-1 / -9	-10 / -19

From the records of The Weather Channel Interactive, Inc.

Good Facts To Know

ABOUT THE PROVINCE

POPULATION: 1,274,000.

AREA: 552,370 sq km (213,270 sq mi.); ranks 8th

CAPITAL: Winnipeg.

HIGHEST POINT: 831 m (2,727 ft.), Baldy Mountain.

LOWEST POINT: Sea level, Churchill.

TIME ZONE(S): Central. DST.

GAMBLING

MINIMUM AGE FOR GAMBLING: 18.

REGULATIONS

TEEN DRIVING LAWS: Teens may not drive between midnight and 5 a.m. and no more than one passenger is permitted unless a supervising licensed driver is seated in the front passenger seat. When driving with a supervising driver, no more passengers than the number of backseat seat belts are permitted. The minimum age for an unrestricted driver's license is 17 years, 6 months. Phone (204) 985-7000 or (800) 665-2410 for more information about Manitoba driver's license regulations.

SEAT BELT/CHILD RESTRAINT LAWS: Seat belts are required for the driver and all passengers ages 18 and over. Children ages 5-18 and over 23 kilograms (50 lbs.) are required to be in a child restraint or seat belt; children must remain in a booster seat until age 9 or over 145 centimetres (57 in.) tall or 36 kilograms (80 lbs.); child restraints are required for children under age 5 and under 23 kilograms (50 lbs.). AAA recommends the use of seat belts and appropriate child restraints for the driver and all passengers.

CELLPHONE RESTRICTIONS: The use of handheld cellphones and text messaging while driving are prohibited.

HELMETS FOR MOTORCYCLISTS: Required for all riders.

MOVE OVER LAW: Driver is required to slow down and vacate the lane nearest stopped police, fire or rescue vehicles when those vehicles are using audible or flashing signals. The law also applies to tow trucks or other recovery vehicles.

RADAR DETECTORS: Not permitted.

FIREARMS LAWS: By federal law, all nonresidents entering Canada with a firearm must declare their weapon in writing and pay a fee of $25 (Canadian). Contact the Canadian Firearms Program at (800) 731-4000 to receive a declaration form or for additional information.

ALCOHOL CONSUMPTION: Legal age 18.

SPECIAL REGULATIONS: Dogs and cats transported from the United States must have proof of rabies vaccination. No person may smoke tobacco or have lighted tobacco in a motor vehicle while anyone under 16 is in the vehicle.

HOLIDAYS

HOLIDAYS: Jan. 1 ■ Louis Riel Day (3rd Mon. in Feb.) ■ Good Friday ■ Easter ■ Easter Monday ■ Victoria Day, Mon. prior to May 25 ■ Canada Day, July 1 ■ Civic Holiday, Aug. (1st Mon.) ■ Labour Day, Sept. (1st Mon.) ■ Thanksgiving, Oct. (2nd Mon.) ■ Remembrance Day, Nov. 11 ■ Christmas, Dec. 25 ■ Boxing Day, Dec. 26.

MONEY

TAXES: In addition to Manitoba's provincial sales tax of 8 percent, there is a national 5 percent Goods and Services Tax (GST).

VISITOR INFORMATION

INFORMATION CENTERS: Free travel information is available at these locations: Canada/United States border, Hwy. 75 at Emerson ■ Manitoba/Ontario boundary, Hwy. 1E just east of West Hawk Lake ■ Manitoba/Saskatchewan boundary on Hwy. 1W west of Kirkella ■ Manitoba/Saskatchewan boundary at Hwys. 16W and 83 near Russell ■ and the Travel Manitoba Visitor Information Centre at The Forks National Historic Site in Winnipeg.

FURTHER INFORMATION FOR VISITORS:
The Forks National Historic Site
401-25 Market Rd.
Winnipeg, MB R3C 4S8
Canada
(204) 983-6757
(888) 773-8888 Parks Canada
Travel Manitoba Visitor Information Centre
21 Forks Market Rd.
Winnipeg, MB R3C 4T7
Canada
(204) 927-7800
(800) 665-0040

RECREATION INFORMATION:
Manitoba Conservation and Water Stewardship
200 Saulteaux Crescent
Winnipeg, MB R3J 3W3
Canada
(204) 945-6784
(800) 214-6497

Manitoba Annual Events
Please call ahead to confirm event details.

JANUARY

- Lieutenant Governor's Winter Festival / Brandon 888-799-1111
- Manitoba AgDays / Brandon 204-534-2010
- Dakota Nation Winterfest Brandon 204-512-0847

FEBRUARY

- Festival du Voyageur Winnipeg 204-237-7692
- Master Playwright Festival Winnipeg 204-956-1340, ext. 415
- Optimist Clubs of Winnipeg Concert Band Festival Winnipeg 204-663-1226

MARCH

- Aurora Winterfest Churchill 888-389-2327
- Royal Manitoba Winter Fair Brandon 204-726-3590
- Cluster: New Music + Integrated Arts Festival Winnipeg 204-223-9939

APRIL

- Rodarama Car Show Winnipeg 204-479-4104
- Brandon Home & Leisure Show / Brandon 204-727-4837
- Winnipeg Comedy Festival Winnipeg 204-284-9477

MAY

- Teddy Bears' Picnic Bear Rescue / Winnipeg 204-787-4000
- Pride Winnipeg Festival Winnipeg 204-803-7849
- Doors Open Winnipeg Winnipeg 204-942-2663

JUNE

- Red River Exhibition Winnipeg 204-888-6990
- Manitoba Summer Fair Brandon 204-726-3590
- TD Winnipeg International Jazz Festival / Winnipeg 204-989-4656

JULY

- Manitoba Stampede and Exhibition / Morris 204-746-2552
- Manitoba Sunflower Festival Altona 204-324-9005
- Winnipeg Fringe Festival Winnipeg 204-943-7464

AUGUST

- Winkler Harvest Festival and Exhibition / Winkler 204-325-5600
- Virden Indoor Rodeo and Wild West Daze / Virden 204-748-2710
- Morden Corn and Apple Festival / Morden 204-823-2676

SEPTEMBER

- ManyFest: All Together Downtown / Winnipeg 204-958-4640
- Fall on the Farm Steinbach 204-326-9661
- Manitoba Mega Train Show / Winnipeg 204-837-4776

OCTOBER

- Wheat City Stampede Brandon 888-501-3021
- Scattered Seeds Craft Market / Winnipeg 204-222-0111
- International Wine Festival of Manitoba / Winnipeg 204-956-4613

NOVEMBER

- Signatures Craft Show & Sale / Winnipeg 888-773-4444
- All That Glows: Then and Now / Winnipeg 204-260-7905
- Grey Cup Festival Winnipeg 204-784-2583

DECEMBER

- Winter Wonderland Winnipeg 204-888-6990
- Island of Lights / Portage la Prairie 204-239-8334
- Christmas at the Fort Dauphin 204-638-6630

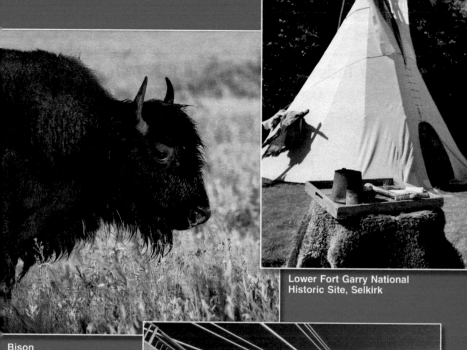

Bison

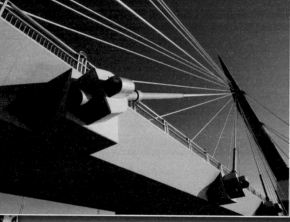

Lower Fort Garry National Historic Site, Selkirk

Eskimo Museum, Churchill

Esplanade Riel footbridge, Winnipeg

Winnipeg skyline

Index: Great Experience for Members

AAA editor's picks of exceptional note

Eskimo Museum

Riding Mountain
National Park

Canadian Museum for
Human Rights

Lower Fort Garry
National Historic Site

See Orientation map on p. 362 for corresponding grid coordinates, if applicable.
*Indicates the GEM is temporarily closed.

Churchill (A-4)
Eskimo Museum *(See p. 367.)*

Inglis (F-1)
Inglis Grain Elevators National Historic Site
(See p. 370.)

International Peace Garden (H-1)
International Peace Garden *(See p. 370.)*

Riding Mountain National Park (F-1)
Riding Mountain National Park *(See p. 372.)*

Selkirk (G-5)
Lower Fort Garry National Historic Site
(See p. 373.)

Winnipeg (G-4)
Canadian Museum for Human Rights (CMHR)
(See p. 386.)

Children's Museum *(See p. 387.)*

The Forks *(See p. 386.)*

The Manitoba Museum *(See p. 388.)*

Royal Canadian Mint *(See p. 389.)*

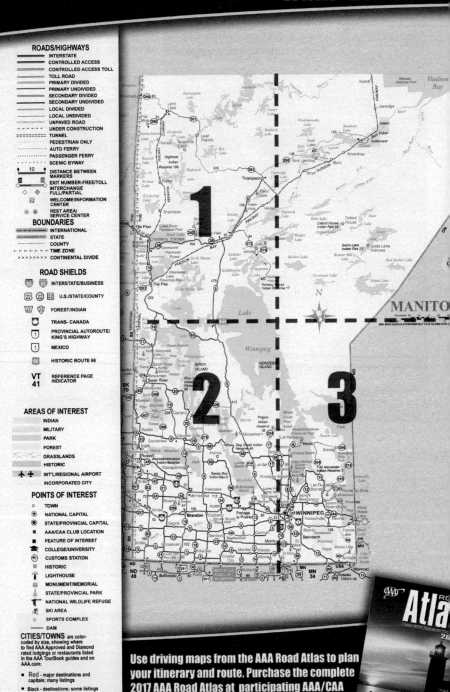

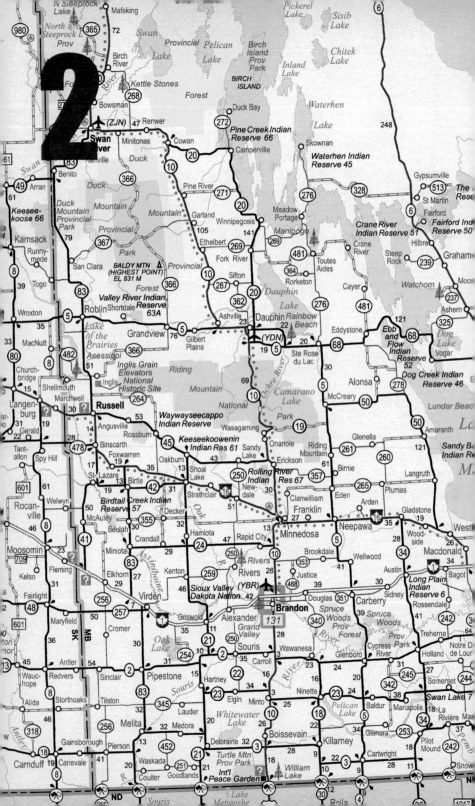

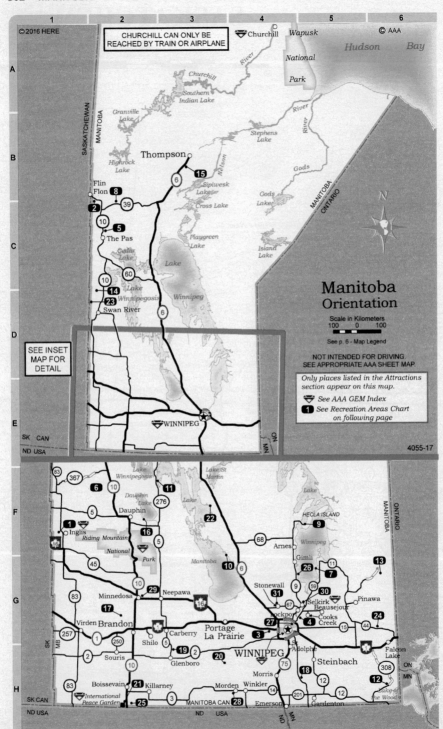

© 2016 HERE

CHURCHILL CAN ONLY BE
REACHED BY TRAIN OR AIRPLANE

Churchill

© AAA

Wapusk

Hudson Bay

National

Park

River

Churchill

Southern
Indian Lake

River

Granville
Lake

Stephens
Lake

River

Highrock
Lake

Thompson

6

15

Nelson

Gods

MANITOBA

ONTARIO

Flin
Flon

8

Sipiwesk
Lake

2

39

Gods
Lake

10

Cross Lake

5

The Pas

Playgreen
Lake

Cedar
Lake

Lake

Island
Lake

10

60

Lake
Winnipegosis

Lake
Winnipeg

Manitoba
Orientation

14

23

Swan River

6

Scale in Kilometers
100   0   100

See p. 6 - Map Legend

NOT INTENDED FOR DRIVING.
SEE APPROPRIATE AAA SHEET MAP.

SEE INSET
MAP FOR
DETAIL

Only places listed in the Attractions
section appear on this map.

See AAA GEM Index

1 See Recreation Areas Chart
on following page

WINNIPEG

SK CAN
ND USA

ON

MN

4055-17

83

367

Lake
Winnipegosis

Lake St
Martin

6

10

11

Dauphin
Lake

276

MANITOBA

ONTARIO

5

Dauphin

22

Lake

HECLA ISLAND

1

Inglis

16

Winnipeg

9

Riding Mountain

5

68

Arnes

Gimli

11

13

National

Park

Manitoba

10

26

7

45

6

59

30

SK
MB

10

29

Neepawa

Stonewall

9

Pinawa

83

Minnedosa

16

31

67

Selkirk

Beausejour

24

17

Lockport

44

15

Virden Brandon

Carberry

Portage
La Prairie

27

4

Cooks
Creek

257

1

250

Shilo

5

3

WINNIPEG

Falcon
Lake

2

19

St. Adolphe

Steinbach

308

Souris

20

75

ON

MN

10

Glenboro

18

12

Morris

12

21

Killarney

14

12

83

Boissevain

25

3

Morden

Winkler

MANITOBA CAN

28

201

Gardenton

Lake
of
the
Woods

SK CAN
ND USA

International
Peace Garden

ND   USA

NS

Emerson

Recreation Areas Chart

The map location numerals in column 2 show an area's location on the preceding map.

	MAP LOCATION	CAMPING	PICNICKING	HIKING TRAILS	BOATING	BOAT RAMP	BOAT RENTAL	FISHING	SWIMMING	PETS ON LEASH	BICYCLE TRAILS	WINTER SPORTS	VISITOR CENTER	LODGE/CABINS	FOOD SERVICE
NATIONAL PARKS *(See place listings.)*															
Riding Mountain (F-1) 2,978 square kilometres. Backpacking, cross-country skiing, golf, hiking, horseback riding, scuba diving, tennis, water skiing, wind surfing; boat cruises, paddleboats.		•	•	•	•	•	•	•	•	•	•	•	•	•	•
PROVINCIAL															
Asessippi (F-1) 2,330 hectares 13 km from Shellmouth Dam on Hwy. 83. Cross-country skiing, fishing, snowmobiling; nature trail.	❶	•	•	•	•	•	•	•	•	•		•		•	•
Bakers Narrows (C-2) 145 hectares 27 km s. of Flin Flon on Hwy. 10. Board sailing, canoeing, wildlife viewing; playground.	❷	•	•	•	•	•	•	•	•	•		•		•	•
Beaudry (G-5) 939 hectares 10 km w. of Winnipeg on Roblin Blvd./Hwy. 241.	❸		•	•				•			•	•	•		
Birds Hill (G-5) 3,550 hectares 24 km n.e. of Winnipeg on Hwy. 59. Cross-country skiing, horseback riding, snowmobiling, wildlife viewing; interpretive programs, playground.	❹	•	•	•				•	•	•	•	•	•		
Clearwater Lake (C-2) 59,265 hectares 19 km n. of The Pas on Hwy. 10, then 2.5 km e. on Hwy. 287. Cross-country skiing, snowmobiling; interpretive trail.	❺	•	•	•	•	•	•	•	•	•		•		•	
Duck Mountain (F-2) 142,430 hectares 56 km n. of Roblin off Hwy. 83. Canoeing, cross-country skiing, snowmobiling.	❻	•	•	•	•	•	•	•	•	•		•		•	•
Grand Beach (G-5) 2,490 hectares 80 km n.e. of Winnipeg on Hwy. 59, then 6 km w. on Hwy 12. Cross-country skiing, sailing, snowmobiling, tennis, windsurfing; interpretive programs, sand beaches.	❼	•	•	•	•	•	•	•	•	•		•	•	•	•
Grass River (B-2) 228,018 hectares at Cranberry Portage off Hwy. 10. Canoeing; interpretive trail.	❽	•	•	•	•	•	•	•	•	•				•	•
Hecla/Grindstone (F-5) 108,440 hectares 165 km n. of Winnipeg via Hwy. 8. Cross-country skiing, golf, sailing, snowmobiling, tennis, windsurfing; interpretive programs.	❾	•	•	•	•	•	•	•	•	•		•	•	•	•
Lundar Beach (G-3) 23 hectares 18 km w. of Lundar on Hwy. 419.	❿				•	•		•	•	•					
Manipogo (F-3) 61 hectares 47 km n. of Dauphin on Hwy. 20. Board sailing, wildlife viewing; playground.	⓫	•	•		•	•		•	•	•					•
Moose Lake (H-6) 956 hectares 30 km n.e. of Sprague on Hwy. 308. Board sailing, canoeing, snowmobiling, wildlife viewing; playground.	⓬	•	•		•	•		•	•	•				•	•
Nopiming (G-6) 142,910 hectares 70 km n.e. of Lac du Bonnet. Canoeing; interpretive trail.	⓭	•	•	•	•	•	•	•	•	•				•	•
North Steeprock Lake (D-2) 13 hectares 3 km n. of Birch River on Hwy. 10, then 40 km w. on Hwy. 365.	⓮	•	•		•	•		•	•	•					
Paint Lake (B-3) 8,848 hectares 32 km s. of Thompson on Hwy. 6. Canoeing, cross-country skiing, ice skating, snowmobiling, tobogganing, windsurfing.	⓯	•	•	•	•	•	•	•	•	•		•		•	•
Rainbow Beach (F-2) 52 hectares 17 km e. of Dauphin on Hwy. 20. Board sailing, golf, wildlife viewing; playground.	⓰	•	•	•	•	•		•	•	•	•				
Rivers (G-2) 37 hectares 14 km n. of Brandon on Hwy. 10, then 26 km w. on Hwy. 25. Playground.	⓱	•	•	•	•	•		•	•	•					
St. Malo (H-5) 148 hectares 64 km s. of Winnipeg on Hwy. 59. Motorized boats not allowed.	⓲	•	•	•	•		•	•	•	•		•			•
Spruce Woods (H-3) 26,950 hectares 25 km s.e. of Carberry on Hwy. 5. Canoeing, cross-country skiing, ice skating, snowmobiling, tobogganing; horse trails, interpretive programs.	⓳	•	•	•	•	•	•	•	•	•		•	•	•	•
Stephenfield (H-3) 94 hectares 10 km w. of Carman on Hwy. 245. Board sailing, golf; playground.	⓴	•	•	•	•	•		•	•	•					•
Turtle Mountain (H-2) 18,570 hectares 23 km s. of Boissevain off Hwy. 10. Cross-country skiing, ice skating, snowmobiling, tobogganing; interpretive trail, horse trails.	㉑	•	•	•	•	•		•	•	•	•	•			
Watchorn (F-3) 10 hectares 11 km w. of Moosehorn on Hwy. 237. Playground.	㉒	•	•		•	•		•	•	•					
Whitefish Lake (D-2) 24 hectares 13 km n. of Swan River, then 28 km w. on Hwy. 279. Playground.	㉓	•	•		•	•		•	•	•					

Recreation Areas Chart

The map location numerals in column 2 show an area's location on the preceding map.

	MAP LOCATION	CAMPING	PICNICKING	HIKING TRAILS	BOATING	BOAT RAMP	BOAT RENTAL	FISHING	SWIMMING	PETS ON LEASH	BICYCLE TRAILS	WINTER SPORTS	VISITOR CENTER	LODGE/CABINS	FOOD SERVICE
Whiteshell (G-6) 272,090 hectares off Hwy. 1 at Falcon Lake, near the Ontario border. Cross-country skiing, downhill skiing, golf, horseback riding, sailing, snowmobiling, tennis, tobogganing, windsurfing; interpretive programs, museum.	24	•	•	•	•	•	•	•	•	•	•	•	•	•	•
William Lake (H-2) 199 hectares 7 km e. of Horton, then 8 km s. Amphitheater, playground.	25	•	•	•	•	•			•	•	•				
Winnipeg Beach (G-5) 41 hectares 45 km n. of Winnipeg on Hwy. 8, then 5 km e. on PR 229. Soccer, tennis, volleyball, wildlife viewing; playground.	26	•	•	•	•	•			•	•	•	•			•
OTHER															
Kildonan (G-4) 39 hectares at 2015 Main St. in Winnipeg. Cross-country skiing, ice skating, tobogganing; pool.	27		•	•					•	•	•	•	•		•
Lake Minnewasta (H-4) 125 hectares 2 km w. of Morden on Hwy. 3, then 1 km s. on Hwy. 434.	28	•	•	•	•	•		•	•	•		•			•
Minnedosa Lake and Beach (G-2) 8 hectares 1.5 km e. of Minnedosa on Beach Dr. (PR 262). Cross-country skiing, ice fishing, ice hockey, snowmobiling; beach, playgrounds. Note: concessions are only offered in summer.	29	•	•	•	•	•	•	•	•		•			•
Selkirk Park (G-5) 81 hectares on the banks of the Red River at Eveline St. in Selkirk. Cross-country skiing, ice fishing; bird sanctuary.	30	•	•	•	•	•			•	•		•			•
Stonewall Quarry (G-4) 30 hectares 4 blks. n. on Main St. in Stonewall. Nature programs. Cross-country skiing, ice skating, tobogganing.	31	•	•	•					•	•		•			•

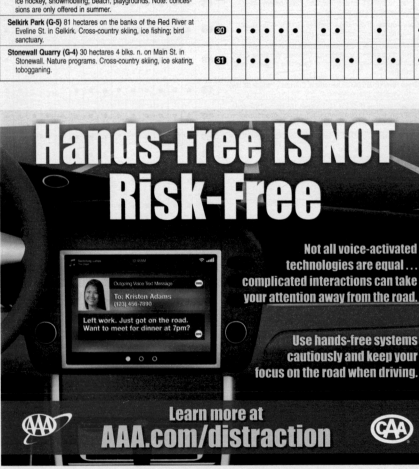

ARNES (F-4) elev. 225m/739'

An old fishing village, Arnes today offers sandy beaches, a marina and a nine-hole golf course. A monument to writer and explorer Vilhjalmur Stefansson is inscribed "I know what I have experienced, and I know what it has meant to me," a statement from his autobiography. Born in 1879, Stefansson traveled by boat and dog sled across the Arctic, mapping large areas of the archipelago and collecting ethnological data from the central Arctic coast. He proved through his explorations that it was possible to live off the land in this forbidding area.

BEAUSEJOUR (G-5) pop. 3,126, elev. 247m/810'

Just 46 kilometres (29 mi.) northeast of Winnipeg, Beausejour is on one of the main roads to Whiteshell Provincial Park. Nature enthusiasts take advantage of the walking, hiking and cross-country ski trails available at Wally Chryplywy Nature Park on First Street.

Town of Beausejour: 639 Park Ave., Beausejour, MB, Canada R0E 0C0. **Phone:** (204) 268-7550.

BOISSEVAIN (H-2) pop. 1,572

Nearby Turtle Mountain Provincial Park *(see Recreation Areas Chart)* is named for the western painted turtle, which lives in the park's many shallow lakes. The park is the year-round home of a large number of waterfowl and of migratory birds in spring and fall. A wildlife center also is available.

As a connection to the park, the town has adopted as its symbol an 8.5-metre-tall (28-ft.) statue known as Tommy Turtle, which can be seen beside the visitor center on Hwy. 10.

An outdoor art gallery throughout the town depicts area history by way of more than 20 colorful wall-size murals, including a large scene painted on a grain elevator in downtown Boissevain. Scenic Hwy. 10 leads south to the North Dakota border and the International Peace Garden *(see place listing p. 370).*

Boissevain Tourism Information Centre: 298 Mountain St., Boissevain, MB, Canada R0K 0E0. **Phone:** (204) 534-6662 or (800) 497-2393.

Self-guiding tours: Literature for a self-guiding walking tour of the city's historic buildings is available at the Boissevain Tourism Information Centre.

BRANDON (G-2) pop. 46,061, elev. 409m/1,300'
• Restaurants p. 366

An agricultural and industrial center, Brandon is the second largest city in the province after Winnipeg and is known for its small-town warmth and big-city amenities.

The Riverbank Discovery Centre, in addition to providing information about Brandon and the surrounding region, is the starting point for the Assiniboine Riverbank Trail System, 17 kilometres (10.5 mi.) of trails that wind throughout Brandon, linking the downtown area with parks, picnic spots and sports venues.

The Keystone Centre, sitting on some 36.4 hectares (90 acres) and offering 540,000 square feet of multi-use space, plays host to some of Manitoba's larger events, concerts and sports competitions; phone (204) 726-3500. Brandon's Community Sportsplex offers both winter and summer recreational activities. Built for the 1979 Canada Winter Games, the structure houses racquetball courts, an ice arena, swimming pool, indoor water slide and an outdoor running track; phone (204) 729-2470.

The Brandon Hills Wildlife Management Area, just a short drive south of the city on Hwy. 10 and east along Beresford Road, provides a setting for a variety of recreational pursuits such as hiking, mountain bicycling, cross-country skiing and bird-watching.

Regional Tourism Centre/Riverbank Discovery Centre: #1-545 Conservation Dr., Brandon, MB, Canada R7A 7L8. **Phone:** (204) 729-2141 or (888) 799-1111.

Self-guiding tours: A historical walking tour of the residential area between 10th and 18th streets offers interesting architecture and turn-of-the-20th-century homes; a booklet describing the tour is available for $3.50 from the tourism center.

BEST WESTERN PLUS BRANDON INN   (204)727-7997

Hotel
$150-$205

AAA Benefit: Save 10% or more every day and earn 10% bonus points!

Address: 205 Middleton Ave R7A 1A8 **Location:** Jct Trans-Canada Hwy 1 and 10; access via north service road. **Facility:** 79 units, some efficiencies. 3 stories, interior corridors. **Parking:** winter plug-ins. **Terms:** check-in 4 pm. **Amenities:** safes. **Pool(s):** heated indoor. **Activities:** hot tub, exercise room. **Guest Services:** valet and coin laundry. **Featured Amenity:** continental breakfast.

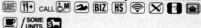

CANAD INNS DESTINATION CENTRE BRANDON
(204)727-1422

Hotel
$122-$259

Address: 1125 18th St R7A 7C5 **Location:** On Hwy 10 (18th St); jct Brandon Ave. **Facility:** 159 units. 11 stories, interior corridors. **Parking:** winter plug-ins. **Amenities:** *Some:* video games. **Dining:** 3 restaurants, nightclub. **Pool(s):** heated indoor. **Activities:** hot tub, exercise room. **Guest Services:** valet laundry.

COMFORT INN BRANDON (204)727-6232

Motel
$105-$190

Address: 925 Middleton Ave R7C 1A8 **Location:** Trans-Canada Hwy 1; between Hwy 10 (18th St) N and 10 S; on north side of service road. Located in a commercial area. **Facility:** 79 units. 2 stories (no elevator), interior corridors. **Parking:** winter plug-ins. **Guest Services:** valet laundry. **Featured Amenity:** full hot breakfast.

SAVE ECO 📶 CALL 🛗 BIZ 📶
❌ 🛏 📷 💻 / SOME UNITS 🐕

DAYS INN & SUITES BRANDON (204)727-3600
Hotel. **Address:** 2130 Currie Blvd R7B 4E7

LAKEVIEW INNS & SUITES BRANDON 204-728-1880
Hotel. **Address:** 1880 18th St N R7C 1A5 *(See ad opposite inside front cover.)*

WHERE TO EAT

CLAY POT CAFE 204-726-9467
American. Casual Dining. **Address:** 2604 Victoria Ave R7B 0M8

JOEY'S ONLY SEAFOOD RESTAURANT 204-729-3700
Seafood. Casual Dining. **Address:** 1212 18th St R7A 5C3

LADY OF THE LAKE SHOP, CAFE & PUB 204-726-8785
International. Casual Dining. **Address:** 135-B 17th St N R7A 1G6

MARINO'S PIZZA 204-578-5555
Pizza. Casual Dining. **Address:** 441 10th St R7A 4G3

MUM'S FAMILY RESTAURANT 204-717-6867
American. Casual Dining. **Address:** 3500 McDonald Ave R7B 0B9

MUM'S FAMILY RESTAURANT 204-725-0888
American. Casual Dining. **Address:** 505 24th St R7B 1X6

CARBERRY (G-3) pop. 1,669, elev. 369m/1,210'

The forests and sand dunes of nearby Spruce Woods Provincial Park *(see attraction listing)* inspired many of the works of artist, naturalist and writer Ernest Thompson Seton, including his stories "The Trail of the Sandhill Stag" and "Wild Animals I Have Known." He was appointed naturalist to the Manitoba government in 1892. A small highway park 15 kilometres (9 mi.) east of Carberry on Hwy. 1 has been dedicated to Seton.

Carberry Municipal Offices: 316 4th Ave., Carberry, MB, Canada R0K 0H0. **Phone:** (204) 834-6600.

SPRUCE WOODS PROVINCIAL PARK is 25 km (16 mi.) s. on Hwy. 5. The 26,950-hectare (66,593-acre) park, a mosaic of geographic features, includes deciduous forests, creeping sand dunes, white spruce-covered sand hills and mixed grass prairie. The park is bisected by the Assiniboine River as it winds its way east.

The desertlike area known as Spirit Sands was formed by an ancient river delta which left behind a 5-kilometre (3-mi.) tract of open sand dunes that tower 30 metres (98 ft.) above the surrounding prairie. The eerie blue-green pond color of Devil's Punch Bowl, near the Spirit Sands, can be observed from several viewpoints; the bowl-shaped depression was caused by the currents of an underground stream.

A 7-kilometre (4.3-mi.) roundtrip self-guiding trail leads through the dunes to the Punch Bowl, and a 4-kilometre (2.5-mi.) trail meanders through the sands. The trails are found in the Spirit Sands trail system located just north of the Assiniboine River off Hwy. 5. Interpretive signs along the trails provide insight into the cultural and natural surroundings.

Spruce Woods is home to the western plains hognose snake; the northern prairie skink, Manitoba's only lizard; wapiti (elk); white-tailed deer; coyotes; and pin cushion and prickly pear cacti.

Interpretive programs about park resources and natural and cultural history are offered. The Park Centre building contains displays introducing the area's significant natural and cultural resources. Family events, campfire and amphitheater programs and guided hikes are offered weekends all year. *See Recreation Areas Chart.* Comfortable walking shoes, a hat and drinking water are recommended. **Time:** Allow 2 hours minimum. **Hours:** Park open daily 24 hours. **Cost:** One-day pass $4.76 per private vehicle. Three-day pass $11.43. An annual pass is available. **Phone:** (204) 827-8850 Park Centre, or (204) 834-8800 District Office.

🏕 🍴 ❌ 🎣 🛏

Spirit Sands Wagon Outfitters, 27 km (17 mi.) s.e. on Hwy. 5 in Spruce Woods Provincial Park, offers 90-minute covered wagon rides through the Spirit Sands and Devil's Punch Bowl, providing views of sand dunes, cactuses, rare snakes and lizards, rolling grasslands and marshes. **Hours:** Trips depart daily at 10, noon and 2, July-Aug.; Sat.-Sun. at noon and 2, by appointment only, mid-May through June 30. **Cost:** $13.33; $7.62 (ages 3-16). Cash only. **Phone:** (204) 827-2800 for wagon office, or (204) 526-7727 in the off-season.

CHURCHILL (A-4) pop. 813, elev. 29m/100'

Churchill, on the shore of Hudson Bay, is Canada's northernmost subarctic sea port. It also is the site of the Hudson's Bay Co.'s Prince of Wales Fort National Historic Site, a partially restored ruin across from Churchill and Cape Merry Battery at the mouth of the Churchill River. Built over a period of 40 years during the 1700s to hold as many as 400 soldiers, the impressive stone fortress housed only 39 untrained men when three French warships mounted a surprise attack in 1782. The fort's governor wisely surrendered without engaging in battle.

After spending 3 unsuccessful days trying to demolish the 12-metre-thick (40-ft.) outer walls, the

French abandoned the fort; it was never occupied again. The site is accessible by boat July through August (weather and tides permitting).

The area around Churchill holds an attraction for two giant mammals: the polar bear and the beluga whale. In fact, the Churchill region is said to have the greatest concentration of accessible polar bears in the world. Having spent the winter hunting on the frozen bay, the bears come to shore south of Churchill as the ice melts, scatter along the coast and up to 50 kilometres (31 mi.) inland, and then return to the ice in autumn when the bay refreezes. Beluga whales are often sighted off the coast of Cape Merry during July and August.

Other natural features include flowers, arctic plant life, various wildlife and some 200 species of birds, which nest or pass through Churchill on their annual migrations. An excellent spot for bird-watching is Bird Cove, on the coast 16 kilometres (9 mi.) east of Churchill. The aurora borealis (northern lights) seen from Churchill during the fall and winter months are among the most brilliant in the world.

Churchill can be reached only by train or airplane. Via Rail Canada trains run from Winnipeg and Thompson to Churchill; phone (888) 842-7245. Calm Air offers flights from Winnipeg to Churchill; phone (800) 839-2256.

The Parks Canada Visitor Reception Centre offers information, interpretive displays and programs, and historical exhibits June through November; by appointment rest of year. Phone (204) 675-8863.

Churchill Chamber of Commerce: 211 Kelsey Blvd., Churchill, MB, Canada R0B 0E0. **Phone:** (204) 675-2022 or (888) 389-2327.

▼GEM **ESKIMO MUSEUM,** 242 La Verendrye Ave., contains exhibits that depict the history and culture of the northern region of Canada. Founded in 1944 by Roman Catholic missionaries, it pays tribute to the creativity and beliefs of the Canadian Inuits. Highlights of the museum are Inuit carvings in bone, ivory, stone and antler as well as wildlife specimens, artifacts and tools dating from 1700 B.C. **Hours:** Mon. 1-5, Tues.-Sat. 9-noon and 1-5, June-Nov.; Mon.-Sat. 1-4:30, rest of year. Closed major holidays. **Cost:** Donations. **Phone:** (204) 675-2030.

NORTH STAR TOURS office is at 12 Hearne St. but guests are picked up from their hotel. Guides conduct historical, cultural and wilderness adventure and birding tours of the Churchill area by school bus covering such topics as Fort Churchill, the Hudson's Bay Co., natural history, geology, and polar bears and other wildlife. During summer beluga whale sightings are the highlight, and polar bear season runs October 1 to November. February, March and August are the months for aurora borealis viewing.

Time: Allow 6 hours minimum. **Hours:** Daily 9-5, June-Aug., Oct.-Nov. and Feb.-Mar. (weather permitting). **Cost:** $110-$175; free (ages 1-12). **Phone:** (204) 675-2356 or (800) 665-0690.

SEA NORTH TOURS LTD., 153 Kelsey Blvd., offers boat tours to Prince of Wales Fort National Historic Site in craft ranging in size up to the 30-passenger *Sea North II.* This vessel is equipped with stereo hydrophones so that passengers can listen to the sounds made by the beluga whales that swim within feet of the boat. Tours also offer chances of sighting polar bears, ice formations and indigenous birds. Kayak tours and snorkeling also are available.

Time: Allow 3 hours minimum. **Hours:** Daily dawn-dusk (times may vary depending on tides), mid-June to late Aug. **Cost:** $115; $57.50 (ages 6-12). Prices may vary; phone ahead. **Phone:** (204) 675-2195 or (888) 348-7591.

POLAR INN & SUITES   204/675-8878
▼▼ Hotel. **Address:** 153 Kelsey Blvd R0B 0E0

THE TUNDRA INN   (204)675-8831
▼▼ Hotel. **Address:** 34 Franklin St R0B 0E0

WHERE TO EAT

GYPSY RESTAURANT & BAKERY   204/675-2322
▼ American. Casual Dining. **Address:** 253 Kelsey Blvd R0B 0E0

THE REEF RESTAURANT & DINING ROOM   204/675-8807
▼▼ American. Casual Dining. **Address:** 299 Kelsey Blvd R0B 0E0

THE TUNDRA INN PUB & DINING ROOM   204/675-8831
▼▼ Canadian. Casual Dining. **Address:** 23 Franklin St R0B 0E0

COOKS CREEK (G-5) elev. 238m/780'

COOK'S CREEK HERITAGE MUSEUM, jct. Hwy. 212 and Sapton Rd., houses artifacts pertaining to the life of the early settlers from Poland, Ukraine and other eastern European countries. Highlights include religious artifacts, folk art, clothing, a blacksmith shop, pioneer houses furnished in period and farm machines. **Time:** Allow 1 hour minimum. **Hours:** Wed.-Sun. 10-5, mid-May through Aug. 31. **Cost:** $5.71; $3.81 (ages 6-17). **Phone:** (204) 444-4448.

DAUPHIN (F-2) pop. 8,251, elev. 293m/960'
• Hotels p. 368 • Restaurants p. 368

Dauphin (DAW-fin) lies in a fertile farming valley between Duck Mountain Provincial Park *(see Recreation Areas Chart)* and Riding Mountain National Park *(see place listing p. 372).* Lake Dauphin, 15 kilometres (9 mi.) east of Dauphin, is a popular place for watersports and offers camping, fishing and wildlife tours.

Parkland Recreation Complex, 200 1st Ave. S.E., includes two arenas, a playground, a curling rink and an aquatic center with an indoor wave pool; phone (204) 622-3150.

Meet your partner or watch as square dancers from across Manitoba compete in the ▼Dauphin Friendship Centre Square Dance Competition in late May at the Rotary Arena. If dancing isn't your forte, you can compete in the fiddling competition.

In late June and early July, more than 14,000 country music fans flock to 🌾 Dauphin's Countryfest, a 4-day music festival held at Selo Ukraina, a heritage village 12 kilometres (7.5 mi.) south of Dauphin near Riding Mountain National Park.

The nation's rich Ukrainian culture and heritage are celebrated in late July at Selo Ukraina during 🌾 Canada's National Ukrainian Festival, a 3-day event featuring Ukrainian music, food and dance.

Dauphin Economic Development & Tourism: 100 Main St. S., Dauphin, MB, Canada R7N 1K3. **Phone:** (204) 622-3216 or (877) 566-5669.

FORT DAUPHIN MUSEUM, 140 Jackson St., is surrounded by a wooden palisade suggestive of an 18th-century fur trading fort of the North West Co. A trapper's cabin, schoolhouse, church, blacksmith shop, trading post and pioneer house inside the fort are furnished in the style of the early settlers. Archeological, fur trade and pioneer artifacts also are featured.

Time: Allow 1 hour minimum. **Hours:** Tues.-Sun. 9-5, July-Aug.; Mon.-Fri. 9-5, May-June and in Sept.; by appointment rest of year. **Cost:** $3.81; $2.86 (students with ID); free (ages 0-12 with adult). **Phone:** (204) 638-6630.

SUPER 8 DAUPHIN   (204)638-0800
🌽🌽 Hotel. **Address:** 1457 Main St S R7N 3B3

WHERE TO EAT

MR MIKES STEAKHOUSECASUAL   204/701-6453
🌽🌽 American. Casual Dining. **Address:** 10 Main St R7N 1N4

EMERSON (H-4) pop. 671

Emerson was named after American poet Ralph Waldo Emerson. When Manitoba became a province in 1870, this town on the border of the United States and Canada was the site of the province's first customs house. The original log buildings still stand just north of the Customs Port of Entry.

In 1874 the North West Mounted Police, later renamed the Royal Canadian Mounted Police, organized at Fort Dufferin, thus beginning their career of maintaining law and order in the untamed western areas of Canada. A 5-metre (15-ft.) bronze statue of a North West Mounted Police Officer and his horse is located next to the Tourist Information Centre on Hwy. 75. The statue is a tribute to the members of the force who made the historic "Trek West" from Emerson to Fort Macleod, Alberta.

The Boundary Commission Trail provides 3 kilometres (1.9 mi.) of hiking along the Red River north to the Historic Fort Dufferin Site. At the fort are the remains of old buildings, grave sites and a memorial to the North West Mounted Police.

Town of Emerson: 104 Church St., Emerson, MB, Canada R0A 0L0. **Phone:** (204) 373-2002.

FALCON LAKE (G-6) pop. 277, elev. 305m/1,001'

As it winds its way across the country, the Trans Canada Trail enters Manitoba from Ontario at West Hawk Lake in Whiteshell Provincial Park, crossing the park diagonally as it heads westward to Pinawa. Incorporating many existing trails and utilizing abandoned railway lines, the trail offers hikers a diverse sampling of the province's topography.

RECREATIONAL ACTIVITIES
Horseback Riding

• **Falcon Beach Riding Stables and Guest Ranch** is off Hwy. 1 Falcon Lake exit (No. 301). **Hours:** Horseback rides offered daily 9-5, July-Aug.; by appointment rest of year. **Phone:** (204) 349-2410, or (877) 949-2410 in Canada.

FLIN FLON (B-2) pop. 5,363, elev. 304m/1,000'

Flin Flon was founded in 1915 when Tom Creighton, one of six prospectors, discovered an ore body which led to the development of Flin Flon as a mining town.

The community owes its name to Josiah Flintabbatey Flonatin, the major character of "The Sunless City," a dime novel found in the area by the discoverers of the mineral deposits. Off Hwy. 10 is a humorous 7.5-metre (25-ft.) statue of Flintabbatey Flonatin ("Flinty" for short) designed by the American cartoonist Al Capp, of "L'il Abner" fame. A boardwalk around Ross Lake, a walking trail and a park also remember the city's namesake; the park features a smaller statue of Flinty.

The Flin Flon Station Museum, north on Hwy. 10A, is open Monday to Friday 10-6 seasonally and displays artifacts collected from mining, transportation and cultural sources; phone (204) 681-7511. Bordering Saskatchewan, Flin Flon is the northern terminus of the Manitoba stretch of scenic Hwy. 10.

Flin Flon and District Chamber of Commerce: 228-35 Main St., Flin Flon, MB, Canada R8A 1J7. **Phone:** (204) 687-4518.

GARDENTON (H-5) elev. 298m/979'

Some of the earliest Ukrainian settlers in Manitoba came to Gardenton in 1896. St. Michael's Ukrainian Orthodox Historical Church, 4 kilometres (2.5 mi.) west, is purportedly North America's first Ukrainian Orthodox church; the church was built 1897-99. Lithographed icons from St. Petersburg, Moscow and Kiev ornament the sanctuary. A pilgrimage is held in summer. Phone (204) 339-2285 for an appointment to tour the church.

The Ukrainian Museum contains articles of clothing and hand tools depicting life in the late 1800s and early 1900s, a one-room schoolhouse and a thatched roof house. Also in the area is a tall-grass prairie. For further information about the museum phone (204) 425-3072 in summer, or (204) 425-8197 rest of year.

GIMLI (G-4) pop. 5,845, elev. 220m/723'

Established in 1875, Gimli was the site of Canada's first permanent Icelandic settlement, the largest outside Iceland. The town's name, derived from Norse mythology, means "home of the gods." A Viking statue designed by Gissur Eliasson and the oldest Icelandic cemetery in Canada testify to Gimli's Nordic heritage. Gimli is located on the western shore of Lake Winnipeg, one of the largest freshwater lakes in the world.

Lake Winnipeg Visitor Centre: 1 Centre Ave., Gimli, MB, Canada R0C 1B0. Open May-Sept. **Phone:** (204) 642-7974.

GLENBORO (H-3) pop. 645, elev. 375m/1,230'

Glenboro is known as the gateway to Spruce Woods Provincial Park *(see Carberry p. 366)* and the Manitoba Desert. At the junction of hwys. 2 and 5 in Camel Park stands Sara the Camel, a 7-metre-high (24-ft.) symbol of the Spirit Sands. The Glenboro Walking Tour takes visitors on a self-guiding stroll which points out many of the sights. Brochures are available at the village office; phone (204) 827-2083.

Slightly northwest of Glenboro on Hwy. 2 is the Stockton Ferry, purported to be the last cable river ferry in Manitoba; phone (204) 827-2252 or (204) 827-2250.

HEADINGLEY pop. 3,215

BEST WESTERN PLUS WINNIPEG WEST
(204)594-2200

Hotel
$120-$140

Best Western PLUS. AAA Benefit: Save 10% or more every day and earn 10% bonus points!

Address: 4140 Portage Ave R4H 1C5 **Location:** Jct Trans-Canada Hwy 1 (Portage Ave) and 101 just w; entrance through travel plaza. **Facility:** 110 units, some efficiencies. 4 stories, interior corridors. **Parking:** winter plug-ins. **Pool(s):** heated indoor. **Activities:** hot tub, exercise room. **Guest Services:** valet and coin laundry. **Featured Amenity:** full hot breakfast.

HECLA

LAKEVIEW HECLA RESORT   204/279-2041
Resort Hotel. **Address:** Hwy 8 R0C 2R0 *(See ad opposite inside front cover.)*

SEAGULLS RESTAURANT & LOUNGE   204/279-2041
American. Casual Dining. **Address:** Hwy 8 R0C 2R0

HECLA ISLAND (F-5) elev. 210m/690'

HECLA/GRINDSTONE PROVINCIAL PARK, 165 km (103 mi.) n. of Winnipeg, or 54 km (34 mi.) n. of Riverton, on Hwy. 8, is comprised of several islands in Lake Winnipeg, the largest of which is Hecla Island. The original settlers were Icelanders displaced from their homeland in 1876, fleeing poverty and Danish rule. Guided walks through the restored buildings of Hecla Village—a church, school, community hall, period house, dockside fish station, a tool display and a partially completed boarding house—are offered. *See Recreation Areas Chart.*

Interpretive programs also are available, as are camping facilities, cabins, hiking trails, snowmobile trails, picnic areas, bicycling, cross-country skiing, fishing and swimming. For further information, contact the Department of Conservation, P.O. Box 70, Riverton, MB, Canada R0C 2R0. **Hours:** Daily 24 hours. **Cost:** One-day pass $4.76 per private vehicle. Three-day pass $11.43. An annual pass is available. **Phone:** (204) 279-2056 May-Sept. or (204) 378-2261.

Grassy Narrows Marsh and Wildlife Viewing Tower, at Hecla/Grindstone Provincial Park, offers wildlife viewing from trails and boardwalks along the marsh as well as from towers along the trails. Some trails are designated bicycling trails. The marsh, a nesting area for Canada geese and other waterfowl, is named after the Narrows, a channel between Hecla Island and the mainland. The tower was built for viewing moose as they feed in the marsh. **Note:** Visitors should bring drinking water and wear comfortable walking shoes. **Hours:** Daily 24 hours. **Cost:** One-day pass $4.76 per private vehicle. Three-day pass $11.43. An annual pass is available. **Phone:** (204) 279-2056 May-Sept., or (204) 378-2261 rest of year.

Hecla Fish Station, at Hecla/Grindstone Provincial Park, is in an old ice house, or "fish station." The site provides a look at the commercial fishing industry of Lake Winnipeg through artifacts, wall plaques and a small museum. During June and September visitors may view fishermen bringing in the day's catch. **Hours:** Daily 11:30-4:30, June 10-Aug. 30. **Cost:** Free. **Phone:** (204) 279-2056 May-Sept. or (204) 378-2261.

Hecla Island Heritage Home Museum, at Hecla/Grindstone Provincial Park, depicts the lifestyle of an Icelandic family from the 1920s to the 1940s. The restored 1928 house is furnished in period with items donated by descendants of the original owners and by other islanders. Walking tours are available. **Hours:** Wed.-Sun. 10-4, June 26-Sept. 2. **Cost:** Donations. **Phone:** (204) 279-2056 May-Sept. or (204) 378-2261.

INGLIS (F-1)

INGLIS GRAIN ELEVATORS NATIONAL HISTORIC SITE is along Railway Ave.

These five vintage grain elevators, once a common sight on western Canadian prairies, have been restored and are now the last remaining row of standard wooden grain elevators in Canada. Dating to the 1920s, similar rows of elevators, built by grain companies and agricultural cooperatives, once stood along rail lines in most small Canadian communities.

An interpretive center in the Paterson elevator explains the importance of these structures to the nation's agricultural history. Exhibits and displays complement a video presentation, which shows how the elevators operated, transporting wheat into storage bins. A walking tour of the grounds provides further insights into the development of Canada's grain industry.

Time: Allow 1 hour minimum. **Hours:** Mon.-Sat. 10-6, Sun. noon-6, June 1-early Sept.; otherwise by appointment. **Cost:** $4.76-$9.52; free (ages 0-7). **Phone:** (204) 564-2243, or (204) 773-4231 for appointments.

INTERNATIONAL PEACE GARDEN (H-1)

On scenic Hwy. 10 and on US 281, the International Peace Garden consists of 1,451 acres (586 hectares) in Manitoba and an adjoining 888 acres (360 hectares) in North Dakota. Set among the lakes and streams of the wooded Turtle Mountains, the botanical garden and park commemorates the friendship between these two countries on the longest unfortified border in the world.

Points of interest include the 120-foot Peace Tower, which represents immigrants from the four corners of the world coming together with high hopes for the common purpose of peace; the Peace Chapel, which includes quotations etched in limestone walls; more than 150,000 flowering annuals in the formal gardens that line the boundary; a floral clock; the Carillon Bell Tower, which chimes every 15 minutes; and the 9/11 Memorial, constructed of steel salvaged from the ruins of the World Trade Center, commemorating the tragic events of Sept. 11, 2001.

The Interpretive Centre and Conservatory houses a retail store, a café, small prairie lands library and a conservatory with more than 6,000 cacti, succulents and orchids. The North American Game Warden Museum is dedicated to officers who died in the line of duty.

Facilities include campgrounds, hiking and bicycling trails and picnic areas. Self-guiding walking and driving tours are available. Flowers are in full bloom mid-July to early September (weather permitting).

The International Music Camp Summer School of Fine Arts is held at the garden June through July.

The Legion Athletic Camp, held July through August, attracts coaches and athletes from many countries.

After leaving the garden all visitors are required to go through customs (U.S. and Canadian customs stations are a short distance from the entrance gate). Allow 2 hours minimum to visit the site. The garden is open daily 24 hours, and the entrance gate is staffed Mon.-Fri. 9-5, Sat.-Sun. 9-7, late May to mid-Sept. Interpretive Centre daily 10-7. Game Warden Museum Tues.-Sun. 10-4, June 7-early Sept.; daily 11-4, early Sept. to mid-Sept.; Sat.-Sun. 11-4, in May; by appointment rest of year. Daily vehicle permit $14.29; pedestrian permit $9.52; season permit $28.57. Game Warden Museum admission is free. Phone (204) 534-2510 in Canada, (701) 263-4390 in the United States, or (888) 432-6733.

KILLARNEY (H-2) pop. 3,233, elev. 495m/1,625'

The area's resemblance to Ireland's Killarney Lakes prompted John Sidney O'Brien to change the name of the town of Oak Lake to Killarney. Green fire engines and a replica of the Blarney Stone are further evidence of the town's Irish heritage.

LOCKPORT (G-4) pop. 754, elev. 313m/1,000'

At Lockport Provincial Heritage Park, on Hwy. 44 just east of the Lockport bridge, is St. Andrews Lock and Dam. This rare structure on Canada's flat prairies was completed in 1910 to allow access and permit navigation on the Red River from Lake Winnipeg to the city of Winnipeg; it is purportedly the only lock and dam of its kind still standing in North America. Picnic sites and footpaths overlook the dam.

ST. ANDREW'S CHURCH is 2 km (1.2 mi.) s. on Hwy. 9, then just e. to 3 St. Andrews Rd. (Hwy. 410). Designed by its first rector 1844-49, this stone Gothic-Revival Anglican church is the oldest house of worship in continuous use in western Canada. It retains many of its original fixtures. The church's cemetery is adjacent. **Time:** Allow 30 minutes minimum. **Hours:** Tours Sun. 1-3, July-Aug. **Cost:** Donations. **Phone:** (204) 334-5700.

St. Andrew's Heritage Centre is 2 km (1.2 mi.) s. on Hwy. 9, then just e. on St. Andrews Rd. (Hwy. 410) to 374 River Rd. (Hwy. 238), across from St. Andrew's Church. The two-story stone building was constructed in 1854 for the church's rectors and represents Red River architecture. Displays include farm equipment and utensils used by early settlers. Hands-on exhibits allow visitors to try a crosscut saw and cook bannock (a flat, quick bread) over an open fire. **Hours:** Mon.-Sat. 10-5, Sun. noon-5, July-Aug. **Cost:** Donations. **Phone:** (204) 339-6396.

MINNEDOSA (G-2) pop. 2,587

A walking trail surrounds the fenced-in Bison Park on Hwy. 262 (Beach Road). The Little Saskatchewan River runs beside the animal viewing area, which is open dawn to dusk May through October. Visitors are not permitted to feed the bison.

Minnedosa Lake and Beach offers ample summer and winter recreational options *(see Recreation Areas Chart)*.

Minnedosa Area Community Development Office: 39 Main St. S., Minnedosa, MB R0J 1E0. **Phone:** (204) 867-3885 or (866) 577-2968.

Self-guiding tours: The Minnedosa Area Community Development Office has brochures about local self-guiding tours. One guides visitors along Main Street to see the 12 Founders Parks, each with historical aesthetic touches and a plaque detailing a town founder. Another brochure showcases the town's historic stone buildings.

MORDEN (H-4) pop. 7,812, elev. 302m/990'

Named after the area's first settler, Alvey Morden, the town grew almost overnight when the Canadian Pacific Railroad arrived in 1882. Located near the Boundary Commission-NWMP Trail in the Boundary Trail Heritage Region, Morden has a progressive industrial and business sector. Abundant recreational activities at Lake Minnewasta *(see Recreation Areas Chart)* and Colert Beach include camping, swimming, fishing, water skiing, canoeing, sailing, bicycling and hiking in the summer. Winter activities include cross-country skiing, snowmobiling and ice fishing.

A mural on the corner of Stephen and Nelson streets is a re-creation of one of the earliest known photographs taken in the area. The scene depicts the supply train for Her Majesty's British North American Boundary Commission at Dead Horse Creek in June 1873.

Another mural, at the corner of Stephen and 7th streets, remembers the visit of Canada's first prime minister, Sir John A. MacDonald, to the town on July 15, 1886. The depiction features Sir John speaking from the rear of his railcar and Philip Locke presenting him with a bouquet of prairie flowers; a version of First Nations war dance also is depicted.

A third mural, at 306 N. Railway St., depicts the original uniform of the North West Mounted Police and provides a history of the force, now known as the Royal Canadian Mounted Police.

Morden and District Chamber of Commerce: 100-379 Stephen St., Morden, MB, Canada R6M 1V1. **Phone:** (204) 822-5630.

Self-guiding tours: Heritage Series Brochures, available at the chamber of commerce, describe self-guiding walking tours of Morden's turn-of-the-20th-century homes and buildings.

CANADIAN FOSSIL DISCOVERY CENTRE is in the lower level of the Access Event Centre at 111-B Gilmour St. Fossil displays chronicle regional paleontology and geology. Marine reptile fossils, such as mosasaurs and plesiosaurs, date from 80 million

years ago when the Western Interior Seaway covered much of North America. A highlight of the exhibits is Bruce, a 43-foot mosasaur and said to be the largest discovered in Canada. The process of finding, excavating and displaying the fossils also is depicted. Fossil Dig Adventure Tours offer a chance to excavate fossils at a site nearby.

Time: Allow 1 hour minimum. **Hours:** Daily 10-5, Apr.-Aug.; Mon.-Fri. 10-5, Sat.-Sun. 1-5, rest of year. Closed Christmas. **Cost:** $8; $5 (ages 5-17); $18 (family, two adults and up to three children). A fee is charged for Fossil Dig. Reservations are recommended 1 week in advance for fossil dig. **Phone:** (204) 822-3406.

MORRIS (H-4) pop. 1,797, elev. 236m/775'

Two rival fur-trading companies—the North West Co. and the Hudson's Bay Co.—set up shop on the Morris River in 1801. Not until 1874 did a permanent settlement take hold; incorporation took place in 1883. Both the town and the river on which it grew were named for Alexander Morris, the second lieutenant governor of Manitoba during the 1870s.

You'll enjoy fair favorites including entertainment, exhibits, fair food and midway rides at the ▼ Manitoba Stampede and Exhibition in mid-July. Highlights include the heart-pounding action of a seven event pro rodeo, and chuck wagon and chariot racing. Kids can take part in the action at the mutton busting and the pig scramble.

Morris Town Office: 1-380 Stampede Grounds, Box 28, Morris, MB, Canada R0G 1K0. **Phone:** (204) 746-2531.

MORRIS & DISTRICT CENTENNIAL MUSEUM, on Main St. at jct. hwys. 75 and 23, consists of two buildings. The main building is the original Carleton School, which contains pioneer-era displays of farm tools and a laundry and dairy section. The second building contains five rooms featuring furniture and artifacts from the turn of the 20th century. A mural depicts the history of the Red River Valley. **Hours:** Thurs.-Tues. noon-5, Wed. 2-8, June-Aug. (or late Sept., if weather permits). **Cost:** Donations. **Phone:** (204) 746-2169.

NEEPAWA (G-3) pop. 3,629, elev. 400m/1,300'

Neepawa, whose name derives from a native word for plenty, is a service center for the surrounding grain and livestock farms on the fertile plains northwest of Winnipeg. This community of tree-lined streets, well-known as the birthplace of author Margaret Laurence, offers many pleasant diversions for residents and travelers alike, including Riverbend Park, a fitness trail, a camping area, a golf course and opportunities for bird-watching.

The city calls itself the World Lily Capital. This claim is bolstered by the annual ▼ Neepawa Lily Festival held over three days in late July. More than 2,000 varieties of lilies are grown in the Neepawa area, and the community celebrates their beauty with live entertainment, music, street vendors and food kiosks, a quilt show, a parade, tours by bus and horse-drawn vehicles and a photography contest.

Neepawa and District Chamber of Commerce: 282 Hamilton St., Neepawa, MB, Canada R0J 1H0. **Phone:** (204) 476-5292.

BEAUTIFUL PLAINS MUSEUM, 91 Hamilton St., is housed in a former CNR station. The museum features several rooms of historical items. A children's room contains antique toys and books, and a military room has uniforms and pictures of local residents involved in World Wars I and II. Other rooms include items dedicated to nature, stores, Masonic lodges, sports and vintage clothing. An extensive doll collection also is displayed. Railroad artifacts and history displays are housed in an antique railroad car.

Time: Allow 30 minutes minimum. **Hours:** Mon.-Fri. 9-5, Sat.-Sun. 1-5, July-Aug.; Mon.-Fri. 9-5, mid-May through June 30. **Cost:** Donations. **Phone:** (204) 476-3896, or (204) 841-9050 in the off-season.

PINAWA (G-5) pop. 1,444, elev. 282m/925'

Named "Pinnawak," meaning calm waters, by the aboriginal people, Pinawa was first settled by families who operated one of the earliest hydroelectric power dams built between Sault Ste. Marie, Ontario, and the Rockies. The townsite was abandoned in 1951, and the historic site is now Pinawa Dam Provincial Heritage Park. The new Pinawa was built in 1963 when the Federal Crown Corp., Atomic Energy of Canada Limited (AECL) built its research center near the old townsite.

PORTAGE LA PRAIRIE (G-3) pop. 12,996, elev. 332m/1,100'

The city's name is derived from the prairie portage between the Red and Assiniboine rivers and Lake Manitoba. In the heart of the city at Crescent Road and Royal Road S. is Island Park. Surrounded by horseshoe-shaped Crescent Lake, this scenic park has a deer sanctuary, a large captive flock of Canada geese and offers opportunities for other bird-watching. Park features include playground areas, exhibition grounds, seasonal harness racing, a golf course, a campground, a water park, a swimming pool, an arboretum, tennis courts, picnic areas, an arena and bicycling and hiking trails.

Portage la Prairie City Hall, built in 1898, was designed by one of Canada's foremost architects, Thomas Fuller.

Portage and District Chamber of Commerce: 56 Royal Rd. N., Portage la Prairie, MB, Canada R1N 1R8. **Phone:** (204) 857-7778.

FORT LA REINE MUSEUM, PIONEER VILLAGE AND TOURIST BUREAU is at jct. hwys. 26 and 1A E. The central museum includes pioneer household articles and implements, a log fort, school, doctor's office, trading post, furnished homestead and

church as well as railway, farming and military displays. Canadian railway official Sir William Van Horne's business car also is displayed. A tourist bureau is available.

Time: Allow 1 hour minimum. **Hours:** Daily 9:30-5:30, mid-May to Aug. 31 and for occasional special events. **Cost:** $9.52; $7.62 (ages 13-18, 60+ and students with ID); $4.76 (ages 5-12); $23.81 (family, two adults and three children). **Phone:** (204) 857-3259. 🅰️

BILL'S STICKY FINGERS   204/857-9999

American
Casual Dining
$9-$36

AAA Inspector Notes: This comfortable, casual, older restaurant offers a wide-ranging menu that includes ribs, chicken, steak, lasagna, gyros and pizza, as well as daily specials. The service is friendly and prompt. **Features:** full bar. **Address:** 210 Saskatchewan Ave E R1N 0K9 **Location:** Just w of Main St.

Ⓛ Ⓓ 🅛🅐🅣🅔 CALL 🅖🅜

💎 RIDING MOUNTAIN NATIONAL PARK (F-1)

Elevations in the park range from 230 metres (755 ft.) at Henderson Creek in the northeastern area to 756 metres (2,480 ft.) at Bald Hill in the eastern side of the park. Refer to CAA/AAA maps for additional elevation information.

Accessible from the north and south via scenic Hwy. 10, or from the east via Hwy. 19, Riding Mountain National Park lies on the plateau of the Manitoba escarpment, 197 kilometres (123 mi.) north of the U.S. border and 259 kilometres (162 mi.) northwest of Winnipeg. The park also encompasses the historic resort town of Wasagaming on Clear Lake, which offers the amenities of a resort destination. The park's 2,978-square-kilometre (1,150-sq.-mi.) area is blanketed with forests, lakes and meadows. It was officially dedicated in 1933 and is home to elk, moose, deer, bears and a wide variety of birds and vegetation. Waterfowl and beavers populate the waterways, and a herd of bison grazes in a large enclosure near Lake Audy. Driving hwys. 10 and 19 as well as Lake Audy Road offer scenic views and opportunities to spot wildlife. Self-guiding bison tour brochures are available at various park facilities.

During the Depression of the 1930s, the Depression Relief Program created jobs for the unemployed, 1,200 of whom were put to work constructing buildings for the park 1934-35. As is the case with much of the architecture found in the country's national parks, the style widely used was a rustic design that incorporated local materials. Perhaps the most eye-catching of their projects here is the East Gate Complex on Hwy. 19, which includes a registration building, two staff buildings and an overhead entrance sign. (Northern and southern complexes had been built but no longer exist.)

Another major international event the following decade further influenced the site's development, when World War II changed the site's focus from recreation to a source of attaining fuelwood. During the war the park was used as a minimum security POW camp, housing German prisoners from North Africa to cut cordwood. When the prisoners were released in late 1945, the function of the park turned once again to recreation.

General Information and Activities

Although the park is open year-round, complete facilities are available only from mid-May to mid-October. Recreational activities available within the park include bicycling, boating, camping, tennis, golfing, lawn bowling, swimming, hiking, fishing, canoeing, sailing, horseback riding, swimming, skateboarding, ice-skating, cross-country skiing and snowshoeing. Snowmobiling is permitted on Clear Lake and around the park's perimeter. Clear Lake has a beach and boat launches, and scuba diving is possible; divers must register with the park. More than 400 kilometres (250 mi.) of hiking, bicycling and horseback trails lead to lakes, meadows and evergreen forests. Bicycle and boat rentals are available. The park has more than a dozen picnic sites.

Note: Except for in Wasagaming, water must be boiled for all uses. Swimming areas are unsupervised; lifeguards are not available. Due to the presence of a parasite in most of the bodies of water in the park, developing swimmer's itch is a concern; take proper precautions. Camping permits and fishing licenses are required.

Several forms of recreation can be pursued nearby. Guides and outfitters offer horseback riding and wagon excursions along with other wilderness activities. *See Recreation Areas Chart.*

ADMISSION is free in 2017 to celebrate Canada's 150th anniversary of Confederation. Otherwise admission is $7.43; $6.24 (ages 65+); $3.71 (ages 6-16); free (ages 0-5); $18.67 (family, up to seven people). An annual pass is available.

PETS are allowed in the park. Dogs must be leashed at all times.

ADDRESS inquiries to Visitor Information, Riding Mountain National Park, Wasagaming, MB, Canada R0J 2H0; phone (204) 848-7275 or (204) 848-7272.

VISITOR INFORMATION CENTRE OF WASAGAMING is on the s. shore of Clear Lake. The center maintains exhibits and displays about the natural and human history of the area. Interpretive programs include nature walks, campfires, theater programs and guided hikes. **Hours:** Daily 9:30-8, June 30-early Sept.; 9:30-5:30, mid-May to June 29 and early Sept. to mid-Oct. **Cost:** Free. **Phone:** (204) 848-7275 or (204) 848-7272. ▲

RUSSELL pop. 1,669

THE RUSSELL INN HOTEL & CONFERENCE CENTRE
(204)773-2186
◆◆ Hotel. **Address:** Hwy 16 R0J 1W0

WHERE TO EAT

RUSSELL INN DINING ROOM   204/773-7507
◆◆ American. Casual Dining. **Address:** Hwy 16 R0J 1W0

SCANTERBURY

SOUTH BEACH CASINO & RESORT   (204)766-2100

Hotel
$87-$299

Address: One Ocean Dr R0E 1W0 **Location:** On Rt 59, just s of town. **Facility:** A half hour north of Winnipeg, near the shores of Lake Winnipeg, this Art Deco-style property offers spacious and very comfortable up-to-date accommodations. 95 units. 6 stories, interior corridors. **Parking:** winter plug-ins. **Terms:** cancellation fee imposed. **Pool(s):** heated indoor.

SELKIRK (G-5) pop. 9,834, elev. 231m/800'

Selkirk's name honors Lord Selkirk, the Scottish philanthropist whose 1812 settlement in the Red River Valley to the south laid the foundation for Winnipeg. During the late 19th- and early 20th centuries, Selkirk's position on the Red River made it a base for commerce and communication with communities on Lake Winnipeg. The Manitoba Marine Museum, at the entrance to Selkirk Park, harbours five of the original lake boats.

Chuck the Channel Catfish, a 9-metre (30-ft.) fiberglass statue, greets visitors on Main Street. The oversize catfish is an apt representation of the live version: Catfish weighing more than 9 kilograms (20 lbs.) abound in the Red River between Selkirk and Lockport.

St. Peter's Dynevor Church, 6.5 kilometres (4 mi.) northeast off Hwy. 59, was built in 1853. The original church, erected in 1836, was the center for Anglican missionary work among the Saulteaux First Nation.

Selkirk Biz : 200 Eaton Ave., Selkirk, MB, Canada R1A 0W6. **Phone:** (204) 482-7176.

◆GEM◆ **LOWER FORT GARRY NATIONAL HISTORIC SITE,** 5 km (3 mi.) s. on Hwy. 9, is purportedly the oldest intact stone fur-trading post in North America. Farm produce constituted the majority of trade that went on between the locals and the Hudson's Bay Co. The 19th-century buildings have been restored and are furnished as they might have been in their early days. Costumed staff members perform tasks and reenact events that re-create the early 1850s atmosphere of the fort in its heyday. In the 1870s the site served other purposes, including as a training base for the North-West Mounted Police.

The grounds contain an impressive collection of early stone buildings; an exhibit showcases the historic architectural styles. The Visitor Reception Centre offers exhibits about the fort's history. Special events are held occasionally throughout the season.

Time: Allow 2 hours minimum. **Hours:** Daily 9:30-5, early May-Labour Day (limited services on weekends early May-June 30). **Cost:** Free in 2017 to celebrate Canada's 150th anniversary of Confederation. Otherwise $7.43; $6.24 (ages 65+); $3.71 (ages 6-16); $18.67 (family, two adults and five children). **Phone:** (204) 785-6050 or (888) 773-8888.

SHILO (G-2)

THE ROYAL REGIMENT OF CANADIAN ARTILLERY MUSEUM is on the Canadian Forces Base Shilo via Hwy. 340. One of the largest military museums in Canada, this indoor-outdoor museum exhibits more than 10,000 articles of dress, technical instruments, ammunition, small arms, guns and vehicles dating from World War II to the present. Among the more than 150 pieces of major military equipment dating to 1796 are German, Russian and French guns. The outdoor Gun Park features more than 30 exhibits and a picnic area.

Time: Allow 1 hour minimum. **Hours:** Daily 10-5, Victoria Day-Labour Day; Mon.-Fri. 10-5, rest of year. **Cost:** $5.71; $3.81 (veterans, including RCMP, ages 6-18 and 65+); free (ages 0-5). Guided tour $23.81. Cash only. **Phone:** (204) 765-3000, ext. 3570 or 3331 for information; ext. 4563 for tour reservations.

SOURIS (H-2) pop. 1,837, elev. 396m/1,300'

The free-swinging 177-metre (581-ft.) footbridge built in 1904 over the Souris (SIR-iss) River is considered the second longest free-suspension footbridge in Canada. The bridge was reconstructed after being destroyed by a flood in 1976. Victoria Park has more than 6 kilometres (4 mi.) of walking trails, a viewing tower and a bird sanctuary; phone (204) 483-5200.

Rockhounding in nearby agate pits yields agate, dendrite, jasper, petrified wood and epidote; the area offers one of the largest varieties of semiprecious stones found in North America. Permits are required and cost $21.52 per private vehicle. Contact the Rock Shop, 8 First St. S., Souris, MB, Canada R0K 2C0; phone (204) 483-2561.

STEINBACH (H-5) pop. 13,524, elev. 261m/900'

SAVE **MENNONITE HERITAGE VILLAGE,** 3 km (1.9 mi.) n. on Hwy. 12, centers on a replica of a Mennonite village with more than 20 completely furnished buildings that were moved to the site. On the 16-hectare (40-acre) grounds are a fruit garden, stock pens, a steam engine, gas tractors and other machinery. The village windmill is said to be one of only two of its kind in Canada. A museum displays antiques and manuscripts.

Time: Allow 2 hours minimum. **Hours:** Mon.-Sat. 9-6, Sun. 11:30-6, July-Aug.; Mon.-Sat. 9-5, Sun. 11:30-5, May-June and in Sept.; Mon.-Fri. 9-4 or by appointment, rest of year. **Cost:** $9.52; $7.62 (ages 13-22 and 65+); $3.81 (ages 6-12); $28.57 (family, two adults and children under 17). **Phone:** (204) 326-9661 or (866) 280-8741.

DAYS INN   (204)320-9200
♥♥ Hotel. **Address:** 75 Hwy 12 N R5G 1T3

STONEWALL (G-4) pop. 4,536

Nobody knows for sure if Stonewall was named after founding father S.J. "Stonewall" Jackson or the limestone ridge on which the town is built. The name fits well, though, since limestone quarrying sustained the area's economy from the early 1880s until 1967. Stonewall's past is captured through the old stone buildings dotting its streets.

Town of Stonewall: 293 Main St., Box 250, Stonewall, MB, Canada R0C 2Z0. **Phone:** (204) 467-7979.

SWAN RIVER (D-2) pop. 3,907, elev. 340m/1,116'

During the last 13 years of the 18th century, control of the Swan River Valley was sought by both the North West Co. and the Hudson's Bay Co. Each company built fur-trading posts in the area, but by 1800 the concentrated trapping generated by the rivalry had depleted the number of fur-bearing animals. The Hudson's Bay Co. abandoned the area until the two companies joined in 1821.

The Swan River Valley, nestled between the Duck and Porcupine mountains, offers fishing, hunting, boating, camping, swimming and picnicking. Scenic Hwy. 10 passes just east of town.

Swan Valley Chamber of Commerce: 1500 Main St., Swan River, MB, Canada R0L 1Z0. **Phone:** (204) 734-3102.

SWAN VALLEY SUPER 8   (204)734-7888
♥♥ Hotel. **Address:** 115 Kelsey Tr R0L 1Z0

THE PAS (C-2) pop. 5,513, elev. 274m/900'

A riverfront lookout in Devon Park at The Pas (pronounced "the paw") honors travelers of the Saskatchewan River including Henry Kelsey, the first known European to see the northern prairies in 1691. It is rumored that the first wheat on the prairies was planted in the area in 1734.

Christ Church (Anglican), on Edwards Avenue, was founded in 1840 by Henry Budd, the first Native American ordained to the Anglican ministry. The church contains hand-hewn furnishings made by ships' carpenters in 1847. Tours are offered by appointment; phone (204) 623-2119.

SAM WALLER MUSEUM is at 306 Fischer Ave. Housed in what is said to be northern Manitoba's oldest brick edifice, the museum originally was the town's Courthouse and Community building. On display are natural history exhibits, local historical materials and First Nations and fur-trading artifacts. The basement features original jail cells and a children's discovery room. Historic walking tours of the downtown and riverfront areas also are offered.

Time: Allow 1 hour minimum. **Hours:** Daily 10-5, July-Aug.; 1-5, rest of year. Historic walking tours by appointment. Closed major holidays. **Cost:** $4.76; $2.86 (ages 65+ and students with ID); $9.52 (family). Admission Wed. by donation. **Phone:** (204) 623-3802.

ANDERSEN INN & SUITES   (204)623-1888
♦♦♦♦ Hotel. **Address:** 1717 Gordon Ave R9A 1K3

KIKIWAK INN   204/623-1800
♦♦ ♦♦ Hotel. **Address:** Hwy 10 N R0B 2J0

THOMPSON (B-3) pop. 12,829, elev. 206m/675'

Thompson sprang up after the discovery of one of the world's largest nickel deposits and is a major mining, communications, transportation, medical and retailing center. The King Miner statue sits atop underground mines and honors men and women miners at the southern entrance to town, 2.5 kilometres (1.5 mi.) south on Hwy. 6.

Lakes and rivers abound in this rugged, picturesque area. Paint Lake Provincial Recreation Park *(see Recreation Areas Chart)* is 32 kilometres (20 mi.) south on Hwy. 6.

Also south of Thompson on Hwy. 6 is the starting point for a 10 kilometre (6-mi.) hiking trail that will take you over a bridge to Kwasitchewan Falls, the highest waterfall in the province. Between Wabowden and Thompson, within Pisew Falls Provincial Park, is Pisew Falls, the second-highest waterfall in Manitoba accessible by road. A 1.3-kilometre (.8-mi.) trail leads from the highway through the dense foliage to a platform overlooking the 12.8-metre (42-ft.) falls. Twelve site plaques describe the flora and fauna of this boreal forest. Picnic facilities are available.

Thompson Spirit Way is a combination gravel and pavement path that offers 16 points of interest. Designed for bicycling or walking, the route starts at the Heritage North Museum and ends at Miles Hart Bridge. Though hiking boots are not required, it is essential to wear comfortable walking shoes. The route stretches for 2 kilometres (1 mi.) and highlights include an 86-foot-tall wolf mural that is said to be the largest lighted mural in the world as well as a restored Norseman floatplane and a tribute to firefighters. Display panels share information about the

sites and vantage points present scenic views. Official Spirit Way guide books may be purchased from the museum or the chamber of commerce.

Thompson Chamber of Commerce: 79 Selkirk Ave., Thompson, MB, Canada R8N 1M2. **Phone:** (204) 677-4155 or (888) 307-0103.

BEST WESTERN THOMPSON HOTEL & SUITES
(204)778-8887

 Best Western. **AAA Benefit:** Save 10% or more every day and earn 10% bonus points!

Address: 205 Mystery Lake Rd R8N 1Z8 **Location:** Hwy 6 exit Mystery Lake Rd. **Facility:** 80 units, some efficiencies. 4 stories, interior corridors. **Parking:** winter plug-ins. **Terms:** cancellation fee imposed. **Amenities:** safes. **Activities:** sauna, exercise room. **Guest Services:** valet and coin laundry. **Featured Amenity:** breakfast buffet.

DAYS INN & SUITES   (204)778-6000
♦♦ ♦♦ Hotel. **Address:** 21 Thompson Dr N R8N 2B5

VIRDEN (G-1) pop. 3,114, elev. 439m/1,440'

About 1,200 oil wells dot the landscape in and around Virden—the richest source of petroleum in Manitoba. The first oil-producing well was sunk in the 1950s in the Rosalee field northwest of Virden.

Many original fieldstone buildings, such as the 1892 St. Mary's Anglican Church at the corner of Queen Street and 9th Avenue, are still in use today. The site of Fort Montagne à la Bosse, built by the North West Co. in 1790, is northeast of Virden on the old Trans-Canada Highway. To help cool things off in the summer, the fairgrounds has a public pool and a waterslide.

Virden Community Chamber of Commerce: 425 6th Ave., Virden, MB, Canada R0M 2C0. **Phone:** (204) 851-1551.

WAPUSK NATIONAL PARK (A-4)

Elevations in the park range from sea level along the Hudson Bay coastal areas to 94 metres (308 ft.) at Silcox Creek. Refer to CAA/AAA maps for additional elevation information.

South and east of Churchill on the shore of Hudson Bay, Wapusk (pronounced to rhyme with tusk) was established in 1996. The park consists of 11,475 square kilometres (7,119 sq. mi.). Translated from the Cree language, Wapusk means "white bear," a fitting name for a park that has an area where polar bears den and produce offspring.

Much of the national park, part of the Hudson Bay and James Bay lowlands, is a flat plain covered by an extensive layer of peat; a layer of permafrost lies underneath. The treeless tundra consists mainly of wetlands—lakes, streams, bogs and rivers.

Polar bears congregate in the northern part of the park near Churchill around October, as they wait for freezing weather and the time when they can return to the ice in search of seals, their main food. The females dig their dens, and their young are born in late November and in December. The area around Churchill *(see place listing p. 366)* is one of the world's best places for viewing polar bears in their native habitat. Specialized tundra vehicles take visitors for close-up encounters.

The park, along a migratory flyway, also is a popular spring and fall feeding spot for waterfowl and shorebirds, including such rare species as the king eider, Ross' gull and gyrfalcon. Many build their nests here on the coast of Hudson Bay during the summer.

Churchill, in a somewhat remote location in northern Manitoba, can be reached by air and rail from Winnipeg. Since Wapusk is a wilderness park, it has no roads or trails. In order to visit the park, it is necessary to be part of an organized tour group, and several commercial operators provide tours into the park by plane or helicopter. The park office can provide a list. Park admission is free. For additional information contact Wapusk National Park, P.O. Box 127, Churchill, MB, Canada R0B 0E0; phone (204) 675-8863 or (888) 773-8888.

WINKLER (H-4) pop. 10,670, elev. 271m/890'

PEMBINA THRESHERMEN'S MUSEUM, 5 km (3 mi.) w. on Hwy. 3, features guided tours through displays of agricultural machinery, tools and household items as well as a steam threshing unit, a working sawmill and a seed elevator. **Time:** Allow 1 hour minimum. **Hours:** Mon.-Fri. 9-5, Sat.-Sun. and holidays 1-5, May-Sept. **Cost:** $7.14; $4.76 (ages 9-15 and 65+); free (ages 0-8). Prices may vary for special events. **Phone:** (204) 325-7497.

Winnipeg

Then & Now

The real estate agent's cry of "Location!" could have been invented in Winnipeg; the position of Manitoba's capital has determined the city's past and present. Archeological evidence shows that Winnipeg has been an important place of settlement for more than 6,000 years.

The confluence of the Red River, which flows south to north, and the Assiniboine River, whose eastward flowing waters were a main route of Western exploration, led to the founding of fur-trading posts in the early 18th century near Winnipeg's present site. The fertile lands created by the rivers later drew farmers and other settlers.

Still later, the area's position south of the peaks of the Canadian Shield meant that roads and railroads were forced to converge at Winnipeg, making it the point through which the eastbound raw materials of the West and the

westbound manufactured goods of the East passed. Profiting by the hydroelectric power generated from its rivers, the city emerged in the 20th century as a manufacturing center in its own right.

French Canadian explorer and trader Pierre Gaultier de la Vérendrye founded Fort Rouge at the confluence of the rivers in 1738. This fur-trading post was succeeded by Fort Gibraltar, built by the North West Co. in 1804, and Fort Garry, founded by the Hudson's Bay Co. in 1821. In the same year, Lord Selkirk brought a party of Scottish settlers to these fertile lands, a move that greatly disturbed the trappers and voyageurs who feared their livelihoods would be destroyed.

The settlement managed to survive, shifting from trapping and hunting to agriculture. Because of aggressive Canadian advertising campaigns in Europe and a homestead policy similar to that being used to settle the plains of the United States, large numbers of immigrants began to flow into the area in the 1860s.

In 1873 the village about a half mile north of Fort Garry was incorporated and named for the Cree Nation words *win* ("muddy") and *nipee* ("water"). The railroad aided Winnipeg's growth still further: In 1876 the city began to ship wheat east, and when the Canadian Pacific Railway connected the coasts in 1885, freight and passengers began to flow through the city in both directions.

The diversity of today's Winnipeg mirrors the many nationalities of the people who settled it, drawn by agriculture, the railroad or industry. From countries throughout Great Britain and Europe they came, creating a cultural mix reflected in the city's skyline, which includes the neoclassical splendor of the Manitoba Legislative Building, the century-old buildings of Old Market Square and the rounded spires of the Ukrainian Greek Orthodox Cathedral.

Archeological digs have uncovered evidence that The Forks' current site was an aboriginal peoples' seasonal meeting place more than 6,000 years ago. Tools, bones, footprints and pottery

Winnipeg skyline

(Continued on p. 378.)

Fast Facts

ABOUT THE CITY

POP: 663,617 ▪ ELEV: 229 m/763 ft.

MONEY

SALES TAX: Manitoba's provincial sales tax is 8 percent. A 5 percent Goods and Services Tax (GST) is levied in Canada on most sales and services. There is a 5 percent accommodations tax on hotel/motel rooms where there are four or more letting rooms.

WHOM TO CALL

EMERGENCY: 911

POLICE (non-emergency): (204) 986-6222

TEMPERATURE: (204) 983-2050

HOSPITALS: Concordia Hospital, (204) 667-1560 ▪ Grace Hospital, (204) 837-0111 ▪ Health Sciences Centre, (204) 787-3661 ▪ St. Boniface Hospital, (204) 233-8563 ▪ Seven Oaks General Hospital, (204) 632-7133 ▪ Victoria General Hospital, (204) 269-3570.

WHERE TO LOOK AND LISTEN

NEWSPAPERS: Winnipeg has three daily newspapers, the *Winnipeg Free Press*, the *Winnipeg Sun* and *Metro Winnipeg*, all distributed in the morning.

RADIO: The Canadian Broadcasting Corporation (CBC) has both AM (990) and FM (89.3 and 98.3) stations in Winnipeg as well as an AM (1050) station broadcasting in French.

VISITOR INFORMATION

Tourism Winnipeg: 300-259 Portage Ave., Winnipeg, MB, Canada R3B 2A9. Phone: (204) 943-1970 or (855) 734-2489.
Tourism Winnipeg is open Mon.-Fri. 8:30-4:30. A second branch, at Winnipeg James Armstrong Richardson International Airport, is open daily 8 a.m.-9:45 p.m.; phone (204) 982-7543.

Travel Manitoba Visitor Information Centre at The Forks: 21 Forks Market Rd., Winnipeg, MB, Canada R3C 4T7. Phone: (204) 927-7800 or (800) 665-0040.

Travel Manitoba is staffed with on-site travel counselors daily 9-6. The telephones are manned daily 8:30-4:30. The 24-hour Forks Hot Line, (204) 957-7618, also provides information. The center features dioramas depicting the various regions of the province.

TRANSPORTATION

AIR TRAVEL: Winnipeg James Armstrong Richardson International Airport (YWG) is about 8 kilometres (5 mi.) northwest of downtown off Metro Rte. 90. Daily bus service between the airport and downtown is provided by Winnipeg Transit routes 15 and 20 between 5:50 a.m. and 12:49 a.m. The one-way fare is $2.65; $2.15 (ages 6-16 and 65+); passengers must have exact change. Phone 311 or (877) 311-4974 for information. Taxis to downtown cost around $18 and a sedan costs around $32. Major hotels offer limousine service to and from the airport.

RENTAL CARS: Hertz, (800) 263-0600 in Canada, or (800) 654-3080 out of Canada, offers discounts to AAA and CAA members. Winnipeg locations are at Winnipeg James Armstrong Richardson International Airport, phone (204) 925-6625, and 1577 Erin St., phone (204) 925-6629.

RAIL SERVICE: The VIA Rail Canada depot is downtown at Union Station, 123 Main St.; phone (888) 842-7245.

TAXIS: Cab companies include Blueline, (204) 925-8888 ▪ Duffy's, (204) 925-0101 ▪ and Unicity, (204) 925-3131. Winnipeg rates start at $3.50 plus an average rate of $1.71 per kilometre or $2.02 per mile.

PUBLIC TRANSPORTATION: Winnipeg Transit, the public bus system, serves downtown Winnipeg and its suburbs. Route maps and route information are available by phoning 311 (within Winnipeg) or visiting the Winnipeg Transit website. Bus fare is $2.65, $2.10 (ages 6-16, ages 65+ and students with ID); riders must have exact change. More than 500 of the buses have accessibility features including low floors, electric ramps and priority accessible seating.

(Continued from p. 377.)

have been unearthed at the site located at the confluence of the Red and Assiniboine rivers. Still a meeting place, this site has modern amenities like shopping, dining and entertainment venues as well as a playground, garden, amphitheater and beautiful views. The Assiniboine Riverwalk, the Children's Museum and the Canadian Museum for Human Rights are three highlights.

The Golden Boy, sculpted by Georges Gardet of Paris, is a 5.25-metre-tall (17.2-ft.), 1,650-kilogram (3,638-lb.) statue sheathed in 24 karat gold leaf atop the Legislative Building dome. In many ways it symbolizes the past and the future of Winnipeg residents. The statue was diverted on its journey from a French foundry during World War I, while the vessel carrying it transported troops for 2 years. After crossing the Atlantic many times, the golden immigrant was finally placed where he stands today, one hand holding aloft the torch of progress, the other cradling a symbolic sheaf of wheat. High above the city, he strides toward the increasingly important natural resources of the north, his color echoing the golden hue of the rolling fields of grain that brought the city below population and prosperity.

Must Do: AAA Editor's Picks

- Roam 7 kilometres of mulch and limestone trails and make your way across floating wetland boardwalks at **FortWhyte Alive** (1961 McCreary Rd.), where you can spot all sorts of critters—from bison to songbirds to prairie dogs—in their natural habitat.

- Salute the province's beloved "Golden Boy" statue at the **Manitoba Legislative Building** (450 Broadway). The 5.25-metre-tall statue, gilded with 23.75-karat gold, stands atop the building's dome. A torch in one hand represents economic development and a sheaf of wheat in the other symbolizes agriculture. Take a guided Hermetic Code Tour to see if you can identify the hieroglyphic inscriptions and secret number codes hidden in the building's architecture.

- Contemplate sculptures made of caribou antlers and dozens of handmade Inuit stone carvings at the **Winnipeg Art Gallery** (300 Memorial Blvd.), a strikingly designed Modernist building housing one of the world's largest collections of contemporary Inuit art. Browse European and Canadian collections and then head up to the rooftop sculpture garden, where you'll find the upscale **Storm Bistro** and live jazz music on select summer nights.

- Try lifting a solid gold bar worth more than $600,000 at the interactive coin museum inside the 🐝 **Royal Canadian Mint** (520 Lagimodiere Blvd.), where as many as 20 million Canadian coins roll off the assembly line each day.

- Survey the city skyline and the spot where the Red and Assiniboine rivers meet from a six-story-high viewing platform atop **The Forks Market** (201-1 Forks Market Rd.) at 🐝 **The Forks,** one of the city's most popular gathering places. Wind your way through the eight-story-high 🐝 **Canadian Museum for Human Rights (CMHR)** (85 Israel Asper Way) via crisscrossing ramps with glowing walls that culminate in a glass spire offering panoramic views of downtown. Explore the area on a narrated boat ride with **Splash Dash Guided River Tours** (see Sightseeing p. 390).

- Hunt for eclectic treasures and cosmopolitan threads in the **Exchange District** (just north of Portage and Main), a historic neighborhood bursting with hip boutiques and eateries. For indoor shopping, you'll find more stores and restaurants off Main Street at **The Forks Market** and in **Johnston Terminal** (25 Forks Market Rd.).

- Chant "GO Jets GO" like a true Jets fan at the **MTS Centre** (300 Portage Ave.), where you can cheer on the Peg City's home team during a fast-paced hockey game. Just don't forget to wear your blue and white.

- Stroll on winding paths around flower beds in the English Gardens at **Assiniboine Park** (2355 Corydon Ave.), then explore the **Leo Mol Sculpture Garden**, where bronze statues and a year-round water feature are highlights. If wildlife viewing is more your style, visit **Assiniboine Park Zoo** for a peek at lions, tigers and bison. Snap a selfie with the statue of Winnie the Bear and his owner located by the Nature Playground; the lovable black bear cub was the inspiration for A.A. Milne's character Winnie the Pooh. The 10-acre Arctic species exhibit, Journey to Churchill, includes polar bears, musk ox, wolves, ringed seals and harbor seals.

- Pack a picnic basket and head to **Kildonan Park** (2015 Main St.) for a stroll along the Red River on a tree-shaded path. Catch a Broadway-caliber musical on summer nights at the park's outdoor theater, Rainbow Stage, and don't miss the Witch's Hut (think "Hansel and Gretel") at the park's northern end.

- Cross the Esplanade Riel footbridge and step into **St. Boniface,** the French-speaking district where some of Winnipeg's oldest buildings lie. Visit **Le Musée de Saint-Boniface Museum** (494 Taché Ave.) for a history lesson on Louis Riel and other early Red River settlers and stop by Riel's gravesite marked by a red granite tombstone in the nearby **St. Boniface Basilica** (190 Cathedrale Ave.) churchyard.

Royal Canadian Mint

Winnipeg 1-day Itinerary

AAA editors suggest these activities for a great short vacation experience.

Morning

- Kick off your tour of the Peg City with an early start at **Stella's Café** (166 Osborne St.) just across the Assiniboine River in Osborne Village. This casual-yet-trendy eatery serves up yummy homemade breakfast foods all day, with options like heart-shaped waffles, baked eggs and fluffy banana pancakes topped with wild blueberries. Put in a to-go order for grilled cinnamon buns.

- After breakfast, a walking tour of vibrant and artsy **Osborne Village** is a must. Hunt for chic shoes, vintage threads or secondhand records in the dozens of boutiques along Osborne Street. The Village is a charming mix of old and new, with modern high-rises standing alongside turn-of-the-20th-century stone buildings.

- One of the best ways to get acquainted with Winnipeg is by boat aboard **Splash Dash Guided River Tours.** Relax as your guide shares entertaining stories about city history on a 30-minute sightseeing cruise of the Red and Assiniboine rivers. Tours depart every 15 minutes from the dock at The Forks, but a water taxi can pick you up from any of seven city docks, including one at Osborne Street Bridge at the north end of Osborne Village.

Esplanade Riel footbridge from St. Boniface

Afternoon

- A great place to disembark is ⌖ **The Forks,** the popular outdoor gathering spot where the Red and Assiniboine rivers meet. Wander the grounds and make your way to **The Forks Market** (201-1 Forks Market Rd.) and **Johnston Terminal** (25 Forks Market Rd.) where you'll find souvenir shops, candy stores, an antique mall and a fresh food market housed in renovated buildings from the railway era. For a casual sit-down lunch, **the Beachcomber** (162-1 Forks Market Rd.) and **Muddy Waters Smokehouse** (15 Forks Market Rd.) are sure bets.

- Follow the river walk north along the Red River to the Provencher Bridge. Look for the strikingly designed Esplanade Riel footbridge and cross the river to **St. Boniface,** Winnipeg's historic French district. At Tache and Cathedral avenues next to St. Boniface Cathedral is the grave of Louis Riel, the Métis leader celebrated as Manitoba's founder. Constructed in 1908 and severely damaged by fire in 1968, the beautiful stone façade of the cathedral is a magnificent photo spot. A stop at **Le Musée de Saint-Boniface Museum** (494 Taché Ave.) can provide a good overview of local history.

- Back in downtown Winnipeg, spend the rest of the afternoon at ⌖ **The Manitoba Museum** (190 Rupert Ave.). Climb aboard a full-size replica of the "Nonsuch," the British ship whose 1668 voyage to Hudson Bay opened western Canada to commerce. In the Urban Gallery, walk the streets of Winnipeg circa the 1920s in a recreated streetscape, complete with wooden boardwalks and boomtown-era storefronts.

Evening

- Treat yourself to a fancy meal at a fine dining restaurant. **Hy's Steakhouse** (1 Lombard Pl.) serves up perfectly prepared steaks in an upscale atmosphere. **Sydney's At The Forks** (215 One Forks Market Rd.) offers lovely views of the rivers as well as a seasonal patio. The creative, five-course menu inspired by Asian, French and Italian cuisines, changes monthly.

- Looking for the nightlife hotspots? When the sun goes down, the place to be is Winnipeg's **Exchange District** (just north of Portage and Main). The 20-block historic area gets its name from the Winnipeg Grain & Produce Exchange that formed here in the late 1800s. Today the district is chock-full of shops, bars and live music venues known to attract a high-energy nighttime crowd. Find a bench in **Old Market Square** (Bannatyne Avenue and King Street) for prime people-watching or, if you're lucky, watch an outdoor performance on the cube stage during summer months.

- If indoor performances are more your style, take in an evening show at the **Royal Manitoba Theatre Centre (MTC) Mainstage** (174 Market Ave.). The theater presents classics, comedies and modern dramas October through May. Or, reserve seats at **Centennial Concert Hall** (555 Main St.) for a jaw-dropping performance by the **Canada's Royal Winnipeg Ballet.** For schedule information and tickets, phone (204) 942-6537 for the MTC Mainstage or (204) 956-2792 for the Royal Winnipeg Ballet.

Arriving

By Car

Forming a circle around Winnipeg is a perimeter highway. To the north of the Trans-Canada Highway, the major approach from the east and west, this perimeter road is designated Hwy. 101. To the south of the Trans-Canada Highway it is numbered Hwy. 100.

There are three major approaches to the perimeter highway: the Trans-Canada Highway, which approaches from both the east and west, and Hwy. 75, which approaches from the south. To the west of the city the Trans-Canada Highway is posted Hwy. 1W; from the east, Hwy. 1E.

Within the perimeter highway all three major approaches change designation: Hwy. 1W becomes Metro Rte. 85, Hwy. 1E becomes Metro Rte. 135, and Hwy. 75 becomes Metro Rte. 42.

Getting Around

Generally, rush hour in Winnipeg is from 7:30 to 9 a.m. and 3:30 to 5:30 p.m. As in most cities, stress can be alleviated if driving during rush hour is avoided. If driving during these times, be careful and be patient; the city's speed limit is 50 kilometres per hour (30 mph) unless otherwise posted.

Note the pedestrian crosswalks marked by pavement stripes and illuminated overhead signs. All vehicles must stop if the crosswalk is occupied by a pedestrian or if a pedestrian on the curb indicates an intention to cross. No vehicle may pass another that is stopped or slowing to yield to a pedestrian. Right turns on red are permitted after a stop, unless otherwise posted.

Street System

Winnipeg's streets are laid out in a number of grids, but each is oriented to a different compass direction. Visitors will find it easiest to orient themselves to the major thoroughfares, which have signs carrying the word "Route" and a number. Routes ending in even numbers designate north-south thoroughfares, and those ending in odd numbers designate major east-west arteries.

The primary north-south routes that cross the downtown area are 42, 52 and 62. The major east-west highways include 105, 115, 57 and 85. A good street map will enable drivers to see how the various grids of named streets connect with the main numbered routes.

Parking

Visitors will do best to park in a commercial lot, where rates average $1-$3 per hour. Daily rates are about $10. Parking meters downtown cost $1-$2 per hour, but most carry a 2-hour limit. Free 2-hour parking in designated metered areas downtown is offered on Saturday while parking is free all day on Sunday.

Parking is strictly controlled along major downtown streets. Cars parked between signs reading "No Parking Between" from 7 to 9 a.m. and 3:30 to 5:30 p.m. will be towed. Re-metering is not allowed. Once a vehicle has been parked at a meter for the maximum time for which a fee can be paid, it must be moved through an intersection before parking at a different meter.

Shopping

The intersection of **Portage Avenue and Main Street** is a good starting point for a shopping excursion. Just one block north of the intersection is the **Exchange District**, a vibrant and historic area filled with more than 40 restaurants and 80 stores including clothing boutiques, vintage shops and toy stores. **Portage Place** connects the Hudson's Bay store to other department stores with an extensive system of skywalks.

Winnipeg has a historic area where shoppers can browse through merchandise of today amid structures of the past. **The Forks Market** *(see attraction listing p. 387)* is behind Union Station, off Main Street (near Portage and Main). The shops and restaurants are located in an indoor market with more than 80 vendors selling everything from fresh fish and baked goods to arts and crafts items. **Johnston Terminal**, across from the market, offers specialty boutiques and eateries.

Shopping for Western wear and accessories is possible at such factory outlet stores as **Canada West Boots**, 1250 Fife St., or **MWG Factory Outlet**, 1147 Notre Dame Ave.

More than 70 shops and restaurants can be found at **Osborne Village**, between River and Wardlaw avenues 2 blocks south of the Manitoba Legislative Building.

Travelers in search of a truly representative souvenir may want to examine the native arts and crafts

The Forks Market

Musical instruments at Folklorama

and western wear available at **Winnipeg Outfitters Inc.** at 250 McPhillips St.

Visitors who like their shopping climate-controlled and under one roof can visit the malls at **cityplace**, 333 St. Mary Ave. at Hargrave Street; **Garden City**, 2305 McPhillips St., with Sears and Winners as its anchor stores; **Grant Park**, 1120 Grant Ave., with McNally Robinson Booksellers and Canadian Tire; **Kildonan Place**, 1555 Regent Ave. W., with Sears and Mountain Warehouse; **Polo Park**, 1485 Portage Ave., which has Hudson's Bay and Sears for anchors; **Portage Place**, 393 Portage Ave.; or **St. Vital Centre**, 1225 St. Mary's Rd., with Hudson's Bay and Sears as its anchor stores.

On Saturdays from 8 to 3 mid-May through October and Wednesdays from 11 to 3 mid-May through September, the **St. Norbert Farmers' Market**, 16 kilometres (10 mi.) south of downtown at 3514 Pembina Hwy., offers baked goods, fresh produce, flowers, furniture, jewelry and other locally made items from more than 70 vendors. It also hosts a bi-weekly indoor market on Saturdays from 10-1, November to Victoria Day.

Big Events

Winnipeg's calendar of events, with more than 170 days of festivals, reflects more than 43 nationalities that have made the city home. The *joie de vivre* spirit of the French voyageurs is revived each February during **Festival du Voyageur,** a 10-day-long celebration including winter sports, ice-sculpting contests, music and food. With the 18th-century fur trade as its theme, the event takes place in St. Boniface, Winnipeg's French quarter.

In early April, crowds yuk it up at the **Winnipeg Comedy Festival** featuring humor-industry headliners. In May, **Manito Ahbee** celebrates Aboriginal music, art and culture. The name, which means "where the creator sits," honors a sacred site in Whiteshell Provincial Park where Aboriginal people gathered for hundreds of years to teach and share wisdom. Events include music awards, an indigenous market and an international powwow.

Fly the rainbow flag at the **Pride Winnipeg Festival** in late May through early June. A week of sports tournaments, dance parties, coffeehouse performances and other events lead up to the annual Pride Parade through the streets of downtown. The city plays host to the 4-day **Winnipeg International Children's Festival** at **The Forks** in early June. Music, theater, dance and comedy performances are offered as well as hands-on workshops and evening shows.

The **TD Winnipeg International Jazz Festival** in mid-June features jazz performers on an outdoor stage in Old Market Square as well as at other indoor venues across the city. The **Red River Exhibition**, known locally as "The Ex" is held during mid- and late June. The Ex's many rides, midway activities and games of chance as well as nightly concerts take place at **Red River Exhibition Park** off Perimeter Highway behind Assiniboia Downs. The event also includes a petting zoo and agricultural displays.

Early July brings the 4-day **Winnipeg Folk Festival** to nearby **Birds Hill Provincial Park,** where more than 200 concerts, children's activities, music workshops and food are highlights. In mid- and late July is the **Winnipeg Fringe Festival,** with various independent theater performances in the Exchange District and other locations throughout the city.

Early August brings the 2-week **Folklorama** multicultural celebration, Winnipeg's largest event and reputedly the largest and longest-running multicultural festival of its kind. The costumes, dances and food of more than 40 cultures are showcased.

Celebrate the holidays from early December through early January in Red River Exhibition Park at **Winter Wonderland**, one of Manitoba's largest drive-through light displays. Illuminated by more than 1 million lights, the 2.25-kilometre route features 26 theme areas and a 75-foot-tall Christmas tree. Ice-skating and sleigh rides are offered on the weekends.

Sports & Rec

Devotees of organized sports will find many opportunities to indulge themselves in Winnipeg. Canadians love **hockey**, and those who fancy flying sticks and flashing skates will find the National Hockey League's **Winnipeg Jets** facing off against their opponents downtown at the **MTS Iceplex** on Race Track Road at the Portage Avenue site, just off Perimeter Highway. Also at this venue, after a few years' absence, the **Manitoba Moose** have returned to Winnipeg and play in the American Hockey League; phone (204) 987-7825.

Football fans can watch the Canadian Football League's **Winnipeg Blue Bombers** play at **Investors Group Field** at the University of Manitoba from June to November; phone (204) 784-2583 for office. The American Association of Independent Professional **Baseball**'s **Winnipeg Goldeyes** play at **Shaw Park** at The Forks from May to late August; phone (204) 982-2273 for tickets.

Sports car racing enthusiasts converge at the **Red River Co-op Speedway**, (204) 582-0527, on Cartier Road, Ste. Adolphe, off Hwy. 75, 8 kilometres (5 mi.) south of St. Norbert, from May through October (weather permitting).

Assiniboia Downs, 3975 Portage Ave. at the Perimeter Highway, offers **Thoroughbred racing** early May to late September. Simulcast races are offered year-round; phone (204) 885-3330.

Note: Policies concerning admittance of children to pari-mutuel betting facilities vary. Phone for information.

Other spectator sports include minor league hockey, **curling** and **ringette** games, held at municipal skating rinks, and **cricket** played in Assiniboine Park. Ringette, similar to hockey, is a popular women's sport developed in Canada.

There are 27 **golf** courses in the Winnipeg area. Nine-hole public courses include **Crescent Drive**, 781 Crescent Dr., (204) 986-5911; **Harbour View**, 1867 Springfield Rd., (204) 222-2751; **The Players Course**, 2695 Inkster Blvd., (204) 697-4976; and **Winnipeg Canoe Club**, 50 Dunkirk Dr., (204) 233-1105. Among the 18-hole public courses are **Kildonan Park**, 2021 Main St., (204) 986-5679; **Tuxedo**, 400 Shaftesbury Blvd., (204) 888-2867; **Meadows at East St. Paul**, 2511 McGregor Farm Rd. N. (adjacent to Hwy. 59), (204) 667-4653; **Shooters Family Golf Centre**, 2731 Main St., (204) 339-2326; and **Windsor Park**, 10 Des Meurons St., (204) 986-3006. **John Blumberg**, 4540 Portage Ave., (204) 986-3490, offers both nine- and 18-hole layouts.

Winnipeg has 115 **tennis** courts, some lighted for night matches. Many courts are at community centers. Championship matches are held during the summer at various locations throughout the city. **Squash**, **handball** and **racquetball** players can avail themselves of courts at a number of athletic clubs and local universities. For information contact Sport Manitoba; phone (204) 925-5600.

Fans of **bicycling** and **in-line skating** take to the marked paths in Winnipeg's city parks. Bicycle trails along less-traveled side streets in and around Winnipeg also have been established. **Cross-country skiing**, **tobogganing** and **ice-skating** facilities are available at Assiniboine, Kildonan and St. Vital parks; facilities for ice-skating also are found at numerous schools and community clubs.

Downhill skiing is available at **Springhill Winter Park Ski Area**, (204) 224-3051, near **Birds Hill Provincial Park** at the junction of Hwy. 59N at the Floodway; and **Stony Mountain Ski Area**, (204) 344-5977, 11 kilometres (6 mi.) north of the Perimeter Highway on Hwy. 7. Birds Hill Provincial Park, (204) 654-6730, also is a site for **snowmobiling** and cross-country skiing.

Swimming can be pursued all year in Winnipeg, where numerous indoor pools include those at four YM-YWCAs; phone (204) 947-3044. The **Pan Am Pool**, 25 Poseidon Bay, is one of the largest indoor bodies of water in Canada and is open all year; phone (877) 311-4974.

Many recreational activities are available at the **Harbour View Recreation Complex** in the northeastern section of Winnipeg in **Kilcona Park**, 1867 Springfield Rd. At this 162-hectare (400-acre) park are facilities for **miniature golf**, **lawn bowling**, **shuffleboard** and **horseshoes** as well as tennis courts, a 27-hole golf course and a driving range during the summer. Golf and tennis lessons are available April to October. Ice-skating, tobogganing and cross-country skiing are available during the winter. Phone (204) 222-2751.

Performing Arts

Canada's **Royal Winnipeg Ballet**, Winnipeg Symphony Orchestra and Manitoba Opera perform in Centennial Concert Hall, 555 Main St., opposite City Hall. The oldest company in Canada and the second oldest in North America, Canada's Royal Winnipeg Ballet is known for its versatile style and performs an eclectic mix of classical and contemporary ballets. At-home performances are from October through May. For ticket information phone (204) 956-2792.

Curling at The Forks

Assiniboine Park Conservatory

The **Winnipeg Symphony Orchestra** performs mid-September to May and offers classical, contemporary and popular orchestral music; for concert information phone (204) 949-3999. The **Manitoba Opera** performs October through May; phone (204) 942-7479, or (204) 944-8824 for tickets.

Modern dance is presented by **Winnipeg's Contemporary Dancers** from October through April at the **Rachel Browne Theatre**, 211 Bannatyne Ave.; for information phone (204) 452-0229.

Theater lovers can enjoy performances of the classics, comedies and modern dramas at the **Royal Manitoba Theatre Centre (Royal MTC) John Hirsch Mainstage**, 174 Market St., from October to May; for general information or tickets phone (204) 942-6537. The **Royal MTC Tom Hendry Warehouse Theatre**, 140 Rupert Ave., (204) 942-6537, features alternative theater performances from November to April. **The Lyric Theatre**, 55 Pavilion Crescent, just east of the Pavilion in Assiniboine Park, (204) 927-6000, is an outdoor theater showcasing performances by the Winnipeg Pops Orchestra, the Winnipeg Symphony Orchestra and other musical groups.

For both adults and young people, the **Prairie Theatre Exchange**, at Portage Place, 393 Portage Ave., (204) 942-5483 for ticket information, presents a season of modern Canadian plays from October to April. **Rainbow Stage** in Kildonan Park offers musicals in a covered outdoor theater from June through August; phone (204) 989-0888 or (888) 989-0888. **Celebrations Dinner Theatre**, 1824 Pembina Hwy. in the Canad Inns Destination Centre Fort Garry, combines an original, three-act musical comedy with a four-course dinner for a one-stop evening out; phone (204) 982-8282.

A variety of theatrical productions for children of all ages is presented at The Forks by the **Manitoba Theatre for Young People**; for information phone (204) 942-8898.

The **Burton Cummings Theatre for the Performing Arts** (The Burt), 364 Smith St., was constructed in 1906-07. Originally named Walker Theatre, it was designed to host ballets, Broadway shows and operas. The Burt now offers touring shows and concerts by top-name performers; phone (204) 987-7825.

The French Canadian heritage of St. Boniface, in the heart of the French district, is remembered through the support of the **Centre Culturel Franco-Manitobain** at 340 Provencher Blvd.; phone (204) 233-8972. The center is the home of such cultural groups as **Le Cercle Molière** theater company (North America's longest running theater company), phone (204) 233-8053; the dance group **L'Ensemble Folklorique de la Rivière Rouge**, phone (204) 233-7440; and the choral groups **L'Alliance Chorale Manitoba** and **La Chorale des Intrépides**; phone (204) 233-7423 for more information.

ATTRACTIONS

ASSINIBOINE PARK is at jct. Park Blvd. and Corydon Ave.; it also may be accessed from Portage Ave. via a footbridge over the Assiniboine River. The 153-hectare (378-acre) park has the Citizens Hall of Fame, a conservatory, a duck pond, gardens, a miniature railway, the Pavilion Gallery Museum (currently closed for renovations), the Qualico Family Centre, a sculpture garden, an outdoor theater where concerts are held in summer and a zoo. Baseball diamonds, a nature playground, soccer fields, and walking and biking paths provide recreational opportunities; tobogganing, cross-country skiing and ice-skating are available in the winter. Winnipeg's only cricket tournaments are played in the park.

Assiniboine Forest, south of the park off Grant Avenue, is one of the largest urban nature parks in Canada. The 283-hectare (700-acre) forest of aspen and oak is home to more than 39 species of mammals, including deer and foxes, and more than 80 species of birds. The 1-kilometre (.6-mi.) Saginay Trail leads hikers to Eve Werier Pond, where a variety of waterfowl can be seen. **Hours:** The park is open daily 24 hours. Nature Playground daily 8-dusk. **Cost:** Free. **Phone:** (204) 927-6000 or (877) 927-6006. 🍽 ✂ ⛲

Assiniboine Park Conservatory, in Assiniboine Park, features indoor gardens and changing floral and plant displays. A tropical palm house contains orchids, ferns and banana plants. **Hours:** Daily 9-5, Easter-Thanksgiving; 9-4, rest of year. **Cost:** Donations. **Phone:** (204) 927-6000 or (877) 927-6006. 🍽

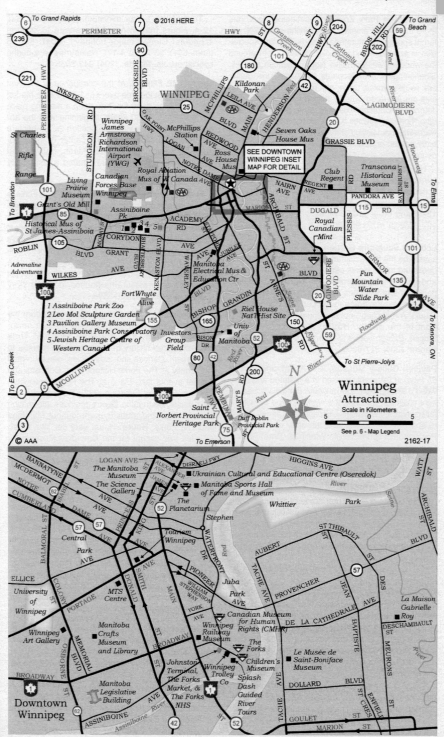

© 2016 HERE

To Grand Rapids

To Grand Beach

PERIMETER   HWY

WINNIPEG

LAGIMODIERE BLVD

St Charles
Rifle
Range

To Brandon

Winnipeg James Armstrong Richardson International Airport (YWG)

Kildonan Park

Seven Oaks House Mus

SEE DOWNTOWN WINNIPEG INSET MAP FOR DETAIL

To Elma

Living Prairie Museum

Grant's Old Mill

Canadian Forces Base Winnipeg

Royal Aviation Mus of W Canada

McPhillips Station

Ross House Mus

Club Regent

Transcona Historical Museum

PANDORA AVE

To Kenora, ON

Historical Mus of St James-Assiniboia

Assiniboine Pk

DUGALD

Royal Canadian Mint

ROBLIN   BLVD   GRANT   AVE

Adrenaline Adventures

WILKES

Manitoba Electrical Mus & Education Ctr

Fun Mountain Water Slide Park

To St Pierre-Jolys

FortWhyte Alive

1 Assiniboine Park Zoo
2 Leo Mol Sculpture Garden
3 Pavilion Gallery Museum
4 Assiniboine Park Conservatory
5 Jewish Heritage Centre of Western Canada

Investors Group Field

Riel House Nat'l Hist Site

Univ of Manitoba

To Elm Creek

MCGILLIVRAY

Saint Norbert Provincial Heritage Park

Duff Roblin Provincial Park

To Emerson

Winnipeg Attractions

Scale in Kilometers

See p. 6 - Map Legend

© AAA

2162-17

Downtown Winnipeg

LOGAN AVE
The Manitoba Museum
The Science Gallery

Ukrainian Cultural and Educational Centre (Oseredok)

Manitoba Sports Hall of Fame and Museum

The Planetarium

Stephen

Whittier Park

Central Park

Tourism Winnipeg

University of Winnipeg

Winnipeg Art Gallery

MTS Centre

Manitoba Crafts Museum and Library

Juba Park

Canadian Museum for Human Rights (CMHR)

Winnipeg Railway Museum

La Maison Gabrielle Roy

Johnston Terminal, The Forks Market, & The Forks NHS

Winnipeg Trolley Co

The Children's Museum

Le Musée de Saint-Boniface Museum

Manitoba Legislative Building

Splash Dash Guided River Tours

Assiniboine Park Zoo, in Assiniboine Park, has more than 1,500 animals representing some 200 different species in naturalistic settings. The zoo specializes in animals found in cooler climates from around the world as well as native North American species. Siberian tigers, snow leopards, two Asian lions, Stellar sea eagles, lynxes, bison, and many other hardy species can be seen outside throughout the year. The Journey to Churchill exhibit features polar bears and other northern species. Large indoor facilities provide warm-weather viewing of many tropical animals. A butterfly garden is open in the summer months. A 360-degree theater also is on site.

Hours: Daily 9-5, Easter weekend-Thanksgiving weekend; 9-4, rest of year. Phone ahead for schedule on Nov. 11, Christmas Eve and Dec. 31. Closed Christmas. **Cost:** $19.75; $17.50 (ages 13-17 and 60+); $10.50 (ages 3-12). **Phone:** (204) 927-6000 or (877) 927-6006. 🍴 🎢

Leo Mol Sculpture Garden, in Assiniboine Park, is said to be the first sculpture garden in North America dedicated to the works of a single artist. The garden and gallery feature bronze sculptures, porcelains, paintings and sketches by the Winnipeg artist. The gardens also are home to the Leo Mol Schoolhouse Studio. A reflecting pool and fountain are located in front of the gallery. **Hours:** Grounds open daily 9-dusk, Easter weekend-Oct. 31. **Cost:** Donations. **Phone:** (204) 927-6000.

Pavilion Gallery Museum is in Assiniboine Park at 55 Pavilion Crescent. Housed in a restored and renovated 1929 pavilion, the museum contains a permanent collection featuring the work of three prominent artists: Ivan Eyre, Walter J. Phillips and Clarence Tillenius. The Pooh Gallery tells the story of Winnie the Pooh and his connection to Winnipeg. **Time:** Allow 1 hour minimum. **Hours:** Daily 9-5 (also Wed. 5-9), Easter-Thanksgiving; daily 10-5 (also Wed. 5-9), rest of year. **Cost:** Free. **Phone:** (204) 927-6000.

DALNAVERT MUSEUM, .5 blk. s. of Broadway at 61 Carlton St., is the former home of Sir Hugh John Macdonald, prominent lawyer and politician and son of John A. Macdonald, the first prime minister of Canada. Built in 1895, it was one of the first houses in Winnipeg to have hot-water heating, electric lighting and indoor plumbing.

Named after the Scottish birthplace of Macdonald's grandmother, the red brick Queen Anne Revival-style house features stained-glass windows and a wraparound verandah. The restored house, which was saved from demolition in 1969, is opulently furnished with Victorian antiques. Tours include a guided tour of the house and a self-guiding audio tour providing a glimpse into the lifestyles of early 20th-century Winnipeg society and the Macdonald family.

The visitor center at the rear of museum has been designed as a "green" building, incorporating reclaimed and recycled materials during its construction and utilizing geothermal energy to heat and cool the building.

Time: Allow 1 hour minimum. **Hours:** Wed.-Sat. 12-4. Hours may vary; phone ahead to confirm schedule. Closed major holidays. **Cost:** $6; $5 (ages 65+); $3 (ages 4-17). Rates may vary during special events. **Phone:** (204) 943-2835.

◤◢ **THE FORKS,** at the confluence of the Red and Assiniboine rivers at 1-201 Forks Market Rd. at jct. Waterfront Dr., has been a meeting place for more than 6,000 years, beginning with the aboriginal peoples. By virtue of location the 23-hectare (56-acre) site evolved into the center of the European fur trade in the 1730s. Métis, natives and eventually European settlers created a community along the rivers.

Now Winnipeg's main gathering spot, The Forks is a favorite place for shopping, dining and entertainment. Attractions include the Canadian Museum for Human Rights, The Forks Market, The Forks National Historic Site, The Plaza skateboarding park, Children's Museum and Variety Heritage Adventure Park for children. Johnston Terminal, 25 Forks Market Rd., is a renovated railway cold storage warehouse with shops, boutiques and restaurants housed in a four-story building; phone (204) 956-5593.

The Riverwalk follows the water's edge from the Manitoba Legislature to The Forks through downtown Winnipeg, and the Wall Through Time chronicles area history from glacial Lake Agassiz to the present. Canoes and "sea cycles" can be rented seasonally at The Forks Historic Port. Concerts and special events take place at The Forks throughout the year *(see Big Events p. 382)*. The Travel Manitoba Visitor Information Centre provides information about events and attractions throughout Manitoba and The Forks. **Hours:** Hours vary per site. **Cost:** All sites free except for the Canadian Museum for Human Rights and the Children's Museum. **Phone:** (204) 957-7618 for an events hotline, (204) 942-6302, or (888) 942-6302 for information.

◤◢ **Canadian Museum for Human Rights (CMHR)** is at The Forks, 85 Israel Asper Way. On a self-guiding audio tour you can leisurely stroll up the glowing ramps from floor to floor to view 12 galleries housing art, artifacts, film, photography and interactive digital exhibits that encourage visitors to discuss and take action to promote human rights. A highlight of the museum is a circular theater in which you can view a 360-degree film featuring four generations of indigenous people sharing stories about responsibilities and rights.

The eight-story building features four main parts: the Roots, the Mountain, the Cloud and the Tower of Hope. The journey of discovery begins at the Roots, where you will find temporary galleries and the entrance to the Great Hall. The Mountain galleries display the museum's core exhibits, and the three-story glass Cloud wraps around an interior Garden of Contemplation, a space with basalt rock and pools of water. The Cloud's wall, made up of 1,300 panes of glass, allows visitors to observe employees at work. The glass-spire Tower of Hope provides panoramic views of Winnipeg and surrounding areas. Guided and self-guiding tours are available. **Time:** Allow 2 hours minimum. **Hours:** Daily 10-5 (also Wed. 5-9), Victoria Day-Labour Day; Tues.-Sun. and Mon. holidays 10-5 (also Wed. 5-9), rest of year. Architectural and gallery tours are offered; phone for schedule. Closed Christmas and one week in mid-Jan. Phone ahead to confirm schedule. **Cost:** $17.14; $13.33 (ages 65+ and students with ID); $8.57 (ages 7-17); $47.62 (family, two adults and four children). **Phone:** (204) 289-2000 or (877) 877-6037. GT ¶↑

Children's Museum, at The Forks, 45 Forks Market Rd., occupies Manitoba's oldest train repair facility. The museum houses a dozen colorful galleries offering a wide variety of educational and fun hands-on activities. Junction 9161 and the Engine House galleries immerse visitors in train history with a 1910 Pullman passenger coach and a 1952 diesel locomotive. A walk through the Illusion Tunnel will test perceptions. Tot Spot caters to little ones. Other areas include Splash Lab, Pop m'Art, Story Line, Tumble Zone, Lasagna Lookout and Milk Machine.

During the holiday season (mid-November to mid-January), visitors can reminisce with a trip to Eaton's Fairytale Vignettes, the original holiday display from downtown's Eaton's department store. The setup features 15 scenes from various fairytales. Special events, public programs and workshops are offered throughout the year.

Time: Allow 1 hour minimum. **Hours:** Daily 9:30-6, July 1-Labour Day; Sun.-Thurs. and holidays 9:30-4:30, Fri.-Sat. 9:30-6, rest of year. Closed Tues.-Fri. following Labour Day, Christmas Eve and Christmas. **Cost:** $11. Children must be accompanied by an adult. **Phone:** (204) 924-4000. ⌂

The Forks Market, is at The Forks, 201-1 Forks Market Rd., jct. Israel Asper Way. Housed in refurbished stable buildings, the market contains shops that offer jewelry and crafts; fresh, specialty and ethnic foods; produce; and baked goods. A six-story glass tower affords a view of the rivers and the downtown area. **Hours:** Daily 7 a.m.-9 p.m. (also Thurs.-Fri. 9-11 p.m.). **Cost:** Free. **Phone:** (204) 957-7618 (events hotline), or (888) 942-6302 (information).

The Forks National Historic Site, at The Forks, 401-25 Forks Market Rd., is a 3.5-hectare (9-acre) park that offers an outdoor playground and a riverside amphitheater with a view of historic St. Boniface. Arctic Glacier Winter Park provides cold-weather fun with a snowboard fun park, a toboggan run and ice skating on trails and a rink. Interpretive programs and festivals are held Victoria Day through Labour Day. A variety of guided tours and theatrical presentations are available July through August. The Parks Canada Information desk is located in the Travel Manitoba Visitor Information Centre at The Forks. **Hours:** Daily 24 hours. Adventure Park daily 10-8, Victoria Day weekend-Thanksgiving weekend. Water Park daily 10-8, June-Labour Day. **Cost:** Free. **Phone:** (204) 983-6757.

FUN MOUNTAIN WATER SLIDE PARK, off Hwy. 1E on Murdock Rd., offers 10 waterslides, a swimming area, a hot tub, bumper boats, miniature golf, ziplining and locker and changing facilities. **Hours:** Wed.-Sun. 11-6 (also Wed. and Sun. 6-10 p.m. for ages 18+), Mon.-Tues. noon-6, mid-June to late Aug. (weather permitting). **Cost:** $20.95; $19.05 (under 48 inches tall). All-inclusive ticket (includes boat tour, bumper boats, miniature golf and unlimited sliding); $23.81 (all heights); All-inclusive Plus ticket (includes the all-inclusive features plus hot dog or burger) $28.57 (all heights); Fast Pass VIP (to bypass lines at slides; 200 per day available) $37.14 (all heights). Ziplining $14.29. **Phone:** (204) 255-3910. ¶↑

HISTORICAL MUSEUM OF ST. JAMES-ASSINIBOIA, 3180 Portage Ave., houses a collection of artifacts relating to the history of the St. James-Assiniboia area and a display building of pioneer activities. Guided interpretive tours through the mid-19th-century William Brown Red River Log House offer a glimpse of the pioneer lifestyle. **Time:** Allow 1 hour minimum. **Hours:** Daily 10-5, mid-May through Labour Day; Mon.-Fri. 10-5, rest of year. **Cost:** Donations. **Phone:** (204) 888-8706.

JEWISH HERITAGE CENTRE OF WESTERN CANADA, 123 Doncaster St., site of the Fort Osborne Barracks, shares the history, experiences, achievements and culture of Jewish people in Western Canada. The Corridor Museum exhibit depicts the settlement of Jews in Western Canada through artifacts, photographs and archival material. The Holocaust Education Centre features items from the

Canadian Museum for Human Rights (CMHR)

Manitoba Legislative Building

and free milkweed. **Time:** Allow 1 hour minimum. **Hours:** Trail open daily dawn-dusk. Interpretive center daily 10-5, July-Aug.; Sun. 10-5, May-June and Sept. to mid-Oct.; by appointment rest of year. **Cost:** Free. **Phone:** (204) 832-0167.

MANITOBA ELECTRICAL MUSEUM & EDUCATION CENTRE is 1 blk. w. of jct. Pembina Hwy. and Stafford St. at 680 Harrow St. The museum's six galleries tell the story of hydroelectric development in the province beginning in the 1870s. The lower-level discovery area features interactive electrical and natural gas safety exhibits and films, seasonal exhibits and a Van de Graaff static electricity generator.

Themed areas such as The Light Goes On 1882-1900, Energizing Manitoba 1900-1960 and Powering up the Farm 1942-1960 provide an idea of the museum's offerings. A yellow turbine runner from one of the oldest hydroelectric stations in Manitoba is outside the 1931 building. **Time:** Allow 1 hour minimum. **Hours:** Mon.-Thurs. 1-4, or by appointment. Closed major holidays. **Cost:** Free. **Phone:** (204) 360-7905. GT

MANITOBA LEGISLATIVE BUILDING, bordered by Broadway Ave., Kennedy and Osborne sts. and the Assiniboine River, reflects neoclassical design in native Tyndall limestone. The Italian marble grand staircase is guarded at its base by two life-size bronze bison, the emblems of Manitoba.

Atop the dome is Golden Boy by Parisian sculptor Georges Gardet. The torch, in the right hand, points to economic development and progress in the north; the sheaf of wheat in the left arm represents agriculture. This 5.25-metre-tall (17.2-ft.) statue weighs 1,650 kilograms (3,638 lbs.) and is sheathed in 24 karat gold leaf. The statue represents eternal youth and the province's spirit of enterprise. Plots on the site's 12 hectares (30 acres) contain flowers, foliage and ornamental plants.

Hours: Guided tours are conducted daily on the hour 9-4, July 1-Labour Day; by appointment rest of year. Self-guiding tours are available daily 8-8, year-round. **Cost:** Free. **Phone:** (204) 945-5813.

Holocaust and stories and artifacts from local survivors.

Time: Allow 30 minutes minimum. **Hours:** Mon.-Thurs. 9-4. Closed major Jewish holidays; phone ahead to confirm. **Cost:** Donations. **Phone:** (204) 477-7460 for tours or appointments.

LE MUSÉE DE SAINT-BONIFACE MUSEUM, s.e. on Main St. (Hwy. 1), then n. to 494 Taché Ave., was built 1846-51 as the first convent and hospital in western Canada. Displays depict the Red River Settlement and early French and Métis Manitoba; an exhibit is dedicated to Louis Riel, leader of the Red River Resistance. Visitors also can view the nearby ruins of the cathedral as well as the cemetery where Riel is buried.

Time: Allow 30 minutes minimum. **Hours:** Mon.-Fri. 10-4 (11-4 on Canada Day), Sat. noon-4. Additional hours may vary; phone ahead. Closed major holidays. **Cost:** $6.43; $5.24 (ages 60+ and students with ID); $4.29 (ages 6-17 and physically impaired); free (ages 0-5); $14.24 (family, two adults and all children). Reservations are required for tours. **Phone:** (204) 237-4500, ext. 400. GT

LIVING PRAIRIE MUSEUM is at 2795 Ness Ave. This 13-hectare (32-acre) unplowed tract supports more than 160 native plant species and is a remnant of the prairie that once covered much of North America. An interpretive center features displays of plants and animals of the tall grass prairie. Nature talks and guided hikes are offered, and a self-guiding trail brochure is available. The annual Butterfly Festival is held in mid-July and includes workshops, family-friendly crafts, a butterfly release

THE MANITOBA MUSEUM, 190 Rupert Ave. at jct. Main St., illustrates the relationship of people and their environment in Manitoba's history through nine permanent galleries and a Discovery Room that changes every six months. The recently upgraded Earth History Gallery shows geologic and organic evolution, the Arctic/Sub-Arctic Gallery explores Inuit culture and the zone's flora and fauna, and the Boreal Forest Gallery features a diorama of a granite cliff, waterfall, marsh, Cree family and a wandering moose. A bat cave, snake pit and a Ukrainian rye farm can be seen at the Parklands/Mixed Woods Gallery.

Visitors can see a replica of the ketch *Nonsuch;* the ship's 1668 voyage to Hudson Bay opened western Canada to commerce and European settlement. The Hudson's Bay Company Gallery highlights fur trading and early exploration. A teepee and a sod house are part of the Grasslands Gallery, and the Urban Gallery shows a 1920s boom-town Winnipeg.

The museum also houses a planetarium and science gallery. **Time:** Allow 1 hour minimum. **Hours:** Daily 10-5, Victoria Day-Labour Day; Tues.-Fri. 10-4, Sat.-Sun. and some holidays 11-5, rest of year (New Year's Day and day after Christmas 10-5, Remembrance Day 1-5, Christmas Eve 10-1). Closed Christmas. **Cost:** $10.48; $8.57 (ages 12-17, ages 60+ and students 18+ with ID); $7.14 (ages 3-11). Combination ticket with The Planetarium or The Science Gallery $18.10; $14.76 (ages 12-17, ages 60+ and students 18+ with ID); $12.38 (ages 3-11). Combination ticket with The Planetarium and The Science Gallery $24.76; $20 (ages 12-17, ages 60+ and students 18+ with ID); $16.67 (ages 3-11). **Phone:** (204) 956-2830 or (204) 943-3139.

The Planetarium, on the lower level of The Manitoba Museum at 190 Rupert Ave., presents interactive and multimedia shows about science and our universe. **Time:** Allow 1 hour minimum. **Hours:** Shows are presented six times per day. Show times vary; phone ahead to confirm schedule. **Note:** Latecomers cannot be admitted after the show has begun. **Cost:** $10.48; $8.57 (ages 12-17, ages 60+ and students 18+ with ID); $7.14 (ages 3-11). Combination ticket with The Manitoba Museum or The Science Gallery $18.10; $14.76 (ages 12-17, ages 60+ and students 18+ with ID); $12.38 (ages 3-11). Combination ticket with The Manitoba Museum and The Science Gallery $24.76; $20 (ages 12-17, ages 60+ and students 18+ with ID); $16.67 (ages 3-11). **Phone:** (204) 956-2830, or (204) 943-3139 for show times.

The Science Gallery, on the lower level of The Manitoba Museum at 190 Rupert Ave., has more than 100 hands-on exhibits. **Time:** Allow 1 hour minimum. **Hours:** Daily 10-5, June-Aug.; Tues.-Fri. 10-4, Sat.-Sun. and most holidays 11-5, rest of year (New Year's Day and day after Christmas 10-5, Remembrance Day 1-5, Christmas Eve 10-1). Closed Christmas. **Cost:** $10.48; $8.57 (ages 12-17, ages 60+ and students 18+ with ID); $7.14 (ages 3-11). Combination ticket with The Manitoba Museum or The Planetarium $18.10; $14.76 (ages 12-17, ages 60+ and students 18+ with ID); $12.38 (ages 3-11). Combination ticket with The Manitoba Museum and The Planetarium $24.76; $20 (ages 12-17, ages 60+ and students 18+ with ID); $16.67 (ages 3-11). **Phone:** (204) 956-2830 or (204) 943-3139.

RIEL HOUSE NATIONAL HISTORIC SITE, 330 River Rd., was the home of the mother of Louis Riel. Although this leader of the Métis and founder of the provisional government of Manitoba never lived in the house, his body lay in state for several days after his execution in 1885. Interpretive panels near the walkway to the house explain the history of the

Métis and of the Riel family. **Time:** Allow 30 minutes minimum. **Hours:** Fri.-Wed. 10-5, Thurs. 1-8, July-Aug. **Cost:** Entry and self-discovery program is free in 2017 to celebrate Canada's 150th anniversary of Confederation. Otherwise $3.71; $3.24 (ages 65+); $1.81 (ages 6-16); $9.33 (family, two adults and five children). **Phone:** (204) 983-6757.

SAVE **ROYAL AVIATION MUSEUM OF WESTERN CANADA,** in an aircraft hangar off Ellice Ave. at 958 Ferry Rd., displays numerous vintage aircraft. All aspects of aviation are exhibited, from bush planes to commercial airliners to military planes and homemade aircraft. Children can explore the interactive Skyways exhibit. A research library and archives can be seen by appointment.

Guided tours are available by appointment. **Time:** Allow 1 hour minimum. **Hours:** Mon.-Fri. 9:30-4:30, Sat. 10-5, Sun. and holidays noon-5. Closed Jan. 1, Good Friday, Easter, Christmas and day after Christmas. **Cost:** $7.14; $4.76 (students with ID and senior citizens); $2.86 (ages 3-12); $17.14 (family, two adults and three children). **Phone:** (204) 786-5503.

GEM **ROYAL CANADIAN MINT** is at 520 Lagimodière Blvd. at jct. Trans-Canada Hwy. and Hwy. 59. This high-tech, high-volume manufacturing facility is considered one of the world's most modern mints; its high-speed coining presses can each strike 750 coins per minute. The Winnipeg Plant produces all of the circulation coinage for Canada as well as coinage for more than 75 foreign countries.

The building includes a landscaped interior courtyard and a glass tower overlooking the manufacturing plant. At the mint's interactive museum visitors can lift a gold bar worth more than $600,000.

Hours: Daily 9-4. Phone ahead to confirm schedule. **Cost:** Museum free. Guided tour (Mon.-Fri.) $5.71; $4.76 (ages 65+); $2.86 (ages 5-17); $14.29 (family, two adults and up to four children). Guided tour (Sat.-Sun.) $4.29; $3.81 (ages 65+); $2.14 (ages 5-17); $10.71 (family, two adults and up to four children). Reservations are recommended. **Phone:** (204) 983-6429 or (877) 974-6468. GT

TRANSCONA HISTORICAL MUSEUM is at 141 Regent Ave. W. In a 1925 bank building, the museum explores the origins of Transcona, a railroad town amalgamated into Winnipeg, and the accomplishments of its residents. Exhibits rotate yearly, showcasing the museum's collection and the history and community spirit of Transcona.

Time: Allow 30 minutes minimum. **Hours:** Daily 9-4 (also Wed.-Sat. 4-7), June-Aug.; Tues.-Sat. 9-4, rest of year. Closed holiday weekends. Hours may vary; phone ahead. **Cost:** Donations. **Phone:** (204) 222-0423.

WINNIPEG ART GALLERY is at 300 Memorial Blvd. Nine galleries contain contemporary and historical works by Manitoba, Canadian and international artists, from the gallery's collection of almost

24,000 works of art. The Inuit art collection is reputed to be the largest public collection of contemporary Inuit art in the world; a small portion of the collection is always on display. Guided tours are offered; phone for scheduled tours and talks.

Time: Allow 1 hour minimum. **Hours:** Tues.-Sun. 11-5 (also Fri. 5-9 or 5-11 on first Fri. of the month). Closed Good Friday, Easter Monday, Thanksgiving and Christmas. **Cost:** $11.43; $7.62 (ages 60+ and students with ID); free (ages 0-5 and for all from 5 p.m. on first Fri. of every month); $26.67 (family, two adults and up to four children). **Phone:** (204) 786-6641 or (204) 789-1760. 🍴

WINNIPEG RAILWAY MUSEUM is at 123 Main St. inside the historic VIA Rail Union Station, on tracks 1 and 2, making it one of only a few North American railroad museums in an active railway station. Highlights on the two sections of 750-foot-long tracks include steam, electric and diesel locomotives, baggage cars, boxcars and cabooses. A 1920 Ford Model T truck and two antique fire trucks also can be seen. Museum exhibits feature a model train display as well as historic items and photos related to the city of Winnipeg, the Canadian National and Canadian Pacific railways and women's roles in railway history.

Time: Allow 45 minutes minimum. **Hours:** Daily 11-4 (also Mon., Thurs. and Sat. 9-11), Apr.-Oct.; Mon. and Thurs. 9-1, Sat.-Sun. 11-4, rest of year. Phone ahead to confirm schedule and for additional hours Dec.-Feb. **Cost:** $4.76; $2.86 (ages 6-15); free (ages 0-5). **Phone:** (204) 942-4632.

Sightseeing

The intersection of Portage Avenue and Main Street, a few blocks from the juncture of Winnipeg's two rivers, has been the major crossroads since the city's earliest days and is a good place to start a sightseeing foray.

Although now part of Winnipeg, the early settlement of St. Boniface has retained its French Canadian identity. A monument honoring the explorer Pierre Gaultier de la Vérendrye is on Taché Avenue opposite St. Boniface Hospital. Also in St. Boniface is the grave of Louis Riel, leader of the Métis and of the provisional government 1869-70. The grave is at Taché and Cathedral avenues in the churchyard of the St. Boniface Basilica.

Boat Tours

SPLASH DASH GUIDED RIVER TOURS departs from the bottom of the river walk at The Forks. The boats provide 30-minute guided historical tours of a section of the Red and Assiniboine rivers. Points of interest are noted along the way. **Time:** Allow 30 minutes minimum. **Hours:** Departures daily every 15 minutes 10 a.m.-sunset, May 15-Aug. 31; noon-sunset, Sept. 1-Oct. 15 (weather permitting). **Cost:** $10.48; $8.57 (ages 4-18 and 55+). **Phone:** (204) 783-6633.

Bus and Trolley Tours

WINNIPEG TROLLEY COMPANY departs from The Forks Market, 1 Forks Market Rd. Guides aboard the orange and cream trolleys share stories including why the River City was once called the wickedest city in Canada, the local hockey team that became the first world Olympic champions and Winnipeg's connection to the famous spy, James Bond.

More than 85 sites along the Heart of a Nation City Tour include the Exchange District National Historic Site where you'll learn about corruption and heroes and see the largest intact collection of turn-of-the-century commercial architecture in North America; The Forks, a gathering place for more than 6,000 years and a great place for shopping, dining and entertainment; and St. Boniface, Winnipeg's historic French district and the final resting place of Louis Riel, the Métis leader and founder of Manitoba.

Time: Allow 1 hour, 30 minutes minimum. **Hours:** Tours depart Tues. and Fri. at 10:30, Wed. and Thurs. at 10:30 and 1, Sat. and Sun. at 1, June 1-Sept. 5. **Cost:** $26.25; $24 (students with ID); $14 (ages 5-12). Reservations are recommended. **Phone:** (204) 226-8687.

Train Tours

Antique rail cars pulled by a vintage locomotive take passengers on 3-hour trips departing from a 1910 station at Inkster Junction, 3 kilometres (1.9 mi.) west of Hwy. 90 off Inkster Boulevard. The Prairie Dog Central Railway makes a stop at a country market in Grosse Isle. The scenic ride operates weekends and holidays, May through September; phone (204) 832-5259.

Walking Tours

Take a self-guiding tour of the city's urban areas that begins and ends at The Forks Market. A guide with maps that highlights more than 50 cultural, historical and modern places of interest along the Downtown Winnipeg Loop and Old St. Boniface Loop is available at visitor centers at ✈ The Forks, Tourisme Riel (219 Provencher Blvd.), Tourism Winnipeg (259 Portage Ave.), Downtown Winnipeg BIZ (426 Portage Ave.) and The Exchange District BIZ (2, Old Market Square, 133 Albert St.). Other themed tours also are available; phone (204) 958-4640.

Guided walking tours of the 20-block Historic Winnipeg area near Portage Avenue and Main Street in the Exchange District are available June through Labour Day weekend. Departing from Old Market Square at the corner of King St. and Bannatyne Ave., these tours visit many of Manitoba's finest historical buildings; for schedule information phone (204) 942-6716.

Guided walking tours of the old St. Boniface area are available Victoria Day through Labour Day or on request; phone (204) 233-8343 or (866) 808-8338 for information and reservations.

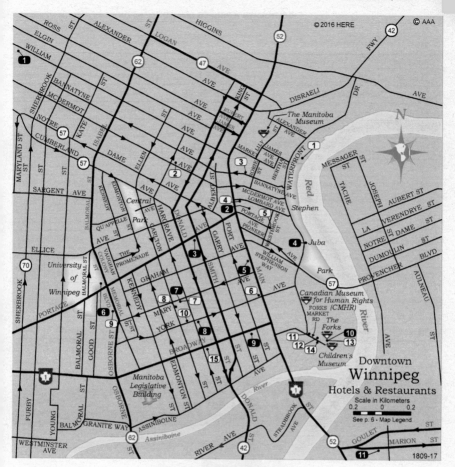

© 2016 HERE   © AAA

Downtown Winnipeg
Hotels & Restaurants
Scale in Kilometers
0.2   0   0.2
See p. 6 · Map Legend

1809-17

Downtown Winnipeg

This index helps you "spot" where approved hotels and restaurants are located on the corresponding detailed maps. Hotel daily rate range is for comparison only. Restaurant price range is a combination of lunch and/or dinner. Turn to the listing page for more information and consult display ads for special promotions.

DOWNTOWN WINNIPEG

Map Page	Hotels	Diamond Rated	Rate Range	Page
1 this page	**Canad Inns Destination Centre Health Sciences Centre**	◆◆◆	$129-$329 SAVE	395
2 this page	**The Fairmont Winnipeg**	◆◆◆	$129-$309 SAVE	395
3 this page	**Radisson Hotel Winnipeg Downtown**	◆◆◆	$160-$265 SAVE	396
4 this page	Mere Hotel	◆◆◆	Rates not provided	396
5 this page	Humphry Inn & Suites	◆◆	$109-$259	396
6 this page	**Holiday Inn & Suites Winnipeg Downtown**	◆◆◆	$109-$399 SAVE	396
7 this page	Delta Winnipeg	◆◆◆	$120-$239	395
8 this page	**Best Western Plus Charter House Hotel Downtown Winnipeg**	◆◆	$129-$159 SAVE	395
9 this page	The Fort Garry Hotel, Spa & Conference Centre	◆◆◆	Rates not provided	396
10 this page	**Inn at the Forks**	◆◆◆	$190-$397 SAVE	396

DOWNTOWN WINNIPEG (cont'd)

Map Page	Hotels (cont'd)	Diamond Rated	Rate Range	Page
11 p. 391	Norwood Hotel	◆◆	$129-$199	396

Map Page	Restaurants	Diamond Rated	Cuisine	Price Range	Page
1 p. 391	Cibo Waterfront Cafe	◆◆	Mediterranean	$15-$35	396
2 p. 391	deer + almond	◆◆◆	New World	$12-$32	396
3 p. 391	Hermanos Restaurant & Wine Bar	◆◆◆	Latin American	$9-$39	396
4 p. 391	Hy's Steakhouse	◆◆◆	Steak	$17-$60	396
5 p. 391	Clay Oven East Indian/Hakka Restaurant	◆◆	Indian	$15-$28	396
6 p. 391	Ivory Restaurant & Bar	◆◆	Indian	$14-$25	396
7 p. 391	Blaze Restaurant & Lounge	◆◆◆	American	$9-$35	396
8 p. 391	Ichiban Japanese Steak House & Sushi Bar	◆◆	Japanese	$26-$42	396
9 p. 391	Storm Bistro	◆◆	American	$9-$14	396
10 p. 391	East India Company Pub & Eatery	◆◆	Indian	$15-$18	396
11 p. 391	Sydney's At The Forks	◆◆◆	New American	$12-$55	396
12 p. 391	the Beachcomber	◆◆	American	$12-$38	396
13 p. 391	Smith	◆◆◆	Canadian	$11-$37	396
14 p. 391	Muddy Waters Smokehouse	◆◆	Barbecue Burgers	$11-$29	396
15 p. 391	Amici	◆◆◆	Italian	$12-$52	396

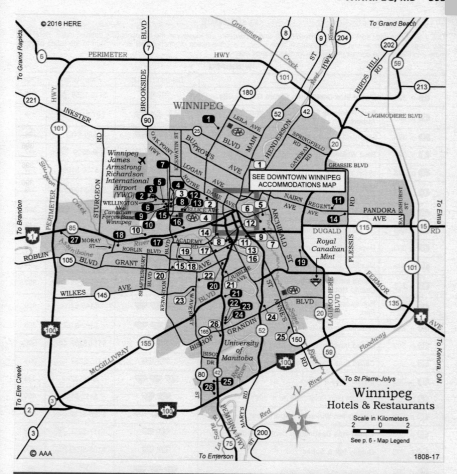

✈ Airport Hotels

Map Page	**WINNIPEG JAMES ARMSTRONG RICHARDSON INTERNATIONAL AIRPORT** (Maximum driving distance from airport: 1.8 mi (2.9 km))	Diamond Rated	Rate Range	Page
④ this page	**Best Western Plus Winnipeg Airport Hotel,** 1.8 mi (2.9 km)	▽▽▽	$99-$209 SAVE	397
⑦ this page	**Comfort Inn Airport,** 1.3 mi (2.1 km)	▽▽	$99-$145 SAVE	398
③ this page	**Courtyard by Marriott Winnipeg Airport,** 0.8 mi (1.4 km)	▽▽▽	$89-$167	398
⑨ this page	**Days Inn & Suites Winnipeg Airport,** 1.2 mi (1.9 km)	▽▽▽	$130-$200	398
② this page	**Four Points by Sheraton Hotel Winnipeg Airport,** on airport property	▽▽▽	$97-$153 SAVE	399
⑥ this page	**Hampton Inn by Hilton Winnipeg Airport/Polo Park,** 1.2 mi (1.9 km)	▽▽▽	$149-$199 SAVE	399
⑤ this page	**Hilton Winnipeg Airport Suites,** 1.1 mi (1.7 km)	▽▽▽	$129-$199	399
⑩ this page	**MainStay Suites Winnipeg,** 1.4 mi (2.2 km)	▽▽▽	$120-$220	400
⑧ this page	**Sandman Hotel & Suites Winnipeg Airport,** 1.4 mi (2.3 km)	▽▽▽	$151	400

Winnipeg

This index helps you "spot" where approved hotels and restaurants are located on the corresponding detailed maps. Hotel daily rate range is for comparison only. Restaurant price range is a combination of lunch and/or dinner. Turn to the listing page for more information and consult display ads for special promotions.

WINNIPEG

Map Page		Hotels	Diamond Rated	Rate Range	Page
1	p. 393	**Canad Inns Destination Centre Garden City**	◈◈	$119-$259 SAVE	398
2	p. 393	**Four Points by Sheraton Hotel Winnipeg Airport**	◈◈◈	$97-$153 SAVE	399
3	p. 393	Courtyard by Marriott Winnipeg Airport	◈◈◈	$89-$167	398
4	p. 393	**Best Western Plus Winnipeg Airport Hotel**	◈◈◈	$99-$209 SAVE	397
5	p. 393	Hilton Winnipeg Airport Suites	◈◈◈	$129-$199	399
6	p. 393	**Hampton Inn by Hilton Winnipeg Airport/Polo Park**	◈◈◈	$149-$199 SAVE	399
7	p. 393	**Comfort Inn Airport**	◈◈	$99-$145 SAVE	398
8	p. 393	Sandman Hotel & Suites Winnipeg Airport	◈◈◈	$151	400
9	p. 393	Days Inn & Suites Winnipeg Airport	◈◈◈	$130-$200	398
10	p. 393	MainStay Suites Winnipeg	◈◈◈	$120-$220	400
11	p. 393	**Canad Inns Destination Centre Club Regent Casino Hotel**	◈◈	$129-$299 SAVE	397
12	p. 393	Homewood Suites by Hilton Winnipeg Airport-Polo Park	◈◈◈	$149-$209	400
13	p. 393	Fairfield Inn & Suites by Marriott	◈◈◈	$102-$166	398
14	p. 393	**Canad Inns Destination Centre Transcona**	◈◈	$114-$239 SAVE	398
15	p. 393	**Canad Inns Destination Centre Polo Park**	◈◈	$115-$259 SAVE	398
16	p. 393	Clarion Hotel & Suites	◈◈◈	$151-$269	398
17	p. 393	Viscount Gort Hotel *(See ad p. 399.)*	◈◈	$117-$149	400
18	p. 393	**Holiday Inn Winnipeg Airport West**	◈◈◈	$126-$139 SAVE	399
19	p. 393	**Canad Inns Destination Centre Windsor Park**	◈◈	$117-$211 SAVE	398
20	p. 393	**Quality Inn & Suites**	◈◈	$103-$220 SAVE	400
21	p. 393	Holiday Inn Winnipeg South	◈◈◈	Rates not provided	399
22	p. 393	**Best Western Plus Pembina Inn & Suites** *(See ad p. 397.)*	◈◈◈	$130-$189 SAVE	397
23	p. 393	**Express by Canad Inns**	◈◈	$105-$165 SAVE	398
24	p. 393	**Canad Inns Destination Centre Fort Garry**	◈◈	$115-$234 SAVE	397
25	p. 393	**Four Points by Sheraton Winnipeg South**	◈◈◈	$109-$309 SAVE	399
26	p. 393	**Comfort Inn Winnipeg South**	◈◈	$107-$180 SAVE	398
27	p. 393	Howard Johnson Express Inn	◈◈	Rates not provided	400

Map Page		Restaurants	Diamond Rated	Cuisine	Price Range	Page
1	p. 393	Santa Lucia Pizza	◈◈	Italian	$10-$24	401
2	p. 393	Ducky's English Style Fish & Chips	◈	Fish & Chips	$8-$19	400
3	p. 393	Chop Steakhouse & Bar	◈◈◈	Steak Seafood	$14-$37	400
4	p. 393	India Palace	◈◈	Indian	$9-$16	400
5	p. 393	Resto Gare	◈◈◈	French	$15-$34	400
6	p. 393	Beaujena's	◈◈◈	French	$39-$49	400
8	p. 393	Bistro Dansk Restaurant	◈◈	European	$12-$24	400

Map Page	Restaurants (cont'd)	Diamond Rated	Cuisine	Price Range	Page
⑨ p. 393	Santa Lucia Pizza	▼▼	Italian	$10-$24	401
⑩ p. 393	Joe Black Coffee Bar	▼	Coffee/Tea	$7-$16	400
⑪ p. 393	Buccacino's Cucina Italiana	▼▼	Italian	$11-$35	400
⑫ p. 393	Segovia Tapas Bar & Restaurant	▼▼▼	New Spanish Small Plates	$12-$28	401
⑬ p. 393	Naru Sushi	▼▼	Japanese	$14-$28	400
⑭ p. 393	529 Wellington	▼▼▼	Steak Seafood	$11-$56	400
⑮ p. 393	Fusion Grill	▼▼▼	Canadian	$12-$45	400
⑯ p. 393	Confusion Corner Bar & Grill	▼▼▼	American	$13-$27	400
⑰ p. 393	Santa Lucia Pizza	▼▼	Italian	$10-$24	401
⑱ p. 393	Mona Lisa Ristorante	▼▼	Northern Italian	$5-$32	400
⑲ p. 393	Bonfire Bistro	▼▼	Mediterranean	$15-$29	400
⑳ p. 393	Stella's Cafe	▼▼	International Breakfast	$9-$16	401
㉑ p. 393	The Round Table Steak House & Pub	▼▼	Steak	$14-$50	400
㉒ p. 393	Wasabi Sabi	▼▼▼	New Sushi	$14-$35	401
㉓ p. 393	Bellissimo Restaurant & Lounge	▼▼▼	Italian	$10-$30	400
㉔ p. 393	Maxime's Restaurant & Lounge	▼▼	Continental	$11-$32	400
㉕ p. 393	La Fiesta Cafecito	▼▼	Salvadoran	$9-$22	401
㉖ p. 393	Nicolino's Restaurant	▼▼	Italian	$19-$30	400

DOWNTOWN WINNIPEG
• Restaurants p. 396
• Hotels & Restaurants map & index p. 391

BEST WESTERN PLUS CHARTER HOUSE HOTEL DOWNTOWN WINNIPEG
(204)942-0101 **8**

Hotel
$129-$159

AAA Benefit: Save 10% or more every day and earn 10% bonus points!

Address: 330 York Ave R3C 0N9 **Location:** Between Hargrave and Donald sts. Located in business district. **Facility:** 87 units. 5 stories, interior corridors. **Parking:** on-site (fee), winter plug-ins. **Dining:** 2 restaurants. **Activities:** exercise room. **Guest Services:** valet and coin laundry, area transportation.

Ask about AAA/CAA
Associate membership to
share the benefits you value

CANAD INNS DESTINATION CENTRE HEALTH SCIENCES CENTRE
(204)594-9472 **1**

▼▼▼▼
Hotel
$129-$329

Address: 720 William Ave R3E 3J7 **Location:** Between Sherbrook and Tecumseh sts. Attached to Health Sciences Centre. **Facility:** 191 units. 16 stories, interior corridors. **Parking:** on-site (fee), winter plug-ins. **Amenities:** Some: safes. **Dining:** 2 restaurants. **Activities:** exercise room. **Guest Services:** valet laundry.

DELTA WINNIPEG
(204)942-0551 **7**

▼▼▼ Contemporary Hotel. **Address:** 350 St. Mary Ave R3C 3J2

AAA Benefit: Members save 5% or more!

THE FAIRMONT WINNIPEG
(204)957-1350 **2**

▼▼▼▼
Hotel
$129-$309

Address: 2 Lombard Pl R3B 0Y3 **Location:** Just e of Portage Ave and Main St. Located in a commercial area. **Facility:** 340 units. 21 stories, interior corridors. **Parking:** on-site (fee) and valet, winter plug-ins. **Terms:** cancellation fee imposed. **Amenities:** safes. **Dining:** 2 restaurants. **Pool(s):** heated indoor. **Activities:** hot tub, steamroom, bicycles, exercise room, massage. **Guest Services:** valet laundry.

(See map & index p. 391.)

THE FORT GARRY HOTEL, SPA & CONFERENCE CENTRE
204/942-8251 **9**

◈◈◈ Historic Hotel. **Address:** 222 Broadway R3C 0R3

HOLIDAY INN & SUITES WINNIPEG DOWNTOWN
(204)786-7011 **6**

◈◈◈
Hotel
$109-$399

Address: 360 Colony St R3B 2P3 **Location:** Corner of Portage Ave. **Facility:** 140 units. 11 stories, interior corridors. **Parking:** on-site (fee), winter plug-ins. **Terms:** cancellation fee imposed. **Amenities:** video games. **Pool(s):** heated indoor. **Activities:** hot tub, exercise room. **Guest Services:** valet and coin laundry.

SAVE ⬛ ⬛ ⬛ CALL ⬛ ⬛
BIZ HS ⬛ ⬛ ⬛ ⬛ ⬛
/ SOME UNITS ⬛

HUMPHRY INN & SUITES (204)942-4222 **5**

◈◈ Hotel. **Address:** 260 Main St R3C 1A9

INN AT THE FORKS (204)942-6555 **10**

◈◈◈
Hotel
$190-$397

Address: 75 Forks Market Rd R3C 0A2 **Location:** At The Forks. Located in a park and entertainment area. **Facility:** 117 units. 5 stories, interior corridors. **Parking:** on-site (fee) and valet, winter plug-ins. **Terms:** cancellation fee imposed, resort fee. **Amenities:** video games, safes. **Dining:** Smith, see separate listing. **Activities:** exercise room, spa. **Guest Services:** valet laundry, area transportation.

SAVE ECO ⬛ ⬛ ⬛ CALL ⬛
BIZ HS ⬛ ⬛ ⬛ ⬛ ⬛

MERE HOTEL 204/594-0333 **4**

◈◈◈ Boutique Contemporary Hotel. **Address:** 333 Waterfront Dr R3C 0A2

NORWOOD HOTEL (204)233-4475 **11**

◈◈ Hotel. **Address:** 112 Marion St R2H 0T1

WHERE TO EAT

AMICI 204/943-4997 **15**

◈◈◈ Italian. Fine Dining. **Address:** 326 Broadway R3C 0S5

THE BEACHCOMBER 204/948-0020 **12**

◈◈◈ American. Casual Dining. **Address:** 162-1 Forks Market Rd R3C 4L8

BLAZE RESTAURANT & LOUNGE 204/944-7259 **7**

◈◈◈ American. Casual Dining. **Address:** 350 St. Mary Ave R3C 3J2

CIBO WATERFRONT CAFE 204/594-0339 **1**

◈◈◈ Mediterranean. Casual Dining. **Address:** 339 Waterfront Dr R3B 0V1

CLAY OVEN EAST INDIAN/HAKKA RESTAURANT
204/982-7426 **5**

◈◈ Indian. Casual Dining. **Address:** 1 Portage Ave R3B 3N3

DEER + ALMOND 204/504-8562 **2**

◈◈◈ New World. Casual Dining. **Address:** 85 Princess St R3B 1K6

EAST INDIA COMPANY PUB & EATERY 204/947-3097 **10**

◈◈ Indian. Casual Dining. **Address:** 349 York Ave R3C 3S9

HERMANOS RESTAURANT & WINE BAR 204/947-5434 **3**

◈◈◈ Latin American. Casual Dining. **Address:** 179 Bannatyne Ave R3B 0R4

HY'S STEAKHOUSE 204/942-1000 **4**

◈◈◈ Steak. Fine Dining. **Address:** 1 Lombard Pl R3B 0X3

ICHIBAN JAPANESE STEAK HOUSE & SUSHI BAR
204/925-7400 **8**

◈◈ Japanese. Casual Dining. **Address:** 189 Carlton St R3C 3H7

IVORY RESTAURANT & BAR 204/944-1600 **6**

◈◈ Indian. Casual Dining. **Address:** 200 Main St R3C 4V9

MOXIE'S CLASSIC GRILL 204/926-5757

◈◈ American. Casual Dining. **Address:** 300 Portage Ave R3C 5S4

MUDDY WATERS SMOKEHOUSE 204/947-6653 **14**

◈◈ Barbecue Burgers. Casual Dining. **Address:** 15 Forks Market Rd R3C 0A2

SMITH 204/944-2445 **13**

◈◈◈ Canadian. Casual Dining. **Address:** 75 Forks Market Rd R3C 0A2

STORM BISTRO 204/948-0085 **9**

◈◈◈ American. Casual Dining. **Address:** 300 Memorial Blvd R3C 1V1

SYDNEY'S AT THE FORKS 204/942-6075 **11**

◈◈◈ New American. Fine Dining. **Address:** 215 One Forks Market Rd R3C 4L9

WINNIPEG

- Restaurants p. 400
- Hotels & Restaurants map & index p. 393

BEST WESTERN PLUS PEMBINA INN & SUITES
(204)269-8888 **22**

Hotel
$130-$189

Best Western PLUS

AAA Benefit: Save 10% or more every day and earn 10% bonus points!

Address: 1714 Pembina Hwy R3T 2G2 **Location:** 0.6 mi (1 km) n of jct Bishop Grandin Blvd. Located in a commercial area. **Facility:** 104 units. 4 stories, interior corridors. **Parking:** winter plug-ins. **Terms:** resort fee. **Amenities:** safes. **Pool(s):** heated indoor. **Activities:** hot tub, exercise room. **Guest Services:** valet and coin laundry. **Featured Amenity:** full hot breakfast. *(See ad this page.)*

BEST WESTERN PLUS WINNIPEG AIRPORT HOTEL
(204)775-9889 **4**

Hotel
$99-$209

Best Western PLUS

AAA Benefit: Save 10% or more every day and earn 10% bonus points!

Address: 1715 Wellington Ave R3H 0G1 **Location:** Jct Century St. Located in a commercial area. **Facility:** 213 units. 6 stories, interior corridors. **Parking:** winter plug-ins. **Pool(s):** heated indoor. **Activities:** hot tub, exercise room. **Guest Services:** valet and coin laundry.

CANAD INNS DESTINATION CENTRE CLUB REGENT CASINO HOTEL
(204)667-5560 **11**

Hotel
$129-$299

Address: 1415 Regent Ave W R2C 3B2 **Location:** 1.3 mi (2.1 km) e of Lagimodiere Blvd (Hwy 20); between Plessis Rd and Lagimodiere Blvd (Hwy 20). **Facility:** With direct access to an adjacent casino, this hotel offers pleasant rooms with comfortable seating. The bathrooms are on the basic side. 146 units. 6 stories, interior corridors. **Parking:** winter plug-ins. **Activities:** exercise room. **Guest Services:** valet laundry.

CANAD INNS DESTINATION CENTRE FORT GARRY
(204)261-7450 **24**

Hotel
$115-$234

Address: 1824 Pembina Hwy R3T 2G2 **Location:** Just n of Bishop Grandin Blvd. **Facility:** 106 units, some two bedrooms. 2 stories, interior corridors. **Parking:** winter plug-ins. **Dining:** 2 restaurants. **Pool(s):** heated indoor. **Activities:** hot tub, exercise room. **Guest Services:** valet laundry.

Visit the AAA and CAA senior

driving websites for tips

to help you drive safely longer

▼ See AAA listing this page ▼

(See map & index p. 393.)

CANAD INNS DESTINATION CENTRE GARDEN CITY
(204)633-0024 **1**

Hotel
$119-$259

Address: 2100 McPhillips St R2V 3T9 **Location:** At Jefferson Ave. Located in a commercial area. **Facility:** 72 units, some two bedrooms. 3 stories, interior corridors. **Parking:** winter plug-ins. **Dining:** 2 restaurants. **Pool(s):** heated indoor. **Activities:** hot tub.

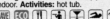

CANAD INNS DESTINATION CENTRE POLO PARK
(204)775-8791 **15**

Hotel
$115-$259

Address: 1405 St. Matthews Ave R3G 0K5 **Location:** Just e of St James St. **Facility:** 107 units. 6 stories, interior corridors. **Parking:** winter plug-ins. **Dining:** 3 restaurants. **Pool(s):** heated indoor. **Activities:** hot tub, exercise room. **Guest Services:** valet and coin laundry, area transportation.

CANAD INNS DESTINATION CENTRE TRANSCONA
(204)224-1681 **14**

Hotel
$114-$239

Address: 826 Regent Ave W R2C 3A8 **Location:** 1.9 mi (3 km) e of Lagimodiere Blvd (Hwy 20); between Plessis Rd and Lagimodiere Blvd (Hwy 20). **Facility:** 50 units, some two bedrooms. 2 stories, interior corridors. **Parking:** winter plug-ins. **Dining:** 2 restaurants, nightclub. **Pool(s):** heated indoor. **Activities:** hot tub. **Guest Services:** valet laundry.

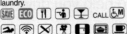

CANAD INNS DESTINATION CENTRE WINDSOR PARK
(204)253-2641 **19**

Hotel
$117-$211

Address: 1034 Elizabeth Rd R2J 1B3 **Location:** Just s of Maginot St and w of Lagimodiere Blvd (Hwy 20). Located in a residential/commercial area. **Facility:** 52 units, some two bedrooms. 2 stories (no elevator), interior corridors. **Parking:** winter plug-ins. **Dining:** nightclub. **Pool(s):** heated indoor. **Activities:** hot tub. **Guest Services:** valet laundry.

CLARION HOTEL & SUITES
(204)774-5110 **16**

Hotel. **Address:** 1445 Portage Ave R3G 3P4

COMFORT INN AIRPORT
(204)783-5627 **7**

Hotel
$99-$145

Address: 1770 Sargent Ave R3H 0C8 **Location:** At King Edward St. Located in a commercial area. **Facility:** 79 units. 2 stories (no elevator), interior corridors. **Parking:** winter plug-ins. **Guest Services:** valet laundry. **Featured Amenity: full hot breakfast.**

COMFORT INN WINNIPEG SOUTH
(204)269-7390 **26**

Hotel
$107-$180

Address: 3109 Pembina Hwy R3T 4R6 **Location:** Just n of jct Perimeter Hwy 100 and 75. Located in a residential/commercial area. **Facility:** 83 units. 2 stories (no elevator), interior corridors. **Parking:** winter plug-ins. **Guest Services:** valet laundry. **Featured Amenity: full hot breakfast.**

COURTYARD BY MARRIOTT WINNIPEG AIRPORT
(204)505-8600 **3**

Contemporary Hotel. **Address:** 780 Powerhouse Rd R3H 1C7

AAA Benefit: Members save 5% or more!

DAYS INN & SUITES WINNIPEG AIRPORT
(204)505-1500 **9**

Hotel. **Address:** 695 Berry St R3H 0S4

EXPRESS BY CANAD INNS
(204)269-6955 **23**

Hotel
$105-$165

Address: 1792 Pembina Hwy R3T 2G2 **Location:** Just n of Bishop Grandin Blvd. **Facility:** 36 units. 2 stories (no elevator), interior corridors. **Parking:** winter plug-ins. **Dining:** nightclub.

FAIRFIELD INN & SUITES BY MARRIOTT
(204)783-7900 **13**

Hotel. **Address:** 1301 Ellice Ave R3G 0N5

AAA Benefit: Members save 5% or more!

(See map & index p. 393.)

FOUR POINTS BY SHERATON HOTEL WINNIPEG AIRPORT
(204)775-5222

Hotel
$97-$153

FOUR POINTS BY SHERATON

AAA Benefit: Members save up to 15%, plus Starwood Preferred Guest® benefits!

Address: 1999 Wellington Ave R3H 1H5 **Location:** At Winnipeg James Armstrong Richardson International Airport. **Facility:** 149 units. 7 stories, interior corridors. **Parking:** on-site (fee), winter plug-ins. **Amenities:** safes. **Activities:** exercise room. **Guest Services:** valet laundry, area transportation.

FOUR POINTS BY SHERATON WINNIPEG SOUTH
(204)275-7711 **25**

Hotel
$109-$309

FOUR POINTS BY SHERATON

AAA Benefit: Members save up to 15%, plus Starwood Preferred Guest® benefits!

Address: 2935 Pembina Hwy R3T 2H5 **Location:** Jct Perimeter Hwy 100 and 75, 0.7 mi (1.1 km) n. **Facility:** 75 units. 5 stories, interior corridors. **Parking:** winter plug-ins. **Pool(s):** heated indoor. **Activities:** hot tub, exercise room. **Guest Services:** valet laundry.

Pick up colorful, top-quality travel guides and atlases at AAA/CAA offices

HAMPTON INN BY HILTON WINNIPEG AIRPORT/POLO PARK
(204)772-3000 **6**

Hotel
$149-$199

 Hampton by HILTON

AAA Benefit: Members save up to 10%!

Address: 730 Berry St R3H 0S6 **Location:** Jct Wellington Ave, just s. **Facility:** 135 units. 6 stories, interior corridors. **Parking:** winter plug-ins. **Terms:** 1-7 night minimum stay, cancellation fee imposed. **Pool(s):** heated indoor. **Activities:** hot tub, exercise room. **Guest Services:** valet and coin laundry, area transportation. **Featured Amenity:** breakfast buffet.

HILTON WINNIPEG AIRPORT SUITES (204)783-1700 **5**
Hotel. **Address:** 1800 Wellington Ave R3H 1B2

AAA Benefit: Members save 5% or more!

HOLIDAY INN WINNIPEG AIRPORT WEST
(204)885-4478 **18**

Hotel
$126-$139

Address: 2520 Portage Ave R3J 3T6 **Location:** Just e of Moray St. Located in a residential/commercial area. **Facility:** 228 units, some two bedrooms and efficiencies. 15 stories, interior corridors. **Parking:** winter plug-ins. **Terms:** cancellation fee imposed. **Pool(s):** heated indoor. **Activities:** hot tub, playground, exercise room. **Guest Services:** valet and coin laundry, area transportation.

HOLIDAY INN WINNIPEG SOUTH 204/452-4747 **21**
Hotel. **Address:** 1330 Pembina Hwy R3T 2B4

▼ See AAA listing p. 400 ▼

(See map & index p. 393.)

HOMEWOOD SUITES BY HILTON WINNIPEG AIRPORT-POLO PARK
(204)515-1941 **12**
▼▼▼ Extended Stay Hotel. **Address:** 1295 Ellice Ave R3G 0N5

AAA Benefit:
Members save up to 10%!

HOWARD JOHNSON EXPRESS INN
204/837-5831 **27**
▼▼ Motel. **Address:** 3740 Portage Ave R3K 0Z9

MAINSTAY SUITES WINNIPEG
(204)594-0500 **10**
▼▼▼ Extended Stay Hotel. **Address:** 670 King Edward St R3H 0P2

QUALITY INN & SUITES
(204)453-8247 **20**

Hotel
$103-$220

Address: 635 Pembina Hwy R3M 2L4 **Location:** Just s of Grant Ave. **Facility:** 69 units. 4 stories, interior corridors. **Parking:** winter plug-ins. **Activities:** game room, exercise room. **Guest Services:** valet and coin laundry. **Featured Amenity:** breakfast buffet.

[SAVE] [▐▌] [▭] [Y] [BIZ] [📶] [📶]
[🖵] /SOME UNITS [S▼] [HS] [▤]

SANDMAN HOTEL & SUITES WINNIPEG AIRPORT
(204)775-7263 **8**
▼▼▼ Hotel. **Address:** 1750 Sargent Ave R3H 0C7

VISCOUNT GORT HOTEL
(204)775-0451 **17**
▼▼▼ Hotel. **Address:** 1670 Portage Ave R3J 0C9 *(See ad p. 399.)*

WHERE TO EAT

529 WELLINGTON
204/487-8325 **14**
▼▼▼ Steak Seafood. Fine Dining. **Address:** 529 Wellington Cres R3M 0A5

BEAUJENA'S
204/233-4841 **6**
▼▼▼ French. Fine Dining. **Address:** 302 Hamel Ave R2H 0K9

BELLISSIMO RESTAURANT & LOUNGE
204/489-0495 **23**
▼▼ Italian. Casual Dining. **Address:** 877 Waverly St, #1 R3T 5V3

BISTRO DANSK RESTAURANT
204/775-5662 **8**
▼▼ European. Casual Dining. **Address:** 63 Sherbrook St R3C 2B2

BONFIRE BISTRO
204/487-4440 **19**
▼▼ Mediterranean. Casual Dining. **Address:** 1433 Corydon Ave R3N 0J2

BUCCACINO'S CUCINA ITALIANA
204/452-8251 **11**
▼▼ Italian. Casual Dining. **Address:** 155 Osborne St R3L 1Y7

CHEZ CORA
▼▼ Breakfast Sandwiches. Casual Dining.
LOCATIONS:
Address: 840 Waverley St R3T 5Z7 **Phone:** 204/928-1200
Address: 101C-1440 Jack Blick Ave R3G 0L4
Phone: 204/415-7730

CHOP STEAKHOUSE & BAR
204/788-2015 **3**
▼▼▼ Steak Seafood. Casual Dining. **Address:** 1750 Sargent Ave R3H 0C7

CONFUSION CORNER BAR & GRILL
204/284-6666 **16**
▼▼▼ American. Casual Dining. **Address:** 500 Corydon Ave R3L 0P1

DUCKY'S ENGLISH STYLE FISH & CHIPS
204/772-5600 **2**
▼ Fish & Chips. Casual Dining. **Address:** 884 Notre Dame Ave R3E 0M7

EARLS KITCHEN + BAR
204/975-1845
▼▼ American. Casual Dining. **Address:** 1455 Portage Ave R3G 0W4

FUSION GRILL
204/489-6963 **15**
▼▼▼ Canadian. Casual Dining. **Address:** 550 Academy Rd R3N 0E3

INDIA PALACE
204/774-6061 **4**
▼▼▼ Indian. Casual Dining. **Address:** 770 Ellice Ave R3G 0B8

JOE BLACK COFFEE BAR
204/415-1660 **10**
▼ Coffee/Tea. Quick Serve. **Address:** 2037 Portage Ave R3K 0K6

JOEY RESTAURANTS
▼▼ American. Casual Dining.
LOCATIONS:
Address: 1550 Kenaston Blvd R3P 0Y4 **Phone:** 204/477-5639
Address: 635 St. James St R3G 3R4 **Phone:** 204/339-5639

LA FIESTA CAFECITO
204/257-7108 **25**
▼▼ Salvadoran. Casual Dining. **Address:** 730 St. Anne's Rd, Unit M R2N 0A2

MAXIME'S RESTAURANT & LOUNGE
204/257-1521 **24**
▼▼ Continental. Casual Dining. **Address:** 1131 St. Mary's Rd R2M 3T9

MONA LISA RISTORANTE
204/488-3687 **18**
▼▼ Northern Italian. Casual Dining. **Address:** 1697 Corydon Ave R3N 0J9

MOXIE'S CLASSIC GRILL
204/783-1840
▼▼ American. Casual Dining. **Address:** 1485 Portage Ave, 234B R3G 0W4

NARU SUSHI
204/888-0028 **13**
▼▼ Japanese. Casual Dining. **Address:** 159 Osborne St R3L 1Y7

NICOLINO'S RESTAURANT
204/269-5004 **26**
▼▼ Italian. Casual Dining. **Address:** 4-2077 Pembina Hwy R3T 5J9

RESTO GARE
204/237-7072 **5**
▼▼▼ French. Casual Dining. **Address:** 630 rue Des Meurons St R2H 2P9

THE ROUND TABLE STEAK HOUSE & PUB
204/453-3631 **21**
▼▼ Steak. Casual Dining. **Address:** 800 Pembina Hwy R3M 2M7

(See map & index p. 393.)

SANTA LUCIA PIZZA   204/237-4134 ⑨
♦♦♦ Italian. Casual Dining. **Address:** 4 St Mary's Rd R2H
1H1

SANTA LUCIA PIZZA   204/488-8090 ⑰
♦♦♦ Italian. Casual Dining. **Address:** 905 Corydon Ave R3M
0W8

SANTA LUCIA PIZZA   204/586-8171 ①
♦♦♦ Italian. Casual Dining. **Address:** 1473 Main St R2W
3V9

SEGOVIA TAPAS BAR & RESTAURANT   204/477-6500 ⑫
♦♦♦ New Spanish Small Plates. Casual Dining. **Address:**
484 Stradbrook Ave R3L 0J9

STELLA'S CAFE   204/453-8562 ⑳
♦♦ International Breakfast. Casual Dining. **Address:** 166
Osborne St R3L 1Y8

WASABI SABI   204/415-7878 ㉒
♦♦♦ New Sushi. Casual Dining. **Address:** 1360 Taylor Ave,
#3 R3M 3Z1

Boreal forest, Northwest Territories

Take a journey into northern Canada and you may be surprised at your options for enjoyment.

Residents joke that the four seasons in the Northwest Territories and Nunavut—June, July, August and winter—are a bit unlike seasons in the rest of the world. The absence of a "real" spring or fall leaves busy summers and extra-long winters.

Arrive in June, July or August and you can dip your toes in the Arctic Ocean and marvel at the wildflower-dotted tundra under a midnight sun.

Or visit during the 6 months of winter and you can choose from activities involving snow and ice: snowmobiling, building an igloo, ice fishing, riding on a paw-powered sled or driving on an "ice highway," made of hard-packed snow piled on frozen lakes.

Celebrate the end of a long, dark winter by living it up at Inuvik's Sunrise Festival—held in January in honor of the sun's appearance after months of hiding.

Tundra flowers, Northwest Territories

Northwest Territories and Nunavut

Canada's Newest Territory

On April Fools' Day, 1999, in the eastern Northwest Territories, Inuit people celebrated the birth of Nunavut, Canada's newest territory.

Twenty-four years after a separation was proposed, Nunavut (meaning "our land" in the Inuktitut language) officially seceded from the Northwest Territories to form its own territory. A new line on the Canadian map allows its approximately 29,474 residents—85 percent of whom are Inuit—the chance to govern their homeland.

Nunavut is a giant chunk of arctic earth stretching so far northeast it almost tickles the shores of Greenland, and yet it contains only one road within its nearly 2 million square kilometres (772,204 sq. mi.). Above the tree line it's a place where animals outnumber humans; where brightly colored rhododendron, yellow buttercups and mountain avens sprinkle treeless tundra; and where it may be easier to hook a trout for dinner than pick up a burger at a drive-thru.

Despite the recent division of Nunavut and Northwest Territories, the two still share similar features. During summer above the Arctic Circle, days have no end. A shining sun never dips below the horizon, and the sky is illuminated 24 hours a day. In winter the opposite occurs as days and nights melt together under a cold, dark sky.

Picture a black sky pin-pricked with stars surrounding a full, glowing moon, its light sprawling across wide, snow-covered tundra and frozen lakes. On such a clear winter night the flat, stark-white landscape glistens.

Bright Lights, Small Cities

The northern lights, or "aurora borealis," painting the winter sky are no less impressive. A faint glow slightly above the horizon serves as the show's opening act. When the lights rise, they resemble curtains in shades of red, lavender and green. Feather-shaped and stretching across the night sky, the lights ripple to form watercolor waves.

In the Northwest Territories you'll have a good chance to catch this dazzling display October through March. A spot void of city lights is best; try giant Great Slave Lake near Yellowknife. Frozen in winter, this fifth largest freshwater lake in North America provides a fine view of the vivid night sky.

Then visit Yellowknife, on the lake's north arm. Once glittering with gold, this former 1930s mining camp now flaunts its colorful past in Old Town, where shops and quaint neighborhoods nestle against the shore.

West of the city is Nahanni National Park Reserve, where Virginia Falls plummets 90 metres (295 ft.) into South Nahanni River. The falls, arguably more spectacular than Niagara, form a pool of eddies and perilous rapids surrounded by cliffs taller than Toronto's CN Tower.

Recreation

Welcome to the top of the world. The vast Northwest Territories and Nunavut boast an area filled with wild rivers, icy seas, lofty mountains and Arctic tundra. Summer days, typically June through August, are long and surprisingly mild. Hikers can check out a variety of topography, from steep mountain trails to frozen tundra. The Canol Heritage Trail, en route to the Yukon, offers some challenging terrain.

Snowmobiling, snowshoeing, dog sledding and cross-country skiing are a way of life that can extend into May—the warmer air and long days make this the perfect time for such outdoor pursuits. Many outfitters offer snowmobile tours or flights to remote areas to observe the spectacular northern lights. Hint: The best time for viewing this brilliant display is October through March.

Travel anywhere in the territories can include aircraft, boat, automobile, snowmobile, Inuit qomatiq (sled) and even dogsled. Of the Northwest Territories' five national parks, only Wood Buffalo can be reached by road. Nahanni's rugged beauty is accessible solely by air. One of the newest parks, Tuktut Nogait, is a hiker's paradise where float planes begin landing on the Homaday River in mid-June.

Water challenges come in varying degrees of difficulty. Arctic rivers can offer the ultimate thrill if explored cautiously. Sea kayakers can flow beside towering icebergs, while the many rivers stemming off the Mackenzie are a canoeist's dream. Paddlers will be dazzled by the breathtaking scenery on the Nahanni. Hoist your sails on Great Slave Lake, or if you are brave enough, scuba dive in the frigid waters.

Cold northern waters yield excellent fishing. Plenty of spots are full of prize catches, from the feisty arctic char to the fierce northern pike. Some of the area's waters are ranked the best in the world for angling, including Great Slave, Great Bear and Murky lakes and the Stark and Snowdrift rivers.

The land's beauty, combined with unspoiled wilderness and vast game selections, makes hunting a rewarding experience. And for those who like to shoot with a camera, wildlife viewing also is rewarding. Bird-watchers flock to the Mackenzie River delta, one of the world's biggest nesting grounds.

Alexandra Falls, Twin Falls Gorge Territorial Park, Enterprise

Historic Timeline

1576	Sir Martin Frobisher, searching for the Northwest Passage to the Orient, arrives.
1763	The Treaty of Paris grants Canada to the British.
1771	Hudson's Bay Co. explorer-trader Samuel Hearne arrives at Great Slave Lake.
1789	Alexander Mackenzie leads an expedition along a westward-flowing river, unearthing another route to the Arctic Ocean.
1850	Capt. Robert John Le Mesurier McClure discovers the Northwest Passage.
1870	Hudson's Bay Co. cedes the region to Canada.
1920	Oil is discovered at Norman Wells.
1934	Gold is discovered at Yellowknife on Great Slave Lake.
1978	A Soviet nuclear-powered satellite crashes into the Great Slave Lake area; debris is spread over 124,000 square kilometres.
1993	The Nunavut Land Claims Agreement, under which the Inuit gain the power to govern their own territory, is passed.
1999	Northwest Territories divides into two territories; the eastern, Inuit-governed territory becomes Nunavut.

What To Pack

Temperature Averages Maximum/Minimum (Celsius)	JANUARY	FEBRUARY	MARCH	APRIL	MAY	JUNE	JULY	AUGUST	SEPTEMBER	OCTOBER	NOVEMBER	DECEMBER
Fort Liard	-20 / -28	-8 / -19	-2 / -15	9 / -4	15 / 2	21 / 8	23 / 11	21 / 9	15 / 3	3 / -4	-8 / -15	-15 / -23
Fort Smith	-19 / -28	-14 / -25	-5 / -19	6 / -6	15 / 1	20 / 7	22 / 10	20 / 8	13 / 2	4 / -3	-7 / -15	-16 / -25
Iqaluit, Nunavut	-7 / -22	-8 / -24	-1 / -19	14 / -3	30 / 18	43 / 32	52 / 38	50 / 38	40 / 31	28 / 18	16 / 1	3 / -15
Inuvik	-24 / -33	-23 / -33	-18 / -30	-8 / -20	4 / -6	16 / 4	19 / 8	16 / 5	7 / -1	-5 / -12	-17 / -26	-21 / -31
Tulita	-24 / -30	-21 / -27	-13 / -24	0 / -10	11 / -1	20 / 7	22 / 10	19 / 11	11 / 4	-1 / -2	-15 / -15	-21 / -24
Yellowknife	-24 / -32	-19 / -29	-13 / -24	-1 / -12	10 / -1	18 / 8	21 / 12	18 / 10	10 / 3	1 / -4	-11 / -19	-20 / -28

From the records of The Weather Channel Interactive, Inc.

Good Facts To Know

ABOUT THE TERRITORIES

POPULATION: Northwest Territories 41,462. Nunavut 31,906.

AREA: Northwest Territories 140,835 sq km (440,479 sq mi.); ranks 3rd. Nunavut 1,932,255 sq km (746,048 sq mi.); ranks 1st.

CAPITAL: Yellowknife, Northwest Territories; Iqaluit, Nunavut.

HIGHEST POINT: 2,762 m (9,062 ft.), Cirque of the Unclimbables Mountain in Nahanni National Park Reserve.

LOWEST POINT: Sea level, Beaufort Sea.

TIME ZONE(S): Mountain/Central/Eastern/Atlantic. DST.

REGULATIONS

TEEN DRIVING LAWS: Minimum age for an unrestricted driver's license is 17. Phone (867) 873-7406 for more information about Northwest Territories driver's license regulations.

SEAT BELT/CHILD RESTRAINT LAWS: Seat belts are required for driver and all passengers 18 kilograms (40 lbs.) and over; children under 18 kilograms (40 lbs.) are required to be in a child restraint; children less than 9 kilograms (20 lbs.) must be in a rear-facing seat. AAA recommends the use of seat belts and appropriate child restraints for the driver and all passengers.

CELLPHONE RESTRICTIONS: Text messaging and handheld cellphone use while driving is prohibited in Northwest Territories.

HELMETS FOR MOTORCYCLISTS: Required for all riders.

RADAR DETECTORS: Not permitted.

MOVE OVER LAW: In the Northwest Territories, drivers must reduce their speed to the posted limit or 60 kph, whichever is less, and must vacate the lane closest to a stopped emergency or law enforcement vehicle with lights flashing. In Nunavut there is no requirement to slow down or move to an adjacent lane when passing stopped emergency vehicles.

FIREARMS LAWS: By federal law, all nonresidents entering Canada with a firearm must declare their weapon in writing and pay a fee of $25 (Canadian).

ALCOHOL CONSUMPTION: Legal age 19.

HOLIDAYS

HOLIDAYS: Jan. 1 ▪ Good Friday ▪ Easter Monday ▪ Victoria Day, May 24 (if a Mon.) or the closest prior Mon. ▪ Aboriginal Day, June 21 ▪ Canada Day, July 1 ▪ Nunavut Day, July 9 ▪ Civic Holiday, Aug. (1st Mon.) ▪ Labour Day, Sept. (1st Mon.) ▪ Thanksgiving, Oct. (2nd Mon.) ▪ Remembrance Day, Nov. 11 ▪ Christmas, Dec. 25 ▪ Boxing Day, Dec. 26.

MONEY

TAXES: The Northwest Territories and Nunavut have no territorial sales tax. However, a 5 percent Goods and Service Tax (GST) is levied.

VISITOR INFORMATION

INFORMATION CENTERS: Territorial welcome centers in the Northwest Territories include an office on Hwy. 1 at the Alberta border (on the 60th parallel) near Enterprise ▪ Dempster/Delta Visitor Information Centre at Km-post 77 on Hwy. 8 near Fort McPherson ▪ the Western Arctic Regional Visitor Information Centre at the termination of the Dempster Hwy. in Inuvik ▪ the Northern Frontier Visitor Centre in Yellowknife.

In Nunavut the Unikkaarvik Visitor Centre is in Iqaluit.

FURTHER INFORMATION FOR VISITORS:
Northwest Territories Tourism
P.O. Box 610
Yellowknife, NT X1A 2N5
Canada
(867) 873-5007
(800) 661-0788
Nunavut Tourism
P.O. Box 1450
IQALUIT, NUNAVUT, NU X0A 0H0
Canada
(866) 686-2888

FISHING AND HUNTING REGULATIONS:
Northwest Territories Environment and Natural Resources
P.O. Box 2668
Yellowknife, NT X1A 2P9
Canada
(867) 873-7184

FERRY AND ROAD INFORMATION:
Northwest Territories Department of Transportation
4510 50 Ave.
P.O. Box 1320
Yellowknife, NT X1A 2L9
Canada
(800) 661-0750

Turn your road trip dreams into reality with the TripTik® Travel Planner

Northwest Territories and Nunavut Annual Events
Please call ahead to confirm event details.

JANUARY	FEBRUARY	MARCH
■ Banff Mountain Film Festival World Tour / Yellowknife 867-873-2474 ■ Sunrise Festival / Inuvik 866-777-8600 ■ Kole Crook Fiddle Association Jamboree Fort Simpson 867-446-1032	■ NWT Ski Day / Yellowknife 867-669-9754 ■ Northwest Territories Badminton Championships Yellowknife 867-669-8332 ■ Yellowknife Heritage Week Yellowknife 867-920-5693	■ Kamba Winter Carnival Hay River 867-874-6701 ■ Long John Jamboree Yellowknife 867-920-0770 ■ Snowking Winter Festival Yellowknife 867-669-1571

APRIL	MAY	JUNE
■ Top of the World Ski Loppet Inuvik 867-777-2303 ■ Yellowknife Music Festival Yellowknife 867-873-4950 ■ Ski Loppet / Yellowknife 867-669-9754	■ Ptarmigan Ptheatrics Spring Musical / Yellowknife 867-766-6101 ■ Freezin' for a Reason Polar Plunge / Yellowknife 867-445-7245 ■ Jayman BUILT MS Walk Yellowknife 867-444-0338	■ Aboriginal Day Yellowknife 867-446-1060 ■ Yellowknife Solstice Festival / Yellowknife 867-873-6762 ■ NorthWords Writers Festival / Yellowknife 867-445-6800

JULY	AUGUST	SEPTEMBER
■ Great Northern Arts Festival Inuvik 867-777-8638 ■ Folk on the Rocks Music Festival / Yellowknife 867-920-7806 ■ Theatre on the Lake Yellowknife 867-873-7551	■ Summer Splash Arts Festival / Fort Smith 867-872-2859 ■ Yellowknife Marathon Yellowknife 867-446-6721 ■ Slave River Paddlefest Fort Smith 867-872-3593	■ Dirt Digger Duathlon Yellowknife 867-669-9724 ■ Yellowknife Golf Club Glow Ball Tournament Yellowknife 867-873-4326 ■ Culture Days / Inuvik 867-920-6370

OCTOBER	NOVEMBER	DECEMBER
■ Halloween Skate Yellowknife 867-920-5676 ■ The Ko K'e Music and Spoken Word Festival Yellowknife 867-873-4950 ■ Yellowknife International Film Festival / Yellowknife 867-766-2586	■ Santa Claus Parade Yellowknife 867-920-5676 ■ Geoscience Forum Yellowknife 867-873-5281 ■ Great Northern Arts Festival Christmas Craft Fair / Inuvik 867-777-8638	■ New Year's Eve Celebrations / Hay River 867-874-6522 ■ New Year's Eve Fireworks Yellowknife 867-920-5676 ■ Santa Claus Parade Inuvik 867-777-2166

Wood Buffalo National Park

Caribou

Iceberg, Nunavut

Aurora borealis, Yellowknife

Kimmirut, Baffin Island, Nunavut

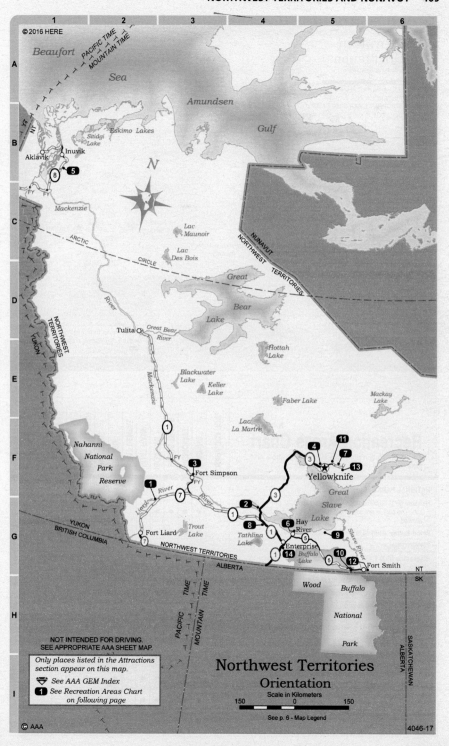

Northwest Territories
Orientation

Scale in Kilometers

See p. 6 - Map Legend

Only places listed in the Attractions
section appear on this map.

See AAA GEM Index

See Recreation Areas Chart
on following page

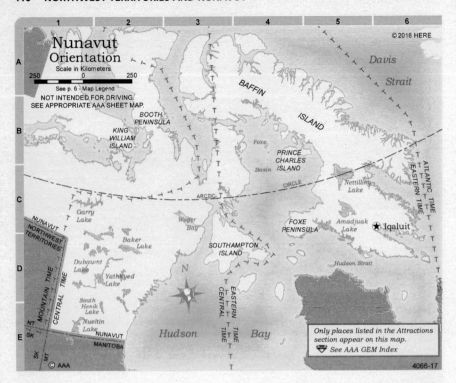

Recreation Areas Chart

The map location numerals in column 2 show an area's location on the preceding map.

	MAP LOCATION	CAMPING	PICNICKING	HIKING TRAILS	BOATING	BOAT RAMP	BOAT RENTAL	FISHING	SWIMMING	PETS ON LEASH	BICYCLE TRAILS	WINTER SPORTS	VISITOR CENTER	LODGE/CABINS	FOOD SERVICE
NATIONAL PARKS *(See place listings.)*															
Nahanni (F-1) 30,000 square kilometres 145 km w. of Fort Simpson. The park is not accessible by road; no motor boats allowed.		•	•	•	•			•	•						
Wood Buffalo (H-5) 44,807 square kilometres on Hwy. 5.		•	•	•	•	•		•	•	•			•	•	•
TERRITORIAL															
Blackstone (F-2) 1,430 hectares 166 km s. of Fort Simpson on Hwy. 7 or 115 km n. of Fort Liard on Hwy. 7.	❶	•	•	•	•			•	•	•				•	
Fort Providence (G-4) 10 hectares at Fort Providence on Hwy. 3.	❷	•	•		•	•		•		•				•	
Fort Simpson (F-3) 18 hectares in Fort Simpson on Hwy. 1.	❸	•	•		•	•		•		•			•		
Fred Henne (F-5) 500 hectares on Hwy. 3 across from Yellowknife airport. Sailing.	❹	•	•	•	•	•		•	•	•			•		
Gwich'in Reserve (B-1) 8,800 hectares s. of Inuvik on Hwy. 8.	❺	•	•	•				•		•					
Hay River (G-4) 11 hectares on Vale Island in Hay River.	❻	•	•		•	•		•	•	•					
Hidden Lake (F-5) 3,000 hectares 45 km e. of Yellowknife along Hwy. 4. Scenic. Canoeing; golf; interpretive displays.	❼	•			•			•	•	•					
Lady Evelyn Falls (G-4) 5 hectares 6.5 km off Hwy. 1 near Kakisa.	❽	•	•	•	•			•	•	•			•		
Little Buffalo River Crossing (G-5) 33 hectares off Hwy. 6, 30 km w. of Fort Resolution.	❾	•	•		•	•		•	•	•					
Little Buffalo River Falls (G-5) 33 hectares off Hwy. 5, 50 km n.w. of Fort Smith.	❿	•	•	•				•		•					

Recreation Areas Chart

The map location numerals in column 2 show an area's location on the preceding map.

	MAP LOCATION	CAMPING	PICNICKING	HIKING TRAILS	BOATING	BOAT RAMP	BOAT RENTAL	FISHING	SWIMMING	PETS ON LEASH	BICYCLE TRAILS	WINTER SPORTS	VISITOR CENTER	LODGE/CABINS	FOOD SERVICE
Prelude Lake (F-5) 95 hectares 29 km w. of Yellowknife on Hwy. 4.	⑪	●	●	●	●	●		●	●	●					
Queen Elizabeth (G-5) 38 hectares off Hwy. 5 in Fort Smith.	⑫	●	●	●				●		●	●		●		
Reid Lake (F-5) 68 hectares 60 km e. of Yellowknife on Hwy. 4.	⑬	●	●	●	●	●		●	●	●					
Twin Falls Gorge (G-4) 673 hectares at Km-post 75 on Hwy. 1.	⑭	●	●	●	●				●			●			

AKLAVIK (B-1) pop. 633

Aklavik, which means "the place of the Barren-land grizzly," was founded in 1912 as the Mackenzie River delta outpost of Hudson's Bay Co. A thriving company base in addition to a trading and trapping center, the town became the administrative center of the Western Arctic region.

However, since the community rested in the middle of the largest delta in Canada, it faced constant change as the powerful Mackenzie River built up new land and flooded the old. These conditions prevented the construction of major roads and airstrips. As a result, the newer town of Inuvik (see place listing p. 413) absorbed Aklavik's administrative role. There are no roads into Aklavik; it is accessible by air from Inuvik or by ice roads during winter.

Many Aklavik residents refuse to move. The descendants of the early traders and trappers work on oil rigs in the Beaufort Sea or trap muskrat in the delta, which is rich in wildlife. A museum, the original company store and restored log cabins serve as reminders of the past.

Just off Main Street is a tree stump in which Albert Johnson, the suspected "Mad Trapper of Rat River," carved his initials. The town also contains his grave. Johnson, who allegedly killed prospectors and trappers for the gold in their teeth, was shot in 1932 after one of the most intensive manhunts in Canadian history. Whether he actually was the "mad trapper" has been a subject explored in both books and film.

BAFFIN ISLAND, NUNAVUT (A-4)

High in Nunavut's Eastern Arctic is Baffin Island, the homeland of the Inuit. It is a land of majestic fiords, icebergs, bountiful wildlife and the midnight sun, which shines until 3 a.m. from March to June. Although Baffin Island is not accessible by car, Iqaluit (see place listing p. 414), Nunavut's capital city, is served by two airlines.

Qaummaarviit Territorial Park, 12 kilometres (7 mi.) west of Iqaluit, can be reached by boat in summer or by dogsled and snowmobile in spring. An easy-to-follow trail links the island's ruins with signs depicting aspects of prehistoric life and culture.

Auyuittuq National Park, 28 kilometres (17 mi.) from Pangnirtung, is accessible by dogsled, snowmobile or boat. The park is notable for its fiords and glaciated valleys and mountains and for being the first national park established above the Arctic Circle. Polar bears, arctic foxes, caribou, seals, walruses, whales and narwhals inhabit the region.

Included in the approximately 40 bird species spotted in the park are the rare gyrfalcon and whistling swan. Remains of the 1,000-year-old Thule Eskimo culture have been found in Cumberland Sound. Hikers and mountain campers traversing Auyuittuq's Akshayuk Pass—commonly known as the "Pang Pass"—will find challenging trails, abundant wildlife and spectacular scenery.

Quttinirpaaq National Park (formerly known as Ellesmere Island National Park Reserve) is the most northerly land mass in Canada and contains 2,604-metre (8,544-ft.) Mount Barbeau, the highest mountain in eastern North America, and Lake Hazen, one of the largest lakes north of the Arctic Circle. The reserve is primarily a polar desert encompassing 39,500 square kilometres (15,250 sq. mi.) of mountain ranges, glaciers, ice shelves and fiords. Remains of buildings from European expeditions can be found on the rocky terrain. Outfitters in Grise Fiord, Iqaluit and Resolute Bay can arrange trips into the park.

Katannilik Territorial Park, between Kimmirut and Iqaluit, is rich with wildlife and unique flora. River tours, hiking and northern survival challenge even the hardiest adventurers. Information can be obtained from Nunavut Tourism, (866) 686-2888, or from the park's visitor center, (867) 939-2416.

In spring and summer licensed guides from Angmarlik Visitor Centre lead expeditions into Kekerten Territorial Park, 50 kilometres (32 mi.) south of Pangnirtung; phone (867) 939-2416. Visitors can see remains of whale lookouts, blubber vats, whalers' houses and Inuit homes. A self-guiding trail connects dozens of ruins.

In the northeasternmost part of Baffin Island is Sirmilik National Park, approximately 22,200 square kilometres (8,572 sq. mi.) of rugged mountains, glaciers, ice fields, ocean fiords and coastal lowlands. In fact Sirmilik translates to "the place of glaciers." Pond Inlet, the closest community to the park, is 25 kilometres (16 mi.) south. Travel to the park—by boat, dogsled or snowmobile (depending on the season)—can be arranged through outfitters in Pond Inlet or Arctic Bay.

The park is accessible year-round, except in October and November when the ice freezes up and in July during ice break up. Popular with mountain climbers, Sirmilik is also a haven for bird-watchers. Colonies of seabirds, including thick-billed murres, black-legged kittiwakes and greater snow geese, inhabit Bylot Island. For additional information contact the park office in Pond Inlet; phone (867) 899-8092.

ENTERPRISE (G-4) pop. 87

Enterprise is the first Northwest Territories community encountered by travelers heading north on Mackenzie Hwy. A major service center for commercial traffic, the town is best known for its spectacular view of Hay River Gorge near the local Esso station.

Scenic 33-metre (108-ft.) Alexandra Falls and 15-metre (50-ft.) Louise Falls in Twin Falls Gorge Territorial Park (see Recreation Areas Chart) are about 9 kilometres (6 mi.) south on Mackenzie Hwy. Camping and picnicking are permitted.

FORT LIARD (G-2) pop. 536

Fort Liard is in the Territories' southwest corner. Nearby archeological digs have revealed strata showing 9,000 years of human occupancy. Prior to 1807 Northwest Co. founded a post that was taken over by Hudson's Bay Co. in 1821 when the companies merged. An earnest fur trade continues.

The opening of Liard Hwy. in the early 1980s put the quiet village on the map. The community is characterized by lush growth and a relatively mild climate, despite its northern location. Bird-watchers will find many songbirds during spring and summer. A small lakefront campground is nearby.

Boat launching is possible on the Petitot River or the Liard River, where visitors can see interesting rock formations and fish for pickerel at the rivers' mouth. Fort Liard is a good jumping-off point for exploring the surrounding mountains or Nahanni National Park Reserve *(see place listing p. 414)*. Chartered flights and a forestry office are available in town.

FORT SIMPSON (F-3) pop. 1,238

Established in 1804 at the fork of the Mackenzie and Liard rivers, Fort Simpson is the oldest continuously occupied trading post in the Mackenzie River Valley. Once a district headquarters for Hudson's Bay Co., the town developed into a center of river trade. Originally Fort of the Forks, the town was renamed to honor Thomas Simpson, first governor of the merged Northwest and Hudson's Bay companies.

Fort Simpson has always been a gathering place for people. It serves as a center for territorial government administration and oil and mining exploration. It also serves as a departure point for air, raft and canoe trips into Nahanni National Park Reserve *(see place listing p. 414)*. A visitor center offers interpretive films, historical walking tours and a native crafts display; phone (867) 695-7750.

The Village of Fort Simpson Tourist Information Centre: P.O. Box 438, Fort Simpson, NT, Canada X0E 0N0. **Phone:** (867) 695-3182.

FORT SMITH (G-5) pop. 2,093

Initially a link in a strategic chain of 19th-century trading posts along the Mackenzie portage route to the Arctic, Fort Smith became an autonomous town in 1966. It is regional headquarters for the government of the Northwest Territories and contains several governmental offices. The town also is the site of the Thebacha Campus of Aurora College. Nearby Wood Buffalo National Park *(see place listing p. 415)* is home to one of the largest buffalo herds in the world.

Fort Smith Visitor Information Centre: 174 McDougal Rd., P.O. Box 147, Fort Smith, NT, Canada X0E 0P0. **Phone:** (867) 872-3065 or (867) 872-8400.

HAY RIVER (G-4) pop. 3,606

Recent archeological finds show that the Slavey Dene have used the area around Hay River for thousands of years, but the first buildings did not appear until 1868 when Hudson's Bay Co. established a trading post. The town's strategic location prompts its occasional reference as the "Hub of the North."

Hay River is the southernmost port of the Mackenzie River system. During the 5-month shipping season barges, fishing boats and Coast Guard craft clog the protected river channels. The town serves as headquarters of the Great Slave Lake commercial fishing industry, which supplies the demand for Great Slave Lake whitefish. Dene Cultural Institute (also known as the Yamozha Kue Society), on the Hay River Dene Reserve, is open for tours mid-May to mid-September. A visitor center on Mackenzie Hwy. is open 9-9, mid-May to mid-September; phone (867) 874-8480.

Hay River Chamber of Commerce: 10K Gagnier St., Hay River, NT, Canada X0E 1G1. **Phone:** (867) 874-2565.

INUVIK (B-1) pop. 3,463

Inuvik, meaning "place of man," was erected in 1958 to replace nearby Aklavik *(see place listing p. 412)*, which appeared to be sinking into the Mackenzie River delta. The town boomed in the 1970s as the center of the Beaufort Sea oil exploration, which since has shifted to other areas. As well as being the communications, commerce and government center for the Western Arctic, the town was the site of a Canadian Forces station until 1986.

Accessible via Dempster Hwy., Inuvik is one of the northernmost points on the North American continent that can be reached by public road. During June and most of July there are 24 hours of daylight. The town also serves as a departure point for plane trips to the Arctic Ocean and the Mackenzie River delta system.

Western Arctic Regional Visitor Centre: 278 Mackenzie Rd., P.O. Box 1160, Bag Service #1, Inuvik, NT, Canada X0E 0T0. **Phone:** (867) 777-7237.

IQALUIT, NUNAVUT (C-6) pop. 6,699

In 1576 British explorer Martin Frobisher arrived at Iqaluit's bay in present-day Nunavut and assumed that he had discovered the Northwest Passage. A discovery he had believed to be gold proved to be iron pyrite, or "fool's gold." The Baffin Island town honored his memory in its name—Frobisher Bay—until 1987, when its name officially was changed back to the traditional Inuit name, Iqaluit (ih-KA-loo-it), which means "place of many fish."

Iqaluit, now the capital of Nunavut, began as a small trading post. During the 19th century European and American whalers frequented the bay waters hoping to supply their home ports with whalebone for women's corsets and blubber for lamp oil. Hiking opportunities are plentiful on the outskirts of town or through the nearby mountains. Inaccessible by car, Iqaluit can be reached by air from Calgary and Edmonton via Yellowknife, Winnipeg via Rankin Inlet, Montréal and Ottawa.

With the construction of the Distant Early Warning (DEW) Line in 1954, the town became an important defense site and a major refueling station for both commercial and military aircraft. Iqaluit is the largest community in Nunavut and the educational, administrative, transportation and economic center for the Baffin region. A focal point for Inuit art, the town boasts numerous galleries.

In 1971 the Astro Hill Complex, which includes retail stores, a hotel, movie theater, high-rise apartments, offices and a swimming pool, was completed using modular precast concrete units. Of architectural interest at the time, the complex was designed to withstand northern climatic extremes.

A kilometre northwest of Iqaluit is Sylvia Grinnell Territorial Park on the Sylvia Grinnell River. Visitors to the park can enjoy a picnic with a view of gentle waterfalls and can survey the tundra scenery from a platform overlooking the river. For more information, phone Iqaluit's Unikkaarvik Visitor Centre at (867) 979-4636.

Nunavut Tourism: P.O. Box 1450, Iqaluit, NU, Canada X0A 0H0. **Phone:** (866) 686-2888.

NAHANNI NATIONAL PARK RESERVE
(F-1)

Elevations in the park range from 1,853 metres (6,079 ft.) at the South Nahanni River to 2,762 metres (9,062 ft.) in the Cirque of the Unclimbables in the park's northwest corner. Refer to CAA/AAA maps for additional elevation information.

About 145 kilometres (90 mi.) west of Fort Simpson and accessible only by air, the park uses Fort Liard and Fort Simpson in the Territories, Muncho Lake in British Columbia, and Watson Lake and Whitehorse in the Yukon as its major supply and jumping-off points. Steeped in myth, mystery and adventure, Nahanni National Park Reserve covers more than 30,000 square kilometres (11,583 sq. mi.) of wilderness in the South Nahanni country.

Liard Highway, linking Fort Nelson and Fort Simpson *(see place listing p. 413)*, passes Blackstone Territorial Park, east of Nahanni National Park Reserve, providing access to Liard River and Nahanni Butte, 30 kilometres (19 mi.) upriver.

A land of rivers, ragged peaks, more than 30 species of mammals and a waterfall twice the height of Niagara Falls, Nahanni National Park Reserve was created in 1972. It was placed on the UNESCO (United Nations Educational, Scientific and Cultural Organization) World Heritage list 6 years later and cited as an "exceptional natural site forming part of the heritage of mankind."

In the early 1900s the area received a reputation for myth and adventure. Gold prospectors, drawn by rumors of placer deposits, began to arrive. When the decapitated bodies of the two MacLeod brothers were found, stories of huge mountain men proliferated.

Although no real mountain men ever were seen, the park remains a place of rugged beauty with little development, including few accommodations for visitors. Those who come to raft and canoe on the rivers and hike the forests, alpine tundra and canyons of Nahanni will find it a bracing experience. Travel by water is an excellent way to enjoy the park; however, it can be dangerous and should be attempted only by those experienced in canoeing and rafting. Reservations are required for river trips. Due to the trips' popularity, reservations should be made well in advance; phone the park office for information.

Less experienced river travelers should hire a licensed outfitter for guided river trips down the South Nahanni River. Tours pass Virginia Falls, where the South Nahanni River plunges more than 90 metres (295 ft.); the Gate, a 90-degree river bend below 213-metre (700-ft.) vertical cliffs; and hot springs such as those at First Canyon and Rabbitkettle. Visitors to Rabbitkettle **must** register at the warden's cabin and have park staff accompany them to the springs. Daytime air trips to Virginia Falls should be prearranged through an air charter company in Fort Simpson, Fort Liard, Watson Lake, Whitehorse or Muncho Lake.

Fishing for arctic grayling, lake and bull trout and northern pike is permitted with a national park fishing license (annual pass $34.30), which can be obtained at the Fort Simpson Administration Office or at the warden's cabin at Rabbitkettle Lake. All national park regulations apply. Firearms are not permitted.

Wildlife species include moose, beavers, woodland caribou, Dall sheep, grizzly and black bears, white-tailed deer and mountain goats. Visitors should take particular care when traveling in areas where they are likely to encounter bears.

The park is open year-round. The park administration office at Fort Simpson is open daily 8:30-noon and 1-5, July-Aug.; Mon.-Fri. 8:30-noon and

1-5, rest of year. Overnight visitors and those planning river rafting or canoe trips must register before entering the park and upon leaving.

One-day admission to the park is $24.50 per person. For route information, park regulations, weather conditions and park activities contact the Superintendent, Nahanni National Park Reserve, P.O. Box 348, Fort Simpson, NT, Canada X0E 0N0; phone (867) 695-7750. *See Recreation Areas Chart.*

Bordering Nahanni National Park Reserve to the northeast, Nááts'ihch'oh National Park Reserve was established in 2012 as Canada's 44th national park. Combined with Nahanni, Nááts'ihch'oh (pronounced naats-each-choh) protects 86 percent of the South Nahanni River watershed including land that is culturally and spiritually important to aboriginal peoples. Trumpeter swans, caribou, mountain goats and grizzly bears live within the park's boundaries.

TULITA (D-2) pop. 478

Because of the lack of roads on the frontier, most towns were founded along rivers. Originally called Fort Norman, Tulita was established in 1810 when Northwest Co. built a trading post at the confluence of the Great Bear and Mackenzie rivers. The town's name means "where two rivers meet."

Later years brought additional industries. In 1920 pitchblende—the chief ore-mineral source of uranium—was discovered, and the early 1980s brought the construction of the Wells-Zama oil pipeline.

Tulita is accessible via air service from Norman Wells. No all-weather roads lead into the community, but a winter road—open from late January to mid-March—connects Tulita to surrounding communities. Nearby is one of the Northwest Territories' oldest Anglican churches, built of squared logs in the 1860s. The restored church can be visited.

About 20 kilometres (12 mi.) away is a bed of low-grade coal that has been burning for centuries. Although the fire likely was ignited by lightning, Dene legend attributes it to a giant's campfire. During the summer the surface of the bed sometimes rises and the coals are exposed. Firefighters' attempts to extinguish the smoldering coals have failed.

Hamlet Office: P.O. Box 91, Tulita, NT, Canada X0E 0K0. **Phone:** (867) 588-4471.

WOOD BUFFALO NATIONAL PARK (H-5)

Elevations in the park range from 183 metres (600 ft.) at the Little Buffalo River to 945 metres (3,100 ft.) in the Caribou Mountains. Refer to CAA/AAA maps for additional elevation information.

Accessible by Hwy. 5, which connects with Mackenzie Hwy. at Hay River, Wood Buffalo National Park is the second largest park in the world. Covering about the same area as the states of Maryland and New Jersey combined, the national park straddles the border between the Northwest Territories and Alberta.

This vast subarctic wilderness contains such remarkable geological features as the Salt Plains, Alberta Plateau, the deltas and lowlands of the Peace River and Athabasca River, and extensive gypsum karst formations. The park was established in 1922 to protect one of the world's largest free-roaming herds of wood bison; approximately 5,000 of these animals now live there. Moose, caribou, muskrats, beavers and black bears are among other park residents.

The Peace Athabasca Delta is an important stopover for North America's four major waterfowl flyways. A large variety of waterfowl as well as hawks, eagles and pelicans, are present for part of the year. The northeastern corner of the park is one of the last nesting grounds in the world for the endangered whooping crane. Some of the park's lakes and rivers contain pike, pickerel, trout, whitefish and goldeye. Wildflowers and berries abound in the rolling meadows.

The 508-kilometre (316-mi.) Fort Chipewyan Winter Road is open mid-December to mid-March (weather permitting). The road runs from Fort McMurray, Alberta, to Fort Smith; part of the road is formed by ice. To check road conditions between Fort Chipewyan and Fort Smith, phone the park office or (867) 872-7962 for recorded information. To check road conditions between Fort Chipewyan and Fort McMurray, phone the Regional Municipality of Wood Buffalo at (780) 697-3600.

Visitors can see such magnificent snow-covered scenery as boreal forest, lakes and wide-open meadows. Before departure travelers should contact the park office for a list of driving regulations and recommended travel supplies.

Boating, picnicking and camping are permitted at Pine Lake. The park has hiking trails, which can be used for snowshoeing and cross-country skiing in winter. Contact the park for information about guided nature hikes and other interpretive events.

The park is open year-round; however, campgrounds and facilities are open Victoria Day weekend through Labour Day. The Fort Smith Visitor Reception Centre at 149 McDougal Rd. is open daily 9-6, June 1 through Labour Day; Mon.-Fri. 9-noon and 1-5, rest of year. Phone (867) 872-7960, or TTY (867) 872-7961. The Fort Chipewyan Visitor Reception Centre on MacKenzie Avenue is open Mon.-Fri. 9-noon and 1-5, year-round. Hours may vary; phone ahead. Phone (780) 697-3662.

Admission to the park is free. For route information, road conditions or details about park activities contact the Superintendent, Wood Buffalo National Park, P.O. Box 750, Fort Smith, NT, Canada X0E 0P0; phone (867) 872-7900. *See Recreation Areas Chart.*

YELLOWKNIFE (F-5) pop. 19,234

Although the Dene hunted the Yellowknife region for thousands of years and Europeans explored it in 1771, a permanent settlement was not established until the discovery of gold in 1934. Taking the name of the copper knives carried by the Chipewyan Indians, the town is now the capital of the Northwest Territories and the site of a gold mine and a booming diamond industry.

In 1967 Yellowknife replaced Ottawa as the seat of government for the Northwest Territories. Tours of the Legislative Assembly are available Mon.-Fri. at 10:30, 1:30 and 3:30, Sun. at 1:30, June-Aug.; Mon.-Fri. at 10:30, rest of year. Phone (867) 669-2200. On the northern shore of Great Slave Lake, this "metropolis" of the north lies less than 500 kilometres (311 mi.) from the Arctic Circle and is an excellent place to shop for Northern arts.

The city's historic Old Town retains the gold rush excitement of the 1930s with quaint restaurants, art galleries, shops, and boat, kayak, canoe and yacht rentals. Planes are available for sightseeing and fishing trips. The visitor center on 49th Street can provide information about rentals and excursions.

Best viewed October through March, the aurora borealis, or northern lights, is produced when atomic particles from outside the atmosphere strike and excite atoms within the upper atmosphere. The lights sweep mysteriously across the clear night sky as luminescent curtains of red, green, pink and purple light in patterns called rayed bands. Guided viewing trips are available.

The scenic 71-kilometre (44-mi.) Ingraham Trail (Hwy. 4) to Tibbitt Lake allows year-round access to several chains of lakes and streams. Seven boat launches and two campgrounds lie along the road. Prelude Nature Trail runs 3 kilometres (1.8 mi.) from Prelude Lake Territorial Park *(see Recreation Areas Chart)* through the wilderness to several lookout points, while another trail leads to Cameron Falls.

Prospector's Trail is in Fred Henne Territorial Park *(see Recreation Areas Chart)*, west near Long Lake. The 4-kilometre (2.5-mi.) loop points out the region's varied geological features and is of interest to rock hounds; sturdy footwear and insect repellent are necessary. Other hiking trails lead from Ingraham Trail; information and brochures are available at the visitor center.

Easily accessible area lakes include Prosperous Lake, Pontoon Lake, Prelude Lake, Reid Lake and Tibbitt Lake. Walsh Lake has good trout fishing, but is accessible only by going through Reid Lake.

The scenic portion of Hwy. 3 runs north from Mackenzie Bison Sanctuary to Edzo, then parallels the northern shore of Great Slave Lake. Driving anywhere in the area, or throughout the Northwest Territories, demands that a vehicle be in top mechanical condition.

Northern Frontier Regional Visitor Center: 4807 49th St., Yellowknife, NT, Canada X1A 3T5. **Phone:** (867) 873-4262 or (877) 881-4262.

Self-guiding tours: The visitor center provides brochures for a walking tour of Old Town and New Town.

COAST FRASER TOWER   (867)873-8700

Hotel
$185-$250

Address: 5303 52nd St X1A 1V1 **Location:** Corner of 52nd St and 53rd Ave. **Facility:** 58 kitchen units, some two bedrooms. 10 stories, interior corridors. **Parking:** winter plug-ins. **Terms:** cancellation fee imposed. **Amenities:** safes. **Activities:** steamroom, exercise room. **Guest Services:** coin laundry. **Featured Amenity: continental breakfast.**

SAVE ECO BIZ 🛜 🅺 🖥 🖨

🖭 / SOME UNITS 🛏 HS

DAYS INN & SUITES YELLOWKNIFE   (867)873-9700
🔷🔷 Hotel. **Address:** 4401 50th Ave X1A 2N2

THE EXPLORER HOTEL   867/873-3531
🔷🔷🔷 Hotel. **Address:** 4825 49th Ave X1A 2R3

SUPER 8 YELLOWKNIFE   (867)669-8888
🔷🔷 Motel. **Address:** 308 Old Airport Rd X1A 3G3

WHERE TO EAT

THE BLACK KNIGHT PUB   867/920-4041
🔷🔷 International. Casual Dining. **Address:** 4910 49th St X1A 2N8

BULLOCK'S BISTRO   867/873-3474
🔷🔷 Regional Canadian. Casual Dining. **Address:** 3534 Weaver Dr X1A 2H2

FUEGO INTERNATIONAL CUISINE   867/873-3750
🔷🔷🔷 American. Casual Dining. **Address:** 4915 50th St X1A 1S1

RED APPLE RESTAURANT   867/766-3388
🔷🔷 Chinese. Casual Dining. **Address:** 4701 50 Ave X1A 2N6

TRADER'S GRILL   867/873-3531
🔷🔷🔷 American. Casual Dining. **Address:** 4825 49th Ave X1A 2R2

Qu'Appelle Valley

Saskatchewan

A visit to Saskatchewan is a perfect escape from the hustle and bustle.

Named after the Plains Cree term *ki-siskatchewan,* meaning "the river that flows swiftly," Saskatchewan boasts more than just a great river with an unusual name.

Along country roads, you'll encounter prairies, mountains, grasslands and even sand dunes. While approximately half the province is covered in pine, white spruce and other trees, a good portion is blanketed with fields of wheat.

Look for signs marked with a barn symbol; they designate bed and breakfast inns and vacation farms, where you can take part in milking cows and enjoy homemade berry preserves or baked goods.

Take a dip into one of more than 100,000 freshwater lakes, including those nestled among resorts and golf courses with rolling fairways in the Qu'Appelle Valley.

For history, head to towns that preserve

the origin of the Mounted Police, the heritage of Métis culture or the rough-and-tumble cowboy lifestyle.

Or visit the Beaver Lodge Cabin on Ajawaan Lake in Prince Albert National Park, residence of naturalist author Grey Owl, who coined the popular belief that "you belong to nature, not it to you."

Colors of the Province

The hues of Saskatchewan's palette were determined both with and without man's help. Painted by nature and the history of the plains, vibrant gold, green and red figure prominently in the province's scheme.

Shimmering fields of grain glint gold in the sunlight. The plains stretch to the horizon in a never-ending series of undulating waves, interrupted only by an occasional silo. More than 50 percent of Canada's wheat crop comes from this land. Proof of the grain's economic importance to the province is the three golden wheat sheaves on its coat of arms. Saskatchewan's flag provides further evidence; its lower half, a solid band of gold, represents the grain fields dominating the province's southern portion.

Color Regina green—the city has more than 350,000 trees. A particularly verdant section of town is Wascana Centre, a 930-hectare urban park that's the heart of Saskatchewan's capital. Lining the rambling shoreline of Wascana Lake, the center is home to cultural and educational institutions and the architecturally impressive Legislative Building, the seat of provincial government. Prince Albert National Park contributes to the

Legislative Building, Regina

emerald color scheme with nearly 1 million acres of spruce, evergreens and grassland.

The Royal Canadian Mounted Police are immediately recognizable by their scarlet tunics. In fact, the route they took in 1874 to establish law and order in western Canada is retraced along Hwy. 13, the Red Coat Trail.

Regina is home to the RCMP Heritage Centre, the RCMP's only training academy. Watch the cadets drill at the Sergeant Major's Parade, usually held Monday, Wednesday and Friday at 12:45 p.m. In July and early August, the province's colors are displayed in the Sunset Retreat Ceremony. The golden glow cast by the setting sun seems especially fitting while you watch crimson-clad cadets proudly march in formation against the backdrop of lush greenery that borders the parade grounds.

Recreation

Contrary to popular belief, Saskatchewan is not all prairie. Even in the southern half, where farming is predominant, lakes and parks overflow with recreational options.

Choose from more than 100,000 lakes, rivers and streams for freshwater fishing. While northern pike, rainbow trout and walleye will take your bait throughout the province, head for northern waters to land trophy-size lake trout, Arctic grayling and other sport fish.

Lake Diefenbaker, south of Outlook, is a favorite destination for walleye or northern pike. The Canadian Shield, in the northern third of the province, is a safe bet for anglers; almost 40 percent of its area consists of H_2O. Try Lac la Ronge for trout. Outfitters will fly you to more remote northern fishing lakes.

Tumbling east to west across the province north of the 55th parallel, the Churchill River provides some of North America's best white-water canoeing. Experience white-water rafting on the Clearwater River.

If the rush of white-water action is too intense, paddle your boat along calmer waters. The Bagwa Canoe Route, in Prince Albert National Park, travels through several pristine lakes. Dip your oars in late May through September, when the lakes are warmest.

For the ultimate in calm, head to Little Manitou Lake, near the resort community of Manitou Beach. The lake is believed to have curative powers; its high concentration of minerals makes sinking impossible.

When winter makes its appearance, go cross-country skiing on groomed and marked trails. Prince Albert National Park has about 150 kilometres (93 mi.) of trails. Moose Mountain Provincial Park, north of Carlyle, adds another 50 kilometres (30 mi.). Thousands of kilometres of groomed trails link towns and parks along Canada's version of Route 66, a cross-country snowmobile route. Put-in points include Nipawin, North Battleford and Yorkton. Snowmobile registration is mandatory; phone Tourism Saskatchewan, (877) 237-2273, for a provincial snowmobile trail map.

When warm weather finally returns, Saskatchewanians and visitors alike head to Prince Albert National Park. Three loop trails—Boundary Bog, Mud Creek and Treebeard—traverse fairly level terrain and put you in touch with some of Mother Nature's creations—a black spruce and tamarack bog; sightings of beavers and great blue herons; and forests of aspens and balsam firs.

Another popular summer playground is the Qu'Appelle Valley, a broad swath of land in southern Saskatchewan bordered by rolling hills. A chain of lakes and three provincial parks are the setting for resort villages where guests enjoy boating, water skiing and swimming.

Churchill River

Historic Timeline

1690	Henry Kelsey, an English fur trader, explores Saskatchewan.
1774	The Hudson's Bay Company builds Saskatchewan's first permanent settlement.
1870	Canada acquires present-day Saskatchewan as part of the Northwest Territories.
1873	The massacre of a band of Assiniboine First Nations by U.S. wolf hunters prompts the creation of the Mounted Police.
1885	Louis Riel leads the Métis tribe's battle for land rights in the Northwest Rebellion.
1905	Saskatchewan becomes a province.
1962	Saskatchewan establishes the first public health insurance program in North America.
1979	John Diefenbaker, Canada's 13th prime minister, is buried at the University of Saskatchewan.
1994	An almost complete Tyrannosaurus rex skeleton is unearthed near Eastend.
2001	Prince Charles makes his first royal visit to Saskatchewan.
2017	Canada marks its 150th birthday with celebrations across the province.

What To Pack

Temperature Averages Maximum/Minimum (Celsius)	JANUARY	FEBRUARY	MARCH	APRIL	MAY	JUNE	JULY	AUGUST	SEPTEMBER	OCTOBER	NOVEMBER	DECEMBER
Maple Creek	-2/-14	1/-12	7/-6	14/0	20/5	25/9	29/12	28/11	22/5	14/-1	5/-7	0/-13
Meadow Lake	-10/-19	-7/-17	-1/-10	10/-2	17/4	21/8	23/11	22/9	16/4	9/-2	-2/-11	-8/-17
Prince Albert	-14/-26	-9/-22	-3/-16	9/-4	18/3	22/8	24/11	23/9	16/3	9/-3	-3/-13	-12/-22
Regina	-11/-22	-8/-18	-1/-12	10/-3	18/4	23/9	26/12	26/11	18/4	12/-2	0/-11	-9/-19
Saskatoon	-13/-23	-9/-19	-2/-13	10/-2	18/4	23/9	25/12	24/10	17/4	11/-2	-2/-11	-10/-19
Yorkton	-13/-23	-9/-21	-3/-14	8/-3	17/3	22/9	24/11	24/9	17/4	10/-2	-2/-11	-11/-20

From the records of The Weather Channel Interactive, Inc.

Good Facts To Know

Saskatchewan Annual Events

Please call ahead to confirm event details.

JANUARY

- Knights of Columbus Saskatchewan Indoor Games / Saskatoon 306-955-4818
- Lieutenant Governor's New Year's Day Levee / Regina 306-787-4070
- Western Canadian Crop Production Show Saskatoon 306-931-7149

FEBRUARY

- Saskatoon Blues Festival Saskatoon 306-345-9587
- Canadian Challenge International Sled Dog Race Prince Albert 306-763-1539
- Prince Albert Winter Festival Prince Albert 306-764-7595

MARCH

- Thunder Creek Model Railroad Club Model Train Show / Moose Jaw 306-693-5989
- Spring Home Show Regina 306-546-5227
- Antiques and Collectibles Swap Meet / Moose Jaw 306-693-7315

APRIL

- Yorkton Spring Expo Yorkton 306-783-4800
- First Nations Spring Celebration Pow Wow Regina 306-790-5950
- GlassArt / Saskatoon 306-343-7450

MAY

- Vesna Festival / Saskatoon 306-652-7717
- Cathedral Village Arts Festival / Regina 306-569-8744
- Saskatchewan Highland Gathering and Celtic Festival / Regina 306-789-6516

JUNE

- SaskTel Saskatchewan Jazz Festival / Saskatoon 306-652-1421
- Humboldt Summer Sizzler Humboldt 306-682-3444
- Mosaic: A Festival of Cultures / Regina 306-757-5990

JULY

- Shakespeare on the Saskatchewan Festival Saskatoon 306-653-2300
- Saskatchewan Festival of Words / Moose Jaw 306-691-0557
- Lloydminster Colonial Days Fair / Lloydminster 306-825-5571

AUGUST

- Saskatoon Folkfest Saskatoon 306-931-0100
- The Saskatoon EX Saskatoon 888-931-9333
- Queen City Exhibition Regina 306-781-9200

SEPTEMBER

- Tapestrama / Prince Albert 306-922-0400
- Goose Festival and Culture Days / Kindersley 306-463-2320
- Maple Creek Cowboy Poetry Gathering and Western Art and Gear Show / Maple Creek 306-662-2434

OCTOBER

- Reflections Art Festival Saskatoon 306-382-3155
- Thanksgiving Pow Wow Prince Albert 306-764-4751
- Haunted Village Moose Jaw 306-692-7798

NOVEMBER

- Canadian Western Agribition Regina 306-565-0565
- Lloydminster Stockade Roundup / Lloydminster 306-825-5571
- Yorkton Grain Miller's Harvest Showdown Yorkton 306-783-4800

DECEMBER

- Enchanted Forest Holiday Light Tour / Saskatoon 306-975-3382
- Sundog Arts and Entertainment Faire Saskatoon 306-384-7364
- Carlyle's Dickens Village Festival / Carlyle 306-453-2363

Fort Walsh National Historic Site, Maple Creek

Saskatoon and the South Saskatchewan River

Kayak in Prince Albert National Park

Grasslands National Park

Canola field

Index: Great Experience for Members

AAA editor's picks of exceptional note

Prince Albert National Park

RCMP Heritage Centre

Royal Saskatchewan Museum

Wanuskewin Heritage Park

See Orientation map on p. 430 for corresponding grid coordinates, if applicable.

*Indicates the GEM is temporarily closed.

Prince Albert National Park (B-3)
Prince Albert National Park *(See p. 441.)*

Regina (E-4)
Government House Museum and Interpretive Centre *(See p. 442.)*

RCMP Heritage Centre *(See p. 442.)*
Royal Saskatchewan Museum *(See p. 443.)*

Saskatoon (D-3)
Wanuskewin Heritage Park *(See p. 448.)*

Get Involved and Keep Teens Safe

Exploring the countryside or visiting nearby cities can be perfect opportunities to teach your teens good habits and rules of the road—before and after they learn to drive.

Get resources from AAA/CAA:

- Tools to improve driving skills
- Information about driver's licensing
- Tips to avoid distracted driving
- Advice for keeping insurance costs down
- A model parent-teen driving agreement

 Visit TeenDriving.AAA.com or DriveRight.CAA.ca

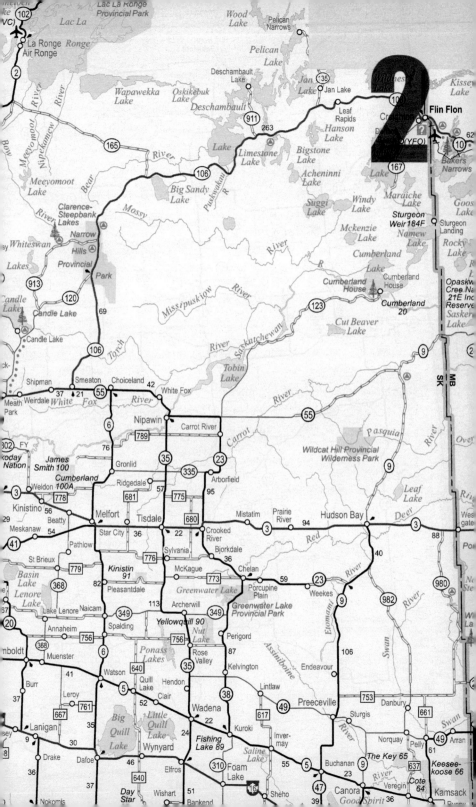

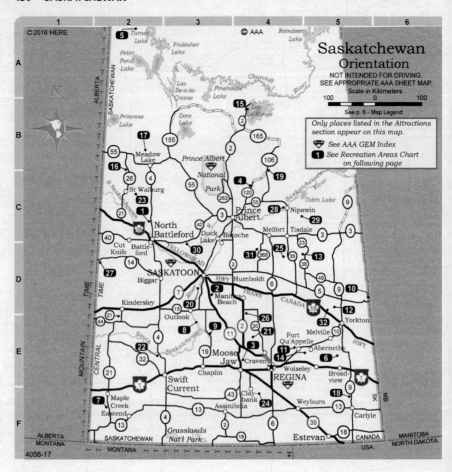

© AAA

Saskatchewan
Orientation
NOT INTENDED FOR DRIVING.
SEE APPROPRIATE AAA SHEET MAP.
Scale in Kilometers

100   0   100

See p. 6 - Map Legend

Only places listed in the Attractions
section appear on this map.

⬥ See AAA GEM Index

1 See Recreation Areas Chart
on following page

4056-17

Recreation Areas Chart
The map location numerals in column 2 show an
area's location on the preceding map.

	MAP LOCATION	CAMPING	PICNICKING	HIKING TRAILS	BOATING	BOAT RAMP	BOAT RENTAL	FISHING	SWIMMING	PETS ON LEASH	BICYCLE TRAILS	WINTER SPORTS	VISITOR CENTER	LODGE/CABINS	FOOD SERVICE
NATIONAL PARKS (See place listings.)															
Grasslands (F-3) 906 square kilometres.		•	•	•						•			•		
Prince Albert (B-3) 3,875 square kilometres. Horse rental.		•	•	•	•	•	•	•	•	•	•	•	•	•	•
PROVINCIAL															
The Battlefords (C-2) 600 hectares 4.75 km n. of Cochin off Hwy. 4. Cross-country skiing, golf.	**1**	•	•	•	•	•	•	•	•	•	•	•	•	•	•
Blackstrap (D-3) 530 hectares 8 km e. of Dundurn via Hwy. 211. Cross-country and downhill skiing; sailboard and water bike rental.	**2**	•	•	•	•	•	•	•	•	•		•			•
Buffalo Pound (E-4) 1,930 hectares 19 km n. of Moose Jaw on Hwy. 2, then 13 km e. on Hwy. 202. Cross-country and downhill skiing, tennis; pool.	**3**	•	•	•	•	•	•	•	•	•	•	•			•
Candle Lake (C-4) 1,270 hectares 60 km n.e. of Prince Albert on hwys. 55 and 120. Cross-country skiing.	**4**	•	•	•	•	•	•	•	•	•		•		•	•

Recreation Areas Chart

The map location numerals in column 2 show an area's location on the preceding map.

	MAP LOCATION	CAMPING	PICNICKING	HIKING TRAILS	BOATING	BOAT RAMP	BOAT RENTAL	FISHING	SWIMMING	PETS ON LEASH	BICYCLE TRAILS	WINTER SPORTS	VISITOR CENTER	LODGE/CABINS	FOOD SERVICE
Clearwater River (A-2) 224,040 hectares 50 km n.e. of La Loche on Hwy. 955 (north of area shown on map). Canoeing (experienced only).	5	•	•	•				•							
Crooked Lake (E-5) 190 hectares 30 km n. of Broadview on Hwy. 605. Golf.	6	•	•	•	•	•	•	•	•	•				•	•
Cypress Hills Interprovincial (F-2) 20,451 hectares 30 km s. of Maple Creek on Hwy. 21. Historic. Canoeing, cross-country skiing, golf, horseback riding, kayaking, sailing, windsurfing; amphitheater; interpretive programs.	7	•	•	•	•	•	•	•	•	•	•	•	•	•	•
Danielson (E-3) 2,910 hectares on n. end of Lake Diefenbaker via hwys. 44, 45 or 219. Geocaching, ice fishing.	8	•	•	•	•	•		•	•	•			•		•
Douglas (E-3) 4,430 hectares 11 km s.e. of Elbow on Hwy. 19. Cross-country skiing, houseboat rental.	9	•	•	•	•	•	•	•	•	•		•		•	•
Duck Mountain (D-5) 26,160 hectares 25 km e. of Kamsack on Hwy. 57. Cross-country and downhill skiing, golf, tennis; horse rental.	10	•	•	•	•	•	•	•	•	•		•	•	•	•
Echo Valley (E-4) 640 hectares 8 km w. of Fort Qu'Appelle off Hwy. 10. Cross-country skiing (ski trails can be used by bicyclists in summer); horse rental.	11	•	•	•	•	•		•	•	•	•	•			•
Good Spirit Lake (D-5) 1,900 hectares 24 km n.e. of Springside via Hwy. 47. Cross-country skiing, tennis.	12	•	•	•	•	•		•	•	•		•			•
Greenwater Lake (D-5) 20,720 hectares 38 km n. of Kelvington on Hwy. 38. Cross-country skiing, ice skating, golf, tennis.	13	•	•	•	•	•	•	•	•	•		•	•	•	•
Katepwa Point (E-4) 8 hectares 10 km s.e. of Lebret on Hwy. 56.	14		•		•	•	•	•	•	•					•
Lac La Ronge (B-4) 344,470 hectares 48.25 km n. of La Ronge on Hwy. 102. Cross-country skiing; houseboat rental.	15	•	•	•	•	•	•	•	•	•		•		•	•
Makwa Lake (B-2) 2,560 hectares n.w. of Loon Lake off Hwy. 26. Cross-country skiing, golf; horse rental.	16	•	•	•	•	•	•	•	•	•		•		•	•
Meadow Lake (B-2) 156,970 hectares 5 km n. of Goodsoil via Hwy. 26. Cross-country skiing, tennis; horse rental, sailboat rental.	17	•	•	•	•	•	•	•	•	•		•		•	•
Moose Mountain (F-5) 40,060 hectares 22.5 km n. of Carlyle on Hwy. 9. Cross-country skiing, golf (18 holes), tennis; horseback riding.	18	•	•	•	•	•	•	•	•	•		•	•	•	•
Narrow Hills (C-4) 53,610 hectares 64.25 km n. of Smeaton on Hwy. 106. Canoeing, cross-country skiing, snowmobiling. ATV trails; playground.	19	•	•	•	•	•	•	•	•	•		•		•	•
Pike Lake (D-3) 500 hectares 30.5 km s. of Saskatoon on Hwy. 60. Golf, tennis; pool. Ten horsepower limit for boats.	20	•	•	•	•	•	•	•	•	•		•	•		•
Rowan's Ravine (E-4) 270 hectares 22.5 km w. of Bulyea on Hwy. 220.	21	•	•	•	•	•	•	•	•	•				•	•
Saskatchewan Landing (E-2) 5,600 hectares 45 km n. of Swift Current via Hwy. 4. Bicycling (park roads only). Horse rental, windsurfing rental, golf (18 holes), geocaching.	22	•	•	•	•	•	•	•	•	•			•	•	•
OTHER															
Brights-Sand Lake (C-2) 648 hectares 27 km e. of St. Walburg off Hwy. 26 on a gravel road. Bird-watching, canoeing, cross-country skiing, golf (nine holes), miniature golf, mountain biking, snowmobiling; beach, canoe rental, nature trails with interpretive signs, playground.	23	•	•	•	•	•	•	•	•	•	•	•	•	•	•
Dunnet (F-4) 50 hectares 7 km s. of Avonlea on Hwy. 334. Cross-country skiing, ice fishing, snowmobiling.	24	•	•	•	•	•		•	•	•		•			•
Kipabiskau (D-4) 16 hectares 35 km s.w. of Tisdale off Hwy. 3 or Hwy. 35. Cross-country skiing, ice fishing, snowmobiling; beach, canoe and kayak rental, nature trails, playground.	25	•	•	•	•	•	•	•	•	•		•		•	•
Last Mountain Lake National Wildlife Area (E-4) 65 hectares 20 km n.w. of Govan off Hwy. 20 on a gravel road. Bird-watching, ice fishing; pool.	26	•	•	•				•	•	•		•		•	•
Macklin Lake (D-2) 154 hectares .4 km s. of Macklin on Hwy. 31. Golf (nine holes); beach, playground, wildlife preserve.	27	•	•	•	•	•	•		•	•	•				•

Recreation Areas Chart

The map location numerals in column 2 show an area's location on the preceding map.

	MAP LOCATION	CAMPING	PICNICKING	HIKING TRAILS	BOATING	BOAT RAMP	BOAT RENTAL	FISHING	SWIMMING	PETS ON LEASH	BICYCLE TRAILS	WINTER SPORTS	VISITOR CENTER	LODGE/CABINS	FOOD SERVICE
Nipawin and District (C-4) 121 hectares 3 km n.w. of Nipawin on Hwy. 55. Cross-country skiing, golf (18 holes), snowmobiling; petting zoo, playground, spray pool.	28	•	•	•	•	•		•	•	•	•	•		•	•
Pasquia (C-5) 65 hectares 12 km n. of Arborfield on Hwy. 23. Cross-country and downhill skiing, golf (9 holes), pool, playground, river canoeing. Road access to Pasquia paleontological site (inquire at the visitor center).	29	•	•	•				•	•	•	•				•
Redberry Lake (D-3) 5,600 hectares 12.8 km e. of Hafford on Hwy. 40. Cross-country skiing, golf (nine holes), playgrounds.	30	•	•	•	•	•		•	•	•		•	•	•	•
St. Brieux (D-4) 65 hectares 1 km w. of St. Brieux on Hwy. 368. Historic. Cross-country skiing, golf (nine holes), miniature golf; beach, playground.	31	•	•	•	•	•		•	•		•				•
Whitesand (E-5) 49 hectares 9 km n.e. of Theodore off Hwy. 16. Golf, miniature golf (nine holes); playground.	32	•	•	•	•	•		•		•	•				•

ABERNETHY (E-5) pop. 196

In 1882, about 2 decades before he began his distinguished career in Canadian politics, William Richard Motherwell arrived in southeastern Saskatchewan from his Ontario birthplace and acquired a 64-hectare (160-acre) homestead grant near Abernethy. He farmed the land using several techniques of scientific agriculture then considered revolutionary.

Motherwell was later instrumental in launching the Territorial Grain Growers Association. His knowledge of the land groomed him for later roles as Saskatchewan's minister of agriculture 1905-18 and federal minister of agriculture during the 1920s.

MOTHERWELL HOMESTEAD NATIONAL HISTORIC SITE is 9 km (5 mi.) s. of jct. hwys. 10 and 22. The site commemorates William Richard Motherwell and his contributions to Canadian agriculture. Motherwell's farmstead, including 3 hectares (8 acres) of landscaped grounds, Ontarian-style barn and six-bedroom fieldstone house, have been restored to the pre-World War I era. **Time:** Allow 1 hour minimum. **Hours:** Mon.-Fri. 10-4, late May-June 30 (also Sat.-Sun., July 1-early Sept.). Phone ahead to confirm schedule. **Cost:** Free in 2017 to celebrate Canada's 150th anniversary of Confederation. Otherwise admission is $3.71; $3.24 (ages 65+); $1.81 (ages 6-16); $9.33 (family, up to seven people with maximum of two adults). **Phone:** (306) 333-2116.

ASSINIBOIA (F-3) pop. 2,418

Assiniboia is an Ojibwa word meaning "one who cooks with stones." Southeast of town off Hwy. 2 is St. Victor Petroglyphs Provincial Historic Park, the site of a sandstone cliff etched with prehistoric First Nations carvings. The carvings at the top of the cliff depict human faces, footprints and animal tracks. Since they have faded with time, the designs are best seen late in the afternoon or on a cloudy day. A picnic site near the base of the cliff is open June 1 through Labour Day. Phone (306) 694-3659 for more information.

The Prince of Wales Cultural and Recreation Centre, 201 3rd Ave. W., was built through volunteer effort; Charles, Prince of Wales turned the sod for the groundbreaking during a visit to Saskatchewan. Performing arts, trade shows and other events take place in the auditorium. The Assiniboia & District Public Library presents rotating monthly displays of works by local artists. The grounds feature xeriscaping, landscaping with plants requiring little water. For information phone (306) 642-3631.

SHURNIAK ART GALLERY is at 122 3rd Ave. W. The gallery, which houses the private collection of international businessman William Shurniak, features paintings and sculptures by Canadian artists as well as art, furniture and rugs from China, Southeast Asia and Australia. Included in the collection are pieces by the Canadian artists known as the Group of Seven. Temporary exhibits also are featured. **Hours:** Tues.-Sat. 10-4:30, Sun. 1-5, Apr.-Dec.; Tues.-Sat. 10-4:30, rest of year. Phone ahead for holiday hours. **Cost:** Donations. **Phone:** (306) 642-5292. ⟦🍴⟧

BATOCHE (C-3)

The Métis—a people of mixed First Nations and French heritage—migrated to the area around Batoche, in the valley of the South Saskatchewan River, around 1870. They built a settlement along the riverbank, but conflict arose with a Canadian government that was determined to settle the country's western reaches. Although the Métis petitioned for rights to the land, their requests were ignored. Batoche National Historic Site chronicles the history behind the events that led to armed conflict in 1885.

BATOCHE NATIONAL HISTORIC SITE is w. on Hwy. 225. The decisive battle of the Northwest Rebellion/Métis Resistance of 1885 was fought at this site, which covers 1,080 hectares (1,650 acres). Features include the ruins of a Batoche village, the St. Antoine de Padoue church and a rectory. The Visitor Reception Centre has an audiovisual presentation and exhibits about the culture and traditions of Métis descendants. Interpretive signs are at key locations throughout the park, and costumed interpreters are on hand to answer questions.

Hours: Daily 9-5, July 1-early Sept.; Mon.-Fri. 9-5, late May-June 30 and early Sept.-early Oct. **Cost:** Free in 2017 to celebrate Canada's 150th anniversary of Confederation. Otherwise admission is $7.43; $6.24 (ages 65+); $3.71 (ages 6-16); $18.67 (family, up to seven people with maximum of two adults). **Phone:** (306) 423-6227.

BATTLEFORD (C-2) pop. 4,065

Once capital of the Northwest Territories, Battleford is one of Saskatchewan's oldest communities. As soon as the Canadian Pacific Railway began construction, citizens made plans for their town to become a western metropolis. But the railroad took a more southerly route, and in 1883 the capital was moved to Regina.

Battleford's hopes revived in 1905 when the Canadian Northern Railway proposed a westward route, but the line was built north of town on the other side of the Saskatchewan River, leading to the establishment of sister city North Battleford *(see place listing p. 439)*.

FORT BATTLEFORD NATIONAL HISTORIC SITE is 2 km (1.2 mi.) off Hwy. 4. The North West Mounted Police district headquarters was established here in 1876 to enforce law and order. The fort became the site of armed confrontations between the First Nations and federal troops in 1885. Five buildings have been preserved; various illustrative exhibits are featured. Costumed staff members provide interpretive information. Historic weapons demonstrations are given, and historic trails also are on site.

Time: Allow 1 hour, 30 minutes minimum. **Hours:** Daily 10-4, July 1-Sept. 5; Mon.-Fri. 10-4, late May-June 30. Phone ahead to confirm schedule. **Cost:** Free in 2017 to celebrate Canada's 150th anniversary of Confederation. Otherwise admission is $3.71; $3.24 (ages 65+); $1.81 (ages 6-16); $9.33 (family, up to seven people with a maximum of two adults). **Phone:** (306) 937-2621. 🏕

FRED LIGHT MUSEUM is at jct. hwys. 4 and 40, just e. on 22nd St., then just s. to 11 20th St. E. Housed in the 1914 St. Vital School, the museum contains a general store, turn-of-the-20th-century furniture, a re-created schoolroom, and displays of farm tools and uniforms from the 1885 Rebellion and World Wars I and II. A firearm collection has more than 300 rifles and pistols dating from 1645. A replica of the Battleford Fire Hall, in operation from 1905-1912 before being destroyed by fire, is also on site. **Time:** Allow 1 hour minimum. **Hours:** Daily 9-8, Victoria Day weekend-Labour Day weekend; by appointment rest of year. **Cost:** Donations. Cash only. **Phone:** (306) 937-7111. 🏕

BIGGAR (D-2) pop. 2,161

Named in honor of W.H. Biggar, General Counsel for the Grand Trunk Pacific Railroad, Biggar is the birthplace of three-time world curling champion and 1998 Olympic curling gold medalist Sandra Schmirler. Sandra Schmirler Olympic Gold Park, at the corner of 8th Avenue E. and King Street, features a wall of fame outlining the athlete's accomplishments. The park also has an interpretive walking trail, picnic areas and a playground.

BROADVIEW (E-5) pop. 574

Broadview began as a division point on the Canadian Pacific Railway. A marker in a park on the west side of town designates the location of the original tracks, laid in 1882.

CARLYLE (F-5) pop. 1,441

North of Carlyle is Moose Mountain Provincial Park *(see Recreation Areas Chart)*, which opened as a resort beach on Lake Kenosee in 1906. The park is home to herds of moose and elk and provides nesting grounds for geese and other birds. There also are more than 450 beaver lodges.

Recreational facilities include an 18-hole golf course, hiking and equestrian trails, riding stables, a clubhouse and a swimming beach. Across from the entrance is Kenosee Superslide, a water park.

CANNINGTON MANOR PROVINCIAL PARK is e. on Hwy. 13 to Grid Rd. 603, then 2 km (1.2 mi.) n. on gravel roads. The village of Cannington Manor, founded in 1882, was an attempt to replicate the upper-middle-class English way of life, right down to cricket matches and fox hunts. A museum and seven buildings contain antiques, artifacts and farming implements used by the original settlers.

Guides in period garb demonstrate typical activities during the last 2 decades of the 19th century. **Hours:** Mon.-Sat. 10-5, Victoria Day-June 30; Wed.-Mon. 10-5, July 1-Labour Day. **Cost:** $3.81; 95c (ages 6-17); $8.57 (family). **Phone:** (306) 739-5251, or (306) 577-2600 (during the off-season). 🏕

RAMADA INN CARLYLE HOTEL   (306)453-2686
▼▼▼ Hotel. **Address:** 110 Turriff Ave E S0C 0R0

CHAPLIN (E-3) pop. 218, elev. 674m/2,214'

CHAPLIN NATURE CENTRE is at the western approach to town via Hwy. 1. The center is in the midst of the Chaplin Lake area, which encompasses some 6,000 hectares (15,000 acres) of inland saline water. More than 30 species of shorebirds, some endangered, either rest and refuel here during migratory journeys or nest and raise their young in the summer, feasting on brine shrimp that teem in the salty, shallow water.

Guided van tours are available; binoculars are provided. **Time:** Allow 1 hour, 30 minutes minimum. **Hours:** Daily 9-5, Victoria Day weekend-Aug. 31. **Cost:** Center displays by donation. Guided 30-minute tour $23.81, 2-hour tour $42.86. Reservations are recommended. **Phone:** (306) 395-2770.

CLAYBANK (F-4) pop. 25

CLAYBANK BRICK PLANT NATIONAL HISTORIC SITE is 1 km (.6 mi.) e. on Hwy. 339. In operation from 1914 to 1989, it is considered to be North America's most intact early 20th-century brick factory complex. The large site, which comprises more than 20 structures, can be seen on a self-guiding tour, and visitors can also hike through the adjacent Massold Clay Canyons. The brick-making process can be observed on special event days.

Time: Allow 1 hour minimum. **Hours:** Daily 10:30-4:30, July-Aug.; Mon.-Thurs. 10:30-4:30, late May-June 30 (also on Heritage Day Sunday); by appointment rest of year. **Cost:** $9.52; $5.71 (ages 65+); $4.76 (ages 6-16); $23.81 (family, up to seven people arriving in a single vehicle with a maximum of two adults). **Phone:** (306) 868-4474. 🍽 🏕

CRAVEN (E-4) pop. 234

Last Mountain House Provincial Park, 8 kilometres (5 mi.) north of town on Hwy. 20, preserves the site of a fur-trade outpost that operated 1869-71. Park interpreters offer guided tours of the site's three reconstructed buildings Thurs.-Sun. 10-5, July 1-Labour Day; phone (306) 725-5200.

CUT KNIFE (C-2) pop. 517

In 1885 Cut Knife was the site of several First Nations uprisings that were inspired by the Métis rebellion *(see Batoche p. 433)*. The Battle of Cut Knife

Hill, between the Cree tribe led by Chief Poundmaker and the North West Mounted Police under Col. W.D. Otter, ended in the retreat of the Mounties to Battleford.

Poundmaker, who stopped his warriors from pursuing and ambushing Otter's troops, later surrendered to the authorities to help restore peace between the First Nations and settlers. A national historic plaque and a framework of tepee poles mark the chief's grave at the Poundmaker Reserve.

A massive tomahawk, constructed in 1971, stands in Tomahawk Park, on the southwest side of town off Hwy. 40. The handle, 17 metres (57 ft.) long and weighing 3,928 kilograms (8,660 lbs.), pierces the top of a 30-foot-tall concrete teepee.

DUCK LAKE (C-3) pop. 577

The town of Duck Lake lies between the North Saskatchewan and South Saskatchewan rivers. The actual lake is a few kilometres west of town. A nearby cairn marks the site of the Battle of Duck Lake, in which the Métis First Nations defeated the North West Mounted Police on Mar. 26, 1885.

EASTEND (F-2) pop. 527

T.REX DISCOVERY CENTRE is at 1 T-rex Dr. In partnership with the Royal Saskatchewan Museum, the center houses fossils and replicas of dinosaurs, a 98-seat theater and interpretive displays. Educational activities also are offered. A nearly complete T. rex skeleton was discovered in the area in 1991.

Time: Allow 1 hour minimum. **Hours:** Daily 10-6, mid-May through Labour Day. **Cost:** Donations. **Phone:** (306) 295-4009. [GT]

ESTEVAN (F-5) pop. 11,054, elev. 570m/1,870'

Estevan is a major center for coal and oil production. Based on records for average annual hours of sunshine, it's also one of the sunniest spots in Canada.

On Hwy. 39 at 118 4th St. is the Estevan Art Gallery & Museum. The museum provides information about local events, presents changing exhibitions and also offers occasional interpretive programs and tours. Museum and gallery open Mon.-Fri. 10-6 (also Thurs. 6-9 p.m.), May-Aug. The museum is also open Sat. 1-4; phone (306) 634-7644.

Adjacent to the museum is the Wood End Building, a former barracks for the North West Mounted Police. It contains artifacts relating to that organization's early days. Nearby Heritage Park contains an oil field display.

Tours to Shand Power Station and Prairie Mines and Royalty can be arranged from June through August at the Estevan Tourism Booth; phone (306) 634-6044.

Southeast of town off Hwy. 39 is Roche Percée, a group of strangely eroded rock formations that were once venerated by local First Nations peoples. Although most of the animals and initials carved on the rocks are no longer discernible, legend maintains that the rocks are visited by spirits whose murmurs can be heard when the wind blows.

Tourism Estevan: 1102 4th St., Estevan, SK, Canada S4A 0W7. **Phone:** (306) 634-6044.

BEST WESTERN PLUS ESTEVAN INN & SUITES
(306)634-7447

Hotel
$129-$199

Best Western PLUS. **AAA Benefit:** Save 10% or more every day and earn 10% bonus points!

Address: 92 King St S4A 2T5 **Location:** Hwy 39, 1 mi (1.6 km) n at Kensington Ave. **Facility:** 94 units, some efficiencies and kitchens. 4 stories, interior corridors. **Parking:** winter plug-ins. **Terms:** cancellation fee imposed. **Pool(s):** heated indoor. **Activities:** hot tub, exercise room. **Guest Services:** valet and coin laundry. **Featured Amenity:** full hot breakfast.

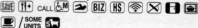

DAYS INN   (306)634-6456
Hotel. **Address:** 1305 9th St S4A 1J1

MICROTEL INN & SUITES BY WYNDHAM ESTEVAN
(306)634-7474
Hotel. **Address:** 120 King St S4A 2T5

MOTEL 6 ESTEVAN   306/634-8666
Motel. **Address:** 88 King St E S4A 2A4

SUPER 8   (306)634-8585
Hotel. **Address:** 134 2nd Ave S4A 2W6

WHERE TO EAT

EDDIE WEBSTER'S NEIGHBOURHOOD GRILL & BAR
306/634-5656
International. Casual Dining. **Address:** 122 4th St S4A 0T4

FORT QU'APPELLE (E-4) pop. 2,034

With the 1874 signing of Treaty Number IV, representatives of the Cree and Saulteaux First Nations gave away legal right to vast tracts of southern Saskatchewan; near the center of Fort Qu'Appelle (kwah-PELL) a cairn marks the site of the signing. The fort for which the town is named was built in 1864 mainly for use as a trading post.

Fort Qu'Appelle is on the Qu'Appelle River, situated in a broad, fertile valley. Berry bushes are grown on the valley's moist, north-facing slopes; in spring the dry, south-facing slopes are carpeted with wildflowers. Hawks soar above the valley floor, while pelicans, herons, ducks and geese nest in riverside marshlands. Near Fort Qu'Appelle the river widens into a chain of lakes.

The unusual name is the French translation of the Cree word *catabuysepu*, or "the river that calls." According to First Nations legend, the river was haunted by a spirit that could be heard crying as it moved up and down the water.

Also taking its name from this Cree expression is nearby Katepwa Point Provincial Park, a lakeside recreation area offering day-use facilities. West of town is Echo Valley Provincial Park, with beaches fronting two lakes, a mini-golf course and volleyball courts. *See Recreation Areas Chart.*

Fort Qu'Appelle Chamber of Commerce: P.O. Box 1273, Fort Qu'Appelle, SK, Canada S0G 1S0. **Phone:** (306) 332-5717.

GRASSLANDS NATIONAL PARK (F-3)

Elevations in the park range from 747 metres (2,450 ft.) at the Frenchman River to 998 metres (3,275 ft.) at Horse Creek. Refer to CAA/AAA maps for additional elevation information.

Grasslands National Park encompasses the grasslands in two separate blocks between Val Marie and Killdeer in the southern part of the province. When completed, the park will preserve 900 square kilometres (350 sq. mi.) of Saskatchewan's original mixed-grass prairie, including such topographic features as buttes, badlands and coulees. Among the wildlife species found in the park are black-tailed prairie dogs, golden eagles, rattlesnakes, short-horned lizards, pronghorn antelopes, mule deer and more recently, reintroduced plains bison and black-footed ferrets.

These grasslands also have a rich history. The first recorded discovery of dinosaur remains in western Canada was made in the badlands in 1875. Proof of early habitation includes remnants of tepee rings, ranch buildings, corrals and old homestead shacks.

Ranching operations exist in the area, and some of the proposed parkland is still under private ownership. Before entering the park, contact or stop at the visitor center located in Val Marie to obtain information, maps and permits. The center also conducts interpretive programs, guided hikes and special events.

Park open year-round. Visitor center open daily 9-5 (also Fri. 5-7), July-Aug.; Thurs.-Mon. 9-5, Victoria Day weekend-June 30 and Sept. 1-Thanksgiving. Admission is free. Write Grasslands National Park, P.O. Box 150, Val Marie, SK, Canada S0N 2T0; phone (877) 345-2257 (West Block Visitor Centre) or (306) 476-2018 (East Block Visitor Centre). *See Recreation Areas Chart.*

HUMBOLDT (D-4) pop. 5,678

Humboldt is on Hwy. 5 about 111 kilometres (69 mi.) east of Saskatoon; the drive takes about 90 minutes. Named for German author, explorer and scientist Baron Friedrich Heinrich Alexander von Humboldt, Humboldt's ethnic heritage is on display

in seven downtown wall murals, and a number of buildings exhibit the German half-timber architectural style. Folk art, utilitarian as well as decorative, is a cottage industry.

Annual events include Polkafest, celebrated the last weekend in May; the Summer Sizzler & Rodeo, held the last weekend in June; and Oktoberfest, which takes place the last Saturday in October.

KINDERSLEY (D-2) pop. 4,678

Kindersley is a popular destination for birdwatchers; the surrounding region is a haven for thousands of migrating geese, more than 10 species of ducks, and occasional whistling swans and whooping cranes. The Kindersley Goose Festival, a community event featuring a parade, a goose-plucking competition, a horse pull, barbecues and family entertainment, is celebrated in late September.

Kindersley Chamber of Commerce: 605 Main St., Box 1537, Kindersley, SK, Canada S0L 1S0. **Phone:** (306) 463-2320.

BEST WESTERN PLUS KINDERSLEY HOTEL

(306)463-3600

Hotel
$139-$149

Best Western PLUS

AAA Benefit: Save 10% or more every day and earn 10% bonus points!

Address: 501 14th Ave E S0L 1S0 **Location:** Jct Hwy 21 and 7, 0.7 mi (1.1 km) e, then just n. **Facility:** 114 efficiencies. 4 stories, interior corridors. **Parking:** winter plug-ins. **Terms:** check-in 4 pm. **Pool(s):** heated indoor. **Activities:** hot tub, exercise room. **Guest Services:** valet and coin laundry.

[SAVE] CALL [GM] [≈] [BIZ] [HS] [�]

[✕] [🛏] [📷] [🖥] / SOME UNITS [S↔]

LLOYDMINSTER pop. 9,772
See also Alberta p. 134

MICROTEL INN & SUITES BY WYNDHAM	(306)825-3820
▼▼ Hotel. **Address:** 4257 44th St S9V 2H1	

SUPER 8 LLOYDMINSTER	(306)825-7988
▼▼ Hotel. **Address:** 4351 41st Ave S9V 2H1	

MANITOU BEACH (D-4) pop. 257

This resort community is on the shore of Little Manitou Lake. First Nations people believed that the 19-kilometre (12 mi.)-long lake's mineral waters possessed curative powers. Three times saltier than the ocean and perfectly buoyant, they allow swimmers to float effortlessly. Visitor facilities include a nine-hole golf course, spa hotel, convention center, mini-mall, tennis courts, drive-in movie theater, indoor heated mineral pool and a 234-site, full-service campground. Cross-country ski trails provide winter recreation.

Camp Easter Seal provides summer recreation for the physically impaired; visitors are welcome. At the east end of town on Hwy. 365 is Danceland, a dance hall with a horsehair-cushioned maple hardwood floor. Ballroom and square dancing to live music takes place Friday and Saturday evenings; gospel shows are presented on Sunday. Phone (866) 756-6665 for tourist information.

MAPLE CREEK (F-2) pop. 2,176

Canadian Pacific Railway workers who spent the winter of 1882 on the banks of Maple Creek named this town, located in Saskatchewan's southwestern corner. The Maple Creek Golf Club's 18-hole layout offers views of the Cypress Hills from every fairway. The course is at 705 Herbert St.; to book a tee time phone (306) 662-2886.

South of town via Hwy. 21 is Cypress Hills Interprovincial Park *(see Recreation Areas Chart)*. This region of lofty hills, forest-covered buttes, plateaus and ridges is also marked by large tracts of ranchland.

The Great Sand Hills region is located about 70 kilometres (44 mi.) north of Maple Creek via Hwy. 21. Covering approximately 190,000 hectares (469,500 acres), it is characterized by fragile native grasslands interspersed with sand dunes up to 25 metres (82 ft.) high, fringed with small clumps of aspen, birch and willow trees, sagebrush and choke cherry. Strong winds blowing from the northwest shift the dunes east at a rate of almost 4 metres (13 ft.) annually.

Maple Creek Visitor Centre: 114 Jasper St., P.O. Box 428, Maple Creek, SK, Canada S0N 1N0. **Phone:** (306) 662-4005.

FORT WALSH NATIONAL HISTORIC SITE is 55 km (34 mi.) s.w. on Hwy. 271. A preserved, early North West Mounted Police fort features reconstructed period buildings housing exhibits of original post artifacts. Guided tours include excursions to the fort and the site of the 1873 Cypress Hills massacre. Visitor activities include bird-watching, walking a self-guiding nature trail and geocaching. A bus trip around the park includes an interpretive commentary.

Time: Allow 2 hours minimum. **Hours:** Daily 9:30-5, Canada Day-Labour Day; Tues.-Sat. 9:30-5, Victoria Day weekend-June 30. Phone ahead to confirm schedule. **Cost:** Free in 2017 to celebrate Canada's 150th anniversary of Confederation. Otherwise admission is $9.33; $7.90 (ages 65+); $4.67 (ages 6-16); $20.95 (family, up to seven people with a maximum of two adults). **Phone:** (306) 662-3590.

THE JASPER CULTURAL AND HISTORICAL CENTRE is at 311 Jasper St. Several rooms of historical displays and art are housed in a two-story brick school building built in 1913. In addition to school memorabilia, there are exhibits pertaining to ranching, rodeo and the railroad. **Time:** Allow 30 minutes minimum. **Hours:** Mon.-Fri. 9-5, Sat.-Sun.

and holidays 1-5, May-Sept.; Mon.-Fri. 10-3, rest of year. **Cost:** $7.14; $4.76 (ages 13-17 and 65+); $2.38 (ages 6-12); $14.29 (family, two adults and children under age 18). **Phone:** (306) 662-2434.

MEADOW LAKE (B-2) pop. 5,045

Meadow Lake, in northwestern Saskatchewan, offers plenty of outdoor recreation, including fishing, hunting for big game, ducks and geese, and winter snowmobiling and cross-country skiing. The 18-hole Meadow Lake Golf Club is a mile south of town on Hwy. 4; phone (306) 236-6388. The Aquatic Centre, 615 Centre St., has a five-lane pool, wading pool, hot tub, climbing wall and an outdoor spray park; phone (306) 236-2686. Lions Regional Campground and RV Park is on 1st St. E., just off Hwy. 55; phone (306) 236-4447.

With 25 sparkling lakes, Meadow Lake Provincial Park *(see Recreation Areas Chart)* is a haven for fishing, swimming, boating and camping. The park offers hiking trails, beaches, interpretive and recreational programs, cabins, a miniature golf course and a 179-kilometre (111-mi.) canoe route stretching along the Waterhen and Beaver rivers.

Of historical interest is Steele Narrows Provincial Historic Park, 72 kilometres (45 mi.) southwest via hwys. 304 and 26. The last armed conflict on Canadian soil occurred between Big Bear and his band of Cree First Nations and Maj. Sam Steele of the North West Mounted Police. The defeat of Big Bear on June 3, 1885, signaled the end of the Métis and First Nations rebellion that began in March 1885 *(see Batoche p. 433)*.

Meadow Lake & District Chamber of Commerce: 9th Avenue W. and Hwy. 4, P.O. Box 847, Meadow Lake, SK, Canada S9X 1Y6. **Phone:** (306) 236-4447 May-Sept., or (306) 236-4061 off-season.

MELFORT (C-4) pop. 5,576, elev. 457m/1,500'

Melfort is also known as the City of Northern Lights due to the visibility of the aurora borealis in the night sky for much of the year. Situated in the Carrot River Valley, an area known for its fertile black loam, agriculture has been an economic mainstay since the days of early settlement in the late 19th century. Melfort was incorporated as a village in 1903, as a town in 1907 and as the province's twelfth city on Sept. 2, 1980.

Melfort & District Chamber of Commerce: Box 2002, Melfort, SK, Canada S0E 1A0. **Phone:** (306) 752-4636.

MELVILLE (E-5) pop. 4,517, elev. 555m/1,820'

Located on the east-west main line of the Canadian National Railway as well as on a major north-south line of the Canadian National Railway, Melville is—appropriately—known as "The Rail Centre." The railway is still the city's largest employer, its presence essential in marketing agricultural products as well as potash from nearby Esterhazy.

Melville & District Chamber of Commerce: 76 Halifax Ave., Melville, SK, Canada S0A 2P0. **Phone:** (306) 728-4177.

MOOSE JAW (E-4) pop. 33,274, elev. 542m/1,778'

Moose Jaw's intriguing name is likely a reference to Moose Jaw Creek. The First Nations called this waterway *moosichappishannissippi,* or "the creek that bends like a moose's jaw." Local legend also attributes it to an early traveler who repaired his cart wheel with a moose's jawbone. Today's visitors are greeted by "Mac," a 9-metre-tall (30 ft.) moose statue said to be the world's largest.

During U.S. Prohibition Moose Jaw was home to an industrious band of bootleggers and American gangsters, earning the town the nickname "Little Chicago of the Prairies." Today Moose Jaw is an industrial center as well as a producer of hard spring wheat. The Canadian Forces base just south of the city is home to one of Canada's busiest airports and headquarters of the Snowbirds, the Canadian armed forces aerobatic team.

Downtown's seasonal roaming "ambassadors" provide visitors with information and brochures. The Murals of Moose Jaw, painted on several downtown buildings, are a collection of more than 50 scenes depicting the town's history. The Moose Jaw Trolley Company provides a tour of the murals and heritage buildings. The Yvette Moore Gallery, downtown at 76 Fairford St. W., exhibits this local artist's work; her paintings are also displayed in Moose Jaw hotels. Phone (306) 693-7600 or (866) 693-7600.

Wakamow Valley is a recreational complex that includes Plaxton's Lake, North River Park, Kiwanis River Park, Kinsmen Wellesley Park, Connor Park, McCaig Gardens, the Ecological Zone and the Devonian Trail, a pedestrian and bicycle trail system. Visitors can picnic, camp, bird-watch, hike, jog and bicycle. For more information phone (306) 692-2717 Mon.-Fri.

Hwy. 2 heading south from the city was once part of the Powder River Trail, which provided access to Denver before the advent of the railroad. About 42 kilometres (26 mi.) north on Hwy. 2 is Buffalo Pound Provincial Park *(see Recreation Areas Chart),* where 350 hectares (865 acres) are set aside as grazing land for a herd of buffaloes.

Moose Jaw Chamber of Commerce: 88 Saskatchewan St. E., Box 1359, Moose Jaw, SK, Canada S6H 0V4. **Phone:** (306) 692-6414.

Self-guiding tours: Brochures outlining a self-guiding tour of downtown Moose Jaw's historic sites are available at the Moose Jaw Art Museum and National Exhibits in Crescent Park.

SUKANEN SHIP, PIONEER VILLAGE AND MU-SEUM is 13 km (8 mi.) s. on Hwy. 2. The large, unfinished ship was built by Tom Sukanen, a Finnish settler who had planned to sail the boat home to his native country by way of the South Saskatchewan River,

Hudson Bay, Greenland and Iceland. The village consists of an old post office, blacksmith shop, school, church, railroad station, a general store, drug store and the Diefenbaker homestead. Also on site is a collection of antique tractors, trucks and cars.

Hours: Mon.-Sat. 9-5, Sun. noon-6, mid-May to mid-Sept. **Cost:** $7.62; $6.67 (students with ID and ages 60+); $4.76 (ages 6-15). **Phone:** (306) 693-7315.

TUNNELS OF MOOSE JAW is at 18 N. Main St. Two themed, 50-minute tours take visitors beneath the streets of Moose Jaw. Miss Fanny and Gus are the guides for the Chicago Connection tour, which explores gangster Al Capone's bootlegging operation and the tunnels he is said to have used to escape American authorities. The Passage to Fortune tour depicts the story of early Chinese immigrants who came to build the Canadian Pacific Railway and their footsteps through adversity and persecution to eventual success.

Hours: Tours depart daily 10-7 (also Fri.-Sat. 7-8 p.m.), July-Aug.; Mon.-Fri. 10-4:30, Sat. 10-5:30, Sun. noon-4:30, Sept.-Oct.; Mon.-Fri. noon-4:30, Sat. 10-5:30, rest of year. Departure times may vary; phone ahead to confirm schedule. Closed Christmas. **Cost:** Individual tour fee $15; $12 (ages 65+); $11.50 (ages 13-18); $8.50 (ages 6-12). Both tours $25; $21 (ages 65+); $20 (ages 13-18); $14 (ages 6-12). Reservations are recommended. **Phone:** (306) 693-5261.

BEST WESTERN PLUS MOOSE JAW   (306)972-3334

Hotel
$139-$149

AAA Benefit: Save 10% or more every day and earn 10% bonus points!

Address: 350 Diefenbaker Dr S6J 1N2 **Location:** Just s of jct Trans-Canada Hwy 1; on Thatcher Dr. Adjacent to Welcome & Information Center. **Facility:** 88 units, some efficiencies. 4 stories, interior/exterior corridors. **Parking:** winter plug-ins. **Terms:** check-in 4 pm. **Pool(s):** heated indoor. **Activities:** hot tub, exercise room. **Guest Services:** valet and coin laundry. **Featured Amenity:** full hot breakfast.

SAVE ⁞⏷ CALL 🄼 ➔ BIZ HS 🛜 ✕ 🖥 🖨 🖵

COMFORT INN   (306)692-2100
Hotel. **Address:** 155 Thatcher Dr W S6J 1M1

HERITAGE INN HOTEL & CONVENTION CENTRE
          (306)693-7550
Hotel. **Address:** 1590 Main St N S6J 1L3

SUPER 8-MOOSE JAW   (306)692-8888
Hotel. **Address:** 1706 Main St N S6J 1L4

TEMPLE GARDENS HOTEL & SPA   306/694-5055
Hotel. **Address:** 24 Fairford St E S6H 0C7

HARWOOD'S   306/693-7778
 Continental. Casual Dining. **Address:** 24 Fairford St E S6H 0C7

HOUSTON PIZZA   306/693-3934
 American. Casual Dining. **Address:** 117 Main St N S6H 0V9

MOOSOMIN pop. 2,485

BEST WESTERN PLUS MOOSOMIN HOTEL
                                        (306)435-4700

Hotel
$149-$179

 AAA Benefit: Save 10% or more every day and earn 10% bonus points!

Address: 405 Moose St S0G 3N0 **Location:** Jct Trans-Canada Hwy 1 and Main St, just s. **Facility:** 79 efficiencies. 3 stories, interior corridors. **Parking:** winter plug-ins. **Pool(s):** heated indoor. **Activities:** hot tub, exercise room. **Guest Services:** coin laundry. **Featured Amenity:** full hot breakfast.

NIPAWIN (C-4) pop. 4,265

The Nipawin Hydroelectric Station, about 5 km (3 mi.) south of town via Hwy. 35, following signs, uses water impounded in Codette Lake by the Francois-Finlay Dam to generate 1.1 billion kilowatt hours of electricity annually. Vista Viewpoint, on a plateau overlooking the dam, offers a spectacular view of the river gorge below.

Nipawin & District Chamber of Commerce: 308 Nipawin Rd. E., Box 177, Nipawin, SK, Canada S0E 1E0. **Phone:** (306) 862-5252.

NORTH BATTLEFORD (C-2) pop. 13,888

On the bank of the North Saskatchewan River, North Battleford is the gateway to the province's vast northwestern wilderness. Agriculture is the backbone of the area's economy; farms produce crops of cereal grains, oil seeds and hay as well as cattle, hogs, poultry and bison. Forestry, manufacturing and heavy crude oil development also are important industries.

The Battlefords Provincial Park *(see Recreation Areas Chart)* is approximately 42 kilometres (26 mi.) north off Hwy. 4 and offers summer fishing, water skiing, boating and hiking. Cross-country skiing and ice fishing are popular winter activities.

Destination Battlefords: 801 River Valley Dr., P.O. Box 1715, North Battleford, SK, Canada S9A 3W2. **Phone:** (306) 445-2000 or (800) 243-0394.

ALLEN SAPP GALLERY is at 1 Railway Ave. This award-winning public gallery features powerful and sensitive images of the Northern Plains Cree by renowned Cree artist Allen Sapp (1928-2015). Sapp's works capture the life and history of the Cree at the turn of the 20th century. Other exhibits include large-screen videos and historical artifacts.

Hours: Daily 11-5, June-Sept.; Wed.-Sun. noon-4, rest of year. **Cost:** Donations. **Phone:** (306) 445-1760.

WESTERN DEVELOPMENT MUSEUM'S HERITAGE FARM AND VILLAGE is at jct. hwys. 16 and 40. A preserved 1920s pioneer village features the exhibit "Winning the Prairie Gamble." Also part of the complex is a working farm where visitors can see demonstrations of early agricultural techniques utilizing vintage equipment.

Time: Allow 2 hours minimum. **Hours:** Daily 9-5, Apr.-Dec.; Tues.-Sun. 9-5, rest of year. Closed provincial holidays Oct.-Apr. Outdoor village closed mid-Oct. through Apr. 30. Hours and admission rates are subject to change; phone to confirm. **Cost:** (good for 2 consecutive days) $9.52; $8.57 (ages 65+); $6.90 (students with ID); $3.81 (ages 6-12); $23.81 (family, parents or guardians and dependent children under age 18). **Phone:** (306) 445-8033.

GOLD EAGLE LODGE HOTEL   (306)446-8877

Hotel
$145-$295

Address: 12004 Railway Ave E S9A 3W3 **Location:** Jct Hwy 4 and 16 (Yellowhead Hwy), just w. **Facility:** 112 units, some two bedrooms and kitchens. 4 stories, interior corridors. **Parking:** winter plug-ins. **Terms:** check-in 4 pm, 3 day cancellation notice-fee imposed, resort fee. **Pool(s):** heated indoor. **Activities:** sauna, hot tub, steamroom, exercise room. **Guest Services:** valet and coin laundry.

LONE STAR HOTEL   (306)446-8888
Hotel. **Address:** 1006 Hwy 16 S9A 3W2

KIHIW RESTAURANT   306/486-3833
American. Casual Dining. **Address:** 11902 Railway Ave S9A 3K7

PORTA BELLA RESTAURANT   306/937-3785
Continental. Casual Dining. **Address:** 2491 99th St S9A 3W8

OUTLOOK (D-3) pop. 2,204

Agriculture sustains Outlook; corn, potatoes, vegetables and sunflowers are among the products grown. The origin of the town name is attributed to two Canadian Pacific Railway officials who stood at an elevated vantage point, mesmerized by the raging South Saskatchewan River gushing below; the silence was broken when one of them exclaimed, "What a wonderful outlook!"

Outlook and District Regional Park, located along the South Saskatchewan River on the west edge of town, has a golf course, swimming pool, campgrounds and hiking trails. Nature enthusiasts will appreciate the numerous birds and venerable elm trees. Phone (306) 867-8846.

A large salt and pepper shaker collection is the highlight of the Outlook & District Heritage Museum, downtown at 100 Railway Ave. E.; phone (306) 867-9485. SkyTrail Pedestrian Bridge, just northwest of the center of town following signs, is one of Canada's longest pedestrian bridges, spanning the South Saskatchewan River 46 metres (150 ft.) above the water and running for a distance of 914 metres (3,000 ft.). Side rails and a safe walking surface allow users to focus their attention on the views.

The South Saskatchewan River Project, on the South Saskatchewan and Qu'Appelle rivers, consists of two dams. Gardiner Dam, midway between Elbow and Outlook, is 5 kilometres (3 mi.) long, 64 metres (210 ft.) high and 1,615 metres (5,300 ft.) wide at its base. The impounded water forms Lake Diefenbaker. The second, smaller structure is Qu'Appelle Dam. A visitor center at Gardiner Dam is open Victoria Day weekend-Labour Day; phone (306) 854-6267 or (306) 857-5500.

Town of Outlook: 400 Saskatchewan Ave., Box 518, Outlook, SK, Canada S0L 2N0. **Phone:** (306) 867-8663.

PRINCE ALBERT (C-3) pop. 35,129

Prince Albert is one of the province's oldest communities. Trapper Peter Pond built a trading post on the north side of the North Saskatchewan River in 1776. The Rev. James Nesbit, credited with founding the town, settled on the south shore in 1866.

The log Presbyterian church that Nisbet built that year stands in Kinsmen Park, on the west side of Central Avenue between 22nd and 28th streets W. A blockhouse next to the church dates from the Northwest Rebellion/Métis Resistance of 1885. The Historical Museum occupies the site of the church built by Nisbet.

Prince Albert Tourism: 3700 2nd Ave. W., Prince Albert, SK, Canada S6W 1A2. **Phone:** (306) 953-4385.

HISTORICAL MUSEUM is at 10 River St. E. at Central Ave. The museum, housed in an old fire hall overlooking the North Saskatchewan River, displays the first fire engine pumper used in the Saskatchewan territory. Other exhibits include First Nations, fur trade and pioneer artifacts as well as a table and benches carved by the Rev. James Nisbet. A tearoom provides a view of the river. **Time:** Allow 1 hour minimum. **Hours:** Daily 9-5, Victoria Day-Sept. 2. **Cost:** $1.90; 95c (ages 6-12). **Phone:** (306) 764-2992.

BEST WESTERN MARQUIS INN & SUITES
(306)922-9595

Hotel
$109-$150

AAA Benefit: Save 10% or more every day and earn 10% bonus points!

Address: 602 Marquis Rd E S6V 7P2 **Location:** Jct Hwy 3 (6th Ave E). **Facility:** 77 units. 2 stories, interior corridors. **Parking:** winter plug-ins. **Terms:** check-in 4 pm. **Amenities:** safes. **Activities:** exercise room. **Featured Amenity: full hot breakfast.**

COMFORT INN PRINCE ALBERT
(306)763-4466

Hotel
$119-$159

Address: 3863 2nd Ave W S6V 1A1 **Location:** On Hwy 2, 1.6 mi (2.6 km) s. **Facility:** 61 units. 2 stories (no elevator), interior corridors. **Parking:** winter plug-ins. **Guest Services:** valet laundry. **Featured Amenity: full hot breakfast.**

DAYS INN PRINCE ALBERT (306)763-8988
Hotel. **Address:** 150 34th St W S6V 8E9

HOLIDAY INN EXPRESS HOTEL & SUITES (306)922-6988
Hotel. **Address:** 3580 2nd Ave W S6V 5G2

SUPER 8-PRINCE ALBERT (306)953-0088
Hotel. **Address:** 4444 2nd Ave W S6V 5R7

TRAVELODGE PRINCE ALBERT (306)764-6441
Motel. **Address:** 3551 2nd Ave W S6V 5G1

WHERE TO EAT

AMY'S ON SECOND 306/763-1515
American. Casual Dining. **Address:** 2990 2nd Ave W S6V 7E9

SHANANIGAN'S COFFEE & DESSERT BAR 306/764-2647
Coffee/Tea Desserts. Quick Serve. **Address:** 2144 6th Ave W S6V 5K6

SIGNATURE 22 RESTAURANT AND LOUNGE 306/764-4497
American. Casual Dining. **Address:** 3245 2nd Ave W S6V 5G1

SMITTY'S 306/764-5627
American. Casual Dining. **Address:** 2995 2nd Ave W, #20 S6V 5V5

SPICY PEPPERCORN 306/763-7755
Chinese. Casual Dining. **Address:** 3590 6th Ave E S6V 7S5

VENICE HOUSE FAMILY RESTAURANT 306/764-6555
Italian. Casual Dining. **Address:** 1498 Central Ave S6V 4W5

ZORBA'S FAMILY RESTAURANT   306/764-2700
▼▼▼ International. Casual Dining. **Address:** 1401 2nd Ave W
S6V 5B3

◢GEM◣ PRINCE ALBERT NATIONAL PARK (B-3)

Elevations in the park range from 488 metres
(1,600 ft.) on the western side of the park to
724 metres (2,375 ft.) on the southern side of
the park. Refer to CAA/AAA maps for
additional elevation information.

The main entrance to Prince Albert National Park
is 81 kilometres (50 mi.) north of the city of Prince
Albert via hwys. 2 and 264.

The park covers 3,875 square kilometres (1,496
sq. mi.) of wilderness in central Saskatchewan. Its
lakes, ponds, streams, bogs and rolling hills are a
legacy of the glacial epoch. Notable are Sandy,
Waskesiu, Kingsmere, Namekus, Crean and the
Hanging Heart lakes. There also are several hundred smaller lakes and ponds and many sand
beaches.

Heavy growths of conifers and several species of
hardwoods surround the lakes, along with numerous
shrubs and wildflowers. Fall foliage is especially colorful. Such wild animals as elk, deer, moose and
bears are plentiful. A herd of bison roams the southwest corner of the park.

Early morning and evening provide the best
chances of seeing wildlife along park roads, especially the Narrows and Kingsmere roads along
Waskesiu Lake. Although some animals may seem
tame, they are wild and should be observed only
from a safe distance.

The park also preserves the legacy of Grey Owl.
Born Archibald Stansfeld Belaney, this controversial
Englishman arrived in Canada in 1905. Adopted by
the Ojibwa First Nations and later married into the
tribe, Grey Owl turned his love of nature to the re-
establishment of the region's beaver population,
which had been decimated by hunters and trappers.
For 7 years he lived at Beaver Lodge on Ajawaan
Lake, where he continued his restoration and conservation efforts.

General Information and Activities

Although the park is open throughout the year,
complete facilities are provided Victoria Day-Labour
Day only. Information is available from the information bureau in the Waskesiu Lake Visitor Services
Centre, 8 kilometres (5 mi.) from the park's main
gate on Hwy. 264.

Roads provide access to Waskesiu, Namekus,
Sandy and the Hanging Heart lakes and to the
Kingsmere River. Although no roads lead directly to
Kingsmere and Crean lakes, access is possible by
boat. A light railway with handcars assists in por-
taging around the unnavigable stretch of the Kingsmere River.

More than 100 kilometres (60 mi.) of hiking trails
traverse the park. Some are suitable for day walks,

while others require an overnight stop. Pamphlets
outlining self-guiding tours are available for the Mud
Creek and Boundary Bog nature trails. From the
boat dock on the north shore of Kingsmere Lake a
3-kilometre (1.9-mi.) trail leads to the home and
grave of Grey Owl.

Park facilities include boat launching and berthing
areas at the Hanging Heart Lakes, the Narrows and
the main marina on Waskesiu Lake. Boats, canoes
and outboard motors can be rented at all three marinas; paddle-wheeler tours are offered daily in
summer. There are bicycle rentals, tennis and volleyball courts and bowling greens at the Waskesiu
Lake Visitor Services Centre.

Waskesiu Lake's 18-hole layout ranks among
Canada's finest golf courses. A 150-kilometre (93-
mi.) network of groomed cross-country ski trails is
open in winter. Snowshoeing and ice fishing also are
permitted. Fishing licenses are required and can be
obtained at the park information center, park en-
trances and campground offices.

Park naturalists offer a free summer interpretive
program that includes car caravans on park roadways and special daily events. Interpretive programs
are regularly presented in the Nature Center theater
on Lakeview Drive, and at the outdoor theaters at
the Narrows and Beaver Glen campgrounds.

Within the Waskesiu Lake Visitor Services Centre
is the Park Nature Centre, which has natural history
exhibits, a bookstore and a theater; it is open in July
and August. *See Recreation Areas Chart.*

ADMISSION to the park is free in 2017 to celebrate
Canada's 150th anniversary of Confederation. Otherwise admission is $7.43; $6.48 (ages 65+); $3.71
(ages 6-16); $18.67 (up to seven people arriving in
a single vehicle).

PETS (dogs and cats) are permitted in the park as
long as they are on leashes.

ADDRESS inquiries to the Superintendent, Prince
Albert National Park, 969 Lakeview Dr., P.O. Box
100, Waskesiu Lake, SK, Canada S0J 2Y0; phone
(306) 663-4522.

REGINA (E-4) pop. 193,100, elev. 578m/1,896'
• Hotels p. 446 • Restaurants p. 447
• Hotels & Restaurants map & index p. 444

First Nations people once used the banks of Wascana Creek for drying buffalo meat and cleaning and
stretching the hides. Thus the area became known
as *Oscana,* a Cree word meaning "pile of bones." In
1882 the Canadian Pacific Railway completed its
track across the plains, and the settlement of Pile-O-
Bones sprang up at the rail terminal on Wascana
Creek.

The seat of government of the Northwest Territories and the headquarters of the North West
Mounted Police were established the same year. A
few years later Princess Louise, the wife of Canada's governor-general, renamed the city Regina

(See map & index p. 444.)

(Latin for queen) to honor her mother, Queen Victoria. In 1905 Saskatchewan became a province, with Regina as its capital.

In the heart of downtown is City Centre, the site of such buildings as the municipal government offices and the public library. The Prairie History Room, which documents local history, and the Dunlop Art Gallery, which displays works by regional artists, are both housed in the library. A glockenspiel imported from Germany stands at 12th Avenue and Scarth Street, at the northeast corner of Victoria Park. The 23 brass bells are mounted on a granite pedestal.

The Globe Theatre in the old City Hall is the home of Regina's professional acting company. Another restored building is Union Station, a transportation hub in the early years of rail travel that is now occupied by Casino Regina. Guided historical tours explore parts of a tunnel system that once stretched beneath downtown streets and also offer a behind-the-scenes look at casino operations. Under 19 are not permitted on the tours; for ticket and schedule information phone the casino at (800) 555-3189.

The Regina Floral Conservatory, 1450B 4th Ave., is a small greenhouse where seasonal floral displays have the backdrop of a waterfall and luxuriant foliage; phone (306) 781-4769.

Following Wascana Creek for about 8 kilometres (5 mi.) is the Devonian Pathway, a paved bicycle trail that passes through six city parks and is used for jogging and walking as well as other activities; in winter it is groomed and lighted for cross-country skiing. The grassland and marsh habitats at the Condie Nature Refuge, just north of the city off Hwy. 11, are crisscrossed by nature trails.

Regina's No. 1 spectator sport is summer football. The Canadian Football League's Saskatchewan Roughriders play at the new Mosaic Stadium, 1734 Elphinstone St. (near the intersection with Saskatchewan Drive). For ticket information phone (888) 474-3377.

Regina Regional Opportunities Commission and Tourism Regina: 1925 Rose St., Regina, SK, Canada S4P 3H1. **Phone:** (306) 789-5099 or (800) 661-5099.

Shopping: Regina's major shopping mall is Cornwall Centre, 2101 11th Ave. Among the more than 60 stores are Hudson's Bay and Sears. The specialty shops and eateries of Scarth Street Mall, downtown between 11th and 12th avenues, line a pedestrian-only street. The Cathedral Village shopping district, another downtown cluster of shops, is centered around 13th Avenue from Albert to Argyle streets and from Saskatchewan Drive to College Avenue.

GOVERNMENT HOUSE MUSEUM AND INTERPRETIVE CENTRE is at 4607 Dewdney Ave. This Italianate-style mansion was the home of the lieutenant governors of the Northwest Territories from 1891 to 1905 and the lieutenant governors of Saskatchewan from 1905 to 1945. From 1945 to the mid-1970s the house served as a rest home for World War II veterans as well as an adult education center.

Flanked by 2.5 hectares (6 acres) of gardens and orchards, the official residence is restored to reflect its original Victorian elegance. Docents dressed in period garb conduct guided house tours. An interpretive center chronicles provincial history and features hands-on exhibits.

Time: Allow 1 hour minimum. **Hours:** Daily 9-5, Victoria Day weekend-Labour Day weekend; Tues.-Sun. 9-4, rest of year. Closed Jan. 10-13, Nov. 14-17, Christmas and day after Christmas. **Cost:** $5; $3 (ages 0-17); $15 (family). **Phone:** (306) 787-5773. ⌂

HOLY ROSARY CATHEDRAL is at 3125 13th Ave., just w. of jct. Cameron St. This Cruciform/Romanesque structure, built in 1912, features 43 stained-glass windows installed in 1951 by French artisan Andre Rault, who designed windows for more than 50 other Canadian churches. Their artistry is best appreciated on a sunny day. A Casavant pipe organ, known for its exceptional sound quality, plays during Sunday services.

Guided tours are available; reservations are required 2 weeks in advance. **Time:** Allow 30 minutes minimum. **Hours:** Tues.-Fri. 9-1. The cathedral is kept locked for security purposes. Phone ahead to confirm schedule. **Cost:** Donations. **Phone:** (306) 565-0909.

RCMP HERITAGE CENTRE is on Dewdney Ave. at the entrance to the RCMP Academy, "Depot" Division. The center tells the story of the Royal Canadian Mounted Police (RCMP), created by an act of Parliament in 1873 to maintain law and order on the Canadian frontier and pave the way for westward settlement. Stretching the length of the main exhibition hall, the sculptural procession "March of the Mounties" anchors the core exhibit areas; graphics trace Canada's geography from west to east and depict the historical evolution of the RCMP from its inception to the present day.

The interactive educational exhibit Maintaining Law and Order in the West chronicles the force's late 19th-century efforts to suppress the whiskey trade, establish amicable relations with Native tribes and ensure the safety of settlers and rail workers. Serving All of Canada is an overview of the RCMP's 20th-century evolution, while Cracking the Case is a hands-on look at the high-tech side of contemporary policing. The 22-minute multimedia presentation "Courage in Red" is shown in the center's SGI Canada Theatre.

Time: Allow 2 hours minimum. **Hours:** Daily 10-5, Canada Day-Labour Day; 11-5, rest of year. A colorful Sergeant Major's Parade is held Mon.-Fri. at 12:45 p.m.; register at the center by noon. Sunset Retreat Ceremonies are held Tues. at 6:30 p.m., Canada Day to mid-Aug. Closed Jan. 1, Good

(See map & index p. 444.)

Friday and Christmas. **Cost:** $9.52; $7.62 (ages 60+ and students with ID); $5.71 (ages 6-17); $28.57 (family, two adults and up to five children); free (military veterans and law enforcement). **Phone:** (306) 719-3000 or (866) 567-7267.

WASCANA CENTRE surrounds Wascana Lake. This 930-hectare (2,300-acre) park complex is the city's recreational and cultural center and includes the Conexus Arts Centre, a performing arts venue. Wascana Place has information about attractions and event listings; on the building's fourth floor is the Joe Moran Gallery, which exhibits photographs from 1882 to the present.

Points of interest include Speakers' Corner, a circular plaza located in the park's southwest corner. Ten vintage gas lamps surround the plaza, which was dedicated in 1966 as a tribute to free speech and the people's right to assemble. Waterfowl display ponds are a haven for geese and ducks. Ferry boats transport visitors to Willow Island, a picnic area. **Hours:** Grounds daily dawn-dusk. Wascana Place Mon.-Fri. 8-4:30. Phone ahead to confirm schedule. **Cost:** Grounds free. **Phone:** (306) 522-3661. 🅰️

Legislative Building (Capitol) is off Albert St. in Wascana Centre. Surrounded by 67 hectares (165 acres) of landscaped grounds, this imposing landmark, topped by a gleaming new copper dome unveiled in May 2016, is the seat of provincial government. Completed in 1912, it is modeled on the architectural style of the English Renaissance and Louis XIV of France.

The building houses several art galleries, including the Cumberland Gallery, a showcase for works of the Native Heritage Foundation of Canada. Green marble columns are among the many handsome decorative accents. The flower gardens just north of the building are at their loveliest in the summer months. On the building's east side is the Trafalgar Fountain, which stood in London's Trafalgar Square from 1845 to 1939.

Guided tours of the building are offered. Tours in French are available. **Time:** Allow 30 minutes minimum. **Hours:** Daily 8 a.m.-9 p.m., Victoria Day-Labour Day; 8-noon and 1-4:30, rest of year. Guided tours are given daily on the half-hour, Victoria Day-Labour Day; on the hour, rest of year. Last tour departs 30 minutes before closing. Closed Jan. 1, Good Friday and Christmas. **Cost:** Free. **Phone:** (306) 787-5358 or (306) 787-5416.

MacKenzie Art Gallery is in the T.C. Douglas Building at Albert St. and 23rd Ave., in the s.w.

corner of Wascana Centre. This major exhibition center features permanent and changing exhibits by Canadian and international artists. **Time:** Allow 1 hour minimum. **Hours:** Mon. and Wed.-Sat. 10-5:30, Sun. and holidays noon-5:30. **Cost:** Free; donations accepted. **Phone:** (306) 584-4250. GT

◤GEM Royal Saskatchewan Museum is at College Ave. and Albert St. in Wascana Centre. The Earth Sciences Gallery focuses on Saskatchewan's geological and paleontological evolution and includes Canada's only resident robotic dinosaur, while the Paleo Pit features hands-on exhibits. Artwork and artifacts in the First Nations Gallery explore the culture and heritage of the province's aboriginal population.

Saskatchewan's natural history is surveyed in the Life Sciences Gallery, which also covers present-day environmental issues. Exhibits depict life in a beaver pond and a Costa Rican rain forest, and address human actions that are affecting global ecosystems. **Time:** Allow 1 hour minimum. **Hours:** Daily 9:30-5 (closes at 3 on Dec. 24 and 31); noon-5, Jan. 1 and day after Christmas. Closed Christmas. **Cost:** $5; $3 (ages 0-11); $15 (family). Cash only for suggested donation amounts under $10. **Phone:** (306) 787-2815.

Saskatchewan Science Centre is at 2903 Powerhouse Dr. in Wascana Centre, on the n. side of Wascana Lake. The Powerhouse of Discovery houses more than 100 permanent hands-on science exhibits and features live stage shows and demonstrations. Visitors who want to test their physical skills can tackle one of the tallest climbing walls in Canada. The 165-seat Kramer IMAX Theatre presents science and nature films on a five-story screen enhanced by a digital sound system, as well as selected classic movies at the monthly After Dark Film Series event.

Time: Allow 2 hours minimum. **Hours:** Mon.-Fri. 9-6; Sat.-Sun. and statutory holidays 10-6, Victoria Day-Labour Day; Tues.-Fri. 9-5, Sat.-Sun. and statutory holidays noon-6, rest of year. Kramer IMAX Theater Tues.-Fri. 9-5, Sat.-Sun. noon-6; show times vary. Phone ahead to confirm schedule. **Cost:** Science center $9.52; $8.57 (ages 13-17); $7.62 (ages 3-12 and 60+). IMAX film showing $9.52; $8.57 (ages 13-17); $7.62 (ages 3-12 and 60+). Combination science center and IMAX theater ticket (or IMAX double feature) $17.14; $15.24 (ages 13-17); $13.33 (ages 3-12 and 60+). IMAX feature-length film $15.24; $14.24 (ages 13-17); $13.33 (ages 3-12 and 60+). **Phone:** (306) 791-7900, or (306) 522-4629 for the IMAX box office. 🍴

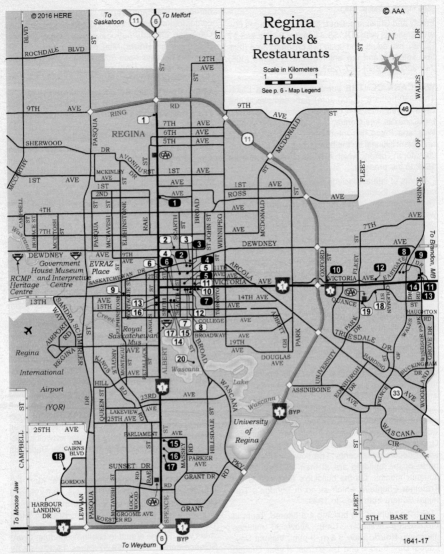

Regina

Regina

Hotels & Restaurants

Scale in Kilometers
1   0   1

See p. 6 - Map Legend

© 2016 HERE

© AAA

1641-17

Regina

This index helps you "spot" where approved hotels and restaurants are located on the corresponding detailed maps. Hotel daily rate range is for comparison only. Restaurant price range is a combination of lunch and/or dinner. Turn to the listing page for more information and consult display ads for special promotions.

REGINA

Map Page	Hotels	Diamond Rated	Rate Range	Page
❶ this page	**Best Western Seven Oaks Inn**	▼▼	$160-$170 SAVE	446
❷ this page	**Delta Regina**	▼▼▼	$85-$207 SAVE	446
❸ this page	Wingate by Wyndham	▼▼	$149-$189	447
❹ this page	Holiday Inn Express Hotel & Suites Regina	▼▼▼	Rates not provided	446
❺ this page	DoubleTree by Hilton Hotel & Conference Centre Regina	▼▼▼	$119-$189	446

REGINA (cont'd)

Map Page	Hotels (cont'd)	Diamond Rated	Rate Range	Page
6 p. 444	**The Hotel Saskatchewan, Autograph Collection**	◇◇◇◇	$152-$237 SAVE	446
7 p. 444	**Quality Hotel**	◇◇	$99-$219 SAVE	446
8 p. 444	Country Inn & Suites By Carlson	◇◇	$115-$199	446
9 p. 444	Holiday Inn Hotel & Suites	◇◇◇	$130-$220	446
10 p. 444	Sandman Hotel Suites & Spa Regina	◇◇◇	Rates not provided	446
11 p. 444	**Best Western Plus Eastgate Inn & Suites**	◇◇◇	$160-$209 SAVE	446
12 p. 444	Super 8 Regina	◇◇	$115-$140	446
13 p. 444	HomeSuites Hotel Regina East	◇◇◇	$154-$199	446
14 p. 444	Days Inn Regina	◇◇◇	$127-$149	446
15 p. 444	Executive Royal Hotel Regina	◇◇◇	Rates not provided	446
16 p. 444	Travelodge Hotel & Conference Centre	◇◇◇	$165-$180	446
17 p. 444	Holiday Inn Express & Suites	◇◇◇	Rates not provided	446
18 p. 444	Days Inn-Regina Airport West	◇◇◇	$130-$169	446

Map Page	Restaurants	Diamond Rated	Cuisine	Price Range	Page
1 p. 444	Luiggi's Pasta House & Lounge	◇◇	Italian	$14-$40	447
2 p. 444	Bushwakker Brewpub	◇◇	Sandwiches Pizza	$13-$20	447
3 p. 444	The Last Spike	◇◇	American	$8-$23	447
4 p. 444	Beer Bros. Bakery & Cuisine	◇◇	American	$12-$25	447
5 p. 444	Siam Authentic Thai Restaurant	◇◇	Thai	$9-$18	447
6 p. 444	The Dining Room	◇◇◇	American	$13-$39	447
7 p. 444	Golf's Steak House	◇◇◇	Steak	$14-$71	447
8 p. 444	Crave Kitchen & Wine Bar	◇◇	International	$15-$35	447
9 p. 444	Creek In Cathedral Bistro	◇◇◇	American	$13-$31	447
10 p. 444	Memories Fine Dining & Lounge	◇◇◇	International	$11-$43	447
11 p. 444	The Rooftop Bar & Grill	◇◇	American	$12-$37	447
12 p. 444	The Diplomat Steakhouse	◇◇	Steak	$14-$70	447
13 p. 444	Slow Brew Pub & Sports Bar	◇◇	American	$6-$14	447
14 p. 444	Henry's Cafe	◇◇	American	$8-$13	447
15 p. 444	Tangerine the food bar	◇◇	American	$9-$14	447
16 p. 444	La Bodega Tapas Bar & Grill	◇◇◇	Mediterranean	$14-$75	447
17 p. 444	Fireside Bistro	◇◇◇	American	$14-$42	447
18 p. 444	Houston Pizza	◇◇	American	$10-$40	447
19 p. 444	Smokin' Okies BBQ	◇	Barbecue	$6-$32	447
20 p. 444	The Willow on Wascana	◇◇◇	Regional Canadian	$12-$39	447

Enjoy great member rates and benefits at AAA/CAA Preferred Hotels

(See map & index p. 444.)

BEST WESTERN PLUS EASTGATE INN & SUITES
(306)352-7587 **11**

Hotel
$160-$209

Best Western PLUS

AAA Benefit: Save 10% or more every day and earn 10% bonus points!

Address: 3840 Eastgate Dr S4Z 1A5 **Location:** Trans-Canada Hwy 1, 1.5 mi (2.4 km) e of Ring Rd, just n. **Facility:** 100 units, some efficiencies. 4 stories, interior corridors. **Parking:** winter plug-ins. **Terms:** check-in 4 pm, resort fee. **Pool(s):** heated indoor. **Activities:** hot tub, exercise room. **Guest Services:** valet and coin laundry. **Featured Amenity:** full hot breakfast.

BEST WESTERN SEVEN OAKS INN
(306)757-0121 **1**

Hotel
$160-$170

Best Western

AAA Benefit: Save 10% or more every day and earn 10% bonus points!

Address: 777 Albert St S4R 2P6 **Location:** On Hwy 6; jct 2nd Ave. **Facility:** 157 units, some two bedrooms. 3 stories, interior corridors. **Parking:** winter plug-ins. **Terms:** resort fee. **Dining:** Ricky's All Day Grill, see separate listing. **Pool(s):** heated indoor. **Activities:** hot tub, exercise room. **Guest Services:** valet and coin laundry.

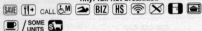

COUNTRY INN & SUITES BY CARLSON   (306)789-9117 **8**
Hotel. **Address:** 3321 Eastgate Bay S4Z 1A4

DAYS INN REGINA   (306)522-3297 **14**
Hotel. **Address:** 3875 Eastgate Dr E S4Z 1A4

DAYS INN-REGINA AIRPORT WEST   (306)584-3297 **18**
Hotel. **Address:** 4899 Harbour Landing Dr S4N 0B7

DELTA REGINA
(306)525-5255 **2**

Hotel
$85-$207

DELTA HOTELS

AAA Benefit: Members save 5% or more!

Address: 1919 Saskatchewan Dr S4P 4H2 **Location:** At Rose St; center. Across from Casino Regina. **Facility:** 274 units. 10-25 stories, interior corridors. **Parking:** on-site (fee), winter plug-ins. **Pool(s):** heated indoor. **Activities:** hot tub, exercise room, spa. **Guest Services:** valet laundry.

/ SOME UNITS

DOUBLETREE BY HILTON HOTEL & CONFERENCE CENTRE REGINA   (306)525-6767 **5**
Hotel. **Address:** 1975 Broad St S4P 1Y2

AAA Benefit: Members save 5% or more!

EXECUTIVE ROYAL HOTEL REGINA   306/586-6755 **15**
Hotel. **Address:** 4025 Albert St S S4S 3R6

HOLIDAY INN EXPRESS & SUITES   306/789-5888 **17**
Hotel. **Address:** 4255 Albert St S4S 3R6

HOLIDAY INN EXPRESS HOTEL & SUITES REGINA   306/569-4600 **4**
Hotel. **Address:** 1907 11th Ave S4P 0J2

HOLIDAY INN HOTEL & SUITES   (306)789-3883 **9**
Hotel. **Address:** 1800 Prince of Wales Dr S4Z 1A4

HOMESUITES HOTEL REGINA EAST   (306)522-4434 **13**
Extended Stay Hotel. **Address:** 3841 Eastgate Dr E S4Z 1A5

THE HOTEL SASKATCHEWAN, AUTOGRAPH COLLECTION
(306)522-7691 **6**

Historic Hotel
$152-$237

AUTOGRAPH COLLECTION HOTELS

AAA Benefit: Members save 5% or more!

Address: 2125 Victoria Ave S4P 0S3 **Location:** At Scarth St; center. Opposite Victoria Park. **Facility:** Built in 1927, this hotel has a majestic, richly decorated lobby. Request a north-facing room for a great view of Victoria Park. A full renovation was completed in 2016. 227 units, some two bedrooms. 10 stories, interior corridors. **Parking:** on-site (fee) and valet, winter plug-ins. **Terms:** 3 day cancellation notice, resort fee. **Amenities:** *Some:* safes. **Dining:** The Dining Room, see separate listing. **Activities:** hot tub, steamroom, spa. **Guest Services:** valet laundry.

QUALITY HOTEL
(306)569-4656 **7**

Hotel
$99-$219

Address: 1717 Victoria Ave S4P 0P9 **Location:** Just e of Broad St; downtown. **Facility:** 126 units. 7 stories, interior corridors. **Parking:** winter plug-ins. **Amenities:** video games. **Dining:** Memories Fine Dining & Lounge, see separate listing. **Activities:** sauna, exercise room. **Guest Services:** valet and coin laundry.

/ SOME UNITS

SANDMAN HOTEL SUITES & SPA REGINA   306/757-2444 **10**
Hotel. **Address:** 1800 Victoria Ave E S4N 7K3

SUPER 8 REGINA   (306)789-8833 **12**
Hotel. **Address:** 2730 Victoria Ave E S4N 6M5

TRAVELODGE HOTEL & CONFERENCE CENTRE   (306)586-3443 **16**
Hotel. **Address:** 4177 Albert St S S4S 3R6

(See map & index p. 444.)

WINGATE BY WYNDHAM   (306)584-7400 **3**
▼▼▼▼ Hotel. **Address:** 1700 Broad St S4P 1X4

WHERE TO EAT

BEER BROS. BAKERY & CUISINE   306/586-2337 **4**
▼▼ ▼▼ American. Casual Dining. **Address:** 1801A Scarth St S4P 2G9

BUSHWAKKER BREWPUB   306/359-7276 **2**
▼▼ Sandwiches Pizza. Casual Dining. **Address:** 2206 Dewdney Ave S4R 1H2

CRAVE KITCHEN & WINE BAR   306/525-8777 **8**
▼▼ International. Casual Dining. **Address:** 1925 Victoria Ave S4P 0R3

CREEK IN CATHEDRAL BISTRO   306/352-4448 **9**
▼▼▼▼ American. Casual Dining. **Address:** 3414 13th Ave S4T 1P7

THE DINING ROOM   306/337-4311 **6**
▼▼▼▼ American. Fine Dining. **Address:** 2125 Victoria Ave S4P 0S3

THE DIPLOMAT STEAKHOUSE   306/359-3366 **12**
▼▼ ▼▼ Steak. Fine Dining. **Address:** 2032 Broad St S4P 1Y3

EARLS KITCHEN + BAR
▼▼ ▼▼ American. Casual Dining.
LOCATIONS:
Address: 2606 28th Ave S4S 6P3 **Phone:** 306/584-7733
Address: 1875 Victoria Ave E S4N 6E6 **Phone:** 306/949-4955

FIRESIDE BISTRO   306/761-2305 **17**
▼▼▼▼ American. Casual Dining. **Address:** 2305 Smith St S4P 2P7

GOLF'S STEAK HOUSE   306/525-5808 **7**
▼▼▼▼ Steak. Fine Dining. **Address:** 1945 Victoria Ave S4P 0R3

HENRY'S CAFE   306/791-7889 **14**
▼▼▼▼ American. Casual Dining. **Address:** 2175 Smith St S4P 2P3

HOUSTON PIZZA   306/585-6888 **18**
▼▼ American. Casual Dining. **Address:** 2815 Quance St S4V 3B7

LA BODEGA TAPAS BAR & GRILL   306/546-3660 **16**
▼▼▼▼ Mediterranean. Casual Dining. **Address:** 2228 Albert St S4P 2V2

THE LAST SPIKE   306/781-7000 **3**
▼▼▼▼ American. Casual Dining. **Address:** 1880 Saskatchewan Dr S4P 0A8

LUIGGI'S PASTA HOUSE & LOUNGE   306/949-7427 **1**
▼▼ ▼▼ Italian. Casual Dining. **Address:** 470 Albert St N S4R 3C1

MEMORIES FINE DINING & LOUNGE   306/522-1999 **10**
▼▼▼▼ International. Fine Dining. **Address:** 1717 Victoria Ave S4P 0P9

MOXIE'S CLASSIC GRILL   306/781-5655
▼▼ ▼▼ American. Casual Dining. **Address:** 1800A Victoria Ave S4N 7K3

RICKY'S ALL DAY GRILL   306/775-3000
▼▼ American. Casual Dining. **Address:** 777 Albert St S4R 2P6

THE ROOFTOP BAR & GRILL   306/359-7663 **11**
▼▼▼▼ American. Casual Dining. **Address:** 1845 Victoria Ave S4P 1Y2

SIAM AUTHENTIC THAI RESTAURANT   306/352-8424 **5**
▼▼ ▼▼ Thai. Casual Dining. **Address:** 1946 Hamilton St S4P 2C4

SLOW BREW PUB & SPORTS BAR   306/751-0000 **13**
▼▼▼▼ American. Gastropub. **Address:** 2124 Albert St S4P 2T9

SMOKIN' OKIES BBQ   306/347-2800 **19**
▼ Barbecue. Quick Serve. **Address:** 2547 Quance St E S4V 2X7

TANGERINE THE FOOD BAR   306/522-3500 **15**
▼▼▼▼ American. Quick Serve. **Address:** 2234 14th Ave S4P 0X8

THE WILLOW ON WASCANA   306/585-3663 **20**
▼▼▼▼ Regional Canadian. Casual Dining. **Address:** 3000 Wascana Dr S4P 3B2

ST. WALBURG (C-2) pop. 716, elev. 634m/2,083'

IMHOFF GALLERY is 2.5 mi. (4 km) s. on Hwy. 26 to the jct. with a gravel road (the turnoff is signed "RGE RD 3224"), then 4 km w. on the gravel road to the farmstead turnoff on the right (TWP RD 532). Born in Germany, religious artist Berthold Von Imhoff moved to St. Walburg in 1913, residing there until his death in 1939. Imhoff's works adorn more than 100 churches throughout Canada and the United States; he was knighted by the pope in 1937.

The artist's original working studio holds many original large canvases and photos. Two rooms in the original homestead are filled with antiques, including a sculpture of Custer, and several mounted game heads attest to Imhoff's prowess as a hunter. Visitors also can watch a 20-minute video about his life.

Time: Allow 1 hour minimum. **Hours:** Daily 10-5, July 1-Labour Day; Mon.-Sat. 10-5, in June. **Cost:** $7.62; $4.76 (students ages 6-18 with ID). **Phone:** (306) 248-3812. GT ⌂

SASKATOON (D-3) pop. 222,189, elev. 487m/1,598'
• Hotels p. 449 • Restaurants p. 451

Saskatoon was founded in 1882 as a temperance colony under leader John Lake. According to legend, a member of the Cree tribe brought Lake a handful of the purple berries that grew in abundance alongside the river. Lake was so taken with the fruit that he named his settlement Saskatoon, after *mis-askquatoomina*, the First Nations name for the wild berries. A slice of pie made with Saskatoon berries (known as serviceberries in the U.S.) is a traditional, fruity treat.

Straddling the South Saskatchewan River, Saskatoon is known as "The City of Bridges" because of the seven spans connecting its banks. It also is home to the University of Saskatchewan, which is building a reputation for research and development in science, medicine and agriculture. The Diefenbaker Canada Centre on campus showcases memorabilia pertaining to Canada's 13th prime minister.

The Local History Room on the second floor of the Frances Morrison Library, 311-23rd St. E., serves as a research facility for information that focuses on prairie history relating to Saskatoon in particular and western Canada in general. Collections include more than 60,000 historic photographs and thousands of books, pamphlets, maps, artifacts and periodicals. An art gallery is adjacent to the room. Phone (306) 975-7558.

The Saskatchewan Railway Museum, 6 kilometres (4 mi.) west on Hwy. 7, then 2 kilometres (1.2 mi.) south on Hwy. 60, is operated by the Saskatchewan Railroad Historical Association. Displays include old railroad buildings and artifacts, including locomotives, cabooses and streetcars; phone (306) 382-9855 May through September.

TCU Place—Saskatoon's Art & Convention Centre, 35 22nd St., is home to the Saskatoon Symphony and the site of concerts and events throughout the year; phone (306) 975-7777. Rock concerts, trade shows, hockey games and other sporting events take place at the SaskTel Centre, on the city's north side next to hwys. 2 and 16; phone (306) 938-7800.

The Meewasin Valley Trail, following the South Saskatchewan River through the heart of the city, has bicycle and jogging trails, picnic areas and playgrounds; winter activities include cross-country skiing and ice-skating. More recreational opportunities are available at nearby Pike Lake and Blackstrap provincial parks *(see Recreation Areas Chart)*.

Racing fans can enjoy horse racing at Marquis Downs, 503 Ruth St., from late May to early September. Races are held Fri.-Sat. 7-10 p.m.; phone (306) 242-6100. Drag racing heats up the Saskatchewan International Raceway, 13 kilometres (8 mi.) s. on Hwy. 11, from early May to mid-September; phone (306) 955-3724. Stock car racing takes place at the Wyant Group Raceway, north on Hwy. 12, from May through September; phone (306) 651-3278.

Note: Policies concerning admittance of children to pari-mutuel betting facilities vary. Phone for information.

Tourism Saskatoon: 101-202 4th Ave. N., Saskatoon, SK, Canada S7K 0K1. **Phone:** (306) 242-1206 or (800) 567-2444.

Shopping: Midtown Plaza, downtown at 1st Avenue and 21st Street, is a two-level mall with more than 130 shops, including anchor stores Hudson's Bay and Sears. The Centre, at Circle Drive and 8th Street, has more than 90 stores and services in "East" and "West" sections connected by an underground walkway.

DIEFENBAKER CANADA CENTRE is at 101 Diefenbaker Pl. on the University of Saskatchewan campus. The archives and personal belongings of Prime Minister John Diefenbaker are housed in the only Prime Ministerial center in Canada; his grave site is on the grounds. The museum also offers changing national and international exhibits about Canadian history, citizenship, leadership, art, politics, science, culture, current affairs and Canada's role in the international community.

Hours: Mon.-Thurs. 9:30-8, Fri. 9:30-4:30, Sat.-Sun. and holidays noon-4:30. Reservations are recommended for guided tours. Closed Family Day (third Mon. in Feb.), Good Friday, Labour Day, Thanksgiving, Nov. 11 and mid-Dec. to early Jan. Phone ahead to confirm schedule. **Cost:** Donations. **Phone:** (306) 966-8384. GT

MUSEUM OF ANTIQUITIES is on the University of Saskatchewan campus at 107 Administration Pl., Room 106 in the Peter MacKinnon Building. Exhibits include original antiquities and pieces of art; a collection of original Greek, Roman and medieval coins; and replicas of Greek, Roman, Egyptian and Near Eastern sculptures. **Hours:** Mon.-Fri. 9-4, Sat. noon-4:30. Guided tours are available by appointment. Closed late Dec.-early Jan. **Cost:** Free; donations accepted. **Phone:** (306) 966-7818.

WANUSKEWIN HERITAGE PARK is 5 km (3.1 mi.) n. on Hwy. 11, 3 km (1.9 mi.) s. on Warman Rd., then 2 km (1.2 mi.) e. on Penner Rd., following signs. This First Nations park traces more than 6,000 years of area history. The park's interpretive center contains a DVD theater and features state-of-the-art exhibits and art pertaining to Northern Plains culture. Cultural offerings include storytelling, children's activities and traditional dance performances.

Self-guiding trails take visitors through the 360-acre (146-hectare) park's prairie landscape, with interpretive signs explaining past uses of the land. Trails lead to 19 sites representing the Northern Plains peoples, including summer and winter campsites, archeological sites, four bison kill sites, a tipi ring site and a boulder alignment known as a medicine wheel.

Time: Allow 2 hours minimum. **Hours:** Daily 9-4:30 (11-4 on statutory holidays), Victoria Day-Labour Day; Mon.-Fri. 9-4:30, Sat. 11-3 (closed statutory holidays), rest of year. Dance performances take place daily at 2, May-Aug. **Cost:** $8.10; $7.14 (ages 65+); $6.19 (students with ID); $3.81 (ages 6-16); $23.81 (family). **Phone:** (306) 931-6767 or (877) 547-6546. GT

WESTERN DEVELOPMENT MUSEUM'S 1910 BOOMTOWN is at 2610 Lorne Ave. This indoor representation of a typical prairie town features more than 30 buildings. Displays include transportation artifacts and vintage agricultural equipment. **Time:** Allow 2 hours minimum. **Hours:** Daily 9-5, Apr.-Dec. (closes at 3 on Dec. 24 and 31); Tues.-Sun. 9-5, rest of year. Closed Jan. 1, Family Day (third Mon. in Feb.), Thanksgiving (second Mon. in Oct.), Nov. 11,

Nov. 20, Christmas and day after Christmas. **Cost:** $9.52; $8.57 (ages 65+); $6.67 (students with ID); $3.81 (ages 6-12); $23.81 (family, parents or guardians and dependent children under age 18). **Phone:** (306) 931-1910.

BEST WESTERN PLUS BLAIRMORE   (306)242-2299

Hotel
$150-$173

AAA Benefit:
Save 10% or more every day and earn 10% bonus points!

Address: 306 Shillington Crescent S7M 1L2 **Location:** Jct Hwy 7 and 14. **Facility:** 100 units. 4 stories, interior corridors. **Parking:** winter plug-ins. **Terms:** check-in 4 pm, resort fee. **Amenities:** Some: safes. **Pool(s):** heated indoor. **Activities:** hot tub, exercise room. **Guest Services:** valet and coin laundry. **Featured Amenity:** full hot breakfast.

Best Western PLUS.

Saltwater Pool, Waterslide & Whirlpool Tub. Business Centre & Meeting Rooms. Free Hot Breakfast.

BEST WESTERN PLUS EAST SIDE   (306)986-2400

Hotel
$160-$175

Best Western PLUS.

AAA Benefit:
Save 10% or more every day and earn 10% bonus points!

Address: 3331 8th St E S7H 4K1 **Location:** Hwy 16 exit 8th St E, just e. **Facility:** 101 units. 4 stories, interior corridors. **Parking:** winter plug-ins. **Terms:** check-in 4 pm, resort fee. **Amenities:** safes. **Pool(s):** heated indoor. **Activities:** hot tub, exercise room. **Guest Services:** valet and coin laundry. **Featured Amenity:** full hot breakfast.

COLONIAL SQUARE INN & SUITES   (306)343-1676

Hotel
$109-$129

Address: 1301 8th St E S7H 0S7 **Location:** 1.5 mi (2.4 km) e of jct Hwy 11 (Idylwyld Dr S); 1.4 mi (2.3 km) w of jct Circle Dr. Opposite Cumberland Park. **Facility:** 78 units. 2 stories (no elevator), interior/exterior corridors. **Parking:** winter plug-ins. **Terms:** cancellation fee imposed. **Dining:** 3 restaurants. **Activities:** exercise room. **Guest Services:** coin laundry.

COMFORT INN   (306)934-1122

Motel
$99-$270

Address: 2155 Northridge Dr S7L 6X6 **Location:** Just ne of jct Hwy 11 (Idylwyld Dr N) and Circle Dr. **Facility:** 78 units. 2 stories (no elevator), interior corridors. **Parking:** winter plug-ins. **Terms:** check-in 4 pm. **Guest Services:** valet laundry. **Featured Amenity:** full hot breakfast.

COUNTRY INN & SUITES BY CARLSON   (306)934-3900

Hotel. **Address:** 617 Cynthia St S7L 6B7

DAYS INN-SASKATOON   (306)242-3297

Hotel
$139-$155

Address: 2000 Idylwyld Dr N S7L 7M7 **Location:** Just nw of jct Circle Dr. **Facility:** 101 units. 4 stories, interior corridors. **Parking:** winter plug-ins. **Amenities:** Some: safes. **Pool(s):** heated indoor. **Activities:** hot tub, exercise room. **Guest Services:** valet and coin laundry.

Days Inn.
INNS • HOTELS • SUITES

Free: Deluxe Continental Breakfast, WI-FI/High-Speed Internet, Airport Shuttle and Local Calls.

DELTA BESSBOROUGH   (306)244-5521

Boutique Vintage Hotel
$139-$229

DELTA HOTELS

AAA Benefit:
Members save 5% or more!

Address: 601 Spadina Crescent E S7K 3G8 **Location:** Jct 21st St E; center. **Facility:** This lovely castle on the river has grand public spaces and beautifully appointed rooms with a modern elegance. It has been a local landmark since the 1930s. 225 units. 6 stories, interior corridors. **Parking:** on-site (fee) and valet, winter plug-ins. **Amenities:** video games. **Dining:** 3 restaurants, also, The Garden Court Café, Samurai Japanese Restaurant, see separate listings. **Pool(s):** heated indoor. **Activities:** sauna, hot tub, steamroom, spa. **Guest Services:** valet laundry.

FOUR POINTS BY SHERATON SASKATOON

(306)933-9889

Hotel
$139-$159

AAA Benefit: Members save up to 15%, plus Starwood Preferred Guest® benefits!

Address: 503 Cope Way S7T 0G3 **Location:** Hwy 11 (Louis Riel Tr) exit Clarence Ave S, just s, then just e. **Facility:** 119 units. 4 stories, interior corridors. **Parking:** winter plug-ins. **Terms:** 5 day cancellation notice-fee imposed. **Pool(s):** heated indoor. **Activities:** hot tub, exercise room. **Guest Services:** valet and coin laundry.

HAMPTON INN/SASKATOON SOUTH

(306)665-9898

Hotel
$119-$189

AAA Benefit: Members save up to 10%!

Address: 105 Stonebridge Blvd S7T 0G3 **Location:** Hwy 11 (Louis Riel Tr) exit Clarence Ave S, just s, then just e. **Facility:** 100 units. 4 stories, interior corridors. **Parking:** winter plug-ins. **Terms:** 1-7 night minimum stay, cancellation fee imposed. **Pool(s):** heated indoor. **Activities:** exercise room. **Guest Services:** valet and coin laundry. **Featured Amenity:** breakfast buffet.

HILTON GARDEN INN SASKATOON DOWNTOWN

(306)244-2311

 Hotel. **Address:** 90 22nd St E S7K 3X6

AAA Benefit: Members save up to 10%!

HOLIDAY INN EXPRESS HOTEL & SUITES SASKATOON

306/384-8844

Hotel. **Address:** 315 Idylwyld Dr N S7L 0Z1

THE JAMES HOTEL SASKATOON

306/244-6446

Boutique Contemporary Retro Hotel. **Address:** 620 Spadina Crescent E S7K 3T5

MOTEL 6 SASKATOON

306/665-6688

Hotel. **Address:** 231 Marquis Dr S7R 1B7

QUALITY INN & SUITES

306/244-5552

Hotel
Rates not provided

Address: 1715 Idylwyld Dr N S7L 1B4 **Location:** On Hwy 11 (Idylwyld Dr), 0.4 mi (0.7 km) s of jct Circle Dr. **Facility:** 106 units, some efficiencies. 2 stories, interior/exterior corridors. **Parking:** winter plug-ins. **Dining:** Ricky's All Day Grill, see separate listing. **Activities:** exercise room. **Guest Services:** valet and coin laundry. **Featured Amenity:** breakfast buffet.

Ricky's All Day Grill & Lounge, Banquet & Meeting Rooms, Cold Beer & Wine Store.

RADISSON HOTEL SASKATOON

306/665-3322

Hotel
Rates not provided

Address: 405 20th St E S7K 6X6 **Location:** At 4th Ave S; center. **Facility:** 291 units. 19 stories, interior corridors. **Parking:** on-site (fee) and street, winter plug-ins. **Amenities:** *Some:* safes. **Dining:** AROMA Resto Bar, see separate listing. **Pool(s):** heated indoor. **Activities:** hot tub, exercise room. **Guest Services:** valet laundry.

RAMADA HOTEL-SASKATOON

(306)665-6500

Hotel
$119-$139

Address: 806 Idylwyld Dr N S7L 0Z6 **Location:** On Hwy 11 (Idylwyld Dr), 2.5 mi (4 km) s of jct Circle Dr. **Facility:** 148 units. 6 stories, interior corridors. **Parking:** winter plug-ins. **Pool(s):** heated indoor. **Activities:** hot tub, miniature golf. **Guest Services:** complimentary laundry.

SANDMAN HOTEL SASKATOON

306/477-4844

Hotel. **Address:** 310 Circle Dr W S7L 2Y5

SHERATON CAVALIER SASKATOON HOTEL

(306)652-6770

Hotel
$139-$289

Sheraton

AAA Benefit:
Members save up to 15%, plus Starwood Preferred Guest® benefits!

Address: 612 Spadina Crescent E S7K 3G9 **Location:** Jct 21st St E; center. **Facility:** 237 units. 8 stories, interior corridors. **Parking:** on-site (fee), winter plug-ins. **Amenities:** safes. **Dining:** Carver's Steakhouse, see separate listing. **Pool(s):** heated indoor. **Activities:** hot tub, exercise room. **Guest Services:** valet laundry.

SAVE ECO ❙❙ ☷ CALL &M 🏊

BIZ HS 📶 ✕ 🛫 🔒 💻 / SOME UNITS 🐾 🖼

SUPER 8 EAST-SASKATOON   (306)384-8989

▼▼ Hotel. **Address:** 706 Circle Dr E S7K 3T7

WHERE TO EAT

2ND AVE GRILL   306/244-9899

▼▼▼ International. Casual Dining. **Address:** 10 123 2nd Ave S S7K 7E6

ALEXANDER'S RESTAURANT & BAR   306/956-7777

▼▼▼ International. Casual Dining. **Address:** 414 Cumberland Ave N S7N 1M6

AMIGOS CANTINA   306/652-4912

▼▼ Tex-Mex. Casual Dining. **Address:** 806 Dufferin Ave S7H 2B8

AROMA RESTO BAR   306/665-9080

▼▼ American. Casual Dining. **Address:** 405 20th St E S7K 6X6

BLISS FINE FOOD   306/477-2077

▼▼▼ Northern American. Casual Dining. **Address:** 1002 Broadway Ave S7N 1B9

CALORIES BAKERY & RESTAURANT   306/665-7991

▼▼▼ International Desserts. Casual Dining. **Address:** 721 Broadway Ave S7N 1B3

CARVER'S STEAKHOUSE   306/652-8292

▼▼▼ Steak. Casual Dining. **Address:** 612 Spadina Cres E S7K 3G9

CHIANTI   306/665-8466

▼▼ Italian. Casual Dining. **Address:** 102 Idylwyld Dr N S7L 0Y7

CHRISTIES IL SECONDO BAKERY PIZZERIA   306/384-0506

▼ Breads/Pastries Pizza. Quick Serve. **Address:** 802C Broadway Ave S7N 1B6

EARLS KITCHEN + BAR   306/664-4060

▼▼ American. Casual Dining. **Address:** 610 2nd Ave N S7K 2C8

THE GARDEN COURT CAFÉ   306/683-6912

▼▼▼ Regional Canadian. Casual Dining. **Address:** 601 Spadina Cres E S7K 3G8

GENESIS FAMILY RESTAURANT   306/244-5516

▼▼ Chinese. Casual Dining. **Address:** 901 22nd St W S7M 0R9

GOLDEN PAGODA BURMESE ASIAN RESTAURANT

306/668-9114

▼▼ Burmese. Casual Dining. **Address:** 411 2nd Ave N S7K 2C1

THE IVY DINING & LOUNGE   306/384-4444

▼▼▼ International. Fine Dining. **Address:** 301 Ontario Ave S7K 1S3

KEO'S KITCHEN   306/652-2533

▼▼ Thai. Casual Dining. **Address:** 1013 Broadway Ave S7N 1C1

LAS PALAPAS RESORT GRILL   306/244-5556

▼▼ Mexican. Casual Dining. **Address:** 910 Victoria Ave S7N 0Z6

MOXIE'S CLASSIC GRILL   306/374-9800

▼▼ American. Casual Dining. **Address:** 3134 8th St E S7H 0W2

RICKY'S ALL DAY GRILL   306/652-3222

▼▼ American. Casual Dining. **Address:** 1715 Idylwyld Dr N S7L 1B4

ST. TROPEZ BISTRO   306/652-1250

▼▼▼ International. Casual Dining. **Address:** 238 2nd Ave S S7K 1K9

SAMURAI JAPANESE RESTAURANT   306/683-6926

▼▼ Japanese. Casual Dining. **Address:** 601 Spadina Cres E S7K 3G8

THE SPADINA FREEHOUSE   306/668-1000

▼▼ International. Gastropub. **Address:** 608 Spadina Cres E S7K 3G9

SUSHIRO   306/665-5557

▼▼ Sushi. Casual Dining. **Address:** 737B Broadway Ave S7N 1B3

TRUFFLES BISTRO   306/373-7779

▼▼▼ New Canadian. Casual Dining. **Address:** 230 21st St E S7K 0B9

SWIFT CURRENT (E-3) pop. 15,503
• Hotels p. 452 • Restaurants p. 452

Swift Current's beginnings date to the establishment of a North West Mounted Police encampment on Swift Current Creek in 1874. Soon after, the Canadian Pacific Railway built a depot, and the settlement became the freight terminus for western Canada. Beyond this point goods were hauled by wagon on overland trails; deep ruts still exist along the old North Battleford Trail north of the city.

Turn-of-the-20th-century farmers and ranchers bolstered the local economy. Oil was discovered in 1952, and in the succeeding decades Swift Current became a business hub for the oil, gas and agricultural industries as well as the major health care center for southwestern Saskatchewan.

Swift Current Creek runs through town, and two nearby lakes offer recreational facilities. At Saskatchewan Landing Provincial Park *(see Recreation Areas Chart)*, a plaque marks the spot where pioneers once forded the South Saskatchewan River on their way into the wilds of the northern province.

In the park's hills are several First Nations grave sites and tepee rings.

Doc's Town Heritage Village, 17th Avenue S.E. and S. Railway Street in Kinetic Park, has a collection of buildings typical of early 20th-century prairie towns, including a blacksmith shop, church and school. Costumed staff are on hand to answer questions. It's open Fri.-Sun. 1-5, Father's Day-Labour Day; phone (306) 773-2944.

Tourism Swift Current: 44 Robert St. W., Swift Current, SK, Canada S9H 4M9. **Phone:** (306) 778-9174.

Self-guiding tours: A brochure with details about a walking tour of historic buildings in downtown Swift Current is available at the Swift Current Museum and from downtown merchants.

ART GALLERY OF SWIFT CURRENT is at 411 Herbert St. E. This public gallery offers exhibitions spotlighting local, provincial and national artists. Cultural events and festivals are scheduled throughout the year. Guided tours are given upon request. **Hours:** Open Mon.-Thurs. 1-5 and 7-9 p.m., Fri.-Sun. 1-5, Sept.-May; Mon.-Thurs. 1-5 and 7-9 p.m., Fri.-Sat. 1-5, rest of year. Closed major holidays and during exhibition changes. Phone ahead to confirm schedule. **Cost:** Free. **Phone:** (306) 778-2736.

BEST WESTERN INN   (306)773-4660

Hotel
$119-$179

Best Western
AAA Benefit: Save 10% or more every day and earn 10% bonus points!

Address: 105 George St W S9H 0K4 **Location:** Jct Trans-Canada Hwy 1 and Central Ave. **Facility:** 86 units. 2 stories (no elevator), interior/exterior corridors. **Parking:** winter plug-ins. **Terms:** check-in 4 pm. **Pool(s):** heated indoor. **Activities:** sauna, hot tub, exercise room. **Guest Services:** valet and coin laundry.

COMFORT INN SWIFT CURRENT   (306)778-3994

Hotel
$88-$150

Address: 1510 S Service Rd E S9H 3X6 **Location:** Trans-Canada Hwy 1, just w of 22nd Ave NE. **Facility:** 73 units. 2 stories (no elevator), interior corridors. **Parking:** winter plug-ins. **Guest Services:** valet laundry. **Featured Amenity: full hot breakfast.**

DAYS INN-SWIFT CURRENT   (306)773-4643
Hotel. **Address:** 905 N Service Rd E S9H 3V1

HOLIDAY INN EXPRESS & SUITES   306/773-8288
Hotel. **Address:** 1301 N Service Rd E S9H 3X6

MOTEL 6 SWIFT CURRENT   (306)778-6060
Hotel. **Address:** 1185 5th Ave NE S9H 5N7

SUPER 8   (306)778-6088
Hotel. **Address:** 405 N Service Rd E S9H 3T7

WHERE TO EAT

AKROPOL FAMILY RESTAURANT   306/773-5454
International. Casual Dining. **Address:** 133 Central Ave N S9H 0K9

HORIZONS RESTAURANT   306/778-5759
American. Casual Dining. **Address:** 1401 N Service Rd E S9H 3X6

MISO HOUSE   306/778-4411

Japanese Casual Dining $9-$24

AAA Inspector Notes: This restaurant offers a good selection of reasonably priced entrées. Most dishes include miso soup, rice and kimchi. Favorites include bento boxes, nigiri sushi and beef, chicken or salmon teriyaki. Tempura dishes include vegetable, prawn, fish and chips and gyoza. **Features:** beer & wine. **Address:** 285 N Service Rd W S9H 3S8 **Location:** Trans-Canada Hwy 1, 0.4 mi (0.6 km) w of Hwy 4 (Central Ave). L D

SPRINGS GARDEN   306/773-2021
Comfort Food. Casual Dining. **Address:** 1 Springs Dr, Suite 323 S9H 3X6

TNT FAMILY RESTAURANT   306/773-6002
American. Casual Dining. **Address:** 83 N Service Rd W S9H 5E7

WONG'S KITCHEN   306/773-4636
Chinese. Casual Dining. **Address:** 320 S Service Rd E S9H 3T6

TISDALE (C-4) pop. 3,180

This rural community in northeastern Saskatchewan provides easy access to several provincial parks offering recreational activities from fishing and boating in summer to skiing in winter. A roadside attraction, allegedly the world's largest honeybee, stands on the south side of Hwy. 3 in town.

Greville Jones Wildlife Sanctuary is reached by a gravel access road about 6.4 kilometres (4 mi.) southwest of Tisdale off Hwy. 3, following signs. The site of an old farmstead, it's a pleasant spot for a summer picnic or a hike along one of several nature trails.

Another scenic route is the Doghide River Trail, a system of walking, cycling and skiing trails that run along several sections of the riverbank. The trail can be accessed from Kinsmen McKay Park; from the junction of Hwys. 3 and 35, proceed east .8 kilometre (.5 mi.), then north .5 kilometre (.3 mi.) and turn right into the park.

WEYBURN (F-4) pop. 10,484

Weyburn's name was coined in 1893 by Scottish railroad workers, who called the surrounding marshy area at the headwaters of the Souris River "wee burn." Weyburn is the southeastern terminus of scenic Hwy. 39, which continues to Moose Jaw.

W.O. Mitchell, author of the popular novel "Who Has Seen the Wind," was born and raised in Weyburn. His works often dealt with life on the Canadian prairie, and in them he immortalized the town as "Crocus, Saskatchewan." Local history is depicted on the "Wheel of Progress" at the Weyburn Public Library, 45 Bison St. Between the spokes of this brass-rimmed mahogany wheel, which weighs 909 kilograms (2,000 lbs.) and has a diameter of 3.9 metres (13 ft.), are 10 mosaic panels showing past city highlights.

Weyburn Chamber of Commerce: 11 3rd St. N.E., Weyburn, SK, Canada S4H 0W1. **Phone:** (306) 842-4738.

SOO LINE HISTORICAL MUSEUM is e. on Hwy. 39 at 411 Industrial Ln. In addition to pioneer and Native artifacts, there is a collection of more than 5,000 pieces of silver—everything from opera glasses to a full tea service—dating from 1750 to 1970. The collection was willed to the museum by local resident Charles Wilson, who spent a lifetime attending auction sales in order to amass his treasures. The museum also houses the Weyburn Visitor Centre. **Time:** Allow 30 minutes minimum. **Hours:** Daily 10-6, Victoria Day weekend-Aug. 31; Sat. 1-5, rest of year. Guided tours are available by appointment. **Cost:** $4.76; $2.86 (ages 13-17 and 65+); $1.90 (ages 6-12). Tours include an audio handset. **Phone:** (306) 842-2922.

CANALTA HOTEL   (306)842-8000
▼▼▼ Hotel. **Address:** 1360 Sims Ave S4H 3N9

MICROTEL INN & SUITES BY WYNDHAM WEYBURN
                                                (306)842-5700
▼▼ Hotel. **Address:** 88 Grace St S4H 3N9

RAMADA INN & SUITES   (306)842-4994
▼▼▼ Hotel. **Address:** 1420 Sims Ave S4H 3N9

TRAVELODGE HOTEL WEYBURN   (306)842-1411
▼▼ Motel. **Address:** 53 Government Rd S S4H 2A2

WHERE TO EAT

T & C FAMILY RESTAURANT/DALLAS PIZZA   306/842-2933
▼▼ International. Casual Dining. **Address:** 72 3rd St NE S4H 0V9

WOLSELEY (E-5) pop. 864

Amiable little Wolseley earned the nickname "The Town With the Swinging Bridge" when just such a contraption was built over man-made Fairly Lake in the center of town. The bridge, which connected homes on the north side of the lake with businesses on the south side, has had a checkered history: It was destroyed by a storm in 1954, rebuilt 10 years later, collapsed in 1993 during repairs and reopened again in 2004 thanks to the fund-raising efforts of the Heritage Canada Foundation.

The Romanesque-style Town Hall & Opera House, at the corner of Richmond and Varennes streets, was completed in 1907. The two-tone brick building (brick was imported from Manitoba when the local supply ran out) housed the town's administrative offices, fire hall, library, jail cell and community hall—commonly known as an Opera House—where touring vaudeville, theatrical and opera companies would perform. The building was extensively refurbished in the early 1990s.

YORKTON (E-5) pop. 15,669

In 1882 some 200 settlers from Ontario bought land in the Northwest Territories in what is now southeastern Saskatchewan. They called the community around their trading post York City. In 1890 the railroad arrived; York City settlers relocated to be near the railroad line and chose the name Yorkton. A plaque marks the site of York City; millstones from the original settlement's gristmill can still be seen.

Good Spirit Lake Provincial Park offers summer recreation. The park, a Hudson's Bay Co. post in the 1880s, is noted for miles of sandy beaches and dunes. *See Recreation Areas Chart.*

Tourism Yorkton Visitor Information Centre: Hwys. 9 and 16, Box 460, Yorkton, SK, Canada S3N 2W4. **Phone:** (306) 783-8707.

Self-guiding tours: The Yorkton Historical Walking Tour route includes gardens and historic buildings. The City Cemetery Walking Tour features the grave sites of many early pioneers, while the Art Walk highlights public art installations, monuments and murals. A nature trail winds through the Ravine Ecological Reserve. Tour brochures are available at the information center.

WESTERN DEVELOPMENT MUSEUM – YORKTON is .4 km (.25 mi.) w. on Hwy. 16A. Exhibits focus on the cultural roots of western Canadian settlers. **Time:** Allow 1 hour minimum. **Hours:** Daily 9-5, mid-June to mid-Aug.; Mon.-Fri. 9-5, Sat.-Sun. noon-5, rest of year (closes at 3 on Dec. 24 and 31). Closed national holidays and Saskatchewan Family Day. Phone ahead to confirm schedule. **Cost:** $9.52; $8.57 (ages 65+); $6.67 (students with ID); $3.81 (ages 6-12); $19.05 (family, parents or guardians and dependent children under age 18). **Phone:** (306) 783-8361. 🏛

DAYS INN & SUITES YORKTON   (306)782-3112
▼▼▼ Hotel. **Address:** 1-275 Broadway St E S3N 0N5

QUALITY INN & SUITES YORKTON   (306)783-3297
▼▼ Hotel. **Address:** 2 Kelsey Bay S3N 3Z4

WHERE TO EAT

MR MIKES STEAKHOUSECASUAL   306/783-6453
▼▼ American. Casual Dining. **Address:** 275 Broadway St E S3N 3G7

Bennett Lake at Carcross

Yukon

To find gleaming gifts of topaz in out-croppings of rock. To wander trails once trodden by miners and trappers. To cry "Mush!" behind a stalwart team of sturdy Alaskan huskies.

To do any of these is to begin to understand the allure of the endless Yukon.

The roughly triangular territory is a place of majesty and adventure; a lonely wilderness; a rugged, pristine land of splendor and beauty.

Klondike or Bust

"Thick between the flaky slabs, like cheese sandwiches"—this was how prospector George Washington Carmack described the gold he saw glimmering between rocks in Bonanza Creek near Dawson City in 1896.

In 1897 the steamship *Excelsior* arrived in San Francisco carrying a treasure worth more than $500,000; a few days later the *Portland* docked in Seattle with a ton of gold piled on its deck. News of these recently discovered riches spread like wildfire.

Gold panning, Dawson City

That winter 100,000 prospectors hopeful of getting rich quick began a long, arduous journey to the Yukon to seek their fortunes. While the rush only lasted about 5 years, history was left in its trampled tracks.

If stampeders survived the trek through Chilkoot Pass—a climb over frozen mountains with heavy backpacks full of supplies—they crossed the border into the Yukon Territory at Bennett Lake.

The lake, surrounded by mighty peaks and woodlands, links to the Yukon River. Most fortune seekers waited out the harsh winter in a crowded tent city. Transients built boats, temporary shelter and a little log church out of timber hewn from the forest. When the lake's ice broke, 7,000 handmade vessels headed across its waters.

Today, those miners' cabins still line Bennett Lake at Carcross, a town full of gold rush history. The 1898 Caribou Hotel, built to welcome gold rushers, is downtown, and graves of early pioneers dot the cemetery.

From Carcross the gold route followed the Yukon River to Miles Canyon, south of Whitehorse. Dangerous currents here caused hundreds of boats to capsize, and licensed guides were a must for piloting would-be miners with smaller vessels through the rocks and whirlpools.

Cheechakos (newcomers) relied upon their own floating devices until stern-wheelers became a popular means of travel. Though boats were specifically designed for the river, many still ran aground or were smashed by rapids or rocks.

The River to Riches

After stopping to relax and dry out in Whitehorse, miners pressed on, traversing Lake Laberge to a stretch of the Yukon called Thirty Mile. Due to swift currents and rocks, it was perhaps the route's most dangerous portion. Historical sites along Thirty Mile include abandoned Northwest Mounted Police posts, grave markers, woodcutters' cabins, telegraph stations, old log buildings and remains of beached paddlewheelers.

More dangerous eddies remained at Five Finger Rapids, outside Carmacks, before exhausted voyagers reached Dawson City.

Downtown Dawson City looks much as it did when prospectors arrived, since codes require that fronts of new buildings be reminiscent of the gold rush era. And old buildings have been restored: Cancan dancing takes place at Diamond Tooth Gertie's Casino and author Jack London's and poet Robert Service's log cabins remain as examples of gold rush housing.

Recreation

Hiking the Chilkoot Trail, Yukon's original inroad, is the best way to understand the challenges faced by gold-rush stampeders. Beginning in Dyea, Alaska, the trail is a 53-kilometre (33-mi.), one-way walk through history that can take 3 to 5 days.

Preparation—proper gear, provisions, permits and registration—is key to this demanding trip through boreal forests, alpine tundra and snow-patched mountains. You must reserve a campsite for each night on the trail through the Trail Centre in Skagway, Alaska. The center offers maps, safety tips and a few words about bears; phone Parks Canada year-round at (800) 661-0486.

Camping in summer (June to mid-September) is a true wilderness experience. Firewood is free, but you'll have to pump your own water. Government campgrounds are spread throughout the Yukon roughly 81-121 kilometres (50-75 mi.) apart, many beside lakes, rivers or streams where you might hook Arctic graylings for dinner. Of the 10 campgrounds along the Alaska Highway (Hwy. 1), Watson Lake is one of the first as you enter Yukon from British Columbia. Farther west is Congdon Creek, one of Yukon's largest. You can fish, swim and hike at both.

Take scenic Dempster Highway (Hwy. 5) from Dawson City to Rock River Campground, the northernmost public facility. Congratulate yourself: You've crossed the Continental Divide—twice—and the Arctic Circle! There's no well water, so get supplies in Dawson City or Eagle Plains (your last chance).

The Klondike Highway (Hwy. 2), open all year, has roadside respites for camping and picnicking. You also can camp just off the Robert Campbell and Silver Trail highways (Hwys. 4 and 11). Travelers can get daily road condition reports from the Department of Highways and Public Works hotline, (877) 456-7623 within the Yukon or (867) 456-7623 outside the Yukon. Watch for wildlife, especially near viewing areas identified with a sign picturing binoculars.

With almost 7 months of winter (October through April), snow skiing is a way of life. Near Whitehorse a chalet and night lighting draw cross-country skiers to Mount McIntyre's trails, while Mount Sima, one of Yukon's largest ski areas, appeals to downhill skiers. Snowboarding is a favorite at Mount Sima as well as on groomed trails around Whitehorse, or over more rugged terrain out of Dawson City, Yukon's snowmobiling capital.

Whitehorse offers kayaking or white-water rafting on the Tatshenshini's Class III and IV rapids, or through Kluane National Park and Reserve on the Alsek, a designated heritage river. Many sections of the Yukon River are easily navigated by canoe.

Kayak in Whitehorse

Historic Timeline

1800	The Hudson's Bay Co. sets up trading posts in the Yukon.
1895	Yukon Territory becomes a provisional district of the Northwest Territories.
1898	More than $100 million in gold is mined in the region over a 6-year span beginning just before the turn of the 20th century.
1942	The Alaska Highway is constructed, creating a new overland transportation route.
1953	Yukon's capital is moved from Dawson City to Whitehorse.
1959	At a cost of $1 million, a large fish ladder is built at the Whitehorse Rapids for migrating chinook salmon.
1979	Kluane National Park is declared a Natural World Heritage Site.
1993	The Council for Yukon Indians and the Canadian and Yukon governments agree on final territorial land claim settlements.
1999	Yukon's accord with the Vuntut Gwitchin marks the territory's first recognition of a First Nation tribe as a valid government.
2003	The name of the Yukon Territory is officially changed to Yukon.
2015	Yukon to spend an additional $1.4 million on mining exploration.

What To Pack

Temperature Averages Maximum/Minimum (Celsius)	JANUARY	FEBRUARY	MARCH	APRIL	MAY	JUNE	JULY	AUGUST	SEPTEMBER	OCTOBER	NOVEMBER	DECEMBER
Burwash Landing	-16 / -29	-11 / -26	-3 / -19	4 / -9	12 / -2	17 / 3	19 / 6	17 / 4	11 / -2	2 / -9	-9 / -21	-14 / -26
Dawson City	-21 / -30	-16 / -27	-3 / -20	8 / -8	15 / 1	21 / 6	23 / 8	20 / 5	11 / -1	-1 / -10	-14 / -22	-20 / -29
Faro	0 / -5	1 / -5	5 / -2	11 / 1	14 / 5	18 / 9	19 / 11	18 / 10	14 / 6	9 / 3	3 / -3	0 / -6
Mayo	-22 / -32	-13 / -26	-3 / -18	6 / -6	14 / 1	20 / 7	22 / 8	19 / 6	12 / 1	2 / -7	-13 / -21	-18 / -28
Watson Lake	-19 / -30	-12 / -25	-3 / -18	6 / -7	13 / 0	19 / 6	21 / 8	19 / 7	13 / 2	4 / -5	-11 / -20	-18 / -28
Whitehorse	-14 / -23	-8 / -18	-2 / -13	6 / -6	12 / 0	18 / 5	20 / 7	18 / 6	12 / 2	4 / -3	7 / -14	-12 / -20

From the records of The Weather Channel Interactive, Inc.

Good Facts To Know

ABOUT THE TERRITORY

POPULATION: 33,897.

AREA: 482,443 sq km (186,271 sq mi.); ranks 9th.

CAPITAL: Whitehorse.

HIGHEST POINT: 5,959 m (19,545 ft.), Mount Logan.

LOWEST POINT: Sea level, Beaufort Sea.

TIME ZONE(S): Pacific.

GAMBLING

MINIMUM AGE FOR GAMBLING: 19.

REGULATIONS

TEEN DRIVING LAWS: Driving is not permitted midnight-5 a.m. unless with a qualified co-driver or if a teen has been granted a work exception. A novice driver may not transport more than one passenger under 13 or a combination of passengers including a passenger under 13 and a passenger under 20 unless accompanied by a passenger over 20. Minimum age for an unrestricted driver's license is 17 years, 6 months. For more information about Yukon driver's license regulations, phone (867) 667-5315.

SEAT BELT/CHILD RESTRAINT LAWS: Seat belts are required for driver and all passengers ages 6 and older. Child restraints are required for children under age 6 and under 22 kilograms (48 lbs.). AAA recommends the use of seat belts and appropriate child restraints for the driver and all passengers.

CELLPHONE RESTRICTIONS: Drivers may not use a cellphone, text or send emails with any kind of hand-held electronic device while driving.

HELMETS FOR MOTORCYCLISTS: Required for all riders.

RADAR DETECTORS: Not permitted.

FIREARMS LAWS: By federal law, all nonresidents entering Canada with a firearm must declare their weapon in writing and pay a fee of $25 (Canadian). Contact the Canadian Firearms Centre at (800) 731-4000 to receive a declaration form or for additional information.

ALCOHOL CONSUMPTION: Legal age 19.

HOLIDAYS

HOLIDAYS: Jan. 1 ■ Heritage Day, Feb. 27 ■ Good Friday ■ Easter Monday ■ Victoria Day, May 24 or the closest prior Mon. ■ Canada Day, July 1 ■ Discovery Day, Aug. (3rd Mon.) ■ Labour Day, Sept. (1st Mon.) ■ Thanksgiving, Oct. (2nd Mon.) ■ Remembrance Day, Nov. 11 ■ Christmas, Dec. 25 ■ Boxing Day, Dec. 26.

MONEY

TAXES: Yukon has no territorial sales tax. The federal Goods and Services Tax (GST) is 5 percent.

VISITOR INFORMATION

INFORMATION CENTERS: Territorial information centers in Beaver Creek ■ Carcross ■ Dawson City ■ Haines Junction ■ Watson Lake ■ and Whitehorse are open 12 hours a day, mid-May to mid-Sept., with reduced hours early to mid-May and mid- to late Sept. The Whitehorse Visitor Information Centre also is open daily 8-8, May 5-Sept. 20 ■ Mon.-Fri. 8:30-5, Sat. 10-2, rest of year

ROAD CONDITIONS: Through its Yukon Network the Canadian Broadcasting Corporation reports road conditions on the Alaska Highway and all other Yukon highways. Major participating stations, with their frequencies in kilohertz (kHz), are listed from south to north: Watson Lake, 990; Swift River, 970; Teslin, 940; Whitehorse, 570; Haines Junction, 860; Destruction Bay, 940; Beaver Creek, 690; Carmacks, 990; Mayo, 1230; Elsa, 560; Dawson City, 560; Faro, 105.1 FM; and Ross River, 990.

ROAD CONDITIONS: For changes in Yukon road conditions, phone (867) 456-7623, (877) 456-7623 or 511 within Yukon.

FERRY SCHEDULES AND INFORMATION: The Department of Highways runs ferries along Dempster Highway and at Dawson City; phone (867) 667-3710.

FURTHER INFORMATION FOR VISITORS:
Department of Tourism & Culture
100 Hanson St.
Whitehorse, YT Y1A 2C6
Canada
(867) 667-5036
(800) 661-0494

FISHING AND HUNTING REGULATIONS:
Environment Yukon
10 Burns Rd.
Whitehorse, YT Y1A 2C6
Canada
(867) 667-5652
(800) 661-0408ext. 5652 in Canada

Upgrade to Plus or Premier membership
for *more* of the benefits you need most

Yukon Annual Events
Please call ahead to confirm event details.

JANUARY

- Women's and Men's Curling Championship / Whitehorse
  867-667-2875
- New Year's Day Snowmobile Poker Run Haines Junction
  867-634-2432
- Pivot Theatre Festival Whitehorse
  867-393-6040

FEBRUARY

- Yukon Quest International Sled Dog Race / Whitehorse
  907-452-7954
- Kiki Karnival / Watson Lake
  867-536-7469
- Yukon Sourdough Rendezvous / Whitehorse
  867-393-4467

MARCH

- Percy DeWolfe Memorial Mail Race / Dawson City
  867-993-5320
- Thaw-Di-Gras Spring Carnival / Dawson City
  867-993-5575
- Burning Away the Winter Blues / Whitehorse
  867-633-4844

APRIL

- Rotary Music Festival Whitehorse
  867-633-3755
- A Celebration of Swans Whitehorse
  867-667-8291
- Education Week Whitehorse
  867-393-7102

MAY

- Sounds of Spring Whitehorse
  867-667-8044
- Crane and Sheep Viewing Festival / Faro
  867-994-2728
- Dawson City International Gold Show / Dawson City
  867-993-5274

JUNE

- Aboriginal Day Celebrations / Dawson City
  867-993-5385
- Solstice and Saint-Jean-Baptiste Celebrations / Whitehorse
  867-668-2663, ext. 232
- Yukon River Quest Canoe and Kayak Race Whitehorse
  867-333-5628

JULY

- Pelly Valley Arts Festival Faro
  867-994-2288
- Canada Day Festivities Watson Lake
  867-536-2246
- Yukon Gold Panning Championships Dawson City
  867-993-5575

AUGUST

- Discovery Days Festival Dawson City
  867-993-2353
- Discovery Days Watson Lake
  867-536-8020
- YukomiCon / Whitehorse
  867-668-3555

SEPTEMBER

- Klondike Trail of '98 International Road Relay Whitehorse
  867-393-8330
- Labour Day Slo-Pitch Classic / Dawson City
  867-993-5575
- Terry Fox Run Watson Lake
  867-536-8020

OCTOBER

- Halloween Bonfire and Fireworks / Watson Lake
  867-536-8022
- Halloween Spooktacular Whitehorse
  867-668-8677
- Halloween Dance Watson Lake
  867-536-8022

NOVEMBER

- Spruce Bog Christmas Craft Sale / Whitehorse
  867-633-2416
- Cranberry Fair / Whitehorse
  867-393-2389
- Onde de Choc / Whitehorse
  867-668-2663, ext. 560

DECEMBER

- City Lights Festival Whitehorse
  867-668-8394
- Christmas Lights Tour Whitehorse
  867-668-8394
- TH (Tr'ondek Hwech'in) Last Minute Christmas Bazaar / Dawson City
  867-993-7100

Tombstone Territorial Park, Dawson City

Red fox

Miles Canyon, Whitehorse

Whitehorse

Sign Post Forest, Watson Lake

Index: Great Experience for Members

AAA editor's picks of exceptional note

The SS *Klondike*
National Historic Site

Yukon Beringia
Interpretive Centre

See Orientation map on this page for corresponding grid coordinates, if applicable.

* Indicates the GEM is temporarily closed.

Whitehorse (D-2)
The SS *Klondike* National Historic Site
(See p. 466.)

Yukon Beringia Interpretive Centre
(See p. 466.)

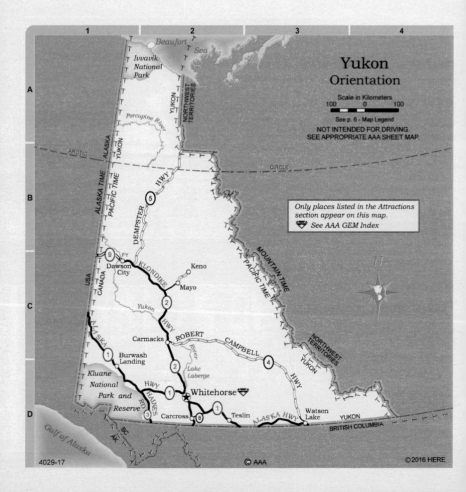

BURWASH LANDING (D-1) pop. 95

In 1904, a year after gold was discovered in Fourth of July Creek, Morley Bones staked a discovery claim on Burwash Creek. Soon after the small community of Burwash sprang up around a trading post. Burwash Landing, with an airstrip, lies between the Kluane Lake and Kluane Game Sanctuary.

CARCROSS (D-2) pop. 289

Carcross, 74 kilometres (46 mi.) from Whitehorse on the S. Klondike Highway, originally was called Caribou Crossing. The town's current name is a combination of the first syllable of each word. From this settlement George Carmack's party set out on the prospecting trip that began the gold rush of 1898. On July 29, 1900, the railroad's final spike was driven, marking the completion of the White Pass & Yukon Route, which linked Alaska and the Yukon Territory by rail.

Today the White Pass & Yukon Route *(see attraction listing in Alaska p. 533)* transports passengers between Carcross and Bennett, British Columbia; phone (907) 983-2217 or (800) 343-7373 for schedule and reservations.

Near the town's train depot is the "Duchess," a tiny locomotive that ran the 6.4-kilometre (4-mi.) line from Taku Arm on Tagish Lake to Atlin Lake in the early 1900s. It supposedly was the shortest and most expensive rail trip in the world—one-way fare was $2—and passengers had to sit on their baggage in the cramped compartment.

Recalling the feverish gold rush days is the Caribou Hotel. Regarded as the Yukon's oldest operating hotel, the historic building, which opened in 1898 to accommodate gold seekers heading north, is a Yukon Historic Site. **Note:** Hotel renovations are expected to continue into 2017; phone (867) 393-4551.

The Carcross Visitor Information Centre is at the Carcross Pavilion, adjacent to the historic White Pass & Yukon Route train depot. The center provides extensive information about Carcross, one of the Yukon's most picturesque areas; phone (867) 821-4431.

Just north of town along the Klondike Highway lies the Carcross Desert, considered the smallest desert in the world. The 260-hectare (650-acre) area was created by retreating glaciers that left a sandy lake bottom; today winds from Lake Bennett constantly shift the sand, limiting vegetation to such plants as kinnikinnick and lodgepole pine.

CARMACKS (C-2) pop. 503

Carmacks, named for George Washington Carmack, one of the discoverers of gold in the Klondike, was an important stopover point on the Overland Trail that linked Whitehorse and Dawson City before the Klondike Highway was built. Items from early travelers still can be found along the trail near town.

About 22 kilometres (14 mi.) north of Carmacks are the Five Fingers Rapids, which claimed the lives of many prospectors trying to reach Dawson City by way of the Yukon River.

DAWSON CITY (C-1) pop. 1,319
• Hotels p. 463 • Restaurants p. 463

Dawson City was the center of the excitement caused by one of the world's most fabulous gold strikes. On Aug. 16, 1896, George Washington Carmack and his companions Skookum Jim and Tagish Charlie made the first strike on Bonanza Creek, a tributary of the Klondike River.

In the summer of 1897 miners from Dawson City arrived in Seattle and San Francisco with nearly $2 million as they carried word of the discovery to the United States, then in the midst of a depression. By the next spring more than 60,000 men and women had passed through Seattle and Alaska's Chilkoot and White passes on their way to the Klondike.

The Dawson settlement, which sprang up at the confluence of the Yukon and Klondike rivers, became a thriving city with some 30,000 inhabitants by the summer of 1898, making it the largest city west of Winnipeg and north of San Francisco.

All the creeks in the area had been staked by the spring of 1899. Hillside and bench claims were made, some yielding rich gold finds in the White Channel gravels. Between 1896 and 1904 Klondike creeks brought in more than $100 million in gold.

This period of Dawson City's history has been preserved by Rex Beach, Jack London, Robert W. Service and others who wrote colorful tales of personal experiences.

It was in Dawson City that London became acquainted with a large dog that he named Buck, a cross between a St. Bernard and a German shepherd that became the prototype for the dog in "Call of the Wild." Daily readings from the works of Jack London are given at a replica of his cabin on Eighth Avenue at Firth Street, part of the Jack London Museum.

A fire destroyed the town center after residents' 1897 Thanksgiving Day celebrations. The Dawson City Firefighters Museum, across from the ferry landing, displays artifacts, early fire extinguishers, gear, and historic vehicles in order to preserve Dawson City's firefighting heritage; a gallery showcases pictures and art created for the museum. Phone (867) 993-7407 or (867) 993-7400 for more information.

However, many historic buildings—some still in use—do survive from the days when Dawson City was the gold capital of the world. The Downtown and Eldorado hotels conjure memories of a lively past.

Harrington's Store, Princess Street and Third Avenue, has a free photographic exhibit titled "Dawson as They Saw It," open June through September. The post office and other restored buildings can be seen as part of various Parks Canada tours. Tickets for the tours are available at the visitor information center at Front and King streets.

The summit of Midnight Dome, 7 kilometres (4 mi.) southeast via Front Street, offers a panorama of Dawson City, the Yukon and Klondike rivers and the gold fields. Many Dawson City pioneers are buried in cemeteries on the hillsides flanking the dome.

The *Klondike Spirit* runs daily paddlewheeler trips up and down the Yukon River; phone (867) 993-5323 for schedule and information.

South on Bonanza Creek Road is the Discovery Claim National Historic Site, the place of the gold discovery that started the great rush. Panning for gold is possible at several locations along the Klondike Highway: Claim 33, Free Claim #6 and Gold Bottom Mine Tours.

The Dawson City Visitor Information Centre features exhibits about Klondike history and is open daily 8-8, May-Sept.

The town celebrates its gold mining heritage during ⚜ Discovery Days Weekend, a weeklong event held at various locations in mid-August.

Dawson City Visitor Information Centre: Front and King streets, Dawson City, YT, Canada Y0B 1G0. **Phone:** (867) 993-5566.

Self-guiding tours: A brochure describing walking tours of historic sites is available at the visitor information center.

INSIDER INFO:
Sourdoughs and Cheechakos

To distinguish between the fortune seekers who entered the Yukon Territory during the 1897-98 Klondike Gold Rush, veterans of the '49 California Rush labeled the seasoned arrivals "Sourdoughs" and the greenhorns "Cheechakos" (CHE-cha-kos). Named after the staple bread of the frontier, Sourdoughs were prospectors who had survived a Yukon winter. The term Cheechako came from the Chinook Indian word for "new to come."

Once off the steamer at Skagway, Alaska, these newcomers had to transport thousands of pounds of survival gear—the Northwest Mounted Police wisely required each prospector to bring a year's supply of food—over the precipitous Chilkoot Pass. After that they had to float their unwieldy cargo over the treacherous rapids of the Yukon River.

More obstacles awaited the greenhorns at the gold sites. By the time the Cheechakos arrived, much of the gold field already was depleted or staked. To make things worse, Cheechakos were often directed to the hills by unscrupulous Sourdoughs who knew the gold nuggets tended to settle in creek beds. Nonetheless, some did tap into a channel of an ancient gold-bearing stream on Cheechako Hill.

Those who had survived to see the ice melt were dubbed Sourdoughs; the graveyards of those who had not succeeded dotted the route all the way back to Skagway. As one cynical Sourdough put it: "We were SOUR on the Yukon and didn't have enough DOUGH to get out."

DANOJA ZHO CULTURAL CENTRE is at 1131 Front St., across from the Dawson City Visitor Information Centre. Guided tours, exhibits, video presentations, dance performances and hands-on activities give visitors an interesting perspective into the culture of the Tr'ondek Hwech'in First Nations peoples. Displays include archeological artifacts, traditional costumes and reproduction tools. Special events also are featured. **Time:** Allow 30 minutes minimum. **Hours:** Mon.-Sat. 10-5, June-Sept. **Cost:** $6; $2.50 (ages 12-18); free (ages 0-11). **Phone:** (867) 993-7100.

DAWSON CITY'S *KLONDIKE SPIRIT* CRUISE departs at Front Street Dock. During 90-minute tours downriver from Dawson City, passengers aboard the paddlewheeler-style *Klondike Spirit* have a choice of barrier-free views from the observation deck or main deck. A 2-hour evening outing with an option for dinner takes in a few areas north of the city, including the Stern-wheeler Graveyard with its decaying watercrafts, Mooshide Village and a cave occupied by one of the local characters before the tour heads south for a scenic segment.

Inquire about weather policies. **Time:** Allow 2 hours minimum. **Hours:** Dawson City's *Klondike Spirit* departs daily at 6:45, late May-early Sept. Dinner cruise departures require a minimum of 15 people. Phone ahead to confirm schedule. **Cost:** $68.25; free (ages 0-12). Fare with dinner $110.25; $10.50 (ages 0-12). Reservations are required for dinner cruise. **Phone:** (867) 993-5323, or (800) 764-3555 in Canada. GT ❙❙

DAWSON HISTORICAL COMPLEX NATIONAL HISTORIC SITE comprises more than a dozen restored buildings scattered throughout Dawson City. The structures evoke the time and place of the Klondike Gold Rush of the 1890s. Visitors may explore the richly appointed Palace Grand Theatre where the interactive presentation, Greatest Klondiker Contest, is offered Sunday through Thursday; the Commissioner's Residence mansion and gardens where themed talks take place along with such activities as flower-pressing and croquet; the Robert Service Cabin, where the Bard of the Yukon lived and wrote many of his ballads and poems 1909-12; and Harrington's Store, which displays photographs and letters from the gold rush.

Self-guiding audio tours and guided tours led by costumed site interpreters are available. A hike with the Poetry of Robert Service is offered daily. Tour tickets are available at the visitor information center. **Hours:** Programs offered daily 9:30-8, Victoria Day-Labour Day. Tour departure times vary. Palace Grand Theatre tours offered daily. Commissioner's Residence tours open daily; hours vary. Robert Service Cabin program offered daily in the afternoon.

Phone for additional tours and departure times. **Cost:** All programs $6.30 each; free (children). **Phone:** (867) 993-7200.

TOMBSTONE TERRITORIAL PARK is 71 km (44 mi.) n. of jct. Dempster and Klondike hwys. This park spans an area of more than 2,164 square kilometres (836 sq. mi.) and features a diversity of wildlife and bird species as well as a variety of vegetation. This is a remote park with few established hiking trails, but there are accessible portions off the highway that offer short hikes and challenging backpacking and ridge walking excursions. The park's arctic tundra environment creates a landscape with spectacular views. The interpretive center offers campfire programs, guided walks and hikes and special events.

Note: When traveling to the park have enough gas and spare tires since there are no roadside services available until Eagle Plains, which is 369 kilometres (229 mi.) north of the Klondike Highway. Once in the park, be aware that it is an isolated and potentially hazardous environment. Rough terrain, drastic weather changes and encounters with wildlife are factors to consider. Use leave-no-trace etiquette when hiking and travel lightly on this sensitive environment. **Time:** Allow 3 hours minimum. **Hours:** Park is open daily 24 hours. Interpretive center open daily 9-5, mid-May to mid-Sept. Phone ahead to confirm schedule. **Cost:** Free. **Phone:** (867) 667-5648.

THE ELDORADO HOTEL   (867)993-5451

Motel
$159-$229

Address: 902 3rd Ave Y0B 1G0 **Location:** Jct 3rd Ave and Princess St; center. **Facility:** 40 units, some kitchens. 2 stories (no elevator), interior/exterior corridors. **Parking:** winter plug-ins. **Terms:** cancellation fee imposed. **Guest Services:** coin laundry.

KLONDIKE KATE'S CABINS   867/993-6527
◆◆ Cabin. **Address:** 1102 3rd Ave Y0B 1G0

WESTMARK INN DAWSON CITY   (867)993-5542
◆◆ Hotel. **Address:** 813 5th Ave Y0B 1G0

YUKON HOTEL   867/993-5451
◆ Hotel. **Address:** 702 Front St Y0B 1G0

WHERE TO EAT

THE DRUNKEN GOAT TAVERNA   867/993-5868
◆◆ Traditional Greek. Casual Dining. **Address:** 952 2nd Ave Y0B 1G0

KLONDIKE KATE'S RESTAURANT   867/993-6527

Canadian
Casual Dining
$10-$35

AAA Inspector Notes: *Historic.* Get a sense of Dawson City's history and the gold rush era at this restaurant located across the street from the theater. The menu features a good variety of appetizers and enticing fish and meat entrées. Rather than dining inside, opt for a seat on the covered, heated patio in the summer. Off-season hours and meal openings can vary, so it is a good idea to check with the restaurant. **Features:** full bar, patio dining, Sunday brunch, happy hour. **Reservations:** suggested. **Address:** 1102 3rd Ave Y0B 1G0 **Location:** Corner of 3rd Ave and King St; center; in Klondike Kate's Cabins. [B] [L] [D] CALL [&M] [Ⓚ]

RIVER WEST BISTRO   867/993-6339
◆ American. Quick Serve. **Address:** 958 Front St Y0B 1G0

SOURDOUGH JOE'S RESTAURANT   867/993-6590
◆◆ Seafood. Casual Dining. **Address:** 902 Front St Y0B 1G0

IVVAVIK NATIONAL PARK (A-1)

Ivvavik National Park is in the extreme northwestern corner of the Yukon. Virtually untouched by humans, the Arctic wilderness is of great geologic interest; it is one of the few regions in Canada that contains areas never covered by glaciers.

Every spring it becomes the calving grounds of Porcupine caribous that arrive after a long, difficult migration from the south and west. From mid-June to early July the park offers 5-day, catered base camp trips led by Parks Canada staff and Inuvialuit cultural hosts. The only access to the park is by air. Phone (867) 777-8800.

KENO (C-2) elev. 812m/2,667'

In 1919 silver and lead ore were discovered in Keno Hill, and by 1920 Keno became a busy community with cabins, a stable and a hotel. The following year, the city was the center of a thriving mining district. The town's name comes from the popular gambling game played at casinos. Today, Keno is home to artists who are inspired by the area's natural beauty.

No matter the season, outdoor recreational opportunities abound and include hiking, bicycling, cross-country skiing, snowmobiling, fishing and canoeing. The awe-inspiring northern lights may be seen from late August through April. A must-see is the often-photographed signpost at the top of Keno Hill, showing mileage to such cities as London, Paris and Rome. The 1,829-metre (6,000-ft.) hill also plays host to a breathtaking view.

Self-guiding tours: This historic walking tour starts from Tolmie Cabin on Duncan Creek Road and includes the Beer Bottle House, Keno City Mining Museum and All Saints Anglican Church. Brochures are available from the Keno City Mining Museum. Phone (867) 995-3103.

KLUANE NATIONAL PARK AND RESERVE (D-1)

Elevations in the park range from 400 metres (1,300 ft.) in the Alsek River to 5,959 m (19,545 ft.) at Mount Logan. Refer to CAA/AAA maps for additional elevation information.

Kluane (kloo-AH-nee) National Park and Reserve is bounded by the Haines (Hwy. 3) and Alaska (Hwy. 1) highways along its northeastern border. The park covers 21,980 square kilometres (8,487 sq. mi.) of wilderness.

The land has drawn a number of people, including the indigenous Southern Tutchone, who have lived in the area for generations. Near the park's southeastern boundary was the Dalton Trail, a route used during the Klondike Rush of 1898. In 1904 a North West Mounted Police post was established on the south shore of Kluane Lake, and in 1942 the lake became a meeting place for crews building the Alaska Highway.

During the building of the highway the wilderness area was preserved as the Kluane Game Sanctuary. In 1979 Kluane was declared a World Heritage Site for its impressive topographical features and its massive nonpolar ice fields. Today the Kluane First Nation and Champagne and Aishihik First Nations peoples cooperatively manage the park with Parks Canada.

The park is dominated by the Saint Elias Mountains, which run through the park in a southeasterly direction. Mount Logan, Canada's highest peak at 5,959 m (19,545 ft.), and Mount St. Elias at 5,489 metres (18,008 ft.) dominate the range. The Saint Elias Mountains hold extensive ice fields that date from the last ice age and constitute the largest nonpolar glacier systems in the world.

An extensive network of glaciers, together with the ice fields, covers more than half of the park's area throughout the year. Notable are the Steele Glacier, which moves sporadically at a relatively rapid rate, and the Kaskawulsh and Lowell glaciers, which are flanked by moraines—accumulations of earth and stones carried and deposited by the glaciers. The movement and debris of the glaciers contribute to such park features as sand dunes and dust storms.

The park has a variety of flora. Such coniferous species as white spruce characterize the boreal forest of the river valleys. Lichens, dwarf birch trees and low shrubs distinguish the tundra uplands in the northern section, and colorful Arctic flowers cling to the crevices and ledges of the mountains. In the southeastern section, where the Pacific Ocean's moderating influence is felt in the climate, the vegetation is more luxuriant.

Arctic grayling, lake trout, northern pike and kokanee salmon are found in lakes and streams. Other park species include golden eagles, ptarmigans, Dall sheep, mountain goats, caribou, moose and wolves. Kluane has one of the largest populations of grizzly bears and subspecies of moose in the world.

General Information and Activities

The park is open all year, but access may be limited in the winter, depending on weather conditions. The Kluane National Park and Reserve Visitor Centre, at Km-post 1635 in Haines Junction, is open daily 9-7, early June to early September; 9-5, mid-May to early June and early September to late September. The Tachäl Dhäl (Sheep Mountain) Visitor Centre at Km-post 1707 is open daily 9-4, mid-May to early September.

The park primarily is a wilderness area, so there are no roads except on the eastern and northern perimeters, traversed by Hwy. 3 and Hwy. 1, respectively. Hiking is the most popular activity in the park, with approximately 250 kilometres (155 mi.) of hiking trails. Hiking is possible along a few old mining roads, creekside paths and marked trails. Some trails are self-guiding. All overnight hikers must register at one of the information centers before and after hikes.

Mountain climbing should be done only by well-trained climbers, who must obtain a climbing permit and register before and after climbs.

Other recreational pursuits include fishing, backpacking, boating, cross-country skiing and ice fishing. All anglers within the park must obtain a national park fishing license, available at the park visitor centers and from area stores and lodges. Camping, fishing and picnic facilities are available at Kathleen Lake, 27 kilometres (17 mi.) south of Haines Junction.

During the summer the park sponsors interpretive activities including campfire talks and guided walks. A relief map, interactive computer touch screens and a video are available. Information about recreational opportunities, sightseeing by small aircraft and other guided tours is available.

ADMISSION to the park is free.

PETS are permitted in the park if kept on a leash.

ADDRESS inquiries about the park to Kluane National Park and Reserve, P.O. Box 5495, Haines Junction, YT, Canada Y0B 1L0; phone (867) 634-7207.

MAYO (C-2) pop. 226

Mayo lies 53 kilometres (33 mi.) northeast of the Klondike Highway at the confluence of the Stewart and Mayo rivers. Both the town and the river were named for the pioneer prospector and trader Alfred Mayo. In the early 1900s Mayo Landing became a shipping point for the gold and silver that was mined farther north in Elsa.

Mayo Lake to the northeast provides excellent fishing. The summit of nearby 1,890-metre (6,200-ft.) Keno Mountain provides a scenic view of the mining village of Keno. This once bustling community has a mining museum.

Further details about the silver mining towns of Mayo, Elsa and Keno, known collectively as the Silver Trail, are available at the information booth at Stewart Crossing.

TESLIN (D-2) pop. 122

The Nisutlin Bay Bridge, the longest water span on the Alaska Highway, crosses an arm of Teslin Lake at Teslin. The highway parallels the 116-kilometre (72-mi.) lake for about 55 kilometres (34 mi.), providing a scenic drive bordered on both sides by mountains. The area is noted for abundant game, and the fjord-like lake provides excellent fishing. The economy of the community depends heavily on hunting, fishing and trapping.

Teslin has one of the largest indigenous populations in the Yukon, with many of its residents descended from the coastal Tlingit tribe. The original settlement is reached by a loop road. In the old village are Catholic and Anglican missions as well as a Royal Canadian Mounted Police station.

TESLIN TLINGIT HERITAGE CENTRE is 4 km (2.5 mi.) w. on Hwy. 1. Totem poles, hand-carved masks, crafts, artifacts and photographs provide insight into the life and culture of the Teslin Tlingit people. **Time:** Allow 30 minutes minimum. **Hours:** Daily 9-5, June-Aug. **Cost:** $5; $4 (ages 55+); free (ages 0-5); $15 (family). **Phone:** (867) 390-2532 ext. 333.

WATSON LAKE (D-3) pop. 802

At Km-post 1016.8 on the Alaska Highway, Watson Lake is an important transportation, distribution and communication center for the southern Yukon. The town was named for Frank Watson, a trapper from England who settled there in 1898.

Watson Lake is known as the Sign Post Forest for its signpost collection that was begun by a homesick soldier during construction of the Alaska Highway in 1942. Over the years, tourists have continued adding signs showing the names of their hometowns, and now the collection includes more than 70,000 signs.

From Watson Lake the historic Robert Campbell Highway loops north and west through the wilderness of southeastern Yukon.

WHITEHORSE (D-2) pop. 23,276,
elev. 689m/2,260'
• Hotels p. 466 • Restaurants p. 467

Whitehorse began during the Klondike gold rush when thousands of prospectors journeyed by ship to Skagway, Alaska, then climbed the rugged mountain passes to the headwaters of the Yukon River. They constructed nearly anything floatable for the more than 900-kilometre (559-mi.) trip to Dawson City via Whitehorse. Above Whitehorse many prospectors died in the dangerous Whitehorse Rapids.

When stern-wheeler service to Dawson became available, the trip from Whitehorse took 2.5 days; the return trip against the current took 5 days. The first rails of the White Pass & Yukon Route were laid at Skagway in May 1898, and the line to Whitehorse opened in July 1900.

During World War II Canadian and United States Army personnel building the Alaska Highway moved to Whitehorse, which became the capital of the Yukon Territory in 1953.

Evolving into the transportation, communication and distribution center of the Yukon, Whitehorse also became the territorial headquarters of the Royal Canadian Mounted Police as well as the heart of the territorial government and federal departments.

Attractions on a much larger scale include Lake Laberge, the setting for Robert W. Service's "The Cremation of Sam McGee," and the Robert Lowe Suspension Bridge across Miles Canyon.

The Whitehorse Power Dam features one of the world's longest wooden fish ladders; the salmon, running in late July or early August, can be seen from viewing windows. Lake Schwatka, impounded by the power dam, was named after Frederick Schwatka, the first U.S. army lieutenant to navigate the entire length of the Yukon River.

Visible from the Alaska Highway, 24 kilometres (15 mi.) south of Whitehorse, is Marsh Lake Lock, the northernmost lock in the Western Hemisphere. It is used by small craft navigating the upper Yukon River.

Guided tours of the town and surrounding area are available through Whitehorse City Tour. A few companies provide Yukon River cruises, guided hikes, and canoe, boat and raft trips on area rivers. The Yukon Conservation Society gives guided nature walks in the summer. For a self-guided walk, there's the City of Whitehorse Millennium Trail, a 5-kilometre (3.1-mi.) paved path along the Yukon River.

The Swan Haven Interpretive Centre, on the shores of M'Clintock Bay, affords bird enthusiasts the opportunity to learn about migratory birds, in particular trumpeter swans. The center is open Mon.-Fri. 5-9 p.m., Sat.-Sun. noon-7, in April. Phone (867) 667-8291.

Yukon Visitor Information Centre, 100 Hanson St., features exhibits and audiovisual presentations about the Yukon. The center is open daily 8-8, early May-Sept. 30; Mon.-Fri. 8:30-noon and 1-5, Sat. 10-2, rest of year. Phone (867) 667-3084.

Whitehorse is the terminus for the 1,000-mile Yukon Quest International Sled Dog Race, which starts in Fairbanks, Alaska, and takes place over a 2-week period from early to mid-February.

Yukon Visitor Information Centre: 100 Hanson St., Whitehorse, YT, Canada Y1A 1E7. **Phone:** (867) 667-3084.

Self-guiding tours: Guidebooks are available from the Yukon Historical and Museums Association, 3126 Third Ave., P.O. Box 4357, Whitehorse, YT, Canada Y1A 1E7; phone (867) 667-4704. Self-guiding audio walking tour podcasts can be downloaded from the association's website.

 THE SS _KLONDIKE_ NATIONAL HISTORIC SITE is next to the river at Second Ave. and Robert Campbell Bridge. One of the largest stern-wheelers on the Yukon River, the _Klondike_ ran its route 1937-55. The original _Klondike_ struck a gravel bar in 1936; a replacement was built the same year. The video, "In the Days of the Riverboats," is presented continuously. Both guided and self-guiding tours are available. **Time:** Allow 30 minutes minimum. **Hours:** Daily 9:30-5, late May-Labour Day. **Cost:** Free. $3 for self-guiding brochure. **Phone:** (867) 667-4511.

WATERFRONT TROLLEY departs northbound from Rotary Peace Park and southbound from Spook Creek Station. Visitors may ride a restored narrow-gauge 1925 trolley originally from Portugal. The bright yellow car seats 24 passengers and travels along the waterfront in downtown Whitehorse, making stops along the way at Rotary Peace Park, the visitor center, White Pass Train Depot, the Roundhouse, Jarvis Street, Black Street, Shipyards Park, Kishwoot Island and Spook Creek. The conductor provides narration about the waterfront and the development of Whitehorse.

Hours: Trips depart daily on the hour 10-5 from Rotary Peace Park and on the half-hour 10:30-5:30 p.m. from Spook Creek Station, mid-May to mid-Sept. **Cost:** Fare $5 (roundtrip); $3 (one-way); free (ages 0-5). **Phone:** (867) 667-6355.

 YUKON BERINGIA INTERPRETIVE CENTRE is 2 km (1.2 mi.) e. on the Alaska Hwy. to Km-post 1473 (mi. 886) by Whitehorse Airport. An area of the Yukon, Alaska and Siberia never covered by glaciers during the ice age, Beringia is believed to be the route traveled by the first peoples who entered the Americas from Asia.

Fossils, life-size animal and first peoples exhibits, interactive computer kiosks, and murals and dioramas of Beringia's landscape illustrate the area's history, geographical events and culture, from the ice age to the present. Highlights include fossils of woolly mammoths, scimitar cats, giant beavers, short-faced bears and steppe bison. A diorama depicts the Bluefish Caves, an important North American archeological site.

Hours: Daily 9-6, mid-May through Sept. 30; Sun.-Mon. noon-5, rest of year. Phone ahead to confirm schedule. **Cost:** $6; $5 (ages 55+); $4 (ages 6-12 and students with ID); $25 (family, yearly pass). Combination pass with Yukon Transportation Museum $12. **Phone:** (867) 667-8855.

BEST WESTERN GOLD RUSH INN   (867)668-4500

Hotel
$150-$185

 AAA Benefit: Save 10% or more every day and earn 10% bonus points!

Address: 411 Main St Y1A 2B6 **Location:** Between 4th and 5th aves; center. **Facility:** 99 units, some two bedrooms and kitchens. 4 stories, interior corridors. **Parking:** winter plug-ins. **Activities:** exercise room, spa. **Guest Services:** coin laundry.

COAST HIGH COUNTRY INN   (867)667-4471

Hotel
$150-$185

Address: 4051 4th Ave Y1A 1H1 **Location:** 0.4 mi (0.6 km) e of Main St. **Facility:** 82 units, some efficiencies. 4 stories, interior corridors. **Parking:** winter plug-ins. **Terms:** cancellation fee imposed. **Activities:** exercise room. **Guest Services:** coin laundry.

MIDNIGHT SUN BED & BREAKFAST   867/667-2255

 Bed & Breakfast. **Address:** 6188 6th Ave Y1A 1N8

SKKY HOTEL   (867)456-2400

Hotel
$110-$250

Address: 91622 Alaska Hwy Y1A 3E4 **Location:** Across from airport. **Facility:** 32 units. 2 stories (no elevator), interior corridors. **Parking:** winter plug-ins. **Terms:** cancellation fee imposed. **Featured Amenity:** continental breakfast.

TOWN & MOUNTAIN HOTEL   (867)668-7644

Motel
$129-$169

Address: 401 Main St Y1A 2B6 **Location:** Center. Located in downtown area. **Facility:** 30 units. 3 stories (no elevator), interior corridors. **Parking:** on-site and street, winter plug-ins. **Terms:** 3 day cancellation notice-fee imposed. **Dining:** nightclub.

WESTMARK WHITEHORSE HOTEL & CONFERENCE CENTER   867/393-9700

 Hotel. **Address:** 201 Wood St Y1A 2E4

Stay connected with #AAA and #CAA on your favorite social media sites

WHERE TO EAT

ALPINE BAKERY 867/668-6871

Breads/Pastries
Vegetarian
Quick Serve
$8-$15

AAA Inspector Notes: A short walk from the downtown core, this organic bakery/café is housed in its own two-story log building and features a hand-crafted, authentic masonry oven. A wide variety of wholesome breads, pastries, pizza, soup, raw foods and sushi—all organic and vegetarian—are offered. Homemade, fair-trade dark chocolates speckled with wild, Yukon cranberries are a specialty. A sunny deck with an organic herb and edible flower garden is out back. Repeat customers should pre-order favorite breads. **Features:** patio dining. **Address:** 411 Alexander St Y1A 2L8 **Location:** Jct 4th Ave.

B L D D

ANTOINETTE'S 867/668-3505
New International. Casual Dining. **Address:** 4121 4th Ave Y1A 1H7

BAKED CAFE & BAKERY 867/633-6291
American. Quick Serve. **Address:** 108-100 Main St Y1A 2A8

BURNT TOAST 867/393-2605
American. Casual Dining. **Address:** 2112 2nd Ave Y1A 1B9

THE CHOCOLATE CLAIM 867/667-2202
American. Quick Serve. **Address:** 305 Strickland St Y1A 2J9

THE DELI 867/667-7583
Deli. Quick Serve. **Address:** 203 Hanson St Y1A 1Y3

GIORGIO'S CUCCINA 867/668-4050
Italian. Casual Dining. **Address:** 206 Jarvis St Y1A 2H1

KLONDIKE RIB & SALMON BBQ 867/667-7554
Seafood. Casual Dining. **Address:** 2116 2nd Ave Y1A 2B9

SANCHEZ CANTINA 867/668-5858
Mexican. Casual Dining. **Address:** 211 Hanson St Y1A 1Y3

TOKYO SUSHI 867/633-4567
Sushi. Casual Dining. **Address:** 204B Main St Y1A 2A9

Bears fishing, Katmai National Park and Preserve

Alaska

Natives didn't call this state *Alyeska*—the Great Land—for nothing. There are approximately 3 million lakes, 3,000 rivers, 1,800 islands and 100,000 glaciers in Alaska's 586,000 square miles of untamed wilderness. And if that isn't enough, nine national parks and preserves and two expansive national forests total about 66 million acres of undisturbed land.

Alaska's diversity is illustrated through its distinct natural features. The state is home to towering Denali—so high that it's cloaked in clouds most of the time. Long, bright days are typical during the summer solstice, when the sun never completely disappears.

Options for excitement in The Land of the Midnight Sun seem endless. Walk on an ice field and feel the crunch of ice under your boots; peer over chunky glaciers and sweeping mountain ranges from a helicopter; gaze at a sky painted with brilliant northern lights; ride on a boat navigating through blue-green

waters packed with bobbing icebergs; marvel at 25-foot-tall sand dunes; or board a bush plane to catch a glimpse of steam from an active volcano.

Tribe members, ingenious at adapting to their variable and sometimes hostile surroundings, made the most of the state's natural offerings, which includes the creatures portrayed in their art. Salmon and orcas are just a couple of animals that appear on totem poles. Used for sustenance, they were often depicted in oral tales; today animals remain the focus of many pictures and the subjects of travelogues. Visitors relish the opportunity to snap a photograph of a moose cow nibbling grass alongside her twins or grizzly cubs wrestling under the protective watch of mama bear.

For many residents Alaska's riches are liquid: The creation of the Trans-Alaska Pipeline made it possible to transport crude oil almost 800 miles from Prudhoe Bay south to Valdez. The pipeline, an amazing engineering feat crossing three mountain ranges and three fault lines, can withstand an earthquake measuring up to 8.5 on the Richter scale as well as temperatures as low as minus 80 F.

Oil isn't Alaska's only rich resource. Discoveries of gold in Fairbanks, Fort Yukon, Juneau, Nome, Skagway and Wrangell lured prospectors from the "Lower 48" to seek their fortune. Visit abandoned gold dredges, camps and mines and imagine the fervor that once pervaded these sites. And there

Moose cow and calf, Cooper Landing

was more money to be made; Russian trappers came in search of valuable sea otter pelts.

But Alaska's native tribes have left the most enduring impact. Traditions of the Aleut, Alutiiq, Athabascan, Cup'ik, Haida, Inupiaq, Tlingit, Tsimpshian and Yup'ik tribes can be appreciated through the acts of proud dancers and storytellers who keep family legacies alive. Artisans create soapstone and whalebone carvings, clothing adorned with intricate beading and baskets made from white birch bark.

And totem poles, Alaska's silent, symbolic sentries, are just one reminder of what makes this land truly great.

Recreation

In the Land of the Midnight Sun, chances for wildlife viewing are as plentiful as snowflakes during winter.

Alaska has one of the largest bald eagle populations in the world. They aren't difficult to spot at the Chilkat Bald Eagle Preserve near Haines; more than 3,500 visit the area to feed from October to February.

Many wildlife cruises headed for the Inside Passage depart from Juneau. Arm yourself with some good binoculars, a camera and a journal to record your sightings. Entries might include descriptions of huge, barking Steller sea lions lounging on top of each other; Dall's porpoises frolicking in a boat's wake; or Sitka black- or white-tailed deer sipping from a stream.

Black bears fish for salmon in Anan Creek near Wrangell Island, and the west coast of Prince of Wales Island (near Ketchikan) is a great spot for watching tufted puffins. It's no "fluke" to see a whale tail; humpbacks often make appearances in Prince William Sound, and wherever there's an iceberg, you can find harbor seals resting upon floating ice chunks.

Day cruises depart from Seward and Whittier to explore Prince William Sound and Kenai Fjords National Park, home to sea mammals galore. Along the Kenai Peninsula, both humpback and beluga whales perform aquatic acrobatics near the Turnagain Arm. Nearby, Dall sheep can be seen grazing atop steep cliffs that grace Cook Inlet.

Looking for bears? The Kodiak National Wildlife Refuge is home to some 2,300 Kodiak bears, and Brooks Camp in Katmai National Park and Preserve safeguards one of the world's largest brown bear populations.

Grizzlies as well as caribou and moose roam the desertlike tundra of Denali National Park and Preserve; take a narrated bus tour to catch a glimpse. Near the park entrance, forest rangers give a demonstration of sled dogs at work. Even better, hang on tight for a sled ride pulled by Iditarod huskies in Seward.

Many activities in Alaska include a magnificent view: Try rafting in Denali on the Nenana River Gorge or canoeing near Admiralty Island National Monument. Kayakers also enjoy the Sarkar Lake Canoe Route in Tongass National Forest. Winter options include cross-country skiing, dog sledding or snowmobiling on the Twin Ridge or Upper Twin ski trails in Tongass National Forest, or downhill skiing at Mount Alyeska in Girdwood.

Want to stand on a glacier? Hikers in Kenai Fjords National Park follow rangers on nature walks to a nearby ice field. Floatplane or helicopter sightseeing is an excellent way to see glaciers, ice fields, mountain ranges, waterfalls, lakes or stark tundra. Nearly every city has flightseeing tour operators.

A fishing charter from one of various harbors is a good way to hook steelhead, grayling or rainbow trout. Sport fishing yields red snapper or cod—and Resurrection Bay (near Seward), Sitka and Wrangell are home to world-class halibut and salmon.

Chilkat Bald Eagle Preserve

Historic Timeline

1741	Russian explorer Vitus Bering, sent by Peter the Great to explore the North Pacific, is the first European to set foot on Alaskan soil.
1867	In a deal known as "Seward's Folly," Secretary of State William Seward buys Alaska from Russia for 2 cents per acre.
1880	"Seward's Folly" becomes a gold mine as vast deposits of precious metals are discovered in Juneau and other cities.
1903	A submarine cable links Seattle to Sitka and Sitka to Valdez, increasing communication between Alaska and the world.
1942	Japan attacks Dutch Harbor and consequently occupies the Aleutian Islands for nearly a year during World War II.
1964	A Good Friday earthquake severely damages Anchorage, Valdez, the Northwest Panhandle and Cook Inlet.
1968	Oil is discovered on Prudhoe Bay, spurring the construction of an 800-mile pipeline to transport the oil to Valdez.
1989	The *Exxon Valdez* spills some 11 million gallons of crude oil into Prince William Sound.
2004	Mitch Seavey of Seward wins the Iditarod Trail Sled Dog Race on his 11th attempt.
2008	Gov. Sarah Palin is the first woman to be on a Republican presidential ticket after Sen. John McCain names her his running mate.
2015	President Barack Obama announces Mount McKinley will be renamed Denali—what it originally was called in the Athabascan Native language.

What To Pack

Temperature Averages Maximum/Minimum (Fahrenheit)	JANUARY	FEBRUARY	MARCH	APRIL	MAY	JUNE	JULY	AUGUST	SEPTEMBER	OCTOBER	NOVEMBER	DECEMBER
Anchorage	22 / 9	26 / 12	34 / 18	44 / 29	55 / 39	62 / 47	65 / 52	63 / 49	55 / 41	40 / 28	28 / 16	24 / 11
Barrow	-8 / -20	-10 / -22	-7 / -20	6 / -7	25 / 15	40 / 30	47 / 34	44 / 34	35 / 28	19 / 10	5 / -6	-5 / -16
Fairbanks	2 / -13	10 / -10	26 / 1	44 / 19	61 / 35	71 / 47	73 / 50	67 / 45	55 / 34	32 / 16	12 / -2	5 / -9
Juneau	31 / 21	34 / 24	39 / 28	48 / 33	56 / 40	62 / 46	64 / 49	63 / 48	56 / 44	47 / 38	38 / 29	33 / 24
Kotzebue	4 / -9	3 / -10	7 / -8	20 / 3	38 / 25	51 / 39	60 / 49	57 / 47	46 / 37	28 / 19	13 / 3	6 / -6
Nome	13 / -2	14 / -2	18 / 1	27 / 12	43 / 31	54 / 41	59 / 47	56 / 45	49 / 37	34 / 23	23 / 11	16 / 1

From the records of The Weather Channel Interactive, Inc.

Good Facts To Know

ABOUT THE STATE

POPULATION: 626,932.

AREA: 665,384 square miles; ranks 1st.

CAPITAL: Juneau.

HIGHEST POINT: 20,310 ft., Denali.

LOWEST POINT: Sea level, Pacific Ocean.

TIME ZONE(S): Alaska for most of the state; Hawaii-Aleutian for the extreme western portion of the Aleutian Islands. DST.

REGULATIONS

TEEN DRIVING LAWS: Driving is not permitted 1 a.m.-5 a.m. No passengers under age 21, with the exception of family members, are permitted for the first 6 months. The minimum age for an unrestricted driver's license is 16 years and 6 months. Phone (907) 269-5551 for more information about Alaska driver's license regulations.

SEAT BELT/CHILD RESTRAINT LAWS: Seat belts are required for driver and all passengers 16 and over. Children under age 1 must be in rear-facing child restraints. Children ages 8-15 are required to be in a child restraint or seat belt; appropriate child restraints are required for children under age 8 unless they are at least 4 feet, 9 inches tall or weigh more than 65 pounds. AAA recommends the use of seat belts and appropriate child restraints for the driver and all passengers.

CELLPHONE RESTRICTIONS: All drivers are prohibited from text messaging while driving.

HELMETS FOR MOTORCYCLES: Required for all passengers, drivers under 18 years old and those with instructional permits.

RADAR DETECTORS: Permitted. Prohibited for use by commercial vehicles.

MOVE OVER LAW: Driver is required to slow down and vacate the lane nearest stopped police, fire and rescue vehicles and tow trucks using audible or flashing signals.

FIREARMS LAWS: Vary by state and/or county. Contact the Division of State Troopers, Headquarters, 5700 E. Tudor Rd., Dept. P, Anchorage, AK 99507; phone (907) 269-5511.

HOLIDAYS

HOLIDAYS: Jan. 1 ▪ Martin Luther King Jr. Day, Jan. (3rd Mon.) ▪ Washington's Birthday/Presidents Day, Feb. (3rd Mon.) ▪ Seward's Day, Mar. (last Mon.) ▪ Memorial Day, May (last Mon.) ▪ July 4 ▪ Labor Day, Sept. (1st Mon.) ▪ Columbus Day, Oct. (2nd Mon.) ▪ Alaska Day, Oct. 18 ▪ Veterans Day, Nov. 11 ▪ Thanksgiving ▪ Christmas, Dec. 25.

MONEY

TAXES: Alaska does not have a statewide sales tax, but cities and boroughs may levy a sales tax of up to 7 percent, plus special taxes on goods and services. A 10 percent tax is levied on rental cars.

VISITOR INFORMATION

INFORMATION CENTERS: Tourist literature and reports on highway and weather conditions are available at the Log Cabin Visitor Information Center, jct. F St. and 4th Ave. in Anchorage ▪ the Fairbanks Visitor Information Center, 101 Dunkel St. in Fairbanks ▪ the Southeast Alaska Discovery Center, 50 Main St. in Ketchikan ▪ and the Tok Information Center, jct. SR 2 (Alaska Hwy.) and SR 1 in Tok.

ROAD CONDITIONS: Information about road conditions or construction can be obtained from the Alaska Department of Transportation & Public Facilities; phone 511 or, outside of the state, (866) 282-7577.

FURTHER INFORMATION FOR VISITORS:
Alaska Travel Industry Association
610 E. 5th Ave., Suite 200
Anchorage, AK 99501
(907) 929-2842

NATIONAL FOREST INFORMATION:
U.S. Forest Service
8510 Mendenhall Loop Rd.
Juneau, AK 99801
(907) 586-8800
(877) 444-6777 (reservations)

NATIONAL PARK INFORMATION:
Alaska Public Lands Information Center
101 Dunkel St., Suite 110
Fairbanks, AK 99701
(907) 459-3730

FISHING & HUNTING REGULATIONS:
Alaska Department of Fish and Game
1255 W. 8th St.
Juneau, AK 99811
(907) 465-4180 (Division of Sport Fishing)
(907) 465-4190 (Division of Wildlife Conservation)

ALASKA FERRY INFORMATION:
Alaska Marine Highway
6858 Glacier Hwy.
Juneau, AK 99811-2505
(907) 465-3941
(800) 642-0066

Alaska Annual Events
Please call ahead to confirm event details.

JANUARY

- Anchorage Folk Festival
  Anchorage
  907-276-4118
- Alcan 200 Road Rally
  Haines
  907-766-2051
- Polar Bear Jump Off
  Seward
  907-224-5230

FEBRUARY

- Valdez Ice Climbing Festival
  Valdez
  907-835-5182
- Homer Winter Carnival
  Homer
  907-235-7740
- Tent City Festival / Wrangell
  800-367-9745

MARCH

- Fur Rendezvous (Rondy)
  Winter Festival
  Anchorage
  907-274-1177
- World Ice Art
  Championships / Fairbanks
  907-451-8250
- Iditarod Trail Sled Dog
  Race / Anchorage
  907-376-5155

APRIL

- Alaska Hummingbird
  Festival / Ketchikan
  907-228-6220
- NYO Games / Anchorage
  907-793-3267
- Stikine River Birding
  Festival / Wrangell
  907-874-2381

MAY

- Little Norway Festival
  Petersburg
  907-772-3646
- Juneau Jazz and Classics
  Juneau
  907-463-3378
- Kodiak Crab Festival
  Kodiak
  907-486-5557

JUNE

- Sitka Summer Music
  Festival / Sitka
  907-277-4852
- Nome Salmonberry Jam
  Folk Fest / Nome
  907-443-6555
- Alaskan Scottish Highland
  Games / Eagle River
  907-770-4967

JULY

- Girdwood Forest Fair
  Girdwood
  800-880-3880
- Bear Paw Festival
  Eagle River
  907-694-4702
- Southeast Alaska State Fair
  Haines
  907-766-2476

AUGUST

- Alaska State Fair / Palmer
  907-745-4827
- Tanana Valley State Fair
  Fairbanks
  907-452-3750
- Seward Silver Salmon
  Derby / Seward
  907-224-8051

SEPTEMBER

- Kachemak Bay Wooden
  Boat Festival / Homer
  907-235-2628
- Kodiak Rodeo and State
  Fair / Kodiak
  907-487-4440
- Seward Music and Arts
  Festival / Seward
  907-362-1131

OCTOBER

- Alaska Native Arts and
  Crafts Fair / Anchorage
  907-274-3611
- Alaska Day Festival / Sitka
  907-747-5124
- Make It Alaskan Festival
  Anchorage
  907-279-0618

NOVEMBER

- GCI Great Alaska
  Basketball Shootout
  Anchorage
  907-786-1293
- Crafts Weekend and
  ReadAlaska Book Fair
  Anchorage
  907-929-9200

DECEMBER

- New Year's Eve Torchlight
  Parade and Fireworks
  Anchorage
  907-754-2111
- Anchorage International
  Film Festival / Anchorage
  907-338-3690
- Colony Christmas / Palmer
  907-745-2880

Fly over Cook Inlet and Anchorage

Denali National Park and Preserve

Iceberg from Mendenhall Glacier, Juneau

Puffins

Chena River, Fairbanks

Index: Great Experience for Members

AAA editor's picks of exceptional note

Alaska Native
Heritage Center

Riverboat Discovery

Mendenhall Glacier

Sitka National
Historical Park

See Orientation map on p. 486 for corresponding grid coordinates, if applicable.
*Indicates the GEM is temporarily closed.

GET YOUR DRIVE TRIP BACK ON TRACK

When a drive trip takes an unexpected turn, use the **MOBILE APP** or go **ONLINE** to quickly request roadside service.

- App GPS identifies your location

- Maps show the service vehicle en route to your location

- Status notifications keep you updated

AAA.com/mobile
CAA.ca/mobile

Alaska, Yukon and

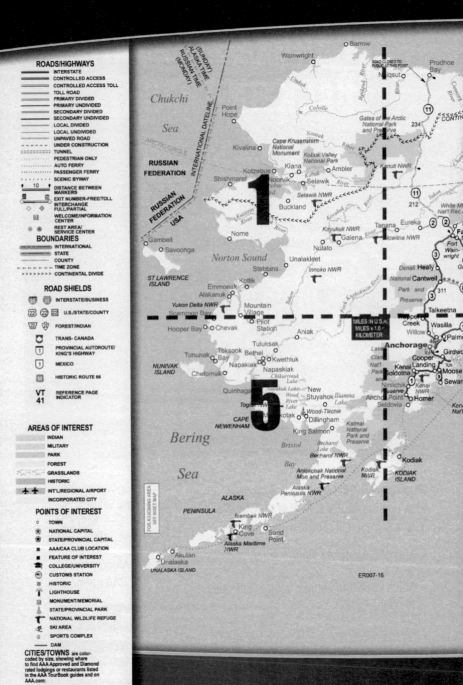

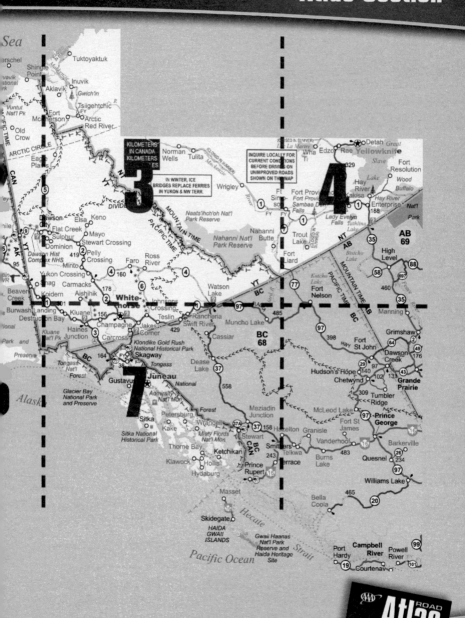

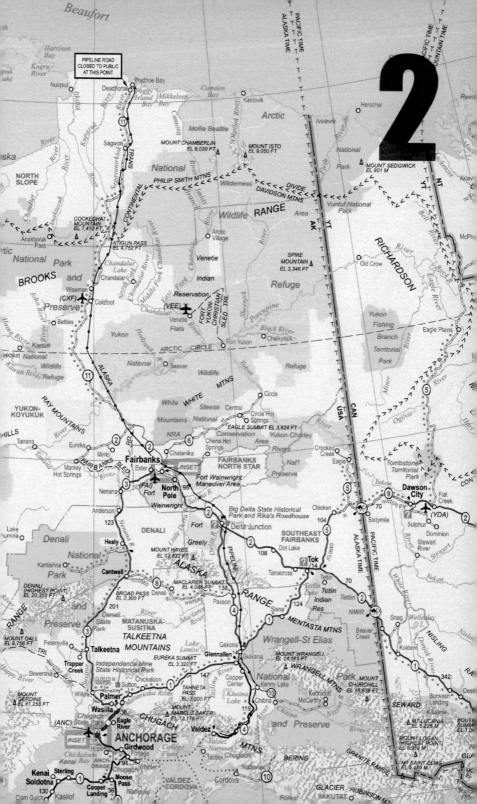

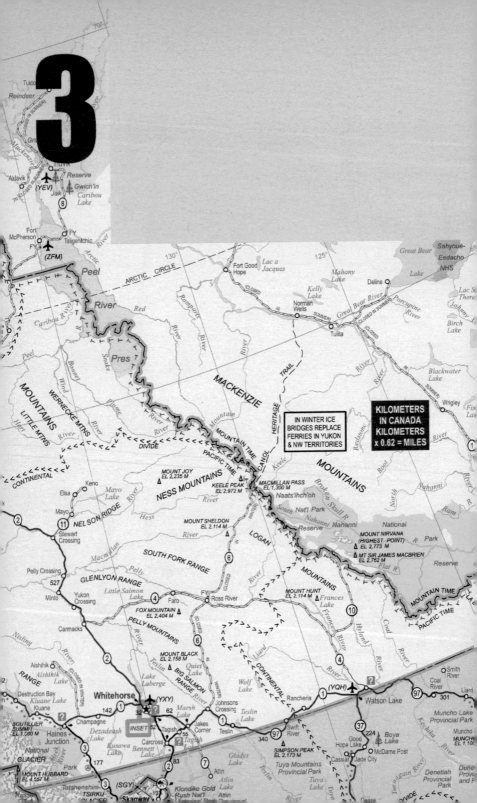

5

Stebbins
(WBB) St Michael
Kodlik
Emmonak
Alakanuk
Yukon
Scammon Bay
Mountain Village
Pilot Station
Hooper Bay
Chevak
Delta
Marshall
Russian Mission

Nunavaktuk Lake
Kuskokwim River
Andreafsky River
Anvik River

Sound
National
Wildlife
Refuge

Grayling
Shageluk
Anvik
Holy Cross
Ophir
Takotna
Iditarod
Crooked Creek

VON FR
EL 4,50

Medfra
McGrath
Nikolai

KUSILVAK

Sea

National
Newtok
(EWU)
Tununak
Mekoryuk
Toksook Bay
**NUNIVAK
ISLAND**
Wilderness

Baird
Kwethluk **(Z13)**
Bethel **(KWT)**
Napakiak Napaskiak
Tuluksak

Lower Kalskag
Aniak
Sleetmute
Stony River
Lime Village

BETHEL

Cairn Mountain
EL 3,799 FT

Mount Plummer
EL 3,623 FT

**LAKE AND
PENINSULA**

Redoubt Volcano El
Preser

Port Alsworth
Nondalton
Newhalen
Koliganek

Eek
Quinhagak
Togiak
Goodnews Bay
Platinum
Togiak
Manokotak
Dillingham **(DLG)**
Aleknagik

Mount Oratia
EL 4,658 FT
Mt Waskey
EL 5,026 FT

DILLINGHAM

Chikuminuk
Lake

Wood River
Lake

New Stuyahok

Bering

Eek River
Eek
Kipnuk
Kwigillingok

Wildlife

National

Refuge

Bristol

Naknek
UNPAVED
King Salmon **(AKN)**
Egegik
Becharof
Mount Katmai
EL 6,715 FT

**KENAI
PENINSULA**

Sea

Bay

Pilot Point

Alaska
**KODIAK
ISLAND**
Larsen Bay
Old Harbor
Akhiok

Karluk
Indian
Reservation

Bristol

Port Heiden
Aniakchak
Nat'l Mon &
Pres
Chignik

Mount
Veniaminof
EL 7,075 FT
**ALEUTIANS
EAST**
Mt Veniaminof
Icefield
Refuge
Nelson
Lagoon
Hague
Channel

**FOR ADJOINING AREA
SEE INSET MAP**

ALEUTIAN ISLANDS

1:11,088,000
Scale in Miles
100   0   100
100   0   100
Scale in Kilometers

Alaska

Bering

Sea

Pacific

Kiska Volcano
EL 4,004 FT
Maritime

National

Ocean

Adak
Wildlife
Korovin Volcano
EL 5,030 FT
ALEUTIANS WEST
Atka
Refuge

Tulik
Volcano
EL 4,111 FT
Unalaska
Nikolski

Aleutian World War II
National Historic Area

INTERNATIONAL DATE LINE
HAWAII-ALEUTIAN TIME
ALASKA

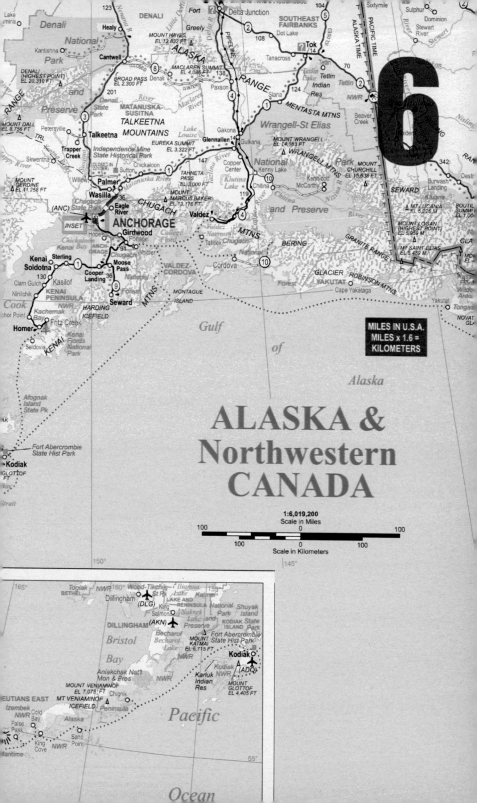

ALASKA & Northwestern CANADA

MILES IN U.S.A.
MILES x 1.6 = KILOMETERS

1:6,019,200
Scale in Miles
Scale in Kilometers

Be Vacation Ready
Know Before You Go

Before setting out on your trip, have your car checked out by a dependable AAA/CAA Approved Auto Repair facility.

AAA.com/Repair

AAA Mobile
CAA Mobile

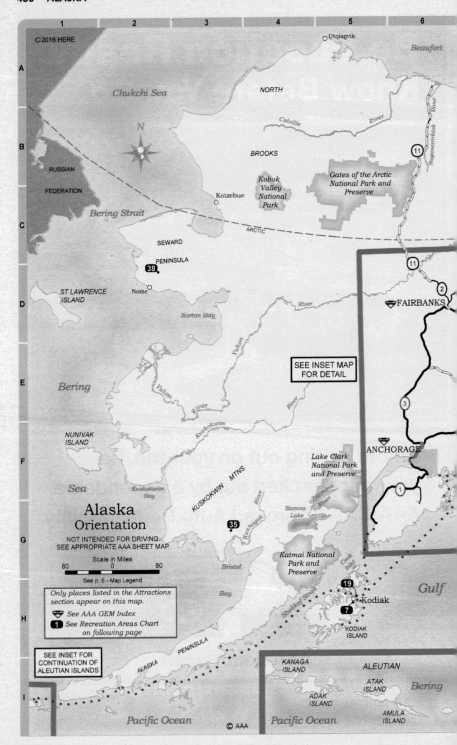

©2016 HERE

Beaufort

Utqiagvik

Chukchi Sea

NORTH

Colville   River

BROOKS

11

RUSSIAN

FEDERATION

Kotzebue

Kobuk
Valley
National
Park

Gates of the Arctic
National Park and
Preserve

Bering Strait

ARCTIC

SEWARD

PENINSULA

38

ST LAWRENCE
ISLAND

Nome

11

2

FAIRBANKS

River

Norton Bay

Bering

Yukon

River

SEE INSET MAP
FOR DETAIL

3

Yukon

River

Kuskokwim

NUNIVAK
ISLAND

Lake Clark
National Park
and Preserve

ANCHORAGE

1

Sea

Kuskokwim
Bay

KUSKOKWIM MTNS

Nushagak   River

Tazimina
River

Alaska
Orientation

NOT INTENDED FOR DRIVING.
SEE APPROPRIATE AAA SHEET MAP

35

Iliamna
Lake

Scale in Miles

80   0   80

See p. 6 - Map Legend

Katmai National
Park and
Preserve

Cook Inlet

Gulf

*Only places listed in the Attractions
section appear on this map.*

See AAA GEM Index

1 *See Recreation Areas Chart
on following page*

Bristol

Bay

Shelikof Strait

19

7

Kodiak

KODIAK
ISLAND

SEE INSET FOR
CONTINUATION OF
ALEUTIAN ISLANDS

PENINSULA

ALASKA

KANAGA
ISLAND

ALEUTIAN

ATAK
ISLAND

Bering

ADAK
ISLAND

Pacific Ocean

Pacific Ocean

AMULA
ISLAND

© AAA

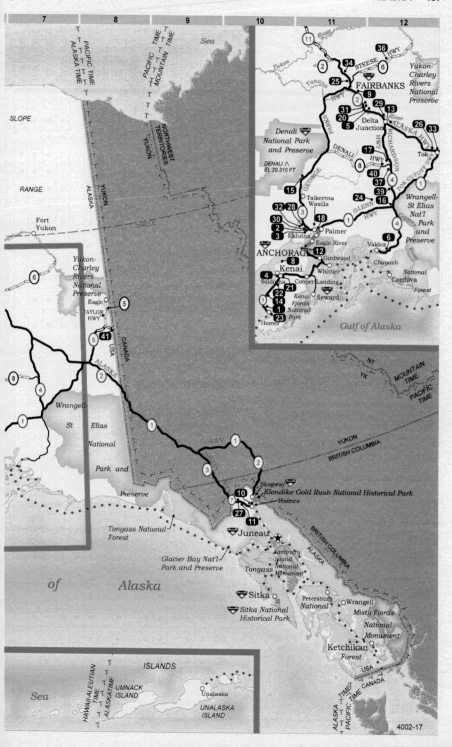

Recreation Areas Chart

The map location numerals in column 2 show an area's location on the preceding map.

	MAP LOCATION	CAMPING	PICNICKING	HIKING TRAILS	BOATING	BOAT RAMP	BOAT RENTAL	FISHING	SWIMMING	PETS ON LEASH	BICYCLE TRAILS	WINTER SPORTS	VISITOR CENTER	LODGE/CABINS	FOOD SERVICE
NATIONAL PARKS AND PRESERVES *(See place listings.)*															
Denali (B-10) 6,028,203 acres. Cross-country skiing, dog mushing, snowmobiling, snowshoeing.		•	•	•				•		•		•	•	•	•
Gates of the Arctic (B-5) 8,500,000 acres. Bird-watching.		•		•	•			•				•	•		
Glacier Bay (G-9) 3,283,168 acres. Bird-watching, hunting, kayaking, rafting.		•		•	•	•	•	•		•			•	•	•
Katmai (G-4) 4,159,097 acres. Canoeing, hunting, kayaking.		•	•	•	•	•	•	•					•	•	•
Kenai Fjords (D-11) 600,000 acres. Cross-country skiing, kayaking, snowmobiling.		•	•	•	•			•		•		•	•	•	
Kobuk Valley (C-4) 1,710,000 acres. Sand dunes.		•		•	•			•					•		
Lake Clark (F-4) 4,000,000 acres. Bird-watching, hunting, kayaking, rafting.		•		•	•			•		•			•	•	
Wrangell-St. Elias (C-12, F-8) 3,000,000 acres. Hunting, sea kayaking; all-terrain vehicle trails.		•	•	•	•			•		•			•	•	
Yukon-Charley Rivers (A-12, D-7) 500,000 acres. Historic. Hunting.		•		•	•			•					•		
NATIONAL FORESTS *(See place listings.)*															
Chugach (D-12) 5,500,000 acres in south-central Alaska. Cross-country skiing, hunting, snowboarding, snowmobiling.		•	•	•	•	•		•		•	•	•	•	•	•
Tongass (G-10) 17,000,000 acres in southeastern Alaska. Canoeing, cross-country and downhill skiing, ice skating, kayaking, snowboarding, snowmobiling.		•	•	•	•			•	•	•	•	•	•	•	•
STATE															
Anchor River (D-10) 264 acres near Anchor Point on Sterling Hwy., Milepost 157.	❶	•	•	•				•		•					
Big Lake (North) (C-10) 19 acres 10 mi. w. of Wasilla on Parks Hwy., then 6 mi. s.w. on Big Lake Rd.	❷	•	•		•	•		•	•	•		•			
Big Lake (South) (C-10) 16 acres 10 mi. w. of Wasilla on Parks Hwy., then 4 mi. s.w. on Big Lake Rd. and 2 mi. s.	❸	•	•		•	•		•	•	•					
Bings Landing (D-10) 126 acres e. of Soldotna on Sterling Hwy., Milepost 79.	❹	•	•		•	•		•		•					
Birch Lake (B-11) 191 acres n.e. of Delta Junction on Richardson Hwy., Milepost 305.5. Ice fishing, jet skiing, water skiing; ice fishing huts.	❺	•	•		•	•		•	•	•		•			
Blueberry Lake (C-12) 192 acres e. of Valdez on Richardson Hwy., Milepost 23.	❻	•	•	•				•		•					
Buskin River (H-5) 168 acres 4 mi. s.e. on Base-Town Rd. in Kodiak. Historic.	❼	•	•	•				•		•	•				
Captain Cook (C-10) 3,460 acres 24 mi. n. of Kenai on N. Kenai Rd., Milepost 36. Beachcombing, berry picking (in season), bird-watching, canoeing, hunting, ice fishing.	❽	•	•	•	•	•		•	•	•			•		
Chena River (A-12) 254,000 acres 27 mi. e. of Fairbanks on Chena Hot Springs Rd. Canoeing, cross-country skiing, kayaking, rock climbing, snowmobiling.	❾	•	•	•	•			•		•	•	•	•		•
Chilkat (F-10) 9,837 acres 7 mi. s. of Haines on Haines Hwy.	❿	•	•	•	•	•		•		•			•		
Chilkoot Lake (G-10) 80 acres 11 mi. n. of Haines on Lutak Rd., Milepost 10.	⓫	•	•		•	•		•	•	•					
Chugach (C-11) 495,204 acres just e. of Eagle River on Glenn Hwy. Numerous access points. Rafting; horse rental.	⓬	•	•	•	•			•		•		•	•	•	
Clearwater (B-12) 27 acres 11 mi. s.e. of Delta Junction on Alaska Hwy., Milepost 1415, then 8 mi. n.e. on side road.	⓭	•	•		•	•		•		•					
Deep Creek (D-10) 155 acres near Ninilchik on Sterling Hwy., Milepost 137.3. Bird-watching, clam digging.	⓮	•	•		•	•		•		•					
Denali (C-10) 325,240 acres n. of Talkeetna on Parks Hwy., Milepost 135-164.	⓯	•	•	•	•	•	•	•		•			•	•	
Dry Creek (C-12) 372 acres n. of Glennallen on Richardson Hwy., Milepost 117.5.	⓰	•	•	•				•		•					

Recreation Areas Chart

The map location numerals in column 2 show an area's location on the preceding map.

	MAP LOCATION	CAMPING	PICNICKING	HIKING TRAILS	BOATING	BOAT RAMP	BOAT RENTAL	FISHING	SWIMMING	PETS ON LEASH	BICYCLE TRAILS	WINTER SPORTS	VISITOR CENTER	LODGE/CABINS	FOOD SERVICE
Fielding Lake (B-12) 300 acres s. of Delta Junction on Richardson Hwy., Milepost 201.	17	•		•	•	•		•		•					
Finger Lake (C-11) 47 acres 4 mi. w. of Palmer on Palmer-Wasilla Rd., then 1 mi. n. and .5 mi. w.	18	•	•	•	•	•	•	•	•	•			•		
Fort Abercrombie (H-5) 182 acres 4.5 mi. s.e. of Kodiak on Miller Point. Historic.	19	•	•					•	•	•				•	
Harding Lake (B-11) 169 acres .5 mi. n.e. from Milepost 321 on the Richardson Hwy. Canoeing, jet skiing.	20	•	•	•	•	•	•	•	•	•			•		
Izaak Walton (D-10) 8 acres e. of Soldotna off Glenn Hwy.	21	•	•		•	•		•	•		•				
Johnson Lake (D-10) 332 acres 16 mi. s. of Soldotna on Glenn Hwy.	22	•	•		•	•		•		•					
Kachemak Bay (D-10) 368,290 acres near Seldovia, at the end of Sterling Hwy., then by boat or plane across Kachemak Bay. Bird-watching, kayaking.	23	•	•	•				•		•				•	
Lake Louise (C-11) 90 acres n.w. of Glennallen on Glenn Hwy., Milepost 160.	24	•	•		•	•		•	•	•					
Lower Chatanika River (A-11) 120 acres n.w. of Fairbanks off SR 2, Milepost 9.	25	•	•		•	•		•		•					
Moon Lake (B-12) 22 acres 18 mi. w. of Tok on Alaska Hwy., near Milepost 1332. Water skiing.	26	•	•		•	•		•	•	•					
Mosquito Lake (G-10) 10 acres 27.5 mi. w. of Haines on Haines Hwy., then 2.5 mi. on Mosquito Lake Rd.	27	•	•		•	•		•	•	•			•		
Nancy Lake (C-10) 22,685 acres 3.5 mi. s. of Willow on Parks Hwy., then 7 mi. w. on side road.	28	•	•		•			•		•				•	
Quartz Lake (A-12) 600 acres 2 mi. n.w. of Delta Junction on Alaska Hwy.	29	•	•	•	•	•	•	•	•	•			•		•
Rocky Lake (C-10) 48 acres 28 mi. w. of Palmer via Wasilla off Parks Hwy. at Milepost 3.5 of Big Lake Rd.	30	•	•		•			•		•					
Salcha River (B-11) 61 acres s.e. of North Pole on Alaska Hwy., Milepost 323. Canoeing.	31	•	•		•	•		•		•			•		
South Rolly Lake (C-10) 200 acres just w. of Wasilla off Parks Hwy. at Milepost 6.5 of Nancy Lake Pkwy.	32	•	•		•			•	•	•			•		
Tok River (B-12) 9 acres 5 mi. e. of Tok Junction on Alaska Hwy., Milepost 1309.	33	•	•		•	•		•	•	•					
Upper Chatanika River (A-11) 73 acres n.e. of Fairbanks off Steese Hwy.	34	•	•		•			•		•					
Wood-Tikchik (G-3) 1,600,000 acres n. of Dillingham.	35	•						•						•	
OTHER															
Cripple Creek (A-12) 5 acres 50 mi. n.e. of Fairbanks on Steese Hwy., Milepost 60.	36	•	•	•				•		•					
Paxson Lake (B-12) 80 acres 10 mi. s. of Paxson on Richardson Hwy., Milepost 175.	37	•	•		•	•		•		•					
Salmon Lake (D-2) 20 acres 40 mi. n. of Nome.	38	•	•		•	•		•							
Sourdough (C-12) 140 acres 35 mi. n. of Glennallen on the Richardson Hwy., Milepost 148.	39	•	•	•	•	•		•		•					
Tangle Lakes (B-12) 100 acres 22 mi. w. of Paxson on Denali Hwy., Milepost 22.	40	•	•		•	•		•		•					
Walker Fork (D-8) 10 acres 80 mi. n.e. of Tok on Taylor Hwy., Milepost 82.	41	•	•	•				•		•					

Ask about AAA/CAA Associate membership

to share the benefits you value

ADMIRALTY ISLAND NATIONAL MONUMENT (G-10)

Accessible by floatplane from Juneau and Sitka or via ferries of the Alaska Marine Highway to Angoon, Admiralty Island is part of Tongass National Forest *(see place listing p. 535)*. Between the rocky beaches and high mountain peaks lie a million acres of coastal rain forests, freshwater lakes and streams, alpine meadows and dense thickets of wild currants and other berries.

Alaskan brown bears outnumber human beings, and the greatest concentration of bald eagles in North America nests along the coast. Beavers, martens, minks, river otters, Sitka black-tailed deer and weasels share the island with Vancouver Canada geese and trumpeter and whistling swans. Offshore are harbor seals, sea lions and whales.

Motorboating and sea kayaking are popular in protected saltwater bays, and a canoe portage trail connects nine interior lakes to bays on the east and west shores. Rustic cabins can be reserved, and campsites and open shelters are available on a first-come, first-served basis. Most of the island is a wilderness area; be prepared for rain and follow no-trace camping practices.

For more information contact the U.S. Forest Service at (907) 586-8800, TTY (907) 790-7444 or (877) 444-6777 (reservations).

ANCHORAGE (F-6) pop. 291,826, elev. 118'

- Hotels p. 499 • Restaurants p. 502
- Attractions map p. 493
- Hotels & Restaurants map & index p. 496

Anchorage, on a high bluff enfolded by the two branches of Cook Inlet, lies as far west as the Hawaiian Islands and as far north as Helsinki, Finland. The tides in the inlet rise from 30 to 33 feet, and the surrounding mountains loom several thousand feet overhead. The protective mountain barrier and the proximity of the ocean afford Anchorage a surprisingly moderate climate, relative to most of Alaska.

Anchorage is Alaska's largest city and is home to almost half of the state's residents. While not a dazzling metropolis, each summer the city is beautifully decorated with almost 100,000 hanging flower baskets brimming with brightly-colored blooms.

Established in 1915 as the construction headquarters for the Alaska Railroad *(see attraction listing)*, it is the transportation and business center of south-central Alaska and a major winter recreation area. Anchorage's heritage as a road town is recalled by a number of historic buildings, notably the Pioneer Schoolhouse in Ben Crawford Memorial Park and two nearby one-room log cabins.

Reminders of Native American and even Russian influences can be found. In downtown, several landmarks denote Alaska Native heritage. For Russian-heritage with a distinct Dena'ina Athabascan

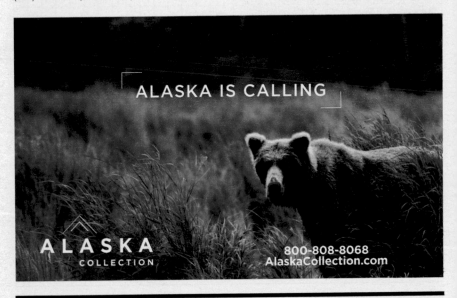
Visit the AAA and CAA senior driving websites
for tips to help you drive safely longer

▼ *See AAA listing p. 494* ▼

YOUR TICKET

TO EXPLORING ALASKA

The Alaska Railroad showcases
the pure scenic beauty of Alaska with
rail vacations and tours in every season.
Request a FREE 2017 vacation planner today!

Now Departing Ordinary ❯ AlaskaRailroad.com ❯ 800.544.0552

© Glenn Aronwits

ALASKA
RAILROAD

Alaska - It's waiting for you.
Potter Marsh, Anchorage

Lodging • Tours • Transportation

Custom vacations to
Alaska's most spectacular
destinations! Call us or visit
our website and see what's
waiting for you.

Alaska
TOUR & TRAVEL

1-800-208-0200 | AlaskaTravel.com

(See map & index p. 496.)

influence, Eklutna Historical Park *(see Eklutna p. 509)*—30 miles from downtown—is a good bet mid-May through September; phone (907) 688-6026 for more information.

Anchorage suffered from the effects of the 1964 Good Friday earthquake, one of the strongest in history, which destroyed much of downtown. Earthquake Park, at the west end of Northern Lights Boulevard, has a walking trail and interpretive signs that provide information about the massive temblor. The park also provides a stunning vista of Cook Inlet.

The dramatic beauty of the nearby mountains, inlets and glaciers offers an easily accessible sampling of Alaska's natural splendors. Two roads affording beautiful views link to Anchorage; scenic SR 1/9 (Seward Highway) extends south to Seward, and SR 1 (Glenn Highway) extends north to Glennallen.

From Anchorage visitors also can take various sightseeing tours of the area, including the Kenai Peninsula and places of interest inaccessible by road. Among the more novel sightseeing trips are dog sled tours, which leave from the Alyeska Resort and Ski Area *(see Girdwood p. 515)* December through March. Trolley tours given by Anchorage City Trolley Tours depart daily May through September from the Log Cabin Visitor Information Center at Fourth Avenue and F Street; phone (907) 276-5603 or (888) 917-8687.

The Park Connection offers twice-daily shuttle service from Anchorage to Denali National Park and Preserve and Seward mid-May to mid-September; phone (907) 344-8775 or (800) 266-8625.

Float trips on the Matanuska River depart by van from Anchorage to the launch point. Panning for gold is available an hour from downtown. For a different perspective, try flightseeing—operators can be found at the airport and Lake Hood.

Gray Line of Alaska and Princess Tours offer a float adventure on Eagle River; tours to Barrow, Juneau, Kodiak Island, Kotzebue, Matanuska Valley, Nome, Portage Glacier and Prudhoe Bay; fishing on the Kenai River; cruises on Prince William Sound to Columbia Glacier; and a city tour of Anchorage. There's also Alaska Tour & Travel, which offers transportation and tours across Alaska, including Fairbanks, Whittier and various national parks.

Most agencies offer 2-, 3- and 4-day round trips between Anchorage and Denali National Park and Preserve. The trips include travel in railway cars equipped with glass ceiling panels. Many of these companies also offer longer excursions to the interior and cruises up the Inside Passage.

Then there are places to explore independently. Ship Creek, with multiple access points along East Ship Creek Drive, is a popular sport salmon fishery and salmon viewing area. King salmon run in June and silver salmon from mid-July to late September. During these months, fishermen line the banks from the mouth of Ship Creek upstream to the Chugach Power Plant Dam. Several viewing platforms span the creek between Whitney Road and the Ship Creek walking trail. The Bait Shack, 212 W. Whitney Rd., sells fishing licenses and rents tackle and fishing gear. The William Jack Hernandez Sport Fish Hatchery is 2 miles upstream from the mouth of the creek at the corner of Reeve Boulevard and Post Road. The hatchery's visitor corridor is open 8 a.m. to 4 p.m.; phone (907) 269-2000 for more information.

Bring the outdoors inside: The Alaska Center for the Performing Arts Sydney Laurence Theatre, at 621 W. 6th Ave., presents a 40-minute, large-screen slide show called "AurorA" that displays a series of

(See map & index p. 496.)

stunning images of the aurora borealis synchronized to classical music. Shows are offered daily late May through August; tickets are available at the door. Phone (907) 263-2993 to confirm schedule information

Anchorage serves as the starting line for the 1,049-mile 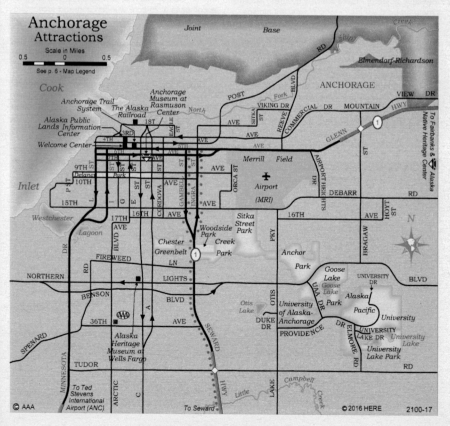 Iditarod Trail Sled Dog Race, which begins the first Saturday in March. The actual mileage of the 2015 race was 1,131 miles; however, 1,049 is often used as a symbolic figure because the distance is always more than 1,000 miles, and 49 was added to symbolize Alaska's place as the 49th state to enter the Union. Dogs and mushers travel over the Alaska Range and across frozen Norton Bay, arriving in Nome nearly 2 weeks later.

The Bear & Raven Adventure Theater, 315 E St., offers "The Amazing Trail," a 30-minute multimedia presentation relating the history of the Iditarod race as well as interactive sledding, ballooning and fishing exhibits. The theater is open mid-May to mid-September and during the Iditarod; phone (907) 277-4545.

Visit Anchorage: 524 W. Fourth Ave., Anchorage, AK 99501-2212. **Phone:** (907) 276-4118, or (800) 446-5352 to request a visitors guide.

Self-guiding tours: A guide outlining a walking tour and driving tours north and south of the city is available at Log Cabin Visitor Information Center, Fourth Avenue and F Street; phone (907) 257-2363.

26 GLACIER CRUISE BY PHILLIPS CRUISES— see Whittier p. 538.

[SAVE] **ALASKA AVIATION MUSEUM,** on Lake Hood at 4721 Aircraft Dr., displays more than 26 vintage aircraft and a flight simulator. Visitors also can observe restorations in progress. Memorabilia and photographs chronicle the history of civilian and military aviation in Alaska; films are shown continuously. **Time:** Allow 30 minutes minimum. **Hours:** Daily 9-5, May 1 to mid-Sept.; Wed.-Sat. 9-5, Sun. noon-5, rest of year. Closed major holidays in winter. **Cost:** $15; $12 (ages 65+ and active military and veterans with ID); $8 (ages 5-17). **Phone:** (907) 248-5325.

ALASKA BOTANICAL GARDEN is 3 mi. e. of New Seward Hwy. on Tudor Rd., then just s. to 4601 Campbell Airstrip Rd. Arctic horticulture is showcased in a 110-acre birch and spruce woodland replete with more than 1,100 varieties of perennials, 150 species of native Alaskan plants as well as herb and alpine rock gardens. The garden includes a wildflower walk, a

Anchorage Attractions

(See map & index p. 496.)

1-mile interpretive nature trail and a creek where salmon spawn in the summer. The peak blooming season commences in late May and culminates in mid-September, occasionally lasting into October.

Note: Though the garden is open in winter, it is often snow-covered. **Time:** Allow 1 hour, 30 minutes minimum. **Hours:** Daily dawn-dusk. **Cost:** Admission May-Sept. $12; $10 (ages 5-18, senior citizens, students and military with ID). Admission rest of year $7; $5 (ages 5-18). **Phone:** (907) 770-3692. GT

ALASKA NATIVE HERITAGE CENTER is about 3 mi. e. on Glenn Hwy. to N. Muldoon Rd. exit, then 1 mi. e. on Heritage Center Dr. Situated on 26 wooded acres, the center presents information about the five regional, Alaska Native groups that inhabit Alaska: the Aleut and Alutiiq; Athabascan; Eyak, Tlingit, Haida and Tsimshian; Inupiaq and St. Lawrence Island Yup'ik; and Yup'ik and Cup'ik cultures.

The main building offers the Gathering Place for storytelling, Alaska Natives dance and games and musical performances as well as a theater for cultural films. The Hall of Cultures exhibit is divided into five areas with changing multimedia displays about the ways of life of Alaska Natives cultures. Artisans create and display their crafts in adjacent studios.

Outside, five village sites surround Lake Tiulana, and guided village site tours are available to explain each dwelling, aspects of daily life and customs. **Time:** Allow 2 hours minimum. **Hours:** Daily 9-5, early May-early Sept. **Cost:** $24.95; $21.15 (ages 62+ and military with ID); $16.95 (ages 7-16); $71.50 (family, two adults and two children). Combination ticket with Anchorage Museum at Rasmuson Center $29.95. **Phone:** (907) 330-8000 or (800) 315-6608. GT TI

THE ALASKA RAILROAD departs from 411 W. First Ave. Narrated sightseeing tours on the Denali Star Train are offered northward between Anchorage and Fairbanks with stops at Wasilla, Talkeetna and Denali National Park and Preserve. The Glacier Discovery Train travels south from Anchorage to Whittier following the Turnagain Arm of Cook Inlet. Stops include Girdwood, Portage and Spencer Glacier, a whistle stop where passengers can take a 1.5-mile ranger-guided hike to see the glacier. The Coastal Classic Train runs from Anchorage to Seward and offers a glimpse of wildlife and glaciers.

Domed cars with glass-covered viewing platforms allow for 180-degree views. Special winter routes as well as excursions and connections to air, rail and boat tours are available. **Hours:** Trips depart daily, mid-May to mid-Sept.; trains depart Sat.-Sun., rest of year. Phone ahead to confirm schedule. **Cost:** One-way fares $63-$239 (an extra fee applies for first-class seating). Reservations are required. **Phone:** (907) 265-2494, (800) 544-0552 or TTY (907) 265-2620. *(See ad p. 491.)*

ALASKA ZOO is 7.5 mi. s. on SR 1 (Seward Hwy.), then 2 mi. e. to 4731 O'Malley Rd.; a shuttle provides transportation from the Log Cabin Visitor Information Center mid-May to mid-Sept. The grounds encompass a 25-acre wooded home to arctic, sub-arctic and Alaskan native animals, including Amur (Siberian) tigers, seals, snow leopards, Tibetan yaks, wolves and black, brown and polar bears. Visitors may interact with selected animals during the 2-hour Discovery Tour.

Time: Allow 1 hour, 30 minutes minimum. **Hours:** Daily 9-9, June-Aug.; 9-6, May and Sept.; 10-5, Mar.-Apr. and in Oct.; 10-4, rest of year (weather permitting). Discovery Tour departs daily at 12:15, late May to mid-Sept. Closed Thanksgiving and

▼ *See AAA listing p. 528* ▼

(See map & index p. 496.)

Christmas. Phone ahead to confirm schedule. **Cost:** $15; $10 (ages 65+ and military with ID); $7 (ages 3-17). Discovery Tour $28; $20 (ages 3-17). **Phone:** (907) 346-2133. 🍴 🎡

 ANCHORAGE MUSEUM AT RAS-MUSON CENTER, 625 C St., has exhibits focusing on the art, history, science and cultures of Alaska and the Circumpolar North. The Alaska Gallery includes objects dating from prehistoric times through European exploration, Russian settlement, the gold rush era, World War II and statehood. The state-of-the-art Smithsonian Arctic Studies Center has multimedia exhibits and displays more than 600 Alaska Native artifacts. Contemporary Alaska Native artists blend traditional and contemporary techniques to examine what it means to be an Alaska Native today.

"Art of the North" explores life in the Arctic through multiple perspectives and visual narratives. The interactive Discovery Center offers exhibits that explore nature, science and technology, including a marine wildlife area, reptile exhibits and a bubble lab. Spark!Lab Smithsonian allows kids and families to create, innovate, collaborate and problem-solve. Other highlights include the Thomas Planetarium and traveling exhibitions.

Note: The Alaska Gallery is closed for renovations until fall 2017; the rest of the museum will remain open. **Time:** Allow 1 hour minimum. **Hours:** Daily 9-6, May-Sept.; Tues.-Sat. 10-6, Sun. noon-6, rest of year. Closed Jan. 1, Thanksgiving and Christmas. **Cost:** $15; $10 (ages 65+, military and students with ID); $7 (ages 3-12). Combination ticket with Alaska Native Heritage Center $29.95. **Phone:** (907) 929-9200. 🍴

MAJOR MARINE TOURS—see Seward p. 528.

PORTAGE GLACIER RECREATION AREA—see Chugach National Forest p. 504.

TRANS ARCTIC CIRCLE TREKS—see Fairbanks p. 513.

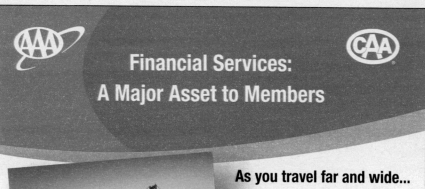

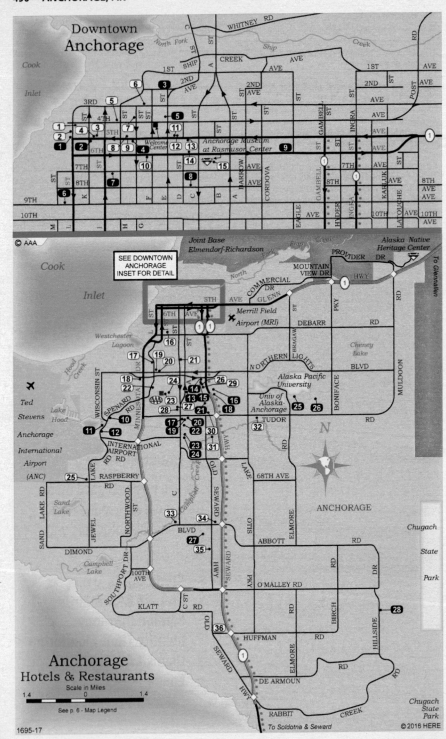

Downtown Anchorage

Anchorage
Hotels & Restaurants

Scale in Miles

1.4   0   1.4

See p. 6 - Map Legend

© AAA

1695-17   ©2016 HERE

✈ Airport Hotels

Map Page	ANCHORAGE INTERNATIONAL (Maximum driving distance from airport: 2.2 mi)	Diamond Rated	Rate Range	Page
12 p. 496	Courtyard by Marriott Anchorage Airport, 1.7 mi	◆◆◆	$113-$247	499
10 p. 496	Holiday Inn Express Anchorage Airport, 2.1 mi	◆◆◆	$109-$359	501
11 p. 496	The Lakefront Anchorage, 2.2 mi	◆◆◆	Rates not provided	501

Anchorage

This index helps you "spot" where approved hotels and restaurants are located on the corresponding detailed maps. Hotel daily rate range is for comparison only. Restaurant price range is a combination of lunch and/or dinner. Turn to the listing page for more information and consult display ads for special promotions.

ANCHORAGE

Map Page	Hotels	Diamond Rated	Rate Range	Page
1 p. 496	Copper Whale Inn	◆◆	$99-$289	499
2 p. 496	The Voyager Inn	◆◆	Rates not provided SAVE	501
3 p. 496	Anchorage Grand Hotel	◆◆	Rates not provided SAVE	499
4 p. 496	Westmark Anchorage	◆◆	$89-$329	501
5 p. 496	Historic Anchorage Hotel	◆◆	$119-$309 SAVE	501
6 p. 496	Clarion Suites Downtown	◆◆◆	$110-$250 SAVE	499
7 p. 496	Anchorage Marriott Downtown	◆◆◆	$123-$355	499
8 p. 496	Quality Suites Historic Downtown	◆◆◆	$121-$250	501
9 p. 496	Sheraton Anchorage Hotel & Spa	◆◆◆	$159-$449 SAVE	501
10 p. 496	Holiday Inn Express Anchorage Airport	◆◆◆	$109-$359	501
11 p. 496	The Lakefront Anchorage	◆◆◆	Rates not provided	501
12 p. 496	Courtyard by Marriott Anchorage Airport	◆◆◆	$113-$247	499
13 p. 496	SpringHill Suites by Marriott Midtown	◆◆◆	$113-$271	501
14 p. 496	Embassy Suites by Hilton Anchorage	◆◆◆	$149-$309	500
15 p. 496	TownePlace Suites by Marriott Anchorage Midtown	◆◆◆	$110-$294	501
16 p. 496	Residence Inn by Marriott	◆◆◆	$136-$265	501
17 p. 496	Home2 Suites by Hilton Anchorage Midtown	◆◆◆	$109-$339	501
18 p. 496	Best Western Golden Lion Hotel	◆◆	$89-$229 SAVE	499
19 p. 496	Hilton Garden Inn Midtown	◆◆◆	$139-$339 SAVE	501
20 p. 496	Aspen Suites Hotel Anchorage Midtown	◆◆	Rates not provided	499
21 p. 496	My Place Hotel Anchorage Midtown	◆◆	$165-$175	501
22 p. 496	Homewood Suites by Hilton Midtown	◆◆◆	$129-$399 SAVE	501
23 p. 496	Fairfield Inn & Suites by Marriott Midtown	◆◆◆	$98-$286	500
24 p. 496	Crowne Plaza Anchorage Midtown	◆◆◆	$129-$299	499
25 p. 496	SpringHill Suites by Marriott University Lake	◆◆◆	$108-$237	501
26 p. 496	Camai Bed & Breakfast	◆◆◆	$85-$179	499
27 p. 496	Dimond Center Hotel	◆◆◆	$189-$499 SAVE	499

ANCHORAGE (cont'd)

Map Page	Hotels (cont'd)	Diamond Rated	Rate Range	Page
28 p. 496	**Highland Glen Lodge Bed & Breakfast**	▽▽▽	$120-$189 SAVE	500

Map Page	Restaurants	Diamond Rated	Cuisine	Price Range	Page
1 p. 496	Snow City Cafe	▽▽	American	$10-$17	502
2 p. 496	Simon & Seafort's Saloon & Grill	▽▽▽	Regional American	$18-$47	502
3 p. 496	**Crow's Nest Restaurant**	▽▽▽▽	New American	$36-$58	502
4 p. 496	Bangkok Cafe	▽▽	Thai	$10-$15	502
5 p. 496	Haute Quarter Grill	▽▽▽	American	$20-$50	502
6 p. 496	**Marx Bros. Café**	▽▽▽▽	New American	$35-$40	502
7 p. 496	Sack's Cafe & Restaurant	▽▽▽	International	$12-$36	502
8 p. 496	Glacier Brewhouse	▽▽	American	$9-$34	502
9 p. 496	Orso	▽▽▽	Italian	$19-$40	502
10 p. 496	Humpy's Great Alaskan Ale House	▽▽	American	$10-$45	502
11 p. 496	Ginger	▽▽▽	Pacific Northwest	$9-$31	502
12 p. 496	Club Paris	▽▽	Steak Seafood	$13-$45	502
13 p. 496	Sullivan's Steakhouse	▽▽▽	Steak	$14-$65	503
14 p. 496	Crush Wine Bistro and Cellar	▽▽	Small Plates	$9-$34	502
15 p. 496	Muse	▽▽	Regional Pacific Northwest	$15-$37	502
16 p. 496	Fire Island Rustic Bakeshop	▽	Breads/Pastries	$3-$14	502
17 p. 496	Ray's Place	▽▽	Vietnamese	$9-$25	502
18 p. 496	City Diner	▽▽	American	$6-$20	502
19 p. 496	Spenard Roadhouse	▽▽▽	American	$10-$32	502
20 p. 496	Sweet Basil Cafe	▽	American	$6-$15	503
21 p. 496	Kriner's Diner	▽▽	American	$8-$16	502
22 p. 496	Yak and Yeti Himalayan Restaurant	▽▽	Indian	$8-$17	503
23 p. 496	Jens' Restaurant	▽▽▽	Pacific Northwest	$13-$45	502
24 p. 496	Campobello Bistro	▽▽	Italian	$11-$28	502
25 p. 496	Kincaid Grill	▽▽▽	Regional Alaskan	$28-$36	502
26 p. 496	Kinley's Restaurant & Bar	▽▽▽	Fusion	$12-$36	502
27 p. 496	Pepper Mill	▽▽	American	$10-$40	502
28 p. 496	Sea Galley	▽▽	Seafood	$10-$40	502
29 p. 496	Moose's Tooth Pub & Pizzeria	▽▽	American	$10-$28	502
30 p. 496	Aladdin's	▽▽	Mediterranean	$15-$29	502
31 p. 496	Sourdough Mining Co	▽▽	American	$14-$56	502
32 p. 496	Fu Do Chinese Restaurant	▽▽	Chinese	$8-$22	502
33 p. 496	Las Margaritas	▽▽	Mexican	$9-$20	502
34 p. 496	Sushi Ya Japanese Restaurant	▽▽	Japanese	$8-$23	503
35 p. 496	China Lights Oriental Cuisine	▽▽	Asian	$11-$20	502
36 p. 496	Southside Bistro	▽▽▽	American	$8-$33	502

(See map & index p. 496.)

ANCHORAGE GRAND HOTEL   907/929-8888 **3**

Extended Stay Hotel

Rates not provided

Address: 505 W 2nd Ave 99501 **Location:** Corner of 2nd Ave and E St. Across from Anchorage Market. **Facility:** 31 kitchen units. 5 stories, interior corridors. **Parking:** street only. **Terms:** check-in 4 pm. **Guest Services:** valet and coin laundry. **Featured Amenity: continental breakfast.**

ANCHORAGE MARRIOTT DOWNTOWN   (907)279-8000 **7**
Hotel. **Address:** 820 W 7th Ave 99501

AAA Benefit: Members save 5% or more!

ASPEN SUITES HOTEL ANCHORAGE MIDTOWN
907/770-3400 **20**
Extended Stay Hotel. **Address:** 100 E Tudor Rd 99503

BEST WESTERN GOLDEN LION HOTEL
(907)561-1522 **18**

Hotel
$89-$229

Best Western. AAA Benefit: Save 10% or more every day and earn 10% bonus points!

Address: 1000 E 36th Ave 99508 **Location:** SR 1 (Seward Hwy) and 36th Ave. **Facility:** 83 units. 3 stories, interior corridors. **Parking:** winter plug-ins. **Activities:** exercise room. **Guest Services:** valet and coin laundry.

CAMAI BED & BREAKFAST   (907)333-2219 **26**
Bed & Breakfast. **Address:** 3838 Westminster Way 99508

CLARION SUITES DOWNTOWN   (907)222-5005 **6**

Hotel
$110-$250

Address: 1110 W 8th Ave 99501 **Location:** Corner of L St and W 8th Ave. **Facility:** 112 units. 3 stories, interior corridors. **Terms:** 3 day cancellation notice. **Amenities:** safes. **Pool(s):** heated indoor. **Activities:** hot tub, limited exercise equipment. **Guest Services:** valet and coin laundry, area transportation. **Featured Amenity: full hot breakfast.**

COPPER WHALE INN   (907)258-7999 **1**
Bed & Breakfast. **Address:** 440 L St 99501

COURTYARD BY MARRIOTT ANCHORAGE AIRPORT
(907)245-0322 **12**
Hotel. **Address:** 4901 Spenard Rd 99517

AAA Benefit: Members save 5% or more!

CROWNE PLAZA ANCHORAGE MIDTOWN
(907)433-4100 **24**
Hotel. **Address:** 109 W International Airport Rd 99518

DIMOND CENTER HOTEL   (907)770-5000 **27**

Hotel
$189-$499

Address: 700 E Dimond Blvd 99515 **Location:** SR 1 (Seward Hwy) exit Dimond Blvd, just w, then s on Dimond Center Dr. Adjacent to Dimond Center Mall. **Facility:** 109 units. 3 stories, interior corridors. **Terms:** 3 day cancellation notice-fee imposed. **Activities:** exercise room. **Guest Services:** valet and coin laundry. **Featured Amenity: full hot breakfast.**

▼ See AAA listing p. 537 ▼

(See map & index p. 496.)

EMBASSY SUITES BY HILTON ANCHORAGE
ᗩᗩᗩᗩ Hotel. **Address:** 600 E Benson Blvd 99503

(907)332-7000 **14**

AAA Benefit:
Members save 5%
or more!

FAIRFIELD INN & SUITES BY MARRIOTT MIDTOWN
ᗩᗩᗩᗩ Hotel. **Address:** 5060 A St 99503

(907)222-9000 **23**

AAA Benefit:
Members save 5%
or more!

HIGHLAND GLEN LODGE BED & BREAKFAST

(907)336-2312 **28**

ᗩᗩᗩᗩ
Bed & Breakfast
$120-$189

Address: 11651 Hillside Dr 99507 **Location:** SR 1 (Seward Hwy) exit O'Malley Rd, 3.8 mi e, then 0.5 mi s. **Facility:** Ideal for families, vacationers, anniversaries or mini retreats, this English estate is a short drive from the city and airport. For relaxation, play bocce ball, cornhole, horseshoes or the piano. 5 units. 2 stories (no elevator), interior corridors. **Terms:** check-in 4 pm, 30 day cancellation notice-fee imposed. **Activities:** lawn sports, picnic facilities. **Featured Amenity:** full hot breakfast.

[SAVE] [BIZ] 🛜 ⊠ 🄺 🖵
/ SOME UNITS [▷〡] [Ⓩ] 🎁

▼ See AAA listing p. 515 ▼

(See map & index p. 496.)

HILTON GARDEN INN MIDTOWN   (907)729-7000   19

Hotel
$139-$339

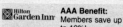
AAA Benefit: Members save up to 10%!

Address: 4555 Union Square Dr 99503 **Location:** SR 1 (Seward Hwy) exit Tudor Rd, 0.8 mi w, U-turn at C St, then just s. **Facility:** 125 units. 4 stories, interior corridors. **Terms:** 1-7 night minimum stay, cancellation fee imposed. **Pool(s):** heated indoor. **Activities:** hot tub, picnic facilities, exercise room. **Guest Services:** valet and coin laundry, area transportation.

[SAVE] [✈] [¶] [Y] CALL [&M] [≈] [BIZ] [HS] [🛜] [✕] [▯] [▭] [▱]

HISTORIC ANCHORAGE HOTEL   (907)272-4553   5

Historic Hotel
$119-$309

Address: 330 E St 99501 **Location:** Between 3rd and 4th aves. **Facility:** Established in 1916, this hotel retains its Old World charm, but with modern amenities. The standard rooms are on the compact side and meant for one or two people while suites are more spacious. 26 units. 3 stories, interior corridors. **Parking:** on-site (fee). **Terms:** 7 day cancellation notice-fee imposed. **Activities:** exercise room. **Guest Services:** valet laundry. **Featured Amenity:** continental breakfast.

[SAVE] [¶→] [BIZ] [🛜] [✕] [✗] [▱] / SOME UNITS [▯]

HOLIDAY INN EXPRESS ANCHORAGE AIRPORT
(907)248-8848   10

▽▽▽ Hotel. **Address:** 4411 Spenard Rd 99517

HOME2 SUITES BY HILTON ANCHORAGE MIDTOWN
(907)561-5618   17

▽▽▽ Extended Stay Contemporary Hotel. **Address:** 4700 Union Square Dr 99503

AAA Benefit: Members save up to 10%!

HOMEWOOD SUITES BY HILTON MIDTOWN
(907)762-7000   22

Extended Stay Hotel
$129-$399

HOMEWOOD SUITES BY HILTON
AAA Benefit: Members save up to 10%!

Address: 101 W 48th Ave 99503 **Location:** SR 1 (Seward Hwy) exit Tudor Rd, 0.8 mi w, U-turn at C St, then just s on Union Square Dr. **Facility:** 122 efficiencies. 4 stories, interior corridors. **Terms:** 1-7 night minimum stay, cancellation fee imposed. **Pool(s):** heated indoor. **Activities:** hot tub, picnic facilities, exercise room. **Guest Services:** valet and coin laundry, area transportation. **Featured Amenity:** breakfast buffet.

[SAVE] [✈] [¶→] CALL [&M] [≈] [BIZ] [HS] [🛜] [▯] [▭] [▱]

THE LAKEFRONT ANCHORAGE   907/243-2300   11

▽▽▽ Hotel. **Address:** 4800 Spenard Rd 99517

MY PLACE HOTEL ANCHORAGE MIDTOWN
(907)929-3500   21

▽▽ Extended Stay Hotel. **Address:** 729 E 40th Ave 99503

QUALITY SUITES HISTORIC DOWNTOWN
(907)274-1000   8

▽▽▽ Hotel. **Address:** 325 W 8th Ave 99501

RESIDENCE INN BY MARRIOTT   (907)563-9844   16

▽▽▽ Extended Stay Hotel. **Address:** 1025 E 35th Ave 99508

AAA Benefit: Members save 5% or more!

SHERATON ANCHORAGE HOTEL & SPA
(907)276-8700   9

Hotel
$159-$449

Sheraton

AAA Benefit: Members save up to 15%, plus Starwood Preferred Guest® benefits!

Address: 401 E 6th Ave 99501 **Location:** Jct 6th Ave and Denali St. **Facility:** 370 units. 16 stories, interior corridors. **Parking:** on-site (fee). **Activities:** exercise room, spa. **Guest Services:** valet and coin laundry.

[SAVE] [¶] [Y] [BIZ] [sHS] [🛜] [✕] [▯] [▭] / SOME UNITS [🐾]

SPRINGHILL SUITES BY MARRIOTT MIDTOWN
(907)562-3247   13

▽▽▽ Hotel. **Address:** 3401 A St 99503

AAA Benefit: Members save 5% or more!

SPRINGHILL SUITES BY MARRIOTT UNIVERSITY LAKE
(907)751-6300   25

▽▽▽ Hotel. **Address:** 4050 University Lake Dr 99508

AAA Benefit: Members save 5% or more!

TOWNEPLACE SUITES BY MARRIOTT ANCHORAGE MIDTOWN   (907)334-8000   15

▽▽▽ Extended Stay Contemporary Hotel. **Address:** 600 E 32nd Ave 99503

AAA Benefit: Members save 5% or more!

THE VOYAGER INN   907/277-9501   2

Hotel
Rates not provided

Address: 501 K St 99501 **Location:** At K St and 5th Ave. **Facility:** 40 units. 4 stories, interior corridors. **Parking:** on-site (fee). **Amenities:** safes. **Guest Services:** valet laundry. **Featured Amenity:** full hot breakfast.

[SAVE] [¶→] [🛜] [✕] [♞] [▯] [▭] [▱] / SOME UNITS [🔌]

WESTMARK ANCHORAGE   (907)276-7676   4

▽▽ Hotel. **Address:** 720 W 5th Ave 99501

(See map & index p. 496.)

WHERE TO EAT

ALADDIN'S   907/561-2373   (30)
♦♦ Mediterranean. Casual Dining. **Address:** 4240 Old Seward Hwy 99503

BANGKOK CAFE   907/274-2233   (4)
♦♦ Thai. Casual Dining. **Address:** 930 W 5th Ave 99501

CAMPOBELLO BISTRO   907/563-2040   (24)
♦♦ Italian. Casual Dining. **Address:** 601 W 36th Ave 99503

CHINA LIGHTS ORIENTAL CUISINE   907/522-5888   (35)
♦♦ Asian. Casual Dining. **Address:** 9220 Old Seward Hwy 99515

CITY DINER   907/277-2489   (18)
♦♦ American. Casual Dining. **Address:** 3000 Minnesota Dr 99503

CLUB PARIS   907/277-6332   (12)
♦♦ Steak Seafood. Casual Dining. **Address:** 417 W 5th Ave 99501

CROW'S NEST RESTAURANT   907/276-6000   (3)
♦♦♦ ♦♦♦
New American Fine Dining
$36-$58
AAA Inspector Notes: A visit to this restaurant and lounge is a must while in Anchorage. Perched high on the 20th floor of The Hotel Captain Cook, the eatery affords one of the best panoramic views of mountains and Cook Inlet, especially on long summer days. The menu features fresh seafood and beef dishes served in an old world dining room with lots of wood accent walls. **Features:** full bar. **Reservations:** suggested. **Address:** 939 W 5th Ave 99501 **Location:** Between I and K sts; downtown; in The Hotel Captain Cook. **Parking:** on-site and valet.
D CALL ⊙M

CRUSH WINE BISTRO AND CELLAR   907/865-9198   (14)
♦♦ Small Plates. Casual Dining. **Address:** 343 W 6th Ave 99501

FIRE ISLAND RUSTIC BAKESHOP   907/569-0001   (16)
♦ Breads/Pastries. Quick Serve. **Address:** 1343 G St 99501

FU DO CHINESE RESTAURANT   907/561-6611   (32)
♦♦ Chinese. Casual Dining. **Address:** 2600 E Tudor Rd 99507

GINGER   907/929-3680   (11)
♦♦♦ Pacific Northwest. Fine Dining. **Address:** 425 W 5th Ave 99501

GLACIER BREWHOUSE   907/274-2739   (8)
♦♦ American. Gastropub. **Address:** 737 W 5th Ave, Suite 110 99501

HAUTE QUARTER GRILL   907/622-4745   (5)
♦♦♦ American. Casual Dining. **Address:** 525 W 4th Ave 99501

HUMPY'S GREAT ALASKAN ALE HOUSE   907/276-2337   (10)
♦♦ American. Casual Dining. **Address:** 610 W 6th Ave 99501

JENS' RESTAURANT   907/561-5367   (23)
♦♦♦ Pacific Northwest. Fine Dining. **Address:** 701 W 36th Ave 99503

KINCAID GRILL   907/243-0507   (25)
♦♦♦ Regional Alaskan. Fine Dining. **Address:** 6700 Jewel Lake Rd 99502

KINLEY'S RESTAURANT & BAR   907/644-8953   (26)
♦♦♦ Fusion. Casual Dining. **Address:** 3230 Seward Hwy 99503

KRINER'S DINER   907/929-8257   (21)
♦♦ American. Casual Dining. **Address:** 2409 C St 99503

LAS MARGARITAS   907/349-4922   (33)
♦♦ Mexican. Casual Dining. **Address:** 541 W Dimond Blvd 99515

MARX BROS. CAFÉ   907/278-2133   (6)
♦♦♦ ♦♦♦
New American Fine Dining
$35-$40
AAA Inspector Notes: Historic. For a truly exquisite meal, look no further than the dining rooms of this renovated 1916 home. Innovative and artistic selections of Alaskan seafood highlight the menu, and the locally renowned Caesar salad is prepared tableside. Choices include not only a wide selection of seafood, such as oysters, salmon and halibut, but also lamb, elk and other meats. Save room for one of the divine desserts. The atmosphere is delightful, and the service friendly and genuine. **Features:** beer & wine. **Reservations:** suggested. **Address:** 627 W 3rd Ave 99501 **Location:** Between F and G sts; downtown. **Parking:** street only. D ⊠

MOOSE'S TOOTH PUB & PIZZERIA   907/258-2537   (29)
♦♦ American. Casual Dining. **Address:** 3300 Old Seward Hwy 99503

MUSE   907/929-9210   (15)
♦♦ Regional Pacific Northwest. Casual Dining. **Address:** 625 C St 99501

ORSO   907/222-3232   (9)
♦♦♦ Italian. Casual Dining. **Address:** 737 W 5th Ave 99501

PEPPER MILL   907/561-0800   (27)
♦♦ American. Casual Dining. **Address:** 4101 Credit Union Dr 99503

RAY'S PLACE   907/279-2932   (17)
♦♦ Vietnamese. Casual Dining. **Address:** 2412 Spenard Rd 99503

SACK'S CAFE & RESTAURANT   907/274-4022   (7)
♦♦♦ International. Fine Dining. **Address:** 328 G St 99501

SEA GALLEY   907/563-3520   (28)
♦♦ Seafood. Casual Dining. **Address:** 4101 Credit Union Dr 99503

SIMON & SEAFORT'S SALOON & GRILL   907/274-3502   (2)
♦♦♦ Regional American. Casual Dining. **Address:** 420 L St 99501

SNOW CITY CAFE   907/272-2489   (1)
♦♦ American. Casual Dining. **Address:** 1034 W 4th Ave 99501

SOURDOUGH MINING CO   907/563-2272   (31)
♦♦ American. Casual Dining. **Address:** 5200 Juneau St 99518

SOUTHSIDE BISTRO   907/348-0088   (36)
♦♦♦ American. Casual Dining. **Address:** 1320 Huffman Park Dr 99515

SPENARD ROADHOUSE   907/770-7623   (19)
♦♦♦ American. Casual Dining. **Address:** 1049 W Northern Lights Blvd 99503

(See map & index p. 496.)

SULLIVAN'S STEAKHOUSE   907/258-2882   13
💎💎💎 Steak. Fine Dining. **Address:** 320 W 5th Ave, Suite 100 99501

SUSHI YA JAPANESE RESTAURANT   907/522-2244   34
💎💎 Japanese. Casual Dining. **Address:** 1111 E Dimond Blvd 99515

SWEET BASIL CAFE   907/274-0070   20
💎 American. Quick Serve. **Address:** 1021 W Northern Lights Blvd 99503

YAK AND YETI HIMALAYAN RESTAURANT
    907/743-8078   22
💎💎 Indian. Casual Dining. **Address:** 3301 Spenard Rd 99503

BARROW (A-5) pop. 4,212, elev. 2'

The northernmost settlement in Alaska, Barrow is 340 miles north of the Arctic Circle on the edge of the omnipresent Arctic icepack. The sun does not go below the horizon for 82 days from early May to early August or rise above the horizon for 51 days between November and January. The town is reached by daily scheduled flights from Anchorage and Fairbanks. Husky sled dogs still are used, but snowmobiles have become more popular.

In 2016 voters approved changing the town's name to the traditional Utqiagvik (oot-ghar-vik) by a vote of 381 to 375; the community is one of the world's largest Inupiat Eskimo settlements. Although to some extent the people continue to follow their old traditions, the trend is toward a more modern way of life: The North Slope oil discovery created great wealth in the area.

The Post-Rogers Memorial, at the airport, commemorates the deaths of Will Rogers and his pilot, Wiley Post, who were killed in a 1935 plane crash 12 miles down the coast.

INUPIAT HERITAGE CENTER is at 5421 N. Star St. Historical exhibits as well as traditional craft demonstrations offer a comprehensive look at Inupiat culture. **Hours:** Mon.-Fri. 8:30-5, Sat.-Sun. 11-3, mid-May to mid-Sept.; otherwise varies. Phone ahead to confirm schedule. **Cost:** $10; $5 (ages 7-17 and college students with ID); free (ages 0-6 and 60+). **Phone:** (907) 852-0422.

CANTWELL pop. 219

BACKWOODS LODGE   907/987-0960
💎 Motel. **Address:** Denali Hwy MP 133.8 99729

CHUGACH NATIONAL FOREST (D-12)

Elevations in the forest range from sea level at the Pacific Ocean at Prince William Sound to 13,176 ft. at Mount Marcus Baker. Refer to AAA maps for additional elevation information.

Extending along the Gulf of Alaska from Cape Suckling to Seward, Chugach (CHEW-gatch) National Forest covers 5,500,000 acres, roughly as large as New Hampshire. It is second in size only to the Tongass National Forest (see place listing p. 535) and includes many of the islands and much of the land bordering Prince William Sound and the northeastern portion of the Kenai Peninsula.

Within the 700,000-acre Copper River Delta Wildlife Management Area just east of Cordova is one of the largest concentrations of trumpeter swans in North America. Also in abundance are dusky Canada geese, short-billed dowitchers, red-throated loons and green-winged teal. Prince William Sound has spectacular scenic opportunities with its 3,500 miles of coastline as well as dramatic tidewater glaciers and marine life that includes many species of whale.

Both saltwater and freshwater fishing are available in abundance in the forest. Halibut, red snapper, salmon and crabs are plentiful along the more than 3,500 miles of saltwater shoreline. Popular spots are Resurrection Bay at Seward and in Prince William Sound around Valdez and Cordova. Freshwater lakes and streams provide red salmon, Dolly Varden char and rainbow trout. A sportfishing license is required for all types of fishing within the forest.

For photographers and sport hunters, the forest offers a variety of big game, including black and brown bears, moose and Dall sheep. Hunting is subject to Alaska's fish and game management laws, seasons and bag limits.

Seward Highway offers 127 miles of scenic driving along saltwater bays, ice-blue glaciers and valleys dotted with native wildlife. The highway connects the cities of Anchorage and Seward. Bordering the forest on the northwest is SR 4; its scenic portion extends from Valdez to the junction of SR 10 west of Chitina. Portions of one of the most famous trails, The Historic Iditarod Trail, can be hiked, skied, dog sledded or explored on snowmobile.

In addition to 14 road-accessible campgrounds and 200 miles of hiking trails, the Forest Service operates 40 cabins in remote areas near lakes, bays and streams. Accessible by trail, boat or floatplane, the cabins are equipped with bunks, tables, chairs, wood or oil stoves and outdoor sanitary facilities, but not electricity.

The fee is $35-$45 per night per party. Reservations are required and can be made up to six months in advance. Further information also can be obtained from the Chugach National Forest, 161 E. 1st Ave., #8, Anchorage, AK 99501; phone (907) 743-9500. The U.S. Forest Service (8510 Mendenhall Loop Rd., Juneau, AK 99802) also can provide information; phone (907) 586-8800, (877) 444-6777 for reservations or TTY (907) 790-7444. See Recreation Areas Chart.

ALASKA WILDLIFE CONSERVATION CENTER, Seward Hwy. Milepost 79, is a 200-acre, drive-through wildlife refuge. Musk oxen, red foxes, lynx, wood bison, Sitka black-tailed deer, caribous, eagles, moose, reindeer, elk and bears may be seen on the drive. **Time:** Allow 30 minutes minimum. **Hours:** Daily 8-8, mid-May to mid-Sept.; daily 10-6, mid-Feb. to mid-May; daily 10-5, mid-Sept. through Nov. 30; daily 10-4 in Dec.; Sat.-Sun. 10-5, rest of year. Last admission is 30 minutes before closing. Phone ahead to confirm schedule. **Cost:** $12.50; $9 (ages 12-18, 65+ and active military with ID); free (ages 0-11). The maximum fee is $35 per carload. Pets are not permitted. **Phone:** (907) 783-2025.

PORTAGE GLACIER CRUISES depart 1.5 mi. s. of the Begich-Boggs Visitor Center in the Portage Glacier Recreation Area *(see attraction listing).* A 1-hour narrated cruise aboard the MV *Ptarmigan* takes passengers to the face of Portage Glacier. Sections of the glacier "calving" or breaking away into the lake below often can be seen. The 149-passenger ship has a climate-controlled cabin with oversize windows and an open-air observation deck. Shuttle and tour packages from Anchorage also are available.

Inquire about weather policies. **Time:** Allow 1 hour, 30 minutes minimum. **Hours:** Cruises depart daily at 10:30, noon, 1:30, 3 and 4:30, mid-May to mid-Sept. **Cost:** Fare $39; $19 (ages 2-12). **Phone:** (907) 277-5581 or (888) 425-1737.

PORTAGE GLACIER RECREATION AREA is 5.5 mi. e. from Milepost 79 of the Seward-Anchorage Hwy. Large icebergs calve off the face of the glacier into 650-foot-deep Portage Lake. An observation platform and a wayside exhibit are at the entrance to Williwaw Campground. Wayside exhibits also are available at Explorer Glacier. Iceworm safaris—hikes centered on spotting the elusive worms living in the glacier ice—are offered. **Hours:** The road to and within the area is open all year. **Phone:** (907) 783-3242. GT 🍴 🏕️

Begich-Boggs Visitor Center, off the Seward-Anchorage Hwy. on Portage Valley Rd., contains an observatory, orientation area, exhibit hall and learning center. A 20-minute film titled "Voices from the Ice" is shown every half hour. **Hours:** Daily 9-6, Memorial Day weekend to mid-Sept.; hours vary rest of year. Phone ahead to confirm schedule. **Cost:** Visitor center and film $5; free (ages 0-15). **Phone:** (907) 783-3242 (Oct.-Apr.), or (907) 783-2326 (May-Sept.).

COOPER LANDING (D-11) pop. 289

RECREATIONAL ACTIVITIES
Boating
- **Alaska Wildland Adventures** departs for Kenai River trips from the launch site on Sterling Hwy. (SR 1) Milepost 50.1. Other activities are offered. **Hours:** Daily May-Sept. **Phone:** (907) 783-2928 or (800) 334-8730.

KENAI PRINCESS WILDERNESS LODGE   (907)595-1425
▼▼▼▼ Hotel. **Address:** 17245 Frontier Cir 99572

WHERE TO EAT

EAGLE'S CREST DINING ROOM   907/595-1425
▼▼ ▼▼ American. Casual Dining. **Address:** 17245 Frontier Cir 99572

CORDOVA (D-12) pop. 2,239, elev. 100'

Cordova is located on the eastern shores of Prince William Sound and is surrounded by the Chugach Mountain Range and the Chugach National Forest. The town can be reached by air from Juneau and Anchorage or via the Alaska Marine Highway from Valdez and Whittier. In the early 1900s, Cordova was the terminus of the Copper River Northwest Railroad that carried copper ore from the Kennecott Mines in McCarthy. Today the town's industry focuses on commercial fishing.

Cordova Chamber of Commerce: 404 First St., Cordova, AK 99574. **Phone:** (907) 424-7260.

DELTA JUNCTION (B-12) pop. 958

The official northern terminus of the Alaska Highway, Delta Junction is one of the state's strongest agricultural producers. The town offers panoramic views of the Alaska Range as well as the Trans-Alaska Pipeline, the Delta Bison Range and glaciers.

DENALI NATIONAL PARK AND PRESERVE (B-10)
- **Hotels p. 508** • **Restaurants p. 509**

Elevations in the park and preserve range from 626 ft. at the northwest corner of the park at Chilcukabena Lake to the 20,310 ft. Denali. Refer to AAA maps for additional elevation information.

In the interior of Alaska, primitive and wild Denali National Park and Preserve covers 9,419 square miles and offers spectacular views of quiet lakes, snowcapped peaks and varicolored tundra. In addition to 20,310-foot Denali, the highest peak in North America, the park encompasses 17,400-foot Mount Foraker, 13,220-foot Silverthrone and 11,670-foot Mount Russell.

Denali, "the high one" in the Athabascan Indian language, was known for a time as Mount McKinley. It has two peaks: South Peak, the true summit, and 2 miles away, 19,470-foot North Peak. Most of the mountain is covered by ice and snow all year. Excellent views of the mountain are possible along the park road (weather permitting); clouds hide the summit about 75 percent of the time in summer and 60 percent the rest of the year.

The park's many glaciers originate on the slopes of the Alaska Range. Muldrow Glacier, the largest northward-flowing glacier in Alaska, stretches from between Denali's twin peaks to within a few miles of the park road; it can be seen from several vantage points.

More than 167 species of birds and 39 kinds of mammals inhabit the park; grizzly bears, moose, Dall sheep, wolves and caribous are some of the larger mammals. Equally varied is the vegetation. The chief conifers are black and white spruce, while dwarf birch grow in thickets on the lower slopes and along the intermountain valleys. Low, boggy meadows are the habitat of stunted, twisted black spruce.

Above the river valleys, forests give way to vast stretches of wet tundra supporting shrubby plants and often underlain by permafrost. Dry alpine tundra blankets the slopes and ridges at the higher elevations.

General Information and Activities

From Anchorage and Fairbanks, the George Parks Highway (SR 3) provides access to the park all year, and SR 8 from Paxson is usually open from early June to mid-October. The park also is accessible from Anchorage or Fairbanks via the Alaska Railroad; there is daily service from late May to mid-September. Trains run northbound to Fairbanks on Saturday and southbound to Anchorage on Sunday the rest of the year. Charter flights are available from principal airports. Visitors often stay in the year-round community of Healy *(see place listing p. 517),* which is 11 miles from the park entrance.

Denali Park Road, beginning at SR 3 at the park's eastern boundary, runs about 90 miles westward through the park, terminating at a partly abandoned mining town, Kantishna. Only the first 14.8 miles to Savage River are paved, and most of the road is narrow with many sharp curves. It is usually open from early June to mid-September. The George Parks Highway (SR 3) runs along the eastern border of the park and offers sweeping views of the park's alpine scenery from Willow to Nenana.

Private vehicles may be used only on the first 14.8 miles of Denali Park Road unless you have a registered campsite at Teklanika Campground. Transportation beyond Savage River or to Sanctuary, Igloo and Wonder Lake campgrounds is provided by shuttle buses that operate to Toklat, Wonder Lake and other points in the park.

Fare for the shuttle varies with destination. Fare to Kantishna $51; free (ages 0-15). Fare to Wonder Lake $46.75; free (ages 0-15). Fare to Toklat and Polychrome $26.50; free (ages 0-15). Fare to Eielson Visitor Center $34; free (ages 0-15). Three- and 6-day trip passes are available; prices vary by destination. These fares do not include the park admission fees.

More than half of the shuttle seats can be reserved by telephone and Internet; phone (907) 272-7275 or (800) 622-7275 in advance. The rest of the spaces can be reserved only in person within 2 days of departure; phone (907) 683-9274 for more information. Buses depart approximately every half-hour beginning at 5:15 a.m. from the Wilderness Access Center near the entrance at Milepost 0.5 on Denali Park Road. The bus stops to view wildlife when conditions are safe. Shuttle buses also drop off and pick up passengers along the park road on a space-available basis. The center houses a small theater.

The Denali Visitor Center, Milepost 1.5 on Denali Park Road, has an information desk, exhibits, a 20-minute film, a bookstore and interpretive programs. It is open daily 8-6, mid-May to mid-September. Only accessible by shuttle bus, the Eielson Visitor Center, Milepost 66 on Denali Park Road, displays "Seasons of Denali," a quilt by fabric artist Ree Nancarrow. The center is open daily 9-7, June 1 to mid-September.

The Murie Science and Learning Center, at Milepost 1.4 on Denali Park Road, is dedicated to research and education about America's eight northernmost national parks and offers field seminars and educational programs. It is open daily 9-4:30; closed major winter holidays. Phone (907) 683-6432.

The Talkeetna Ranger Station, Milepost 98 on George Parks Highway (SR 3), also offers interpretive programs and is open daily 8-5:30, mid-April through Labor Day; Mon.-Fri. 8-4:30, rest of year. Phone (907) 733-2231.

To camp outside the established campgrounds, stop at the Wilderness Access Center for a backcountry permit. Reservations for all campgrounds may be made here.

Sled dog demonstrations are given by rangers at the park kennels, Milepost 3 on Denali Park Road. The 40-minute presentations are offered daily at 10, 2 and 4, June through August; phone ahead for availability. Ranger-naturalists also present various lectures, hikes and other activities daily at various campgrounds. Information about activities is available at the park Visitor Center and ranger stations, or pick up a copy of the park's informational newspaper, *Denali Alpenglow.*

Guided and self-guiding hikes are available along several nature trails with trailheads along the paved portion of the park road. Throughout the rest of the park, hiking is generally cross-country. The Spruce Forest Trail loop takes about 15 minutes, while the Morino Trail takes 30 minutes to complete. Backcountry permits are available from the Backcountry Information Center, adjacent to the Wilderness Access Center. The park offers several ranger-guided hikes. The hikes are free; however, hikers must purchase shuttle bus tickets to reach the various trails that do not originate at the Denali Visitor Center. Fares are $26.50-$51; free (ages 0-15) depending on the trailhead.

Do not feed or disturb wildlife. Grizzly bears in particular can be dangerous; inquire at the Visitor Center about how to avoid close encounters with grizzlies. Firearms must be declared and made inoperative when you enter the park; hunting and shooting are forbidden.

Most fishing is poor in the park; only streams that are free of glacial silt are good fishing spots. No license is required within the national park; the daily creel limit is 10 fish, only two of which may be lake trout. An Alaska fishing license is required in the national preserve areas. Check at a ranger station for further information.

Temperatures during the park season can vary from 40 to 80 degrees Fahrenheit, with an average of 50 to 54 degrees June through August. Daylight generally lasts for more than 18 hours during the summer months.

Morino Grill, a cafeteria-style restaurant, is next to the Denali Visitor Center. A store near the park entrance contains supplies, but no gas is available; the store is open approximately 7 a.m.-9 p.m. during peak season, shorter hours at other times. A gas station north of the park entrance on George Parks Highway (SR 3) is open in the summer. Food and supplies also are available at Riley Creek campground just inside the park boundaries. *See Recreation Areas Chart.*

ADMISSION , valid for 7 days, is $10 per person; free (ages 0-15).

PETS are permitted in the park only if they are leashed or otherwise physically restrained; they are not allowed on trails, shuttle buses or in the backcountry.

ADDRESS inquiries to the Superintendent, Denali National Park and Preserve, P.O. Box 9, Denali Park, AK 99755; phone (907) 683-9532 or (800) 622-7275 for reservations.

ALASKA CABIN NITE DINNER THEATER is 1.7 mi. n. of the park entrance on George Parks Hwy. (SR 3) at Milepost 239. The theater presents a 1915-style dinner show that highlights Alaska's goldmining history. A pre-show dinner is served familystyle. **Time:** Allow 2 hours minimum. **Hours:** Shows Mon.-Fri. at 5 and 7:30 p.m., mid-May to mid-Sept. Phone ahead to confirm schedule. **Cost:** $75; $37.50 (ages 3-15). Reservations are required. **Phone:** (907) 683-8200, or (800) 276-7234 for reservations. [TI]

DENALI AIR is 10 mi. s. on George Parks Hwy. (SR 3) at Milepost 229.5. Commentary about history, scenery and topography complements an hour-long flight along the Alaska Range and around Denali. **Time:** Allow 1 hour minimum. **Hours:** Flights depart every even hour daily 8-8 (weather permitting), mid-May to mid-Sept. **Cost:** Fare $405; $205 (ages 2-12). Reservations are recommended. **Phone:** (907) 683-2261.

DENALI BACKCOUNTRY ADVENTURE departs from Denali Cabins, Milepost 229, George Parks Hwy. (SR 3), 9 mi. s. of park entrance or from the Alaska Railroad Depot. This narrated bus tour travels along the 95-mile Denali Park Road to Denali Backcountry Lodge in Kantishna. Along the route, the guide points out wildlife such as moose and caribou, and makes stops at various times for photography. The complete trip lasts 13 hours and includes either gold panning or a guided nature walk to Fannie Quigley's historic pioneer cabin. Lunch and snacks are provided.

Allow a full day. **Hours:** Tours depart daily at 6 a.m., early June to mid-Sept. **Cost:** Fee $184 (plus $10 per person park entrance fee). **Phone:** (907) 376-1992 or (877) 376-1992. *(See ad p. 490, p. 508, p. 507.)* [GT] [TI]

DENALI NATURAL HISTORY TOUR, departing from area hotels, takes visitors on a bus tour across sections of the park where they can enjoy views of the Alaska Range from Denali to Mount Deborah. Driverguides explain the region's natural history, unusual geological formations and local flora and fauna. A stop at the Wilderness Access Center allows time to view the film "Across Time and Tundra."

Time: Allow 4 hours, 45 minutes minimum. **Hours:** Trips depart daily 6-9 a.m. and 1:30-3:30, mid-May to mid-Sept. Phone ahead to confirm schedule. **Cost:** Fare (includes park admission and a snack) $81.10; $35.45 (ages 0-15). **Phone:** (907) 272-7275 or (800) 276-7234. [GT]

DENALI WILDERNESS SAFARIS, at Milepost 216 on George Parks Hwy. (SR 3), offers 3-hour heated jet boat rides or 3-hour sled dog-pulled cart rides to a camp in the Alaskan "bush" country, where locals share their methods of hunting, prospecting and trapping. Gold panning opportunities are presented. Free transportation is provided from all area hotels. **Hours:** Wilderness boat trips and dog sled rides depart daily at 8, 2:30 and 6, mid-May to mid-Sept. **Cost:** Boat fare $129; $89 (ages 0-12); free (active military with ID). Dog sled $99; $69 (ages 0-12); free (active military with ID). Fees include a snack. Reservations are recommended. **Phone:** (907) 768-2550.

ERA HELICOPTERS FLIGHTSEEING TOURS, 1 Glacier Way, offers a narrated 35-minute aerial flight over Denali National Park. A 70-minute glacier landing tour consists of 50 minutes in the air and 20 minutes on the ice. Five-hour heli-hiking excursions also are available. Caribous, moose and Dall sheep can often be seen in the valleys. Free transportation is provided from area hotels. **Hours:** Daily 7-7, May-Sept. **Cost:** Tours range from $375-$560. Flights require a minimum of four passengers. **Phone:** (907) 683-2574 or (800) 843-1947.

FLY DENALI departs from the entrance of Denali National Park and Preserve, 224 George Parks Hwy., for scenic flightseeing tours, and provides complimentary shuttle service around the park. Its specialty tour features a 2-hour trip around Denali, including the Great Gorge of the Ruth and Ruth Amphitheater, and glacier landing. Departing Healy River State Airport, the 60-minute Denali Quest and Park flight explores the eastern end of the park.

Note: Inquire about weather policies and weight restrictions. **Time:** Allow 3 hours minimum. **Hours:** Tours depart daily at 8:30, noon, 3:15 and 6:15, May 10 to mid-Sept. **Cost:** Denali Glacier Landing $524; $393 (ages 0-9). Denali Quest and Park Flight $399; $299.25 (ages 0-9). Reservations are required. **Phone:** (907) 683-2359, or (877) 770-2359 Sales.

KANTISHNA EXPERIENCE TOUR departs from local hotels. This bus tour takes visitors along the Gold Rush trails once traveled by pioneer Fannie

Quigley to Kantishna. An interpretive park ranger explains in detail the region's geology, flora and fauna as well as the history of Kantishna on the 11- to 12-hour tours. The trip is 92 miles each way. Guests may bring binoculars for a better view of such wildlife as moose, caribou and bears.

Note: Guests are advised to dress in layers. The tour is not recommended for the physically impaired. **Time:** Allow 12 hours minimum. **Hours:** Trips depart daily 6:15 and 7:30 a.m. from area hotels, early June to mid-Aug.; daily 7:30 a.m., late Aug. to mid-Sept. Phone ahead to confirm schedule. **Cost:** Fare (includes park admission, lunch, beverages and snacks) $203.70; $96.60 (ages 0-15). Reservations are required. **Phone:** (907) 272-7275 or (800) 276-7234. 🍴

TUNDRA WILDERNESS TOURS picks up visitors at local hotels. Buses travel to Toklat River, making frequent stops en route for photography. Driver-guides explain in detail the region's geology, flora and fauna on the 7- to 8-hour tours. Binoculars are recommended for spotting moose, caribous, bears and other wildlife.

Inquire about weather policies. **Hours:** Trips depart daily 5-9 a.m. and 1:30-3:30 p.m., mid-May to mid-Sept. Phone ahead to confirm schedule. **Cost:** Fare (includes park admission and a box lunch)

$69.85-$136.75; $29.65-$63.25 (ages 0-15). Reservations are recommended. **Phone:** (907) 272-7275 or (800) 276-7234.

RECREATIONAL ACTIVITIES
White-water Rafting
- **Alaska Raft Adventures** departs from the McKinley Chalet at Milepost 238 on George Parks Hwy. (SR 3). **Hours:** Trips depart daily at 7:30, 1:30 and 6, mid-May to mid-Aug.; daily 7:30, 1:30 and 5:30, late Aug. to mid-Sept. **Phone:** (907) 276-7234 or (800) 276-7234.
- **Denali Raft Adventures, Inc.** is .5 mi. n. of the park entrance at Milepost 238.6 on George Parks

Hwy. (SR 3). **Hours:** Trips depart daily mid-May to mid-Sept.; check-in times vary depending on trip. **Phone:** (907) 683-2234 or (888) 683-2234.

DENALI BLUFFS HOTEL   907/683-7000
◆◆ Hotel. **Address:** Milepost 238.4 Parks Hwy 99755

DENALI CABINS   (907)376-1900
◆ Cabin. **Address:** Milepost 229 Parks Hwy 99755 *(See ad p. 490, this page, p. 507.)*

DENALI PRINCESS WILDERNESS LODGE   (907)683-2282
◆◆◆ Hotel. **Address:** Milepost 238.5 Parks Hwy 99755

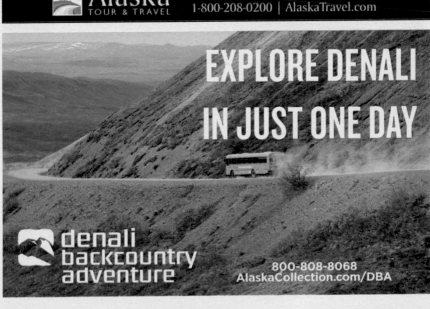

GRANDE DENALI LODGE   907/683-5100
 Hotel. **Address:** Milepost 238.2 Parks Hwy 99755

MCKINLEY CHALET RESORT   (907)683-6450
 Hotel. **Address:** Milepost 238.9 Parks Hwy 99755

MCKINLEY CREEKSIDE CABINS & CAFE
    (907)683-2277

Cabin
$229-$369

Address: Milepost 224 Parks Hwy 99755 **Location:** 13 mi s; Milepost 224, on SR 3 (Parks Hwy). **Facility:** 32 cabins. 1 story, exterior corridors. **Terms:** closed 9/15-5/15, check-in 4 pm, 14 day cancellation notice-fee imposed. **Dining:** Creekside Cafe, see separate listing.

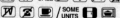

DENALI BACKCOUNTRY LODGE   907/376-1900
(fyi) Not evaluated; located in remote area. **Address:** MM 95 Denali Park Rd 99755 *(See ad p. 490, p. 508, p. 507.)*

WHERE TO EAT

CREEKSIDE CAFE   907/683-2277
 American. Casual Dining. **Address:** Milepost 224 Parks Hwy 99755

KING SALMON   907/683-2282
 American. Casual Dining. **Address:** Milepost 238.5 Parks Hwy 99755

MORINO GRILL   907/683-9225
 American. Quick Serve. **Address:** Denali Visitor Center 99755

THE PERCH   907/683-2523
 Regional American. Casual Dining. **Address:** Milepost 224 (Parks Hwy) 99755

PROSPECTORS PIZZERIA & ALEHOUSE   907/683-7437
 American. Casual Dining. **Address:** Milepost 238.9 Parks Hwy 99755

DENALI STATE PARK

MT. MCKINLEY PRINCESS WILDERNESS LODGE
    (907)733-2900
 Resort Hotel. **Address:** Milepost 133.1 Parks Hwy 99683

DOUGLAS

THE ISLAND PUB   907/364-1595
 Pizza. Gastropub. **Address:** 1102 2nd St 99824

EAGLE (D-8) pop. 86

Eagle was settled in 1897 by 28 miners who named the town after the bald eagles that nested on the nearby bluff. In 1899, the Army established Fort Egbert and within several years, some 37 military buildings were constructed. Founded along the Yukon River near the Canadian border, Eagle is the only planned town of the gold rush.

Eagle Historical Society: P.O. Box 23, Eagle, AK 99738. **Phone:** (907) 547-2325.

EAGLE MUSEUMS are all within 1 sq. mi. of town. Tours depart from the courthouse at First and Berry sts. Visitors can join a walking tour that includes six restored buildings, including Judge James Wickersham's original courthouse, the Army Mule Barn, Redman Lodge, Customs House, St. Paul's Log Church and the Waterwagon Shed. Each building contains memorabilia portraying the small town's history. **Time:** Allow 2 hours minimum. **Hours:** Tours depart Mon.-Sat. at 9 and 1, Sun. at 9 and 2:30, Memorial Day-Labor Day. Phone ahead to confirm schedule. **Cost:** $7; free (ages 0-11). **Phone:** (907) 547-2325.

EAGLE RIVER (C-11)

CHUGACH STATE PARK is e. on Glenn Hwy. Wildlife populations flourish within the park's 700 square miles of mountains, rivers, lakes and glaciers, providing many opportunities for viewing moose and beavers as well as the occasional bear or wolf. Major areas are Eklutna Lake, Eagle River, Anchorage Hillside and Turnagain Arm. A number of recreational activities are available. The park's headquarters is in the historic Potter Section House, at Milepost 115 of the Seward Highway. *See Recreation Areas Chart.*

Hours: Headquarters open Mon.-Fri. 10-noon and 1-4:30. **Cost:** Free. **Parking:** $5 at many trailheads. **Phone:** (907) 345-5014.

EKLUTNA (C-11)

About 30 miles north of Anchorage, the village of Eklutna has been home to the Dena'ina Athabascan Indians for more than 350 years. In the 1840s, Russian Orthodox missionaries came to convert the natives, and today the village exhibits traits of both Russian and Dena'ina Athabascan cultures.

The circa 1830 St. Nicholas Russian Orthodox Church was reconstructed in the 1970s. Next to the 1830 structure is a newer church; built in the 1960s, the diminutive white building is topped by a cupola, two small onion-shaped domes and two three-bar crosses. The church still holds religious services and also houses Russian icons.

Adjacent to the church, colorfully painted spirit houses adorn gravesites at the Eklutna Cemetery, which dates to the 1650s and remains in use. Built to hold the souls of the deceased, the shapes and colors of the spirit houses denote their family and status. The churches and cemetery are located at the Eklutna Historical Park, Milepost 26 on Glenn Highway, where you can see religious relics and historic artifacts at the Eklutna Village Heritage House. The park is open Mon.-Sat. 10-5, mid-May through Sept. 30. A small admission fee is charged; phone (907) 688-6026 to confirm schedule.

FAIRBANKS (D-6) pop. 31,535, elev. 432'
• Hotels p. 513 • Restaurants p. 514
• Attractions map p. 510

Fairbanks, near the geographical center of Alaska, is a major visitor center and the northern terminus of the Alaska Railroad. The military, transportation and market nucleus of the Alaskan interior, Fairbanks is a supply point for arctic oil operations and a departure point for airlines statewide.

In 1901 Capt. E.T. Barnette founded a trading post where Fairbanks now stands—a riverboat captain refused to ferry him any farther up the Chena River due to the low water level. Gold was discovered nearby a year later, and the first wave of prospectors flooded up the river. The settlement was named for Charles Warren Fairbanks of Indiana, a U.S. senator who later became vice president to Theodore Roosevelt.

The construction of the Alaska Highway and the influx of the military into Fairbanks heralded a second boom. And in 1968 the discovery of oil in Prudhoe Bay, 390 miles north, triggered a third wave of development.

Fairbanks offers a variety of winter sports and other activities, including aurora viewing, cross-country and downhill skiing, curling, ice hockey and dog mushing. The city's geographical location allows the semiprofessional Alaska Goldpanners team to play its ⬥ Midnight Sun Baseball Game at 10:30 p.m. on June 21 without using artificial lighting.

The Robert G. White Large Animal Research Station, 2220 Yankovich Rd., is a 134-acre facility offering .25-mile narrated walking tours of its grounds, allowing visitors to observe caribou, musk oxen and reindeer. Tours are conducted June-Aug. Phone (907) 474-5724.

Local sightseeing tours to Alaska's arctic zone and other remote places are available from Fairbanks. Using railway cars with skylights, Gray Line of Alaska and Princess Tours offer trips between Anchorage and Fairbanks via Denali National Park and Preserve. Canoes for trips on the Chena River can be rented from several outfitters.

Interesting drives include visits to Chena Hot Springs and the town of Ester. Abandoned gold dredges can be seen outside of Fairbanks along the roads to Chatanika and Ester. The Alaska Public Lands Information Center, at the Morris Thompson Cultural and Visitors Center at 101 Dunkel St., has museum exhibits, shows free movies and offers information about public lands and parks; phone (907) 459-3700 or (866) 869-6887.

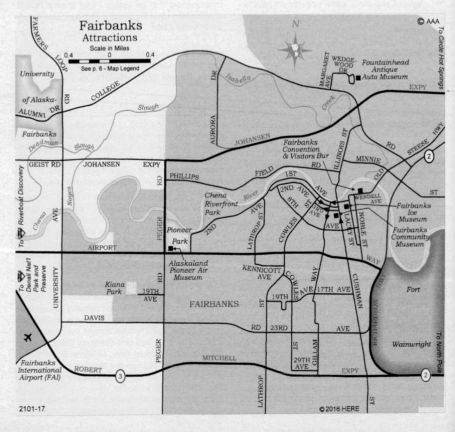

Fairbanks Attractions

Scale in Miles
0.4   0   0.4

See p. 6 - Map Legend

© 2016 HERE

Be inspired by the light of the Aurora Borealis.
Renew your energy under the Midnight Sun.
Experience the warmth of Fairbanks—Alaska's
Golden Heart—and the gateway to Denali, Interior
and Arctic Alaska. Make the Morris Thompson
Cultural and Visitors Center your first stop to
planning your Alaskan adventure.

Morris Thompson Cultural and Visitors Center
101 Dunkel Street • Downtown Fairbanks
8am – 9pm Summer • 8am – 5pm Winter

www.explorefairbanks.com
(907) 456-5774
info@explorefairbanks.com

Explore Fairbanks: 101 Dunkel St., Suite 111, Fairbanks, AK 99701. **Phone:** (907) 456-5774 or (800) 327-5774. *(See ad p. 511.)*

Self-guiding tours: Information about a historical walking tour is available from the Fairbanks Visitor Information Center, 101 Dunkel St.

FOUNTAINHEAD ANTIQUE AUTO MUSEUM is off Johansen Expwy. exit 4 (College Rd.), just w. on College Rd., then .2 mi. n. on Margaret Ave.; the museum is at 212 Wedgewood Dr. on the grounds of the Wedgewood Resort. The museum's collection of more than 85 pristine working condition automobiles, which date from the turn of the 20th century to the late 1930s, includes the only surviving 1920 Argonne; a 1917 Owen-Magnetic M-25 Touring, a gas hybrid; and series of early and rare examples that explain the expanding technical changes.

Other exhibits include historical photographs and vintage clothing displays. One-hour guided tours of the vehicles, 55 of which are displayed at any given time, are offered.

Time: Allow 1 hour minimum. **Hours:** Sun.-Thurs. 10-8, Fri.-Sat. 11-6, mid-May to mid-Sept.; Sun. noon-6, rest of year. Phone ahead to confirm schedule. **Cost:** $10; $5 (ages 6-12 and Fountainhead Hotel guests). Guided tour prices vary; phone ahead. Reservations and a minimum of 2 people are required for guided tours. **Phone:** (907) 450-2100 or (800) 528-4916.

NORTHERN ALASKA TOUR COMPANY departs from the e. ramp of the Fairbanks International Airport. Tours highlight the natural and cultural aspects of Alaska's arctic region. Excursions, which last a full day to multiple days, explore the arctic circle by plane, or bus along the Dalton Highway. Other trips visit the Anaktuvuk Pass, Beaver Village, Brooks Range, Barrow and the Arctic Ocean. Guides offer insight along the route. **Time:** Allow 1 hour minimum. **Hours:** Tours depart daily, mid-May to mid-Sept.; Mon.-Sat., rest of year. Hours vary by trip. **Cost:** Fare $219-$1,599. Reservations are required. **Phone:** (907) 474-8600 or (800) 474-1986. *(See ad this page.)*

PIONEER PARK is at 2300 Airport Way. The pioneer theme park offers four museums; the Kitty Hensley and Wickersham houses, two restored early 20th-century dwellings; the renovated *S.S. Nenana,* one of the largest wooden sternwheelers ever constructed; Red & Roela's Carousel; and a train that travels and offers unique views of the park. Such activities as miniature golf are provided; bocce courts as well as horseshoe and volleyball areas also are on the premises. A revue show at The Palace Theatre and The Big Stampede show at Pioneer Hall also are offered.

Hours: Park open daily 24 hours, year-round. Vendors open noon-8, Memorial Day-Labor Day. Train trips depart every 15 minutes noon-4 and 5-7:45. Palace Theater show nightly at 8:15. Theater show is not recommended for children under 13. Big Stampede shows are presented daily at 11:30, 1, 2:30 and 4. **Cost:** Park free. Train ride $2; $1 (ages 4-13). Palace Theater show $19.95; $9 (ages 4-13). Big Stampede show $4; $2 (ages 6-16). Carousel $3. Train $2; $1 (ages 0-12). A small fee is applicable at several of the attractions and museums. **Phone:** (907) 459-1087. 🍴 🎡

Alaskaland Pioneer Air Museum, in Pioneer Park, is housed in a gold-domed building and offers an aeronautical collection consisting of 14 intact aircraft, including a Stinson SR-5 Junior and a UH-1 Iroquois "Huey" helicopter, as well as a variety of recovered plane wrecks. A large assortment of flight

▼ *See AAA listing this page* ▼

records, newspaper articles, pilot manuscripts and some 500 photographs details the history of solo aviators, early flight and selected airlines. Such items as engines, propellers, model aircraft and memorabilia also are displayed.

Time: Allow 1 hour minimum. **Hours:** Daily noon-8, mid-May to mid-Sept. **Cost:** $4; free (ages 0-12); $8 (four adults). **Phone:** (907) 451-0037. GT

RIVERBOAT DISCOVERY, departing from a pier on Discovery Rd. off Airport Way, provides 3.5-hour trips on the Chena and Tanana rivers aboard the stern-wheeler *Discovery III*. Guides discuss area wildlife, history, anthropology, geology and customs. Views vary from wilderness to elegant houses, and the trip includes a guided walking tour of the Chena Indian village. **Hours:** Trips depart daily at 9 and 2, mid-May to mid-Sept. Phone ahead to confirm schedule. **Cost:** Fare $62.95; $39.95 (ages 3-12). Reservations are required. **Phone:** (907) 479-6673 or (866) 479-6673. *(See ad this page.)*

TRANS ARCTIC CIRCLE TREKS is at 3820 University Ave. This tour company offers a variety of guided excursions including day trips to the Arctic Circle and multi-day trips to the Arctic Ocean, Brooks Range, Prudhoe Bay and Point Barrow. Visitors on the 1-day tour can enjoy mountain scenery, a walk through alpine tundra and a hands-on Trans-Alaska Pipeline demonstration. Add-on land and air excursions are available.

Hours: One-day tour departs daily June-Aug.; departs 3-5 days per week in May and Sept. Other tours depart throughout the year. Phone ahead to confirm schedule. **Cost:** Fare for 1-day tour $219. Rates vary according to tour; phone ahead. Reservations are required. **Phone:** (907) 479-5451 or (800) 336-8735.

A TASTE OF ALASKA LODGE 907/488-7855
 Bed & Breakfast. **Address:** 551 Eberhardt Rd 99712

BEST WESTERN PLUS CHENA RIVER LODGE
(907)328-3500

 Hotel $75-S304   Best Western PLUS. **AAA Benefit:** Save 10% or more every day and earn 10% bonus points!

 Address: 1255 Tvsa Way 99709 **Location:** Jct Airport and Sportsman ways, just w on Boat St. **Facility:** 67 units. 3 stories, interior corridors. **Parking:** winter plug-ins. **Terms:** check-in 4 pm. **Activities:** exercise room. **Guest Services:** coin laundry, area transportation. **Featured Amenity:** full hot breakfast.

BEST WESTERN PLUS PIONEER PARK INN
(907)479-8080

 Hotel $89-S129 Best Western PLUS. **AAA Benefit:** Save 10% or more every day and earn 10% bonus points!

 Address: 1908 Chena Landings Loop Rd 99701 **Location:** From airport, exit Peger Rd, 1 mi n, just e on Phillips Field Rd, then just s. **Facility:** 74 units. 3 stories, interior corridors. **Parking:** winter plug-ins. **Terms:** check-in 4 pm, resort fee. **Pool(s):** heated indoor. **Activities:** exercise room. **Guest Services:** complimentary laundry, area transportation.

BRIDGEWATER HOTEL (907)452-6661
 Hotel. **Address:** 723 1st Ave 99701

▼ See AAA listing this page ▼

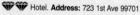

FAIRBANKS HAMPTON INN & SUITES (907)451-1502

▼▼▼ Hotel. **Address:** 433 Harold Bentley Ave 99701

FAIRBANKS PRINCESS RIVERSIDE LODGE (907)455-4477

▼▼ Hotel. **Address:** 4477 Pikes Landing Rd 99709

HOLIDAY INN EXPRESS 907/328-1100

▼▼▼ Hotel. **Address:** 400 Merhar Ave 99701

MINNIE STREET INN 907/456-1802

▼▼ Boutique Bed & Breakfast. **Address:** 345 Minnie St 99701

PIKE'S WATERFRONT LODGE 907/456-4500

▼▼▼▼ Hotel
Rates not provided

Address: 1850 Hoselton Dr 99709 **Location:** Waterfront. Jct Airport Way and Hoselton Dr. **Facility:** 208 units, some cabins. 1-3 stories, interior/exterior corridors. **Parking:** winter plug-ins. **Amenities:** *Some:* safes. **Dining:** Pike's Landing Restaurant, see separate listing. **Activities:** steamroom, boat dock, fishing, miniature golf, lawn sports, exercise room. **Guest Services:** valet and coin laundry, boarding pass kiosk, area transportation. **Featured Amenity:** breakfast buffet.

SAVE ✈ ♦ ▼ BIZ 🛜 ✕
🔌 📷 💻 /SOME UNITS 🛏 HS

RIVER'S EDGE RESORT (907)474-0286

▼▼▼ Cottage $159-$259

Address: 4200 Boat St 99709 **Location:** Waterfront. Airport Way, just n on Sportsman Way, 0.5 mi w. **Facility:** 94 units, some cottages. 1-2 stories (no elevator), interior/exterior corridors. **Terms:** closed 9/16-5/14, cancellation fee imposed. **Dining:** Chena's Alaskan Grill, see separate listing. **Guest Services:** coin laundry, area transportation.

SAVE ✈ ♦ ▼ CALL 🅼
BIZ 🛜 ✕ 💻

♦RIVER'S EDGE ♦RESORT *A most unique hotel*

Restaurant & bar on-site serving breakfast & dinner on the Chena River. Alaska at its Finest.

SOPHIE STATION SUITES (907)479-3650

▼▼ Extended Stay Hotel. **Address:** 1717 University Ave S 99709

SPRINGHILL SUITES BY MARRIOTT (907)451-6552

▼▼▼ Hotel. **Address:** 575 1st Ave 99701

WEDGEWOOD RESORT (907)452-1442

▼▼ Extended Stay Hotel. **Address:** 212 Wedgewood Dr 99701

WESTMARK FAIRBANKS HOTEL & CONFERENCE CENTER (907)456-7722

▼▼ Hotel. **Address:** 813 Noble St 99701

WHERE TO EAT

ALASKA COFFEE ROASTING CO 907/457-5282

▼ Coffee/Tea Desserts. Quick Serve. **Address:** 4001 Geist Rd 99709

ALASKA SALMON BAKE 907/452-7274

▼ Seafood. Casual Dining. **Address:** 3175 College Rd, #1 99709

BOBBY'S DOWNTOWN 907/456-3222

▼▼ Greek. Casual Dining. **Address:** 609 2nd Ave 99701

CHENA'S ALASKAN GRILL 907/474-3644

▼▼ American. Casual Dining. **Address:** 4200 Boat St 99709

THE COOKIE JAR RESTAURANT 907/479-8319

▼▼ American. Casual Dining. **Address:** 1006 Cadillac Ct 99701

GERALDO'S ITALIAN RESTAURANT 907/452-2299

▼▼ Italian. Casual Dining. **Address:** 701 College Rd 99701

HOT LICKS 907/479-7813

▼ Desserts. Quick Serve. **Address:** 372 Old Chena Pump Rd 99708

LAVELLE'S BISTRO 907/450-0555

▼▼▼ Regional American. Casual Dining. **Address:** 575 1st Ave 99701

LEMONGRASS 907/456-2200

▼▼ Thai. Casual Dining. **Address:** 388 Chena Pump Rd, Suite K 99709

LULU'S BREAD & BAGELS 907/374-3804

▼ Breads/Pastries. Quick Serve. **Address:** 388 Chena Pump Rd, Suite A 99709

PIKE'S LANDING RESTAURANT 907/479-6500

▼▼ American. Casual Dining. **Address:** 1850 Hoselton Dr 99709

THE PUMP HOUSE RESTAURANT & SALOON
907/479-8452

▼▼ ▼▼
American
Casual Dining
$14-$48

AAA Inspector Notes: *Historic.* An authentic former tin pump house used in gold-mining operations, this restaurant is listed on the National Register of Historic Places. The décor exudes a warm Victorian mining era charm. The large deck and glassed-in dining area afford great views of the Chena River. Fresh oysters feature on the menu, as do a variety of Alaskan seafood, steaks and other game meats. It's closed Mondays during the winter. **Features:** full bar, patio dining, Sunday brunch. **Reservations:** suggested. **Address:** 796 Chena Pump Rd 99708 **Location:** Jct Parks Hwy and Geist Rd, just e to Chena Pump Rd, 1.3 mi s. L D CALL 🅼

THAI HOUSE RESTAURANT 907/452-6123

▼▼ Thai. Casual Dining. **Address:** 412 5th Ave 99701

THE TURTLE CLUB 907/457-3883

▼▼ American. Casual Dining. **Address:** 2098 Old Steese Hwy 99712

WOLF RUN RESTAURANT 907/458-0636

▼▼ American. Casual Dining. **Address:** 3360 Wolf Run 99709

FORT YUKON (C-7) pop. 583

Just 8 miles north of the Arctic Circle at a point where the Yukon River is almost 3 miles wide, the Athabascan Indian village of Fort Yukon was established as a trading post by the Hudson's Bay Co. in 1847. The village was an important port during the gold rush days, and the post office has remained popular for those who wish to mail from above the Arctic Circle.

Fort Yukon is reached by daily air service from Fairbanks; flight time is approximately 1 hour. Visitors travel here for spectacular viewings of the northern lights and may also see fish wheels in operation and purchase craftwork and fine furs. Temperatures have ranged as high as 100 degrees Fahrenheit in the summer and as low as minus 78 degrees Fahrenheit in winter.

GATES OF THE ARCTIC NATIONAL PARK AND PRESERVE (B-5)

Elevations in the park and preserve range from 300 ft. along the Kobuk River to 8,510 ft. at Mount Igikpak. Refer to AAA maps for additional elevation information.

Lying north of the Arctic Circle, Gates of the Arctic National Park and Preserve's 8.5 million acres features a raw, austere landscape of sparse vegetation and jagged spires. The rocky spine of the Brooks Range forms the park's backbone, and a boreal forest, or taiga, of spruce, birch and poplar meets the almost treeless tundra that rolls uninterrupted to the Arctic Ocean.

Despite being four times the size of Yellowstone National Park, Gates of the Arctic is a meager larder for the caribou, moose, wolves and bears that roam the park in search of food. Fortunately much of their arctic range is protected, as Gates of the Arctic is joined on either side by Noatak National Preserve and nearby Arctic National Wildlife Refuge.

It was a forester on leave, Bob Marshall, who, in exploring this uncharted region in the late 1930s, christened this land Gates of the Arctic. The term both describes and evokes the grandeur of this wilderness—the soaring immensity of sky and mountains, the burst of wildflowers in summer and the cyclical abundance of wildlife.

But as Marshall remarked, the greatest pleasure is its undeveloped and wild character, which gives the visitor the sense of being the first to visit the tundra foothills or one of the park's nameless peaks. Today a good way to enjoy the park is to follow Marshall's example and hike the park's rugged terrain, which offers challenging backpacking. A popular alternative is to canoe or raft the network of rivers and lakes.

Most visitors use various air charter services from Fairbanks and Bettles Field to reach the park's interior. The Dalton Highway skirts the park's eastern edge and is the only road that approaches the park. Because of Gates of the Arctic's fragile ecology,

there are no park facilities, trails or campgrounds within the park.

Bettles Ranger Station and Visitor Center open daily 8-5, mid-June through Sept. 30; Mon.-Fri. 1-5, rest of year. For trip planning assistance and a list of outfitters, guides and air taxi operators, write Gates of the Arctic National Park and Preserve, P.O. Box 30, Bettles, AK 99726; phone (907) 692-5494. *See Recreation Areas Chart.*

GIRDWOOD (C-11) elev. 23'

Initially called Glacier City, Girdwood was established at the turn of the 20th century as a gold mining town. The community prospered until mine closures in the 1930s reduced it to a virtual ghost town. Misfortune struck again when the 1964 Good Friday earthquake caused massive destruction along the coast, forcing residents to move the town 2.5 miles inland to its present location. Today Girdwood thrives as a year-round recreation destination.

Girdwood is on Turnagain Arm, a fjord carved by glaciers and known for its dramatic bore tides, which can be 6 feet high and travel at speeds of up to 15 miles an hour. The town also is located at the base of 3,939-foot Mount Alyeska; a 60-passenger tramway ascends to the 2,300-foot level and offers a panorama of the valley and Turnagain Arm.

RECREATIONAL ACTIVITIES

Skiing

- **Alyeska Resort and Ski Area** is on SR 1 (Seward Hwy.). Other activities are offered. **Hours:** Mid-Nov. to mid-Apr., weather permitting. **Phone:** (907) 754-2111.

WHERE TO EAT

SAKURA ASIAN BISTRO 907/754-1111

▼▼▼▼▼

Asian
Casual Dining
$12-$39

AAA Inspector Notes: This restaurant makes the most of its cozy space with seating at the sushi bar and family-style at long granite tables. The temptations are endless—fresh white king salmon, black cod, eel, octopus or king crab presented as sushi, sashimi, nigiri or maki. Bento box meals also are available. For those who may want their fish cooked, the chef expertly grills your choice for a mouthwatering meal. **Features:** full bar. **Address:** 1000 Arlberg Ave 99587 **Location:** SR 1 (Seward Hwy), 3 mi n on Alyeska Blvd, 1 mi e; in The Hotel Alyeska. **Parking:** on-site and valet.

D CALL &M K

SEVEN GLACIERS RESTAURANT 907/754-2237

▼▼▼ ▼▼▼

Regional
American
Fine Dining
$29-$75

AAA Inspector Notes: This phenomenal mountaintop eatery is accessible by an aerial tram from the hotel. The menu centers on creative Alaskan and West Coast preparations such as seafood, beef, dry-aged pork chops, exotic game and a nightly chef's tasting menu. The crab cakes and scallop bisque are extraordinary. The wow factor begins the moment the elevator doors open to the Northern Lights display on the reception desk and continues while you dine surrounded by the spectacular, panoramic view of the seven glaciers. **Features:** full bar. **Reservations:** suggested. **Address:** 1000 Arlberg Ave 99587 **Location:** SR 1 (Seward Hwy), 3 mi n on Alyeska Blvd, 1 mi e; in The Hotel Alyeska. **Parking:** on-site and valet. *(See ad p. 500.)*

D CALL &M K

GLACIER BAY NATIONAL PARK AND PRESERVE (G-9)

Elevations in the park and preserve range from sea level at Glacier Bay to 15,320 ft. at Mount Fairweather. Refer to AAA maps for additional elevation information.

Stretching northward from Cross Sound to the Canadian border, Glacier Bay National Park is one of the most scenic spots in Alaska. In this 3,283,168-acre park, blue-white glaciers flow from the snow-clad peaks of the Fairweather Range to fiordlike inlets.

The park features 15,320-foot Mount Fairweather and Glacier Bay. The bay, about 65 miles long and 2.5 to 10 miles wide, was filled with ice 5,000 feet thick as recently as 200 years ago. The park contains some of the world's most impressive tidewater glaciers. Icebergs that crack off, or calve, from the nearly vertical ice cliffs dot the waters of the upper bay. Boaters are likely to encounter numerous harbor seals and an occasional whale.

This spectacular region is accessible only by plane, boat or cruise ship. Alaska Airlines offers flights from Juneau daily late May through early September. A 10-mile road connects the park headquarters with the small community of Gustavus, where charter vessels and air and boat service to Juneau are available.

An 8-hour boat tour of the bay departs at 7:30 a.m. from Glacier Bay Lodge May 23-Sept. 7 (weather permitting). Phone ahead for schedule and rates. Reservations are strongly recommended; phone (888) 229-8687.

Due to concern for the endangered humpback whale, permits are required from June through August for private vessels to enter Glacier Bay. An

Alaska fishing license is required for fishing. Boaters should contact the National Park Service for current regulations; phone (907) 697-2627. A visitor center for boaters and campers, at head of the public-use dock in Bartlett Cove, open daily 7-7, June-Aug.; daily 8-5, in May and Sept. Phone (907) 697-2627.

Glacier Bay National Park Visitor Center, in Glacier Bay Lodge, open daily 11-8, late May-early Sept. Phone (907) 697-2661.

For further information about the park contact the Superintendent, Glacier Bay National Park and Preserve, P.O. Box 140, Gustavus, AK 99826; phone (907) 697-2230. *See Recreation Areas Chart.*

GLENNALLEN pop. 483

LAKE LOUISE LODGE 907/822-3311
▼ Motel. **Address:** Mile 16.1 Lake Louise Rd 99588

GUSTAVUS pop. 442

ANNIE MAE LODGE (907)697-2346
▼▼ Country Inn. **Address:** 2 Grandpa's Farm Rd 99826

GLACIER BAY LODGE 907/697-4000
▼▼ Motel. **Address:** 179 Bartlett Cove 99826

GLACIER BAY'S BEAR TRACK INN (907)697-3017
▼▼▼ Country Inn. **Address:** 255 Rink Creek Rd 99826

WHERE TO EAT

FAIRWEATHER DINING ROOM 907/697-4000
▼▼ American. Casual Dining. **Address:** 179 Bartlett Cove 99826

HAINES (G-10) pop. 1,713, elev. 66'

Haines lies in a spectacular setting on the Chilkat Peninsula near the northern end of Lynn Canal between the waters of the Inside Passage and the Chilkat River. The Alaska Marine Highway links Haines with Prince Rupert, British Columbia, and Bellingham, Wash., and enables visitors to connect with the Alaska Highway at Haines Junction, Milepost 1016, via SRs 7 and 4. For information about the Alaska Marine Highway phone (907) 465-3941 or (800) 642-0066.

The 40-acre Kroschel Wildlife Center, 27 miles north on scenic Haines Highway, is home to reindeer, wolverines, bears, falcons and other native species. Reservations are required for tours; phone (907) 767-5464.

Nearby, from late October through February the 48,000-acre Chilkat Bald Eagle Preserve, between Mileposts 9 and 31 on Haines Highway, harbors one of the largest congregations of bald eagles in the world. More than 3,500 of the birds gather to feed on the salmon in the Chilkat River; sometimes as many as 30 eagles roost in a tree during this time. Use roadside pull-offs for viewing; stopping on the road is prohibited. Tour information is available at Haines Visitor Center.

Other interesting drives near Haines include Lutak Road, leading to Chilkoot Lake, and Mud Bay Road, which passes Pyramid Harbor and an old cannery with its salmon boats before approaching Chilkat State Park *(see Recreation Areas Chart).* Davidson and Rainbow glaciers also are visible from this route.

Buildings that once comprised Fort William H. Seward, the site of the first permanent Army post in Alaska, have been restored and contain several inns, private residences and galleries. A historic area at the south end of Haines Highway, the fort also contains a replica of a tribal house. The old hospital houses carvers who use traditional Tlingit Indian methods. Phone (907) 766-2234 for fort information.

Fjord Express, (800) 320-0146, and Haines-Skagway Fast Ferry, (907) 766-2100 or (888) 766-2103, provide efficient transportation between Haines, Skagway and Juneau.

Haines Convention & Visitors Bureau: 122 Second Ave., P.O. Box 530, Haines, AK 99827. **Phone:** (907) 766-2234 or (800) 458-3579.

Self-guiding tours: Brochures featuring walking tours of Haines and Fort William H. Seward are available from Haines Visitor Center and Hotel Halsingland.

ASPEN SUITES HOTEL   907/766-2211
◆◆ Extended Stay Contemporary Hotel. **Address:** 409 Main St 99827

CAPTAIN'S CHOICE MOTEL   (907)766-3111

◆
Motel
$155

Address: 108 2nd Ave N 99827 **Location:** Jct 2nd Ave and Dalton St. **Facility:** 37 units. 2 stories (no elevator), exterior corridors. **Terms:** cancellation fee imposed. **Guest Services:** coin laundry, rental car service, area transportation. **Featured Amenity:** continental breakfast.

WHERE TO EAT

CHILKAT RESTAURANT & BAKERY   907/766-3653
◆◆ American. Casual Dining. **Address:** 25 5th Ave 99827

LIGHTHOUSE RESTAURANT   907/766-2442
◆◆
American
Casual Dining
$8-$34

AAA Inspector Notes: Overlooking the boat harbor marina, guests can dine in a casual setting and watch the ferry and cruise ships come in. Fresh seafood is available in season. The rest of the year diners can enjoy great burgers and sandwiches. **Features:** full bar. **Address:** 101 N Front St 99827 **Location:** Waterfront; next to marina. Ⓛ Ⓓ Ⓚ

HEALY pop. 1,021

This small community in the interior of Alaska originated from what was once a mining and hunting camp circa 1904. Many of the current residents still work in the nearby Usibelli Coal Mine. Recreational opportunities range from hiking in summer to dog-sledding in winter.

DENALI DOME HOME BED & BREAKFAST   (907)683-1239
◆◆◆ Bed & Breakfast. **Address:** 137 Healy Spur Rd 99743

DENALI LAKEVIEW INN   907/683-4035
◆◆
Bed & Breakfast
$99-$229

Address: Milepost 1.2 Otto Lake Rd 99743 **Location:** SR 3 (Milepost 247), 1.2 mi w. **Facility:** 21 units. 2-3 stories (no elevator), interior/exterior corridors. **Parking:** winter plug-ins. **Terms:** check-in 4 pm, 14 day cancellation notice-fee imposed. **Guest Services:** coin laundry. **Featured Amenity:** continental breakfast.

HEALY HEIGHTS FAMILY CABINS   907/683-2639
◆◆ Cabin. **Address:** Hill Top Rd 99743

WHERE TO EAT

BLACK DIAMOND GRILL   907/683-4653
◆◆ American. Casual Dining. **Address:** 1 Mile Otto Lake Rd 99743

HOMER (D-10) pop. 5,003, elev. 67'
• Hotels p. 518 • Restaurants p. 518

Homer Pennock landed a party of gold and coal prospectors in the schooner *Excelsior* in 1896 and established Homer. Gold was not found, but an abundance of coal was and the settlement remained.

Healthy fishing and tourism industries support Homer's economy. Kachemak Bay, a 30-mile arm of lower Cook Inlet, provides a usually ice-free deep-water harbor for Homer. A small boat harbor has launching facilities and charter boats. Charter planes are available in town for hunting, fishing, wildlife viewing and sightseeing expeditions. Cross-country skiing is popular in winter. The city is linked by daily air service with Anchorage and once a month in the summer with Juneau, and by the Alaska Marine Highway with Kodiak and Seldovia.

Skyline Drive, accessible from West and East Hill roads, follows the rim of the plateau behind the town and offers access to ski slopes and views of the bay, Homer Spit and the Kenai Mountains. Chartered bush flights afford panoramas of the bay, open coal seams and Harding Icefield to the southeast.

Homer Chamber of Commerce: 201 Sterling Hwy., Homer, AK 99603. **Phone:** (907) 235-7740.

ALASKA ISLANDS & OCEAN VISITOR CENTER

is at 95 Sterling Hwy. The center presents an overview of the area through interpretive exhibits about Kachemak Bay; local estuaries; research ships; and the seabird and marine inhabitants of the Alaska Maritime National Wildlife Refuge. Outdoor nature trails link the 60-acre site with Bishop's Beach Park on Kachemak Bay. Naturalist-led tours are offered, and a short movie about the Aleutian Islands is shown.

Time: Allow 2 hours minimum. **Hours:** Daily 9-5, Memorial Day-Labor Day; Tues.-Sat. noon-5, rest of year. Closed major holidays. **Cost:** Free. **Phone:** (907) 235-6961.

RECREATIONAL ACTIVITIES

Fishing

- SAVE **Homer Ocean Charters** is at Cannery Row boardwalk on Homer Spit Rd. **Hours:** Trips depart daily by appointment, May-Sept. **Phone:** (907) 235-6212 or (800) 426-6212.

BEST WESTERN BIDARKA INN   (907)235-8148

Hotel
$100-$200

Best Western. **AAA Benefit:** Save 10% or more every day and earn 10% bonus points!

Address: 575 Sterling Hwy 99603 **Location:** Just n of Pioneer Ave on SR 1 (Sterling Hwy). **Facility:** 74 units. 2 stories (no elevator), interior/exterior corridors. **Parking:** winter plug-ins. **Terms:** check-in 4 pm. **Activities:** exercise room. **Guest Services:** coin laundry, area transportation. **Featured Amenity:** breakfast buffet.

SAVE ⟵ ¶¶ ⛶ CALL ⟍M BIZ

HS ⟋ ⟡ ⬛ ⟠ ⬛ / SOME UNITS ⟱

LAND'S END RESORT   907/235-0400

Hotel. **Address:** 4786 Homer Spit Rd 99603

PIONEER INN   (907)235-5670

Motel. **Address:** 244 W Pioneer Ave 99603

WHERE TO EAT

CAFE CUPS   907/235-8330

American. Fine Dining. **Address:** 162 W Pioneer Ave 99603

CAPTAIN PATTIE'S FISH HOUSE   907/235-5135

Seafood. Casual Dining. **Address:** 4241 Homer Spit Rd 99603

THE CHART ROOM RESTAURANT & LOUNGE   970/235-0406

American. Casual Dining. **Address:** 4786 Homer Spit Rd 99603

DON JOSE'S MEXICAN RESTAURANT & CANTINA   907/235-7963

Mexican. Casual Dining. **Address:** 127 W Pioneer Ave 99603

DUNCAN HOUSE DINER   907/235-5344

Breakfast Sandwiches. Casual Dining. **Address:** 125 E Pioneer Ave 99603

FAT OLIVES RESTAURANT & ESPRESSO   907/235-8488

Pizza Sandwiches. Casual Dining. **Address:** 276 Ohlson Ln 99603

FRESH SOURDOUGH EXPRESS BAKERY & CAFE
907/235-7571

Natural/Organic Sandwiches. Casual Dining. **Address:** 1316 Ocean Dr 99603

THE HOMESTEAD RESTAURANT   907/235-8723

Seafood Steak. Casual Dining. **Address:** Mile 8.2 East End Rd 99603

LA BALEINE CAFE   907/299-6672

Sandwiches Soup. Casual Dining. **Address:** 4460 Homer Spit Rd, Suite A 99603

MAURA'S CAFE & DELICATESSEN   907/235-1555

Breakfast Sandwiches. Casual Dining. **Address:** 106 W Bunnell #B 99603

TWO SISTERS BAKERY   907/235-2280

American. Casual Dining. **Address:** 233 E Bunnell Ave 99603

JUNEAU (G-10) pop. 31,275, elev. 12'

- Hotels p. 520 • Restaurants p. 521
- Attractions map p. 519

Juneau, Alaska's capital city, lies along the beautiful Gastineau Channel at the foot of snowcapped mounts Roberts and Juneau. The borough of Juneau covers 3,108 square miles of towering mountains, islands, saltwater bays, forested valleys and residential flatlands. Its road system extends from Thane, 6 miles southeast of downtown, northwest to Echo Cove at Milepost 40.2 on the Glacier Highway. The city is accessible by air or by sea.

When Joe Juneau and Richard Harris discovered gold in 1880, they started the first rush in American Alaska. At one time the Alaska-Juneau and Treadwell mines were producing about 20,000 tons of ore daily. Not until 1944, when the low price of gold and the high cost of extraction rendered it impractical, did mining operations cease.

The Alaska State Capitol offers free 30-minute guided tours mid-May to mid-September; the immense building lies between 4th and 5th streets and Main and Seward streets. The State Office Building, one block west of the capitol at 333 Willoughby Ave., contains a century-old totem pole and a Kimball Theatre pipe organ equipped with such accessories as a glockenspiel, sleigh bells and bird whistles. Free concerts are held Friday at noon May through September in the eighth-floor atrium. Also on the eighth floor, a terrace affords panoramas of the harbor and the surrounding mountains.

Impromptu, informal tours of one of the oldest churches in southeastern Alaska are available in summer. Built in 1894, St. Nicholas Russian Orthodox Church is at Fifth and Gold streets; inquire at the church gift shop, or phone (907) 586-1023. The Shrine of St. Therese, near Milepost 23 on the Glacier Highway, is a stone chapel on an island connected to shore by a gravel causeway.

There are many ways to tour Juneau. Nearby hiking trails, which vary in length and difficulty, lead to fishing spots, scenic mountain areas, old mine ruins and points near Mendenhall Glacier. Bus tours circle points of interest in Juneau and visit Mendenhall Glacier and the log Chapel-by-the-Lake at Auke Lake. Tours depart from the cruise ship docks during the summer. Visitors also can charter boats for sightseeing or fishing.

A good way to see the ice field is to take a charter flight. Companies that offer flightseeing tours from Juneau are Alaska Fly 'n' Fish Charters, (907) 790-2120; Alaska Seaplane Service, (907) 789-3331; Ward Air, (907) 789-9150; and Wings of Alaska, (907) 789-0790. Helicopter tours, float trips, gold-panning excursions and several tours of nearby and more distant points of interest are available through Gray Line of Alaska, (907) 586-9825; and Princess Tours, (907) 463-3900.

Travel Juneau: 800 Glacier Ave., Suite 201, Juneau, AK 99801. **Phone:** (907) 586-2201 or (888) 581-2201.

Self-guiding tours: Free walking tour maps of the historical and governmental districts are available at the Travel Juneau office.

ALASKA STATE MUSEUM, w. of Egan Dr. at 395 Whittier St., chronicles the state's history and preserves and exhibits Tlingit and Athabascan Indian, Eskimo and Aleut culture. There are wildlife, timber, maritime and mining displays; Russian-American historical exhibits; and fine art. Highlights include an 18-ton locomotive.

Guided tours are available in summer. **Time:** Allow 1 hour minimum. **Hours:** Daily 9-5, mid-May to late Sept.; Tues.-Sat. 9-5, rest of year. Closed state holidays. **Cost:** Mid-May to mid-Sept. $12; $11 (ages 65+); free (ages 0-18). Rest of year $5; $4 (ages $65); free (ages 0-18 and first Fri. of the month 4:30-7). Admission and schedule may vary; phone ahead. **Phone:** (907) 465-2901. GT ⓘ

DOLPHIN JET BOAT TOURS provides pick-up downtown at the tram parking area. Three-hour tours on a jet boat offer the opportunity to view humpback and killer whales, porpoises, sea lions, seals and eagles. Other tours are available. **Hours:** Tours depart daily at 8, 10, noon, 2 and 4, May-Sept. **Cost:** Fare $95-$110. Phone ahead to confirm fare and schedule. Reservations are recommended. **Phone:** (907) 463-3422 or (800) 719-3422.

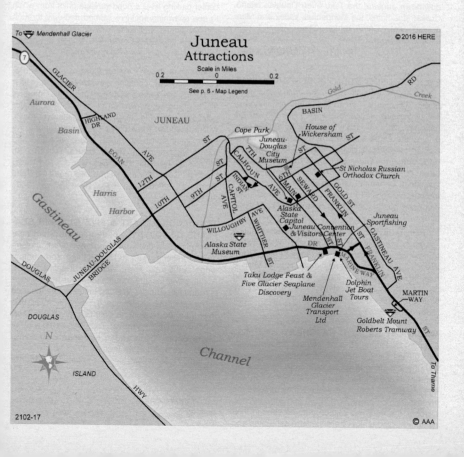

Juneau
Attractions

© 2016 HERE

Scale in Miles

See p. 6 - Map Legend

© AAA

ERA HELICOPTERS FLIGHTSEEING TOURS depart from the North Douglas Heliport. Narrated, 1-hour tours (with 30 minutes of flight time) offer views of the capital city, the pristine Alaskan backcountry and four glaciers in the Juneau Icefield. Highlights include a 25-minute glacier landing to explore the blue ice. A 95-minute tour (with 30 minutes in the air) visits a dog sled camp on the Norris Glacier where passengers learn hands-on how to mush a team of dogs across a snow-capped glacier. **Time:** Allow 2 hours minimum. **Hours:** Daily 8-5, May-Sept. **Cost:** Fare $420-$735. Flights require a minimum of four passengers. **Phone:** (907) 586-2030 or (800) 843-1947. GT

GLACIER GARDENS RAINFOREST ADVENTURE is at 7600 Glacier Hwy. A motorized shuttle takes passengers on a guided tour up Thunder Mountain through temperate botanical gardens nestled in a lush Alaskan rain forest. Guests travel past streams, ponds, waterfalls and such flora as rhododendrons, Japanese maples, ferns, and upside-down Flower Tower planters, which are inverted Sitka spruce and Western hemlock trees with various flowers planted in the root ball of the trees. A scenic overlook, 600 feet above sea level offers a spectacular view of downtown Juneau, the Taku Inlet, Douglas Island, Chilkat Mountains, the Mendenhall Valley and Mendenhall State Game refuge. **Time:** Allow 1 hour minimum. **Hours:** Daily 9-6, May-Sept. **Cost:** $24.95; $15.95 (ages 6-12). **Phone:** (907) 790-3377.

GOLDBELT MOUNT ROBERTS TRAMWAY, 490 S. Franklin St. on the cruise ship dock, offers a 5-minute ride to the 1,800-foot level of Mount Roberts. At the top, visitors can stop at the nature center, view native and historical artwork, see a live bald eagle displayed by the Juneau Raptor Center, take wildlife or nature walks to a rainforest and alpine meadow and view the spectacular scenery, including the Chilkat Mountains and Gastineau Channel. Common wildlife sightings from the outlooks include marmots, ravens, eagles, deer, mountain goats, black bear and a variety of song birds.

"Seeing Daylight," a movie about Alaska's native Tlingit, is presented in the Chilkat Theater. Entertainment and demonstrations are offered. **Time:** Allow 1 hour, 30 minutes minimum. **Hours:** Daily 8 a.m.-9 p.m., May-Sept. Hours may vary in May and Sept. Phone ahead to confirm schedule. **Cost:** Fare $33; $16 (ages 6-12). **Phone:** (907) 463-3412 or (888) 461-8726. [TI]

MACAULAY SALMON HATCHERY is at 2697 Channel Dr. During 15- to 20-minute presentations, tour guides explain hatchery processes, beginning with the imprinting of young salmon to ensure a return at the end of their lifespan and concluding with egg retrieval. In May-June, visitors may observe the juvenile salmon pre-release; from mid-June through October, the returning salmon may be seen in their outdoor holding tanks where they are separated and prepared for egg harvesting. Indoor aquariums contain more than 100 species of southeast Alaska sea life, including anemones, crabs and octopi. Visitors may feel such animals as starfish in touch tanks.

Time: Allow 30 minutes minimum. **Hours:** Mon.-Fri. 10-6, Sat.-Sun. 10-5, May-Sept.; by appointment rest of year. **Cost:** $5; $3 (ages 2-12). **Phone:** (907) 463-4810 or (877) 463-2486. GT

MENDENHALL GLACIER, 13 mi. n.w. via SR 7 and Mendenhall Loop Rd., is an impressive river of blue ice, 13 miles long and 1.5 miles wide at its widest point. The glacier is fed by the 1,500-square-mile Juneau Icefield, part of the Tongass National Forest (see place listing p. 535).

Trails on either side of the glacial valley afford scenic views. To the east are Mendenhall Lake and Nugget Creek Falls; the west trail ascends above the glacier. Camping and picnic facilities are available at Mendenhall Lake. An easily traversable .5-mile nature trail begins near the visitor center; brochures are available.

The Steep Creek viewing platform near the visitor center parking lot is a good vantage point from which to see spawning sockeye salmon mid-July through mid-September. The salmon run attracts bald eagles and black bears mid-September through November. **Hours:** Trails open daily 6 a.m.-midnight.

Mendenhall Glacier Visitor Center, at the end of Glacial Spur Rd., contains a model depicting glacier dynamics, dioramas and display cases that interpret five evolving ecosystems at the glacier and a naturalistic salmon-filled stream that tumbles over rocks. A film is shown three times every hour during the summer, otherwise by request. Interpretive talks and nature hikes also are offered. **Hours:** Daily 8-7:30, May-Sept.; Fri.-Sun. 10-4, Oct.-Mar. Closed winter holidays. **Cost:** $5 (May-Sept.); free (ages 0-15 and Oct.-Mar.). **Phone:** (907) 789-0097 or (907) 789-6640.

TAKU LODGE FEAST & FIVE GLACIER SEAPLANE DISCOVERY departs from the wharf near the cruise ship docks. A Wings Airways floatplane takes passengers to a 1923 fishing and hunting lodge in the Taku River Valley for a salmon feast. Aerial views include mountains, Taku Inlet, waterfalls and five glaciers. Walking trails explore the area surrounding the historic lodge, which is across the river from the Hole-in-the-Wall Glacier. **Time:** Allow 3 hours minimum. **Hours:** Trips depart daily, May 1-late Sept. Phone ahead to confirm schedule. **Cost:** Fare $309; $265 (ages 2-11); free (ages 0-1 on lap). Reservations are recommended. **Phone:** (907) 586-6275.

ASPEN SUITES HOTELS   907/500-7700
▼▼▼ Extended Stay Hotel. **Address:** 8400 Airport Blvd 99801

BEST WESTERN COUNTRY LANE INN   (907)789-5005

Motel
$119-$195

Best Western. **AAA Benefit:** Save 10% or more every day and earn 10% bonus points!

Address: 9300 Glacier Hwy 99801 **Location:** Just e off Egan Dr. **Facility:** 55 units, some efficiencies. 2 stories (no elevator), exterior corridors. **Guest Services:** valet and coin laundry, area transportation.

SAVE ✈ ❙❙✚ BIZ 🛜 ✕ ⓚ
🔋 🖻 🖵 / SOME UNITS HS

BEST WESTERN GRANDMA'S FEATHER BED
(907)789-5566

Country Inn
$139-$205

Best Western. **AAA Benefit:** Save 10% or more every day and earn 10% bonus points!

Address: 2358 Mendenhall Loop Rd 99801 **Location:** Just e off Egan Dr. **Facility:** 14 units. 2 stories (no elevator), interior corridors. **Guest Services:** valet laundry, area transportation.

SAVE ✈ ❙❙ BIZ HS 🛜 ✕
🔋 🖻 🖵

PEARSON'S POND LUXURY INN AND ADVENTURE SPA
(907)789-3772

Bed & Breakfast
$239-$599

Address: 4541 Sawa Cir 99801 **Location:** From Egan Dr, 3.5 mi n on Mendenhall Loop Rd. Located in a quiet residential area. **Facility:** A tranquil pond beautifies the lovely grounds, which feature gazebos and sitting areas where you can view the Mendenhall Glacier or soak in an outdoor hot tub. Every whim is taken care of. 5 efficiencies. 2 stories (no elevator), interior/exterior corridors. **Terms:** check-in 4 pm, 2 night minimum stay - seasonal, 30 day cancellation notice-fee imposed, resort fee. **Activities:** sauna, hot tub, boat dock, bicycles, exercise room, massage. **Guest Services:** complimentary laundry.

SAVE ❙❙✚ BIZ HS 🛜 ✕ ⓩ 🔋 🖻 🖵

WESTMARK BARANOF HOTEL   (907)586-2660
Hotel. **Address:** 127 N Franklin St 99801

WHERE TO EAT

THE HANGAR ON THE WHARF   907/586-5018
Regional American. Casual Dining. **Address:** 2 Marine Way, Suite 106 99801

MI CASA RESTAURANT   907/789-3636
Mexican. Casual Dining. **Address:** 9200 Glacier Hwy 99801

THE ROOKERY   907/463-3013
Breads/Pastries Coffee/Tea. Casual Dining. **Address:** 111 Seward St 99801

SALT   907/780-2221
Mediterranean. Casual Dining. **Address:** 200 Seward St 99801

SUWANNA CAFE   907/789-1250
Thai. Quick Serve. **Address:** 8800 Glacier Hwy 99801

TIMBERLINE BAR & GRILL   907/463-1338
American. Casual Dining. **Address:** 490 S Franklin St 99801

TWISTED FISH COMPANY   907/463-5033
Seafood. Casual Dining. **Address:** 550 S Franklin St 99801

KATMAI NATIONAL PARK AND PRESERVE (G-4)

Elevations in the park and preserve range from sea level at the Shelikof Strait to 7,606 ft. at Mount Dennison. Refer to AAA maps for additional elevation information.

On the northern portion of the Alaska Peninsula, 4.1-million-acre Katmai National Park and Preserve displays an outstanding example of volcanism. In 1912 one of the greatest volcanic explosions in recorded history turned a nameless green valley into what became known as the Valley of Ten Thousand Smokes. For more than 45 years the eruption was attributed to Mount Katmai, but recent studies indicate that the source was a new volcanic vent called Novarupta, some 6 miles distant.

During or shortly after the eruption, the peak of Mount Katmai collapsed, forming a caldera that subsequently filled with water. Molten material released from Novarupta and surrounding vents flowed down the valley, and thousands of holes from which smoke and gases arose formed as gases and vaporized surface water percolated through the volcanic deposits. These fumaroles, which gave the valley its name, lasted only about 20 years.

Although nearly all of the "smokes" have died out, steam columns from nearby volcanoes sometimes can be seen. By air it is possible to see the jade-green lake in the crater of Mount Katmai and to circle over still-active mounts Trident, Mageik and Martin.

In addition to its superlative scenery—large lakes, rivers, glaciers and active volcanoes—the park is noted for its abundant wildlife. The most prominent mammal is the Alaskan brown bear, the world's largest carnivore, averaging 500 pounds with some reaching 1,200 pounds. It is recommended that visitors maintain at least 50 yards from individual bears and 100 yards from sows with young. Visitors also should make noises while walking or hiking.

Katmai National Park can be reached only by boat or plane. A boat ramp is at Lake Camp, 10 miles by dirt road from King Salmon. Commercial airlines serve King Salmon, 35 miles from Brooks Camp. Amphibious aircraft make daily scheduled flights between King Salmon and Brooks Camp. Bush planes can be chartered.

Daily 7-hour bus and hiking tours to the Valley of Ten Thousand Smokes begin at Brooks Camp at 9 a.m., early June to mid-Sept. Fare $96 (with bag lunch); $88 (no lunch); $51 (one way). Departures require a minimum of 2 people. Other tours are available; for more information phone Katmailand, Inc., (800) 544-0551. For further information about the park contact the Superintendent, Katmai National Park and Preserve, P.O. Box 7, King Salmon, AK 99613; phone (907) 246-3305. *See Recreation Areas Chart.*

KENAI (D-10) pop. 7,100, elev. 86'

Established as Fort St. Nicholas by Russian fur traders in 1791, Kenai (KEEN-eye) is one of the oldest permanent settlements in Alaska. Until 1953 the town grew under a squatters' rights policy. Kenai is the closest settlement to the south-central region's most promising oil-development fields and is the site of major petrochemical plants.

Kenai's Russian Orthodox Church, established in 1894, contains religious and art objects brought from Russia in 1841.

A popular, colorful pastime during the summer months in Kenai is berry picking. Such berries as Alaska blueberries (a smaller version of its common cousin), nagoonberries (reddish purple in color), cloudberries and salmonberries (both peach in color), crowberries (black in color), northern red currants, wild raspberries and cranberries grow on the peninsula.

Kenai Chamber of Commerce and Visitors Center: 11471 Kenai Spur Hwy., Kenai, AK 99611. **Phone:** (907) 283-1991.

KENAI NATIONAL WILDLIFE REFUGE—see Soldotna p. 533.

ASPEN SUITES HOTEL KENAI   907/283-2272
▼▼▼▼ Extended Stay Hotel. **Address:** 10431 Kenai Spur Hwy 99611

WHERE TO EAT

CHARLOTTE'S CAFE   907/283-2777
▼▼ ▼▼ Sandwiches Soup. Casual Dining. **Address:** 115 S Willow Cir, Suite 102 99611

FLATS BISTRO   907/335-1010
▼▼▼▼ American. Casual Dining. **Address:** 39847 Kalifornsky Beach Rd 99611

VERONICA'S CAFE   907/283-2725
▼▼ Sandwiches Soup. Quick Serve. **Address:** 602 Petersen Way 99611

KENAI FJORDS NATIONAL PARK (D-11)

Elevations in the park range from sea level at Nuka Bay to 6,400 ft. at a peak on the Harding Icefield. Refer to AAA maps for additional elevation information.

On the southeastern side of the Kenai Peninsula, Kenai Fjords National Park covers more than 600,000 acres. Access to the park is by private vehicle, plane or boat from Seward. Air charters also are available from other communities on the Kenai Peninsula. Scheduled bus service is available between Seward and Anchorage. Several tour companies offer trips to Exit Glacier and boat trips to the fjords.

The park encompasses a coastal mountain range that includes most of Harding Icefield, one of the four largest ice fields in the United States. A remnant of the ice age, it blankets all but the top of the Kenai Mountains. Along the coast is the rugged shoreline of the glacier-carved Kenai Fjords. Seals, porpoises, whales and sea otters are some of the 23 marine mammal species that inhabit the coastal waters.

Exit Glacier is the most accessible of the glaciers that flow from Harding Icefield. Three miles north of Seward via the Seward Highway and Exit Glacier Road, the glacier is reached by a .7-mile trail that begins at the Exit Glacier parking area; guided tours depart daily at 10, 2 and 4, mid-May to mid-September. A strenuous 8.2-mile round-trip journey from the base of Exit Glacier to Harding Icefield departs from the Exit Glacier Nature Center on Saturdays at 9, July through August. Bald eagles, bears, moose, mountain goats and Steller sea lions inhabit the area.

Picnicking and backcountry camping are permitted; a 12-site walk-in tent campground and three rustic cabins are available. Winter activities at Exit Glacier include skiing, snowmobiling, snowshoeing and dog sledding. Boat and air charters provide access to the coast during the summer.

Both park headquarters and a visitor center are in Seward. Park headquarters is at 500 Adams St., Suite 103, and the visitor center is at 1212 4th Ave. next to the harbormaster's office. The Exit Glacier Nature Center is inside the park at the Exit Glacier parking area. Slide shows, exhibits and information about ranger-conducted activities are available.

The visitor center in Seward is open daily 9-7, Memorial Day-Labor Day; 9-5, mid- to late May and early to mid-Sept. The Exit Glacier Nature Center is open daily 9-7, Memorial Day-Labor Day; 9-5, day after Labor Day-Sept. 27. Admission to Exit Glacier is free. For information write the Superintendent, Kenai Fjords National Park, P.O. Box 1727, Seward, AK 99664; phone (907) 422-0535 or (907) 422-0573 for recorded information. *See Recreation Areas Chart.*

KETCHIKAN (H-12) pop. 8,050
• Restaurants p. 524

Alaska's southernmost city sits on stilts at the base of the Tongass National Forest *(see place listing p. 535).* On Revillagigedo Island, separated from the mainland by Behm Canal, Ketchikan claims to be the salmon capital of the world. An average annual rainfall of 156 to 162 inches makes it the wettest community in North America. The city's economic base relies on fishing, canning, mineral exploration, tourism and logging and cold-storage operations.

The town is populated with native culture and contains the largest concentration of Tlingit (KLINK-it), Haida (HY-dah), and Tsimshian (SIMP-shee-ane) people in Alaska. This heritage can be seen in the many totem poles that populate the area. Totem poles—tall cedar logs carved with eagles, ravens, wolves, bears, whales and other figures—depict stories or designate clans or lineage, and Ketchikan is reputed to contain the most in the world.

Creek Street is a relic of Ketchikan's rough-and-tumble past. Built on stilts over Ketchikan Creek, the street was once the site of a thriving red-light district. Highlights include art galleries, shops and a museum. The creek is a spawning ground for salmon.

Gray Line of Alaska, (907) 225-2404, and Princess Tours, (800) 774-6237, are among the companies that offer tours of the city. Ketchikan Visitor Information Center (on the waterfront at the corner of Front and Mission streets) can provide a more complete list; phone (907) 225-6166 or (800) 770-3300. Information about charter aircraft, boats, rental cars, buses and taxis is available at the Visitor Information Center, the airport and the ferry terminal.

Southeast Alaska Discovery Center: 50 Main St., Ketchikan, AK 99901. **Phone:** (907) 228-6220 or TTY (907) 228-6237.

Self-guiding tours: Information about a 2-hour walking tour of downtown is provided at the Ketchikan Visitors Bureau, 131 Front St., Ketchikan, AK 99901; phone (907) 225-6166 or (800) 770-3300.

Shopping: The Creek Street boardwalk area in downtown contains a number of specialty shops and boutiques.

ALASKA AMPHIBIOUS TOURS is inside the Ketchikan Visitor Center on the cruise ship dock, booth # 10, 131 Front St. Take a 90-minute historic tour through downtown Ketchikan, passing by Ketchikan Creek and then splashing into the Tongass Narrows waterway, where you can see fishing boats and sea planes in the harbor as well as nearby canneries where bald eagles are known to visit. Passengers ride on an amphibious vehicle which is driven on dry land and becomes a boat in the water. **Time:** Allow 1 hour, 30 minutes minimum. **Hours:** Tours depart daily 7:30-3, May-Sept. Phone ahead to confirm schedule. **Cost:** $49; $29 (ages 3-12). **Phone:** (907) 225-9899 or (866) 341-3825.

BERING SEA CRAB FISHERMEN'S TOUR departs from the Tender Float at the main downtown dock. This 3-hour excursion on the waters of the Metlakatla Indian Reservation is conducted on the *Aleutian Ballad* — a vessel featured on season two of the TV show "Deadliest Catch" — and offers passengers a firsthand look at the king crab fishing industry and its techniques. As the tour proceeds, passengers are regaled with tales of life at sea and educated about the state's fishing history and the variety of fishing vessels used. A heated and sheltered amphitheater allows passengers to observe the ship's crew as it unloads 700-pound crab pots.

Often seen among the ship's catch are such sea creatures as octopus, prawns, sharks and wolf eels; many animals are placed in an on-deck tank for observation and photo opportunities prior to release back into the sea. Such local wildlife as bald eagles,

sea lions, seals and humpback whales may be seen during the tour.

Note: Prior to boarding, potential passengers should seek to locate a tour representative on the dock at least 30 minutes before the scheduled departure time. Passengers should dress in comfortable and warm layers of clothing. Each passenger should be of sufficient age (minimum age 5) and capacity to remain in the ship's passenger-designated zones and outside its working areas as well as be able to navigate the ship's aisles and stairs. Limited storage space is available.

Time: Allow 3 hours, 15 minutes minimum. **Hours:** Tours depart once or twice daily (departure times vary), early May to mid-Sept. The schedule is designed to accommodate cruise ship passengers; phone ahead to verify departure times. **Cost:** Fare $169; $109 (ages 5-12). Children ages 0-4 are not permitted on the tour. Reservations are recommended. **Phone:** (907) 821-2722 or (888) 239-3816.

TOTEM BIGHT STATE HISTORICAL PARK, 10 mi. n. on N. Tongass Hwy., displays 14 poles by Haida and Tlingit clans and a model of a Tlingit clan house. The site is reached by a short trail through a forest from the parking area. A brochure describes typical totem characters and gives insight to the art of totem carving. More totem poles are in Saxman Native Village, 2.5 miles south on S. Tongass Highway. **Time:** Allow 30 minutes minimum. **Hours:** Daily 6 a.m.-10 p.m., May-Sept.; Mon.-Fri. 10-4, rest of year. **Cost:** Free. **Phone:** (907) 247-8574.

BEST WESTERN PLUS LANDING HOTEL

(907)225-5166

Hotel
$164-$270

Best Western PLUS
AAA Benefit: Save 10% or more every day and earn 10% bonus points!

Address: 3434 Tongass Ave 99901 **Location:** Across from Alaska Marine Hwy ferry terminal. **Facility:** 107 units. 2-4 stories, interior/exterior corridors. **Dining:** The Landing, see separate listing. **Activities:** exercise room. **Guest Services:** valet and coin laundry, area transportation.

CAPE FOX LODGE

907/225-8001

Hotel
Rates not provided

Address: 800 Venetia Way 99901 **Location:** Above Creek St (tramway from Creek St). **Facility:** 72 units. 3 stories, interior/exterior corridors. **Dining:** Cape Fox Lodge Dining Room & Lodge, see separate listing. **Guest Services:** valet and coin laundry, area transportation.

WHERE TO EAT

ANNABELLE'S FAMOUS KEG & CHOWDER HOUSE
907/225-6009
♦♦♦♦ Regional Seafood. Casual Dining. **Address:** 326 Front St 99901

BAR HARBOR RESTAURANT   907/225-2813
♦♦♦♦ Alaskan. Casual Dining. **Address:** 2813 Tongass Ave 99901

CAPE FOX LODGE DINING ROOM & LODGE   907/225-8001
♦♦♦♦ American. Casual Dining. **Address:** 800 Venetia Way 99901

THE EDGEWATER INN   907/247-2600
♦♦♦♦ American. Casual Dining. **Address:** 4871 N Tongass Hwy 99901

THE LANDING   907/225-5166
♦♦♦♦ American. Casual Dining. **Address:** 3434 Tongass Ave 99901

SALMON FALLS RESORT   907/225-2752
♦♦♦♦ Regional American. Casual Dining. **Address:** 16707 N Tongass Hwy 99901

◆ KLONDIKE GOLD RUSH NATIONAL HISTORICAL PARK—
See Skagway p. 434

KOBUK VALLEY NATIONAL PARK (B-4)

Elevations in the park range from 100 ft. at the point where the Kobuk River flows out of the southwest corner of the park to 4,700 ft. in the Brooks Range, which forms the park's northern border. Refer to AAA maps for additional elevation information.

Some 25 miles north of the Arctic Circle, Kobuk Valley National Park covers 1,710,000 acres in the heart of the arctic wildlands, where the boreal forest gives way to the frozen tundra. The broad Kobuk Valley is enclosed almost completely by the Baird Mountains to the north and the Waring Mountains to the south. Traversing the valley from east to west, the wide and placid Kobuk River offers good fishing and idyllic float trips. The swifter Salmon River, a designated Wild and Scenic River, flows south from the Baird Mountains.

Preserved within the park are the 25-square-mile Great Kobuk Sand Dunes, the largest active dunes in the Arctic. Created by the grinding action of ancient glaciers, the sand was carried by wind and water to a wide area south of the Kobuk River. The 100-foot dunes are accessible by a difficult hike from the river along Kavet Creek.

Home to seminomadic tribes for more than 12,500 years, the region still supports the native Inupiats; they are granted by law the right to continue subsistence hunting, trapping and other practices. Important to their survival is North America's largest caribou herd, numbering some 500,000. Many can be seen crossing the Kobuk River in September during their migration southward.

Other wildlife common to the region include moose, grizzly and black bears, wolves, red foxes, lynxes, wolverines and martens. Golden eagles can be seen in the northern latitudes; other birds include sandhill cranes, arctic loons, American golden plovers and arctic terns.

The park attracts experienced backpackers, campers and river travelers. Though the park is open year-round, the elements limit most visits to June through September. Fishing is good when the rivers are clear of silt; catches include salmon, pike, arctic char, whitefish and grayling. An Alaska fishing license is required. Hunting is not permitted, but it is legal to carry a firearm for protection from bears.

Access to the region is by daily commercial flights from Anchorage and Fairbanks to Kotzebue *(see place listing p. 525)*, where connections to the villages of Kiana and Ambler can be made. Air taxi service into the park is available from Kotzebue, Kiana and Ambler. There are no facilities, services, trails or campgrounds in the park. Park headquarters is at the Northwest Arctic Heritage Center in Kotzebue and is open Mon.-Fri. 8:30-noon and 1-6:30, Sat. 10-6:30, Sat. 10-6:30, June-Sept.; Tues.-Fri. 9-noon and 1-6, Sat. noon-4, rest of year. The visitor center has museum exhibits and can provide information about the park; phone (907) 442-3890.

Due to its location, the area is subject to harsh weather and high winds. It is advisable to carry protection against hypothermia, mosquitoes and biting flies.

For trip planning assistance and a list of authorized outfitters, guides and air taxi operators, write the Superintendent, Western Arctic National Parklands, P.O. Box 1029, Kotzebue, AK 99752; phone (907) 442-3890. *See Recreation Areas Chart.*

KODIAK (H-5) pop. 6,130

One of the oldest towns in Alaska, Kodiak is on the northeastern tip of Kodiak Island and is home to the Kodiak brown bear. A Russian explorer-trader's quest for sea otter pelts led to the European settlement of the island in 1784. The community was established about 1792 when Alexander Baranov moved his headquarters from the original 1784 settlement at Three Saints Bay, making Kodiak the first capital of Russian America.

Kodiak was nearly destroyed twice; in June 1912, an eruption from Mount Novarupta covered the town with ash. On Good Friday in 1964 an earthquake in south central Alaska created tsunamis that enveloped the islands. Citizens found refuge on nearby Pillar Mountain and returned with the task of rebuilding the city.

Kodiak is a leading commercial fishing port. Several cruise lines dock at the Port of Kodiak for shore excursions. On days when cruise ships are in port, visitors can enjoy performances by the Kodiak

Alutiiq Dancers at 11 a.m. at the Kodiak Tribal Council building, 312 W. Marine Way; phone (907) 486-4449. The blue, onion-shaped domes of the Holy Resurrection Russian Orthodox Church recall the days when the Russian Empire in the North Pacific was administered from Kodiak.

Kodiak can be reached by air service from Anchorage or by the Alaska Marine Highway, a passenger/vehicle ferry, from Homer and Seward. Reservations are required well in advance for the ferry; write Alaska Marine Highway, P.O. Box 703, Kodiak, AK 99615, or phone (907) 486-3800 or (800) 642-0066.

Discover Kodiak: 100 Marine Way, Suite 200, Kodiak, AK 99615. **Phone:** (907) 486-4782 or (800) 789-4782.

ALUTIIQ MUSEUM is at 215 Mission Rd. in the Alutiiq Center building across from Holy Resurrection Russian Orthodox Church. Permanent exhibits tell the 7,500-year history, lifestyle and cultural traditions of the Alutiiq people through archeological artifacts, photographs, petroglyph rubbings, oral histories, videos and contemporary art. **Time:** Allow 1 hour minimum. **Hours:** Tues.-Fri. 10-4, Sat. noon-4, by appointment on Mon. Closed major holidays. **Cost:** $7; free (ages 0-16). **Phone:** (907) 486-7004. [GT]

FORT ABERCROMBIE STATE HISTORICAL PARK, 4 mi. n.e. on Rezinof Dr., is a National Historic Landmark due to World War II fortification. The 182-acre park offers a view of the rocky coastline and nearby islands. Interpretive displays and a self-guiding walking tour highlight the remnants and remaining bunkers of the coastal defense system, reflecting Alaska's participation in World War II. Scheduled interpretive tide pool and historical programs are given, and approximately 7 miles of hiking trails are available. There are generally abundant views of birds, wildlife and marine mammals in the area. *See Recreation Areas Chart.*

Hours: Park open daily 24 hours. Visitor center daily 8-4, May-Sept. **Cost:** Free. $5 (day use). **Phone:** (907) 486-6339. [A] [X] [img] [img]

KODIAK LABORATORY AQUARIUM & TOUCH TANK is at the Kodiak Fisheries Research Center at 301 Research Ct. The 3,500-gallon aquarium displays specimens collected from Kodiak Island's waters, including crabs, mollusks and other invertebrates as well as such echinoderms as urchins, sea cucumbers and starfish. A giant Pacific octopus also can be seen while a touch tank allows visitors to interact with selected intertidal organisms.

Time: Allow 30 minutes minimum. **Hours:** Mon.-Sat. 8-4:30, Memorial Day-Labor Day; Mon.-Fri. 8-4:30, rest of year. Phone ahead to confirm schedule and availability. Closed major holidays. **Cost:** Free. **Phone:** (907) 481-1800.

BEST WESTERN KODIAK INN & CONVENTION CENTER
(907)486-5712

Hotel
$106-$235

AAA Benefit: Save 10% or more every day and earn 10% bonus points!

Address: 236 W Rezanof Dr 99615 **Location:** Just w of ferry terminal; downtown. Across from St. Paul's Harbor. **Facility:** 82 units, some efficiencies. 3 stories, interior/exterior corridors. **Dining:** Chart Room Restaurant & Lounge, see separate listing. **Activities:** hot tub, exercise room. **Guest Services:** coin laundry, area transportation. **Featured Amenity:** full hot breakfast.

[SAVE] [+] [TI] [Y] CALL[&M] [BIZ] [wifi] [X] [X] [H]
[img] [img] /SOME UNITS [S] [HS]

WHERE TO EAT

CHART ROOM RESTAURANT & LOUNGE   907/486-5712
Regional American. Casual Dining. **Address:** 236 W Rezanof Dr 99615

HENRY'S GREAT ALASKAN RESTAURANT   907/486-8844
American. Casual Dining. **Address:** 512 Marine Way 99615

MONK'S ROCK COFFEEHOUSE & CAFE   907/486-0905
Deli Breads/Pastries. Quick Serve. **Address:** 202 E Rezanof Dr 99615

OLD POWER HOUSE RESTAURANT   907/481-1088
Sushi Seafood. Casual Dining. **Address:** 516 E Marine Way 99615

OLDS RIVER INN RESTAURANT   907/486-6040
American. Casual Dining. **Address:** 32233 Pasagshak Rd 99615

SPARROWS PIZZA-GYROGRILL   907/512-2800
Pizza Specialty. Casual Dining. **Address:** 113 Lower Mill Bay Rd 99615

KOTZEBUE (C-3) pop. 3,201, elev. 20'

Kotzebue, on the Baldwin Peninsula, sits on glacial moraine on the eastern edge of Kotzebue Sound. It was named after Otto Von Kotzebue, a German sailor exploring for Russia around 1818. Inhabited by the Kikiktagruk Inupiat Eskimos since the early 19th century, the area later became a seasonal trading center for the various Eskimo tribes due to its position at the confluence of the Noatak and Kobuk rivers. Its establishment as a permanent city began in 1899 with a Quaker mission.

Kotzebue is situated 33 miles above the Arctic Circle in the treeless tundra; the sun rises each year in early June and remains above the horizon for only 38 days. A spectacular ice breakup takes place for 2 weeks between mid-May and mid-June.

The second-largest Eskimo village in Alaska, Kotzebue is reached only by daily air service from Anchorage, Nome and Fairbanks. Arrangements for bush plane flights over the surrounding tundra and to the Kobuk River for hunting and fishing expeditions can be made at the airport. Short air and boat excursions to most of the surrounding villages also are available through independent operators. Northwest Arctic Heritage Center, near the airport, is the visitor center for Kobuk Valley National Park *(see place listing p. 524).* The center has an exhibit hall and also provides information about the surrounding area; phone (907) 442-3890.

LAKE CLARK NATIONAL PARK AND PRESERVE (F-4)

Elevations in the park and preserve range from sea level along Cook Inlet to 10,197 ft. at Mount Redoubt. Refer to AAA maps for additional elevation information.

West of Cook Inlet, Lake Clark National Park and Preserve is an almost 4-million-acre mountainous crossroads where ice and fire meet. The Pacific crust grinds beneath the North American plate, creating the Chigmit Mountains, a jagged array of spires and two steaming volcanoes, Mount Redoubt and Mount Iliamna. Mount Redoubt, the more active, last erupted in March 2009; it continues to emit steam.

Covered by massive ice fields, the seemingly impenetrable Chigmit Mountains are formed by the linkage of two great ranges, the Alaska and the Aleutian. Together the ranges divide the park into distinct areas: the eastern flank's coastal plain bordering Cook Inlet and the lake and tundra region on the western flank. Lake Clark, 50 miles long, juts in from the southwest.

Moisture abounds along the park's coastal area, which is characterized by rocky cliffs along its southern portion, giving way to tidal marshes and grasslands in the north. In contrast to the luxuriant alder thickets and Sitka spruce along Cook Inlet, lakes, boreal forests and rolling tundra highlands distinguish the park's western landscape.

Numerous glacier-fed rivers and creeks are channeled through Lake Clark, creating one of the richest sockeye salmon spawning grounds in the world. The park was created primarily to protect this fruitful breeding area.

Although the park is open all year, most people visit during the peak of the summer season, late June through August. Even in summer months, weather conditions vary in the interior; it is advisable to bring protection against insects as well as clothing for sunny, wet or freezing weather. Visitors should outfit themselves in Kenai, Homer or Anchorage, as the communities closer to the park have limited supplies.

For anglers the rivers and lakes on the park's western side provide a variety of trophy-size fish, including salmon, arctic grayling and trout. A 2- to 3-mile trail to Tanalian Falls and Kontrashibuna Lake is accessible from Port Alsworth, near Lake Clark. The open foothills are ideal for backpacking. River-running also is popular on the Mulchatna, Tlikakila and Chilikadrotna rivers, all federally designated wild and scenic rivers.

As there are no roads in the park, access is almost exclusively by air. Most travelers charter aircraft; the closest airport is south of the park in Iliamna. A 1- to 2-hour flight from Anchorage, Homer or Kenai will provide access to most points within the park and preserve.

The National Park Service facility is at Port Alsworth and contains a visitor center with displays regarding natural history topics; phone (907) 781-2117. The center is open daily 9-5:30, Memorial Day-Labor Day; Mon.-Fri. 9-5, day after Labor Day-Sept. 30. While there are minimal National Park facilities—staffed patrol cabins at Telaquana Lake, Twin Lakes, Crescent Lake and Chinitna Bay—there are a number of private lodges and cabins in the park.

For information about accommodations as well as a list of outfitters and maps, write the Superintendent, Lake Clark National Park and Preserve, 240 W. 5th Ave., Suite 236, Anchorage, AK 99501; phone (907) 644-3626. *See Recreation Areas Chart.*

MISTY FIORDS NATIONAL MONUMENT (H-11)

East of Ketchikan and within the Tongass National Forest *(see place listing p. 535),* Misty Fiords National Monument covers about 3,580 square miles of wilderness. The area is accessible by float plane from Ketchikan and other communities near the national forest. An information center and cruises to the monument are available in Ketchikan *(see place listing p. 522).*

Behm Canal, a deep inlet of the Pacific Ocean, leads to the interior of the monument, where rock walls that rise 3,000 feet surround Walker Cove and Rudyerd Bay. Geological features include mineral springs, 237-foot-tall New Eddystone Rock, 3,150-foot-tall Punchbowl Face, lava flows, five major rivers and hundreds of small streams. The region receives more than 120 inches of precipitation each year. Bald eagles, brown and black bears, wolves and mountain goats inhabit the area; whales, porpoises, seals and sea lions can be sighted in Behm Canal or in the ocean nearby.

Recreational activities include backpacking, picnicking, bird-watching, hunting, fishing and crabbing. Rustic cabins are available for $25-$45 per day; reservations may be made by calling Reserve America, (877) 444-6777. Four free Adirondack-type shelters are available on a first-come, first-served basis. For further information contact the Southeast Alaska Discovery Center, 50 Main St., Ketchikan, AK 99901; phone (907) 228-6220, or TTY (907) 228-6237.

MOOSE PASS pop. 219

TRAIL LAKE LODGE   907/288-3101

◆ Motel. **Address:** 33654 Depot Rd 99631

NOME (D-2) pop. 3,598, elev. 13'

Placer gold washed from the hillsides to the beaches at Nome lured thousands to the remote shores of the Bering Sea in 1898. At the height of the gold rush, 20,000 people lived in Nome, once the largest settlement in Alaska.

On the Seward Peninsula, Nome is the judicial and commercial center of northwestern Alaska and the main supply point for nearby mining districts and Eskimo villages. The city is accessible daily by plane from Anchorage. Regularly scheduled and charter flights are available to various Eskimo villages.

Cruise ships serve Nome during the summer, and rental cars provide visitors with opportunities for self-guiding trips to nearby villages.

When a diphtheria epidemic threatened the town in 1925, the necessary serum was delivered by dog team. The annual ⬦ Iditarod Trail Sled Dog Race commemorates this emergency mission. The race, which begins in Anchorage *(see place listing p. 490)* the first Saturday in March, encompasses treacherous climbs, river passages and bone-chilling blizzards. Mushers cross the finish line in Nome after traveling roughly 1,112 miles, exhausted but invigorated by cheers from supporters lining the chute on Front Street.

One of the activities during the final week of the race is the Bering Sea Ice Classic, a six-hole golf tournament played on frozen Norton Sound.

The Midnight Sun Folk Fest celebrates the summer solstice, the longest day of the year with almost 24 hours of sunlight. The mid-June festival lasts several days and includes a parade, live music and The Nome River Raft Race.

Nome Convention and Visitors Bureau: 301 Front St., Nome, AK 99762. **Phone:** (907) 443-6555.

INSIDER INFO:
The Last Great Race

To commemorate the 1925 event in which 20 mushers relayed serum to Nome to save children who contracted diphtheria, the first Iditarod Trail Sled Dog Race took place on Mar. 3, 1973.

Beginning in Anchorage and culminating in Nome, the race trail covers some 1,112 miles of rugged terrain, takes between 9-17 days to complete and can reach temperatures of minus 60 F.

In preparation for the great race, the trail is broken and marked with reflector tape, and checkpoints are chosen where teams stop to eat and rest. Since it's not feasible for mushers to carry all of their provisions in their sleds, the bulk of food and supplies is shipped to the checkpoints prior to the race.

To aid in endurance, dogs ingest 5,000 calories or more each day, gobbling such delicacies as moose, caribou or even seal meat. Concern for the dogs'

health is strong: Booties are worn for paw protection, and about 25 veterinarians man the checkpoints to examine each dog.

While teams may begin the race with as many as 16 dogs, some drop from the race. "Dropped dogs"—dogs that do not finish the race due to dehydration, flu or fatigue—are carried to the nearest checkpoint and flown back to Anchorage. A musher must finish the race with at least five dogs.

Teams travel at night as well as during the day, and dogs rest about 10-12 hours per 24-hour period. But mushers don't enjoy that luxury: Responsible for feeding and caring for the dogs (including changing their booties every 100 miles), they rarely sleep more than 2 hours per night.

The goal? Nome's Burled Arch on Front Street. At this finish line, teams are greeted by cheering crowds and the sounding of the city's fire siren.

NORTH POLE pop. 2,117

PAGODA   907/488-3338
♦♦ ♦♦ Chinese. Casual Dining. **Address:** 431 Santa Claus Ln 99705

PALMER (C-11) pop. 5,937, elev. 240'

The peaks of the Chugach and Talkeetna mountains rise above Palmer, a city surrounded by the lush pastures and dairy and vegetable farms of the fertile Matanuska Valley, where cabbages can grow to weigh more than 70 pounds. A drive to Wasilla *(see place listing p. 537)* provides a good view of the valley and its farms. The Matanuska Agricultural Experimental Farm, 7 miles southwest, is operated by the University of Alaska Fairbanks' School of Natural Resources and Agricultural Sciences and welcomes visitors; phone (907) 746-9495.

Palmer lies near the intersection of the Glenn and George Parks highways (SRs 1 and 3), both of which are scenic highways. An interesting drive is along a narrow, rough, winding road that follows Willow Creek through formerly rich gold areas. The road crosses Hatcher Pass en route to Willow.

The Palmer Museum and Visitor Center, 723 S. Valley Way, contains a historical museum featuring items from the city's pioneer era. The 2-acre Agricultural Showcase Garden is on the center's grounds and features a variety of perennials; phone (907) 745-8878. Garden open daily 24 hours. Visitor Center open daily 9-6, May-Sept.

Mat-Su Convention & Visitors Bureau: 610 S. Bailey St., Suite 201, Palmer, AK 99645. **Phone:** (907) 746-5000.

THE INN CAFE AND STEAKHOUSE   907/746-6118
♦♦ ♦♦ American. Casual Dining. **Address:** 325 E Elmwood Ave 99645

PETERSBURG (H-11) pop. 2,948, elev. 28'

Petersburg, at the north end of Mitkof Island, is an Alaska Marine Highway port. In 1897 Norwegian Peter Buschmann decided to build a cannery on Mitkof Island at the head of picturesque Wrangell Narrows. The facility at the north end of Nordic Drive was completed in 1900 and packed 32,750 cases of salmon during its first production year. Now Petersburg Fisheries, the firm is a pioneer in Alaska's expanding bottom-fishing and salmon industries.

Nicknamed "Little Norway," Petersburg boasts brightly painted wooden houses decorated with hand-painted floral designs, a traditional craft called rosemaling.

Among the nearby points of interest is LeConte Glacier, the southernmost of its kind in the northern hemisphere; just south of Petersburg; it can be reached via chartered plane, helicopter or boat. In nearby Frederick Sound whale-watching is popular; the area is home to orca and humpback whales as well as other sea mammals.

Petersburg Visitor Information Center: First and Fram sts., P.O. Box 649, Petersburg, AK 99833. **Phone:** (907) 772-4636.

SEWARD (D-11) pop. 2,693, elev. 70'
• Hotels p. 530 • Restaurants p. 530

Named for William H. Seward, who negotiated the purchase of Alaska, Seward is an ice-free port in a setting of great beauty. At the northeast end of a bay named Resurrection by Russians who arrived in its waters on Easter, the city is surrounded by lush, tall mountains and ice fields.

Charter boats and planes can be hired for fishing, hunting and sightseeing trips. Seward is the southern terminus of the Seward Highway, a national scenic byway extending north to Anchorage through an alpine terrain of glaciers and lakes. Seward also is the main access point to Kenai Fjords National Park *(see place listing p. 522)*, which includes Exit Glacier, one of the few accessible glaciers.

Seward Community Library, 238 5th Ave., shows a movie about the havoc wreaked by the 1964 Good Friday earthquake. The movie is screened Memorial Day-Labor Day; phone (907) 224-4082 for schedule information.

Seward Chamber of Commerce: 2001 Seward Hwy., Seward, AK 99664. **Phone:** (907) 224-8051.

Self-guiding tours: Information about a walking tour is available at the chamber of commerce's visitor information center, 2001 Seward Hwy.; phone (907) 224-8051 for details.

ALASKA SEALIFE CENTER, on Seward Hwy. (SR 9) at Milepost 0, generates and shares scientific knowledge to promote understanding and stewardship of Alaska's marine ecosystems. Highlights include Steller sea lions, harbor seals, Giant Pacific octopus and a sea

bird habitat that allows visitors to get up close to puffins, red-legged kittiwakes and other Alaskan avian wonders.

Exhibits also include a jellyfish display, the hands-on Discovery touch pool and the Lifecycles of Pacific Salmon, which examines the life stages of all five species of Pacific salmon. More than 300 of the fish may be observed in 2,200- to 6,000-gallon tanks. Guided behind-the-scenes tours are available in addition to marine mammal, octopus and puffin encounters. Reservations for tours and encounters are recommended.

Time: Allow 1 hour, 30 minutes minimum. **Hours:** Mon.-Thurs. 9-9, Fri.-Sun. 8 a.m.-9 p.m., Memorial Day-Labor Day; otherwise varies, rest of year. Behind-the-scenes tours depart daily at 10, 1:30 and 4:30, Memorial Day-Labor Day; otherwise varies, rest of year (under 12 not permitted). Marine mammal encounters depart daily at noon and 3, Memorial Day–Labor Day; otherwise varies, rest of year (under 10 are not permitted). Puffin encounters depart daily at 11 and 2, Memorial Day-Labor Day; otherwise varies, rest of year (under 10 are not permitted). Octopus encounter tours depart daily at 1, Memorial Day–Labor Day; otherwise varies, rest of the year (under 6 are not permitted). Closed Thanksgiving and Christmas. **Cost:** $21.95; $19.95 (ages 65+); $11.95 (ages 4-12). Behind-the-scenes tours $14.95. Marine mammal and puffin encounters $74.95. Octopus encounters $74.95. **Phone:** (907) 224-6300, (888) 378-2525 for reservations or (800) 224-2525. **GT**

KENAI FJORDS TOURS depart from the Seward Small Boat Harbor. The company offers glacier and wildlife cruises into the waters of Kenai Fjords National Park. Cruises also explore Resurrection Bay and the Northwestern Fjords, where active tidewater glaciers are a highlight. A variety of marine mammals can be seen; gray whales often are spotted on whale-watching tours. Six- and 8.5-hour Kenai Fjords National Park tours; 9-hour Northwestern Fjords tours; and 3.5- and 4.5-hour Resurrection Bay wildlife cruises with a wild Alaska salmon bake and prime rib buffet at Fox Island, are available.

Inquire about weather policies. **Hours:** Tours depart daily, mid-May to mid-Sept. Kenai Fjords National Park 6-hour tours depart at 8 and 11:30; 8.5-hour tour departs at 10. Northwestern Fjord tour departs at 8:30. Resurrection Bay wildlife cruises depart at noon and 5. Phone ahead to confirm schedule. **Cost:** National Park tour $154-$172; $77-$86 (ages 2-11). Northwestern Fjord tour $189; $92 (ages 2-11). Bay tour $99; $49.50 (ages 2-11). Reservations are recommended. **Phone:** (907) 224-8068 or (877) 777-4051. *(See ad p. 494.)*

MAJOR MARINE TOURS depart from the Seward Small Boat Harbor, 1 blk. e. of Seward Hwy. A park ranger narrates full- and half-day glacier and wildlife cruises in Kenai Fjords National Park. Passengers may spot bald eagles, otters, porpoises, puffins, sea lions and whales.

Inquire about weather policies. Full-day cruise not recommended for infants and toddlers. **Hours:** Cruises depart daily, early Mar. to mid-October. Half-day cruises depart at 9, noon, 1:30 and 6; full-day cruises depart at 9, 10 and 11:30. **Cost:** Half-day fare $79-$84; $39.50-$42 (ages 2-11). Full-day fare $154-$214; $77-$84.50 (ages 2-11). Reservations are recommended. **Phone:** (907) 274-7300 or (800) 764-7300. *(See ad this page.)*

SCENIC MOUNTAIN AIR (FLIGHTSEEING) operates wheeled planes from Seward Airport and float planes from Trail Lake in Moose Pass. Sights on the varied tours include Harding Icefield, Kenai Fjords and wildlife. Fly-in fishing tours also are available. **Hours:** Flights depart daily 8 a.m.-7 p.m., early May to mid-Sept. (weather permitting). **Cost:** Fares $50-$1,650, depending on length of tour. Reservations are recommended. **Phone:** (907) 288-3646 or (800) 478-1449.

BEST WESTERN PLUS EDGEWATER HOTEL
(907)224-2700

Hotel
$129-$429

 Best Western PLUS

AAA Benefit: Save 10% or more every day and earn 10% bonus points!

Address: 202 5th Ave 99664 **Location:** Downtown; just e of Alaska SeaLife Center. Across from Resurrection Bay. **Facility:** 76 units. 3 stories, interior corridors. **Parking:** street only. **Terms:** closed 9/15-4/30, check-in 4 pm, 3 day cancellation notice. **Guest Services:** coin laundry, area transportation.

BOX CANYON CABINS
(907)224-5046

Cabin. **Address:** 31515 Lois Way 99664

HARBOR 360 HOTEL
907/865-6224

Hotel. **Address:** 1412 4th Ave 99664

HARBORVIEW INN
(907)224-3217

Motel. **Address:** 804 3rd Ave 99664

HOTEL SEWARD
(907)224-8001

Hotel
$59-$399

Address: 221 5th Ave 99664 **Location:** Downtown; just n of Alaska SeaLife Center. **Facility:** 38 units. 3 stories, interior corridors. **Parking:** on-site and street. **Terms:** check-in 4 pm, 3 day cancellation notice-fee imposed. **Dining:** Ms. Gene's Place, see separate listing. **Activities:** fishing, recreation programs in summer. **Guest Services:** coin laundry, area transportation.

SEWARD WINDSONG LODGE
(907)224-7116

Motel
$276

Address: 31772 Herman Leirer Rd 99664 **Location:** 3.5 mi n on SR 9 (Seward Hwy) to exit Glacier Rd/Herman Leirer Rd, 0.8 mi w. **Facility:** 180 units. 2 stories (no elevator), exterior corridors. **Terms:** closed 9/19-5/17, 14 day cancellation notice. **Dining:** Resurrection Roadhouse, see separate listing. **Guest Services:** area transportation. (See ad p. 529.)

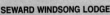

SEWARD
WINDSONG LODGE

Secluded lodge minutes from Seward; fresh Alaska cuisine, local brews, wine; guided glacier hikes.

WHERE TO EAT

CHINOOKS WATERFRONT RESTAURANT   907/224-2207
Alaskan. Casual Dining. **Address:** 1404 4th Ave 99664

CHRISTO'S PALACE   907/224-5255
American. Casual Dining. **Address:** 133 4th Ave 99664

THE COOKERY & OYSTER BAR   907/422-7459
Seafood Small Plates. Casual Dining. **Address:** 209 5th Ave 99664

EXIT GLACIER SALMON BAKE   907/224-2204
Alaskan. Casual Dining. **Address:** 1/4 Mile Exit Glacier Rd 99664

MS. GENE'S PLACE   907/224-8001
American. Casual Dining. **Address:** 221 5th Ave 99664

RESURRECTION ROADHOUSE   907/224-7116
Regional American. Fine Dining. **Address:** 31772 Herman Leirer Rd 99664

SEWARD BREWING COMPANY   907/422-0337
American. Gastropub. **Address:** 139 4th Ave 99664

SITKA (H-10) pop. 8,881

Surrounded by high peaks and small wooded islands, historic Sitka is accessible by air or the Alaska Marine Highway.

In 1804 Russians led by Alexander Baranov established a settlement on the site of an ancient Tlingit (KLINK-it) village; that settlement became the capital of Russian America. Originally named New Archangel, it was a thriving port of nearly 3,000 when San Francisco was just a mission village. Castle Hill marks the site of Baranov's headquarters and commemorates the 1867 ceremony that transferred ownership of Alaska from Russia to the United States. St. Michael's Cathedral, a restored Russian church with an onion-shaped dome, contains a collection of religious icons and artwork; phone (907) 747-8120.

The colorfully costumed New Archangel Dancers perform Russian dances in the Harrigan Centennial Hall auditorium, 330 Harbor Dr., during summer when large ships are in port; phone (907) 747-3225. Performances by the Sheet'ka Kwáan Naa Kahidi Native Dancers are given at the Tribal Community House on Katlian Street; phone (907) 747-7290.

For cruise ship and ferry passengers, Sitka Tribal Tours offers a short bus tour of Sitka, which includes guide service and round-trip transportation from the port; its native Alaskan guides all live in the Sitka community. The company also offers performances by native dancers as well as walking tours of the town and Sitka National Historical Park; phone (907) 747-0110.

Visit Sitka: 104 Lake St., Sitka, AK 99835. **Phone:** (907) 747-8604 or (800) 557-4852.

ALASKA RAPTOR CENTER, .8 mi. e. of Lake St. at 1000 Raptor Way, is home to more than 20 "raptors in residence," including bald and golden eagles, hawks, falcons and owls. The 17-acre rehabilitation center, surrounded by muskeg, mountains and the Indian River, provides medical treatment to more than 100 eagles and other birds of prey each year. A stage presentation, a video, live demonstrations of birds in flight training and a .25-mile nature trail are available.

Raptors unable to be released into the wild help educate visitors and travel to schools nationwide to raise awareness of wild birds and their habitats. Feathers, bones, photographs and a national map indicating where birds have been released are displayed. Visitors can view raptors in their natural habitats outside the center as well as in the clinic's treatment room and recuperation areas.

Time: Allow 1 hour, 30 minutes minimum. **Hours:** Daily 8-4, May-Sept. **Cost:** $12; $6 (ages 6-12). **Phone:** (907) 747-8662 or (800) 643-9425. GT

SUPER 8-SITKA (907)747-8804
♦♦ Hotel. **Address:** 404 Sawmill Creek Rd 99835

TOTEM SQUARE HOTEL & MARINA 907/747-3693
♦♦ Hotel. **Address:** 201 Katlian St 99835

WESTMARK SITKA (907)747-6241
♦♦ Hotel. **Address:** 330 Seward St 99835

WILD STRAWBERRY LODGE FISHING RESORT
907/747-3232
♦♦ Resort Motel. **Address:** 724 Siginaka Way 99835

WHERE TO EAT

ASIAN PALACE 907/966-4600
♦♦ Asian. Casual Dining. **Address:** 327 Seward St 99835

CHANNEL CLUB 907/747-7440
♦♦♦ Regional American. Fine Dining. **Address:** 2906 Halibut Point Rd 99835

LARKSPUR CAFE 907/966-2326
♦♦ American. Casual Dining. **Address:** 2 Lincoln St, Suite 1A 99835

LITTLE TOKYO 907/747-5699
♦ Sushi. Casual Dining. **Address:** 315 Lincoln St 99835

LUDVIG'S BISTRO 907/966-3663
♦♦♦ Mediterranean. Casual Dining. **Address:** 256 Katlian St 99835

RAVEN DINING ROOM 907/747-6241
♦♦ American. Casual Dining. **Address:** 330 Seward St 99835

VAN WINKLE & SONS 907/747-7652
♦♦ American. Casual Dining. **Address:** 205 Harbor Dr 99835

SITKA NATIONAL HISTORICAL PARK (H-10)

Near downtown Sitka on Lincoln Street, this urban park commemorates the Battle of Sitka, fought in 1804 between the Kiksadi Tlingit Indians and the fur hunters and Aleut natives of the Russian-American Co. The battle marked the last major armed resistance by Alaska Natives to European domination. The 113-acre park preserves the Tlingit fort site, the battlefield and the 1842 Russian Bishop's House.

A fine collection of Tlingit (KLINK-it) and Haida (HY-dah) totem poles, some more than a century old, is displayed along a 1-mile trail through the park's temperate rain forest and coastal intertidal area. During August and September visitors may view salmon spawning in the Indian River.

The visitor center contains exhibits and audio-visual presentations about the area's Tlingit Indian heritage as well as its Russian legacy. Within the visitor center skilled Alaska Natives artisans demonstrate traditional crafts at the Cultural Center, which is open most weekdays.

Trails open daily 6 a.m.-10 p.m., May-Sept.; 7 a.m.-8 p.m., rest of year. Visitor center open daily 8-5, May-Sept.; Sun.-Fri. noon-3, rest of year. Closed winter holidays. Park and visitor center free. Address inquiries to the Superintendent, Sitka National Historical Park, 103 Monastery St., Sitka, AK 99835; phone (907) 747-0110.

THE RUSSIAN BISHOP'S HOUSE, 501 Lincoln St. across from Crescent Harbor, is a two-story log structure completed in 1842. It is one of the last surviving colonial Russian buildings in North America. Restored to its 1853 appearance, the building reflects the influence of the Russian Orthodox Church and the traders of the Russian-American Co., who made Sitka the economic center of colonial Russian America.

Time: Allow 30 minutes minimum. **Hours:** Daily and holidays 9-5, mid-May to late Sept.; Tues.-Fri. by appointment rest of year. Tours are offered on the half-hour. Last tour begins 30 minutes before closing. **Cost:** Guided tour of second floor during summer $4; free (ages 0-16, for first floor and during winter season). **Phone:** (907) 747-0110. GT

SKAGWAY (F-10) pop. 920, elev. 2'
• Hotels p. 533 • Restaurants p. 533

During the icy winter of 1897-98 hordes of enthusiastic would-be prospectors who had heard of the Klondike gold strike swarmed ashore at Dyea. They assembled their gear and began the trek over treacherous mountains and down raging rivers to the Klondike. Within 3 months of the first gold strike, the settlement at Skagway grew from one cabin into a thriving city of more than 20,000 people. But the gold rush ended suddenly, and those who had come to Skagway moved on.

The notorious outlaw Jefferson R. "Soapy" Smith and Frank Reid, who represented the outraged citizenry, shot it out in a battle that cost both men their lives. Gold Rush Cemetery, 1.5 miles from town, contains the graves of both "Soapy" Smith and Frank Reid.

A stop on many summer cruises along the Inside Passage, Skagway is the northern terminus of the Alaska Marine Highway. Sightseeing opportunities include visits to Reid Falls and flower gardens; tours of the city and the harbor; flightseeing tours to Glacier Bay, gold rush trails and the Juneau Ice Cap; bus excursions to Dyea and Carcross, Yukon; and hiking trips to AB Mountain and the Dewey Lakes.

Gray Line of Alaska offers historical points-of-interest tours daily; phone (907) 983-2241 or (800) 452-1737.

Skagway Convention & Visitors Bureau: 245 Broadway, P.O. Box 1029, Skagway, AK 99840. **Phone:** (907) 983-2854 or (888) 762-1898.

JEWELL GARDENS & GLASSWORKS is 1.5 mi. n. on Klondike Hwy. Once the site of a late 19th-century vegetable farm known best for its rhubarb, the gardens feature such spectacular flowers as begonias, delphiniums, lilacs, nasturtiums and poppies. The mountains along the Lynn Canal serve as a backdrop to the site, which also is home to organic herb and vegetable gardens and a greenhouse. At the glassblowing theater, visitors may observe daily demonstrations.

Time: Allow 3 hours minimum. **Hours:** Daily 9-5, early May-late Sept. **Cost:** $12.50; $6 (ages 0-12). **Phone:** (907) 983-2111. 🍴 🎦

🔻 **KLONDIKE GOLD RUSH NATIONAL HISTORICAL PARK** includes the Skagway Historic District and Chilkoot and White Pass trails, over which each prospector was required to haul nearly a ton of supplies during the gold rush of 1897-98. It was during this stampede that Skagway's population boomed from 5 to more than 10,000.

The park visitor center at Broadway and Second Avenue is in the original White Pass and Yukon Route Railroad Depot, one of Alaska's oldest. Highlights include the 25-minute film "Gold Fever: Race for the Klondike." The Jeff Smith Parlor Museum contains exhibits and interpretive programs about the era. The Moore House belonged to Skagway's first homesteading family. The Junior Ranger Activity Center, in the Pantheon Saloon at 4th and Broadway streets, features animal furs, Victorian dress-up clothes, coloring sheets, historic artifacts and other activities for kids to enjoy. Walking tours led by a park ranger explore the Skagway Historic District, where many restored buildings represent a colorful history. The Chilkoot Trail Center provides information about day hikes and backpacking on the Chilkoot Trail.

Hours: Visitor center and museum daily 8:30-5:30. Film is shown on the hour at 9 and 11-5. Moore House daily 10-5. Junior Ranger Activity Center Mon.-Fri. 10-noon and 1-3. Walking tours depart the visitor center daily on the hour 9-11 and 2-3, early May-late Sept. Trail center daily 8-5, June-Labor Day weekend. Phone ahead to confirm schedule. **Cost:** Visitor center (including exhibits), Moore House, walking tours and trail center free.

▼ *See AAA listing p. 533* ▼

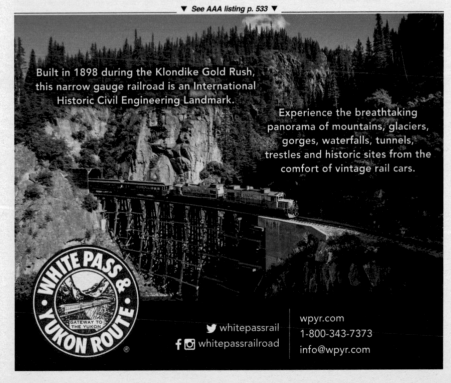

Built in 1898 during the Klondike Gold Rush, this narrow gauge railroad is an International Historic Civil Engineering Landmark.

Experience the breathtaking panorama of mountains, glaciers, gorges, waterfalls, tunnels, trestles and historic sites from the comfort of vintage rail cars.

WHITE PASS & YUKON ROUTE · GATEWAY TO THE YUKON

🐦 whitepassrail
f 📷 whitepassrailroad

wpyr.com
1-800-343-7373
info@wpyr.com

Jeff Smith Parlor Museum $5. Fees apply, and reservations are recommended for Chilkoot Trail backpacking. **Phone:** (907) 983-9223 for the visitor center, (907) 983-9234 for trail information June-Aug., or (800) 661-0486 for trail information rest of year.

WHITE PASS & YUKON ROUTE is at Second Ave. and Spring St. A vintage train chugs across mountain rivers and chasms during fully narrated narrow-gauge rides. The rail line was built in 1898 to carry people and supplies to the Klondike gold rush. Passengers travel round-trip in a period parlor car to the summit of White Pass or Fraser Meadows, past granite gulches, cascading waterfalls and spectacular scenery. A narrator tells the story of the stampede north into the gold fields through some of the most rugged terrain in the United States and Canada.

The 3-hour White Pass Summit Excursion rises from tidewater elevations to 2,865 feet in 20 miles. The 4-hour steam excursion to Fraser Meadows rises from tidewater elevation to 3,000 feet in 26 miles. One-way and round-trip excursions to Lake Bennett and Fraser, British Columbia, as well as to Carcross, Yukon, also are available.

Hours: Ticket office open daily 7:30-4:30, May-Sept. White Pass Summit Excursion departs daily at 8:15 and 12:45, also Tues.-Wed. at 4:30, late May-early Sept. Fraser Meadows Steam Excursion departs Thurs.-Fri. at noon and Mon. at 8 or noon, mid-May to mid-Sept. Phone ahead to confirm schedule. **Cost:** White Pass Summit Excursion fare $119; $59.50 (ages 3-12). Fraser Meadows Steam Excursion fare $159; $79.50 (ages 3-12). Reservations are required. **Phone:** (800) 343-7373. *(See ad p. 532.)*

WESTMARK INN SKAGWAY   (907)983-6000
▼▼ Motel. **Address:** 3rd Ave & Spring St 99840

WHERE TO EAT

BONANZA BAR & GRILL   907/983-6214
▼▼ American. Casual Dining. **Address:** 3rd Ave & Spring St 99840

STARFIRE   907/983-3663
▼▼ Thai. Casual Dining. **Address:** 230 4th St 99840

SWEET TOOTH CAFE   907/983-2405
▼ American. Casual Dining. **Address:** 315 Broadway St 99840

SOLDOTNA (D-10) pop. 4,163

Soldotna's location on the Kenai Peninsula at the junction of Sterling and Kenai Spur highways has ensured its steady growth since homesteading began in 1947. World War II veterans were among the first homesteaders; they were given a 90-day preference right in choosing and filing for land.

The area is rich with opportunities for year-round recreation—hiking, fishing, camping, canoeing and ice fishing are favored activities. Nearby Kenai River yields record catches of salmon and rainbow trout.

Soldotna Chamber of Commerce and Visitor Information Center: 44790 Sterling Hwy., Soldotna, AK 99669. **Phone:** (907) 262-9814.

KENAI NATIONAL WILDLIFE REFUGE, with its headquarters in Soldotna, 1 mi. s.e. of the Kenai River Bridge to 1 Ski Kill Rd., covers about 1,920,000 acres. The refuge was established in 1941 by President Franklin D. Roosevelt to preserve the area's large moose population. Other wildlife include Dall sheep, coyotes, black bears and bald eagles. Fishing and hunting are subject to state and federal regulations. Boat ramps, camping and hiking trails from one-quarter mile to more than 2 miles are available. **Hours:** The refuge is open all year, except when roads are impassable. Daily 9-5, Memorial Day-Labor Day; Tues.-Sat. 10-5, rest of year. **Phone:** (907) 262-7021 or TTY (907) 260-2803.

Visitor Center, 1 mi. s.e. of the Kenai River Bridge on Ski Hill Rd., exhibits wildlife dioramas and presents films. **Hours:** Mon.-Fri. 8-4:30, Sat. 9-5, June 1-Labor Day; Mon.-Fri. 8-4:30, Sat. 10-5, rest of year. Phone ahead to confirm schedule. **Cost:** Free.

ASPEN HOTEL SOLDOTNA   907/260-7736
▼▼ Hotel. **Address:** 326 Binkley Cir 99669

BEST WESTERN KING SALMON MOTEL   (907)262-5857

▼▼ ◆
Motel
$79-$179

Best Western. **AAA Benefit:** Save 10% or more every day and earn 10% bonus points!

Address: 35546A Kenai Spur Hwy 99669 **Location:** Jct Sterling Hwy (SR 1), 1 mi n. **Facility:** 45 units. 2 stories (no elevator), exterior corridors. **Parking:** winter plug-ins. **Terms:** check-in 4 pm. **Guest Services:** coin laundry.

SAVE ⓣⓘ BIZ HS 📶 ✕ ▤ ▥ / SOME UNITS ⓚ

ORCA LODGE ON THE KENAI RIVER   907/262-5649
▼▼ Cabin. **Address:** 44240 Oehler Dr 99669

WHERE TO EAT

BUCKETS SPORTS GRILL   907/262-7220
▼▼ American. Casual Dining. **Address:** 43960 Sterling Hwy (SR 1) 99669

FINE THYME CAFE   907/262-6620
▼▼ Sandwiches Desserts. Casual Dining. **Address:** 43977 Sterling Hwy 99669

FROSO'S FAMILY DINING   907/262-7797
▼▼ American. Casual Dining. **Address:** 35433 Kenai Spur Hwy 99669

ST. ELIAS BREWING COMPANY   907/260-7837
▼▼   Pizza   Sandwiches.   Casual   Dining.   **Address:** 434
Sharkathmal Ave 99669

SENOR PANCHO'S MEXICAN RESTAURANT   907/260-7777
◆ Mexican. Quick Serve. **Address:** 44096 Sterling Hwy 99669

STERLING pop. 5,617, elev. 198'

SUZIE'S CAFE   907/260-5751
▼▼   American. Casual Dining. **Address:** 38515 Barbara St
99672

TALKEETNA (C-11) pop. 876, elev. 355'

Situated at the confluence of the Talkeetna, Susitna and Chulitna rivers, Talkeetna takes its name
from the Tanaina Indian word for "river of plenty."
The village was an important supply station for gold
prospectors from the late 1800s to 1940, but is now
a popular staging area for outdoors enthusiasts.

Self-guiding tours: A map of a downtown walking
tour is available at Talkeetna Historical Society Museum *(see attraction listing)* and the visitor center
next to Village Park on Main Street.

DENALI SUMMIT FLIGHTS depart from Talkeetna
State Airport, off Talkeetna Spur Rd., and Healy
River Airport near Denali National Park and Preserve. Passengers are treated to views of Denali
National Park and Preserve, and the flights are
oxygen-equipped to aim for the 21,000-foot summit
of Denali. Flights from Fairbanks to Denali National
Park and Preserve are available in winter. **Time:**
Allow 2 hours minimum. **Hours:** Daily 6 a.m.-
midnight, mid-May to mid-Sept.; 9-5, rest of year
(weather permitting). **Cost:** Fare $429; other tours
are available. **Phone:** (907) 474-8600 or (800)
474-1986.

K-2 AVIATION is at Talkeetna State Airport off Talkeetna Spur Rd. Flightseeing tours of varying types
and lengths include the 1-hour Denali Experience,
which offers views of Denali (formerly called Mount
McKinley) and Ruth Glacier; the 75-minute Denali
Climber & Summit Tour to the mountain's summit;
the Denali Flyer Tour, which lasts 75 minutes and offers views of the mountain range's south side; and
the 90-minute Denali Grand Tour, which encircles
the mountain and offers views of Kahiltna and Ruth
glaciers. Glacier landings are available for an additional fee.

Note: A fuel surcharge of 5 percent is added to
the cost of each trip. **Hours:** Daily 7 a.m.-9 p.m.,
mid-May to late-Sept.; Mon.-Fri. 8:30-4, rest of year
(weather permitting). **Cost:** Denali Climber &
Summit Tour fare $345; $460 (with glacier landing).
Denali Grand Tour fare $335; $420 (with glacier
landing). Denali Flyer Tour fare $285; $370 (with glacier landing). Denali Experience fare $220; $305
(with glacier landing). Reservations are recommended. **Phone:** (907) 733-2291 or (800) 764-2291.

MAHAY'S RIVERBOAT SERVICE departs from
Milepost 14 on Talkeetna Spur Rd. The company offers three excursions: a 2-hour, 20-mile Wilderness
Jetboat Adventure; a 3.5-hour, 50-mile three-river
tour on the Chulitna, Susitna and Talkeetna rivers;
and a 5-hour Devil's Canyon tour. Tours offer a leisurely .25-mile nature walk to a Dena'ina Indian encampment and a view into the lives of turn-of-the-
century trappers.

Time: Allow 2 hours minimum. **Hours:** Office
open daily 7 a.m.-9 p.m., mid-May to mid-Sept. Wilderness Jetboat Adventure departs daily at 8:45,
noon, 2:30 and 6:30, mid-May to mid-Sept. Three-
river tour departs daily at 3:30, mid-May to mid-
Sept. Canyon tour departs daily at 9:30, mid-May to
mid-Sept. **Cost:** Wilderness Jetboat Adventure $70;
$53 (ages 0-12). Three-river tour $120; $90 (ages
0-12). Canyon tour $165; $124 (ages 0-12). **Phone:**
(907) 733-2223 or (800) 736-2210.

TALKEETNA AIR TAXI, at Talkeetna State Airport
off Talkeetna Spur Rd., offers flightseeing tours: a
1-hour South Face McKinley Tour, with views of
Ruth Gorge; a 75-minute McKinley Base Camp
Tour, which circles over Kahiltna Glacier; a 90-
minute Grand Denali Tour, which offers views of active gold mines, Kahiltna base camp and
Wickersham Wall; and a 2-hour Summit Flight Tour,
which takes in the summits of Denali (formerly Mc-
Kinley), Foraker and Hunter. Other activities such as
mountain climbing, glacier landing, support and wilderness touring, and scenic helicopter touring also
are offered. **Note:** Full mobility is required for the
2-hour Summit Flight Tour.

Hours: Daily 7 a.m.-8 p.m., May-Sept.; 9-4, Mar.-
Apr. and in Oct.; 9-3, rest of year (weather permitting). Phone ahead to confirm schedule. **Cost:**
South Face McKinley Tour fare May-Sept. $210;
$147 (ages 0-10 and under 100 lbs.); with glacier
landing $305; $213.50 (ages 0-10 and under 100
lbs.). McKinley Base Camp Tour fare May-Sept.
$275; $192.50 (ages 0-10 and under 100 lbs.); with
glacier landing $370; $259 (ages 0-10 and under
100 lbs.). Grand Denali Tour fare May-Sept. $325;
$227.50 (ages 0-10 and under 100 lbs.); with glacier
landing $420; $294 (ages 0-10 and under 100 lbs.).
Summit Flight Tour fare with glacier landing May-
Sept. $450 (ages 12+). Phone ahead for helicopter
fares and winter rates. Reservations are recommended. **Phone:** (907) 733-2218 or (800) 533-2219.

TALKEETNA HISTORICAL SOCIETY MUSEUM, in
five buildings at the corner of First Alley and Village
Airstrip Rd., displays a wealth of local history memorabilia within re-creations of a log cabin, a one-room
schoolhouse, a railroad depot and section house. Of
interest is a large-scale model of Denali (formerly
called Mount McKinley) and the surrounding area.
Time: Allow 30 minutes minimum. **Hours:** Daily
10-6, May 15-Sept. 15; Sat.-Sun. 11-4, Mon.-Fri. by
appointment, rest of year. Phone ahead to confirm
schedule. **Cost:** $3; free (ages 0-12). **Phone:** (907)
733-2487.

TALKEETNA ALASKAN LODGE   907/733-9500

◆◆◆◆◆
Hotel
Rates not provided

Address: 23601 S Talkeetna Spur Rd 99676 **Location:** 3.5 mi s of town. **Facility:** 212 units. 3 stories, interior/exterior corridors. **Dining:** Foraker Dining Room, see separate listing. **Activities:** bicycles, trails, exercise room. **Guest Services:** coin laundry, area transportation.

TALKEETNA
ALASKAN LODGE

Lodge offers stunning views of Denali, casual & fine dining, and local brews. An outdoor adventure.

WHERE TO EAT

FORAKER DINING ROOM   907/733-9500
◆◆◆ Continental. Casual Dining. **Address:** 23601 S Talkeetna Spur Rd 99676

TALKEETNA ROADHOUSE   907/733-1351
◆ Breakfast Breads/Pastries. Casual Dining. **Address:** 13550 E Main St 99676

WILD FLOWER CAFE   907/733-2695
◆◆ American. Casual Dining. **Address:** 13578 E Main St 99676

TOK (B-12) pop. 1,258

On the Alaska Highway 93 miles from the Canadian border, Tok is a trade center for nearby Athabascan villages. Some claim that Tok's name derives from the native word meaning "peace crossing"; others say Tok was the name of a survey crew's dog.

A center for dog breeding, training and mushing, Tok claims the title "Dog Capital of Alaska."

Tok Chamber of Commerce: P.O. Box 389, Tok, AK 99780. **Phone:** (907) 883-5775.

TETLIN NATIONAL WILDLIFE REFUGE is in e. central Alaska, directly s. of the Alaska Hwy. and n. of Wrangell-St. Elias National Park and Preserve; the visitor center is at Milepost 1229 on Alaska Hwy. The gateway to Alaska, the refuge occupies 682,604 acres along a major bird migration corridor. At least 115 of the 186 bird species stop to nest in the vast wetlands. Abundant waterfowl such as ducks, geese, swans and loons can be seen on the many streams and lakes. Black and grizzly bears, moose, wolves and caribou are year-round residents.

A visitor center—built in a log trapper's cabin style with a sod roof—contains an observation deck with telescopes overlooking the vast valley as well as Alaska Native cultural exhibit and demonstrations. Ranger-led interpretive programs are offered in the

visitor center and evening programs are presented at Deadman Campground at 7 p.m. Recreational activities include bird-watching, canoeing, fishing, hiking, photography and hunting.

The refuge operates two seasonal, public campgrounds: Deadman Campground, at Milepost 1249.5 on Alaska Hwy., and Lakeview Campground, at Milepost 1256.6 on Alaska Hwy. Both are located on a lake with a boat ramp and are fee-free with only nine spots available. Larger rigs are limited as the road is narrow. Nine pullouts along the highway offer interpretive signs. Historic Seaton Roadhouse has a small pond, wildlife viewing and 4 miles of short-loop hiking trails available. **Hours:** Refuge open daily 24 hours. Visitor center open daily 8-4:30, May 15-Sept. 15. Schedule may vary; phone ahead to confirm. **Cost:** Free. **Phone:** (907) 883-5312 or (907) 883-9404. 🅐

CLEFT OF THE ROCK BED & BREAKFAST   907/883-4219
◆◆ Bed & Breakfast. **Address:** 0.5 Sundog Tr 99780

WHERE TO EAT

FAST EDDY'S RESTAURANT   907/883-4411
◆◆ American. Casual Dining. **Address:** 1313 Alaska Hwy 99780

TONGASS NATIONAL FOREST (G-10)

Elevations in the forest range from sea level at the Pacific Ocean to 10,290 ft. at Mount Ratz. Refer to AAA maps for additional elevation information.

In southeastern Alaska, Tongass National Forest covers about 17 million acres, making it the largest national forest. In 1907 Teddy Roosevelt created the forest, taking the name from the "Tongass" clan of Tlingit Indians that lived along the southern edge of the forest's present-day boundaries. It boasts more than 5 million acres of preserved wilderness, including Misty Fiords National Monument *(see place listing p. 526)* and Admiralty Island National Monument *(see place listing p. 490).*

Consisting mostly of islands, the forest also includes a mountainous mainland strip deeply cleft by rock-walled fiords, bays, inlets and channels with glaciers, ice fields and waterfalls. The abundant wildlife includes trumpeter swans, bald eagles and Alaskan brown (grizzly) and black bears. Licenses are required for hunting and fishing.

The largest island within the National Forest and one of the largest islands in the United States is Prince of Wales Island. Long inlets and deep bays mark its 1,000-mile coastline, while U-shaped valleys and low mountains rising up to 3,800 feet distinguish its interior. Thanks to a moist climate, a dense forest of spruce and hemlock blankets the landscape.

One of the most interesting features of the island is its caves, including El Capitan, a large limestone cave system with 11,000 feet of mapped passages.

Grizzly bear bones more than 12,000 years old have been found inside. The Forest Service provides free 2-hour tours of El Capitan from mid-May to early September; reservations are required. Access to the cave entrance is via a steep 1,100-foot-long trail and visitors need to bring their own equipment for the tour, including flashlights and sturdy footgear. The underground temperature is a constant 40 degrees Fahrenheit. Phone (907) 828-3304 for information and reservations.

The Forest Service provides cabins at several locations within Tongass National Forest. Many rental cabins are near lakes and streams or high in alpine meadows. Although a few can be reached by boat or trail, most are accessible only by charter plane from Craig, Hoonah, Juneau, Ketchikan, Petersburg, Sitka, Wrangell and Yakutat. Charter planes seating two to five people cost about $325-$550 an hour.

A $25-$45 per-party, per-night fee is charged for cabins. There is a 7-night limit May through September; a 10-night limit the rest of the year. Cabin permits are necessary and can be requested up to 180 days prior to use; full payment is required at the time the reservation is made. Forest information centers with exhibits, films and cabin reservation information are in Juneau *(see place listing p. 518)*, Ketchikan *(see place listing p. 522)* and Petersburg *(see place listing p. 528)*.

For further information write Southeast Alaska Discovery Center, 50 Main St., Ketchikan, AK 99901; phone (907) 228-6220, TTY (907) 228-6237, or (877) 444-6777 for camping and cabin reservations. *See Recreation Areas Chart.*

 MENDENHALL GLACIER—see Juneau p. 520.

TRAPPER CREEK pop. 481

GATE CREEK CABINS   (907)733-1393
♦♦ Cabin. **Address:** 21800 Townes Pl 99683

TRAPPER CREEK INN & RV PARK   907/733-2302
♦ Motel. **Address:** Mile 114.6 Parks Hwy 99683

VALDEZ (C-12) pop. 3,976, elev. 15'

Called the "Switzerland of Alaska," Valdez (val-DEEZ) is ringed by snowcapped mountains. As the northernmost ice-free port, the town was established in 1898 as an outfitting point for miners taking the hazardous pack trail over Valdez Glacier to the northern gold fields.

In addition to the gold rush, Valdez's rich history includes the 5-minute, 9.2-magnitude Good Friday earthquake in 1964; construction of the Trans-Alaska Pipeline and Marine Terminal in the 1970s; and the 1989 *Exxon Valdez* oil spill and cleanup.

Access into Valdez is by scheduled air service, ferry or via the scenic Richardson Highway. Near Milepost 16 are Bridal Veil and Horsetail falls and the Historic 1899 Trans-Alaska Military Trail & Wagon Road. Thompson Pass, Milepost 26, offers a spectacular view of the Chugach Mountains, valley rivers and historic Keystone Canyon. At Milepost 29 is Worthington Glacier State Park, which has walking trails.

Nearby glaciers in Prince William Sound include Mears, Shoup and Columbia, the second largest tidewater glacier in North America.

Valdez Convention and Visitors Bureau: 309 Fairbanks Dr., Valdez, AK 99686. **Phone:** (907) 835-2984.

▼ See AAA listing p. 537 ▼

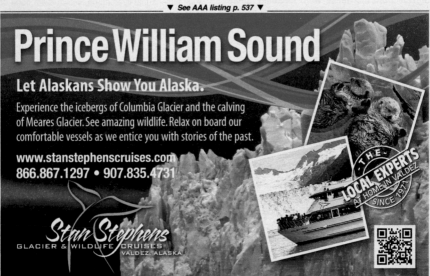

MAXINE & JESSE WHITNEY MUSEUM is on the grounds of Prince William Sound Community College at 303 Lowe St. The museum's collection of Alaskan native art, artifacts, beadwork, dolls and furs comprises one of the largest of its kind. Its pieces were collected over more than 50 years of travel to Alaskan villages by Jesse Whitney and wife Maxine after the couple moved to Alaska in 1947. The Paul Kulik History of Transportation Collection features to-scale vehicle models made of Eskimo ivory and that interpret the state's aviation history.

Time: Allow 30 minutes minimum. **Hours:** Daily 9-7, Memorial Day-Labor Day; by appointment rest of year. Closed major holidays. **Cost:** Donations. **Phone:** (907) 834-1690.

STAN STEPHENS GLACIER & WILDLIFE CRUISES departs from 112 N. Harbor Dr., 3 blks. e. of jct. Richardson Hwy. and Meals St. The outfit offers 6- and 9-hour narrated sightseeing cruises on Prince William Sound to Columbia and Meares glaciers. Along the way, guests might glimpse bald eagles, Dall's porpoises, black bears, sea otters, Steller sea lions, puffins, mountain goats and humpback, minke and orca whales. A narrator details area history and information about the Trans-Alaska Pipeline. A light meal is included.

Hours: Columbia Glacier trips depart daily at 11, mid-May to mid-Sept. Meares Glacier trips depart daily at 10, early June-Aug. 31. Meares Glacier trips are not available on some days. Phone ahead to confirm schedule. **Cost:** Fare $132-$165; $66-$82 (ages 3-12). Reservations are recommended. **Phone:** (907) 835-4731 or (866) 867-1297. *(See ad p. 536.)*

BEST WESTERN VALDEZ HARBOR INN   (907)835-3434

WWW
Hotel
$99-$249

BW Best Western. **AAA Benefit:** Save 10% or more every day and earn 10% bonus points!

Address: 100 N Harbor Dr 99686 **Location:** Just s at Meals Ave. Located at small boat harbor. **Facility:** 88 units. 2 stories (no elevator), interior corridors. **Terms:** check-in 4 pm, resort fee. **Dining:** Off the Hook Grill, see separate listing. **Activities:** exercise room. **Guest Services:** coin laundry, area transportation. **Featured Amenity:** breakfast buffet.

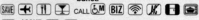

WHERE TO EAT

ALASKA HALIBUT HOUSE   907/835-2788
W Fish & Chips. Quick Serve. **Address:** 208 Meals Ave 99686

FU KUNG   907/835-5255
WW Chinese Sushi. Casual Dining. **Address:** 207 Kobuk St (Box 263) 99686

MIKE'S PALACE   907/835-2365
WW Regional International. Casual Dining. **Address:** 205 N Harbor Dr 99686

OFF THE HOOK GRILL   907/835-8114
WW International. Casual Dining. **Address:** 100 N Harbor Dr 99686

WASILLA (C-11) pop. 7,831
• Restaurants p. 538

Founded in 1917 with the construction of the Alaska Railroad, the community of Wasilla is contiguous to the junction of SRs 1 and 3, both of which are scenic highways, and rests in the Matanuska-Susitna Valley. The area's name originates from that of a respected Native American chief and has varying interpretations; some believe the word is defined as "breath of air" in the Dena'ina Athabascan Indian dialect, while others attribute it to a variation of the Russian word for the name William, "Vasili."

Gold miners from nearby Knik and Willow Creek flocked to Wasilla in the early 1900s due to its proximity to the gold fields and newly constructed railroad. With the advent of Anchorage in 1915 and Wasilla's founding two years later, Knik and other neighboring communities were rapidly abandoned. Mining in Wasilla played an integral role through much of World War II and the mid-20th century; a handful of the area's mines, which once numbered more than 50, remain active to this day.

The Dorothy G. Page Museum, 323 N. Main St., contains historical artifacts and relates the heritage of Wasilla, Knik and Willow Creek. The museum is open year-round; phone (907) 373-9071. Adjoining the museum is the Old Wasilla Town Site, which preserves Wasilla's first school, two log cabins, a post office, a smithy and the town's first public bath.

In August 2008, former Alaska Gov. Sarah Palin, who served two terms as mayor of Wasilla 1996-2002, was chosen by Arizona Sen. John McCain as his running mate in the November presidential election. Her GOP nomination set several precedents as Palin became the first Alaskan and only the second woman—and the first woman as a Republican—to appear on a major party's presidential ticket.

Greater Wasilla Chamber of Commerce: 415 E. Railroad Ave., Wasilla, AK 99654. **Phone:** (907) 376-1299.

AGATE INN   (907)373-2290
WWW Hotel. **Address:** 4725 Begich Cir 99654

BEST WESTERN LAKE LUCILLE INN   (907)373-1776

WWW
Hotel
$100-$300

BW Best Western. **AAA Benefit:** Save 10% or more every day and earn 10% bonus points!

Address: 1300 W Lake Lucille Dr 99654 **Location:** SR 3 (George Parks Hwy), just w on Hallea Ln; center. **Facility:** 54 units. 2 stories (no elevator), interior corridors. **Parking:** winter plug-ins. **Activities:** sauna, boat dock, exercise room. **Guest Services:** coin laundry. *(See ad p. 499.)*

EVANGELO'S TRATTORIA   907/376-1212
♦♦ Italian. Casual Dining. **Address:** 2530 E Parks Hwy 99654

WHITTIER (D-11) pop. 220

Nearly surrounded by mountains and perched at the edge of beautiful Prince William Sound, Whittier remained relatively isolated until June 2000 when a 2.5-mile railroad tunnel was converted to accommodate automobile traffic. The unusual Anton Anderson Memorial Tunnel is a single-lane combination highway and railway that enables cars and trains to take turns passing through the tunnel. Because the tunnel has only one lane, the direction of traffic alternates, ceasing altogether while trains travel through.

Phone (877) 611-2586 for the tunnel's traffic schedule. Tunnel information also is broadcast by radio on 530 AM in Whittier and 1610 AM in Portage and Bear Valley. A toll of $12 per car is charged at the tunnel's western entrance; toll increases with size of vehicle.

26 GLACIER CRUISE BY PHILLIPS CRUISES departs from the port of Whittier. Cruises explore the calm, protected waters of Prince William Sound. Passengers aboard the company's high-speed catamaran can see tidewater glaciers plus an array of wildlife on this 5-hour tour. A 3.75-hour Glacier Quest cruise also is available. All cruises are narrated by a Chugach National Forest Service Ranger.

Hours: 26 Glacier Cruise departs daily at 12:30, May-Sept. Glacier Quest Cruise departs daily at 1, May-Sept. **Cost:** 26 Glacier Cruise (includes onboard lunch) $149; $89 (ages 2-11). Glacier Quest Cruise (includes onboard lunch) $99; $59 (ages 2-11). Bus or rail service is offered from Anchorage, Girdwood or Whittier at an additional cost. Reservations are recommended. **Phone:** (907) 276-8023 or (800) 544-0529. *(See ad p. 492.)*

MAJOR MARINE TOURS depart from the marina day-cruise dock. A 4.5-hour or 5.25-hour sightseeing cruise narrated by a Chugach forest ranger takes passengers to see spectacular 700-foot-tall active tidewater glaciers and picturesque waterfalls in Prince William Sound. Eagles, otters, sea lions, whales and shorebirds may be spotted.

Inquire about weather policies. **Hours:** Departures daily at 12:15 (5.25-hour cruise) and 12:45 (4.5-hour cruise), mid-May to mid-Sept. **Cost:** Fare for 4.5-hour cruise $119; $59.50 (ages 2-11). Fare for 5.25-hour cruise $149; $74.50 (ages 2-11). Onboard lunch available for an additional $19. Reservations are recommended. **Phone:** (907) 274-7300 or (800) 764-7300. *(See ad this page.)* 🍽

RECREATIONAL ACTIVITIES
Kayaking
• **Alaska Sea Kayakers** depart from the Whittier Boat Harbor. **Hours:** Daily 8-7, May-Sept. **Phone:** (907) 472-2534 or (877) 472-2534.

▼ *See AAA listing this page* ▼

WRANGELL (H-11) pop. 2,369, elev. 37'

Petroglyphs pecked into shale rock and elaborately carved totem poles, cedar monuments of the Stikine (STIK-een) and Tlingit (KLINK-it) Indians, are interesting aspects of Wrangell. Although European and American explorers visited the area in the late 1700s, Russians began trading here by 1811 and established a redoubt in Wrangell in 1834. The only Alaskan town to have existed under Russian, British and American rule, it also survived three gold rushes in 1861, 1872 and 1898, when the lure of riches brought an onslaught of miners and settlers.

Petroglyphs can be seen on a beach at the north end of Wrangell Island. Of undetermined age, some carvings face the water, others the shore or sky. They are best viewed at low tide. Nearby Anan Creek allows the opportunity to observe sea lions and seals and watch black bear fish for salmon.

Other attractions include the nine totem poles (some are replicas carved by the Civilian Conservation Corps in the late 1930s) on Shakes Island in Wrangell Harbor, as well as the four totem poles in Kiksadi Totem Park at Front and Episcopal streets. Artifacts are displayed in Chief Shakes Tribal House, also on the island. A large concentration of bald eagles gather in the borough from January to mid-April waiting for smelt to run up the Stikine River.

Wrangell Chamber of Commerce: 107 Stikine Ave., P.O. Box 49, Wrangell, AK 99929. **Phone:** (907) 874-3901.

WRANGELL MUSEUM is at 296 Campbell Dr. The collection describes the colorful history of the Wrangell area. Of note are four beautiful Tlingit houseposts—carved in the 1700s, they are believed to be the oldest complete set in existence. A variety of displays detail early Russian and English settlement and the city's role in the 1861 Stikine gold rush. Spruceroot and cedarbark baskets, beadwork, stone tools and other artifacts crafted by Alaskan natives are shown.

Time: Allow 30 minutes minimum. **Hours:** Mon.-Sat. 10-5, Apr. 15-Oct. 15; Fri.-Sat. noon-5, rest of year. Phone ahead to confirm schedule. **Cost:** $7; $5 (ages 60+); $4 (ages 6-12). **Phone:** (907) 874-3770.

WRANGELL-ST. ELIAS NATIONAL PARK AND PRESERVE (C-12, E-7)

Elevations in the park and preserve range from sea level at the Gulf of Alaska to 18,008 ft. at Mount St. Elias. Refer to AAA maps for additional elevation information.

In southeast Alaska bordering Canada's Yukon, Wrangell-St. Elias National Park and Preserve is the country's largest national park. It is a place of overpowering dimensions, embracing an area larger than Massachusetts, Rhode Island and Connecticut combined; glaciers five times the size of Manhattan; and nine of the 16 highest peaks in North America.

In this 13-million-acre park, the collision of two continental plates has produced some of the world's highest coastal ranges. Forming a barrier along the Gulf of Alaska are the Chugach Mountains, and paralleling them to the north are the Wrangell Mountains.

Between these two ranges are the St. Elias Mountains, extending like the stem of the letter "Y" into Canada's Kluane National Park. Atop these towering peaks are ice fields so immense that they act as a natural cooling system, affecting areas as far south as Chicago and the Central Plains.

As imposing as its ice fields are, it was another commodity traded by the Ahtna Dene or "people of the Copper River" that caught the world's attention. These and other tribes forged tools of locally mined copper. The first person of European descent to verify the source of the copper trading was Lt. Henry Allen, who in 1885 explored much of Alaska's interior.

Fifteen years later two miners discovered the malachite cliffs above the Kennicott Glacier, which became one of the world's richest sources of copper. The subsequent founding of the Kennecott Mine became one of the most significant events in Alaska's history: The great wealth and development it spawned affected not only Alaska but the entire nation. Currently the ruined mine, a 14-story mill building and a few historic structures are all that remain of this immense enterprise, preserved as the Kennecott Mines National Historic Landmark. St. Elias Alpine Guides offers two-hour guided tours of the mill building daily at 9:30, 1:30 and 3:30, late May to mid-Sept.; the cost is $27.50 per person. The Kennicott Visitor Center is open daily 9:30-6:30, Memorial Day-Labor Day; phone (907) 554-1105 for ranger-guided program information. Phone (907) 554-4445 for mill building tour information, or inquire in person at the visitor center.

Legacies of the Kennecott Mine and the Yukon gold fields are some of the area's roads, which provide limited access to the park. One of Alaska's oldest roadways is the Richardson Highway, which was completed in 1919 and was the first all-Alaska route to the Yukon gold fields. Both the Richardson and Glenn highways follow the curve of the park's western boundary and offer several spectacular views of 12,010-foot Mount Drum, 14,163-foot Mount Wrangell and 16,237-foot Mount Sanford.

Two other roads penetrate the park's interior—the Chitina-McCarthy and the Nabesna. Both of these gravel roads offer good views of the mountains and are convenient jumping-off places for hiking and river-running. The 60-mile McCarthy Road follows an abandoned railroad bed. Visitors should allow a minimum of 3 hours to drive between Chitina and McCarthy. Before using either of these routes, check with the ranger stations in Slana and Chitina.

The park's headquarters and visitor center, 3 miles north of Copper Center on Richardson

Highway at Milepost 106.8, provides trip-planning assistance and information about park activities. Fishing, hiking, rafting and wildlife- viewing, especially of the park's large population of Dall sheep, are just some of the activities pursued in the park; phone (907) 822-7250.

On the southeastern edge of the park and accessible only by sea is Hubbard Glacier on Disenchantment Bay. In 1986 this vast, active tidewater glacier advanced so quickly that for several months it blocked the entrance to Russell Fjord behind a dam of ice, briefly turning it into a lake.

For more information write the Superintendent, Wrangell-St. Elias National Park and Preserve, P.O. Box 439, Copper Center, AK 99573; phone (907) 822-5234. *See Recreation Areas Chart.*

YUKON-CHARLEY RIVERS NATIONAL PRESERVE (A-12, D-7)

Elevations in the preserve range from 600 ft. on the Yukon River where it leaves the preserve near Circle to 6,435 ft. in the Cirque Lakes area on the Charley River drainage. Refer to AAA maps for additional elevation information.

Near the Canadian border in east central Alaska, more than 140 miles of the Yukon River and the entire watershed of the Charley River are encompassed within the 2.5 million acres of the Yukon-Charley Rivers National Preserve. John McPhee remarked in his book "Coming into the Country" that New Jersey could easily fit into this vast emptiness between Eagle and Circle.

Although only 10 year-round residents now live within the preserve's boundaries, it was not always so sparsely populated. During the gold rush, the Yukon—a summer waterway and winter highway—was thronged with people who briefly transformed such communities as Circle and Dawson City, Canada into the "Paris of the North." This rough-and-tumble gold rush region was the grist of Robert Service's poetry and Jack London's stories.

Now quiet has returned, and where riverboats once departed from Eagle, river runners make the 5- to 7-day float down the river to Circle. One of the pleasures of this trip is the opportunity to see Peregrine falcons, a threatened species that makes its home in the bluffs along the river. Hikers can catch a glimpse of caribou and Dall sheep in the preserve's upland regions and moose in the lowlands.

The Taylor and Steese highways are the primary summer access routes to the national preserve, terminating respectively in Eagle and Circle just outside the preserve's boundaries. The scenic portion of the Taylor Highway from Chicken to Eagle runs through mountains, rolling tundra and river valleys. Most people, however, reach the park by boat or float on the Yukon River and its tributaries.

The preserve has no roads and no established trails or maintained public airstrips. Seven public-use cabins are available on a first-come, first-served basis. Food service, basic supplies, lodgings and charter boat and air service are available during the summer months in nearby Eagle and Circle. A list of authorized guides can be obtained from the preserve headquarters and visitor center in Eagle.

In addition, the Bureau of Land Management administers Fort Egbert and a campground in Eagle. The park visitor center is open daily 8-5, mid-May through Labor Day; Mon.-Fri. 8-5, rest of year. The center can be contacted at P.O. Box 167, Eagle, AK 99738; phone (907) 547-2233. For more information write the Superintendent, Yukon-Charley Rivers National Preserve, 4175 Geist Rd., Fairbanks, AK 99707-4718. *See Recreation Areas Chart.*

 *Offices*

Main office listings are shown in **BOLD TYPE** and toll-free member service numbers appear in *ITALIC TYPE*.
All are closed Saturdays, Sundays and holidays unless otherwise indicated.
The addresses, phone numbers and hours for any AAA/CAA office are subject to change.
The type of service provided is designated below the name of the city where the office is located:

✛ Auto travel services, including books and maps, and on-demand TripTik® routings.
● Auto travel services, including selected books and maps, and on-demand TripTik® routings.
▪ Books/maps only, no marked maps or on-demand TripTik® routings.
▲ Travel Agency Services, cruise, tour, air, car and rail reservations; domestic and international hotel reservations; passport photo services; international and domestic travel guides and maps; travel money products; and International Driving Permits. In addition, assistance with travel related insurance products including trip cancellation, travel accident, lost luggage, trip delay and assistance products.
❖ Insurance services provided. If only this icon appears, only insurance services are provided at that office.
◖ Car Care Plus Facility provides car care services.
▣ Electric vehicle charging station on premises.

AAA NATIONAL OFFICE: 1000 AAA DRIVE, HEATHROW, FLORIDA 32746-5063, (407) 444-7000

ALASKA

ANCHORAGE—AAA MOUNTAINWEST, 3565 ARCTIC BLVD STE D5, 99503. WEEKDAYS (M-F) 8:30-5:30. (907) 344-4310, *(888) 460-4222.* ✛ ▲ ❖

ALBERTA

CALGARY—ALBERTA MOTOR ASSOCIATION, #600 85 SHAWVILLE BLVD SE, T2Y 3W5. WEEKDAYS (M-F) 9:00-6:00, SAT 9:00-5:00. (403) 254-6776, *(800) 642-3810.* ● ▲ ❖

CALGARY—ALBERTA MOTOR ASSOCIATION, 220 CROWFOOT CRES NW, T3G 3N5. WEEKDAYS (M-F) 9:00-6:00, SAT 9:00-5:00. (403) 239-6644, *(800) 642-3810.* ● ▲ ❖

CALGARY—ALBERTA MOTOR ASSOCIATION, 3650 20 AVE NE, T1Y 6E8. WEEKDAYS (M-F) 9:00-6:00, SAT 9:00-5:00. (403) 590-0009, *(800) 642-3810.* ● ▲ ❖

CALGARY—ALBERTA MOTOR ASSOCIATION, 4700 17TH AVE SW, T3E 0E3. WEEKDAYS (M-F) 9:00-6:00, SAT 9:00-5:00. (403) 240-5300, *(800) 642-3810.* ● ▲ ❖

CALGARY—ALBERTA MOTOR ASSOCIATION, 524-10816 MACLEOD TRL SE, T2J 5N8. WEEKDAYS (M-F) 9:00-6:00, SAT 9:00-5:00. (403) 278-4840, *(800) 642-3810.* ● ▲ ❖

CAMROSE—ALBERTA MOTOR ASSOCIATION, 6702 48 AVE, T4V 4S3. WEEKDAYS (M-F) 9:00-5:30, SAT 9:00-2:00. (780) 672-3391, *(800) 642-3810.* ● ▲ ❖

EDMONTON—ALBERTA MOTOR ASSOCIATION, 10310 GA MACDONALD AVE NW, T6J 6R7. WEEKDAYS (M-F) 9:00-6:00. (780) 430-5555, *(800) 642-3810.* ● ▲ ❖

EDMONTON—ALBERTA MOTOR ASSOCIATION, 10310 GA MACDONALD AVE NW, T6J 6R7. WEEKDAYS (M-F) 9:00-6:00, SAT 9:00-5:00. (780) 430-5468 ● ▲ ❖

EDMONTON—ALBERTA MOTOR ASSOCIATION, 11220 109 ST NW, T5G 2T6. WEEKDAYS (M-F) 9:00-6:00, SAT 9:00-5:00. (780) 474-8700, *(800) 642-3810.* ● ▲ ❖

EDMONTON—ALBERTA MOTOR ASSOCIATION, 5040 MANNING DR NW, T5A 5B4. WEEKDAYS (M-F) 9:00-6:00, SAT 9:00-5:00. (780) 473-3123, *(800) 642-3810.* ● ▲ ❖

EDMONTON—ALBERTA MOTOR ASSOCIATION, 9938 170 ST, T5T 6G7. WEEKDAYS (M-F) 9:00-6:00, SAT 9:00-5:00. (780) 484-1221, *(800) 642-3810.* ● ▲ ❖

FORT MCMURRAY—ALBERTA MOTOR ASSOCIATION, 4 HOSPITAL ST, T9H 5E4. WEEKDAYS (M-F) 9:00-5:30. (780) 743-2433, *(800) 642-3810.* ● ▲ ❖

GRANDE PRAIRIE—ALBERTA MOTOR ASSOCIATION, 11401 99 ST, T8V 2H6. WEEKDAYS (M-F) 9:00-5:30, SAT 9:00-2:00. (780) 532-4421, *(800) 642-3810.* ● ▲ ❖

LETHBRIDGE—ALBERTA MOTOR ASSOCIATION, 120 SCENIC DR S, T1J 4R4. WEEKDAYS (M-F) 9:00-5:30, SAT 9:00-2:00. (403) 328-7921, *(800) 642-3810.* ● ▲ ❖

MEDICINE HAT—ALBERTA MOTOR ASSOCIATION, 2710 13 AVE SE, T1A 3P8. WEEKDAYS (M-F) 9:00-5:30, SAT 9:00-2:00. (403) 527-1166, *(800) 642-3810.* ● ▲ ❖

RED DEER—ALBERTA MOTOR ASSOCIATION, 141 2004 50TH AVE, T4R 3A2. WEEKDAYS (M-F) 9:00-5:30, SAT 9:00-5:00. (403) 342-6633 ● ▲ ❖

SHERWOOD PARK—ALBERTA MOTOR ASSOCIATION, #19 101 BREMNER DR, T8H 0M5. WEEKDAYS (M-F) 9:00-6:00, SAT 9:00-5:00. (780) 467-8074, *(800) 642-3810.* ● ▲ ❖

ST. ALBERT—ALBERTA MOTOR ASSOCIATION, 200 665 ST ALBERT TRL, T8N 3L3. WEEKDAYS (M-F) 9:00-6:00, SAT 9:00-5:00. (780) 418-8900, *(800) 642-3810.* ● ▲ ❖

BRITISH COLUMBIA

ABBOTSFORD—CAA BRITISH COLUMBIA, 33338 S FRASER WAY, V2S 2B4. WEEKDAYS (M-F) 9:00-5:30, SAT 9:00-5:00. (604) 870-3850, *(800) 663-1956.* ✛ ❖

BURNABY—CAA BRITISH COLUMBIA, 4480 LOUGHEED HWY, V5C 3Z3. WEEKDAYS (M-F) 9:00-6:00, SAT 9:00-5:00. (604) 268-4060 ✛ ❖ ▣

BURNABY—CAA BRITISH COLUMBIA, 4567 CANADA WAY, V5G 4T1. WEEKDAYS (M-F) 8:30-5:00. (604) 268-5000 ✛ ❖ ▣

BURNABY—CAA BRITISH COLUMBIA, 4567 CANADA WAY, V5G 4T1. WEEKDAYS (M-F) 9:00-5:30, SAT 9:00-5:00. (604) 268-5500, *(800) 663-1956.* ✛ ❖

CHILLIWACK—CAA BRITISH COLUMBIA, #1-45609 LUCKAKUCK WAY, V2R 1A3. WEEKDAYS (M-F) 9:00-6:00, SAT 9:00-5:00. (604) 824-2720, *(800) 663-1956.* ✛ ❖

COQUITLAM—CAA BRITISH COLUMBIA, 50-2773 BARNET HWY, V3B 1C2. WEEKDAYS (M-F) 9:00-6:00, SAT 9:00-5:00. (604) 268-5750, *(800) 663-1956.* ✛ ❖

COURTENAY—CAA BRITISH COLUMBIA, UNIT 17-1599 CLIFFE AVE, V9N 2K6. WEEKDAYS (M-F) 8:30-5:30, SAT 9:00-5:00. (250) 703-2328, *(800) 663-1956.* ✛ ❖

DELTA—CAA BRITISH COLUMBIA, 7343 120TH ST, V4C 6P5. WEEKDAYS (M-F) 9:00-6:00, SAT 9:00-5:00. (604) 268-5900, *(800) 663-1956.* ✛ ❖

KAMLOOPS—CAA BRITISH COLUMBIA, 400-500 NOTRE DAME DR, V2C 6T6. WEEKDAYS (M-F) 9:00-6:00, SAT 9:00-5:00. (250) 852-4600, *(800) 663-1956.* ✛ ❖

KELOWNA—CAA BRITISH COLUMBIA, #18-1470 HARVEY AVE, V1Y 9K8. WEEKDAYS (M-F) 9:00-6:00, SAT 9:00-5:00. (250) 870-4900, *(800) 663-1956.* ✛ ❖

KELOWNA—CAA BRITISH COLUMBIA, 1545 KEEHN RD, V1X 5T3. WEEKDAYS (M-F) 7:30-6:00, SAT 8:30-5:00. (250) 979-4950 ◄

LANGLEY—CAA BRITISH COLUMBIA, #10 -20190 LANGLEY BYPASS, V3A 9J9. WEEKDAYS (M-F) 9:00-6:00, SAT 9:00-5:00. (604) 268-5950, *(800) 663-1956.* ✚ ✿

MAPLE RIDGE—CAA BRITISH COLUMBIA, #500 20395 LOUGHEED HWY, V2X 2P9. WEEKDAYS (M-F) 9:00-6:00, SAT 9:00-5:00. (604) 205-1200, *(800) 633-1956.* ✚

NANAIMO—CAA BRITISH COLUMBIA, #400 6581 AULDS RD, V9T 6J6. WEEKDAYS (M-F) 9:00-6:00, SAT 9:00-5:00. (250) 390-7700, *(800) 663-1956.* ✚ ✿

NANAIMO—CAA BRITISH COLUMBIA, #600-6581 AULDS RD, V9T 6J6. WEEKDAYS (M-F) 7:30-6:00, SAT 8:30-5:00. (250) 390-7380 ◄

NELSON—CAA BRITISH COLUMBIA, 596 BAKER ST, V1L 4H9. WEEKDAYS (M-F) 9:00-5:00, SAT 9:00-5:00. (250) 505-1720, *(800) 663-1956.* ✚ ✿

NEW WESTMINSTER—CAA BRITISH COLUMBIA, 501 SIXTH ST, V3L 3B9. WEEKDAYS (M-F) 9:00-6:00, SAT 9:00-5:00. (604) 268-5700, *(800) 663-1956.* ✚ ✿

NORTH VANCOUVER—CAA BRITISH COLUMBIA, 1527 LONSDALE AVE, V7M 2J2. WEEKDAYS (M-F) 9:00-6:00, SAT 9:00-5:00. (604) 205-1050, *(800) 663-1956.* ✚ ✿

PENTICTON—CAA BRITISH COLUMBIA, #162-2111 MAIN ST, V2A 1A3. WEEKDAYS (M-F) 7:30-6:00, SAT 8:30-5:00. (250) 487-2430 ◄

PENTICTON—CAA BRITISH COLUMBIA, 100-2100 MAIN ST, V2A 5H7. WEEKDAYS (M-F) 9:00-6:00, SAT 9:00-5:00. (250) 487-2450, *(800) 663-1956.* ✚ ✿

PRINCE GEORGE—CAA BRITISH COLUMBIA, 100 - 2324 FERRY AVE, V2N 0B1. WEEKDAYS (M-F) 9:00-6:00, SAT 9:00-5:00. (250) 649-2399, *(800) 663-1956.* ✚ ✿

RICHMOND—CAA BRITISH COLUMBIA, #618-5300 NO 3 RD, V6X 2X9. WEEKDAYS (M-F) 9:00-6:00, SAT 9:00-5:00. (604) 268-5850, *(800) 663-1956.* ✚ ✿

SURREY—CAA BRITISH COLUMBIA, #D1-15251 101 AVE, V3R 9V8. WEEKDAYS (M-F) 9:00-6:00, SAT 9:00-5:00. (604) 205-1000, *(800) 663-1956.* ✚ ✿

SURREY—CAA BRITISH COLUMBIA, 130 2655 KING GEORGE BLVD, V4P 1H7. WEEKDAYS (M-F) 9:00-6:00, SAT 9:00-5:00. (604) 205-1150, *(800) 663-1956.* ✚ ✿

VANCOUVER—CAA BRITISH COLUMBIA, 2301 CAMBIE ST, V5Z 2T9. WEEKDAYS (M-F) 9:00-6:00, SAT 9:00-5:00. (604) 268-5600, *(800) 663-1956.* ✚ ✿

VANCOUVER—CAA BRITISH COLUMBIA, 2347 W 41ST AVE, V6M 2A3. WEEKDAYS (M-F) 9:00-6:00, SAT 9:00-5:00. (604) 268-5800, *(800) 663-1956.* ✚ ✿

VANCOUVER—CAA BRITISH COLUMBIA, 289 DAVIE ST, V6B 0H8. WEEKDAYS (M-F) 9:00-6:00, SAT 9:00-5:00. (604) 801-7130 ✚ ✿

VANCOUVER—CAA BRITISH COLUMBIA, 428 SW MARINE DR, V5X 0C4. WEEKDAYS (M-F) 9:00-6:00, SAT 9:00-5:00. (604) 268-4000 ✚ ✿ ▢

VERNON—CAA BRITISH COLUMBIA, #103-5710 24TH ST, V1T 9T3. WEEKDAYS (M-F) 9:00-6:00, SAT 9:00-5:00. (250) 550-2400, *(800) 663-1956.* ✚ ✿

VERNON—CAA BRITISH COLUMBIA, 5460 ANDERSON WAY, V1T 9W2. WEEKDAYS (M-F) 7:30-6:00. (250) 558-2340 ◄

VICTORIA—CAA BRITISH COLUMBIA, #120-777 ROYAL OAK DR, V8X 4V1. WEEKDAYS (M-F) 9:00-6:00, SAT 9:00-5:00, SUN 11:00-5:00. (250) 704-1750, *(800) 663-1956.* ✚ ✿

VICTORIA—CAA BRITISH COLUMBIA, UNIT 115 1644 HILLSIDE AV, V8T 2C5. WEEKDAYS (M-F) 9:30-5:30, SAT 9:30-5:30, SUN 11:00-5:30. (250) 414-8320, *(800) 663-1956.* ✚ ✿

WEST VANCOUVER—CAA BRITISH COLUMBIA, 710 MAIN ST PARK ROYAL S, V7T 0A5. WEEKDAYS (M-F) 9:00-6:00, SAT 9:00-5:00, SUN 11:00-5:00. (604) 268-5650, *(800) 663-1956.* ✚ ✿

WESTBANK—CAA BRITISH COLUMBIA, 301 3550 CARRINGTON RD, V4T 2Z1. WEEKDAYS (M-F) 9:00-6:00, SAT 9:00-5:00. (250) 707-4800, *(800) 663-1956.* ✚ ✿

MANITOBA

ALTONA—CAA MANITOBA, 61 2ND AVE NE, R0G 0B0. WEEKDAYS (M-F) 9:00-5:00, SAT 9:00-1:00. (204) 324-8474 ●▲✿

BRANDON—CAA MANITOBA, 305 - 18TH ST N, R7A 6Z2. WEEKDAYS (M-F) 9:00-5:00, THU 9:00-8:00, SAT 9:00-4:00. (204) 571-4111, *(877) 222-1321.* ✚▲✿

WINNIPEG—CAA MANITOBA, 2211 MCPHILLIPS ST UNIT C, R2V 3M5. WEEKDAYS (M-F) 9:00-6:00, SAT 9:00-4:00. (204) 262-6223, *(800) 222-4357.* ●▲✿

WINNIPEG—CAA MANITOBA, 501 ST ANNES RD, R2M 3E5. WEEKDAYS (M-F) 9:00-6:00, SAT 9:00-4:00. (204) 262-6201, *(800) 222-4357.* ●▲✿

WINNIPEG—CAA MANITOBA, 870 EMPRESS ST, R3G 3H3. WEEKDAYS (M-F) 9:00-6:00, SAT 9:00-4:00. (204) 262-6166, *(800) 222-4357.* ✚▲✿

WINNIPEG—CAA MANITOBA, 987 MILT STEGALL DR, R3G 3H7. WEEKDAYS (M-F) 8:30-4:00. (204) 262-6166

SASKATCHEWAN

ESTEVAN—CAA SASKATCHEWAN, 1208 4TH ST, S4A 0W9. WEEKDAYS (M-F) 9:00-5:30. (306) 637-2185, *(800) 564-6222.* ✚▲✿

MOOSE JAW—CAA SASKATCHEWAN, 80 CARIBOU ST W, S6H 2J6. WEEKDAYS (M-F) 9:00-5:30, SAT 9:00-5:30. (306) 693-5195, *(800) 564-6222.* ✚▲✿

NORTH BATTLEFORD—CAA SASKATCHEWAN, 2002-100TH ST, S9A 0X5. WEEKDAYS (M-F) 9:00-5:30, SAT 9:00-5:30. (306) 445-9451, *(800) 564-6222.* ✚▲✿

PRINCE ALBERT—CAA SASKATCHEWAN, #29 2995 2ND AVE W, S6V 5V5. WEEKDAYS (M-F) 9:00-5:30, SAT 9:00-5:30. (306) 764-6818, *(800) 564-6222.* ✚▲✿

REGINA—CAA SASKATCHEWAN, 200 ALBERT ST, S4R 2N4. WEEKDAYS (M-F) 9:00-5:30, SAT 9:00-5:30. (306) 791-4337, *(800) 564-6222.* ✚▲✿

REGINA—CAA SASKATCHEWAN, 200 ALBERT ST N, S4R 5E2. WEEKDAYS (M-F) 8:30-5:00. (306) 779-6635, *(800) 564-6222.*

REGINA—CAA SASKATCHEWAN, 2510 E QUANCE ST, S4V 2X5. WEEKDAYS (M-F) 9:00-5:30, SAT 9:00-5:30 (306) 791-4323, *(800) 564-6222.* ✚▲✿

REGINA—CAA SASKATCHEWAN, 4528 ALBERT ST, S4S 6B4. WEEKDAYS (M-F) 9:00-5:30, SAT 9:00-5:30. (306) 791-4322, *(800) 564-6222.* ✚▲✿

REGINA—CAA SASKATCHEWAN, 980 DEWDNEY AVE, S4N 0G8. WEEKDAYS (M-F) 7:30-5:00. (306) 791-9500 ◄

SASKATOON—CAA SASKATCHEWAN, 150 - 1ST AVE S, S7K 1K2. WEEKDAYS (M-F) 9:00-5:30, SAT 9:00-5:30. (306) 668-3737, *(800) 564-6222.* ✚▲✿

SASKATOON—CAA SASKATCHEWAN, 2112 MILLAR AVE, S7K 6P4. WEEKDAYS (M-F) 7:30-5:00. (306) 668-3768 ◄

SASKATOON—CAA SASKATCHEWAN, 3110 8TH ST E #1, S7H 0W2. WEEKDAYS (M-F) 9:00-5:30, SAT 9:00-5:30. (306) 668-3770, *(800) 564-6222.* ✚▲✿

SWIFT CURRENT—CAA SASKATCHEWAN, 15 DUFFERIN ST W, S9H 5A1. WEEKDAYS (M-F) 9:00-5:30, SAT 9:00-5:30. (306) 773-3193, *(800) 564-6222.* ✚▲✿

WEYBURN—CAA SASKATCHEWAN, 110 SOURIS AVE, S4H 2Z8. WEEKDAYS (M-F) 9:00-5:30, SAT 9:00-5:30. (306) 842-6651, *(800) 564-6222.* ✚▲✿

YORKTON—CAA SASKATCHEWAN, 159 BROADWAY ST E, S3N 3K6. WEEKDAYS (M-F) 9:00-5:30, SAT 9:00-5:30. (306) 783-6536, *(800) 564-6222.* ✚▲✿

Border Information

U.S. Residents Traveling to Canada

Border crossing requirements: Travelers are required to present proper travel documents in order to enter Canada and return to the U.S.

Air travel: A U.S. passport is required.

Land or sea travel: Proof of citizenship and proof of identity are required. Approved documents include a passport or passport card, Enhanced Driver's License or NEXUS trusted traveler program card. Visit the U.S. Department of State website travel.state.gov for the most current information on these requirements. Canadian citizens should refer to the Canada Border Services Agency website www.cbsa-asfc.gc.ca.

U.S. resident aliens: An Alien Registration Receipt Card (Green Card) as well as a passport from the country of citizenship is required.

Children: All children must provide their own travel documents. In lieu of a U.S. passport or passport card, children under 16 traveling to Canada by land or sea may present an original or copy of their birth certificate, a Report of Birth Abroad obtained from a U.S. Consulate or a Naturalization Certificate. Minors must be accompanied by both parents; if one parent is absent, a notarized

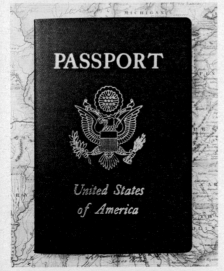

letter of consent from the absent parent giving permission to go on the trip is required.

Legal Issues: Persons with felony convictions, DUI convictions or other offenses may be denied entry into Canada.

Firearms: Canada has strict laws regarding the importing, exporting, possession, use, storage, display and transportation of firearms. These are federal laws that apply across the country. Firearms are divided into classes: non-restricted (most ordinary rifles and shotguns); restricted (mainly handguns) and prohibited (full and converted automatics and certain handguns, among others).

To bring a non-restricted or restricted firearm into Canada you must:
- Be 18 years of age or older
- Declare firearm(s) in writing at the first point of entry
- Obtain an Authorization to Transport (ATT) from a provincial or territorial Chief Firearms Officer prior to arrival at the point of entry; contact the Canadian Firearms Centre at (800) 731-4000 for additional details.

Hunters may bring in, duty-free, 200 rounds of ammunition; a valid license or declaration to purchase ammunition is required. Those planning to hunt in multiple provinces or territories must obtain a hunting license from each one.

Firearms are forbidden in many of Canada's national and provincial parks, game reserves and adjacent areas. For additional information regarding the temporary importation and use of firearms consult the Canada Border Services Agency website.

Personal items: Clothing, personal items, sports and recreational equipment, automobiles, snowmobiles, cameras, personal computers and food products appropriate for the purpose and duration of the visit may be brought into Canada duty and tax-free. Customs may require a refundable security deposit at the time of entry.

Tobacco products: Those meeting age requirements (18 years in Alberta, Manitoba, Northwest Territories, Nunavut, Saskatchewan, Quebec and Yukon; 19 years in other provinces) may bring in up to 50 cigars, 200 cigarettes, 200 grams of tobacco and 200 tobacco sticks.

Alcohol: Those meeting age requirements (18 years in Alberta, Manitoba and Quebec; 19 years in other provinces and territories) may bring in limited alcoholic beverages: 40 fluid ounces (1.14 litres) of liquor, 53 fluid ounces (1.5 litres) of wine (about two 750-ml bottles) or 287 fluid ounces (8.5 litres) of beer or ale (the equivalent of 24 12-ounce bottles or cans).

- Amounts exceeding the allowable quantities are subject to federal duty and taxes, and provincial/territorial liquor fees.
- Provincial fees are paid at customs at the time of entry in all provinces and Yukon.
- It is illegal to bring more than the allowable alcohol quantity into the Northwest Territories or Nunavut.

Purchases: Articles purchased at Canadian duty-free shops are subject to U.S. Customs exemptions and restrictions; those purchased at U.S. duty-free shops before entering Canada are subject to duty if brought back into the United States.

Prescription drugs: Persons requiring medication while visiting Canada are permitted to bring it for their own use. Medication should be in the original packaging with a label listing the drug and its intended use. Bring a copy of the prescription and the prescribing doctor's phone number.

Gifts: Items not exceeding $60 (CAN) in value (excluding tobacco, alcoholic beverages and advertising matter) taken into or mailed to Canada are allowed free entry. Gifts valued at more than $60 are subject to regular duty and taxes on the excess amount.

Pets: You must have a certificate for a dog or cat 3 months and older. It must clearly describe the animal, declare that the animal is currently vaccinated against rabies and include a licensed veterinarian signature.

- Collar tags are not sufficient proof of immunization.
- Be sure the vaccination does not expire while traveling in Canada.
- The certificate is also required to bring the animal back into the U.S.

Exemptions: Service animals; healthy puppies and kittens under 3 months old with a health certificate signed by a licensed

veterinarian indicating that the animal is too young to vaccinate.

Vehicles

- Vehicles entering Canada for leisure travel, including trailers not exceeding 8 feet 6 inches (2.6 m) in width, are generally subject to quick and routine entry procedures.
- To temporarily leave or store a car, trailer or other goods in Canada if you must leave the country, you must pay an import duty and taxes or present a valid permit. Canadian Customs officials issue vehicle permits at the point of entry.
- You are required to carry your vehicle registration document when traveling in Canada.
- If driving a car other than your own, you must have written permission from the owner.
- If driving a rented car, you must provide a copy of the rental contract.
- A valid U.S. driver's license is valid in Canada.
- In all Canadian provinces and territories except Alberta, British Columbia and Saskatchewan, it is illegal to use radar detectors, even if unplugged.
- Seat belt use is required for the driver and all passengers.

Financial Responsibility Laws in Canada: When an accident involves death, injury or property damage, Canadian provinces and territories require evidence of financial responsibility.

U.S. motorists should check with their insurance company regarding whether they are required to obtain and carry a yellow Non-Resident Inter-Province Motor Vehicle Liability Insurance Card (accepted as evidence of financial responsibility throughout Canada). Those not carrying proper proof may be subject to a substantial fine. If renting a vehicle, check with the rental car company.

U.S. Residents Returning to the U.S.

U.S. citizens returning to the U.S. from Canada by air must have a valid passport. Those returning by land or sea are required to present the appropriate travel documents outlined above.

Every individual seeking entry into the United States—foreign visitors, U.S. citizens or lawful permanent residents—must be inspected at the point of entry and each family (persons living in the same household related by blood, marriage, domestic partnership or adoption) must complete a declarations form. Random searches may be conducted by U.S. Customs and Border Protection agents.

U.S. Exemptions for a Stay in Canada of 48 Hours or More

- Each individual may bring back tax- and duty-free articles not exceeding $800 in retail value.
- Any amount over the $800 exemption is subject to duty.
- The exemption is allowed once every 31 days.
- A family may combine purchases to avoid exceeding individual exemption limits.
- Exemptions are based on fair retail value (keep receipts of all purchases as proof).
- Exemptions apply to articles acquired only for personal or household use or as gifts and not intended for sale.
- The exemption may include 100 cigars, 200 cigarettes and 1 litre (33.8 fluid ounces) of liquor per person over age 21. Customs enforces state liquor laws.
- All articles must accompany you on your return.

U.S. Exemptions for a Stay in Canada Less Than 48 Hours

- Each individual may bring back tax- and duty-free articles not exceeding $200 in retail value.
- The exemption may include no more than 10 cigars, 50 cigarettes, 150 millilitres (5 fluid ounces) of alcohol or 150 millilitres of perfume containing alcohol.
- A family may not combine purchases.
- If purchases exceed the $200 exemption, you forfeit the exemption and all purchases become subject to duty.
- All articles must be declared and accompany you upon return.

Gifts

- Gifts up to $100 fair retail value may be sent to friends or relatives in the United States provided no recipient receives more than one gift per day (gifts do not have to be included in the $800 exemption).
- Gifts of tobacco products, alcoholic beverages or perfume containing alcohol valued at more than $5 retail are excluded from this provision.

- Mark the contents, retail value and "Unsolicited Gift" on the outside of the package.

Prohibited: Narcotics and dangerous drugs, drug paraphernalia, obscene articles and publications, seditious or treasonable matter, lottery tickets, hazardous items (fireworks, dangerous toys, toxic or poisonous substances) citrus products and switchblade knives. Also prohibited are any goods originating in embargoed countries.

Canadian Residents Traveling to the U.S.

Canadian citizens entering the U.S. by air must have a valid passport. Canadian citizens entering the U.S. by land or sea are required to present the appropriate travel documents; refer to the Canada Border Services Agency website www.cbsa-asfc.gc.ca or travel.state.gov for the most current information on these requirements.

If traveling to the United States with a minor 15 years or younger, carry documentation proving your custodial rights. A person under age 18 traveling to the United States alone or with only one parent or another adult must carry certified documentation proving that the trip is permitted by both parents.

U.S. Customs permits Canadian residents to bring—duty-free for personal use and not intended for sale—the following: clothing, personal items and equipment appropriate to

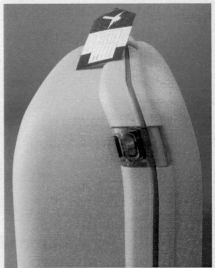

the trip, up to 200 cigarettes, 50 cigars or 2 kilograms of tobacco, and 1 litre of liquor.

Canadian Residents Returning to Canada

There are no exemptions for same-day cross-border shoppers.

Canadian residents may claim a $200 (CAN) exemption on goods, excluding alcoholic beverages and tobacco products, if returning after less than 48 hours and not using any other exemption. This exemption may apply any number of times in a year. No tobacco or alcohol may be brought back if returning from a visit of less than 48 hours.

For each absence of 48 hours or more (but fewer than seven days), residents may bring back, free of duty and taxes, goods valued up to $800 (CAN) any number of times a year, provided the visit to the United States is 48 hours or more and all goods accompany the purchaser (a written declaration may be required).

If returning after 7 days or more (not counting the departure day from Canada) you may claim up to a $800 (CAN) exemption, but goods other than alcohol and tobacco products need not accompany you (a written declaration may be required).

Permitted within the $200 and $800 exemptions: up to 50 cigars, 200 cigarettes, 200 tobacco sticks and 200 grams of tobacco; and up to 1.14 litres (40 fluid ounces) of liquor, 1.5 litres (53 fluid ounces) of wine (about two 750-ml bottles) or 8.5 litres (287 fluid ounces) of beer or ale (the equivalent of 24 12-ounce bottles or cans). You must meet the minimum age requirement of the province or territory entered to claim alcohol or tobacco products.

While AAA makes every effort to provide accurate and complete information, AAA makes no warranty, express or implied, and assumes no legal liability or responsibility for the accuracy or completeness of any information contained herein.

Photo Credits

Page numbers are in bold type. Picture credit abbreviations are as follows:
- (i) numeric sequence from top to bottom, left to right ▪ (AAA) AAA Travel library.

(cont'd)

- **275** © RM USA / Alamy Stock Photo
- **282** © AAA. Photo by AAA associate Diana Beyer for AAA
- **316** © Jose Moya / age fotostock
- **319** © Wolfgang Kaehler / age fotostock
- **320** © iStockphoto.com / Frank Leung
- **321** © Jose Moya / age fotostock
- **322** © Josh McCulloch / age fotostock
- **323** © Jamey Ekins / Shutterstock.com
- **325** © Chris Cheadle / age fotostock
- **326** © Chris Cheadle / age fotostock
- **350** (i) © Ken Gillespie / age fotostock
- **350** (ii) © Eric Baccega / age fotostock
- **351** © Alan Dyer / age fotostock
- **352** (i) Courtesy of Wikimedia Commons
- **352** (ii) © John Todd / Alamy Stock Photo
- **355** (i) © Keith Levit / Alamy Stock Photo
- **355** (ii) © Yvette Cardozo / Alamy Stock Photo
- **355** (iii) © Ken Gillespie / age fotostock
- **355** (iv) © Keith Levit / age fotostock
- **355** (v) © Ken Gillespie / age fotostock
- **356** (i) © Cindy Hopkins / Alamy Stock Photo
- **356** (ii) © Keith Levit / Alamy Stock Photo
- **356** (iii) © All Canada Photos / Alamy Stock Photo
- **356** (iv) © Design Pics Inc / Alamy Stock Photo
- **377** © Dave Reede / age fotostock
- **379** © Bilderbuch / age fotostock
- **380** © Dave Reede / age fotostock
- **381** © Ken Gillespie / age fotostock
- **382** © TOPIC PHOTO AGENCY IN / age fotostock
- **383** © Ken Gillespie / age fotostock
- **384** © Terrance Klassen / age fotostock
- **387** © iStockphoto.com / OlgaRadzikh
- **388** © age fotostock / Rolf Hicker
- **402** (i) © Michael S. Nolan / age fotostock
- **402** (ii) © All Canada Photos / Alamy Stock Photo
- **403** © Ron Erwin / age fotostock
- **404** (i) © National Gallery of Canada / Wikimedia Commons
- **404** (ii) © Ansgar Walk / Wikimedia Commons
- **407** (i) © Mike Grandmaison / age fotostock
- **407** (ii) © John E Marriott / age fotostock
- **407** (iii) © John E Marriott / age fotostock
- **407** (iv) © Wayne Lynch / age fotostock
- **407** (v) © Andrew Stewart / age fotostock
- **418** (i) © Don Johnston / age fotostock
- **418** (ii) © Dereje Belachew / age fotostock
- **419** © Dave Reede / age fotostock
- **420** (i) © H. C. Barley / Wikimedia Commons
- **420** (ii) © Robert McGouey / Alamy Stock Photo
- **423** (i) © Bilderbuch / age fotostock
- **423** (ii) © Dave Reede / age fotostock
- **423** (iii) © Rolf Hicker / age fotostock
- **423** (iv) © Ron Erwin / age fotostock
- **423** (v) © Ron Erwin / age fotostock
- **424** (i) © Terrance Klassen / age fotostock
- **424** (ii) © Finnbarr Webster / Alamy Stock Photo
- **424** (iii) © FOTOSEARCH RM / age fotostock
- **424** (iv) © Eitan Simanor / age fotostock
- **454** (i) © Tom Soucek / age fotostock
- **454** (ii) © Egmont Strigl/imageBROKER / age fotostock
- **455** © Newman Mark / age fotostock
- **456** (i) Courtesy of Wikimedia Commons

LET'S GET SOCIAL

Connect with #AAA and #CAA for the latest updates.

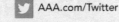 AAA.com/Facebook   AAA.com/Googleplus

AAA.com/Twitter   YouTube.com/AAA

CAA Social Media: CAA.ca/social